CCIE Practical Studies: Security (CCIE Self-Study)

Dmitry Bokotey
Andrew G. Mason
Raymond Morrow

Cisco Press

Cisco Press
201 West 103rd Street
Indianapolis, IN 46290 USA

CCIE Practical Studies: Security (CCIE Self-Study)

Dmitry Bokotey, Andrew G. Mason, and Raymond Morrow

Copyright © 2003 Cisco Press

Published by:
Cisco Press
201 West 103rd Street
Indianapolis, IN 46290 USA

Printed in the United States of America 1 2 3 4 5 6 7 8 9 0

First Printing June 2003

Library of Congress Cataloging-in-Publication Number: 2002105412

ISBN: 1-58705-110-9

Warning and Disclaimer

This book is designed to provide information for CCIE Security candidates looking for hands-on study. Every effort has been made to make this book as complete and accurate as possible, but no warranty or fitness is implied.

The information is provided on an "as is" basis. The authors, Cisco Press, and Cisco Systems, Inc., shall have neither liability nor responsibility to any person or entity with respect to any loss or damages arising from the information contained in this book or from the use of the discs or programs that may accompany it.

The opinions expressed in this book belong to the authors and are not necessarily those of Cisco Systems, Inc.

Trademark Acknowledgments

All terms mentioned in this book that are known to be trademarks or service marks have been appropriately capitalized. Cisco Press or Cisco Systems, Inc., cannot attest to the accuracy of this information. Use of a term in this book should not be regarded as affecting the validity of any trademark or service mark.

Feedback Information

At Cisco Press, our goal is to create in-depth technical books of the highest quality and value. Each book is crafted with care and precision, undergoing rigorous development that involves the unique expertise of members of the professional technical community.

Reader feedback is a natural continuation of this process. If you have any comments regarding how we could improve the quality of this book, or otherwise alter it to better suit your needs, you can contact us through e-mail at feedback@ciscopress.com. Please make sure to include the book title and ISBN in your message.

We greatly appreciate your assistance.

Publisher	John Wait
Editor-in-Chief	John Kane
Executive Editor	Brett Bartow
Cisco Representative	Anthony Wolfenden
Cisco Press Program Manager	Sonia Torres Chavez
Manager, Marketing Communications, Cisco Systems	Scott Miller
Cisco Marketing Program Manager	Edie Quiroz
Production Manager	Patrick Kanouse
Development Editor	Dayna Isley
Project Editor	Marc Fowler
Copy Editor	Gayle Johnson
	Progressive Publishing Alternatives
Technical Editors	Maurilio Gorito
	Randy Ivener
	Martin Walshaw
Team Coordinator	Tammi Ross
Book Designer	Gina Rexrode
Cover Designer	Louisa Adair
Composition	Octal Publishing, Inc.
Indexer	Tim Wright

CISCO SYSTEMS

Corporate Headquarters
Cisco Systems, Inc.
170 West Tasman Drive
San Jose, CA 95134-1706
USA
www.cisco.com
Tel: 408 526-4000
    800 553-NETS (6387)
Fax: 408 526-4100

European Headquarters
Cisco Systems International BV
Haarlerbergpark
Haarlerbergweg 13-19
1101 CH Amsterdam
The Netherlands
www-europe.cisco.com
Tel: 31 0 20 357 1000
Fax: 31 0 20 357 1100

Americas Headquarters
Cisco Systems, Inc.
170 West Tasman Drive
San Jose, CA 95134-1706
USA
www.cisco.com
Tel: 408 526-7660
Fax: 408 527-0883

Asia Pacific Headquarters
Cisco Systems, Inc.
Capital Tower
168 Robinson Road
#22-01 to #29-01
Singapore 068912
www.cisco.com
Tel: +65 6317 7777
Fax: +65 6317 7799

Cisco Systems has more than 200 offices in the following countries and regions. Addresses, phone numbers, and fax numbers are listed on the
Cisco.com Web site at www.cisco.com/go/offices.

Argentina • Australia • Austria • Belgium • Brazil • Bulgaria • Canada • Chile • China PRC • Colombia • Costa Rica • Croatia • Czech Republic
Denmark • Dubai, UAE • Finland • France • Germany • Greece • Hong Kong SAR • Hungary • India • Indonesia • Ireland • Israel • Italy
Japan • Korea • Luxembourg • Malaysia • Mexico • The Netherlands • New Zealand • Norway • Peru • Philippines • Poland • Portugal
Puerto Rico • Romania • Russia • Saudi Arabia • Scotland • Singapore • Slovakia • Slovenia • South Africa • Spain • Sweden
Switzerland • Taiwan • Thailand • Turkey • Ukraine • United Kingdom • United States • Venezuela • Vietnam • Zimbabwe

About the Authors

Dmitry Bokotey, CCIE No. 4460, holds a triple CCIE title in the fields of Routing and Switching, ISP Dial, and Security. He is a network consulting engineer with the U.S. Advanced Engineering Service IP/MPLS Core Technologies department of Cisco Systems. For the past ten years, he has designed and implemented diverse networking environments for various large enterprise and service provider customers. Over the course of his career, he has presented seminars about numerous advanced networking subjects. He is currently working on another Cisco Press book, *CCNP Practical Studies: Remote Access.*

Andrew G. Mason, CCIE No. 7144, CCDP, CSS1, CCNP: Security is the technical director of Boxing Orange (www.boxingorange.com), a UK-based Cisco VPN/Security partner specializing in the design and implementation of Cisco security solutions. He has 12 years of experience in the networking industry and has provided services for many large organizations worldwide.

Raymond Morrow, CCIE No. 4146, CSS1, Cisco IP Telephony Design Specialist, is currently employed at Northrop Grumman. Previously, he was a principal consultant with Computer Solutions, a San Antonio, Texas-based Cisco Silver Partner with Security and VPN Partner specialization. He has 16 years of experience in the networking arena and designs and implements various networking projects to a diverse customer base. Currently he is studying for his CCIE Security Lab exam after having passed the CCIE Security Qualification exam. He is also working on another writing project— *CCNP Practical Studies: Remote Access* for Cisco Press.

About the Technical Reviewers

Maurilio Gorito, CCIE No. 3807, is a triple CCIE, having certified in Routing & Switching in 1998, WAN Switching in 2001, and Security in 2003. Maurilio has more than 16 years of experience in networking including Cisco networks and SNA environments. It covers the planning, designing, implementation, and troubleshooting of large IP networks running IGRP, EIGRP, BGP, OSPF, QoS, and SNA worldwide, including Brazil and the U.S. He also has more than seven years of experience in teaching technical classes at schools and companies. Maurilio is currently a content engineer for Cisco Systems, Inc. He is part of the CCIE team responsible for helping in content development for CCIE lab exams, performing content technical review for CCIE lab exams, contacting candidates as part of the CCIE customer service, and proctoring CCIE Routing & Switching and CCIE Security lab exams at the CCIE Lab in San Jose, CA, U.S. He holds degree in Mathematics and Pedagogy.

Randy Ivener, CCIE No. 10722, is a security specialist with Cisco Systems Advanced Services. He is a Certified Information Systems Security Professional and ASQ Certified Software Quality Engineer. He has spent several years as a network security consultant, helping companies understand and secure their networks. He has worked with many security products and technologies, including firewalls, VPNs, intrusion detection, and authentication systems. Before becoming immersed in security, he spent time in software development and as a training instructor. He graduated from the U.S. Naval Academy and holds a master's degree in business administration.

Martin Walshaw, CCIE No. 5629, CISSP, CCNP, CCDP, is a Systems Engineer working for Cisco Systems in the Enterprise Line of Business in South Africa. His areas of specialty include convergence, security, and content delivery networking, which keeps him busy both night and day. During the last 15 years, Martin has dabbled in many aspects of the IT industry, ranging from programming in RPG III and Cobol to PC sales. When Martin is not working, he likes to spend all of his available time with his patient wife Val, and his sons Joshua and Callum. Without their patience, understanding, and support projects such as this would not be possible.

Dedications

Dmitry Bokotey: To my wife, Alina, for her never-ending patience and support, for being there from the start, and for never doubting any of my "silly" ideas.

To my daughter, Alyssa, for bringing light and meaning to my existence every day.

Andrew Mason: I would like to dedicate this book to my family. Helen, my beautiful wife, has yet again endured the late nights and busy weekends with nothing but support and belief in me. My two wonderful children, Rosie and Jack, keep me going and constantly remind me just what a lucky guy I am.

Raymond Morrow: I would like to dedicate this book to the woman who means the world to me and whose smile can always brighten my day and to the best children a parent could possibly ask for.

Acknowledgments

Dmitry Bokotey: This book is a product of collective effort. I would like to thank my coauthors, Andrew Mason and Raymond Morrow, for introducing me to the world of publishing, for their willingness to synchronize and compromise, and for their professionalism and knowledge. I'm forever grateful to my wife, Alina, for her help with writing and editing my chapters.

I would also like to thank the team at Cisco Press, especially Brett Bartow, for believing in me and keeping all of us on track; all the technical reviewers; and Dayna Isley for their invaluable input in making this a better book.

Big thanks to the Cisco Systems CCIE department, especially Kathe Saccenti, who helped me become a better engineer. Also, I'm thankful for my Cisco Systems colleagues' and managers–Rosa Elena Lorenzana and Sanjay Pal–support and respect.

Finally, I want to thank my parents for letting me spend days and nights beside my computer, no matter how pointless they thought it was.

Andrew Mason: This book was written by me and two authors whom I have never met and who live on the other side of the world. We immediately formed a team and worked together on this project. I would like to thank them both, Dmitry and Raymond, for their immaculate and professional work on this book. It has been a pleasure.

I would like to thank Brett Bartow and Dayna Isley of Cisco Press for all their help and guidance. They add so much value to the whole process and ease the burden on the authors.

Thanks also go out to Max Leitch and all the staff at Boxing Orange for their support and help along the way.

Raymond Morrow: Writing this book is the completion of a lifelong dream. Without the support I have received from my family, friends, coauthors, and the dedicated staff at Cisco Press, I would never have been able to make this dream a reality. Without the encouragement of my wife, Liz, and the understanding of my children as to why I spent so much time in front of my computer, this book would have been only half-completed.

This type of book, as well as the scope of the subject, would be practically impossible for one person to write, so I need to thank my coauthors, Dmitry Bokotey and Andrew Mason, for their willingness to compromise and collaborate on what has resulted in a project we can all be proud of. Of course, someone has to keep us all on track and in the proper direction, so a big thanks goes out to Brett Bartow, who knows when to give in and when not to, and to Dayna Isley for her wonderful suggestions, without which this book would have been one big jumble of words from three separate people.

Contents at a Glance

Table of Contents

Foreword

We are beyond the revolution that can be called "networking." Most employees have become sophisticated in applications that deploy networking, and words that link actions with "i" or "e" are assumed to be tools that are done in conjunction with some type of Internet function. Those who ride on the wake of this movement as networking specialists are confronted with fine-tuning and, in some cases, reengineering network resources, with greater attention paid to security. Now that the networking industry has achieved tremendous popularity, we perceive security breaches as having the potential to impact huge numbers of users. The effort to secure networks now far outweighs any perceived trade-offs in networking efficiency. A networking person who possesses the in-depth knowledge and expertise to implement security practices is highly desirable.

It makes sense that the CCIE Program would follow suit and add a CCIE-level certification to help employers identify and qualify this type of expertise. However, the idea of a Security Track for CCIE is not new. Rather, it has been the opinion of the CCIE department that this direction is long overdue. We have many people inside and outside Cisco Systems to thank for helping us make this track a reality.

The CCIE Security Track started to emerge almost three years ago with the introduction of the CCIE Security written exam. The number of folks attempting this test has steadily grown to the point where it is second in popularity only to the Routing and Switching written exam. As with all CCIE labs, it took many months of careful watch, survey, and rewrites to position a lab that would take the practices most commonly deployed by industry experts and our TAC engineers and build a practical addition to the already-popular written test. It is important to remember that although the written exam is required to qualify a candidate for a CCIE lab, the lab tests for the skills required to build a lab infrastructure before deploying the more-security-specific functions. Because the CCIE program makes every attempt to meet what employers seek in an "internetworking expert," those pursuing a CCIE Security should bear this in mind in their preparation for the CCIE Security Track.

This book is geared toward networking professionals who intend to include practice in their study toward the CCIE Security. From my years as a proctor, I cannot emphasize enough the importance of mastering the concepts behind deploying functions in any network. It is never enough to prepare for a lab without the hands-on practice that helps you drill deep in pursuit of that level of understanding. The more scenarios a candidate can access, the more easily he or she can interpret lab problems. Working through lab activities and practicing with **show** and **debug** commands will better prepare the exam candidate to implement and troubleshoot solutions efficiently and successfully.

Anyone who can combine reading with hands-on practice has a very good chance of obtaining his or her CCIE certification. But it is important to remember that obtaining a CCIE certification should not be the only goal. The CCIE program strives to identify a level of expertise that is recognized by the networking industry. The ability to achieve expertise is marked not only by a badge from Cisco. Ultimately, it is the knowledge of the technology and the ability to perform successful secure network implementations by subscribing to a higher level of preparation and skill. That is the final reward for taking the road to CCIE Security lab preparation.

Kathe Saccenti, CCIE #2099
Life Cycle Manager, CCIE Routing/Switching and co-developer of the CCIE Security exam
Cisco Systems, Inc.

Introduction

In today's ever-changing world of networking technology, as our dependence on this technology to accomplish our everyday tasks increases, securing your network has never been as important as it is right now. Through the use of hardware and software such as firewalls, virtual private networks (VPNs), and Intrusion Detection Systems (IDSs), many corporations are stepping up to the challenges presented by "script kiddies" and "black hat" hackers in today's electronic world and are searching for individuals they can trust to secure their electronic environment.

Cisco Systems, Inc., has developed a specialization track for its popular Cisco Certified Internetworking Expert (CCIE) program specifically designed with the security professional in mind. The CCIE Security track is a prestigious certification designed to identify security professionals who have demonstrated their unique abilities in the continuously changing world of network security. CCIE Security candidates are tested through a written qualification examination of common and obscure security best practices and a demanding one-day hands-on lab exam that requires them to demonstrate their ability to put the theory of security to work in a network environment.

This book is designed to help prepare CCIE Security candidates for the requirements of the one-day lab exam by providing many practice labs. These practice labs are also designed to help security professionals in their everyday job requirements. Because the CCIE Security exam includes routing and switching coverage as well as security concepts and practices, this book begins with a review of networking fundamentals and then builds on this foundation with the more-advanced requirements of modern technology.

Audience

CCIE Practical Studies: Security is intended for network and security administrators and engineers who are studying for the CCIE Security lab examination.

The secondary audience for this book could be other technical staff in the industry who are interested in learning how to configure a specific security technology and who are looking for clear examples of how to achieve this.

This book is intended to help you measure the technical competency required to sit and pass the CCIE Security lab examination. The content in this book assumes that you have passed the CCIE Security written examination and are preparing for the CCIE Security lab examination. If you are preparing for the written examination, it is advisable to refer to certification-related books for the Cisco Certified Network Associate (CCNA) and the Cisco Certified Security Professional (CCSP) to cover the more fundamental concepts of the technologies.

Book Features

This book is primarily designed to help the CCIE candidate prepare for the CCIE Security lab. It offers an organized, step-by-step build-out of a complete security lab environment for you to complete in the final chapter at your own pace. In each chapter, you will find Case Studies and Lessons in which you practice the techniques and methodologies necessary to complete the final security lab. Case Studies usually involve topologies that consist of more than one device. Although the Case Studies are designed to enforce the chapter's topics, they involve all the required configurations, such as IP addressing and routing protocols, to make the scenario work in a networking environment. Lessons are used in place of Case Studies when a Case Study is unnecessary or is impossible to provide. These Case Studies and Lessons are presented in a way that tests your ability to solve and complete the process before the answers are revealed. It is strongly advised that you work through all the Case Studies and Lessons, because each builds on the previous steps. The final lab results in a complete network security solution.

This book focuses on the configuration skills necessary to configure network and security technologies at a level similar to what you will find on the CCIE Security lab examination. The book briefly reviews the theory behind each technology, but this book should not replace detailed reference books that are specific to each technology.

Each chapter ends with a section of review questions that help you assess whether you are ready to move on to the next chapter. Each chapter also has a FAQ section that gives you a glimpse of where the material might fit into your networking environment.

Command Syntax Conventions

The conventions used to present command syntax in this book are the same conventions used in the IOS Command Reference. The Command Reference describes these conventions as follows:

- Vertical bars (|) separate alternative, mutually exclusive elements.
- Square brackets ([ ]) indicate an optional element.
- Braces ({ }) indicate a required choice.
- Braces within brackets ([{ }]) indicate a required choice within an optional element.
- **Bold** indicates commands and keywords that are entered literally as shown. In configuration examples and output (not general command syntax), bold indicates commands that are manually input by the user (such as a **show** command).
- *Italic* indicates arguments for which you supply actual values.

Device Icons Used in the Figures

Cisco uses the following standard icons to represent different networking devices.
You will encounter several of these icons within this book.

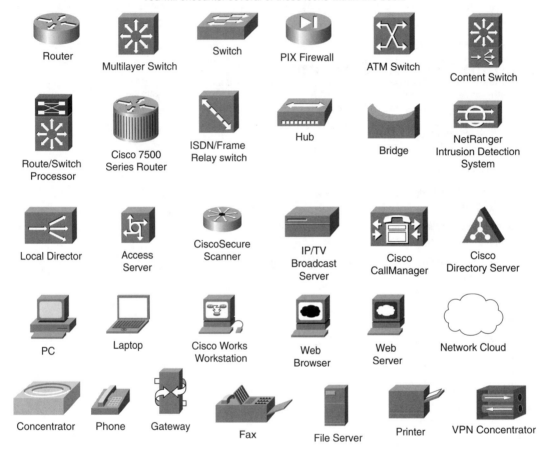

What Is Covered

The book is organized into 26 chapters and 6 appendixes:

- **Chapter 1, "The CCIE Security Program"**—This chapter provides an overview of the CCIE certification program, with special emphasis on the Security track.

- **Chapter 2, "Building a CCIE Mind-Set"**—This chapter covers the attitude and psychology that are required to start the CCIE studies. This chapter also covers motivation and the importance of a structured study plan. This is something that is always overlooked in other books and something that a lot of people find challenging.

- **Chapter 3, "Building the Test Laboratory"**—This chapter covers the required lab equipment for the CCIE Security exam. It covers the required routers, switches, and security devices. It also outlines the best equipment to use and ways to reduce the lab's cost. The lab you build at this point is used throughout the book.

- **Chapter 4, "Layer 2 and Layer 3 Switching and LAN Connectivity"**—This chapter looks at the configuration of the Catalyst 3550 switch. It also covers addressing virtual LANs (VLANs) and applying the correct IP addresses to the LAN interfaces on the lab routers.

- **Chapter 5, "Frame Relay Connectivity"**—This chapter looks at the configuration of Frame Relay and the aspects that relate to the CCIE Security lab.

- **Chapter 6, "ISDN Connectivity"**—This chapter looks at the configuration of ISDN. It covers the basic configuration and then focuses on security aspects such as authentication and callback.

- **Chapter 7, "ATM Connectivity"**—This chapter looks at the configuration of ATM. ATM concepts are covered, as well as the configuration steps necessary to configure classical IP over ATM.

- **Chapter 8, "RIP"**—This chapter provides a brief overview of RIP. You will build some configuration examples showing basic RIP and then add associated security features such as authentication.

- **Chapter 9, "EIGRP"**—This chapter provides a brief overview of EIGRP. You configure simple EIGRP, configure EIGRP options, and troubleshoot your EIGRP configuration.

- **Chapter 10, "OSPF"**—This chapter provides a brief overview of OSPF. You will build some configuration examples showing basic OSPF and then add the associated security features.

- **Chapter 11, "IS-IS"**—This chapter provides a brief overview of IS-IS and examples of configuring, monitoring, and debugging IS-IS.

- **Chapter 12, "BGP"**—This chapter provides a brief overview of BGP and includes configuration examples showing basic BGP and associated security features.

- **Chapter 13, "Redistribution"**—This chapter provides an overview of redistribution and shows scenario-based examples of various redistribution tasks.

- **Chapter 14, "Security Primer"**—This chapter provides an overview of security technologies. It includes an overview of Cisco IOS security and technologies such as VPNs, AAA, and IDS.

- **Chapter 15, "Basic Cisco IOS Software and Catalyst 3550 Series Security"**—This chapter covers basic security such as password management, access lists, and Secure Shell (SSH).

- **Chapter 16, "Access Control Lists"**—This chapter looks at the options available with access lists, including lock and key, reflexive ACLs, and extended ACLs.

- **Chapter 17, "IP Services"**—This chapter looks at services offered by IP, such as configuring the Director Response Protocol (DRP) server agent, logging, configuring Hot Standby Router Protocol (HSRP), and IP accounting.

- **Chapter 18, "AAA Services"**—This chapter covers the configuration of AAA services. It looks at configuring the RADIUS and TACACS+ protocols.

- **Chapter 19, "Virtual Private Networks"**—This chapter covers VPNs. It mainly focuses on IPSec and gives examples of both the PIX and IOS routers.

- **Chapter 20, "Advanced Virtual Private Networks"**—This chapter covers Dynamic Multipoint VPNs (DMVPNs). It looks at multipoint GRE, IPSec profiles, dynamic address spoke routers, and dynamic tunnel creation between the hub and spoke routers.

- **Chapter 21, "Virtual Private Dialup Networks"**—This chapter covers the basics and configuration of VPDNs, including configuring VPDNs with authentication and configuring the default VPDN group template.

- **Chapter 22, "Cisco IOS Firewall"**—This chapter covers the Cisco IOS Firewall, along with configuring TCP intercept, Context-Based Access Control (CBAC), and Port-to-Application Mapping (PAM).

- **Chapter 23, "Cisco PIX Firewall"**—This chapter covers configuring and monitoring Cisco PIX Firewalls.

- **Chapter 24, "IDS on the Cisco PIX Firewall and IOS Software"**—This chapter looks at PIX and IOS IDS—when to implement them and the drawbacks of each.

- **Chapter 25, "Internet Service Provider Security Services"**—This chapter covers security aspects pertaining to the service provider industry, including techniques for preventing denial-of-service (DoS) attacks and configuring L2VPN.

- **Chapter 26, "Sample Lab Scenarios"**—Eight sample lab scenarios are provided in this chapter. These scenarios are based on technologies used throughout the book. These scenarios emulate the type of scenarios you can expect to find on the CCIE Security lab exam.

- **Appendix A, "Basic UNIX Security"**—This appendix covers basic UNIX security and the commands you might require on the CCIE Security lab exam.

- **Appendix B, "Basic Windows Security"**—This appendix covers basic Windows security and the technologies you might need to know for the CCIE Security lab exam.

- **Appendix C, "ISDN Error Codes and Debugging Reference"**—This informative appendix provides the ISDN error codes you can use as a reference when debugging ISDN problems.

- **Appendix D, "Password Recovery on Cisco IOS, CatalystOS, and PIX"**—Password recovery is a very important skill to have. This appendix covers the various password-recovery methods used on Cisco IOS, CatalystOS, and the PIX Firewall.

- **Appendix E, "Security-Related RFCs and Publications"**—This appendix covers security-related RFCs and publications that can help you in your studies and ambitions to become a fully qualified Security CCIE.

- **Appendix F, "Answers to the Review Questions"**—This appendix includes the answers to the review questions that appear at the end of each chapter.

The CCIE Program and Your Lab Environment

This chapter covers the following topics:

- The Cisco CCIE program
- The CCIE Security exam

CHAPTER 1

The CCIE Security Program

This chapter provides an overview of the CCIE Security program. You will start by looking at the whole CCIE program and then concentrate on the development of the CCIE Security exam. You will look at the requirements to pass the CCIE Security exam, and you will learn about online resources that provide more-detailed information on this certification track.

The Cisco CCIE Program

The Cisco Certified Internetworking Expert (CCIE) program is recognized worldwide as the ultimate vendor-based certification in the internetworking field. The CCIE program has earned this reputation based on the grueling study requirements to pass the exam, along with the skill level and quality of the chosen few who obtain the coveted "CCIE #."

Today's business arena is placing more and more emphasis on internetworking and connectivity. The dawn of the Internet in the late 1990s spawned a massive growth in the demand for certified individuals. Combine this with the much-publicized skills gap, and it was not long before everyone jumped on the bandwagon. This explosion in interest in the certification industry had a negative effect on some of the paper-based certifications, but the CCIE stood alone as the pinnacle of networking certifications.

Cisco introduced the CCIE program in 1993 as an expert-level certification to help organizations identify highly skilled technical engineers in the internetworking industry. Today, the CCIE program sets the professional benchmark for internetworking expertise.

Currently, there are four CCIE offerings:

- Routing and Switching
- Security
- Communication and Services
- Voice

The CCIE Security Exam

One byproduct of the impressive growth of the Internet and internetworking is the requirement for skilled security engineers. Every day we hear about some new virus, Trojan horse, or worm that infects corporate networks. You probably have had firsthand experience combating a computer virus or attack. Security problems are now so prominent that they make headlines, partly due to the fear factor and the obvious massive cost to industry. This situation has led to the need for highly qualified security engineers.

The CCIE Security program is a relatively new CCIE qualification that has been offered since early 2001. Many people consider it an ideal "second CCIE" to undertake after the most common Routing and Switching CCIE, although more and more people are focusing solely on the Security CCIE.

The CCIE Security exam focuses on TCP/IP, differing from the multiprotocol Routing and Switching exam. This makes it an ideal choice for students who are newer to the field of internetworking. They do not have to learn about protocols they might never use, because these protocols are in worldwide decline due to the adoption of newer, more efficient technologies. You are tested on IP, its inherent security, and its routing protocols, as well as other IP-based security devices such as firewalls, VPNs, and Intrusion Detection Systems.

The CCIE Security exam also delves into Windows and UNIX operating system security. The IP sections of the CCIE Security exam have distinct similarities to the CCIE Routing and Switching exam. You have to attain an expert level on IP routing issues for the CCIE Security exam in the same way you have to for the CCIE Routing and Switching exam. There are no other desktop protocols apart from TCP/IP on the CCIE Security exam. You only have to learn about TCP/IP and the routing aspects and protocols related to it.

The obvious addition to the CCIE Security exam is the extensive focus on IP security-related topics. The exam covers firewalls, VPNs, and Intrusion Detection Systems. It also has more emphasis on the security configuration of base-level Cisco IOS Software and routing protocols. The next section lists the security protocols covered on the CCIE Security exam.

To pass the CCIE Security exam, you have to pass a 100-question computer-delivered qualification test and a one-day lab exam. It is the one-day lab exam that really separates the CCIE from all other vendor-based certifications.

Qualification Exam

The CCIE Security qualification exam consists of 100 questions covering a wide range of topics. The exam has to be completed within 120 minutes.

Cisco has produced a blueprint for the CCIE Security qualification exam that outlines areas of study. The exam is based on potential questions from the eight sections on the blueprint, which are as follows:

1 Security Protocols

2 Operating Systems

3 Application Protocols

4 General Networking

5 Security Technologies

6 Cisco Security Applications

7 Security General

8 Cisco General

These main sections are broken down into more detail, as described next. It is important to study every topic mentioned in the blueprint when preparing to take the CCIE Security qualification exam. Remember to periodically check Cisco's website (www.cisco.com/en/US/learning/ or www.cisco.com/warp/public/625/ccie/) to see if any changes have been made to this blueprint:

1 Security Protocols

- Remote Authentication Dial-In User Service (RADIUS)
- Terminal Access Controller Access Control System Plus (TACACS+)
- Kerberos
- Virtual Private Dial-up Networks (VPDN/Virtual Profiles)
- Data Encryption Standard (DES)
- Triple DES (DES3)
- IP Secure (IPSec)
- Internet Key Exchange (IKE)
- Certificate Enrollment Protocol (CEP)
- Point to Point Tunneling Protocol (PPTP)
- Layer 2 Tunneling Protocol (L2TP)

2 Operating Systems

- UNIX
- Windows (NT/95/98/2000)

3 Application Protocols

- Domain Name System (DNS)
- Trivial File Transfer Protocol (TFTP)
- File Transfer Protocol (FTP)
- Hypertext Transfer Protocol (HTTP)
- Secure Socket Layer (SSL)
- Simple Mail Transfer Protocol (SMTP)
- Network Time Protocol (NTP)
- Secure Shell (SSH)

- Lightweight Directory Access Protocol (LDAP)
- Active Directory

4 General Networking

- Networking Basics
- TCP/IP
- Switching and Bridging (including VLANs, Spanning Tree, and so on)
- Routed Protocols
- Routing Protocols (including RIP, EIGRP, OSPF, and BGP)
- Point-to-Point Protocol (PPP)
- IP Multicast
- Integrated Services Digital Network (ISDN)
- Async
- Access Devices (such as the Cisco AS 5300 series)

5 Security Technologies

- Concepts
- Packet Filtering
- Proxies
- Port Address Translation (PAT)
- Network Address Translation (NAT)
- Firewalls
- Active Audit
- Content Filters
- Public Key Infrastructure (PKI)
- Authentication Technologies
- Virtual Private Networks (VPNs)

6 Cisco Security Applications

- Cisco Secure UNIX
- Cisco Secure NT
- Cisco Secure PIX Firewall
- Cisco Secure Policy Manager (formerly Cisco Security Manager)
- Cisco Secure Intrusion Detection System (formerly NetRanger)
- Cisco Secure Scanner (formerly NetSonar)
- IOS Firewall Feature Set

7 Security General

- Policies
- Standards Bodies
- Incident Response Teams
- Vulnerability Discussions
- Attacks and Common Exploits
- Intrusion Detection

8 Cisco General

- IOS Specifics

The CCIE Security qualification exam is delivered by either Prometric or VUE. You can schedule the exam online at either www.2test.com or www.vue.com. The code for the exam is 350-018. Visit Cisco's website to learn more about registering for exams: www.cisco.com/en/US/learning/le3/le11/learning_certification_resources_home.html.

After you have passed the qualification exam, you can schedule your lab exam. You have 18 months after passing the CCIE Security qualification exam to schedule and sit for the lab exam. If you do not take the lab exam in this time period, you must retake the CCIE Security qualification exam.

Lab Exam

The CCIE lab exam was traditionally a two-day lab held at locations throughout the world. On October 1, 2001, Cisco changed the format to a new one-day lab after extensive research into how the CCIE was delivered and the industry's changing needs.

In the one-day CCIE Security lab exam, you are presented with a complex design to implement from the physical layer up. You are not required to configure any end-user systems, but you are responsible for any device residing in the internetwork, including routers, switches, and firewalls. Network specifics, point values, and testing criteria used to assess the correctness of the individual configurations are provided.

Each configuration scenario and problem has a preassigned point value. You must obtain a minimum mark of 80% to pass.

The CCIE lab exam is what the CCIE is all about. Over the years there have been many articles and reports on the level of knowledge, skill, and determination required to get through the CCIE lab exam. The pass mark is still very low, and the number of people who pass on their first attempt is also very low. It is an unusual exam because it is hands-on and timed, and it places you under an enormous amount of pressure. Knowing the technical aspects is only 80% of the battle. You must also have a strong positive mental attitude and be able to relax under pressure. Many CCIEs fail the lab exam due to little mistakes that escalate into major problems that then lead to a failure in one section of the lab. Because the lab is fairly progressive, if you fail to get the Layer 2 issues working, you cannot configure the Layer 3 aspects, and you are headed for certain failure.

Luckily, Cisco produces a list of lab equipment, services, and applications covered on the lab. You should use these to build your own test lab, as described in more detail in Chapter 3, "Building the Test Laboratory."

Use the following lab equipment, services, and applications list provided by Cisco to practice for the lab exam:

- 2600 series routers

- 3600 series routers

- Catalyst 3550 series switches

- PIX running PIX software version 6.1

- Certificate Authority Support

- Cisco Secure Access Control System

- Cisco Secure Intrusion Detection System

The focus of the Security lab exam is configuring routers and switches, not servers. Because of this, some of the services and applications might be preconfigured. Other services and applications not listed here might be provided fully configured with a task in which you interact with theses services and applications.

Summary

This opening chapter looked at the development of the CCIE Security exam and what you need to obtain this prestigious certification. This chapter started by covering the CCIE program in general and then looked at the CCIE Security exam. You then learned about the qualification exam and lab exam requirements, including the Security blueprint that you can refer to for both the qualification and lab exams. This chapter also provided a list of the lab equipment, services, and applications you need for the lab exam.

The best resource for up-to-date information about the Security CCIE exam or the CCIE program in general is the CCIE home page, which you can find at www.cisco.com/go/ccie.

This chapter covers the following topics:

- What it takes to become a CCIE
- Developing proper study habits
- Lab experience versus real-world experience

CHAPTER 2

Building a CCIE Mind-Set

Chapter 1, "The CCIE Security Program," provided an overview of the Cisco Certified Internetworking Expert (CCIE) program and, more specifically, the CCIE Security program. Now that you understand what the CCIE is, this chapter looks at the personal attitudes and attributes you need to study for and pass the CCIE Security qualification and lab exams. The CCIE is a very difficult certification. You need a certain mental attitude to commit yourself to the arduous study that is required.

What It Takes to Become a CCIE

The road to becoming a CCIE is long and winding, with a lot of large hills along the way. You need to have a certain mind-set to undertake such a journey. As you travel down the road, you need to adapt to and embrace the challenges that lie ahead.

As you read about in Chapter 1, you must pass two exams to attain the security CCIE qualification: the qualification exam and the lab exam. Each of these requires a slightly different approach. The qualification exam is a prerequisite for the lab exam, so your initial focus needs to be on passing the qualification exam, which contains quite a bit of theory. After passing the qualification exam, you use this theory to build the foundations for the practical lab exam.

The suggested way to prepare for the CCIE Security exam is to study for and pass the CCNA, CCNP, and CCSP before going for the CCIE Security qualification exam. You can learn more about these certifications at the following locations on Cisco's website:

www.cisco.com/go/ccna

www.cisco.com/go/ccnp

www.cisco.com/go/ccsp

> the following link needs to be verified closer to the pub date. It is not yet active.

Short-Term Goals Versus Long-Term Goals

In addition to the technical aspects of passing the Cisco certification exams, you must keep up your motivation and desire to study for and pass the CCIE Security qualification exam.

For most candidates, the CCIE Security qualification is a very difficult exam that covers a vast array of technologies. Passing the CCIE Security qualification exam can be considered a long-term goal because of the time you must take to attain the level of knowledge required. Long-term goals are very important, but it can be hard to stay motivated. When a long-term goal appears too large, we tend to divert our focus from it.

One way to overcome the problem with long-term goals is to split the process into more-manageable chunks, or short-term goals, that lead toward the long-term goal. Passing the CCNA, CCNP, and CCSP can each be thought of as an achievable short-term goal that leads toward the long-term goal of passing the CCIE Security qualification exam. This is especially true of the CCSP certification. Studying for the CCSP helps you pass the CCIE Security qualification, because there is a lot of overlap in topics between the CCSP exams and the CCIE Security qualification exam.

Breaking long-term goals into more-manageable chunks helps you stay focused. Each single exam success can be thought of a step toward your long-term goal.

It is fair to state that the written portion of the CCIE Security exam is considerably easier than the lab portion of the exam.

To pass the CCIE Security lab exam, the most important thing you must do is get as much hands-on experience configuring Cisco routers, switches, and security devices as possible. The importance of hands-on practice for the lab exam cannot be stressed enough.

Chapter 1 covered the hardware equipment list that is used for the CCIE Security lab exam. It is important to obtain a study lab and prepare for the lab exam by getting as much hands-on practice as possible. This topic is covered in depth in Chapter 3, "Building the Test Laboratory."

Developing Proper Study Habits

Numerous books that have been written on the subject of study habits are generic in nature. The study habits required to pass the qualification and lab exams of the Security CCIE are much like those required for obtaining a high school diploma or college degree. This section looks at good study habits to get into, along with common study traps you might encounter.

Good Study Habits

Good study habits are something that is acquired. First and foremost, you must want to study. Without this interest or desire, it's hard to keep up your momentum and motivation. The following pointers help you develop good study habits:

- **Formulate a study plan**—One of the most important parts of study is to formulate a plan. Winston Churchill stated, "If you fail to plan, you plan to fail." This is very true of study. Create a written plan that breaks down the technology areas, and stick with it.

- **Concentrate on difficult tasks first**—One bad habit that is very easy to get into is to put off difficult tasks and concentrate on topics you know or find interesting. When formulating your study plan, try to cover the difficult tasks first. This gives you more time to understand the difficult tasks. You also might find that you gain confidence after completing and mastering the tasks you found difficult.

- **Create a good study environment**—It is very important to create the correct environment to study in. Studying for the CCIE is a long task, and concentration is the key to mastering the very advanced topics you have to learn. Make sure that your study environment is clean, tidy, and free from environmental stresses. It is also very important to ensure that you can study without interruptions. Interruptions break your train of thought, and it can take a considerable amount of wasted time to regain your thought and momentum.

- **Take regular breaks while studying**—Research shows that taking regular breaks while studying improves your capacity to learn and helps your retention of the material. A good habit to get into is to have a 10-minute break every hour. During this time, try to get some fresh air and relax. Ten minutes every hour is only a loose suggestion. If you are in the middle of learning about IPSec, for example, and you are making good progress, it is sometimes better to cover the topic and then take a well-deserved break.

- **Know when to change your study pattern**—Network security can be a tedious and not-always-interesting subject to study. You have to realize when you are becoming bored with your current study patterns or topics. At this point, it is a good idea to change your tactics and study something different. For example, if you have spent three days going over OSPF theory, it might be good idea to give it a rest and perform a hands-on task that proves BGP theories.

- **Know when to "call it a day"**—There will come a time when, because of either mental or physical fatigue, your study will no longer be productive. You have to recognize when you reach this point and when to call it a day. There is no use studying into the early hours of the morning if you are not retaining the material you are studying. You would benefit from getting a good night's sleep and starting again the following morning with a clear mind.

- **Review and take notes**—One excellent way to study is to take notes throughout your studying. These notes should focus on the topics you are covering, and they should be a synopsis of your thoughts on the subject matter. If there are areas you are weak in, be sure to write down your findings after you have mastered the areas. You can use these notes throughout your studying.

- **Get a study partner**—It is excellent if you can team up with a colleague or another person in your area who is also studying for the CCIE Security exam. You can work through solutions together and bounce ideas off each other. You can pool equipment to build a better study lab. Also, your study partner might understand some areas better than you do and might be able to coach you in these areas.

This is by no means an exhaustive list of study habits, but they are all suggestions that make your study for the CCIE Security exam more focused.

Common Study Traps

As well as the good habits outlined in the preceding section, there are also some very easy traps to fall into while studying or planning to study. These traps are pretty common. You probably have experienced some of them:

- **"I don't know where to begin."**—Take control of your study time and plan. Make a list of all the things you have to do. Break your workload into manageable chunks. Prioritize to schedule your time realistically. Interrupt your study time with planned study breaks. Begin studying early, with an hour or two per day, and slowly build as the exam approaches.

- **"I've got so much to study and so little time."**—The most important point here is to plan. Formulate your study plan, and write it down. Prioritize your study topics. Have them correspond to the published exam blueprint from Cisco.com. There is no point in wasting time studying something that is not on the qualification or lab exam. Time is a finite resource. Ensure that you use your time to the best possible effect.

- **"This stuff is so dry, I can't stay awake reading it."**—Get actively involved with the text as you read. Ask yourself, "What is important to remember about this section?" Take notes or underline key concepts. Discuss the material with others, either in person or over the Internet. Try to get a local study partner. Stay on the offensive, especially with material you don't find interesting, rather than reading passively and missing important points. Another strategy is to practice the theory you are learning and implement it in hands-on practice.

- **"I read it. I understand it. But I just can't get it to sink in."**—We remember best the things that are most meaningful to us. As you are reading, try to elaborate upon new information with your own examples. Try to integrate what you're studying with what you already know. You will be able to remember new material better if you can link it to something that's already meaningful to you. Here are some techniques:

— **Chunking**—Chunking can be described as breaking up complicated lists of information into smaller "chunks" that are easier to remember. For example, suppose you wanted to remember the colors in the visible spectrum—red, orange, yellow, green, blue, indigo, violet; you would have to memorize seven "chunks" of information in order. But if you take the first letter of each color, you can spell the name "Roy G. Biv" and reduce the information one "chunk."

— **Mnemonics**—Any memory-assisting technique that helps you associate new information with something familiar is a mnemonic. For example, to remember a formula or equation, you could use letters of the alphabet to represent certain numbers. Then you can change an abstract formula into a more meaningful word or phrase so you can remember it better. Sound-alike associations can be very effective too, especially when you're trying to learn a new language. The key is to create your own links; then you won't forget them. For example, to remember the OSI layers, you can use the phrase "All people seem to need data processing" to remember the seven layers. The first letters of the words in the phrase are the same as the first letters in the OSI layer—application, presentation, session, transport, network, data link, physical.

• **"I guess I understand it."**—The best way to check if you understand a concept is to test yourself. Make up questions about key sections in your notes or reading. Examine the relationships between concepts and sections. Often, by simply changing section headings, you can generate many effective questions.

• **"There's too much to remember."**—You recall information better if it is represented in an organized framework that makes retrieval more systematic. Many techniques can help you organize new information:

— Write chapter outlines or summaries; emphasize relationships between sections.

— Group information into categories or hierarchies where possible.

— Draw up a matrix, or information map, to organize and interrelate material. For example, if you were trying to understand the causes of World War I, you could make a chart listing all the major countries involved across the top, and then list the important issues and events down the side. Next, in the boxes in between, you could describe the impact each issue had on each country to help you understand these complex historical developments.

• **"I knew it a minute ago."**—After reading a section, try to recall the information contained in it. Try answering the questions you made up for that section. If you cannot recall enough, reread the portions you had trouble remembering. The more time you spend studying, the more you tend to recall. Even after the point at which you perfectly recall information, further study makes the material less likely to be forgotten entirely. In other words, you can't overstudy. However, how you organize and integrate new information is still more important than how much time you spend studying.

- **"I like to study in bed."**—Recall is better when your study context (your physical location, as well as your mental, emotional, and physical state) are similar to the test context. The greater the similarity between the study setting and the test setting, the greater the likelihood that during the test you will recall the material you studied. Bed is not the best place to study.

- **"Cramming before a test helps me keep the topics fresh in my mind."**—Start studying now. Keep studying as you go along. Begin with an hour or two a day a few months before the exam, and then increase your study time as the exam approaches. Your recall increases as your study time gets spread out over time.

- **"I'm going to stay up all night until I understand this."**—Avoid mental exhaustion. Take short breaks often when studying. Before the test, have a rested mind. When you take a study break, and just before you go to sleep at night, don't think about academics. Relax and unwind, mentally and physically. Otherwise, your break won't refresh you, and you'll find yourself lying awake at night. It's more important than ever to take care of yourself before an exam! Eat well, sleep, and get enough exercise. A healthy brain retains more information and also functions better.

Lab Experience Versus Real-World Experience

The CCIE Security lab exam can be broken into two main areas—configuration and troubleshooting. In the previous two-day CCIE lab, the afternoon of the second day was dedicated to troubleshooting; the lab proctor would introduce errors into the network. In the one-day exam, troubleshooting is an integral part of the lab exam; errors can be found throughout the lab. This section discusses how you can prepare for both the configuration and troubleshooting aspects of the lab exam.

It is easy to study for the configuration parts of the CCIE lab exam. You can obtain various scenarios to practice configuring the required tasks on the equipment. The Cisco website has numerous configuration and design guides that show you step by step how to configure tasks such as site-to-site IPSec VPNs using a Certificate Authority.

Troubleshooting, on the other hand, is harder to learn. You have to really understand how the protocol or technology works to perform advanced debugging. When working with your own network, it's common to make mistakes during configuration, so some troubleshooting is required. This is good experience, but you have the advantage of knowing the network and technology you are implementing.

Real-world experience from troubleshooting large corporate networks is an excellent way to boost your troubleshooting knowledge. Troubleshooting requires flexibility, skill, and a methodology you perfect over time.

To summarize, you can learn configuration skills from a book. Although you can also learn troubleshooting methods from a book, the best way to learn them is through troubleshooting real problems in real networks.

Summary

This chapter looked at what you must do to achieve the CCIE Security certification. The CCIE is one of the most prestigious networking qualifications, and it does not come easy. The lab exam is renowned as being a tough exam to pass with very low success rates, especially on the first attempt.

This chapter started by looking at what it takes to become a CCIE, including the qualification exam and the feared lab exam. You then looked into developing proper study habits for the lab exam. This section covered good study habits and also common study traps.

The CCIE Security exam includes configuration and troubleshooting. The final section of this chapter looked at how to attain configuration and troubleshooting knowledge through real-world on-the-job experience as opposed to just gaining experience from lab practice.

In closing, as stated throughout this chapter, the CCIE Security is a very tough exam to study for. The breadth of material that you have to master is very daunting and can put a lot of people off studying for the exam. If you are starting out on the CCIE Security journey, you should set out a game plan with attainable short-term goals. One excellent way to achieve this is to go through the Cisco Career Certifications, such as the CCNA and CCNP, and then move on to the CCSP, which covers much of the material that is on the CCIE Security blueprint.

This chapter covers the following topics:

- Study time on a lab

- Planning your home lab

- Designing your practice lab for this book

CHAPTER 3

Building the Test Laboratory

The one thing that makes the CCIE such a sought-after certification is that it is highly respected in the networking community. Unlike other certifications that solely rely on computer-based testing, the CCIE certification includes a one-day hands-on laboratory exam in addition to a computer-based written exam. Computer-based exams are generally easy to prepare for, and the questions come from a limited pool. Therefore, someone could pass the written section of the CCIE purely from reading textbooks. The CCIE lab exam, however, requires an expert level of configuration expertise. The only way to attain this level of expertise is through daily hands-on practice with the equipment.

To practice for the CCIE Security lab exam, you require access to routers, switches, firewalls, and some software applications. This chapter looks at the equipment required to build a lab adequate for you to pass the CCIE Security lab exam. Also in this chapter, you design the lab that is referenced throughout this book. You will go through the various components that are used and see a topology diagram of the lab.

For a list of the equipment used in the CCIE Security lab, refer to Chapter 1, "The CCIE Security Program," or visit the Cisco website at www.cisco.com/en/US/learning/ and navigate to the CCIE Security page.

Study Time on a Lab

From a recent survey, it is estimated that the average CCIE (Routing and Switching) spends a minimum of 350 hours of practical study on a lab. The basic requirement to pass the CCIE Security exam is hands-on practice in a lab environment. Passing the CCIE Security exam without extensive hands-on experience is nearly impossible.

If you haven't already, start an action plan for getting hands-on practice using a study lab. Three options are available to you:

- Use a study lab at your place of work.
- Buy the required equipment to create a study lab at home.
- Use the services of a remote lab provider.

Work-Based Study Lab

If you are employed, it is highly probable that your employer is very interested in your attaining the CCIE designation due to the prestigious and financial benefits it can bring to the business. Cisco runs a first-class partner program. One of the requirements to proceed to Silver or Gold partner status is that you must have a minimum number of qualified CCIEs on staff.

So it is not out of the question for your employer to consider providing you with a lab to practice, because there are mutual benefits. However, in the real world, it is uncommon for all but the largest companies to have the type of equipment required to pass the CCIE Security lab spare and available to use. Even if equipment is available, you have to share it with other employees, or you might have only limited access to it. Your employer might not be happy with your spending time during the day studying, presuming that the study lab would be based at your place of work. These factors can prove difficult, unless you want to spend your nights and weekends in the office studying instead of studying in the comfort of your home.

To give yourself a chance of passing the lab, you need to be able to study on your own terms and use the study lab when your schedule dictates, and from wherever you choose. The work-based study lab is an adequate solution that should never be turned down, but the type of lab covered in the next section, the home lab, is considered the best way to study.

Home-Based Study Lab

Networking equipment is expensive. Most organizations do not have spare equipment available to let you build an adequate test lab. Combined with the fact that most organizations do not allow such equipment to be taken home, this motivates many CCIE candidates to create a home lab. You can then use this home lab to practice and master the technologies required to pass the Security CCIE lab exam.

The benefits of having a home lab are obvious. This is a lab that you own and are free to use whenever you choose. You can build and break labs to your heart's content.

The obvious issue with building a home lab is the cost. The CCIE Security lab exam has more equipment and applications than the CCIE Routing and Switching exam, and these extra components do not come cheap.

One point to consider when designing a home-based study lab is remote access to the lab. For instance, it would be good for you to be able to practice on your home lab from your place of work, such as during breaks. You can accomplish this by connecting a terminal server to the Internet, thus making the lab available to you when you are at work. Another good investment is a remote power device. This allows you to power up, power down, and power-cycle the lab equipment as you wish. This means that you don't have to leave the lab equipment turned on all day, and you can also reboot the equipment in the case of a hardware crash.

If building a home lab is something you would like to pursue, read the "Planning Your Home Lab" section in this chapter.

Remote Lab

The alternative to building a costly home lab is to use a remote lab. A remote lab is a lab full of the required Cisco equipment to study for the CCIE Security lab exam that is located on the premises of the company that is offering the remote lab service.

Remote lab offerings can be a great way to get hands-on experience for the CCIE Security lab exam. Various companies offer time on their lab equipment for a fee. The amount of lab gear, the topology and features, the lab exercises, and of course the cost are all part of your decision about whether these labs are right for you.

The features of the lab pods vary between remote lab offerings. A typical remote lab gives you some level of access to the devices in the lab. All labs provide simple console access to routers and switches. Some offer PCs, with the ability to remotely control the PCs over the Internet, even allowing you to boot them remotely. Power management is also important, in case you need to recover passwords, or if the OS on the PC gets the "blue screen of death." Often, all devices are cabled to the same LAN switch, so with configuration, you can form any LAN topology you need. In some cases, a router might be included in the pod for the purpose of acting as a Frame Relay switch; in other cases, a separate router, not controlled by the user, is cabled and configured as a Frame Relay switch. The real goal of the remote lab is to give you total control of everything that can be done without moving a cable.

A remote lab pod helps, but you need some lab exercises to perform on the pods. Some remote labs offer CCIE Security lab exercises as part of the rental fee. Others do not let you simply buy time on the lab. You buy a lab exercise, and you get the amount of time that the remote lab company thinks you need to work on the lab. In other cases, you can just buy lab time and perform any of the labs offered by the remote lab company while working at your own pace.

Which should you use—a home lab or a remote lab?

Well, you could actually benefit from both. The home lab has some obvious advantages. However, remote labs tend to have a more complete set of devices. If you can afford to duplicate the lab pods in this book in your home lab, that would be better than using remote labs. Short of duplicating the lab topology in this book, it makes sense to do the core practice on your home lab and get specific practice with labs that require a larger topology on remote labs.

Planning Your Home Lab

In the preceding section you looked at the three main lab offerings that are available to people who want to study for and pass the CCIE Security lab exam. In this section, you look at planning a home-based study lab.

Sourcing the Lab Equipment

Building a home lab can be a very costly exercise. The CCIE Security lab consists of roughly seven routers, two PIX Firewalls, and a single 3550 Catalyst switch. You also need at least one PC/server running ACS, CA, and the IDS management platform.

You also need to consider sourcing backbone routers. These backbone routers are used to inject routing information into the lab environment.

You can break the required equipment into four areas:

- Routers
- Switches
- PIX Firewall
- WAN connectivity

The normal way to buy Cisco equipment is from a Cisco Partner that sources the equipment either directly from Cisco or through distribution. This method of purchasing equipment is very costly. You do get new equipment, but you pay close to retail for it. To build your lab, you might be better off buying secondhand equipment. There is a large market for secondhand Cisco equipment. A search on eBay or any other Internet-based auction site will show you exactly what is available.

You can download Cisco ACS for a free 30-day evaluation from the Cisco website.

Routers

Routers are the basic requirement for the CCIE Security lab. Although you should be looking for at least seven routers, five or six with enough interfaces should be enough to let you work through some lab scenarios.

Ideally, you should look for a mix of 2600 and 3600 routers. These routers are Cisco's current product line. They support all the new technologies, such as VoIP and VPN acceleration through hardware. They also have software support to allow current Cisco IOS Software images to be used. These routers are modular (the 2600 has single/dual Ethernet/Fast Ethernet ports), and allow a number of differing modules to be included.

Older routers such as the 2500 and the 4000/4500 might also be an option. These routers are less expensive than the 2600/3600 models and offer a variety of interfaces. Memory restrictions on these models might hinder you from upgrading when newer processor- and memory-intensive Cisco IOS Software releases are introduced.

The key thing to remember is to get routers with as many interfaces as possible. The following interfaces are required for the CCIE Security lab:

- Serial (normally DB60)
- ATM

- ISDN
- Ethernet
- Fast Ethernet

All routers in the lab should have enough DRAM and Flash memory to load and use the Enterprise IOS Software feature set. This feature set has all the software functions required for the CCIE Security lab, including IPSec.

Switches

The CCIE historically was always run on the Cisco Catalyst 5000 range of switches running CatOS. Recently, this was changed to use the Cisco Catalyst 3550 series of switches. Therefore, it is quite important to obtain a Cisco Catalyst 3550 switch as the Layer 2 device for the whole lab. The 3550 currently comes in two versions—24-port and 48-port. The 24-port version is more than adequate for the CCIE Security lab.

PIX Firewall

The CCIE Security lab currently uses version 6.1 of the PIX Firewall software. Any hardware model of the Cisco PIX Firewall will run release 6.1 of the software.

The PIX is currently available in five models: the 501, 506, 515E, 525E, and 535E. The ideal model for CCIE Security lab preparation is the 515E with six interfaces. This is a 1U 19-inch rack-mount PIX that uses the same chassis as a Cisco 2600 router.

The PIX 501 and 506 both run the PIX software, but they are restricted in performance and how many interfaces they can support.

WAN Connectivity

You require three types of WAN connectivity: Frame Relay, ISDN, and ATM.

Frame Relay is easy. You can just configure one of your routers as a frame switch and use this router as the device that simulates the Frame Relay cloud.

ISDN and ATM are harder to emulate, and both require hardware. In the case of ISDN, you require either two ISDN lines from your service provider to practice on or an ISDN simulator. Getting two physical lines can prove costly, because there will be an installation charge for the ISDN circuits as well as ongoing call charges as you use and test ISDN within your lab. ISDN simulators are also expensive, about $1000. You might be able to pick up a secondhand ISDN simulator or even rent one for a couple of months.

ATM is very expensive to simulate. You require an ATM switch such as the Cisco Lightstream LS100 or LS1010 as well as very expensive ATM interfaces in your high-end lab routers. ATM might be a technology that makes the use of a remote lab worthwhile for the ATM sections.

Windows-based Products and UNIX

In addition to the hardware listed in the preceding sections, you also require a PC/server running Windows and UNIX. Ideally, you will have one Windows 2000 Server and one UNIX server. The applications can be spread across these two operating systems.

Designing Your Practice Lab for This Book

Throughout this book, you will use a common lab for all the examples and exercises. This lab is made up of the following components:

- Eleven routers, including eight internal routers, two backbone routers, and one router acting as a Frame Relay switch

- Two PIX Firewalls

- One 3550 switch. All Ethernet VLANs exist on this switch.

- ISDN and ATM connectivity

- One server running ACS and CA

The lab designed for this book provides all the necessary hardware and services that are required for the Security CCIE. The lab topology is shown in Figure 3-1.

Figure 3-1 *Lab Topology*

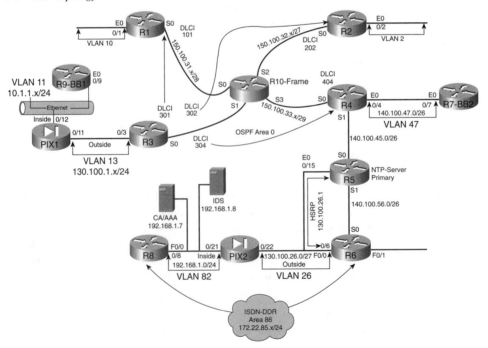

Figure 3-1 is used throughout this book. If you have the right type of equipment, this lab topology is an excellent lab to build to study for your CCIE Security lab exam.

Summary

This chapter covered the requirements of a study lab for the CCIE Security lab exam. The CCIE is different from other certifications in that it has an intense one-day hands-on lab that requires a lot of planning and preparation.

This chapter started by looking at the list of equipment for the CCIE Security lab exam that Cisco publishes on its website. You looked at each piece of hardware and reviewed a brief technical overview of it.

You looked at the requirements for study time on a lab. You also learned about the three options that are available to you as a potential candidate for the Security CCIE—a work lab, a home lab, and a remote lab. You learned that the home lab is an excellent place to start, and you learned about sourcing the correct equipment for your lab. You finally moved on to designing the study lab.

At this point, you saw the lab topology that you will use throughout this book for all the examples and exercises. The lab in this book contains all the required hardware for you to work through the lessons and case studies in this book and to study for the CCIE Security lab exam.

Connectivity

This chapter includes the following topics:

- Catalyst Operating System
- Switching overview
- Spanning tree overview
- Layer 3 switching overview
- Virtual LAN overview
- VLAN Trunking Protocol overview
- Switch interface overview
- EtherChannel overview
- Optional configuration items
- Switched Port Analyzer overview
- Basic Catalyst 3500 switch configuration

CHAPTER 4

Layer 2 and Layer 3 Switching and LAN Connectivity

Cisco Catalyst switches provide a variety of functions in your network environment. In addition to providing switching at Layer 2, the Catalyst family of switches can address the following issues:

- Gigabit scalability

- High availability

- Rich services and multilayer switching in the backbone, distribution, and access layers of your network

These switches are able to address such issues while providing you with support for a wide range of interface densities, performance, and in the case of certain switch lines, integration of powerful services modules.

Catalyst switches can meet most Layer 2 and Layer 3 LAN connectivity needs with the many different models of switches offered. In this chapter, you cover the Cisco 3550 Catalyst series of switches to prepare for the LAN connectivity requirements that you are likely to encounter during the CCIE Security lab exam.

Catalyst Operating System

The Catalyst switch family runs a version of software referred to as CatalystOS (CatOS). Like IOS, CatOS provides common functionality, scalability, and security for all products across the switches that support it. The CatOS line of operating systems currently comes in one of the following types:

- **Hybrid**—The hybrid series is the same operating system that originally shipped with the first Catalysts, with some enhancements.

- **Native**—The native series aims to bring configuration of the Catalyst switch more in line with the commands that are traditionally used in Cisco IOS Software.

In this chapter, you concentrate on Cisco IOS Software version 12.1, which runs on the Catalyst 3550 series of switches.

The following is a quick overview of the command modes that are available with the Catalyst 3550 series switches. Command modes support specific Cisco IOS commands.

For example, the **ip route** *network-number network-mask {ip-address | interface-name}* [*distance*] [**name** *name*] command only works when entered in global configuration mode. The following main command modes are available to you:

- **User EXEC**—Used to display information about your switch and to perform basic tests

- **Privileged EXEC**—Used to verify configuration commands and for troubleshooting

- **Global configuration**—Used to configure global parameters

- **Interface configuration**—Used to configure parameters that apply to interfaces

- **Config-vlan**—Used to configure parameters for virtual LANs (VLANs)

- **VLAN configuration**—Used to configure parameters for VLANs while in the VLAN database

- **Line configuration**—Used to configure parameters for the line

Switching Overview

Switches were originally developed to work at the most fundamental layer of your network. They were designed to give your users the ability to send information over a network at the same time without slowing each other down when compared to a network composed of hubs. Today's switches are blurring the line between switches and routers. Just like routers, which allow different networks to communicate with each other, today's switches not only allow different nodes on your network to communicate directly with each other, but some are also able to route between networks without the use of a router.

In the next sections, you learn about a LAN switch and how transparent bridging works. You also learn about VLANs, trunking, and spanning trees. You learn about switch security in Chapter 15, "Basic Cisco IOS Software and Catalyst 3550 Series Security."

Switching Technologies

As you learned in the previous section, switches were originally developed to work at Layer 2, or the data link layer, of the OSI Reference Model using MAC addresses, whereas routers were developed to work at Layer 3, or network layer, using Layer 3 addresses such as IP, IPX, or AppleTalk, depending on what Layer 3 protocols are being used. Differences still exist between a router and a switch, with most of the differences existing in the algorithm that switches use to decide how to forward packets. One of the major differences is how a switch handles broadcast packets. Recall that a broadcast packet is important to the proper operation of your network. Whenever a device on your network needs to send out information but does not know where the destination is, the device sends out a broadcast packet to locate the destination. One example of a broadcast is as follows: Every time a new computer or other device becomes active on your network, it usually sends out a gratuitous Address Resolution Protocol (ARP), or a broadcast packet that is designed to announce its presence to the other devices on your network.

A hub or Layer 2 switch passes any broadcast packet that is received out to all the other segments in the broadcast domain. This is different than a router or Layer 3 switch because these devices only pass the broadcast packet, unless configured to do otherwise.

LAN switches rely on a packet-switching technology. This means that the switch only establishes a connection between two segments long enough to send the current packet. Incoming packets are saved in a temporary memory area, or buffer, while the MAC address contained in the frame's header is read and compared to a list of addresses that the switch maintains in a lookup table. Packet-based switches are based on one of the following three methods for routing traffic:

- **Cut-through**—Reads the MAC address as soon as a packet is detected by the switch. The cut-through immediately begins sending the packet to the destination node after storing the 6 bytes of information that contain the address information, even though the rest of the packet is coming into the switch.

- **Store and forward**—Saves the entire packet to the buffer and checks it for Cyclic Redundancy Check (CRC) errors or other problems. The packet is discarded if an error is detected; otherwise, the switch looks up the MAC address and sends the packet to the destination node device.

- **Fragment-free**—Works in a fashion that is similar to cut-through but stores the first 64 bytes of the packet before sending the packet to the destination device. This gives the switch a type of error checking because most errors and all collisions occur during the initial 64 bytes of a packet.

LAN switches also vary in their physical design. The following three popular configurations are currently in use:

- **Shared-memory**—Stores all incoming packets in a common memory buffer that is shared by all the switch interfaces and then sends the packets out the correct interface for the destination node.

- **Matrix**—Has an internal grid with the input interfaces and the output interfaces crossing each other. When a packet is detected on an input interface, the MAC address is compared to the lookup table to find the appropriate output interface. The switch then makes a connection on the grid where these two interfaces intersect.

- **Bus-architecture**—An internal transmission path, or common bus—instead of an internal grid—is shared by all the interfaces using time-division multiaccess (TDMA). A switch based on this configuration has a dedicated memory buffer for each interface and an application-specific integrated circuit (ASIC) to control the internal bus access.

Transparent Bridging

You might be wondering why transparent bridging is being discussed in a chapter about switches, but most Ethernet LAN switches use transparent bridging to create their address lookup tables. Transparent bridging allows a switch to learn all the details about how to reach an end destination without requiring you to statically enter the information. Transparent bridging is composed of the following five parts:

- **Learning**—When the switch receives the first packet from a device, the switch reads the MAC address and saves it in its lookup table for that segment.

- **Flooding**—During flooding, the switch sends a packet for an unknown destination to all segments, with the exception of the segment that the packet was received on.

- **Filtering**—Filtering causes the switch to ignore packets that are traveling between nodes on the same segment.

- **Forwarding**—During forwarding, the switch sends a packet to a destination that it knows about on a different segment than the origination segment by briefly connecting the two segments.

- **Aging**—When an entry is added to the lookup table for a device, it is time-stamped. Each time the switch receives a packet from that device, the switch updates the time stamp. The switch uses a user-configurable timer to monitor these time stamps to determine if the entry needs to be removed from the lookup table.

Spanning Tree Overview

As your business requirements place more emphasis on network availability and as your end users depend more on the network to accomplish their everyday tasks, redundancy becomes a major component of the network infrastructure.

One of the most important protocols required to make a redundant network infrastructure operate efficiently is the Spanning Tree Protocol (STP). In the early days of networking, it was discovered, through trial and error, that only one active path can exist between any two stations in a network. When multiple active paths are present, switches can see stations on multiple ports. This results in loops in your network topology. If you were to imagine a large oak tree, you would picture something with a root at the bottom, a trunk in the middle, and individual branches reaching out from the trunk. Each individual branch can function with each other without any question of where to go for the services that are provided by the root.

STP aims to build a virtual tree out of your network topology to provide a loop-free active topology. When STP is complete and everything is assigned its place in the active topology, your network is free from a type of meltdown, also known as a *broadcast storm,* where packets are duplicated across multiple ports and run rampant through the network until their time to live (TTL) expires. The possible roles assigned to the ports are defined as follows:

- **Root port**—A unique forwarding port that is elected for the spanning tree topology

- **Designated port**—A forwarding port that is elected for every switched LAN segment

- **Alternate port**—A blocked port that provides an alternate path to the root port in the spanning tree

- **Backup port**—A blocked port in a loopback configuration

STP can eliminate loops in your network by forcing certain redundant data paths into a standby state. The ports normally selected for this function are ports that are directly in the standby path to the root bridge. STP only activates the standby path if the primary path becomes unreachable or if the spanning-tree costs, or the cost of using a path to reach the root of the primary and/or standby paths, change.

Cisco based the proprietary STP that it developed—Inter-Switch Link (ISL)—on the IEEE 802.1d STP standard. The 802.1d STP standard describes a Layer 2 management protocol that is aimed at providing path redundancy in a network infrastructure while preventing undesirable loops through the use of an algorithm that is capable of calculating the best loop-free path through the network. The Catalyst 3550 switch currently supports the Per-VLAN Spanning Tree (PVST+) Protocol.

Bridge Protocol Data Unit

The Bridge Protocol Data Unit (BPDU) is the heart of the Spanning Tree Protocol. The BPDU is used by all switches that participate in a spanning tree to gather the necessary information about all the other switches in the network. The information that is exchanged through the BPDU is used to perform the following actions:

- Select a unique root switch.

- Select a designated switch for every switched LAN segment.

- Eliminate all loops by placing redundant switch ports in a backup state; all paths that are not needed to reach the root switch from anywhere in the switched network are placed in STP-blocked mode.

When these actions are completed, tracing the selected path through the network results in an appearance much like that of your imaginary oak tree. The root switch is at the base of the path, with each switch having only a single path back to it. The resulting topology of an active switched network is determined by the following:

- The unique bridge ID, composed of the Media Access Control (MAC) address and the switch priority

- The path cost to the root switch

- The port identifier (port priority and MAC address) that is associated with each Layer 2 interface

When you power up the switches in your network, each one functions as the root switch. Each switch transmits a configuration BPDU through all its ports. These BPDUs are used to communicate and compute the spanning-tree topology. Each configuration BPDU contains the following information:

- The unique bridge ID of the switch that the sending switch identifies as the root switch

- The spanning-tree path cost to the root

- The bridge ID of the sending switch

- The message age

- The identifier of the sending interface

- Values for the hello, forward delay, and max-age protocol timers

When a switch receives a configuration BPDU that contains information that is superior to the information it transmitted (lower bridge ID, lower path cost, and so on), the switch stores the information for that port. If this BPDU happens to be received on the identified root port of the switch, the switch also forwards the BPDU with an updated message to all attached LANs for which it is the designated switch.

If a switch receives a configuration BPDU that contains inferior information to that currently stored for that port, the BPDU is ignored and discarded. If the switch is a designated switch for the LAN from which the inferior BPDU was received, the switch sends that LAN a BPDU containing the up-to-date information that is stored for that port.

A BPDU exchange results in the following actions:

1 One switch is elected as the root switch.

2 A root port is selected for each switch (except the root switch). This port provides the best path (lowest cost) when the switch forwards packets to the root switch.

3 The shortest distance to the root switch is calculated for each switch based on the path cost.

4 A designated switch for each LAN segment is selected. The designated switch incurs the lowest path cost when forwarding packets from that LAN to the root switch. The port through which the designated switch is attached to the LAN is called the *designated port*.

5 Interfaces that are included in the spanning-tree instance are selected. Root ports and designated ports are put in the forwarding state.

6 All interfaces that are not included in the spanning tree are blocked.

Following these actions, BPDUs are then sent and received across the active topology at regular intervals to identify the selected path and to determine any failures that might occur.

Election Process

As you know, all switches in your network participate in the spanning tree to gather information about every other switch in your network. This exchange of information is accomplished through the exchange of BPDU data messages. This exchange of messages results in the following actions:

- The election of a unique root switch for each spanning-tree instance

- The election of a designated switch for every switched LAN segment

- The removal of loops in the switched network by blocking Layer 2 interfaces that are connected to redundant links

For each VLAN that you have configured, the switch with the highest switch priority (the lowest numerical priority value) is elected as the root switch. If you leave all switches with the default priority of 32,768, the switch with the lowest MAC address in the VLAN becomes the root switch. The switch priority value occupies the most significant bits of the bridge ID.

One of the biggest drawbacks to using the default method to determine the root switch is that the elected switch might not be the ideal root switch due to traffic patterns, number of forwarding ports, or line types. This could result in suboptimal traffic flow when your traffic must cross the network to talk to another switch that is logically closer than the root switch. Because you are most likely not managing MAC addresses or using them to determine where to place a switch in your environment, CatOS provides a way to influence where the root switch lies in the network. You can force a switch to become the root switch by configuring a lower numerical priority number, using the following command:

```
3550A(config)#spanning-tree vlan vlan-id root [primary | secondary]
```

This command causes the switch to check the switch priority of the root switches for each VLAN. Because Catalyst 3550 switches provide support of the extended system ID support, the switch sets its priority for the specified VLAN to 24,576 if this value causes this switch to become the root for the specified VLAN.

If any root switch for the specified VLAN has a switch priority lower than 24,576, the switch sets its own priority for the specified VLAN to 4096 less than the lowest switch priority. Table 4-1 outlines the switch priorities and Extended System IDs used by the 3550 switches.

Once elected, the root switch becomes the logical center of the spanning-tree topology, using BPDUs to maintain the topology and identify any failures. BPDUs are also used to identify the designated switch and the root port for the switched network. The root port is the port on the switch that received a BPDU with the lowest cost information on how to get back to the root switch. This port is the one that is used to forward traffic toward the root switch. The designated switch is the switch that is one hop closer to the root switch and the switch that the root port forwards its traffic to.

Table 4-1   *Switch Priorities and Extended System IDs*

Switch Priority Value	Bit 16	32768
	Bit 15	16384
	Bit 14	8192
	Bit 13	4096
Extended System ID (Set Equal to the VLAN ID)	Bit 12	2048
	Bit 11	1024
	Bit 10	512
	Bit 9	256
	Bit 8	128
	Bit 7	64
	Bit 6	32
	Bit 5	16
	Bit 4	8
	Bit 3	4
	Bit 2	2
	Bit 1	1

NOTE   Additional parameters carried in a BPDU from the root switch can override parameters that are locally configured on a switch to ensure that the entire network uses consistent timers.

You can also influence what becomes the standby root switch by using the following command:

```
3550A(config)#spanning-tree vlan vlan-id root secondary
```

BPDUs contain valuable information about the sending switch and its ports for use by other switches in your network, including switch and MAC addresses, switch priority, port priority, and path cost.

Spanning-Tree Interface States

The spanning-tree algorithm decides what state a port is placed in depending on the port's function in the network. This algorithm is run whenever a topology change takes place. These changes can be due to a link coming up or a link going down, either by the device on the other end being shut down or by a failure. During a switch port transition from nonparticipation in the topology to the forwarding state, it can create temporary data loops. To prevent this, ports must wait for new topology information to propagate through the switches in the LAN and allow the frame lifetime to expire for frames that were already sent before the ports can start forwarding frames.

A switch port that is entering the topology must go through a series of states to learn its function in the spanning-tree topology. These states are as follows:

- From initialization to blocking

- From blocking to listening or to disabled

- From listening to learning or to disabled

- From learning to forwarding or to disabled

- From forwarding to disabled

Ports in one of these five states perform a certain function, as follows:

- **Blocking**—A switch port that is placed in the blocking state by the spanning tree must not participate in frame forwarding. A switch always places its ports in the blocking state following switch initialization.

- **Listening**—As the first transitional state a port enters after the blocking state, the listening state is used when the spanning tree determines that the port should participate in frame forwarding. While in the listening state, learning of addresses to place in the address database is disabled.

- **Learning**—A port that is placed in the learning state is preparing to participate in frame forwarding. The port enters the learning state from the listening state.

- **Forwarding**—A port that is placed in the forwarding state can actively forward frames onto the network. The port enters the forwarding state from the learning state.

- **Disabled**—A port that is placed in the disabled state does not participate in frame forwarding or STP for any reason. A port in the disabled state is virtually nonoperational in the sense that traffic is not forwarded or received.

One of the problems that you can encounter with every port in your network needing to go through these transition states is the fact that a network with a few hundred machines could effectively bring down the network with broadcasts due to port changes. If you are using Dynamic Host Configuration Protocol (DHCP) for automatic address assignments, STP can cause this step to fail. Cisco has modified the STP implementation with a proprietary command called *PortFast.*

PortFast is applied per port and has the following specific effects on the switch:

- Ports entering the topology are put directly into the forwarding state.

- Topology Change Notifications (TCNs) are never generated for ports that are configured for PortFast.

With this in mind, ports that are connected to a single workstation or server should never receive BPDUs. A port with PortFast enabled undergoes the normal cycle of spanning-tree status changes when the switch is restarted. Use care about where you enable PortFast because ports that connect to another switch can cause a loop in your network if PortFast is enabled.

Use the following command to enable PortFast on an interface:

```
3550B(config)#interface interface-id
3550B(config-if)#spanning-tree portfast [disable | trunk]
3550B(config-if)#end
```

NOTE   Use the PortFast command only on ports that cannot be looped somewhere in the network, such as ports going to workstations.

Spanning-Tree Address Management

The IEEE 802.1d standard specifies 17 unique multicast addresses, ranging from 0x00180C2000000 to 0x0180C2000010, to be used by different bridge protocols. Because these addresses are static addresses, you cannot remove them.

Regardless of which spanning-tree state an interface is in, it can receive, but not forward, packets that are destined for this multicast range of addresses.

If you have enabled STP, these packets are forwarded to the switch CPU for processing; otherwise, the switch forwards those packets as unknown multicast addresses.

STP and IEEE 802.1q Trunks

The IEEE 802.1q standard for VLAN trunks imposes limitations on the spanning-tree strategy that you can use in your network. This standard requires only one spanning-tree instance for *all* VLANs that are allowed on the trunks. However, Cisco switches that are connected through 802.1q trunks allow the switches to maintain a single spanning-tree instance for *each* VLAN that you allow on the trunks by implementing a per-VLAN spanning tree (PVST+) to provide spanning-tree interoperability.

PVST+ can do this by combining the spanning-tree instance of the 802.1q VLAN of the trunk with the spanning-tree instance of the non-Cisco 802.1q switch. At the same time, all PVST+ information is maintained by Cisco switches that are separated by a cloud of non-Cisco 802.1q switches. This cloud of non-Cisco 802.1q switches is treated by the switch as a single trunk link between the switches, allowing you to have a spanning-tree instance per VLAN.

VLAN-Bridge STP

The Cisco VLAN-bridge STP is designed for use with the fallback bridging feature (bridge groups). This feature forwards non-IP protocols, such as DECnet or IPX, between two or more VLAN bridge domains or routed ports. The VLAN-bridge STP forms individual VLAN spanning trees using the bridge groups to provide loop-free operation if multiple connections exist among VLANs. It is also used to prevent the individual spanning trees from the VLANs being bridged from collapsing into a single spanning tree.

STP and Redundant Connectivity

One of the greatest advantages to running STP is your ability to have redundant links in your network without fear of having an unstable network. You can create redundancy by connecting two switch interfaces to another device or to two different devices. STP automatically disables one of the redundant interfaces, but it enables the interface if the other one fails. If one of your redundant links is a high-speed link and the other is low-speed link, the low-speed link is always disabled by STP. If the link speeds are the same, the port priority and port ID are added together, and the spanning tree disables the link with the lower value.

Use the following command to influence which link becomes the forwarding link in a redundant configuration:

```
3550A(config)#interface interface-id
3550A(config-if)#spanning-tree [vlan vlan-id] port-priority priority
```

NOTE   You can also create redundant links through the use of EtherChannel groups.

Accelerated Aging to Retain Connectivity

One of the most catastrophic failures you can encounter in a switched network is an STP reconfiguration. During a reconfiguration, some stations can be unreachable for up to 5 minutes using the default setting of the **mac-address-table aging-time** configuration command of 5 minutes. This behavior is due to the fact that during the reconfiguration, many of your station locations can change as seen by the switch. Because 5 minutes of unreachability is not, in most cases, acceptable, the address-aging time can be accelerated so that station addresses can be dropped from the address table and then relearned. This parameter is the same as the forward-delay parameter value (**spanning-tree vlan** *vlan-id* **forward-time** *seconds* configuration command) when the spanning tree reconfigures.

Address-aging is accomplished on a per-VLAN basis. This means that a spanning-tree reconfiguration on one VLAN can cause the dynamic addresses learned on that VLAN to be subject to accelerated aging while other VLANs remain unaffected.

RSTP and MSTP

The Catalyst 3550 switch supports two other modes of STP: IEEE 802.1W Rapid STP (RSTP) and IEEE 802.1S Multiple STP (MSTP). As its name implies, RSTP provides you with rapid convergence of the spanning tree after an incident. On the other hand, MSTP, which uses RSTP to provide rapid convergence, enables multiple VLANs to be grouped into a spanning tree instance to provide you with multiple forwarding paths for data traffic, and enables load balancing. MSTP improves the fault tolerance of your network because a failure in one instance (forwarding path) does not affect other instances (forwarding paths).

Both RSTP and MSTP improve the operation of a spanning tree in your network while maintaining backward compatibility with equipment that is based on the (original) 802.1D spanning tree, with the existing Cisco per-VLAN spanning tree (PVST+), and with the existing Cisco-proprietary Multiple Instance STP (MISTP). For more information related to these two STPs, refer to the *Configure RSTP and MSTP Configuration Guide* for the particular software version you are running.

Layer 3 Switching Overview

All Catalyst 3550 Gigabit Ethernet switches contain the enhanced multilayer software image (EMI), which provides you with Layer 2 features, full Layer 3 routing, and advanced services. Catalyst 3550 Fast Ethernet switches give you the choice of the standard multilayer software image (SMI) or EMI installed. The SMI provides Layer 2 features and basic Layer 3 routing.

Briefly, when a router receives a packet, it looks at the Layer 3, or the Network layer, source and destination addresses to determine the path that the packet should take. A Layer 3 switch, besides having optimized hardware to pass data as fast as Layer 2 switches, can also make decisions on how to transmit traffic at Layer 3. The pattern matching and caching used by Layer 3 switches is very similar to the pattern matching and caching seen on a router. Both make use of a routing protocol and routing table to determine the best path. However, a Layer 3 switch uses the information from the routing protocol to reprogram the switch hardware dynamically.

Virtual LAN Overview

One problem with early flat networks is the amount of broadcasts that are sent to every networking device. Remember that a flat, bridged network sends all broadcast packets that are generated by any device in the network to all other devices in the network. The ambient level of broadcasts that are generated by the higher-layer protocols in the network, known as *broadcast radiation,* typically restricts the total number of devices that the network can support. In extreme cases, the effects of broadcast radiation can be so severe that an end station spends all of its CPU power on processing broadcasts.

The virtual LAN (VLAN) concept was designed to address the broadcast radiation problem, along with the following problems that are inherent to a flat, bridged network:

- Scalability

- Simplification of network management by facilitating network reconfigurations

VLANs are so common in today's networks that many people do not consider why they use them. VLANs offer you the following features:

- VLANs build on your switch's ability to isolate collision domains for attached hosts and only forward appropriate traffic out a particular port. Your switch will also provide complete isolation between the VLANs configured on it. By doing this, a VLAN is considered a *bridging domain,* and all broadcast and multicast traffic is contained within it.

- VLANs provide security in two ways:

  - High-security users can be isolated from other users into a VLAN that is defined for them so that no users outside of that VLAN are allowed to communicate with them, even if they are on the same physical segment. Note that a higher-security implementation can be achieved if you implement VLANs with different security levels on physically separate switches.

  - Because VLANs are logical groups that are treated as physically separate entities, you can only achieve inter-VLAN communication through the use of a router. Whether this router is physically separate from the switch or one of the many routing-capable modules that are supported on switches, whenever inter-VLAN communication occurs, all the security and filtering functionality that routers traditionally provide can be implemented on the communications because the router is able to see the Layer 3 information.

NOTE	Because a router is required for inter-VLAN communications, nonroutable protocols cannot communicate outside of their VLAN. All communication for these protocols must take place within their VLAN.

- The logical grouping of users allows an increase of performance in the network. Because network-intensive applications or users can be isolated to their own dedicated VLAN, the demands of these network bandwidth consumers can be isolated from other users, resulting in improved performance for both the bandwidth-hungry user and the rest of the users.

- Because a VLAN can exist across all switches in the network, a user is no longer tied to a specific physical location. Adds, moves, and changes can be achieved by simply placing a switch port into the appropriate VLAN. Most of the time, expensive recabling is no longer required. Be aware that trunking VLANs across the entire network infrastructure is usually restricted to a management VLAN and is not generally recommended for user traffic.

You can assign an interface to a VLAN in the following ways:

- **Static access**—A static-access port can belong to one VLAN and is manually assigned.

- **Trunk (ISL or 802.1q)**—A trunk is a member of all VLANs in the VLAN database. You can control which VLANs the trunk is a member of by using the allowed-VLAN list.

- **Dynamic access**—A dynamic-access port can belong to one VLAN like the static-access port, but it is assigned by a Catalyst 5000/6000 acting as a VLAN Membership Policy Server (VMPS) server.

The following special case exists when you are configuring a tunnel port on an edge switch to your service provider:

- **Tunnel (dot1q-tunnel)**—This is a tunnel port that is used for 802.1q tunneling to maintain customer VLAN integrity across a service provider network. A tunnel port can only belong to a single VLAN dedicated to tunneling.

Assigning or Modifying VLANs

Assigning VLANs to the 3550 requires you to enter the VLAN database configuration mode. You can configure many options when you create a new VLAN or modify an existing VLAN. The following is a list of items that you can configure:

- VLAN ID

- VLAN name

- VLAN type [Ethernet, Fiber Distributed Data Interface (FDDI), FDDI network entity title (NET), TrBRF or TrCRF, Token Ring, Token Ring-Net]

- VLAN state (active or suspended)

- Maximum transmission unit (MTU) for the VLAN

- Security Association Identifier (SAID)

- Bridge identification number for TrBRF VLANs

- Ring number for FDDI and TrCRF VLANs

- Parent VLAN number for TrCRF VLANs

- Spanning Tree Protocol (STP) type for TrCRF VLANs

- VLAN number to use when translating from one VLAN type to another

The 3550 comes enabled with a default VLAN with the following parameters:

- VLAN ID: 1
- VLAN name: default
- VLAN state: active
- VLAN SAID: 100001
- MTU size: 1500
- Translational Bridge 1: 0
- Translational Bridge 2: 0

Use the following guidelines when creating or modifying the VLANs in your network:

- 1005 VLANs are supported in VLAN Trunking Protocol (VTP) client, server, and transparent modes. VLANs are identified with a number between 1 and 1001. VLAN numbers 1002 through 1005 are reserved for Token Ring and FDDI VLANs.

- You must configure the switch to be either in VTP server mode or VTP transparent mode before you can configure VLANs. If the switch is a VTP server, you must define a VTP domain.

- Catalyst 3550 switches do not provide support for Token Ring or FDDI media. As such, the switch does not forward FDDI, FDDI-NET, TrCRF, or TrBRF traffic, but it does propagate the VLAN configuration through VTP.

- Only 128 STP instances are supported. If you define more active VLANs than supported STP instances, STP is disabled on the VLANs above the 128-STP limit.

Occasionally you must change a configured item for a VLAN. You can do this by using the same method as adding a VLAN.

Deleting VLANs

To delete a VLAN, use the following command:

```
3550A(vlan)#no vlan vlan-id
```

or

```
3550A(config)#no vlan vlan-id
```

You cannot delete the default media VLANs, which consist of Ethernet VLAN 1 and the FDDI and Token Ring VLANs 1002–1005. When you delete a VLAN, any ports that are assigned to the VLAN are placed in an inactive state until you reassign them to a different VLAN.

Configuring Extended-Range VLANs

If you configure your switch to run in the VTP transparent mode, you can make use of an extended range of VLANs (in the range of 1006 to 4094). You must use the config-vlan mode (accessed by entering the **vlan** *vlan-id* configuration command) to configure your extended range of VLANs.

The extended-range VLAN that you configure is not stored in the VLAN database, but because VTP mode is transparent, the VLAN is stored in the switch running configuration file. You can save the configuration in the startup configuration file by using the **copy running-config startup-config** privileged EXEC command.

VLAN Trunking Protocol Overview

VLAN Trunking Protocol (VTP) is a Layer 2 messaging protocol used to maintain VLAN configuration consistency across your network infrastructure. VTP manages the addition, deletion, and renaming of VLANs throughout the network from a centralized location. VTP introduces the concept of a server switch, which communicates these changes through the VTP to all the other switches in your network.

The VTP Domain

The VTP domain, or the VLAN management domain, is used to group one or more of your interconnected switches together using the same VTP domain name, much like routers can be grouped under a single autonomous system. Unlike a router, you can configure a switch to participate in only one VTP domain. Once the switches are under a single VTP domain, you can make global VLAN configuration changes using either the command-line interface (CLI) or Simple Network Management Protocol (SNMP).

The default configuration for VTP is server mode with a NULL VTP domain name. The switch remains in this condition until it receives a VTP advertisement for a domain over a trunk link or until you manually configure a VTP management domain. If the switch is configured by receiving an advertisement, it inherits both the management domain name and the VTP config-uration revision number. Remember that you cannot create or modify VLANs on a switch that is configured as a VTP server until the management domain name is specified or learned.

VTP Modes

VTP is designed to give you maximum flexibility in the design of your VTP domain. Whether you desire to have centralized management of VLAN configuration or want to configure VLANs on each switch in your network, VTP provides the following VTP modes:

- **Server mode**—When a switch is placed in the VTP server mode, you can create, modify, and delete VLANs and specify other configuration parameters (such as VTP version and VTP pruning) for the entire VTP domain; these parameters are stored in the nonvolatile

RAM (NVRAM). VTP servers advertise their VLAN configuration to other switches in the same VTP domain for inclusion in their configuration and synchronize their VLAN configuration with other switches based on advertisements received over trunk links. VTP server is the default mode.

- **Client mode**—On VTP clients, you cannot create, change, or delete VLANs. A VTP client does not advertise its configurations to other VTP domain members. Because of this, VTP clients only contain default VLAN definitions until receipt of an advertisement from a VTP server. VTP clients do not save the VLAN information in NVRAM.

- **Transparent mode**—VTP-transparent switches are not active participants in VTP. VTP-transparent switches do not advertise their VLAN configuration to other switches and do not synchronize their VLAN configuration based on received advertisements. VTP-transparent switches save their VLAN information in the running configuration. However, when you are using VTP version 2, transparent switches forward VTP advertisements that they receive out their trunk ports.

VTP Passwords

You are given the option of configuring a password for your VTP domain. You are required to configure this same password on all the switches in your management domain. If you do not do this, switches with the wrong password or switches without a password reject all password-protected VTP advertisements.

Use the following command to enter a password for your VTP domain:

```
3550A(vlan)#vtp password word
```

VTP Advertisements

Like most items that are configured on your network devices, VTP consumes bandwidth due to its need to send and receive periodic advertisements out each configured trunk port to a reserved multicast address. Notice that a trunk port is required for the switch to be able to send and receive VTP advertisements. When VTP advertisements are received by a switch that is not configured for VTP transparent mode, the switch updates its VTP and VLAN configurations, if necessary, with the information that is contained in the advertisements.

VTP advertisements distribute the following global domain information:

- VTP domain name
- VTP configuration revision number
- Update identity and update time stamp
- MD5 digest VLAN configuration, including maximum transmission unit (MTU) size for each VLAN
- Frame format

VTP advertisements distribute the following VLAN-specific information for each configured VLAN:

- IDs (ISL and the IEEE standard 802.1q)

- name

- type

- state

- Additional configuration information specific to the VLAN type

VTP Version 2

Following the philosophy that nothing is perfect and that everything can be improved upon, VTP has two separate versions that you can choose from. In most situations, with the exception of Token Ring support, you can run either version 1, which is what you have learned about so far in this chapter, or version 2. Version 2, of course, improves on the list of features provided by version 1 by including the following enhancements:

- **Token Ring support**—VTP version 2 supports Token Ring LAN switching and VLANs [Token Ring Bridge Relay Function (TrBRF) and Token Ring Concentrator Relay Function (TrCRF)].

- **Unrecognized Type-Length-Value (TLV) support**—A VTP server or client propagates configuration changes to its other trunks, even for TLVs, that it cannot parse but are saved in nonvolatile RAM (NVRAM).

- **Version-dependent transparent mode**—VTP version 2 forwards all VTP messages while the switch is in transparent mode.

- **Consistency checks**—In VTP version 2, VLAN consistency checks (such as VLAN names and values) are performed only when you enter new information through the CLI or SNMP. If the digest on a received VTP message is correct, its information is accepted without consistency checks.

NOTE   Even though the 3550 supports VTP version 2, it does not provide support for Fiber Distributed Data Interface (FDDI) or Token Ring.

Use the following command to change the VTP version to version 2:

```
3550A(vlan)#vtp v2-mode
```

or

```
3550A(config)#vtp version [1 - 2]
```

VTP Pruning

Even with the lower cost of bandwidth you are most likely enjoying, eliminating unnecessary broadcast traffic is still one of the first goals of network design. CatOS provides a feature called *VTP pruning,* which can help you enhance network bandwidth use by reducing unnecessary traffic that is normally flooded throughout the network, such as broadcast, multicast, unknown, and flooded unicast packets. VTP pruning can accomplish this task by restricting flooded traffic to those trunk links that the traffic must use to access the appropriate network devices. Unfortunately, VTP pruning is disabled by default.

TIP

You might be wondering why such a useful feature is not enabled by default. All the switches under your management domain might not support VTP pruning. This means that VLANs cannot be pruned from links that might not require them.

Enabling VTP pruning on a VTP server enables pruning for the entire management domain, although it can take several seconds for pruning to take effect after you enable it. By default, VLANs 2 through 1000 are pruning eligible as long as the VLAN is not marked as pruning ineligible. VLAN 1 is, by default, always pruning ineligible, but you can essentially disable them by not assigning interfaces to them and by prohibiting them from crossing a trunk.

Use the following command to enable pruning on your switch:

```
3550A(vlan)#vtp pruning [v2-mode]
```

or

```
3550A(config)#vtp pruning
```

Note that you are also given the option of changing your VTP version with this same command.

Pruning eligibility is configured on the local switch by configuring a list on a trunk. To configure VLAN pruning eligibility, enter the following command:

```
3550A(config-if)#switchport trunk pruning vlan {add | except | none | remove} vlan-atom
[,vlan-atom…]
```

Table 4-2 explains the keyword usage.

Table 4-2   *The **switchport trunk pruning vlan** Keywords*

Keyword	Definition
None	Is an empty list.
Add	Inserts the defined list of VLANs to those currently set instead of replacing the list. Valid IDs are from 2 to 1001. Separate nonconsecutive VLAN IDs with a comma; use a hyphen to designate a range of IDs. Do not enter leading 0s.

continues

Table 4-2   *The* **switchport trunk pruning vlan** *Keywords (Continued)*

Keyword	Definition
Remove	Deletes the defined list of VLANs from those currently set instead of replacing the list. Valid IDs are from 2 to 1001. Separate nonconsecutive VLAN IDs with a comma; use a hyphen to designate a range of IDs. Do not enter leading 0s. You cannot remove VLAN 1 or 1002 to 1005 from the list.
except	Lists the VLANs that should be calculated by inverting the defined list of VLANs. (VLANs are added except the ones you specify in the command.) Valid IDs are from 2 to 1001. Separate nonconsecutive VLAN IDs with a comma; use a hyphen to designate a range of IDs. Do not enter leading 0s.
vlan-atom	Is either a single VLAN number from 1 to 1005 or a continuous range of VLANs described by two VLAN numbers, the lesser one first, separated by a hyphen.

VTP Configuration Guidelines

Like the configuration of a routing protocol, VTP must be configured in a consistent manner for your switching environment to operate in a consistent and expected manner. Use the following guidelines when implementing VTP in your network:

- All switches in a VTP domain must run the same VTP version. When VTP version 2 is disabled on VTP version 2–capable switches, the switches can operate in the same VTP domain as a switch running VTP version 1. If you use VTP version 2, all switches in the VTP must support VTP version 2 because enabling VTP version 2 on a switch causes all the version 2–capable switches in the domain to enable VTP version 2.

- If you plan on implementing VTP in a secure mode, you must configure the same password on each switch in the management domain; otherwise, you can receive unpredictable results.

- VTP version 2 must be enabled in a Token Ring environment for Token Ring VLAN switching to function properly.

- Enabling or disabling VTP pruning on a VTP server enables or disables VTP pruning for the entire management domain.

- Making VLANs pruning eligible or pruning ineligible on a switch affects pruning eligibility for those VLANs on that device only.

Displaying VTP

You can display VTP activity, including VTP advertisements that are sent and received and VTP errors, by using one of the following commands:

```
3550A#show vtp status
3550A#show vtp counters
```

Switch Interface Overview

The 3550 supports many different interface types through the use of *switch ports.* Switch ports can be either an access port or a trunk port. You are also given the option of using Dynamic Trunking Protocol (DTP) on a per-port basis to automatically determine if the port should be an access or a trunk, by negotiating with the port on the other end. Because switch ports are Layer 2 ports, they cannot route or bridge traffic.

Access Ports

You use an access port to carry traffic from a single VLAN. This type of port can be a member of only one VLAN. Traffic is sent and received in native formats with no VLAN tagging. Because the traffic is untagged, any traffic that arrives on an access port is assumed to belong to the VLAN that is assigned to the port.

Currently, the following two different types of access ports are supported:

- **Static**—These access ports are manually assigned to a VLAN.

- **Dynamic**—VLAN membership of dynamic access ports is learned through incoming packets. By default, a dynamic access port is not a member of a VLAN, and forwarding to and from the port is enabled only when the VLAN membership of the port is discovered. In the Catalyst 3550 switch, dynamic access ports are assigned to a VLAN by a VLAN Membership Policy Server (VMPS). The VMPS can be a Catalyst 6000 series switch; the Catalyst 3550 switch does not support the function of a VMPS.

Trunk Ports

When you configure a port as a trunk port, you enable the port to carry traffic from multiple VLANs. Trunk ports, by default, are a member of all VLANs that you have configured in the VLAN database. You have the choice of the following two different types of trunk ports to configure:

- **ISL trunk port**—A trunk where any received packets are expected to be encapsulated with an ISL header, and all transmitted packets are sent with an ISL header. Native (nontagged) frames received from an ISL trunk port are dropped.

- **IEEE 802.1q trunk port**—A trunk that is capable of supporting simultaneous tagged and untagged traffic. An 802.1q trunk port is assigned a default port VLAN ID (PVID), and all untagged traffic travels on the port default PVID. All untagged traffic and tagged traffic with a NULL VLAN ID are assumed to belong to the port default PVID. A packet with a VLAN ID equal to the outgoing port default PVID is sent untagged. All other traffic is sent with a VLAN tag.

Even though the default configuration of a trunk port is that it is a member of every VLAN known to the VTP, you can choose to limit its VLAN membership by configuring an allowed list of VLANs on a per-trunk basis. A trunk port can only become a member of a VLAN if VTP knows of the VLAN and the VLAN is in the enabled state. Any new, enabled VLANs are added to the trunk if that VLAN is in the allowed list for the trunk port. If a new, enabled VLAN that is not in the allowed list for a trunk port is added, the port does not become a member of the VLAN, and no traffic for the VLAN is forwarded to or from the port.

NOTE   VLAN 1, the default Ethernet VLAN, cannot be excluded from the allowed list for a trunk.

Use the commands discussed next in this section to create a trunk interface.

To enter the interface configuration mode and configure the port for trunking, use the following command:

```
3550A(config)#interface interface-id
```

Use the following command to configure the port to support ISL or 802.1q encapsulation or to negotiate (the default) with the neighboring interface for encapsulation type:

```
3550A(config-if)#switchport trunk encapsulation {isl | dot1q | negotiate}
```

To configure the interface as a Layer 2 trunk (required only if the interface is a Layer 2 access port or tunnel port) or to specify the trunking mode, use the following command:

```
3550A(config-if)#switchport mode {dynamic {auto | desirable} | trunk}
```

With this command, you have the following options:

- **dynamic auto**—Set the interface to a trunk link if the neighboring interface is set to trunk or desirable mode.

- **dynamic desirable**—Set the interface to a trunk link if the neighboring interface is set to trunk, desirable, or auto mode.

- **trunk**—Set the interface in permanent trunking mode and negotiate to convert the link to a trunk link, even if the neighboring interface is not a trunk interface.

Specify the native VLAN for 802.1q trunks with the following command:

```
3550A(config-if)#switchport trunk native vlan vlan-id
```

Routed Ports

A *routed port* is a physical port that acts like a port on a router; however, you are not required to have a router connected to it. You do not associate a routed port with any particular VLAN because you create it as an access port. A routed port behaves like a regular router interface, with the exception that you cannot configure VLAN subinterfaces. You can configure a routed port with a Layer 3 routing protocol.

NOTE   The number of routed ports and SVIs that you can configure is not limited by software; however, you can experience high CPU utilization, depending on the number of routed ports and SVIs along with any other features that you might wish to configure.

You configure a routed port by using the following commands:

```
3550A(config)#interface interface-id
3550A(config-if)#no switchport
3550A(config-if)#ip address ip-address netmask
3550A(config-if)#no shutdown
3550A(config)#end
```

By using these commands, you are turning a Layer 2 interface into a Layer 3 interface. You can configure many of the options that are available to you on a Cisco router, including an IP routing protocol (RIP, IGRP, OSPF, and EIGRP), support for subnet zero, IP classless routing, and forwarding of DHCP requests. To configure any of these options, use the following commands:

```
3550A(config)#ip subnet-zero
3550A(config)#ip classless
3550A(config)#interface interface-id
3550A(config-if)#ip helper-address address
3550A(config-if)#exit
3550A(config)#ip routing
3550A(config)#router ip-routing-protocol
3550A(config-router)#end
```

EtherChannel Overview

In some cases, you might want to group multiple switch ports together for them to appear as a single port. EtherChannel port groups provide you with this ability. These port groups behave as a single logical port for high-bandwidth connections between switches or between switches and servers. An EtherChannel balances the traffic load across the links in the channel and provides redundancy in the case of a link failure within the EtherChannel by sending traffic that was previously carried over the failed link to the remaining links. You can create an EtherChannel port group by grouping multiple trunk ports into one logical trunk port or by grouping multiple access ports into one logical access port. When you configure an EtherChannel, you create a port-channel logical interface and assign any number of interfaces to the EtherChannel.

An EtherChannel can be made up of up to eight Fast Ethernet ports or up to eight Gigabit Ethernet ports. Each port in an EtherChannel must be of the same speed, and you must configure all ports as either Layer 2 or Layer 3 interfaces. If you choose to use Fast Ethernet ports, you can obtain full-duplex bandwidth of up to 800 Mbps throughput in each direction. Using Gigabit Ethernet ports can give you up to 8 Gbps of throughput in each direction between your switch and another switch or host.

The following sections take a more in-depth look at the creation and theory behind EtherChannel technology.

Port-Channel Interfaces

The creation of a Layer 2 EtherChannel differs from the creation of a Layer 3 EtherChannel. However, both configurations involve the use of logical interfaces. When you use Layer 3 interfaces, you must manually create the logical interface by using the **interface port-channel** configuration command. When you use Layer 2 interfaces, the logical interface is dynamically created for you. Whichever method you decide to use, with both types of interfaces, you manually assign an interface to the EtherChannel by using the **channel-group** configuration command to bind the physical and logical ports.

Because each EtherChannel is bound to a logical interface, this logical port-channel interface is assigned a number from 1 to 64. The channel groups are also numbered from 1 to 64.

Once you have your EtherChannel configured, any configuration changes that you make to the port-channel interface apply to all the physical interfaces that are assigned to the port-channel interface. Any configuration changes that you apply to the physical interface affect only the interface to which you apply the configuration.

Understanding the Port Aggregation Protocol

The Port Aggregation Protocol (PAgP) enables you to automatically create an EtherChannel through the exchange of packets between Ethernet interfaces. PAgP does this by learning the capabilities of PAgP-capable switches and dynamically grouping similarly configured interfaces into a single logical link (channel or aggregate port); these interfaces are grouped based on hardware, administrative, and port parameter constraints. Once these links are joined into an EtherChannel, PAgP adds the group to the spanning tree as a single switch port.

PAgP supports several user-configurable EtherChannel modes for the **channel-group** interface configuration command, as follows:

- **Auto**—The default setting that places an interface into a passive negotiating state, in which the interface responds to PAgP packets it receives; however, the interface does not start a PAgP packet negotiation.

- **Desirable**—Places an interface into an active negotiating state, in which the interface starts negotiations with other interfaces by sending PAgP packets.

- **On**—Forces the interface to channel without PAgP. With the **on** mode, a usable Ether-Channel exists only when an interface group in the **on** mode is connected to another interface group in the **on** mode.

- **Non-silent**—If you connect your switch to a partner that is PAgP-capable, you can configure the switch interface for non-silent operation. You can only configure an interface with the **non-silent** keyword when you use the auto or desirable mode. If you do not specify **non-silent** with the auto or desirable mode, silent is assumed. The silent setting is for connections to file servers or packet analyzers; this setting allows PAgP to operate, to attach the interface to a channel group, and to use the interface for transmission.

Interfaces form an EtherChannel with one another when they are in different PAgP modes as long as the modes are compatible. For example:

- An interface in desirable mode can form an EtherChannel with another interface that is in desirable or auto mode.

- An interface in auto mode can form an EtherChannel with another interface in desirable mode.

- An interface in auto mode cannot form an EtherChannel with another interface that is also in auto mode because neither interface starts PAgP negotiation.

- An interface in the on mode that is added to a port channel is forced to have the same characteristics as the already-existing on mode interfaces in the channel.

EtherChannel Load Balancing and Forwarding Methods

EtherChannels are capable of providing load balancing across the links in a channel by reducing part of the binary pattern that is formed from the addresses in the frame to a numerical value that selects one of the links in the channel. EtherChannel load balancing can base itself on either the source MAC or destination MAC address forwarding.

When it is using the source MAC address for forwarding, packets are distributed across the ports in the channel based on the source MAC address of the incoming packet. This means that packets from different hosts use different ports in the channel, while packets from the same host use the same port in the channel (assuming that the MAC address learned by the switch does not change).

Source MAC address forwarding also provides load distribution based on whether the source and destination IP address are enabled for routed IP traffic. Packets between two IP hosts always use the same chosen port in the channel, and traffic between any other pair of hosts can select a different port in the channel to use.

When you are using the destination MAC address for forwarding, packets are distributed across the ports in the channel based on the destination host's MAC address of the incoming packet. Packets to the same destination are forwarded over the same port, and packets to a different destination are sent on a different port in the channel.

Use the following command to configure the load balancing and forwarding method:

```
3550A(config)#port-channel load-balance {dst-mac | src-mac}
```

EtherChannel Configuration Guidelines

Improperly configuring an EtherChannel can cause some EtherChannel interfaces to be automatically disabled to avoid network loops and other problems. Follow these guidelines to avoid configuration problems:

- Each EtherChannel can have up to eight compatibly configured Ethernet interfaces.

- Configure all interfaces in an EtherChannel to operate at the same speeds and duplex modes.

- Enable all interfaces in an EtherChannel. A shutdown interface in an EtherChannel is treated as a link failure, and its traffic is transferred to one of the remaining interfaces in the EtherChannel.

- When a group is first created, all ports follow the parameters set for the first port to be added to the group. If you change the configuration of one of these parameters, you must also make the changes to all ports in the group:

  — Allowed-VLAN list

  — STP path cost for each VLAN

  — STP port priority for each VLAN

  — STP Port Fast setting

- An EtherChannel does not form if one of the interfaces is a Switch Port Analyzer (SPAN) destination port.

- A port that belongs to an EtherChannel port group cannot be configured as a secure port.

- Before enabling 802.1X on the port, you must first remove it from the EtherChannel. If you try to enable 802.1X on an EtherChannel or on an active port in an EtherChannel, an error message appears, and 802.1X is not enabled. If you enable 802.1X on a not-yet-active port of an EtherChannel, the port does not join the EtherChannel.

Consider the following additional items when using Layer 2 EtherChannels:

- Assign all interfaces in the EtherChannel to the same VLAN, or configure them as trunks. Interfaces with different native VLANs cannot form an EtherChannel.

- If you configure an EtherChannel from trunk interfaces, verify that the trunking mode (ISL or 802.1q) is the same on all the trunks. Inconsistent trunk modes on EtherChannel interfaces can have unexpected results.

- An EtherChannel supports the same allowed range of VLANs on all the interfaces in a trunking Layer 2 EtherChannel. If the allowed range of VLANs is not the same, the interfaces do not form an EtherChannel, even when PAgP is set to the **auto** or **desirable** mode.

- Interfaces with different STP path costs can form an EtherChannel as long they are otherwise compatibly configured. Setting different STP path costs does not, by itself, make interfaces incompatible for the formation of an EtherChannel.

For Layer 3 EtherChannels, assign the Layer 3 address to the port-channel logical interface, not to the physical interfaces in the channel.

Creating Layer 2 EtherChannels

Configure Layer 2 EtherChannels by using the following commands:

```
3550A(config)#interface interface-id
3550A(config-if)#switchport mode {access | trunk}
3550A(config-if)#switchport access vlan vlan-id
3550A(config-if)#channel-group channel-group-number mode {auto [non-silent] | desirable
  [non-silent] | on}
3550A(config-if)#end
```

Use the following command to remove an interface from a Layer 2 EtherChannel:

```
3550A(config-if)#no channel-group
```

Optional Configuration Items

Many optional configuration items are available to you to fine tune your spanning-tree environment. These options include the following:

- BPDU Guard
- BPDU Filtering
- UplinkFast
- BackboneFast
- Loop Guard

The following sections describe each of these optional items in more detail. Whether you choose to use these options depends on the specific needs of your network.

BPDU Guard

As you know from previous discussions, PortFast-enabled ports are not allowed to receive BPDUs. The BPDU Guard feature puts a port that is receiving a BPDU in the error-disabled state. You can enable the BPDU Guard feature globally on the switch or on a per-interface basis, but be aware that the feature operates with some differences.

When you enable BPDU Guard on a global level, you use the **spanning-tree portfast bpduguard default** configuration command. The spanning tree shuts down ports that you set to a PortFast-operational state. Receiving a BPDU on a PortFast-enabled port signals an invalid configuration, such as the connection of an unauthorized device, and the BPDU Guard feature puts the port in the error-disabled state.

When you enable BPDU Guard at the interface level, you use the **spanning-tree bpduguard enable** interface configuration command without enabling the PortFast feature. When the port receives a BPDU, it is put in the error-disabled state.

The BPDU Guard feature provides a secure response to invalid configurations because you must manually put the port back in service. Use the BPDU Guard feature in a service-provider network to prevent an access port from participating in the spanning tree.

If your switch is running PVST or MSTP, you can enable the BPDU Guard feature for the entire switch or for an interface.

BPDU Filtering

Much like BPDU Guard, you can enable the BPDU Filtering feature globally or on a per-interface basis, but the feature operates with some differences.

When you enable BPDU filtering on a global level, you can use the **spanning-tree portfast bpdufilter default** configuration command on a PortFast-enabled interface. This command is used to prevent ports that are in a PortFast-operational state from sending or receiving BPDUs. The port is still able to send a few BPDUs at linkup before the switch begins to filter outbound BPDUs. You should globally enable BPDU filtering on a switch so that hosts that are connected to these ports do not receive BPDUs. Unlike the BPDU Guard feature, if a BPDU is received on a PortFast-enabled port, the port loses its PortFast-operational status, and BPDU filtering is disabled.

When you enable BPDU filtering at the interface level, you can use the **spanning-tree bpdufilter enable** configuration command without enabling the PortFast feature. This command prevents the port from sending or receiving BPDUs.

Use care when enabling the BPDU Filtering options because it is the same as disabling the spanning tree. As you know, disabling the spanning tree can result in loops inside of your network.

UplinkFast

UplinkFast provides fast STP convergence after a direct link failure in the network access layer. UplinkFast operates without modifying the STP protocol, while reducing the convergence time in specific circumstances to less then 3 seconds, rather than the typical 30-second delay that you encounter without it.

Because this effectively bypasses the normal STP topology change-handling process (listening and learning), an alternate topology correction mechanism is required to inform switches that local end stations are reachable via an alternate path. To accomplish this, the access layer switch that is running UplinkFast also generates frames for each MAC address in its Content Addressable Memory (CAM) to a multicast MAC address (01-00-0c-cd-cd-cd, HDLC protocol 0x200a) to update the CAM table in all switches in the domain with the new topology.

BackboneFast

BackboneFast provides rapid convergence from indirect link failures. By adding functionality to STP, convergence times can typically be reduced from the default of 50 seconds to 30 seconds. The mechanism is initiated when a root port or blocked port on a switch receives "inferior BPDUs" from its designated switch. This can happen when a downstream switch has lost its connection to the root and starts sending its own BPDUs to elect a new root. An inferior BPDU identifies a switch as both the root bridge and the designated switch.

Under normal STP rules, the receiving switch ignores inferior BPDUs for the configured maximum aging time, 20 seconds by default. With BackboneFast configured, the switch sees the inferior BPDU as a signal that the topology might have changed, and tries to determine whether it has an alternate path to the root bridge using Root Link Query (RLQ) BPDUs. This protocol addition allows a switch to determine whether the root is still available, moves a blocked port to forwarding in less time, and notifies the isolated switch that sent the inferior BPDU that the root is still there.

Loop Guard

Loop Guard is used to prevent alternate or root ports from becoming designated ports because of a failure that leads to a unidirectional link. If you are running PVST or Multiple Spanning Tree (MST) on your switches, you can enable this feature by using the **spanning-tree loopguard default** configuration command.

When you are using the PVST mode, Loop Guard prevents alternate and root ports from becoming designated ports, and spanning tree does not send BPDUs on root or alternate ports.

When you are using the MST mode, BPDUs are not sent on nonboundary ports only if the port is blocked by Loop Guard in all MST instances. On a boundary port, Loop Guard blocks the port in all MST instances.

Switched Port Analyzer Overview

At some point, you will need to analyze the network traffic that is passing through ports or VLANs by using the Switched Port Analyzer (SPAN) to send a copy of the traffic to another port on the switch that has been connected to a SwitchProbe device or other Remote Monitoring (RMON) probe. SPAN works by mirroring received or sent (or both) traffic on a source port, or received traffic on one or more source ports or source VLANs, to a destination port for analysis.

Only the traffic that enters or leaves source ports or traffic that enters source VLANs can be monitored by using SPAN.

Although SPAN does not affect the switching of network traffic on source ports or source VLANs, use care so that you do not oversubscribe the destination port. For example, a 10-Mbps port monitoring a 100-Mbps port can cause congestion on the switch. Destination ports do not receive or forward traffic, except that required for the SPAN session.

SPAN Session

A SPAN session is an association of a destination port that you configure with source ports or source VLANs. You should be aware of the following restrictions of traffic monitoring in a SPAN session:

- You can monitor incoming traffic on a series or range of ports or VLANs.

- You can monitor outgoing traffic on a single port; you cannot monitor outgoing traffic on multiple ports.

- You cannot monitor outgoing traffic on VLANs.

- You can configure two separate SPAN sessions with separate or overlapping sets of SPAN source VLANs. You can also configure both switched and routed ports as SPAN sources and destinations. SPAN sessions do not interfere with the normal operation of the switch.

- You can configure SPAN sessions on disabled ports; however, a SPAN session does not become active unless you enable the destination port and at least one source port or VLAN for that session.

- A SPAN session remains inactive after system power up until the destination port is operational.

Configuring SPAN

When you are determining what ports to configure your SPAN on, follow these guidelines:

- Use a network analyzer to monitor ports.

- Only two SPAN sessions can be active on a switch at the same time.

- The destination port cannot be a source port; a source port cannot be a destination port.

- You can have only one destination port per SPAN session. You cannot have two SPAN sessions using the same destination port.

- An EtherChannel port can be a SPAN source port; it cannot be a SPAN destination port.

- An 802.1X port can be a SPAN source port. You can enable 802.1X on a port that is a SPAN destination port; however, 802.1X is disabled until the port is removed as a SPAN destination.

- For a SPAN source port, you can monitor transmitted traffic for a single port or received traffic for a series or range of ports or VLANs.

- When you configure a switch port as a SPAN destination port, it is no longer a normal switch port; only monitored traffic passes through the SPAN destination port.

- A trunk port can be a source port or a destination port. When a destination port is a trunk port, outgoing packets through the SPAN port carry the encapsulation headers configured by the user, either Inter-Switch Link (ISL) or IEEE 802.1q. If no encapsulation type is defined, the packets are sent in native form.

- When you specify a single source port and do not specify a traffic type (Tx, Rx, or both), both is used as the default.

- For received traffic, you can mix multiple source ports and source VLANs within a single SPAN session. You cannot mix source VLANs and filter VLANs within a SPAN session; you can have source VLANs or filter VLANs, but not both at the same time.

- You can limit SPAN traffic to specific VLANs by using the **filter vlan** keyword. If a trunk port is being monitored, only traffic on the VLANs that are specified with this keyword is monitored. By default, all VLANs are monitored on a trunk port.

- The **no monitor session** *session_number* global configuration command removes a source or destination port from the SPAN session or removes a source VLAN from the SPAN session. If you do not specify any options following the **no monitor session** *session_number* command, the entire SPAN session is removed. The **no monitor** global configuration command also clears all SPAN sessions.

- A SPAN destination port never participates in any VLAN spanning tree. SPAN includes BPDUs in the monitored traffic, so any spanning-tree BPDUs received on the SPAN destination port for a SPAN session are copied from the SPAN source ports.

When SPAN is enabled, configuration changes have the following results:

- If you change the VLAN configuration of a destination port, the change is not effective until SPAN is disabled.

- If you disable all source ports or the destination port, the SPAN function stops until both a source and destination port are enabled.

- If the source is a VLAN, the number of ports being monitored changes when you move a switched port into or out of the monitored VLAN.

Use the following commands to create a SPAN session and specify the source (monitored) and destination (monitoring) ports.

Specify the SPAN session and the source port (monitored port) with the following command:

```
3550A(config)#monitor session session_number source interface interface-id [, | -] [both
| rx | tx]
```

- For *session_number*, specify 1 or 2.

- For *interface-id*, specify the source port to monitor. Valid interfaces include physical interfaces and port-channel logical interfaces (port-channel *port-channel-number*).

- For [**,** | **-**] (optional), specify a series or range of interfaces. Enter a space after the comma; enter a space before and after the hyphen.

- (Optional) You can also specify the direction of traffic to monitor. If you do not specify a traffic direction, the source interface sends both sent and received traffic. Only received (rx) traffic can be monitored on additional source ports:

    — **Both**—Monitor both received and sent traffic

    — **rx**—Monitor received traffic

    — **tx**—Monitor sent traffic

To specify the SPAN session and the destination port (monitoring port), use the following command:

```
3550A(config)#monitor session session_number destination interface interface-id
[encapsulation {dot1q | isl}]
```

- For *session_number*, specify 1 or 2.

- For *interface-id*, specify the destination port. Valid interfaces include physical interfaces.

- (Optional) Specify the encapsulation header for outgoing packets. If not specified, packets are sent in native form:

    — **isl**—Use ISL encapsulation

    — **dot1q**—Use 802.1q encapsulation

To remove the entire SPAN session, use the following command:

```
3550B(config)#no monitor session session_number
```

To remove just the source or destination port from the SPAN session, use one of the following commands:

```
3550B(config)#no monitor session session_number source interface interface-id
3550B(config)#no monitor session session_number destination interface interface-id
```

Basic Catalyst 3550 Switch Configuration

The following case studies are dedicated to basic Catalyst switch software configuration methods that are grouped into several scenarios, variations of which you are likely to encounter in the CCIE Security lab exam or in real life.

Case Study 4-1: Basic Network Connectivity

To get the full benefit of this chapter, you need to configure a simple switched network. Figure 4-1 illustrates the topology that you will use in this case study.

Figure 4-1   *Simple Switch Topology*

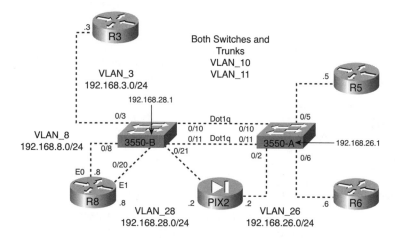

In this case study, you configure your Catalyst 3550 switches for basic connectivity by following these steps:

Step 1   Configure the host name.

Step 2   Configure a VTP domain.

Step 3   Configure the VLANs (as illustrated in Figure 4-1).

Step 4   Configure a management IP address.

Step 5   Configure a default gateway.

The next sections describe each step.

Step 1: Configure the Host Name

Configuring the host name for your switch is much like configuring the host name on a Cisco router. Use the following command:

```
Switch(config)#hostname word
```

Example 4-1 shows you the configuration items that are necessary to give your 3550 a host name. It also shows you the format of the configuration file that you will be using for the rest of this chapter.

Example 4-1 *Setting the Host Name*

```
Switch(config)#hostname 3550A
3550A(config)#
```

Step 2: Configure a VTP Domain

In this step, you run VTP in transparent mode with a VTP domain name of ccie_lab. You can configure the VTP domain name by entering the following commands:

```
3550A#vlan database
3550A(vlan)#vtp domain word
3550A(vlan)#vtp transparent
3550A(vlan)#exit
```

or

```
3550A(config)#vtp mode transparent
3550A(config)#vtp domain word
```

You can return VTP to server mode by using the **no vtp transparent** command. However, once you configure a domain name, you cannot return it to Null; you can only change it to a different name.

Example 4-2 shows the configuration that is necessary to complete this portion of the case study, and Example 4-3 verifies that your VTP configuration is correct.

Example 4-2 *Configuring the VTP Mode and Domain Name*

```
3550A(config)#vtp mode transparent
3550A(config)#vtp domain ccie_lab
```

Example 4-3 *The **show vtp domain** Command Output*

```
3550A#show vtp status
VTP Version                    : 2
Configuration Revision         : 0
Maximum VLANs supported locally : 254
Number of existing VLANs       : 5
VTP Operating Mode             : Transparent
```

Example 4-3 *The **show vtp domain** Command Output (Continued)*

```
VTP Domain Name              : ccie_lab
VTP Pruning Mode             : Disabled
VTP V2 Mode                  : Enabled
VTP Traps Generation         : Disabled
MD5 digest                   : 0xA0 0x8A 0xD0 0x34 0xE8 0xBD 0x3D 0x95
Configuration last modified by 192.168.124.100 at 3-1-93 00:36:35
```

As you can see from the output in Example 4-3, you have successfully configured the VTP domain to ccie_lab and the VTP mode to transparent. You should now configure the 3550B with the same VTP configuration that you placed on the 3550A switch. You should now apply the VTP configuration to your 3550B Catalyst switch.

Example 4-4 shows the configurations that are necessary to complete this step.

Example 4-4 *VTP Configuration for Switch 3550B*

```
3550B#vlan database
3550B(vlan)#vtp domain ccie_lab
3550B(vlan)#vtp transparent
3550B(vlan)#exit
```

Step 3: Configure the VLANs

Each Ethernet VLAN that you configure has a unique 4-digit ID between 1 and 1001. For you to add a VLAN to the VLAN database, you must specify the VLAN number with an optional VLAN name. Use the following command to add a VLAN:

```
3550A#vlan database
3550A(vlan)#vlan vlan-id name vlan-name
3550A(vlan)#exit
```

or

```
3550A(config)#vlan vlan-id
3550A(config)#name vlan-name
```

In this step, you configure VLANs 10, 11, and 26 on 3550A and name them vlan_10, vlan_11, and vlan_26. Example 4-5 shows you the commands that you can use, and Example 4-6 shows you the results of adding VLAN 26 to 3550A.

Example 4-5 *Adding VLANs to Switch 3550A*

```
3550A(config)#vlan 10
3550A(config-vlan)#name vlan_10
3550A(config-vlan)#exit
3550A(config)#vlan 11
3550A(config-vlan)#name vlan_11
```

continues

Example 4-5 *Adding VLANs to Switch 3550A (Continued)*

```
3550A(config-vlan)#exit
3550A(config)#vlan 26
3550A(config-vlan)#name vlan_26
```

Example 4-6 *The* **show vlan name vlan_26** *Command Output*

```
3550A#show vlan name 26
VLAN Name                             Status    Ports
---- -------------------------------- --------- ------------------------------
26   vlan_26                          active

VLAN Type  SAID       MTU   Parent RingNo BridgeNo Stp  BrdgMode Trans1 Trans2
---- ----- ---------- ----- ------ ------ -------- ---- -------- ------ ------
26   enet  100026     1500  -      -      -        -    -        0      0
```

You should now configure the VLANs for 3550B as outlined in Figure 4-1. Example 4-7 shows you the commands that are required to accomplish this.

Example 4-7 *VLAN Configuration for Switch 3550B*

```
3550B#vlan database
3550B(vlan)#vlan 3 name VLAN_3
3550B(vlan)#vlan 8 name VLAN_8
3550B(vlan)#vlan 10 name VLAN_10
3550B(vlan)#vlan 11 name VLAN_11
3550B(vlan)#vlan 28 name VLAN_28
3550B(vlan)#exit
```

Now that you have your VLANs defined, you force 3550A to become the root switch for VLAN 26. You can achieve this by using the **spanning-tree vlan** *vlan-id* **root [primary |**
secondary] command. Switch 3550B becomes the root switch for VLANs 1, 3, 8, and 28. The switches are configured to be the standby root switch for the other VLANs.

Example 4-8 illustrates the results of your configuration efforts.

Example 4-8 *Setting the Root Switch*

```
Configuration items for 3550A:
3550A(config)#spanning-tree vlan 26 root primary
3550A(config)#spanning-tree vlan 1 root secondary
3550A(config)#spanning-tree vlan 3 root secondary
3550A(config)#spanning-tree vlan 8 root secondary

Configuration items for 3550B:
3550B(config)#spanning-tree vlan 1 root primary
3550B(config)#spanning-tree vlan 3 root primary
3550B(config)#spanning-tree vlan 8 root primary
3550B(config)#spanning-tree vlan 26 root secondary
```

Step 4: Configure a Management IP Address

You can assign an IP address to the 3550 switch in one of three ways:

- **Switch setup program**—A program that runs at the first startup of the switch or by issuing the setup command that prompts you for an IP address, a host name, an enable secret, and optionally, a telnet password if your switch is part of a cluster.

- **Automatically**—The switch can obtain an IP address by using the Dynamic Host Configuration Protocol (DHCP).

- **Manual**—You can manually assign an IP address to your switch by using the **ip address** command.

Because most of the time you will use the manual method of assigning an IP address to the switch, this is the only method covered in this chapter. If you need to use any of the other methods, refer to the appropriate *Assigning the Switch IP Address and Default Gateway* technical guide for the CatOS level that you are using.

Assigning an IP address to your switch requires you to decide what VLAN is to manage the switch. Because you have already created VLAN 26, you can now assign an IP address to it. Use the following commands to accomplish this:

```
3550A(config)#interface vlan vlan-id
3550A(config-subif)#ip address ip-address subnet-mask
```

Before configuring an IP address on the switch, be aware of the interface under which you configure the IP address. A switch virtual interface (SVI) is used to provide a single interface for configuration of routing or bridging of a VLAN. This configuration is applied to the physical interfaces, or ports, that you assign to that VLAN. You can only associate a single SVI with a VLAN, but you configure an SVI for a VLAN only when you want to do one of the following:

- Route between VLANs

- Provide a fallback bridge for nonroutable protocols between VLANs

- Provide IP host connectivity to the switch

By default, the only SVI created is for the default VLAN (VLAN 1) to permit remote switch administration. You must explicitly configure all other SVIs. Be aware that in Layer 2 mode, SVIs only provide IP host connectivity to the system; in Layer 3 mode, you can configure routing across SVIs.

SVIs are created when you enter the **vlan interface** configuration command for a VLAN interface. The VLAN corresponds to the VLAN tag that is associated with data frames on an ISL or 802.1q encapsulated trunk or the VLAN ID configured for an access port. You should configure a VLAN interface for each VLAN for which you want to route traffic, and assign it an IP address.

Your next step in the configuration of this case study is to configure 3550A and PIX2 with their respective IP addresses. You must also shut down the default VLAN, VLAN 1. PIX commands and configuration are covered in greater detail in Chapter 23, "Cisco PIX Firewall."

To assign an IP address to the PIX, use the following command:

```
PIX2(enable)#ip address interface_name ip-address netmask
```

Example 4-9 shows the configuration items necessary for you to complete this part of your case study.

Example 4-9 *Configuring the IP Address on Switch 3550A*

```
Configuration items on 3550A:
3550A(config)#interface Vlan1
3550A(config-if)#shutdown
3550A(config-if)#exit
3550A(config)#interface Vlan26
3550A(config-if)#ip address 192.168.26.1 255.255.255.0

Configuration items on PIX2:
PIX2(config)#ip address inside 192.168.26.2 255.255.255.0
```

You should now configure the designated IP address on the rest of the equipment that you use in this example. Example 4-10 illustrates the commands that you can use to complete this requirement.

Example 4-10 *Configuring the IP Address on Switch 3550B*

```
3550B(config)#interface Vlan1
3550B(config-if)#shutdown
3550B(config-if)#exit
3550B(config)#interface Vlan28
3550B(config-if)#ip address 192.168.28.1 255.255.255.0

Configuration items on PIX2:
PIX2(config)#ip address outside 192.168.28.2 255.255.255.0

Configuration items on R3:
R3(config)#interface ethernet0
R3(config-if)#ip address 192.168.3.3 255.255.255.0

Configuration items on R5:
R5(config)#interface ethernet0
R5(config-if)#ip address 192.168.26.5 255.255.255.0

Configuration items on R6:
R6(config)#interface ethernet0
R6(config-if)#ip address 192.168.26.6 255.255.255.0
```

Example 4-10 *Configuring the IP Address on Switch 3550B (Continued)*

```
Configuration items on R8:
R8(config)#interface ethernet0
R8(config-if)#ip address 192.168.8.8 255.255.255.0
R8(config-if)#exit
R8(config)#interface ethernet1
R8(config-if)#ip address 192.168.28.8 255.255.255.0
```

Step 5: Configure a Default Gateway

Because the 3550 does not know where every possible destination for a packet resides, you need to tell it where to send packets for which it does not have a destination. You can tell the switch where to send these packets by configuring a default gateway. The default gateway receives IP packets that have an unresolved or unknown destination from the switch.

Use the following command to configure the default gateway:

```
3550A(config)#ip default-gateway ip-address
```

In this portion of the case study, you configure the default gateway for 3550A as the inside interface of PIX2. Example 4-11 contains the commands that are necessary to finish this step.

Example 4-11 *Setting the Default Gateway of Switch 3550A*

```
3550A(config)#ip default-gateway 192.168.26.2
```

As you can see from the output of the **show ip route** command in Example 4-12, the default gateway of 3550A is pointing to the inside interface of PIX2.

Example 4-12 *Confirming the Default Route of Switch 3550A*

```
3550A#show ip route
Default gateway is 192.168.26.2

Host            Gateway            Last Use    Total Uses    Interface
ICMP redirect cache is empty
```

You can now complete this case study by configuring the default gateway of 3550B as the Ethernet1 interface of R8. Example 4-13 shows the configuration that is required to complete this step.

Example 4-13 *Setting the Default Gateway of Switch 3550B*

```
3550A(config)#ip default-gateway 192.168.28.8
```

Case Study 4-2: Configuring Interfaces

In this case study, you configure the identified interfaces on the Catalyst switches into their respective VLANs.

To configures the VLAN membership mode of the interface, use the following commands:

```
3550A(config)#interface interface-id
3550A(config-if)#description Description
3550A(config-if)#switchport mode {access | dot1q-tunnel | dynamic {auto | desirable} |
   trunk}
3550A(config-if)#switchport access vlan vlan-id
3550A(config-if)#end
```

Example 4-14 shows you the results of using the preceding commands. This configuration should match Figure 4-1, shown in Case Study 4-1.

Example 4-14 *VLAN Assignment Configuration*

```
Configuration items for 3550A:
3550A(config)#interface FastEthernet0/2
3550A(config-if)#description Connection to PIX2 Inside
3550A(config-if)#switchport mode access
3550A(config-if)#switchport access vlan 26
3550A(config-if)#exit
3550A(config)#interface FastEthernet0/5
3550A(config-if)#description Connection to R5
3550A(config-if)#switchport mode access
3550A(config-if)#switchport access vlan 26
3550A(config-if)#exit
3550A(config)#interface FastEthernet0/6
3550A(config-if)#description Connection to R6
3550A(config-if)#switchport mode access
3550A(config-if)#switchport access vlan 26
3550A(config-if)#exit
3550A(config)#interface FastEthernet0/10
3550A(config-if)#description Connection to 3550B 0/10
3550A(config-if)#switchport mode access
3550A(config-if)#switchport access vlan 10
3550A(config-if)#exit
3550A(config)#interface FastEthernet0/11
3550A(config-if)#description Connection to 3550B 0/11
3550A(config-if)#switchport mode access
3550A(config-if)#switchport access vlan 11

Configuration items for 3550B
3550B(config)#interface FastEthernet0/2
3550B(config-if)#description Connection to PIX2 Outside
3550B(config-if)#switchport mode access
3550B(config-if)#switchport access vlan 28
3550B(config-if)#exit
3550B(config)#interface FastEthernet0/3
3550B(config-if)#description Connection to R3
3550B(config-if)#switchport mode access
3550B(config-if)#switchport access vlan 3
```

Example 4-14 *VLAN Assignment Configuration (Continued)*

```
3550B(config-if)#exit
3550B(config)#interface FastEthernet0/8
3550B(config-if)#description Connection to R8
3550B(config-if)#switchport mode access
3550B(config-if)#switchport access vlan 8
3550B(config-if)#exit
3550B(config)#interface FastEthernet0/10
3550B(config-if)#description Connection to 3550A 0/10
3550B(config-if)#switchport mode access
3550B(config-if)#switchport access vlan 10
3550B(config-if)#exit
3550B(config)#interface FastEthernet0/11
3550B(config-if)#description Connection to 3550A 0/11
3550B(config-if)#switchport mode access
3550B(config-if)#switchport access vlan 11
3550B(config-if)#exit
3550B(config)#interface FastEthernet0/20
3550B(config-if)#description Connection to R8
3550B(config-if)#switchport mode access
3550B(config-if)#switchport access vlan 28
3550B(config-if)#exit
```

An examination of the output in Example 4-15 shows you that each of your interfaces was configured with VLANs.

Example 4-15 *The* **show vlan** *Command Output*

```
3550A# show vlan
VLAN Name                             Status    Ports
---- -------------------------------- --------- -------------------------------
1    default                          active    Fa0/1, Fa0/3, Fa0/4, Fa0/7
                                                Fa0/8, Fa0/9, Fa0/12, Fa0/13
                                                Fa0/14, Fa0/15, Fa0/16, Fa0/17
                                                Fa0/18, Fa0/19, Fa0/20, Fa0/21
                                                Fa0/22, Fa0/23, Fa0/24, Gi0/1,
                                                Gi0/2
10   VLAN_10                          active    Fa0/10
11   VLAN_11                          active    Fa0/11
26   VLAN_26                          active    Fa0/2, Fa0/5, Fa0/6
! Output omitted for brevity

3550B# show vlan
VLAN Name                             Status    Ports
---- -------------------------------- --------- -------------------------------
1    default                          active    Fa0/1, Fa0/2, Fa0/4, Fa0/5
                                                Fa0/6, Fa0/7, Fa0/9, Fa0/12
                                                Fa0/13, Fa0/14, Fa0/15, Fa0/16
                                                Fa0/17, Fa0/18, Fa0/19, Fa0/20
                                                Fa0/21, Fa0/22, Fa0/23, Fa0/24,
                                                Gi0/1, Gi0/2
```

continues

Example 4-15 *The **show vlan** Command Output (Continued)*

```
3    VLAN_3                    active    Fa0/3
8    VLAN_8                    active    Fa0/8
10   VLAN_10                   active    Fa0/10
11   VLAN_11                   active    Fa0/11
1002 fddi-default             active
1003 token-ring-default       active
1004 fddinet-default          active
1005 trnet-default            active
! Output omitted for brevity
```

Case Study 4-3: Configuring PortFast

In this case study, you configure FastEthernet 0/24 as a PortFast-enabled interface on 3550B. Example 4-16 illustrates the configuration items that are required to accomplish this task.

Example 4-16 *Enabling PortFast*

```
3550B(config)#interface FastEthernet 0/24
3550B(config-if)#spanning-tree portfast
```

With this configuration, the workstation that is connected to the 3550B switch, interface 0/24, does not undergo the normal spanning-tree process.

Case Study 4-4: Creating a Layer 2 EtherChannel

In the next step, you create an EtherChannel between 3550A and 3550B ports 1/10 and 1/11.

Example 4-17 shows you the configuration that is necessary to create the channel and provides a few **show** commands from 3550A to verify operation. If you examine the configuration of the switches, you notice that the logical interface, Port Channel 1, is created for you.

Example 4-17 *Creation of a Layer 2 EtherChannel*

```
Configuration of 3550A
3550A(config)#interface Port-channel 1
3550A(config-if)#switchport mode access
3550A(config-if)#exit
3550A(config)#interface FastEthernet0/10
3550A(config-if)#channel-group 1 mode desirable
3550A(config-if)#exit
3550A(config)#interface FastEthernet0/11
3550A(config-if)#channel-group 1 mode desirable

Configuration of 3550B
3550B(config)#interface Port-channel 1
3550B(config-if)#switchport mode access
```

Example 4-17 *Creation of a Layer 2 EtherChannel (Continued)*

```
3550B(config-if)#exit
3550B(config)#interface FastEthernet0/10
3550B(config-if)#switchport mode access
3550B(config-if)#channel-group 1 mode desirable
3550B(config-if)#exit
3550B(config)#interface FastEthernet0/11
3550B(config-if)#channel-group 1 mode desirable
```

An examination the output of Example 4-18, which shows the output of the **show interface port-channel 1** command, verifies that your configuration is complete.

Example 4-18 *The* **show interface port-channel 1** *Command Output*

```
3550A#show interface port-channel 1
Port-channel1 is up, line protocol is up
Hardware is EtherChannel, address is 0002.4b28.db02 (bia 0002.4b28.db02)
MTU 1500 bytes, BW 200000 Kbit, DLY 1000 usec,
reliability 255/255, txload 1/255, rxload 1/255
Encapsulation ARPA, loopback not set
Keepalive set (10 sec)
 Full-duplex, 100Mb/s
input flow-control is off, output flow-control is off
 Members in this channel: Fa0/10 Fa0/11
ARP type: ARPA, ARP Timeout 04:00:00
Last input 00:03:27, output 00:00:00, output hang never
Last clearing of "show interface" counters never
Queueing strategy: fifo
Output queue 0/40, 0 drops; input queue 0/75, 0 drops
5 minute input rate 0 bits/sec, 0 packets/sec
5 minute output rate 0 bits/sec, 0 packets/sec
26 packets input, 5344 bytes, 0 no buffer
Received 17 broadcasts, 0 runts, 0 giants, 0 throttles
0 input errors, 0 CRC, 0 frame, 0 overrun, 0 ignored
0 input packets with dribble condition detected
59 packets output, 5050 bytes, 0 underruns
0 output errors, 0 collisions, 2 interface resets
0 babbles, 0 late collision, 0 deferred
0 lost carrier, 0 no carrier
0 output buffer failures, 0 output buffers swapped out
```

Case Study 4-5: Creating Trunks

In this case study, you create two 802.1q trunks between the two 3550s using the same interfaces that were previously used to create the EtherChannels. You are only going to allow certain VLANs across the trunks. For example, you are not going to allow VLAN_26 across to 3550B or allow VLAN_3 or VLAN_8 across to 3550A.

Example 4-19 shows you the results of configuring the trunks.

Example 4-19 *Configuring Trunks*

```
Configuration items for 3550A:
3550A(config)#interface FastEthernet 0/10
3550A(config-if)#switchport trunk encapsulation dot1q
3550A(config-if)#switchport mode trunk
3550A(config-if)#switchport trunk allowed vlan remove 26
3550A(config-if)#exit
3550A(config)#interface FastEthernet 0/11
3550A(config-if)#switchport trunk encapsulation dot1q
3550A(config-if)#switchport mode trunk
3550A(config-if)#switchport trunk allowed vlan remove 26

Configuration items for 3550B:
3550B(config)#interface FastEthernet 0/10
3550B(config-if)#switchport trunk encapsulation dot1q
3550B(config-if)#switchport mode trunk
3550B(config-if)#switchport trunk allowed vlan remove 3,8
3550B(config-if)#exit
3550B(config)#interface FastEthernet 0/11
3550B(config-if)#switchport trunk encapsulation dot1q
3550B(config-if)#switchport mode trunk
3550B(config-if)#switchport trunk allowed vlan remove 3,8
```

Review the results of the **show interface FastEthernet 0/10 trunk** command in Example 4-20 issued on 3550A. These results show that the trunk is up and running as a dot1q trunk. VLAN_26 has also been removed from the allowed list.

Example 4-20 *The* **show interface FastEthernet 0/10 trunk** *Command Output*

```
3550A#show interface FastEthernet 0/10 trunk
Port      Mode          Encapsulation  Status        Native vlan
Fa0/10    on            802.1q         trunking      1

Port      Vlans allowed on trunk
Fa0/10    1-25,27-1005

Port      Vlans allowed and active in management domain
Fa0/10    1,10-11

Port      Vlans in spanning tree forwarding state and not pruned
Fa0/10    1,10-11
```

Case Study 4-6: Configuring Layer 3 EtherChannels

Configuring a Layer 3 EtherChannel is more complicated than creating a Layer 2 EtherChannel. To configure a Layer 3 EtherChannel, you must create the port-channel logical interface and then put the Ethernet interfaces into the port-channel. Follow these steps to configure a Layer 3 EtherChannel:

Step 1   Create port-channel logical interfaces.

Step 2   Configure the physical interfaces.

The next sections describe both steps.

Step 1: Create Port-Channel Logical Interfaces

Use the following commands to create the port-channel:

```
3550A(config)#interface port-channel port-channel-number
3550A(config-if)#no switchport
3550A(config-if)#ip address ip-address netmask
3550A(config-if)#end
```

The **no switchport** command lets you configure a Layer 3 interface instead of a Layer 2 interface. To remove a port-channel interface, use the following command:

```
3550A(config)#no interface port-channel port-channel-number
```

Step 2: Configure the Physical Interfaces

Configuring an interface for participation in a Layer 3 EtherChannel is much the same as configuring a Layer 2 EtherChannel. Follow these steps to add the interface to the port-channel:

```
3550A(config)#interface interface-id
3550A(config-if)#no switchport
3550A(config-if)#no ip address
3550A(config-if)#channel-group channel-group-number mode {auto [non-silent] I desirable
  [non-silent] I on}
3550A(config-if)#end
```

Use the following command to remove an interface from a Layer 3 EtherChannel:

```
3550A(config-if)#no channel-group
```

In this case study, you change the Layer 2 EtherChannel that you created in Case Study 4-4 into a Layer 3 EtherChannel.

Example 4-21 shows you the configuration that is necessary to create the channel and provides a few **show** commands from 3550A to verify operation.

Example 4-21 *Creation of a Layer 3 EtherChannel*

```
Configuration of 3550A
3550A(config)#interface Port-channel 1
3550A(config-if)#no switchport
3550A(config-if)#ip address 192.168.1.1 255.255.255.0
3550A(config-if)#exit
3550A(config)#interface FastEthernet0/10
```

continues

Example 4-21 *Creation of a Layer 3 EtherChannel (Continued)*

```
3550A(config-if)#no switchport
3550A(config-if)#no ip address
3550A(config-if)#channel-group 1 mode desirable
3550A(config-if)#exit
3550A(config)#interface FastEthernet0/11
3550A(config-if)#no switchport
3550A(config-if)#no ip address
3550A(config-if)#channel-group 1 mode desirable

Configuration of 3550B
3550B(config)#interface Port-channel 1
3550B(config-if)#no switchport
3550B(config-if)#ip address 192.168.1.2 255.255.255.0
3550B(config-if)#exit
3550B(config)#interface FastEthernet0/10
3550B(config-if)#no switchport
3550B(config-if)#no ip address
3550B(config-if)#channel-group 1 mode desirable
3550B(config-if)#exit
3550B(config)#interface FastEthernet0/11
3550B(config-if)#no switchport
3550B(config-if)#no ip address
3550B(config-if)#channel-group 1 mode desirable
```

An examination of Example 4-22 shows that your EtherChannel is now a Layer 3 EtherChannel.

Example 4-22 *The* **show etherchannel 1 summary** *Command Output*

```
3550A#show etherchannel 1 summary
Flags:  D - down         P - in port-channel
        I - stand-alone  s - suspended
        R - Layer3       S - Layer2
        U - port-channel in use
Group Port-channel  Ports
-----+------------+--------------------------------------------------------
1    Po1(RU)     Fa/10(P)   Fa0/11(P)
```

Case Study 4-7: EtherChannel Load Balancing

Use the following commands to configure EtherChannel load balancing:

```
3550A(config)#port-channel load-balance {dst-mac | src-mac}
3550A(config)#end
```

Remember that **src-mac** is the default for the command. You can return EtherChannel load balancing to the default configuration by using the following command:

```
3550A(config)#no port-channel load-balance
```

In this case study, you configure EtherChannel load balancing by using the destination-based forwarding method on 3550A and 3550B. Example 4-23 shows you the configuration that is necessary to complete this case study.

Example 4-23 *Configuring EtherChannel Load Balancing*

```
Configuration items for 3550A:
3550A(config)#port-channel load-balance dst-mac

Configuration items for 3550B:
3550B(config)#port-channel load-balance dst-mac
```

Many different **show** commands are available to you regarding EtherChannels and PAgP. This section describes a few of the commands that you can use. For a complete listing of these commands, see "Configuring EtherChannels" in the appropriate *Software Configuration Guide* for your software version. The following are some of the **show** commands that are available to you.

To display EtherChannel information in a brief, detailed, and one-line summary form, use the following command. Note that you can also use this command to display the load balance or frame-distribution scheme, port, and port-channel information:

```
3550A#show etherchannel [channel-group-number] {brief I detail I load-balance I port I
  port-channel I summary}
```

Use the following command to display PAgP information, such as traffic information, the internal PAgP configuration, and neighbor information:

```
3550A#show pagp [channel-group-number] {counters I internal I neighbor}
```

Use the following command to clear the PAgP channel-group information and traffic filters:

```
3550A#clear pagp {channel-group-number I counters}
```

Case Study 4-8: Configuring a Routed Port

In this case study, you configure an interface on 3550B as a routed port, send all DHCP requests to 10.1.1.100, and configure OSPF as your routing protocol to talk to R3 and R8. Example 4-24 shows the results of your configuration efforts.

Example 4-24 *Routed Ports*

```
Configuration items on 3550B:
3550B(config)#interface FastEthernet 0/4
3550B(config-if)#description Layer 3 interface
3550B(config-if)#no switchport
3550B(config-if)#ip address 192.168.1.2 255.255.255.0
3550B(config-if)#ip helper-address 10.1.1.100
3550B(config-if)#no shutdown
```

continues

Example 4-24 *Routed Ports (Continued)*

```
3550B(config-if)#exit
3550B(config)#ip subnet-zero
3550B(config)#ip classless
3550B(config)#ip routing
3550B(config)#router ospf 234
3550B(config[router)#network 192.168.1.0 0.0.0.255 area 0
3550B(config[router)#network 192.168.3.0 0.0.0.255 area 0
3550B(config[router)#network 192.168.8.0 0.0.0.255 area 0

Configuration items for R3:
R3(config)#router ospf 234
R3(config-if)#network 192.168.1.0 0.0.0.255 area0
R3(config-if)#network 192.168.3.0 0.0.0.255 area0
R3(config-if)#network 192.168.8.0 0.0.0.255 area0

Configuration items for R8:
R8(config)#router ospf 234
R8(config-if)#network 192.168.1.0 0.0.0.255 area 0
R8(config-if)#network 192.168.3.0 0.0.0.255 area0
R8(config-if)#network 192.168.8.0 0.0.0.255 area 8
```

As you can see from the output of Example 4-25, you have a routed interface and you have OSPF up and running under process ID 234.

Example 4-25 *The* **show ip protocols** *Command Output*

```
Switch# show ip protocols
<output truncated>
Routing Protocol is "ospf 234"
  Invalid after 0 seconds, hold down 0, flushed after 0
  Outgoing update filter list for all interfaces is
  Incoming update filter list for all interfaces is
  Redistributing: ospf 234
  Maximum path: 4
  Routing for Networks:
    192.168.1.0/24 Area 0
    192.168.3.0/24 Area 0
    192.168.8.0/24 Area 0
  Routing Information Sources:
    Gateway         Distance      Last Update
  Distance: (default is 110)
```

Case Study 4-9: Configuring SPAN

Your last configuration item is to enable the FastEthernet 0/24 interface on the 3550B switch to monitor VLAN 8 through SPAN, as outlined in Figure 4-2.

Figure 4-2   *SPAN Topology*

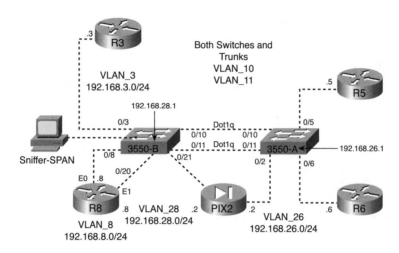

Example 4-26 illustrates the configuration items on the 3550B switch that you need to accomplish this. You can see from the output that you are now monitoring VLAN_8 traffic and sending it to FastEthernet 0/24.

Example 4-26 *SPAN Configuration*

```
Configuration items on 3550B:
3550B(config)#no monitor session 1
3550B(config)#monitor session 1 source vlan 8
3550B(config)#monitor session 1 destination interface fastethernet0/24

3550B#show monitor session 1
Session 1
---------
Source Ports:
    RX Only:      None
    TX Only:      None
    Both:         None
Source VLANs:
    RX Only:      None
    TX Only:      None
    Both:         8
Destination Ports: Fa0/24
    Encapsulation: Native
Filter VLANs:     None
```

Summary

This chapter has reviewed the Catalyst 3550 switch. The 3550 is a multifunction LAN switch that is capable of meeting most of your networking requirements. This chapter began by examining the many items that you can configure on a 3550, including a host name, VLANs, and a spanning tree. The chapter covered the configuration of the many types of interfaces that are available to you, such as the access port, trunk port, and routed port. You also reviewed optional items that are available to you. You finished the chapter with a look at configuring SPAN for traffic monitoring.

Review Questions

1 What is the purpose of the VLAN Trunking Protocol?

2 How are nonroutable protocols affected by VLANs?

3 How does the Catalyst 3550 switch, with Layer 3 software installed, deal with packets that are for an unknown destination?

4 Why would you configure an interface as a trunk?

5 Why would you see an untagged packet on a switch that is configured with VLANs?

6 Why would you use PAgP?

7 What is a routed port?

8 What is a designated port?

9 What can prevent an alternate or root port from becoming the designated port after a unidirectional link failure?

10 What can prevent packets with an unknown destination MAC address from being flooded to every port on a switch?

FAQs

Q — *I want to use extended VLANs. How do I enable this on a 3550 switch?*

A — Extended VLANS, those above 1005, are only supported when you are using the VTP transparent mode.

Q — *I want to be able to support Token Ring and FDDI with a 3550. Is this possible?*

A — Although the 3550 does not support Token Ring or FDDI VLANs, if you are running VTP version 2, the 3550 can pass any Token Ring and FDDI VLAN information that it receives.

Q — *What happens to a physical interface if I assign an IP address to it and disable the switchport?*

A — When you do this, you turn the Layer 2 interface, the switchport, into a Layer 3 interface.

Q — *I want to run a routing protocol on my 3550 switch. What routing protocols are supported?*

A — The 3550 switch supports RIP, OSPF, IGRP, and EIGRP.

Q — *I do not want to configure a VLAN on each access port that I have in my network. What can I do?*

A — The 3550 switch supports the concept of a dynamic access port. This is a port that learns what VLAN it is on by examining incoming packets. In the case of the 3550 switch, a VLAN Membership Policy Server (VMPS) is required. Currently, the VMPS functionality is provided by the Catalyst 6000 series switches.

Q — *I have a trunk in my network that is beginning to become overutilized. What can I do with a 3550 to alleviate this problem?*

A — You can create an EtherChannel to provide high-bandwidth links to network devices. You can group up to eight Fast Ethernet ports together to obtain 800 Mbps of bandwidth or group eight Gigabit Ethernet ports together to obtain 8 Gbps of bandwidth.

Q — *Whenever I look for the root switch in my network, it always seems to be a switch that does not appear to be the best possible choice. How can I fix this?*

A — The 3550 switch offers a command, spanning-tree vlan *vlan-id* root, which can set a switch's priority in such a fashion that it becomes the root switch. Note that this does not work if another switch in your network has a priority of 1.

Q — *I want to add a second link from an access switch to the core switch. Will I expose my network to spanning-tree loops?*

A — Redundancy in links usually causes one link to be placed in the blocked mode to prevent any loops.

This chapter includes the following topics:

- Frame Relay overview
- Frame Relay devices
- Frame Relay topologies
- Frame Relay virtual circuits
- Frame Relay signaling
- Network-to-network interface
- User-network interface
- Congestion-control mechanisms
- The Local Management Interface
- Configuring Frame Relay
- Creating a broadcast queue for an interface
- Transparent bridging and Frame Relay
- Configuring a backup interface for a subinterface
- TCP/IP header compression
- Troubleshooting Frame Relay connectivity

CHAPTER 5

Frame Relay Connectivity

In this chapter, you look at the configuration of Frame Relay. Frame Relay provides the core WAN technology that you use in your pursuit of the CCIE Security certification. You need to understand the configuration tasks that are necessary to complete many requirements and to troubleshoot your implementation.

Frame Relay Overview

Frame Relay is an industry-standard, switched data link layer protocol that is capable of handling multiple virtual circuits (VCs) using High-Level Data Link Control (HDLC) encapsulation between Frame Relay–capable devices. Figure 5-1 illustrates an ANSI T1.618 Frame Relay frame.

Figure 5-1   *The Frame Relay Format*

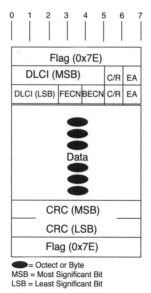

The nine fields of the Frame Relay frame are as follows:

- **Flag**—Used to identify the beginning and end of the frame.

- **Data-Link Connection Identifier (DLCI)**—Identifies the path through the network to a specific destination.

- **Command/Response (C/R)**—Not generally used.

- **Extended Address (EA)**—Identifies whether the header octet is followed by another header octet. A value of 0 means that another octet follows, and 1 identifies the last octet.

- **Forward-Explicit Congestion Notification (FECN)**—Used to inform the connected devices of congestion in the network.

- **Backward-Explicit Congestion Notification (BECN)**—Used to inform the connected devices of congestion in the network.

- **Discard Eligibility (DE)**—Used to identify a packet that is eligible for discard during congestion.

- **Data**—Can be used to carry any type of information.

- **Cyclic redundancy check (CRC)**—Used to detect transmission errors and cover the header and data fields.

The 10-bit DLCI value is a logical number in the range of 16 to 1007 that is used to identify the logical connection. Permanent virtual circuits (PVCs) are multiplexed into the physical circuit. The DLCI only has significance between your customer premises equipment (CPE) and your provider's Frame Relay switch. Because DLCI is used to differentiate between different conversations on the same physical circuit, you can think of it as the heart of the Frame Relay header. Without it, your Frame Relay access device (FRAD) would not be able to identify the different data streams that are passing through it.

Frame Relay does not need to provide the explicit, per-VC flow control that developers implemented in X.25. In its place, Frame Relay uses a simple congestion notification mechanism that allows a network to inform a FRAD that the network resources are close to a congested state. This notification can also be used to alert the higher-layer protocols that flow control might be needed.

By using Frame Relay, you can reduce your network complexity and simplify your network architecture by supporting the three-tiered network model of having separate core, distribution, and access layers. Frame Relay supports many different topologies for the placement of your network equipment, including full, partial, and hybrid meshing.

Frame Relay Devices

All Frame Relay devices that are capable of attaching to a Frame Relay WAN fall into the following two general categories:

- Data terminal equipment (DTE)
- Data circuit-terminating equipment (DCE)

DTEs are commonly the terminating equipment for a specific network that communicates directly to an end user or network. DTEs are typically located on the premises of the customer, usually close to the demarcation (demarc) point of the service provider, and are usually owned and operated by the customer.

DCEs provide you with the clocking and switching services in a Frame Relay network. The DCE converts your user data from your DTE into an acceptable form for the WAN service facility. DCEs are usually the carrier-owned internetworking devices that have the responsibility for transmitting data in the WAN. Figure 5-2 illustrates the relationship between a DCE and DTE.

Figure 5-2 *DCE-to-DTE Relationship*

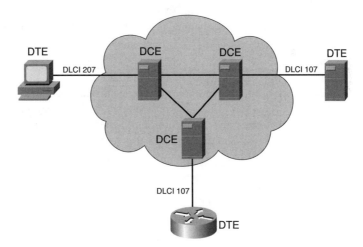

While the connection between the DTE device and the DCE device exists as a physical layer component, it also contains a link layer component. The physical component defines the specifications that are used to connect the devices. The link layer component specifies how the connection is established between the DTE device and the DCE device.

The DTE/DCE interface is typically used to identify the boundary of responsibility, or who has management control of the area, for the traffic that is passing between you and your service provider. The physical standards that are used to specify the DTE/DCE interface include EIA/TIA-232, X.21, EIA/TIA-449, V.24, V.35, and HSSI.

Frame Relay Topologies

One of the first items that you should consider when designing a Frame Relay network, or any type of regional WAN, is how the connectivity is to be laid out. When considering Frame Relay for a WAN media, you can choose from the following three basic design approaches:

- **Star topology**—A topology where end points on a network are connected to a common central switch by point-to-point links.

- **Fully meshed topology**—A topology where devices are organized in a mesh topology, with each network node having either a physical circuit or a virtual circuit that connects it to every other network node.

- **Partially meshed topology**—A topology where devices are organized in a mesh topology, with some network nodes organized in a full mesh but others that are connected only to one or two other nodes in a network. This topology can also be referred to as a hybrid topology.

Each of these topologies has its own characteristics to consider for your overall design.

Star Topologies

The star topology, one of the most popular topologies in use today, features a single internet-working hub, usually the home office, that provides access from leaf internetworks, usually remote offices, into the backbone while still providing access to each other through the core router. Figure 5-3 illustrates a Frame Relay star topology.

Figure 5-3   *Frame Relay Star Topology*

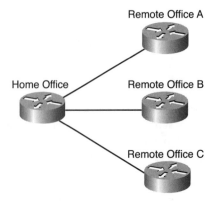

The star topology offers many advantages, such as simplified management and minimized tariff costs, but it has some major drawbacks. The most obvious drawback to this topology that you should see after examining Figure 5-3 is the catastrophic results that can happen in the event that the core router fails. This device represents a single point of failure in an otherwise stable network design. The next shortcoming is that the core router limits overall performance for access to backbone resources because it is the single pipe through which all traffic must pass. The third drawback to this design is the lack of scalability.

Fully Meshed Topologies

A fully meshed topology means that each routing node on the periphery of a given packet-switching network has a direct path to every other node on the cloud. Figure 5-4 illustrates this kind of arrangement.

Figure 5-4   *Fully Meshed Topology*

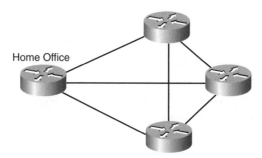

One of the major reasons for deploying a fully meshed topology is the requirement of a high level of redundancy. Although a fully meshed topology can support all major network protocols, it is not a likely solution for deployment in a large Frame Relay cloud. One reason for this is the amount of virtual circuits that you are required to configure and maintain to provide this type of connectivity. When you are required to have one virtual circuit for every connection between routers, problems can also arise due to the large number of packet/broadcast replications required, and the configuration complexity for routers in the absence of multicast support in nonbroadcast environments.

Partially Meshed Topologies

The partially meshed topology combines fully meshed and star topology approaches into a partially meshed environment, giving you an improvement in fault tolerance without the performance and management problems that are associated with a fully meshed approach.

A partially meshed topology allows you to reduce the number of FRADs within a region that has direct connections to all other nodes in that region. All nodes in this environment do not require direct connectivity to all other nodes in the cloud. For a nonmeshed node to communicate with another nonmeshed node, the first node can send its traffic through one of the collection point routers that are meshed. Figure 5-5 illustrates such a situation.

Figure 5-5   *Partially Meshed Topology*

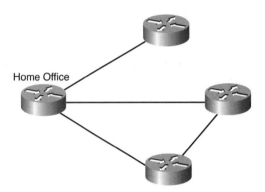

Although a partially meshed topology can take one of many different forms, this topology is generally considered to provide the best balance for Frame Relay topologies in terms of the number of virtual circuits, redundancy, and performance.

Frame Relay Subinterfaces

To provide support of a partially meshed Frame Relay network, you should make use of the subinterface capabilities that are included in Cisco IOS Software. Most protocols in use today need to believe that they have transitivity on a logical network; they assume that if station A can talk to station B, and station B can talk to station C, then station A should be able to directly talk to station C. While this concept of transitivity is mostly true on LANs, it is not true on a Frame Relay network unless station A is also directly connected to station C.

One other item that certain protocols can have difficulty with on partially meshed networks such as RIP, AppleTalk, and transparent bridging, has to do with split horizon. *Split horizon* states that when a packet is received on an interface, it cannot be sent out of the same interface, even if it is received and transmitted on different VCs.

Frame Relay uses subinterfaces to overcome the issues that are raised by split horizon by ensuring that a single physical interface is treated as multiple virtual interfaces. A virtual interface is seen as being separate from every other virtual interface, enabling packets that are received on one virtual interface to be forwarded out another virtual interface, even if the virtual interfaces are configured on the same physical interface.

Subinterfaces also address the limitations of Frame Relay networks by providing you with a way to subdivide your partially meshed Frame Relay network into a number of smaller, fully meshed—or point-to-point—subnetworks. You assign each subnetwork its own network number to make it appear to protocols as if these networks are reachable through a separate interface. If you have transparent bridging configured in your networking environment, each subinterface is viewed as a separate bridge port.

NOTE   A point-to-point subinterface can be implemented as an unnumbered interface when used with IP, reducing the addressing burden that might otherwise result.

You have two choices of subinterface types: the point-to-point subinterface or the multipoint subinterface, neither of which is the default. Use the following command to configure a subinterface for use on a Frame Relay network:

```
R2(config-if)#interface type number.subinterface-number {multipoint | point-to-point}
```

NOTE   If you have configured a subinterface and later decide to change from a multipoint interface to a point-to-point interface, you might need to remove the configurations from the main interface and from the subinterfaces before changing the interface type. You might also have to reload the router before the changes take effect.

Frame Relay Virtual Circuits

One reason for the continued popularity of Frame Relay is its capability to logically create multiple connection-oriented data link layer communication paths between two devices across a single physical interface. These VC provide a bidirectional communications path that can exist between a single pair of equipment, commonly referred to as a *point-to-point connection*, or between multiple pairs of equipment, also known as a *partial mesh* or *full mesh*. Each of these VCs is identified by a locally unique DLCI. The DLCI value is usually assigned by your service provider.

Frame Relay DLCIs only have local significance to the DTE/DCE pair that it is configured on, which means that their values need only be unique in the LAN. Because of this, any Frame Relay DLCIs can be reused throughout the WAN.

Virtual circuits have the added benefit of providing a reduction in the amount of equipment that is required to support the same amount of circuits in a leased-line design. Frame Relay can do this by multiplexing virtual circuits across a physical circuit, which also reduces the complexity of the WAN infrastructure.

VCs can be mapped across any service provider's Frame Relay network, without regard to the amount of hops that the connection crosses. This means that your VC is not limited to three devices—DTE to DCE to DTE—but can have any number of devices between the two DTEs.

VCs can be divided into two categories, switched virtual circuits (SVCs) or permanent virtual circuits (PVCs). The following subsections describe both in more detail.

Switched Virtual Circuits

The SVC provides you with a technology that can automatically create temporary connections between DTE devices in the Frame Relay network for use in on-demand situations, such as those requiring sporadic data transfer. The communication component of an SVC consists of the following four operational states:

- **Call setup**—Indicates that the establishment of the SVC between two Frame Relay DTE devices is currently being negotiated

- **Data transfer**—Indicates that data is being transmitted between DTE devices over an SVC

- **Idle**—Indicates that the SVC between DTE devices is still active, but no data is currently being transferred

- **Call termination**—Indicates that the SVC between DTE devices is being terminated

When an SVC remains in an idle state for a defined period of time, the SVC can be torn down and the call terminated. After termination of an SVC is complete, if additional data needs to be transmitted between the DTE devices, a new SVC is established. Cisco devices use the same signaling protocols that are used in an Integrated Services Digital Network (ISDN) to establish, maintain, and terminate SVCs.

You can use both the SVC and the PVC on the same router and even the same site. This gives you an ability to provide any-to-any communication to your end users without the cost or setup of any-to-any PVCs.

You can also specify quality of service (QoS) parameters on an SVC on a call-by-call basis to request network resources.

To use an SVC in your network, you must have the following services:

- SVCs must be supported by your service provider's switching equipment.

- A leased line or dedicated line must exist between your DTE and your service provider's local Frame Relay switch.

To run SVCs in your environment, you are required to set up the data link layer to run the ITU-T Q.922 Link Access Procedures to Frame (LAPF) mode bearer services before your device can signal for an SVC. When you enable SVC support on your FRAD, and both the line and line protocol are in the up state, Layer 2 configures itself automatically. When the first demand for an SVC occurs, the Q.933 signaling sequence becomes active. Once your FRAD has finished the setup of the SVC, data transfer begins.

The Q.922 LAPF is used to provide a reliable link layer for Q.933 to operate across. Q.933 sends all call control information over DLCI 0, the same DLCI number that is used for the management protocols specified in ANSI T1.617 Annex D or Q.933 Annex A.

You can only enable SVC operation at the interface level. Once you do so, SVC operation is enabled on any subinterfaces under that interface that you configure. One signaling channel, DLCI 0, also configured on the interface level, is used to control all SVCs.

Permanent Virtual Circuits

The PVC, unlike the SVC, establishes a permanent connection between your DTE devices. This type of circuit is typically used for frequent and consistent data transfers across the Frame Relay network. Because PVC establishment does not require a call setup or termination, it is always established. PVCs only have two operational states, as follows:

- **Data transfer mode**—Indicates that data is currently being transmitted between the DTE devices over the PVC.

- **Idle**—Indicates that the connection between DTE devices is active, but no data is transferred between DTE devices.

    Because there is no call setup or termination with a PVC connection, it is not terminated under any circumstances when in an idle state, unlike the SVC idle state.

Once the PVC is established, your DTE devices can transfer data whenever they are ready, without the delay that is associated with the establishment of an SVC.

Frame Relay Signaling

Frame Relay was not designed to include a built-in mechanism to address network outages; instead, the Local Management Interface (LMI) signaling protocol was developed to exchange keepalives and to pass administrative information, such as addition, deletion, or failure of PVCs. These messages are only exchanged between the DTE/DCE pair and are never transmitted across the network in-band of the PVC.

Within Cisco IOS Software, you can assign the LMI type by using a static assignment or by using a feature called LMI autosense. A statically defined LMI type comes in three different standards:

- **ansi**—The Annex D standard defined by the American National Standards Institute (ANSI) Standard T1.617

- **q.933**—The ITU-T Q.933 Annex A standard

- **cisco**—The original LMI type defined by the Gang of Four: Cisco, Digital Equipment Corporation, Northern Telecom, and StrataCom

The term LMI refers to a specific signaling protocol. However, all three of the definable LMI types that are available in IOS are also generally referred to as LMI. Use care when deciding which type you are going to use because, although each of the three LMI types is designed to support the same basic functionality, enough differences exist between them that the interfaces on your DTE/DCE pair must run the same LMI type or you will experience unpredictable results.

One of the most important functions that each of these LMI types must support is a basic handshake mechanism. This mechanism consists of an exchange of status query frames and response status frames. Your FRAD is responsible for starting this exchange by sending inquiries to the network before the network can send any signaling protocol messages to your FRAD.

Each status query frame that is sent by your FRAD contains a sequence number and a request for either a short status frame or a long status frame. Short status frames contain only a sequence number and are normally used as a form of keepalive between the DTE and DCE, often referred to as the LMI keepalive. Long status messages contain event notifications such as the addition, deletion, failure, or modification of one or more PVCs. The long status message also contains a sequence number and the status and relevant information on the PVCs that are currently configured on the port.

By default, the FRAD sends LMI status messages every 10 seconds to the WAN. A full status request is sent as every sixth LMI status query, to which the WAN responds with a long status message, including any new events that have occurred since the last long status message.

LMI also offers a number of extensions for managing complex internetworks. Some of the extensions used by Frame Relay are as follows:

* **Global addressing**—An extension that gives the Frame Relay DLCI values global rather than local significance by making DLCI values the DTE address that remains unique in the Frame Relay WAN

* **Virtual circuit status messages**—Provides communication and synchronization between Frame Relay DTE and DCE devices to periodically report on the status of PVCs, which prevents data from being sent into black holes (that is, over PVCs that no longer exist)

* **Multicasting**—An extension that allows multicast groups to be assigned to save bandwidth by allowing routing updates and address-resolution messages to be sent only to specific groups of routers

LMI Frame Format

Cisco Frame Relay frames conform to the LMI specifications, as shown in Figure 5-6.

Figure 5-6   *Nine Fields of the Frame Relay LMI Frame*

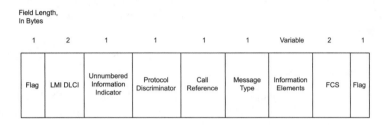

The nine fields of the Frame Relay LMI frame are as follows:

- **Flag**—Delimits the beginning and end of the frame.

- **LMI DLCI**—Identifies the frame as an LMI frame instead of a basic Frame Relay frame.

- **Unnumbered Information Indicator**—Sets the poll/final bit to 0.

- **Protocol Discriminator**—Always contains a value that is used to identify the frame as an LMI frame.

- **Call Reference**—Always contains 0s and is not used at this time.

- **Message Type**—Labels the frame as one of the following message types:

  - **Status-inquiry Message**—Allows a user's device to inquire about the status of the network.

  - **Status Message**—Responds to status-inquiry messages, including keepalives and PVC status messages.

- **Information Elements**—Contains a variable number of individual information elements (IEs). IEs consist of the following fields:

  - **IE Identifier**—Uniquely identifies the IE.

  - **IE Length**—Indicates the length of the IE.

- **Information Elements**—Contains 1 or more bytes of encapsulated upper-layer data.

- **Frame Check Sequence (FCS)**—Ensures the integrity of transmitted data.

LMI Timers

When working with Frame Relay technology, there are several configurable timers and keepalives that you can tune. Each of these items is discussed in its individual section.

You have the option of tuning five configurable parameters to define how signaling information is exchanged between the DTE and DCE. Two of these parameters define how often a FRAD sends a short- and long-status query, while the other three define when an alarm is generated by the WAN. These parameters are as follows:

- **T391**—Used to define the time interval, in seconds, between short-status queries. The default value is 10 seconds.

- **N391**—Used to define the multiplier that is used to calculate the frequency of long-status queries. The default value is 6, resulting in a long-status query being sent every 60 seconds, assuming that T391 is also set to its default value of 10.

- **T392**—Used to define the time interval, in seconds, between expected status queries. The default value is 15 seconds but should be greater then the T391 value defined on the FRAD. If the T392 timer expires and a status query frame has not been received, a timeout is counted.

- **N392**—Used to define the number of timeouts, out of N393 expected queries, that causes an alarm to be generated.

- **N393**—Used to define the number of expected queries that define a window for alarm declaration.

Tuning LMI Timers

You can use one or all of the commands described in this section to fine-tune the operation of the LMI polling and timer intervals on the LMI DTE and DCE devices. You should only change any of these timers when required by your service provider or, in the case that you are your own service provider, when you completely understand the ramifications that changing these times can cause in your network.

Use the following command to set the DCE and Network-to-Network Interface (NNI) error threshold:

```
R2(config-if)#frame-relay lmi-n392dce threshold
```

Use the following command to set the DCE and NNI monitored events count:

```
R2(config-if)#frame-relay lmi-n393dce events
```

Use the following command to set the polling verification timer on a DCE or NNI interface:

```
R2(config-if)#frame-relay lmi-n392dce seconds
```

Use the following command to set a full status polling interval on a DTE or NNI interface:

```
R2(config-if)#frame-relay lmi-n391dte keep-exchanges
```

Use the following command to set the DTE or NNI error threshold:

```
R2(config-if)#frame-relay lmi-n392dte threshold
```

Use the following command to set the DTE and NNI monitored event counts:

```
R2(config-if)#frame-relay lmi-n393dte events
```

LMI Autosense

Cisco FRADs running Cisco IOS Software version 11.2 and later provide support for the LMI autosense feature. LMI autosense gives you the ability to "sense" the LMI sent by one device that has the LMI type configured, usually on your service providers' WAN equipment, preventing possible misconfiguration. LMI autosense is automatically enabled in the following situations:

- The router is powered up or the interface changes state to up.
- The line protocol is down but the line is up.
- The interface is a Frame Relay DTE.
- The LMI type is not explicitly configured on the interface.

When LMI autosense is active, the FRAD sends a full status request in all three LMI message formats to the WAN equipment. The FRAD sends the packets in the following sequence: ANSI, ITU, and finally cisco. LMI information is passed on DLCI 0 for both the Cisco LMI and Q.933a LMI types. LMI information is passed on DLCI 1023 for the ANSI LMI type. LMI autosense can work because the Frame Relay code in IOS can listen to both DLCI 1023 and 0 at the same time.

When the three messages reach the switch, one or more of them elicits a reply, sent back in the form of a status message. Your FRAD then decodes the format of the reply to configure the LMI type of the interface automatically. Accommodating intelligent switches that can support multiple LMI types and send more than one reply is handled by the FRAD configuring itself using the last LMI type received. Now, if you look back at the sequence in which the LMI messages are sent, the order should make more sense.

If LMI autosense fails to detect the correct LMI type, a retry interval is initiated. For every N391 time interval, which has a 60 second default, LMI autosense retries its automatic LMI configuration sequence.

Network-to-Network Interface

One item of concern for a service provider is the possibility that a Frame Relay network can cross between two networks that might not be Cisco equipment. Because each vendor supports Frame Relay standards, these vendors are also given the option of providing customizations to differentiate their product from another vendor's product.

To facilitate intervendor communication, the Network-to-Network Interface (NNI) port was defined as a bidirectional protocol to allow configuration, administration, and control information to be communicated between two networks. NNI consists of two independent unidirectional signaling protocols, one from each network, to provide bidirectional communications.

NNI supports status exchanges between the two networks, much like the exchanges between a DTE/DCE pair. The biggest difference between NNI communications and DTE/DCE pair communications is that both sides are capable of initiating a query message exchange, and both sides can respond with either a short- or long-status message.

User-Network Interface

The User-Network Interface (UNI) port defines a unidirectional protocol that allows your FRAD to request information about all available PVCs on your service provider's Frame Relay equipment. Your FRAD can then use this information to ensure its proper configuration for the transmission or acceptance of any DLCI defined on your service provider's equipment.

Due to the nature of the UNI, it is the signaling protocol used between the DTE and the DCE. It does not allow the full configuration, administration, and control between two peer DTE devices.

Congestion-Control Mechanisms

In networking today, congestion is a problem that plagues the WAN environment more than the LAN environment. With the speed of today's LAN networks, up to 10-gigabit speeds on some interfaces, congestion is less of a problem in the LAN environment than it has been in the past. Congestion usually shows up when you attempt to pass 10 GB of information down a 1.5-Mbps Frame Relay T1.

One reason for congestion still being a problem in today's environment is that the developers of WAN protocols must contend with the overhead that is associated with any type of congestion control. When you are paying a premium for limited speed, you don't want a significant amount of management traffic taking resources away from your critical data that the link was originally purchased for. Frame Relay can reduce this network overhead by implementing simple congestion-notification mechanisms rather than explicit, per-virtual-circuit flow control.

Frame Relay networks provide guaranteed throughput to your critical traffic as long as your data rate falls below the established committed information rate (CIR). If your data rate exceeds the established CIR, the network devices can set the discard eligibility (DE) bit on the excess frames. The DE bit is covered in more detail later in "Frame Relay Discard Eligibility."

Unfortunately, CIR is not an adaptable setting that can provide flexibility when your traffic rates vary. Service providers often offer their customers the option of bursting above CIR for some defined period of time to handle the bursty nature of LAN traffic crossing a serial interface. Committed burst (Bc) size and excess burst (Be) size define the amount of traffic that you can burst above your CIR.

Bc defines the maximum amount of bursty traffic under normal conditions, and Be defines the maximum amount of bursty traffic in excess of Bc that the Frame Relay attempts to transfer over a set period of time. If the number of frames entering the Frame Relay network is greater than Bc+Be and the DE bit is set to 1, these frames are discarded.

NOTE   Be is used to determine the maximum data rate (MaxR) for the Frame Relay circuit. MaxR is measured in bits per second and uses the following formula:

$$MaxR = [(Bc + Be) / Bc] \times CIR$$

For example: If Bc = 64,000, Be = 64,000, and CIR = 64 kbps, then $[(64,000 + 64,000) / 64,000] \times 64,000 = 128$ kbps as the MaxR.

If congestion is encountered in the Frame Relay network, you can use the following two different congestion-notification mechanisms to inform the devices of the congestion:

- Forward-explicit congestion notification (FECN)

- Backward-explicit congestion notification (BECN)

FECN and BECN each use a single bit in the Frame Relay frame header for control of congestion. Frame Relay also uses another bit in the header, the DE bit, to mark traffic that can be discarded in the event of congestion.

The FECN bit is located in the Address field of the Frame Relay header. The FECN mechanism, used when a DTE device sends Frame Relay frames into the network, is set to 1 by the DCE when congestion is present. After the frames reach the destination DTE device, the Address field (with the FECN bit set) can be examined. If the bit is set to 1, this indicates that the frame experienced congestion along its path from source DTE to destination DTE. This information can then be sent to a higher-layer protocol for processing. Depending on the implementation of the higher-layer protocol, FECN can be used to initiate some type of flow control or the indication can be ignored.

The BECN bit is located in the Address field of the Frame Relay header. The value of the BECN is set to 1 by the DCE device for frames that are traveling in the opposite direction of frames with their FECN bit set. This information tells the receiving DTE device that this particular path through the network is currently experiencing congestion. This information can then be sent to a higher-layer protocol for processing as well as for automatically reducing the amount of outbound traffic that is sent by the Frame Relay device. Depending on the implementation, this information can be used to initiate some type of flow control or it can be ignored.

As a quick review, a set FECN bit tells you that a frame encountered congestion, whereas a set BECN bit is used to notify the sender of congestion conditions on the circuit. The BECN frame might have encountered congestion of its own.

Now that you have a clearer understanding of the use of the FECN and BECN bits, you might be wondering how the Frame Relay device can control congestion. One of the functions of the DE bit, discussed in further detail in the next section, is to provide this control.

Frame Relay Discard Eligibility

Just like traffic that transverses your LAN, certain traffic crossing your WAN requires a higher priority than other traffic. The Frame Relay DE bit is designed to be used for this purpose. When the DE bit is set to 1 by a DTE device, it indicates to the network that this is a frame of lower priority that is eligible for discard. Upon notification of congestion, the DCE begins to discard frames that have the DE bit set before discarding those that do not.

You can create DE lists to identify the characteristics of packets that you want to be eligible for discarding, and you can specify DE groups to identify the DLCI that is affected.

Use the following command to define a DE list to specify the packets that can be dropped when the Frame Relay switch is congested:

```
R2(config)#frame-relay de-list list-number {protocol protocol | interface typenumber}
    characteristic
```

You can base your DE lists on the protocol or the interface, and on characteristics such as fragmentation of the packet, a specific TCP or User Datagram Protocol (UDP) port, an ACL number, or a packet size.

Use the following command to define a DE group, specifying the DE list and DLCI affected:

```
R2(config-if)#frame-relay de-group group-number dlci
```

DLCI Priority Levels

You can use a priority level with a DLCI to allow you to separate different types of traffic and to provide a traffic management tool for congestion problems caused by following situations:

- Mixing batch and interactive traffic over the same DLCI

- Traffic from sites with high-speed access being queued at destination sites with lower-speed access

Before you can configure DLCI priority levels, you need to complete the following tasks:

Step 1   Define a global priority list.

Step 2   Enable Frame Relay encapsulation.

Step 3   Define dynamic or static address mapping.

Step 4   Define each of the DLCIs to which you intend to apply levels.

Step 5   Configure the LMI type for your circuit.

NOTE	DLCI priority levels give you a mechanism that you can use to define multiple parallel DLCIs for different types of traffic. DLCI priority levels do not assign priority queues within your FRAD; they are independent queues. However, if you were to enable queuing and use the same DLCIs in these queues, your high-priority DLCIs can be put into high-priority queues.

Use the following command to configure DLCI priority levels:

```
R2(config-if)#frame-relay priority-dlci-group group-number high-dlci medium-dlci
   normal-dlci low-dlci
```

You do not have to explicitly specify a DLCI for each of the priority levels; the last DLCI that you specified in the command line is used as the value of the remaining arguments. At a minimum, you must configure the high-priority and the medium-priority DLCIs.

Frame Relay Error Checking

The CRC, used in many applications such as the file systems used in today's popular operating systems, is used by Frame Relay to provide an error-checking mechanism. The CRC works by comparing two calculated values to determine if errors where encountered along the transmission path from source to destination. Frame Relay uses the CRC to reduce the network overhead caused by error-checking mechanisms by leaving extensive error checking up to the higher-layer protocols that you run. Frame Relay can to do this because of the reliability of today's networks.

Frame Relay ForeSight

ForeSight is another type of traffic control software that is used by some Cisco switches. A Cisco Frame Relay switch can extend messages that are generated by ForeSight over a UNI, passing the BESN for VCs. ForeSight gives your Cisco FRADs the ability to process and react to ForeSight messages and adjust their VC-level traffic shaping in a timely manner.

To use ForeSight, you must explicitly configure it on both the Cisco router and the Cisco switch. ForeSight is enabled on a Cisco FRAD when you configure Frame Relay traffic shaping. However, you must use the **frame-relay adaptive-shaping foresight** command in a VC map-class to allow your FRAD to respond to ForeSight. When ForeSight is enabled on the switch, it periodically send out a ForeSight message based on your configured time value. This time interval can range from 40 to 5000 milliseconds.

When a Cisco FRAD receives a ForeSight message indicating that certain DLCIs are experiencing congestion, the Cisco FRAD reacts by activating its traffic-shaping function to slow the output rate. The FRAD reacts in the same manner as if it received a packet with the BECN bit set.

When you enable ForeSight, Frame Relay traffic shaping adapts to ForeSight messages and BECN messages.

For ForeSight to work with your FRAD, the following conditions must exist on your FRAD:

- Frame Relay traffic shaping must be enabled on the interface.

- The traffic shaping for a circuit must be adapted to ForeSight.

- The UNI that is connecting to the router must be Consolidated Link Layer Management (CLLM) enabled, with the proper time interval specified.

When you use the **frame-relay traffic-shaping** command, you automatically enable Frame Relay ForeSight. However, you must issue the **map-class frame-relay** command and the **frame-relay adaptive-shaping foresight** command before your FRAD can react to ForeSight messages and apply the traffic-shaping effect on a specific interface, subinterface, or VC.

Frame Relay Congestion Notification Methods

The main difference between the BECN and ForeSight congestion-notification methods is that BECN requires a user packet to be sent in the direction of the congested DLCI to convey the signal. This makes the BECN notification unreliable because you cannot predict when a user packet will be sent. By using timed messages in ForeSight, you can guarantee that the FRAD receives notification before congestion becomes a problem. Traffic can then be slowed in the direction of the congested DLCI.

Frame Relay End-to-End Keepalives

By using Frame Relay end-to-end keepalives, you can monitor the status of PVCs on a per-PVC basis for network monitoring or backup applications. This is facilitated by the switch's ability, within the local PVC segment, to deduce the status of the remote PVC segment through an NNI and to report this status to your FRAD.

Two separate keepalive systems must be used because a single PVC can have a different upstream path than its downstream path. One system can send out a request and handle any responses to those requests, the send side, while the other system can handle and reply to any requests from the device at the other end of the PVC, the receive side. The send side on one device communicates with the receive side on the other device, and vice versa.

The send side sends a keepalive request and waits for a reply to that request. If a reply is received before the configurable timer expires, a send side Frame Relay end-to-end keepalive is recorded. If a reply is not received before the timer expires, an error event is recorded. A number of the most recently recorded events are examined and, if enough error events are accumulated, the keepalive status of the VC is changed from up to down, or if enough consecutive successful replies are received, the keepalive status of the VC is changed from down to up. The number of events that are examined is referred to as the *event window*. The receive side uses a similar mechanism to set the status of the VC.

You have the following four different modes to choose from when configuring the end-to-end keepalive:

- **Bidirectional**—Both the send and receive sides are enabled. The FRAD's send side sends out and waits for a reply to its keepalive requests from the receive side of the other PVC device. The FRAD's receive side waits for and replies to the keepalive requests from the send side of the FRAD.

- **Request**—Only the send side is enabled, and the FRAD sends out and waits for replies to its keepalive requests.

- **Reply**—Only the receive side is enabled, and the FRAD waits for and replies to keepalive requests.

- **Passive-reply**—The device only responds to keepalive requests, but it does not set any timers or keep track of any events.

The end-to-end keepalive was developed from the LMI protocol and works between peer Cisco communications devices. The major difference is that end-to-end keepalives are communicated over the individual data channels rather than over the signaling channel, as is the case with LMI.

Because the encapsulation of the keepalive packets is proprietary, the feature is only available on Cisco devices running a Cisco IOS Software version that supports the Frame Relay end-to-end keepalive feature.

Keepalives must be enabled on both ends of a VC. If you configure one end as bidirectional, you must configure the other end as bidirectional as well. If you configure one end as request, you must configure the other end as reply or passive-reply. If you configure one end as reply or passive-reply, you must configure the other end as request.

Use the following two commands to configure Frame Relay end-to-end keepalives.

Use the following command to specify a map class for a VC:

```
R2(config)#map-class frame-relay map-class-name
```

Use the following command to specify the end-to-end keepalive mode:

```
R2(config-map-class)#frame-relay end-to-end keepalive mode {bidirectional | request |
    reply | passive-reply}
```

You also have the option of modifying the end-to-end keepalive default parameter values by using any of the following map-class configuration commands.

Use the following command to modify the number of errors required to change the keepalive state from up to down:

```
R2(config-map-class)#frame-relay end-to-end keepalive error-threshold {send | receive}
    count
```

Use the following command to modify the number of recent events to check for errors:

```
R2(config-map-class)#frame-relay end-to-end keepalive event-window {send I receive}
   count
```

Use the following command to modify the number of success events required to change the keepalive state from down to up:

```
R2(config-map-class)#frame-relay end-to-end keepalive success-events {send I receive}
   count
```

Use the following command to modify the timer interval:

```
R2(config-map-class)#frame-relay end-to-end keepalive timer {send I receive} interval
```

Configuring Frame Relay

You will complete the following three case studies in this chapter:

- Case Study 5-1: Configuring Frame Relay

- Case Study 5-2: Configuring Frame Relay SVCs

- Case Study 5-3: Frame Relay Traffic Shaping

In each of these case studies, you concentrate on a specific aspect of Frame Relay. For instance, Case Study 5-1 concentrates on configuring Frame Relay in the same manner that you can experience in your everyday job duties. Case Study 5-2 takes a look into configuring Frame Relay SVCs and some optional configuration items that you might encounter. The final case study takes you through configuring Frame Relay traffic shaping in a Frame Relay environment.

Case Study 5-1: Configuring Frame Relay

The actual configuration of Frame Relay is fairly simple. Frame Relay only requires that you configure the following Steps 1 and 2, assuming that you are using Inverse ARP, to establish a connection and start passing traffic. The remaining steps are optional and can be used to enhance or customize your Frame Relay. The steps are as follows:

Step 1   Enable Frame Relay encapsulation on an interface.

Step 2   Configure dynamic or static address mapping.

Step 3   Configure the LMI.

Step 4   Configure Frame Relay SVCs.

Step 5   Configure Frame Relay traffic shaping.

Step 6   Configure Frame Relay switching.

Step 7   Customize Frame Relay for your network.

Step 8   Monitor and maintain the frame relay connections.

Step 1: Enable Frame Relay Encapsulation

Your first step in configuring Frame Relay is to enable it on the interface that you use for the connection. Use the following commands to enable Frame Relay encapsulation:

```
R2(config)#interface type number
R2(config-if)#encapsulation frame-relay [ietf]
```

You can configure Frame Relay to support encapsulation of any protocol that conforms to RFC 1490, "Multiprotocol Interconnect over Frame Relay," providing interoperability between multiple vendors. You must use the Internet Engineering Task Force (IETF) form of encapsulation if your device is connected to another vendor's equipment across a Frame Relay network. You can use IETF encapsulation on the interface level or on a per-VC basis.

One item that is often overlooked is the fact that you must shut down your interface prior to changing encapsulation types. By doing this, you ensure that the interface is reset and is using the new encapsulation type.

You are now going to configure a Frame Relay partial-mesh topology. You combine both the point-to-point and point-to-multipoint Frame Relay subinterface to create your partial-mesh Frame Relay topology using R1, R2, R3, and R4. You must configure R10 as your Frame Relay switch.

Your topology for this section is illustrated in Figure 5-7.

Figure 5-7   *Partial-Mesh Frame Relay Topology*

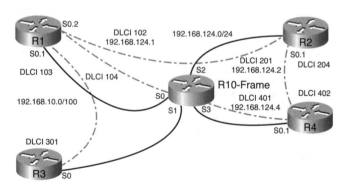

In this case study, you use a point-to-point subinterface on R1 to communicate with R3. You use a multipoint interface on R1, R2, and R4. On R3, you use the physical interface for communications. Example 5-1 shows you the configuration of R10, the Frame Relay switch, and Example 5-2 shows the steps that are necessary to accomplish this task.

Example 5-1 *Frame Relay Switch Configuration*

```
R10(config)#frame-relay switching
R10(config-if)#encapsulation frame-relay
R10(config-if)#frame-relay lmi-type ansi
R10(config-if)#frame-relay intf-type dce
R10(config-if)#frame-relay route 102 interface Serial2 201
R10(config-if)#frame-relay route 103 interface Serial1 301
R10(config-if)#frame-relay route 104 interface Serial3 104
R10(config-if)#exit
R10(config)#interface Serial1
R10(config-if)#encapsulation frame-relay
R10(config-if)#frame-relay lmi-type ansi
R10(config-if)#frame-relay intf-type dce
R10(config-if)#frame-relay route 301 interface Serial0 103
R10(config-if)#frame-relay route 103 interface Serial1 301
R10(config-if)#frame-relay route 104 interface Serial3 401
R10(config-if)#exit
R10(config)#interface Serial2
R10(config-if)#encapsulation frame-relay
R10(config-if)#frame-relay lmi-type ansi
R10(config-if)#frame-relay intf-type dce
R10(config-if)#frame-relay route 201 interface Serial0 102
R10(config-if)#exit
R10(config)#interface Serial3
R10(config-if)#encapsulation frame-relay
R10(config-if)#frame-relay lmi-type ansi
R10(config-if)#frame-relay intf-type dce
R10(config-if)#frame-relay route 401 interface Serial0 104
```

Example 5-2 *Enabling Frame Relay*

```
Configuration items for R1:
R1(config)#interface serial 0
R1(config-if)#encapsulation frame-relay
R1(config-if)#exit
R1(config)#interface serial 0.1 point-to-point
R1(config-if)#ip address 192.168.13.1 255.255.255.252
R1(config-if)#exit
R1(config)#interface serial 0.2 multipoint
R1(config-if)#ip address 192.168.124.1 255.255.255.0

Configuration items for R2:
R2(config)#interface serial
R2(config-if)#encapsulation frame-relay
```

continues

Example 5-2 *Enabling Frame Relay (Continued)*

```
R2(config-if)#exit
R2(config)#interface serial 0.1 multipoint
R2(config-if)#ip address 192.168.124.2 255.255.255.0

Configuration items for R4:
R4(config)#interface serial
R4(config-if)#encapsulation frame-relay
R4(config-if)#exit
R4(config)#interface serial 0.1 multipoint
R4(config-if)#ip address 192.168.124.4 255.255.255.0
R4(config-if)#encapsulation frame-relay

Configuration items for R3:
R3(config)#interface serial 0
R3(config-if)#ip address 192.168.13.2 255.255.255.252
R3(config-if)#encapsulation frame-relay
```

Step 2: Configure Dynamic or Static Address Mapping

When you use point-to-point subinterfaces on the physical interface, the destination is identified or implied by the use of the **frame-relay interface-dlci** command. When you use multipoint subinterfaces, the destinations can be dynamically resolved through the use of Frame Relay Inverse ARP or can be statically mapped through the use of the **frame-relay map** command.

You can use Inverse ARP to build dynamic address mappings in Frame Relay networks running AppleTalk, Banyan VINES, DECnet, IP, Novell IPX, and XNS. Inverse ARP allows your device to discover the protocol address of the remote device. Inverse ARP is able to build the dynamic addressing due to the fact that the service provider's switch advertises the DLCI assigned to your device. Your device can then take this DLCI and advertise to the remote end so that it can create the mapping. This process is reversed from the remote end to your local end.

Inverse ARP is enabled by default, but you have the option of explicitly disabling it for a given protocol and DLCI pair. You should disable or reenable Inverse ARP under the following conditions:

- You should disable Inverse ARP for a selected protocol and DLCI pair when you know that the protocol is not supported on the other end of the connection.

- You should reenable Inverse ARP for a protocol and DLCI pair if conditions or equipment changes and support for the protocol by the other end of the connection begins.

Inverse ARP is not required if you use a point-to-point interface because only a single destination exists and discovery of the destination is not required.

If, for some reason, you disabled Inverse ARP, use the following command to reenable it:

```
R2(config-if)#frame-relay inverse-arp protocol dlci
```

Use the following command to disable Inverse ARP for a specific protocol and DLCI pair:

```
R2(config-if)#no frame-relay inverse-arp protocol dlci
```

Use the following command to clear dynamically created Frame Relay maps:

```
R2(config-if)#clear frame-relay-inarp
```

Use the following command to display information about dynamically created Frame Relay maps:

```
R2(config-if)#show frame-relay map
```

NOTE   If you define a subinterface as a point-to-point subinterface, you cannot reassign the same subinterface number as a multipoint subinterface without first rebooting your device.

When you use a multipoint subinterface, you have a couple of choices on how it is addressed. You can use Inverse ARP to dynamically map the IP-to-DCLI mapping, or you can statically define the IP-to-DLCI mapping. Be aware that not all protocols support dynamic address mapping and must use static address mapping. When you use static mapping, Inverse ARP is automatically disabled for the specified protocol on the specified DLCI.

Because you have a physical interface that is logically divided into multiple subinterfaces, you must provide enough information so that a subinterface can be distinguished from the physical interface and to associate a specific subinterface with a specific DLCI.

To associate a DLCI with a subinterface, use the following command:

```
R2(config-subif)#frame-relay interface-dlci dlci
```

Use the following commands to establish static mapping according to your network needs.

Use the following command to define the mapping between a destination protocol address and the DLCI:

```
R2(config-if)#frame-relay map protocol protocol-address dlci [broadcast] [ietf] [cisco]
[payload-compress {packet-by-packet | frf9 stac [hardware-options] | data-stream stac
[hardware-options]}]
```

Use the following command to forward broadcasts when Connectionless Network Service (CLNS) is used for routing:

```
R2(config-if)#frame-relay map clns dlci [broadcast]
```

Use the following command to specify that broadcasts are to be forwarded during bridging:

```
R2(config-if)#frame-relay map bridge dlci [broadcast] [ietf]
```

Table 5-1 lists all the supported protocols and their corresponding keywords.

Table 5-1   *Supported Protocols for Static Mapping*

Protocol	Keyword
IP	ip
DECnet	decnet
AppleTalk	appletalk
XNS	xns
Novell IPX	ipx
VINES	vines
ISO CLNS	clns
Apollo	apollo
Data Link Switching	dlsw
LLC2	llc2
PPP over Ethernet	pppoe
QLLC	qllc
Remote Source-Route Bridging	rstb
Serial Tunnel	stun

You must use the **broadcast** keyword for routing protocols such as OSI protocols and the Open Shortest Path First (OSPF) Protocol.

You could allow all the interfaces in your case study to use Inverse ARP to discover the appropriate mappings, but this is a learning scenario, so you will use static mappings on the multipoint interfaces between R1, R2, and R4. Example 5-3 shows the commands that are necessary to accomplish this task.

Example 5-3   *Static Mappings Between Multipoint Subinterfaces*

```
Configuration items for R1:
R1(config)#interface serial 0.2
R1(config-if)#frame-relay map 192.168.124.2 102 broadcast
R1(config-if)#frame-relay map 192.168.124.4 104 broadcast

Configuration items for R2:
R2(config)#interface serial 0.1
R2(config-if)#frame-relay map 192.168.124.1 201 broadcast
R2(config-if)#frame-relay map 192.168.124.4 204 broadcast

Configuration items for R4:
R4(config)#interface serial 0.1
R4(config-if)#frame-relay map 192.168.124.1 401 broadcast
R4(config-if)#frame-relay map 192.168.124.2 402 broadcast
```

To finish your configuration, you can create the dynamic mappings for communications across the point-to-point subinterface between R1 and R3. Example 5-4 shows the commands that are necessary to accomplish this task.

Example 5-4 *Dynamic Mappings Between Point-to-Point Subinterfaces*

```
Configuration items for R1:
R1(config)#interface serial 0.1
R1(config-if)#frame-relay interface-dlci 103 broadcast

Configuration items for R3:
R3(config)#interface serial 0
R3(config-if)#frame-relay interface-dlci 301 broadcast
```

Step 3: Configure the LMI

Configuring a FRAD to support LMI autosense is perhaps one of the easiest features that you can configure in Frame Relay. This is because LMI autosense is transparent to you, meaning that configuration options are nonexistent.

It is only when you want to explicitly set the LMI type to one of the three supported types that you actually have to touch the device. Use the following steps to disable the LMI autosense feature:

Step 1 Set the LMI type to one of the three supported types by using the following command:

```
R2(config-if)#frame-relay lmi-type {ansi | cisco | q933a}
```

Step 2 Set the LMI keepalive interval, which by default is 10 seconds and, per the LMI protocol, must be less than the corresponding interval on the switch, by using the following command:

```
R2(config-if)#keepalive number
```

If desired, you can disable keepalives on networks that do not use LMI by using the following command:

```
R2(config-if)#no keepalive
```

Step 3 Set the LMI polling and timer intervals to fine-tune the operation of the LMI DTE and DCE devices by using the timer commands covered in "Tuning LMI Timers."

Continuing with your configuration, you configure the ANSI LMI type for your Frame Relay topology. Example 5-5 shows you the commands that are necessary to complete this step.

Example 5-5 *Configuring an LMI Type*

```
Configuration items for R1:
R1(config)#interface serial 0
R1(config-if)#frame-relay lmi-type ansi

Configuration items for R2:
R2(config)#interface serial 0
R2(config-if)#frame-relay lmi-type ansi

Configuration items for R3:
R3(config)#interface serial 0
R3(config-if)#frame-relay lmi-type ansi

Configuration items for R4:
R4(config)#interface serial 0
R4(config-if)#frame-relay lmi-type ansi
```

After completing this case study, you should have a functioning Frame Relay topology. Although the next few sections are still part of configuring Frame Relay as optional items, you review these features one at a time.

Case Study 5-2: Configuring Frame Relay SVCs

To enable the Frame Relay SVC service and enable the creation and deletion of SVCs, you can perform the following tasks:

Step 1   Enable SVCs on a physical interface.

Step 2   Optionally enable SVCs on a subinterface.

Step 3   Configure a map class.

Step 4   Configure a map group with E.164 or X.121 addresses.

Step 5   Associate the map class to a static protocol address map.

Step 6   Optionally tune the LAPF parameters.

NOTE   Although the tuning of LAPF tasks is optional, you should not attempt any configuration of these items unless you thoroughly understand the possible impact on your network.

Step 1: Enable SVCs on a Physical Interface

You can use the commands that are described in this section to enable SVC operation on a Frame Relay interface.

Use the following command to assign a map group to the interface:

```
R2(config-if)#map-group group-name
```

Use the following command to enable Frame Relay encapsulation on the interface:

```
R2(config-if)#encapsulation frame-relay
```

Use the following command to enable Frame Relay SVC support on the interface:

```
R2(config-if)#frame-relay svc
```

You reuse the topology from Figure 5-7 for this case study. You reconfigure the R1-to-R3 connection to use SVCs after removing the previous configurations. You configure a map-group named ccie_lab for this interface. Example 5-6 shows you the new commands that you add to the physical interface of R3.

Example 5-6 *Enabling SVCs on R3*

```
Configuration items for R3:
R3(config)#interface serial 0
R3(config-if)#ip address 192.168.13.2 255.255.255.252
R3(config-if)#encapsulation frame-relay
R3(config-if)#map-group ccie_lab
R3(config-if)#frame-relay lmi-type ansi
R3(config-if)#frame-relay svc
```

Step 2: Optionally Enable SVCs on a Subinterface

You can configure Frame Relay SVCs to operate on a subinterface by completing all the commands in the previous section, with the exception of assigning a map-group. After you complete these steps, use the following command to complete the configuration:

```
R2(config-subif)#map-group group-name
```

Continuing your case study, you now configure R1 to use SVCs. You use the same map class that was defined on R3 in your previous step, ccie_lab. Example 5-7 shows the new commands that you enter after you remove the previous commands.

Example 5-7 *Enabling SVCs on R1*

```
Configuration items for R1:
R1(config)#interface serial 0
R1(config-if)#encapsulation frame-relay
R1(config-if)#frame-relay lmi-type ansi
R1(config-if)#exit
R1(config)#interface serial 0.1 point-to-point
R1(config-if)#ip address 192.168.13.1 255.255.255.252
R1(config-if)#map-group ccie_lab
```

Step 3: Configure a Map Class

To create a map class, perform the following tasks:

- Specify the map class name.

- Optionally specify a custom queue list for the map class.

- Optionally specify a priority queue list for the map class.

- Optionally enable BECN feedback.

- Optionally set the nondefault QoS values.

Use the commands described in this section to create your map class.

Use the following command to specify a Frame Relay map class name and enter the map class configuration mode:

```
R2(config)#map-class frame-relay map-class-name
```

Use the following command to specify a custom queue list to be used for the map class:

```
R2(config-map-class)#frame-relay custom-queue-list list-number
```

Use the following command to assign a priority queue to VCs that are associated with the map class:

```
R2(config-map-class)#frame-relay priority-group list-number
```

Use the following command to enable the type of BECN feedback to throttle the frame-transmission rate:

```
Router(config-map-class)#frame-relay adaptive-shaping [becn | foresight]
```

Use the following command to specify the inbound CIR, in bits per second:

```
R2(config-map-class)#frame-relay cir in bps
```

Use the following command to specify the outbound CIR, in bits per second:

```
R2(config-map-class)#frame-relay cir out bps
```

Use the following command to set the minimum acceptable incoming CIR, in bits per second:

```
R2(config-map-class)#frame-relay mincir in bps
```

Use the following command to set the minimum acceptable outgoing CIR, in bits per second:

```
R2(config-map-class)#frame-relay mincir out bps
```

Use the following command to set the incoming committed burst size (Bc), in bits:

```
R2(config-map-class)#frame-relay bc in bits
```

Use the following command to set the outgoing Bc, in bits:

```
R2(config-map-class)#frame-relay bc out bits
```

Use the following command to set the incoming excess burst size (Be), in bits:

```
R2(config-map-class)#frame-relay be in bits
```

Use the following command to set the outgoing Be, in bits:

```
R2(config-map-class)#frame-relay be out bits
```

Use the following command to set the idle timeout interval, in seconds:

```
R2(config-map-class)#frame-relay idle-timer seconds
```

You can define multiple map classes. Remember that you associate a map class with a static map. The map class is not associated with an interface or subinterface; the static map is assigned to the interface or subinterface. This gives you the flexibility to define different map classes for different destinations.

You are now going to define your map class called security to associate with your map group. You define a CIR into and out of 128000 for R1 and a CIR into and out of 64000 for R3. Example 5-8 shows you the commands that are necessary to complete this task.

Example 5-8   *Defining a Map Class*

```
Configuration items for R1:
R1(config)#map-class frame-relay security
R1(config-map-class)#frame-relay cir in 128000
R1(config-map-class)#frame-relay cir out 128000

Configuration items for R3:
R3(config)#map-class frame-relay security
R3(config-map-class)#frame-relay cir in 64000
R3(config-map-class)#frame-relay cir out 64000
```

Step 4: Configure a Map Group with E.164 or X.121 Addresses

After you have a map group defined for your interface, the next step is to associate your map group with a specific source and destination address that is to be used. You use either an E.164 addresses or X.121 addresses for the source and destination addresses. To specify the map group to associate with a specific interface, use the following command:

```
R2(config)#map-list map-group-name source-addr {e164 | x121} source-address dest-addr
{e164 | x121} destination-address
```

Step 5: Associate the Map Class with Static Protocol Address Maps

You can use the **class** command to define the protocol addresses that are used under the **map-list** command and associate each protocol address with a specified map class. You must use this command for each protocol address to be associated with a map class. Use the following command to associate a map class with a protocol address:

```
R2(config-map-list)#protocol protocol-address class class-name [ietf] [broadcast
[trigger]]
```

You can use the **ietf** keyword to specify RFC 1490 encapsulation and the **broadcast** keyword to specify that broadcasts must be carried. Use the **trigger** keyword, which can only be configured if **broadcast** is also configured, to enable a broadcast packet to trigger an SVC. If the SVC that uses this map class has already been created, it simply carries the broadcast to the other side.

You are now going to associate your map group of ccie_lab to a map list. R1 has an E.164 address of 123456, and R3 has an E.164 address of 654321. You also configure a static protocol address of the other IP address. Example 5-9 shows you how to define this configuration.

Example 5-9   *Defining a Map List*

```
Configuration items for R1:
R1(config)#map-list ccie_lab source-addr E164 123456 dest-addr E164 654321
R1(config-map-list)#ip 192.168.13.2 class security

Configuration items for R3:
R3(config)#map-list ccie_lab source-addr E164 654321 dest-addr E164 123456
R3(config-map-list)#ip 192.168.13.1 class security
```

Step 6: Configure LAPF Parameters

You can use the configurable parameters of the Frame Relay Link Access Procedure for Frame Relay (LAPF) to tune Layer 2 to operate in the most efficient manner to meet your networking requirements. Although you would normally not be required to use anything other than the default settings, there are cases where you would want to change the parameters, such as when your service provider's network does not support the Frame Reject (FRMR) in the LAPF Frame Reject procedure. To remedy this situation, you can force your equipment to not send this parameter by using the following command:

```
R2(config-if)#no frame-relay lapf frmr
```

You can change other Layer 2 parameters by using one of the following commands.

Use the following command to set the LAPF window size k:

```
R2(config-if)#frame-relay lapf k number
```

Use the following command to set the LAPF maximum retransmission count N200:

```
R2(config-if)#frame-relay lapf n200 retries
```

Use the following command to set the maximum length of the Information field of the LAPF I frame N201:

```
R2(config-if)#frame-relay lapf n201 bytes
```

Use the following command to set the LAPF retransmission timer value T200:

```
R2(config-if)#frame-relay lapf t200 tenths-of-a-second
```

Use the following command to set the LAPF link idle timer value T203 of DLCI 0:

```
R2(config-if)#frame-relay lapf t203 seconds
```

Case Study 5-3: Frame Relay Traffic Shaping

When using traffic shaping to control outbound traffic data flow to the speed of the remote device with Frame Relay, it applies to both PVCs and SVCs. You can configure Frame Relay traffic shaping by performing the following tasks:

Step 1   Define VCs for different types of traffic.

Step 2   Enable Frame Relay traffic shaping on an interface.

Step 3   Enable ELMI (described later).

Step 4   Specify a traffic-shaping map class for an interface.

Step 5   Define a map class with queuing and traffic-shaping parameters.

Step 6   Define an Access Control List (ACL).

Step 7   Define priority queue lists for the map class.

Step 8   Define custom queue lists for the map class.

If you use Cisco IOS Software release 11.2, the following Frame Relay traffic-shaping capabilities are available to you:

- **Rate Enforcement on a Per-VC Basis**—The peak rate for your outbound traffic. This value can be set to match the CIR or another value.

- **Dynamic Traffic Throttling on a Per-VC Basis**—When BECN packets indicate congestion on the network, the outbound traffic rate is automatically stepped down; when congestion eases, the outbound traffic rate is increased.

- **Enhanced Queuing Support on a Per-VC Basis**—Either custom queuing or priority queuing can be configured for individual VCs.

In this case study, you configure Frame Relay traffic shaping between R1, R2, and R4. You want to ensure that communications from R1 do not saturate the 64-kbps port speed of R2. The port speed of both R1 and R4 is 1.544 Mbps, but only a 512-kbps CIR exists between them. The CIR for R2 is set at 32 kbps. Figure 5-8 illustrates the topology that you will use in this case study.

Figure 5-8   *Frame Relay Traffic-Shaping Topology*

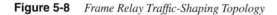
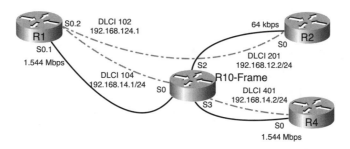

Step 1: Define VCs for Different Types of Traffic

You can perform virtual time-division multiplexing on the same line by defining separate VCs for different types of traffic and by specifying queuing and an outbound traffic rate for each VC. In this manner, you can provide guaranteed bandwidth for each traffic type that crosses that line. This gives you the ability to throttle the outbound traffic from high-speed LAN lines in your central office to the lower-speed WAN lines in your remote locations, easing congestion and data loss in your network; enhanced queuing mechanisms can also prevent congestion-caused data loss.

Step 2: Enable Frame Relay Traffic Shaping on the Interface

By enabling Frame Relay traffic shaping on an interface, you enable both traffic shaping and per-VC queuing on all PVCs and SVCs that are defined on the interface. Remember that traffic shaping gives your FRAD the ability to control the circuit's output rate and, if configured, to react to congestion-notification information.

Use the following command to enable Frame Relay traffic shaping on a specified interface:

```
R2(config-if)#frame-relay traffic-shaping
```

Your first step in configuring the topology that is outlined in the case study is to enable Frame Relay traffic shaping on each router. Remember that this command is issued on the physical interface, not on a subinterface. Example 5-10 shows you the commands that are necessary to complete this step.

Example 5-10 *Enabling Frame Relay Traffic Shaping*

```
Configuration items for R1:
R1(config)#interface serial 0
R1(config-if)#encapsulation frame-relay
R1(config-if)#frame-relay traffic-shaping
```

continues

Example 5-10 *Enabling Frame Relay Traffic Shaping (Continued)*

```
R1(config-if)#frame-relay lmi-type ansi
R1(config-if)#exit
R1(config)#interface serial 0.1 point-to-point
R1(config-if)#ip address 192.168.14.1 255.255.255.252
R1(config-if)#frame-relay map 192.168.14.2 104 broadcast
R1(config-if)#exit
R1(config)#interface serial 0.2 point-to-point
R1(config-if)#ip address 192.168.12.1 255.255.255.252
R1(config-if)#frame-relay map 192.168.12.2 102 broadcast

Configuration items for R2:
R2(config)#interface serial 0
R2(config-if)#ip address 192.168.14.1 255.255.255.252
R2(config-if)#encapsulation frame-relay
R2(config-if)#frame-relay traffic-shaping
R2(config-if)#frame-relay lmi-type ansi
R2(config-if)#frame-relay map 192.168.14.1 201 broadcast

Configuration items for R4:
R4(config)#interface serial 0
R4(config-if)#ip address 192.168.14.1 255.255.255.252
R4(config-if)#encapsulation frame-relay
R4(config-if)#frame-relay traffic-shaping
R4(config-if)#frame-relay lmi-type ansi
R4(config-if)#frame-relay map 192.168.14.1 401 broadcast
```

Step 3: Enable Enhanced Local Management Interface

You can use the Enhanced Local Management Interface (ELMI) feature in conjunction with traffic shaping so that your FRAD can dynamically respond to changes in the network. ELMI allows your FRAD to learn quality of service (QoS) parameters from a Cisco switch and use them for traffic-shaping, configuration, or management purposes. Because of this, ELMI can simplify the process of configuring traffic shaping on your FRAD.

Use the following command to configure ELMI:

```
R2(config-if)#frame-relay QoS-autosense
```

You are not required to configure traffic shaping on the interface that you want to enable ELMI on, but you might want to do so to know the values that are being used by the switch. If you want your FRAD to respond to the QoS information that is received from the switch by adjusting the output rate, you must configure traffic shaping on the interface.

You now enable ELMI on the interfaces on which you are configuring traffic shaping. Example 5-11 shows the commands that are necessary to complete this task.

Example 5-11 *Enabling Enhanced Local Management Information*

```
Configuration items for R1:
R1(config)#interface serial 0
R1(config-if)#frame-relay QoS-autosense

Configuration items for R2:
R2(config)#interface serial 0
R2(config-if)#frame-relay QoS-autosense

Configuration items for R4:
R4(config)#interface serial 0
R4(config-if)#frame-relay QoS-autosense
```

Step 4: Specify a Traffic-Shaping Map Class for the Interface

When specifying a Frame Relay map class for a main interface, all the VCs that you define on its subinterfaces also inherit the traffic-shaping parameters that are defined for the class.

Use the following command to specify a map class for a specified interface:

```
R2(config-if)#frame-relay class map-class-name
```

You can override the default for a specific DLCI on a specific subinterface by using the **class** VC command to explicitly assign the DLCI to a different class.

Your next step is to associate your map class to the appropriate interface/subinterface. In Example 5-12, the map class named ccie64 is assigned to the interfaces that are associated with R1 and R2, while the map class named cciet1 is assigned to the circuit between R1 and R4.

Example 5-12 *Enabling Frame Relay Traffic Shaping*

```
Configuration items for R1:
R1(config)#interface serial 0.1
R1(config-if)#frame-relay class cciet1
R1(config-if)#exit
R1(config)#interface serial 0.2
R1(config-if)#frame-relay class ccie64

Configuration items for R2:
R2(config)#interface serial 0
R2(config-if)#frame-relay class ccie64

Configuration items for R4:
R4(config-if)#interface serial 0
R4(config-if)#frame-relay class cciet1
```

Step 5: Define a Map Class with Queuing and Traffic-Shaping Parameters

You can specify the average and peak rates, in bits per second, that you want to allow on a VC by defining and associating it with a map class. You can also specify a custom queue list *or* a priority queue group for use by the VC that is associated with the map class.

To define a map class, use the commands described in this section.

Use the following command to specify a map class:

```
R2(config)#map-class frame-relay map-class-name
```

Use the following command to define the traffic rate:

```
R2(config-map-class)#frame-relay traffic-rate average [peak]
```

Use the following command to specify a custom queue list:

```
R2(config-map-class)#frame-relay custom-queue-list list-number
```

Use the following command to specify a priority queue list:

```
R2(config-map-class)#frame-relay priority-group list-number
```

Use the following command to select BECN or ForeSight as a congestion backward-notification mechanism to which traffic shaping adapts:

```
R2(config-map-class)#frame-relay adaptive-shaping {becn | foresight}
```

Your next required task is to configure the Frame Relay map class for ccie64 and cciet1. Example 5-13 shows you the commands to complete this task.

Example 5-13 *Defining the Map Classes*

```
Configuration items for R1:
R1(config)#map-class frame-relay ccie64
R1(config-map-class)#frame-relay adaptive-shaping becn mode
R1(config-map-class)#frame-relay cir 1544000
R1(config-map-class)#frame-relay bc 8000
R1(config-map-class)#frame-relay be 64000
R1(config-map-class)#frame-relay mincir 32000
R1(config)#map-class frame-relay cciet1
R1(config-map-class)#frame-relay adaptive-shaping becn mode
R1(config-map-class)#frame-relay cir 1544000
R1(config-map-class)#frame-relay bc 8000
R1(config-map-class)#frame-relay be 64000
R1(config-map-class)#frame-relay mincir 512000
```

Step 6: Define ACLs

When using custom queuing, you can specify an Access Control List (ACL) to identify the traffic that it will use. You associate the lists through the list numbers. For more information about defining ACLs, refer to Chapter 16, "Access Control Lists."

Step 7: Define Priority Queue Lists for the Map Class

You have the option of defining a priority list for a protocol as well as a default priority list. You use the number that you specified for a specific priority list to associate it to the Frame Relay priority group that is defined for a specified map class.

Example 5-14 shows the commands that are necessary to define a priority queue for placing decent traffic.

Example 5-14 *Defining a Priority Queue*

```
Configuration items for R1:
R1(config)#map-class frame-relay fast_vcs
R1(config-map-class)#frame-relay priority-group 2
R1(config-map-class)#frame-relay cir 1544000
R1(config-map-class)#frame-relay bc 8000
R1(config-map-class)#frame-relay be 64000
R1(config-map-class)#exit
R1(config)#priority-list 2 protocol decent high
```

Step 8: Define Custom Queue Lists for the Map Class

You have the option of defining a queue list for a specific protocol and a default queue list for all other traffic. You can also specify the maximum number of bytes to be transmitted in any given cycle. You use the number that you specified for a specific queue list to associate it to the Frame Relay custom queue list that is defined for a specified map class.

Example 5-15 shows you a way to define a custom queue list that allows traffic that matches access list 100 to use the defined queue.

Example 5-15 *Defining a Custom Queue List*

```
Configuration items for R1:
R1(config)#map-class frame-relay slow_vcs
R1(config-map-class)#frame-relay custom-queue-list 1
R1(config-map-class)#frame-relay cir 1544000
R1(config-map-class)#frame-relay bc 8000
R1(config-map-class)#frame-relay be 64000
R1(config-map-class)#exit
R1(config)#queue-list 1 protocol ip list 100
R1(config)#access-list 100 permit ip host 192.168.1.1 host 192.168.2.1
```

Creating a Broadcast Queue for an Interface

In a very large Frame Relay network, you can experience performance issues when you have many DLCIs terminating to a single FRAD that must replicate routing updates and service advertising updates out each DLCI. To avoid this performance issue, you have the option of

creating a special broadcast queue for an interface. This broadcast queue is managed independently of the normal interface queue, has its own buffers, and has a configurable size and service
rate.

You define a maximum transmission rate, or throughput limit, that is measured in both bytes
per second and packets per second. The queue is serviced to ensure that no more than this
maximum is provided. The broadcast queue is given priority when transmitting at a rate less
than your configured maximum and has a guaranteed minimum bandwidth allocation. These
two transmission rate limits are intended to avoid flooding the interface with broadcasts. The
actual transmission rate limit in any measured second is the first rate limit that is reached.

Use the following command to create a broadcast queue:

```
R2(config-if)#frame-relay broadcast-queue size byte-rate packet-rate
```

Transparent Bridging and Frame Relay

You can use transparent bridging (TB) for point-to-point or point-to-multipoint subinterfaces
on Frame Relay encapsulated serial and High Speed Serial Interface (HSSI) interfaces. The
only restriction is that all PVCs that are configured on a subinterface must belong to the same
bridge group.

Use the following command to enable transparent bridging on a point-to-point or a point-to-
multipoint subinterface:

```
R2(config-subif)#bridge-group bridge-group
```

Configuring a Backup Interface for a Subinterface

You can use a backup interface with both a point-to-point and a multipoint Frame Relay subinterface. This allows individual PVCs to be backed up in case of a failure rather than waiting
for the entire Frame Relay connection to fail before any redundancy takes over. You can
configure a subinterface for backup on a failure only, not for backup based on the loading on
the subinterface.

Any backup interface that you configure for the main interface has precedence over any subinterface backup interface that you have configured when a complete loss of connectivity is
experienced. Because of this, a subinterface backup is activated only if the main interface is up
or if the main interface is down and does not have a backup interface defined. If a subinterface
fails while the backup interface is in use, and the main interface goes down, the backup subinterface remains connected.

Use the following two commands to configure a backup interface for a Frame Relay
subinterface.

To specify the backup interface for the subinterface, use the following command:

```
R2(config-if)#backup interface type number
```

To specify the enable and disable delay, use the following command:

```
R2(config-if)#backup delay enable-delay disable-delay
```

TCP/IP Header Compression

RFC 1414 describes a mechanism that can improve the efficiency of bandwidth utilization over low-speed serial links, using features such as TCP/IP header compression. A typical TCP/IP packet has a 40-byte datagram header that, once the connection is established, is fairly redundant in following packets. A compressed header is an average of 10 bytes in length because the receiving end can reconstruct the header by receiving a smaller header that identifies the connection and indicates the fields that changed and the amount of change.

However, for this algorithm to function properly, packets must arrive in order. If the packets were to arrive out of order, the reconstruction appears to work, but the packets do not match the original. Priority queuing, which changes the order in which packets are transmitted, is not recommended for use with TCP/IP header compression.

NOTE   If you use Cisco encapsulation and TCP/IP header compression on an interface, Frame Relay IP maps inherit the compression characteristics of the interface. However, if you use IETF encapsulation on an interface, the interface cannot be configured for compression. Frame Relay maps must be configured individually to support TCP/IP header compression.

Configuring an Individual IP Map for TCP/IP Header Compression

If you must use IETF encapsulation on an interface as a whole, you still have the option of configuring a specific IP map to use Cisco encapsulation and TCP header compression. You can also use a specific IP map to not compress TCP/IP headers.

In addition, you have the option to specify whether TCP/IP header compression is active or passive. When active, every outgoing packet is compressed. When passive, compression is applied only if a packet had a compressed header when it was received.

Use the following command to configure an IP map to use Cisco encapsulation and TCP/IP header compression:

```
R2(config-if)#frame-relay map ip ip-address dlci [broadcast] cisco tcp header-
    compression {active | passive}
```

Configuring an Interface for TCP/IP Header Compression

You can use active, the default, or passive TCP/IP header compression on an interface. Use the following command to apply TCP/IP header compression to an interface:

```
R2(config-if)#frame-relay ip tcp header-compression [passive]
```

Disabling TCP/IP Header Compression

You can disable TCP/IP header compression by using one of two commands. Each command has a different effect, depending on whether you explicitly configured Frame Relay IP maps to configure TCP/IP header compression or have inherited their compression characteristics from the interface. If you used Frame Relay IP maps to explicitly configure TCP/IP header compression, you must also explicitly disable TCP/IP header compression.

Use one of the following commands to disable TCP/IP header compression:

```
R2(config-if)#no frame-relay ip tcp header-compression
```

or

```
R2(config-if)#frame-relay map ip ip-address dlci nocompress
```

Troubleshooting Frame Relay Connectivity

Now that your Frame Relay is configured, at some point, you might need to go back and ensure that it is working correctly. Fortunately, Cisco provides many different ways to verify configurations. Two easy ways to accomplish this through a CLI is the **show** and **debug** suite of commands that are available in Cisco IOS Software.

Becoming familiar with the **show** and **debug** commands that are available for Frame Relay allows you to quickly troubleshoot and correct most problems without overloading you with a lot of excess information. In this chapter, only commands that relate to the information that was already covered is explored. For a complete listing of available **show** and **debug** commands, refer to the *IOS WAN Configuration Guide* for the IOS version that you are using.

The show frame-relay lmi Command

Because all traffic crossing a Frame Relay circuit rides over the LMI that was configured for that circuit, the **show frame-relay lmi** command can provide you with valuable information. The output of this command provides you with a lot of information, but when you are starting to troubleshoot a connectivity problem or are verifying that the circuit is operational, two fields—the Num Status Enq. Sent and Num Status msgs Rcvd—provide you with information about the health of the circuit. Example 5-16 provides you with the output of this command as issued on R2.

Example 5-16 *The* **show frame-relay lmi** *Command Output*

```
R2#show frame-relay lmi
LMI Statistics for interface Serial0 (Frame Relay DTE) LMI TYPE = ANSI
    Invalid Unnumbered info 0           Invalid Prot Disc 0
    Invalid dummy Call Ref 0            Invalid Msg Type 0
    Invalid Status Message 0            Invalid Lock Shift 0
    Invalid Information ID 0            Invalid Report IE Len 0
    Invalid Report Request 0           Invalid Keep IE Len 0
    Num Status Enq. Sent 296           Num Status msgs Rcvd 293
    Num Update Status Rcvd 0           Num Status Timeouts 0
```

Looking at the output in Example 5-16, you can see that the circuit is sending and receiving Status messages without any timeouts, which is vital for the operation of Frame Relay. This output also supplies you with the LMI type that the circuit is using for operation, in this case ANSI. If you were experiencing a problem with the configured LMI type, you would receive an output similar to that shown Example 5-17.

Example 5-17 *Mismatched LMI*

```
R2#show frame-relay lmi
LMI Statistics for interface Serial0 (Frame Relay DTE) LMI TYPE = ANSI
    Invalid Unnumbered info 0           Invalid Prot Disc 0
    Invalid dummy Call Ref 0            Invalid Msg Type 0
    Invalid Status Message 0            Invalid Lock Shift 0
    Invalid Information ID 0            Invalid Report IE Len 0
    Invalid Report Request 0           Invalid Keep IE Len 0
    Num Status Enq. Sent 96            Num Status msgs Rcvd 3
    Num Update Status Rcvd 0           Num Status Timeouts 93
```

As you can see in Example 5-17, your Num Status Timeouts are increasing, indicating a misconfigured circuit.

The show frame-relay pvc Command

Once you have confirmed that your LMI matches the service provider's, you can verify that you have the proper PVC(s) configured. Use the **show frame-relay pvc** [*dlci* | *interface*] command to display information about the DLCIs that the router is aware of. Example 5-18 is an output display of this command.

Example 5-18 *The* **show frame-relay pvc** *Command Output*

```
R2#show frame-relay pvc

PVC Statistics for interface Serial0 (Frame Relay DTE)
```

continues

Example 5-18 *The* **show frame-relay pvc** *Command Output (Continued)*

```
                    Active    Inactive    Deleted    Static
    Local             3          0           0          0
    Switched          0          0           0          0
    Unused            0          0           0          0

DLCI = 110, DLCI USAGE = LOCAL, PVC STATUS = ACTIVE, INTERFACE = Serial0.1

    input pkts 78           output pkts 78          in bytes 21770
    out bytes 22404         dropped pkts 0          in FECN pkts 0
    in BECN pkts 0          out FECN pkts 0         out BECN pkts 0
    in DE pkts 0            out DE pkts 0
    out bcast pkts 63       out bcast bytes 20844
    pvc create time 01:00:23, last time pvc status changed 00:59:45

DLCI = 120, DLCI USAGE = LOCAL, PVC STATUS = ACTIVE, INTERFACE = Serial0.2

    input pkts 10           output pkts 20          in bytes 1040
    out bytes 2080          dropped pkts 0          in FECN pkts 0
    in BECN pkts 0          out FECN pkts 0         out BECN pkts 0
    in DE pkts 0            out DE pkts 0
    out bcast pkts 0        out bcast bytes 0
    pvc create time 01:00:17, last time pvc status changed 00:59:47

DLCI = 130, DLCI USAGE = LOCAL, PVC STATUS = ACTIVE, INTERFACE = Serial0.2

    input pkts 15           output pkts 16          in bytes 1560
    out bytes 1620          dropped pkts 0          in FECN pkts 0
    in BECN pkts 0          out FECN pkts 0         out BECN pkts 0
    in DE pkts 0            out DE pkts 0
    out bcast pkts 0        out bcast bytes 0
    pvc create time 01:00:19, last time pvc status changed 00:59:49
```

NOTE   Notice that the output of the **show frame-relay pvc** command displays information about all PVCs that the router knows about. If you wanted more specific information about a specific interface or DLCI, you can supply the proper keyword to the command and receive only that information.

By analyzing the output of the **show frame-relay pvc** command, you can see that all the configured PVCs are in an active state. PVCs can be in one of the following states at any given time:

- **ACTIVE**—Your PVC is active and can pass traffic.

- **INACTIVE**—Your local connection to the Frame Relay is operational, but the remote router's connection is not operational.

- **DELETED**—You are not receiving LMIs, or the physical layer is encountering a problem.

Other areas of interest in this output are the pvc create time, which tells you when the PVC was created, and the last time pvc status changed time, which tells you the last time that the PVC state time changed. Both of these items can provide invaluable troubleshooting information.

If you need information about congestion, this is also the command to use because it provides you with counters that are related to FECN and BECN packets that the router has processed.

The show frame-relay map Command

You use the **show frame-relay map** command to display information about the static mappings that you have defined. Remember that static mappings are used to statically map network layer addresses to an associated DLCI for each remote destination that you can have. Example 5-19 shows an output of this command.

Example 5-19 *The* **show frame-relay map** *Command Output*

```
R2#show frame-relay map
Serial0.2 (up): ip 192.168.100.3 dlci 120(0x78,0x1C80), static,
               broadcast,
               CISCO, status defined, active
Serial0.2 (up): ip 192.168.100.5 dlci 130(0x82,0x2020), static,
               broadcast,
               CISCO, status defined, active
Serial0.1 (up): point-to-point dlci, dlci 110(0x6E,0x18E0), broadcast
               status defined, active
```

One other use for the **show frame-relay map** command is to verify proper operation of the Inverse ARP operation.

The debug frame-relay lmi Command

Just like most technologies that are supported by Cisco IOS Software, Frame Relay supports debugging of numerous configuration items. The one debug command that this chapter examines, **debug frame-relay lmi**, is useful for the beginning of your troubleshooting steps. If you need to use other debugging commands for Frame Relay, refer to the *IOS WAN Configuration Guide* for your IOS software version. Example 5-20 shows a sample output from the **debug frame-relay lmi** command.

Example 5-20 *The* **debug frame-relay lmi** *Command Output*

```
R2#debug frame-relay lmi
Frame Relay LMI debugging is on
Displaying all Frame Relay LMI data
R2#
01:51:51: Serial0(out): StEnq, myseq 31, yourseen 31, DTE up
```

continues

Example 5-20 *The* **debug frame-relay lmi** *Command Output (Continued)*

```
01:51:51: datagramstart = 0xE30BD8, datagramsize = 14
01:51:51: FR encap = 0x00010308
01:51:51: 00 75 95 01 01 01 03 02 1F 1F
01:51:51:
01:51:51: Serial0(in): Status, myseq 31
01:51:51: RT IE 1, length 1, type 1
01:51:51: KA IE 3, length 2, yourseq 32, myseq 31
01:52:01: Serial0(out): StEnq, myseq 32, yourseen 32, DTE up
01:52:01: datagramstart = 0xE30BD8, datagramsize = 14
01:52:01: FR encap = 0x00010308
01:52:01: 00 75 95 01 01 01 03 02 20 20
01:52:01:
01:52:01: Serial0(in): Status, myseq 32
01:52:01: RT IE 1, length 1, type 1
01:52:01: KA IE 3, length 2, yourseq 33, myseq 32
01:52:11: Serial0(out): StEnq, myseq 33, yourseen 33, DTE up
01:52:11: datagramstart = 0xE30BD8, datagramsize = 14
01:52:11: FR encap = 0x00010308
01:52:11: 00 75 95 01 01 01 03 02 21 21
01:52:11:
01:52:11: Serial0(in): Status, myseq 33
01:52:11: RT IE 1, length 1, type 1
01:52:11: KA IE 3, length 2, yourseq 34, myseq 33
R2#
```

You can see from this output that this router is successfully exchanging LMIs with the service provider's Frame Relay switch by the fact that the myseq and yourseq fields are increasing. The router adds 1 to the received sequence number when each successive message is sent. If the received sequence number field were not increasing, LMI exchanges would not be occurring. If three successive LMI messages are sent without a reply, where only one field is increasing, the link would be reset and the process would restart.

Summary

This chapter has taken a look at the Frame Relay technology as supported by Cisco devices. Cisco IOS Software supports the Frame Relay standard as defined by both ANSI and the ITU-T. First, you reviewed the configuration items necessary to support the example network that was defined at the beginning of the chapter. You learned the theory behind the commands and then put what you learned to use by configuring those items. You then looked at the many different commands that you could use to troubleshoot and maintain your Frame Relay network.

Review Questions

1 What kind of technology is Frame Relay?

2 Describe the difference between SVCs and PVCs.

3 What is the data-link connection identifier (DLCI)?

4 Describe how LMI Frame Relay differs from basic Frame Relay.

FAQs

Q — *Can I ping my own IP address on a multipoint interface?*

A — You cannot ping your own IP address on a multipoint Frame Relay interface because mappings are not made to your own interface. Pings to your own interface address are only successful on point-to-point subinterfaces or High-Level Data Link Control (HDLC) links because the device on the other side of the link returns the ICMP echo and echo reply packets.

You cannot ping from one spoke to another spoke in a hub-and-spoke configuration using multipoint interfaces because no mapping exists for the other spokes' IP addresses. Only the hub's address is learned via Inverse Address Resolution Protocol (IARP). If you configure a static map using the **frame-relay map** command for your IP address or the IP address of a remote spoke to use the local data-link connection identifier (DLCI), you can ping your interface address and the addresses of other spokes.

Q — *Can I use* IP *unnumbered with Frame Relay?*

A — If you do not have the IP address space to use many subinterfaces, you can use IP unnumbered on each subinterface as long as they are point-to-point subinterfaces. You must use static routes or dynamic routing for your traffic to get routed.

Q — *Can I configure a Cisco router to act as a Frame Relay switch?*

A — Yes. You can configure a Cisco router to function as Frame Relay data communication equipment (DCE) or Network-to-Network Interface (NNI) devices (Frame Relay switches). You can also configure a router to support hybrid data terminal equipment/data communication equipment/permanent virtual circuit (DTE/DCE/PVC) switching.

Q — *Is a special configuration necessary to connect Cisco routers to other vendor devices over Frame Relay?*

A — The Internet Engineering Task Force (IETF) encapsulation format must be specified to interact with other vendor devices because Cisco devices use a proprietary encapsulation by default. You can specify the IETF encapsulation on a per-interface or per-DLCI basis.

Q — *Is Frame Relay Inverse ARP on by default? The* **inverse-arp** *command does not show up in the configuration.*

A — Yes, Frame Relay Inverse ARP is on by default.

Q — *Can Frame Relay Inverse ARP be used without LMI?*

A — No, LMI is used to determine which PVCs to map.

Q — *When implementing a* **show frame map** *command, DLCIs are defined and active. This can occur when the DLCIs are not working. What does "defined and active" mean?*

A — The message "defined and active" means that the DLCI can carry data and that the router at the far end is active.

Q — *Can I change subinterfaces from point-to-point to multipoint or vice versa?*

A — No, after a specific type of subinterface is created, the subinterface can only be changed after deleting the subinterface and reloading the router. The deleted subinterface continues to show up in a **show ip interface brief** command until the router is reloaded.

Q — *What are FECN and BECN packets? How do they affect performance?*

A — FECN stands for Forward-Explicit Congestion Notification; BECN stands for Backward-Explicit Congestion Notification. This congestion notification is accomplished by changing a bit in the address field of a frame as it traverses the Frame Relay network. Network DCE devices (switches) change the value of the FECN bit to 1 on packets traveling in the same direction as the data flow. This notifies an interface device (DTE) that congestion avoidance procedures should be initiated by the receiving device. BECN bits are set in frames that travel in the opposite direction of the data flow to inform the transmitting DTE device of network congestion.

Q — *Can I reserve bandwidth for certain applications?*

A — Class-Based Weighted Fair Queuing (CBWFQ) is one classification option that allows you to reserve bandwidth for different applications of flows, depending on access lists or incoming interfaces.

Q — *How is IP split horizon handled on Frame Relay interfaces?*

A — IP split horizon checking is disabled by default for Frame Relay encapsulation to allow routing updates to go into and out of the same interface. An exception is the Enhanced Interior Gateway Routing Protocol (EIGRP), for which split horizon must be explicitly disabled.

Certain protocols, such as AppleTalk, transparent bridging, and IPX, cannot be supported on partially meshed networks because they require split horizon. (A packet received on an interface cannot be transmitted over the same interface, even if the packet is received and transmitted on different virtual circuits.)

Configuring Frame Relay subinterfaces ensures that a single physical interface is treated as multiple virtual interfaces. This capability allows you to overcome split horizon rules so packets that are received on one virtual interface can be forwarded to another virtual interface, even if they are configured on the same physical interface.

Q — *How can I calculate the bandwidth that is consumed by routing updates over Frame Relay?*

A — Reliable estimates can only be calculated for distance vector protocols that send periodic updates. This includes Routing Information Protocol (RIP) and IGRP for IP, RIP for IPX, and Routing Table Maintenance Protocol (RTMP) for AppleTalk.

This chapter covers the following topics:

- ISDN overview
- Point-to-Point Protocol (PPP) overview
- Dial-on-Demand Routing (DDR) overview
- Configuring ISDN

CHAPTER 6

ISDN Connectivity

Integrated Services Digital Network (ISDN) was introduced in the 1960s and was discussed in more detail at the 1968 International Telecommunications Union Telecommunications Standardization Sector (ITU-T) meeting. Before then, network communications took place over analog circuits.

A major advantage of ISDN is its ability to use existing telephone wiring to offer a dependable, cost-effective way to access the World Wide Web and other high-speed services, such as voice, video, and data. ISDN uses digital signaling and data transmission end-to-end. As such, it offers an excellent alternative to analog dialup modems through faster bits-per-second transmission rates and faster call setup.

In this chapter you will learn how to configure ISDN as well as the ISDN-related Point-to-Point Protocol (PPP) and Dial-on-Demand Routing (DDR) parameters. Specifically, this chapter covers material you can expect to be tested on on the CCIE Security lab exam.

ISDN Overview

ISDN was developed to provide integrated access to the widest range of services such as voice, video, and, of course, data. Its ability to effectively connect small offices, home offices, and telecommuters to the central site allows companies specializing in different industrial and service fields to use several new voice and data services that were not available over the traditional network while maintaining their investment in existing technology. Such services could not have been economically accessed in the old basic telephone service/Public Switched Telephone Network (PSTN) environment.

ISDN Standards Support

To communicate from the local terminal equipment to the ISDN switch in the central office, ISDN uses a unique collection of protocols. ITU organizes these protocols in the following manner:

- **E series**—Describes telephone network standards as they relate to ISDN.
- **I series**—Describes theory, terminology, interfaces, and common techniques.

- **Q series**—Describes switching and signaling. For instance, Q.921 deals with Link Access Procedure processes at Layer 2 of the OSI model. Q.931 deals with Layer 3 of the OSI model. D channels use Q.931 signaling. Both of these protocols are important to understand when it comes to troubleshooting ISDN.

After the completion of call setup and connection establishment, the ISDN process is identical to conventional calls. ISDN protocols come into play again when the call is disconnected between the local switch and the terminal equipment. The section, "ISDN Layers and Call Stages," describes these protocols in more detail.

ISDN Digital Channels

ISDN supports the use of several digital channels, including the following:

- **B channel**—Bearer service channel, which is used for voice and data at the rate of 64 kbps or 56 kbps, depending on the switch.

- **D channel**—Data channel, which is used for out-of-band signaling and network messages such as call setup and teardown.

Cisco offers two combinations of B and D channels for the access interface as recommended by ITU-T:

- **Basic Rate Interface (BRI)**—BRI uses two B channels and one 16 kbps D channel, plus framing and synchronization at 48 kbps, for a total of 192 kbps.

- **Primary Rate Interface (PRI)**—PRI joins one 64 kbps D channel and 23 B channels in North America and Japan (T1). In Europe and elsewhere, 30 B channels are used, along with one 64 kbps D channel (E1). Framing and synchronization are carried out at 8 kbps for T1 and 64 kbps for E1.

ISDN Terminal Equipment and Network Termination Devices

Both ISDN terminal equipment and network termination devices are known as *functional groups*. These groups are necessary in certain combinations to access the ISDN network with *customer premises equipment* (*CPE*):

- **Terminal equipment 1 (TE1)**—Specifies a device that has its own ISDN interface, such as a router with an ISDN interface or a digital telephone. It connects to NT1 or NT2.

- **Terminal equipment 2 (TE2)**—Specifies a device that does not have its own ISDN interface. In such cases, a terminal adapter is required.

- **Terminal adapter (TA)**—Analog signals V.35 or EIA/TIA-232 are converted into those that are compatible with ISDN to be used by TE2 devices.

- **Network Termination 1 (NT1)**—Specifies a device that connects four-wire CPE wiring to the two-wire local loop.

- **Network Termination 2 (NT2)**—Specifies a device that performs switching and concentrating. It directs traffic to and from different customer devices and the NT1. PBX is a good example of such a device.

Reference Points

Reference points are arrangements of various connections of which the functional groups are capable. In other words, they are logical points between the previously mentioned devices. Figure 6-1 illustrates the relationship between reference points and ISDN functions. The following list describes each reference point:

- **U (user)**—Between NT1 and the carrier's ISDN network. ITU-T standards for the U interface.

- **T (terminal)**—Between NT1 and NT2.

- **S (system)**—Between NT2 and TE1 or TA.

- **R (rate)**—Between a non-ISDN interface (TE2) and TA.

- **S/T reference point**—Between NT1 and TE1 or TA. Used if NT2 is not implemented. The most common scenario with BRI subscribers.

Figure 6-1 *ISDN Reference Points*

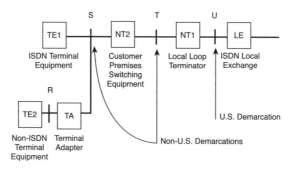

Figure 6-2 shows the S/T interface integrated into the router. NT1 interfaces can also come built in on a Cisco router. In North America, you as a customer are expected to provide NT1, unlike in Europe, where NT1 is a part of the telco-side equipment.

Given the fact that the interface connectors are similar, you must ensure that they are plugged in correctly.

Figure 6-2   *Reference Points for a Router with an Integrated S/T Interface*

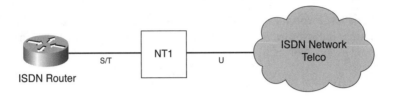

ISDN Layers and Call Stages

ISDN spans the bottom three layers of the OSI reference model. ISDN uses a multitude of protocols that fall under those layers and govern its operation.

ISDN Physical Layer Operation and Frame Format

Layer 1 encompasses the physical connection between the ISDN circuit and the CPE. This layer is shared by the B and D channels. ISDN Layer 1 is controlled by the following protocols:

- **I.430**—For BRI across S/T interface
- **I.431**—For PRI
- **ANSI T1.601**—For BRI U interface (the U interface is not standardized by ITU-T)

The contents of the ISDN I.430 BRI frame depend on which direction the frame is moving: from TE to NT or from NT to TE. Figure 6-3 illustrates both types.

Let's take a closer look at both frame types. They include 4 bits from the D channel and 32 bits from both B channels combined. If no data needs to be sent across the B channels, the framing still takes place so that NT1 can supply the provider with clocking and framing. Within this constant stream of frame exchange, each frame needs to be sequenced in a particular order, with each bit playing a particular role. These bits are as follows:

- **B1**—Belongs to the first B channel
- **B2**—Belongs to the second B channel
- **D**—Belongs to the D channel
- **F**—Framing bit used for synchronization
- **L**—Corrects average bit value
- **E**—Echo of prior D bit
- **A**—Activation bit
- **S**—Spare bit

Figure 6-3   *Layer 1 BRI Frame*

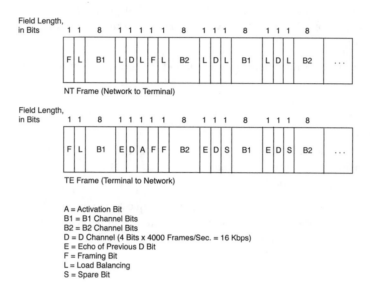

A = Activation Bit
B1 = B1 Channel Bits
B2 = B2 Channel Bits
D = D Channel (4 Bits x 4000 Frames/Sec. = 16 Kbps)
E = Echo of Previous D Bit
F = Framing Bit
L = Load Balancing
S = Spare Bit

ISDN Data Link Layer Operation

Layer 2, the data link layer, deals with the B and D channels separately, offering functions unique to either channel. It specifies the Link Access Procedure on the D channel (LAPD) as the framing protocol used for the D channel. On the other hand, the B channel uses High-Level Data Link Control (HDLC) or PPP encapsulation.

Protocol assignment for Layer 2 is as follows:

- **Q.920**—Specifies the ISDN functions.

- **Q.921**—Specifies signaling over the network.

As is the case with the conventional LAN setting, the ISDN network needs hardware addressing to take place between all the linked devices. ISDN Layer 2 is responsible for such addressing. In addition, there is further discrimination within each device when it comes to different processes running in that device. Therefore, a terminal endpoint identifier (TEI), dynamically assigned to each router by the switch at bootup, is used in tandem with a service access point identifier (SAPI), which is a way to identify the types of messages sent across the network.

ISDN Network Layer Operation

At Layer 3, the D channel is controlled by the Q.931 protocol. The Q.931 protocol is a part of the Digital Subscriber Signaling System 1 (DSS1) protocol suite, which deals with the message exchange.

The B channel specifications include support for network layer protocols such as IP, IPX, and AppleTalk.

ISDN Call Stages

ISDN call setup and teardown reflect the activity of the Layer 3 Q.931 protocol. While an ISDN call is being set up, several messages are exchanged between the called and calling parties that identify the progress of the setup.

As you can see in Figure 6-4, the called party requests a call setup. Some steps and messages that are displayed might not necessarily be a part of your particular call setup. It depends on the type of switches used in the exchange and their requirements.

Figure 6-4   *ISDN Call Setup*

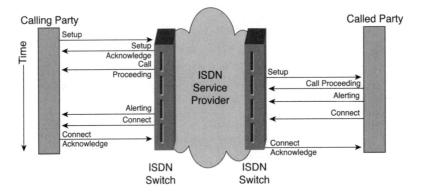

The teardown of a call may be initiated by either of the parties. However, the switch handles the teardown proceedings.

The Disconnect message is transmitted on the D channel. As shown in Figure 6-5, as soon as the switch receives the Disconnect message, it starts the release of the B channel circuit and sends a Release message to the downstream switch. The involved switches eventually transmit the Release message to the final switch.

Figure 6-5   *ISDN Call Teardown*

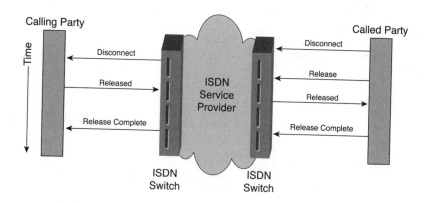

To make sure the call is being disconnected properly, each foregoing switch starts a T12 timer. The switch expects to receive a Release message from the neighbor switch, upon which it issues a Release Complete message back to the neighbor. If the Release Complete message isn't received within the timer period, the Release message is reissued.

As you are consulting Figure 6-5, keep in mind that the call teardown procedure is handled rapidly throughout the network.

Point-to-Point Protocol (PPP) Overview

This section describes Point-to-Point Protocol (PPP) to make you comfortable with the practice of ISDN in general and this book in particular. Even though PPP's application reaches far beyond the realms of ISDN, this section specifically concentrates on the ISDN side of PPP.

PPP is used to frame datagrams for their transport over the link layer. It is by far the preferred protocol when it comes to encapsulation and advanced options in ISDN.

Link Control Protocol (LCP) and Network Control Protocol (NCP) are the functional components of PPP. As implied by their names, LCP deals with establishing and configuring the connection at the data link layer, and NCP dynamically establishes network-layer protocols and bridged data. The following sections describe both protocols in greater depth.

Link Control Protocol (LCP)

The LCP phase is related to aspects that are link-dependent and protocol-independent. Many examples including callback, multilink, and whether authentication should be used, are discussed in Lesson 6-1: Beginning ISDN Configuration.

LCP has several different packet types that are specified in the Cisco **debug** output. Table 6-1 describes the most-used types.

Table 6-1   *LCP Packet Types*

Packet Type	Debug Output	Definition
Configure-Request	CONFREQ	Identifies to the peer the configuration options that are configured on the local device.
Configure-Ack	CONFACK	Acknowledges the received CONFREQ from the peer. Includes all the options specified in the CONFREQ received from the peer.
Configure-Nak	CONFNAK	Negatively acknowledges an option requested by the peer. The options whose values are being NAKed are included in the CONFNAK, along with any acceptable values. The peer may transmit another CONFREQ with new values included, or it may transmit another CONFREQ with the NAKed values omitted.
Configure-Reject	CONFREJ	Rejects an option included in the received CONFREQ. The rejected option(s) are included in the CONFREJ. The peer should transmit another CONFREQ without the rejected options included.
Terminate-Request	TERMREQ	Terminates an existing connection.
Terminate-Ack	TERMACK	Acknowledges the receipt of a TERMREQ from the peer.
Echo-Request	Echo-Request	Confirms connectivity and detects loopback.
Echo-Reply	Echo-Reply	Replies to an echo request from the peer.

During the LCP negotiation, both peers must agree on their options and acknowledge their peer's request to open the LCP process. The PPP negotiation between layers is sequential. Before the subsequent phase can occur, the previous one needs to be completed. Therefore, after LCP is open, authentication takes place followed by the NCP phase.

Network Control Protocol (NCP)

NCP is a Layer 3 protocol that is link-independent and protocol-dependent. Examples of protocol-specific options are a protocol address and protocol compression. Of these options, protocol address is always negotiated. By default, the peer is placed in the routing table as a directly connected route.

The individual type of the negotiated NCP depends on the protocol configured on an interface. For the purposes of the exam, you will concentrate on IP Control Protocol (IPCP). Typical negotiated options for IPCP include the IP address, IP/TCP header compression, and the DNS and WINS primary and secondary servers, which relate to the Microsoft Windows remote nodes only.

Most NCP packet types are the same as those of LCP, except for the absence of Echo-Request and Echo-Reply in NCP. Refer to Table 6-1 for the LCP packet types.

A PPP link terminates when LCP or NCP events are used to close it or when any kind of physical failure occurs. If the link closure is initiated by LCP, all NCP connections close with it. However, if NCP initiates the termination, it might not be able to accomplish it.

Dial-on-Demand Routing (DDR) Overview

DDR determines whether to bring up a connection that is not already active based on interesting and uninteresting traffic coming into the router. Interesting traffic brings up a connection, and uninteresting traffic doesn't.

A router decides which traffic is interesting and which isn't through preconfigured access lists and dialer lists. In Lesson 6-2 later in this chapter, you will learn how to configure interesting traffic.

Figure 6-6 displays the basic process of determining interesting traffic.

Figure 6-6   *Interesting Versus Uninteresting Packets*

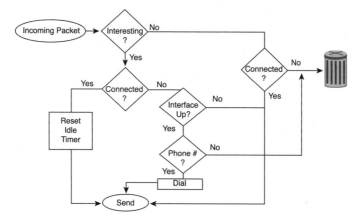

A dialer list specifies interesting traffic that is allowed to make a connection. Numerous dialer list settings can be used in conjunction with access lists to provide more granular control for a dialer list. A dialer list is then assigned to a dial group that refers to it when needed. A physical BRI interface belongs to a dial group and therefore carries out the instructions set up in a dialer list.

It is very important to understand the need for static route entries to prevent routing updates from initiating a call and thus adding unnecessary service charges. You can configure DDR with several different options as well. For instance, an idle timer disconnects a call when no traffic has been transmitted for a predetermined period of time.

You can also use DDR for other valuable purposes, such as backup for a leased line or Frame Relay connection. In this case, an ISDN link may be brought up after a certain load has been reached on the main line or a preconfigured amount of time has lapsed since the line became inactive.

Another DDR concept that is discussed in Lesson 6-2 is legacy DDR versus dialer profiles. You can think of legacy DDR as the configuration that applies to the physical interface, whereas dialer profiles use logical dialer interfaces to accomplish DDR.

Configuring ISDN

Configuring ISDN on a router involves setting up several global and interface parameters. Some of the parameters are mandatory, and others are optional. This chapter specifies both kinds.

The tasks to perform when configuring ISDN include the following:

- **Global parameters**—Specify the switch type used by the central office (CO), set up static routes to various ISDN destinations, and select conditions for initiating an ISDN call—that is, interesting traffic.

- **Interface parameters**—Configure interface options, assign an interface to a dialer group, and map ISDN calls to the appropriate destinations.

- **Optional parameters**—Include options such as idle timer or response time to a call.

Most of these tasks aren't arranged in this particular order. You will probably go back and forth between configuration modes while setting up your ISDN.

Lesson 6-1: Beginning ISDN Configuration

This lesson covers the initial tasks that are part of any ISDN configuration. The following configuration steps are included:

Step 1   Configuring the ISDN switch type

Step 2   Configuring SPIDs

Step 1: Configuring the ISDN Switch Type

When configuring ISDN, the first thing you should do is specify the switch type. Table 6-2 lists several switches and their Cisco IOS command equivalents. As you can see, there are quite a few. The types of switches vary from country to country. Also, most switches are available in either basic or primary implementations for use with BRI or PRI, accordingly.

Table 6-2   *Types of ISDN Switches*

Command	ISDN Switch
basic-1tr6	1TR6 ISDN switches (Germany)
basic-5ess	AT&T basic rate switches (U.S.)
basic-dms100	NT DMS-100 (North America)
basic-net3	NET3, also known as E-DSS1 or DSS1 switches (United Kingdom and Europe)
basic-ni1	National ISDN-1 (North America)
basic-ni2	National ISDN-2 (North America)
basic-nwnet3	NET3 switches (Norway)
basic-nznet3	NET3 switches (New Zealand)
basic-ts013	TS013 and TS014 switches (Australia)
ntt	NTT ISDN switch (Japan)
primary-4ess	AT&T 4ess switch (U.S.)
primary-5ess	AT&T 5ess switch (U.S.)
primary-dms100	NT DMS-100 switch (U.S.)
primary-net5	NET5 switches (Europe)
vn2 to vn5	VN2, VN3, VN4, and VN5 ISDN switches (France)

Find out which switch is used by your service provider. Make sure you are clear on the correct type of switch to avoid numerous problems.

You can configure the switch type in either global or interface configuration mode. Global mode controls the type of switch for all ISDN interfaces. Interface mode commands apply the switch type to that interface only. If two different switches are specified for global and interface configuration, interface takes precedence over global for that particular interface.

To configure your CO's switch type, use one of the following commands:

```
R6(config)#isdn switch-type switch-identifier
```

or

```
R6(config-if)#isdn switch-type switch-identifier
```

Step 2: Configuring SPIDs

After you've specified the switch type, you might need to specify a service profile identifier (SPID) number. Not all switches require a SPID value, especially outside the U.S. Whenever a SPID number is required, you can find out the exact SPID information from your ISDN service provider.

SPIDS are dial-in numbers used by some service providers with certain types of switches (for example, National ISDN1 and DMS-100). These numbers verify the services provided by your contract. SPIDs are available in spid1 and spid2 categories, one for each B channel.

The syntax for the SPID commands is as follows:

```
R6(config-if)#isdn spid1 spid-number [ldn]

R6(config-if)#isdn spid2 spid-number [ldn]
```

Sometimes the keyword *ldn,* which stands for local directory number, might have to be placed at the end of the command line. The LDN is assigned by the service provider and is used to make sure that calls are properly routed to both B channels.

Example 6-1 shows configuration Steps 1 and 2 described in this lesson. You can see the global setup of the ISDN switch type and the assignment of the SPID numbers under interface BRI0/0.

Example 6-1   *BRI Interface with SPID Numbers Set Up*

```
R6_ISDN(config)#isdn switch-type basic-ni
R6_ISDN(config)#interface BRI0/0
R6 ISDN(config)# no cdp enable
R6_ISDN(config-if)#isdn spid1 5556212
R6_ISDN(config-if)#isdn spid2 5556213
```

NOTE   CDP triggers the ISDN call and therefore should be disabled if it isn't needed.

Lesson 6-2: Configuring DDR

This lesson describes the DDR portion of ISDN configuration. It should be configured after the basic steps described in Lesson 6-1. Configuring DDR is a multistep process:

Step 1   Specifying interesting traffic.

Step 2   Assigning an interesting traffic definition to an interface.

Step 3   Charting destination parameters with legacy DDR or dialer profiles.

Step 1: Specifying Interesting Traffic

You might recall the definition of interesting traffic from the earlier section "Dial-on-Demand Routing (DDR) Overview." To identify interesting traffic, use the **dialer-list** command. The **dialer-list** command has two versions: the basic version and the version referring to an access list. The basic version allows or drops only packets belonging to an entire protocol. The access list version adds the richness of all the options that could be defined by the extended access list. Access lists are described in Chapter 16, "Access Control Lists."

The syntax for the basic **dialer-list** command appears first, followed by the access list version of the command:

```
R6(config)#dialer-list dialer-group-number protocol protocol-name [permit | deny]
```

or

```
R6(config)#dialer-list dialer-group-number protocol protocol-name list
    access-list-number
```

dialer-group-number is the dialer list identifier that is used in the next step of DDR configuration to assign this list to an interface. The *access-list-number* argument matches an extended access list that is defined separately for the purposes of being used with the **dialer-list** command.

Step 2: Assigning **dialer-list** to an Interface

The *dialer-group-number* used in the **dialer-list** command needs to match another command's argument that applies it to an actual interface. The **dialer-list** command set up in global configuration mode controls which packets initiate a call through that interface by referencing the same number in the **dialer-group** interface command:

```
R6(config-if)#dialer-group dialer-group-number
```

To better demonstrate how this works, Example 6-2 combines this and the previous steps. You can see that the **dialer-list** command qualifies all IP traffic as interesting, and the **dialer-group** command assigns this definition to the BRI0/0 interface. The **isdn switch-type** and **spid** commands discussed in Lesson 6-1 are included in the output as well.

Example 6-2 *Specifying Interesting Traffic*

```
R6#show run
!
interface BRI0/0
 ip address 150.100.1.1 255.255.255.252
 encapsulation ppp
 no cdp enable
 dialer string 5551212
 dialer-group 1
 isdn switch-type basic-ni
 isdn spid1 5556212
 isdn spid2 5556213
!
dialer-list 1 protocol ip permit → permits all IP traffic
```

Step 3: Charting Destination Parameters with Legacy DDR or Dialer Profiles

To place a call to a destination, a router needs some way of identifying it. The "Dial-on-Demand Routing (DDR) Overview" section mentioned the existence of legacy DDR and its more-advanced successor, dialer profiles. Here you will learn how to configure both. Remember that they are used as substitution for one another, not a combination.

Configuring Legacy DDR with Dialer Maps

Dialer maps associate the destination router's protocol address with a specific telephone number called the *dial string*. The **dialer map** command allows other options to be specified as well. It's important to understand that this command is applied to the physical interface:

```
R6(config-if)#dialer map protocol next-hop-address [name hostname] [broadcast]
  dial-string
```

This syntax does not include all the options available for this command. Here are the options that are included:

- *protocol*—The Layer 3 protocol to which the phone number is mapped

- *next-hop-address*—The Layer 3 protocol address

- *hostname*—The name of the remote router used for authentication

- **broadcast**—Broadcasts, such as routing updates, are forwarded to this address

- *dial-string*—The destination's telephone number

Multiple **dialer map** statements identifying different destinations may be used on the physical interface.

Example 6-3 illustrates the use of legacy DDR with dialer maps configured on router R6. It offers two **dialer map** statements to the same destination, R8, using two different dial strings. R8's configuration includes two **dialer map** statements pointing back to R6.

Example 6-3   **dialer map** *Statements*

```
R6#show run
hostname R6
!
username R8 password cisco
!
isdn switch-type basic-ni
!
interface BRI0/0
 ip address 150.100.1.1 255.255.255.252
 encapsulation ppp
no cdp enable
 dialer map ip 150.100.1.2 name R8 broadcast 5556214
 dialer map ip 150.100.1.2 name R8 broadcast 5556215
 dialer-group 1
```

Example 6-3 **dialer map** *Statements (Continued)*

```
 ppp authentication chap
 isdn switch-type basic-ni
 isdn spid1 5556212
 isdn spid2 5556213
 !
 dialer-list 1 protocol ip permit

 R8#show run
 hostname R8
 username R6 password cisco
 !
 isdn switch-type basic-ni
 !
 interface BRI0/0
 ip address 150.100.1.2 255.255.255.252
 encapsulation ppp
 no cdp enable
 dialer map ip 150.100.1.1 name R6 broadcast 5556212
 dialer map ip 150.100.1.1 name R6 broadcast 5556213
 dialer-group 1
 ppp authentication chao
 isdn switch-type basic-ni
 isdn spid1 5556214
 isdn spid2 5556215
 !
 dialer-list 1 protocol ip permit
```

NOTE If you have a **dialer string** configured, you must remove it from the BRI interface to use **dialer map**. Otherwise, using a **dialer map** with a *string* argument will not work. You would receive this error message:

```
R6_ISDN(config-if)#dialer map ip 150.100.1.2 name R8 broadcast 5556214
%Cannot change dialer map when dialer string present.
```

Dialer Profiles Over Logical Interfaces

Configuring dialer profiles is more complicated than legacy DDR. So why use dialer profiles? The answer is that dialer profiles allow for greater flexibility, and that often is the deciding factor.

Whereas dialer maps are applied to physical interfaces, dialer profiles involve logical interfaces called *dialer interfaces*. The logical interface configurations are then dynamically joined with the physical on a per-call basis. They also enable different configuration for separate B channels.

To configure dialer profiles, you need to remove all legacy DDR settings from the physical interface and then follow these steps:

Step 1   Create a logical interface:

```
R6(config)#interface dialer number-between-0-and-255
```

Step 2   Add interface characteristics such as IP address, encapsulation type, and PPP authentication type (as described in Lesson 6-5).

Step 3   Configure the name of one remote router on the dialer interface:

```
R6(config-if)#dialer remote-name hostname
```

Step 4   Add a dialer string to a logical interface. (Dialer maps work only on physical interfaces.)

Step 5   Bind the physical interface with a logical interface. This is a dual-step process:

(a)   Configure a dialer pool on a logical interface:

```
R6(config-if)#dialer pool number-between-1-and-255
```

(b)   Assign the physical interface to the configured dialer pool:

```
R6(config-if)#dialer pool-member dialer-pool-number
```

Step 6   Assign interesting traffic definition to a dialer interface with the **dialer-group** command.

Example 6-4 demonstrates these configuration steps in action.

Example 6-4   *DDR Dialer Profiles*

```
R6#show run
hostname R6
!
username R8 password <chap_password>
!
isdn switch-type basic-ni
!
interface Ethernet0/0
ip address 172.16.2.6 255.255.255.0
no cdp enable
!
interface BRI0/0
encapsulation ppp
no cdp enable
dialer pool-member 1
isdn switch-type basic-ni
isdn spid1 40855512100101 5551210
isdn spid2 40855512110101 5551211
ppp authentication chap
ppp multilink
```

Example 6-4 *DDR Dialer Profiles (Continued)*

```
!
interface Dialer0
ip address 150.100.1.1 255.255.255.252
encapsulation ppp
no cdp enable
dialer remote-name R8
dialer string 5551212 class R8
dialer load-threshold 128 outbound
dialer pool 1
dialer-group 5
ppp authentication chap
ppp multilink
!
map-class dialer R8
  dialer idle-timeout 180
  dialer fast-idle 5
!
ip route 172.16.1.0 255.255.255.0 Dialer0
ip route 172.16.1.0 255.255.255.0 150.100.1.2
dialer-list 5 protocol ip permit
```

Lesson 6-3: Routing Over ISDN

You already know that if you choose to advertise routing updates and inadvertently don't prevent those updates from bringing up the link, you might be unpleasantly surprised when you receive a bill from your provider.

Do not despair. ISDN technology offers numerous options to successfully accomplish what you need while keeping the charges in check. These options include:

- Static routes and default routes

- Dynamic routing with the **passive-interfaces** command

- Floating static routes

- OSPF demand circuit

The most pertinent options are described in the next sections.

Static Routes and Default Routes

Whenever you implement a stub network, there is no real need to use dynamic routing, because all connections come from and go to the same point. Stub networking is discussed in more detail in Chapter 10, "OSPF." Figure 6-7 illustrates a network in which static routes would come in handy.

Figure 6-7   *Stub Network*

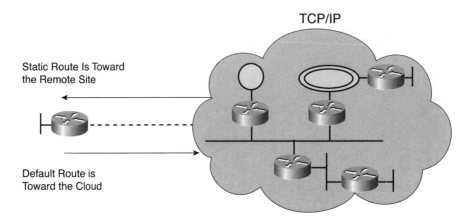

To set up static routing, use the following command:

```
R6(config)#ip route destination-address destination-subnet-mask [local-interface |
  next-hop-address]
```

NOTE   Should you decide to use the local interface instead of the next-hop address, make sure that destination parameters are set up via **dialer-string**. If **dialer map** is used, DDR won't work.

When you configure static routing, you want to include a default route instance as well. This causes all unknown routes that are not part of a routing table to be forwarded to the same address that can make a routing decision for you. To accomplish this task, use the following commands alongside the **ip route** command:

```
R6(config)#ip route 0.0.0.0 0.0.0.0 next-hop-address
```

or

```
R6(config)#ip default-network known-network-address
```

A network address and subnet mask of 0.0.0.0 indicates to the router that a default route is being referenced. Consider Figure 6-8 and Example 6-5 to see how these commands work together.

Figure 6-8   *Static and Default Routing Topology*

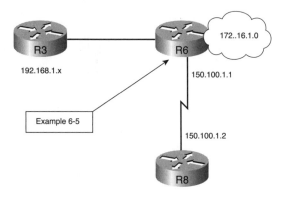

Example 6-5   *Static and Default Routing*

```
R6#config t
Enter configuration commands, one per line.  End with CNTL/Z.
R6(config)#router rip
R6(config-router)#network 172.16.1.0
R6(config-router)#redistribute static
R6(config-router)#version 2
R6(config-router)#exit
R6(config)#ip route 192.168.1.0 255.255.255.0 150.100.1.2
R6(config)#ip route 0.0.0.0 0.0.0.0 150.100.1.2
```

Sometimes a situation occurs in which other networks need to be informed of the stub network's existence. Therefore, the static route is redistributed into a dynamic protocol of your choice. For this purpose, apply the following command:

```
R6(config-router)#redistribute static
```

Passive Interfaces

If you introduce your stub network into your dynamic protocol, you assume your links will be constantly brought up by the routing updates, right? Well, not if you configure passive interfaces. A passive interface listens to routing updates but doesn't forward them. Use the following command to configure a passive interface:

```
R6(config-router)#passive-interface interface
```

Figure 6-9 illustrates a network example, and Example 6-6 shows a way of configuring a passive interface for a routing protocol.

Figure 6-9   **passive-interface** *Command Application*

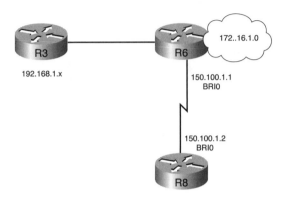

Example 6-6   **passive-interface** *Command*

```
R6#config t
Enter configuration commands, one per line. End with CNTL/Z.
R6(config)#router rip
R6(config-router)#network 172.16.0.0
R6(config-router)#passive-interface bri0
```

Floating Static Routes

Figure 6-10 exemplifies a situation in which you might want your static routes to take the back
burner to dynamic routing and be used only if other routes are unavailable.

To make this possible, you need to configure floating static routes. Normally, static routes have
a default administrative distance of 1. This means that under ordinary circumstances they are
preferred over dynamic routing protocols. To use dynamic routing instead of static routing,
manually assign an administrative distance to the static route that is higher than the one for a
dynamic route. A value above 200 is recommended to ensure that the administrative distance of
your floating static route is higher than the default administrative distance of a dynamic
protocol. Employ the familiar **ip route** command, but this time add an *administrative distance*
argument at the end:

```
R6(config)#ip route destination-network destination-subnet-mask [local-interface |
  next-hop] administrative-distance
```

Figure 6-10 *Floating Static Routes*

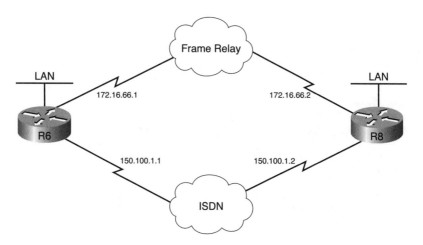

Example 6-7 shows a configuration of a floating static route with the assigned administrative distance of 200.

Example 6-7 *Configuration of a Floating Static Route*

```
R6#show run
hostname r6
!
username r8 password 0 cisco
isdn switch-type basic-ni
!
Interface ethernet 0/0
no cdp enable
ip address 172.16.6.1 255.255.255.0
!
interface serial 0/0
ip address 172.16.66.1 255.255.255.0
encapsulation frame-relay
no cdp enable
frame-relay map ip 172.16.66.2 68 broadcast
!
Interface BRI0/0
ip address 150.100.1.1 255.255.255.0
encapsulation ppp
no cdp enable
isdn spid1 40855512100101 5551210
isdn spid2 40855512110101 5551211
dialer map ip 150.100.1.2 broadcast 5551212
dialer-group 1
ppp authentication chap
```

continues

Example 6-7 *Configuration of a Floating Static Route (Continued)*

```
!
router rip
passive-interface BRI0
network 172.16.0.0
network 150.100.0.0
version 2
!
ip classless
!
ip route 172.16.8.0 255.255.255.0 150.100.1.2 200
!
dialer-list 1 protocol ip permit
R8#show run
hostname r8
!
username r6 password 0 cisco
isdn switch-type basic-ni
!
Interface ethernet 0/0
ip address 172.16.8.1 255.255.255.0
no cdp enable
!
interface serial 0/0
ip address 172.16.66.2 255.255.255.0
encapsulation frame-relay
no cdp enable
frame-relay map ip 172.16.66.1 86 broadcast
!
Interface BRI0/0
ip address 150.100.1.2 255.255.255.0
encapsulation ppp
no cdp enable
isdn spid1 40855512120101 5551212
isdn spid2 40855512130101 5551213
dialer map ip 150.100.1.1 broadcast 5551210
dialer-group 1
ppp authentication chap
!
router rip
passive-interface BRI0
network 172.16.0.0
network 150.100.0.0
version 2
!
ip classless
!
ip route 172.16.6.0 255.255.255.0 150.100.1.1 200
!
dialer-list 1 protocol ip permit
```

OSPF Demand Circuit

This section concentrates on how OSPF demand circuit pertains to ISDN. For a more comprehensive look at OSPF, see Chapter 10.

OSPF demand circuit is yet another feature that enables routing over ISDN without keeping the link constantly open. Perhaps you already know that to maintain neighbor relationships and ensure the accuracy of its link-state databases, OSPF sends hello packets every 10 seconds and link-state advertisements (LSAs) every 30 minutes. Normally, this constant exchange of hellos and LSAs would keep the link up indefinitely.

The OSPF demand circuit option was created to stifle periodic hellos and LSAs. When demand circuit is configured on a router, its hello packets have a Demand Circuit (DC) bit set, and its LSAs have a DoNotAge (DNA) bit set, which suppresses those periodic refreshers. The way this works is at first OSPF creates adjacencies and synchronizes LSA databases in the usual manner. After that process is done, OSPF keeps those adjacencies so that the routing updates can initiate an ISDN call only after a topological change has taken place.

To configure the OSPF demand circuit, use the following command on your ISDN interface:

```
R6(config-if)#ip ospf demand-circuit
```

Some people argue that this command should be placed on routers at both ends of the call. However, it needs to reside on only the calling router. It is of no use to the receiving router that has no dial string configured. Figure 6-11 and Example 6-8 demonstrate just that. In instances where both routers have dial strings pointing to one another, do not use OSPF demand circuit. Otherwise, you might run into a situation where both routers initiate a call simultaneously after the topological change, and the call never gets through. You will get a better feel for this and other routing-over-ISDN options in the hands-on chapter of this book, Chapter 26, "Sample Lab Scenarios."

Figure 6-11 *OSPF Demand Circuit*

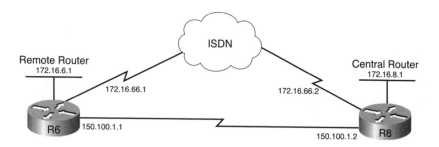

Example 6-8 *OSPF Demand Circuit Configuration on the Remote and Central Routers*

```
R6#show run
hostname r6
!
username r8 password 0 cisco
isdn switch-type basic-ni
!
Interface loopback 0
ip address 172.16.16.1 255.255.255.255
!
Interface ethernet 0/0
ip address 172.16.6.1 255.255.255.0
no cdp enable
!
interface serial 0/0
ip address 150.100.1.1 255.255.255.0
encapsulation ppp
no cdp enable
bandwidth 64
!
Interface BRI0/0
ip address 172.16.66.1 255.255.255.0
encapsulation ppp
no cdp enable
ip ospf demand-circuit
ip ospf cost 9999
isdn spid1 40855512100101 5551210
isdn spid2 40855512110101 5551211
dialer map ip 150.100.1.2 name r8 broadcast 5551212
dialer-group 1
ppp authentication chap
!
router ospf 100
network 150.100.1.0 0.0.0.255 area 0
network 172.16.0.0 0.0.255.255 area 0
!
dialer-list 1 protocol ip permit

R8#show run
hostname r8
!
username r6 password 0 cisco
isdn switch-type basic-ni
!
interface loopback 0
ip address 172.16.18.1 255.255.255.255
!
Interface ethernet 0/0
ip address 172.16.8.1 255.255.255.0
no cdp enable
!
interface serial 0/0
```

Example 6-8 *OSPF Demand Circuit Configuration on the Remote and Central Routers (Continued)*

```
ip address 150.100.1.2 255.255.255.0
encapsulation ppp
no cdp enable
bandwidth 64
!
Interface BRI0/0
ip address 172.16.66.2 255.255.255.0
encapsulation ppp
no cdp enable
isdn spid1 40855512120101 5551212
isdn spid2 40855512130101 5551213
dialer-group 1
ppp authentication chap
!
router ospf
network 150.100.1.0 0.0.0.255 area 0
network 172.16.0.0 0.0.255.255 area 0
!
dialer-list 1 protocol ip permit
```

Several issues are associated with OSPF demand circuit. If you are not careful while redistributing protocols into OSPF, demand circuit might cause routing loops and link flapping. These in turn keep the line up indefinitely because of the constant "change" in topology.

Link flaps can occur when OSPF demand circuit is configured. When you run PPP encapsulation, it installs a host route /32 for the other side of the link. RIPv1 supports classful networks only, so RIP "owns" this /32. When you redistribute RIP into OSPF, this /32 also gets redistributed as an external route. When the link goes down, this /32 disappears, and OSPF recognizes this as a change in topology. Therefore, the DC brings up the link. This process keeps repeating, and route flapping occurs. There are two ways to solve this:

- Use the **no peer neighbor-route** command under the BRI0/0 interface that's running demand circuit. This ensures that /32 is not installed anymore.

- When redistributing RIPv1 into OSPF, use a route map to deny /32.

In addition to link flapping, you might encounter a scenario in which the ISDN interface's bandwidth, which figures into the OSPF metric of cost, equals that of the primary link. OSPF cost is based on the following formula:

cost = 100,000,000/bandwidth (bps)

Lesson 6-4: Configuring the Interface and Backup Interface

Although this chapter has introduced you to several interface mode commands, you haven't concentrated on an interface configuration itself. This lesson explains interface setup and leads you right into the discussion of the interface backup configuration. The discussion revolves around the following configuration parameters:

- Entering interface configuration mode

- Configuring the backup interface

- Configuring the backup interface's optional parameters

- Configuring encapsulation options

Entering Interface Configuration Mode

To specify the interface for use by ISDN, choose one of the two available commands. The first command applies to routers with the native ISDN interface TE1:

```
R6(config)#interface bri number
```

If native TE1 is not a part of your router setup, you need to designate a serial interface for use in ISDN with the following command. The serial interface becomes TE2 with external TA.

```
R6(config)#interface serial number
```

All subsequent commands that govern the interface take place in interface configuration mode. Whether you are using legacy DDR or dialer profiles determines whether most of your interface configuration tasks are applied to a logical or physical interface. Regardless, the ISDN interface is assigned a protocol address, encapsulation option (discussed later in this lesson), dialer group, and, possibly, SPID numbers.

Configuring the Backup Interface

You already know that the ISDN interface might act as a backup to another interface. For instance, when that interface goes down or becomes oversaturated with traffic, the ISDN interface steps in and takes over.

The backup interface is used as an alternative to the floating static routes discussed earlier. When an ISDN interface is configured as the backup, its status changes to "standby" and its line protocol state to "down." They remain that way until something happens to the main link. The command for backup interface is configured under the principal interface (not the ISDN interface!). The syntax for the command is as follows:

```
R6(config-if)#backup interface interface number
```

Configuring the Backup Interface's Optional Parameters

Several optional parameters can be configured under a backup interface setup. The **backup delay** command specifies the amount of time in seconds that lapses after the main interface failure and before the ISDN backup link is brought up. The **backup delay** command also specifies how long after the principal link is repaired the ISDN interface stays up until it becomes inactive again. This command is used in conjunction with the **backup interface** command under the chief interface configuration. If the **backup delay** command is omitted, the ISDN interface kicks in instantaneously after the primary link failure and deactivates after the primary link is back—not a good idea when you are dealing with a flapping connection.

```
R6(config-if)#backup delay activation-time deactivation-time
```

NOTE   Unlike the floating static routes, **backup delay** works only when the principal interface is physically down. It does not work under the "administratively down" status.

The **backup load** command is used in a bandwidth-on-demand scenario. It controls the percentage of main link saturation before activating the ISDN interface as well as the percentage decrease in traffic before bringing down the ISDN link. It is also used with the **backup interface** command.

```
R6(config-if)#backup load activation-percentage deactivation-percentage
```

backup load can be configured alongside the **backup delay** command. Then, each command is responsible for its own sphere of influence. Example 6-9 exhibits a backup interface configuration with **backup delay** and **backup load**.

Example 6-9   *ISDN as a Backup Configuration*

```
R6#show run
hostname r6
!
username r8 password 0 cisco
isdn switch-type basic-ni
!
Interface ethernet 0/0
ip address 172.16.6.1 255.255.255.0
!
interface serial 0/0
backup delay 10 60
backup load 10 30
backup interface BRI0/0
ip address 172.16.66.1 255.255.255.0
encapsulation frame-relay
frame-relay map ip 172.16.66.2 68 broadcast
!
Interface BRI0/0 <- Active only if physical link goes down.
ip address 150.100.1.1 255.255.255.0
encapsulation ppp
no cdp enable
isdn spid1 40855512100101 5551210
isdn spid2 40855512110101 5551211
```

continues

Example 6-9 *ISDN as a Backup Configuration (Continued)*

```
dialer map ip 150.100.1.2 broadcast 5551212
dialer-group 1
ppp authentication chap
!
router rip
no auto-summary
network 172.16.0.0
network 150.100.0.0
version 2
!
dialer-list 1 protocol ip permit
```

Configuring Encapsulation Options

Interface encapsulation is one of the parameters necessary to configure an ISDN interface. Theoretically, BRI interfaces can be encapsulated with HDLC, X.25, LAPB, and Frame Relay. Here you concentrate on PPP encapsulation because it gives you greater control, including Password Authentication Protocol (PAP) and Challenge Handshake Authentication Protocol (CHAP). For more information on PPP, see the earlier section "Point-to-Point Protocol (PPP) Overview."

To configure PPP encapsulation on an ISDN interface, use the following command:

```
R6(config-if)#encapsulation ppp
```

Lesson 6-5: Configuring PPP Options

Example 6-10 is a snapshot of the multitude of PPP options offered on a BRI interface.

Example 6-10 *Options for PPP Under a BRI Interface*

```
R8(config-if)#ppp ?
  authentication  Set PPP link authentication method
  bap             Set BAP bandwidth allocation parameters
  bridge          Enable PPP bridge translation
  callback        Set PPP link callback option
  chap            Set CHAP authentication parameters
  encrypt         Enable PPP encryption
  ipcp            Set IPCP negotiation options
  lcp             PPP LCP configuration
  link            Set miscellaneous link parameters
  max-bad-auth    Allow multiple authentication failures
  multilink       Make interface multilink capable
  pap             Set PAP authentication parameters
  quality         Set minimum Link Quality before link is down
  reliable-link   Use LAPB with PPP to provide a reliable link
  timeout         Set PPP timeout parameters
  use-tacacs      Use TACACS to verify PPP authentications
```

Many of the most widely used PPP options are discussed in this lesson. You might choose to use some of these options in your setup as a matter of personal preference; others might be required.

Lesson 6-6: Configuring Advanced Options

This section covers a few widely used ISDN options. Some of them might be a matter of personal preference in your setup; others might be required.

PPP Authentication

As mentioned earlier in this chapter, PPP figures heavily into many of the optional parameters—and authentication is one of them. Authentication is a way to make your connection more secure. You should use it whenever you want to verify the caller's legitimacy. Authentication takes place when the LCP phase of the PPP negotiation process is complete and the link is open. PAP and CHAP are PPP's authentication protocols.

PAP authenticates a peer using a two-way handshake. First, a router sends its host name and secret to another router. Then the receiving router compares these values against a preconfigured value locally or via an AAA server. If a match is found, the first router is granted access. If not, the connection is terminated.

When PAP is used, the secret is sent over the connection in clear text. There is no safeguard from a "playback" attack that might capture your secret and use it to gain access to your network. This inability to shield itself from a protocol analyzer makes PAP an undesirable method of authentication, but you still need to be familiar with its configuration because it is one of the options available and sometimes is the only option supported.

CHAP's main advantage over PAP is its ability to encrypt the verification process with the Message Digest 5 (MD5) algorithm and periodically recheck a caller's identity with variable value challenges, thus providing protection against "playback."

CHAP uses a three-way handshake process. The authenticating party sends a challenge message to the peer seeking access. In turn, the peer responds with a one-way hash value, the result of an MD5 calculation. The authenticator verifies the received value against its own expected value calculated in the same manner. If a match is found, the peer is authenticated. Otherwise, the connection is terminated.

Both PAP and CHAP configuration presume that you have already configured **encapsulation ppp**. They involve the following commands:

```
R6(config-if)#ppp authentication pap
```

or

```
R6(config-if)#ppp authentication chap
```

The **ppp authentication** command specifies the authentication protocol you choose. The following command must match the remote router's host name and password:

```
R6(config)#username remote-router-name password remote-router-password
```

Examples 6-11 and 6-12 show the output of PAP and CHAP configuration, respectively.

Example 6-11 *PPP PAP Configuration*

```
R6#show run
hostname r6
!
username r8 password 0 cisco
isdn switch-type basic-ni
!
Interface BRI0/0
ip address 150.100.1.1 255.255.255.0
encapsulation ppp
no cdp enable
isdn spid1 40855512100101 5551210
isdn spid2 40855512110101 5551211
dialer map ip 150.100.1.2 name r8 broadcast 5551212
dialer-group 1
ppp authentication pap
!
dialer-list 1 protocol ip permit

R8#show run
hostname r8
!
username r6 password 0 cisco
isdn switch-type basic-ni
!
Interface BRI0/0
ip address 150.100.1.2 255.255.255.0
encapsulation ppp
no cdp enable
isdn spid1 40855512120101 5551212
isdn spid2 40855512130101 5551213
dialer-group 1
ppp authentication pap
!
dialer-list 1 protocol ip permit
```

Example 6-12 *PPP CHAP Configuration*

```
R6#show run
hostname r6
!
username r8 password 0 cisco
isdn switch-type basic-ni
```

Example 6-12 *PPP CHAP Configuration (Continued)*

```
!
Interface BRI0/0
ip address 150.100.1.1 255.255.255.0
encapsulation ppp
no cdp enable
isdn spid1 40855512100101 5551210
isdn spid2 40855512110101 5551211
dialer map ip 150.100.1.2 name r8 broadcast 5551212
dialer-group 1
ppp authentication chap
!
dialer-list 1 protocol ip permit

R8#show run
hostname r8
!
username r6 password 0 cisco
isdn switch-type basic-ni
!
Interface BRI0/0
ip address 150.100.1.2 255.255.255.0
encapsulation ppp
no cdp enable
dialer map ip 150.100.1.1 name r6 broadcast 5551210
isdn spid1 40855512120101 5551212
isdn spid2 40855512130101 5551213
dialer-group 1
ppp authentication chap
!
dialer-list 1 protocol ip permit
```

PPP Authentication with a Different Host Name

You might run into a situation in which a username you set up for a calling router does not match its host name. For instance, not knowing a router's host name, dealing with a rotational host name, or simply shortening the task of storing a multitude of host names with their respective passwords would prompt you to skip the real host name and opt for an alternative. Cisco offers such an option for CHAP in its Cisco IOS software.

To achieve authentication with a different host name, configure the **username password** command on called router R8 using an alternative host name. At the same time, match this alternative host name on calling router R6 with the following command:

```
R6(config-if)#ppp chap hostname alternate-host-name
```

Example 6-13 shows R6 configured with an alternative host name for CHAP authentication and R8 capable of accepting this alternative host name.

Example 6-13 *Using an Alternative Host Name*

```
R6#show run
hostname r6
!
username r8 password 0 cisco
isdn switch-type basic-ni
!
Interface BRI0/0
ip address 150.100.1.1 255.255.255.0
encapsulation ppp
no cdp enable
isdn spid1 40855512100101 5551210
isdn spid2 40855512110101 5551211
dialer map ip 150.100.1.2 name r8 broadcast 5551212
dialer-group 1
ppp authentication chap
ppp chap hostname ccie
!
dialer-list 1 protocol ip permit

R8#show run
!
hostname r8
!
username r6 password 0 cisco
username ccie password 0 cisco
isdn switch-type basic-ni
!
Interface BRI0/0
ip address 150.100.1.2 255.255.255.0
encapsulation ppp
no cdp enable
dialer map ip 150.100.1.1 name r6 broadcast 5551210
isdn spid1 40855512120101 5551212
isdn spid2 40855512130101 5551213
dialer-group 1
ppp authentication chap
!
dialer-list 1 protocol ip permit
```

Unidirectional PPP Authentication

You can use the **ppp authentication [pap | chap]** command with an optional **callin** keyword at the end. This keyword specifies that authentication is to be used only if the router is on the receiving end of the call. Normally, when PPP authentication is used, it is requested by both communicating routers that mutually authenticate one another.

What if one of the routers doesn't support authentication? In the scenario depicted in Figure 6-12, if R6 places a call into R8, it allows R8 to challenge R6, but R6 does not challenge R8 in return. However, if R8 places a call to R6 (a call in), R6 makes an authentication request from R8. The full syntax for the command is as follows:

```
R6(config-if)#ppp authentication [pap | chap] callin
```

Figure 6-12 shows one-way authentication between R6 and R8.

Figure 6-12 *One-Way PPP Authentication*

PPP Multilink

It is possible to combine two or more B channels into one (called a *virtual channel*) by using bandwidth aggregation techniques. The channels are grouped into a bundle of up to 2 links for BRI, 23 for T1, and 30 for E1 PRIs. The Multilink PPP (MLP) technique is described here, but the Cisco proprietary Bandwidth on Demand (BOD), MLP's predecessor, is outside the scope of this book.

MLP provides load balancing by fragmenting packets and sending them simultaneously across multiple physical channels to the same destination, where they are reassembled. The process is specified by an additional 4-byte PPP frame header that controls sequencing for the fragments. Standard DDR should be configured before adding MLP. You can apply MLP settings to the physical or virtual interface depending on whether legacy DDR or dialer profiles are used.

MLP is negotiated between two network devices during the LCP phase. If needed, additional bandwidth is temporarily allocated between them. This happens according to the threshold configured for inbound and/or outbound traffic (outbound is the default). The threshold is a value between 1 and 255 representing two ends of the first channel's utilization spectrum; the lesser the value, the quicker another link comes up. This value is calculated over a 5-minute interval. Preferably, only one end of a link should be configured for load threshold, or different values should be assigned to both ends.

```
R6(config-if)#dialer load-threshold load [outbound | inbound | either]
```

Similarly, the load threshold determines link subtraction as well as addition. When the link saturation falls below the specified percentage for the idle timer interval, the latest channel to have been added to the bundle is dropped. If there is no traffic on the link during the idle timer interval, the entire bundle is terminated. The command to configure the idle timer is as follows:

```
R6(config-if)#dialer idle-timeout seconds
```

Finally, you need to enable MLP itself on an interface. Again, the interface in question may be physical or logical, depending on your layout. The syntax for the command is as follows:

```
R6(config-if)#ppp multilink
```

Example 6-14 displays the coherent configuration of MLP.

Example 6-14 *MLP Configuration*

```
R6#show run
!
hostname r6
!
username r8 password 0 cisco
isdn switch-type basic-ni
!
Interface BRI0/0
ip address 150.100.1.1 255.255.255.0
encapsulation ppp
no cdp enable
isdn spid1 40855512100101 5551210
isdn spid2 40855512110101 5551211
dialer map ip 150.100.1.2 name r8 broadcast 5551212
dialer load-threshold 127 either
dialer idle-timeout 30 inbound
dialer-group 1
ppp authentication chap
ppp multilink
!
dialer-list 1 protocol ip permit
```

ISDN Callback

The ISDN callback feature is implemented when you want central control over all outgoing ISDN calls. This is generally done for billing and various other objectives such as security. The security aspect is achieved by calls made back to preconfigured telephone numbers, as well as mandatory PPP authentication before the callback occurs.

How does a callback work? The method is based on a client/server relationship. During LCP negotiation, the remote end (client) requests a callback from the central site (server). The server acknowledges the request, authenticates the client, and verifies whether this client is approved for callback. If it is, the server disconnects the call from its client, waits for the specified amount of time, and initiates a call back to the client. If callback is not set up for the client, the server continues the original call.

Several commands are used on either side of the call to make the callback operation possible. On the client side, aside from authentication and other standard ISDN and DDR statements, you need to tell the interface that it will be the client of the client/server model. Use the following command:

```
R6(config-if)#ppp callback request
```

Also, you need to specify how long the client is willing to wait for a callback from the server:

```
R6(config-if)#dialer hold-queue packets timeout seconds
```

On the server, you need to configure the flip side of those two commands with the following:

```
R8(config-if)#ppp callback accept

R8(config-if)#dialer enable-timeout seconds
```

The first command is self-explanatory. The second specifies how long the server waits before making a callback. The recommended time is half of whatever is set with the **dialer hold-queue timeout** command on the client. Remember, if the return call hasn't been established, the callback server does not retry the call. Additionally, if you want to maintain a higher level of security and disconnect the client call even if it's not allowed the callback, configure the following command on the server side:

```
R8(config-if)#dialer callback-secure
```

Now, think back to the DDR **dialer map** command. This time it needs to include the **class** keyword along with the case-sensitive *classname* to reference a **map-class** statement for PPP callback. The third command has a keyword **username** that aligns it with the *hostname* in the **dialer map** statement to point it to the dialer string to use when calling back to the client:

```
R8(config-if)#dialer map protocol next-hop-address name hostname class classname
   dial-string
R8(config-map-class)#map-class dialer classname
R8(config-map-class)#dialer callback-server [username]
```

Examples 6-15 and 6-16 demonstrate both sides of the PPP callback configuration.

Example 6-15 *PPP Callback Client Configuration*

```
R6#show run
!
hostname r6
!
username r8 password 0 cisco
isdn switch-type basic-ni
!
Interface BRI0/0
no ip directed-broadcast
dialer wait-for-carrier-time 30
dialer hold-queue 100 timeout 30
isdn switch-type basic-ni
ppp callback request
```

continues

Example 6-15 *PPP Callback Client Configuration (Continued)*

```
 ip address 150.100.1.1 255.255.255.0
 encapsulation ppp
 no cdp enable
 isdn spid1 40855512100101 5551210
 isdn spid2 40855512110101 5551211
 dialer map ip 150.100.1.2 name r8 broadcast 5551212
 dialer-group 1
 ppp authentication chap
 !
 dialer-list 1 protocol ip permit
```

Example 6-16 *PPP Callback Server Configuration*

```
R8#show run
!
hostname r8
!
username r6 password 0 cisco
isdn switch-type basic-ni
!
interface BRI0/0
 ip address 150.100.1.2 255.255.255.0
 encapsulation ppp
no cdp enable
 dialer callback-secure
 dialer enable-timeout 15
 dialer map ip 150.100.1.1 name r6 class callback 5551210
 dialer hold-queue 100
 dialer-group 1
 isdn switch-type basic-ni
 isdn spid1 40855512120101 5551212
 isdn spid2 40855512130101 5551213
 no cdp enable
 ppp callback accept
 ppp authentication chap
 !
map-class dialer callback
 dialer callback-server username
 !
 dialer-list 1 protocol ip permit
```

NOTE   This section concentrated on the router-to-router callback configuration using the Cisco IOS software command-line interface. AAA server techniques are covered in Chapter 18, "AAA Services."

Lesson 6-7: Monitoring and Troubleshooting ISDN

This section explains commands you can use to verify your ISDN configuration and perform troubleshooting. The following **show** and **debug** commands are discussed:

- **show interfaces bri 0/0**
- **show isdn status**
- **show dialer**
- **show isdn active**
- **show ppp multilink**
- **debug dialer events**
- **debug isdn events**
- **debug ppp multilink** [*events*]/[*fragments*]
- **debug ppp authentication**
- **debug ppp negotiation**
- **debug isdn q931**

The show interfaces bri Command

If you want to verify the status of the native ISDN interface (TE1) on your router, you can issue the **show interfaces bri** command.

You may also choose to add 1 and/or 2 at the end of the command to view the status of the first or second B channel or both of them. The syntax for this command is as follows:

```
R6#show interfaces bri number[[:bchannel] | [first] [last]]
```

Example 6-17 shows the command output. Notice that the line protocol state is up and spoofing. This means that the ISDN interface is acting as if it were up so that the traffic can be passed through it if necessary.

Example 6-17 **show interfaces bri 0/0** *Command Output*

```
R8#show interfaces bri 0/0
BRI0/0 is up, line protocol is up (spoofing)
  Hardware is PQUICC BRI with U interface
  Internet address is 150.100.1.2/24
  MTU 1500 bytes, BW 64 Kbit, DLY 20000 usec,
     reliability 255/255, txload 1/255, rxload 1/255
  Encapsulation PPP, loopback not set
  Last input never, output never, output hang never
  Last clearing of "show interface" counters 00:11:56
```

continues

Example 6-17 show interfaces bri 0/0 *Command Output (Continued)*

```
   Input queue: 0/75/0/0 (size/max/drops/flushes); Total output drops: 0
   Queueing strategy: weighted fair
   Output queue: 0/1000/64/0 (size/max total/threshold/drops)
      Conversations  0/0/16 (active/max active/max total)
      Reserved Conversations 0/0 (allocated/max allocated)
      Available Bandwidth 48 kilobits/sec
   5 minute input rate 0 bits/sec, 0 packets/sec
   5 minute output rate 0 bits/sec, 0 packets/sec
      0 packets input, 0 bytes, 0 no buffer
      Received 0 broadcasts, 0 runts, 0 giants, 0 throttles
      0 input errors, 0 CRC, 0 frame, 0 overrun, 0 ignored, 0 abort
      0 packets output, 0 bytes, 0 underruns
      0 output errors, 0 collisions, 1 interface resets
      0 output buffer failures, 0 output buffers swapped out
      0 carrier transitions
```

Example 6-18 shows the output for the **show interfaces bri 0/0 1 2** command.

Example 6-18 show interfaces bri 0/0 1 2 *Command Output*

```
R8#show interfaces bri 0/0 1 2
BRI0/0:1 is up, line protocol is up
  Hardware is PQUICC BRI with U interface
  MTU 1500 bytes, BW 64 Kbit, DLY 20000 usec,
      reliability 255/255, txload 1/255, rxload 1/255
  Encapsulation PPP, loopback not set
  Keepalive set (10 sec)
  LCP Closed
  Closed: IPCP
  Last input never, output never, output hang never
  Last clearing of "show interface" counters never
  Input queue: 0/75/0/0 (size/max/drops/flushes); Total output drops: 0
  Queueing strategy: weighted fair
  Output queue: 0/1000/64/0 (size/max total/threshold/drops)
      Conversations  0/0/16 (active/max active/max total)
      Reserved Conversations 0/0 (allocated/max allocated)
      Available Bandwidth 48 kilobits/sec
  5 minute input rate 0 bits/sec, 0 packets/sec
  5 minute output rate 0 bits/sec, 0 packets/sec
      0 packets input, 0 bytes, 0 no buffer
      Received 0 broadcasts, 0 runts, 0 giants, 0 throttles
      0 input errors, 0 CRC, 0 frame, 0 overrun, 0 ignored, 0 abort
      0 packets output, 0 bytes, 0 underruns
      0 output errors, 0 collisions, 0 interface resets
      0 output buffer failures, 0 output buffers swapped out
      0 carrier transitions
BRI0/0:2 is up, line protocol is up
  Hardware is PQUICC BRI with U interface
  MTU 1500 bytes, BW 64 Kbit, DLY 20000 usec,
      reliability 255/255, txload 1/255, rxload 1/255
```

Example 6-18 show interfaces bri 0/0 1 2 *Command Output (Continued)*

```
  Encapsulation PPP, loopback not set
  Keepalive set (10 sec)
  LCP Closed
  Closed: IPCP
  Last input never, output never, output hang never
  Last clearing of "show interface" counters never
  Input queue: 0/75/0/0 (size/max/drops/flushes); Total output drops: 0
  Queueing strategy: weighted fair
  Output queue: 0/1000/64/0 (size/max total/threshold/drops)
     Conversations  0/0/16 (active/max active/max total)
     Reserved Conversations 0/0 (allocated/max allocated)
     Available Bandwidth 48 kilobits/sec
  5 minute input rate 0 bits/sec, 0 packets/sec
  5 minute output rate 0 bits/sec, 0 packets/sec
     0 packets input, 0 bytes, 0 no buffer
     Received 0 broadcasts, 0 runts, 0 giants, 0 throttles
     0 input errors, 0 CRC, 0 frame, 0 overrun, 0 ignored, 0 abort
     0 packets output, 0 bytes, 0 underruns
     0 output errors, 0 collisions, 0 interface resets
     0 output buffer failures, 0 output buffers swapped out
     0 carrier transitions
```

Some of the details in the output include the PPP encapsulation and the status of LCP and NCP.

NOTE   If your interface is not a native BRI (TE2), use the **show interfaces serial** command.

The **show isdn status** Command

Issue the **show isdn status** command to see whether your router is communicating successfully with the service provider switch. It should be one of the first verification commands you use. The output of this command indicates the current configured switch type, the status of Layers 1, 2, and 3, and the SPIDs' status, among other things.

Example 6-19 shows output from the **show isdn status** command.

Example 6-19 show isdn status *Command Output*

```
r6#show isdn status
Global ISDN Switchtype = basic-5ess
ISDN BRI0 interface
        dsl 0, interface ISDN Switchtype = basic-5ess
    Layer 1 Status:              Layer 1 ISDN is up
        ACTIVE                   Circuit is Active
    Layer 2 Status:
        TEI = 64, Ces = 1, SAPI = 0, State = MULTIPLE_FRAME_ESTABLISHED
```

continues

Example 6-19 show isdn status *Command Output (Continued)*

```
  Layer 3 Status:
       1 Active Layer 3 Call(s)            Connection has been made to another
  Host or Router
         CCB:callid=8010, sapi=0, ces=1, B-chan=1, calltype=DATA
     Active dsl 0 CCBs = 1
     The Free Channel Mask:  0x80000002
     Total Allocated ISDN CCBs = 1
```

The **show isdn status** command can also be employed to zero in on more-specific characteristics. Here is the syntax of this command with its available keywords:

```
R6#show isdn status [dsl | serial number]
```

NOTE Sometimes if you change the already-configured switch type and SPIDs parameters, the changes do not take effect until the interface is reset. Use the **show isdn status** command to view the correct current information.

The **show dialer** Command

The **show dialer** command shows statistics for the DDR interface. Among the information you'll find in the output are the statistics for all B channels. These statistics include a dial string for a destination, the reason the channel has been brought up (on the calling router), and the time until the call is disconnected.

Example 6-20 shows interface BRI0 configured as an ISDN dialer.

Example 6-20 show dialer *Command Output*

```
r6#show dialer

BRI0/0 - dialer type = ISDN

Dial String      Successes       Failures      Last Called    Last status
5551212          28              0             00:00:43       successful
0 incoming call(s) have been screened.

BRI0/0:1 - dialer type = ISDN
Idle timer (120 secs), Fast idle timer (20 secs)
Wait for carrier (30 secs), Re-enable (15 secs)
Dialer reason: ip (s=172.16.6.1, d 172.16.8.23)
Time until disconnect 98 secs
Connected to 5551212 (r8)
BRI0/0:2 - dialer type = ISDN
Idle timer (120 secs), Fast idle timer (20 secs)
Wait for carrier (30 secs), Re-enable (15 secs)
```

Example 6-20 show dialer *Command Output (Continued)*

```
Dialer state is physical layer up
Dialer reason: Multilink bundle overloaded
Time until disconnect 98 secs
Connected to 5551212 (r8)
```

The **show isdn active** Command

Like **status**, **active** is an optional keyword at the end of the **show isdn** command. Adding it creates a valuable monitoring tool. As shown in Example 6-21, this command covers current active calls with the called number, the name of a remote node, time connected, time remaining, idle time, and charge-eligible time units during the call period.

Example 6-21 show isdn active *Command Output*

```
R6#show isdn active
--------------------------------------------------------------------------------
                              ISDN ACTIVE CALLS
--------------------------------------------------------------------------------
Call    Calling      Called     Remote  Seconds Seconds Seconds Charges
Type    Number       Number     Name    Used    Left    Idle    Units/Currency
--------------------------------------------------------------------------------
--------------------------------------------------------------------------------
5551212    r8           12                               0       0       -------Out
--------------------------------------------------------------------
```

The **show ppp multilink** Command

The **show ppp multilink** command demonstrates whether there are any active bundles. If there are, you can find out a bundle's name, the number of member channels, which link was first in a bundle, and the number of fragments of various origin and functions.

Example 6-22 shows the results of the **show ppp multilink** command.

Example 6-22 show ppp multilink *Command Output*

```
r6#show ppp multilink

Virtual-Access1, bundle name is r8
! -- Bundle name is the authenticated name of user on the peer device.
  0 lost fragments, 0 reordered, 0 unassigned, sequence 0x2A/0x20 rcvd/sent
  0 discarded, 0 lost received, 1/255 load
  Member links: 2 (max not set, min not set)
    BRI0/0:1
    BRI0/0:2
```

The **debug dialer events** Command

The facts you can gather from the **debug dialer events** command can be very useful. This command is a great aid to the ISDN failure detective.

First, the **debug dialer events** command lists the cause of call initiation so that you can check whether it occurred for the right reasons. If a call fails, this command shows the reason for the failure. Example 6-23 shows output from the **debug dialer events** command.

Example 6-23 debug dialer events *Command Output*

```
r6#debug dialer events
r6#show debugging
Dial on demand:
  Dial on demand events debugging is on
r6#ping 172.16.8.1

Type escape sequence to abort.
Sending 5, 100-byte ICMP Echos to 172.16.8.1, timeout is 2 seconds:

*May 15 23:28:33.828: BRI0/0 DDR: rotor dialout [priority]
*May 15 23:28:33.832: BRI0/0 DDR: Dialing cause ip (s=172.16.6.1, d=172.16.8.1)
*May 15 23:28:33.836: BRI0/0 DDR: Attempting to dial 5551212*May  15 23:28:34.562:
  %LINK-3-UPDOWN: Interface BRI0:1, changed state to up
! -- r6 initiates the DDR process and uses its first BRI B channel.
*May 15 23:28:34.594: BRI0/0:1: interface must be fifo queue, force FIFO
*May 15 23:28:34.610: %DIALER-6-BIND: Interface BRI0/0:1 bound to profile Dialer1.
!!!!
Success rate is 80 percent (4/5), round-trip min/avg/max = 44/53/76 ms
*May 15 23:28:34.626: isdn_call_connect: Calling lineaction of BRI0/0:1
*May 15 23:28:34.761: Dialer1 DDR: Authenticated host r8 with no matching
  dialer map
*May 15 23:28:34.796: Dialer1 DDR: dialer protocol up
*May 15 23:28:35.741: %LINEPROTO-5-UPDOWN: Line protocol on Interface BRI0/0:1,
  changed state to up
*May 15 23:28:40.574: %ISDN-6-CONNECT: Interface BRI0/0:1 is now connected to
  5551212 r8
```

The **debug isdn events** Command

The **debug isdn events** command is used to troubleshoot Layer 3. It monitors the condition of incoming and outgoing calls through the process of call setup and teardown.

Example 6-24 shows sample output from the **debug isdn events** command.

Example 6-24 debug isdn events *Command Output*

```
r6#debug isdn events
r6#clear interface brI 0
*Mar  6 21:20:23.172: ISDN BR0/0: Physical layer is IF_DOWN
*Mar  6 21:20:23.176: ISDN BR0/0: Recvd MPH_IIC_IND from L1
*Mar  6 21:20:23.176: ISDN BR0/0: Recvd MPH_IIC_IND from L1
```

Example 6-24 debug isdn events *Command Output (Continued)*

```
*Mar  6 21:20:23.180: ISDN BR0/0: Shutting down ME
*Mar  6 21:20:23.184: ISDN BR0/0: Shutting down ISDN Layer 3
*Mar  6 21:20:23.208: ISDN BR0/0: L1 is IF_ACTIVE
*Mar  6 21:20:23.212: ISDN BR0/0: Incoming call id = 0x8, dsl 0
r6#
*Mar  6 21:20:24.276: %ISDN-6-LAYER2UP: Layer 2 for Interface BR0/0, TEI 64
  changed to up

r6#ping 150.100.1.2

Type escape sequence to abort.
Sending 5, 100-byte ICMP Echos to 150.100.1.2, timeout is 2 seconds:
..!!!
Success rate is 60 percent (3/5), round-trip min/avg/max = 112/114/120 ms

r6#
*Mar  6 21:17:54.816: ISDN BR0/0: Outgoing call id = 0x8002, dsl 0
*Mar  6 21:17:54.820: ISDN BR0/0: Event: Call to 5551212 at 64 Kb/s
*Mar  6 21:17:54.820: ISDN BR0/0: process_bri_call(): call id 0x8002, called
  _number 5551212, speed 64, call type DATA
*Mar  6 21:17:54.828: CC_CHAN_GetIdleChanbri: dsl 0
*Mar  6 21:17:54.828:     Found idle channel B1
*Mar  6 21:17:54.948: ISDN BR0/0: received HOST_PROCEEDING call_id 0x8002
*Mar  6 21:17:57.236: ISDN BR0/0: received HOST_CONNECT call_id 0x8002
*Mar  6 21:17:57.240: %LINK-3-UPDOWN: Interface BRI0/0:1, changed state to up
*Mar  6 21:17:57.260: %ISDN-6-CONNECT: Interface BRI0:1 is now connected to
  5551212
*Mar  6 21:17:57.272: ISDN BR0/0: Event: Connected to 5551212 on B1 at 64 Kb/s
*Mar  6 21:17:57.412: %LINK-3-UPDOWN: Interface Virtual-Access1, changed state
  to up
*Mar  6 21:17:58.396: %LINEPROTO-5-UPDOWN: Line protocol on Interface BRI0/0:1,
  changed state to up
*Mar  6 21:17:58.436: %LINEPROTO-5-UPDOWN: Line protocol on Interface
  Virtual-Access1, changed state to up
r6#
*Mar  6 21:18:03.264: %ISDN-6-CONNECT: Interface BRI0:1 is now connected to
  5551212 r8
r6#
```

The **debug ppp multilink** [*events*]/[*fragments*] Command

The **debug ppp multilink** command displays information on individual multilink fragments and important multilink events. Packet sequence numbers and fragment sizes are also shown.

CAUTION   Use this command only as a last resort, because it is memory-intensive and does not explain why connections aren't bundling.

Example 6-25 shows output from the **debug ppp multilink** command.

Example 6-25 **debug ppp multilink** *Command Output*

```
r6#debug ppp multilink
r6#show debug
PPP:
  Multilink fragments debugging is on
  Multilink events debugging is on

r6#ping 150.100.1.2

Type escape sequence to abort.
Sending 5, 100-byte ICMP Echos to 150.100.1.2, timeout is 2 seconds:
..!!!
Success rate is 60 percent (3/5), round-trip min/avg/max = 112/114/120 ms
r6#
*Mar  6 21:30:17.976: %LINK-3-UPDOWN: Interface BRI0/0:1, changed state to up
*Mar  6 21:30:18.000: %ISDN-6-CONNECT: Interface BRI0/0:1 is now connected to
  5551212
*Mar  6 21:30:18.140: BR0/0:1 MLP: Multilink up event pending
*Mar  6 21:30:18.152: Vi1 MLP: Added to huntgroup BR0
*Mar  6 21:30:18.156: Vi1 MLP: Clone from BR0/0
*Mar  6 21:30:18.164: %LINK-3-UPDOWN: Interface Virtual-Access1, changed state
  to up
*Mar  6 21:30:18.188: BR0/0:1 MLP: Hughes, multilink up, first link
*Mar  6 21:30:19.140: %LINEPROTO-5-UPDOWN: Line protocol on Interface BRI0:1,
  changed state to up
*Mar  6 21:30:19.184: %LINEPROTO-5-UPDOWN: Line protocol on Interface
  Virtual-Access1, changed state to up
r6#
```

The **debug ppp authentication** Command

The **debug ppp authentication** command is used when PPP authentication is a suspected reason for the connection failure between two routers, such as if the link keeps coming up and dropping. This command displays phases of the authentication process so that you can find possible misconfiguration problems, as shown in Example 6-26.

Example 6-26 **debug ppp authentication** *Command Output*

```
r6#debug ppp authentication
PPP authentication debugging is on

r6#ping 150.100.1.2

Type escape sequence to abort.
Sending 5, 100-byte ICMP Echos to 150.100.1.2, timeout is 2 seconds:
..!!!
Success rate is 60 percent (3/5), round-trip min/avg/max = 112/114/120 ms
```

Example 6-26 debug ppp authentication *Command Output (Continued)*

```
r6#
*May 15 22:05:31.868: %LINK-3-UPDOWN: Interface BRI0/0:1, changed state to up
*May 15 22:05:31.892: %ISDN-6-CONNECT: Interface BRI0/0:1 is now connected to
  5551212
*May 15 22:05:31.900: BR0/0:1 PPP: Treating connection as a callout
*May 15 22:05:31.900: BR0/0:1 CHAP: Using alternate hostname cisco
*May 15 22:05:31.984: BR0/0:1 CHAP: I CHALLENGE id 50 len 27 from "r8"
*May 15 22:05:31.988: BR0/0:1 CHAP: Using alternate hostname cisco
*May 15 22:05:31.992: BR0/0:1 CHAP: Username r8 not found
*May 15 22:05:31.992: BR0/0:1 CHAP: Using default password
*May 15 22:05:31.996: BR0/0:1 CHAP: O RESPONSE id 50 len 26 from "cisco"
*May 15 22:05:32.040: BR0/0:1 CHAP: I SUCCESS id 50 len 4
*May 15 22:05:32.060: %LINK-3-UPDOWN: Interface Virtual-Access1, changed state
  to up
*May 15 22:05:32.076: Vi1 PPP: Treating connection as a callout
*May 15 22:05:32.080: Vi1 CHAP: Using alternate hostname cisco
*May 15 22:05:33.040: %LINEPROTO-5-UPDOWN: Line protocol on Interface BRI0/0:1,
  changed state to up
*May 15 22:05:33.464: %LINEPROTO-5-UPDOWN: Line protocol on Interface
  Virtual-Access1, changed state to up
*May 15 22:05:37.896: %ISDN-6-CONNECT: Interface BRI0:1 is now connected to
  5551212 r8
```

The **debug ppp negotiation** Command

The **debug ppp negotiation** command is self-explanatory. It describes the process of PPP negotiation. Sent and received packet types are listed in chronological order in an action-result fashion.

The **debug isdn q931** Command

When troubleshooting ISDN call failure issues, the **debug isdn q931** command is very helpful in determining the likely cause of connection failure.

Example 6-27 demonstrates the usage of the **debug isdn q931** command.

Example 6-27 debug isdn q931 *Command Output*

```
R6#debug isdn q931
ISDN Q931 packets debugging is on
R8#ping 150.100.1.2

Type escape sequence to abort.
Sending 5, 100-byte ICMP Echos to 150.100.1.2, timeout is 2 seconds:

1w6d: ISDN BR0/0: TX -> SETUP pd = 8  callref = 0x4A
1w6d:        Bearer Capability i = 0x8890
```

continues

Example 6-27 debug isdn q931 *Command Output (Continued)*

```
1w6d:            Channel ID i = 0x83
1w6d:            Keypad Facility i = '5551212'
1w6d: ISDN BR0/0: RX <-  CALL_PROC pd = 8  callref = 0xCA
1w6d:            Channel ID i = 0x89
1w6d: ISDN BR0/0: RX <-  CONNECT pd = 8  callref = 0xCA
1w6d:            Channel ID i = 0x89
1w6d: %LINK-3-UPDOWN: Interface BRI0/0:1, changed state to up
1w6d: ISDN BR0/0: TX ->  CONNECT_ACK pd = 8  callref = 0x4A
1w6d: %LINK-3-UPDOWN: Interface Virtual-Access1, changed state to up.!!!!
Success rate is 80 percent (4/5), round-trip min/avg/max = 32/34/36 ms
R6#
1w6d: %LINEPROTO-5-UPDOWN: Line protocol on Interface BRI0/0:1, changed state
  to up
1w6d: %LINEPROTO-5-UPDOWN: Line protocol on Interface Virtual-Access1, changed
  state to up
1w6d: %ISDN-6-CONNECT: Interface BRI0/0:1 is now connected to 5551212 R8
```

Summary

This chapter provided a general overview of the multitude of ISDN topics, as well as a more in-depth look at its working configurations and various solutions. ISDN concepts are comprehensive and complex, and many of them are beyond the scope of this book. However, you were introduced to the most important parts of ISDN that give you a solid base in your preparation for the CCIE Security practical exam.

Review Questions

1 Which protocol series does ISDN use to communicate from the local terminal equipment to the ISDN switch in the central office?

2 True or false: The S reference point is an interface between NT1 and NT2.

3 What is an ISDN switch type?

A. A global configuration parameter

B. An interface configuration parameter

C. Either a global or an interface communication parameter

4 True or false: Access lists can be used to define interesting traffic.

5 What is the correct command syntax for assigning interesting traffic to an interface?

6 OSPF demand circuit is designed to stifle what?

A. Hellos

B. Routing updates

C. LSAs

D. All of the above

7 True or false: PAP encapsulation is more secure than CHAP.

FAQs

Q — *Why should I use CHAP instead of PAP?*

A — It is recommended that you use CHAP because of its security superiority over PAP. PAP is sent over the wire in clear text and can be sniffed. CHAP uses the MD5 encryption method and repeated challenges.

Q — *In what situation would I use OSPF demand circuit?*

A — OSPF transmits periodic hellos and LSAs necessary to maintain neighbor relationships and accurate link-state databases. This adds unnecessary connection costs to your ISDN network. OSPF demand circuit solves this problem by suppressing these advertisements until a topological change has occurred. Then and only then can the routing updates be used to initiate an ISDN call.

Q — *Why should I use dialer profiles instead of legacy dialer?*

A — Dialer profiles allow different configurations for different B channels. They also let BRIs belong to multiple dialer pools, eliminating the waste of B channels. Multiple destinations can be mapped to avoid split-horizon problems. Also, some new ISDN features are available only for dialer profiles.

Q — *Why would I use passive interface in DDR?*

A — Passive interface is used to keep routing updates from bringing up the link. Passive interface listens to routing updates but does not forward them.

Q — *Why would I want to use the callin keyword?*

A — The **callin** keyword may be used with the **ppp authentication [pap | chap]** command for one-way authentication. It ensures that a calling router skips the authentication of the router on the receiving end of the call. It makes sense when authentication is not supported.

Q — *Why do I need the callback feature in ISDN?*

A — It is a way of controlling billing, cost savings, and access. As such, it provides certain security capabilities.

This chapter covers the following topics:

- ATM overview
- Configuring ATM

CHAPTER 7

ATM Connectivity

This chapter briefly covers some of the concepts of Asynchronous Transfer Mode (ATM), specifically those related to RFCs 2684 and 2225. Although it is included in the CCIE Security lab exam, a comprehensive knowledge of ATM for the purposes of the exam is not necessary. As a result, the chapter is designed to provide just enough knowledge of the ATM-related topics that you might encounter during your test without overwhelming you with extraneous information.

ATM Overview

Internationally standardized ATM technology is an effective way of providing services for real-time applications such as voice and video as well as data. ATM is able to provide such services due to its underlying cell-switching architecture. With ATM, a sender divides packets into a fixed-size cell format for transfer over the medium. Each ATM cell consists of 53 bytes, 48 of them taken up by a payload and the remaining 5 by a header. The cells are hardware switched and carry an identifying label virtual path identifier (VPI)/virtual channel identifier (VCI) for routing purposes.

An ATM cell header can take on two different formats, User-Network Interface (UNI) and Network-to-Network Interface (NNI). UNI defines private and public ATM network access and connects ATM end users (as hosts and routers). NNI defines ATM interswitch communication. A UNI ATM header contains the following fields:

- **Generic Flow Control (GFC)**—A 4-bit field of local significance that can be used at the UNI, although currently it is not used and is set to all 0s.

- **Virtual Path Identifier (VPI)**—8 bits at UNI and 12 bits at NNI. Another locally significant field, it identifies a particular interface address. It can be thought of as similar in function to data-link connection identifier (DLCI) in Frame Relay.

- **Virtual Channel Identifier (VCI)**—16 bits. As mentioned, it is a part of the locally significant ATM address and can identify 65,536 virtual channels (VCs).

- **Payload Type (PT)**—A 3-bit field with every bit carrying its own function. The first bit specifies whether the cell contains user data or control data, the second indicates the presence of congestion, and the third bit is designated as the last-cell identifier in the stream of cells for a single frame, called end of message.

- **Cell Loss Priority (CLP)**—A 1-bit field that designates the cell priority as low or high so that the cell can be disposed of in case of congestion.

- **Header Error Control (HEC)**—An 8-bit field that performs cyclic redundancy check (CRC) on the header to spot bit errors.

Figure 7-1 displays the contents of the ATM cell UNI header.

Figure 7-1   *ATM UNI Header*

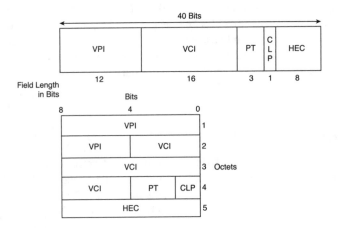

For more in-depth information about ATM theoretical concepts, consult Appendix E, "Security-Related RFCs and Publications."

Configuring ATM

Four implementation methods are used to transmit information over ATM. Briefly, they are as follows:

- **RFC 2684, "Multiprotocol Encapsulation over AAL5 (ATM Adaptation Layer 5)"**—A manual method of mapping upper-layer protocol addresses to the ATM addresses. Updates RFC 1483.

- **RFC 2225, "Classical IP and ARP over ATM"**—A dynamic method of transporting IP over ATM without the need for manual mapping. Updates RFCs 1577 and 1626.

- **Local-Area Network Emulation (LANE)**—Mimics LAN behavior over ATM cloud.

- **Multiprotocol over ATM (MPOA)**—A dynamic method, based on LANE, of transporting all protocols, not just IP.

For the purposes of the exam, this book concentrates on multiprotocol encapsulation over AAL5 and Classical IP and Address Resolution Protocol (ARP) over ATM.

Cisco offers a variety of router series models with ATM interfaces. You will be expected to configure two 36xx Series routers during your practical exam. They are implemented along with one LightStream 1010 switch, which requires no special input from you. However, this chapter includes basic switch configuration information for your benefit.

Lesson 7-1: RFC 2684: Multiprotocol Encapsulation over AAL5

Multiprotocol encapsulation (RFC 2684) is the first of the two methods described here, followed by the discussion of Classical IP and ARP over ATM (RFC 2225). To differentiate the two methods, the main concept to remember is that RFC 2684 (as its name suggests) allows multiple protocols to be transported but is static and, therefore, labor intensive. RFC 2225, on the other hand, is dynamic, but provides for IP only.

The basic premise of RFC 2684 is its ability to encapsulate upper-layer protocol datagrams into a format understood by the lower-layer ATM network. It allows for two different ways of carrying traffic, both routed and bridged, over an ATM network. The first method, AAL5 Subnetwork Access Protocol (AAL5SNAP), establishes multiple protocols over a single ATM virtual circuit by using Logical Link Control (LLC)/Subnetwork Access Protocol (SNAP) encapsulation. The second method, AAL5 Multiplex (AAL5MUX), encapsulates one protocol per single VC using a multiplexer.

The concept of RFC 2684 is straightforward, easy to configure, stable, and has little protocol overhead. However, because it requires a lot of manual configuration, it does not scale well. Also, it does not support ATM to the desktop.

RFC 2684 is most suitable for smaller networks, those campus or WAN backbones that consist of 5–10 end nodes with a few switches in between. As the number of end nodes and protocols increases, it becomes more complex in managing and troubleshooting. Transition from the existing backbone to an ATM backbone is painless. The difficulty is in the maintenance of the ATM backbone as it becomes larger.

You can accomplish encapsulation over permanent virtual circuits (PVCs) and switched virtual circuits (SVCs). PVCs are statically configured and remain open all the time. SVCs are dynamically established and used when sporadic activity is anticipated. This case study covers the PVC method. The SVC method is not included in the CCIE Security exam and therefore is not further discussed in this chapter.

The PVC method uses PVCs to configure point-to-point connections between terminating devices in an ATM network. It calls for individual PVCs for every node in a full-mesh ATM cloud. As you can see, the PVC implementation is a static and laborious task.

You can implement PVC networks in one of the following ways:

- **Static PVC**—Manually assigning VPI/VCI numbers based on the provider's information.

- **Dynamic PVC**—Edge routers dynamically obtaining VPI/VCI numbers from the edge ATM switch.

You can imagine that static assignment entails all-manual effort. If VPI/VCI numbers ever change within the ATM cloud, you have to alter your configurations within the routers accordingly. For example, in only a 3-node network, you need 8 VPI/VCI pairs to be configured plus 3 map statements for each router to form a fully meshed ATM cloud.

The dynamic method of VPI/VCI allocation is somewhat simpler. Here, routers find out the information from their adjacent switches dynamically. The discovered PVCs and their traffic parameters are configured on the specified main ATM interface or subinterface. By using Interim Local Management Interface (ILMI), your router receives the PVC parameter information.

Either way, VPI/VCI numbers are still locally significant. VPI, together with the VCI, identifies the next hop of a cell as it passes through a series of ATM switches on its way to the final destination. ATM switches use those fields to pinpoint the next virtual channel link (VCL), a connection between two ATM devices that a cell needs to transit. As with other instances where addresses are used, you must make sure that the information on the VPI/VCI numbers is correct. Unintentional mistakes can end up causing major chaos.

In this section, you use the same example of ATM topology for both manual and dynamic PVC implementations. Figure 7-2 represents your network. The ATM cloud is one ATM switch that is colocated with two routers: R5 and R11. The routers are physically interconnected by one LightStream 1010 switch. Although, RFC 2684 is capable of carrying multiple protocols, this section concentrates on IP.

Figure 7-2 *RFC 2684 Implementation with PVCs*

Configuring Static PVC

Static PVC configuration is fairly straightforward and requires a fully meshed ATM cloud between the routers. Even though it is awkward and hard to troubleshoot in outsized scenarios, static PVC configuration usually works well in smaller topologies.

Follow these steps to configure static PVCs:

Step 1   Enter an ATM interface configuration mode:

```
R5(config)#interface atm slot/port
```

The exact syntax depends on the router model used. The **interface** command presented here is based on the 3640 model. You can use a major interface or a subinterface. Subinterfaces are not required for the lab, and their usage is a matter of personal preference. In this case, you are using the major interface.

Step 2   Configure protocol addressing information for ATM interfaces on both routers using the following command:

```
R5(config-if)#ip address address mask
```

Step 3   Configure one ATM PVC on each router. In the case of R5, it is for connectivity to R11. The full syntax of the command is as follows:

```
R5(config-if)#pvc [name] vpi/vci [ces | ilmi | qsaal | smds]
```

This statement enables you to configure the PVC, where:

— *name* (optional)—Uniquely identifies the PVC in the router.

— *vpi*—Virtual path identifier.

— *vci*—Virtual channel identifier. Both the *vpi* and *vci* values are provided for you during the exam.

— *ces | ilmi | qsaal | smds* (optional)—Specifies the encapsulation type on an ATM PVC.

Step 4   (Optional) Configuring the **pvc** command places you in the interface-ATM-VC configuration mode, where you can manually assign an encapsulation method to the PVC (could also be **aal5mux**, as previously mentioned).

```
R5(config-if-atm-vc)#encapsulation aal5encap
```

Because **aal5snap**, used in this scenario, is also the global default **encapsulation** value, you can skip the encapsulation command.

When applied to both routers, the configuration steps described enable functional static PVC operation.

Example 7-1 shows the configuration of the R5 static PVC.

Example 7-1 *R5 Static PVC Configuration*

```
R5#show run
hostname R5
!
interface ATM3/0
 ip address 172.100.1.1 255.255.255.0
 no atm enable-ilmi-trap
 no atm ilmi-keepalive
 pvc 1/200
  encapsulation aal5snap
```

Example 7-2 shows the configuration of the R11 static PVC.

Example 7-2 *R11 Static PVC Configuration*

```
R11#show run
hostname R11
!
interface ATM3/0
 ip address 172.100.1.2 255.255.255.0

 no atm enable-ilmi-trap
 no atm ilmi-keepalive
 pvc 1/100
  encapsulation aal5snap
```

To create the PVC on the LS1010, type the following command:

```
LS1010(config)int atm interface
LS1010(config-if)#atm pvc vpi vci int atm exit-interface vpi vci
```

This command creates a bidirectional PVC. When a cell enters on the configured ATM interface with specified VPI and VCI numbers, it exits the switch through the exit interface using another specified VPI/VCI set and vice versa.

Example 7-3 demonstrates the LS1010 switch configuration. It shows incoming 1/200 VPI/VCI pairs from R5 outgoing to interface 3/0/1 with 1/100 VPI/VCI pairs to R11. Also, 1/100 VPI/VCI pairs are coming in from R11 on interface 3/0/1, which is being switched out on interface 3/0/3 with VPI/VCI pairs of 1/200 to R5. Notice that interface 3/0/3 is missing from the configuration. By specifying the entry and exit VPI/VCI pair as well as the mapping direction on one interface, you automatically enable a mapping in the opposite direction. The ATM cloud is now complete.

Example 7-3 *LS1010 Configuration for PVCs*

```
LS1010#show run
hostname LS1010
!
interface ATM3/0/1
no keepalive
atm pvc 1 100 interface ATM3/0/3 1 200
!
interface ATM3/0/3
no keepalive              <----no need to configure ATM 3/0/3
```

NOTE   On the CCIE Security lab exam, you are not required to configure the LS1010 switch. However, the LS1010 configuration is included with this lesson for your benefit.

Configuring Dynamic PVC

To enable the dynamic PVC discovery feature, you need to make certain modifications to the **pvc** command that was described in the previous section, "Configuring Static PVC." These changes are as follows:

Step 1   Specify the **ilmi** type of PVC encapsulation, as follows:

```
R5(config-if)#pvc [name] 0/16 ilmi
```

This is because the dynamic VPI/VCI assignment involves automatic discovery of numbers by using the ILMI. The ATM Forum specifies that you must apply a VPI value of **0** and a VCI value of **16** to the **pvc** command when ILMI is used.

Step 2   Introduce the following new command:

```
R5(config-if)#atm ilmi-pvc-discovery [subinterface]
```

When the router terminates the PVC, and PVC discovery is configured on that PVC, an ATM Inverse ARP request is generated. Therefore, you no longer a need a static map. The PVC can resolve its own network addresses dynamically. The optional **subinterface** keyword results in discovered PVCs being assigned to those ATM subinterfaces with the same subinterface number value as the discovered PVC's VPI number. In other words, if the discovered PVC's VPI value is 1, it is assigned to a subinterface whose number is .1.

Address mappings gathered dynamically age out and are refreshed periodically. Inverse ARP used to be available only for IP with RFC 2225 (discussed later in "RFC 2225: Classical IP and ARP over ATM"), but Cisco IOS Software currently provides Inverse ARP for the IPX protocol as well.

Example 7-4 shows dynamic PVC configuration of R5 and R11.

Example 7-4 *RFC 2684: Dynamic PVC Configuration*

```
R5#show run
hostname R5
!
interface ATM3/0
 pvc 0/16 ilmi
 atm ilmi-pvc-discovery subinterface
!
interface ATM 3/0.1 point-to-point
ip address 172.100.1.1 255.255.255.0
```
```
R11#show run
hostname R11
!
interface ATM3/0
 pvc 0/16 ilmi
 atm ilmi-pvc-discovery subinterface
!
interface ATM 3/0.1 point-to-point
ip address 172.100.1.2 255.255.255.0
```

Even though it is not crucial for this ATM topology, the dynamic method of setting up PVCs is less labor intensive compared to the static method and can be more manageable for the growing ATM environment.

Monitoring and Troubleshooting PVCs

The commands described in this section are used for monitoring and troubleshooting PVC activity. First, examine the following command:

```
R5#show atm vc
```

Example 7-5 shows that one PVC is active on the ATM3/0 interface. The VCs have local significance and show an active connection to the switch. To view VC values on a router-to-router ATM connection, you must go to each device between the two end routers and begin checking the interface status and incoming VPI/VCI pair. The outgoing VPI/VCI pair of the R5 router must match the incoming VPI/VCI pair of the LS1010. In case of a mismatch, the router keeps sending out ATM cells, but the switch drops them because the VPI/VCI pair is unknown.

Example 7-5 *The **show atm vc** Command Output*

```
R5#show atm vc
            VCD /Peak Avg/Min Burst
Interface         Name      VPI  VCI  Type  Encaps    Kbps    Kbps  Cells Sts
ATM3/0              1         1   200  PVC   SNAP    155000  155000         UP
```

To determine if the interface status is up on the switch, use the following command (see Example 7-6):

```
LS1010#show atm status
```

Example 7-6   *The* **show atm status** *Command Output*

```
LS1010#show atm status
NUMBER OF INSTALLED CONNECTIONS: (P2P=Point to Point, P2MP=Point to MultiPoint,
MP2P=Multipoint to Point)

Type     PVCs SoftPVCs     SVCs     TVCs     PVPs SoftPVPs     SVPs     Total
P2P        21        0        0        0        0        0        0        21
P2MP        0        0        0        0        0        0        0         0
MP2P        0        0        0        0        0        0        0         0
                                        TOTAL INSTALLED CONNECTIONS =       21

PER-INTERFACE STATUS SUMMARY AT 14:05:33 UTC Thu May 23 2002:
    Interface        IF       Admin  Auto-Cfg     ILMI Addr    SSCOP     Hello
      Name         Status     Status   Status     Reg State    State     State
------------     --------  ----------- --------  ------------- --------  -------
ATM11/0/1          DOWN       down    waiting          n/a      Idle      n/a
ATM11/0/2          DOWN       down    waiting          n/a      Idle      n/a
ATM11/0/3          DOWN       down    waiting          n/a      Idle      n/a
ATM11/1/0          DOWN       down    waiting          n/a      Idle      n/a
ATM3/0/3           UP         up      done       UpAndNormal    Idle      n/a
ATM3/0/1           UP         up      done       UpAndNormal    Idle      n/a
```

After you check VPI/VCI pairs and mapping statements for each device, ping from one router to the other (see Example 7-7) as follows:

```
R5#ping ip-address
```

Example 7-7   *The* **ping** *Command Results*

```
R5#ping 172.100.1.2
Type escape sequence to abort.
Sending 5, 100-byte ICMP Echos to 172.100.1.2, timeout is 2 seconds:
!!!!!
Success rate is 100 percent (5/5), round-trip min/avg/max = 1/1/4 ms
```

Lesson 7-2: RFC 2225: Classical IP and ARP over ATM

RFC 2225 describes Classical IP and ARP over ATM. Its goal is to allow the operation of an IP network over an ATM network. In an RFC 2225 implementation, each IP subnet forms a Logical IP Subnet (LIS). In turn, each LIS requires a router to travel to another LIS. Each LIS has clients that have IP addresses and ATM addresses. They are directly connected to the ATM network. The advantage of RFC 2225 is that no IP address–to–ATM address mapping is required to go from one router to another. The mapping is done by using an ARP mechanism.

Each LIS has an ATM Address Resolution Protocol (ATMARP) server. The server maintains a database of IP address–to–ATM address mappings. When a LIS client in each subnet has the IP address of another client and needs to locate its ATM address, it contacts the ATMARP server. Once the ATM address is located, a connection is set up over the ATM cloud. All clients must have their ATMARP server's ATM address and contact the server when they come up. The ATMARP server then performs an Inverse ARP, finds the IP address of the clients, and installs the address in its database. If a client needs to talk to a client in another LIS, it needs to go through an IP router that is configured as a member of both LIS groups. Only SVC-based ATM networks feature a client/server relationship. A PVC-based ATM network resolves VC identifiers to the corresponding IP addresses using InATMARP instead. Therefore, it does not require an ARP server. In this chapter, you learn the RFC 2225 implementation of both the SVC- and the PVC-based networks.

Configuring Classical IP with PVC

As previously mentioned, Classical IP with PVCs implements InATMARP. Refer to Figure 7-3 for a representation of Classical IP over PVCs. Each of our routers, R5 and R11, uses the InATMARP technique. InATMARP takes the IP addresses and their associated PVCs and forwards this information to other edge devices. Each router then creates a dynamic ARP table of IP addresses, matching them with the virtual circuit descriptor (VCD) numbers.

Figure 7-3 *RFC 2225 Implementation with PVCs*

The syntax of PVC commands for Classical IP is virtually the same as those you encountered earlier in "RFC 2684: Multiprotocol Encapsulation over AAL5." As a reminder, these commands are as follows:

```
R5(config)#interface atm slot/0
R5(config-if)#ip address address mask
R5(config-if)#pvc [name] vpi/vci
```

By default, Inverse ARP datagrams are sent on each PVC every 15 minutes. To adjust the Inverse ARP time period, use the following command in interface-ATM-VC configuration mode:

```
R5(config-if-atm-vc)#inarp minutes
```

Example 7-8 combines the configuration of the two routers in your topology.

Example 7-8 *RFC 2225 Configuration Using PVCs*

```
R5#show run
hostname R5
!
interface ATM3/0
 no ip address
 no ip directed-broadcast
 no atm enable-ilmi-trap
 no atm ilmi-keepalive
!
interface ATM3/0.1 point-to-point
 ip address 172.100.1.1 255.255.255.0
 pvc 1/200
   inarp 10
!

R11#show run
hostname R11
!
interface ATM3/0
 no ip address
 no ip directed-broadcast
 no atm enable-ilmi-trap
 no atm ilmi-keepalive
!
interface ATM3/0.1 point-to-point
 ip address 172.100.1.2 255.255.255.0
 pvc 1/100
   inarp 10
```

NOTE   The Inverse ATM ARP mechanism works with IP and IPX only, but other protocols are not
included in the CCIE Security exam.

Configuring Classical IP with SVC

The configuration of RFC 2225 includes an ATM ARP server configuration. Cisco routers with
an ATM interface and LightStream 1010 switches can act as an ATM ARP server. In Figure 7-4,
the LS1010 switch is an ARP server.

Figure 7-4 *Classical IP over ATM Topology*

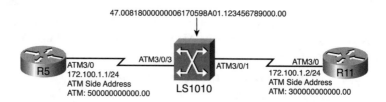

Configuring an ATM ARP Server

You only need the following command to enable the LS1010 switch to act as an ARP server:

```
LS1010(config-if)#atm arp-server self
```

See Example 7-9 for the LS1010 switch acting as an ARP server configuration.

Example 7-9 *RFC 2225 Switch Configuration*

```
LS1010#show run
hostname ls1010
!
logging buffered 16384 debugging
!
interface ATM3/0/3
 ip address 172.100.1.3 255.255.255.0
 no keepalive
 atm nsap-address 47.0081810000000006170598A01.123456789000.00
 atm arp-server self
```

Configuring Routers as ATM ARP Clients

The client's portion of the configuration includes the assignment of the ATM address to the interface involved. Due to the dynamic nature of the SVC setup, its address needs to be globally significant. For this purpose, you use a special SVC ATM address. The address is comprised of 160 bits that are translated into 40 hexadecimal characters or 20 bytes. If you use a private ATM network, you would use a network service access point (NSAP)–based ATM address. This is an ISO-specified network address and signifies the point at which OSI network service is made available to a Layer 4 entity. If a public ATM network is used, you would rely on an E.164-based ATM address.

To manually assign a full NSAP address to an ATM interface, use the following command:

```
R5(config-if)#atm nsap-address nsap-address
```

As an alternative to a 20-byte-long NSAP address, you can choose to assign a shorter end-system identifier (ESI), which has only 12 hexadecimal numbers and 2 hexadecimal selector numbers that form the last 7 bytes of the ATM address. In this example, you also need to use ILMI to automatically obtain a 13-byte prefix from the attached ATM switch.

The **esi-address** statement syntax is as follows:

```
R5(config-if)#atm esi-address esi.selector
```

If you are using ESI, make sure that the signaling and the ILMI PVCs are set up.

Then, you specify the full ATM address of the ATM ARP server. Your router uses this NSAP address to establish a connection to the ARP server when the ATM interface comes up. The syntax for the command is as follows:

```
R5(config-if)#atm arp-server nsap nsap-address
```

Example 7-10 demonstrates the client-side configuration of Classical IP and ARP in an SVC environment.

Example 7-10 *RFC 2225 Client-Side SVC Configuration*

```
R5#show run
hostname r5
!
interface ATM3/0
 ip address 172.100.1.1 255.255.255.0
 no keepalive
 atm esi-address 500000000000.00
 pvc 0/5 qsaal
 pvc 0/16 ilmi
 atm arp-server nsap 47.0081810000000006170598A01.123456789000.00
!
```
```
R11#show run
hostname r11
!
logging buffered 16384 debugging
!
interface ATM3/0
 ip address 172.100.1.2 255.255.255.0
 no keepalive
 atm esi-address 300000000000.00
 pvc 0/5 qsaal
 pvc 0/16 ilmi
 atm arp-server nsap 47.0081810000000006170598A01.123456789000.00
```

Summary

In this chapter, you learned various implementations of Layer 3 protocols over ATM. Specifically targeted toward the CCIE Security lab exam, the chapter concentrated on two methods of ATM deployment: multiprotocol encapsulation (RFC 2684) and Classical IP (RFC 2225). RFC 2684 encompasses multiple protocols, and RFC 2225 focuses on IP only. Both of these implementations included a discussion on permanent virtual circuits (PVCs) and switched virtual circuits (SVCs), their configurations, and monitoring and troubleshooting techniques.

Review Questions

1 How many bits are used for VPI at UNI?

2 What form of addressing does a PVC use?

3 What are two forms of ATM global addresses?

4 Automatic ATM address registration is enabled via what?

5 Specifying an AAL5SNAP encapsulation type is a mandatory configuration step in the RFC 2684 configuration using PVCs. True or false?

FAQs

Q — *What is the difference in the implementation of RFC 2684 between SVCs and PVCs?*

A — The difference is in how addressing is referenced. With PVCs, the VPI/VCI numbers (using VCDs) are referenced. With SVCs, the globally significant NSAP addresses are referenced.

Q — *Are there any VPI/VCI space management guidelines?*

A — Yes. Some of the guidelines are as follows:

- VCIs from 0 to 31 (inclusive) are reserved by the ITU-T and the ATM Forum, and should not be used in a live network.

- On logical ports, the VPI for all VCs should equal the VPI of the tunneling VP. On the CPU port, the VPI should be 0.

- The recommendation for PVCs is to use the VCI numbers in a higher range.

Q — *What is Q.2931, and how is it used?*

A — Q.2931 is the ATM signaling protocol. It is used to set up an SVC connection. In such instances, the edge devices must have a PVC with the VCI of 5 defined for Q.2931 to use.

Q — *What are the valid types of ATM virtual connections?*

A — The valid types are PVC, SVC, and Soft PVC. A PVC is a permanent circuit that is created by the administrator. SVCs are dynamically established. A Soft PVC uses PVCs to access the network that is interconnected through SVCs.

IP Routing

This chapter includes the following topics:

- RIP structure
- Configuring RIP

CHAPTER 8

RIP

This chapter assumes that, in your previous studies and work experience, you have already encountered Routing Information Protocol (RIP) and, therefore, omits some of the basic background information. Nonetheless, concepts that are considered pertinent to the topic are covered. RIP is a part of the routing portion of the CCIE Security lab exam. RIP also has a number of important security-related characteristics. This chapter's discussion of RIP encompasses general configuration of RIP as well as its security parameters.

RIP Structure

The following is an ultra-quick summary of RIP features. When reading this book, keep these features in mind:

- RIP is the oldest routing protocol in use today.

- RIP is an interior gateway protocol that was created for small homogenous networks. You will see the reasoning behind it when you read more about RIP's structure in the next few sections.

- RIP is a distance-vector routing protocol and, subsequently, uses the distance-vector defined path determination and routing update techniques.

- Numerous RIP-like routing protocols exist—some even carry the same name—but only IP RIP is of interest to you here.

- Two versions of RIP exist: RIPv1 and RIPv2. RIPv2 is an enhanced version of RIPv1. You see more about this topic later in the section, "RIPv1 Versus RIPv2."

Routing Updates and Timers

RIP broadcasts User Datagram Protocol (UDP) data packets to send routing information. These routing-update messages are sent at regular intervals and inform you of a network topology change. When the topology change is detected, the router first updates its own routing table and then immediately begins to send out routing updates that reflect the change to other routers on the network.

Unlike the routing updates, periodic updates are transmitted regularly. Various timers control such transmissions. The available timers and their defaults are as follows:

- **Routing-update timer**—The interval between periodic advertisements—about 30 seconds—but varies slightly to prevent all routers from simultaneously trying to update their neighbors.

- **Invalid timer**—180 seconds. If an update for a route is not received for the specified interval, the route is marked as unusable.

- **Hold-down timer**—180 seconds. If a router receives an update with a metric higher than that recorded in its routing table, the route is forced into a hold-down.

- **Route-flush timer**—240 seconds. When the invalid timer expires, the route is not used but it remains in the table. If no update occurs within the flush timer interval, the route is removed from the table.

If timers' defaults are changed on one router, you must change them in the entire RIP domain. Carefully weigh the consequences before making such a change.

Routing Metric

RIP bases its routing decisions on a single metric: hop count. RIP distinguishes among different available routes to a destination by the smallest number of routers (hops) that can be passed through on the way. For example, a directly connected network has a metric of 0, and each additional hop in a path is assigned a value of 1.

The way a router calculates hop count is that when it receives a routing update with a new or changed destination network entry, it uses the IP address of the neighbor that sent an update as the next hop. Next, the router takes the existing metric value contained in the update and adds 1 to it. Then, the router installs the route in its routing table. RIP only keeps the best route to a destination in the table.

Keep in mind that a metric of 16 indicates an unreachable network. RIP is inadequate for large networks with such a small range and the frequency and size of routing updates. This topic is discussed in the next section.

Split-Horizon Issues

By its nature, RIP is prone to routing loops. However, it employs several useful mechanisms to avoid the problem. First, it implements a hop limit, briefly mentioned in the preceding section. The maximum number of hops is set at 15. If a router keeps receiving a routing update with a topology change and keeps increasing the metric value by 1, the metric eventually reaches 16, which is recognized as infinity, marking the network unreachable.

Hold-down timer and split horizon with poison reverse feature are also used to ensure stability in a RIP network. Hold-down timer prevents information on a looped route from being forwarded. Poison reverse rule is simple. It states that once a route is learned via an interface, it cannot be advertised back through that same interface.

RIP and Default Routes

A RIP-enabled router can learn of a default network when it receives an update from another RIP-enabled router or generates the default network itself. Either way, the default network is propagated by RIP to other neighbors. You can establish the default network via redistribution into RIP or explicit configuration statements, which are discussed in Case Study 8-1 and "Step 4: Advertising a Default Route," later in this chapter.

RIPv1 Versus RIPv2

RIPv2 extends RIPv1 capabilities. It does not, however, make the previous version obsolete. RIPv2 adheres to all operational procedures, timers, and stability features of RIPv1. The difference comes from the addition of various information fields to the RIP packet in version 2, which allows it to carry extra information. In short, RIPv2 is able to make use of a plain text or message digest algorithm 5 (MD5) authentication to secure table updates, and it supports classless routing, which, in turn, offers route summarization, classless interdomain routing (CIDR), and variable-length subnet masks (VLSMs). None of these features were previously available in RIPv1.

Another critical update in version 2 is its ability to send multicast updates instead of broadcasts. RIPv2 utilizes the reserved Class D address of 224.0.0.9 to multicast messages to other RIPv2-speaking routers. However, for compatibility with version 1, RIPv2 update packets might have to be broadcast rather than multicast.

Configuring RIP

This section discusses the commands that are necessary to enable proper operation of RIP along with the concepts and issues that can arise as a result of certain implementation and configuration. The configuration tasks are divided into four major categories, as follows:

- Basic RIP configuration
- RIPv1 over router to PIX 5.2 connection
- RIPv2 over router to PIX 6.2 connection with authentication
- Advanced RIP configuration

Case Study 8-1: Basic RIP Configuration

This case study takes you through a step-by-step process of configuring basic RIP. It starts out by introducing you to those commands that apply to both versions of RIP and gradually moves on to the commands that you can only use with version 2. Version application is indicated for each command. The last configuration tasks of this chapter, covered in "Advanced RIP Configuration," follow the same format.

The configuration steps discussed in this case study are as follows:

Step 1   Initial setup, which includes enabling RIP on a router and specifying networks for routing RIP

Step 2   Blocking RIP updates on an interface

Step 3   Route filtering

Step 4   Advertising a default route

Step 5   Specifying a RIP version

Step 6   RIP route summarization, which includes turning off automatic route summarization with RIPv2, creating a summary route, and the issue of split horizon

Step 7   RIP authentication with and without MD5 encryption

Step 8   Troubleshooting RIP

The topology for this section is illustrated in Figure 8-1.

Figure 8-1 demonstrates the full lab topology used in this chapter. This case study involves R4 and R7, which are running RIPv2 over their Ethernet 0 interfaces as well as over their loopback interfaces.

Step 1: Initial Setup

Enabling RIP is not a difficult task. Simply start out in global configuration by executing the following command:

```
R4(config)#router rip
```

The **router rip** command is the same for both versions of RIP. After a **router** command is in place, you are forwarded into a router configuration mode. This is true for any routing protocol, not just RIP.

Now you need to specify networks that are supposed to participate in RIP routing. You need to repeat the following command for every network that you want to include:

```
R4(config-router)#network ip-address
```

Figure 8-1 *Basic RIP Configuration*

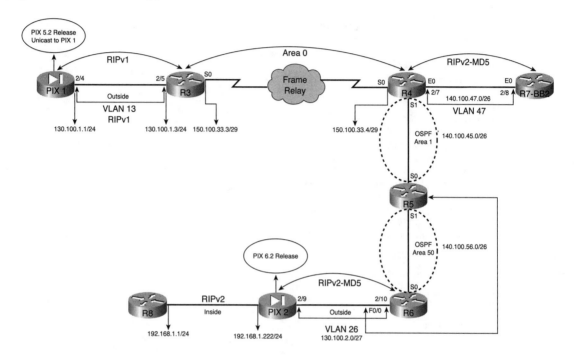

Example 8-1 demonstrates that R4 configuration includes **network** statements for both the 140.100.0.0 network belonging to its Ethernet0 interface and the 4.0.0.0 network of Loopback4. Because R7 is attached to five major networks (which include its loopback interfaces), five **network** statements are included in its router configuration. Notice that networks are summarized at class boundaries, even though Ethernet0 and Loopback444 of R7, for example, belong to different subnets.

Example 8-1 *Enabling RIP Routing on R4 and R7*

```
R4#show run
hostname r4
!
interface Loopback4
 ip address 4.4.4.4 255.255.255.0
!
interface Ethernet0
 ip address 140.100.47.4 255.255.255.192
!
interface Serial0
 ip address 150.100.33.4 255.255.255.248
 encapsulation frame-relay
```

continues

Example 8-1 *Enabling RIP Routing on R4 and R7 (Continued)*

```
 ip ospf network point-to-point
 frame-relay interface-dlci 404
 frame-relay lmi-type ansi
!
interface Serial1
 ip address 140.100.45.6 255.255.255.252
 clockrate 64000
!
router ospf 123
 router-id 4.4.4.4
 log-adjacency-changes detail
 area 1 virtual-link 5.5.5.5
 area 1 virtual-link 6.6.6.6
 redistribute rip metric 1 subnets
 network 4.4.4.4 0.0.0.0 area 0
 network 150.100.33.0 0.0.0.7 area 0
 network 140.100.45.4 0.0.0.3 area 1
 network 140.100.45.0 0.0.0.3 area 1
!
router rip
 redistribute ospf 123 metric 1
 network 4.0.0.0
 network 140.100.0.0

r7#show run
hostname r7
!
interface Loopback1
 ip address 7.1.1.7 255.255.255.0
!
interface Loopback2
 ip address 17.1.1.7 255.255.255.0
!
interface Loopback3
 ip address 27.1.1.7 255.255.255.0
!
interface Loopback4
 ip address 37.1.1.7 255.255.255.0
!
interface Loopback444
 ip address 140.100.9.1 255.255.255.224
!
interface Loopback777
 ip address 7.7.7.7 255.255.255.0
!
interface Ethernet0
 ip address 140.100.47.7 255.255.255.192
!
router rip
 network 7.0.0.0
 network 17.0.0.0
 network 27.0.0.0
```

Example 8-1 *Enabling RIP Routing on R4 and R7 (Continued)*

```
network 37.0.0.0
network 140.100.0.0
```

```
r4#show ip route rip
R    17.0.0.0/8 [120/1] via 140.100.47.7, 00:00:06, Ethernet0
     140.100.0.0/16 is variably subnetted, 3 subnets, 3 masks
R       140.100.9.0/27 [120/1] via 140.100.47.7, 00:00:06, Ethernet0
R    37.0.0.0/8 [120/1] via 140.100.47.7, 00:00:06, Ethernet0
R    7.0.0.0/8 [120/1] via 140.100.47.7, 00:00:06, Ethernet0
R    27.0.0.0/8 [120/1] via 140.100.47.7, 00:00:06, Ethernet0

r7#show ip route rip
     4.0.0.0/8 is variably subnetted, 2 subnets, 2 masks
R    4.0.0.0/8 [120/1] via 140.100.47.4, 00:00:22, Ethernet0
R    4.4.4.0/24 [120/1] via 140.100.47.4, 00:01:20, Ethernet0
     140.100.0.0/16 is variably subnetted, 3 subnets, 3 masks
R    140.100.45.4/30 [120/1] via 140.100.47.4, 00:00:22, Ethernet0
```

Step 2: Blocking RIP Updates on an Interface

You already familiarized yourself with the method of blocking a routing protocol process on an interface in Chapter 6, "ISDN Connectivity." The syntax for the command is as follows:

```
R7(config-if)#passive-interface interface-type number
```

The **passive-interface** command does not apply to RIP only. You can use it with any IP routing protocol except BGP, and it applies to both RIPv1 and RIPv2. An interface configured with the **passive-interface** command still listens to RIP broadcasts and updates its routing table. However, it does not respond to a RIP request received on that interface.

In your topology, R7 has the Serial0 interface. Its IP address of 140.100.48.1/24 is not on the same subnet as Ethernet0. However, as far as RIP is concerned, Serial0 is a member of the same Class B network as Ethernet0 and, therefore, is included in the RIP process with the **network 140.100.0.0** command discussed previously. The same is true for the Loopback777 interface. Its IP address of 7.7.7.7/24 is included with the Loopback1 interface because of their common Class A network root. To prevent Serial0 and Loopback444 from participating in the RIP updates process, you need to specify a **passive-interface** statement for each of them, as shown in Example 8-2.

Example 8-2 *Using the* **passive-interface** *Command on R7*

```
R7#show run
hostname r7
!
interface Loopback1
 ip address 7.1.1.7 255.255.255.0
```

continues

Example 8-2   *Using the* **passive-interface** *Command on R7 (Continued)*

```
!
! Output omitted for brevity
!
interface Loopback444
 ip address 140.100.9.1 255.255.255.224
!
interface Loopback777
 ip address 7.7.7.7 255.255.255.0
!
interface Ethernet0
 ip address 140.100.47.7 255.255.255.192
!
interface Serial0
 ip address 140.100.48.1 255.255.255.0
!
router rip
 passive-interface Loopback444
 passive-interface Serial0
 network 7.0.0.0
 network 17.0.0.0
 network 27.0.0.0
 network 37.0.0.0
 network 140.100.0.0
```

Step 3: Route Filtering

To prevent certain routes from being advertised in routing updates to other routers, you can
create a filter that blocks these routes from leaving a router. At the same time, you can choose
to avoid processing certain routes that are listed in incoming updates. You can accomplish both
tasks with one command. The only variation depends on its incoming or outgoing application,
as follows:

```
R7(config-router)#distribute-list [access-list-number | name] out | in [interface-type
    number]
```

Suppose that you want to suppress the Loopback1 subnet on R7 from being advertised in R7's
routing updates. First, you create an access list, which denies the 7.1.1.0/24 subnet and permits
all else. Then, in the router configuration mode, you call up your newly created access list
with the **distribute-list** command and specify that it applies to the outgoing advertisements.
Example 8-3 demonstrates this configuration in action.

Example 8-3   *Filtering of Routes in Outgoing Updates*

```
R7#show run
hostname r7
!
interface Loopback1
 ip address 7.1.1.7 255.255.255.0
```

Example 8-3 *Filtering of Routes in Outgoing Updates (Continued)*

```
!
! Output omitted for brevity
!
interface Loopback777
 ip address 7.7.7.7 255.255.255.0
!
! Output omitted for brevity
!
router rip
passive-interface Loopback444
 passive-interface Serial0
 network 7.0.0.0
 network 17.0.0.0
 network 27.0.0.0
 network 37.0.0.0
 network 140.100.0.0
 distribute-list 1 out
!
access-list 1 deny  7.1.1.0 0.0.0.255 log
access-list 1 permit any

r7#show access-lists
Standard IP access list 1
    deny   7.1.1.0, wildcard bits 0.0.0.255 log (101 matches) check=1230
    permit any log (1230 matches)
```

Step 4: Advertising a Default Route

The following command generates a default route into RIP. You can use it with or without a route map for more granularity, as follows:

```
R4(config-router)#default-information originate [route-map mapname]
```

For example, you might want R7 to dynamically learn a default route from R4. You can do so by placing **default-information originate** on R4, as shown in Example 8-4.

Example 8-4 *Default Route on R4*

```
R4#show run
hostname r4
!
! Output omitted for brevity
!
router rip
 network 4.0.0.0
 network 140.100.0.0
 default-information originate          → Sends a default route to R7
```

When the **show ip route rip** command is executed on R7 and displayed in Example 8-5, you can see that the default route is known via R4's Ethernet0 interface.

Example 8-5 *The **show ip route rip** Output on R7*

```
r7#show ip route rip
     4.0.0.0/24 is subnetted, 1 subnets
R       4.4.4.0 [120/1] via 140.100.47.4, 00:00:06, Ethernet0
R*    0.0.0.0/0 [120/1] via 140.100.47.4, 00:00:06, Ethernet0
```

Step 5: Specifying a RIP Version

In the topology depicted in Figure 8-1, RIPv2 is running between R4 and R7. However, the default behavior of a Cisco router is to listen to both RIPv1 and RIPv2 messages, but to send only RIPv1. This, of course, needs to change to fit your particular scenario. Enter the following command to change the default:

```
R4(config-router)#version [1 | 2]
```

As shown in Example 8-6, both routers specify version 2 in the router configuration mode as their version of choice.

Example 8-6 *Specifying the RIP Version*

```
R4#show run
hostname r4
!
! Output omitted for brevity
!
router rip
 version 2
 network 4.0.0.0
 network 140.100.0.0
 default-information originate


R7#show run
hostname r7
!
! Output omitted for brevity
!
router rip
 version 2
 passive-interface Loopback444
 passive-interface Serial0
 network 7.0.0.0
 network 17.0.0.0
 network 27.0.0.0
 network 37.0.0.0
 network 140.100.0.0
```

Note that the **version** command governs the global RIP version in the router. To exercise more control or override the global behavior on a per-interface basis, you can specify which RIP version messages an interface sends or receives with the following commands:

```
R4(config-if)#ip rip send version [1 | 2 | 1 2 ]
R4(config-if)#ip rip receive version [1 | 2 | 1 2]
```

In Example 8-7, R4 and R7 Ethernet0 interfaces display version 2 for both send and receive options in their configurations.

Example 8-7   *Interface-Level RIP Version*

```
R4#show run
hostname r4
!
! Output omitted for brevity
!
interface Ethernet0
 ip address 140.100.47.4 255.255.255.192
 ip rip send version 2
 ip rip receive version 2
!
router rip
 version 2
 network 4.0.0.0
 network 140.100.0.0
 default-information originate

r7#show run
hostname r7
!
! Output omitted for brevity
!
interface Ethernet0
 ip address 140.100.47.7 255.255.255.192
 ip rip send version 2
 ip rip receive version 2
!
router rip
 version 2
 passive-interface Loopback444
 passive-interface Serial0
 network 7.0.0.0
 network 140.100.0.0
```

Step 6: RIP Route Summarization

Now you have reached the part of the basic RIP configuration tasks where all commands apply to RIPv2 only. From the previous discussion, you know that RIPv2, unlike RIPv1, is a classless protocol that understands VLSM, CIDR, and route summarization. However, the default behavior of RIPv2 is the same as RIPv1, that is, to summarize at major network boundaries.

Example 8-8 displays the output of the **show ip route rip** command on R4 and R7. You can see that with your current configuration, all existing subnets are summarized into their major networks, with the exception of Loopback444, which is showing its true subnet of /27, as explained later in this section.

Example 8-8   *The* **show ip route rip** *Command Output of R4 and R7*

```
r4#show ip route rip
R       17.0.0.0/8 [120/1] via 140.100.47.7, 00:00:03, Ethernet0
        140.100.0.0/16 is variably subnetted, 2 subnets, 2 masks
R       140.100.9.0/27 [120/1] via 140.100.47.7, 00:00:03, Ethernet0
R       37.0.0.0/8 [120/1] via 140.100.47.7, 00:00:03, Ethernet0
R       7.0.0.0/8 [120/1] via 140.100.47.7, 00:00:03, Ethernet0
R       27.0.0.0/8 [120/1] via 140.100.47.7, 00:00:03, Ethernet0


r7#show ip route rip
R       4.0.0.0/8 [120/1] via 140.100.47.4, 00:00:00, Ethernet0
R*      0.0.0.0/0 [120/1] via 140.100.47.4, 00:00:00, Ethernet0
```

To turn off summarization and allow subnets to be advertised for both routers, issue the following command on each router:

```
R7(config-router)#no auto-summary
```

Example 8-9 shows the configuration of R7 with the **no auto-summary** command and indicates how the RIP routing tables of both routers have changed as a result. (Assume that the same configuration statement has been applied to R4). Specific subnets are now advertised.

Example 8-9   *The* **no auto-summary** *Configuration and the Resulting Routing Tables*

```
r4#show ip route rip
        17.0.0.0/8 is variably subnetted, 2 subnets, 2 masks
R          17.1.1.0/24 [120/1] via 140.100.47.7, 00:00:17, Ethernet0
R          17.0.0.0/8 [120/1] via 140.100.47.7, 00:00:47, Ethernet0
        140.100.0.0/16 is variably subnetted, 2 subnets, 2 masks
R          140.100.9.0/27 [120/1] via 140.100.47.7, 00:00:17, Ethernet0
        37.0.0.0/8 is variably subnetted, 2 subnets, 2 masks
R          37.1.1.0/24 [120/1] via 140.100.47.7, 00:00:17, Ethernet0
R          37.0.0.0/8 [120/1] via 140.100.47.7, 00:00:47, Ethernet0
        7.0.0.0/8 is variably subnetted, 2 subnets, 2 masks
R          7.7.7.0/24 [120/1] via 140.100.47.7, 00:00:17, Ethernet0
R          7.0.0.0/8 [120/1] via 140.100.47.7, 00:00:47, Ethernet0
        27.0.0.0/8 is variably subnetted, 2 subnets, 2 masks
R          27.1.1.0/24 [120/1] via 140.100.47.7, 00:00:17, Ethernet0
R          27.0.0.0/8 [120/1] via 140.100.47.7, 00:00:47, Ethernet0
_____

r7#show ip route rip
        4.0.0.0/8 is variably subnetted, 2 subnets, 2 masks
```

Example 8-9 *The* **no auto-summary** *Configuration and the Resulting Routing Tables (Continued)*

```
R       4.4.4.0/24 [120/1] via 140.100.47.4, 00:00:17, Ethernet0
R       4.0.0.0/8 [120/1] via 140.100.47.4, 00:01:14, Ethernet0
R*   0.0.0.0/0 [120/1] via 140.100.47.4, 00:00:17, Ethernet0
```

If you look closely at the RIP routing tables in Example 8-9, you see that the incorrect summary routes, such as 4.0.0.0/8, are still showing up along with the subnetted routes. This occurs because the following command has not been issued yet:

```
R7#clear ip route *
```

Example 8-10 presents the **show ip route rip** command output after the **clear ip route** * command is issued. Notice that all incorrectly summarized routes are gone.

Example 8-10 *The* **clear ip route** * *Command and the Resulting Routing Tables*

```
r7#show ip route rip
     4.0.0.0/24 is subnetted, 1 subnets
R       4.4.4.0 [120/1] via 140.100.47.4, 00:00:02, Ethernet0
R*   0.0.0.0/0 [120/1] via 140.100.47.4, 00:00:02, Ethernet0
r7#
```

Remember the detail that was mentioned earlier: Even before the **no auto-summary** command has been issued, R7's Loopback444 interface already had its subnet 140.100.9.0/27 advertised. This occurred because the Loopback444's subnet happens to be on the same Class B network as R7's Ethernet0 interface. RIPv2 recognizes the subnet information of Loopback444 and separates it from the directly connected advertising Ethernet0 interface. If RIPv1 had been used instead of RIPv2, the network 140.100.0.0 would have been excluded from the RIP routing table.

Suppose you do not want to advertise the separate route for Loopback444 and would like to summarize it into a common subnet. The method of summarization is used to improve scalability and efficiency because fewer routes need to be included in the routing table. This reduces the size of the table and lets it handle more routes. The way summary routes are handled by RIP reduces processing time as well. The summary route command is placed in the interface configuration of the forwarding interface, or Ethernet0 in this case. The syntax for the command is as follows:

```
R7(config-if)#ip summary-address rip ip-address ip-network-mask
```

Example 8-11 demonstrates the change in the R7 configuration to include the summary route of 140.100.0.0 255.255.0.0. If you later remember to issue the **clear ip route** * command, your RIP routing table on R4 should look like the one shown in Example 8-12. The subnet 140.100.9.0/27 is no longer there.

Example 8-11 *Summary Route Configuration on R7*

```
R7#show run
hostname r7
!
interface Ethernet0
 ip address 140.100.47.7 255.255.255.192
 ip rip send version 2
 ip rip receive version 2
 no ip split-horizon
 ip summary-address rip 140.100.0.0 255.255.0.0
!
router rip
 version 2
 passive-interface Loopback444
 passive-interface Serial0
 network 7.0.0.0
 network 17.0.0.0
 network 27.0.0.0
 network 37.0.0.0
 network 140.100.0.0
 distribute-list 1 out
 no auto-summary
```

Example 8-12 *RIP Routing Table of R4*

```
r4#show ip route rip
     17.0.0.0/24 is subnetted, 1 subnets
R       17.1.1.0 [120/1] via 140.100.47.7, 00:00:03, Ethernet0
     140.100.0.0/16 is variably subnetted, 2 subnets, 2 masks
R       140.100.0.0/16 [120/1] via 140.100.47.7, 00:00:03, Ethernet0
     37.0.0.0/16 is subnetted, 1 subnets
R       37.1.0.0 [120/1] via 140.100.47.7, 00:00:03, Ethernet0
     7.0.0.0/24 is subnetted, 1 subnets
R       7.7.7.0 [120/1] via 140.100.47.7, 00:00:03, Ethernet0
     27.0.0.0/24 is subnetted, 1 subnets
R       27.1.1.0 [120/1] via 140.100.47.7, 00:00:03, Ethernet0
r4#
```

Another issue related to route summarization is split horizon in RIP networks. RIP is a broadcast-type protocol and is prone to routing loops. Therefore, split horizon is normally a very useful feature that minimizes the possibility of routing loops and is enabled by default. However, when a RIP interface is connected to a nonbroadcast network such as Frame Relay, split horizon can prevent routers from communicating properly.

Example 8-13 illustrates the Serial 0 interface of R4 connected to a Frame Relay network and configured as point-to-multipoint. In such instances, you need to disable split horizon.

Conversely, the Serial 1 interface is linked to R5 as a point-to-point connection with split horizon enabled.

Example 8-13 *Absence of Split Horizon on a Frame Relay Interface*

```
Frame-Relay Interface Point-to-Multipoint Interface

r4#show ip interface serial 0                          → Frame Relay
Serial0 is up, line protocol is up
  Internet address is 150.100.33.4/29
  Broadcast address is 255.255.255.255
  Directed broadcast forwarding is disabled
  Multicast reserved groups joined: 224.0.0.5 224.0.0.6
  Outgoing access list is not set
  Inbound  access list is not set
  Proxy ARP is enabled
  Security level is default
  Split horizon is disabled
  ICMP redirects are always sent
  ICMP unreachables are always sent
  ICMP mask replies are never sent
! Output omitted for brevity


Point-to-Point Interface Encapsulation HDLC

r4#show ip interface serial 1                  → HDLC
Serial1 is up, line protocol is up
  Internet address is 140.100.45.6/30
  Broadcast address is 255.255.255.255
  Directed broadcast forwarding is disabled
  Multicast reserved groups joined: 224.0.0.5 224.0.0.6 224.0.0.9
  Outgoing access list is not set
  Inbound  access list is not set
  Proxy ARP is enabled
  Security level is default
  Split horizon is enabled
  ICMP redirects are always sent
  ICMP unreachables are always sent
! Output omitted for brevity
```

Also, if you refer to Example 8-11, you notice that split horizon is manually disabled on the Ethernet0 interface. This is because split horizon does not allow the summary route to be advertised out Ethernet0 because it was learned via Ethernet0. If split horizon is enabled, interface summary address does not work. To disable split horizon, use the following command:

```
R7(config-if)#no ip split-horizon
```

Step 7: RIP Authentication

RIPv2 is the only RIP version to support authentication. You must explicitly enable authentication because it is not provided for RIP packets by default.

The first step in the authentication-configuration process is to define a key chain with a name. The key chain specifies the key or set of keys to be used on the interface. Authentication does not work without a defined key chain. To create a key chain, use the following global command:

```
R4(config)#key chain name-of-chain
```

Keep in mind that the key chain name is locally significant and need not be the same on both authenticating routers. To simplify the configuration in Example 8-14, the name ccie is used for both R4's and R7's key chains. The next step is to select and number a key. Both routers have key 6727 assigned. Now, you need to define a password or key-string of alphanumeric characters for the key. In this case, that is also 6727. Key-string must be the same for both sides participating in authentication. The syntax for key definition is as follows:

```
R4(config-keychain)#key key-number
R4(config-keychain)#key-string password
```

Example 8-14 *Key Chain Configuration*

```
r4#show run
service password-encryption
!
hostname r4
!
key chain ccie
 key 6727
  key-string 7 0759761E19
!
! Output omitted for brevity


r7#show run
service password-encryption
!
hostname r7
!
key chain ccie
 key 6727
  key-string 7 03520C5951
!
! Output omitted for brevity
```

Notice in the output in Example 8-14 that R4's key-string is different from the key-string on R7. This is because the **service password-encryption** command has been applied to R4, so the key-string no longer appears in cleartext. It is a security test, after all.

Finally, you are ready to configure the RIP-related portion of authentication. RIPv2 authentication is enabled on an interface by assigning the newly configured key-chain to it, as follows:

```
R4(config-if)#ip rip authentication key-chain name-of-chain
```

As you know, two modes of authentication are supported for RIP on Cisco routers: plain text and MD5. The default is plain text authentication, so if you omit the next command, plain text is assumed. However, plain text is obviously not recommended for security purposes. Always specify the MD5 authentication mode, as follows, unless it is absolutely necessary to do otherwise.

```
R4(config-if)#ip rip authentication mode [text | md5]
```

Example 8-15 shows the entire authentication configuration for R4 and R7. You can see that authentication mode MD5 and key-chain ccie have been assigned to Ethernet0 interfaces.

Example 8-15 *RIPv2 Authentication Configuration*

```
r4#show run
service password-encryption
!
hostname r4
!
key chain ccie
 key 6727
  key-string 7 0759761E19
!
! Output omitted for brevity
!
interface Ethernet0
 ip address 140.100.47.4 255.255.255.192
 ip rip send version 2                          → MD5 Only in RIPv2
 ip rip receive version 2                       → MD5 Only in RIPv2
 ip rip authentication mode md5
 ip rip authentication key-chain ccie


r7#show run
service password-encryption
!
hostname r7
!
key chain ccie
 key 6727
  key-string 7 03520C5951
!
! Output omitted for brevity
!
interface Ethernet0
 ip address 140.100.47.7 255.255.255.192
 ip rip send version 2                          → MD5 Only in RIPv2
```

continues

Example 8-15 *RIPv2 Authentication Configuration (Continued)*

```
ip rip receive version 2                    → MD5 Only in RIPv2
ip rip authentication mode md5
ip rip authentication key-chain ccie
no ip split-horizon
ip summary-address rip 140.100.0.0 255.255.0.0
```

Also, you have the option of configuring key management to make the router use different keys at different times. This concept, however, is irrelevant to the task at hand and is not covered in this book.

Step 8: Troubleshooting RIP

Example 8-16 demonstrates a useful technique of verifying whether your authentication is working properly with the **debug ip rip events** command. You see that the last line of the output states *invalid authentication*. The authentication process can fail for a couple of reasons. First, the key chain could be misconfigured on one or both sides of the link. Remember, the key-string must be identical, including case sensitivity and any extra spaces. The misconfiguration can be almost invisible to the naked eye, but the router picks up on it and your authentication does not succeed.

Another reason that the authentication process can fail is that RIP might not update itself with the key-chain information. In this instance, you should remove your RIP configuration and then paste it back again.

Example 8-16 *The* **debug ip rip events** *Command Output with Failed Authentication*

```
r4#debug ip rip events
05:18:49: RIP: sending v2 update to 224.0.0.9 via Ethernet0 (140.100.47.4)
05:18:49: RIP: build update entries
05:18:49:       0.0.0.0/0 via 0.0.0.0, metric 1, tag 0
05:18:49:       4.4.4.0/24 via 0.0.0.0, metric 1, tag 0
05:18:49: RIP: sending v2 update to 224.0.0.9 via Loopback4 (4.4.4.4)
05:18:49: RIP: build update entries
05:18:49:       0.0.0.0/0 via 0.0.0.0, metric 1, tag 0
05:18:49:       140.100.47.0/26 via 0.0.0.0, metric 1, tag 0
05:18:49: RIP: ignored v2 packet from 4.4.4.4 (sourced from one of our addresses)
05:18:54: RIP: received packet with MD5 authentication
05:18:54: RIP: ignored v2 packet from 140.100.47.7 (invalid authentication)
```

The working authentication debug output looks like the output shown in Example 8-17. The comment *received v2 update* at the end indicates a successful exchange.

Example 8-17 *The* **debug ip rip events** *Command Output with Successful Authentication*

```
r4#debug ip rip events
02:09:23: RIP: sending v2 update to 224.0.0.9 via Loopback777 (7.7.7.7)
02:09:23: RIP: build update entries
02:09:23:      0.0.0.0/0 via 0.0.0.0, metric 2, tag 0
02:09:23:      4.4.4.0/24 via 0.0.0.0, metric 2, tag 0
02:09:23:      17.1.1.0/24 via 0.0.0.0, metric 1, tag 0
02:09:24:      27.1.1.0/24 via 0.0.0.0, metric 1, tag 0
02:09:24:      37.1.1.0/24 via 0.0.0.0, metric 1, tag 0
02:09:24:      140.100.9.0/27 via 0.0.0.0, metric 1, tag 0
02:09:24:      140.100.47.0/26 via 0.0.0.0, metric 1, tag 0
02:09:24: RIP: ignored v2 packet from 7.1.1.7 (sourced from one of our addresses)
02:09:24: RIP: ignored v2 packet from 17.1.1.7 (sourced from one of our addresses)
02:09:24: RIP: ignored v2 packet from 27.1.1.7 (sourced from one of our addresses)
02:09:24: RIP: ignored v2 packet from 37.1.1.7 (sourced from one of our addresses)
02:09:24: RIP: ignored v2 packet from 7.7.7.7 (sourced from one of our addresses)
02:09:24: RIP: received packet with MD5 authentication        →MD5 is working
02:09:24: RIP: received v2 update from 140.100.47.4 on Ethernet0
```

Besides **debug ip rip events**, a few other commands are used to verify the operation of RIP. Example 8-18 displays the output of the **show ip route rip** command, which you encountered earlier in this chapter. It is a good way to ensure that all the routes you expect to see are, in fact, there, and those you don't, aren't.

Example 8-18 *The* **show ip route rip** *Command Output*

```
r4#show ip route rip
     17.0.0.0/24 is subnetted, 1 subnets
R       17.1.1.0 [120/1] via 140.100.47.7, 00:00:13, Ethernet0
     140.100.0.0/16 is variably subnetted, 3 subnets, 3 masks
R       140.100.0.0/16 [120/1] via 140.100.47.7, 00:00:13, Ethernet0
     37.0.0.0/16 is subnetted, 1 subnets
R       37.1.0.0 [120/1] via 140.100.47.7, 00:00:13, Ethernet0
     7.0.0.0/24 is subnetted, 1 subnets
R       7.7.7.0 [120/1] via 140.100.47.7, 00:00:13, Ethernet0
     27.0.0.0/24 is subnetted, 1 subnets
R       27.1.1.0 [120/1] via 140.100.47.7, 00:00:13, Ethernet0
```

Example 8-19 illustrates the output of the **show ip protocols** command for R4 and R7.

Example 8-19 *The* **show ip protocols** *Command Output*

```
r4#show ip protocols
Routing Protocol is "rip"
  Sending updates every 30 seconds, next due in 5 seconds
  Invalid after 180 seconds, hold down 180, flushed after 240
  Outgoing update filter list for all interfaces is
```

continues

Example 8-19 *The* **show ip protocols** *Command Output (Continued)*

```
  Incoming update filter list for all interfaces is
  Redistributing: rip
  Default version control: send version 2, receive version 2
    Interface           Send  Recv  Triggered RIP  Key-chain
    Ethernet0            2     2                    ccie
    Loopback4            2     2
    Serial1             2     2
  Automatic network summarization is not in effect
  Routing for Networks:
    4.0.0.0
    140.100.0.0
  Routing Information Sources:
    Gateway         Distance      Last Update
    140.100.47.7        120       00:00:22
  Distance: (default is 120)
```

```
r7#show ip protocols
Routing Protocol is "rip"
  Sending updates every 30 seconds, next due in 3 seconds
  Invalid after 180 seconds, hold down 180, flushed after 240
  Outgoing update filter list for all interfaces is 1
  Incoming update filter list for all interfaces is not set
  Redistributing: rip
  Default version control: send version 2, receive version 2
    Interface           Send  Recv  Triggered RIP  Key-chain
    Ethernet0            2     2                    ccie
    Loopback1            2     2
    Loopback2            2     2
    Loopback3            2     2
    Loopback4            2     2
    Loopback777          2     2
  Automatic network summarization is not in effect
  Address Summarization:
    140.100.0.0/16 for Loopback444, Ethernet0              → Summary address
  Maximum path: 4
  Routing for Networks:
    7.0.0.0
    17.0.0.0
    27.0.0.0
    37.0.0.0
    140.100.0.0
  Passive Interface(s):
    Loopback444
    Serial0
  Routing Information Sources:
    Gateway         Distance      Last Update
    140.100.47.4        120       00:00:18
  Distance: (default is 120)
```

Case Study 8-2: RIPv1 over Router to PIX 5.2 Connection

The topology for RIPv1 over router to PIX 5.2 scenario is illustrated in Figure 8-2. It is yet another portion of the full lab used in Figure 8-1. R3 is receiving routes via OSPF from R4. R3 Ethernet0 interface is connected to the Catalyst port 2/5 on VLAN 13. PIX1 Ethernet outside is also connected to Catalyst VLAN 13 on port 2/4. The goal of this section is to advertise the redistributed OSPF routes to PIX1.

Figure 8-2   *RIPv1 Router to PIX 5.2 Topology*

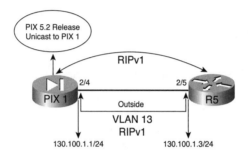

The steps discussed in this case study are as follows:

Step 1   Enabling RIPv1 on a router

Step 2   Configuring OSPF routing and redistribution on a router

Step 3   Configuring RIP routing on the PIX firewall

Step 4   Enabling unicast updates

Step 1: Enabling RIPv1 on a Router

The first step involves enabling RIPv1 on R3. The commands discussed in the previous section apply here as well. In Example 8-20, the **router rip** command begins the RIP routing process. Version 1 and network 130.100.0.0 statements are placed in the router configuration mode. RIPv1 is also assigned to the Ethernet0 interface for sending and receiving packets.

Example 8-20 *Enabling RIPv1 on R3*

```
R3#show run
hostname r3
!
interface Loopback0
 ip address 3.3.3.3 255.255.255.0
!
interface Ethernet0
 ip address 130.100.1.3 255.255.255.0
```

continues

Example 8-20 *Enabling RIPv1 on R3 (Continued)*

```
 ip rip send version 1
 ip rip receive version 1
 !
interface Serial0.4 point-to-point
 description Connection to R4
 ip address 150.100.33.3 255.255.255.248
 frame-relay interface-dlci 304
 !
router rip
 version 1
 network 130.100.0.0
```

Step 2: Configuring OSPF Routing and Redistribution on a Router

Next, you need to configure OSPF routing on R3. Then, redistribute OSPF into RIP and
vice versa. For more information on redistribution and OSPF routing, refer to Chapter 13,
"Redistribution," and Chapter 10, "OSPF," respectively. See Example 8-21 for the configuration
output. The **redistribute rip metric 1 subnets** statement injects the RIP routes into OSPF and
redistribute ospf 123 metric 1 redistributes OSPF routes into RIP.

Example 8-21 *RIP Route Redistribution*

```
R3#show run
hostname r3
!
router ospf 123
 router-id 3.3.3.3
 log-adjacency-changes detail
 redistribute rip metric 1 subnets
 network 3.3.3.0 0.0.0.255 area 0
 network 150.100.33.0 0.0.0.7 area 0
!
router rip
 version 1
 redistribute ospf 123 metric 1
 network 130.100.0.0
```

Example 8-22 shows the results of redistribution configuration on R3. Use the **show ip rip
database** command to verify the correct route information.

Example 8-22 *The* **show ip rip database** *Command Output*

```
r3#show ip rip database
0.0.0.0/0     auto-summary
0.0.0.0/0
    [1] via 130.100.1.1, 00:00:15, Ethernet0
3.0.0.0/8     auto-summary
```

Example 8-22 *The* **show ip rip database** *Command Output (Continued)*

```
3.3.3.0/24     redistributed
   [1] via 0.0.0.0,
4.0.0.0/8     auto-summary
4.4.4.4/32     redistributed
   [1] via 4.4.4.4,                              → From R4
5.0.0.0/8     auto-summary
5.5.5.5/32     redistributed
   [1] via 4.4.4.4,
6.0.0.0/8     auto-summary                       → Because of RIPv1 /8
6.6.6.0/24     redistributed
   [1] via 5.5.5.5,
7.0.0.0/8     auto-summary
7.7.7.0/24     redistributed
   [1] via 4.4.4.4,
130.100.0.0/16     auto-summary
130.100.1.0/24     directly connected, Ethernet0
130.100.2.0/24     redistributed
   [1] via 5.5.5.5,
140.100.0.0/16     auto-summary
140.100.45.4/30     redistributed
   [1] via 4.4.4.4,
150.100.0.0/16     auto-summary
150.100.33.0/29     redistributed
   [1] via 0.0.0.0,
```

NOTE   Incidentally, you might have noticed the redistribution statements for R4 presented in Example 8-1 of Case Study 8-1. Although they were not discussed in Case Study 8-1, they are important elements of configuration that enable reachability across the network. Now that you know how to configure RIP redistribution, you can go back to R4 and add these statements to the R4's setup.

Step 3: Configuring RIP Routing on the PIX Firewall

Now, it's time to prepare PIX1 for RIP routing. You can activate the outside interface with the following command:

```
PIX1(config)#interface ethernet0 auto
```

Assign the IP address of 130.100.1.1/24 to the outside interface. The syntax for the command is as follows:

```
PIX1(config)#ip address interface-name ip-address subnet-mask
```

Finally, enable the RIP process on the PIX. The following command facilitates IP routing table updates from received RIP broadcasts:

```
PIX1(config)#rip interface-name default | passive [version [1 | 2]]
```

The **default** keyword signifies the broadcast of a default route on the interface, and the **passive** keyword means that the firewall listens for RIP routing broadcasts and uses that information to populate its routing tables. In your configuration, you need to specify both. Verify that your configuration matches Example 8-23. Note the statements **rip outside passive version 1** and **rip outside default version 1**, which are at the end of the output.

Example 8-23 *RIPv1 PIX Configuration*

```
PIX1#write terminal
PIX Version 5.2(3)
nameif ethernet0 outside security0
nameif ethernet1 inside security100
nameif ethernet2 dmz security10

hostname PIX1

interface ethernet0 auto
interface ethernet1 auto
interface ethernet2 auto
interface ethernet3 auto

ip address outside 130.100.1.1 255.255.255.0
! Output omitted for brevity

rip outside passive version 1
rip outside default version 1
```

It seems that all the necessary steps have been taken and the configuration should work. Use the **show route** command on the firewall to display the available routes. Examine Example 8-24 for the results. Notice that the expected routes are missing. What happened?

Example 8-24 *The* **show route** *Command Output on PIX1*

```
PIX1# show route
        inside 127.0.0.1 255.255.255.255 127.0.0.1 1 CONNECT static
        outside 130.100.1.0 255.255.255.0 130.100.1.1 1 CONNECT static
PIX1#
```

Step 4: Enabling Unicast Updates

PIX version 5.2.*x* and earlier implementations of RIP do not understand broadcast or multicast updates received from a router. To fix this problem, you must enable the unicast packet exchange. You can achieve this with the following statement:

```
R3(config-router)#neighbor ip-address
```

Example 8-25 demonstrates the updated configuration of R3, which includes the **neighbor 130.100.1.1** statement in its RIP configuration.

Example 8-25 *Enabling Unicast Updates on R3*

```
r3#show run
! Output omitted for brevity
router rip
 version 1
 redistribute ospf 123 metric 1
 network 130.100.0.0
 neighbor 130.100.1.1
```

Now if you repeat the **show route** command on PIX1, you see that all routes are there, as demonstrated in Example 8-26.

Example 8-26 *The* **show route** *Command Output on PIX1*

```
PIX1(config)# show route
  outside 3.0.0.0 255.0.0.0 130.100.1.3 2 RIP
  outside 4.0.0.0 255.0.0.0 130.100.1.3 2 RIP
  outside 5.0.0.0 255.0.0.0 130.100.1.3 2 RIP
  outside 6.0.0.0 255.0.0.0 130.100.1.3 2 RIP
  outside 7.0.0.0 255.0.0.0 130.100.1.3 2 RIP
  outside 130.100.1.0 255.255.255.0 130.100.1.1 1 CONNECT static
  outside 130.100.2.0 255.255.255.0 130.100.1.3 2 RIP
  outside 140.100.0.0 255.255.0.0 130.100.1.3 2 RIP
  outside 150.100.0.0 255.255.0.0 130.100.1.3 2 RIP
```

NOTE   The **neighbor** command is not just applicable in RIP for PIX 5.2.*x*. For RIP updates to reach nonbroadcast networks such as Frame Relay, you would also have to explicitly permit the point-to-point exchange of unicast updates with the **neighbor** command. You can use this command in conjunction with the **passive-interface** command. To specify additional neighbors, use multiple **neighbor** commands.

Case Study 8-3: RIPv2 over Router to PIX 6.2 Connection with Authentication

The goal of this section is to teach you to use authentication techniques, not only for router-to-router authentication but also for router-to-PIX. The topology involves PIX2 using version 6.2, R5, R6, and, in a way, R8. R5 and R6 are running RIPv2 and OSPF in two different areas: area 1 and area 50. R5's Ethernet0 interface is connected to VLAN 26 along with R6's FastEthernet0/0 interface and PIX2 outside interface. R5 is also connected to R6 back-to-back via their serial interfaces. This has no particular significance in this exercise, but it will become useful in other chapters of this book. The inside interface of PIX2 is connected to Ethernet0 of R8. R8 is only of interest to you here because it is injecting a loopback route of 8.8.8.8 into PIX2.

Figure 8-3 illustrates the current topology, which is a part of the full lab shown in Figure 8-1.

Figure 8-3 *RIPv2 over Router to PIX 6.2 with Authentication*

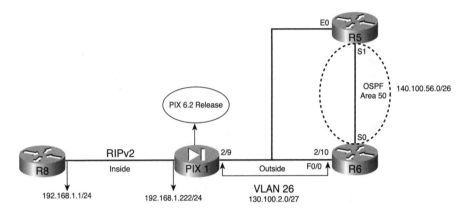

The steps discussed in this case study are as follows:

Step 1   Configuring RIPv2 on two routers

Step 2   Configuring MD5 authentication between two routers

Step 3   Configuring the PIX firewall

Step 1: Configuring RIPv2 on Two Routers

To successfully accomplish RIPv2 over router to PIX 6.2 with authentication, you first need to go through the familiar steps of enabling RIP on a router, which were discussed in the previous sections. Example 8-27 shows the initial setup of R5 and R6. You see that the OSPF-RIP redistribution is configured in a similar manner to R3. However, unlike the preceding section, this configuration implements RIPv2. This is done so that you can make use of the authentication techniques that are not available in version 1. Also, note the presence of the RIPv2-specific **no auto-summary** command and the absence of the **neighbor** statement. Because you are using version 6.2 on the PIX, this command is not necessary.

Example 8-27 *RIP Configuration on R5 and R6*

```
r5#show run
hostname r5
!
interface Loopback5
 ip address 5.5.5.5 255.255.255.0
```

Example 8-27 *RIP Configuration on R5 and R6 (Continued)*

```
!
interface Ethernet0
 ip address 130.100.2.5 255.255.255.224
!
interface Serial0
 ip address 140.100.45.5 255.255.255.252
 ip ospf network point-to-point
!
interface Serial1
 ip address 140.100.56.5 255.255.255.192
 clockrate 64000
!
router ospf 123
 router-id 5.5.5.5
 log-adjacency-changes detail
 area 1 virtual-link 4.4.4.4
 network 5.5.5.0 0.0.0.255 area 1
 network 140.100.45.4 0.0.0.3 area 1
 network 140.100.56.0 0.0.0.63 area 50
!
router rip
 version 2
 redistribute ospf 123 metric 1
 network 130.100.0.0
 no auto-summary


r6#show run
hostname r6
!
interface Loopback6
 ip address 6.6.6.6 255.255.255.0
!
interface FastEthernet0/0
 ip address 130.100.2.6 255.255.255.224
 duplex auto
 speed auto
!

interface Serial0/0
 ip address 140.100.56.6 255.255.255.192

!
interface FastEthernet0/1
 no ip address
 duplex auto
 speed auto
!
router ospf 123
 router-id 6.6.6.6
```

continues

Example 8-27 *RIP Configuration on R5 and R6 (Continued)*

```
log-adjacency-changes detail
redistribute rip metric 1 subnets
network 6.6.6.0 0.0.0.255 area 50
network 140.100.56.0 0.0.0.63 area 50!
router rip
version 2
redistribute ospf 123 metric 1
network 130.100.0.0
no auto-summary
```

Step 2: Configuring MD5 Authentication Between Two Routers

The next step is to configure the MD5 authentication between R5 and R6. You follow the same order as described in Step 7 of Case Study 8-1. Example 8-28 shows the key chain ccie and key 1 set up on both routers as the assigned ccie password. Ethernet interface configurations contain **ip rip authentication key-chain** and **ip rip authentication mode md5** statements, which enable RIP authentication between routers.

Example 8-28 *RIPv2 Authentication Between R5 and R6*

```
r5#show run
hostname r5
!
key chain ccie
 key 1
  key-string ccie
!
! Output omitted for brevity
!
interface Ethernet0
 ip address 130.100.2.5 255.255.255.224
 ip rip send version 2
 ip rip receive version 2
 ip rip authentication mode md5
 ip rip authentication key-chain ccie


r6#show run
hostname r6
!
key chain ccie
 key 1
  key-string ccie
!
! Output omitted for brevity
!
interface FastEthernet0/0
 ip address 130.100.2.6 255.255.255.224
 ip rip send version 2
```

Example 8-28 *RIPv2 Authentication Between R5 and R6 (Continued)*

```
ip rip receive version 2
ip rip authentication mode md5
ip rip authentication key-chain ccie
duplex auto
speed auto
```

To verify that the authentication between routers is working, issue the **show ip protocols** command on both routers. The output of this command, shown in Example 8-29, proves that the key chain ccie has been applied.

Example 8-29 *The* **show ip protocols** *Command Output*

```
r5#show ip protocols
Routing Protocol is "ospf 123"
  Invalid after 0 seconds, hold down 0, flushed after 0
  Outgoing update filter list for all interfaces is
  Incoming update filter list for all interfaces is
  Redistributing: rip
  Routing for Networks:
    5.5.5.0/24
    140.100.45.4/30
    140.100.56.0/26
  Routing Information Sources:
    Gateway        Distance      Last Update
    3.3.3.3             110      00:40:43
    4.4.4.4             110      00:40:43
  Distance: (default is 110)

Routing Protocol is "rip"
  Sending updates every 30 seconds, next due in 25 seconds
  Invalid after 180 seconds, hold down 180, flushed after 240
  Outgoing update filter list for all interfaces is
  Incoming update filter list for all interfaces is
  Redistributing: ospf 123 (internal, external 1 & 2, nssa-external 1 & 2)

  Redistributing: rip
  Default version control: send version 2, receive version 2
    Interface           Send  Recv  Triggered RIP  Key-chain
    Ethernet0           2     2                     ccie
  Automatic network summarization is not in effect
  Routing for Networks:
    130.100.0.0
  Routing Information Sources:
    Gateway        Distance      Last Update
    130.100.2.6         120      00:00:05
    130.100.2.2         120      00:00:21
  Distance: (default is 120)
```

continues

Example 8-29 *The* **show ip protocols** *Command Output (Continued)*

```
r6#show ip protocols
Routing Protocol is "ospf 123"
  Invalid after 0 seconds, hold down 0, flushed after 0
  Outgoing update filter list for all interfaces is
  Incoming update filter list for all interfaces is
  Redistributing: rip
  Routing for Networks:
    6.6.6.0/24
    140.100.56.0/26
  Routing Information Sources:
    Gateway         Distance      Last Update
  Distance: (default is 110)

Routing Protocol is "rip"
  Sending updates every 30 seconds, next due in 10 seconds
  Invalid after 180 seconds, hold down 180, flushed after 240
  Outgoing update filter list for all interfaces is
  Incoming update filter list for all interfaces is
  Redistributing: ospf 123 (internal, external 1 & 2, nssa-external 1 & 2)

  Redistributing: rip
  Default version control: send version 2, receive version 2
    Interface            Send  Recv  Triggered RIP  Key-chain
    FastEthernet0/0      2     2                     ccie
    Interface            Send  Recv  Triggered RIP  Key-chain
  Automatic network summarization is not in effect
  Routing for Networks:
    130.100.0.0
  Routing Information Sources:
    Gateway         Distance      Last Update
    130.100.2.5          120      00:00:14
    130.100.2.2          120      00:00:02
  Distance: (default is 120)
```

Step 3: Configuring the PIX Firewall

After you establish RIP authentication between routers, move on to the PIX configuration. Just as in the previous case study, you first activate interfaces and assign IP addresses to them. In Example 8-30, you find that in addition to activating the outside interface as in Case Study 8-2, you have to activate the inside interface connected to R8.

In this case, RIPv1 is assigned to the inside interface to allow it to provide the default route to R8 and receive R8's routes, such as 8.8.8.8, in return. The outside interface, on the other hand, is now labeled as RIPv2 with authentication option. The syntax for the command is as follows:

```
PIX2(config)#rip interface-name default I passive version 2 authentication [text I md5]
    key key-number
```

Example 8-30 *PIX2 Configuration for RIPv2 with Authentication*

```
PIX2#show run
PIX Version 6.2(1)
nameif ethernet0 outside security0
nameif ethernet1 inside security100

hostname pix2

interface ethernet0 auto
interface ethernet1 auto

ip address outside 130.100.2.2 255.255.255.224
ip address inside 192.168.1.222 255.255.255.0

rip outside passive version 2 authentication md5 ccie 1
rip outside default version 2 authentication md5 ccie 1
rip inside passive version 1
rip inside default version 1
```

Example 8-31 demonstrates the **show route** PIX command output so that you see all the routes being advertised to the firewall, including 8.8.8.8.

Example 8-31 *The* **show route** *Command Output on PIX2*

```
PIX2# show route
        inside 0.0.0.0 0.0.0.0 192.168.1.1 1 RIP
        outside 3.3.3.3 255.255.255.255 130.100.2.5 1 RIP
        outside 4.4.4.4 255.255.255.255 130.100.2.5 1 RIP
        outside 5.5.5.0 255.255.255.0 130.100.2.5 1 RIP
        outside 6.6.6.0 255.255.255.0 130.100.2.6 1 RIP
        outside 7.7.7.0 255.255.255.0 130.100.2.5 1 RIP
        inside 8.0.0.0 255.0.0.0 192.168.1.1 1 RIP
        inside 10.0.0.0 255.0.0.0 192.168.1.1 1 RIP
        inside 65.0.0.0 255.0.0.0 192.168.1.1 1 RIP
        intf2 127.0.0.1 255.255.255.255 127.0.0.1 1 CONNECT static
        outside 130.100.1.0 255.255.255.0 130.100.2.5 1 RIP
        outside 130.100.2.0 255.255.255.224 130.100.2.2 1 CONNECT static
        outside 140.100.45.4 255.255.255.252 130.100.2.5 1 RIP
        outside 150.100.33.0 255.255.255.248 130.100.2.5 1 RIP
        inside 192.168.1.0 255.255.255.0 192.168.1.222 1 CONNECT static
```

Now if you type **show ip route** or **show ip route rip** on either router, you see the default route that is learned via the PIX2 outside interface. Example 8-32 proves that the route exchange is working.

Example 8-32 *Routing Table of R5 and R6*

```
r5#show ip route rip
     6.0.0.0/24 is subnetted, 1 subnets
R       6.6.6.0 [120/1] via 130.100.2.6, 00:00:08, Ethernet0
R*   0.0.0.0/0 [120/1] via 130.100.2.2, 00:00:17, Ethernet0

r6#show ip route rip
     5.0.0.0/24 is subnetted, 1 subnets
R       5.5.5.0 [120/1] via 130.100.2.5, 00:00:26, FastEthernet0/0
R*   0.0.0.0/0 [120/1] via 130.100.2.2, 00:00:03, FastEthernet0/0
```

To verify whether the authentication process is truly operational between the routers and PIX, execute the **debug ip rip** command on both routers and the **debug rip** command on the PIX. Example 8-33 validates your configuration by displaying the successful MD5 packet exchange.

Example 8-33 *The* **debug rip** *Command Output of PIX2*

```
PIX2# debug rip
RIP trace on
PIX2# 1: RIP: interface inside received v1 update from 192.168.1.1
2: RIP: update contains 3 routes
3: RIP: Advertise network 8.0.0.0 mask 255.0.0.0 gateway 192.168.1.1 metric 1
4: RIP: Advertise network 10.0.0.0 mask 255.0.0.0 gateway 192.168.1.1 metric 1
5: RIP: Advertise network 65.0.0.0 mask 255.0.0.0 gateway 192.168.1.1 metric 1
6: RIP: interface outside received v2 update from 130.100.2.6
7: RIP: update contains 12 routes
8: RIP: Advertise network 3.3.3.3 mask 255.255.255.255 gateway 130.100.2.6 metric 1
9: RIP: Advertise network 4.4.4.4 mask 255.255.255.255 gateway 130.100.2.6 metric 1
10: RIP: Advertise network 5.5.5.5 mask 255.255.255.255 gateway 130.100.2.6 metric 1
11: RIP: Advertise network 6.6.6.0 mask 255.255.255.0 gateway 130.100.2.6 metric 1
12: RIP: Advertise network 7.7.7.0 mask 255.255.255.0 gateway 130.100.2.6 metric 1
13: RIP: Advertise network 130.100.1.0 mask 255.255.255.0 gateway 130.100.2.6 metric 1
14: RIP: Advertise network 130.100.2.0 mask 255.255.255.0 gateway 130.100.2.6 metric 1
15: RIP: Advertise network 140.100.45.4 mask 255.255.255.252 gateway 130.100.2.6 metric 1
16: RIP: Advertise network 140.100.56.0 mask 255.255.255.192 gateway 130.100.2.6 metric 1
19: RIP: Advertise network 150.100.33.0 mask 255.255.255.248 gateway 130.100.2.6 metric 1
20: RIP: interface outside received v2 update from 130.100.2.5
21: RIP: update contains 12 routes
22: RIP: Advertise network 3.3.3.3 mask 255.255.255.255 gateway 130.100.2.5 metric 1
23: RIP: Advertise network 4.4.4.4 mask 255.255.255.255 gateway 130.100.2.5 metric 1
24: RIP: Advertise network 5.5.5.0 mask 255.255.255.0 gateway 130.100.2.5 metric 1
25: RIP: Advertise network 6.6.6.6 mask 255.255.255.255 gateway 130.100.2.5 metric 1
26: RIP: Advertise network 7.7.7.0 mask 255.255.255.0 gateway 130.100.2.5 metric 1
27: RIP: Advertise network 130.100.1.0 mask 255.255.255.0 gateway 130.100.2.5 metric 1
28: RIP: Advertise network 130.100.2.0 mask 255.255.255.224 gateway 130.100.2.5 metric 1
29: RIP: Advertise network 140.100.45.4 mask 255.255.255.252 gateway 130.100.2.5 metric 1
30: RIP: Advertise network 140.100.56.0 mask 255.255.255.192 gateway 130.100.2.5 metric 1
33: RIP: Advertise network 150.100.33.0 mask 255.255.255.248 gateway 130.100.2.5 metric 1
```

Lesson 8-1: Advanced RIP Configuration

This section explains some of the optional RIP configuration tasks. No specific topology is necessary to demonstrate them. Their implementation depends on your personal preferences or operation requirements.

In this lesson, you learn how to perform the following tasks:

- Adjusting RIP timers

- Configuring RIP on a WAN

- Enabling broadcasts with RIPv2

Adjusting Timers

Previously, in "Routing Updates and Timers," you learned that RIP uses the following types of timers to control its operation:

- An update timer

- A time-out or invalid timer

- A hold-down timer for split horizon

- A flush timer to rid a routing table of an invalid route

All of these timers have default settings, which you do not need to set. However, to change any of the defaults, you must invoke the following command:

```
R1(config-router)#timers basic update invalid holddown flush
```

NOTE   In this lesson, R1 refers to any router, rather than a specific router.

All the timers are measured in seconds. All four timers comprise the command. If you need to make a change to just one of them, you still need to retype the values for all. Another drawback to this command is the fact that once you have modified the defaults on one router, you must also alter all routers in the RIP routing domain.

Example 8-34 shows the implementation of the **timers basic** command on a router.

Example 8-34 *Adjusting RIP Timers on a Router*

```
R1#show run
!
router rip
 version 2
```

continues

Example 8-34 *Adjusting RIP Timers on a Router*

```
timers basic 90 180 260 320
redistribute ospf 123 metric 1
network 130.100.0.0
no auto-summary
```

RIP's Application on a WAN

RIP's broadcast-type nature of periodic advertisements makes its application impractical with remote connectivity. Updates every 30 seconds keep the on-demand links forever up, and the amount of information carried in those advertisements interrupts the normal data flow on the expensive point-to-point leased lines.

RIP tries to conquer this nuisance by allowing only triggered updates to pass over the WAN links. Whenever the change to its routing database occurs or the update is requested, RIP sends an update out of its serial interface where this special feature is enabled. Otherwise, all periodic-type updates are suppressed. You can think of this feature as being similar in function to the OSPF demand circuit discussed in Chapter 6. The configuration involves two steps, as follows:

Step 1 Specify a WAN interface.

Step 2 Enable the command under the interface configuration, as follows:

```
R1(config)#interface serial number
R1(config-if)#ip rip triggered
```

Example 8-35 illustrates the application of the **ip rip triggered** command on a router.

Example 8-35 *Enabling Triggered Updates on the RIP WAN Interface*

```
R6#show run
interface Serial0/0
 ip address 140.100.56.6 255.255.255.192
 ip rip triggered
```

Enabling Broadcasts in RIPv2

In earlier sections of this chapter, you learned that RIPv2 on a Cisco router sends its advertisements to a multicast address of 224.0.0.9. However, some vendors' firewall equipment, as well as PIX software versions prior to 5.3, does not understand RIPv2 multicasts and would only accept broadcast updates. So, for multivendor interoperability, you can force RIPv2 into a broadcast mode with the following command:

```
R6(config-if)#ip rip v2-broadcast
```

Example 8-36 exhibits the **debug ip rip** command output before and after the **ip rip v2-broadcast** command has been enabled. The difference is clear: The address of 224.0.0.9 has changed to 255.255.255.255.

Example 8-36 *The* **debug ip rip** *Command Output*

```
02:53:56: RIP: sending v2 flash update to 224.0.0.9 via Loopback3 (27.1.1.7)
02:53:56: RIP: build flash update entries


02:53:54: RIP: received packet with MD5 authentication
02:53:54: RIP: received v2 update from 140.100.47.4 on Ethernet0
! Output omitted for brevity
02:53:54:       140.100.45.4/30 via 0.0.0.0 in 1 hops
02:53:54:       150.100.33.0/29 via 0.0.0.0 in 5 hops
02:53:55: RIP: sending v2 flash update to 255.255.255.255 via Ethernet0 (140.100.47.7)
```

Summary

RIP is the oldest routing protocol out there, but it has proven resiliency. It is still widely used and is an integral part of networking. The CCIE Security lab exam is not based solely on RIP, but a good understanding of RIP theory and a knowledge of configuration are required.

In this chapter, you learned some of the most vital RIP concepts such as the mechanics of RIPv1 and RIPv2, configuration tasks for basic and advanced RIP networking, and some of the security-related issues, such as RIP authentication and RIP router-to-PIX communication.

Review Questions

1 Manual summarization is supported in which version of RIP?

2 he invalid timer's default period, in seconds?

3 What is the correct syntax for creating an authentication key?

4 Fill in the blanks: By default, a Cisco router listens to _____ messages but sends _____ messages.

5 When RIP is used for routing in nonbroadcast network environments, do you need to turn split horizon on or off?

FAQs

Q — *What is the major difference between RIPv1 and RIPv2?*

A — The most critical difference between the two is RIPv2's extended capabilities. RIPv2's major advantage over RIPv1 is its capacity to support authentication and to understand subnet masks.

Q — *What is the diameter limit of a RIP network?*

A — A valid RIP network diameter can have up to 15 hops. A value of 16 is regarded as infinity and indicates a routing loop.

Q — *What is the purpose of key authentication?*

A — Key authentication is used for security purposes. It ensures that the communication is established only with a legitimate peer.

Q — *What is the advantage of summarization?*

A — Route summarization was designed to minimize the size of a routing table, where instead of numerous separate routes, only one route, representing a group of other routes, is installed. When implemented properly, summarization drastically reduces processing time and memory requirements and enables expansion to large-size networks.

This chapter covers the following topics:

- An EIGRP overview
- Configuring EIGRP
- EIGRP Building Blocks
- Configuring EIGRP options
- Troubleshooting EIGRP

CHAPTER 9

EIGRP

The Interior Gateway Routing Protocol (IGRP) is a proprietary distance vector routing technology developed by Cisco Systems. IGRP is designed for deployment in TCP/IP and OSI-compliant networks and is regarded as an Interior Gateway Protocol (IGP), but it has been used successfully as an Exterior Gateway Protocol (EGP) for interdomain routing. IGRP technology is based on the concept that each router in the network does not need to know about all the router/link relationships in the entire network. Each router advertises destinations with a corresponding distance. Upon receiving this information, each router adjusts the distance and propagates this information to neighboring routers.

If you examined a routing update sent by IGRP, you would notice that it is a composite of four items:

- Available bandwidth

- Delay

- Load utilization

- Link reliability

For a more in-depth explanation of IGRP, refer to the *Cisco IOS IP and IP Routing Protocols Configuration Guide* for your particular Cisco IOS software version. It is available on the Cisco website (www.cisco.com).

Enhanced Interior Gateway Routing Protocol (EIGRP) uses the same distance vector technology found in IGRP; the underlying distance information is unchanged. However, EIGRP improves on IGRP's convergence properties and operating efficiency by allowing architecture improvement while retaining your existing investment in IGRP.

This chapter examines the many features of EIGRP and how you can configure them in preparation for the CCIE Security lab exam.

An EIGRP Overview

EIGRP has many features:

- **Variable-Length Subnet Mask (VLSM) support**—EIGRP is a classless protocol and carries subnet information in its updates.

- **Incremental updates**—EIGRP sends only information that has changed. It doesn't require full routing updates, unlike other routing protocols such as Routing Information Protocol (RIP).

- **Rapid convergence**—By using Diffusing Update Algorithm (DUAL) and the concept of a feasible successor, EIGRP can preselect the next best path to a destination.

- **MD5 route authentication**—Since Cisco IOS software Release 11.3, EIGRP supports MD5 password authentication on routing updates.

- **Automatic route summarization**—Route summarization is done automatically on major bit boundaries.

- **Multiple protocol support**—EIGRP provides support for IPX and AppleTalk along with its support of IP.

EIGRP uses DUAL to obtain a loop-free network at any time throughout its route computation. By providing this loop-freedom, every router in your network topology can synchronize its tables at the same time. One important benefit of EIGRP is that routers that are not affected by topology changes do not have to recompute their routing tables.

Another benefit of EIGRP is that it is network layer protocol-independent, thereby allowing DUAL to support other protocol suites.

IP-EIGRP is composed of four basic components:

- **Neighbor discovery/recovery**—The process that routers use to dynamically learn of other routers on their directly attached networks. This process uses a hello mechanism that has the added benefit of allowing the router to know when a neighbor has become unreachable.

- **Reliable Transport Protocol**—This protocol is responsible for guaranteed, ordered delivery of EIGRP packets to all neighbors. It supports transmissions of multicast or unicast packets with or without reliability.

- **DUAL Finite State Machine (FSM)**—The DUAL FSM is responsible for the decision process for all route computations. It tracks metrics advertised by all neighbors so that it can select the routes to be added to the route table. DUAL selects these routes through a concept known as *feasible successors*. A successor is a neighboring router used for packet forwarding that has a least-cost path to a destination that is guaranteed not to be part of a routing loop. When there are no more feasible successors but there are neighbors advertising the destination, a recomputation must occur to select a new successor. The amount of time it takes to recompute the route affects the convergence time even though it is not processor-intensive. Even so, you should try to avoid recomputation if it is not necessary.

- **Protocol-dependent modules**—These modules are responsible for network layer protocol-specific requirements. For example, the IP-EIGRP module is responsible for sending and receiving EIGRP packets encapsulated in IP.

Configuring EIGRP

Before we discuss the functionality of EIGRP in more detail, you need to complete Lesson 9-1, in which you configure a simple EIGRP topology between R1 and R10 on an Ethernet network.

Lesson 9-1: Configuring Simple EIGRP

To see EIGRP routes in the routing table, you will configure two loopback interfaces on each router. You will then configure each router to advertise these routes to its neighbor in the same autonomous system. Figure 9-1 shows the network topology and IP addressing you will use in this lesson.

Figure 9-1   *Simple EIGRP Topology*

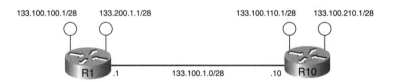

To configure simple EIGRP, follow these steps first on R1 and then on R10:

Step 1   To enable EIGRP, you must start the EIGRP autonomous system process on your router. The syntax is

```
R1(config)#router eigrp autonomous-system
```

EIGRP sends updates out an interface only if its network is listed under the EIGRP autonomous system.

Step 2   Because all the networks you will configure are included in a single Class B network, you need to configure only a single network entry. You could optionally configure three network commands by specifying the subnet mask to be used for each **network** statement. The syntax you use is

```
R1(config-router)#network network-number [network-mask]
```

Step 3 Next, you need to configure the two loopback interfaces on R1. This step is needed for output in later examples. Configuring a loopback interface is a two-step process:

(a) Activate the loopback interface using the following syntax:

```
R1(config)#interface loopback 0-2147483647
```

(b) Apply an IP address to the loopback interface you just created:

```
R1(config-if)#ip address ip-address mask [secondary]
```

Repeat these two steps to create your second loopback interface.

Remember to follow these steps on R10 to complete your basic EIGRP configuration.

You can verify that the EIGRP process is running by using the **show ip protocols** command. Example 9-1 shows you the output of this command from R1.

Example 9-1 **show ip protocols** *Command Output from R1*

```
R1#show ip protocol
Routing Protocol is "eigrp 234"
  Outgoing update filter list for all interfaces is
  Incoming update filter list for all interfaces is
  Default networks flagged in outgoing updates
  Default networks accepted from incoming updates
  EIGRP metric weight K1=1, K2=0, K3=1, K4=0, K5=0
  EIGRP maximum hopcount 100
  EIGRP maximum metric variance 1
  Redistributing: eigrp 234
  Automatic network summarization is in effect
  Routing for Networks:
    133.100.0.0
  Routing Information Sources:
    Gateway         Distance      Last Update
    133.100.1.10          90      00:01:03
  Distance: internal 90 external 170
```

A few items to note from Example 9-1 are the networks that EIGRP is routing for and the default distance in use.

Example 9-2 displays a configuration you can use to complete your simple EIGRP network topology between the two routers.

Example 9-2 *Simple EIGRP Configuration of R1 and R10*

```
Configuration items for R1:
R1(config)#interface Loopback0
R1(config-if)#ip address 133.100.100.1 255.255.255.240
R1(config-if)#exit
R1(config)#interface Loopback1
```

Example 9-2 *Simple EIGRP Configuration of R1 and R10 (Continued)*

```
R1(config-if)#ip address 133.100.200.1 255.255.255.240
R1(config-if)#exit
R1(config)#interface Ethernet0
R1(config-if)#ip address 133.100.1.1 255.255.255.240
R1(config-if)#exit
R1(config)#router eigrp 234
R1(config-router)#network 133.100.0.0

Configuration items for R10:
R10(config)#interface Loopback0
R10(config-if)#ip address 133.100.110.1 255.255.255.240
R10(config-if)#exit
R10(config)#interface Loopback1
R10(config-if)#ip address 133.100.210.1 255.255.255.240
R10(config-if)#exit
R10(config)#interface Ethernet0
R10(config-if)#ip address 133.100.1.10 255.255.255.240
R10(config-if)#exit
R10(config)#router eigrp 234
R10(config-router)#network 133.100.0.0
```

EIGRP Building Blocks

Now that you have a functioning EIGRP topology, you can quickly review how EIGRP operates to get the necessary background to troubleshoot it efficiently. This section is designed to give you enough information about EIGRP to complete the lessons in this chapter. For an in-depth description of any concept in this chapter, refer to the *Cisco IOS IP and IP Routing Protocols Configuration Guide* for your particular Cisco IOS software version. Another excellent source of information on both IGRP and EIGRP is *Routing TCP/IP,* Volume I by Jeff Doyle (Cisco Press, 1998).

Packet Formats

EIGRP uses five different packet types:

- **Hellos/acknowledgments**—Hellos are the multicast neighbor discovery/recovery mechanism used by EIGRP. A hello packet is sent to the multicast address of 224.0.0.10. An acknowledgment is actually a hello packet that does not contain any data. Unlike the hello, an acknowledgment is always sent using a unicast address and contains a nonzero acknowledgment number.

- **Update**—Update packets are used to convey reachability information. In the case of new neighbors, update packets are sent to a unicast address and are used to build the topology table. In other cases, update packets are sent to a multicast address and are usually used to convey updated information, such as link cost. In either case, update packets are sent reliably.

- **Query**—Query packets are sent when a destination goes into the active state. Queries are always multicast unless they are in response to a query. A response query is sent to the successor that sent the original query through a unicast. Queries are also sent reliably.

- **Reply**—Reply packets are always sent unicast in response to queries to tell the originator that it does not need to go into an active state because it has a feasible successor. Replies are always sent reliably.

- **Request**—Request packets are used to request specific information from one or more neighbors, usually from a route server application. Requests can be either multicast or unicast and are transmitted unreliably.

TIP   If you adjust the hello interval, the holdtime must be adjusted manually to three times the hello interval, or you might receive unpredictable results.

EIGRP Tables

For EIGRP to provide a loop-free topology, it employs two separate tables to store routing information along with the routing table:

- Neighbor table
- Topology table

The following sections describe both tables in more detail.

Neighbor Table

Each EIGRP router in your network is required to keep state information about its adjacent neighbors. EIGRP uses a hello mechanism to form adjacencies with its neighbors. Unlike IGRP, EIGRP does not need to send full routing updates on a periodic basis. It sends information about link changes only to the neighbors who need to know the change information. The neighbor table, one for each protocol-dependent module you enable, is used to record the address and interface of each neighboring router in the neighbor data structure. When a neighbor sends a hello packet to your network on multicast address 224.0.0.10, it advertises the amount of time that a router treats a neighbor as reachable and operational.

By default, hellos are sent every 5 seconds on high-bandwidth links such as LAN interfaces, serial interfaces greater than T1 speed, point-to-point serial links, and ATM and Frame Relay point-to-point links. Hellos on nonbroadcast multiaccess (NBMA) media, such as serial links with a speed less than T1, ATM and Frame Relay multipoint interfaces, ATM SVCs, and ISDN BRIs, are sent every 60 seconds. If a hello packet isn't heard within the defined holdtime—by default, three times the hello interval, 15 seconds for high-bandwidth links, or 180 seconds for low-speed multipoint links—the holdtime expires and DUAL is informed of the topology change.

The neighbor table contains the following fields:

- **H**—The handle. A Cisco IOS number used to identify a neighbor.

- **Address**—The IP address of the router it received the hello from.

- **Interface**—The interface the hello was received on.

- **Hold**—The hold timer agreed on by both neighbors.

- **Uptime**—How long the adjacency has been operational.

- **SRTT**—Smooth Round-Trip Time. The round-trip time.

- **RTO**—Retransmission Timeout. How long EIGRP waits before retransmitting a packet from the retransmission queue.

- **Q Cnt**—The count of messages in the queue waiting to be sent.

- **Seq Num**—The last sequence number seen.

The neighbor table also includes information required by the reliable transport mechanism. The neighbor table contains a listing of the last sequence numbers seen so that EIGRP can match acknowledgments with data packets and identify out-of-order packets. EIGRP stores the sequence number along with a transmission list to queue packets for possible retransmission on a per-neighbor basis in the neighbor table. EIGRP also stores round-trip timers in this table, which are used by EIGRP to estimate an optimal retransmission interval. This piece of important information will aid you in your troubleshooting efforts.

If you are using secondary addressing in your network, keep in mind that EIGRP does not build peer relationships over secondary addresses. All EIGRP traffic is sourced by the interface's primary address.

NOTE   Because EIGRP uses the multicast hello packet to communicate with other EIGRP neighbors, you might receive the "not on common subnet" error message. This message appears when EIGRP receives an EIGRP hello packet sourced from an IP address on a subnet that is different from the subnet configured on its receiving interface:

```
timestamp: IP-EIGRP: Neighbor neighbor IP address not on common subnet for interface
```

When using secondary addressing, remember to configure the IP address that EIGRP will use as its primary address on the same subnet as its neighbor. For example, the following configuration results in this error:

```
R1:
interface ethernet0
 ip address 10.1.1.1 255.255.255.0
 !
router eigrp 1
 network 10.0.0.0
```

```
R2:
interface ethernet0
 ip address 10.1.2.2 255.255.255.0
!
router eigrp 1
 network 10.0.0.0
```

The following configuration does not result in an error:

```
R1:
interface ethernet0
 ip address 10.1.1.1 255.255.255.0
!
router eigrp 1
 network 10.0.0.0

R2:
interface ethernet0
 ip address 10.1.1.2 255.255.255.0
!
router eigrp 1
 network 10.0.0.0
```

Example 9-3 shows the output of a **show ip eigrp neighbors** command issued on R1.

Example 9-3   **show ip eigrp neighbors** *Command Output from R1*

```
R1#show ip eigrp neighbors
IP-EIGRP neighbors for process 234
H   Address              Interface   Hold Uptime    SRTT   RTO  Q  Seq
                                     (sec)          (ms)        Cnt Num
0   133.100.1.10         Et0          14 00:08:20    1    4500  0  1
```

As you can see, R1 has formed an adjacency with R10 across its Ethernet 0 interface. This adjacency is the first step in the creation of the neighbor table.

Topology Table

The next table that EIGRP builds on your router is the topology table. It is populated by protocol-dependent modules and is used by the DUAL finite state machine in its decision-making process. It contains a list of all destinations advertised by neighboring routers with an association of destination addresses to all neighbors that advertised the destination. For each neighbor, the advertised metric that the neighbor is using in its routing table is recorded. One rule that a distance vector routing protocol must follow is that it is not allowed to advertise a route unless it is using that route in its own routing table to forward packets.

You should also notice that the destination is associated with the metric that the router uses to reach the destination. This metric is the sum of the best-advertised metrics from all neighbors plus the link cost to the best neighbor. This is the metric that your router will use in its routing table and for advertisements to other routers.

The topology table contains the following information:

- **Lowest bandwidth**—Expressed in kilobits, this is the lowest bandwidth along the path to this destination as reported by the upstream neighbor. If you use anything other than the default bandwidth on an interface, you should explicitly configure it to ensure proper calculation of this metric.

- **Total delay**—Expressed in microseconds, total delay is the sum of the delays along the path to the destination.

- **Path reliability**—A number between 1 and 255, computed dynamically, where a setting of 255 indicates a fully reliable link and 1 indicates an unreliable link. Although it is included, it is not used in the default metric calculation.

- **Path loading**—A number between 1 and 255, calculated dynamically, where a setting of 1 indicates a minimally loaded link and 255 indicates a 100 percent loaded link. Like path reliability, path loading is not used in the default EIGRP path selection process.

- **Minimum path Maximum Transmission Unit (MTU)**—MTU is not used in metric calculations.

- **Feasible distance**—The best metric along the path to the destination, including the metric to the neighbor advertising the path.

- **Reported distance**—The total metric along the path to the destination as advertised by the upstream neighbor.

- **Route source**—External routes are tagged.

EIGRP uses a composite metric that is calculated using the following formula:

composite metric = $256 \times ([k1 \times BW_{min} + (k2 \times BW_{min}) / (256 - LOAD) + k3 \times DELAY_{sum}] \times X)$

where:

$BW_{min} = 10^7$ / bandwidth of slowest link

$DELAY_{sum}$ = (delays along the path)

$X = k5 / \Sigma(reliability + k4)$ if and only if $k1 <> 1$; if $k1 = 1$, $X = 1$

Because $k1 = k3 = 1$ and $k2 = k4 = k5 = 0$, EIGRP reduces this complex formula to metric = 256(delay + bandwidth) for its default calculation, but remember that EIGRP cannot perform any floating-point mathematical formulas. The previously complex formula now becomes

composite metric = $256(BW_{min} + DELAY_{sum})$

Example 9-4 is the output of the **show ip eigrp topology** command issued on R1 followed by a detailed listing for a single route.

Example 9-4 **show ip eigrp topology** *Command Output from R1*

```
R1#show ip eigrp topology
IP-EIGRP Topology Table for AS(234)/ID(133.100.1.1)

Codes: P - Passive, A - Active, U - Update, Q - Query, R - Reply,
       r - reply Status, s - sia Status

P 133.100.200.0/28, 1 successors, FD is 128256
        via Connected, Loopback1
P 133.100.210.0/28, 1 successors, FD is 409600
        via 133.100.1.10 (409600/128256), Ethernet0
P 133.100.100.0/28, 1 successors, FD is 128256
        via Connected, Loopback0
P 133.100.110.0/28, 1 successors, FD is 409600
        via 133.100.1.10 (409600/128256), Ethernet0
P 133.100.1.0/28, 1 successors, FD is 281600
        via Connected, Ethernet0

R1#show ip eigrp topology 133.100.210.0 255.255.255.240
IP-EIGRP topology entry for 133.100.210.0/28
  State is Passive, Query origin flag is 1, 1 Successor(s), FD is 409600
  Routing Descriptor Blocks:
  133.100.1.10 (Ethernet0), from 133.100.1.10, Send flag is 0x0
      Composite metric is (409600/128256), Route is Internal
      Vector metric:
        Minimum bandwidth is 10000 Kbit
        Total delay is 6000 microseconds
        Reliability is 255/255
        Load is 1/255
        Minimum MTU is 1500
        Hop count is 1
```

By examining Example 9-4, you will notice that it contains information on all routes that EIGRP knows about, both its local routes and routes learned from neighbors. The **show ip eigrp topology** output contains a code field that defines the route's state. You should pay attention to the following codes:

- **P**—The EIGRP route is in the passive state. This is the ideal state, because EIGRP is not performing any computations on the route.

- **A**—The EIGRP route is in the active state. This is not an ideal state, because the EIGRP process is currently performing computations on the route.

- **U**—The EIGRP route is in the update state. This means that an update packet has been sent to this destination.

- **Q**—The EIGRP route is in the query state. This means that a query packet has been sent to this destination.

- **R**—The EIGRP route is in the reply state. This means that a reply packet was sent to this destination.

You should also note that the output contains information about the route itself:

- **Network address/mask**—The IP address of the network that EIGRP knows about. You will notice that the subnet mask information is included in this output, making EIGRP a classless routing protocol.

- **Successors**—The number of successors for this route.

- **FD**—The feasible distance to the destination.

- **Originating information**—Identifies where the route was learned. In this case, only routes from directly connected interfaces and from R10 are listed.

Example 9-5 illustrates an output of the **show ip route** command issued on R1. This example is the product of EIGRP after the completion of DUAL computations. These routes identify where EIGRP can send packets.

Example 9-5 show ip route *Command Output from R1*

```
R1#show ip route
Codes: C - connected, S - static, I - IGRP, R - RIP, M - mobile, B - BGP
       D - EIGRP, EX - EIGRP external, O - OSPF, IA - OSPF inter area
       N1 - OSPF NSSA external type 1, N2 - OSPF NSSA external type 2
       E1 - OSPF external type 1, E2 - OSPF external type 2, E - EGP
       i - IS-IS, L1 - IS-IS level-1, L2 - IS-IS level-2, ia - IS-IS inter area
       * - candidate default, U - per-user static route, o - ODR
       P - periodic downloaded static route

Gateway of last resort is not set

     133.100.0.0/28 is subnetted, 5 subnets
C       133.100.200.0 is directly connected, Loopback1
D       133.100.210.0 [90/409600] via 133.100.1.10, 01:08:22, Ethernet0
C       133.100.100.0 is directly connected, Loopback0
D       133.100.110.0 [90/409600] via 133.100.1.10, 01:08:22, Ethernet0
C       133.100.1.0 is directly connected, Ethernet0
```

The output in Example 9-5 lists where the routes come from; the D identifies the router as an EIGRP route. The IP address identifies the network, followed by the administrative distance; 90 is the default for an internal EIGRP route, and 170 is the default for an external EIGRP route. The administrative distance is followed by the 32-bit composite metric. The **via** entry identifies the neighbor the route was learned from, when the route was last updated, and the interface the router learned the route from.

Feasible Successors

As soon as your router has its tables populated with the information it needs, it starts the selection of feasible successors to populate its own routing table. A destination entry is moved from the topology table to the routing table only when a feasible successor is identified and the route is identified as the successor. EIGRP does this by taking all minimum-cost paths to the destination and forming them into a set. From this set, EIGRP can identify neighbors that have an advertised metric less than the current routing table metric, and it considers them feasible successors.

Your router views a feasible successor as any neighbor that is downstream with respect to the destination. If the neighbors meet all the requirements, they are placed in the forwarding table along with their associated metrics.

You might be wondering what happens when a neighbor changes the metric it has been advertising or if a topology change occurs in your network and EIGRP still has feasible successors. If EIGRP has remaining entries in its set of feasible successors, they may be reevaluated to avoid a new route recomputation.

Route States

When an entry is placed in the topology table, it can be in only one of two states: passive or active. You want to see every route known by EIGRP put into the passive state. The passive state tells you that EIGRP has a feasible successor and is not actively performing a route computation. When a route is in the active state, it does not have a feasible successor, and the router undergoes a route computation. If a feasible successor is always identified, a route never has to be placed in the active state and avoids a route recomputation.

If for some reason a route doesn't have a feasible successor, the route is placed in the active state, and route recomputation must occur. When the router starts the route recomputation process, a query packet is sent to all the router's neighbors to see if they have a feasible successor for the route in question. If the neighboring routers have a feasible successor, they can either send a reply for the route in question or optionally return a query indicating that they are also performing a route recomputation. One rule that you need to be aware of is while a route is in the active state, the router cannot change the next-hop neighbor it is using to forward packets. However, as soon as all replies are received for a given query, the destination can be transitioned to the passive state, and a new successor can be selected.

NOTE   If a link to a neighbor goes down and it is the only feasible successor, all routes with that neighbor as the next hop start a route recomputation and enter the active state.

Route Tagging

Like many other routing protocols, EIGRP categorizes routes as internal or external. A route is considered *internal* when it originates within your EIGRP autonomous system. A route is considered *external* when it is learned from another routing protocol or is a static route in the routing table. External routes are tagged individually with the identity of their origination.

External route tags are composed of the following information:

- The router ID of the EIGRP router that redistributed the route

- The autonomous system number where the destination resides

- A configurable administrator tag

- The protocol ID of the external protocol

- The metric from the external protocol

- Bit flags for default routing

By using the route tagging EIGRP offers, you are given flexibility in your policy controls, which helps you customize your routing environment.

IGRP and EIGRP Interoperability

If you are migrating from IGRP to EIGRP, EIGRP provides compatibility and seamless interoperation with IGRP routers. Cisco incorporated an automatic redistribution mechanism so that IGRP routes are imported into EIGRP and vice versa. The metrics for both protocols are directly translatable, making them easy to compare, as if they were routes that originated in their own autonomous system. IGRP routes are treated as external routes in EIGRP, so you can use EIGRP's tagging capabilities to customize your environment. The only requirement for automatic redistribution is that the autonomous system numbers defined by both IGRP and EIGRP must be the same. By default, EIGRP routes always take precedence over IGRP routes.

An Example of DUAL in Action

Figure 9-2 shows a sample topology to help you understand how DUAL converges. It focuses on routing to Router Z only. As a preliminary, each node shows its cost to Router Z in hops. The arrows show the node's successor. For example, Router C uses Router A to reach Router Z, and the cost is 2.

Figure 9-2   *DUAL Sample Topology*

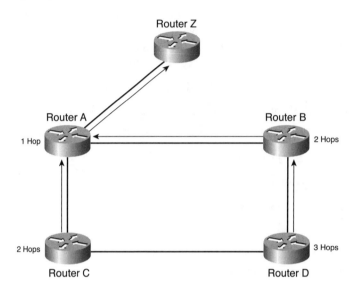

If the link between Router A and Router B fails, Router B sends a query informing its neighbors that it has lost its feasible successor. Router D receives Router B's query and determines whether it has any other feasible successors. If it does not, it must start its own route computation and place the destination route in the active state. However, in this case, Router C is a feasible successor, because its cost of 2 is less than Router D's current cost of 3 to Router Z. Router D can switch to Router C as its successor instead of starting a recomputation. Note that Router A and Router C do not actively participate in this process, because they are unaffected by the change.

By changing the scenario so that the link between Router A and Router C fails instead, you can see that the sample topology has no choice but to rerun the computation. Router C determines that it has lost its successor and has no other feasible successors. In this case, Router D is not be considered a feasible successor because its advertised metric of 3 is greater than Router C's current cost of 2 to reach Router Z. Router C must perform a route computation to obtain a new route to Router Z. Router C sends a query to its only neighbor, Router D in this case, and Router D sends a reply because its successor has not changed. Note that Router D does not need to perform a route computation. When Router C receives the reply, it knows that all neighbors have processed the news about the failure to Router Z. At this point, Router C can choose its new feasible successor, Router D, with a cost of 4 to reach Router Z. Note that Routers A and B are unaffected by the topology change and that Router D simply needs to reply to Router C.

Configuring EIGRP Options

The next step in your examination of EIGRP is to look into optional items you can use to fine-tune the routing process:

- Logging neighbor adjacency changes
- Disabling route summarization
- Configuring manual route summarization
- Configuring default routing
- EIGRP route control
- EIGRP redistribution with route control
- Configuring EIGRP route authentication
- Configuring EIGRP stub routing
- Configuring EIGRP over Generic Routing Encapsulation (GRE) tunnels
- Disabling EIGRP split horizon

After you learn how to reconfigure your topology to add a WAN connection, the next sections outline how to configure each of these options in your network.

Lesson 9-2: Adding a WAN Connection

You first need to reconfigure your topology by adding a WAN connection, as shown in Figure 9-3.

Figure 9-3   *EIGRP Across a WAN*

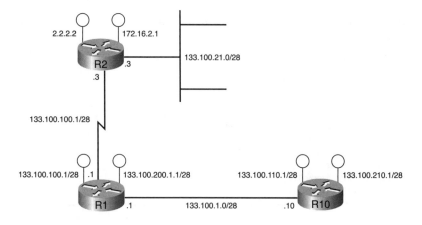

As you can see from the figure, you will connect R2 to R1 with a simple Frame Relay connection. You will also define two loopback interfaces on R2 and add them to the EIGRP routing process to provide entries into the routing table. To add R2 to your EIGRP topology, follow these steps on R1 and R2:

Step 1   Configure the required Frame Relay items on R1. You need to enter the following on R1:

```
R1(config)#interface serial number
R1(config-if)#ip address ip-address mask
R1(config-if)#encapsulation frame-relay [cisco | ietf]
R1(config-if)#frame-relay interface-dlci dlci [ietf | cisco]
  [voice-encap size] [voice-cir cir] [ppp virtual-template-name]
R1(config-if)#frame-relay lmi-type {ansi | cisco | q933a}
```

Enter the following on R2:

```
R2(config)#interface serial number
R2(config-if)#no ip address
R2(config-if)#encapsulation frame-relay [cisco | ietf]
R2(config-if)#frame-relay lmi-type {ansi | cisco | q933a}
R2(config-if)#exit
R2(config)#interface serial number.subinterface number {multipoint |
  point-to-point}
R2(config-subif)#ip address ip-address mask
R2(config-subif)#frame-relay interface-dlci dlci [ietf | cisco]
  [voice-encap size] [voice-cir cir] [ppp virtual-template-name]
```

Step 2   Complete the configuration of R2 by adding two loopback interfaces as outlined in Step 3 of Lesson 9-1.

NOTE   For an explanation of Frame Relay commands, including syntax, refer to Chapter 5, "Frame Relay Connectivity."

Example 9-6 illustrates the relevant commands entered into R1 and R2 to run EIGRP across a serial interface.

Example 9-6   *EIGRP Across a WAN*

```
Configuration items for R1:
R1(config)#interface serial0
R1(config-if)#ip address 150.100.31.1 255.255.255.240
R1(config-if)#encapsulation frame-relay
R1(config-if)#frame-relay interface-dlci 101
R1(config-if)#frame-relay lmi-type ansi
R1(config-if)#exit
R1(config)#router eigrp 234
R1(config-router)#network 150.100.31.0
```

Example 9-6 *EIGRP Across a WAN (Continued)*

```
Configuration items for R2:
R2(config)#interface loopback0
R2(config-if)#ip address 2.2.2.2 255.255.255.0
R2(config-if)#exit
R2(config)#interface loopback1
R2(config-if)#ip address 172.16.2.1 255.255.255.240
R2(config-if)#exit
R2(config)#interface ethernet0
R2(config-if)#ip address 130.100.21.3 255.255.255.0
R2(config-if)#exit
R2(config)#interface serial0
R2(config-if)#encapsulation frame-relay
R2(config-if)#frame-relay lmi-type ansi
R2(config-if)#exit
R2(config)#interface serial0.1 point-to-point
R2(config-if)#ip address 150.100.31.3 255.255.255.240
R2(config-if)#frame-relay interface-dlci 301
R2(config-if)#exit
R2(config)#router eigrp 234
R2(config-router)#network 2.0.0.0
R2(config-router)#network 150.100.31.0
R2(config-router)#network 130.100.1.0
R2(config-router)#network 172.16.0.0
```

Lesson 9-3: Logging Neighbor Adjacency Changes

Because the complexity of your network is increasing, the ability to tell when a neighbor adjacency is formed or broken can be invaluable. The router's default configuration does not alert you to these state changes, but you can configure it to do so by entering the following commands:

```
R1(config)#router eigrp autonomous-system
R1(config-router)#eigrp log-neighbor-changes
```

After you enter the following commands on each of your routers, when a neighbor becomes unreachable for any reason, you see a message similar to the following in your log:

```
03:14:09: %DUAL-5-NBRCHANGE: IP-EIGRP 234: Neighbor 133.100.1.10 (Ethernet0) is
  down: holding time expired
```

When a new adjacency is built, you should see a message similar to the following in your log:

```
03:15:54: %DUAL-5-NBRCHANGE: IP-EIGRP 234: Neighbor 133.100.1.10 (Ethernet0) is
  up: new adjacency
```

NOTE   To enable the logging of neighbor changes, you should complete this step for all three routers.

Lesson 9-4: Disabling Route Summarization

EIGRP autosummarizes routes advertised to its neighbors under two conditions:

- At major class boundaries during redistribution of classful routing protocols. It is important to note that this action cannot be disabled.

- At major class boundaries when the neighbor is on an interface that is in a different major class. You can disable this default action by entering the **no auto-summary** command while in the configuration for the EIGRP autonomous system.

While this at first might seem to be a benefit, in fact it makes EIGRP enforce the discontinuous subnet rule where major bit boundaries meet. This means that EIGRP forms a route to null for each major bit boundary it has configured. When a packet is received that EIGRP does not have a specific route for, it is discarded instead of being forwarded anywhere else.

You can see this behavior by following these steps:

Step 1   Disable automatic route summarization on R1 by entering the following commands:

```
R1(config)#router eigrp 234
R1(config-router)#auto-summary
```

Step 2   Issue the following command on R1:

```
R1#show ip route
```

As you can see by examining the output in Example 9-7, R1 has two major bit boundaries configured on it, 133.100.0.0/16 and 150.100.0.0/16. If you deploy your network so that discontinuous subnets are nonexistent, this default behavior should not be a problem. Unfortunately, in most networks, avoiding discontinuous networks is not possible because of demands placed on you, such as rapid deployment of resources, migrations of IP addressing, and mergers of companies.

Example 9-7   **show ip route** *with Auto-Summary Enabled*

```
R1#show ip route
Codes: C - connected, S - static, I - IGRP, R - RIP, M - mobile, B - BGP
       D - EIGRP, EX - EIGRP external, O - OSPF, IA - OSPF inter area
       N1 - OSPF NSSA external type 1, N2 - OSPF NSSA external type 2
       E1 - OSPF external type 1, E2 - OSPF external type 2, E - EGP
       i - IS-IS, L1 - IS-IS level-1, L2 - IS-IS level-2, ia - IS-IS inter area
       * - candidate default, U - per-user static route, o - ODR
       P - periodic downloaded static route

Gateway of last resort is not set

     2.0.0.0/8 is variably subnetted, 2 subnets, 2 masks
D       2.2.2.0/28 [90/409600] via 133.100.100.3, 00:29:29, Serial0
D       2.0.0.0/16 is a summary, 01:46:39, Null0
     133.100.0.0/16 is variably subnetted, 7 subnets, 2 masks
D       133.100.31.0/28 [90/409600] via 133.100.100.3, 00:29:29, Serial0
```

Example 9-7 **show ip route** *with Auto-Summary Enabled (Continued)*

```
C        133.100.200.0/28 is directly connected, Loopback1
D        133.100.210.0/28 [90/409600] via 133.100.1.10, 00:29:29, Ethernet0
C        133.100.100.0/28 is directly connected, Loopback0
D        133.100.110.0/28 [90/409600] via 133.100.1.10, 00:29:29, Ethernet0
C        133.100.1.0/28 is directly connected, Ethernet0
D        133.100.0.0/16 is a summary, 01:46:39, Null0
     150.100.0.0/16 is variably subnetted, 4 subnets, 4 masks
D        150.100.32.0/27 [90/2681856] via 150.100.31.3, 01:46:38, Serial0
D        150.100.33.0/29 [90/2681856] via 150.100.31.3, 01:14:49, Serial0
C        150.100.31.0/28 is directly connected, Serial0
D        150.100.0.0/16 is a summary, 01:46:40, Null0
     172.16.0.0/16 is variably subnetted, 2 subnets, 2 masks
D        172.16.2.0/28 [90/409600] via 133.100.100.3, 00:29:29, Serial0
D        172.16.0.0/16 is a summary, 01:46:39, Null0
```

By using the **no auto-summary** command, you prevent null routes from being created and prevent summarized routes from being propagated.

You can see this behavior by following these steps:

Step 1   Disable automatic route summarization on R1 by entering the following commands:

```
R1(config)#router eigrp 234
R1(config-router)#no auto-summary
```

Step 2   Issue the following command on R1:

```
R1#show ip route
```

Now, examining the routing table on R1, as shown in Example 9-8, you no longer see null routes in your routing table, permitting you to have discontinuous subnets in your network. Just remember that you should avoid using discontinuous subnets whenever possible.

Example 9-8 **show ip route** *with Auto-Summary Disabled*

```
Configuration items for R1:
R1(config)#router eigrp 234
R1(config-router)#no auto-summary

R1#show ip route
Codes: C - connected, S - static, I - IGRP, R - RIP, M - mobile, B - BGP
       D - EIGRP, EX - EIGRP external, O - OSPF, IA - OSPF inter area
       N1 - OSPF NSSA external type 1, N2 - OSPF NSSA external type 2
       E1 - OSPF external type 1, E2 - OSPF external type 2, E - EGP
       i - IS-IS, L1 - IS-IS level-1, L2 - IS-IS level-2, ia - IS-IS inter area
       * - candidate default, U - per-user static route, o - ODR
       P - periodic downloaded static route
```

continues

Example 9-8 **show ip route** *with Auto-Summary Disabled (Continued)*

```
Gateway of last resort is not set

     2.0.0.0/8 is variably subnetted, 1 subnets, 1 masks
D       2.2.2.0/28 [90/409600] via 133.100.100.3, 00:29:29, Serial0
     133.100.0.0/28 is subnetted, 6 subnets
D       133.100.31.0/28 [90/409600] via 133.100.100.3, 00:29:29, Serial0
C       133.100.200.0 is directly connected, Loopback1
D       133.100.210.0 [90/409600] via 133.100.1.10, 00:00:47, Ethernet0
C       133.100.100.0 is directly connected, Loopback0
D       133.100.110.0 [90/409600] via 133.100.1.10, 00:00:47, Ethernet0
C       133.100.1.0 is directly connected, Ethernet0
     150.100.0.0/16 is variably subnetted, 3 subnets, 3 masks
D       150.100.32.0/27 [90/2681856] via 150.100.31.3, 00:00:20, Serial0
D       150.100.33.0/29 [90/2681856] via 150.100.31.3, 00:00:21, Serial0
C       150.100.31.0/28 is directly connected, Serial0
     172.16.0.0/16 is variably subnetted, 1 subnets, 1 masks
D       172.16.2.0/28 [90/409600] via 133.100.100.3, 00:29:29, Serial0
```

Lesson 9-5: Configuring Manual Route Summarization

Route summarization can be critical to the success of your routing protocol, but you should have more control over what is summarized and how it is summarized. Route summarization provides a mechanism to control EIGRP queries and helps you control the size of your routing table.

EIGRP provides you with two ways to create manual route summarizations:

- Advertising a summary or aggregate address by using the following command:

  ```
  R1(config-if)#ip summary-address eigrp as_number summary_address address_mask
  ```

- Advertising a default route by using the following command:

  ```
  R1(config-if)#ip summary-address eigrp as_number 0.0.0.0 0.0.0.0
  ```

The interesting thing about these commands is, because they are configured on an interface basis, you can customize summaries to the needs of your network. For instance, a summary sent from R1 to R2 can be completely different from the summary sent from R1 to R10.

You can summarize the routes learned from R1 for the 150.100.0.0/16 network on R10 to a single entry by following these steps on R1:

Step 1 Summarize the three routes advertised out of R1's Ethernet 0 interface by adding the following commands to the configuration of R1:

```
Configuration changes on R1:
R1(config)#interface Ethernet0
R1(config-if)#ip summary-address eigrp 234 150.100.0.0 255.255.0.0
```

Step 2 Issue the **show ip route** command on R10 to see the results.

Example 9-9 shows the result of configuring manual route summarization.

Example 9-9 *Manual Route Summarization*

```
R10#show ip route
Codes: C - connected, S - static, I - IGRP, R - RIP, M - mobile, B - BGP
       D - EIGRP, EX - EIGRP external, O - OSPF, IA - OSPF inter area
       N1 - OSPF NSSA external type 1, N2 - OSPF NSSA external type 2
       E1 - OSPF external type 1, E2 - OSPF external type 2, E - EGP
       i - IS-IS, L1 - IS-IS level-1, L2 - IS-IS level-2, ia - IS-IS inter area
       * - candidate default, U - per-user static route, o - ODR

Gateway of last resort is not set

     2.0.0.0/8 is variably subnetted, 1 subnets, 1 masks
D       2.2.2.0/28 [90/409600] via 133.100.100.3, 00:29:29, Serial0
     133.100.0.0/28 is subnetted, 5 subnets
D       133.100.31.0/28 [90/409600] via 133.100.1.1, 00:29:29, Ethernet0
D       133.100.200.0 [90/409600] via 133.100.1.1, 00:00:17, Ethernet0
C       133.100.210.0 is directly connected, Loopback1
D       133.100.100.0 [90/409600] via 133.100.1.1, 00:00:17, Ethernet0
C       133.100.110.0 is directly connected, Loopback0
C       133.100.1.0 is directly connected, Ethernet0
D    150.100.0.0/16 [90/2195456] via 133.100.1.1, 00:00:17, Ethernet0
     172.16.0.0/16 is variably subnetted, 1 subnets, 1 masks
D       172.16.2.0/28 [90/409600] via 133.100.1.1, 00:29:29, Ethernet0
```

As you can see from Example 9-9, after the summary is configured on R1, the routing table on R10 is decreased by three entries.

Lesson 9-6: Configuring Default Routing

At some point, your company will want to connect its network to the Internet if it has not done so already. Because you probably won't run Border Gateway Protocol (BGP) across your internal network, you need a mechanism that allows packets to be routed for destinations your router does not know about.

EIGRP offers several such mechanisms to inject a default route into your EIGRP network:

- By summarizing a default route of 0.0.0.0 using the manual summary address examined in the previous network. You can use the following command to allow a summary address to be used as a default route:

  ```
  R1(config-if)#ip summary-address eigrp autonomous-systems 0.0.0.0 0.0.0.0
  ```

- By redistributing a default static route into EIGRP. You can create the default static route by using the **ip route 0.0.0.0 0.0.0.0** *next_hop_IP_address* command in global configuration mode. You also must enter the **redistribute static** command and a default metric under the EIGRP autonomous system process. You can use the following commands to accomplish this:

```
R1(config)# ip route prefix mask {address | interface} [distance] [tag tag]
  [permanent]
R1(config)#router eigrp autonomous-system
R1(config-router)#redistribute static
R1(config-router)# default-metric bandwidth delay reliability loading mtu
```

- By marking a route as the default route. You can use the following command to specify the default network to use:

```
R1(config)#ip default-network network-number
```

NOTE   If you are working with Cisco IOS software earlier than Release 12.0, you also need to enable classless routing before the router will forward packets it does not have explicit routes for. You can enable classless routing by entering the **ip classless** command in global configuration mode.

In this lesson, you will configure your EIGRP topology so that R1 advertises a default route of 150.100.32.2 to the other routers. Follow these steps to complete this task:

Step 1   Create a static route to network 0.0.0.0 0.0.0.0 using the following command:

```
R1(config)#ip route 0.0.0.0 0.0.0.0 150.100.32.2
```

Step 2   Configure EIGRP to redistribute the default route to the rest of the network using the following commands:

```
R1(config)#router eigrp 234
R1(config-router)#redistribute static
R1(config-router)#default-metric 100000 100 255 1 1500
```

Step 3   Verify your configuration by issuing the **show ip route** command on R10.

NOTE   Because summarizing a default route is applied on a per-interface basis, you can advertise a different route on an interface without having to use a distribute list or another mechanism to prevent this route from being propagated to your core. You must have a static route for the other interfaces to use for a default route, or your router will drop all packets to destinations it does not have a route for.

Example 9-10 shows R10's routing table to verify the result after default routing is configured on R1.

Example 9-10 *Default Routing Results from R10*

```
R10#show ip route
Codes: C - connected, S - static, I - IGRP, R - RIP, M - mobile, B - BGP
       D - EIGRP, EX - EIGRP external, O - OSPF, IA - OSPF inter area
       N1 - OSPF NSSA external type 1, N2 - OSPF NSSA external type 2
       E1 - OSPF external type 1, E2 - OSPF external type 2, E - EGP
       i - IS-IS, L1 - IS-IS level-1, L2 - IS-IS level-2, ia - IS-IS inter area
       * - candidate default, U - per-user static route, o - ODR

Gateway of last resort is 133.100.1.1 to network 0.0.0.0

     2.0.0.0/8 is variably subnetted, 1 subnets, 1 masks
D       2.2.2.0/28 [90/409600] via 133.100.100.3, 00:29:29, Serial0
     133.100.0.0/28 is subnetted, 5 subnets
D       133.100.31.0/28 [90/409600] via 133.100.1.1, 00:29:29, Ethernet0
D       133.100.200.0 [90/409600] via 133.100.1.1, 00:00:17, Ethernet0
C       133.100.210.0 is directly connected, Loopback1
D       133.100.100.0 [90/409600] via 133.100.1.1, 00:00:17, Ethernet0
C       133.100.110.0 is directly connected, Loopback0
C       133.100.1.0 is directly connected, Ethernet0
D    150.100.0.0/16 [90/2195456] via 133.100.1.1, 00:00:17, Ethernet0
     172.16.0.0/16 is variably subnetted, 1 subnets, 1 masks
D       172.16.2.0/28 [90/409600] via 133.100.1.1, 00:29:29, Ethernet0
D*EX 0.0.0.0/0 [170/307200] via 133.100.1.1, 00:00:33, Ethernet0
```

You should notice in Example 9-10 that EIGRP has added a gateway of last resort to the routing table and also an external route to the gateway of last resort.

Lesson 9-7: Controlling EIGRP Routes

You can control where routes can be propagated by using a distribute list. You fine-tune these distribute lists using either an extended or standard access list. You can use the following commands to associate a distribute list with an access list:

```
R10(config)# access-list access-list-number {deny | permit} source
  [source-wildcard] [log]
R10(config)#router eigrp autonomous-system
R10(config-router)# distribute-list {access-list-number | access-list-name}
  [in | out] [interface-type interface-number]
```

The **in** and **out** keywords are applied from the view of the interface. To prevent a routing update from being sent out an interface, use the **out** keyword. If you want to prevent an update from coming into an interface, use the **in** keyword.

In this lesson, you will use a distribute list on R10 to deny the 133.100.200.0/28 route from being placed in R10's routing table without any configuration changes to R1. You can follow these steps to complete this task:

Step 1   Create an access list to deny the route from R1:

```
R1(config)#access-list 10 deny    133.100.200.0
R1(config)#access-list 10 permit any
```

Note that a **permit** statement is required as the last statement for any EIGRP routes to be included in the routing table.

Step 2   Associate the access list to your EIGRP autonomous system in the "in" direction:

```
R1(config)#router eigrp 234
R1(config-router)#distribute-list 10 in
```

Step 3   Verify the configuration on R10.

Example 9-11 gives the results of using a distribute list on R10.

Example 9-11 **show ip route** *Command After a Distribute List is Applied on R10*

```
R10#show ip route
Codes: C - connected, S - static, I - IGRP, R - RIP, M - mobile, B - BGP
       D - EIGRP, EX - EIGRP external, O - OSPF, IA - OSPF inter area
       N1 - OSPF NSSA external type 1, N2 - OSPF NSSA external type 2
       E1 - OSPF external type 1, E2 - OSPF external type 2, E - EGP
       i - IS-IS, L1 - IS-IS level-1, L2 - IS-IS level-2, ia - IS-IS inter area
       * - candidate default, U - per-user static route, o - ODR

Gateway of last resort is 133.100.1.1 to network 0.0.0.0

     2.0.0.0/8 is variably subnetted, 1 subnets, 1 masks
D       2.2.2.0/28 [90/409600] via 133.100.100.3, 00:29:29, Serial0
     133.100.0.0/28 is subnetted, 5 subnets
D       133.100.31.0/28 [90/409600] via 133.100.1.1, 00:29:29, Ethernet0
C       133.100.210.0 is directly connected, Loopback1
D       133.100.100.0 [90/409600] via 133.100.1.1, 00:00:17, Ethernet0
C       133.100.110.0 is directly connected, Loopback0
C       133.100.1.0 is directly connected, Ethernet0
D    150.100.0.0/16 [90/2195456] via 133.100.1.1, 00:00:17, Ethernet0
     172.16.0.0/16 is variably subnetted, 1 subnets, 1 masks
D       172.16.2.0/28 [90/409600] via 133.100.1.1, 00:29:29, Ethernet0
D*EX 0.0.0.0/0 [170/307200] via 133.100.1.1, 00:00:33, Ethernet0
```

Examining the output in Example 9-11, notice that the route for 133.100.200.0/28 no longer appears in your router table, verifying that your distribute list is functioning correctly.

Lesson 9-8: Redistributing EIGRP with Route Controls

Often you will need to redistribute one routing protocol into another, whether it is for a migration or after an acquisition. Redistribution offers the option of supplying a metric for routes originating from another routing protocol that uses a different metric. Remember that IGRP redistribution is built into EIGRP, so in most cases you do not need to adjust these metrics or the use of a route map to provide route control.

One of the easiest ways to adjust the metrics is through the **default-metric** command, although you can supply the metric with the **redistribute** command. One important point to remember is that if you redistribute routes from one protocol to another, in most cases you need to redistribute the second protocol into the first for IP connectivity to remain unbroken. This is called *mutual redistribution*. Redistribution is covered in greater detail in Chapter 13, "Redistribution."

Lesson 9-9: Configuring EIGRP Route Authentication

If your company security policy dictates it, EIGRP provides a mechanism for authenticating routing updates. EIGRP uses an MD5 keyed digest to sign each packet to prevent unauthorized devices from introducing a routing update or spoofing an update to your routers.

You can use the following commands to enable EIGRP authentication:

```
R1(config-if)#ip authentication mode eigrp autonomous-system md5
R1(config-if)#ip authentication key-chain eigrp autonomous-system key-chain
```

To use EIGRP authentication, you must use a key chain. Each key has its own key identifier, which is used in combination with the interface to uniquely identify the authentication algorithm and MD5 authentication in use.

You can configure multiple keys with different lifetimes. The router examines the configured keys from the lowest to the highest until it encounters the first valid key. Here are a few points to remember about authentication:

- A trailing space is a valid character for the key string. If you configure the space on one router, it must be configured on all routers.

- Lifetimes should overlap to prevent a time in which authentication is not in effect.

- The routers must be synchronized with the same time for lifetimes to behave as expected. You may use the Network Time Protocol (NTP) to accomplish this synchronization.

Use the following commands to enable the key chain and define the key string to be used for authentication:

```
R1(config)#key chain name-of-chain
R1(config-keychain)#key number
R1(config-keychain-key)#key-string text
R1(config-keychain-key)#accept-lifetime start-time {infinite | end-time | duration
  seconds}
R1(config-keychain-key)#send-lifetime start-time {infinite | end-time | duration
  seconds}
```

After your key chain is defined, you can use the following commands to associate it with an interface and specify the MD5 authentication mode for EIGRP:

```
R1(config-if)#ip authentication mode eigrp as-number md5
R1(config-if)#ip authentication key-chain eigrp as-number key-chain
```

To complete this lesson, configure R1 and R10 to use EIGRP MD5 authentication for your autonomous system. You will configure a key chain called ccie with a key of 6727 and a string of ccie_string. Follow these steps to configure this:

Step 1 Configure your key chain, and assign your key using the following commands:

```
R1(config)#key chain ccie
R1(config-keychain)#key 6727
R1(config-keychain-key)#key-string ccie_string
```

Step 2 Specify the EIGRP authentication mode, and enable authentication of EIGRP packets by issuing the following commands:

```
R1(config-if)#ip authentication mode eigrp 234 md5
R1(config-if)#ip authentication key-chain eigrp 234 ccie
```

Step 3 Verify proper operation of your EIGRP MD5 authentication by issuing the **show key chain** command and debugging EIGRP packets.

Example 9-12 shows the results of configuring the key chain on R1.

Example 9-12 show key chain *Output*

```
R1#show key chain ccie
Key-chain ccie:
    key 6727 -- text "ccie_string"
        accept lifetime (always valid) - (always valid) [valid now]
        send lifetime (always valid) - (always valid) [valid now]

R1#debug eigrp packet
00:09:26: EIGRP: received packet with MD5 authentication
00:09:26: EIGRP: Received HELLO on Ethernet0 nbr 133.100.1.10
00:09:26:    AS 234, Flags 0x0, Seq 0/0 idbQ 0/0 iidbQ un/rely 0/0 peerQ un/rely
0/0
```

If you used multiple keys in the key chain, you would need to configure the accept and send lifetimes, but for this lesson, you do not need to.

Lesson 9-10: Configuring EIGRP Stub Routing

EIGRP stub routing can be used to improve the stability of and minimize the configuration required on the stub router. You use EIGRP stub routing mostly in a hub-and-spoke topology. An EIGRP stub router has only one exit point from the routing domain and forms an adjacency with one or more distribution routers. The stub router responds to queries for summaries, connected routes, redistributed static routes, external routes, and internal routes marked as "inaccessible." Like most stub domains, an EIGRP stub router can be configured to advertise static and connected routes at the same time. The options you can choose from include the following:

- **receive-only**—The stub router only receives updates. It does not send any to its neighbors.

- **connected**—The stub router advertises all connected routes to a single neighbor.

- **static**—The stub router advertises all static routes to a single neighbor.

- **summary**—The stub router advertises summary routes.

You are required to configure EIGRP stub routing only on the remote or spoke routers. The distribution routers are still required to run EIGRP. The remote routers inform other routers that they are stub routers.

To configure EIGRP stub routing, use the following command:

```
R10(config-router)#eigrp stub [receive-only | connected | static | summary]
```

You can use the following command to verify stub routing:

```
R10#show ip eigrp neighbor detail
```

In this lesson, you will turn R10 into an EIGRP stub router. You will configure it so that it advertises connected, static, and summary routes that R10 knows about. Follow these steps to accomplish this task:

Step 1 You need to configure stub routing only on the router that is actually the stub router—in this case, R10. You can use the following commands to do this:

```
R10(config)#router eigrp 234
R10(config-router)#eigrp stub connected static summary
```

Step 2 Verify proper operation of stub routing through the use of the **show ip eigrp neighbor detail** command on R1, the stub router's neighbor.

Example 9-13 shows the results of Step 2.

Example 9-13 *Stub Routing Verification on R1*

```
R1#show ip eigrp neighbor detail
IP-EIGRP neighbors for process 234
H   Address                Interface    Hold Uptime    SRTT    RTO  Q  Seq Type
                                        (sec)          (ms)         Cnt Num
1   133.100.1.10           Et0             12 00:00:07   12    200  0  8
    Version 12.0/1.1, Retrans: 1, Retries: 0
    Stub Peer Advertising ( CONNECTED STATIC SUMMARY ) Routes
0   150.100.31.3           Se0             10 00:03:17   67    402  0  48
    Version 12.1/1.2, Retrans: 3, Retries: 0
```

Lesson 9-11: Configuring EIGRP Over GRE Tunnels

Sometimes you must run EIGRP across a medium that might not be secure. IPSec can provide the security you need, but it does not provide a built-in mechanism to run routing protocols on top of it, such as EIGRP or OSPF, nor does it provide security for non-IP protocols. Cisco provides a way for you to accomplish this—by running these protocols encapsulated in a GRE tunnel.

When you are considering implementing GRE tunnels, regard the following items:

- Ensure that the tunnel is functional before applying a crypto map.

- Crypto access lists should have GRE as the protocol to permit.

- Use loopback IP addresses to identify the Internet Key Exchange (IKE) peers, tunnel source, and tunnel destination to improve availability.

- Make sure that the MTU of all devices complies with the extra overhead of IPSec.

- GRE tunnels are point-to-point only. You must configure separate tunnels for each link.

You can create a GRE tunnel by using the following commands:

```
R1(config)#interface tunnel number
R1(config-if)#ip address ip-address mask [secondary]
R1(config-if)#ip mtu mtu_size
R1(config-if)#tunnel source {ip-address | type number}
R1(config-if)#tunnel destination {hostname | ip-address}
R1(config-if)#tunnel mode {aurp | cayman | dvmrp | eon | gre ip | nos}
```

You will configure a GRE tunnel between Router R1 and Router R10. You will configure the tunnel to use the loopback 1 interfaces on each router as the destination. You will configure the tunnel to use ISAKMP with a preshared key of cisco123. You will configure IPSec to run in tunnel mode and allow GRE traffic to pass through it. For a complete explanation of the ISAKMP and IPSec commands, see Chapter 19, "Virtual Private Networks."

You can use the following steps to complete this scenario:

Step 1   Identify the interesting traffic to pass over the tunnel. Do this by defining an access list that matches the traffic type you are interested in using the following command:

```
R1(config)#access-list 101 permit gre host 133.100.100.1 host 133.100.110.1
```

Step 2   Create the ISAKMP policy to be used with your GRE tunnel using the following commands:

```
R1(config)#crypto isakmp policy 25
R1(config-isakmp-group)#hash md5
R1(config-isakmp-group)#authentication pre-share
```

Step 3 Because you defined your authentication to use preshare, issue the following commands to identify the peer and set the preshare key:

```
R1(config)#crypto isakmp key cisco123 address 133.100.110.1
```

Step 4 Create a transform set for use with IPSec using the following commands:

```
R1(config)#crypto ipsec transform-set ccielab esp-3des esp-sha-hmac
R1(cfg-crypto-trans)#mode transport
```

Step 5 Define your crypto map for IPSec using the following commands:

```
R1(config)#crypto map GRE 50 ipsec-isakmp
R1(config-crypto-map)#set peer 133.100.110.1
R1(config-crypto-map)#set transform-set ccielab
R1(config-crypto-map)#match address 101
```

Step 6 Because you are using a loopback interface instead of the physical interface, issue the following command so that IPSec will use the loopback as the identifying interface:

```
R1(config)#crypto map GRE local-address Loopback0
```

Step 7 Create the tunnel interface you will use to start and terminate the GRE tunnel using the following commands:

```
R1(config)#interface tunnel 0
R1(config-if)#ip address 10.1.1.1 255.255.255.252
R1(config-if)#ip mtu 1440
R1(config-if)#tunnel source loopback 0
R1(config-if)#tunnel destination 133.100.110.1
R1(config-if)#tunnel mode gre ip
```

Step 8 Define the crypto map you will use for the GRE tunnel. Issue the following command on both the tunnel 0 interface and the Ethernet 0 interface:

```
R1(config-if)#crypto map GRE
```

Step 9 Before your tunnel becomes established, your router needs to know where the destination IP address resides. You can use the following command to accomplish this:

```
R1(config)#ip route 133.100.110.0 255.255.255.240 133.100.1.10
```

Step 10 Set the authentication mode and key chain for EIGRP that were defined in Lesson 9-9:

```
R1(config-if)#ip authentication mode eigrp 234 md5
R1(config-if)#ip authentication key-chain eigrp 234 ccie
```

Step 11 Enter the following commands on R10 to configure its tunnel interface:

```
R10(config)#crypto isakmp policy 25
R10(config-isakmp-group)#hash md5
R10(config-isakmp-group)#authentication pre-share
R10(config-isakmp-group)#crypto isakmp key cisco123 address 133.100.100.1.1
R10(config-isakmp-group)#exit
R10(config)#crypto ipsec transform-set ccielab esp-des esp-md5-hmac
```

```
R10(cfg-crypto-trans)#mode transport
R10(cfg-crypto-trans)#exit
R10(config)#crypto map GRE local-address Loopback0
R10(config-crypto-map)#crypto map GRE 50 ipsec-isakmp
R10(config-crypto-map)#set peer 133.100.100.1
R10(config-crypto-map)#set transform-set ccielab
R10(config-crypto-map)#match address 101
R10(config-crypto-map)#exit
R10(config)#interface tunnel0
R10(config-if)#ip address 10.1.1.2 255.255.255.252
R10(config-if)#ip mtu 1440
R10(config-if)#tunnel source loopback0
R10(config-if)#tunnel destination 133.100.100.1
R10(config-if)#crypto map GRE
R10(config-if)#ip authentication mode eigrp 234 md5
R10(config-if)#ip authentication key-chain eigrp 234 ccie
R10(config-if)#exit
R10(config)#interface ethernet0
R10(config-if)#crypto map GRE
R10(config-if)#exit
R10(config)#ip route 133.100.100.0 255.255.255.240 133.100.1.1
R10(config)#access-list 101 permit gre host 133.100.110.1 host 133.100.100.1
```

Step 12 Verify the GRE tunnel by issuing the **show interfaces** command.

Example 9-14 shows the results of issuing the **show interfaces tunnel 0** command on R1.

Example 9-14 **show interfaces tunnel 0** *Command Output on R1*

```
R1#show interfaces tunnel 0
Tunnel0 is up, line protocol is up
  Hardware is Tunnel
  Internet address is 10.1.1.1/30
  MTU 1440 bytes, BW 9 Kbit, DLY 500000 usec,
      reliability 255/255, txload 1/255, rxload 1/255
  Encapsulation GRE-IP, loopback not set
  Keepalive set (10 sec)
  Tunnel source 133.100.100.1 (Loopback0), destination 133.100.110.1
```

You can see that your tunnel is functioning correctly.

You might see the error message "%TUN-5-RECURDOWN: Tunnel0 temporarily disabled due to recursive routing" when working with GRE tunnels. This error message means that your GRE tunnel router has discovered a recursive routing problem. This condition is usually caused by either of the following:

- A misconfiguration that causes your router to try to route to the tunnel destination address using the tunnel interface itself (recursive routing)

- A temporary instability caused by route flapping elsewhere in the network

When your router detects a recursive routing failure for the tunnel destination, it shuts down the tunnel interface for a few minutes to allow the situation causing the problem to resolve itself as routing protocols converge. If the problem is caused by misconfiguration, the link might oscillate indefinitely.

One other symptom of this problem is continuously flapping neighbors when the neighbors reside across a GRE tunnel. To avoid this problem, configure static routes for your tunnel destinations.

Lesson 9-12: Disabling EIGRP Split Horizon

One last item you might want to configure is the disabling of EIGRP split horizon. Split horizon is used to control the sending of EIGRP update and query packets. With split horizon enabled on an interface, to prevent routing loops, packets are not sent to destinations for which the interface is the next hop. In most cases this is the preferred behavior, but when you use secondary addresses, they are not advertised by EIGRP.

One other area in which split horizon might need to be disabled is in the use of EIGRP in NBMA networks, such as Frame Relay and ATM. To disable split horizon, use the following command:

```
R10(config-if)#no ip split-horizon eigrp autonomous-system
```

In this lesson, you will configure a secondary address of 10.10.10.10/24 on R10 and advertise the network to the rest of the EIGRP autonomous system. To accomplish this task, follow these steps:

Step 1   Configure the secondary address on R10 using the following command:

```
R10(config-if)# ip address 10.10.10.10 255.255.255.0 secondary
```

Step 2   Disable split horizon on the physical interface so that EIGRP can advertise the network using the following command:

```
R10(config-router)#network 10.10.10.0 0.0.0.255
```

Step 3   Verify the proper operation by checking the routing table on R1.

Example 9-15 illustrates the effects of disabling split horizon for EIGRP.

Example 9-15 **show ip route** *Command Output on R1 After Split Horizon Is Disabled on R10*

```
R1#show ip route
Codes: C - connected, S - static, I - IGRP, R - RIP, M - mobile, B - BGP
       D - EIGRP, EX - EIGRP external, O - OSPF, IA - OSPF inter area
       N1 - OSPF NSSA external type 1, N2 - OSPF NSSA external type 2
       E1 - OSPF external type 1, E2 - OSPF external type 2, E - EGP
       i - IS-IS, L1 - IS-IS level-1, L2 - IS-IS level-2, ia - IS-IS inter area
       * - candidate default, U - per-user static route, o - ODR
       P - periodic downloaded static route

Gateway of last resort is not set

    2.0.0.0/8 is variably subnetted, 1 subnets, 1 masks
```

continues

Example 9-15 show ip route *Command Output on R1 After Split Horizon Is Disabled on R10 (Continued)*

```
D       2.2.2.0/28 [90/409600] via 133.100.100.3, 00:29:29, Serial0
     10.0.0.0/8 is variably subnetted, 2 subnets, 2 masks
D       10.10.10.0/24 [90/297295616] via 133.100.1.10, 00:00:27, Tunnel0
     133.100.0.0/28 is subnetted, 6 subnets
!Output omitted for brevity
```

As you can see, the secondary address you configured on R10 is now being sent to the rest of the EIGRP autonomous system.

Troubleshooting EIGRP

When you are troubleshooting EIGRP, it helps to think about the process EIGRP uses in its operation:

Step 1   EIGRP neighbor adjacencies must be established.

Step 2   Each router with EIGRP enabled—the EIGRP speaker—must build its topological database.

Step 3   The feasible distance entries in a given router's topology table must be greater than the directly connected EIGRP neighbor's advertised metric.

Step 4   The optimal topology table entries are used in the IP routing table.

If you need to reinitialize the EIGRP routing process, you can enter the following command:

```
R1#clear ip eigrp neighbors [ip-address | interface]
```

Example 9-16 shows the message you receive when clearing an EIGRP neighbor.

Example 9-16 clear ip eigrp neighbors *Command Output*

```
R10#clear ip eigrp neighbors
R10#
02:32:15: %DUAL-5-NBRCHANGE: IP-EIGRP 234: Neighbor 133.100.1.1 (Ethernet0) is
  down: manually cleared
02:32:15: %DUAL-5-NBRCHANGE: IP-EIGRP 234: Neighbor 133.100.1.1 (Ethernet0) is
  up: new adjacency
```

As you can see, the adjacency R10 had with R1 was cleared and then rebuilt.

CAUTION   The **clear ip eigrp neighbors** command should be used with caution in a production environment, because each adjacency your router has established with a neighbor needs to be reestablished. This could cause dropped packets while the adjacency is established.

Many of the **show** commands you use with EIGRP have already been covered, but as a quick reminder, here are the recommended **show** commands available to you:

- **show ip eigrp neighbors** [*type number*]—Shows the status of all neighbors.

- **show ip eigrp topology** [*autonomous-system-number* | [[*ip-address*] *mask*]]—Lists the contents of the EIGRP topology table.

- **show ip eigrp interfaces** [*interface*] [*as-number*]—Displays information about interfaces configured to run EIGRP.

- **show ip eigrp traffic** [*autonomous-system-number*]—Displays the number of packets sent and received for EIGRP.

- **show ip route** [[*ip-address* [*mask*] **longer-prefixes**]] | [*protocol* [*process-id*]] | [*list access-list-number* | *access-list-name*]—Lists the router's current route table.

- **show ip protocols**—Displays all routing protocols, detailed timer and metric information, and routing update information.

You should be careful when debugging EIGRP in a production environment. The information provided by debugging can quickly overwhelm you and your router. One of the most useful **debug** commands is **debug eigrp packets**. To control what is debugged, enable logging and use the optional keywords available with the **debug ip eigrp** command. The syntax of this command is as follows:

```
R1#debug eigrp packets
R1#debug ip eigrp [neighbor as_neighbor IP_address_of_neighbor]
```

Example 9-17 shows a sample truncated output of debugging EIGRP neighbors.

Example 9-17 *Debugging EIGRP Neighbors on R10*

```
02:34:03: IP-EIGRP: 133.100.110.0/28 - do advertise out Ethernet0
02:34:03: IP-EIGRP: Int 133.100.110.0/28 metric 128256 - 256 128000
02:34:03: IP-EIGRP: 133.100.210.0/28 - do advertise out Ethernet0
02:34:03: IP-EIGRP: Int 133.100.210.0/28 metric 128256 - 256 128000
!Output omitted for brevity
02:34:05: IP-EIGRP: Processing incoming UPDATE packet
02:34:05: IP-EIGRP: Ext 0.0.0.0/0 M 307200 - 256000 51200 SM 51200 - 25600 25600
!Output suppressed
02:34:05: IP-EIGRP: 0.0.0.0/0 - denied by stub
!Output suppressed
```

This sample output gives you an idea of the process EIGRP uses in operation—in this case, between routers R1 and R10. You can see the router deciding which routes it will send to the EIGRP neighbors, accepting routes in an incoming update, and an extra step that an EIGRP stub router goes through—denying all the incoming routes except for the routes allowed to be stored on a stub router.

Example 9-18 demonstrates debugging EIGRP packets, showing the hello mechanism used by EIGRP.

Example 9-18 *Debugging EIGRP Packets on R10 for Hello Processing*

```
02:38:26: EIGRP: Sending HELLO on Loopback1
02:38:26:   AS 234, Flags 0x0, Seq 0/0 idbQ 0/0 iidbQ un/rely 0/0
02:38:26: EIGRP: Received HELLO on Loopback1 nbr 133.100.210.1
02:38:26:   AS 234, Flags 0x0, Seq 0/0 idbQ 0/0
02:38:26: EIGRP: Packet from ourselves ignored
02:38:28: EIGRP: Sending HELLO on Ethernet0
02:38:28:   AS 234, Flags 0x0, Seq 0/0 idbQ 0/0 iidbQ un/rely 0/0
02:38:30: EIGRP: Received HELLO on Ethernet0 nbr 133.100.1.1
02:38:30:   AS 234, Flags 0x0, Seq 0/0 idbQ 0/0 iidbQ un/rely 0/0 peerQ un/rely
0/0
```

Note that in Example 9-18, because EIGRP is enabled on two loopback interfaces, EIGRP sends hellos out every configured interface. Fortunately, EIGRP is smart enough to discard packets sent to itself and to not try to form additional adjacencies.

Summary

This chapter looked at EIGRP support of Cisco IOS software. EIGRP is a classless routing protocol that provides enhancements to the IGRP protocol originally developed by Cisco. You started out by examining EIGRP's need to form adjacencies with neighbors to create the tables required by DUAL. These tables—the neighbor table and the topology table—and the routing table can be viewed with the appropriate **show** command. You read about many optional configuration items such as route control, redistribution, and split horizon. The chapter ended with a look at EIGRP by examining commands used for troubleshooting.

Review Questions

1 What algorithm does EIGRP use to decide which route is put into the routing table?

2 Besides the routing table, what other tables does EIGRP use in its operation?

3 What default metric values does EIGRP use?

4 Why does EIGRP use protocol-dependent modules?

5 How do you update automatic redistribution between IGRP and EIGRP?

6 What is a passive route in EIGRP?

7 What is the default hello interval for a low-speed T1 circuit?

8 When using authentication with EIGRP, what is protected, and how is it protected?

9 Are GRE tunnels point-to-point or point-to-multipoint?

FAQs

Q — *What does the eigrp log-neighbor-changes command do when you're configuring EIGRP?*

A — This command makes it easier for you to determine why an EIGRP neighbor was reset by logging error messages to wherever you have logging enabled.

Q — *Does EIGRP support secondary addresses or only primary addressing?*

A — EIGRP provides support for both primary and secondary addressing. However, it is recommended that you configure all routers on a particular subnet with a primary address that belongs to the same subnet because of EIGRP's need to source data packets from the primary address. Routers do not form EIGRP neighbors over secondary networks because of the rules of split horizon. Therefore, if all routers' primary IP addresses do not agree, problems can arise with neighbor adjacencies.

Q — *Is a default network required for EIGRP to propagate a default route?*

A — EIGRP redistributes default routes directly; therefore, a default network is not required.

Q — *Does EIGRP support route aggregation and VLSM?*

A — Yes.

Q — *Is more than one EIGRP autonomous system possible on the same router?*

A — Although you can configure more than one EIGRP autonomous system on the same router, this is not recommended. The recommended way to deploy EIGRP is to use a single autonomous system as the internal routing protocol and use an external router protocol, such as BGP, to connect two different EIGRP autonomous systems. This is because multiple EIGRP autonomous systems on the same router using mutual redistribution can cause discrepancies in the EIGRP routing tables.

Q — *What does the EIGRP "stuck in active" message mean?*

A — The EIGRP "stuck in active" (SIA) message means that EIGRP hasn't received a reply to a query it sent when it lost a route without having another feasible route in its topology table. When the SIA error message occurs, your EIGRP routing protocol has failed to converge for the specified route. Usually this is caused by a flapping interface, a configuration change, or dialup clients (the route loss is normal). Your routing to other destinations is unaffected while the EIGRP process is in the active state for the specified route. When the SIA timer for the neighbor that didn't reply expires, the neighbor is cleared (EIGRP doesn't trust the state of a neighbor that exceeds the timer). As a consequence, routes in the topology table beyond that neighbor are cleared and must then reconverge. This means that the forwarding table can be affected by an SIA and that packets can be dropped while the network is converging.

Q — *Why would I need a neighbor statement when configuring EIGRP?*

A — You should not use the **neighbor** statement when configuring EIGRP. Although you are allowed to configure a **neighbor** statement, it will not behave as you intended, and it can have a negative effect on your EIGRP neighbors.

Q — *What happened to my neighbors after I configured a passive-interface command?*

A — The **passive-interface** command disables the transmission and receipt of all EIGRP hello packets on an interface. If you had neighbors before using this command, they no longer can form an adjacency for the interface configured.

Q — *Will a route for a passive interface be propagated to other routers?*

A — Although the interface specified in the **passive-interface** command does not participate in the routing protocol, any interface that is not configured as passive still propagates the information necessary to reach the interface to its adjacent neighbors. The route for the passive interface is still included in the routing table that the passive interface is configured on so that the router can pass this information to any neighbors not residing on a passive interface.

This chapter includes the following topics:

- Configuring OSPF
- Monitoring and maintaining OSPF

CHAPTER 10

OSPF

The Open Shortest Path First (OSPF) Protocol offers you many configurable features and parameters. Because of this, it has a position of importance in most Cisco lab scenarios. This chapter is designed to provide the information that is needed to bring your network topology online with any-to-any connectivity.

OSPF is an Interior Gateway Protocol (IGP) designed for IP networks. OSPF supports IP subnetting, tagging of externally derived routing information, packet authentication, and makes use of IP multicast when sending and receiving packets.

Cisco's OSPF implementation conforms to the specifications outlined in RFC 2328, "OSPF Version 2." Some of the features supported in this implementation of OSPF include the following:

- **Stub areas**—You can define stub areas. Remember that a stub area is an area where information on external routes is not sent.

- **Route redistribution**—You can allow redistribution of routes learned via any IP routing protocol into any other IP routing protocol.

- **Authentication**—You can implement authentication between neighbors within an area using plain text or message digest algorithm 5 (MD5).

- **Routing interface parameters**—You have several configurable parameters that you can change, including interface output cost, retransmission interval, interface transmit delay, router priority, router dead and Hello intervals, and authentication key.

- **Virtual links**—You can define virtual links. A virtual link is used to connect an area to the backbone, whether it is due to a break in connectivity or because you have purposely added a partition.

- **Not-so-stubby areas (NSSAs)**—You can define NSSAs as described in RFC 1587, "The OSPF NSSA Option."

- **OSPF over demand circuit**—You can define demand circuits as described in RFC 1793, "Extending OSPF to Support Demand Circuits."

Configuring OSPF

Configuring OSPF can be a complex process. In a minimal configuration, you can configure an OSPF router with all the default parameter values, no authentication, and interfaces assigned to an area. However, if you decide to customize your OSPF environment, you have to ensure the configurations of your Area Border Routers (ABRs), which are routers connected to multiple areas, and Autonomous System Boundary Routers (ASBRs), which are routers running multiple routing protocols to connect an OSPF autonomous system to a non-OSPF autonomous system, are compatible.

OSPF external routes fall into two categories: external Type 1 and external Type 2. The difference between the two is the way the cost, or metric, of the route is calculated. The cost of a Type 2 route is always the external cost, irrespective of the interior cost to reach that route. A Type 1 cost is the addition of the external cost and the internal cost used to reach that route. A Type 1 route is always preferred over a Type 2 route for the same destination.

OSPF uses a link-state advertisement (LSA) packet to describe routes to its neighbors. Table 10-1 lists the different type codes used by OSPF.

Table 10-1   *OSPF Type Codes*

Type Code	Description
1	Router LSA
2	Network LSA
3	Network Summary LSA
4	ASBR Summary LSA
5	AS External LSA
6	Group Membership LSA
7	NSSA External LSA
8	External Attributes LSA
9	Opaque LSA (link-local scope)
10	Opaque LSA (area-local scope)
11	Opaque LSA (AS scope)

This section discusses the commands necessary to enable proper operation of OSPF along with the concepts and issues that can arise as a result of certain implementations and configurations. The configuration tasks are divided into four major categories, as follows:

- Basic OSPF configuration
- OSPF and route summarization

- OSPF filtering
- OSPF and non-IP traffic over GRE

Case Study 10-1: Basic OSPF Configuration

This case study takes you through a step-by-step process of configuring basic OSPF. Figure 10-1 illustrates the topology that you will use while configuring OSPF.

Figure 10-1 *OSPF Beginning Topology*

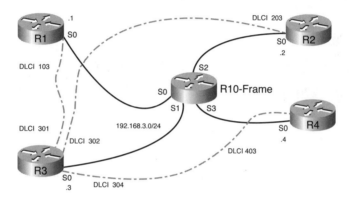

This case study involves routers R1, R2, R3, and R4. The routers are configured in a hub-and-spoke topology, with R3 being the hub and the remaining routers performing the spoke functionality.

The configuration steps discussed in this case study are as follows (Step 1 is required and the others are optional):

Step 1 Enable OSPF

Step 2 Configure OSPF interface parameters

Step 3 Configure OSPF area parameters

Step 4 Configure OSPF NSSA

Step 5 Configure route summarization between areas or when redistributing routes into OSPF

Step 6 Create virtual links

Step 7 Generate a default route

Step 8 Configure DNS lookup

Step 9   Use loopback interfaces for the router ID

Step 10   Control default metrics

Step 11   Change administrative distances

Step 12   Configure OSPF on Simplex Ethernet Interfaces

Step 13   Configure route calculation timers

Step 14   Configure OSPF over demand circuits

Step 15   Log neighbor adjacency changes

Step 16   Change the LSA group pacing

Step 17   Block or reduce LSA flooding

Step 18   Ignore multicast OSPF (MOSPF) LSA packets

The following sections describe each of these tasks

Step 1: Enabling OSPF

You can enable OSPF by creating an OSPF routing process, specifying the range of IP addresses to be associated with the routing process, and assigning area IDs to be associated with your range of IP addresses.

To enable OSPF routing, use the following command:

```
R2(config)#router ospf process-id
```

NOTE   The *process-id* that you use when defining the OSPF process on a router is an arbitrary number that matches across the OSPF autonomous system and is not related to OSPF area IDs.

To define an interface on which OSPF runs and define the area ID for that interface, use the following command:

```
R2(config-router)#network ip-address wildcard-mask area area-id
```

Your first step in this case study is to configure your routers to enable Frame Relay, as diagramed in Figure 10-1. You need to add the appropriate IP addressing and enable OSPF as process-id 1. Example 10-1 shows the relevant configuration items that are required to complete this step.

Example 10-1 *Enabling OSPF on a Point-to-Multipoint, Nonbroadcast Network*

```
Configuration items for R3:
R3(config)#interface Serial0
R3(config-if)#ip address 133.100.300.3 255.255.255.0
R3(config-if)#ip ospf network point-to-multipoint non-broadcast
R3(config-if)#encapsulation frame-relay
R3(config-if)#frame-relay local-dlci 201
R3(config-if)#frame-relay map ip 133.100.300.1 301
R3(config-if)#frame-relay map ip 133.100.300.2 302
R3(config-if)#frame-relay map ip 133.100.300.4 304
R3(config-if)#exit
R3(config)#router ospf 1
R3(config-router)#network 133.100.300.0 0.0.0.255 area 0

Configuration items for R1:
R1(config)#interface Serial0
R1(config-if)#ip address 133.100.300.1 255.255.255.0
R1(config-if)#encapsulation frame-relay
R1(config-if)#ip ospf network point-to-multipoint non-broadcast
R1(config-if)#frame-relay local-dlci 103
R1(config-if)#frame-relay map ip 133.100.300.3 103
R1(config-if)#exit
R1(config)#router ospf 1
R1(config-router)#network 133.100.300.0 0.0.0.255 area 0

Configuration items for R2:
R2(config)#interface Serial0
R2(config-if)#ip address 133.100.300.2 255.255.255.0
R2(config-if)#encapsulation frame-relay
R2(config-if)#ip ospf network point-to-multipoint non-broadcast
R2(config-if)#frame-relay local-dlci 203
R2(config-if)#frame-relay map ip 133.100.300.3 203
R2(config-if)#exit
R2(config)#router ospf 1
R2(config-router)#network 133.100.300.0 0.0.0.255 area 0

Configuration items for R4:
R4(config)#interface Serial0
R4(config-if)#ip address 133.100.300.4 255.255.255.0
R4(config-if)#encapsulation frame-relay
R4(config-if)#ip ospf network point-to-multipoint non-broadcast
R4(config-if)#frame-relay local-dlci 403
R4(config-if)#frame-relay map ip 133.100.300.3 403
R4(config-if)#exit
R4(config)#router ospf 1
R4(config-router)#network 133.100.300.0 0.0.0.255 area 0
```

Step 2: Configuring OSPF Interface Parameters

Although you can make OSPF work in your environment by using the default parameter values, you can choose to customize your configuration for certain interface-specific OSPF parameters. If you choose to alter any parameter, such as those controlled by the **ip ospf hello-interval** command, the **ip ospf dead-interval** command, or the **ip ospf authentication-key** command, you must ensure consistency across all the routers under your administrative control.

Use the commands that are described in this section to tune any interface parameters you choose for your network.

To explicitly specify the cost of sending a packet on an OSPF interface, use the following command:

```
R2(config-if)#ip ospf cost cost
```

To specify the number of seconds between LSA retransmissions for adjacencies belonging to an OSPF interface, use the following command:

```
R2(config-if)#ip ospf retransmit-interval seconds
```

To set the estimated number of seconds required to send a link-state update packet on an OSPF interface, use the following command:

```
R2(config-if)#ip ospf transmit-delay seconds
```

To set the priority used to determine the OSPF-designated router for a network, use the following command:

```
R2(config-if)#ip ospf priority number-value
```

To specify the length of time between the Hello packets that the Cisco IOS Software sends on an OSPF interface, use the following command:

```
R2(config-if)#ip ospf hello-interval seconds
```

To set the number of seconds that a device must wait before it places a neighbor OSPF router in the down state because it has not received a Hello packet, use the following command:

```
R2(config-if)#ip ospf dead-interval seconds
```

To assign a password to be used by neighboring OSPF routers on a network segment that is using the OSPF simple password authentication, use the following command:

```
R2(config-if)#ip ospf authentication-key key
```

To enable OSPF MD5 authentication, the values for the *key-id* and *key* arguments must match values specified for other neighbors on a network segment, as follows:

```
R2(config-if)#ip ospf message-digest-key key-id md5 key
```

To specify the authentication type for an interface, use the following command:

```
R2(config-if)#ip ospf authentication [message-digest | null]
```

OSPF performs a check to determine if its neighbor is using the same maximum transmission unit (MTU) on its interface. This check is performed when neighbors exchange their Database

Descriptor (DBD) packets. If it receives an MTU in the DBD packet that is higher then the IP MTU configured on the incoming interface, the OSPF adjacency is not established. Use the following command to modify this behavior:

```
R2(config-if)#ip ospf mtu-ignore
```

In this section of the case study, you assign R3 to have a cost of 100, R1 has a cost of 10, and R4 has a cost of 15. One additional command, the **neighbor** command, is introduced here. The syntax of the **neighbor** command, used to assign a cost to a neighbor is as follows:

```
R3(config-router)#neighbor ip-address [cost number]
```

All configurations are to be completed on R3. Example 10-2 illustrates the commands that you need to add to R3.

Example 10-2 *OSPF Cost*

```
Configuration items for R3:
R3(config)#interface Serial0
R3(config-if)#ip ospf cost 100
R3(config-if)#exit
R3(config)#router ospf 1
R3(config-router)#neighbor 192.168.3.1 cost 10
R3(config-router)#neighbor 192.168.3.4 cost 15
```

You can display the neighbor relationships by using the **show ip ospf neighbor** command. Example 10-3 shows the result of running this command on R3.

Example 10-3 *The* **show ip ospf neighbor** *Command Output Using Broadcast*

```
R3#show ip ospf neighbor
Neighbor ID     Pri   State       Dead Time   Address       Interface
192.168.3.2     1     FULL/  -    00:01:50    192.168.3.2   Serial0
192.168.3.1     1     FULL/  -    00:01:47    192.168.3.1   Serial0
192.168.3.4     1     FULL/  -    00:01:45    192.168.3.4   Serial0
```

Configuring OSPF over Different Physical Networks

One of the most useful features that is available with OSPF is its support of multiple interface categories. Currently, OSPF classifies different media into one of the following three types of networks by default:

- Broadcast networks such as Ethernet, Token Ring, and Fiber Distributed Data Interface (FDDI).

- Nonbroadcast multiaccess (NBMA) networks such as Switched Multimegabit Data Service (SMDS), Frame Relay, and X.25.

- Point-to-point networks such as High-Level Data Link Control (HDLC) and PPP.

Even though OSPF supports NBMA networks, you are given the option of configuring your network as a broadcast network. This statement also applies to both the X.25 and Frame Relay network types when you configure the optional **broadcast** keyword in their respective map statements. The following sections cover several different types of networks.

OSPF Point-to-Multipoint Nonbroadcast

In this portion of the case study, you also use the topology illustrated in Figure 10-1. You re-create this topology using a nonbroadcast layout. You assign a cost of 5 to R1, 10 to R2, and 15 to R4. Example 10-4 demonstrates one example of possible configurations to complete this task.

Example 10-4 *Point-to-Multipoint, Nonbroadcast Example*

```
Configuration items for R3:
R3(config)#interface Serial0
R3(config-if)#ip address192.168.3.3 255.255.255.0
R3(config-if)#ip ospf network point-to-multipoint non-broadcast
R3(config-if)#encapsulation frame-relay
R3(config-if)#frame-relay local-dlci 201
R3(config-if)#frame-relay map ip 192.168.3.1 301
R3(config-if)#frame-relay map ip 192.168.3.2 302
R3(config-if)#frame-relay map ip 192.168.3.4 304
R3(config-if)#exit
R3(config)#router ospf 1
R3(config-router)#network 192.168.3.0 0.0.0.255 area 0
R3(config-router)#neighbor 192.168.3.1 cost 5
R3(config-router)#neighbor 192.168.3.2 cost 10
R3(config-router)#neighbor 192.168.3.4 cost 15

Configuration items for R1:
R1(config)#interface Serial0
R1(config-if)#ip address 192.168.3.1 255.255.255.0
R1(config-if)#encapsulation frame-relay
R1(config-if)#ip ospf network point-to-multipoint non-broadcast
R1(config-if)#frame-relay local-dlci 103
R1(config-if)#frame-relay map ip 192.168.3.3 103
 R1(config-if)#exit
R1(config)#router ospf 1
R1(config-router)#network 192.168.3.0 0.0.0.255 area 0

Configuration items for R2:
R2(config)#interface Serial0
R2(config-if)#ip address 192.168.3.2 255.255.255.0
R2(config-if)#encapsulation frame-relay
R2(config-if)#ip ospf network point-to-multipoint non-broadcast
R2(config-if)#frame-relay local-dlci 203
R2(config-if)#frame-relay map ip 192.168.3.3 203
 R2(config-if)#exit
R2(config)#router ospf 1
R2(config-router)#network 192.168.3.0 0.0.0.255 area 0
```

Example 10-4 *Point-to-Multipoint, Nonbroadcast Example (Continued)*

```
Configuration items for R4:
R4(config)#interface Serial0
R4(config-if)#ip address 192.168.3.4 255.255.255.0
R4(config-if)#encapsulation frame-relay
R4(config-if)#ip ospf network point-to-multipoint non-broadcast
R4(config-if)#frame-relay local-dlci 403
R4(config-if)#frame-relay map ip 192.168.3.3 403
 R4(config-if)#exit
R4(config)#router ospf 1
R4(config-router)#network 192.168.3.0 0.0.0.255 area 0
```

Once again, you can use the **show ip ospf neighbor** command to display the neighbor relationships. Example 10-5 shows the output of this command when issued on R3.

Example 10-5 *The* **show ip ospf neighbor** *Command Output from Nonbroadcast*

```
R3#show ip ospf neighbor
Neighbor ID     Pri   State         Dead T
ime    Address       Interface
192.168.3.1     1   FULL/  -        00:01:52   192.168.3.1   Serial0
192.168.3.2     1   FULL/  -        00:01:52   192.168.3.2   Serial0
192.168.3.4     1   FULL/  -        00:01:52   192.168.3.4   Serial0
```

OSPF VLSM Support

One of the features of OSPF is its ability to support variable-length subnet masks (VLSMs). With VLSM support, you can use different masks for the same network number on different interfaces, giving you the ability to conserve IP addresses and efficiently use your address space.

In this portion of the case study, you configure VLSM on a serial interface for router R5. You use a 24-bit subnet mask on R5's Ethernet 0 interface. You use 30-bit subnet masks on R5's Serial interfaces. You configure OSPF to include all of these networks. Example 10-6 gives one solution to this scenario.

Example 10-6 *VLSM Example*

```
Configuration items for R5:
R5(config)#interface ethernet 0
R5(config-if)#ip address 192.168.5.5 255.255.255.0
 R5(config-if)#exit
R5(config)#interface serial 0
R5(config-if)#ip address 192.168.54.1 255.255.255.252
 R5(config-if)#exit
```

continues

Example 10-6 *VLSM Example (Continued)*

```
R5(config)#interface serial 1
R5(config-if)#ip address 192.168.56.1 255.255.255.252
 R5(config-if)#exit
R5(config)#router ospf 1
R5(config-router)#network 192.168.0.0 0.0.255.255 area 0
```

Configuring Your OSPF Network Type

Choosing to configure your OSPF network as either a broadcast or NBMA network type is not limited to the default media type you are using. One example of why you would choose to alter the network type is when you have devices in your network that are not capable of sending or receiving multicast packets. Under these circumstances, you can choose to use the NBMA network type.

You can also choose to convert your NBMA networks into broadcast networks to ease configuration of your devices. One restriction when configuring NBMA networks as either broadcast or nonbroadcast is that you need to have virtual circuits (VCs) from every router to every router or fully meshed network. Cost constraints can limit your ability to provide a fully meshed network, so you are also given the option of configuring a partially meshed network as a point-to-multipoint network. This causes all routing packets passed between two routers that are not directly connected to each other to go through the router that has VCs to both routers. This configuration also eliminates your need to configure neighbor statements for peer routers.

The OSPF point-to-multipoint interface can be defined as a numbered point-to-point interface having one or more neighbor routers. This also causes it to create multiple host routes in its routing table. An OSPF point-to-multipoint network can provide you with the following benefits when compared to NBMA and point-to-point networks:

- A point-to-multipoint network is easier to configure because you do not have to configure neighbor commands, it consumes only one IP subnet, and it requires no designated router election.

- You can implement point-to-multipoint on a partially meshed network topology, reducing your costs when compared to a fully meshed network topology.

- Point-to-multipoint provides you with more reliability because it can maintain connectivity in the event of VC failure.

Use the following command to configure your OSPF network type:

```
R2(config-if)#ip ospf network {broadcast | non-broadcast | {point-to-multipoint [non-
  broadcast] | point-to-point}}
```

Configuring Point-to-Multipoint, Broadcast Networks

OSPF is a flexible routing protocol, as far as its configuration is concerned. Even though you are not required to specifically configure neighbors on a point-to-multipoint broadcast network, you can optionally configure them using the **neighbor** router configuration command. Just remember that if you choose to do this, you must also specify a cost to that neighbor.

Before support of the **point-to-multipoint** keyword was added in Cisco IOS Software to the **ip ospf network** interface configuration command, some OSPF point-to-multipoint protocol traffic was treated as multicast traffic. In particular, the Hello, update, and acknowledgment messages were sent using multicasting. This enabled the multicast Hello to dynamically discover all its neighbors dynamically, eliminating the need to use the **neighbor** router command.

Use the commands that are described in this section to treat an interface as a point-to-multipoint broadcast type and optionally assign a cost to each neighbor.

To configure an interface as point-to-multipoint for broadcast media, use the following command:

```
R2(config-if)#ip ospf network point-to-multipoint
```

To exit and return to global configuration mode so that you can enter the rest of the commands, use the following command:

```
R2(config-if)#exit
```

To configure an OSPF routing process, use the following command:

```
R2(config)#router ospf process-id
```

To specify a neighbor and assign a cost to that neighbor, use the following command:

```
R2(config-router)#neighbor ip-address cost number
```

In this section, you create a network that enables R3 to communicate to R1 using data-link connection identifier (DLCI) 301, to R2 using DLCI 302, and to R4 using DLCI 304 (refer to Figure 10-1 for your topology). R1 uses DLCI 103 to communicate with R3 and DLCI 102 to communicate with R2. R2 uses DLCI 203 to communicate with R3 and DLCI 201 to communicate with R1. R4 uses DLCI 403 to communicate with R3. Example 10-7 shows you the configuration items that are required to complete this portion of the case study.

Example 10-7 *Point-to-Multipoint Broadcast Configuration*

```
Configuration items for R3:
R3(config)#interface serial 0
R3(config-if)#ip address 192.168.3.3 255.255.255.0
R3(config-if)#ip ospf network point-to-multipoint
R3(config-if)#encapsulation frame-relay
```

continues

Example 10-7 *Point-to-Multipoint Broadcast Configuration (Continued)*

```
R3(config-if)#frame-relay map ip 192.168.3.1 301 broadcast
R3(config-if)#frame-relay map ip 192.168.3.2 302 broadcast
R3(config-if)#frame-relay map ip 192.168.3.4 304 broadcast
 R3(config-if)#exit
R3(config)#router ospf 1
R3(config-router)#network 192.168.3.0 0.0.0.255 area 0

Configuration items for R1:
R1(config)#interface serial 0
R1(config-if)#ip address 192.168.3.1 255.255.255.0
R1(config-if)#ip ospf network point-to-multipoint
R1(config-if)#encapsulation frame-relay
R1(config-if)#frame-relay map ip 192.168.3.3 103 broadcast
R1(config-if)#frame-relay map ip 192.168.3.2 102 broadcast
R1(config-if)#exit
R1(config)#router ospf 1
R2(config-router)#network 192.168.3.0 0.0.0.255 area 0

Configuration items for R2:
R2(config)#interface serial 0
R2(config-if)#ip address 192.168.3.2 255.255.255.0
R2(config-if)#ip ospf network point-to-multipoint
R2(config-if)#encapsulation frame-relay
R2(config-if)#frame-relay map ip 192.168.3.3 203 broadcast
R2(config-if)#frame-relay map ip 192.168.3.1 201 broadcast
R2(config-if)#exit
R2(config)#router ospf 1
R2(config-router)#network 192.168.3.0 0.0.0.255 area 0

Configuration items for R4:
R4(config)#interface serial 0
R4(config-if)#ip address 192.168.3.4 255.255.255.0
R4(config-if)#ip ospf network point-to-multipoint
R4(config-if)#encapsulation frame-relay
R4(config-if)#frame-relay map ip 192.168.3.3 403 broadcast
R4(config-if)#exit
R4(config)#router ospf 1
R4(config-router)#network 192.168.3.0 0.0.0.255 area 0
```

Configuring OSPF for Nonbroadcast Networks

In a large OSPF network, a designated router (DR) and backup designated router (BDR) are elected using the multicast Hello packets. The router with the highest OSPF priority on the segment becomes the DR. The same process is used to select the BDR. In the event of a tie, the router with the highest router ID wins the election. The default value for an interface is 1, but if you want to prohibit a router from the election process, you can set this value to 0.

The DR is used to reduce the number of adjacencies required in large networks. The OSPF router is responsible for generating the LSAs used in the multiaccess network, along with other special functions. The BDR assumes the responsibilities in the event of a DR failure. If your network does not use the broadcast capabilities that are available, you must configure special parameters for the DR selection process to function correctly.

You are only required to configure these parameters on devices that are eligible to become the DR or BDR, or any router with a nonzero router priority value.

To configure a router that interconnects to nonbroadcast networks, use the following command:

```
R2(config-router)#neighbor ip-address [priority number] [poll-interval seconds]
```

You have the option of specifying the following neighbor parameters:

- The priority of a neighboring router
- The interval used in a nonbroadcast poll

As in a broadcast network, on a point-to-multipoint nonbroadcast network, now use the **neighbor** command to identify your neighbors. You also have the option of assigning a cost to your neighbor.

When you use a point-to-multipoint interface, whether you configured it with the broadcast keyword or not, the cost to each neighbor is assumed to be equal. Because, in most cases, the bandwidth you have going to each neighbor is not necessarily the same, you can modify this cost using the **ip ospf cost** configuration command. You can only use this feature when you use the point-to-multipoint interfaces command.

Use the commands that are described in this section to treat an interface as point-to-multipoint when your media does not support broadcast.

To set an interface for use with nonbroadcast media, use the following command:

```
R2(config-if)#ip ospf network non-broadcast
```

To exit and return to the global configuration mode to enter the rest of the commands, use the following command:

```
R2(config-if)#exit
```

To configure an OSPF routing process, use the following command:

```
R2(config)#router ospf process-id
```

To specify a neighbor and assign a cost to that neighbor, use the following command:

```
R2(config-router)#neighbor ip-address [cost number]
```

You can repeat the last configuration item for each neighbor that you want to specify a cost for. Otherwise, neighbors use the cost of the interface, which you can specify with the **ip ospf cost** configuration command.

Step 3: Configuring OSPF Area Parameters

You have the option of configuring several area parameters when using OSPF. These parameters include the following:

- **Authentication**—Allows you to assign passwords to provide protection against unauthorized access to an area. You can send authentication using plain text or MD5, a more secure alternative.

- **Stub areas**—Allows you to create areas into which information on external routes is not sent. Instead, a default external route is generated by the ABR into the stub area for destinations outside the autonomous system. You must enable default routing to take advantage of the OSPF stub-area support. You have the option of further reducing the number of LSAs sent into a stub area by configuring the **no-summary** keyword of the **area stub** command on the ABR to prevent it from sending summary link advertisements (Type 3 LSAs) into the stub area.

- **Summary route costs**—You can assign specific costs to the default summary route.

Use the commands that are described in this section to specify an area parameter for your network.

To enable authentication for an OSPF area, use the following command:

```
R2(config-router)#area area-id authentication
```

To enable MD5 authentication for an OSPF area, use the following command:

```
R2(config-router)#area area-id authentication message-digest
```

To define an area to operate as a stub area, use the following command:

```
R2(config-router)#area area-id stub [no-summary]
```

To assign a specific cost to the default summary route used for the stub area, use the following command:

```
R2(config-router)#area area-id default-cost cost
```

For OSPF to operate correctly, coordination must exist between your internal routers, ABRs, and ASBRs. At a minimum, you can accomplish this coordination by configuring your OSPF-based routers with all default parameter values, with no authentication, and with interfaces assigned to areas.

In this section, you configure a stand-alone router, R8, with a simple OSPF configuration that enables OSPF and attaches Fast Ethernet interfaces 0/0 and 0/1 to area 0. Example 10-8 shows a configuration example.

Example 10-8 *Redistribution of RIP into OSPF*

```
Configuration items for R8:
R8(config)#interface fastethernet 0/0
R8(config-if)#ip address 192.168.8.8 255.255.255.0
```

Example 10-8 *Redistribution of RIP into OSPF (Continued)*

```
R8(config-if_#ip ospf cost 1
R8(config-if)#exit
R8(config)#interface fastethernet 0/1
R8(config-if)#ip address 192.168.86.8 255.255.255.0
 R8(config-if)#exit
R8(config)#router ospf 1
R8(config-router)#network 192.168.0.0 0.0.255.255 area 0
```

Each **network area** command entered is evaluated sequentially, so the order in which you enter them is important. The address/wildcard-mask pair that you enter is also evaluated sequentially.

Consider the configuration shown in Example 10-9. In this example, four area IDs are assigned to four IP address ranges.

Example 10-9 *The* **network area** *Command*

```
Router(config)#router ospf 1
Router(config-router)#network 192.168.20.0 0.0.0.255 area 192.168.20.0
Router(config-router)#network 192.168.108.0 0.0.0.255 area 2
Router(config-router)#network 192.168.109.0 0.0.0.255 area 3
Router(config-router)#network 0.0.0.0 255.255.255.255 area 0
Router(config-router)#exit
Router(config)#interface ethernet 0
Router(config-if)#ip address 192.168.20.5 255.255.255.0
Router(config-if)#exit
Router(config)#interface ethernet 1
Router(config-if)#ip address 192.168.108.5 255.255.255.0
Router(config-if)#exit
Router(config)#interface ethernet 2
Router(config-if)#ip address 192.168.109.1 255.255.255.0
Router(config-if)#exit
Router(config)#interface ethernet 3
Router(config-if)#ip address 192.168.1.1 255.255.255.0
Router(config-if)#exit
Router(config)#interface ethernet 4
Router(config-if)#ip address 10.1.0.1 255.255.0.0
```

Looking at the first **network area** command that you configured, area ID 192.168.20.0 is configured for the interface on which subnet 192.168.20.0 is located. This condition should cause a match for Ethernet interface 0. Ethernet interface 0 is then attached to area 192.168.20.0 only.

The second **network area** command that you entered is evaluated next. For area 2, the same evaluation process is applied to all interfaces, with the exception of Ethernet interface 0. Evaluation of the list results in OSPF being enabled for that interface and it being attached to area 2.

OSPF repeats this process of attaching interfaces to OSPF areas for all your **network area** commands. You might wonder whether the format of the last **network area** command, **network 0.0.0.0 255.255.255.255 area 0**, in this example, is a typo. It is a special case that attaches all available interfaces that are not explicitly attached to another area to area 0.

Step 4: Configuring OSPF NSSAs

In some cases, the OSPF stub area cannot meet all your requirements, but the area in question does not require the full capabilities of OSPF. You have the option of creating a not-so-stubby area (NSSA), which can import autonomous system external routes without flooding Type 5 LSA external routes from the core into the area.

You can implement these external routes in the NSSA by redistributing LSA Type 7 LSA autonomous system external routes. These Type 7 LSA routes are translated into Type 5 LSAs by your NSSA ABRs, which, in turn, are flooded throughout the whole routing domain. You can still implement summarization and filtering during the translation of the LSAs.

Use the following command to specify area parameters as needed to configure your OSPF NSSA:

```
R2(config-router)#area area-id nssa [no-redistribution] [default-information-originate]
```

Use the following command to control summarization and filtering of Type 7 LSAs into Type 5 LSAs:

```
R2(config-router)#summary address prefix mask [not advertise] [tag tag]
```

You should consider the following items before you implement the OSPF NSSA feature:

- You are allowed to create a Type 7 default route that can be used to reach external destinations. If you choose to do this, your router then generates a Type 7 default into the NSSA or the NSSA ABR.

- You need to configure every router within the same area to be of the NSSA type; if not, your router cannot communicate.

Figure 10-2 illustrates the topology that you will use for the next step in your case study.

In this step, you configure a basic OSPF network with three areas: area 0, area 2, and area 3. This step assumes that you have a configured and operational Frame Relay network between the routers. You configure authentication for each area. You create a stub area with area ID 2. Finally, you configure authentication between routers on area 0, with a key of abcdefgh, and routers on area 3, with a key of ijklmnop. Example 10-10 gives you solution for this scenario.

Figure 10-2 *Authentication and Redistribution Topology*

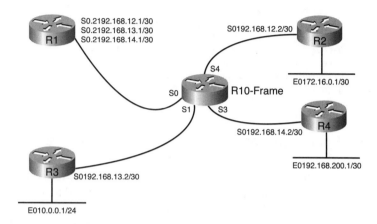

Example 10-10 *Authentication and Redistribution Example*

```
Configuration items for R1:
R1(config)#interface serial 0.2 point-to-point
R1(config-subif)#ip address 192.168.12.1 255.255.255.252
R1(config-subif)#ip ospf message-digest-key 1 md5 abcdefgh
R1(config-subif)#ip ospf cost 10
 R1(config-subif)#exit
R1(config)#interface serial 0.3 point-to-point
R1(config-subif)#ip address 192.168.13.1 255.255.255.252
R1(config-subif)#ip ospf message-digest-key 1 md5 ijklmnop
R1(config-subif)#ip ospf cost 20
R1(config-subif)#ip ospf retransmit-interval 10
R1(config-subif)#ip ospf transmit-delay 2
R1(config-subif)#ip ospf priority 4
 R1(config-subif)#exit
R1(config)#interface serial 0.4 point-to-point
R1(config-subif)#ip address 192.168.14.1 255.255.255.252
R1(config-subif)#ip ospf message-digest-key 1 md5 abcdefgh
R1(config-subif)#ip ospf cost 10
 R1(config-subif)#exit
R1(config-subif)#router ospf 1
R1(config-router)#network 192.168.14.0 0.0.0.3 area 3
R1(config-router)#network 192.168.13.0 0.0.0.3 area 2
R1(config-router)#network 192.168.12.0 0.0.0.3 area 0
R1(config-router)#area 0 authentication message-digest
```

continues

Example 10-10 *Authentication and Redistribution Example (Continued)*

```
R1(config-router)#area 2 stub
R1(config-router)#area 2 authentication message-digest
R1(config-router)#area 2 default-cost 20
R1(config-router)#area 3 authentication message-digest
R1(config-router)#area 2 range 10.0.0.0 255.0.0.0
R1(config-router)#area 3 range 192.168.200.0 255.255.255.0
R1(config-router)#area 0 range 172.16.0.0 255.255.240.0
```

Step 5: Configuring Route Summarization Between OSPF Areas

When you need to consolidate advertised addresses, you can use route summarization. With route summarization, you cause a single summary route to be advertised to your other areas by your ABR. Remember that you use an ABR to advertise networks from one area into another area. If you configure your network numbers in an area to be contiguous, you can use the ABR to advertise a summary route that covers all the individual networks within the area that fall into the specified range.

To specify an address range for which a single route is advertised, use the following command:

```
R2(config-router)#area area-id range ip-address mask [advertise | not-advertise]
```

In this section, you set up the minimum configuration required to summarize the IP range of 192.168.16.0 through 192.168.31.0 to area 1.

Example 10-11 shows one solution.

Example 10-11 *Route Summarization Between OSPF Areas*

```
Router(config)#router ospf 1
Router(config-router)#area 1 range 192.168.16.0 255.255.255.240
```

When routes from other protocols are redistributed into OSPF (as described in Chapter 13, "Redistribution"), each route is advertised individually in an external LSA. However, you can configure the Cisco IOS Software to advertise a single route for all the redistributed routes that are covered by a specified network address and mask. Doing so helps decrease the size of the OSPF link-state database.

To specify an address and mask that cover redistributed routes so that only one summary route is advertised, use the following command (you can use the optional **not-advertise** keyword to filter out a set of routes):

```
R2(config-router)#summary-address {{ip-address mask} | {prefix mask}} [not-
  advertise][tag tag]
```

You have the ability to redistribute routes from other protocols into your OSPF autonomous system, with or without the use of route maps. The next few examples demonstrate how to redistribute routes from IP and Connectionless Network Service (CLNS) routing protocols.

Example 10-12 shows you a redistribution scheme where OSPF external routes with tags 1, 2, 3, and 5 are redistributed into RIP with metrics of 1, 1, 5, and 5, respectively. OSPF routes with a tag of 4 are not redistributed into RIP.

Example 10-12 *OSPF to RIP Redistribution*

```
Router(config)#router rip
Router(config-router)#redistribute ospf 1 route-map 1
Router(config-router)#exit
Router(config)#route-map 1 permit 10
Router(config-route-map)#match tag 1 2
Router(config-route-map)#set metric 1
Router(config-route-map)#exit
Router(config)#route-map 1 permit 11
Router(config-route-map)#match tag 3
Router(config-route-map)#set metric 5
Router(config-route-map)#exit
Router(config)#route-map 1 deny 12
Router(config-route-map)#match tag 4
Router(config-route-map)#exit
Router(config)#route map 1 permit 13
Router(config-route-map)#match tag 5
Router(config-route-map)#set metric 5
```

Step 6: Creating Virtual Links

OSPF has a requirement that all areas that you have must be connected in some fashion to your backbone area. If your backbone suffers a break in continuity, or you purposefully partition your backbone, you can still maintain continuity by establishing a *virtual link.* The two endpoints of your virtual link must be an ABR and must be configured in both routers. The configuration you use in each router consists of information such as the other virtual endpoint, the other ABR, and the nonbackbone area that the two routers have in common, referred to as the *transit area.* One restriction is that a virtual link cannot be configured through stub areas.

Use the commands that are described in this section to establish a virtual link.

To establish a virtual link, use the following command:

```
R2(config-router)#area area-id virtual-link router-id [authentication [message-digest |
   null]] [hello-interval seconds] [retransmit-interval seconds] [transmit-delay
   seconds] [dead-interval seconds] [[authentication-key key] | [message-digest-key
   key-id md5 key]]
```

Use the following command to display information about virtual links:

```
R2#show ip ospf virtual-links
```

Use the following command to display the router ID of an OSPF router:

```
R2#show ip ospf
```

Figure 10-3 illustrates the topology that you will use to create a virtual link.

Figure 10-3 *Virtual Link Topology*

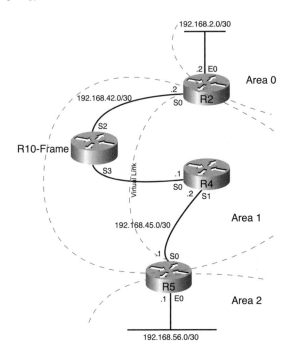

In this step, you configure router R5 to virtually connect to area 0. R5 is considered to be a virtual ABR because it connects to area 0 through R4. Area 0 uses authentication for OSPF. Example 10-13 shows one solution to this problem.

Example 10-13 *Virtual Link with Plain Text Authentication*

```
Configuration items for R2:
R2(config)#interface Ethernet0
R2(config-if)#ip address 192.168.2.2 255.255.255.252
R2(config-if)#ip ospf authentication-key ccie_lab
R2(config-if)#exit
R2(config)#interface Serial0
R2(config-if)#ip address 192.168.42.2 255.255.255.252
R2(config-if)#exit
R2(config)#router ospf 2
R2(config-router)#network 192.168.2.0 0.0.0.255 area 0
R2(config-router)#network 192.168.42.0 0.0.0.3 area 1
R2(config-router)#area 0 authentication
R2(config-router)#area 1 virtual-link 192.168.45.1 authentication-key ccie_lab
```

Example 10-13 *Virtual Link with Plain Text Authentication (Continued)*

```
Configuration items for R5:
R5(config)#interface Ethernet0
R5(config-if)#ip address 192.168.56.1 255.255.255.0
R5(config-if)#exit
R5(config)#interface Serial 0
R5(config-if)#ip address 192.168.45.1 255.255.255.252
R5(config-if)#exit
R5(config)#router ospf 2
R5(config-router)#network 192.168.56.0 0.0.0.255 area 2
R5(config-router)#network 192.168.45.0 0.0.0.3 area 1
R5(config-router)#area 0 authentication
R5(config-router)#area 1 virtual-link 192.168.45.2 authentication-key ccie_lab
```

The next part of your case study requires you to reconfigure your routers to enable MD5 authentication for OSPF. MD5 authentication is more secure than plain-text authentication. Example 10-14 shows the commands that are required to make the change in authentication methods.

Example 10-14 *Virtual Link with MD5 Authentication*

```
Configuration items for R2:
R2(config)#interface Ethernet0
R2(config-if)#ip address 192.168.2.2 255.255.255.252
R2(config-if)#ip ospf message-digest-key 1 md5 ccie_lab
R2(config-if)#exit
R2(config)#interface Serial0
R2(config-if)#ip address 192.168.42.2 255.255.255.252
R2(config-if)#exit
R2(config)#router ospf 2
R2(config-router)#network 192.168.2.0 0.0.0.255 area 0
R2(config-router)#network 192.168.42.0 0.0.0.3 area 1
R2(config-router)#area 0 authentication message-digest
R2(config-router)#area 1 virtual-link 192.168.45.1 message-digest-key 1 md5 ccie_lab

Configuration items for R5:
R5(config)#interface Ethernet0
R5(config-if)#ip address 192.168.56.1 255.255.255.0
R5(config-if)#exit
R5(config)#interface Serial 0
R5(config-if)#ip address 192.168.45.1 255.255.255.252
R5(config-if)#exit
R5(config)#router ospf 2
R5(config-router)#network 192.168.56.0 0.0.0.255 area 2
R5(config-router)#network 192.168.45.0 0.0.0.3 area 1
R5(config-router)#area 0 authentication message-digest
R5(config-router)#area 1 virtual-link 192.168.45.2 message-digest-key 1 md5 ccie_lab
```

Step 7: Generating a Default Route

You can use your ASBR to generate a default route for your OSPF routing domain. You can create an ASBR by configuring redistribution of routes into your OSPF routing domain. However, this does not generate a default route for your OSPF routing domain.

Use the following command to force your ASBR to generate a default route:

```
R2(config-router)#default-information originate [always] [metric metric-value] [metric-
   type type-value] [route-map map-name]
```

Example 10-15 shows how to use a route map to redistribute default information, such as a default route. When used with the **default-information** command, this technique is referred to as a *conditional default origination*. OSPF originates the selected default route with a Type 2 metric of 5 if 140.222.0.0 is in the routing table.

Example 10-15 *Redistributing Default Information with a Route Map*

```
Router(config)#route-map ospf-default permit
Router(config-route-map)#match ip address 1
Router(config-route-map)#set metric 5
Router(config-route-map)#set metric-type type-2
Router(config-route-map)#exit
Router(config)#access-list 1 140.222.0.0 0.0.255.255
Router(config)#router ospf 1
Router(config)#default-information originate route-map ospf-default
```

Step 8: Configuring DNS Lookup

If you would prefer to use a Domain Name System (DNS) name in your OSPF show commands, you can configure OSPF to use DNS for name lookup. One advantage of this method, assuming that you have configured your DNS correctly, is that all routers are displayed with their name instead of their router ID or neighbor ID.

Use the following command to configure DNS name lookup:

```
R2(config)#ip ospf name-lookup
```

Step 9: Using a Loopback Interface for the Router ID

By default, when OSPF is enabled on your router, it uses the highest IP address configured on the interfaces as its router ID. If the interface associated with this IP address is ever brought down, or if the address is removed, the OSPF process must recalculate a new router ID and resend all its routing information out its interfaces.

You can use a loopback interface to overcome this because a loopback interface never goes down. If you have configured a loopback interface with an IP address, Cisco IOS Software uses this IP address as its router ID, even if other interfaces have higher IP addresses. This functionality of using a loopback as the router ID has the added benefit of allowing you to use an IP address that is locally significant, making it easier to facilitate troubleshooting. If you have multiple loopback interfaces configured, OSPF chooses the highest IP address among all loopback interfaces. However, you do not have the ability to configure OSPF to use any particular interface.

Use the commands that are described in this section to configure an IP address on a loopback interface.

To create a loopback interface, use the following command:

```
R2(config)#interface loopback 0
```

To assign an IP address to this interface, use the following command:

```
R2(config-if)#ip address ip-address mask
```

In this case study, you configure a loopback interface with an IP address of 10.10.10.10 with a subnet mask of 255.255.255.255. Example 10-16 shows one solution to this case study.

Example 10-16 *Configuring a Loopback Interface*

```
Router(config)#interface loopback 0
Router(config-if)#ip address 10.10.10.10 255.255.255.255
```

Step 10: Controlling Default Metrics

By default, Cisco IOS Software uses the bandwidth of the interface to calculate the OSPF metric that is to be used by the interface. This metric value is calculated as the *ref-bw* value divided by the *bandwidth* value, with the *ref-bw* value equal to 10^8 by default and the *bandwidth* value determined by the **bandwidth** command. The calculation is designed to give an FDDI a metric of 1. Because of this, when you have multiple links with high bandwidth, you might want to specify a higher number to differentiate the cost on those links.

To differentiate high-bandwidth links, use the following command:

```
R2(config-router)#ospf auto-cost reference-bandwidth ref-bw
```

In this step, change the auto-cost to 1000 instead of the default value to give an FDDI link a cost of 10, while leaving a Gigabit Ethernet link with its value of 1.0 to area 1. Example 10-17 shows one solution to this task.

Example 10-17 *Auto-cost Configuration*

```
Router(config)#router ospf 1
Router(config-router)#ospf auto-cost reference-bandwidth 1000
```

Step 11: Changing Administrative Distances

A router uses an administrative distance value to apply a rating of the trustworthiness of a routing information source, such as an individual router or a group of routers. The administrative distance can be an integer value from 0 to 255. In most cases, the higher the value, the lower the trust rating of the source.

You can have the following three types of administrative distance with OSPF:

- **Intra-area**—Routes within an area

- **Inter-area**—Routes to another area

- **External**—Routes from another routing domain that are learned via redistribution

The default distance assigned for each type of route is 110.

Use the following command to change any of the default OSPF distance values:

```
R2(config-router)#distance ospf {[intra-area dist1] [inter-area dist2] [external
  dist3]}
```

Figure 10-4 illustrates the topology that you will use for the next step in your case study.

Figure 10-4 *Administrative Distance Topology*

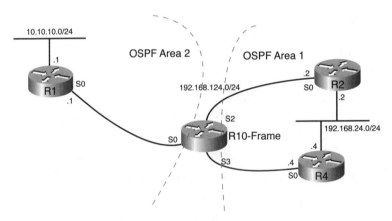

You can use the administrative distance tag to influence the preference of a routing path. In this step, you configure the links from R1 and R2 to have an external distance to 200, making this path less trustworthy. Example 10-18 provides a possible solution for this step.

Example 10-18 *Administrative Distance*

```
Configuration items for R1:
router ospf 1
 redistribute ospf 2 subnet
```

Example 10-18 *Administrative Distance (Continued)*

```
 distance ospf external 200
!
router ospf 2
 redistribute ospf 1 subnet
 distance ospf external 200

Configuration items for R2:
router ospf 1
 redistribute ospf 2 subnet
 distance ospf external 200
!
router ospf 2
 redistribute ospf 1 subnet
 distance ospf external 200
```

Step 12: Configuring OSPF on Simplex Ethernet Interfaces

A Simplex Ethernet interface between two devices represents only one network segment. When you use OSPF with simplex interfaces, you must configure the sending interface to be a passive interface. This prevents OSPF from sending Hello packets to the sending interface. Both devices are still able to see each other via the Hello packet that was generated for the receiving interface.

To suppress the sending of Hello packets through the specified interface, use the following command:

```
R2(config-router)#passive-interface interface-type interface-number
```

Step 13: Configuring Route Calculation Timers

You can configure the delay time between when OSPF receives a topology change and when it starts a shortest path first (SPF) calculation. You can also configure the hold time between two consecutive SPF calculations. Setting these timers low can cause your router to switch paths quickly in the event of a failure but causes a higher CPU load during SPF calculations. Use the following command to accomplish this task:

```
R2(config-router)#timers spf spf-delay spf-holdtime
```

In this step, you change the SPF timers that your router uses by default. You change the delay from the 5-second default to a 10-second delay. You also change your hold-down time from the default of 10 seconds to 20 seconds. Example 10-19 shows you one solution to this step.

Example 10-19 *SPF Timer Tuning*

```
Router(config)#router ospf 1
Router(config-router)#timers spf 10 20
```

Step 14: Configuring OSPF over Demand Circuits

You must make certain considerations when running OSPF over low-bandwidth lines that are typically used for backup scenarios. The OSPF on-demand circuit is an enhancement to the OSPF Protocol that allows efficient operation over these circuits, which include ISDN, X.25 switched virtual circuits (SVCs), and dial-up lines. OSPF over on-demand circuits provides support of RFC 1793.

When you use this feature, the periodic OSPF Hellos that would normally be exchanged between the routers are suppressed and the periodic refreshes of LSAs are not flooded over the demand circuit. Because of this, these packets now only bring up the link when they are exchanged for the first time, or when a change occurs in the information that they contain. This simple change in operation allows the underlying data link layer to be closed when the network topology is stable.

Critical changes to your topology that require OSPF to run a new SPF calculation are still sent to maintain network topology integrity. Only the periodic refreshes that do not include topology change information are not sent across the link.

Use the following commands to configure OSPF for on-demand circuits.

To enable OSPF operation, use the following command:

```
R2(config)#router ospf process-id
```

To enter the interface configuration mode, use the following command:

```
R2(config)#interface interface-type interface-number
```

To configure OSPF over an on-demand circuit, use the following command:

```
R2(config-if)#ip ospf demand-circuit
```

If your router is part of a point-to-point topology, you are only required to configure one end of the demand circuit with the **ip ospf demand-circuit** command. The one requirement is that all your routers must have this feature loaded.

If your router is part of a point-to-multipoint topology, you are only required to configure the multipoint end with this command.

You should consider the following caveats before implementing the OSPF over on-demand circuits feature:

- You should place demand circuits in NSSAs or OSPF stub areas to isolate the demand circuit from topology changes. Remember that LSAs that included topology changes are flooded over your on-demand circuit.

- If you deploy your on-demand circuits within a stub area or NSSA, all of your routers in the area must have this feature loaded. If you choose to deploy this feature within a regular area, all other regular areas must also support this feature before the demand circuit functionality can take effect, because Type 5 external LSAs are flooded throughout all areas.

- Implementing this feature on a broadcast-based network topology causes your link to remain up because you cannot successfully suppress the overhead protocols, such as Hello and LSA packets.

For further information on using the OSPF on-demand feature, refer to Chapter 6, "ISDN Connectivity."

Step 15: Logging Neighbor Adjacency Changes

By default, an OSPF neighbor that is going up or down causes the system to send a syslog message. If, for some reason, you have turned off this feature and desire to restore it, use the following command:

```
R2(config-router)#log-adj-changes [detail]
```

You can also use the **debug ip ospf adjacency** command to display neighbor adjacency changes. However, the **log-adj-changes** command provides you with a higher-level view of the peer relationship with less output than the **debug** command displays. You can use the **detail** keyword to display messages for each state change.

Step 16: Changing the LSA Group Pacing

The OSPF LSA group-pacing feature allows your router to group OSPF LSAs and pace the refreshing, checksumming, and aging functions. This group-pacing feature should result in a more efficient use of your router.

With LSA group pacing, your router can use the groups to combat sudden increases in CPU usage and network resources. Although this feature provides the most benefits in large OSPF networks, it is enabled by default.

Original LSA Behavior

Each OSPF LSA is tracked by its age to ensure its validity. Once the maximum age—1 hour—is reached, the LSA is discarded. During this aging process, the LSA's originating router sends a refresh packet every 30 minutes to refresh the LSA age. It sends these refresh packets to keep the LSA from expiring, regardless of whether a change in the network topology has occurred. Every 10 minutes, checksumming is performed on every LSA. Your router keeps track of each LSA that it generates and each LSA that it receives from other routers. Your router sends refreshes for the LSAs that it generates; it ages the LSAs that it received from other routers.

Prior to inclusion of the LSA group-pacing feature in Cisco IOS Software, the software would perform refreshing based on a single timer, while checksumming and aging were based on another timer. For example, the software would scan its entire database every 30 minutes, sending refreshes for every LSA the router generated, no matter how old the LSA was. This process wasted CPU resources because, in most cases, only a small portion of the database needed to be refreshed. Sending refreshes based on this single timer resulted in the age of all LSAs becoming synchronized, creating a large amount of CPU processing at once. It could also result in a sudden increase of network traffic when generating refreshes for a large OSPF topology, consuming a large amount of network resources in a short period of time.

LSA Group Pacing with Multiple Timers

Cisco IOS Software configures each LSA with its own timer. This means that each LSA is refreshed when it is 30 minutes old, regardless of the age of the other LSAs. This results in your CPU being used only when necessary. The downside is that LSAs being refreshed at frequent, random intervals require many packets for the few refresh LSAs that your router must send out, which is an inefficient use of bandwidth.

To overcome this inefficiency, your router delays the LSA refresh function for an interval of time instead of performing it when the individual timers are reached. This accumulation of LSAs creates a group, which can then be sent out in one or more packets. Checksumming and aging are also paced in this manner.

The pacing interval is user configurable, with a default interval of 4 minutes, and is inversely proportional to the number of LSAs that your router is refreshing. A large number of LSAs obtain more benefit from a lower value than a small number of LSAs. You can configure this value to be between 10 seconds to 30 minutes. The pacing interval is also randomized to further avoid synchronization.

Use the following command to change the LSA group-pacing interval:

```
R2config-router)#timers lsa-group-pacing seconds
```

Example 10-20 shows how to change the OSPF pacing between LSA groups to 60 seconds.

Example 10-20 *Changing OSPF Pacing*

```
Router(config)#router ospf 1
Router(config-router)#timers lsa-group-pacing 60
```

Step 17: Blocking or Reducing LSA Flooding

Whenever a router receives a new OSPF LSA, by default, it floods the LSA over all interfaces that belong to the same area as the LSA, with the exception of the interface that the LSA was received on. This behavior can result in a waste of bandwidth and could eventually destabilize your network due to excessive link and CPU usage in certain topologies, such as the fully meshed topology.

You have the option of blocking OSPF flooding of LSAs in the following two ways, depending on your type of network:

- On broadcast, nonbroadcast, and point-to-point networks, you can block flooding over specified OSPF interfaces by using the following command:

  ```
  R2(config-if)#ospf database-filter all out
  ```

- On point-to-multipoint networks, you can block flooding to a specified neighbor by using the following command:

  ```
  R2(config-router)#neighbor ip-address database-filter all out
  ```

Example 10-21 shows how to prevent flooding of OSPF LSAs to broadcast, nonbroadcast, or point-to-point networks that are reachable through Ethernet interface 0.

Example 10-21 *Preventing LSA Flooding Through an Interface*

```
Router(config)#interface ethernet 0
Router(config-if)#ospf database-filter all out
```

Example 10-22 shows how to prevent flooding of OSPF LSAs to point-to-multipoint networks to the neighbor at IP address 1.2.3.4.

Example 10-22 *Preventing LSA Flooding to a Neighbor*

```
Router(config)#router ospf 1
Router(config-router)#neighbor 1.2.3.4 database-filter all out
```

One hindrance to the scalability of OSPF is its need to refresh routes as they expire after 3600 seconds. To overcome this, some implementations of OSPF have reduced the frequency to refresh from every 30 minutes to about every 50 minutes. This enhancement results in a reduction in the amount of refresh traffic but still requires at least one refresh before the LSA expires. The OSPF flooding reduction feature further refines this concept by reducing unnecessary refreshing and flooding of already known and unchanged information. To achieve this, the LSAs are now flooded with the higher bit set, so the LSAs are now marked as "do not age."

Use the following command to reduce unnecessary refreshing and flooding of LSAs on your network:

```
R2(config-if)#ip ospf flood-reduction
```

Step 18: Ignoring Multicast OSPF LSA Packets

LSA Type 6 multicast OSPF (MOSPF) is not supported by your Cisco router. When your router receives one of these packets, it generates a syslog message. If you are receiving many of these

MOSPF packets, you have the option to configure your router to ignore the packets, preventing the syslog message from being generated. Use the following command to ignore MOSPF LSA packets:

```
R2(config-router)#ignore lsa mospf
```

Example 10-23 shows how to configure the router to suppress the sending of syslog messages when it receives MOSPF packets.

Example 10-23 *Preventing MOSPF Error Messages*

```
Router(config)#router ospf 109
Router(config-router)#ignore lsa mospf
```

Case Study 10-2: OSPF and Route Summarization

You can use route summarization in your OSPF implementation to consolidate multiple routes into one single advertisement. You would normally implement this function at the boundaries of your ABRs, but it can be implemented in two areas. When making this decision, remember that you should configure summarization in the direction of your backbone. By doing this, you ensure that your backbone only receives aggregate addresses and can then inject them, already summarized, into other areas. With OSPF, you can use the following two types of summarization:

- Inter-area route

- External route

The following sections describe both types of summarization in more detail.

Inter-Area Route Summarization

When using inter-area route summarization, configuration is done on the ABR and applied to routes from within the autonomous system. Summarization does not apply to external routes injected into OSPF via redistribution. You must design your network with your network numbers assigned in contiguous order to gain a major benefit from this feature.

Use the following command to consolidate and summarize routes at an area boundary:

```
R2(config-router)#area area-id range ip-address mask [advertise | not-advertise] [cost
    cost]
```

When you use the **area** command, you can summarize routes for the targeted area. The **area** command produces a single summary route that can be advertised to other areas by your ABR. In this manner, your routing information is condensed at area boundaries so that external to the area, a single route is advertised for each address range. You can configure summarization addresses for sets of areas by configuring multiple **area** commands with the **range** keyword.

To take advantage of summarization, you should assign network numbers in areas contiguously to be able to lump these addresses into one range. To specify an address range, perform the following task in router configuration mode:

```
R2(config-router)#area area-id range address mask
```

In this command, the *area-id* is the area containing the networks that you want to be summarized. The *address* and *mask* are used to specify the range of addresses to be summarized in one range.

Figure 10-5 illustrates the topology that you will use for the inter-area route summarization.

Figure 10-5 *Inter-Area Route Summarization Topology*

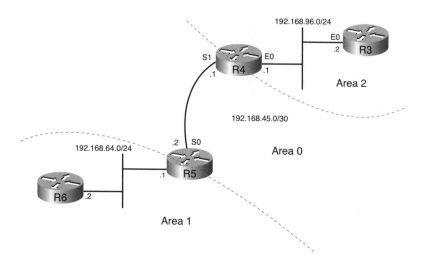

In this portion of the case study, you configure inter-area route summarization on R5 for the range of subnets from 192.168.64.0 to 192.168.95.0 into one range: 192.168.64.0 255.255.224.0. You also configure R4 to generate summary address 192.168.96.0 255.255.224.0 into the backbone using the same technique. Example 10-24 shows a solution to this complex problem.

Example 10-24 *Inter-Area Route Summarization*

```
Configuration items for R4:
R4(config)#interface ethernet 0
R4(config-if)#ip address 192.168.96.1 255.255.255.0
R4(config-if)#exit
R4(config)#interface serial 1
R4(config-if)#ip address 192.168.45.1 255.255.255.252
R4(config-if)#exit
```

continues

Example 10-24 *Inter-Area Route Summarization (Continued)*

```
R4(config)#router ospf 201
R4(config-router)#network 192.168.45.0 0.0.0.3 area 0
R4(config-router)#network 192.168.96.0 0.0.0.255 area 2
R4(config-router)#area 2 range 192.168.96.0 255.255.224.0

Configuration items for R5:
R5(config)#interface ethernet 0
R5(config-if)#ip address 192.168.64.1 255.255.255.0
R5(config-if)#exit
R5(config)#interface serial 0
R5(config-if)#ip address 192.168.45.2 255.255.255.252
R5(config-if)#exit
R5(config)#router ospf 100
R5(config-router)#network 192.168.45.0 0.0.0.3 area 0
R5(config-router)#network 192.168.64.0 0.0.0.255 area 1
R5(config-router)#area 1 range 192.168.64.0 255.255.224.0
```

After working through this scenario, it should be apparent that it would be difficult to configure the summarization required if the subnets between area 1 and area 2 overlapped. Your backbone area would receive summary ranges that overlap and would not know where to correctly send the traffic based on the summary address. Also, note that the summary addresses are sent from an area and not to an area.

If you use summarization with a Cisco IOS Software release prior to 12.1(6), you should manually configure a discard static route for your summary address on your ABR to prevent any possible routing loops. For example, using one of the summary routes from your case study, use the following command:

```
R5(config)#ip route 128.213.64.0 255.255.224.0 null0
```

With Cisco IOS Software release 12.1(6) and higher, this discard route is generated automatically by default. You still have the option of not using a discard route by using either of the following commands:

```
R4(config-router)#[no] discard-route internal
R4(config-router)#[no] discard-route external
```

External Route Summarization

External route summarization follows the same concept as inter-area route summarization, with the exception that it is applied to external routes that are injected into OSPF via redistribution. Use the following command on your ASBR that is performing redistribution into OSPF to summarize external routes:

```
R4(config-router)#summary-address ip-address mask
```

Figure 10-6 shows the topology that you will use to configure external route summarization in this case study.

Figure 10-6 *External Route Summarization Topology*

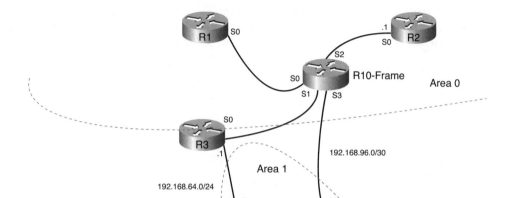

In this portion of the case study, you configure R4 and R8 to inject external routes received from routers R4 and R8 into your OSPF autonomous system. R8 is injecting routes in the range of 192.168.64–95, and R4 is injecting routes in the range of 192.168.96–127. For an explanation of the **redistribute** command used in this example, refer to Chapter 13. Example 10-25 shows one solution to this scenario.

Example 10-25 *External Route Summarization Example*

```
Configuration items for R8:
R8(config)#router ospf 100
R8(config-router)#summary-address 192.168.64.0 255.255.224.0
R8(config-router)#redistribute bgp 50 metric 1000 subnets

Configuration items for R4:
R4(config)#router ospf 100
R4(config-router)#summary-address 192.168.96.0 255.255.224.0
R4(config-router)#redistribute bgp 20 metric 1000 subnets
```

As in the previous example, this configuration causes R5 to generate one external route 192.168.64.0 255.255.224.0 and causes R6 to generate 192.168.96.0 255.255.224.0.

Case Study 10-3: OSPF Filtering

You can control routing update information on OSPF updates through the use of filtering. This gives you the ability to optimize and control the routes that are included in your routing table. Cisco IOS Software supports the following types of filtering:

- OSPF ABR Type 3 LSA filtering
- LSA filtering on an interface
- LSA filtering on a neighbor

OSPF ABR Type 3 LSA Filtering

Cisco IOS Software provides a feature that allows you to filter Type 3 LSAs sent between different OSPF areas by extending the functionality of the ABR, giving improved control over route redistribution. With this feature, you can allow only packets with specified prefixes to be sent from one area to another area, and restrict all packets with other prefixes. You can apply this type of area filtering into or out of a specific OSPF area or into and out of the same OSPF areas at the same time.

Use the next two commands to filter inter-area routes into a specified area.

To configure the router to filter inter-area routes into the specified area, use the following command:

```
R2(config-router)#area area-id filter-list prefix prefix-list-name in
```

To create a prefix list with the name specified for the list-name argument, use the following command:

```
R2(config-router)#ip prefix-list list-name [seq seq-value] deny | permit network/len [ge
  ge-value] [le le-value]
```

Use the next two commands to filter inter-area routes out of a specified area.

To configure the router to filter inter-area routes out of the specified area, use the following command:

```
R2(config-router)#area area-id filter-list prefix prefix-list-name out
```

To create a prefix list with the name specified for the list-name argument, use the following command:

```
R2(config-router)#ip prefix-list list-name [seq seq-value] deny | permit network/len [ge
  ge-value] [le le-value]
```

In this portion of the case study, you configure R2 to filter inter-area routes in both incoming and outgoing directions. You filter two routes in the outward direction, 10.25.0.0/8 and 172.16.0.0/20, and a single route on the inbound direction, 172.16.0.0/20. Example 10-26 shows a solution to this task.

Example 10-26 *Inter-Area Filtering of Private Networks*

```
Configuration items for R2:
R2(config)#router ospf 100
R2(config-router)#log-adjacency-changes
R2(config-router)#area 1 filter-list prefix AREA_1_OUT out
R2(config-router)#area 3 filter-list prefix AREA_3_IN in
R2(config-router)#network 10.0.0.0 0.255.255.255 area 3
R2(config-router)#network 172.16.0.0 0.0.15.255 area 0
R2(config-router)#network 192.168.0.0 0.0.255.255 area 1
R2(config-router)#exit
R2(config)#ip prefix-list AREA_1_OUT seq 10 permit 10.25.0.0/8
R2(config)#ip prefix-list AREA_1_OUT seq 20 permit 172.16.0.0/20
R2(config)#ip prefix-list AREA_3_IN seq 10 permit 172.16.0.0/20
```

LSA Filtering on an Interface

OSPF has a feature that allows you to filter outgoing LSAs to a specified interface configured to run OSPF. Use the following command to filter LSAs on an interface:

```
R2(config-if)#ip ospf database-filter all out
```

In this portion of the case study, you configure R2 to prevent the flooding of LSAs to broadcast, nonbroadcast, or point-to-point networks that are reachable through Ethernet interface 0. Example 10-27 illustrates the commands that are necessary to complete this task.

Example 10-27 *LSA Filtering for an Interface*

```
Configuration items for R2:
R2(config)#interface ethernet 0
R2(config-if)#ip ospf database-filter all out
```

LSA Filtering to a Neighbor

OSPF allows you to filter outgoing LSAs to a configured OSPF neighbor. Use the following command to filter LSAs to an OSPF neighbor:

```
R2(config-router)#neighbor ip-address database-filter all out
```

In this portion of the case study, you configure R2 to filter LSAs going to R3 at address 133.100.23.2. Example 10-28 shows the commands that are necessary to do this.

Example 10-28 *LSA Filtering to an OSPF Neighbor*

```
Configuration items for R2:
R2(config)#router ospf 100
R2(config-if)#neighbor 133.100.23.2 database-filter all out
```

Case Study 10-4: OSPF and Non-IP Traffic over GRE

When you run a normal IP Security (IPSec) configuration, you will find that it does not support the transfer of routing protocols, such as OSPF, or support non-IP traffic, such as Internetwork Packet Exchange (IPX) and AppleTalk. In this section, you learn how to route between different networks using a routing protocol and non-IP traffic with IPSec. More specifically, you see how to use generic routing encapsulation (GRE) to accomplish routing between the different networks.

Before considering this scenario, you must remember the following:

* Ensure that your tunnel is fully functional before applying your crypto maps.

* If required, adjust the MTU to eliminate any possible issues, as described in Chapter 17, "IP Services."

To complete the following case study requirements, you must read and work through the lessons outlined in Chapter 22, "Cisco IOS Firewall." For questions regarding any of the configuration items, refer to the appropriate *Cisco PIX Firewall Command Reference* for your PIX OS level.

Figure 10-7 illustrates the components that you will use in creating your case study topology.

Figure 10-7 *OSPF and Non-IP Traffic over GRE*

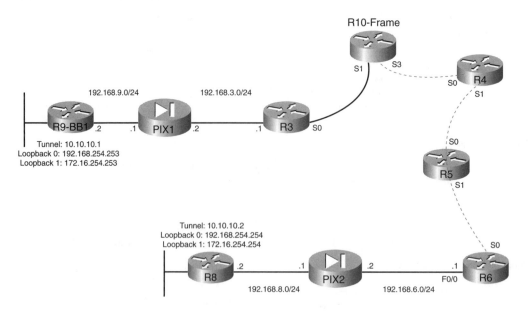

In this case study, you configure a preshared key Virtual Private Network (VPN) between PIX1 and PIX2. Once this tunnel is established, you can run OSPF across the resulting GRE tunnel between R8 and R9. Remember that you must configure a static route for the other router because your routing protocol cannot exchange routes until the tunnel is established. R3, R5, and R6 are considered to be service provider connections and are not required to run OSPF. The configuration of these three routers is not covered in this section because they are transparent to the OSPF protocol. Example 10-29 illustrates one configuration for successful completion of this task.

Example 10-29 *OSPF over a GRE Tunnel*

```
Configuration items for PIX1:
PIX1(config)#access-list nonat permit ip 192.168.9.0 255.255.255.0 192.168.8.0
  255.255.255.0
PIX1(config)#ip address outside 192.168.3.2 255.255.255.252
PIX1(config)#ip address inside 192.168.9.1 255.255.255.0
PIX1(config)#global (outside) 1 interface
PIX1(config)#nat (inside) 0 access-list nonat
PIX1(config)#nat (inside) 1 0.0.0.0 0.0.0.0 0 0
PIX1(config)#route outside 0.0.0.0 0.0.0.0 192.168.3.1 1
PIX1(config)#sysopt connection permit-ipsec
PIX1(config)#crypto ipsec transform-set pixset esp-des esp-md5-hmac
PIX1(config)#crypto map pixmap 20 ipsec-isakmp
PIX1(config)#crypto map pixmap 20 match address nonat
PIX1(config)#crypto map pixmap 20 set peer 192.168.6.2
PIX1(config)#crypto map pixmap 20 set transform-set pixset
PIX1(config)#crypto map pixmap interface outside
PIX1(config)#isakmp enable outside
PIX1(config)#isakmp key ccie-pre-share address 192.168.6.2 netmask 255.255.255.255
PIX1(config)#isakmp identity address
PIX1(config)#isakmp policy 20 authentication pre-share
PIX1(config)#isakmp policy 20 encryption des
PIX1(config)#isakmp policy 20 hash md5
PIX1(config)#isakmp policy 20 group 1
PIX1(config)#isakmp policy 20 lifetime 86400

Configuration items for PIX2:
PIX2(config)#access-list nonat permit ip 192.168.8.0 255.255.255.0 192.168.9.0
  255.255.255.0
PIX2(config)#ip address outside 192.168.6.2 255.255.255.252
PIX2(config)#ip address inside 192.168.8.1 255.255.255.0
PIX2(config)#global (outside) 1 interface
PIX2(config)#nat (inside) 0 access-list nonat
PIX2(config)#nat (inside) 1 0.0.0.0 0.0.0.0 0 0
PIX2(config)#conduit permit icmp any any
PIX2(config)#route outside 0.0.0.0 0.0.0.0 192.168.6.1 1
PIX2(config)#sysopt connection permit-ipsec
PIX2(config)#crypto ipsec transform-set pixset esp-des esp-md5-hmac
PIX2(config)#crypto map pixmap 20 ipsec-isakmp
PIX2(config)#crypto map pixmap 20 match address nonat
PIX2(config)#crypto map pixmap 20 set peer 192.168.3.2
PIX2(config)#crypto map pixmap 20 set transform-set pixset
PIX2(config)#crypto map pixmap interface outside
PIX2(config)#isakmp enable outside
PIX2(config)#isakmp key ccie-pre-share address 192.168.3.2 netmask 255.255.255.255
```

continues

Example 10-29 *OSPF over a GRE Tunnel (Continued)*

```
PIX2(config)#isakmp identity address
PIX2(config)#isakmp policy 20 authentication pre-share
PIX2(config)#isakmp policy 20 encryption des
PIX2(config)#isakmp policy 20 hash md5
PIX2(config)#isakmp policy 20 group 1
PIX2(config)#isakmp policy 20 lifetime 86400

Configuration items for R8:
R8(config)#interface Loopback0
R8(config-if)#ip address 192.168.254.254 255.255.255.255
R8(config-if)#exit
R8(config)#interface Loopback1
R8(config-if)#ip address 172.16.254.254 255.255.255.255
R8(config-if)#exit
R8(config)#interface Tunnel0
R8(config-if)#ip address 10.10.10.2 255.255.255.0
R8(config-if)#tunnel source Ethernet0
R8(config-if)#tunnel destination 192.168.9.2
R8(config-if)#exit
R8(config)#interface Ethernet0
R8(config-if)#ip address 192.168.8.2 255.255.255.0
R8(config-if)#exit
R8(config)#router ospf 22
R8(config-router)#log-adjacency-changes
R8(config-router)#network 10.10.10.0 0.0.0.255 area 0
R8(config-router)#network 172.16.254.254 0.0.0.0 area 0
R8(config-router)#exit
R8(config)#ip route 0.0.0.0 0.0.0.0 192.168.8.1
R8(config)#ip route 192.168.254.253 255.255.255.255 Tunnel0

Configuration items for R9:
R9(config)#interface Loopback0
R9(config-if)#ip address 192.168.254.253 255.255.255.255
R9(config-router)#exit
R9(config)#interface Loopback1
R9(config-router)#ip address 172.16.254.253 255.255.255.255
R9(config-router)#exit
R9(config)#interface Tunnel0
R9(config-router)#ip address 10.10.10.1 255.255.255.0
R9(config-router)#tunnel source Ethernet0
R9(config-router)#tunnel destination 192.168.8.2
R9(config-router)#exit
R9(config)#interface Ethernet0
R9(config-router)#ip address 192.168.9.2 255.255.255.0
R9(config-router)#exit
R9(config)#router ospf 11
R9(config-router)#log-adjacency-changes
R9(config-router)#network 10.10.10.0 0.0.0.255 area 0
R9(config-router)#network 192.168.254.253 0.0.0.0 area 0
R9(config-router)#exit
R9(config)#ip route 0.0.0.0 0.0.0.0 192.168.9.1
R9(config)#ip route 192.168.254.254 255.255.255.255 Tunnel0
```

Monitoring and Maintaining OSPF

When running OSPF, you can display specific statistics such as the contents of your IP routing tables, caches, and databases. You can use this information to determine resource utilization and to solve network problems. You can also display information about node reachability and can discover the routing path that your device packets are taking through your network.

Use the following commands to display various routing statistics.

To display general information about OSPF routing processes, use the following command:

```
R2#show ip ospf [process-id]
```

To display the internal OSPF routing table entries of the ABR and ASBR, use the following command:

```
R2#show ip ospf border-routers
```

To display lists of information related to the OSPF database, use the following commands:

```
R2#show ip ospf [process-id [area-id]] database
R2#show ip ospf [process-id [area-id]] database [database-summary]
R2#show ip ospf [process-id [area-id]] database [router] [self-originate]
R2#show ip ospf [process-id [area-id]] database [router] [adv-router [ip-address]]
R2#show ip ospf [process-id [area-id]] database [router] [link-state-id]
R2#show ip ospf [process-id [area-id]] database [network] [link-state-id]
R2#show ip ospf [process-id [area-id]] database [summary] [link-state-id]
R2#show ip ospf [process-id [area-id]] database [asbr-summary] [link-state-id]
R2#show ip ospf [process-id [area-id]] database [external] [link-state-id]
R2#show ip ospf [process-id [area-id]] database [nssa-external] [i]
R2#show ip ospf [process-id [area-id]] database [opaque-link] [link-state-id]
R2#show ip ospf [process-id [area-id]] database [opaque-area] [link-state-id]
R2#show ip ospf [process-id [area-id]] database [opaque-as] [link-state-id]
```

To display a list of LSAs waiting to be flooded over an interface to observe OSPF packet pacing, use the following command:

```
R2#show ip ospf flood-list interface interface-type
```

To display OSPF-related interface information, use the following command:

```
R2#show ip ospf interface [interface-type interface-number]
```

To display OSPF neighbor information on a per-interface basis, use the following command:

```
R2#show ip ospf neighbor [interface-name] [neighbor-id] detail
```

To display a list of all LSAs requested by a router, use the following command:

```
R2#show ip ospf request-list [neighbor] [interface] [interface-neighbor]
```

To display a list of all LSAs waiting to be re-sent, use the following command:

```
R2#show ip ospf retransmission-list [neighbor] [interface] [interface-neighbor]
```

To display a list of all summary address redistribution information configured under an OSPF process, use the following command:

```
R2#show ip ospf [process-id] summary-address
```

To display OSPF-related virtual links information, use the following command:

```
R2#show ip ospf virtual-links
```

To clear redistribution based on the OSPF routing process ID, use the following command. If the *pid* option is not specified, all OSPF processes are cleared:

```
R2#clear ip ospf [pid] {process | redistribution | counters [neighbor [neighbor-interface]
  [neighbor-id]]}
```

Verifying OSPF ABR Type 3 LSA Filtering

Use the following command to verify that the OSPF ABR Type 3 LSA Filtering feature has been configured:

```
R2#show ip ospf [process-id]
```

Example 10-30 shows a typical output from this command.

Example 10-30 *The show ip ospf Command Output*

```
Router#show ip ospf 1
  Routing Process "ospf 1" with ID 172.16.0.1
  Supports only single TOS(TOS0) routes
  Supports opaque LSA
  It is an area border router
  SPF schedule delay 5 secs, Hold time between two SPFs 10 secs
  Minimum LSA interval 5 secs. Minimum LSA arrival 1 secs
  Number of external LSA 0. Checksum Sum 0x0
  Number of opaque AS LSA 0. Checksum Sum 0x0
  Number of DCbitless external and opaque AS LSA 0
  Number of DoNotAge external and opaque AS LSA 0
  Number of areas in this router is 2. 2 normal 0 stub 0 nssa
  External flood list length 0
    Area BACKBONE(0)
        Number of interfaces in this area is 2
        Area has no authentication
        SPF algorithm executed 6 times
        Area ranges are
           10.0.0.0/8 Passive Advertise
        Area-filter AREA_0_IN in
        Area-filter AREA_0_OUT out
        Number of LSA 5. Checksum Sum 0x29450
        Number of opaque link LSA 0. Checksum Sum 0x0
        Number of DCbitless LSA 0
        Number of indication LSA 0
        Number of DoNotAge LSA 0
        Flood list length 0
```

By examining the output from Example 10-30, you can see that the feature is properly configured because it has been enabled for the area filter in both the in and out directions.

To display information about a prefix list or prefix list entries, use the following command:

```
R2#show ip prefix-list
```

Displaying OSPF Update Packet Pacing

The older method of sending OSPF update packets needed to be made more efficient. Some of these update packets were getting lost in cases where the link was slow, a neighbor could not receive updates quickly enough, or the router ran out of buffer space.

Newer implementations of OSPF allow update packets to be automatically paced so that they are not sent less than 33 milliseconds apart. This pacing is also added between resends to increase efficiency and minimize lost retransmissions. You can display the LSAs that are waiting to be sent out an interface. Because there are no configuration tasks for this feature, remember that it occurs automatically; it is one of the easiest OSPF features to use.

Use the following command to observe OSPF packet pacing by displaying a list of LSAs waiting to be flooded over a specified interface:

```
R2#show ip ospf flood-list interface-type interface-number
```

Summary

This chapter has reviewed the OSPF implementation that Cisco supports. OSPF is an Interior Gateway Protocol (IGP) designed for IP networks that supports IP subnetting, tagging of externally derived routing information, and packet authentication; it makes use of IP multicast when sending and receiving packets. You began by examining the many items that you need to make your OSPF design function in your environment. You covered the many features and parameters that you can "tune" to make your OSPF implementation more robust in your environment. You finished the chapter with a look at different ways that you can monitor and maintain your OSPF configuration.

Review Questions

1 Why are loopback interfaces advertised as /32 in OSPF?

2 What are the route types used with OSPF?

3 Why do I receive the "cannot allocate router id" error message?

4 Why do I receive the "unknown routing protocol" error message?

5 What do the states DR, BDR, and DROTHER mean in the **show ip ospf** interface command output?

6 Which router is responsible for generating the network LSA?

7 Why do neighbors show a state of 2-WAY/DROTHER when issuing the **show ip ospf neighbor** command?

8 Why is it difficult to identify the DR or BDR on a serial link?

FAQs

Q — *Is there a way to change the reference bandwidth in OSPF to more accurately reflect my bandwidth?*

A — Yes, you can use the **ospf auto-cost reference-bandwidth** command to change the reference bandwidth from 100 Mbps to your bandwidth.

Q — *Why would it be important to change the reference bandwidth?*

A — OSPF uses the reference bandwidth to calculate the cost of a route. This formula is reference bandwidth divided by interface bandwidth. If you were to use the **ip ospf cost <cost>** command on your interface, it overrides this formulated cost.

Q — *Can I enable the OSPF routing protocol to authenticate routing exchanges?*

A — Yes, you can authenticate packets through simple passwords or through MD5 cryptographic checksums. You can use the **ip ospf authentication-key** command to configure simple passwords of up to eight octets for authentication of an area. You must then enter the **area <x> authentication** command, where **x** is the area number, under your OSPF router process to enable authentication.

Q — *Can I change the link-state retransmit interval?*

A — Use the **ip ospf retransmit-interval** command to change the retransmit interval from the default value of 5 seconds.

Q — *I have an area that cannot be physically connected to the backbone area. How can I make this work?*

A — Virtual links in OSPF maintain connectivity to the backbone from nonbackbone areas, whether by design or during times of network instability.

Q — *I implemented OSPF and now I am seeing multicast IP address on my network. Why is this?*

A — OSPF sends all of its advertisements using multicast addressing. With the exception of Token Ring, the multicast IP addresses are mapped to MAC-level multicast addresses. Cisco uses MAC-level broadcast addresses for Token Ring implementations.

Q — *I want to implement IP type of service (ToS)–based routing in my OSPF environment. Can I do this?*

A — Yes and no. Cisco OSPF only provides support for ToS 0. This means that routers route all packets on the ToS 0 path, eliminating the need to calculate nonzero ToS paths.

Q — *How does OSPF generate a default route that is based on external information on a router that does not itself have a default?*

A — OSPF generates a default only if you configure it using the **default-information originate** command and OSPF is redistributing a default network from a different routing process on the device. The default route in OSPF is 0.0.0.0. Use the **default-information originate always** command to enable your router to generate a default route, even if it does not have a default route itself.

Q — *I want to filter routes into or out of my OSPF routing process. Can I use the **distribute-list in/out** command to do this?*

A — You cannot filter OSPF routes from entering your OSPF database. The **distribute-list in** command only filters routes from entering your routing table, but it does not prevent link-state packets from being propagated.

The **distribute-list out** command only works on the routes being redistributed by the ASBR into OSPF. This means that you apply it to external Type 2 and external Type 1 routes, but not to intra-area and inter-area routes.

Q — *How does Cisco compensate for a partial-mesh topology when running OSPF on Frame Relay networks?*

A — You can tell OSPF whether to try to use its multicast facilities on a multiaccess interface. If multicast is available, OSPF uses it for its normal multicasts.

You can also use subinterfaces with Frame Relay to tie a set of virtual circuits (VCs) together to form a virtual interface. This causes the VCs to act as a single IP subnet. You can also consider using the point-to-multipoint subinterface.

This chapter includes the following topics:

- Integrated IS-IS overview
- Configuring IS-IS
- IS-IS building blocks
- The IS-IS state machine
- Pseudonodes
- IS-IS addressing
- Limiting LSP flooding
- Configuring IS-IS authentication
- Using **show** and **debug** commands

CHAPTER 11

IS-IS

The *Intermediate System-to-Intermediate System (IS-IS)* link-state protocol, specified in ISO 10589, is a dynamic routing protocol designed for use with Connectionless Network Service (CLNS) to facilitate hop-by-hop path selection. IS-IS is a standard intra-domain routing protocol in the OSI protocol suite.

IS-IS provides a means to implement a hierarchical topology based on areas. Unlike OSPF, which also uses the concept of areas, IS-IS only provides two areas—Level-1 and Level-2—although you can have a router that is part of both the Level-1 and Level-2 areas, much like the Area Border Router in OSPF. You can use a Level-1 area to break a large network into more manageable sections, also known as *Level-1 routing areas.* You can use a Level-2 area to provide the interconnections among different Level-1 areas, frequently referred to as the *backbone area.*

This chapter provides an overview of IS-IS, followed by configuration tasks and troubleshooting techniques.

Integrated IS-IS Overview

Cisco adapted the Open System Interconnection (OSI) IS-IS Protocol into a protocol that is capable of carrying IP prefixes in addition to CLNS routing information. You might know this protocol as either *Integrated IS-IS* or *Dual IS-IS.* Most routing protocols use a "ships in the night" approach in their operation, meaning that they only work with a single protocol, but Integrated IS-IS overcomes this by providing concurrent processing of reachability information for multiple network layer protocols. The standard IS-IS packet is modified so that it can support multiple network-layer protocols. Fortunately, IS-IS packet formats were originally designed to support the addition of new fields without a loss of compatibility with nonintegrated versions of IS-IS. Some capabilities added to IS-IS include the following:

- Tells ISs which network-layer protocols are supported by other ISs

- Tells ISs whether end stations running other protocols can be reached

- Includes any other required network-layer, protocol-specific information

As a result, Integrated IS-IS can support three different IS configurations:

- Those running IP only

- Those running the Connectionless Network Protocol (CLNP) only

- Those running both IP and CLNP

If you configure your IS to run only one of the two protocols, it ignores information concerning the other protocol. In fact, your IS refuses to recognize other ISs as neighbors unless they have at least one protocol in common. If you configure your IS to run both protocols, it can become a neighbor with the other IS types.

This chapter only covers the IP-only configuration of IS-IS. For a configuration guide of the other two configurations that are possible with IS-IS, refer to the appropriate *Cisco IOS IP and IP Routing Configuration Guide* for your version of Cisco IOS Software or *IS-IS Network Design Solutions,* written by Abe Martey and published by Cisco Press (February 2002).

Configuring IS-IS

To configure IS-IS, you are only required to enable the IS-IS process and assign areas and to enable IS-IS for IP routing for an interface. Once you have IS-IS up and running, you can configure several optional items and, if you choose to do so, implement filtering of routing information or specify route redistribution.

Case Study 11-1: Configuring IS-IS for IP

In this case study, you configure IS-IS for IP routing between routers R3, R4, and R7. You use an area ID of 49.0001, and you configure each router as a Level-1/Level-2 router with no optional parameters. You configure each router to have a loopback interface that is advertised by IS-IS. Figure 11-1 illustrates the IS-IS topology, as well as IP addressing, that you use throughout this case study.

Figure 11-1 *IS-IS Topology*

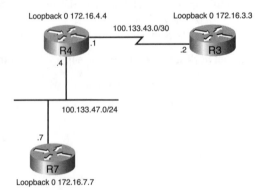

Use the following steps to configure IS-IS for your case study:

Step 1   Enable IS-IS and define areas.

Step 2   Assign IS-IS to an interface.

The following sections guide you through each of these steps in more detail.

Step 1: Enable IS-IS and Define Areas

The first step in your design of an IS-IS–capable network should be deciding what network service access point (NSAP) definitions you are going to use, similar to when you decide on a subnetting scheme for IP. Like the subnet, the NSAP defines the area that an IS-IS–capable router operates in. This means that you must configure an NSAP, even when you only want to route IP prefixes.

Network entity titles (NETs) configure the NSAP for a router, providing the address for the entire router, not per interface, as you would do in IP addressing. Much like other routing protocols, IS-IS uses the concepts of areas, a group of routers that know how to reach all the system IDs in their local area, and a system ID for the router, a unique ID for each system, much like an IP address. IS-IS can also use a backbone area when used in a multi-area IS-IS configuration. In this case, area systems still know how to reach the system IDs in their local area. The systems also know how to reach the backbone area for IDs out of their local area and the backbone knows how to reach other areas. The NET contains both the area address used for IS-IS and the system ID of the router.

In IS-IS, the borders between areas are defined as the interconnecting links between the routers, not the router itself. See Figure 11-2 for an example of this.

Figure 11-2 *IS-IS Borders*

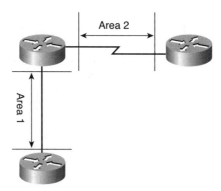

When you enable IS-IS on a router, you can tell that IS-IS is not like other routing protocols. Enabling IS-IS is unique in one aspect: After you create the IS-IS routing process, you assign interfaces to the process instead of assigning networks to the process. You are also given the option of implementing a multi-area IS-IS configuration by specifying more than one IS-IS routing process per router, with each process receiving its own options. You enable the IS-IS process by entering the following commands:

```
R1(config)#router isis [area tag]
R1(config-router)#net network-entity-title
```

You use the *area tag* argument to identify the area to which this IS-IS router instance is assigned. You are only required to enter a value for the *area tag* if you are going to configure multiple IS-IS areas.

You should now complete the first step in configuring your case scenario. Example 11-1 shows one example configuration.

Example 11-1 *Enabling IS-IS for Case Study 1*

```
Configuration items for R3:
R3(config)#router isis ccie_lab
R3(config-router)#net 49.0001.1234.5678.0003.00

Configuration items for R4:
R4(config)#router isis ccie_lab
R4(config-router)#net 49.0001.1234.5678.0004.00

Configuration items for R7:
R7(config)#router isis ccie_lab
R7(config-router)#net 49.0001.1234.5678.0007.00
```

Levels and Adjacencies

Once you have your IS-IS process up and running, you need to decide what function your router is to provide. Small networks are usually built as a single area that includes all the routers in your network. When your network grows large enough, you usually reorganize your routers to include a backbone area, which is made up of Level-2 routers connected to all your local areas. Within a local area, your routers are required to know how to reach all system IDs. Between areas, your routers know how to reach your backbone, and your backbone routers know how to reach all your other areas.

To provide this connectivity, your routers establish Level-1 adjacencies to perform routing within a local area (*intra-area routing*). Your backbone routers establish Level-2 adjacencies to perform routing between Level-1 areas (*inter-area routing*).

You might be wondering what determines which type of adjacency a router forms with its neighbors. IS-IS uses areas to make this determination. In IS-IS, a group of interconnected intermediate systems (ISs) and end systems (ESs) with the same area address define the area, unlike OSPF, where IP subnets define areas. ISs form adjacencies by sending and receiving Intermediate System-Intermediate System Hellos (IIHs). ISs usually form Level-1 adjacencies with other ISs in the same area but could be configured to form Level-2 adjacencies. A router-to-router connection, where each router belongs to different areas, can only be a Level-2 adjacency, but each router is still able to form Level-1 adjacencies with other routers in their respective areas. Note that the default behavior of interconnected Cisco routers is to form both Level-1 and Level-2 adjacencies. This is done to prevent you from inadvertently partitioning an area or even the backbone due to any type of misconfiguration.

If you implement multi-area IS-IS, your router can participate in routing in one of up to 29 Level-1 areas, as well as perform Level-2 routing for a single backbone area. The first IS-IS instance that you configure is Level-1-2 by default. Any later instances are created automatically as a Level-1.

You are given the option of configuring your router to act as a Level-1 router, as both a Level-1 router and a Level-2 router, or as a Level-2 router only.

To specify the router level that you are going to use, enter the following command:

```
R10(config-router)#is-type {level-1 | level-1-2 | level-2-only}
```

Your next step in creating your case study scenario is to assign each router to act as a Level-1-2 router. Because this is the default behavior for the first IS-IS area you create on a router, this step is only included for completeness. Example 11-2 lists the steps that are necessary for this task.

Example 11-2 *Creating the Area Levels for Case Study 11-1*

```
Configuration items for R3:
R3(config-router)#is-type level-1-2

Configuration items for R4:
R4(config-router)#is-type level-1-2

Configuration items for R7:
R7(config-router)#is-type level-1-2
```

Step 2: Assign IS-IS to an Interface

The next step in the configuration of your case study is to enable IP routing and specify the area for the IS-IS routing process. Use the following commands to accomplish this:

```
R1(config)#interface type number
R1(config-if)#ip router isis [area tag]
R1(config-if)#ip address ip-address-mask
```

Note that you are required to configure an IP address on all interfaces that are in an IS-IS–enabled area, even if they are not going to be configured to run IS-IS across them.

Now you can assign the IP addresses outlined in Figure 11-1 as well as enable IS-IS on the respected interfaces. Example 11-3 illustrates the items that you need to configure to complete the case study configuration.

Example 11-3 *Assigning Interfaces to IS-IS*

```
Configuration items for R3:
R3(config)#interface loopback 0
R3(config-if)#ip address 172.16.3.3 255.255.255.0
R3(config-if)#exit
R3(config)#interface serial 0
R3(config-if)#ip address 100.133.43.2 255.255.255.252
R3(config-if)#ip router is-is ccie_lab

Configuration items for R4:
R4(config)#interface loopback 0
R4(config-if)#ip address 172.16.4.4 255.255.255.0
R4(config-if)#exit
R4(config)#interface serial 0
R4(config-if)#ip address 100.133.43.1 255.255.255.252
R4(config-if)#ip router is-is ccie_lab
R4(config-if)#exit
R4(config)#interface ethernet 0
R4(config-if)#ip address 100.133.47.4 255.255.255.0
R4(config-if)#ip router is-is ccie_lab

Configuration items for R7:
R7(config)#interface loopback 0
R7(config-if)#ip address 172.16.7.7 255.255.255.0
R7(config-if)#exit
R7(config)#interface ethernet 0
R7(config-if)#ip address 100.133.47.7 255.255.255.0
R7(config-if)#ip router is-is ccie_lab
```

Once you have your loopback interfaces created, you need to make them passive under the IS-IS process. Example 11-4 illustrates the commands that are necessary for this task.

Example 11-4 *Making the Loopback Interfaces Passive in Case Study 11-1*

```
Configuration items for R3:
R3(config-router)#passive-interface loopback0

Configuration items for R4:
R4(config-router)#passive-interface loopback0

Configuration items for R7:
R7(config-router)#passive-interface loopback0
```

Note that you did not enable IS-IS on the loopback interfaces that you created. By enabling the IS-IS process on your router, you place all interfaces that you do not specifically assign to an IS-IS area in passive mode. This means that IS-IS routing information is not sent out of these interfaces, but they are advertised to neighboring routers.

You can use the **show clns neighbor** command to see the adjacencies that are formed by your IS-IS–enabled router. Example 11-5 shows you the output that you receive from this command on R3 and R7.

Example 11-5 *The* **show clns neighbor** *Command Output from R3 and R7*

```
R7#show clns neighbor
System Id   Interface  SNPA            State  Holdtime  Type Protocol
R4          Et0        0000.0c47.b947  Up     24        L1L2 ISIS

R4#show clns neighbor
System Id   Interface  SNPA            State  Holdtime  Type Protocol
R7          Et0        0000.0c09.9fea  Up     24        L1L2 ISIS
R3          Se0        *HDLC*          Up     28        L1L2 ISIS
```

From the output in Example 11-5, you can see that R7 recognizes R4 on its Ethernet 0 interface with the adjacency type of L1/L2. Because they are both sending and receiving both Level-1 and Level-2 hellos, this satisfies the adjacency requirements that were outlined in your case study. R4 recognizes R7 on its Ethernet 0 interface, and R3 on its Serial 0 interface. Because R4 and R7 both reside on the same Ethernet interface, there is a Designated IS (DIS) for both Level-1 and Level-2. You can use the **show clns interface [int]** command on R7 to verify this, as shown in Example 11-6.

Example 11-6 *The* **show clns interface [int]** *Command Output from R7*

```
R7#show clns interface ethernet 0
Ethernet0 is up, line protocol is up
  Checksums enabled, MTU 1497, Encapsulation SAP
  Routing Protocol: ISIS
    Circuit Type: level-1-2
    Interface number 0x0, local circuit ID 0x1
    Level-1 Metric: 10, Priority: 64, Circuit ID: R4.01
    Number of active level-1 adjacencies: 1
    Level-2 Metric: 10, Priority: 64, Circuit ID: R4.01
    Number of active level-2 adjacencies: 1
    Next ISIS LAN Level-1 Hello in 5 seconds
    Next ISIS LAN Level-2 Hello in 1 seconds
```

In the output of Example 11-6, R4 is the DIS. The DIS is responsible for generating the pseudonode link-state packet (LSP) and is denoted with a nonzero LSP-ID: R4.01. This is similar to the designated router (DR) in the Open Shortest Path First (OSPF) routing protocol, with the exception that a backup DIS in not elected.

You can also examine the following items:

- Circuit type: Level-1-2.

- L1 and L2 metrics and priorities are at default values of 10 and 64.

- L1 and L2 adjacencies: 1 (from R7's perspective on the Ethernet interface).

- IS-IS LAN hellos for L1 and L2.

- Maximum transmission unit (MTU) 1497. This is because the OSI IS-IS header is encapsulated inside a 3-byte 802.2 header.

IS-IS Building Blocks

Now that you have a functioning IS-IS network, you are ready for a more detailed examination of the IS-IS routing protocol.

A Level-1 IS delivers and receives adjacency information packets from other ISs and also route based on their ID portion of their address, or within their native areas. Level-1 ISs forward other area traffic to the nearest Level-2 router in the local area. A Level-2 IS routes data traffic based on its area address toward other areas in the same domain or to other domains. Level-2 routers do not need to know anything about the internal structure of an area to route toward them. Level-1 routing occurs between Level-1 ISs, and Level-2 routing occurs between Level-2 ISs.

Internodal connections are referred to as *adjacencies,* much like Enhanced Interior Gateway Routing Protocol (EIGRP). However, IS-IS organizes its adjacencies into a link-state database and uses hierarchy to control the scope of distribution of the database between ISs.

Because IS-IS is a link-state protocol, ISs are required to maintain the same view of the area as other ISs in the area. They achieve this through the exchange of link-state packets (LSPs) in a process known as *flooding.* Flooding of the link-state advertisement (LSA) goes out all IS ports except those ports on which the LSA was received. The LSA includes the remaining lifetime and sequence number fields. These fields are used to help determine whether a received LSA is a duplicate, too old, or otherwise inappropriate. ISs send LSAs at regular intervals and when the following special events occur:

- When an IS discovers that its link to a neighbor is not available

- When an IS discovers a new neighbor

- When an IS discovers that the cost of a link to an existing neighbor has increased or decreased

The LSPs are then stored in the link-state database. Each IS can then calculate path information from its own perspective, building what is known as the *shortest path tree.* Example 11-7 illustrates the output of the **show isis database** command from router R4.

Example 11-7 *The* **show isis database** *Command Output from R4*

```
R4#show isis database
ISIS Level-1 Link State Database:
LSPID           LSP Seq Num  LSP Checksum  LSP Holdtime   ATT/P/OL
R7.00-00        0x0000008B   0x6843        55             0/0/0
R4.00-00      * 0x00000083   0x276E        77             0/0/0
R4.01-00      * 0x00000004   0x34E1        57             0/0/0
R3.00-00        0x00000086   0xF30E        84             0/0/0
ISIS Level-2 Link State Database:
LSPID           LSP Seq Num  LSP Checksum  LSP Holdtime   ATT/P/OL
R7.00-00        0x00000092   0x34B2        41             0/0/0
R4.00-00      * 0x0000008A   0x7A59        115            0/0/0
R4.01-00      * 0x00000004   0xC3DA        50             0/0/0
R3.00-00        0x0000008F   0x0766        112            0/0/0
```

Note the following items about the output from Example 11-7:

- You can divide the LSP-ID, R7.00-00, into three sections: R7, 00, and 00.

    — R7 is the system ID.

    — The first 00 is the nonzero value for the pseudonode. Notice that R4.01-00 is the pseudonode LSP.

    — The second 00 represents the fragment number. In this case, 00 indicates that all the data fits into a single LSP fragment, with no need to create more fragments. If all the information had not fit into the first LSP, IS-IS would have created more LSP fragments, such as 01, 02, and so on.

- The asterisk (*) indicates that the LSPs are being generated by R3. Also, because R4 is running IS-IS as a Level-1 and Level-2 router, it contains both a Level-1 and Level-2 database.

Use the **detail** keyword to obtain more specific LSP information. See Example 11-8.

Example 11-8 *The* **show isis database [lspid] detail** *Command Output from R4*

```
R3#show isis database R4.00-00 detail
ISIS Level-1 LSP R4.00-00
LSPID           LSP Seq Num  LSP Checksum  LSP Holdtime   ATT/P/OL
R4.00-00      * 0x00000093   0x077E        71             0/0/0
  Area Address: 49.0001
  NLPID:        0xCC
  Hostname: R3
  IP Address:   172.16.4.4
  Metric: 0          IP 172.16.4.4 255.255.255.255
  Metric: 10         IS R4.01
  Metric: 10         IS R3.00
```

continues

Example 11-8 *The* **show isis database [lspid] detail** *Command Output from R4 (Continued)*

```
ISIS Level-2 LSP R4.00-00
LSPID            LSP Seq Num  LSP Checksum  LSP Holdtime  ATT/P/OL
R4.00-00    * 0x0000009A    0x5A69         103            0/0/0
  Area Address: 49.0001
  NLPID:        0xCC
  Hostname: R4
  IP Address:   172.16.4.4
  Metric: 10        IS R4.01
  Metric: 10        IS R3.00
  Metric: 10        IP 172.16.7.7 255.255.255.255
  Metric: 10        IP 172.16.3.3 255.255.255.255
  Metric: 0         IP 172.16.4.4 255.255.255.255
```

Example 11-8 shows that the loopback address is advertised with a value of 0 because it is advertised with a **passive-interface** command under the router IS-IS process, and the loopback interface by itself is not enabled for IS-IS. All other IP prefixes have a value of 10, which is the default cost on the interfaces that run IS-IS.

The calculation against the database is done by running the shortest path first (SPF) algorithm, which is commonly known as the *Dijkstra algorithm*. The Dijkstra algorithm iterates on the length of a path, examining the LSAs of all ISs, working outward from the host IS. The end result of this computation is a connectivity tree that yields the shortest paths to each IS.

The IS-IS State Machine

The IS-IS state machine is responsible for the flow of information in the IS-IS architecture. The state machine is comprised of four processes: receive, update, decision, and forward. IS-IS also includes a Routing Information Base (RIB), which is composed of two databases, the link-state database and the forwarding database, and is essentially the routing table.

The receive process is responsible for receiving the LSAs and passing them onto the other three processes.

The following sections describe each process in more detail.

The Receive Process

The state machine is located at the input of the receive process. This process is the entry point for all datagrams including user data, error reports, and routing and control packets. The receive process then forwards these packets to the appropriate area. As you might expect, the user data packets and error report are passed on to the forward process, while datagrams that pertain to routing and control are directed to the update process.

The Update Process

The process that generates local link-state information, for distribution to neighboring nodes, falls under the update process. This process also receives, processes, and forwards similar information to and from neighboring ISs. The update process builds and manages the link-state database.

The Decision Process

The forwarding database is created by the decision process by running the SPF algorithm on the link-state database. If you are running redundancy, this process also computes the equal-cost paths to each destination in the form of an adjacency set for load balancing.

The Forward Process

Once the receive process forwards a data packet to the forward process, it uses the forwarding database to forward the packet toward its destination. The forward process also performs load sharing, redirection, and error report generation for nonroutable packets.

Pseudonodes

IS-IS has potential drawbacks when running it over a LAN. One of these drawbacks results from the fact that each router on the LAN needs to announce a link to every other router on the LAN. This could result in your IS-IS router having a table containing n*(n–1) links. Another potential drawback is the fact the each router on the LAN reports the same list of end systems (ESs) to each other, resulting in an enormous amount of duplication.

To combat these situations, IS-IS introduced a concept of virtual nodes, known as *pseudonodes (PSNs)*. A PSN is an IS on a link whose purpose is to reduce the number of full-mesh adjacencies required between nodes on a multiaccess link. This node is called the *Designated IS (DIS)*. All routers on the multiaccess link, including the one elected to be the DIS, form adjacencies with the PSN instead of forming n*(n–1)–order adjacencies with each other in a full mesh. Only the PSN LSP includes the list of ESs on the LAN, eliminating the potential duplication problems.

Figure 11-3 shows a logical view of a network, with the PSN identified.

The election process for the DIS is based on the interface priority; the default is 64. The node with the highest interface priority is elected the DIS. In the case of a tie in interface priorities, the router with the highest subnetwork point of attachment (SNPA) is selected. In IS-IS, the MAC addresses are used as SNPAs on LANs. On nonbroadcast networks such as Frame Relay, the SNPA is the local data-link connection identifier (DLCI). In the case of multipoint Frame Relay scenarios that have the DLCI value, the highest system ID is used as a tiebreaker, independent of area ID.

Figure 11-3 *The Pseudonode*

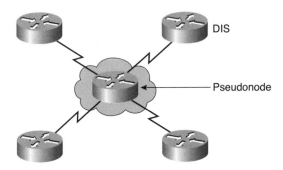

You are given the option of influencing the election by configuring the priority used by your router. You can also configure these priorities for Level-1 and Level-2 elections separately.

Use the following command to specify the value to use in the designated router election:

```
R3(config-if)#isis priority value {level-1 | level-2}
```

For your case study, you can set the priority of R4 so that it is always the DIS for both the Ethernet and the LAN. Example 11-9 shows you how to do this.

Example 11-9 *Setting the DIS Priority*

```
Configuration items for R4:
R4(config)#interface serial 0
R4(config-if)#isis priority 128 level-1
R4(config-if)#isis priority 128 level-2
R4(config-if)#exit
R4(config)#interface ethernet 0
R4(config-if)#isis priority 128 level-1
R4(config-if)#isis priority 128 level-2
```

When a router with a higher priority comes online, the DIS election is preemptive, meaning that a newly connected router with a higher interface priority than the current DIS immediately takes over and assumes the PSN functionality. One important restriction is that there is no dedicated interface priority value for making a router ineligible to be the DIS. Preemptive assumption of the DIS role is nondisruptive due to periodic synchronization on broadcast links.

The DIS's responsibilities include the following:

- Generating PSN link-state packets, for reporting links to all systems on the broadcast subnetwork

- Carrying out flooding over the LAN

A separate DIS is elected for Level-1 routing and for Level-2 routing.

IS-IS Addressing

CLNP uses a format of addressing, referred to as the network service access point (NSAP) address, to identify individual nodes on a network. Figure 11-4 illustrates the NSAP packet. The NSAP address has a maximum size of 160 bits (20 bytes) and is composed of the following major parts:

- **The initial domain part (IDP)**—Made of a 1-byte authority and format identifier (AFI) and a variable-length initial domain identifier (IDI)

- **The domain specific part (DSP)**—Composed of fields such as the area ID, system ID, and the N-selector

Figure 11-4 *The NSAP Packet*

The Simplified NSAP Format

The NSAP format was designed with a hierarchical addressing structure in mind. While the NSAP format contains multiple fields, only the following three main components are required:

- NSAP selector (NSEL)

- System ID

- Area address

The following sections describe each component in detail.

NSEL

The NSEL is known as the NSAP selector, but it is also referred to as the N-selector or the SEL. If you were to look as an NSAP frame, the NSEL is the last byte of the packet. The NSEL is used to identify a network service user, most often a transport entity. An NSAP with an NSEL value of 0 indicates that this is the network entity title (NET). The NET denotes that this is the network entity or the routing layer.

System ID

The system ID can be referred to as the SysID. The system ID is used as the system identifier of an IS in an area. The system ID can be of variable length, between 1 and 8 octets; however,

Cisco implements it as a fixed length in compliance with version 2.0 of U.S. Government OSI Profile (GOSIP).

Area Address

The area address is a variable-length field that is composed of high-order octets of the NSAP, excluding the system ID and NSEL fields. You use the area address to associate a single area within the routing domain. You can see the area address for the router by issuing the **show clns protocol** command.

Example 11-10 shows the output of the **show clns protocol** command from R1. R1 is configured with a manual area of 49.0001 with two loopback interfaces and a subinterface on Serial 0.

Example 11-10 *The* **show clns protocol** *Command Output from R1*

```
R1#show clns protocol
IS-IS Router: 234
  System Id: 0000.0000.0003.00   IS-Type: level-2
  Manual area address(es):
        49.0001
  Routing for area address(es):
        49.0001
  Interfaces supported by IS-IS:
        Loopback1 - IP
        Loopback0 - IP
        Serial0.1 - IP
  Redistribute:
    static (on by default)
  Distance for L2 CLNS routes: 110
  RRR level: none
  Generate narrow metrics: level-1-2
  Accept narrow metrics:   level-1-2
  Generate wide metrics:   none
  Accept wide metrics:     none
```

As you can see from the output in Example 11-10, R1 has a manual area assigned and is routing for this area.

Addressing Requirements

When designing an IS-IS addressing scheme, you must abide by the following requirements:

- All routers must use the same area address to be considered to be in the same area.

- An end system can be adjacent to a Level-1 router only if they both share a common area address.

- Each node in an area must have its own unique system ID.

- All Level-2 routers in a domain must have their own unique system ID.

- All systems in a given domain must have system IDs of the same length in their NSAP addresses.

- At a minimum, in a Cisco implementation, you must have at least 8 bytes to define the NSAP on a router: 1 byte for area, 6 bytes for system ID, and 1 byte for the N-selector field. The maximum size of an NSAP remains at 20 bytes.

- At least one NSAP is required per node.

- All NETs on the same router must have the same system ID.

Limiting LSP Flooding

As with any routing protocol, IS-IS can consume a large amount of your bandwidth under certain conditions. If you plan on implementing a network with a large amount of redundant links, flooding of LSPs can limit network scalability. You have the option of reducing LSP flooding in the following ways:

- **Blocking flooding on specific interfaces**—This method offers an advantage over using mesh groups because it is easier to configure and understand, and fewer LSPs are flooded. Blocking flooding on all links can give you the best scaling performance but often results in a less robust network structure.

- **Configuring mesh groups**—This method offers an advantage over full blocking in that mesh groups allow LSPs to be flooded over one hop to all your routers on the mesh, while full blocking allows only some of your routers to receive LSPs over multiple hops. This delay in flooding can have an impact on your convergence times, but the delay is negligible compared to the overall convergence times that you experience.

The following sections describe both of these options in detail.

Blocking Flooding on Specific Interfaces

You can enable the complete blocking of all new LSPs that would normally be flooded out an interface. You should not implement this on too many interfaces because if all nonblocking links fail, your routers cannot synchronize their link-state databases, even if you still have connectivity to the rest of the network. If your link-state database becomes unsynchronized, you will most likely have routing loops to contend with.

If you are implementing blocking on a point-to-point link, you have the option of configuring the complete sequence number PDU (CSNP) data unit interval. Using the **isis csnp-interval** command controls the sending of CSNPs, by the designated router, that are used to maintain synchronization of your link-state databases. You should only consider using CSNP for this purpose as a last resort.

Configuring Mesh Groups

You can help to limit the redundant flooding that occurs in your network by configuring a mesh group, which is a set of interfaces on a router. This means that all the routers that are reachable over one of the interfaces in a particular mesh group are assumed to be densely connected, that is, IS-IS can assume that many links can fail without isolating one or more routers from the network.

This configuration alters the normal operation of IS-IS. Because a new LSP is received on an interface that is part of the mesh group, it is not flooded out other interfaces that are part of the same mesh group. This means that you must have a full mesh of links between the routers in a mesh group. If you fail to implement this mesh, and one or more links in the full mesh goes down, the full mesh is broken, and some routers might miss new LSPs, even though there is connectivity to the rest of the network. Use care to select alternative paths over which to flood in case interfaces in the mesh group go down.

To minimize the possibility of incomplete flooding, you should allow unrestricted flooding over at least a minimal set of links in the mesh. You should ideally select enough links to ensure that LSP flooding is not detrimental to your scaling plans, but you should have enough links so that under most failure scenarios, no router is logically disconnected from the rest of the network.

Selecting the smallest set of logical links that covers all physical paths can result in very low flooding of LSAs, but this could result in less robustness in your network design.

For a simple exercise, you can configure R1 with two loopback interfaces and add them to the IS-IS process. Once you have this completed, you can configure a mesh group and add the loopback interfaces to a mesh group. Example 11-11 illustrates the configuration items on R1.

Example 11-11 *Mesh Group Configuration*

```
Configuration Changes on R1:
R1(config)#interface Loopback0
R1(config-if)#ip address 133.100.110.1 255.255.255.240
R1(config-if)#ip router isis 234
R1(config-if)#isis mesh-group blocked
R1(config-if)#exit
R1(config)#interface Loopback1
R1(config-if)#ip address 133.100.210.1 255.255.255.240
R1(config-if)#ip router isis 234
R1(config-if)#isis mesh-group blocked
```

Generating a Default Route

Just like any routing protocol that you are likely to deal with, IS-IS provides a means for you to introduce a default route into the IS-IS routing domain. Remember though, whenever you specifically configure redistribution of routes into an IS-IS routing domain, the Cisco IOS Software does not, by default, redistribute the default route into your IS-IS routing domain.

Optionally, you can use a route map to conditionally advertise the default route, depending on the existence of another route in the routing table of the router.

To configure a default route, use the following command:

```
R1(config-router)#default-information originate [route-map map-name]
```

In the next exercise, you configure R1 to originate a default route to 3.3.3.3. You configure R3 with a loopback interface with the 3.3.3.3 address and configure IS-IS to talk to R1. Example 11-12 shows you the relevant configuration items that are needed for R1 to generate a default route pointing to R3.

Example 11-12 *Default Router Configuration*

```
Configuration Changes on Router R1:
R1(config)#router isis 234
R1(config-router)#default-information originate
R1(config)#exit
R1(config)#ip route 0.0.0.0 0.0.0.0 3.3.3.3

R1#show ip route
Codes: C - connected, S - static, I - IGRP, R - RIP, M - mobile, B - BGP
       D - EIGRP, EX - EIGRP external, O - OSPF, IA - OSPF inter area
       N1 - OSPF NSSA external type 1, N2 - OSPF NSSA external type 2
       E1 - OSPF external type 1, E2 - OSPF external type 2, E - EGP
       i - IS-IS, L1 - IS-IS level-1, L2 - IS-IS level-2, ia - IS-IS inter area
       * - candidate default, U - per-user static route, o - ODR
       P - periodic downloaded static route

Gateway of last resort is 3.3.3.3 to network 0.0.0.0

     1.0.0.0/24 is subnetted, 1 subnets
C       1.1.1.0 is directly connected, Loopback2
     3.0.0.0/8 is variably subnetted, 1 subnets, 1 masks
i L2    3.3.3.0/24 [115/20] via 150.100.31.3, Serial0.1
     133.100.0.0/28 is subnetted, 4 subnets
C       133.100.200.0 is directly connected, Loopback1
C       133.100.100.0 is directly connected, Loopback0
C    192.168.1.0/24 is directly connected, Ethernet0
     150.100.0.0/16 is variably subnetted, 1 subnets, 1 masks
C       150.100.31.0/28 is directly connected, Serial0.1
S*   0.0.0.0/0 [1/0] via 3.3.3.3
```

Route Redistribution

Most of the time, you are not building your network from the ground up, or you are absorbing a network from a purchased company into yours, so you must face redistributing one routing protocol into another. Your routers support this sharing of routing information, known as *route redistribution,* between multiple routing protocols and even between multiple instances of the same routing protocol.

IS-IS supports enhanced route redistribution to provide you with improved administrative control over methods by which routing information moves between your routing domains. One of the most important features that you work with is the route map. A *route map* is a set of instructions that you define to tell the router how routing information is to be redistributed between two routing protocols or between two instances of the same routing protocol.

Route maps are based on a user-defined, ordered list of match conditions. The route map then steps through each defined item in the list to see if any item matches the route being considered for redistribution. If it finds a match, whatever action you defined for the match is performed against the route. You are given the option to permit the route, deny the route, or attach additional information, called *route tags,* to the route. You can also mandate the use of certain route metrics or route types and even modify the route's destination in outgoing advertisements. You can also use the same route map for different routing protocols.

Your next configuration task is to redistribute the default route that you generated in the last example configuration using a route map if the route to 3.3.3.3 is in router R1's routing table.

In this exercise, you configure R1 to redistribute the default route that you configured in your last exercise to R10. Example 11-13 illustrates the relevant configuration items that are necessary for R1 to redistribute the default route.

Example 11-13   *Redistributing a Default Route*

```
Configuration Changes on Router R1:
R1(config)#router isis 234
R1(config-router)#default-information originate route-map isis-default
R1(config)#exit
R1(config)#access-list 1 permit 3.3.3.3 0.0.0.0
R1(config)#route-map isis-default permit 10
R1(config-route-map)#match ip address 1
R1(config-route-map)#set metric 5
R1(config-route-map)#set metric-type type-2
```

Setting IS-IS Optional Parameters

IS-IS offers many parameters that you can customize to fit your particular networking needs. These parameters include the following:

- Setting the advertised hello interval to refine the time between hellos

- Setting the advertised CSNP interval to determine when database synchronization takes place

- Setting the retransmission interval in the case of lost LSPs

- Setting the LSP transmission interval to adjust the time between successive LSP transmissions

Each of these options is reviewed in greater detail in the following sections.

Setting the Advertised Hello Interval

If the default hello time needs to be adjusted because your network is stable (not a likely scenario) or you have slow links (a more likely scenario), you have the option to specify the length of time (in seconds) between hello packets that are sent on the interface.

You can specify the length of time between hello packets for the specified interface by using the following command:

```
R1(config-if)#isis hello-interval seconds {level-1 | level-2}
```

You are allowed to configure the hello interval independently for Level-1 and Level-2, except when you are using serial point-to-point interfaces. (Because only a single type of hello packet is sent on serial links, it is independent of Level-1 or Level-2.)

Setting the Advertised CSNP Interval

In IS-IS, the CSNPs are sent by the designated router to maintain synchronization of the databases used by the routers. You can configure the IS-IS CSNP interval on a per-interface basis.

You can configure the CSNP interval for a specified interface by using the following command:

```
R1(config-if)#isis csnp-interval seconds {level-1 | level-2}
```

The one drawback to this command is that it does nothing when applied to serial point-to-point interfaces; it is only in effect if the WAN connection is seen as a multiaccess meshed network.

Setting the Retransmission Interval

You are given the option of tuning the number of seconds between retransmission of IS-IS link-state packets (LSPs) for point-to-point links. To configure this setting, use the following command:

```
R1(config-if)#isis retransmit-interval seconds
```

The value that you specify needs to be an integer greater than the expected round-trip delay between any two routers on the attached network.

Setting the LSP Transmission Interval

You can change the delay between successive IS-IS LSP transmissions by using the following command:

```
R1(config-if)#isis lsp-interval milliseconds
```

Configuring IS-IS Authentication

IS-IS gives you three options for authentication of LSPs—authentication of a specified interface or link, of an area, or of a domain—and can be used in combinations of the three. Routers that want to become neighbors must exchange the same password for the level of authentication that is configured on the router. Currently, IS-IS supports only a simple password mechanism that does not guarantee against hostile attacks. However, authentication functions are extensible, so a stronger cryptographically based security scheme can be added in the future.

The authentication information is encoded as a Type Length Value (TLV) triple in the LSP. The type of the authentication TLV is 10, the length of the TLV is variable, and the value of the TLV depends on the authentication type that you select.

Case Study 11-2: IS-IS Authentication

Case Study 11-2 is a collection of exercises in which you build all three levels of authentication into a topology that consists of four routers. You begin by building interface authentication between routers R1 and R8 on the topology that is illustrated in Figure 11-5.

Figure 11-5 *Interface Authentication Topology 1*

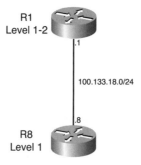

You then configure area authentication and domain authentication on the topology that is illustrated in Figure 11-6. You finish the case study by combining all the authentications on the same topology, as illustrated in Figure 11-6.

Interface Authentication

When you configure IS-IS authentication on an interface level, you are given the option of enabling the password support for Level-1, Level-2, or both Level-1/Level-2 routing. If you do not specify a level, Level-1 is selected as the default authentication level. Use the following command to enable interface authentication:

```
R1(config-if)#isis password password level
```

Figure 11-6 *Interface Authentication Topology 2*

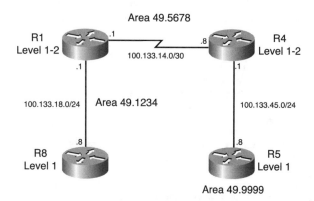

Your first step in this case study is to configure routers R1 and R8 to use interface authentication between them. You use a password of isis-ia for this authentication and define your IS-IS to run under the tag of ccie_lab. Example 11-14 illustrates a solution to this step.

Example 11-14 *Interface Authentication Between R1 and R8*

```
Configuration items for R1:
R1(config)#interface ethernet 0
R1(config-if)#ip address 100.133.18.1 255.255.255.0
R1(config-if)#ip router isis ccie_lab
R1(config-if)#isis password isis-ia level-1
R1(config-if)#isis password isis-ia level-2
R1(config-if)#exit
R1(config)#router isis ccie_lab
R1(config-if)#net 49.0000.0000.0000.0001.00

Configuration items for R8:
R1(config)#interface ethernet 0
R1(config-if)#ip address 100.133.18.8 255.255.255.0
R1(config-if)#ip router isis ccie_lab
R1(config-if)#isis password isis-ia level-1
R1(config-if)#isis password isis-ia level-2
R1(config-if)#exit
R1(config)#router isis ccie_lab
R1(config-if)#net 49.0000.0000.0000.0008.00
```

Area Authentication

When you configure IS-IS using area authentication, all the routers within that area must have the same password configured on them. Use the following command to enable area authentication:

```
R1(config-router)#area-password password
```

The next step in your case study is to configure area authentication between all the routers in the area. Use a password of isis-aa for your area authentication and define your IS-IS to run under the tag of ccie_lab. Example 11-15 illustrates a solution to this step.

Example 11-15 *Area Authentication*

```
Configuration items for R1:
R1(config)#interface ethernet 0
R1(config-if)#ip address 100.133.18.1 255.255.255.0
R1(config-if)#ip router isis ccie_lab
R1(config-if)#exit
R1(config)#interface serial 0
R1(config-if)#ip address 100.133.14.1 255.255.255.252
R1(config-if)#ip router isis ccie_lab
R1(config-if)#exit
R1(config)#router isis ccie_lab
R1(config-if)#net 49.0000.0000.0000.0001.00
R1(config-if)#area password isis-aa

Configuration items for R4:
R4(config)#interface ethernet 0
R4(config-if)#ip address 100.133.45.4 255.255.255.0
R4(config-if)#ip router isis ccie_lab
R4(config-if)#exit
R4(config)#interface serial 0
R4(config-if)#ip address 100.133.14.2 255.255.255.252
R4(config-if)#ip router isis ccie_lab
R4(config-if)#exit
R4(config)#router isis ccie_lab
R4(config-if)#net 49.0000.0000.0000.0005.00
R4(config-if)#area password isis-aa

Configuration items for R5:
R5(config)#interface ethernet 0
R5(config-if)#ip address 100.133.45.5 255.255.255.0
R5(config-if)#ip router isis ccie_lab
R5(config-if)#exit
R5(config)#router isis ccie_lab
R5(config-if)#net 49.0000.0000.0000.0005.00
R5(config-if)#area password isis-aa

Configuration items for R8:
R8(config)#interface ethernet 0
R8(config-if)#ip address 100.133.18.8 255.255.255.0
R8(config-if)#ip router isis ccie_lab
R8(config-if)#exit
R8(config)#router isis ccie_lab
R8(config-if)#net 49.0000.0000.0000.0008.00
R8(config-if)#area password isis-aa
```

Domain Authentication

When you configure IS-IS using domain authentication, all the routers within that domain must have the same password configured on them. Use the following command to enable area authentication:

```
R1(config-router)#domain-password password
```

The next task in your case study is to create three separate IS-IS domains and to configure domain authentication between them. Routers R1 and R8 are in the IS-IS area 49.1234, R4 is in the IS-IS area 49.5678, and R5 is in the IS-IS area 49.9999. You use the domain password of isis-da. Example 11-16 shows one solution to this scenario.

Example 11-16 *Domain Authentication*

```
Configuration items for R1:
R1(config)#interface ethernet 0
R1(config-if)#ip address 100.133.18.1 255.255.255.0
R1(config-if)#ip router isis ccie_lab
R1(config-if)#exit
R1(config)#interface serial 0
R1(config-if)#ip address 100.133.14.1 255.255.255.252
R1(config-if)#ip router isis ccie_lab
R1(config-if)#exit
R1(config)#router isis ccie_lab
R1(config-if)#net 49.1234.0000.0000.0001.00
R1(config-if)#domain password isis-da

Configuration items for R4:
R4(config)#interface ethernet 0
R4(config-if)#ip address 100.133.45.4 255.255.255.0
R4(config-if)#ip router isis ccie_lab
R4(config-if)#exit
R4(config)#interface serial 0
R4(config-if)#ip address 100.133.14.2 255.255.255.252
R4(config-if)#ip router isis ccie_lab
R4(config-if)#exit
R4(config)#router isis ccie_lab
R4(config-if)#net 49.5678.0000.0000.0005.00
R4(config-if)#domain password isis-da

Configuration items for R5:
R5(config)#interface ethernet 0
R5(config-if)#ip address 100.133.45.5 255.255.255.0
R5(config-if)#ip router isis ccie_lab
R5(config-if)#exit
R5(config)#router isis ccie_lab
R5(config-if)#net 49.9999.0000.0000.0005.00
R5(config-if)#domain password isis-da

Configuration items for R8:
R8(config)#interface ethernet 0
```

continues

Example 11-16 *Domain Authentication (Continued)*

```
R8(config-if)#ip address 100.133.18.8 255.255.255.0
R8(config-if)#ip router isis ccie_lab
R8(config-if)#exit
R8(config)#router isis ccie_lab
R8(config-if)#net 49.1234.0000.0000.0008.00
R8(config-if)#domain password isis-da
```

Combining Domain, Area, and Interface Authentication

You are also given the option of enabling any combinations of all three authentication types in your IS-IS environment. If you decide to do this, you must follow the rules for each of the three authentication types.

Your last task in the configuration of your case study is to combine all three types of authentication into your topology. R1 and R2 are in the same area and are configured with the area password of isis-aa. All routers are in the same domain and share the domain-level password of isis-da. R1 and R4 have an interface configuration for the Serial link between them with a password of isis-ia for Level-2. Example 11-17 shows one solution to this scenario.

Example 11-17 *Domain Authentication*

```
Configuration items for R1:
R1(config)#interface ethernet 0
R1(config-if)#ip address 100.133.18.1 255.255.255.0
R1(config-if)#ip router isis ccie_lab
R1(config-if)#exit
R1(config)#interface serial 0
R1(config-if)#ip address 100.133.14.1 255.255.255.252
R1(config-if)#ip router isis ccie_lab
R1(config-if)#isis password isis-ia level-2
R1(config-if)#exit
R1(config)#router isis ccie_lab
R1(config-if)#net 49.1234.0000.0000.0001.00
R1(config-if)#domain password isis-da
R1(config-if)#area password isis-aa

Configuration items for R4:
R4(config)#interface ethernet 0
R4(config-if)#ip address 100.133.45.4 255.255.255.0
R4(config-if)#ip router isis ccie_lab
R4(config-if)#exit
R4(config)#interface serial 0
R4(config-if)#ip address 100.133.14.2 255.255.255.252
R4(config-if)#ip router isis ccie_lab
R4(config-if)#isis password isis-ia level-2
R4(config-if)#exit
R4(config)#router isis ccie_lab
R4(config-if)#net 49.5678.0000.0000.0005.00
```

Example 11-17 *Domain Authentication (Continued)*

```
R4(config-if)#domain password isis-da
R4(config-if)#area password isis-aa

Configuration items for R5:
R5(config)#interface ethernet 0
R5(config-if)#ip address 100.133.45.5 255.255.255.0
R5(config-if)#ip router isis ccie_lab
R5(config-if)#exit
R5(config)#router isis ccie_lab
R5(config-if)#net 49.9999.0000.0000.0005.00
R5(config-if)#domain password isis-da
R5(config-if)#area password isis-aa

Configuration items for R8:
R8(config)#interface ethernet 0
R8(config-if)#ip address 100.133.18.8 255.255.255.0
R8(config-if)#ip router isis ccie_lab
R8(config-if)#exit
R8(config)#router isis ccie_lab
R8(config-if)#net 49.1234.0000.0000.0008.00
R8(config-if)#domain password isis-da
R8(config-if)#area password isis-aa
```

Authentication Problems

Sometimes when you are using IS-IS authentication in your network, you run across links that do not appear to work correctly. One possible solution to this problem is to examine the output of a **show clns neighbor** command, from one router's perspective, which can show the adjacency to be in the INIT state with type IS-IS while the other router has a full ES-IS adjacency.

When you configure domain authentication, your router rejects the LSPs from routers that do not have the same domain authentication configured. However, routers that do not have authentication configured can accept the LSPs from the routers that have authentication configured. You encounter the same scenario when you are using area authentication. Because only routers configured for domain or area authentication reject LSPs from routers that do not have (the same) authentication configured, these routers can have differing views of the network topology because their link-state databases are not in sync.

One way you can tell that IS-IS authentication is working is to examine the output from the **show clns neighbor** detail command. The protocol field shows up as ES-IS instead of IS-IS if authentication is not working.

Using show and debug Commands

IS-IS has a wide selection of **show** and **debug** commands that are available for monitoring and troubleshooting purposes. Because the display of **show** commands can give you a lot of information, IS-IS includes a useful command to make these displays easier to read when your IS-IS is running in multi-area mode. Use the following command to enable this feature:

```
R1(config)#isis display delimiter [return cnt | char cnt]
```

For example, the following command causes information about individual areas to be separated by 14 dashes (-) in the display:

```
R1#isis display delimiter - 14
```

Monitoring IS-IS

You already covered most of the commands that are available for monitoring the tables and databases. For your review, the following is a summary of the available commands:

```
R1#show isis database [level-1] [level-2] [l1] [l2] [detail] [lspid]
R1#show isis area-tag route
R1#show isis spf-log
R1#show isis area-tag topology
```

If you need to clear the state of your IS-IS adjacency, use the following command:

```
R1#clear isis *
```

Example 11-18 gives you a typical output that you should receive when entering the **clear isis *** command on router R1.

Example 11-18 *The* **clear isis *** *Command Output from R1*

```
R1#clear isis *
03:48:27: %CLNS-5-ADJCLEAR: ISIS: All adjacencies cleared
03:48:30: %CLNS-5-ADJCHANGE: ISIS: Adjacency to R10 (Ethernet0) Up, new adjacency
03:48:35: %CLNS-5-ADJCHANGE: ISIS: Adjacency to R3 (Serial0.1) Up, new adjacency
```

As you can see from this output, the adjacency to routers R3 and R10 was cleared, and then each router re-formed its adjacency with router R1.

Debugging IS-IS

In some cases, you must debug IS-IS to determine if your configurations are correct.

When you are examining problems related to building adjacencies, IS-IS offers you the following command:

```
R1#debug isis adj-packets
```

Example 11-19 shows the output when running the **debug** command on router R1.

Example 11-19 *The* **debug isis adj-packets** *Command Output for R1*

```
R1#debug isis adj-packets
03:46:35: ISIS-Adj: Sending L1 LAN IIH on Ethernet0, length 1497
03:46:35: ISIS-Adj: Sending L2 LAN IIH on Loopback0, length 1514
03:46:36: ISIS-Adj: Rec serial IIH from DLCI 101 (Serial0.1), cir type L2, cir i
d 00, length 1499
03:46:36: ISIS-Adj: rcvd state UP, old state UP, new state UP
03:46:36: ISIS-Adj: Action = ACCEPT
```

You can see from this output that R1 is receiving and sending IIHs out all interfaces that IS-IS is currently running over.

Excessive SPF calculations can be a sign that a problem exists with your IS-IS environment. IS-IS offers you the following **debug** command, which can show you the steps that SPF goes through during its calculations:

```
R1#debug isis spf-events
```

Example 11-20 illustrates the output from router R1 after enabling the **debug isis spf-events** command.

Example 11-20 *The* **debug isis spf-events** *Command Output from Router R1*

```
R1#debug isis spf-events
IS-IS SPF events debugging is on
R1#
03:47:36: ISIS-Spf:  Compute L2 SPT
03:47:36: ISIS-Spf: Move 0000.0000.0001.00-00 to PATHS, metric 0
03:47:36: ISIS-Spf: Aging L1 LSP 1 (0000.0000.0001.00-00), version 30
03:47:36: ISIS-Spf: Deleted NDB
03:47:41: ISIS-Spf:  Compute L1 SPT
03:47:41: ISIS-Spf: Move 0000.0000.0001.00-00 to PATHS, metric 0
03:47:41: ISIS-Spf: Add 0000.0000.0001.01-00 to TENT, metric 10
03:47:41: ISIS-Spf: considering adj to 0000.0000.0010 (Ethernet0) metric 10, lev
el 1, circuit 1, adj 1
03:47:41: ISIS-Spf:    (accepted)
03:47:41: ISIS-Spf: Add 0000.0000.0010.00-00 to TENT, metric 10
03:47:41: ISIS-Spf:    Next hop 0000.0000.0010 (Ethernet0)
03:47:41: ISIS-Spf: Move 0000.0000.0010.00-00 to PATHS, metric 10
03:47:41: ISIS-Spf: Add 192.168.1.0/255.255.255.0 to IP RIB, metric 20
03:47:41: ISIS-Spf: Next hop 0000.0000.0010/192.168.1.110 (Ethernet0) (rejected)
03:47:41: ISIS-Spf: Redundant IP route 133.100.110.0/255.255.255.240, metric 20,
 not added
03:47:41: ISIS-Spf: Redundant IP route 133.100.210.0/255.255.255.240, metric 20,
 not added
```

By examining the output from the **debug isis spf-events** command, you can determine what routes IS-IS is installing into the routing table and what neighbors it is accepting routes from.

Summary

In this chapter, you reviewed the configuration options that are available to you with the IS-IS routing protocol. You covered three options that are available for running IS-IS in your environment: CLNS only, IP only, and CLNS with IP. You created a lab environment that went from configuring simple IS-IS to a lab that included multiple IS-IS areas and configuration of optional parameters. You concluded the chapter by looking at the available **show** and **debug** commands.

Review Questions

1   What is IS-IS?

2   What is Dual IS-IS?

3   What is the difference between a NET and an NSAP?

4   Which of the following packets are used in IS-IS?

   A. IIHs—IS-to-IS hellos

   B. EIHs—ES-to-IS hellos

   C. LSPs—link-state packets

   D. FSNPs—fragmented sequence number packets

   E. CSNPs—complete sequence number packets

   F. PSNPs—partial sequence number packets

5   What algorithm does IS-IS use to determine "best" routes?

6   Which of the following are the three modes of operation that Integrated IS-IS can run in?

   A. CLNS only

   B. OSI only

   C. IP only

   D. Hybrid—CLNS with IP

   E. IPX only

7   How can I tell who is acting as the PSN in a multiaccess network?

8   How many Level-2 IS-IS areas can I configure on a single router?

FAQs

Q — *When would you implement multiple NETs on a box?*

A — Multiple NETs can be used when you are in the process of merging or splitting areas. You should only use multiple NETs on a temporary basis.

Q — *If I implement Dual IS-IS for IP only, do I still need to configure CLNS?*

A — No, but you must still configure an NSAP for the router to determine its area.

Q — *Can I use IS-IS for load balancing?*

A — Yes, you can use IS-IS to support equal-cost load balancing. IP supports up to 6 equal cost paths, with 4 being the default. CLNS only supports a maximum of 4 equal-cost paths.

Q — *What is the process for electing the DIS?*

A — The DIS election is based on the interface priority. The default priority is 64. In the case of a tie, the IS with the higher SNAP (MAC address) is elected.

Q — *Can I clear the IS-IS adjacency with a neighbor without affecting all the other adjacencies?*

A — Yes, by using the clear isis command in privileged mode, you can clear individual adjacencies or an adjacency that you specify.

Q — *Can I specify multiple areas in IS-IS like I can in OSPF?*

A — No, IS-IS uses only two levels: Level-1 for intra-area routing and Level-2 for inter-area routing.

This chapter covers the following topics:

- Understanding BGP concepts
- Configuring BGP

CHAPTER 12

BGP

This chapter is dedicated to the Border Gateway Protocol (BGP) portion of the CCIE Security lab exam and introduces concepts necessary to understand and implement BGP. You will concentrate on BGP's fundamental setup and security-related features.

Understanding BGP Concepts

BGP currently is in its fourth version, introduced in 1993 and defined in RFC 1771, *Border Gateway Protocol 4 (BGP4)*. BGP is robust and incredibly scalable, with new features constantly being developed and added. It is generally viewed as an exterior routing protocol, and as such it supports loop-free interdomain routing between autonomous systems.

Autonomous Systems

As far as BGP is concerned, an *autonomous system* is a group of networks under a single technical administration, which implies using the same routing protocols and the same routing policy. There can be multiple Interior Gateway Protocols (IGPs) for internal autonomous system routing and an Exterior Gateway Protocol (EGP), such as BGP, for routing outside the autonomous system.

The ARIN assigns public numbers to autonomous systems that need to appear unique on the Internet. These numbers are in the form of 2 bytes and range from 1 to 65536. Also, some private autonomous system numbers (64512 to 65535) have been allocated for use in private networks. If private autonomous system numbers are used, they need to be translated into globally unique numbers for Internet connectivity.

An autonomous system may fall into three general categories:

- **Single-homed or stub**—Connects to a single Internet service provider (ISP). In this case, BGP is mostly used for future growth; otherwise, static routes are sufficient.

- **Multihomed**—Connects to two or more ISPs and requires the use of BGP for full redundancy. Users in a multihomed network may reach other destinations on the Internet via either an ISP through basic load sharing of traffic or through a policy that determines the best route to any particular destination. When one ISP connection fails, the other maintains full availability.

- **Transit**—Is itself an ISP. It provides connectivity between other autonomous systems, both its customers and other ISPs, by allowing the BGP updates to flow from customers to the rest of the Internet and back.

BGP Functionality

BGP is an enhanced distance vector protocol. It carries a list of the BGP autonomous system numbers as an indication of the path to a destination network. Each BGP speaker adds its own autonomous system to the list and then forwards it to a peer. This process is done for loop detection purposes: If the same autonomous system number appears more than once in a path, a loop exists. Routing policies can be used based on the autonomous system numbers in the path.

BGP bases its forwarding decisions on IP destination address only. The source IP address does not play a role in this. For instance, packets created in another autonomous system that use the local autonomous system as a transit and packets created inside the local autonomous system are treated equally and use the same next hop as long as they are destined for the same network. Therefore, the shortest path does not necessarily mean the best path. Although a BGP router can maintain multiple paths to a particular destination, only the best path is forwarded. When it comes to BGP, the best path involves a complex metric consisting of various attributes and is determined through a policy (you'll read more about that in the "Configuring BGP" section).

Another important BGP fact is that it uses TCP as its transport protocol (port 179). TCP means reliable transport. When a router running BGP sends an update, it is always acknowledged. This eliminates the need for periodic updates; only information about a change is transmitted. This makes BGP highly scalable and capable of handling colossal-sized networks, such as the Internet. The drawback is the extra load on the CPU of the BGP-speaking routers and a slight increase in network traffic, so convergence is somewhat an issue. However, scalability is more important to BGP functionality, and it takes precedence over convergence.

EBGP and IBGP

Up to this point in the chapter, the BGP discussion has revolved around exterior BGP (EBGP), which is used between different autonomous systems. EBGP is the "classic" BGP application and the reason BGP was created in the first place. However, the need to transmit attributes to implement a routing policy inside the autonomous system as well as its scalable nature made BGP an attractive choice for an interior protocol. This type of BGP is called IBGP, or internal BGP.

To create full reachability within an autonomous system, several techniques can be used. IBGP peering is a valid solution. Also, redistributing IGP into IBGP is a common choice. There is, of course, much more to the issue of IBGP and its interconnectivity with EBGP. You will be presented with the necessary information in Case Study 12-2.

BGP Updates

BGP routers exchange their full BGP routing tables when the session is first established. As mentioned, the use of reliable TCP ensures that the sender is aware of the receiver actually receiving and transmitting the information. Periodic updates are, therefore, unnecessary. After the initialization, only incremental updates are sent, reflecting a change in the network topology or a routing policy.

BGP maintains a BGP table version number. This number should be the same for all the BGP peers. Whenever a new update is received, the version number is revised.

When BGP is in idle state, a peer can go down without TCP's noticing because such an event is detected only when traffic needs to be passed through that peer. To resolve this, BGP periodically sends small keepalive packets to ensure that the connection exists between the BGP peers. You can manipulate a keepalive period to suit your particular topology. Keepalive packets are also transmitted reliably. As a result, the peer router must reply with its own keepalive packet.

Configuring BGP

Figure 12-1 represents the complete topology used for BGP in this chapter. This topology will be further broken down to better illustrate each case study. As you go along, you will notice how section by section the case studies cover all nine routers and both PIX Firewalls.

Figure 12-1 *BGP Topology*

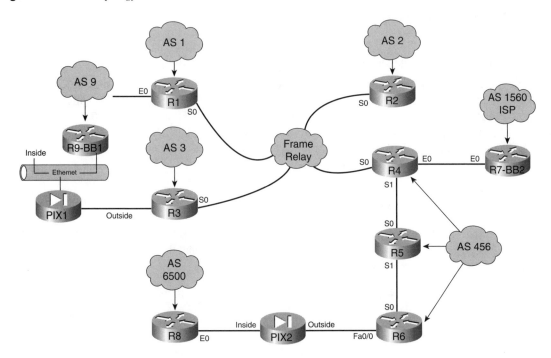

Case Study 12-1: Single-Homed Autonomous System Setup

The topology for this case study is shown in Figure 12-2. The entire configuration in this section is applied to two routers: R4 in autonomous system 456, and R7, the second backbone router, in autonomous system 1560. AS 456 has only one connection to an ISP, so it acts as a single-homed autonomous system. Also, because both routers are in different autonomous systems, the type of BGP used in this section is EBGP.

Figure 12-2   *Single-Homed Autonomous System Topology*

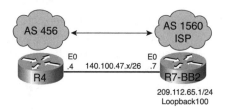

To successfully complete this case study, follow these steps:

Step 1   Enable the BGP process

Step 2   Specify BGP neighbors

Step 3   Advertise networks

Step 4   Verify your configuration

Step 1: Enabling the BGP Process

The first step needed to enable BGP is to start a BGP routing process on the participating routers. In the given scenario, you have two routers—R7-BB2 and R4—to configure to talk BGP. The routers are in different autonomous systems, AS 456 and AS 1560. You begin by defining the router process along with the autonomous system number that the routers are a part of. Remember that a router can have only one BGP process, and it should be assigned the local autonomous system number.

To enable BGP on a router, use the following command:

```
R4(config)#router bgp autonomous-system
```

Example 12-1 shows the **router bgp** command issued on R4 and R7. The highlighted lines indicate that R4 is running BGP and belongs to AS 456 and that R7-BB2 is also running BGP and belongs to AS 1560.

Example 12-1 *Enabling BGP on Routers*

```
R4#show run
hostname R4
!
! Output omitted for brevity
!
interface Loopback4
ip address 4.4.4.4 255.255.255.0
!
interface Ethernet0
ip address 140.100.47.4 255.255.255.192
!
router bgp 456
R7#show run
hostname R7
!
interface Loopback1
 ip address 7.1.1.7 255.255.255.0
!
interface Loopback2
 ip address 17.1.1.7 255.255.255.0
!
interface Loopback3
 ip address 27.1.1.7 255.255.255.0
!
interface Loopback4
 ip address 37.1.1.7 255.255.255.0
!
interface Loopback100
 ip address 209.112.65.1 255.255.255.0
!
interface Loopback101
 ip address 209.112.66.1 255.255.255.0
!
interface Loopback102
 ip address 209.112.67.1 255.255.255.0
!
interface Loopback103
 ip address 209.112.68.1 255.255.255.0
!
interface Loopback104
 ip address 209.112.69.1 255.255.255.0
!
interface Loopback105
 ip address 209.112.70.1 255.255.255.0
!
interface Loopback200
 ip address 156.46.1.1 255.255.255.0
!
```

continues

Example 12-1 *Enabling BGP on Routers (Continued)*

```
interface Loopback201
 ip address 156.46.2.1 255.255.255.0
!
interface Loopback202
 ip address 156.46.3.1 255.255.255.0
!
interface Loopback203
 ip address 156.46.4.1 255.255.255.0
!
interface Loopback204
 ip address 156.46.100.1 255.255.252.0
!
interface Loopback444
 ip address 140.100.9.1 255.255.255.224
!
interface Loopback777
 ip address 7.7.7.7 255.255.255.0
!
interface Ethernet0
 ip address 140.100.47.7 255.255.255.192
!
interface Serial0
 ip address 140.100.48.1 255.255.255.0
 no keepalive!
!
router bgp 1560
```

The next section explains how to configure a valid BGP peering.

Step 2: Specifying BGP Neighbors

This step defines BGP neighbors. In other words, this process indicates to R4 and R7-BB2 that they should be communicating with each other through BGP.

BGP peers or neighbors are defined as two BGP routers that have formed a TCP connection. The TCP session is opened from one router to the other. If R4 is trying to open a session with R7-BB2, it must have knowledge of the IP address to which it can direct its attempts. In turn, R7-BB2 needs to verify the source address of the TCP SYN packet from R4 against the list of IP addresses that it itself can open a connection with. So, for a TCP session to be established between the two routers, they need to be aware of one another.

BGP differs from other routing protocols because it can't auto-detect its neighbors. Neighbors have to be manually configured. Otherwise, the connection is not opened.

The command syntax for adding a neighbor is as follows:

```
R4(config-router)#neighbor ip-address remote-as number
```

The **remote-as** *number* argument indicates to which autonomous system the specified neighbor belongs. As shown in Example 12-2, both routers have neighbor statements pointing to one another. To peer with R7, R4 associates R7's E0 IP address of 140.100.47.7 with AS 1560, of which R7 is a member.

Example 12-2 *BGP Peer Configuration*

```
R4#show run
hostname R4
!
! Output omitted for brevity
!
router bgp 456
bgp router-id 4.4.4.4
bgp log-neighbor-changes
neighbor 140.100.47.7 remote-as 1560
neighbor 140.100.47.7 description R7-BB2

R7#show run
hostname r7
!
! Output omitted for brevity
!
router bgp 1560
bgp router-id 7.7.7.7
bgp log-neighbor-changes
neighbor 140.100.47.4 remote-as 456
neighbor 140.100.47.4 description R4
```

A number of optional commands can be associated with a neighbor. After the **neighbor** command has been set, you can input these commands. In Example 12-2 the description of R7 and R4 has been added to their neighbor configuration. The syntax for the **description** command is as follows:

```
R4(config-router)#neighbor [ip-address | peer-group-name] description text
```

Another useful command you might have noticed in Example 12-2 is

```
R4(config-router)#bgp log-neighbor changes
```

The **bgp log-neighbor changes** command is helpful because it logs a line indicating a change in a neighbor status, such as the neighbor's coming up or going down.

Before you get to the next step of advertising networks, you might want to assign a router ID to the BGP process, as in Example 12-2. The router ID uniquely identifies each BGP router. This number is normally selected from IP addresses available on a router. The highest numerical address is the one chosen as the router ID. This can be a random, nondescriptive number that is hard to troubleshoot because you can't easily associate it with any particular router in your mind.

To overwrite the router's default behavior, assign the following command with an IP address of your choosing:

```
R4(config-router)#bgp router-id ip-address
```

To verify whether your neighbor configuration is working properly and you are receiving the information from your peer, issue the **show ip bgp neighbors** [*ip-address*] command, used in Example 12-3.

Example 12-3 show ip bgp neighbors *Output*

```
R4#show ip bgp neighbors 140.100.47.7
BGP neighbor is 140.100.47.7,  remote AS 1560, external link
Description: R7-BB2
BGP version 4, remote router ID 7.7.7.7
BGP state = Established, up for 00:12:36
Last read 00:00:35, hold time is 180, keepalive interval is 60 seconds
Neighbor capabilities:
Route refresh: advertised and received(new)
Address family IPv4 Unicast: advertised and received
Received 57 messages, 0 notifications, 0 in queue
Sent 65 messages, 0 notifications, 0 in queue
Route refresh request: received 0, sent 0
Default minimum time between advertisement runs is 30 seconds
!
! Output omitted for brevity

R7#show ip bgp neighbors 140.100.47.4
BGP neighbor is 140.100.47.4,  remote AS 456, external link
Description: R4
BGP version 4, remote router ID 4.4.4.4
BGP state = Established, up for 00:15:28
Last read 00:00:28, hold time is 180, keepalive interval is 60 seconds
Neighbor capabilities:
Route refresh: advertised and received(new)
Address family IPv4 Unicast: advertised and received
Received 68 messages, 0 notifications, 0 in queue
Sent 60 messages, 0 notifications, 0 in queue
Route refresh request: received 0, sent 0
Default minimum time between advertisement runs is 30 seconds
!
! Output omitted for brevity
```

Notice that both routers display the correct information on their neighbor. The IP address you specified is associated with the autonomous system. The description for the neighbor you entered locally and the router ID received from the neighbor are also displayed.

A common mistake when configuring new neighbor statements or making a change to existing ones is to forget to reset the old neighbor connection. In this scenario, the neighbor configuration on R4 and R7 is new. Had there been a previous configuration and you changed it, you would need to reset the connection with one of the following commands:

```
R4#clear ip bgp neighbor-address
```

or

```
R4#clear ip bgp *
```

The first command clears the connection to a particular neighbor, and the second resets all neighbor connections. If you don't reset the previous neighbor connection, your new configuration changes won't take effect.

Step 3: Advertising Networks

The final step in this scenario's BGP configuration is advertising the networks from one router to another. There are several ways to accomplish this task. In this particular example, a **network** command is used to inject routes. The purpose of this command is to indicate which networks originate in a router. This works only if the networks you are advertising are known to a router through direct connection or are learned, meaning that they appear in the forwarding table.

The command syntax is as follows:

```
R4(config-router)#network ip-address [mask subnet-mask]
```

You have the option of specifying a subnet mask if your particular subnet differs from the major network boundary. For instance, Example 12-4 omits the mask from the Class C 209 network on R7 but includes it for all other **network** statements.

Example 12-4 *Using the* **network** *Statement in BGP*

```
R4#show run
hostname R4
!
! Output omitted for brevity
!
router bgp 456
 bgp router-id 4.4.4.4
 bgp log-neighbor-changes
 network 140.100.47.0 mask 255.255.255.192
 neighbor 140.100.47.7 remote-as 1560
 neighbor 140.100.47.7 description R7-BB2

R7#show run
hostname R7
!
! Output omitted for brevity
```

continues

Example 12-4 *Using the* **network** *Statement in BGP (Continued)*

```
!
router bgp 1560
bgp router-id 7.7.7.7
bgp log-neighbor-changes
network 140.100.47.0 mask 255.255.255.192
neighbor 140.100.47.4 remote-as 456
neighbor 140.100.47.4 description R4
network 7.1.1.0 mask 255.255.255.0
network 7.7.7.0 mask 255.255.255.0
network 17.1.1.0 mask 255.255.255.0
network 27.1.1.0 mask 255.255.255.0
network 37.1.1.0 mask 255.255.255.0
network 156.46.1.0 mask 255.255.255.0
network 156.46.2.0 mask 255.255.255.0
network 156.46.3.0 mask 255.255.255.0
network 156.46.4.0 mask 255.255.255.0
network 156.46.100.0 mask 255.255.252.0
network 209.112.65.0
network 209.112.66.0
network 209.112.67.0
network 209.112.68.0
network 209.112.69.0
network 209.112.70.0
```

Step 4: Verification

After your configuration is complete, you need to verify the BGP operation and troubleshoot it if necessary. You learned about the **show ip bgp neighbors** command in Step 2 of this case study. You can use other helpful commands in a logical step-by-step order for the most efficient verification and troubleshooting.

Use the following command to display the list of neighbors and the status of all BGP connections:

```
R4#show ip bgp summary
```

In Example 12-5, the **show ip bgp summary** command is issued on R7 three times consecutively. Each time, the state of the peer changes from idle to active to the number of advertised prefixes.

Example 12-5 **show ip bgp summary** *Output of R7*

```
R7#show ip bgp summary
BGP router identifier 7.7.7.7, local AS number 1560
BGP table version is 18, main routing table version 18
17 network entries and 17 paths using 2261 bytes of memory
1 BGP path attribute entries using 120 bytes of memory
1 BGP AS-PATH entries using 24 bytes of memory
0 BGP route-map cache entries using 0 bytes of memory
0 BGP filter-list cache entries using 0 bytes of memory
```

Example 12-5 show ip bgp summary *Output of R7 (Continued)*

```
BGP activity 34/51 prefixes, 36/19 paths, scan interval 60 secs

Neighbor        V    AS MsgRcvd MsgSent   TblVer   InQ OutQ Up/Down State/PfxRcd
140.100.47.4    4   456      22      22       0     0    0 00:00:19 Idle

R7#show ip bgp summary
BGP router identifier 7.7.7.7, local AS number 1560
BGP table version is 18, main routing table version 18
17 network entries and 17 paths using 2261 bytes of memory
1 BGP path attribute entries using 60 bytes of memory
0 BGP route-map cache entries using 0 bytes of memory
0 BGP filter-list cache entries using 0 bytes of memory
BGP activity 34/51 prefixes, 36/19 paths, scan interval 60 secs

Neighbor        V    AS MsgRcvd MsgSent   TblVer   InQ OutQ Up/Down State/PfxRcd
140.100.47.4    4   456      22      22       0     0    0 00:00:39 Active

R7#show ip bgp summary
BGP router identifier 7.7.7.7, local AS number 1560
BGP table version is 18, main routing table version 18
17 network entries and 18 paths using 2297 bytes of memory
2 BGP path attribute entries using 120 bytes of memory
1 BGP AS-PATH entries using 24 bytes of memory
0 BGP route-map cache entries using 0 bytes of memory
0 BGP filter-list cache entries using 0 bytes of memory
BGP activity 34/51 prefixes, 37/19 paths, scan interval 60 secs

Neighbor        V    AS MsgRcvd MsgSent   TblVer   InQ OutQ Up/Down State/PfxRcd
140.100.47.4    4   456      27      27      18     0    0 00:00:02        1
```

The number of received prefixes is a very useful clue in troubleshooting. Note the number of networks R4 receives from R7 in Example 12-6. Compare it to the number of network statements in R7's BGP configuration, and confirm that these numbers match. Seventeen network statements are configured on R7 (as shown in Example 12-4), and 17 prefixes are received by R4.

Example 12-6 show ip bgp summary *Output of R4*

```
R4#show ip bgp summary
BGP router identifier 4.4.4.4, local AS number 456
BGP table version is 18, main routing table version 18
17 network entries and 18 paths using 2297 bytes of memory
2 BGP path attribute entries using 120 bytes of memory
1 BGP AS-PATH entries using 24 bytes of memory
0 BGP route-map cache entries using 0 bytes of memory
0 BGP filter-list cache entries using 0 bytes of memory
BGP activity 51/180 prefixes, 54/36 paths, scan interval 60 secs

Neighbor        V    AS MsgRcvd MsgSent   TblVer   InQ OutQ Up/Down State/PfxRcd
140.100.47.7    4  1560      36      36      18     0    0 00:09:21       17
```

After checking the number of prefixes received from the neighbors, display the detailed information on those routes in the BGP database with the following command:

```
R4#show ip bgp
```

Example 12-7 displays the **show ip bgp** command issued on R4.

Example 12-7 show ip bgp *Output*

```
R4#show ip bgp
BGP table version is 18, local router ID is 4.4.4.4
Status codes: s suppressed, d damped, h history, * valid, > best, i -
internal
Origin codes: i - IGP, e - EGP, ? - incomplete

   Network          Next Hop         Metric LocPrf Weight Path
*> 7.1.1.0/24       140.100.47.7          0             0 1560 i
*> 7.7.7.0/24       140.100.47.7          0             0 1560 i
*> 17.1.1.0/24      140.100.47.7          0             0 1560 i
*> 27.1.1.0/24      140.100.47.7          0             0 1560 i
*> 37.1.1.0/24      140.100.47.7          0             0 1560 i
*  140.100.47.0/26  140.100.47.7          0             0 1560 i
*>                  0.0.0.0               0         32768 i
*> 156.46.1.0/24    140.100.47.7          0             0 1560 i
*> 156.46.2.0/24    140.100.47.7          0             0 1560 i
*> 156.46.3.0/24    140.100.47.7          0             0 1560 i
*> 156.46.4.0/24    140.100.47.7          0             0 1560 i
*> 156.46.100.0/22  140.100.47.7          0             0 1560 i
*> 209.112.65.0     140.100.47.7          0             0 1560 i
*> 209.112.66.0     140.100.47.7          0             0 1560 i
*> 209.112.67.0     140.100.47.7          0             0 1560 i
*> 209.112.68.0     140.100.47.7          0             0 1560 i
*> 209.112.69.0     140.100.47.7          0             0 1560 i
*> 209.112.70.0     140.100.47.7          0             0 1560 i
```

Issuing the **debug ip bgp updates** command shows you exactly what's going on with your updating process. Example 12-8 shows R7 receiving routes from R4.

Example 12-8 debug ip bgp updates *Output of R7*

```
01:08:03: BGP: 140.100.47.7 went from Idle to Active
01:08:03: BGP: 140.100.47.7 open active, delay 18404ms
01:08:09: BGP: Applying map to find origin for 140.100.47.0/26
01:08:22: BGP: 140.100.47.7 open active, local address 140.100.47.4
01:08:22: BGP: 140.100.47.7 went from Active to OpenSent
01:08:22: BGP: 140.100.47.7 sending OPEN, version 4, my as: 456
01:08:22: BGP: 140.100.47.7 send message type 1, length (incl. header) 45
01:08:22: BGP: 140.100.47.7 rcv message type 1, length (excl. header) 26
01:08:22: BGP: 140.100.47.7 rcv OPEN, version 4
01:08:22: BGP: 140.100.47.7 rcv OPEN w/ OPTION parameter len: 16
01:08:22: BGP: 140.100.47.7 rcvd OPEN w/ optional parameter type 2 (Capability)
   len 6
```

Example 12-8 debug ip bgp updates *Output of R7 (Continued)*

```
01:08:22: BGP: 140.100.47.7 OPEN has CAPABILITY code: 1, length 4
01:08:22: BGP: 140.100.47.7 OPEN has MP_EXT CAP for afi/safi: 1/1
01:08:22: BGP: 140.100.47.7 rcvd OPEN w/ optional parameter type 2 (Capability)
  len 2
01:08:22: BGP: 140.100.47.7 OPEN has CAPABILITY code: 128, length 0
01:08:22: BGP: 140.100.47.7 OPEN has ROUTE-REFRESH capability(old) for all address
  families
01:08:22: BGP: 140.100.47.7 rcvd OPEN w/ optional parameter type 2 (Capability)
  len 2
01:08:22: BGP: 140.100.47.7 OPEN has CAPABILITY code: 2, length 0
01:08:22: BGP: 140.100.47.7 OPEN has ROUTE-REFRESH capability(new) for all
  address-families
01:08:22: BGP: 140.100.47.7 went from OpenSent to OpenConfirm
01:08:22: BGP: 140.100.47.7 send message type 4, length (incl. header) 19
01:08:22: BGP: 140.100.47.7 rcv message type 4, length (excl. header) 0
01:08:22: BGP: 140.100.47.7 went from OpenConfirm to Established
01:08:22: %BGP-5-ADJCHANGE: neighbor 140.100.47.7 Up
01:08:22: BGP: 140.100.47.7 send message type 4, length (incl. header) 19
01:08:22: BGP: 140.100.47.7 rcv message type 4, length (excl. header) 0
01:08:22: BGP: 140.100.47.7 rcv message type 4, length (excl. header) 0
```

Case Study 12-2: Transit Autonomous System Setup

In Figure 12-3, R4, R5, and R6 belong to the same autonomous system, AS 456. This qualifies the type of BGP that runs between them as IBGP. R4 has also peered with R7 from AS 1560; therefore, an EBGP relationship has been established between R4 and R7.

Figure 12-3 *Transit Autonomous System Topology*

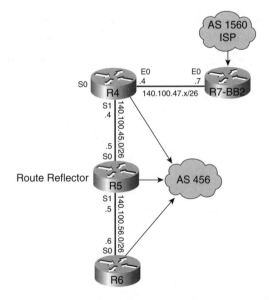

This case study follows these steps:

Step 1   Disable synchronization

Step 2   IBGP peering and route reflectors

Step 3   Change the next-hop attribute

Step 4   Configure aggregate addresses

Step 5   Route map filtering

Step 6   Distribute list filtering

Step 1: Disabling Synchronization

Before you start configuring anything related to IBGP functionality, you need to understand the concept of synchronization. Synchronization is a BGP feature. Basically, it means that if your autonomous system is acting as a transit autonomous system, BGP doesn't advertise a route until all routers in your autonomous system have learned about that route through IGP. BGP waits as long as it takes until this occurs. Only then does it advertise the route to the outside. Synchronization was intended for use in the days when transit autonomous systems relied on BGP route redistribution into IGP.

It is unreasonable to expect modern autonomous systems to inject the number of routes carried in the Internet into an IGP. So if your autonomous system is not passing the outside traffic through, or if all routers are running IBGP and redistribution is no longer applicable, you can and should disable synchronization. This results in faster convergence and fewer routes to burden your IGP. Otherwise, a router will forever be expecting an IGP update about a certain route and will never send it to external peers.

All routers in AS 456 are talking BGP, so redistribution into OSPF is unneeded. If synchronization isn't disabled on all routers, the traffic exchange won't work.

Synchronization is automatically enabled. To disable it, you need to manually reverse it using the following command:

```
R4(config-router)#no synchronization
```

Check Example 12-9 to see how synchronization is disabled on R5. R4 and R6 have identical synchronization disabling configurations applied.

Example 12-9 *Disabling the Synchronization Feature*

```
R5#show run
!
! Output omitted for brevity
!
router bgp 456
no synchronization
```

If for any reason you need to reenable synchronization, repeat this command without the **no**.

Step 2: IBGP Peering and Route Reflectors

AS 456 is functioning as a transit system, so it has to pass the routes from one autonomous system to another. To forward traffic from one exit point in the autonomous system to another, a path over the intermediate routers needs to exist. In the preceding step, you learned that redistributing BGP routes into IGP isn't a viable solution, so you need to route external information using IBGP.

Here, you need to understand a very important difference between EBGP and IBGP behavior. When a BGP speaker receives an update from other BGP speakers via IBGP, the receiving BGP speaker passes that information along to other outside BGP speakers using EBGP. However, it never forwards that update to another IBGP peer in its own autonomous system.

This behavior is the result of IBGP's implementation of the split-horizon rule you learned about in Chapter 8, "RIP." Because each route BGP includes the path of autonomous systems traversed on the way with its routing updates, an IBGP router can't add its own autonomous system number and update another IBGP peer that belongs to the same autonomous system. Otherwise, a loop occurs.

When applied to the network shown in Figure 12-3, the BGP split-horizon rule acts in the following manner:

- Let's assume that you went through the configuration steps in Case Study 12-1 and that you configured the neighbor relationships between R4 and R7 and R4 and R6.

- After R4 receives the information from R7, it forwards it in the direction of R6 based on the information discovered from R6. In this case, the packets need to pass through R5.

- When the packets arrive at R5, the router checks its routing table for a matching entry, but there isn't one. Consequently, it drops the packet, because it has no knowledge of how to reach R6.

R5 must have some way of passing the information to R6. Therefore, all IBGP routers must maintain neighbor relationships with all other IBGP routers to ensure that the information about external networks is known throughout. Such knowledge results in the necessary full-mesh IBGP within an autonomous system. However, the full mesh of IBGP sessions is fairly impractical. In a small network, such as the one shown in Figure 12-3, this doesn't pose much of a problem. What if there were many more routers inside that autonomous system?

A solution to the growing number of IBGP sessions is a route reflector. The IBGP design with route reflectors alleviates the inconvenience of a full mesh. Unlike "classic" IBGP, in which a full mesh is defined between R4, R5, and R6 within AS 456, a route reflector allows the routes learned via IBGP to be forwarded to other IBGP speakers. This is possible because a router configured as a route reflector passes the updates received over an IBGP session to another IBGP session.

The route reflector communicates with two types of routers: *clients* and *nonclients*. At least one route reflector and its clients create a cluster. Nonclients are routers that are not part of the cluster (such as other route reflectors, external routers, and routers) that don't understand the route-reflector concept. The clients in a cluster form IBGP sessions only with their route reflector. A cluster can have more than one route reflector. In this situation, clients need to peer with all their route reflectors, and route reflectors need to peer with each other. An autonomous system can also be divided into multiple clusters.

Cluster formation and route-reflector selection are dictated by the topology. In this case, R4, R5, and R6 are combined into a single cluster with one route reflector within AS 456. It makes sense to elect R5 as a route reflector so that it has a separate IBGP peering with R4 and R6. First, you configure neighbor statements on R4 with R5 and configure neighbor statements on R6 with R5. R5, as route reflector, peers with both R4 and R6. The need for peering between R4 and R6 is eliminated, because R5 relays the updates coming from R4 and R6.

The route reflector is configured using the **neighbor** statement with an additional argument:

```
R5(config-router)#neighbor ip-address router-reflector-client
```

Example 12-10 shows the neighbor-as-client definition on route reflector R5.

Example 12-10 *R5 as a Route Reflector Configuration*

```
R5#show run
hostname R5
!
interface Loopback5
 ip address 5.5.5.5 255.255.255.0
!
interface Serial0
 ip address 140.100.45.5 255.255.255.192
!
interface Serial1
 ip address 140.100.56.5 255.255.255.192
 clockrate 64000
!
router bgp 456
 no synchronization
 bgp router-id 5.5.5.5
 bgp log-neighbor-changes
 network 140.100.45.0 mask 255.255.255.192
 network 140.100.56.0 mask 255.255.255.192
 neighbor 140.100.45.4 remote-as 456
 neighbor 140.100.45.4 description R4
 neighbor 140.100.45.4 route-reflector-client
 neighbor 140.100.56.6 remote-as 456
 neighbor 140.100.56.6 description R6
 neighbor 140.100.56.6 route-reflector-client
```

Having the highlighted commands placed on it, R5 becomes the route reflector, and R4 and R6 become its clients. Clients don't require any special configuration.

Step 3: Changing the Next-Hop Attribute

Another example of IBGP's tricky behavior is the way it handles the next-hop attribute. This attribute is carried in BGP updates, and in EBGP it's automatically set to the sender's IP address. When R4 receives an update from R7, it knows that to reach the networks advertised by R7, it needs to go through R7, whose IP address is specified as the next hop.

However, the rules that govern IBGP state that the next hop advertised by EBGP isn't changed after it gets into the IBGP environment. So, when R5 receives an update from R4 of the networks advertised by R7, the next hop's address is still R7, not R4. This poses a problem, because now it seems that besides establishing peering within the autonomous system, an internal router needs to know how to reach an outside router as well.

To solve this problem, BGP lets you tweak this default behavior. If explicitly configured to do so, an autonomous system border router may change the next hop from the external router's IP address to its own. This means that when an internal router receives an update, it knows that to reach a network in another autonomous system it needs to direct its traffic to another IBGP router. It already knows how to reach that router because of the full-mesh or cluster relationships configured inside the autonomous system.

The command syntax for changing the next-hop attribute on the border router is

```
R4(config-router)#neighbor [ip-address | peer-group-name] next-hop-self
```

Example 12-11 shows how this command works on R4 and R6. R4 advertises R7's networks to R5 with itself as the next hop. Consequently, this information is passed on to R6 as well. Now, R6 is also a border router connected to AS 65000. As such, it has the **next-hop-self** statement directed to R5.

Example 12-11 *Changing the Next-Hop Attribute*

```
R4#show run
hostname R4
!
! Output omitted for brevity
!
interface Serial0
 ip address 150.100.33.4 255.255.255.248
 encapsulation frame-relay
 frame-relay map ip 150.100.33.3 404 broadcast
 frame-relay interface-dlci 404
 frame-relay lmi-type ansi
!
interface Serial1
 ip address 140.100.45.6 255.255.255.192
```

continues

Example 12-11 *Changing the Next-Hop Attribute (Continued)*

```
  clockrate 64000
 !
 router bgp 456
  no synchronization
  bgp router-id 4.4.4.4
  bgp log-neighbor-changes
  network 140.100.45.0 mask 255.255.255.192
  network 140.100.47.0 mask 255.255.255.192
  network 150.100.33.0 mask 255.255.255.248
  neighbor 140.100.45.5 remote-as 456
  neighbor 140.100.45.5 description R5_Route_Reflector

  neighbor 140.100.45.5 next-hop-self
  neighbor 140.100.47.7 remote-as 1560
  neighbor 140.100.47.7 description R7-BB2

 R6#show run
 hostname R6
 !
 interface Loopback6
  ip address 6.6.6.6 255.255.255.0
 !
 interface FastEthernet0/0
  ip address 130.100.26.6 255.255.255.224
  speed 10
  half-duplex
 !
 interface Serial0/0
  ip address 140.100.56.6 255.255.255.192
 !
 router bgp 456
  no synchronization
  bgp router-id 6.6.6.6
  bgp log-neighbor-changes
  network 140.100.56.0 mask 255.255.255.192
  neighbor 140.100.56.5 remote-as 456
  neighbor 140.100.56.5 description R5_Route_Reflector
  neighbor 140.100.56.5 next-hop-self
```

NOTE   If you issue **show ip bgp route** on R6, you will notice that R7's networks can be reached via R4's IP address, as you have configured it. For your troubleshooting techniques in the lab environment, you might prefer to see the actual next hop, R5. In this case, you need to place the **next-hop-self** statement on R5 as well.

Step 4: Configuring Aggregate Addresses

The concept and benefits of summarization were discussed in previous chapters, so here the discussion focuses on the summarization techniques used in BGP. The summarization of BGP routes is called *aggregation*.

It is appropriate to summarize routes at border routers to minimize the impact that these routes could have when brought into or announced out of an autonomous system. In this scenario, the goal is to suppress specific routes coming in from the outside networks in AS 1560 and AS 1234, as shown in Figure 12-1.

Before proceeding with summarization configuration, you need to disable automatic summarization, because it takes the finer control out of your hands. Recall that the command for disabling auto-summary is

```
R4(config-router)#no auto-summary
```

The next step is to decide on the subnet boundary for the summarization. You will use /16 for all three summarized networks: 150.100.0.0, 156.46.0.0, and 209.112.0.0. The syntax for the route aggregation contains many optional keywords. The syntax of the command that is of use to you here is

```
R4(config-router)#aggregate-address address mask [summary-only]
```

You need to realize the difference between inclusion and exclusion of the **summary-only** keyword. When **summary-only** is omitted, BGP creates an aggregate address as specified but also includes the more-specific routes that were there in the first place. In Example 12-12, **aggregate-address 150.100.0.0 255.255.0.0** is missing **summary-only**. On the other hand, networks 156.46.0.0 and 209.112.0.0 aren't. This means that for networks 156.46.x.x and 209.112.x.x, only aggregate addresses are propagated, and for network 150.100.x.x, all routes, including the summary, are forwarded.

Example 12-12 **aggregate-address** *Application*

```
R4#show run
hostname R4
!
! Output omitted for brevity
!
router bgp 456
no synchronization
bgp router-id 4.4.4.4
bgp log-neighbor-changes
network 140.100.45.0 mask 255.255.255.192
network 140.100.47.0 mask 255.255.255.192
network 150.100.33.0 mask 255.255.255.248
aggregate-address 150.100.0.0 255.255.0.0
aggregate-address 156.46.0.0 255.255.0.0 summary-only
aggregate-address 209.112.0.0 255.255.0.0 summary-only
neighbor 140.100.45.5 remote-as 456
```

continues

Example 12-12 **aggregate-address** *Application (Continued)*

```
neighbor 140.100.45.5 description R5_Route_Reflector
neighbor 140.100.45.5 next-hop-self
neighbor 140.100.47.7 remote-as 1560
neighbor 140.100.47.7 description R7-BB2
no auto-summary
```

If you issue the **show ip bgp** command on R4, as shown in Example 12-13, you will see that the routes that are being summarized are still there but are marked with a letter "s." This means that they are suppressed from R4's routing updates to other peers.

Example 12-13 **show ip bgp** *Command on R4*

```
R4#show ip bgp
BGP table version is 40, local router ID is 4.4.4.4
Status codes: s suppressed, d damped, h history, * valid, > best, i - internal
Origin codes: i - IGP, e - EGP, ? - incomplete

   Network          Next Hop         Metric LocPrf Weight Path
*> 7.1.1.0/24       140.100.47.7          0             0 1560 i
*> 7.7.7.0/24       140.100.47.7          0             0 1560 i
*> 17.1.1.0/24      140.100.47.7          0             0 1560 i
*> 27.1.1.0/24      140.100.47.7          0             0 1560 i
*> 37.1.1.0/24      140.100.47.7          0             0 1560 i
*  i140.100.45.0/26 140.100.45.5          0    100      0 i
*>                  0.0.0.0               0         32768 i
*    140.100.47.0/26 140.100.47.7         0             0 1560 i
*>                  0.0.0.0               0         32768 i
*>i140.100.56.0/26  140.100.45.5          0    100      0 i
*> 150.100.0.0      0.0.0.0                         32768 i
*> 156.46.0.0       0.0.0.0                         32768 i
s> 156.46.1.0/24    140.100.47.7          0             0 1560 i
s> 156.46.2.0/24    140.100.47.7          0             0 1560 i
s> 156.46.3.0/24    140.100.47.7          0             0 1560 i
s> 156.46.4.0/24    140.100.47.7          0             0 1560 i
s> 156.46.100.0/22  140.100.47.7          0             0 1560 i
*> 209.112.0.0/16   0.0.0.0                         32768 i
s> 209.112.65.0     140.100.47.7          0             0 1560 i
s> 209.112.66.0     140.100.47.7          0             0 1560 i
s> 209.112.67.0     140.100.47.7          0             0 1560 i
s> 209.112.68.0     140.100.47.7          0             0 1560 i
s> 209.112.69.0     140.100.47.7          0             0 1560 i
s> 209.112.70.0     140.100.47.7          0             0 1560 I
```

Step 5: Route Map Filtering

In Example 12-12, **summary-only** was not used for the 150.100.0.0/16 aggregate address, and all routes with the 150.100 prefix were forwarded. This creates more information in the BGP table and seems to defeat the purpose of aggregation.

There are, however, other ways of suppressing routes such as through route filtering. You can use route maps to filter updates. Only those routes permitted in the route map are propagated. To begin configuring a route map, give it a case-sensitive name, such as PERMIT_SUMMARY, in global configuration mode. Then you need to assign it a **match** statement that references conditions set in an access list. The access list used here is numbered 10 and permits the summarized routes of 150.100.x.x, 156.46.x.x, and 209.112.x.x and makes all other routes not welcome.

Finally, you associate the route map with the specific neighbor and specify whether it is applied to incoming or outgoing routes. Example 12-14 shows how the route map filtering is resolved on R4. The route map configured is designed to filter all specific routes from entering R5 via R4.

Example 12-14 *Route Map Filtering*

```
router bgp 456
neighbor 140.100.45.5 route-map PERMIT_SUMMARY out
!
route-map PERMIT_SUMMARY permit 10
 match ip address 10
 !
access-list 10 permit 150.100.0.0 0.0.255.255 log
access-list 10 permit 156.46.0.0 0.0.255.255 log
access-list 10 permit 209.112.0.0 0.0.255.255 log
```

The task of suppressing the specific routes of network 150.100.0.0 is now accomplished. Take a look at Example 12-15, though. This is the output of the **show ip route bgp** and **show ip bgp** commands on R5. Notice how only summary routes are displayed for all networks in the routing table, but the BGP database still shows every route for 150.100.x.x. This is because in the previous section, **summary-only** wasn't included in the aggregate statement of 150.100.0.0.

Example 12-15 **show ip route bgp** *and* **show ip bgp** *Commands on R5*

```
R5#show ip route bgp
     150.100.0.0/16 is variably subnetted, 4 subnets, 4 masks
B       150.100.0.0/16 [200/0] via 140.100.45.4, 00:02:30

R5#show ip bgp
BGP table version is 100, local router ID is 5.5.5.5
Status codes: s suppressed, d damped, h history, * valid, > best, i - internal
Origin codes: i - IGP, e - EGP, ? - incomplete
   Network          Next Hop            Metric LocPrf Weight Path
*> 140.100.45.0/26  0.0.0.0                  0          32768 i
* i140.100.56.0/26  140.100.56.6             0    100      0 i
*>                  0.0.0.0                  0          32768 i
*>i150.100.0.0      140.100.45.4                  100      0 i
*>i150.100.33.0/29  140.100.45.4             0    100      0 1234 i
!
! Output omitted for brevity
!
```

Step 6: Distribute List Filtering

As far as this scenario is concerned, the distribute list method of filtering updates can achieve the same results as the route map, but in a somewhat simpler way. In R4, access list 11 permits only the summarized route of 150.100.0.0/16. This access list is then referred to in a **neighbor** statement to R7 and is applied to the outgoing updates, as shown in Example 12-16.

Example 12-16 *Distribute List Filtering*

```
R4#show run
hostname R4
!
router bgp 456
no synchronization
bgp router-id 4.4.4.4
neighbor 140.100.47.7 remote-as 1560
neighbor 140.100.47.7 description R7-BB2
!
! Output omitted for brevity
!
neighbor 140.100.47.7 distribute-list 11 out
!
access-list 11 permit 150.100.0.0 0.0.255.255 log
```

Example 12-17 shows the output of R7's routing table after the distribute list has been applied to R4. You can see that all routes that would have come from R4, aside from 150.100.0.0/16, are gone.

Example 12-17 **show ip route bgp** *Command on R7*

```
R7#show ip route bgp
B      150.100.0.0/16 [20/0] via 140.100.47.4, 00:00:08
```

Case Study 12-3: BGP Confederations

BGP confederations is a method of combining several smaller autonomous systems into one common autonomous system, called a *confederation*. The confederation number, not the separate autonomous system number, is propagated to other autonomous systems. This concept works well for IBGP as an alternative to full mesh and route reflectors. With IBGP, a large autonomous system is broken into smaller autonomous system-like structures to avoid a full mesh. Full-mesh relationships are required only for each separate mini-autonomous system, but inter-autonomous system relationships within a confederation take on EBGP characteristics.

The confederation concept can be used with EBGP as well. For instance, in the situation depicted in Figure 12-4, R1, R2, R3, and R4 are communicating through Frame Relay. All of these routers belong to different autonomous systems. The challenge is to combine R1 in AS 1, R2 in AS 2, and R3 in AS 3 into one confederation so that R3's peer, R4 in AS 456, sees them as members of AS 1234.

Figure 12-4 *BGP Confederations*

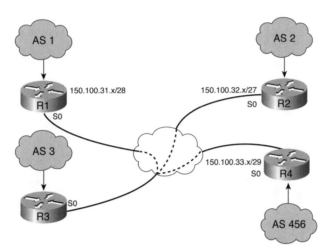

During this case study, you will accomplish the following tasks:

Step 1 Configure R1, R2, and R3 for BGP routing

Step 2 Create a confederation

Step 3 Verify your configuration

Step 1: Beginning Configuration of R1, R2, and R3

The first steps of confederation setup for R1, R2, and R3 are general EBGP configuration steps, as shown in Example 12-18. Notice the **next-hop-self** statement on R3 directed at R1 and R2. R1, R2, R3, and R4 are connected via Frame Relay. Frame Relay is a nonbroadcast multiaccess (NBMA) technology, so R1 and R2 don't have a direct path to R4. If R3 didn't have **next-hop-self** configured, routing would fail.

Example 12-18 *BGP Configuration of R1, R2, and R3*

```
R1#show run
hostname R1
!interface Serial0.1 point-to-point
 ip address 150.100.31.1 255.255.255.240
 frame-relay interface-dlci 101
!
router bgp 1
 network 150.100.31.0 mask 255.255.255.240
 neighbor 150.100.31.3 remote-as 3                    ←R3
 neighbor 150.100.31.3 description R3
```

continues

Example 12-18 *BGP Configuration of R1, R2, and R3 (Continued)*

```
    no auto-summary

R2#show run
hostname R2!
interface Loopback2
 ip address 2.2.2.2 255.255.255.0
 !
interface Serial0.1 point-to-point
 ip address 150.100.32.2 255.255.255.224
 frame-relay interface-dlci 202
 !
router bgp 2
 network 150.100.32.0 mask 255.255.255.224
 neighbor 150.100.32.3 remote-as 3                          ←R3
 no auto-summary

R3#show run
hostname R3
 !
interface Serial0.1 point-to-point
 description Connection to R1
 ip address 150.100.31.3 255.255.255.240
 frame-relay interface-dlci 301
 !
interface Serial0.2 point-to-point
 description Connection to R2
 ip address 150.100.32.3 255.255.255.224
 frame-relay interface-dlci 302
 !
interface Serial0.4 point-to-point
 description Connection to R4
 ip address 150.100.33.3 255.255.255.248
 frame-relay interface-dlci 304
 !
router bgp 3
 network 150.100.31.0 mask 255.255.255.240
 network 150.100.32.0 mask 255.255.255.224
 network 150.100.33.0 mask 255.255.255.248
 neighbor 150.100.31.1 remote-as 1
 neighbor 150.100.31.1 description R1
 neighbor 150.100.31.1 next-hop-self
 neighbor 150.100.32.2 remote-as 2
 neighbor 150.100.32.2 description R2
 neighbor 150.100.32.2 next-hop-self
 neighbor 150.100.33.4 remote-as 456
 neighbor 150.100.33.4 description R4 IBGP -Link to AS456
 no auto-summary
```

Step 2: Creating a Confederation

After the initial BGP configuration, two commands are required on each participating router to enable confederation. The first command identifies the confederation ID, the common denominator for all three routers. The second command specifies the router's confederation peers. The syntax for both commands is as follows:

```
R1(config-router)#bgp confederation identifier autonomous-system
```

and

```
R1(config-router)#bgp confederation peers autonomous-system [autonomous-system]...
```

Example 12-19 demonstrates the application of the preceding commands on each router. Every router is identified as a member of confederation 1234. R1 is peered with AS 2 and AS 3, R2 with AS 1 and AS 3, and R3 with AS 1 and AS 2.

Example 12-19 *Confederation Setup*

```
R1#show run
hostname R1
!
! Output omitted for brevity
!
router bgp 1
bgp log-neighbor-changes
bgp confederation identifier 1234
bgp confederation peers 2 3
network 150.100.31.0 mask 255.255.255.240
neighbor 150.100.31.3 remote-as 3
neighbor 150.100.31.3 description R3
no auto-summary

R2#show run
hostname R2
!
! Output omitted for brevity
!
router bgp 2
no synchronization
bgp log-neighbor-changes
bgp confederation identifier 1234
bgp confederation peers 1 3
network 150.100.32.0 mask 255.255.255.224
redistribute connected route-map loopback
neighbor 150.100.32.3 remote-as 3
no auto-summary
!
access-list 1 permit 2.2.2.0 0.0.0.255 log
route-map loopback permit 10
 match ip address 1
```

continues

Example 12-19 *Confederation Setup (Continued)*

```
R3#show run
hostname R3
!
! Output omitted for brevity
!
router bgp 3
no synchronization
bgp log-neighbor-changes
bgp confederation identifier 1234
bgp confederation peers 1 2
network 150.100.31.0 mask 255.255.255.240
network 150.100.32.0 mask 255.255.255.224
network 150.100.33.0 mask 255.255.255.248
neighbor 150.100.31.1 remote-as 1
neighbor 150.100.31.1 description R1
neighbor 150.100.31.1 next-hop-self
neighbor 150.100.32.2 remote-as 2
neighbor 150.100.32.2 description R2
neighbor 150.100.32.2 next-hop-self
neighbor 150.100.33.4 remote-as 456
neighbor 150.100.33.4 description R4 IBGP -Link to AS456
no auto-summary
```

When you configure R4's peer relationship with R3, everything stays the same, except instead
of associating R3's IP address with AS 3, R4 uses AS 1234. Example 12-20 shows R4's
configuration.

Example 12-20 *Peering R4 with R3*

```
R4#show run
hostname R4
!
router bgp 456
no synchronization
bgp router-id 4.4.4.4
bgp log-neighbor-changes
!
! Output omitted for brevity
!
neighbor 150.100.33.3 remote-as 1234
neighbor 150.100.33.3 description R3_Confederation peer
neighbor 140.100.47.7 distribute-list 11 out


!
access-list 11 permit 150.100.0.0 0.0.255.255 log
access-list 11 permit 2.2.2.0 0.0.0.255 log
access-list 11 permit 8.8.8.0 0.0.0.255 log
```

Step 3: Verification

Issue **show ip bgp** on R4, and you'll notice that all routes arriving by way of R3 display 1234 as their autonomous system path attribute, not AS 3. This was the intended result of the configuration scenario, as shown in Example 12-21.

Example 12-21 show ip bgp *Command on R4*

```
R4#show ip bgp | include 1234
*> 2.2.2.0/24       150.100.33.3                     0 1234 ?
*> 150.100.31.0/28  150.100.33.3          0          0 1234 i
*> 150.100.32.0/27  150.100.33.3          0          0 1234 i
*> 150.100.33.0/29  150.100.33.3          0          0 1234 i
```

However, if you issue the same command on any of the confederation member routers, you'll see that routes coming from other members preserve their real autonomous system number in parentheses under the autonomous system path, as shown in Example 12-22. This is done so that routing information loops can be avoided inside the confederation.

Example 12-22 show ip bgp *Command on R3*

```
R3#show ip bgp
BGP table version is 98, local router ID is 172.16.3.1
Status codes: s suppressed, d damped, h history, * valid, > best, i - internal
Origin codes: i - IGP, e - EGP, ? - incomplete

   Network          Next Hop         Metric LocPrf Weight Path
*> 2.2.2.0/24       150.100.32.2          0    100      0 (2) ?
*> 7.7.7.0/24       150.100.33.4                        0 456 1560 i
! Output omitted for brevity
*> 140.100.45.0/26  150.100.33.4          0             0 456 i
*> 140.100.47.0/26  150.100.33.4          0             0 456 i
*> 140.100.56.0/26  150.100.33.4                        0 456 i
*> 150.100.0.0      150.100.33.4                        0 456 i
*  150.100.31.0/28  150.100.31.1          0    100      0 (1) i
*>                  0.0.0.0               0         32768 i
*  150.100.32.0/27  150.100.32.2          0    100      0 (2) i
*>                  0.0.0.0               0         32768 i
*> 150.100.33.0/29  0.0.0.0               0         32768 i
*> 156.46.0.0       150.100.33.4                        0 456 i
*> 209.112.0.0/16   150.100.33.4                        0 456 i
```

Case Study 12-4: BGP Over a Firewall with a Private Autonomous System

Figure 12-5 shows the topology of this case study. R8 belongs to private autonomous system 65000. It needs to peer with R6 in AS 456 over the PIX2 firewall. The goal of this exercise is to be able to propagate AS 65000 into AS 456 but to hide it from the service provider, AS 1560.

Figure 12-5 *BGP Over PIX with a Private Autonomous System*

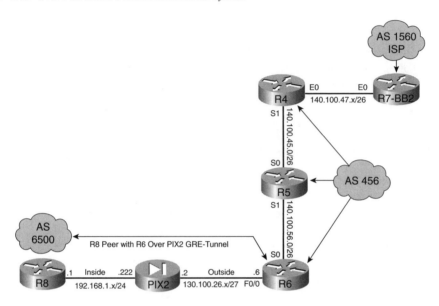

The configuration steps for this case study are as follows:

Step 1   Basic PIX configuration

Step 2   Static routing via a GRE tunnel

Step 3   BGP peering between R6 and R8

Step 4   Route redistribution on R8

Step 5   MD5 authentication

Step 6   Conceal the private autonomous system from service providers

Step 1: Initial PIX Configuration

The first step in the process is to configure the firewall. You start by activating the inside and outside interfaces and assigning IP addresses to both. Specifying **static (inside,outside) 192.168.1.1 192.168.1.1 netmask 255.255.255.255 0 0** allows R8's FastEthernet0/1 interface to be visible outside.

Access list acl-bgp placed on the outside interface allows ICMP requests and GRE tunneling originated in R6 destined for R8. Static routes point to R6 as the source of any route and to R8 as the source of network 192.168.0.0/16. The necessary PIX2 configuration is shown in Example 12-23. For more information on the commands and PIX Firewalls in general, refer to Chapter 23, "Cisco PIX Firewall."

Example 12-23 *PIX2 Configuration*

```
PIX2#show run
PIX Version 6.2.(2)
nameif ethernet0 outside security0
nameif ethernet1 inside security100
hostname PIX2

interface ethernet0 auto
interface ethernet1 auto

ip address outside 130.100.26.2 255.255.255.224
ip address inside 192.168.1.222 255.255.255.0

static (inside,outside) 192.168.1.1 192.168.1.1 netmask 255.255.255.255 0 0

access-list acl-bgp permit icmp host 130.100.26.6 host 192.168.1.1
access-list acl-bgp permit gre host 130.100.26.6 host 192.168.1.1

access-group acl-bgp in interface outside

route outside 0.0.0.0 0.0.0.0 130.100.26.6 1            ← To R6
route inside 192.168.0.0 255.255.0.0 192.168.1.1 1      ← To R8
```

Step 2: Static Routing Via a GRE Tunnel

The next step is to configure static routes on R6 and R8 to each other via PIX2 and then configure a GRE tunnel between R6's and R8's Ethernet interfaces. The GRE tunnel allows R6 and R8 to simulate a back-to-back connection as if PIX2 weren't there.

In Example 12-24, you can see that R6 points to R8's FastEthernet0/1 interface IP address through PIX2's outside interface and that R8 reverses it by pointing to R6 through PIX2's inside interface. The GRE tunnel is created by establishing a logical interface on each router belonging to the 192.168.118.0/24 subnet and identifying the tunnel's source and destination as actual physical Ethernet interfaces.

Example 12-24 *Static Routes and GRE Tunneling*

```
R6#show run
hostname r6
!
! Output omitted for brevity
!
interface Tunnel6
ip address 192.168.118.6 255.255.255.0
tunnel source 130.100.26.6
tunnel destination 192.168.1.1                  ←R8
!
interface FastEthernet0/0
```

continues

Example 12-24 *Static Routes and GRE Tunneling (Continued)*

```
ip address 130.100.26.6 255.255.255.224
!
ip route 192.168.1.1 255.255.255.255 130.100.26.2
hostname R8
!
interface Tunnel8
ip address 192.168.118.8 255.255.255.0
tunnel source 192.168.1.1
tunnel destination 130.100.26.6                    ←R6
!
interface FastEthernet0/1
ip address 192.168.1.1 255.255.255.0
!
ip route 130.100.26.6 255.255.255.255 192.168.1.222


R8#show interfaces tunnel 8
Tunnel8 is up, line protocol is up
Hardware is Tunnel
Internet address is 192.168.118.8/24
MTU 1514 bytes, BW 9 Kbit, DLY 500000 usec,
reliability 255/255, txload 1/255, rxload 1/255
Encapsulation TUNNEL, loopback not set
Keepalive not set
Tunnel source 192.168.1.1, destination 130.100.26.6
Tunnel protocol/transport GRE/IP, key disabled, sequencing disabled
Checksumming of packets disabled,  fast tunneling enabled
Last input 00:00:01, output 00:00:02, output hang never
Last clearing of "show interface" counters never
Input queue: 0/75/0/0 (size/max/drops/flushes); Total output drops: 286
Queueing strategy: fifo
Output queue :0/0 (size/max)
5 minute input rate 0 bits/sec, 0 packets/sec
5 minute output rate 0 bits/sec, 0 packets/sec
209 packets input, 20938 bytes, 0 no buffer
Received 0 broadcasts, 0 runts, 0 giants, 0 throttles
0 input errors, 0 CRC, 0 frame, 0 overrun, 0 ignored, 0 abort
588 packets output, 49129 bytes, 0 underruns
0 output errors, 0 collisions, 0 interface resets
0 output buffer failures, 0 output buffers swapped out

R8#ping 192.168.118.6                      ←Testing the GRE tunnel

Type escape sequence to abort.
Sending 5, 100-byte ICMP Echos to 192.168.118.6, timeout is 2 seconds:
!!!!!
Success rate is 100 percent (5/5), round-trip min/avg/max = 1/2/4 ms
```

Step 3: BGP Peering Between R6 and R8

To establish peering between R6 and R8, you need to go through the usual BGP configuration steps, as shown in Example 12-25. Pay special attention to the IP addresses in the **neighbor** statements of both routers. The IP address associated with the **neighbor** statement on each router is the IP address of the GRE interface, not the physical interface.

Example 12-25 *Establishing Peering Between R6 and R8*

```
R6#show run
hostname r6
!
interface Loopback6
ip address 6.6.6.6 255.255.255.0
!
interface Tunnel6
ip address 192.168.118.6 255.255.255.0
tunnel source 130.100.26.6
tunnel destination 192.168.1.1
!
interface FastEthernet0/0
ip address 130.100.26.6 255.255.255.224
!
interface Serial0/0
ip address 140.100.56.6 255.255.255.192
!
! Output omitted for brevity
!
router bgp 456
no synchronization
bgp router-id 6.6.6.6
bgp log-neighbor-changes
network 130.100.26.0 mask 255.255.255.224
network 140.100.56.0 mask 255.255.255.192
network 192.168.118.0                              ←Tunnel Interface Network
neighbor 140.100.56.5 remote-as 456
neighbor 140.100.56.5 description R5_Route_Reflector
neighbor 140.100.56.5 next-hop-self
neighbor 192.168.118.8 remote-as 65000
neighbor 192.168.118.8 description R8_Private_AS
no auto-summary
!
ip classless
ip route 192.168.1.1 255.255.255.255 130.100.26.2

R8#show run
hostname R8
!
```

continues

Example 12-25 *Establishing Peering Between R6 and R8 (Continued)*

```
interface Loopback8
ip address 8.8.8.8 255.255.255.0
!
interface Tunnel8
ip address 192.168.118.8 255.255.255.0
tunnel source 192.168.1.1
tunnel destination 130.100.26.6
!
interface Serial0/0
ip address 10.1.1.2 255.255.255.0
!
interface FastEthernet0/1
ip address 192.168.1.1 255.255.255.0
!
router bgp 65000
no synchronization
bgp router-id 8.8.8.8
bgp log-neighbor-changes
network 192.168.1.0
network 192.168.118.0
neighbor 192.168.118.6 remote-as 456
neighbor 192.168.118.6 description R6
no auto-summary
!
ip route 130.100.26.6 255.255.255.255 192.168.1.222          ←PIX2 Inside
```

Step 4: Route Redistribution on R8

As mentioned, injecting networks into BGP with the **network** statement isn't the only way to reach the objective. Routes may also be redistributed into BGP, as is the case with R8's Loopback8 interface. The command syntax for redistribution is

```
R8(config-router)# redistribute protocol [process-id] {level-1 | level-1-2 |
   level-2} [metric metric-value] [metric-type type-value] [match {internal |
   external 1 | external 2}] [tag tag-value] [route-map map-tag] [weight weight]
   [subnets]
```

The full syntax of this command is explained in Chapter 13, "Redistribution." Of all the available arguments for this command, the ones of interest to you here are *protocol* and **route-map**. Because Loopback8 is configured on the router, it qualifies as connected; therefore, when specifying redistribution, instruct the router to use **connected** as the keyword.

You learned about the concept of a BGP route map earlier, in Step 2 of Case Study 12-2. However, in this case the route map is applied to redistribution instead of to a neighbor. The route map loopback shown in Example 12-26 calls up access list 10, which names 8.8.8.0/24 as the allowed network. When route map loopback is used in conjunction with the **redistribution** command, it makes sure that only 8.8.8.0/24 is redistributed into BGP.

Example 12-26 *Redistributing the Connected Routes on R8*

```
R8#show run
hostname R8
!
! Output omitted for brevity
!
interface Loopback8
ip address 8.8.8.8 255.255.255.0
!
router bgp 65000
no synchronization
bgp router-id 8.8.8.8
bgp log-neighbor-changes
network 192.168.1.0
network 192.168.118.0
redistribute connected route-map Loopback
no auto-summary
!
route-map Loopback permit 10
match ip address 10
!
access-list 10 permit 8.8.8.0 0.0.0.255 log
```

Step 5: MD5 Authentication

MD5 authentication with BGP is a very useful security tool that can prevent spoofing, denial-of-service attacks, and man-in-the-middle attacks. When authentication is configured between two BGP peers, it forces each segment sent on the TCP connection between the peers to be verified. The password on both BGP peers must be identical, and it's never transmitted on the network.

The authentication feature uses the MD5 algorithm, which works by two BGP neighbors signing every TCP segment with an MD5 checksum based on the segment's contents and a shared secret. If the receiver using the same secret calculates the same checksum from the TCP segment, the source is validated. The syntax for the command is

```
R6(config-router)#neighbor [ip-address | peer-group-name] password string
```

In Example 12-27, both R6 and R8 **neighbor** statements are configured with the ccie4460 password. On R8, it appears encrypted because of the **service-password encryption** command.

Example 12-27 *MD5 Authentication*

```
R6#show run
hostname R6
!
! Output omitted for brevity
!
```

continues

Example 12-27 *MD5 Authentication (Continued)*

```
router bgp 456
 no synchronization
 bgp router-id 6.6.6.6
 bgp log-neighbor-changes
 network 130.100.26.0 mask 255.255.255.224
 network 140.100.56.0 mask 255.255.255.192
 network 192.168.118.0
 neighbor 140.100.56.5 remote-as 456
 neighbor 140.100.56.5 description R5_Route_Reflector
 neighbor 140.100.56.5 password ccie4460
 neighbor 140.100.56.5 next-hop-self
 neighbor 192.168.118.8 remote-as 65000
 neighbor 192.168.118.8 description R8_Private_AS
 neighbor 192.168.118.8 password ccie4460

R8#show run
hostname R8
service password-encryption          ← Encrypts password "ccie4460"
!
! Output omitted for brevity
!
router bgp 65000
 no synchronization
 bgp router-id 8.8.8.8
 bgp log-neighbor-changes
 network 192.168.1.0
 network 192.168.118.0
 redistribute connected route-map Loopback
 neighbor 192.168.118.6 remote-as 456
 neighbor 192.168.118.6 description R6
 neighbor 192.168.118.6 password 7 15110805017E7F7278
 no auto-summary
```

NOTE   Adding a password to an existing session triggers it to be torn down, after which a new session is set up.

Step 6: Concealing Private Autonomous Systems from Service Providers

AS 65000 is a private autonomous system and should never be forwarded to a service provider. Yet, if you issue **show ip bgp** on R7 in AS 1560, you will see that network 8.8.8.0/24 is advertised from AS 456 and AS 65000 provided that you permit this network in access list 11 on R4, as shown in Example 12-28. This is unacceptable, and AS 65000 needs to be removed from the autonomous system path.

Example 12-28 show ip bgp *Output on R7*

```
R7#show ip bgp
BGP table version is 33, local router ID is 7.7.7.7
Status codes: s suppressed, d damped, h history, * valid, > best, i - internal
Origin codes: i - IGP, e - EGP, ? - incomplete

   Network          Next Hop          Metric LocPrf Weight Path
*> 2.2.2.0/24       140.100.47.4                        0 456 1234 ?
*> 7.1.1.0/24       0.0.0.0                0      32768 i
*> 7.7.7.0/24       0.0.0.0                0      32768 i
*> 8.8.8.0/24       140.100.47.4                        0 456 65000
```

To hide private autonomous systems from service providers, issue the following command on the border router, R4:

```
R4(config-if)#neighbor ip-address remove-private-as
```

Example 12-29 displays the portion of R4's running configuration where this command has been applied.

Example 12-29 *Suppressing the Private Autonomous System*

```
router bgp 456
no synchronization
bgp router-id 4.4.4.4
bgp log-neighbor-changes
network 140.100.45.0 mask 255.255.255.192
network 140.100.47.0 mask 255.255.255.192
neighbor 140.100.47.7 remote-as 1560
neighbor 140.100.47.7 description R7-BB2
neighbor 140.100.47.7 remove-private-AS
neighbor 140.100.47.7 distribute-list 11 out
```

Now if you view R7's BGP database, shown in Example 12-30, you'll observe that AS 65000 no longer appears under the autonomous system path attribute.

Example 12-30 *R7's BGP Database After the Removal of the Private Autonomous System*

```
R7#show ip bgp
BGP table version is 63, local router ID is 7.7.7.7
Status codes: s suppressed, d damped, h history, * valid, > best, i - internal
Origin codes: i - IGP, e - EGP, ? - incomplete

   Network          Next Hop          Metric LocPrf Weight Path
*> 2.2.2.0/24       140.100.47.4                        0 456 1234 ?
*> 7.1.1.0/24       0.0.0.0                0      32768 i
*> 7.7.7.0/24       0.0.0.0                0      32768 i
*> 8.8.8.0/24       140.100.47.4                        0 456 ? ←6500 is gone
```

Case Study 12-5: BGP Through a Firewall with Prepend

Figure 12-6 illustrates R9 in AS 9 and R3 in AS 3 connected via PIX1. The goal is to enable BGP peering between the two routers and to force R9's autonomous system number to be propagated as something else.

Figure 12-6 *BGP Through a Firewall with Autonomous System Prepend*

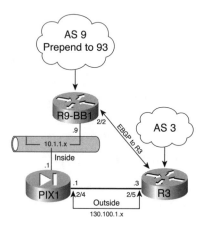

Here are the configuration steps covered in this case study:

Step 1 Initial PIX1 configuration

Step 2 Add static routes on R3 and R9

Step 3 BGP configuration of R3 and R9

Step 4 The **ebgp-multihop** command

Step 5 The **as-path prepend** command

Step 6 Limit a number of routes

Step 7 Verification

Step 1: Initial PIX1 Configuration

You need to configure a PIX Firewall to make this scenario work. Again, you go through the now-familiar steps of the initial configuration. You can see from Example 12-31 that both the inside and outside interfaces have been activated and assigned IP addresses. The **static (inside, outside)** command with the **norandomseq** keyword at the end specifies that network 10.1.1.0 is visible on the outside.

NOTE   The **norandomseq** option disables randomization of the TCP/IP packet sequence numbers. Without it, there would be an issue with proper BGP operation through the PIX. Unfortunately, in most cases the use of the **norandomseq** option diminishes security in the PIX Firewall.

Example 12-31 *PIX1 Configuration*

```
PIX1#write terminal
PIX Version 5.2(3)
nameif ethernet0 outside security0
nameif ethernet1 inside security100

hostname PIX1

access-list bgpin permit tcp host 130.100.1.3 host 10.1.1.9 eq bgp
access-list bgpin permit icmp any any
access-list bgpin permit tcp host 130.100.1.3 host 10.1.1.9 eq telnet
access-list bgpin permit udp any any gt 33000

interface ethernet0 auto
interface ethernet1 auto

ip address outside 130.100.1.1 255.255.255.0
ip address inside 10.1.1.1 255.255.255.0

static (inside,outside) 10.1.1.9 10.1.1.9 netmask 255.255.255.255 0 0 norandomseq
access-group bgpin in interface outside

route outside 0.0.0.0 0.0.0.0 130.100.1.3 1
route inside 9.9.9.0 255.255.255.0 10.1.1.9 1
```

Observe that static routes are indicated for all routes sourced from R3 and network 9.9.9.0/24 sourced from R9. An access list allowing BGP routing, ICMP requests, Telnet, and traceroute has been specified and applied to the incoming traffic on the outside interface. For a more comprehensive explanation of PIX topics, read Chapter 23.

Step 2: Static Routes on R3 and R9

After you configure the PIX Firewall, the static routes on both routers come into play, as shown in Example 12-32. The static route on R3 directs traffic destined for R9 to the PIX1 outside interface. Consequently, R9 points to PIX1's inside interface for traffic going toward R3.

Example 12-32 *Static Routes on R3 and R9*

```
R9#show run
!
! Output omitted for brevity
!
ip route 130.100.1.0 255.255.255.0 10.1.1.1


R3#show run
!
! Output omitted for brevity
!
ip route 10.1.1.0 255.255.255.0 130.100.1.1

R3#ping 10.1.1.9

Type escape sequence to abort.
Sending 5, 100-byte ICMP Echos to 10.1.1.9, timeout is 2 seconds:
!!!!!
Success rate is 100 percent (5/5), round-trip min/avg/max = 4/5/8 ms
R3#
```

Step 3: BGP Configuration of R3 and R9

The next configuration steps repeat the ones from Case Study 12-4. Because R3 was configured in Case Study 12-3, the only thing that still needs to be added on R3 is the **neighbor** statement for R9. Note that because there is no GRE tunnel here, the IP address of R9 is the actual Ethernet0 address.

You can trace the same steps for R9 that will result in the configuration shown in Example 12-33. Interestingly, the **neighbor** statement for R3 on R9 names autonomous system 1234 instead of 3. This is because R3 is a member of confederation 1234 set up in Case Study 12-3.

Example 12-33 *BGP Configuration of R3 and R9*

```
R3#show run
hostname R3
!
interface Loopback0
 ip address 3.3.3.3 255.255.255.0
!
interface Ethernet0
 ip address 130.100.1.3 255.255.255.0
!
interface Serial0
 encapsulation frame-relay
 frame-relay lmi-type ansi
!
```

Example 12-33 *BGP Configuration of R3 and R9 (Continued)*

```
interface Serial0.1 point-to-point
 description Connection to R1
 ip address 150.100.31.3 255.255.255.240
frame-relay interface-dlci 301
!
interface Serial0.2 point-to-point
 description Connection to R2
 ip address 150.100.32.3 255.255.255.224
frame-relay interface-dlci 302
!
interface Serial0.4 point-to-point
 description Connection to R4
 ip address 150.100.33.3 255.255.255.248
frame-relay interface-dlci 304
!
router bgp 3
no synchronization
bgp log-neighbor-changes
bgp confederation identifier 1234
bgp confederation peers 1 2
network 150.100.31.0 mask 255.255.255.240
network 150.100.32.0 mask 255.255.255.224
network 150.100.33.0 mask 255.255.255.248
neighbor 10.1.1.9 remote-as 9
neighbor 10.1.1.9 description R9 Behind Firewall
neighbor 10.1.1.9 password ccie4460
neighbor 150.100.31.1 remote-as 1
neighbor 150.100.31.1 description R1
neighbor 150.100.31.1 next-hop-self
neighbor 150.100.32.2 remote-as 2
neighbor 150.100.32.2 description R2
neighbor 150.100.32.2 next-hop-self
neighbor 150.100.33.4 remote-as 456
neighbor 150.100.33.4 description R4 IBGP -Link to AS456
no auto-summary
!
ip route 10.1.1.0 255.255.255.0 130.100.1.1

R9#show run
hostname r9
!
interface Loopback9
ip address 9.9.9.9 255.255.255.0
!
interface Ethernet0
ip address 10.1.1.9 255.255.255.0
!
router bgp 9
bgp log-neighbor-changes
network 10.10.10.0 mask 255.255.255.0
redistribute connected
```

continues

Example 12-33 *BGP Configuration of R3 and R9 (Continued)*

```
neighbor 130.100.1.3 remote-as 1234
neighbor 130.100.1.3 description R3 over Pix1
neighbor 130.100.1.3 password ccie4460
no auto-summary
!
ip route 130.100.1.0 255.255.255.0 10.1.1.1
```

Step 4: The **ebgp-multihop** Command

So far, the new configuration has been almost identical to Case Study 12-4. However, the important difference is that, unlike in that case study, the routers do not communicate over a tunnel, but rather through a direct link of their physical interfaces to PIX1. This introduces an extra hop between them.

Typically, EBGP neighbors are directly connected, and because they both use the same IP subnet, they know how to reach one another. That's why in Case Study 12-4 a GRE tunnel was introduced, creating a logical subnet that both routers shared. However, in this case the routers are not directly connected and have no tunnel in between.

To solve this dilemma, EBGP allows the following command to indicate that the neighbor connection is to be established between two non-directly connected external peers:

```
R3(config-router)#neighbor [ip-address | peer-group-name] ebgp-multihop [ttl]
```

Without **ebgp-multihop**, the neighbor session will not move forward to the active state from its idle state. Example 12-34 demonstrates application of this command on both routers. The optional TTL value of 2 signifies that two neighbors are one hop distant from each other. Otherwise, the default value of 1 indicates that no packet routing takes place between the two neighbors, because they are directly connected. The default TTL value is automatically changed with the **ebgp-multihop** command and is set to a new default of 255 whenever it isn't explicitly specified.

Example 12-34 **ebgp-multihop** *Command Configuration*

```
R9#show run
hostname r9
!
! Output omitted for brevity
!
router bgp 9
neighbor 130.100.1.3 ebgp-multihop 2              ←to R3

R3#show run
!
! Output omitted for brevity
!
router bgp 3
neighbor 10.1.1.9 ebgp-multihop 2                 ←to R9
```

Whenever the neighbors are separated by another hop, some kind of IGP or static routing should also be configured so that the neighbors can reach one another. If you recall, a static route has been configured on each router and PIX1 right before the BGP configuration. If you miss this important step, you receive the error shown in Example 12-35.

Example 12-35 *Result of No Available Routing*

```
03:54:22: BGP: 10.1.1.9 multihop open delayed 13680ms (no route)
R3#
```

Step 5: The **as-path prepend** Command

The next step demonstrates the use of a route map with the **neighbor** statement. You have seen its application before, but here a route map is created in a new way. Instead of matching filtering conditions preset with a filter list, this route map sets its own parameters.

Sometimes, in a real-life BGP setup you might need to make the autonomous system path appear longer than it is. In the present scenario, the path information needs to be modified to add a nonexistent autonomous system number to routes coming from AS 9. You do this by adding (prepending) autonomous system numbers to the existing path statistics advertised from AS 9 to AS 3.

The route map command syntax is

```
R9(config-route-map)#set as-path prepend as-path-number [as-path-number]...
```

Example 12-36 shows the application of **route-map prepend** outgoing to R3. The route map's **set** statement specifies the add-on of autonomous system 93 to AS 9's updates.

Example 12-36 *Prepending an Autonomous System to the Autonomous System Path*

```
R9#show run
!
! Output omitted for brevity
!
router bgp 9
neighbor 130.100.1.3 route-map Lilo out
!
route-map Lilo permit 10
  set as-path prepend 93
```

Step 6: Limiting a Number of Routes

Suppose that R3 is injecting a large number of routes into AS 9, and AS 9 wants to protect itself against this. You can configure a limit on how many prefixes a BGP router is willing to receive from its peer. This is yet another filtering tool made possible by BGP. The command syntax is

```
R9(config-router)#neighbor [ip-address | peer-group-name] maximum-prefix maximum
  [threshold] [warning-only]
```

Example 12-37 shows how this command is implemented on R9. R9 allows R3 to send up to 100 networks in its routing updates to AS 9. When the preset maximum is exceeded, R9 terminates the peering. If you wanted to bring up the peering again, you would need to issue the **clear ip bgp** command. However, if the **warning-only** keyword were specified, the router would only send a log message; it wouldn't drop the session.

Example 12-37 *Setting the Maximum Number of Incoming Routes*

```
R9#show run
hostname R9
!
! Output omitted for brevity
!
router bgp 9
neighbor 130.100.1.3 maximum-prefix 100
```

Step 7: Verification

Because of the configuration steps taken in this case study, autonomous system 3 receives updates about 9.9.9.0 and 10.1.1.0 with the path information of 9, 93. Compare the output of the **show ip bgp** command on R9 and R3 shown in Example 12-38. On R9, networks 9.9.9.0 and 10.1.1.0 don't indicate a path, because they are local. On the other hand, R3 displays the path for these networks through a real AS 9 and a fictitious AS 93.

Example 12-38 *BGP Databases of R3 and R9*

```
R3#show ip bgp
Origin codes: i - IGP, e - EGP, ? - incomplete

   Network          Next Hop          Metric LocPrf Weight Path
*> 9.9.9.0/24       10.1.1.9               0             0 9 93 ?
*> 10.1.1.0/24      10.1.1.9               0             0 9 93 ?
```

To ensure a successful configuration, issue the **show ip bgp summary** command on R9 and R3. Check if you are receiving the accurate number of routes from all configured neighbors. Example 12-39 shows the output of **show ip bgp summary** issued on R9. You can see that R9 is receiving 13 prefixes from its neighbor R3.

Example 12-39 show ip bgp summary *Command on R3 and R9*

```
R9#show ip bgp summary
BGP router identifier 9.9.9.9, local AS number 9
BGP table version is 158, main routing table version 158
15 network entries and 15 paths using 1995 bytes of memory
7 BGP path attribute entries using 420 bytes of memory
4 BGP AS-PATH entries using 96 bytes of memory
0 BGP route-map cache entries using 0 bytes of memory
0 BGP filter-list cache entries using 0 bytes of memory
```

Example 12-39 **show ip bgp summary** *Command on R3 and R9 (Continued)*

```
BGP activity 54/99 prefixes, 86/71 paths, scan interval 15 secs

Neighbor        V    AS MsgRcvd MsgSent   TblVer  InQ OutQ Up/Down  State/PfxRcd
130.100.1.3     4  1234    306     252      158   0    0 00:01:32       13
```

Then verify whether these routes appear correctly in the routing table, as shown in Example 12-40.

Example 12-40 **show ip route bgp** *Command on R3 and R9*

```
R9#show ip route bgp
     2.0.0.0/24 is subnetted, 1 subnets
B       2.2.2.0 [20/0] via 130.100.1.3, 00:03:37
     140.100.0.0/26 is subnetted, 3 subnets
B       140.100.45.0 [20/0] via 130.100.1.3, 00:03:37
B       140.100.47.0 [20/0] via 130.100.1.3, 00:03:37
B       140.100.56.0 [20/0] via 130.100.1.3, 00:03:37
B    156.46.0.0/16 [20/0] via 130.100.1.3, 00:03:37
     7.0.0.0/24 is subnetted, 1 subnets
B       7.7.7.0 [20/0] via 130.100.1.3, 00:03:37
     8.0.0.0/24 is subnetted, 1 subnets
B       8.8.8.0 [20/0] via 130.100.1.3, 00:03:37
B    192.168.118.0/24 [20/0] via 130.100.1.3, 00:03:37
     150.100.0.0/16 is variably subnetted, 4 subnets, 4 masks
B       150.100.32.0/27 [20/0] via 130.100.1.3, 00:03:37
B       150.100.33.0/29 [20/0] via 130.100.1.3, 00:03:37
B       150.100.31.0/28 [20/0] via 130.100.1.3, 00:03:37
B       150.100.0.0/16 [20/0] via 130.100.1.3, 00:03:37
B    209.112.0.0/16 [20/0] via 130.100.1.3, 00:03:37

R3#show ip route bgp | include 10.1.1.9
B       9.9.9.0 [20/0] via 10.1.1.9, 00:03:57
```

Finally, you need to confirm that inter-autonomous system reachability is working properly throughout the full case study topology shown in Figure 12-1. By pinging R7 and R8 from R9 and tracing a route from R2 to AS 9, you can make certain that the autonomous systems that are farthest away are still accessible.

Example 12-41 *ICMP Requests and Traceroute Verification*

```
R2#traceroute 10.1.1.9

Type escape sequence to abort.
Tracing the route to 10.1.1.9

  1 150.100.32.3 24 msec 24 msec 24 msec
  2 10.1.1.9 [AS 93] 56 msec 32 msec *
```

Summary

This chapter presented some general information on Border Gateway Protocol (BGP). The "Configuring BGP" section dealt with the important underlying BGP setup and advanced security aspects.

BGP is a highly scalable protocol with numerous configuration and filtering features, some of which are impossible and unnecessary to cover in this book. However, this chapter was designed to give you a firm grasp of many security concepts achieved with the help of BGP and also some of the necessary and common configuration tasks without which BGP simply wouldn't work. Reading and understanding the material covered here and completing the exercises suggested in Chapter 26, "Sample Lab Scenarios," should make you very comfortable with the level of BGP offered in the CCIE Security lab exam.

Review Questions

1 What are the applications of a route map in BGP?

2 What is the purpose of MD5 authentication in BGP?

3 Why is the **maximum-prefix** command needed?

4 Why should private autonomous system filtering be used?

5 Where do you use the **next-hop-self** command?

FAQ

Q — *When a route reflector is configured, does it change the next-hop information for a route it's reflecting?*

A — No. Not unless the **next-hop-self** command is specified.

Q — *When the **show ip bgp** command is issued, what does a next hop of 0.0.0.0 mean?*

A — 0.0.0.0 shows that a network is of local origin. The means by which a network can be locally originated include redistributing Interior Gateway Protocol (IGP) into BGP and a **network** or **aggregate** command in the BGP configuration.

Q — *What are the rules for resetting a particular BGP session?*

A — When you make a change to the inbound/outbound policy for a BGP session, you should clear that session. There are several ways of doing this. To clear a BGP session for outbound changes, issue the **clear ip bgp** *neighbor-address* **soft out** command. To clear a BGP session for inbound changes, issue the **clear ip bgp** *neighbor-address* command or the **clear ip bgp** *neighbor-address* **soft in** command if the neighbor supports it.

Q — *In what order are filtering techniques applied to a BGP neighbor?*

A — It depends on whether they are applied to inbound or outbound updates. For inbound updates, the route map is tried first, and then the distribute list. For outbound updates, this order is reversed.

This chapter includes the following topics:

- Metrics
- Administrative distance
- Avoiding problems due to redistribution
- Configuring redistribution of routing information

CHAPTER 13

Redistribution

In this chapter, you look at the redistribution of routes from one protocol or autonomous system to another. Redistribution of routes from one routing protocol or autonomous system into another is an integral part of the CCIE Security lab exam. You will be asked to redistribute the routes from one protocol into another and to possibly modify their metrics and/or filter the routes injected into or from a routing protocol.

Redistribution occurs whenever you use a routing protocol to advertise routes that are learned by some other means such as by another routing protocol, static routes, or directly connected routes. Many reasons exist for the use of redistribution, including some of the most common reasons for running multiprotocol routing, mergers, multiple departments managed by multiple network administrators, and multivendor environments.

Each routing protocol in use can have different characteristics such as metrics, administrative distance, and classful and classless capabilities, which can have a distinct effect on redistribution. You must take these differences into consideration to ensure success in your redistribution efforts.

Metrics

Protocol metrics play an important role in redistribution of routes. Each routing protocol can make use of different metrics. For example, Routing Information Protocol (RIP) uses hop count as its metric, while Interior Gateway Routing Protocol/Enhanced Interior Gateway Routing Protocol (IGRP/EIGRP) bases its metric on bandwidth and delay. Because these differences exist, when you distribute routes, you must define an artificial metric that the receiving protocol can understand and use. With Cisco IOS Software, two ways of defining metrics when redistributing routes are as follows:

- You can define the metric for that specific redistribution only.
- You can use the same metric as a default for all redistributions.

The supported automatic metric translations between the routing protocols, assuming that you have not defined a default redistribution metric, are as follows:

- RIP can automatically redistribute static routes and assigns them a metric of 1.

- Border Gateway Protocol (BGP) does not normally send metrics in its routing updates.

- IGRP can automatically redistribute static routes, with the same metric as a directly connected route, and information from other IGRP-routed autonomous systems. IGRP does not change the metrics of routes derived from IGRP updates from other autonomous systems.

- Automatic metric translation occurs between IGRP and EIGRP.

Administrative Distance

The following is an area of concern when redistributing routes: What happens when your router learns a route to the same destination using both routing protocols? Which route will be selected over the other, or is it possible to create a routing loop? Adding to this dilemma is the fact that each protocol uses its own metric type to determine the best route, making it impossible to compare routes with different metric types. To alleviate this problem, Cisco IOS Software uses the administrative distance of the route to determine which one is placed in the routing table. Administrative distances are assigned so that the routing table can ensure that the route from the most preferred source is chosen as the best path.

While administrative distances are helpful with route selection among different routing protocols, they can cause problems when you configure your network to use redistribution. Some of these problems take the form of routing loops, convergence issues, or inefficient routing.

Classless and Classful Capabilities

A routing protocol can be classless or classful. You might be wondering why this has any bearing on how a router builds its routing table. If a routing protocol is classful, such as RIP and IGRP, it does not carry subnet masks in its routing updates. However, classless routing protocols, such as EIGRP and OSPF, do carry subnet masks. When a classful routing protocol receives a routing update in the same major network as the interface it is received on, the interface must have the same subnet mask as the one in the update. If the update is in a different class, it is automatically summarized at that class's major bit boundary. This means that if you were to redistribute a classless routing protocol into a classful protocol and the same major network crosses the boundaries of both routing protocols, the classful routing protocol does not install the subnets into its routing table. You must configure static routes to these networks on the classful routers.

Avoiding Problems Due to Redistribution

Because redistribution can potentially cause problems on your network, such as less-than-optimal routing, routing loops, or slow convergence, elimination of these problems is imperative. Fortunately, you can avoid these issues by simply following this rule: Never announce the information originally received from routing process X back into routing process X.

The easiest way to accomplish this is to filter these updates. You can add a distribute list to your configuration to filter any updates that can be reintroduced to the same routing protocol that originated it from the receiving routing protocol. A route must pass the criteria defined in the associated access list to be permitted by the distribute list. Note that even if one of the routing protocols has a higher administrative distance than the other, it still might not be the installed route.

Another technique that is available to you is to use route maps to set tags for various routes. Your routing processes can then redistribute routes based on these tags. You cannot use this method of control with RIP version 1 or IGRP.

Configuring Redistribution of Routing Information

As you learned in the preceding section, you can accomplish conditional control of the redistribution of routes between routing domains by using route maps. Due to the wide range of routing protocols that you can choose from, some of the **match** and **set** commands that you use with your route maps are specific to a particular protocol.

Use the following command to define a route map for redistribution:

```
R2(config)#route-map map-tag [permit | deny] [sequence-number]
```

Once you have the route map defined, you have the option of defining one or more **match** commands and one or more **set** commands to control traffic. If you do not define a **match** command, then everything matches. If you do not define a **set** command, nothing else is done to the routes.

Use at least one of the following **match** commands to define conditions for redistributing routes from one routing protocol into another.

To match a BGP autonomous system path access list, use the following command:

```
R2(config-route-map)#match as-path path-list-number
```

To match a BGP community list, use the following command:

```
R2(config-route-map)#match community-list community-list-number [exact]
```

To match a standard access list, use the following command:

```
R2(config-route-map)#match ip address {access-list-number | access-list-name}
   [...access-list-number | ...access-list-name]
```

To match the specified metric, use the following command:

```
R2(config-route-map)#match metric metric-value
```

To match a next-hop router address passed by one of the access lists specified, use the following command:

```
R2(config-route-map)#match ip next-hop {access-list-number | access-list-name} [access-
   list-number | access-list-name]
```

To match the specified tag value, use the following command:

```
R2(config-route-map)#match tag tag-value [tag-value]
```

To match the specified next-hop route out one of the interfaces specified, use the following command:

```
R2(config-route-map)#match interface interface-type interface-number [interface-type
   interface-number]
```

To match the address specified by the advertised access lists, use the following command:

```
R2(config-route-map)#match ip route-source {access-list-number | access-list-name}
   [access-list-number | access-list-name]
```

To match the specified route type, use the following command:

```
R2(config-route-map)#match route-type {local | internal | external [type-1 | type-2] |
   level-1 | level-2}
```

Use at least one of the following **set** commands to define conditions for redistributing routes from one routing protocol into another.

To set the communities attribute, use the following command:

```
R2(config-route-map)#set community {community-number [additive]} | none
```

To set BGP route dampening factors, use the following command:

```
R2(config-route-map)#set dampening halflife reuse suppress max-suppress-time
```

To assign a value to a local BGP path, use the following command:

```
R2(config-route-map)#set local-preference number-value
```

To specify the BGP weight for the routing table, use the following command:

```
R2(config-route-map)#set weight weight
```

To set the BGP origin code, use the following command:

```
R2(config-route-map)#set origin {igp | egp as-number | incomplete}
```

To modify the BGP autonomous system path, use the following command:

```
R2(config-route-map)#set as-path {tag | prepend as-path-string}
```

To specify the address of the next hop, use the following command:

```
R2(config-route-map)#set next-hop next-hop
```

To enable automatic computing of the tag table, use the following command:

```
R2(config-route-map)#set automatic-tag
```

To specify the areas in which to import routes, use the following command:

```
R2(config-route-map)#set level {level-1 | level-2 | level-1-2 | stub-area | backbone}
```

To set the metric value to give the redistributed routes for any protocol except IGRP or EIGRP, use the following command:

```
R2(config-route-map)#set metric metric-value
```

To set the metric value to give the redistributed routes for IGRP or EIGRP only, use the following command:

```
R2(config-route-map)#set metric bandwidth delay reliability loading mtu
```

To set the metric type to give redistributed routes, use the following command:

```
R2(config-route-map)#set metric-type {internal | external | type-1 | type-2}
```

To set the Multi-Exit Discriminator (MED) value on prefixes advertised to exterior BGP neighbors to match the Interior Gateway Protocol (IGP) metric of the next hop, use the following command:

```
R2(config-route-map)#set metric-type internal
```

To set the tag value to associate with the redistributed routes, use the following command:

```
R2(config-route-map)#set tag tag-value
```

Use the following commands to distribute routes from one routing domain into another and to control route redistribution.

To redistribute routes from one routing protocol to another routing protocol, use the following command:

```
R2(config-router)#redistribute protocol [process-id] {level-1 | level-1-2 | level-2}
   [metric metric-value] [metric-type type-value] [match internal | external type-value]
   [tag tag-value] [route-map map-tag] [weight number-value] [subnets]
```

To cause the current routing protocol to use the same metric value for all redistributed routes (BGP, OSPF, RIP), use the following command:

```
R2(config-router)#default-metric number
```

To cause the IGRP or EIGRP routing protocol to use the same metric value for all non-IGRP redistributed routes, use the following command:

```
R2(config-router)#default-metric bandwidth delay reliability loading mtu
```

To disable the default redistribution of default information between IGRP processes, use the following command:

```
R2(config-router)#no default-information {in | out}
```

Redistributing Connected Networks into OSPF

When redistributing connected networks into OSPF, you must know what version of Cisco IOS Software you are running.

Whenever you have a major network that you have allocated into subnets, you use the **subnet** keyword to redistribute protocols into OSPF. If you do not use the keyword, OSPF only redistributes any major networks that have not been divided into subnets.

Prior to Cisco IOS Software Release 12.1(3)

Before the introduction of Cisco IOS Software Release 12.1(3), when you redistributed connected routes into OSPF, a connected network that you included in a network statement under your router OSPF configuration is advertised in Type 1, Type 2, or Type 3 link-state advertisements (LSAs), along with Type 5 LSAs. Storing these Type 5 LSAs consumes memory and requires the CPU to process the LSAs during full or partial shortest path first (SPF) runs and to flood them when some instability occurs.

Cisco IOS Software Release 12.1(3) and Later

With the introduction of Cisco IOS Software Release 12.1(3) and later, Type 5 LSAs were no longer created for connected networks that are included in the network statements under your OSPF configuration.

Lesson 13-1: Redistributing OSPF into Border Gateway Protocol

RFC 1403, "BGP OSPF Interaction," outlines the proper behavior of OSPF to BGP redistribution. You can override the default behavior of not redistributing any routes from OSPF to BGP through the use of route maps. This means that using the **redistribute ospf 1** command under the **router bgp 1** command does not work; specific keywords such as **internal**, **external**, and **nssa-external**, are required to enable the redistribution of the respective routes.

Figure 13-1 illustrates the topology that you will use for your OSFP-to-BGP redistribution lesson.

In this lesson, you configure BGP autonomous system 100 to redistribute the routes it learns from redistributing OSPF. Autonomous system 200 should see the internal routes (intra- and inter-area) of 133.108.1.0/24 and 133.108.2.0/24 from autonomous system 100. Example 13-1 shows the configuration of R5 that you need to complete this lesson.

Figure 13-1 *OSPF-to-BGP Redistribution Topology*

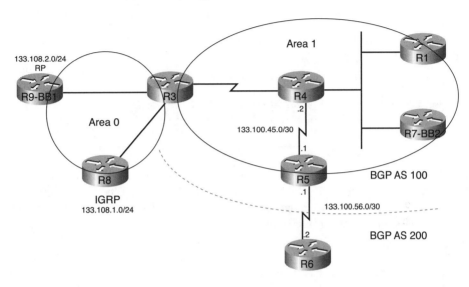

Example 13-1 *Internal Route Redistribution, OSPF to BGP*

```
Configuration items for R5:
R5(config)#interface Serial0
R5(config-if)#ip address 133.100.145.1 255.255.255.252
R5(config-if)#exit
R5(config)#interface Serial1
R5(config-if)#ip address 133.100.56.1 255.255.255.252
R5(config-if)#exit
R5(config)#router ospf 1
R5(config-router)#network 133.100.145.0 0.0.0.255 area 1
R5(config-router)#exit
R5(config)#router bgp 100
R5(config-router)#redistribute ospf 1 match internal
R5(config-router)#neighbor 133.100.56.2 remote-as 200
```

By looking at the routing table of R6, you can see that it is learning these two routes from BGP, as shown in Example 13-2.

Example 13-2 *The* **show ip route** *Command Output from R6 for Internal Routes*

```
R6#show ip route
Codes: C - connected, S - static, I - IGRP, R - RIP, M - mobile, B - BGP
       D - EIGRP, EX - EIGRP external, O - OSPF, IA - OSPF inter area
```

continues

Example 13-2 *The* **show ip route** *Command Output from R6 for Internal Routes (Continued)*

```
          N1 - OSPF NSSA external type 1, N2 - OSPF NSSA external type 2
          E1 - OSPF external type 1, E2 - OSPF external type 2, E - EGP
          i - IS-IS, L1 - IS-IS level-1, L2 - IS-IS level-2, * - candidate default
          U - per-user static route, o - ODR

Gateway of last resort is not set

B    133.108.1.0/24 [20/20] via 133.100.56.1, 00:01:43
B    133.108.2.0/24 [20/20] via 133.100.56.1, 00:01:43
C    133.100.56.0/30 is directly connected, Serial0
```

Now you need to change the configuration of router R5 so that it only redistributes OSPF external routes into BGP. You redistribute the OSPF external Type 1 route 100.1.1.0/24 and the OSPF external Type 2 route 100.1.2.0/24 into BGP. Example 13-3 shows a possible configuration to make this lesson work.

Example 13-3 *Redistributing Type 1 and Type 2 External Routes into BGP*

```
Configuration changes required on R5:
R5(config)#router bgp 100
R5(config-router)#redistribute ospf 1 match external 1 external 2
```

After completing these configuration changes, reissuing the **show ip route** command on R6 shows that it is learning these two OSPF external routes from BGP, as shown in Example 13-4.

Example 13-4 *The* **show ip route** *Command Output from R6 for External Routes*

```
R6#show ip route
Codes: C - connected, S - static, I - IGRP, R - RIP, M - mobile, B - BGP
          D - EIGRP, EX - EIGRP external, O - OSPF, IA - OSPF inter area
          N1 - OSPF NSSA external type 1, N2 - OSPF NSSA external type 2
          E1 - OSPF external type 1, E2 - OSPF external type 2, E - EGP
          i - IS-IS, L1 - IS-IS level-1, L2 - IS-IS level-2, * - candidate default
          U - per-user static route, o - ODR

Gateway of last resort is not set

B    100.1.1.0/24 [20/20] via 133.100.56.1, 00:01:43
B    100.1.2.0/24 [20/20] via 133.100.56.1, 00:01:43
C    133.100.56.0/30 is directly connected, Serial0
```

Note that you could have entered the following command under your BGP configuration and seen the same results:

```
R5(config-router)#redistribute ospf 1 match external
```

This is because redistribution of external routes, by default, includes both Type 1 and Type 2. If you only want to redistribute one type, you must specify it when you define your redistribution command.

In this lesson, you configure redistribution of OSPF internal and external routes into BGP. Example 13-5 shows the changes required for R5 to make this operational.

Example 13-5 *Redistributing Internal and External OSPF Routes into BGP*

```
Configuration changes on R5:
R5(config)#router bgp 100
R5(config-router)#redistribute ospf 1 match internal external 1 external 2
R5(config-router)#neighbor 133.100.56.2 remote-as 200
```

Upon completion of these changes, router R6 shows that it is learning all OSPF routes from BGP, as shown in Example 13-6.

Example 13-6 *The* **show ip route** *Command Output from R6 for Internal and External Routes*

```
R6#show ip route
Codes: C - connected, S - static, I - IGRP, R - RIP, M - mobile, B - BGP
       D - EIGRP, EX - EIGRP external, O - OSPF, IA - OSPF inter area
       N1 - OSPF NSSA external type 1, N2 - OSPF NSSA external type 2
       E1 - OSPF external type 1, E2 - OSPF external type 2, E - EGP
       i - IS-IS, L1 - IS-IS level-1, L2 - IS-IS level-2, * - candidate default
       U - per-user static route, o - ODR

Gateway of last resort is not set

B       133.108.1.0/24 [20/20] via 133.100.56.1, 00:01:43
B       133.108.2.0/24 [20/20] via 133.100.56.1, 00:01:43
B       100.1.1.0/24 [20/20] via 133.100.56.1, 00:01:43
B       100.2.2.0/24 [20/20] via 133.100.56.1, 00:01:43
C       133.100.56.0/30 is directly connected, Serial0
```

Lesson 13-2: Redistributing OSPF Not-So-Stubby Area External Routes into BGP

When you choose to redistribute OSPF routes from a not-so-stubby area (NSSA) into BGP, you must treat it as a special case. While it is not significantly different from redistributing OSPF external routes into BGP, the main difference is that BGP is now matching NSSA external routes instead of just external routes.

Figure 13-2 shows the topology that you will use for the following lessons.

Figure 13-2 *Redistribution of OSPF NSSA Routes into BGP*

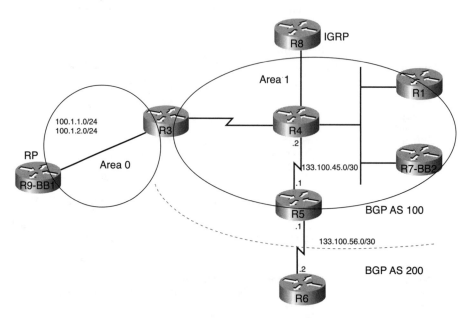

In this lesson, you configure router R5 to redistribute routes learned from the NSSA (100.1.1.0/24 and 100.1.2.0/24). Example 13-7 shows a possible solution to this lesson.

Example 13-7 *Redistribution of NSSA Routes into BGP*

```
Configuration items for R5:
R5(config)#router ospf 1
R5(config-router)#network 133.100.45.1 0.0.0.3 area 1 nssa
R5(config-router)#exit
R5(config)#router bgp 100
R5(config-router)#redistribute ospf 1 match nssa-external 1 nssa-external 2
R5(config-router)#neighbor 133.100.56.2 remote-as 200
```

After completion of the lesson, examining the **show ip route** command output from router R6 shows you that it is learning the routes from the NSSA, as expected. Example 13-8 shows this output.

Example 13-8 *The* **show ip route** *Command Output from R6 Showing NSSA Routes*

```
R6#show ip route
Codes:  C - connected, S - static, I -    IGRP, R - RIP, M - mobile, B - BGP
        D -    EIGRP, EX - EIGRP external, O - OSPF, IA - OSPF inter area
        N1 - OSPF NSSA external type 1, N2 - OSPF NSSA external type 2
        E1 - OSPF external type 1, E2 - OSPF external type 2, E - EGP
```

Example 13-8 *The* **show ip route** *Command Output from R6 Showing NSSA Routes (Continued)*

```
          i - IS-IS, L1 - IS-IS level-1, L2 - IS-IS level-2, * - candidate default
          U - per-user static route, o - ODR

Gateway of last resort is not set

B     100.1.1.0/24 [20/20] via 133.100.56.1, 00:01:43
B     100.1.2.0/24 [20/20] via 133.100.56.1, 00:01:43
C     133.100.56.0/30 is directly connected, Serial0
```

Note that you could have entered the following command under your BGP configuration and seen the same results:

```
R5(config-router)#redistribute ospf 1 match nssa-external
```

This is because redistribution of NSSA external routes, by default, includes both Type 1 and Type 2. If you only want to redistribute one type, you must specify it when you define your redistribution command.

Lesson 13-3: Redistributing Routes Between OSPF and RIP Version 1

When redistributing routes between OSPF and RIP version 1, a problem arises when OSPF has a different mask than RIP version 1. Because RIP is a classful routing protocol, it does not redistribute these routes. One way around this is to create a static route with a mask that matches the RIP version 1 mask in use and that points to the OSPF domain with a classful mask, but points to a next hop of null.

Figure 13-3 illustrates the topology that you will use for this lesson.

Figure 13-3 *OSPF-to-RIP Redistribution Topology*

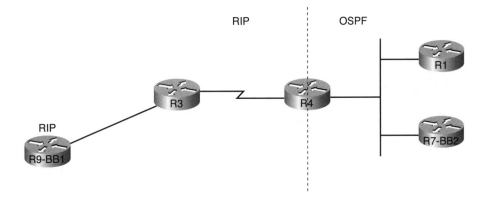

For this lesson, you assume that OSPF is using a longer subnet mask for the same network that RIP is using. Configure router R4 so that you can inform RIP of the routes that OSPF is using in the 200.100.0.0 network. Example 13-9 shows the configuration items on R4 that make this possible.

Example 13-9 *OSPF with Longer Subnet Mask Redistributed to RIP*

```
Configuration items for R4:
R4(config)#ip route 200.100.0.0 255.255.255.0 null0
R4(config)#router rip
R4(config-router)#redistribute static
R4(config-router)#default metric 1
```

This configuration still works, even though you pointed the static route to null0, because router R4 has more specific routes to the destination networks through information obtained through OSPF.

You can also use this method of tricking the classful routing protocol when you use EIGRP instead of OSPF, and IGRP instead of RIP. You do not see this problem if the masks of both protocols are the same or if all the protocols that you are using support variable-length subnet masks (VLSMs).

Lesson 13-4: Redistributing Between Two EIGRP Autonomous Systems

When advertising EIGRP routes from two separate autonomous systems, you must use filtering to keep routes from the same autonomous system from being reintroduced into it. This can cause a routing loop to occur on your network.

Figure 13-4 illustrates the new topology that you will use with the following lesson.

Figure 13-4 *Redistribution Between Two EIGRP Autonomous Systems*

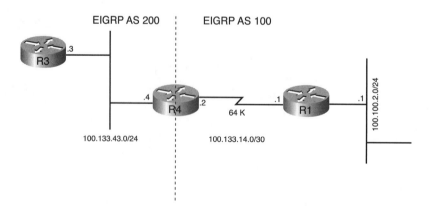

In this lesson, router R1 is configured to advertise the network 100.100.2.0/24 to router R4 through autonomous system 100. Router R4 is configured to redistribute this route into autonomous system 200 and advertise it to router R3. Example 13-10 shows you one solution to this lesson.

Example 13-10 *Redistributing Two EIGRP Autonomous Systems*

```
Configuration items for R3:
R3(config)#router eigrp 200
R3(config-router)#network 133.100.34.0 0.0.0.255

Configuration items for R4:
R4(config)#router eigrp 200
R4(config)#redistribute eigrp 100 route-map to-eigrp200
R4(config-router)#network 133.100.34.0 0.0.0.255
R4(config-router)#exit
R4(config)#router eigrp 100
R4(config-router)#redistribute eigrp 200 route-map to-eigrp100
R4(config-router)#network 133.100.41.0 0.0.0.255
R4(config-router)#exit
R4(config)#route-map to-eigrp100 deny 10
R4(config-route-map)#match tag 100
R4(config-route-map)#exit
R4(config)#route-map to-eigrp100 permit 20
R4(config-route-map)#set tag 200
R4(config-route-map)#exit
R4(config)#route-map to-eigrp200 deny 10
R4(config-route-map)#match tag 200
R4(config-route-map)#exit
R4(config)#route-map to-eigrp200 permit 20
R4(config-route-map)#set tag 100

Configuration items for R1:
R1(config)#router eigrp 100
R1(config-router)#network 133.100.41.0 0.0.0.255
R1(config-router)#network 100.100.2.0 0.0.0.255
```

Lesson 13-5: Redistributing Routes Between EIGRP and IGRP in Two Different Autonomous Systems

When you redistribute IGRP routes into an EIGRP autonomous system that has a different autonomous system number, the IGRP metrics are preserved but are scaled by multiplying the original IGRP metric by the constant 256. There is one exception to this rule: If the network is directly connected to the router doing the redistribution, it advertises the route with a metric of 1.

Remember that when you redistribute between EIGRP and IGRP, no metric conversion is required, so you do not need to define any metrics or use the **default-metric** command.

Figure 13-5 shows the updated topology that you will use for the following lesson.

Figure 13-5 *Redistributing IGRP into a Different EIGRP Autonomous System*

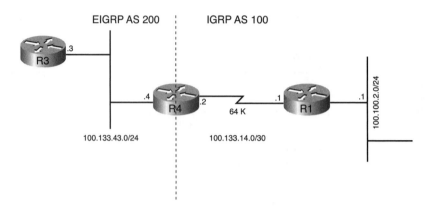

In this lesson, R1 is configured to advertise the network 100.100.2.0/24 to R4 through autonomous system 100. Router R4 is configured to redistribute this route into autonomous system 200 and advertise it to R3. Example 13-11 shows you one solution to this lesson.

Example 13-11 *Redistributing Between IGRP and EIGRP of Different Autonomous Systems*

```
Configuration items for R3:
R3(config)#router eigrp 200
R3(config-router)#network 133.100.34.0 0.0.0.255

Configuration items for R4:
R4(config)#router eigrp 200
R4(config-router)#redistribute igrp 100 route-map to-eigrp200
R4(config-router)#network 133.100.34.0 0.0.0.255
 R4(config-router)#exit
R4(config)#router igrp 100
R4(config-router)#redistribute eigrp 200 route-map to-igrp100
R4(config-router)#network 133.100.41.0 0.0.0.255
R4(config-router)#exit
R4(config)#route-map to-igrp100 deny 10
R4(config-route-map)#match tag 100
R4(config-route-map)#exit
R4(config)#route-map to-igrp100 permit 20
R4(config-route-map)#set tag 200
R4(config-route-map)#exit
R4(config)#route-map to-eigrp200 deny 10
R4(config-route-map)#match tag 200
R4(config-route-map)#exit
R4(config)#route-map to-eigrp200 permit 20
R4(config-route-map)#set tag 100
```

Example 13-11 *Redistributing Between IGRP and EIGRP of Different Autonomous Systems (Continued)*

```
Configuration items for R1:
R1(config)#router igrp 100
R1(config-router)#network 133.100.41.0 0.0.0.255
R1(config-router)#network 100.100.2.0 0.0.0.255
```

Lesson 13-6: Redistributing Routes Between EIGRP and IGRP in the Same Autonomous System

Configuring redistribution between EIGRP and IGRP when they are on the same autonomous system is similar to redistributing between two different autonomous systems running IGRP and EIGRP. Note the following two caveats with EIGRP/IGRP redistribution within the same autonomous system:

- Internal EIGRP routes are always preferred over external EIGRP or IGRP routes.

- External EIGRP route metrics are compared to scaled IGRP metrics (the administrative distance is ignored).

Figure 13-6 shows the new topology for use with this lesson.

Figure 13-6 *Redistribution Between EIGRP and IGRP in the Same Autonomous System*

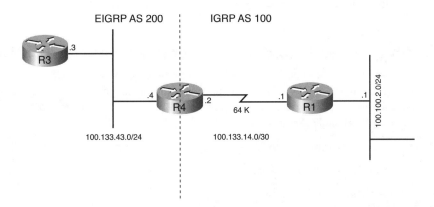

In this lesson, R1 is configured to advertise the network 100.100.2.0/24 to R4 through autonomous system 100. R4 is configured to redistribute this route into autonomous system 200 and advertise it to R3. Example 13-12 shows you one solution to this lesson.

Example 13-12 *Redistribution Between IGRP and EIGRP on the Same Autonomous System*

```
Configuration items for R3:
R3(config)#router eigrp 200
R3(config-router)#network 133.100.34.0

Configuration items for R4:
R4(config)#router eigrp 200
R4(config-router)#network 133.100.34.0
R4(config-router)#exit
R4(config)#router igrp 200
R4(config-router)#network 133.100.41.0

Configuration items for R1:
R4(config)#router igrp 200
R4(config-router)#network 133.100.41.0
R4(config-router)#network 100.100.2.0
```

R4 is redistributing the IGRP route into EIGRP. When reviewing the configuration in Example 13-12, remember that IGRP and EIGRP can automatically redistribute routes into each other if you define the same autonomous system numbers as the process ID. If two routes, one from IGRP and one from EIGRP, have the same metric, after scaling the IGRP route by 256, the router prefers the EIGRP route. This is because the router always prefers the path with the lowest-cost metric and ignores the administrative distance.

Redistributing Routes to and from Other Protocols from EIGRP

Although redistribution between EIGRP and other protocols, such as OSPF and RIP, works in the same manner as redistribution between other protocols, you should use the default metric whenever possible. Be aware of the following caveats when you are redistributing routes between EIGRP and other protocols:

- Routes redistributed into EIGRP are not always summarized.

- External EIGRP routes have an administrative distance of 170.

Lesson 13-7: Redistributing Static Routes to Interfaces with EIGRP

When EIGRP redistributes a static route that you define with a next hop of an interface and with a network statement, it redistributes it as if it were a directly connected interface.

Figure 13-7 shows the topology that you will use for the next lesson.

Figure 13-7 *Redistributing Static Routes to Interfaces with EIGRP*

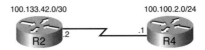

100.133.42.0/30   100.100.2.0/24

R2 .2   .1 R4

In this lesson, R4 is configured with a static route to network 100.100.2.0/24 configured through interface Serial 0. R4 needs to advertise this route to R2 without distributing any other static routes it can have. Example 13-13 shows a solution to this scenario.

Example 13-13 *Redistributing Static Routes to Interfaces with EIGRP*

```
Configuration items for R4:
R4(config)#ip route 100.100.2.0 255.255.255.0 Serial0
R4(config)#router eigrp 200
R4(config-router)#network 133.100.42.0
R4(config-router)#network 100.100.2.0
R4(config-router)#no auto-summary
```

Now you can examine the output on R2 to see that the route is included in the routing table as an internal EIGRP route. Example 13-14 shows the output of the **show ip route** command issued on R2.

Example 13-14 *The* **show ip route** *Command Output on R2*

```
R2#show ip route
    ....
        100.0.0.0/8 is variably subnetted, 2 subnets, 2 masks
    C       100.100.42.0/304 is directly connected, Serial0
    D       100.100.2.0 [90/2169856] via 100.100.42.1, 00:00:47, Serial0
```

Lesson 13-8: Redistributing Directly Connected Networks

The redistribution of directly connected networks into a routing protocol is not a common practice, but you should be aware that it can be done, both directly and indirectly. Use the following command to directly redistribute connected routes:

```
R4(config-router)#redistribute connected
```

When you use this command, you should also specify a metric to be used.

The second method of redistribution of directly connected routes involves the use of a routing protocol. As long as the directly connected route is defined in one of the routing protocols and mutual redistribution is in use, both protocols can learn the routes through the redistribution.

Figure 13-8 illustrates the topology that you will use for this lesson.

Figure 13-8 *Redistributing Directly Connected Networks*

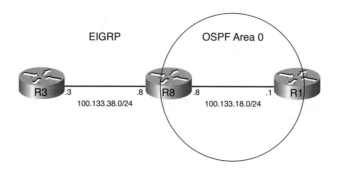

In this lesson, you use a routing protocol to redistribute your connected networks. Because R8 has two Ethernet interfaces, you configure Ethernet 0 in network 100.133.38.0/24 and Ethernet 1 in network 100.133.18.0/24. You ensure that R8 is running EIGRP with R3, and OSPF with R1. You configure R8 so that it is mutually redistributing between the EIGRP and OSPF processes. Example 13-15 shows you only the pertinent configuration information for R8.

Example 13-15 *Redistributing Directly Connected Networks*

```
Configuration items for R8:
R8(config)#interface Ethernet0
R8(config-if)#ip address 100.133.38.8 255.255.255.0
R8(config-if)#exit
R8(config)#interface Ethernet1
R8(config-if)#ip address 100.133.18.8 255.255.255.0
R8(config-if)#exit
R8(config)#router eigrp 7
R8(config-router)#redistribute ospf 7 metric 10000 100 255 1 1500
R8(config-router)#network 100.133.38.0 0.0.0.255
R8(config-router)#auto-summary
R8(config-router)#no eigrp log-neighbor-changes
R8(config-router)#exit
R8(config)#router ospf 7
R8(config-router)#log-adjacency-changes
R8(config-router)#redistribute eigrp 7 subnets
R8(config-router)#network 100.133.18.0 0.0.0.255 area 0
```

Now, if you issue the **show ip route** command on your routers, you get an output similar to the one shown in Example 13-16.

Example 13-16 *The* **show ip route** *Command Output for Redistributing Directly Connected Networks*

```
R8#show ip route
Codes: C - connected, S - static, I - IGRP, R - RIP, M - mobile, B - BGP
       D - EIGRP, EX - EIGRP external, O - OSPF, IA - OSPF inter area
```

Example 13-16 *The* **show ip route** *Command Output for Redistributing Directly Connected Networks (Continued)*

```
              N1 - OSPF NSSA external type 1, N2 - OSPF NSSA external type 2
              E1 - OSPF external type 1, E2 - OSPF external type 2, E - EGP
              i - IS-IS, L1 - IS-IS level-1, L2 - IS-IS level-2, ia - IS-IS inter area
              * - candidate default, U - per-user static route, o - ODR
              P - periodic downloaded static route

Gateway of last resort is not set

     100.0.0.0/8 is subnetted, 2 subnets
C       100.133.18.0 is directly connected, Ethernet1
C       100.133.38.0 is directly connected, Ethernet0

R3#show ip route
Codes: C - connected, S - static, I - IGRP, R - RIP, M - mobile, B - BGP
       D - EIGRP, EX - EIGRP external, O - OSPF, IA - OSPF inter area
       N1 - OSPF NSSA external type 1, N2 - OSPF NSSA external type 2
       E1 - OSPF external type 1, E2 - OSPF external type 2, E - EGP
       i - IS-IS, L1 - IS-IS level-1, L2 - IS-IS level-2, * - candidate default
       U - per-user static route, o - ODR

Gateway of last resort is not set

     100.0.0.0/8 is subnetted, 2 subnets
C       100.133.38.0 is directly connected, Ethernet0
D EX    100.133.18.0 [170/2560025856] via 100.133.38.8, 00:07:26, Ethernet0

R1#show ip route
Codes: C - connected, S - static, I - IGRP, R - RIP, M - mobile, B - BGP
       D - EIGRP, EX - EIGRP external, O - OSPF, IA - OSPF inter area
       N1 - OSPF NSSA external type 1, N2 - OSPF NSSA external type 2
       E1 - OSPF external type 1, E2 - OSPF external type 2, E - EGP
       i - IS-IS, L1 - IS-IS level-1, L2 - IS-IS level-2, ia - IS-IS inter area
       * - candidate default, U - per-user static route, o - ODR
       P - periodic downloaded static route

Gateway of last resort is not set

     100.0.0.0/8 is subnetted, 2 subnets
C       100.133.18.0 is directly connected, Ethernet0
O E2    100.133.38.0 [110/20] via 100.133.18.8, 00:07:32, Ethernet0
```

From the configuration and the routing table output from R8, you should notice the following:

- The networks in question are in R8's routing table as directly connected networks.

- Network 100.133.38.0/24 is part of the EIGRP process, and network 100.133.18.0/24 is part of the OSPF process.

- R8 is mutually redistributing between EIGRP and OSPF.

Now, examining the routing tables for routers R1 and R3, you should see the following:

* R1 is learning the network 100.133.18.0/24 via EIGRP.

* R3 is learning the network 100.133.38.0/24 via OSPF.

This means that although R8 is not configured with the **redistribute connected** command, it does advertise the network 100.133.38.0/24, which is part of the EIGRP process redistributed into OSPF. Similarly, R8 advertises network 100.133.18.0/24, which is part of the OSPF process redistributed into EIGRP.

Lesson 13-9: Filtering Routing Information

You can filter routing protocol information by performing the following steps:

Step 1   Prevent routing updates through an interface

Step 2   Optionally control the advertising of routes in routing updates

Step 3   Optionally control the processing of routing updates

Step 4   Optionally filter sources of routing information

Because route filtering works by controlling the routes that are entered into or advertised out of your route table, it has a different effect when used on link-state routing protocols than when used on distance-vector protocols. If your router is running a distance-vector protocol, which advertises routes based on what is in its route table, a route filter influences which routes your router advertises to its neighbors.

If your router is running a link-state protocol, which determines routes based on information in its link-state database, a route filter has no effect on link-state advertisements or on the link-state database.

Step 1: Preventing Routing Updates Through an Interface

By keeping routing update messages from being sent through a router interface, you can prevent other routers on your LAN from learning about routes dynamically. You can use this feature with all IP-based routing protocols with the exception of the BGP routing protocol.

Keep in mind that OSPF and IS-IS behave somewhat differently with this feature. When used with OSPF, the interface address that you specify as passive appears as a stub network in the OSPF domain. OSPF routing information is neither sent nor received through the specified router interface. When used with IS-IS, the specified IP addresses are advertised without IS-IS actually having to run on those interfaces.

Use the following command to prevent routing updates through a specified interface:

```
R2(config-router)#passive-interface interface-type interface-number
```

In an Internet service provider (ISP) or large enterprise network, the distribution routers can have more than 200 interfaces. Before the Default Passive Interface feature was introduced, two possibilities for obtaining routing information from these interfaces existed:

- You could configure a routing protocol such as OSPF on the backbone interfaces and redistribute the connected interfaces.

- You could configure the routing protocol on all interfaces and manually set most of them as passive.

Problems existed in these large networks with either of these scenarios. The first scenario could allow the flooding of a large number of Type 5 LSAs, because you could not always summarize these LSAs at your router level, where your redistribution occurs.

The second scenario could allow flooding of large Type 1 LSAs into the area. Your Area Border Router (ABR) creates a Type 3 LSA for each Type 1 LSA and floods them onto your backbone. With this scenario, it is possible to inject a unique summary route into the backbone at your ABR level.

By introducing the Default Passive Interface feature, it eliminated the requirement to manually configure a passive interface command on each interface (by using a single **passive-interface default** command) and then enable individual interfaces where an adjacency is desired) by using the **no passive-interface** command).

Use the following commands to set all interfaces as passive by default and then activate only those interfaces that need to have adjacencies set.

To configure the routing protocol on the network, use the following command:

```
R2(config)#router protocol process-id
```

To set all interfaces as passive by default, use the following command:

```
R2(config-router)#passive-interface default
```

To activate only those interfaces that need to have adjacencies set, use the following command:

```
R2(config-router)#no passive-interface interface-type
```

To specify the list of networks for the routing process, use the following command:

```
R2(config-router)#network network-address [options]
```

Use one of the next two commands to verify your configuration.

To verify that interfaces on your network have been set to passive, use the following command:

```
R2#show ip ospf interface
```

To verify that the interfaces you enabled as active, use the following command:

```
R2#show ip interface
```

Step 2: Controlling the Advertising of Routes in Routing Updates

You can suppress routes from being advertised in a routing update to prevent other routers from learning one or more routes. By suppressing routes in route updates, you prevent other routers from learning about the suppressed routes from this router. One caveat to this is that when you redistribute routes from any other protocol into OSPF, they are converted to OSPF external routes.

Use the following command to suppress routes from being advertised in routing updates:

```
R2(config-router)#distribute-list {access-list-number | access-list-name} out
    [interface-name | routing-process | as-number]
```

Step 3: Controlling the Processing of Routing Updates

You have the option to avoid processing certain routes listed in incoming updates for installation into your routing table. This feature does not apply to OSPF or IS-IS, although an LSA blocked by this method is still installed in the OSPF database. Use the following command to suppress routes in incoming updates:

```
R2(config-router)#distribute-list {access-list-number | access-list-name} in [interface-
    type interface-number]
```

You use the **distribute-list in** command to control which routes are processed in incoming routing updates. Note that the access list that you are referencing is applied to the contents of the update, not to the source or destination of the routing update packets. Your router decides whether to include the contents in its routing table based on the access lists, for example, if you have the following configuration on a router:

```
access-list 1 permit 100.0.0.0 0.255.255.255
router rip
distribute-list 1 in
```

Any inbound RIP update received is checked against access-list 1, and only routes that match a 100.xxx.xxx.xxx format are placed in your routing table.

For every routing process that is defined on your router, you can define one inbound interface-specific distribute list per interface and define one globally defined distribute list. In this case, if the route is denied by either distribute list, it is not allowed into the routing table. The route must be allowed by both lists. For example, you can configure the following combination on one of your routers:

```
access-list 1 permit 100.0.0.0 0.255.255.255
access-list 2 permit 100.133.3.0 0.0.0.255
router rip
distribute-list 2 in ethernet 0
distribute-list 1 in
```

In this case, your router checks the interface on which the update comes in. If the update comes in on Ethernet 0, access-list 2 is applied before it is allowed into the routing table. If the network is denied by access-list 2, no further checking is needed. However, if distribute-list 2 allows the network, then distribute-list 1 is also checked. If both distribute lists allow the network, it is placed into your routing table. The following algorithm is followed when multiple distribute lists are used:

1 Extract the next network from the inbound update.

2 Check the interface that it came into.

3 Is a distribute list applied to that interface?

   a. If yes, is the network denied by that list? If yes, the network does not make it; return to Step 1. If no, the network is allowed; continue to Step 4.

   b. If no, continue to Step 4.

4 Does a global distribute list exist?

   a. If yes, is the network denied by that list? If yes, the network does not make it; return to Step 1. If no, the network is allowed; return to Step 1.

   b. If no, return to Step 1.

You use the **distribute-list out** command to control which routes are included in outgoing routing updates. For example, assume that you have the following configuration on a router:

```
access-list 1 permit 100.0.0.0 0.255.255.255
router rip
default-metric 1
redistribute igrp 20
distribute-list 1 out igrp 20
```

Now you have routes from the IGRP 20 routing process being redistributed into RIP. Any outbound routing update originally sourced from the IGRP 20 routing process is checked against access-list 1. Only routes that match a 100.xxx.xxx.xxx format are sent.

As with the **distribute list in** command, you can specify multiple distribute lists for a given routing process if they are applied to different interfaces, or globally. So, for any given routing protocol, you can define one interface-specific distribute list per interface and one protocol-specific distribute list for each process/autonomous system pair. For example, you can configure the following combination on one of your routers:

```
access-list 1 permit 100.0.0.0 0.255.255.255
access-list 2 permit 100.133.3.0 0.0.0.255
router rip
distribute-list 2 in ethernet 0
distribute-list 1 in
```

In this case, your router only sends routes pertaining to network 100.133.3.0 out of its Ethernet 0 interface. It also sends any routes pertaining to network 100.0.0.0 out all its other interfaces, including the 100.133.0.0 network. The following algorithm is used when multiple distribute lists are used:

1 Select the next network to receive an outbound update.

2 Check the interface it is being sent out on.

3 Is a distribute list applied to that interface?

    a. If yes, is the network denied by that list? If yes, the network does not go out; return to Step 1. If no, the network is allowed; continue to Step 4.

    b. If no, continue to Step 4.

4 Check the routing process or autonomous system from which you derive the route.

5 Is a distribute list applied to that process or autonomous system?

    a. If yes, is the network denied by that list? If yes, the network does not go out; return to Step 1. If no, the network is allowed, continue to Step 6.

    b. If no, continue to Step 6.

6 Does a global distribute list exist?

    a. If yes, is the network denied by that list? If yes, the network does not go out; return to Step 1. If no, the network is allowed, return to Step 1.

    b. If no, return to Step 1.

NOTE A router performs many different checks, not just against a distribute list but also against distance-vector routes, before it includes it in the routing table or in an update. Some of these checks include tests for desirability, policies, split horizon, and other factors.

Step 4: Filtering Sources of Routing Information

You can prioritize routing information from different sources, based on the fact that some routing information is more accurate from one source than the other, by filtering the source of the routing information. One piece of routing information is the administrative distance, a system used to rate the trustworthiness of a routing information source. By specifying this value, you enable your router to intelligently discriminate between sources of routing information. The router can then choose the route whose routing protocol has the lowest administrative distance.

Use the following command to filter sources of routing information:

```
R2(config-router)#distance weight {ip-address {ip-address mask}} [ip-standard-list]
    [ip-extended]
```

While no general guidelines exist for assigning the administrative distances that you use, you must determine a reasonable matrix of administrative distances for your individual network requirements. Table 13-1 lists the default administrative distances assigned by Cisco IOS Software for various routing information sources.

Table 13-1   *Default Administrative Distances*

Route Source	Default Distance
Connected interface	0
Static route	1
EIGRP summary route	5
Exterior Border Gateway Protocol (BGP)	20
Internal EIGRP	90
IGRP	100
OSPF	110
IS-IS	115
RIP	120
EIGRP external route	170
Interior BGP	200
Unknown	255

You can also use the administrative distance value to rate the routing information from routers running the same routing protocol. Be careful when using administrative distance values in this application because unfamiliarity with it can result in inconsistent routing information, including forwarding loops. In the following example, you want the default metric assigned to IS-IS to be reassigned to a value of 90. More preference is given to these IP routes compared to the routes with the default administrative distance value of 110:

```
router isis
  distance 90 ip
```

Summary

In this chapter, you learned about redistribution between routing protocols. You looked at such items as metrics, administrative distances, and avoiding problems with redistribution. While redistribution usually occurs without problems, there are a few exceptions such as redistribution between OSPF and BGP. You looked at the EIGRP routing protocol as the template for other routing protocols and stepped through many scenarios involving mutual redistribution. You concluded the chapter with a look at filtering routing updates in both the in and out directions.

Review Questions

1   What metric is used by RIP?

2   Which routing protocols can redistribute static routes automatically without any additional configuration?

3   What happens if you do not include a match statement with a route map?

4   Which RFC is written to cover redistribution between OSPF and BGP?

5   Why do you need to filter routes when redistributing between two EIGRP autonomous systems?

FAQs

Q — *Why would I want to redistribute a routing protocol instead of running a single routing protocol in my network?*

A — While a goal for many network administrators is to simplify their network configuration through the use of a single routing protocol, many reasons still exist in today's networks for the use of redistribution, including some of the most common reasons for running multiprotocol routing, mergers, multiple departments managed by multiple network administrators, and multivendor environments.

Q — *Why do I loose the metrics when I redistribute BGP routes?*

A — Unlike other routing protocols, BGP does not automatically redistribute metrics with routes.

Q — *What are some of the problems that can arise from incorrect redistribution of routes?*

A — Some of the problems you can see include routing loops, slow convergence, and suboptimal routing paths. You can use filtering to avoid many of these problems.

Q — *What is the access list used for when I define a route map?*

A — The access list is used to match routing updates for further processing by the route map. It does not match the source of the routing updates, as you might expect.

Q — *I cannot see any of my subnets when I redistribute from EIGRP into OSPF. Why is this happening?*

A — You must use the subnet keyword when you define the redistribution with OSPF or it only redistributes any major networks that have not been divided into subnets.

Q — *Why is RIP not redistributing my OSPF routes?*

A — When redistributing routes between OSPF and RIP, a problem arises if OSPF has a different mask than RIP. Because RIP is a classful routing protocol, it does not redistribute these routes. You can use static routing as a patch for this problem.

Security Practices

This chapter includes the following topics:

- Important security acronyms
- White hats versus black hats
- Cisco security implementations
- VPN overview
- AAA overview
- IDS fundamentals

CHAPTER 14

Security Primer

In this chapter, you are given a brief overview of the security technologies that you might be exposed to throughout your career. Many topics related to security are covered, including an overview of security in Cisco IOS and CatalystOS (CatOS) and technologies such as VPNs, AAA, and IDS. Some of the topics that are included in this chapter are not required for the CCIE Security lab exam but are covered for completeness of the subject.

One of the most exciting times in the career of a network administrator is the introduction of new technology into their infrastructure. This is also the time that some of the worst security nightmares begin. While today's technology revolution continues to improve productivity in work and enhances quality of life, it also introduces new and unique ways for unauthorized people to gain access to privileged and private information. The previously happy network administrator must now spend more time trying to keep this information secure in the face of these overwhelming odds. The administrator must now spend more time analyzing network traffic that is coming to and going from the network, trying to keep one step ahead of the latest vulnerability, patching devices for things never heard of before, reading mailing lists, and so on.

Today's security specialist must be able to sort through mounds of information to determine what type of threat to his organization is real and what type of threat is only an urban legend. This is done through continuing education, participation in security groups and/or mailing lists, the CIA website at www.cia.gov, and most of all, personal experience. Many forums exist where the administrator can express opinion or get answers to questions, but like anything else that is free, some of the advice and answers should be taken for what they are worth.

Good security practices result in minimizing the chance of a security incident occurring and minimizing the impact of a security incident through the protection of information, systems, and services against mistakes, disasters, and manipulation. While many ways exist to ensure security, the components that make up excellent security practices include integrity, confidentiality, and availability.

Integrity requires that some type of control must exist to ensure that business-critical items are accurate and in a workable condition. No one wants to find out that the Intrusion Detection System (IDS) server was compromised by an attacker and now cannot be trusted to report accurate and complete information. Integrity practices apply to almost any device that is capable of running a TCP/IP stack.

Confidentiality, on the other hand, requires controls to ensure that access restrictions are enforced so that only authorized personal are allowed to see or use sensitive items. Confidentiality is one of the harder items in security to implement due to the curious nature of humans. While everyone agrees that security is needed, no one wants to believe that it should personally apply.

While availability does not seem like it would apply to security, it is in fact one of the bigger targets on the Internet today. Many different types of threats exist to undermine the controls that a company puts in place to ensure that services are available when needed. Redundancy in the design of the network and systems, UPS power backup, and a verified system backup routine are integral components of availability.

Important Security Acronyms

The following is a brief introduction to the terms and acronyms that you can see throughout the network security field. Most of the acronyms that are associated with security can be associated to an encryption algorithm or a technology. The following are important security terms and acronyms:

- **Authentication, authorization, and accounting (AAA, or Triple A)**—AAA provides a key part of enforcing your security policy by providing centralized access control and accounting in addition to router and switch access management. The components that make up AAA are discussed in further detail later in "AAA Overview."

- **Access Control List (ACL)**—ACLs are commonly used to control access to a file, folder, system, or network. An ACL can be a great asset to secure your network, but if misconfigured, it can be a nightmare to troubleshoot.

- **Authentication Header (AH)**—An AH is a security protocol that is used as part of an IPSec VPN that is designed to provide data authentication and optional antireplay services for data. AH is embedded in the data to be protected in the form of a one-way keyed hash that is used to detect changes in the IP datagram.

- **Audit log and audit trail**—Usually sent to a syslog server of some type, the audit log and audit trail are used to provide information on what was done or who accessed a system or device and, in some cases, can be required by law or regulations. This enables you to verify proper use of the system and proper operation and configuration of security measures, and to identify any misuse of the system. While the audit log and audit trail introduce overhead to both the system generating the messages and the system responsible for compiling them, their use usually far outweighs the extra demand that is placed on the systems. Automated tools are available to help you manage audit logs, and you can also use these logs as a type of passive intrusion detection.

- **Authentication**—Authentication refers to the verification of the authenticity of a person, data, application, device, or IP address through the use of a validation system. This system could be as simple as a user ID/password combination or as complex a biometric match of some physical characteristic of the individual and, if you believe what you see on TV, a quick DNA testing of the prospective user. Authentication is usually the first step that is performed in all forms of access control to a system or its data.

- **Authorization**—Authorization is a methodology that uses a person or process to ensure that a user or process has sufficient right or permission to perform a specific event or action. However, in the case of a person that can authorize an action, it is an unacceptably high-risk situation for that person to be given the power to create new actions and then to authorize those same entries. The scenario could be disastrous.

- **Certificate Authority (CA)**—A CA is a trusted third-party clearinghouse that issues digital certificates and digital signatures, which are commonly used for nonrepudiation of transactions. These certificates include your organization's name and public key, a serial number, and an expiry date. The CA is also responsible for issuing the Certificate Revocation List (CRL) of expired or compromised certificates.

- **Cipher**—Cipher describes either the means of encrypting data or the encrypted text itself. Encryption ciphers use one of many different algorithms that can, along with a key of some type, create cipher text from clear text. The receiver must also have knowledge of the same key and algorithm that are used to create the cipher text to decipher the text back to clear text, which is much easier for most people to read and understand.

- **Confidentiality**—Confidentiality, a synonym for encryption, is the assurance that information is transmitted securely so that it is not altered or tampered with and is accessed only by authorized individuals or applications.

- **Cryptography**—The primary function of cryptography is to maintain the privacy of communications by ensuring the confidentiality of the data. This book does not discuss cryptography in detail. For more details, refer to *Cryptography and Network Security: Principles and Practice,* Second Edition, by Dr. William Stallings (ISBN: 0138690170, Prentice Hall, 1998).

- **Data Encryption Standard (DES)**—DES is a data encryption standard that was developed by IBM, in cooperation with the National Security Agency (NSA) in 1974, that is used in the scrambling of data to protect its confidentiality. In 2000, restrictions that were originally imposed by the U.S. Government regarding export from the United States were lifted for the countries of the European Union (EU) and a number of other countries. Export restrictions still exist for a number of countries. See also Triple DES (3DES), later in this section.

- **Diffie-Hellman (DH)**—DH is a public-key cryptography protocol that allows the establishment of a shared secret key over an insecure communications channel between two parties. DH is a component of the Oakley key exchange, a key establishment protocol based on the DH algorithm, that is used by Internet Key Exchange (IKE) to establish session keys. DH is available on Cisco platforms in a 768-bit, 1024-bit, or 1536-bit DH group.

- **Digital certificate**—A digital certificate electronically establishes credentials and authenticates connection when performing transactions across a network. A digital certificate is obtained from a CA, which validates and authenticates the requesting individual or organization. The digital certificate identifies the name of the individual or organization, a serial number, the validity dates, and the individual's or organization's public key where encryption is required. The X.509 Public Key Infrastructure for the Internet defines the requirements for digital certificates.

- **Digital signature**—A digital signature is the electronic equivalent of an individual's written signature, used to authenticate and validate the data, usually an e-mail, to which it is appended. When you sign a message with a digital signature, the signature provides proof that the data is the same data that was sent by the user, because any alteration to the data results in a message where the signature does not match the contents. A digital signature also provides a digital time stamp for confirmation of the time and date of the signing. This feature makes repudiation of data signed with a digital signature very difficult. A CA issues digital signatures in much the same manner as a digital certificate; the identity of the individual must be verified through some medium. Digital signatures can be accompanied by the certificate of the CA to provide greater trust in the digital signature.

- **Encapsulating Security Payload (ESP)**—ESP, a part of IPSec VPNs, is a security protocol that provides privacy services, optional authentication, and antireplay services for IP datagrams. ESP encapsulates the data to be protected by encrypting the IP packet using a variety of encrypting algorithms.

- **Hashed-based Message Authentication Code (HMAC)**—HMAC is a mechanism for message authentication using cryptographic hash functions. HMAC can be used with any iterative cryptographic hash function in combination with a secret shared key. The cryptographic strength of HMAC depends on the properties of the underlying hash function.

- **Internet Key Exchange (IKE)**—IKE establishes authentication keys and security associations for other services such as IPSec. Cisco supports both a preshared key and a CA to establish the verification of its peer's identity.

- **Information security policy**—An information security policy is a document, usually ratified by senior management and distributed to anyone with access rights to the organization's IT systems or information resources, that aims to reduce the risk of, and minimize the effect of, any type of security incident.

- **Integrity**—In data, integrity is the assurance that the information received is authentic and complete without alteration. Integrity is also a synonym for authentication.

- **Intrusion Detection System (IDS)**—The IDS is a complex software/hardware application/appliance that monitors network activity to detect misuse of the network. Some IDSs can also identify a known pattern of attack or attack scenario through the matching of a pattern at the packet level.

- **IP Security (IPSec)**—IPSec is a framework supporting open standards that provides authentication, confidentiality, and integrity of data, at the IP level, between two peers.

- **Masquerading**—Masquerading is the act of trying to identify yourself to someone or something as someone else.

- **Message Digest 5 (MD5)**—MD5 authenticates the origin, verifies the integrity, and checks for timeliness of communications by using a one-way hashing algorithm to produce a 128-bit hash. Cisco implements an HMAC version with MD5, HMAC-MD5, that is in compliance with RFC 2104, "HMAC: Keyed-Hashing for Message Authentication." HMAC-MD5 is a keyed version of MD5 that enables two parties to validate transmitted information using a shared secret.

- **Nonrepudiation**—Nonrepudiation is based on the use of a digital signature that not only validates the sender but also time stamps the transaction so that it cannot be claimed or disputed at a later time that the transaction was not authorized by the sender or was not a valid transaction. Nonrepudiation works both ways by using two distinct messages: the first from one entity to another and the second in reverse of the first.

- **Public Key Infrastructure (PKI)**—PKI is the use and management of a public and private cryptographic key combination that, among many other uses—such as certificate management, archive management, key management, and token management—provides secure transmission and authentication of data across public networks. A public key infrastructure generally consists of the following:

  - A CA that issues and assures the authenticity of digital certificates. A digital certificate includes the public key or other information about the public key.

  - An optional *registration authority (RA)* that validates requests for the issuance of digital certificates. The RA authorizes the issuance of the keys to the requestor by the CA. The RA can be used to record and verify certain information for the CA but does not sign digital signatures or Certificate Revocation Lists (CRLs).

  - A *certificate management system* that is a software application developed and provided by the vendor of the PKI system.

  - A *physical directory* where the certificates, together with their public keys, are stored, usually conforming to the X.500 standards. The certificate management system is responsible for managing the certificates that are stored here.

- **Risk assessment**—Assessing risk is the process that is used to identify what to protect, who or what to protect it from, and how to go about protecting it. You can use risk assessment to determine the cost of the information that you are trying to protect versus the cost of implementing the required level of security required to protect it.

- **Rivest, Shamir, and Adleman (RSA)**—RSA is a public-key encryption and authentication algorithm that generates a variable key length. Cisco's IKE implementation uses a Diffie-Hellman exchange to get the secret keys. You can then use RSA to authenticate the Diffie-Hellman exchange. RSA is not public domain and must be licensed from RSA Data Security.

- **Security Hash Algorithm 1 (SHA-1)**—SHA-1 authenticates the origin, verifies the integrity, and checks for timeliness of communications by using a one-way hashing algorithm to produce a 160-bit hash. Cisco implements an HMAC version with SHA, HMAC-SHA, that is in compliance with RFC 2104. HMAC-SHA is a keyed version of MD5 that enables two parties to validate transmitted information using a shared secret.

- **Triple DES (3DES)**—3DES is a variant of DES that takes 64 bits of data and processes the data three times with a different independent 56-bit key each pass. *See also* Data Encryption Standard (DES), earlier in this section.

- **Virtual Private Network (VPN)**—A VPN is a network that uses hardware and software to provide encryption and tunneling, which emulates a private network, even when it is run over public network lines and infrastructure such as the Internet.

White Hats Versus Black Hats

The world of security experts is divided into *black hats,* often referred to as *hackers* or *crackers,* and *white hats,* or your information security officer (ISO) or chief security officer (CSO). Both sides are interested in finding the latest security vulnerability in either a device or application. However, black hats typically use this information for personal gain, while white hats use the information for protection of the device or application from the other. The black hats are interested in these vulnerabilities because they can use them to gain unauthorized access to devices. With that access, they can appropriate proprietary information or deface a corporate website. White hats, however, are interested in finding vulnerabilities to put countermeasures in place before a hole can be exploited.

Some people claim to be one hat color or the other; however, a person could also wear a *gray hat.* A gray hat is a hacker who exploits a security weakness in a computer system or product with the intent of bringing the weakness to the attention of the owners. Unlike a black hat, a gray hat acts without malicious intent. While the goal of a gray hat is to improve system and network security, he can, by publicizing the vulnerability, give other hackers the opportunity to exploit it.

Cisco Security Implementations

Cisco offers many types of devices that can help the security expert secure his network such as the built-in support of security standards and practices in the IOS and CatOS, and software packages and appliances that are designed specifically for security.

Cisco IOS Security Overview

Cisco developed IOS software to provide intelligent network services on a flexible network infrastructure that provides the rapid deployment of Internet applications. Cisco IOS Software provides the administrator with common functionality, scalability, and security for all products under the CiscoFusion architecture, including routers and an increasing number of LAN switches that run a native IOS software.

NOTE   Cisco IOS Software is based on over 200 industry standards and provides support of multiple protocols such as TCP/IP, AppleTalk, IPX, and SNA.

Cisco IOS Software performs sophisticated classification, encoding, prioritization, and route selection of network traffic. Moreover, it can recognize a particular application as the application requests network resources and ensures that the resources are provided through the use of intelligent network services. This section focuses on the VPN and security portions of Cisco's Intelligent Network Services, which offer a comprehensive suite of network services such as security, quality of service (QoS), voice, video, and replication, among many others, as outlined in Figure 14-1.

Figure 14-1 *Cisco's Intelligent Network Services*

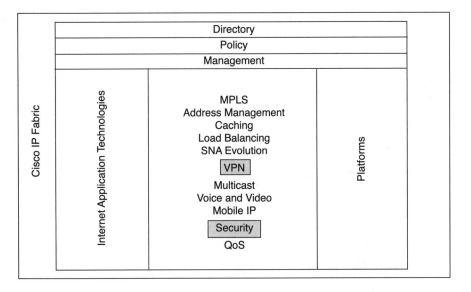

IOS provides its security services through the use of items such as ACLs, AAA, IPSec, and the Cisco IOS firewall feature set.

The security that is provided by IOS is designed to enable secure communications either between two parties or between an administrator and the network device itself. IOS provides this confidentiality by supporting features such as link-layer encryption, IPSec, VPN, and SSL to protect the communications between two parties. The recent addition of support for secure shell (SSH) in IOS software enables the administrator to establish secure communications from the workstation to the network device. Use Table 14-1 as a cross reference for further information regarding Cisco IOS Software security features.

Table 14-1   *Cisco IOS Security Features*

Chapter	Topic
15	Basic Cisco IOS Software and Catalyst 3550 Series Security
16	Access Control Lists
17	IP Services
22	Cisco IOS Firewall

CatalystOS Security Overview

Cisco's CatOS is implemented on the Catalyst line of LAN switches. Like IOS, CatOS provides common functionality, scalability, and security for all products across the switches that support it. Cisco classifies its CatOS into two separate categories, as follows:

- **Hybrid**—The Hybrid series of CatOS is the same interface that was introduced with the Catalyst line of switches.

- **Native** —The Native CatOS takes on a more IOS-like interface.

The Catalyst series of switches support many different security options, including the following:

- Passwords

- VLAN Trunking Protocol (VTP)

- Port security

- Private VLANs

- Dynamic VLANs with VPMS

- VLAN ACLs (VACLs)

- Router ACLs (RACLs)

- IP Permit Lists

- SPAN and RSPAN

- Support of AAA services

Many people overlook these features, often not realizing that security should be implemented both as close to the sources as possible and enforced at any point in the network that is capable of supporting security enforcement. Use Table 14-2 as a cross reference for further information regarding CatalystOS security features.

Table 14-2   *CatalystOS Security Features*

Chapter	Topic
4	Layer 2 and Layer 3 Switching and LAN Connectivity
15	Basic Cisco IOS Software and Catalyst 3550 Series Security
16	Access Control Lists
18	AAA Services
24	IDS on the Cisco PIX Firewall and IOS Software

VPN Overview

As external connections to your internal networks become an everyday occurrence instead of the exception and as more of your business colleagues work from home, you must establish a new, cost-effective method of extending your security and management policies to these connections. One way to accomplish this is through the use of the Virtual Private Network (VPN) technology, which can offer a secure, reliable connection over a shared public network infrastructure, such as the Internet, at a lower cost than over dedicated private networks. Cisco VPNs can be established across most networking infrastructure platforms, security environments, network services, network appliances, and management scenarios that you are likely to encounter.

A VPN can be simply defined as an enterprise network deployed on a shared infrastructure that uses the same security, management, and throughput policies that are applied in a private network. VPNs provide an alternative to the WAN infrastructure that you can use to replace or augment your existing private networks. VPNs are not meant to change your WAN requirements, such as support for multiple protocols, high reliability, and extensive scalability, but VPNs give you a means to meet these requirements in a more cost-effective manner and to provide greater flexibility. The functionality of a VPN is defined primarily by the equipment that is deployed at the edge of your network and feature integration across the WAN, not by the WAN transport protocol itself.

VPNs can be segmented into three separate categories, as follows:

- **Remote access**—Remote-access VPNs provide connectivity to telecommuters, mobile users, or even smaller remote offices.

- **Intranets**—An intranet VPN provides connectivity to fixed locations and branch and home offices.

- **Extranets**—An extranet extends limited access of your computing resources to business partners, enabling access to shared information.

Each type of VPN has different security and bandwidth management issues for you to consider.

Use Table 14-3 as a cross reference for further information regarding VPN features.

Table 14-3   *VPN Features*

Chapter	Topic
16	Access Control Lists
18	AAA Services
19	Virtual Private Networks
21	Virtual Private Dial-Up Networks

AAA Overview

AAA is a framework that is designed to implement authentication, authorization, and accounting (AAA) in a consistent but modular fashion. You can configure authentication without the use of an external AAA server, such as a Cisco Secure ACS, but if you need to implement a backup authentication method or use one of the security protocols (RADIUS, TACACS+, or Kerberos), you must use the external AAA server.

Detailed configuration of AAA services is covered in Chapter 18, "AAA Services." Cisco recommends the use of AAA services whenever possible for more granular control of network devices.

IDS Fundamentals

Intrusion detection is the ability to detect different types of attacks launched against your network infrastructure. These attacks can be divided into three distinct types:

- **Access attacks**—When an intruder attacks networks or systems to retrieve data, gain access, or escalate his access privilege

- **Denials of service (DoS) attacks**—Designed to attack the network in way that damages or corrupts your computer system, or denies you and others access to your networks, systems, or services

- **Reconnaissance attacks**—An attempt to discover and map systems, services, or vulnerabilities

The Cisco Secure Intrusion Detection System (IDS) is designed to prevent, detect, and react to activity that matches configured signatures. The IDS then has the choice of logging the activity, resetting the connection, applying a dynamic Access Control List to a device that can support it, or any combination of these three items. The Cisco Secure IDS line of IDS appliances and software can meet the needs of small, medium, and large businesses.

Use Table 14-4 as a cross reference for further information regarding Cisco IDS features.

Table 14-4   *Cisco IDS Features*

Chapter	Topic
22	Cisco IOS Firewall
23	Cisco PIX Firewall
24	IDS on the Cisco PIX Firewall and IOS Software

Summary

This chapter took you through a high-level overview of the many security offerings that Cisco has implemented throughout its line of security products. You took a brief look at the reasons behind the need for network security and defined the roles of the security players. You learned terms such at black hat, white hat, and gray hat and defined each of the roles they play in security. You looked at the many built-in security features of the IOS and the Catalyst Operating System (CatOS). This chapter also defined a VPN and briefly touched on the services that AAA can give in your efforts to provide authentication, authorization, and accounting in your network.

The chapter wrapped up with a brief overview of an Intrusion Detection System (IDS) and how the IDS accomplishes its task of network traffic analysis. Throughout the rest of this book, you learn in detail and with examples how these technologies and products are brought together in the CCIE Security lab exam.

Review Questions

1 What are the three ways to ensure security in your network environment?

2 What two security protocols provide data authentication?

3 What three types of VPNs are supported by Cisco devices?

4 What three types of security server protocols are currently supported by Cisco devices?

5 What product is the same as an electronic ID?

6 What three types of attacks is an IDS designed to protect against?

7 What two types of traffic analysis procedures are available on Cisco's IDS products?

8 Why would a company need a risk assessment?

FAQs

Q — *Why do I need to consider availability as part of my overall security policy?*

A — Confidentiality, integrity, and availability all help ensure the security of your network environment. Availability is included because a service that is not available when needed is as harmful to a company as that company being hacked. A denial-of-service attack is one example of an attack aimed at availability.

Q — *Why would I use a digital signature?*

A — Digital signatures are a way for an individual to electronically sign an electronic transaction. The digital signature provides the nonrepudiation service of an electronic transaction through the validation of the sender as well as places a time stamp on the message.

Q — *Why would I use an Intrusion Detection System?*

A — An Intrusion Detection System (IDS) is designed to give you a mechanism to detect misuse of your network resources.

Q — *Why would my company choose to implement VPNs instead of private WANs?*

A — Virtual Private Networks (VPNs) provide you with a secure, reliable connection over a shared public network infrastructure, such as the Internet, at a lower cost than you would pay for dedicated private networks.

This chapter includes the following topics:

- Cisco IOS Software security and configuration
- Catalyst 3550 security and configuration

CHAPTER 15

Basic Cisco IOS Software and Catalyst 3550 Series Security

Routers and Catalyst 3550 series switches are the predominant hardware components used in the CCIE Security lab exam. This chapter covers some of the basic security features that are available in Cisco IOS Software for routers and 3550 switches. The chapter is divided into two major parts:

- Cisco IOS Software security
- Catalyst 3550 security

The first part deals with the introduction and configuration of some of the basic router security features. The second part discusses configuration of basic security features on the 3550 switches. Although many more basic security features are available for routers and switches than those included in this chapter, here you concentrate on those features that are most likely to appear on the CCIE Security exam.

Cisco IOS Software Security

Routers are an important part of any network, and successful implementation of Cisco IOS Software security features increases router efficiency and, by association, the efficiency of the entire network. Cisco IOS Software includes a number of useful services. Unfortunately, many of them present a security concern. In this chapter, you find a short explanation of some of these services, their functionality, and how they can be misused by an attacker. Then you learn how to use the various Cisco IOS Software basic mechanisms that are designed to protect information.

Network Time Protocol Security

Network Time Protocol (NTP) is used for automatic time synchronization. Cisco networks use NTP to make timekeeping accurate and coordinated across the board. The use of NTP is highly recommended for security because having accurate time is important for intrusion and forensic analysis. NTP is typically deployed in a hierarchical fashion. All routers on the network should be made a part of the hierarchy, if possible. If an NTP hierarchy is not feasible, you should disable NTP. To prevent NTP from traversing the router altogether, apply an access list to an appropriate interface.

HTTP Server Security

To enable configuration and management of network devices remotely, Cisco IOS Software offers web-based Hypertext Transfer Protocol (HTTP) administration. Though the web-access features are quite common on Cisco routers, they facilitate not only a mechanism for monitoring and configuring but also for attacking a router. The HTTP traffic needs to be protected by securing the communication between the HTTP client and the HTTP server. Several security technologies are available for this task (HTTPS, SSL, SSH, and IPSec) which are discussed throughout this book. Of course, if web-based remote administration is not necessary, you should disable this feature.

Password Management

To control who can access the router command prompt, you can set various passwords for various access points to the router. You can configure the passwords for local console access or remote access via Telnet. This is done to prevent unauthorized changes to a router's behavior and also to protect information that can be learned by looking at the network statistics on a router. This chapter's password discussion concentrates on three types of passwords:

- Enable password
- Per-user passwords and privilege levels
- Line passwords

Enable Password

Enable password secures the privileged EXEC mode of a router. At this level, an administrator can view and change anything on the router. That is why such access needs to be closely guarded.

Privilege Levels

Additional controls are available in Cisco IOS Software to limit administrative access with various privilege levels. You can define different privilege levels for different passwords that permit a certain subset of commands to be configured by a user. Once the password is entered, the user is able to operate at the corresponding level. Cisco IOS Software supports a total of 16 privilege levels, ranging from 0 to 15. The default levels are 1 and 15. Level 1 is basic (or nonprivileged), and 15 is the privileged EXEC mode that was discussed in the preceding section.

Line Passwords

For remote administration, you can access Cisco routers via Telnet. Telnet occurs over virtual terminal lines (vty). Most Cisco IOS Software versions have five virtual terminals—0 through 4—

that support five simultaneous Telnet sessions. You should explicitly configure all the virtual terminals for security purposes. No password is configured on vty ports by default to deny all attempts to log in to a router remotely.

Access Lists

Cisco IOS Software uses *access lists*, also known as *Access Control Lists (ACLs)*, as security filters to permit or deny specific traffic from entering or exiting parts of the network. Access lists are used heavily on Cisco routers for restricting access to a router's services and for filtering traffic passing through the router. The router looks at each packet and determines whether to forward or drop the packet, based on the conditions that are specified in the access lists.

Access lists can include the source and destination addresses of the traffic, the protocol type, and so on. Access lists contain a list of statements that are arranged in sequential order that establishes the matching criteria. Each packet is checked against the list in the same order that the statements are positioned. When a match is found, the router processes the packet accordingly and does not go through the remainder of the statements. Therefore, you need to call out specific conditions before the more general ones. For more on access lists, refer to Chapter 16, "Access Control Lists."

Secure Shell

Secure Shell (SSH) service is a newer Cisco IOS Software feature that is intended for use in secure remote administration. To create a secure link between a client and a server, SSH uses Rivest, Shamir, and Adelman (RSA) public key cryptography. Therefore, the communication between the administrator's host and the router is encrypted. SSH is also used to prevent various kinds of network attacks. Currently, Cisco implements only version 1 of SSH, but remember to check for future updates.

| NOTE | The SSH client has been available since the Cisco IOS Software 12.1.3.T release. |

Basic IOS Security Configuration

The following lessons and case studies are dedicated to basic Cisco IOS Software security configuration methods and are grouped into several scenarios, variations of which you are likely to encounter in the CCIE Security lab exam or in real life.

Lesson 15-1: Configuring Passwords, Privileges, and Logins

In this lesson, R8 is the router that needs to have basic Cisco IOS Software security features configured. Once R8 is configured, a remote host attempts to log in and perform some tasks.

This lesson covers the following configuration steps:

Step 1 Setting passwords

Step 2 Limiting connection time

Step 3 Configuring vtys and accessing the network remotely

Step 4 Creating user accounts

Step 5 Assigning privileges

Step 6 Local authentication, authorization, and accounting

Step 7 Remote administration with FTP

Step 8 Hiding Telnet addresses

Step 9 Verification

Step 1: Setting Passwords

First, you have to protect access to a router by setting various passwords. Prevent unauthorized login by configuring passwords on the console and virtual terminal lines. The syntax for both of them is identical, as follows:

```
R8(config-line)#password string
```

After the line passwords are set, you need to take care of the privileged EXEC level. You should not use the **enable password** command because it is not secure and can give away a system password. Instead, opt for the following command:

```
R8(config)#enable secret string
```

The **enable secret** command, as well as the username passwords described in "Creating User Accounts," later in this lesson, can be up to 25 characters long, including spaces, and are case sensitive. Example 15-1 demonstrates the application of passwords on R8. Note that both the console and the vty passwords appear scrambled. This is because **service password-encryption** is enabled on the router to hide the real string from a passerby.

Example 15-1 *Password Application on a Router*

```
R8#show run
version 12.2
service timestamps debug uptime
service timestamps log uptime
service password-encryption
```

continues

Example 15-1 *Password Application on a Router (Continued)*

```
!
hostname R8
!
enable secret 5 $1$uKVI$j1Y9WEzw7YIAWSkFwZZZB.
!
line vty 0 4
 password 7 1511021F0725
!
line con 0
 password 7 060506324F41
```

Step 2: Limiting Connection Time

For security reasons, you do not want to leave the connection to any port, be it console or remote connection, logged in indefinitely. If the connections are configured to time out automatically, the administrator is logged out by a router after a specified period if he forgets to do it himself. The syntax is the same for any line and is as follows:

```
R8(config-line)#exec-timeout minutes seconds
```

In Example 15-2, the console and auxiliary (aux) port are both configured to time out after a 5-minute interval.

Example 15-2 *Configuring a Timeout Period*

```
R8#show run
!
! Output omitted for brevity
!
line con 0
exec-timeout 5 0
password 7 05080F1C2243185E4B52
line aux 0
transport input all
exec-timeout 5 0
```

NOTE   When you are in a lab-testing environment, a constant timeout can turn into a nuisance. If security is not an immediate concern, you can choose to set the timeout interval to infinity by using the **exec-timeout 0 0** command. However, you should never do so in real-world networking.

Step 3: Configuring vtys and Accessing the Network Remotely

As you know, vtys are used for remote network connections to the router. Generally, all the router's vtys have the same configuration. If there are extra vtys that are not used, it is a good practice to disable them with the **no line vty** command.

Applying an access list to vtys can effectively limit access to the router by specifying which connections are allowed. The command for assigning an access list to vtys is as follows:

```
R8(config-line)#access-class access-list in
```

Some of the protocols supported by the vtys (for example, rlogin and web) are not secure. To minimize the security risk, you can confine the acceptable type of connection to Telnet only with the following command:

```
R8(config-line)#transport input [telnet]
```

Example 15-3 shows IP access-list 5, which permits host 192.168.1.8. Applying access-list 5 to vty lines for inbound connections means that only one particular host can Telnet to R8.

Example 15-3 *The vty Configuration*

```
R8#show run
!
! Output omitted for brevity
!
access-list 5 permit 192.168.1.8
!
line vty 0 4
 access-class 5 in
 exec-timeout 5 0
 password 7 01302F377824
 transport input telnet
```

NOTE   While configuring these commands, make sure that you are connected via an aux or console port. If you perform the commands while logged in to the router via Telnet, you might inadvertently disconnect yourself.

Step 4: Creating User Accounts

In this scenario, administrators log in according to the local router database. Each administrator receives his own username, password, and privilege level assigned, which indicates the level of control an administrator has over the router. The following command places a user in a local database:

```
R8(config)#username name privilege level password string
```

In Example 15-4, five administrators are assigned to the database. When they attempt to log in, they are authenticated by their username and corresponding password and are authorized to operate on the prescribed level.

Example 15-4 *Creating a Local Database*

```
R8#show run
!
! Output omitted for brevity
!
hostname R8
!
username admin privilege 3 password 7 02100A175809
username Sam privilege 15 password 7 05080F1C2243
username Jessie privilege 15 password 7 13061E010803
username Terry privilege 15 password 7 030752180500
username Joe privilege 5 password 7 01100F175804
```

Step 5: Assigning Privileges

Now that you have specified privilege levels for your users, you can assign a set of commands to a privilege level. Every user at the same privilege level can execute the same set. By default, every command in the Cisco IOS Software is designated for either level 1 or level 15. Level 0 exists, but it is rarely used. It includes following five commands:

- **disable**
- **enable**
- **exit**
- **help**
- **logout**

To change the default level and sign up certain commands to another level, use the following command:

```
R8(config)#privilege exec level level available-command
```

Keep in mind that for security reasons, you should move some commands that allow too much freedom for a lower level to a higher level, not the other way around. If you move higher-level commands, such as the **configure** command, down, you might enable a user to make unauthorized changes by letting him modify his own level to a higher one. Example 15-5 shows how privilege level 3 is limited to three commands:

- **telnet**
- **show ip route**
- **show startup**

Example 15-5 *Designating a Privilege Level*

```
R8(config)#privilege exec level 3 show start
R8(config)#privilege exec level 3 show ip route
R8(config)#privilege exec level 3 telnet
```

Step 6: Local Authentication, Authorization, and Accounting (AAA)

AAA technology is discussed in detail in Chapter 18, "AAA Services." Here, you are shown just a few AAA commands that make use of the local database that is configured in Steps 4 and 5 of this lesson. AAA has the following three separate functions:

- **Authentication**—Authentication identifies users before admitting them into a network.

- **Authorization**—Once a user is authenticated, authorization dictates what a user can accomplish on the network.

- **Accounting**—Accounting tracks the user's actions and logs them to monitor resource usage.

Example 15-6 illustrates the AAA commands configured on R8. To start an AAA process, the **aaa new-model** command is defined. The next command, **aaa authentication login default local**, names a local database as the one that is used for authentication on R8. The **aaa authorization config-commands** command enables AAA authorization of configuration commands specified by the **aaa authorization commands** statement that follows. The **aaa authorization exec default local** command specifies the local database as the source of authorization information, and the **aaa authorization commands 3 default local if-authenticated** command means that provided the user has been authenticated successfully, he is authorized by the router, after looking up the local database, to use the specified privilege level 3 commands. The latter command is helpful in the debugging process. Its practical usage is discussed in "Verification," later in this lesson.

Example 15-6 *AAA Configuration*

```
R8#show run
!
! Output omitted for brevity
!
hostname R8
!
aaa new-model
aaa authentication login default local
aaa authorization config-commands
aaa authorization exec default local
aaa authorization commands 3 default local if-authenticated
!
username admin privilege 3 password 7 02100A175809
```

NOTE	User admin is authorized to operate at privilege level 3 only if the user accesses the router via vty. If the same user attempted to access R8 via console, the user would receive privilege level 15.

Step 7: Remote Administration with FTP

You can use File Transfer Protocol (FTP) to transfer configuration files to and from the router for remote administration. FTP is preferred because Trivial File Transfer Protocol (TFTP) does not support authentication and is, therefore, less secure and should not be used to transfer configuration files. The following commands are used to make the router FTP ready:

```
R8(config)#ip ftp source-interface interface-type number
R8(config)#ip ftp username name
R8(config)#ip ftp password string
```

The first command specifies the local interface that is set up for the FTP connection. The two subsequent commands create the username and password for authentication on the FTP server. Example 15-7 shows the FTP configuration on R8.

Example 15-7 *Configuring FTP*

```
R8#show run
!
! Output omitted for brevity
!
ip ftp source-interface FastEthernet0/0
ip ftp username anonymous
ip ftp password 7 1511021F0725
```

Step 8: Hiding Telnet Addresses

Normally, when you try to Telnet to a device, the router displays the address to which the connection is attempted along with other connection messages. This allows an unauthorized passerby to see it. To suppress the Telnet address, issue the following command:

```
R8(config)#service hide-telnet-address
```

Step 9: Verification

Example 15-8 demonstrates the output of the **debug aaa authentication** command followed by the **debug aaa authorization** command. The combination of these two commands shows the process a router goes through while authenticating and authorizing a user admin logging in from the remote host 192.168.1.6, permitted by access-list 5.

Example 15-8 *Debugging AAA*

```
R8#debug aaa authentication
R8#debug aaa authorization
Feb 28 17:48:46: AAA: parse name=tty66 idb type=-1 tty=-1
Feb 28 17:48:46: AAA: name=tty66 flags=0x11 type=5 shelf=0 slot=0 adapter=0 port=66
channel=0
Feb 28 17:48:46: AAA/MEMORY: create_user (0x8270E0D0) user='NULL' ruser='NULL' ds0=0
port='tty66' rem_addr
='130.100.26.2' authen_type=ASCII service=LOGIN priv=15 initial_task_id='0'
Feb 28 17:48:46: AAA/AUTHEN/START (1304267484): port='tty66' list='' action=LOGIN
service=LOGIN
Feb 28 17:48:46: AAA/AUTHEN/START (1304267484): using "default" list
Feb 28 17:48:46: AAA/AUTHEN/START (1304267484): Method=LOCAL
Feb 28 17:48:46: AAA/AUTHEN (1304267484): status = GETUSER
Feb 28 17:48:48: AAA/AUTHEN/CONT (1304267484): continue_login (user='(undef)')
Feb 28 17:48:48: AAA/AUTHEN (1304267484): status = GETUSER
Feb 28 17:48:48: AAA/AUTHEN/CONT (1304267484): Method=LOCAL
Feb 28 17:48:48: AAA/AUTHEN (1304267484): status = GETPASS
Feb 28 17:48:49: AAA/AUTHEN/CONT (1304267484): continue_login (user='admin')
Feb 28 17:48:49: AAA/AUTHEN (1304267484): status = GETPASS
Feb 28 17:48:49: AAA/AUTHEN/CONT (1304267484): Method=LOCAL
Feb 28 17:48:49: AAA/AUTHEN (1304267484): status = PASS
Feb 28 17:48:49: tty66 AAA/AUTHOR/EXEC (1491533337): Port='tty66' list='' service=EXEC
Feb 28 17:48:49: AAA/AUTHOR/EXEC: tty66 (1491533337) user='admin'
Feb 28 17:48:49: tty66 AAA/AUTHOR/EXEC (1491533337): send AV service=shell
Feb 28 17:48:49: tty66 AAA/AUTHOR/EXEC (1491533337): send AV cmd*
Feb 28 17:48:49: tty66 AAA/AUTHOR/EXEC (1491533337): found list "default"
Feb 28 17:48:49: tty66 AAA/AUTHOR/EXEC (1491533337): Method=LOCAL
Feb 28 17:48:49: AAA/AUTHOR (1491533337): Post authorization status = PASS_ADD
Feb 28 17:48:49: AAA/AUTHOR/EXEC: Processing AV service=shell
Feb 28 17:48:49: AAA/AUTHOR/EXEC: Processing AV cmd*
Feb 28 17:48:49: AAA/AUTHOR/EXEC: Processing AV priv-lvl=3
Feb 28 17:48:49: AAA/AUTHOR/EXEC: Authorization successful
```

Note that the **aaa authorization config-commands** commands and **aaa authorization commands 3 default local if-authenticated** commands of this scenario's AAA configuration were not yet set at the time the **debug** commands from Example 15-8 were issued. This resulted in the debug output not displaying the user's activity after the user has been authorized.

Example 15-9 shows the **debug** command output after **aaa authorization config-commands** commands and **aaa authorization commands 3 default local if-authenticated** commands have been applied. You can see that the user has issued the **show startup-config** command authorized for their privilege level.

Example 15-9 *Debugging AAA after the* **authorization config-commands** *Commands*

```
R8#show debug
General OS:
  AAA Authentication debugging is on
  AAA Authorization debugging is on
```

Example 15-9 *Debugging AAA after the* **authorization config-commands** *Commands (Continued)*

```
Sep 28 17:40:45: AAA/AUTHEN (1358087791): status = GETUSER
Sep 28 17:40:45: AAA/AUTHEN/CONT (1358087791): Method=LOCAL
Sep 28 17:40:45: AAA/AUTHEN (1358087791): status = GETPASS
Sep 28 17:40:47: AAA/AUTHEN/CONT (1358087791): continue_login (user='admin')
Sep 28 17:40:47: AAA/AUTHEN (1358087791): status = GETPASS
Sep 28 17:40:47: AAA/AUTHEN/CONT (1358087791): Method=LOCAL
Sep 28 17:40:47: AAA/AUTHEN (1358087791): status = PASS
Sep 28 17:40:47: tty66 AAA/AUTHOR/EXEC (1731500233): Port='tty66' list='' service=EXEC
Sep 28 17:40:47: AAA/AUTHOR/EXEC: tty66 (1731500233) user='admin'
Sep 28 17:40:47: tty66 AAA/AUTHOR/EXEC (1731500233): send AV service=shell
Sep 28 17:40:47: tty66 AAA/AUTHOR/EXEC (1731500233): send AV cmd*
Sep 28 17:40:47: tty66 AAA/AUTHOR/EXEC (1731500233): found list "default"
Sep 28 17:40:47: tty66 AAA/AUTHOR/EXEC (1731500233): Method=LOCAL
Sep 28 17:40:47: AAA/AUTHOR (1731500233): Post authorization status = PASS_ADD
Sep 28 17:40:47: AAA/AUTHOR/EXEC: Processing AV service=shell
Sep 28 17:40:47: AAA/AUTHOR/EXEC: Processing AV cmd*
Sep 28 17:40:47: AAA/AUTHOR/EXEC: Processing AV priv-lvl=3
Sep 28 17:40:47: AAA/AUTHOR/EXEC: Authorization successful
Sep 28 17:40:55: tty66 AAA/AUTHOR/CMD (1039984762): Port='tty66' list='' service=CMD
Sep 28 17:40:55: AAA/AUTHOR/CMD: tty66 (1039984762) user='admin'
Sep 28 17:40:55: tty66 AAA/AUTHOR/CMD (1039984762): send AV service=shell
Sep 28 17:40:55: tty66 AAA/AUTHOR/CMD (1039984762): send AV cmd=show
Sep 28 17:40:55: tty66 AAA/AUTHOR/CMD (1039984762): send AV cmd-arg=startup-config
Sep 28 17:40:55: tty66 AAA/AUTHOR/CMD (1039984762): send AV cmd-arg=<cr>
Sep 28 17:40:55: tty66 AAA/AUTHOR/CMD (1039984762): found list "default"
Sep 28 17:40:55: tty66 AAA/AUTHOR/CMD (1039984762): Method=LOCAL
Sep 28 17:40:55: AAA/AUTHOR (1039984762): Post authorization status = PASS_ADD
```

Lesson 15-2: Disabling Services

Many services are offered by Cisco IOS Software. Although each service carries a useful function, it could present a potential security risk. When services are not used, you need to disable them. Otherwise, they open a security hole for an attacker to manipulate. This lesson is devoted to disabling unnecessary services on R8. Keep in mind that different Cisco IOS Software releases maintain different services on or off by default. If a service is off by default, disabling it does not appear in the running configuration. It is best, however, not to make any assumptions and to explicitly disable all unneeded services, even if you think they are already disabled.

The services covered in this lesson are as follows:

- Router name and DNS name resolution
- Cisco Discovery Protocol (CDP)
- TCP and UDP small servers
- Finger server

- NTP service

- BOOTP server

- Configuration auto-loading

- Proxy ARP

- IP source routing

- IP directed broadcast

- IP unreachables, redirects, and mask replies

Router Name and DNS Name Resolution

If no Domain Name System (DNS) server is specifically mentioned in the router configuration, by default all the name queries are sent to the broadcast address of 255.255.255.255. To alter the default behavior and turn off the automatic lookup, use the following command:

```
R8(config)#no ip domain-lookup
```

Cisco Discovery Protocol

The Cisco Discovery Protocol (CDP) is a proprietary protocol that Cisco devices use to identify their directly connected neighbors. CDP is not frequently used and, like any other unnecessary local service, is considered potentially harmful to security. You can use the following commands to turn off CDP—globally and per interface:

```
R8(config)#no cdp run
R8(config-if)#no cdp enable
```

Disabling CDP per interface is a nice feature because it allows you to still run CDP for the parts of the network that need it.

TCP and UDP Small Servers

Another two services that you should also turn off are the Transmission Control Protocol (TCP) and User Datagram Protocol (UDP) small servers. They are included in the list of standard TCP and UDP services that hosts should provide but are seldom needed. Use the following commands to disable TCP and UDP small servers:

```
R8(config)#no service tcp-small-servers
R8(config)#no service udp-small-servers
```

Finger Server

Next, you need to make sure that the Cisco IOS Software support for the UNIX finger protocol is disabled. Having the finger service enabled allows a user to view other active users. There are many known ways that the service can be misused and the information can fall into the wrong hands. To keep your network security in full force, you should consider turning off the finger service. After all, those who are not authorized to log in to the router have no business looking up those who do. Use the following command to disable the finger service:

```
R8(config)#no ip finger
```

NTP Service

If NTP, described earlier in "Network Time Protocol Security," is not used in the network, disable it with the following interface command:

```
R8(config-if)#ntp disable
```

BOOTP Server

In theory, BOOTP service might sound like a good idea. It is meant for use in networks where a centralized strategy of Cisco IOS Software deployment is implemented. One router can be used by other routers to load its operating system. However, the BOOTP protocol is seldom used, and it gives a hacker an opportunity to steal an IOS image. Therefore, in most situations, you should disable it using the following command:

```
R8(config)#no ip bootp server
```

Configuration Auto-Loading

The routers can find their startup configuration either in their own NVRAM or load it over the network. Obviously, loading in from elsewhere is taking a security risk. To disable the router's ability to get its configuration from the network, apply the following commands:

```
R8(config)#no boot network
R8(config)#no service config
```

Proxy ARP

Proxy Address Resolution Protocol (ARP) replies are sent to an ARP request destined for another device. When an intermediate Cisco device knows the MAC address of the destination device, it can act as a proxy. When an ARP request is destined for another Layer 3 network, a proxy ARP device extends a LAN perimeter by enabling transparent access between multiple LAN segments. This presents a security problem. An attacker can issue multiple ARP requests and use up the proxy ARP device's resources when it tries to respond to these requests in a denial-of-service (DoS) attack.

Proxy ARP is enabled on Cisco router interfaces. Disable it with the following interface command whenever it is not needed:

```
R8(config-if)#no ip proxy-arp
```

NOTE   If, however, static routes use the interface as the destination instead of a next-hop router, proxy ARP is required.

IP Source Routing

An option is found in the header of every IP packet. The Cisco IOS Software examines the option and acts accordingly. Sometimes an option indicates source routing. This means that the packet is specifying its own route. Even though it is the default, this feature has several drawbacks. First, to allow source routing in the ISP environment means that a customer selects a route as they please. Also, this feature poses a known security risk, such as a hacker taking control of a packet's route and directing it through his network. So, if source routing is not necessary in your network, you should disable it on all routers by using the following command:

```
R8(config)#no ip source-route
```

IP-Directed Broadcast

If IP directed broadcast is enabled on a router's interface, it allows the interface to respond to the Internet Control Message Protocol (ICMP) requests directed to a broadcast address of its subnet. This can cause excessive traffic and possibly bring a network down, which is a tool often used by hackers in a smurf attack.

NOTE   During a *smurf attack,* the ping requests sent to a broadcast address are forwarded to up to 255 hosts on a subnet. Because the return address of the ping request is spoofed to be the address of the attack target, all hosts that receive the ping requests reply to the attack target, flooding it with replies.

You can turn off IP directed broadcast capability on every interface with the following command:

```
R8(config-if)#no ip directed-broadcast
```

IP Unreachables, Redirects, and Mask Replies

ICMP messages that are automatically sent by Cisco routers in response to various actions can give away a lot of information, such as routes, paths, and network conditions, to an unauthorized individual. Attackers commonly use the following three types of ICMP message response features:

- **Unreachable**—A response to a nonbroadcast packet that uses an unknown protocol known as Protocol Unreachable, or a response to a packet that a responding device failed to deliver because there is no known route to a destination (Host Unreachable)

- **Redirect**—A response to a packet that notifies the sender of a better route to a destination

- **Mask Reply**—A response from a network device that knows a subnet mask for a particular subnet in an internetwork to a Mask Request message from a device that requires such knowledge

To disable the automatic messaging feature on interfaces, use the following commands:

```
R8(config-if)#no ip unreachables
R8(config-if)#no ip redirects
R8(config-if)#no ip mask-reply
```

Verification

Example 15-10 shows that all the services discussed in this lesson are disabled on R8. You do not see some of them in the running configuration output because of the default settings in this particular version of Cisco IOS Software.

Example 15-10 *Disabling Unnecessary Services*

```
R8#show run
version 12.2
hostname R8
!
! Output omitted for brevity
!
!
username admin privilege 3 password 7 02100A175809
username Sam privilege 15 password 7 05080F1C2243
username Jessie privilege 15 password 7 13061E010803
username Terry privilege 15 password 7 030752180500
username Joe privilege 5 password 7 01100F175804
no ip source-route
!
ip ftp source-interface FastEthernet0/0
ip ftp username anonymous
ip ftp password 7 1511021F0725
no ip domain-lookup
!
interface FastEthernet0/0
ntp disable
no cdp enable
!
interface FastEthernet0/1
```

continues

Example 15-10 *Disabling Unnecessary Services (Continued)*

```
ip address 192.168.1.1 255.255.255.0
no ip unreachables
no ip redirects
no ip mask-reply
no cdp enable
!
```

Lesson 15-3: Setting up a Secure HTTP Server

In this scenario, R8 needs to be configured as the HTTP server so that it allows remote management through the Cisco web browser interface. The syntax for the HTTP server command is as follows:

```
R8(config)#ip http server
```

Specifying the Port Number

You should change the HTTP port number from the default of 80 to something else to hide the HTTP server from an intruder. To modify the default, use the following command:

```
R8(config)#ip http port port-number
```

Specifying Authentication Technique

Next, you need to set up basic user authentication on your HTTP server. Although, you can use AAA services for this purpose, this example queries for the local database. The configuration of usernames and passwords in the database was discussed in the first lesson in "Configuring Passwords, Privileges, and Logins." Use the following command to set up basic user authentication on your local HTTP server:

```
R8(config)#ip http authentication [local]
```

Limiting Access to the Server

To limit access to the server, you can create an access list and then apply it to the HTTP configuration. To associate the list with the HTTP server access, generate the following command:

```
R(config)#ip http access-class access-list
```

Syslog Logging

You can choose to enable the logging of a router's events to a syslog server, including the HTTP-related activity. To specify syslog logging, use the following set of commands:

```
R8(config)#logging on
R8(config)#logging facility [syslog]
R8(config)#logging source-interface local-interface
R8(config)#logging syslog-server-address
R8(config)#logging trap [alerts]
```

The first command on the list, **logging on**, turns the logging on. The **logging facility [syslog]** command names a syslog server as the logging monitor. The **logging source-interface** *local-interface* command identifies local interface that forwards logs to the server. The **logging** *syslog-server-address* command points to the syslog server's IP address. The **logging trap** command sets up the trap level.

Verification

Example 15-11 displays the running configuration of R8. Notice the resolution of the HTTP commands. For example, the port number is changed to 8080. Access-list 11, permitting host 192.168.1.8, was created on R8. FastEthernet0/1 forwards logs to the server.

Example 15-11 *HTTP Configuration*

```
R8#show run
!
! Output omitted for brevity
!
ip http server
ip http port 8080
ip http access-class 1
ip http authentication local
access-list 11 permit 192.168.1.8
!
logging facility syslog
logging source-interface FastEthernet0/1
logging 192.168.1.7
logging trap alerts
```

Now that the HTTP server has been successfully configured, an authorized user can log in. Figures 15-1 and 15-2 show the browser login prompt and the postlogin screen, respectively.

Figure 15-1 *HTTP Login Prompt*

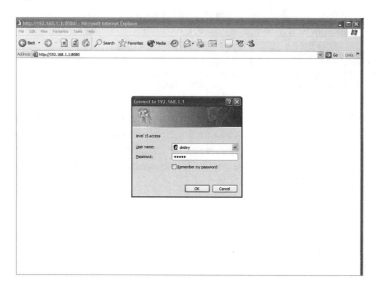

Figure 15-2 *Administrator's Browser Screen*

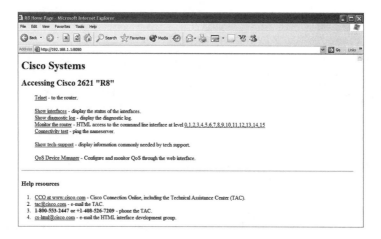

Case Study 15-1: Secure NTP Configuration

Figure 15-3 describes the network topology where R6 is a client of two NTP masters: R5 and R8. To throw in a twist, PIX2 is placed between R8 and R6. This case study is not meant as an in-depth demonstration of the NTP protocol. The main goal is to achieve a functional, secure NTP configuration between the three routers using MD5 authentication.

Figure 15-3 *Network Topology for NTP Configuration*

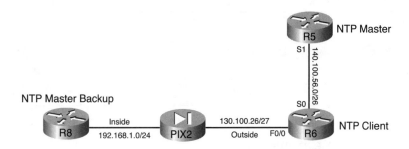

This case study covers the following steps:

Step 1   Setting up time

Step 2   Setting up NTP relationships

Step 3   Configuring PIX2

Step 4   Restricting NTP access

Step 5   Configuring NTP authentication

Step 6   Verification

Step 1: Setting up Time

If you are using a local router as your time synchronization source, the first task you need to complete is to set the clock on the router that is to be your server, R5 in this case. The following command establishes the time (in military format) and date on the router:

```
R5>clock set hh:mm:ss day month year
```

Then, on all participating routers, set the time zone as compared to the Coordinated Universal Time (UTC). Also, configure the routers to automatically switch to daylight-saving time when appropriate. The following two commands identify the time zone and configure daylight-saving time for that zone:

```
R5(config)#clock timezone zone hours [minutes]
R5(config)#clock summer-time zone recurring [week day month hh:mm week day month hh:mm
  [offset]]
```

This scenario uses Pacific Standard Time (PST), offset 8 hours from the UTC. The summertime clock comes into effect on the first and ends on the second specified day every year, as shown in Example 15-12.

Example 15-12 *Coordinating Clocks*

```
R5#show run
!
! Output omitted for brevity
!
clock timezone PST -8
clock summer-time PDT recurring
```

Step 2: Setting Up NTP Relationships

When an external NTP source is not available, as is the case with this NTP configuration scenario, you need to designate a local router as the master that is to be the source of time in the network. To appoint a router as the NTP master, use the following command:

```
R5(config)#ntp master [stratum]
```

To implement redundancy, two routers act as masters: R5 and R8. When an NTP client is configured with several NTP masters, the *stratum level* of a master is the deciding factor. The stratum level of R5 is 1, and the stratum level of R8 is 3; this means that R5 takes precedence over R8.

Next, you need to set up peering between routers for clock synchronization. Use the following command:

```
R5(config)#ntp peer ip-address
```

Each router in the network has been peered up with the two other routers, as shown in Example 15-13.

Example 15-13 *NTP Router Relationships*

```
R5#show run
!
! Output omitted for brevity
!
ntp peer 130.100.26.8                    ←R8
ntp peer 140.100.56.6                    ←R6
```

Step 3: Configuring PIX2

Because R8 is separated from R6 by PIX2, the configuration is not fully functional without the firewall's involvement. For a comprehensive reference on the PIX functions and commands, see Chapter 23, "Cisco PIX Firewall." In this case study, you are offered a short explanation of the commands that are necessary to enable NTP between the routers.

In Example 15-14, you can see that inside and outside interfaces have been assigned their IP addresses. R6 was associated with IP address 130.100.26.6 with the **name 130.100.26.6 R6** statement. Inside-to-outside Network Address Translation (NAT) has been enabled with the **global (outside) 10 interface** and **nat (inside) 10 0.0.0.0 0.0.0.0 0 0** commands. The **static (inside,outside) 130.100.26.8 192.168.1.1 netmask 255.255.255.255 0 0** command specifies the outside IP address to be translated to the inside for packet forwarding to R8. The **route outside 0.0.0.0 0.0.0.0 R6 1** command designates R6 as the default gateway to the outside. Finally, the access list permitting NTP traffic destined for R8 has been applied to the inbound traffic of the outside interface.

Example 15-14 *PIX2 Configuration for NTP*

```
PIX2#show run
!
! Output omitted for brevity
!
nameif ethernet0 outside security0
nameif ethernet1 inside security100
name 130.100.26.6 R6
interface ethernet0 10full
interface ethernet1 auto
access-list outside_access_in permit udp any host 130.100.26.8 eq ntp
ip address outside 130.100.26.2 255.255.255.224
ip address inside 192.168.1.222 255.255.255.0
static (inside,outside) 130.100.26.8 192.168.1.1 netmask 255.255.255.255 0 0
access-group outside_access_in in interface outside
global (outside) 10 interface
nat (inside) 10 0.0.0.0 0.0.0.0 0 0
route outside 0.0.0.0 0.0.0.0 R6 1
```

Step 4: Restricting NTP Access

You can assign an access list to the NTP process to exercise better control over your NTP synchronization. For example, R6 needs to limit the sources of its NTP updates to R5 and R8 only. To allow NTP traffic from the two routers, specify an access list, such as the one in Example 15-15, allowing 140.100.56.5 and 130.100.26.8, and apply it to NTP with the following command:

```
R6(config)#ntp access-group [query-only | serve-only | serve | peer] access-list-number
```

Example 15-15 *NTP Access List*

```
R6#show run
!
! Output omitted for brevity
!
interface FastEthernet0/0
 ip address 130.100.26.6 255.255.255.224
```

continues

Example 15-15 *NTP Access List (Continued)*

```
 ip access-group 110 in
 ip auth-proxy auth
 duplex auto
 speed auto
 ntp broadcast
!
interface Serial0/0
 ip address 140.100.56.6 255.255.255.192
 ip ospf network point-to-point
 ntp broadcast
 no cdp enable
!
ntp access-group peer 1
access-list 1 permit 140.100.56.5
access-list 1 permit 130.100.26.8
 !
ntp peer 130.100.26.8
ntp peer 140.100.56.5
```

Step 5: Configuring NTP Authentication

You have reached the final step of this configuration. NTP supports MD5 authentication, which is useful for preserving your network's security. When MD5 authentication is enforced, your router can be sure that the NTP updates that arrived are from the authorized source. To configure NTP MD5 authentication, perform the following tasks on all the participating routers:

Step 1 Start the NTP authentication process.

Step 2 Specify the NTP authentication-key, MD5 authentication type and string.

Step 3 Set up an NTP trusted key that matches the authentication-key.

Step 4 Add the authentication-key to the peer statements.

To accomplish these tasks, use the following commands and review their application on the routers shown in Example 15-16:

```
R5(config)#ntp authenticate
R5(config)#ntp authentication-key number md5 value
R5(config)#ntp trusted-key key-number
R5(config)#ntp peer ip-address [key keyid]
```

Example 15-16 *MD5 Authentication of NTP*

```
R5#show run
hostname R5
!
! Output omitted for brevity
!
ntp authentication-key 6727 md5 cisco
ntp authenticate
```

Example 15-16 *MD5 Authentication of NTP (Continued)*

```
ntp trusted-key 6727
ntp clock-period 17179922
ntp access-group peer 1
access-list 1 permit 130.100.26.2
access-list 1 permit 140.100.56.6
ntp master 1
ntp peer 130.100.26.8 key 6727
ntp peer 140.100.56.6 key 6727
```

Step 6: Verification

To verify that your NTP configuration is working properly, issue the following commands on any of the routers (see Example 15-17):

```
R5#show ntp associations
R5#show ntp status
R5#show clock
```

Example 15-17 *Verifying NTP Operation*

```
R5#show ntp associations

        address         ref clock      st  when  poll reach  delay  offset   disp
*~127.127.7.1      .LOCL.           0   540   64    0    0.0    0.00  16000.
*~130.100.26.8     140.100.56.5     2  1143   64    0   21.2  -11.17  16000.
*~140.100.56.6     140.100.56.5     2   236   64    0   33.1   -5.71  16000.
*master (synced), # master (unsynced), + selected, - candidate, ~ configured

R5#show ntp status
Clock is synchronized, stratum 1, reference is 127.127.7.1
nominal freq is 250.0000 Hz, actual freq is 249.9992 Hz, precision is 2**19
reference time is AF3BF47D.EBB36EC2 (18:33:33.920 PST Sun Sep 28 2002)
clock offset is -11.1668 msec, root delay is 0.00 msec
root dispersion is 0.02 msec, peer dispersion is 0.02 msec

R5#show clock
.21:14:12.900 PDT Sat Sep 28 2002


R8#show clock
.21:14:14.600 PDT Sat Sep 28 2002
```

NOTE   If you make any changes to the master or the client NTP configuration, they do not take effect until you restart the router in question.

Case Study 15-2: Configuring SSH

In this case study, R5 has been selected as an SSH server. After you complete the necessary configuration tasks, an SSH-enabled client—R6 in this case—can securely connect to the router for administration. (Refer to Figure 15-3 to see the topology.)

The preliminary tasks for configuring SSH are specifying a host name and a domain name for a router. As a result, two statements—**hostname R5** and **ip domain-name cisco.com**—have been placed on R5. After taking this non-SSH-specific step, you can begin the SSH configuration procedure, which includes the following steps:

Step 1   Allowing access for a client

Step 2   Setting up usernames

Step 3   Generating RSA keys

Step 4   Fine-tuning SSH

Step 5   Verification

Step 1: Allowing Access for a Client

To limit SSH access to a known client only, create an access list that specifies the IP address of R6. The **access-list 15 permit 140.100.56.6 log** command is a standard access list that helps achieve the desired outcome.

The syntax for the command that assigns an inbound access list to the vtys was discussed in Lesson 15-1. When applied to this scenario, it results in the following line-mode command:

```
access-class 15 in
```

Step 2: Setting Up Usernames

The next step is to create user accounts, as described in Lesson 15-1. However, instead of using AAA, a local login has been specified here, as follows:

```
R5(config-line)#login local
```

In other words, the **login local** command indicates to the router that when a user is trying to connect via SSH, the router uses the local database configured with the **username admin privilege 15 password cisco** command to authenticate the said user.

Step 3: Generating RSA Keys

For R5 to become an SSH server, it needs to get an RSA key pair. To generate a new RSA key pair for R5, use the following command:

```
R5(config)#crypto key generate rsa
```

At the next prompt, specify **R5.cisco.com** as the name for the keys and the default of 512 bits accepted for the key modulus. By generating the RSA key pair, you automatically enabled SSH on the router. To exercise further control over your SSH, use the commands described in the next step.

Step 4: Fine-Tuning SSH

Authentication timeout is the interval, measured in seconds, that the server waits until a client responds with a password. The default and the maximum are both 120 seconds. In this configuration, the timeout stands at 60 seconds. The syntax for configuring the authentication timeout is as follows:

```
R5(config)#ip ssh timeout seconds
```

If a user logs in incorrectly several times, the router drops the connection. The default for authentication attempts is 3, and the maximum is 5. In this example, the default is kept, but the syntax for the command is as follows:

```
R5(config)#ip ssh authentication-retries number
```

In Lesson 15-1, you allowed Telnet as the type of connection over vtys on R8. Here, you specify SSH as the connection of choice in the following manner:

```
R5(config-line)#transport input ssh
```

Step 5: Verification

Example 15-18 shows the output of the running configuration of R5. All the steps that have been covered in this case study are displayed.

Example 15-18 *SSH Configuration*

```
R5(config)#hostname R5
R5(config)#ip domain-name cisco.com
R5(config)#access-list 15 permit 140.100.56.6 log                ← Only R6

R5(config)#line vty 0 4
R5(config-line)#access-class 15 in
R5(config-line)#login local
R5(config-line)#transport input ssh
R5(config-line)#exit

R5(config)#username admin privilege 15 password cisco
R5(config)#crypto key generate rsa
The name for the keys will be: R5.cisco.com
Choose the size of the key modulus in the range of 360 to 2048 for your
  General Purpose Keys. Choosing a key modulus greater than 512 may take
  a few minutes.
```

continues

Example 15-18 *SSH Configuration (Continued)*

```
How many bits in the modulus [512]:512 "or hit ENTER"
Generating RSA keys ...
[OK]

R5(config)#
Sep 29 22:26:42: %SSH-5-ENABLED: SSH 1.5 has been enabled


R5(config)#ip ssh authentication-retries 3
R5(config)#ip ssh time-out 60
R5(config)#
```

To determine whether the configuration is working, the next logical step is to try to connect to R5 from R6 via SSH. Issue the following statement on R6, as shown in Example 15-19:

```
ssh -c des -l admin 140.100.56.5
```

Type in the password at the prompt.

Example 15-19 *Connecting from R6 to R5 via SSH*

```
r6#ssh -c des -l admin 140.100.56.5               ← R5
Trying 140.100.56.5...Open
password:cisco
```

Once you are successfully connected, you can input **show ssh** on R5 to verify that SSH has been successfully enabled and check that your session is using SSH. Example 15-20 shows the output of the **show ssh** command, which displays the status of SSH server connections, and the **show ip ssh** command, which demonstrates the version and configuration data for SSH.

Example 15-20 *The* **show ssh** *and* **show ip ssh** *Commands on R5*

```
R5#show ssh
Connection     Version Encryption     State                 Username
    0            1.5      DES          Session started         cisco

R5#show ip ssh
SSH Enabled - version 1.5
Authentication timeout: 60 secs; Authentication retries: 3
```

If you use the Cisco IOS Software **debug ip ssh** command, you can monitor the SSH operation. Example 15-21 illustrates the output of the **debug ip ssh client** command. The first part of the output is the display of user activity, and the second is the log line that was recorded after the user exited the SSH server.

Example 15-21 *The* **debug ip ssh client** *Command Output*

```
R5#debug ip ssh client

Sep 29 22:36:52: SSH1: sent protocol version id SSH-1.5-Cisco-1.25
Sep 29 22:36:52: SSH1: protocol version id is - SSH-1.5-Cisco-1.25o
!
User exits ssh router
Sep 29 22:37:37: SSH1: Session terminated normally
```

Catalyst 3550 Security

Because the 3550 family of Catalyst switches uses the IOS-based command-line interface, the handling of the basic security features on the switch is virtually the same as it is on the router. By the time this book is released, the 3550 switches will even offer full support of routing protocol security. For now, use Access Control Lists (ACLs), covered in Chapter 16, to enforce remote administration security.

A few security concepts, however, remain specific to the Catalyst switch. Among them is the network security configuration with ACLs, mentioned in the preceding paragraph, and L2VPN, covered in Chapter 25, "Internet Service Provider Security Services." In this lesson, you concentrate on port-based traffic control configuration.

Lesson 15-4: Port-Based Traffic Control

This lesson discusses how to configure the port-based traffic control features on your switch. The lesson consists of the following configuration tasks:

- Configuring storm control
- Configuring protected ports
- Configuring port blocking
- Configuring port security
- Port security aging

Configuring Storm Control

A *LAN storm* takes place when packets overflow the LAN, causing unnecessary traffic and diminishing network stability. Storm control or the traffic suppression feature configured on a physical interface prevents switchports on a LAN from being overwhelmed by a broadcast, multicast, or unicast storm. Storm control screens the incoming traffic over a period of 1 second and compares the amount with the control level threshold if one exists. If the threshold is exceeded, additional traffic is blocked until the continuing monitoring determines that incoming traffic fell below the threshold level, and traffic is then allowed to be forwarded again.

The switch handles separate storm control thresholds for broadcast, multicast, and unicast traffic. Interestingly, when broadcast or unicast thresholds are reached, traffic is suppressed for only that specific type. On the other hand, when the multicast traffic rate exceeds the threshold, all incoming traffic, except spanning-tree packets, including broadcast and unicast, is throttled until the level drops below the specified threshold.

Storm control on an interface is enabled separately for each type of traffic. The configured threshold level is the percentage of total available bandwidth that you want to serve as a limit indicator. The percentage can be from 1 to 100, with an optional fraction. The higher the level, the more packets are allowed to pass through. The default is no storm control, which translates into 100 percent threshold. In contrast, a value of 0.0 means that all port traffic is blocked for a particular type. The syntax for configuring traffic suppression is as follows:

```
3550-A(config-if)#storm-control [broadcast | multicast | unicast] level level [.level]
```

Configuring Protected Ports

A protected port feature is used in those environments where no traffic can be forwarded between two ports on the same switch. This way, one neighbor connected to one port does not see the traffic that is generated by another neighbor connected to the second port. The blocking of traffic (unicast, broadcast, or multicast) only works when both ports are protected. When a protected port is communicating with an unprotected port, the traffic is forwarded in the usual manner. Once the ports are protected, traffic between them can only be forwarded by a Layer 3 device.

By default, the protected port feature is not enabled. You can configure protected ports on either a physical interface or an EtherChannel group. Once you enable the protected port feature on the latter, it is extended to all the group's ports. The following command sets port protection:

```
3550-A(config-if)#switchport protected
```

Configuring Port Blocking

The default behavior of a switch is to forward the packets with unknown destination MAC addresses to all its ports. This might not always be desirable, especially in terms of security. If you configure a port block feature, then depending on what type of traffic you specified, unicast or multicast packets are not forwarded from one port to another. Blocking unicast or multicast traffic is not automatically enabled, even on a protected port; you must manually define it.

As with the protected interface, you can configure blocking on a physical interface and an EtherChannel group. If blocking is configured on an EtherChannel, it applies to all ports in the group. To block unknown multicast or unicast packets from a port, use the following command:

```
3550-A(config-if)#switchport block [multicast | unicast]
```

Configuring Port Security

The port security feature is used to limit access to an interface to only those devices whose MAC address is identified as allowed and as long as the maximum number of allowed addresses is not already reached. In other words, if a port that is configured as secure recognizes that a station is trying to gain access, it checks whether the configured maximum number of secure MAC addresses has been exceeded. If it has not, the port checks the table of secure MAC addresses, and if the MAC address in question is not there yet, the port learns it and marks it as secure. If the preset maximum number has been reached, and the MAC address is not a member of the secure addresses, a security violation is noted. Similarly, the violation occurs when a device whose MAC address is known as secure on one secure port tries to access another secure port.

To configure a secure port, first set the physical interface's mode to "access" because an interface in the default mode cannot be configured as a secure port:

```
3550-B(config-if)#switchport mode access
```

Then, enable port security on that interface by using the following command:

```
3550-B(config-if)#switchport port-security
```

Placement of the following three commands is optional because the exact commands you choose depend on the desired functional effect. The following command specifies the maximum number of secure MAC addresses for the interface (the number ranges from 1 to 128, with 128 being default):

```
3550-B(config-if)#switchport port-security maximum value
```

Next, you can configure the interface to take one of the following actions in case of a security violation:

- The **protect** keyword causes the packets with unknown source addresses to be dropped when the maximum threshold is reached.

- The **restrict** keyword increments a violation counter.

- The **shutdown** keyword, the default, deactivates the port immediately and sends an SNMP trap notification.

```
3550-B(config-if)#switchport port-security violation [protect | restrict | shutdown]
```

NOTE   If a secure port has been shut down as a result of a security violation, you can bring it out of this state by entering the **errdisable recovery cause** *psecure-violation* global configuration command, or you can manually reenable it by entering the **shutdown** and **no shut down** interface configuration commands.

Finally, to enter a secure MAC address for the interface, use the following command. If the number of manually defined addresses is less than the configured maximum, the rest are learned dynamically.

```
3550-B(config-if)#switchport port-security mac-address mac-address
```

Port Security Aging

You can define an optional security-aging feature to cause all secure addresses to become obsolete without having to manually remove each of them. The types of aging mechanisms are as follows:

- **Absolute**—Specifies an aging period after which the secure addresses on that port are deleted

- **Inactivity**—Discards secure addresses only if they have been inactive for the specified aging time

The **aging time** command includes a number of arguments. The **static** keyword involves the manually configured addresses for the interface. The **time** keyword specifies the aging time, ranging from 0 to 1440 minutes. The *type* identifier indicates either absolute or inactivity, as follows:

```
3550-B(config-if)#switchport port-security aging [static] time time type [absolute |
    inactivity]
```

Verification

The following examples display the outputs from a number of **show** commands on both switches that assist in the verification and monitoring of port-based traffic control.

Example 15-22 captures a portion of the 3550-A running configuration for interface FastEthernet0/1.

Example 15-22 *Running Configuration of 3550-A*

```
interface FastEthernet0/1
switchport mode access
switchport port-security maximum 2
switchport port-security mac-address 1000.2000.3000
switchport port-security violation protect
switchport port-security aging time 600
no ip address
storm-control broadcast level 10.00
storm-control multicast level 10.00
storm-control unicast level 10.00
```

Example 15-23 shows a portion of the 3550-B running configuration for interface FastEthernet0/2.

Example 15-23 *Running Configuration of 3550-B*

```
interface FastEthernet0/2
switchport mode dynamic auto
switchport block multicast
switchport block unicast
no ip address
```

Example 15-24 shows the output of the **show interfaces fastEthernet switchport** command for the 0/1 and 0/2 ports.

Example 15-24 *The* **show interfaces fastEthernet switchport** *Command Output*

```
3550-A#show interfaces fastEthernet 0/1 switchport
Name: Fa0/1
Switchport: Enabled
Administrative Mode: static access
Operational Mode: up
Administrative Trunking Encapsulation: negotiate
Negotiation of Trunking: Off
Access Mode VLAN: 1 (default)
Trunking Native Mode VLAN: 1 (default)
Trunking VLANs Enabled: ALL
Pruning VLANs Enabled: 2-1001
Protected: false

Unknown unicast blocked: disabled
Unknown multicast blocked: disabled
Voice VLAN: none (Inactive)
Appliance trust: none

3550-A#show interfaces fastEthernet 0/2 switchport
Name: Fa0/2
Switchport: Enabled
Administrative Mode: dynamic auto
Operational Mode: down
Administrative Trunking Encapsulation: negotiate
Negotiation of Trunking: On
Access Mode VLAN: 1 (default)
Trunking Native Mode VLAN: 1 (default)
Trunking VLANs Enabled: ALL
Pruning VLANs Enabled: 2-1001

Protected: false
Unknown unicast blocked: enabled
Unknown multicast blocked: enabled
```

Example 15-25 shows the output of the **show storm-control** command. You can use this command to view your storm control configuration per port.

Example 15-25 *The* **show storm-control** *Command Output*

```
3550-A#show storm-control
Interface  Filter State   Level    Current
---------- -------------- -------- --------
Fa0/1      Forwarding      10.00%    0.00%
Fa0/2      inactive       100.00%   N/A
Fa0/3      inactive       100.00%   N/A
Fa0/4      inactive       100.00%   N/A
Fa0/5      inactive       100.00%   N/A
Fa0/6      inactive       100.00%   N/A
Fa0/7      inactive       100.00%   N/A
Fa0/8      inactive       100.00%   N/A
Fa0/9      inactive       100.00%   N/A
Fa0/10     inactive       100.00%   N/A
```

Example 15-26 shows the ports configured as secure.

Example 15-26 *The* **show port-security** *Command Output*

```
3550-A#show port-security address

          Secure Mac Address Table
------------------------------------------------------------

Vlan    Mac Address      Type             Ports
----    -----------      ----             -----
   1    1000.2000.3000   SecureConfigured   Fa0/1
```

Summary

In this chapter, you were introduced to several features of basic Cisco IOS Software and Catalyst 3550 security. On routers, these features include the following:

- Password management

- Disabling unnecessary services

- Setting up secure HTTP and NTP services

- SSH

On 3550 switches, controlling traffic on ports was also discussed.

For some of you, the basic IOS security features might have seemed too basic. Remember, however, that these service features are essential to overall network security and are, or might become, an integral part of the CCIE Security lab exam. Likewise, the HTTP and NTP case studies were included to demonstrate how you can apply security to various Cisco IOS Software services. You can consult plenty of references to find out more information. Some of them are suggested in the Appendix E, "Security-Related RFCs and Publications."

This chapter was designed to make you comfortable with basic IOS security and to help you realize that network security can be enhanced with as few as one or two commands.

Review Questions

   1 What is the NTP standard time zone?

   2 What is the secure alternative to Telnet?

   3 Which command(s) protect(s) the privileged EXEC mode on a router?

   4 How many privilege levels exist?

   5 What does the **exec-timeout 0 0** command indicate?

   6 You can disable the Cisco Discovery Protocol (CDP) globally or per interface. True or false?

   7 You can exercise storm control on the 3550 switch ports for which type(s) of traffic?

FAQs

Q — *What is basic Cisco IOS Software security?*

A — Basic IOS security comprises the features that are available in Cisco IOS Software to protect your router and, in turn, your network from unauthorized activities. It is the first line of software defense that is relatively easy to implement and should always be used unless your particular circumstances dictate otherwise.

Q — *How do I protect my NTP services?*

A — You can protect your NTP services by applying an access list to NTP for access restriction. You can also apply an access list that specifies NTP services to an interface. MD5 encryption is used for authenticating NTP peers to ensure their identity.

Q — *Why do I need HTTP services on the router?*

A — To simplify the tasks of router access and management, HTTP offers web-based services with a browser look and feel.

Q — *What kind of password-management techniques does Cisco IOS Software have?*

A — Cisco IOS Software supports enable passwords, which control access to administrative-level commands on a router. There are also line passwords, which control access to a router, be it locally via a console port or remotely through an auxiliary port or virtual terminal access.

Q — *What is the purpose of SSH?*

A — SSH is an alternative to Telnet service. Telnet service sends traffic in cleartext and can easily be intercepted by an attacker. SSH is implemented to provide security by encrypting traffic between the SSH server and a client. It is available in the newer versions of Cisco IOS Software.

Q — *Why do I need to disable some services on the router?*

A — Unused services on the router always present a security risk. They can be manipulated in a variety of ways to aid an attacker in his pursuit. If a service is not used, you should turn it off. If you must use the service, make securing that service one of your primary concerns.

Q — *Why do I need port security on the switch?*

A — Port security on the switch is a way to limit access to a port to only those devices whose MAC addresses are explicitly allowed, either through manual configuration or by being dynamically learned.

This chapter includes the following topics:

- Overview of Access Control Lists (ACLs)
- ACLs on the IOS router and Catalyst 3550 switch
- Time-of-day ACLs
- Lock-and-key ACLs
- Reflexive ACLs
- Router ACLs
- Port ACLs
- Defining ACLs
- Maintaining ACLs
- Unsupported features on the Catalyst 3550 switch

CHAPTER 16

Access Control Lists

The Access Control List (ACL) provides you with basic traffic-filtering capabilities to filter the packets of all routed network protocols such as TCP/IP. This allows you to control what traffic is permitted to enter or exit your network.

For the CCIE Security exam, you are expected to know the different types of ACLs that are available on Cisco equipment, how to implement them, and how to monitor and trouble-shoot them. Don't be surprised if you are required to design, implement, and troubleshoot one or more types of ACLs during the lab portion of the exam.

Overview of Access Control Lists

ACLs are used to filter network traffic, often referred to as *packet filtering,* by deciding whether routed packets are forwarded or blocked at your router's interfaces. An ACL contains an ordered list of access control entries (ACEs). Each ACE specifies whether to *permit* or *deny* a packet based on a set of conditions that the packet must satisfy to match the ACE. The meaning of permit or deny depends on the context in which the ACL is used. The router examines each packet as it enters or before it exits an interface to determine whether to forward or drop the packet.

Use crypto access lists to define which IP traffic you want to be protected by crypto and which traffic you do not want to be protected by crypto. The access lists that you define are not specific to IPSec. It is only through a crypto map entry referencing the specific access list that defines whether IPSec processing is applied to the traffic matching a permit in the access list. Crypto access lists that are associated with IPSec crypto map entries have the following four primary functions:

- Select the outbound traffic that you want to be protected by IPSec (permit = protect).

- Indicate the data flow to be protected by the new security associations (specified by a single permit entry) when initiating negotiations for IPSec associations.

- Process inbound traffic to filter out and discard traffic that should have been protected by IPSec.

- Determine whether to accept requests for IPSec associations on behalf of the requested data flows when processing Internet Key Exchange (IKE) negotiation from the peer.

The router tests packets against the conditions in an ACL one by one. It uses the first match to determine whether to accept or reject the packets. If no matching condition exists, an implied deny at the end of the ACL rejects the packets.

You can use a packet's source or destination address, the upper-layer protocol, or many other types of information to define the criteria to use for matching. Just remember that ACLs are not the magic answer where security is concerned; a sophisticated user or application might be able to successfully evade or fool basic ACLs because no authentication is required. ACLs can also have an impact on the performance of the device when it is required to compare a packet to a lengthy ACL. One other drawback to using ACLs to define your network security is that typical ACLs do not maintain state information on traffic flows, possibly allowing a crafted packet to bypass the access control defined by the ACL.

While switches traditionally operate at Layer 2 only, the Catalyst 3550 switch has the capability to perform Layer 3 operations with an enhanced multilayer software image installed. This means that the switch first bridges the packet, then routes the packet internally, and then bridges the packet again to send it along the way to its destination. During this process, the switch can apply ACLs that you define against all packets it switches, including packets that are bridged within a virtual LAN (VLAN).

NOTE   By using the Catalyst 3550 switch along with routers in your network design, you can configure your ACLs on either your routers or switches to provide basic security for your network.

Where to Configure an ACL

Because there can be many entrance and exit points in your network, or at least the portion that needs protection, one of the hardest things to choose is where and why to implement a certain type of ACL. Some of the reasons to implement an ACL include restricting routing updates, providing traffic flow control as part of a traffic-shaping design, or even coloring packets for a quality of service (QoS) implementation. However, the reason that most people implement an ACL is for use as part of their network security solution. You are going to focus on this last reason throughout this chapter.

The simplest implementation that you can use for an ACL is to provide a basic level of security, guarding access to your network. If you choose not to implement an ACL where needed, beware that all packets entering your network are allowed by default, possibly to all parts of your network. One example that seems to be prevalent throughout the Internet is allowing access to one web server while preventing access to another. Figure 16-1 demonstrates this by allowing IP addresses A and B to access Web_Server while preventing access to SQL_Server, which resides on the same subnet.

Figure 16-1 *Preventing Server Access with ACLs*

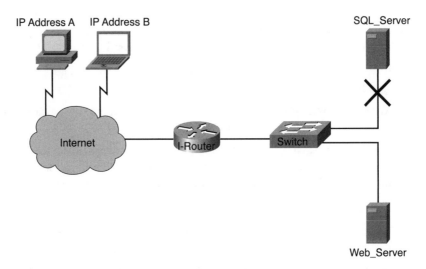

You can use ACLs for security purposes, such as allowing only certain hosts to access a device via Simple Network Management Protocol (SNMP) or Telnet, to a more complex implementation where you allow a host to connect to e-mail on a server, but not allow it to view the server through NetBIOS.

When to Configure an ACL

In most cases, you want to use an ACL on a firewall router that is as close to the entry or exit point of the network that you are concerned with. This usually means that you must position this router between your internal network and an external network such as the Internet or a business-to-business connection. One other place that you might want to use an ACL is between a secure area and a nonsecure area, such as access to the human resources or finance areas of your company.

At a minimum, you should consider implementing ACLs on your border routers. A *border router* is any router that provides an entry into or exit out of your network. On border routers, you should configure an ACL for each network protocol that is configured on the router interfaces, which, in most cases, would be TCP/IP. You should configure the ACLs so that both inbound traffic and outbound traffic are filtered on an interface, although you can choose to only filter traffic inbound or outbound.

ACLs on the IOS Router and the Catalyst 3550 Switch

You can select from many different types of ACLs when implementing them on the Cisco IOS series of devices. Cisco IOS Software uses ACLs for its traffic-filtering implementation with both a basic and advanced ACL capability, as follows:

- **Basic ACLs**—Filter traffic based on source and destination address and protocol type of each packet

- **Advanced ACLs**—Provide you with a means to configure sophisticated and dynamic traffic-filtering capabilities for a stronger, more flexible network security

The Catalyst 3550 also has a rich selection of ACLs that you can configure. Like ACLs in IOS software, the ACLs that are used by the 3550 allow you to filter traffic depending on your individual needs. The 3550 switch also gives you the ability to configure basic and advanced ACLs.

Basic ACLs

You can use basic ACLs to allow only specified traffic through the device; other traffic is simply dropped. You have the capability to specify individual hosts or subnets that should be allowed into your network, and you can specify what type of traffic they should be allowed to use on your network.

Basic ACLs accomplish access control by using the packet's source and destination address and protocol type to determine which traffic to filter. At a minimum, you should implement a basic ACL for all network protocols that are to be routed through your networking device such as IP, IPX, AppleTalk, and so on. However, be aware that the Catalyst 3550 switch is not capable of filtering some types of network protocols, even though you can configure them.

Basic ACLs for IOS software and the 3550 switch include the following:

- **Standard IP ACL**—Uses the source address for matching operations. This can be a numbered or named ACL.

- **Extended IP ACL**—Uses the source and destination addresses for matching operations and uses optional protocol type information for finer granularity of control. This can be a numbered or named ACL.

- **MAC Extended ACL**—Used to match source and destination MAC addresses and optional protocol type information.

The following sections discuss the ACLs that you can configure in greater detail.

Numbered Standard IP ACLs

You can use the numbered standard ACL to match the source address of an IP packet. Once the packet is matched, you can permit or deny the packet depending on your requirements.

When you configure a standard ACL, if you omit the mask, a mask of 0.0.0.0 is assumed. One thing to remember about ACLs on a 3550 switch is the fact that a switch always rewrites the order of standard ACLs so that entries with host matches and entries with matches having a *"don't care" mask* (which is a mask that matches any other mask) of 0.0.0.0 are moved to the top of the list, above any entries with nonzero masks.

Numbered Extended IP ACLs

You can use an extended ACL to match the source and destination address and, optionally, use the protocol type information for finer granularity of control. An extended IP ACL supports any IP protocol from 0 through 255 as well as the following IP protocols, which you can reference by protocol keywords, in parentheses in bold:

- Authentication Header Protocol (**ahp**)
- Enhanced Interior Gateway Routing Protocol (**eigrp**)
- Encapsulation Security Payload (**esp**)
- Generic routing encapsulation (**gre**)
- Internet Control Message Protocol (**icmp**)
- Internet Group Management Protocol (**igmp**)
- Interior Gateway Routing Protocol (**igrp**)
- Internet Protocol (**ip**)
- IP in IP tunneling (**ipinip**)
- KA9Q NOS-compatible IP over IP tunneling (**nos**)
- Open Shortest Path First routing (**ospf**)
- Payload Compression Protocol (**pcp**)
- Protocol Independent Multicast (**pim**)
- Transmission Control Protocol (**tcp**)
- User Datagram Protocol (**udp**)

Named Standard IP ACLs

A named standard IP ACL uses the same information to filter traffic that a numbered standard IP ACL uses, but the named standard IP ACL has the advantage of providing you with a primitive editing capability.

You can use a named ACL to configure more IP ACLs than you would if you were to use numbered ACLs. You can give a named ACL a number that is in the supported range of ACL numbers, such as naming a standard IP ACL 1 to 99 or naming an extended IP ACL 100 to 199.

Using a number with a named ACL provides the ability to delete individual ACEs without having to first remove the entire ACL, as you would have to with a numbered ACL. After you create a named ACL, any additions are placed at the end of the list. While you cannot selectively add ACEs to a specific ACL, you can use the **no permit** and **no deny** commands to remove entries from a named ACL.

Named Extended IP ACLs

A named extended IP ACL uses the same information to filter traffic that a number extended IP ACL uses but also gives you the ability of primitive editing.

Named MAC Extended ACLs

On a 3550 switch, you can filter non-IP traffic on a VLAN and on a physical Layer 2 interface by using MAC addresses and named MAC extended ACLs. The procedure you use for this is similar to that of configuring other extended named ACLs. You can also use a number to name your MAC ACL, but you cannot use the MAC ACL numbers from 700 through 799. You cannot apply a named MAC extended ACL to a Layer 3 interface.

Because the MAC extended ACL is a named ACL, you can also delete individual ACEs from it.

After you create a MAC ACL, you need to apply it to a Layer 2 interface to filter non-IP traffic that is coming into that interface. Consider the following guidelines when you apply the MAC ACL:

- If your switch already has an input Layer 3 ACL or a VLAN map applied to it, you cannot apply your ACL to a Layer 2 interface. You can apply an ACL to a Layer 2 interface if the switch has output Layer 3 ACLs applied.

- You can only have one MAC ACL applied to a Layer 2 interface.

Advanced ACLs

The advanced ACLs that you can configure provide sophisticated and dynamic traffic-filtering capabilities for a stronger, more flexible network security implementation.

Advanced ACLs for IOS software include the following:

- **Dynamic extended IP ACL**—Grants access per user to a specific source or destination host basis through a user authentication process.

- **Lock-and-key ACL**—Uses dynamic ACLs to grant temporary access to users who would normally be denied access.

- **Reflexive ACL**—Allows IP packets to be filtered based on session information. Reflexive ACLs contain temporary entries and are nested within extended named IP ACLs.

On a 3550 switch, advanced ACLs include the following:

- **Router ACLs**—Used to control routed traffic between VLANs and are applied to Layer 3 interfaces. Note that you must be running the enhanced multilayer software image on your switch to apply an ACL to a Layer 3 interface and to filter packets routed between VLANs.

- **Port ACLs**—Used to control traffic that is entering a Layer 2 interface. The 3550 switch does not support port ACLs in the outbound direction. You can only apply one IP access list and one MAC access list to a Layer 2 interface.

- **VLAN ACLs or VLAN maps**—Used to control bridged and routed packets. You can use VLAN maps to filter traffic between devices in the same VLAN. VLAN maps are configured to provide access control based on Layer 3 addresses for IP. Unsupported protocols are access controlled through MAC addresses by using Ethernet ACEs. Once a VLAN map is applied to a VLAN, all packets, whether routed or bridged, that enter the VLAN are checked against the VLAN map. Packets can enter the VLAN through either a switch port or a routed port after being routed.

Time-of-Day ACLs

You have the option of implementing ACLs based on the time of day and week using the **time-range** configuration command. You would first define the name and times of the day and week of the time range, and then reference the time range by name in an ACL to apply the restrictions.

You are currently restricted to using only a named or numbered extended ACL to implement time ranges. The time range function allows you to define when the permit or deny statements in your ACL are active.

The time range function can provide the following benefits:

- You have greater control over permitting or denying a user access to resources such as an application, policy routing, or on-demand link.

- You can set time-based security policies, including the following:

  — Perimeter security using the Cisco IOS Firewall feature set or ACLs.

  — Data confidentiality with Cisco Encryption Technology or IP Security Protocol (IPSec).

- Policy-based routing (PBR) and queuing functions are enhanced.

- When provider access rates vary by time of day, you can automatically reroute traffic cost effectively.

- Service providers can dynamically change a committed access rate (CAR) configuration to support the quality of service (QoS) service level agreements (SLAs) that are negotiated for certain times of the day.

- You can control logging messages. ACL list entries can log traffic at certain times of the day, but not constantly.

Lock-and-Key ACLs

Lock-and-key is a traffic-filtering security feature that you can use to dynamically filter IP traffic. You configure lock-and-key by using IP dynamic extended ACLs. You can use lock-and-key in conjunction with other standard ACLs and static extended ACLs.

When you configure lock-and-key, you designate which users, whose IP traffic is normally blocked, can gain temporary access through the device. When lock-and-key is triggered, it reconfigures the interface's existing IP ACL to permit designated users to reach their designated host(s). Afterward, lock-and-key reconfigures the IP ACL to its original state until its next use.

A user can trigger lock-and-key to obtain temporary access by first using a standard Telnet session to the device. When the Telnet session reaches the device, lock-and-key automatically attempts to authenticate the user. If the user is granted access, temporary access is then gained through the device and can reach the destination host.

Lock-and-key uses the following process in its operation:

1 The user opens a Telnet session to a border (firewall) router configured for lock-and-key. The user connects via one of the virtual terminal ports on the router.

2 The software receives the Telnet packet, opens a Telnet session, prompts for a password, and completes a user authentication process. The user must pass authentication before access through the router is permitted. The authentication process can be done locally by the router or by a central access security server such as a TACACS+ or RADIUS server.

3 When the user passes authentication, the user is logged out of the Telnet session and the software creates a temporary ACE statement in the dynamic ACL. (Per your configuration, this temporary ACE can limit the range of networks to which the user is given temporary access.)

4 The user exchanges data through your firewall.

5 The software deletes the temporary ACL ACE when a configured timeout is reached or when the system administrator manually clears it. The configured timeout can be either an idle timeout or an absolute timeout.

Why You Should Use Lock-and-Key

Although lock-and-key provides the same benefits as standard and static extended ACLs, lock-and-key also has the following security benefits:

- Lock-and-key uses a challenge mechanism in its authentication of individual users.

- Lock-and-key provides you with simpler management in large internetworks.

- In many cases, lock-and-key reduces the amount of processing that is required for ACLs.

- Lock-and-key reduces the opportunity for network break-ins by network hackers.

- One often-overlooked use is as an authentication method. For example, once a user is authenticated, the user can access another service, such as initiating an ISDN connection.

Lock-and-key provides the ability to specify which users are permitted access to which source/destination hosts. These users must pass a user authentication process before they can gain access to their designated host(s). Lock-and-key creates dynamic user access through a firewall, without compromising other configured security restrictions.

When You Should Use Lock-and-Key

Deciding when to use lock-and-key is easier if you follow these two examples:

- If you have a scenario where you have a specific remote user (or group of remote users) that needs access to a host within your network, connecting from the remote host via the Internet

- If you want a subset of hosts on a local network to access a host on a remote network that is protected by a firewall

Source-Address Spoofing and Lock-and-Key

One danger that is associated with lock-and-key is that it is susceptible to source-address spoofing. When lock-and-key is triggered, it creates a dynamic opening in your firewall by temporarily reconfiguring the ACL that is associated with an interface to grant the user access. As you know, anytime an opening exists in your security, another host can spoof the authenticated user's address to gain access behind the firewall. Spoofing is an inherent problem with any ACL, and lock-and-key does not specifically address this problem. You should consider configuring another security measure, such as network data encryption, to prevent spoofing from occurring.

Lock-and-Key Configuration Tips

Before you consider configuring lock-and-key, understand the tips for dynamic access lists, lock-and-key authentication, and using the autocommand feature discussed in the following sections.

Dynamic Access List Tips

Follow these tips when configuring dynamic access lists:

- Do not create more than one dynamic ACL for any one ACL. The software can only refer to the first dynamic ACL that you define.

- Do not assign the same *dynamic-name* to another ACL. This causes the software to reuse the existing list name. You must use a globally unique name with all named ACLs.

- Assign attributes to the dynamic ACL in the same manner that you assign attributes for a static ACL. The temporary ACEs inherit the attributes that you assign to this list.

- Configure Telnet as the protocol of choice, forcing the user to Telnet into the router to be authenticated before he can gain access through the router.

- Either define an idle timeout with the **timeout** keyword in the **access-enable** command in the **autocommand** command or define an absolute timeout value with the **access-list** command. You must define one or the other; otherwise, the temporary ACE remains configured indefinitely on the interface (even after the user has terminated his session) until you manually remove the entry. You can configure both idle and absolute timeouts if you desire.

- If you configure an idle timeout, the idle timeout value should be equal to any WAN idle timeouts that you have defined on your WAN interfaces.

- If you configure both idle and absolute timeouts, the idle timeout value must be less than the absolute timeout value.

- The only values that are replaced in the temporary entry are the source or destination address, depending on whether the ACL was applied to the input or output ACL. All other attributes, such as port, are inherited from the main dynamic ACL.

- Each addition to the dynamic list is always put at the beginning of the dynamic list. You cannot specify the order of temporary ACE entries.

- Temporary ACEs are never written to NVRAM.

Lock-and-Key Authentication Tips

You have three possible methods when configuring an authentication query process. These three methods are described as follows:

- **Security server**—You can use a network access security server to authenticate users. While this method requires additional configuration steps, it allows you to configure stricter authentication queries and have more sophisticated tracking capabilities. This is the recommended method for authentication.

- **Local authentication**—You can use a local database for authentication by using the **username** command. This method provides authentication on a per-user basis.

- **password and login**— You can use the **password** and **login** commands to provide authentication. This method is the least effective because the password is configured for the port, not for the user. Therefore, any user who knows the password can authenticate successfully.

The **autocommand** Command Tips

You can use the autocommand feature to automatically execute a command when a user connects to a particular line. Follow these tips when configuring the **autocommand** command:

- When using a TACACS+ server for authentication, you should configure the **autocommand** command on the TACACS+ server as a per-user autocommand. When using local authentication, use the **autocommand** command on the line.

- Configure all virtual terminal (VTY) ports with the same **autocommand** command. Omitting an **autocommand** command on a VTY port allows a random host to gain EXEC mode access to your router and does not create a temporary ACE in the dynamic ACL.

- If you did not previously define an idle timeout with the **autocommand access-enable** command, you must define an absolute timeout using the **access-list** command.

- If you configure both idle and absolute timeouts, the absolute timeout value must be greater than the idle timeout value.

Verifying Lock-and-Key Configuration

You are able to verify that lock-and-key is successfully configured on your router by Telnetting to the router, allowing the Telnet session to close, and then attempting to access a designated host on the other side of the router.

You can then use the **show access-lists** command at the router to view the dynamic ACL, which should include an additional ACE entry that permits the user access through the router.

Maintaining Lock-and-Key

The dynamic ACL that is used with lock-and-key can grow and shrink as entries are added and deleted. You should ensure that these entries are being deleted in a timely manner because, while these dynamic entries exist, your risk of a spoofing attack is increased. A large amount of entries in your dynamic ACL can also have a bigger performance impact on your router.

Manually Deleting Dynamic Access List Entries

If you choose to manually delete a temporary ACE or decide not to use a timeout, use following command to delete the entry:

```
R2#clear access-template [access-list-number | name] [dynamic-name] [source]
   [destination]
```

Reflexive ACLs

You can use the *reflexive ACL*, also known as *IP session filtering*, to filter network traffic based on IP upper-layer protocol session information. You can use reflexive ACLs to permit only sessions that originate from within your network while denying sessions that originate from outside your network.

You can only define a reflexive ACL through an extended named IP ACL. You cannot use the numbered or standard named IP ACLs with other protocol ACLs. However, you can use reflexive ACLs in conjunction with other standard and static extended ACLs.

Reflexive ACLs are similar to any other ACL that you can use. Reflexive ACLs contain condition statements that you use to define the criteria for permitting IP packets into your network. Just like other ACLs, these entries are evaluated in order, and when a match occurs, no more entries are evaluated.

However, reflexive ACLs have some significant differences that set them apart from other types of ACLs. Reflexive ACLs only contain temporary entries that are automatically created when a new IP session begins, and the entries are removed when the session ends. You do not apply reflexive ACLs directly to an interface, but "nest" them within an extended named IP ACL that you apply to the interface. Finally, reflexive ACLs do not have the usual implicit "deny all traffic" statement at the end of the list, due to the nesting with an extended named IP ACL.

NOTE You can approximate the session-filtering capabilities of the reflexive ACL with the static extended ACLs, when you use the **established** keyword with the **permit** command. The **established** keyword filters TCP packets based on whether the ACK or RST bits are set. This type of filter criterion would be part of an ACL that is applied permanently to an interface. Be aware that the **established** keyword is available only for the TCP upper-layer protocol and can pose a security risk because the ACL is always present. This means that, for the other upper-layer protocols (such as UDP, ICMP, and so on), you need to either permit all incoming traffic or define all possible permissible source/destination host/port address pairs for each protocol. (Besides being an unmanageable task, this could exhaust NVRAM space.)

You trigger the reflexive ACL when a new IP upper-layer session is initiated from inside your network to an external network. Once triggered, the reflexive ACL generates a new, temporary entry. This entry permits returning traffic that is part of a previously established session to enter your network, but does not permit any traffic to enter your network if the traffic is not part of the session.

The characteristics of these temporary ACEs are as follows:

- The entry is always a **permit** entry.
- The entry must specify the same protocol as the original outbound TCP packet.

- The entry must specify the same source and destination addresses as the original outbound TCP packet, except that the addresses are swapped.

- The entry must specify the same source and destination port numbers as the original outbound TCP packet, except that the port numbers are swapped. These characteristics apply only to TCP and UDP packets. Other protocols, such as ICMP and IGMP, do not have port numbers, and other criteria are specified. For example, for ICMP, type numbers are used instead.

- Inbound TCP traffic is evaluated against the entry, as long as the entry is valid.

Temporary reflexive ACEs are removed at the end of the session. For TCP sessions, the entry is removed by default 5 seconds after 2 set FIN bits are detected, or immediately after matching a TCP packet with the RST bit set. Or, the temporary entry is removed after no packets of the session have been detected for a configurable length of time (the timeout period).

Because UDP and other protocols do not use port numbers, the end of the session is determined differently than for TCP. The end of a session is determined when there are no longer any detectable packets in the session for a configurable length of time (the timeout period).

Reflexive ACL Benefits and Restrictions

Because you would configure a reflexive ACL on your border router, it can provide you with an important tool in securing your network against network hackers, and it can be included in a firewall defense. Reflexive ACLs provide you with a level of security against spoofing and certain denial-of-service (DoS) attacks. Reflexive ACLs are simple to use and, compared to basic ACLs, provide you with greater control over which packets are allowed to enter your network.

Reflexive ACLs, however, cannot work with applications that use, change, or dynamically allocate port numbers during a session. Because of this, if a port number for a return packet is different from the port number of the originating packet, the return packet is denied by the reflexive ACL, even though the packet is actually part of the same session.

Reflexive ACL Design Considerations

You must consider a few items before you configure a reflexive ACL. Your first item for consideration is whether to configure your reflexive ACL on an internal or external interface.

You most commonly use reflexive ACLs with one of two basic network topologies: with a DMZ interface (complex topology) and without a DMZ interface (simple topology). Determining which of these two topologies fits your requirements can help you decide whether to use your reflexive ACL with an internal interface (with a DMZ interface) or with an external interface (without a DMZ interface).

Router ACLs

You can configure a router ACLs for use on a Switch Virtual Interface (SVI), which is the Layer 3 interface to a VLAN; on a physical Layer 3 interface; and on a Layer 3 EtherChannel interface. Just like the ACLs that you would use on a router, router ACLs on a 3550 switch are applied on interfaces for either the inbound or outbound direction.

You are restricted to only applying one IP ACL in each direction, although you can define an ACL to be used with multiple features for a given interface and you can use one feature for multiple ACLs. Be aware though, when you use a single router ACL with multiple features, it is examined multiple times.

The router ACL uses the standard IP ACL for matching the source address and the extended IP ACL for matching the source and destination address as well as optional protocol type information.

Your switch examines ACLs associated with features that are configured on a given interface and a direction. As these packets enter your switch on an interface, any ACLs that you associate with all inbound features configured on that interface are examined. After the packets are routed and before they are forwarded to the next hop, all ACLs associated with outbound features that are configured on the egress interface are examined.

Port ACLs

The 3550 switch also supports an ACL that you can associate with a Layer 2 interface on your switch. These ACLs, referred to as *port ACLs,* are only supported on a physical interface and not on EtherChannel interfaces. You can apply port ACLs only on an interface in the inbound direction. You can define the following types of ACLs on a Layer 2 interface:

- Standard IP ACLs
- Extended IP ACLs
- MAC extended ACLs

If you apply a port ACL to a trunk port, the ACL filters traffic on every VLAN that is present on that trunk port. If you apply a port ACL to a port with voice VLAN, the ACL filters traffic on both data and voice VLANs.

NOTE   When you configure a port ACL, you can filter IP traffic by using IP ACLs and non-IP traffic on the same Layer 2 interface, by using MAC addresses or by applying both an IP ACL and a MAC ACL to the interface. However, you cannot apply more than one IP ACL and one MAC ACL to a Layer 2 interface.

VLAN Maps

The 3550 switch offers you a powerful feature, called the *VLAN map,* that you can use to access control all traffic on a switch. You can apply a VLAN map to examine all packets that are routed into or out of a VLAN or are bridged within a VLAN. You would use a VLAN map strictly for security packet filtering. Unlike the router ACL, a VLAN map is not defined by the input or output direction.

You can configure a VLAN map to match a Layer 3 address for IP traffic. You can configure access control for all non-IP protocols through their MAC address and Ethertype using a MAC VLAN map. You can only enforce a VLAN map on packets that are going through the switch; you cannot enforce a VLAN map on traffic between hosts on a hub or on another switch that is connected to this switch.

You configure filtering in a VLAN through the use of a VLAN map. The VLAN map does not have a direction associated with it. To filter your traffic in a specific direction by using a VLAN map, you must include an ACL with specific source or destination addresses.

Follow these guidelines when configuring VLAN maps:

- If you do not define a router ACL to deny traffic on a routed VLAN interface, whether it is for input or output traffic, and you have not configured a VLAN map, all traffic is permitted.

- Each VLAN map that you create consists of a series of entries. The order of entries for a VLAN map is important. Just like an ACL, a packet that comes into the switch is tested against the first entry in the VLAN map. If it results in a match, the action specified for that part of the VLAN map is taken. If it does not result in a match, the packet is tested against the next entry in the map.

- If you define at least one match clause for a particular type of packet, IP or MAC, and the packet does not match any of these match clauses, the default is to drop the packet. If no match clause exists for that type of packet in the VLAN map, the default is to forward the packet.

- Your switch can take longer to boot if you configure a very large number of ACLs on it.

- If you have an IP ACL or a MAC ACL applied to a Layer 2 interface, you are allowed to create VLAN maps, but you are not allowed to apply a VLAN map to any of the switch VLANs.

Using VLAN Maps with Router ACLs

You can control access to both bridged and routed traffic through the use of VLAN maps or in combination with a router ACL. Using these two in combination gives you the ability to define a router ACL for both input and output routed VLAN interfaces and a VLAN map to control access of bridged traffic.

When you use VLAN maps in combination with a router ACL, if one of your packet flows matches a deny statement of a VLAN, regardless of the router ACL configuration, the packet flow is denied.

When you configure router ACLs in conjunction with VLAN maps on the same VLAN, you should consider a few guidelines. These guidelines do not apply to cases where you configure router ACLs and VLAN maps on different VLANs:

- Because the switch hardware can only provide one lookup for security ACLs for each direction, input and output, you must merge a router ACL and a VLAN map when you place them on the same VLAN. This merging of the router ACL with the VLAN map can significantly increase the number of ACEs.

- If possible, write the ACL with all entries having a single action except for the final, default action of the other type. That is, write the ACL using one of these two forms:

  — **permit...**

  — **permit...**

  — **permit...**

  — **deny ip any any**

  or

  — **deny...**

  — **deny...**

  — **deny...**

  — **permit ip any any**

- Group each action type together when you are defining multiple actions in an ACL (permit, deny) to reduce the number of entries.

- Due to complications in the merging process, try to avoid including Layer 4 information in an ACL. Your best merge results can be obtained if the ACLs are filtered based on IP addresses (source and destination) and not on the full flow (source IP address, destination IP address, protocol, and protocol ports). You can also use "don't care" bits in the IP address, whenever possible.

- If you must specify the full-flow mode and the ACL contains both IP ACEs and TCP/UDP/ICMP ACEs with Layer 4 information, place the Layer 4 ACEs at the end of the list. This gives priority to the filtering of traffic based on IP addresses.

Fragmented and Unfragmented Traffic

One inherent problem with IP ACLs is the fact that IP packets can be fragmented as they cross your network. When this happens, only the first fragment contains the beginning of the packet that contains the Layer 4 information such as TCP or UDP port numbers, ICMP type and code, and so on. All the other fragments do not contain this information.

Some ACEs are not capable of checking the Layer 4 information, making them ideal for application to all packet fragments. The ACEs that can test Layer 4 information cannot be applied in a standard manner to most of the fragments in a fragmented IP packet. When a fragment contains no Layer 4 information and your ACE is configured to test some Layer 4 information, the matching rules are modified as follows:

- Permit ACEs that check the Layer 3 information in the fragment are considered to match the fragment, regardless of what the missing Layer 4 information might have been.

- Deny ACEs that check Layer 4 information never match a fragment unless the fragment contains Layer 4 information.

You can specify whether your device is to examine noninitial IP fragments of packets when used with IP extended named and numbered ACLs, allowing you more granularity of control over noninitial packets.

Because noninitial fragments do not contain any Layer 4 information (they only contain Layer 3 information), ACEs that are defined with only Layer 3 information can be applied to noninitial fragments. The fragment contains enough information to filter a packet, allowing ACEs with the optional **fragments** keyword to be applied only to noninitial fragments of packets; the fragment is either permitted or denied accordingly. Table 16-1 shows the behavior of ACEs regarding the presence or absence of the **fragments** keyword.

You should not add the **fragments** keyword to all your ACEs because the first fragment of the IP packet is considered to be nonfragmented and is treated independently of the subsequent fragments. This means that the initial fragment will not match an ACL **permit** or **deny** entry that contains the **fragments** keyword but must continue the comparison of the ACL until it is either permitted or denied by an ACE that does not contain the **fragments** keyword. Because of this, you might need to define two ACEs for every **deny** entry that you require. The first **deny** entry should not include the **fragments** keyword so that it applies to the initial fragment. The second **deny** entry of the pair should have the **fragments** keyword and is applied to any subsequent fragments. You can also use the **fragments** keyword with dynamic ACLs.

Table 16-1   *Behavior With and Without the* **fragments** *Keyword*

If the Access List Entry . . .	Then . . .

. . . does not have the **fragments** keyword, and assuming that all the access list entry information matches . . .	For an ACL that only contains Layer 3 information, the entry is applied to nonfragmented packets, initial fragments, and noninitial fragments.
	
	For an access list entry that contains Layer 3 and Layer 4 information:
	
	• The entry is applied to nonfragmented packets and initial fragments:
	
	  — If the entry matches and is a **permit** statement, the packet or fragment is permitted.
	
	  — If the entry matches and is a **deny** statement, the packet or fragment is denied.
	
	• The entry is also applied to noninitial fragments in the following manner. Because noninitial fragments only contain Layer 3 information, only the Layer 3 portion of an ACE can be applied:
	
	  — If the Layer 3 portion of the access list entry matches, and if the entry is a **permit** statement, the noninitial fragment is permitted.
	
	  — If the Layer 3 portion of the access list entry matches, and if the entry is a **deny** statement, the next access list entry is processed.

. . . has the **fragments** keyword and all of the ACE information matches . . .	The ACE is applied only to noninitial fragments.

Logging ACLs

When working with any kind of ACL, consider the fact that a router or switch can provide logging messages about packets that are permitted or denied by the ACL. This logging could provide you with invaluable information when you are trying to determine what happened or if you are trying to get real-time alerts about what is currently happening on your network.

When using logging, because routing is done in hardware and logging is done in software, if a large number of packets match a permit or deny ACE that contains a **log** keyword, the software might not be able to match the hardware processing rate, and not all packets will be logged. The first packet that triggers the ACL causes a message to be logged immediately, while subsequent packets are collected over 5-minute intervals before they are displayed or logged. The logging message includes the access list number, whether the packet was permitted or denied, the source IP address of the packet, and the number of packets from that source that were permitted or denied in the prior 5-minute interval. Your performance can also be impacted, depending on the level of logging that you enable. Logging at a level of debugging can have a larger impact on your performance than logging at the informational level. A few restrictions to this are that an output ACL cannot log multicast packets and logging is not supported for ACLs that are applied to a Layer 2 interface.

Logging for router and regular ACLs on the 3550 switch is supported in two variations. You can use the **log** keyword to send an informational logging message to the console about the packet that matches the entry, or you can use the **log-input** keyword to include the input interface information in the log entry. Logging is not supported for the port ACL.

Defining ACLs

Although you can create an ACL for many types of protocols that you might want to filter, you are only going to concentrate on IP ACLs in this chapter. For a complete explanation of ACLs that are used by other protocols, refer to either the *Cisco IOS Security Configuration Guide* for your appropriate IOS level or *Configuring Network Security with ACLs* for your appropriate 3550 software release.

Your first consideration when creating an ACL is to decide whether the ACL is to be applied to inbound traffic or outbound traffic. The direction is referenced as to whether the packet is entering or exiting an interface.

When creating your ACL, you are defining logically ordered ACEs that comprise the ACL. The ACEs are what your device uses when evaluating whether to forward or block each packet. Typically, your ACEs are based on a packet's source address, destination address, or the upper-layer protocol of the packet.

When defining a single ACL, you can define multiple matching criteria in multiple, separate ACE statements. You tie these ACEs together by referencing the same identifying name or number. You can define as many ACEs as you want; however, you are limited by the available memory of the device and can experience a performance impact with an ACL that has a large amount of ACEs defined. Remember that the more ACE statements you create, the more difficult it is to comprehend and manage your ACLs at a later date.

The Implied "Deny All Traffic" ACE Statement

One item that you often have trouble with when working with ACLs is the fact that anything that you do not explicitly allow is denied. This is because at the end of every ACL, the software automatically places an implied "deny all traffic" ACE statement. Even if you were to place an "allow all traffic" ACE at the end of the ACL, the implied "deny all traffic" entry is still there, although all traffic is allowed to pass.

CAUTION   When you define an inbound ACL for traffic filtering, you should include explicit ACE statements to permit routing updates. If you fail to do this, you can lose communication from the interface when routing updates are blocked by the implicit "deny all traffic" statement at the end of the ACL.

ACE Entry Order

You should be aware that when a device starts the evaluation of the ACEs in an ACL, it tests the packet against each ACE in the order that you entered it. Not only is the order of the ACEs important, in some cases, such as the numbered ACL, you cannot delete individual ACE statements after you enter them; you must delete the entire ACL and reenter the ACE statements in the order that you want them.

After a matching ACE statement is found, your device does not test any more ACEs, no matter how many more exist. This means that you should define the more explicit commands first, usually a deny or an entry for a specific host or service, with general statements later in the ACL.

Using a TFTP Server to Create and Edit ACLs

You might find that creating and editing your ACLs on the device can be confusing at best. One option that you have is to use a Trivial File Transfer Protocol (TFTP) server to accomplish this task. Because there seems to be a TFTP server for virtually every operating system in use today, and because most operating systems have some kind of text editor included with them, creating or editing an ACL can be as simple as creating a document. You can then tweak your ACL by reordering or deleting entries to meet your requirements without fear of rendering your device inoperable due to an empty ACL that denies everything until you can gain physical access to correct it. Once you have the ACL in the format that you need it and save it in an ASCII format, you can then download the entire ACL to your device.

Remember, the first command of an edited ACL file should delete the previous ACL (for example, type a **no access-list** command at the beginning of the file). If you forget to first delete the previous version of the ACL, when you copy the edited file to your device, you are merely appending additional criteria statements to the end of the existing access list.

A few other suggestions for managing ACLs are as follows:

- Create or edit the ACL in your favorite text editor and cut and paste it into your device through a console session or Telnet session.

- Change the ACL name or number when editing the ACL so that you can paste it in your configuration or use a TFTP program to retrieve it into your configuration without affecting the defined ACLs. When you are ready to use the newly defined ACL, change the references to match the name or number of the new ACL. Then you can delete the previous ACL after you have determined that it is no longer required.

Applying ACLs to Interfaces

Now that you have your ACL with the ACE statements in the order that you want, you need to apply the ACL to something on your device. The most common way to do this is to apply the ACL to some type of interface.

When you are using Cisco IOS Software, follow these guidelines:

- IP allows you to apply up to two ACLs on an interface: one inbound ACL and one outbound ACL.

- If you apply the ACL inbound, when the device receives a packet, it checks the ACL's ACE statements for a match. If the packet is permitted by the ACL, the software continues to process the packet. If the packet is denied by the ACL, the software discards the packet.

- If you apply the ACL outbound, after receiving and routing a packet to the outbound interface, the device checks the ACL's ACE statements for a match. If the packet is permitted by the ACL, the software transmits the packet. If the packet is denied by the ACL, the software discards the packet.

With the Catalyst 3550 switch, you can associate ACLs with Layer 2 or Layer 3 interfaces. You can apply these ACLs either outbound or inbound on Layer 3 interfaces, but you can only apply them inbound on Layer 2 interfaces.

Use the following guidelines when applying your IP ACLs to your 3550 switch:

- When using an ACL to control access to a line, you must use a numbered ACL.

- When using an ACL to control access to an interface, you can use a name or number.

- Use identical restrictions on all the virtual terminal lines to prevent possible security issues.

- If you apply an ACL to a Layer 3 interface and the enhanced multilayer software image is not installed on your switch, the ACL only filters packets that are intended for the CPU such as SNMP, Telnet, or web traffic. The enhanced image is not required when applying ACLs to Layer 2 interfaces.

- You cannot use port ACLs on the same switch with input router ACLs and VLAN maps.

- You cannot apply an ACL to a Layer 2 interface on a switch that has an input Layer 3 ACL or a VLAN map applied to it; you can apply an ACL to a Layer 2 interface if the switch has output Layer 3 ACLs applied.

- You cannot apply an ACL to an input Layer 3 interface on a switch that has a Layer 2 ACL applied to it; you can apply an ACL to an output Layer 3 interface if the switch has Layer 2 ACLs applied.

- You can apply one IP ACL to the input of a Layer 2 interface; a single IP ACL can be applied to the input and a single IP ACL can be applied to the output of a Layer 3 interface.

- You can apply a port ACL only to a physical Layer 2 interface; you cannot apply port ACLs to EtherChannel interfaces.

Lesson 16-1: Configuring an ACL

When you configure an ACL, you only need to complete two basic steps:

Step 1   Create the ACL criteria through ACEs.

Step 2   Apply the ACL to an interface.

One important security item to note is that, by default, a router sends an Internet Control Message Protocol (ICMP) unreachable message, ICMP message type 3, when a packet is denied by an access group. When someone is attempting a reconnaissance attack against your network, these messages can provide them with invaluable information. If you do not have a specific requirement for these messages, they should be disabled on any exposed interfaces. For an IOS software device or Catalyst 3550 switch, use the following commands:

```
3550A(config)#interface vlan number
3550A(config-if)#no ip unreachables
```

or

```
R2(config)#interface type number
R2(config-if)#no ip unreachables
```

In the case of the Catalyst 3550 switch, access group denied packets are not dropped in hardware but are bridged to the switch CPU so that it can generate the ICMP unreachable message. To drop access group denied packets in hardware, you must disable ICMP unreachables.

Step 1: Create the ACL Criteria through ACEs

Creating the criteria to use for an ACL depends on the type of ACL that you are defining. Refer to the following commands to determine which commands are appropriate for your particular ACL.

To create a numbered standard IP ACL in IOS or a 3550, use the following command:

```
3550A or R2(config)#access-list access-list-number {permit | deny} source [source-
  wildcard] [log]
```

To create a numbered extended IP ACL in IOS or a 3550 switch, use one of the following commands:

```
3550A or R2(config)#access-list access-list-number {deny | permit} protocol
  source source-wildcard destination destination-wildcard [precedence precedence]
  [tos tos] [fragments] [log] [log-input] [time-range time-range-name] [dscp dscp]
```

or, for TCP:

```
3550A or R2(config)#access-list access-list-number {deny | permit} tcp source
  source-wildcard [operator [port]] destination destination-wildcard [operator
  [port]] [established] [precedence precedence] [tos tos] [fragments] [log]
  [log-input] [time-range time-range-name] [dscp dscp] [flag]
```

or, for UDP:

```
3550A or R2(config)#access-list access-list-number {deny | permit} udp source
    source-wildcard [operator [port]] destination destination-wildcard [operator
    [port]] [precedence precedence] [tos tos] [fragments] [log] [log-input]
    [time-range time-range-name] [dscp dscp]
```

or, for ICMP:

```
3550A or R2(config)#access-list access-list-number {deny | permit} icmp source
    source-wildcard destination destination-wildcard [icmp-type | [[icmp-type
    icmp-code] | [icmp-message]] [precedence precedence] [tos tos] [fragments]
    [log] [log-input] [time-range time-range-name] [dscp dscp]
```

or, for IGMP:

```
3550A or R2(config)#access-list access-list-number {deny | permit} igmp source
    source-wildcard destination destination-wildcard [igmp-type] [precedence
    precedence] [tos tos] [fragments] [log] [log-input] [time-range
    time-range-name] [dscp dscp]
```

You can use the **remark** keyword to include your comments about any entries that you place in any IP standard or extended ACL. Each of your remark lines is limited to 100 characters and can be placed before or after the statement that you are commenting about.You can apply a remark to a numbered IP ACL in IOS or a 3550 switch by using the following command:

```
3550A or R2(config)#access-list access-list-number remark remark
```

To create a named standard IP ACL in IOS or a 3550 switch, use the following command:

```
3550A or R2(config)#ip access-list standard name
3550A or R2(config-std-nacl)# deny source [source-wildcard]
```

or

```
3550A or R2(config-std-nacl)# permit source [source-wildcard]
```

Use the following commands to delete an ACE from a named standard IP ACL in IOS or a 3550 switch:

```
3550A or R2(config)#ip access-list standard name
3550A or R2(config-std-nacl)#no deny source [source-wildcard]
```

or

```
3550A or R2(config-std-nacl)#no permit source [source-wildcard]
```

To create a named extended IP ACL in IOS or a 3550 switch, use the following command:

```
3550A or R2(config)#ip access-list extended name
3550A or R2(config-ext-nacl)#deny protocol source source-wildcard destination
    destination-wildcard [precedence precedence] [tos tos] [log]
```

or

```
3550A or R2(config-ext-nacl)#permit protocol source source-wildcard destination
    destination-wildcard [precedence precedence] [tos tos] [log]
```

Use the following commands to delete an ACE from a named extended IP ACL in IOS or a 3550 switch:

```
3550A or R2(config)#ip access-list extended name
3550A or R2(config-ext-nacl)#no deny protocol source source-wildcard destination
  destination-wildcard [precedence precedence] [tos tos] [log]
```

or

```
3550A or R2(config-ext-nacl)#no permit protocol source source-wildcard destination
  destination-wildcard [precedence precedence] [tos tos] [log]
```

You can also apply a remark to a named IP ACL in IOS or a 3550 switch by using the following command:

```
3550A or R2(config-ext-nacl)#remark remark
```

Use the following commands to create a named MAC extended ACL:

```
3550A(config)#mac access-list extended name
3550A(config-ext-macl)#{deny | permit} {any | host source MAC address | source
  MAC address mask} {any | host destination MAC address | destination MAC address
  mask} [type mask | lsap lsap mask | aarp | amber | dec-spanning | decnet-iv |
  diagnostic | dsm | etype-6000 | etype-8042 | lat | lavc-sca | mop-console |
  mop-dump | msdos | mumps | netbios | vines-echo |vines-ip | xns-idp | 0-65535]
  [cos cos]
```

The following list specifies features that you can optionally enable, depending on the individual requirements of your organization:

- *type mask*

- **lsap** *lsap mask*

- **aarp | amber | dec-spanning | decnet-iv | diagnostic | dsm | etype-6000 | etype-8042 | lat | lavc-sca | mop-console | mop-dump | msdos | mumps | netbios | vines-echo |vines-ip | xns-idp**

- **cos** *cos*

Use the following command to remove a MAC extended ACL:

```
3550A(config)#no mac access-list extended name
```

In this lesson, you define a fictitious named extended access list called ccie_lab on a router of your choice. You allow the host at 10.10.10.10 to talk to 192.168.10.10 on TCP port 1023. Example 16-1 shows you the commands that are necessary to complete these requirements.

Example 16-1 *Named Extended Access List*

```
Configuration items for R2:
R2(config)#ip access-list extended ccie_lab
R2(config-ext-nacl)#remark Lesson 17-1 ACL
R2(config-ext-nacl)#permit tcp host 10.10.10.10 host 192.168.10.10 eq 1023
```

Step 2: Apply the ACL to an Interface

Use the following commands to apply an IP ACL to a virtual terminal line in IOS software or a 3550 switch:

```
3550A or R2(config)#line [console | vty] line-number
3550A or R2(config-line)#access-class access-list-number {in | out}
```

Use the following commands to remove access restrictions on a terminal line in IOS software or a 3550 switch:

```
3550A or R2(config)#line [console | vty] line-number
3550A or R2(config-line)#no access-class access-list-number {in | out}
```

Use the following commands to apply an IP ACL to an interface in IOS software or a Layer 2 or Layer 3 interface on a 3550 switch:

```
R2(config)#interface interface-id
R2(config-if)#ip access-group {access-list-number | name} {in | out}
```

Use the following commands to remove the IP ACL from an interface in IOS software or a Layer 2 or Layer 3 interface on a 3550 switch:

```
3550A(config)#interface interface-id
3550A(config-if)#no ip access-group {access-list-number | name} {in | out}
```

Use the following commands to apply a MAC ACL to a Layer 2 interface:

```
3550A(config)#interface interface-id
3550A(config-if)#mac access-group {name} {in}
```

Use the following commands to remove the MAC ACL from an interface:

```
3550A(config)#interface interface-id
3550A(config-if)#no mac access-group {name} {in}
```

In this lesson, you apply the fictitious ccie_lab IP ACL to filter packets that are entering FastEthernet 0/3 on the 3550A switch.

Example 16-2 demonstrates the configuration items that are needed on the 3550A switch.

Example 16-2 *Applying a Named IP ACL to Switch 3550A*

```
Configuration items for 3550A:
3550A(config)#interface fastethernet 0/3
3550A(config-if)#ip access-group ccie_lab in
```

If you were applying this IP ACL to a Layer 3 interface, a Switched Virtual Interface (SVI), a Layer 3 EtherChannel, or a routed port, you must have an IP address already configured on the interface. Layer 3 access groups filter packets that are routed or are received by Layer 3 processes on the CPU. These IP ACLs do not affect packets that are bridged within a VLAN. Example 16-3 shows the steps that are necessary to add the ccie_lab access list to the VLAN 1 Layer 3 interface.

Example 16-3 *Applying a Named IP ACL to a Layer 3 Interface on Switch 3550A*

```
Configuration items for 3550A:
3550A(config)#interface vlan1
3550A(config-if)#ip access-group ccie_lab in
```

Lesson 16-2: Creating a Numbered Standard IP ACL

Figure 16-2 illustrates the topology that you will use to deny the host at 192.168.1.10 on 3550A while permitting other IP hosts to access the network.

Figure 16-2 *Simple ACL Topology*

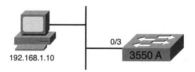

As you can see from the output of the **show access-lists** command in Example 16-4, the IP host 133.100.3.102 is now denied access while other IP hosts are allowed access.

Example 16-4 illustrates the configuration items and displays the results on the 3550 switch.

Example 16-4 *Standard IP ACL on Switch 3550A*

```
Configuration items on 3550A:
3550A(config)#access-list 2 deny host 192.168.1.10
3550A(config-std-nacl)#access-list 2 permit any
3550A(config-std-nacl)#exit
3550A(config)#interface FastEthernet 0/3
3550A(config-if)#ip access-group 2 in
3550A(config-if)#exit
3550A#show access-lists
Standard IP access list 2
    deny   192.168.1.10
    permit any
```

As you can see from the output of the **show access-lists** command in Example 16-4, the IP host 133.100.3.102 is now denied access while other IP hosts are allowed access.

Lesson 16-3: Creating a Numbered Extended IP ACL

In this lesson, you create a numbered extended ACL to deny Telnet access from any host in the 192.168.3.0 network to any host in the 192.168.30.0 network while permitting any other hosts to Telnet to the 192.168.30.0 network.

Example 16-5 illustrates this configuration and displays the resulting ACL.

Example 16-5 *Numbered Extended ACL on R3*

```
Configuration items on R3:
R3(config)#access-list 102 deny tcp 192.168.3.0 0.0.0.255 192.168.30.0 0.0.0.255 eq
   telnet
R3(config)#access-list 102 permit ip any any
R3(config)#interface Ethernet 0
R3(config-if)#ip access-group 102 in
R3(config-if)#exit
R3(config)#exit
R3#show access-lists

Extended IP access list 102
    deny tcp192.168.3.0 0.0.0.255192.168.30.0 0.0.0.255 eq telnet
    permit ip any any
```

As you can see from the output of the **show** command in Example 16-5, the numbered extended IP ACL 102 is denying exactly what you desired while permitting all other traffic.

Lesson 16-4: Creating a Named Standard IP ACL

In this lesson, you create a named standard ACL, named telnet_allowed, that permits all traffic from 192.168.10.100 to Telnet to R3 while denying everyone else from Telnetting to the router. Example 16-6 shows the commands that are required to complete this task.

Example 16-6 *Named Standard ACL on R3*

```
Configuration items on R3:
R3(config)#ip access-list standard telnet_allowed
R3(config-std-nacl)#permit tcp 192.168.10.100
R3(config)#line vty 0 4
R3(config-line)#access-class telnet_allowed in
```

Lesson 16-5: Creating a Named Extended IP ACL

In this lesson, you define a named extended ACL, named ccie, on 3550A that allows any TCP Telnet traffic to the destination address and wildcard of 172.31.0.0 0.0.255.255 and denies any other TCP traffic. You need to permit any ICMP traffic, deny UDP traffic from any source to the destination address range 172.31.0.0 through 172.31.255.255 with a destination port less than 1024, deny any other IP traffic, and provide a log of the result. You apply it to the outgoing direction on FastEthernet 0/4. Example 16-7 shows you how to configure this lesson.

Example 16-7 *Named Extended IP ACL*

```
Configuration items for 3550A:
3550A(config)#ip access-list extended ccie
3550A(config-ext-nacl)#permit tcp any 172.31.0.0 0.0.255.255 eq telnet
3550A(config-ext-nacl)#deny tcp any any
3550A(config-ext-nacl)#permit icmp any any
3550A(config-ext-nacl)#deny udp any 172.31.0.0 0.0.255.255 lt 1024
3550A(config-ext-nacl)#deny ip any any log
3550A(config-ext-nacl)#exit
3550A(config)#interface fastethernet 0/4
3550A(config-if)#ip access-group ccie out
```

Lesson 16-6: Implementing Time of Day and ACLs

Use the following commands to define a time range in IOS or a 3550 switch:

```
3550A or R2(config)#time-range time-range-name
3550A or R2(config-time-range)#absolute [start time date] [end time date]
```

or

```
3550A or R2(config-time-range)#periodic days-of-the-week hh:mm to
  [days-of-the-week] hh:mm
```

You can repeat these steps to create multiple items so that you can have the desired effect at different times.

In this lesson, you configure time ranges for your company's work hours, 8:00 a.m. to noon and 1:00 p.m. to 5:00 p.m. on weekdays, and for your company holidays, which include the following days:

- New Year's Day, January 1

- Thanksgiving Day, November 22

- Christmas Eve and Christmas Day, December 24–25

You complete this lesson by verifying your configuration.

Example 16-8 shows you the output of your lesson.

Example 16-8 *Time-Based ACLs Using Numbered ACLs on Switch 3550A*

```
Configuration items on 3550A:
3550A(config)#time-range workhours
3550A(config-time-range)#periodic weekdays 8:00 to 12:00
3550A(config-time-range)#periodic weekdays 13:00 to 17:00
3550A(config-time-range)#exit3550A(config)#time-range new_year_day_2000
3550A(config-time-range)#absolute start 00:00 1 Jan 2000 end 23:59 1 Jan 2000
3550A(config-time-range)#exit3550A(config)#time-range thanksgiving_2000
3550A(config-time-range)#absolute start 00:00 22 Nov 2000 end 23:59 23 Nov 2000
3550A(config-time-range)#exit3550A(config)#time-range christmas_2000
```

Example 16-8 *Time-Based ACLs Using Numbered ACLs on Switch 3550A (Continued)*

```
3550A(config-time-range)#absolute start 00:00 24 Dec 2000 end 23:50 25 Dec 2000
3550A(config-time-range)#exit
3550A(config)#access-list 188 deny tcp any any time-range new_year_day_2000
3550A(config)#access-list 188 deny tcp any any time-range thanskgiving_2000
3550A(config)#access-list 188 deny tcp any any time-range christmas_2000
3550A(config)#access-list 188 permit tcp any any time-range workhours
3550A(config)#exit
3550A#show time-range
time-range entry: christmas_2000 (inactive)
   absolute start 00:00 24 December 2000 end 23:50 25 December 2000
time-range entry: new_year_day_2000 (inactive)
   absolute start 00:00 01 January 2000 end 23:59 01 January 2000
time-range entry: thanksgiving_2000 (active)
   absolute start 00:00 22 November 2000 end 23:59 23 November 2000
time-range entry: workhours (inactive)
   periodic weekdays 8:00 to 12:00
   periodic weekdays 13:00 to 17:00

3550A#show access-lists
Extended IP access list 188
   deny tcp any any time-range new_year_day_2000 (inactive)
   deny tcp any any time-range thanskgiving_2000 (active)
   deny tcp any any time-range christmas_2000 (inactive)
   permit tcp any any time-range workhours (inactive)
```

As you can see from the output of the **show** commands in Example 16-8, your time ranges are behaving correctly. Because the time and date on the 3550 switch is configured for November 22 at 6:00 a.m., the Thanksgiving ACL is active.

Example 16-9 illustrates the same configuration, but uses the named ACL instead.

Example 16-9 *Time-Based ACLs Using Named ACLs on Switch 3550A*

```
Configuration items on 3550A:
3550A(config)#time-range workhours
3550A(config)#periodic weekdays 8:00 to 12:00
3550A(config)#periodic weekdays 13:00 to 17:00
3550A(config)#time-range new_year_day_2000
3550A(config)#absolute start 00:00 1 Jan 2000 end 23:59 1 Jan 2000
3550A(config)#time-range thanksgiving_2000
3550A(config)#absolute start 00:00 22 Nov 2000 end 23:59 23 Nov 2000
3550A(config)#time-range christmas_2000
3550A(config)#absolute start 00:00 24 Dec 2000 end 23:50 25 Dec 2000
3550A(config)#ip access-list extended deny_access
3550A(config-ext-nacl)#deny tcp any any time-range new_year_day_2000
3550A(config-ext-nacl)#deny tcp any any time-range thanksgiving_2000
3550A(config-ext-nacl)#deny tcp any any time-range christmas_2000
3550A(config-ext-nacl)#exit
3550A(config)#exit
```

continues

Example 16-9 *Time-Based ACLs Using Named ACLs on Switch 3550A (Continued)*

```
3550A#show ip access-lists

Extended IP access list deny_access
    deny tcp any any time-range new_year_day_2000 (inactive)
    deny tcp any any time-range thanksgiving_2000 (active)
    deny tcp any any time-range christmas_2000 (inactive)
```

As you can see from the output of Example 16-9, the Thanksgiving time range is once again active.

Lesson 16-7: Configuring Lock-and-Key

To configure lock-and-key using TACACS+, use the following commands:

```
R2(config)#access-list access-list-number [dynamic dynamic-name [timeout minutes]]
   {deny | permit} telnet source source-wildcard destination destination-wildcard
   [precedence precedence] [tos tos] [established] [log]
R2(config)#interface type number
R2(config-if)#ip access-group access-list-number
R2(config-if)#exit
R2(config)#tacacs-server host address
R2(config)#tacacs-server key key_string
R2(config)#line vty line-number [ending-line-number]
R2(config-line)#login tacacs
```

In this lesson, you configure lock-and-key to use a TACACS+ server. Example 16-10 illustrates the required configuration to accomplish this.

Example 16-10 *Lock-and-Key Using TACACS+*

```
Configuration items on R2:
R2(config)#aaa authentication login default group tacacs+ enable
R2(config)#aaa accounting exec stop-only group tacacs+
R2(config)#aaa accounting network stop-only group tacacs+
R2(config)#interface ethernet0
R2(config-if)#ip address 172.16.23.9 255.255.255.0
 R2(config-if)#exit
R2(config)#interface serial0
R2(config-if)#ip address 172.16.21.1 255.255.255.0
R2(config-if)#ip access-group 102 in
R2(config-if)#exit
R2(config)#access-list 102 permit tcp any host 172.16.21.1 eq telnet
R2(config)#access-list 102 dynamic testlist timeout 5 permit ip any any
R2(config)#ip route 172.16.250.0 255.255.255.0 172.16.21.2
R2(config)#tacacs-server host 172.16.23.21
R2(config)#tacacs-server host 172.16.23.14
R2(config)#tacacs-server key test1
R2(config)#line VTY 0 4
R2(config-line)#autocommand access-enable timeout 5
R2(config-line)#login tacacs
```

To configure lock-and-key using local authentication, use the following commands:

```
R2(config)#username name password secret
R2(config)#line [aux | console | tty | vty] line-number [ending-line-number]
R2(config-line)#login local
```

or

```
R2(config)#line [aux | console | tty | vty] line-number [ending-line-number]
R2(config-line)#password password
R2(config-line)#autocommand access-enable host [timeout minutes]
```

Lesson 16-8: Configuring Reflexive ACLs

Figure 16-3 illustrates the simplest topology in which you can implement reflexive ACLs. In this simple topology, you configure reflexive ACLs for the external interface of your router. This prevents IP traffic from entering your internal network through the router, unless the traffic is part of an already established session.

Figure 16-3 *Simple Reflexive ACL Topology*

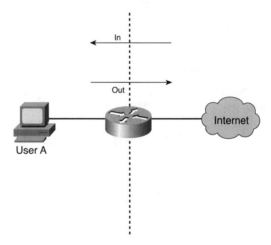

To configure a reflexive ACL for your external interface, follow these steps:

Step 1 Define the reflexive ACL in an outbound IP extended named ACL. You should apply this extended named IP ACL to the outbound traffic. Use the following commands to accomplish this:

```
R2(config)#ip access-list extended nameR2(config-ext-nacl)#permit protocol any
any reflect name [timeout seconds]
```

You can repeat this step for each IP upper-layer protocol; you can use the same *name* for multiple protocols. Note that you must use the **reflect** keyword in this application.

NOTE   When you mix reflexive ACLs with other **permit** or **deny** statements, if the packet matches an entry prior to the reflexive **permit** entry, the packet is not evaluated by the reflexive **permit** entry, and no temporary entry is created for the reflexive ACL (reflexive filtering is not triggered).

If your extended named IP ACL is not applied to the selected interface, you must also apply the extended named IP ACL to the interface.

Use the following command to apply the extended named IP ACL to your designated interface:

```
R2(config-if)#ip access-group name out
```

Step 2   Nest the reflexive ACL in an inbound IP extended named ACL.

After your reflexive ACL is defined in an IP extended ACL, you need to "nest" the reflexive ACL within a different extended named IP ACL.

When configuring the reflexive ACL, remember to nest the reflexive ACL within the extended named IP ACL that you apply to the inbound traffic. Once you nest the reflexive ACL, packets that are heading into your internal network can be evaluated against any reflexive ACE temporary entries, along with the other entries in the extended named IP ACL.

Use the following commands to nest the reflexive ACL:

```
R2(config)#ip access-list extended name
R2(config-ext-nacl)#evaluate name
```

Use the **evaluate** command after each reflexive ACL to point to each reflexive ACL name that you previously defined.

The order in which you place your entries is important. Under normal circumstances, when a packet is evaluated against ACEs in an ACL, the ACEs are evaluated in sequential order, with no more ACEs evaluated once a match occurs. When a reflexive ACL is nested within an extended ACL, the extended ACL ACEs are evaluated sequentially up to the nested entry, then the reflexive ACEs are evaluated sequentially, and then the remaining entries in the extended ACL are evaluated sequentially.

If your extended named IP ACL has never been applied to the interface, use the following command to apply the ACL to the selected interface:

```
R2(config-if)#ip access-group name in
```

Step 3 Set a global timeout value.

The reflexive ACL uses a timeout period, a certain length of time during which no packets are detected for a session, to remove its temporary ACEs. You are given the option of specifying the timeout for a particular reflexive ACL when you define the reflexive ACL. However, if you do not specify the timeout for a given reflexive ACL, the list instead uses the global timeout value, 300 seconds by default.

To change the global timeout value, use the following command to set it to a positive value from 0 to 2,147,483:

```
R2(config)#ip reflexive-list timeout seconds
```

Figure 16-4 illustrates the second possible topology that you can use. In this topology, you would configure your reflexive ACLs for the internal interface. This allows external traffic to access the services that are offered in your demilitarized zone (DMZ) but prevents IP traffic from entering your internal network, unless the traffic is part of a session that is already established from within your internal network.

Figure 16-4 *Complex Reflexive ACL Topology*

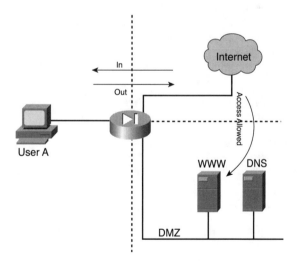

To configure a reflexive ACL for your internal interface, follow these steps:

Step 1   Define the reflexive ACL in an inbound IP extended named ACL.

Step 2   Nest the reflexive ACL in an outbound IP extended named ACL.

Step 3   Set a global timeout value.

Figure 16-5 illustrates the topology that you will use to configure reflexive ACLs. In this lesson, configure a reflexive ACL on your external interface of R1 so that it only allows inbound and outbound TCP traffic at interface Serial 0, but only if the first packet of the session originates from inside of your network. You should also allow EIGRP and BGP without requiring evaluation. You should deny any ICMP packet from your network. Interface Serial 0 connects to R3 through the Frame Relay for testing purposes.

Figure 16-5 *Reflexive ACL Topology*

Example 16-11 shows the configuration that is necessary and demonstrates its functionality through the use of **show** commands.

Example 16-11 *Reflexive ACL External Interface Configuration*

```
Configuration items applied to R1:
R1(config)#interface Serial 0
R1(config-if)#ip access-group inboundfilters in
R1(config-if)#ip access-group outboundfilters out
 R1(config-if)#exit
R1(config)#ip reflexive-list timeout 120
R1(config)#ip access-list extended outboundfilters
R1(config-ext-nacl)#permit tcp any any reflect tcptraffic
 R1(config-ext-nacl)#exit
R1(config)#ip access-list extended inboundfilters
R1(config-ext-nacl)#permit tcp any any eq bgp
R1(config-ext-nacl)#permit eigrp any any
R1(config-ext-nacl)#deny icmp any any
R1(config-ext-nacl)#evaluate tcptraffic

! The following show command is before the reflexive ACL has been triggered:
R1#show access-list
Extended IP access list inboundfilters
 permit tcp any any eq bgp
 permit eigrp any any
 deny icmp any any
 evaluate tcptraffic
```

Example 16-11 *Reflexive ACL External Interface Configuration (Continued)*

```
Extended IP access list outboundfilters
 permit tcp any any reflect tcptraffic

! The following show command was issued after a Telnet connection is initiated
! from within your network to R3:
R1#show access-list
Extended IP access list inboundfilters
 permit tcp any any eq bgp (2 matches)
 permit eigrp any any
 deny icmp any any
 evaluate tcptraffic
Extended IP access list outboundfilters
 permit tcp any any reflect tcptraffic
Reflexive IP access list tcptraffic
 permit tcp host 172.19.99.67 eq telnet host 192.168.60.185 eq 11005 (5 matches)
 (time left 115 seconds)
```

As you can see from the shaded text in Example 16-11, the reflexive ACL *tcptraffic* now appears
and displays the temporary entry that is generated when the Telnet session initiated with an
outbound packet. Before this, the output did not show any reflexive ACL entries.

Lesson 16-9: Logging ACLs

In this example, you configure the 3550A to log debugging-level messages to the internal buffer,
the console, a syslog server at 192.168.1.254, and any Telnet session. You configure a named
standard ACL named ccie1 that denies traffic from the 10.1.1.0/24 network and apply it to
FastEthernet 0/6. Example 16-12 shows the configuration that is necessary to complete
these tasks.

Example 16-12 *Enabling Logging*

```
Configuration items for 3550A:
3550A(config)#ip access-list standard ccie1
3550A(config-std-nacl)#deny ip 10.1.1.0 0.0.0.255 log
3550A(config-std-nacl)#permit ip any any log
3550A(config-std-nacl)#exit
3550A(config)#interface fastethernet 0/6
3550A(config-if)#access-group ccie1 in
3550A(config-if)#exit
3550A(config)#logging buffered debugging
3550A(config)#logging console debugging
3550A(config)#logging monitor debugging
3550A(config)#logging trap debugging
```

Example 16-13 illustrates logging is enabled by using a **show** command to view the
buffered log.

Example 16-13 *The* **show logging** *Command Output on Switch 3550A with* **log**

```
3550A#show logging

Syslog logging: enabled (0 messages dropped, 0 flushes, 0 overruns)
    Console logging: level debugging, 37 messages logged
    Monitor logging: level debugging, 0 messages logged
    Buffer logging: level debugging, 37 messages logged
    File logging: disabled
    Trap logging: level debugging, 39 message lines logged

Log Buffer (4096 bytes):

00:00:48: NTP: authentication delay calculation problems

<output truncated>

00:09:34:%SEC-6-IPACCESSLOGS:list ccie1 permitted 0.0.0.0 1 packet
00:09:59:%SEC-6-IPACCESSLOGS:list ccie1 denied 10.1.1.15 1 packet
00:10:11:%SEC-6-IPACCESSLOGS:list ccie1 permitted 0.0.0.0 1 packet
00:15:33:%SEC-6-IPACCESSLOGS:list ccie1 denied 10.1.1.15 2009 packets
```

You can see from the shaded text in Example 16-13 that your ACL is denying the correct traffic. You should also notice that each entry has a hit count that is appended to the end of the line. You could use a permit access list entry to give you a rough estimate of traffic flow through an interface, if desired.

Example 16-14 demonstrates the use of the **log-input** keyword when used with logging.

Example 16-14 *The* **show logging** *Command Output on Switch 3550A with* **log-input**

```
R1#show logging
00:04:21:%SEC-6-IPACCESSLOGDP:list ccie1 permitted icmp 10.1.1.10
  (Vlan1 0001.42ef.a400) -> 10.1.1.61 (0/0), 1 packet
```

You can see from the preceding output that the interface, in this case VLAN1, is now included in the output.

Lesson 16-10: Configuring a Named MAC Extended ACL

In this lesson, configure your topology so that all NetBIOS traffic is denied from the host 192.168.3.102 to any host using a MAC extended ACL called no_netbios.

Example 16-15 shows you how this is accomplished on the 3550A switch. It includes a **show** command to verify proper operation.

Example 16-15 *MAC Extended ACL to Block NetBIOS*

```
Configuration items for 3550A:
3550A(config)#mac access-list extended no_netbios
3550A(config-ext-nacl)#deny host 00e0.183d.cc92 any netbios
3550A(config-ext-nacl)#permit any any
 3550A(config-ext-nacl)#exit
3550A(config)#interface fastethernet0/3
3550A(config)#mac access-group mac1 in

3550A#show access-lists

Extended MAC access list mac1
    deny   host 00e0.183d.cc92 any netbios
    permit any any
```

Creating a VLAN Map

Use the following commands to create, add to, or delete a VLAN map entry:

```
3550A(config)#vlan access-map name [number]
3550A(config-access-map)#action {drop | forward}
3550A(config-access-map)#match {ip | mac} address {name | number} [name | number]
```

When you create a VLAN map, you have the option of specifying a number after the name. This number represents the sequence number of the entry that is assigned to it within the map. If you do not assign a number to it, the switch assigns a number to the entry sequentially in increments of 10. You can then reference this number when modifying or deleting map entries.

To remove a VLAN map, or one of its entries, use one of the next three commands.

Use the following command to delete the entire map:

```
3550A(config)#no vlan access-map name
```

Use the following command to delete a single sequence entry from within the map:

```
3550A(config)#no vlan access-map name number
```

Use the following command to return to the default action:

```
3550A(config-access-map)#no action
```

Lesson 16-11: Using ACLs with VLAN Maps

To deny packets while using VLAN maps, you must create an ACL that matches the packet and then use the VLAN map to set the action to drop. To permit packets while using VLAN maps, you must create an ACL that matches the packet and then use the VLAN map to set the action to forward. Remember that a permit statement in the ACL counts as a match, while a deny statement in the ACL means no match.

After you have your VLAN map defined, you must associate it with a VLAN. Use the following commands to accomplish this:

```
3550A(config)#vlan filter mapname vlan-list list
```

Use the following command to remove a VLAN map from a VLAN:

```
3550A(config)#no vlan filter mapname vlan-list list
```

In this lesson, you create two separate ACLs and a VLAN map to deny any packet that is not TCP or UDP. In the first ACL, any TCP packets match the VLAN_TCP ACL. The second ACL matches any UDP packets using the VLAN_UDP ACL. You then apply the VLAN map to VLAN 8.

Example 16-16 illustrates the creation of these two ACLs.

Example 16-16 *VLAN Map with a Named Extended IP ACL*

```
Configuration items for 3550A:
3550A(config)#ip access-list extended VLAN_TCP
3550A(config-ext-nacl)#permit tcp any any
3550A(config-ext-nacl)#exit
3550A(config)#ip access-list extended VLAN_UDP
3550A(config-ext-nacl)#permit udp any any
3550A(config-ext-nacl)#exit
3550A(config)#vlan access-map 1 10
3550A(config-access-map)#match ip address VLAN_TCP
3550A(config-access-map)#action forward
3550A(config-access-map)#exit
3550A(config)#vlan access-map 1 20
3550A(config-access-map)#match ip address VLAN_UDP
3550A(config-access-map)#action forward
3550A(config-access-map)#exit
3550A(config)#vlan filter map 1 vlan-list 8
```

In this scenario, any IP packets that do not match either of your defined ACLs are dropped.

Maintaining ACLs

After you have defined and applied ACLs, you can display various information about them, such as what ACLs are configured on the switch, what interfaces and VLANs an ACL is applied to, and information about configuration conflicts or resource usage related to your ACLs.

To display the contents of one or all current IP and MAC address ACLs or a specific ACL, numbered or named, use the following command:

```
3550A#show access-lists [number | name]
```

To display detailed configuration and status information of an interface, use the following command. Note that if IP is enabled on the interface and ACLs have been applied by using the **ip access-group** interface configuration command, the access groups are included in the display.

```
3550A#show ip interface interface-id
```

To display the contents of the configuration file for the switch or the specified interface, including all configured MAC and IP ACLs and which access groups are applied to an interface, use the following command:

```
3550A#show running-config [interface interface-id]
```

To display MAC ACLs that are applied to all Layer 2 interfaces or the specified Layer 2 interface, use the following command:

```
3550A#show mac access-group [interface interface-id]
```

You can also display information about VLAN access maps or VLAN filters.

To display information about all VLAN access maps or the specified access map, use the following command:

```
3550A#show vlan access-map [mapname]
```

To display information about all VLAN filters or about a specified VLAN or VLAN access map, use the following command:

```
3550A#show vlan filter [access-map name | vlan vlan-id]
```

Displaying ACL Resource Usage

The 3550 switch offers a switch feature manager that you can use to allocate resources to your configured ACLs. When there is a lack of hardware resources for a configuration or when a configuration conflict exists, the switch feature manager generates an error message.

You are offered several commands to display ACL resource usage.

To display feature-manager information for the interface or the VLAN, including the hardware port-label or vlan-label number for the interface and feature-manager problems that have occurred, use one of the following commands:

```
3550A#show fm vlan vlan-id
```

or

```
3550A#show fm interface interface-id
```

To display information about the identified label, including which of the configured ACL features fit into hardware, use one of the following commands:

```
3550A#show fm vlan-label label-id
```

or

```
3550A#show fm port-label label-id
```

To display information about the input or output ACL regions of Ternary Content Addressable Memory (TCAM), use the following command. Note that you might not be able to interpret the results of this command without help from the Cisco Technical Assistance Center (TAC).

```
3550A#show tcam {inacl | outacl} tcam-id {{port-labels [label-id]} | size |{statistics
  [entries | hits | labels | masks]} | {vlan-labels [label-id]}}
```

Troubleshooting Configuration Issues

When you attempt to enter an ACL configuration that you are not allowed to complete, for example, applying a port ACL to an interface on a switch that has router ACLs already configured, an error message is logged.

Example 16-17 shows the results of attempting to apply an ACL to a Layer 2 interface when an ACL is already applied to a Layer 3 interface.

Example 16-17 *Failed Attempt to Apply an ACL to a Layer 2 Interface*

```
3550A(config)# interface fastethernet0/1
3550A(config-if)# ip access-group bad_acl in
3550A(config-if)#
  1d18h:%FM-3-CONFLICT:Port ACL bad_acl conflicts with input router ACLs
```

When an attempt to apply an ACL to a Layer 2 interface has failed, use the **show fm interface** command for an interface to determine if a possible ACL configuration conflict exists or to learn the port-label number for the port. You can then use the **show fm port-label** command to display more details, as shown in Example 16-18.

Example 16-18 *Troubleshooting Failed ACL Association to a Layer 2 Interface*

```
3550A# show fm interface fastethernet0/1
Conflicts exist with layer 3 access groups.
Input Port Label:2

3550A# show fm port-label 2
Conflicts exist with layer 3 access groups.
Needed in CAM(s):1
Loaded into CAM(s):1
Sent to CPU by CAM(s):
Interfaces: Fa0/1
IP Access Group:bad_acl 0 VMRs
DHCP Broadcast Suppression Disabled.
MAC Access Group:(None) 0 VMRs
```

As you can see from the output of the **show** commands in Example 16-18, you are able to identify the conflict.

Example 16-19 shows the result of trying to apply ACL 101 to an SVI, VLAN 10, when the switch already has ACLs applied to Layer 2 interfaces.

Example 16-19 *Failed Attempt to Apply an ACL to an SVI Interface*

```
3550A(config)# interface vlan 10
3550A(config-if)# ip access-group 101 in
3550A(config-if)#
  1d18h:%FM-3-CONFLICT:Input router ACL 101 conflicts with port ACLs
```

You can look further into this error by entering the **show fm vlan** command for a VLAN to display the conflict and to determine the VLAN *label-ids*, and then enter the **show fm vlan-label** command to obtain more detailed information, as shown in Example 16-20.

Example 16-20 *Troubleshooting Failed ACL Association to a Layer 2 Interface*

```
3550A# show fm vlan 10
Conflicts exist with layer 2 access groups.
Input VLAN Label:1
Output VLAN Label:0 (default)
Priority:normal

3550A# show fm vlan-label 1
Conflicts exist with layer 2 access groups.
Input Features:
  Interfaces or VLANs: Vl1
  Priority:normal
  Vlan Map:(none)
  Access Group:101, 0 VMRs
  Multicast Boundary:(none), 0 VMRs
Output Features:
  Interfaces or VLANs:
  Priority:low
  Bridge Group Member:no
  Vlan Map:(none)
  Access Group:(none), 0 VMRs
```

Once again, you can examine the output of the **show** commands and identify what is in conflict.

ACL Configuration Size

One problem with ACLs is that they can quickly grow in size. As you know, ACL processing in the Catalyst 3550 switch is accomplished mostly in its hardware. When you configure complex ACLs on the 3550 switch, its hardware can reach its capacity to store your ACL configurations.

Once this happens, the switch software attempts to fit a simpler configuration into the hardware, but this simpler configuration does not do all the filtering that has been configured; instead, the configuration sends some or all packets to the CPU to be filtered by software. By doing this, all of your configured filtering is still accomplished, but the performance of the 3550 switch can be greatly decreased when the filtering is done in software.

For example, if the combination of an input router ACL that is applied to a VLAN interface and a VLAN map that is applied to the same VLAN does not fit into the hardware, the following results might occur:

- If your VLAN map alone fits in the hardware, the software sets up the hardware to send to the CPU all packets that need to be routed for filtering and possible routing. Packets that only require bridging within the input VLAN are still handled entirely by the hardware and are not sent to the CPU.

- If your VLAN map does not fit in the hardware, all packets on that VLAN must be both filtered and forwarded by the software.

Any problem that the switch encounters in fitting the configuration into the hardware is logged. You can use the **show fm** commands to determine if any interface configuration or VLAN configuration did not fit into the allocated hardware.

To allocate the maximum hardware resources for ACL configuration, use the **sdm prefer access** configuration command to set the Switch Database Management feature to the access template. The access template is typically used on an access switch in which your route table size might not be substantial.

Unsupported Features on the Catalyst 3550 Switch

While the Catalyst 3550 switch supports many types of ACLs, it does not provide support for these IOS router ACL-related features:

- Non-IP protocol ACLs.

- Bridge-group ACLs.

- IP accounting.

- Inbound and outbound rate limiting (except with QoS ACLs).

- IP packets with a header length of less than 5 are not access controlled (an ICMP parameter error results).

- Reflexive ACLs.

- Dynamic ACLs (except for certain specialized dynamic ACLs that are used by the switch-clustering feature).

- For Layer 2 port ACLs, the switch does not support logging or outbound ACLs.

Summary

This chapter has reviewed traffic filtering with ACLs. The ACL is a powerful tool that you can use in your pursuit of a secure network environment. The chapter began by examining the many different types of ACLs that are available, including the numbered and named IP ACLs that you can use on both the 3550 switch and an IOS software device, the lock-and-key and reflexive ACLs that you can use on IOS, and the router, port, and VLAN ACLs for use on the 3550 switch. The chapter covered the configuration of these ACLs and discussed how to associate them to an interface along with the VLAN mapping feature that is available on the 3550 switch. You looked at optional items such as logging of ACLs. The chapter concluded with a look at monitoring and troubleshooting VLANs and the unsupported items on the 3550 switch.

Review Questions

1 What feature allows you to provide access control on a network device that determines what traffic is permitted to enter or exit your network?

2 How is the 3550 switch able to filter IP packets?

3 How are entries in an ACL processed?

4 What type of ACL is used to control traffic entering a Layer 2 interface?

5 Which ACL grants a user access to a specific source or destination based on a user authentication process?

6 What is a Switched Virtual Interface?

7 What criteria are used to define an ACL?

8 When you use a VLAN map with a router ACL and one of your packet flows matches a deny statement of a VLAN, what happens to the packet flow?

9 What is the function of a VLAN map?

10 Which ACL can provide filtering based on the IP upper-layer protocol "session" information?

FAQs

Q — *I have an ACL with an unusually large amount of entries in it. How many entries should I have in one ACL?*

A — The number of entries that you can define in a single ACL is limited only by the amount of available memory of your device. Other factors that are a result of large ACLs include the processing time used to send a packet, the amount of time that your device takes to load its configuration at bootup or reboot, the ability of someone to comprehend the ACL, and the troubleshooting of a large ACL.

Q — *I want to define an ACL that denies access to a host but allows access to the rest of the subnet. Does it matter what order I place the entries in the ACL?*

A — Yes, ACLs use the first match to determine the disposition of a packet. If you were to allow the subnet first and deny the host second, the host would still be allowed access due to the first match. When designing your ACLs, it is best to define more specific and frequently used matches first and then generalized matches last.

Q — *After applying an ACL to my interface, my routing table gets corrupted. When I remove the ACL, my routing table returns to normal. Why is this happening?*

A — At the end of an ACL is an implied deny all traffic ACE. This implied statement is placed there by the software automatically, perhaps to prevent a misconfiguration from compromising your network security. You must explicitly permit routing protocol traffic to correct this situation. You can also add an explicit deny any any log statement to the end of your ACL to help troubleshoot situations like this.

Q — *I have an existing ACL that I need to edit. How do I accomplish this task?*

A — If your ACL is a numbered ACL, you must completely remove the ACL and reapply it with the desired changes. One way to make this easier is to complete your changes on a TFTP server and then retrieve it from the TFTP server. Remember that your first statement should delete the existing ACL, or all of your new entries will be placed at the end of the existing ACL. If your ACL is a named ACL, you have some editing functionality that you can use; however, if you are making a large number of editing changes, it can be easier to use the TFTP method previously discussed.

Q — *I defined a named ACL to control Telnet access to my 3550 switch. Whenever I try to associate it with a line, I get an error message. Why does this occur?*

A — You are only allowed to associate a numbered ACL to a VTY. Remember to use the same security restrictions across all VTYs or you might open an unexpected hole into your switch. You can associate a numbered or named ACL to an interface.

Q — *My company provides Internet access to our customers. We need a means to dynamically change access rates based on the negotiated QoS and SLA for the different times of day. Can we use an extended named IP ACL to accomplish this?*

A — Yes, by defining a time range and associating it to either a standard or extended ACL, you can dynamically change your ACLs based on the time of day.

Q — *Why do I need to allow Telnet when I am configuring lock-and-key access control?*

A — The user uses a Telnet session to the router to gain access to the network. The user is authenticated through the Telnet session, and temporary ACEs are entered into the ACL for the user.

Q — *I need to control access from my network based on the upper-layer session information. How can I do this?*

A — By using a reflexive ACL, also known as session filtering, you can control which traffic is allowed out of your network based on the upper-layer information while denying access into the network.

Q — *I want to provide access control on my 3550 switch across a Layer 3 EtherChannel. Is there an ACL that I can use?*

A — Yes, you can use a router ACL to provide access control by applying it to an SVI, a Layer 3 physical interface, or a Layer 3 EtherChannel.

Q — *I know that a VLAN map does not have the concept of direction. Is there a way to use a VLAN map that can monitor traffic on the input of an interface?*

A — Yes, you can use a VLAN map in conjunction with an appropriate ACL. However, if the VLAN map denies a certain traffic flow, the packet is dropped, regardless of what your ACL allows.

This chapter includes the following topics:

- Managing IP connections
- Filtering IP packets using access lists
- Hot Standby Router Protocol (HSRP) overview
- IP accounting overview
- Configuring TCP performance parameters
- Configuring the MultiNode Load Balancing Forwarding Agent
- Network Address Translation (NAT) overview
- Configuring IP services
- Monitoring and maintaining IP services

CHAPTER 17

IP Services

In this chapter, you review many of the IP services that you need to make your lessons, case studies, and eventually, your CCIE lab function correctly.

The following optional IP services are available:

- Managing IP connections
- Hot Standby Router Protocol (HSRP)
- IP accounting
- TCP performance parameters
- IP over WANs
- MultiNode Load Balancing Forwarding Agent
- Network Address Translation (NAT)

Each of these items is optional, and each can be configured to better customize your network according to your needs. Remember that certain features are not available in all releases of Cisco IOS Software; consult the release notes to determine their availability.

Managing IP Connections

With the IP suite that is available in Cisco IOS Software, a number of services are available to help control and manage your IP connections. Internet Control Message Protocol (ICMP) provides many of these services. ICMP does this by sending messages to hosts or other routers when a problem is discovered with the Internet header. For more detailed information about ICMP, refer to RFC 950, "Internet Standard Subnetting Procedure."

Some of the services that can help you manage various aspects of IP connections include the following:

- ICMP unreachable messages
- ICMP redirect messages
- ICMP mask reply messages
- IP Path MTU Discovery
- MTU packet size

- IP source routing

- Simplex Ethernet interfaces

- Director Response Protocol (DRP) server agents

The next sections describe these services in more detail.

ICMP Unreachable Messages

The ICMP unreachable message is used to notify the sender that a nonbroadcast packet that is destined for the device used an unknown protocol. ICMP also notifies the sender if your router receives a packet that it cannot deliver to the ultimate destination because it does not have a route to the destination address. This feature is enabled by default in Cisco IOS Software.

Use the following command to reenable the sending of ICMP protocol unreachable and host unreachable messages, if you previously disabled it using the **no ip unreachables** command:

```
R2(config-if)#ip unreachables
```

Use the following command to limit the rate of ICMP destination unreachable messages that are generated:

```
R2(config)#ip icmp rate-limit unreachable [df] milliseconds
```

NOTE   ICMP unreachables can be used by unauthorized individuals to gain valuable information about your network, such as what hosts are available. You should only enable this service after you have a complete understanding of this service.

ICMP Redirect Messages

The ICMP redirect message is used when a router receives a packet that has a more optimal route to a destination through another path. This could happen when a router is forced to resend a packet through the same interface on which it was received. This condition causes the router to send an ICMP redirect message to the originator of the packet, telling the originator that the router is not the best route to the receiving device. This device can be on the same subnet that the sender is on or it can be reached through a different gateway. This process is designed to inform the originator of the packet that it can presumably send it to the next hop without involving your router. The ICMP redirect message feature is enabled in Cisco IOS Software by default.

Use the following command to reenable the sending of ICMP redirect messages if you have previously disabled it using the **no ip redirects** command:

```
R2(config-if)#ip redirects
```

ICMP Mask Reply Messages

The ICMP mask reply message is sent when a network device uses the ICMP mask request message to find out the subnet mask for a particular subnetwork in your internetwork. Cisco IOS Software responds to ICMP mask request messages if you enable this feature.

Use the following command to enable the sending of ICMP mask reply messages:

```
R2(config-if)#ip mask-reply
```

IP Path MTU Discovery

The IP Path MTU Discovery mechanism, as defined in RFC 1191, "Path MTU Discovery," allows a host to dynamically discover and cope with differences in the maximum allowable maximum transmission unit (MTU) size of the various links along its path. If a router is unable to forward a datagram because it requires fragmentation, but it has the "don't fragment" (DF) bit set, it sends an ICMP message to the originating host with its Code field indicating "Fragmentation needed and DF set," which informs the host of the failure. The host can then fragment the packets so that they fit the smallest MTU along the path to the destination.

You can also use IP Path MTU Discovery after a failure of a link forces rerouting through another link that possibly has different MTU-sized links. When a router sends the ICMP message back to the host and has IP Path MTU Discovery enabled, it can include the MTU of the next-hop network link in the low-order bits of an unused header field.

IP Path MTU Discovery is also used during the establishment of a connection when the sender has no information about the intervening links. Because efficiency is important in networking, you should always use the largest MTU that the links can bear; the larger the MTU, the fewer the packets the host must send.

NOTE	IP Path MTU Discovery is a process that is initiated by end hosts. If an end host does not support IP Path MTU Discovery, the receiving device cannot avoid fragmenting datagrams generated by the end host, as long as the DF bit is not set in the packet, in which case, the packet is discarded.

Fragmenting packets can slow the performance of your router. By enabling IP Path MTU Discovery on all the hosts in your network and configuring the largest possible MTU on the interfaces of your router, you can prevent this slowdown on your router.

You only need to enable IP Path MTU Discovery for your router when it acts as a host.

MTU Packet Size

Whenever a device sends a packet, it only sends the amount of information that does not exceed the interface's default MTU packet size. With Cisco IOS Software, you can adjust the IP MTU size so that any IP packet that exceeds the MTU set for an interface is fragmented.

However, be aware that changing the MTU value can affect the IP MTU value. If your current IP MTU value is set to the same value as the MTU value and you change the MTU value, the IP MTU value is automatically modified to match the new MTU. However, the reverse of this is not true; changing the IP MTU value has no effect on the value for the **mtu** command.

You must also have the same protocol MTU as the physical medium in order to operate. Use the following command to set the MTU packet size for a specified interface:

```
R2(config-if)#ip mtu bytes
```

IP Source Routing

You router examines all the IP header options that are included in every packet. It supports the following IP header options, as defined in RFC 791, "IP Protocol":

- **Strict Source Route**—Used to route a packet based on information supplied by the source, without any deviation in the path

- **Loose Source Route**—Used to route a packet based on information supplied by the source, with deviation allowed so that a gateway can choose any path to reach the next address specified

- **Record Route**—Used to record, in the packet, the route that a packet takes to a destination

- **Time Stamp**—Used to record a time stamp

If your router discovers a packet with one of these options enabled, it performs the appropriate action. If your router discovers a packet with an invalid option, it sends an ICMP parameter problem message to the source of the packet and discards the packet.

Source routing is an IP option that allows the source IP host to specify a route through the IP network. If source routing is enabled on your router, it forwards the packet according to the specified source route. Source routing is almost never used with legitimate traffic and can be used to bypass security mechanisms that you have in place. The default in Cisco IOS Software is to perform source routing.

Use the following command to enable the IP source-route header option if you have previously disabled it:

```
R2config)#ip source-route
```

Simplex Ethernet Interfaces

A *simplex interface*, not to be confused with setting an interface to half-duplex, is an interface that either sends or receives, but not both. You can use a simplex Ethernet interface in setting up dynamic IP routing over a simplex circuit. When a route is learned on a receive-only interface, the interface designated as the source of the route is converted to the interface that you specify. When packets are routed out this specified interface, they are sent to the IP address of the source of the routing update. You must statically define the Address Resolution Protocol (ARP) entry on a transmit-only Ethernet link to map this IP address to the hardware address of the other end of the link.

Use the following command to assign a transmit interface to a receive-only interface:

```
R2config-if)#transmit-interface type number
```

DRP Server Agents

Director Response Protocol (DRP) is a User Datagram Protocol (UDP)–based application that enables the Cisco DistributedDirector product to query routers (considered the DRP Server Agent) for Border Gateway Protocol (BGP) and Interior Gateway Protocol (IGP) routing table metrics between distributed servers and clients. DistributedDirector can then use this information to transparently redirect end-user service requests to the topologically closest responsive server. DRP gives DistributedDirector the ability to provide dynamic, scalable, and "network intelligent" Internet traffic load distribution between multiple geographically dispersed servers.

The DRP Server Agents are border routers, or peers to border routers, that support the geographically distributed servers for which DistributedDirector service distribution is desired. Note that because DistributedDirector makes decisions based on BGP and IGP information, your DRP Server Agents must have access to full BGP and IGP routing tables.

Filtering IP Packets Using Access Lists

Packet filtering can help control packet movement through your network. This control can help limit network traffic and restrict network use by certain users or devices. To permit or deny packets from crossing specified interfaces, you can use access lists. For more information concerning the use and implementation of access lists, refer to Chapter 16, "Access Control Lists."

Hot Standby Router Protocol Overview

Hot Standby Router Protocol (HSRP) can provide high network availability because it has the ability to route IP traffic for your hosts, whether it is on Ethernet, Fiber Distributed Data Interface (FDDI), or Token Ring networks, without relying on the availability of any single router. You use HSRP to group routers so that they can select an active router and a standby router. The active router is the router that is used to route packets; the standby router is a router that can take over the routing duties when an active router fails or when your predefined conditions are met.

HSRP is most useful when used with hosts that do not support a router discovery protocol, such as ICMP Router Discovery Protocol (IRDP), and do not have the ability to switch to a new router when their selected router reloads or loses power. One other benefit of HSRP is that existing TCP sessions can survive the HSRP failover, providing a more transparent recovery for hosts than dynamically choosing a next hop for routing IP traffic.

HSRP works because it provides a virtual MAC address and an IP address, referred to as the *virtual IP,* which is shared among a group of routers running it. One device out of the group is selected by HSRP to function as the active router. The active router receives and routes packets that are destined for the MAC address of the group. For *n* routers running HSRP, *n*+1 IP and MAC addresses are assigned.

HSRP can detect a failure of the active router and select a standby router to assume control of the MAC and IP addresses that are assigned to the HSRP group. If applicable, a new standby router is selected at this time.

A multicast UDP-based hello mechanism is used by the devices that are running HSRP to detect router failure and to designate active and standby routers.

You can configure multiple HSRP groups on an interface, enabling you to make full use of redundant routers and load sharing. You do this by specifying a unique group number for each HSRP command that you configure for the interface.

NOTE   You can only assign three HSRP groups on a Token Ring interface: 0, 1, and 2.

Before configuring HSRP, the next section provides the information that you need to understand how ICMP redirect messages are handled on interfaces that are configured to run HSRP.

HSRP and ICMP Redirects

In previous implementations of HSRP, ICMP redirect messages were automatically disabled on interfaces that were configured with HSRP. When running HSRP, it is important that your hosts are unable to discover the interface (or real) MAC address of routers in your HSRP group. If one of your hosts is redirected by ICMP to the real MAC address of one of the routers, and it later fails, packets from that host are lost.

With Cisco IOS Software release 12.1(3)T and later, the ICMP redirect messages are automatically enabled on interfaces that are configured with HSRP. This works by filtering outgoing

ICMP redirect messages through HSRP, where the next-hop IP address can be changed to an HSRP virtual IP address.

Redirects to Active HSRP Routers

The next-hop IP address in the ICMP redirect is compared to the list of active HSRP routers on that network. If a match is found, the real next-hop IP address is replaced with a corresponding virtual IP address, and the redirect message is allowed to continue.

If a match is not found, the ICMP redirect message is sent only if the router that corresponds to the new next-hop IP address is not running HSRP. Note that redirects to passive HSRP routers, which are routers that are running HSRP but do not contain an active HSRP group on the interface, are not allowed. Redundancy can be lost if hosts learn the real IP addresses of HSRP routers.

A network that is configured with passive HSRP routers is considered a misconfiguration. You should have at least one active HSRP group for every router on your network that is running HSRP for HSRP ICMP redirection to operate optimally.

Redirects to Non-HSRP Routers

ICMP redirects to routers that are not running HSRP on their local interface are permitted. Redundancy does not become an issue in this case if your hosts learn the real IP address of non-HSRP routers.

Passive HSRP Router Advertisements

A router that is running passive HSRP sends out HSRP advertisement messages periodically and when entering/leaving the passive state. Because of this, all your HSRP routers can determine the HSRP group state of any HSRP router on your network. These advertisements provide information to the other HSRP routers on your network of their HSRP interface state, as follows:

- **Dormant**—Interface has no HSRP groups; single advertisements are sent once when the last group is removed.

- **Passive**—Interface has at least one nonactive group and no active groups; advertisements are sent out periodically.

- **Active**—Interface has at least one active group; a single advertisement is sent out when the first group becomes active.

Redirects Not Sent

If an HSRP router cannot uniquely determine the IP address that is used by a host when it sends a packet that causes a redirect, the redirect message is not sent. The router uses the destination

MAC address in the original packet to make this determination. Under certain conditions, such as when you use the **standby use-bia** command, ICMP redirects cannot be sent. In this case, the HSRP groups use the interface MAC address as their virtual MAC address and are unable to determine if the default gateway of the host is the real IP address or one of the HSRP virtual IP addresses that are active on the interface.

IP Accounting Overview

IP accounting can provide you with basic IP accounting functions, such as seeing the number of bytes and packets that are switched through the Cisco IOS Software based on the source and destination IP address. One limitation of this is that only IP traffic that is using the device as a transition point can be measured and then, only on the outbound direction; traffic that is generated by the software or that terminates in the software is not included in the accounting statistics. Two accounting databases are used to maintain accurate accounting totals: the active and the checkpointed database.

When you use IP accounting, you can also obtain information that identifies IP traffic that fails your IP Access Control Lists (ACLs). This feature requires you to enable IP accounting of ACL violations by using the **ip accounting access-violations** command. Your users can then display the number of bytes and packets from a single source that attempted to breach security against the ACL for the source destination pair. By default, IP accounting displays the number of packets that have passed access lists and were routed.

IP MAC Accounting

MAC address accounting provides you with accounting information for IP traffic based on the source and destination MAC addresses on LAN interfaces. MAC accounting calculations can provide the total packet and byte counts for a LAN interface that receives or sends IP packets to or from a unique MAC address. This information is time stamped for the last packet that is received or sent.

Use the next two commands to configure the interface for IP accounting based on the MAC address.

Use the following command to specify the interface (or subinterface) and enter interface configuration mode:

```
R2(config)# interface type number
```

Use the following command to configure IP accounting based on the MAC address of received (input) or transmitted (output) packets:

```
R2(config-if)#ip accounting mac-address {input | output}
```

Use the **show interface mac** command to display MAC accounting information for interfaces that are configured for MAC accounting.

IP Precedence Accounting

Precedence accounting provides you with accounting information for IP traffic based on the precedence on any interface. Precedence accounting calculates the total packet and byte counts for an interface that receives or sends IP packets and sorts the results based on the IP precedence that is assigned to the packets.

Use the commands that are described in this section to configure the interface for IP accounting based on IP precedence.

To specify the interface (or subinterface) and enter interface configuration mode, use the following command:

```
R2(config)#interface type number
```

To configure IP accounting based on the precedence of received (input) or transmitted (output) packets, use the following command:

```
R2(config-if)#ip accounting precedence {input | output}
```

Use the **show interface precedence** command to display precedence accounting information for interfaces that are configured for precedence accounting.

Configuring TCP Performance Parameters

Tuning certain parameters on your router can help TCP performance in your network. You can use the following options to tune your IP performance:

- Compressing TCP packet headers
- Setting the TCP connection attempt time
- Using TCP path MTU discovery
- Using TCP selective acknowledgments
- Using TCP time stamps
- Using the TCP maximum read size
- Setting the TCP window size
- Setting the TCP outbound queue size

The next sections describe each of these options in more detail.

Compressing TCP Packet Headers

By using compression on headers, you can reduce the size of your TCP/IP packets to increase the performance of your network devices. This feature provides the most benefits on networks that have a large percentage of small packets. Use the following command to enable TCP header compression:

```
R2(config-if)#ip tcp header-compression [passive]
```

Remember that this command only compresses the TCP header; it has no effect on UDP packets or other protocol headers. You can use the TCP header compression technique on serial lines using High-Level Data Link Control (HDLC) or PPP encapsulation, but it must be enabled on both ends of the connection.

To optionally specify outgoing packets to be compressed only if TCP incoming packets on the same interface are compressed, you can specify the **passive** keyword.

Expressing TCP Header Compression

If you used TCP header compression with Cisco IOS Software release 12.0(7)T or earlier, the compression was performed in the process-switching path. This meant that any compression that was performed in the process-switching path that traversed TCP compression-enabled interfaces caused the packets to be queued and passed up to the processor to be switched. This resulted in a slower transmission time of the packet.

With the release of Cisco IOS Software release 12.1, TCP header compression occurs by default in the fast-switched path or the Cisco Express Forwarding (CEF)–switched path, depending on which switching method you enable on your interface. If you do not enable either switching path, TCP compression occurs in the process-switched path, as described in the preceding paragraph.

You can use the Express TCP Header Compression feature to reduce network overhead and speed transmission of TCP packets. This faster speed provides a greater benefit when used on slower links than when used on faster links.

The following conditions must be met before you can use Express TCP Header Compression:

- CEF switching or fast switching must be enabled on the interface.

- HDLC, PPP, or Frame Relay encapsulation must be configured.

- TCP header compression must be enabled.

Changing the Number of TCP Header Compression Connections

Depending on the underlying technology that you choose to implement, you might need to specify the total number of header compression connections that can exist on your interface. At a minimum, you should configure one connection for each TCP connection through that interface.

Some of the reasons that you might need to specify the total number of header compression connections that can exist on your interface are as follows:

- By default, when using Frame Relay encapsulation, there can be only 128 two-way header compression connections, or 256 one-way header compression connections. This maximum value is fixed; you cannot configure it.

- By default, when using PPP or HDLC encapsulation, there are only 16 two-way header compression connections or 32 one-way header compression connections allowed by the software. You can change this default, up to a maximum of 256 header compression connections.

To specify the total number of TCP header compression connections that can exist on an interface, use the following command:

```
R2(config-if)#ip tcp compression-connections number
```

Setting the TCP Connection Attempt Time

TCP connections that originate from your router wait a set amount of time for the three-way handshake to be completed. You can change the default amount of time, 30 seconds, during which Cisco IOS Software waits. Because the connection attempt time is a host parameter, it does not apply to traffic that is traversing your router.

To set the amount of time that Cisco IOS Software waits to attempt to establish a TCP connection, use the following command:

```
R2(config)#ip tcp synwait-time seconds
```

Using TCP Path MTU Discovery

Path MTU Discovery was developed to maximize the use of your available network bandwidth between the two endpoints of a TCP connection. This feature is further described in RFC 1191. By default, this feature is disabled in Cisco IOS Software.

Use the following command to enable Path MTU Discovery:

```
R2(config)#ip tcp path-mtu-discovery [age-timer {minutes | infinite}]
```

You can use the **ip tcp path-mtu-discovery** command to enable Path MTU Discovery for connections that are initiated by your router when it is acting as a host.

The **age-timer** keyword represents the time interval for how often TCP should reestimate the path MTU with a larger maximum segment size (MSS). The default Path MTU Discovery is 10 minutes, with a maximum configurable value of 30 minutes. You can use the **infinite** setting to turn off this timer.

Using TCP Selective Acknowledgment

You can use the TCP selective acknowledgment feature to improve performance in the event that multiple packets are lost from one TCP window of data. This feature enables the receiving TCP host to return selective acknowledgment packets to the sender, informing the sender of data that has been received. This means that the receiver now has the ability to acknowledge packets that are received out of order, allowing the sender to resend only the missing data segments (instead of everything since the first missing packet). Because of this, the feature is only used when multiple packets are dropped within one TCP window, with no performance impact when it is not used.

Refer to RFC 2018, "TCP Selective Acknowledgment Options," for more detailed information on TCP selective acknowledgment.

Use the following command to enable TCP selective acknowledgment:

```
R2(config)#ip tcp selective-ack
```

Using TCP Time Stamps

If you require a mechanism that can be used to measure TCP round-trip time, you can use the TCP time-stamp feature. One caveat to this feature is that because time stamps are always sent and echoed in both directions and the time-stamp value in the header is always changing, TCP header compression does not compress the outgoing packet. When you use TCP header compression over a serial link, the TCP time-stamp option is disabled.

Refer to RFC 1323, "TCP Extensions for High Performance," for more detailed information on the TCP time stamp.

Use the following command to enable TCP time stamp:

```
R2(config)#ip tcp timestamp
```

Setting the TCP Maximum Read Size

The maximum number of characters that TCP can read from the input queue at one time is a large number, by default, when using Telnet and rlogin, which generally send small packets. This number is the largest possible 32-bit positive number. Although you should not change this value, you can use the following command to set the TCP maximum read size for Telnet or rlogin:

```
R2(config)#ip tcp chunk-size characters
```

Setting the TCP Window Size

The default TCP window size used by your router is 2144 bytes. You should not change this value unless your router is sending packets larger than 536 bytes. Use the following command to change the default window size:

```
R2(config)#ip tcp window-size bytes
```

Setting the TCP Outgoing Queue Size

The default TCP outgoing queue size per TTY-associated connection is 5 segments. If no TTY connection, such as a Telnet session, is associated with it, the default queue size is 20 segments. Use the following command to change the 5-segment default value:

```
R2(config)#ip tcp queuemax packets
```

Configuring the MultiNode Load Balancing (MNLB) Forwarding Agent

The *MultiNode Load Balancing (MNLB) Forwarding Agent* is the Cisco IOS Software–based packet redirector component that is included in the MNLD Feature Set built for the Local-Director, a product that is used for load balancing.

The Forwarding Agent discovers the destination of a connection request and forwards its packets between the client and the chosen destination. This received request is forwarded to the MNLB services manager, the LocalDirector-based component of the MNLD Feature Set for LocalDirector. The services manager makes a decision on load balancing and informs the Forwarding Agent of the optimal destination. Upon the specification of the destination, the session data is directly forwarded to that destination, without requiring further participation by the services manager. The MNLD Feature Set for LocalDirector has no limit to the number of Forwarding Agents that you can configure.

The MNLD Feature Set for LocalDirector is comprised of hardware and software that runs on multiple network components. The services manager runs on the LocalDirector chassis and makes all the load-balancing decisions. The Forwarding Agent is implemented on Cisco IOS router and switch platforms and forwards packets to and from the selected destination. This separation of decision making and packet forwarding allows a much faster packet throughput. The underlying Cisco architecture used in this solution, ContentFlow architecture, enables the following features:

- High availability

- Unbounded scalability

- Application-aware balancing

- No single point of failure

Configuring the MNLB Forwarding Agent

To configure the MNLB Forwarding Agent, perform the following tasks:

Step 1   Enable CEF.

Step 2   Optionally enable NetFlow switching.

Step 3   Enable IP multicast routing.

Step 4   Configure the router as a Forwarding Agent.

The following sections describe each of these steps in greater detail.

Step 1: Enable CEF

Cisco Express Forwarding (CEF) is one of the advanced Layer 3 IP switching technologies that is available with Cisco IOS Software. CEF provides optimization of network performance and scalability for networks with large and dynamic traffic patterns, such as the Internet, on networks that are characterized by intensive web-based applications, or interactive sessions.

Use the following command to enable CEF on devices that do not support distributed CEF (dCEF):

```
R2(config)#ip cef
```

Use the following command to enable CEF on devices that support dCEF:

```
R2(config)#ip cef distributed
```

This command enables CEF globally, but you can still disable CEF on a particular interface if you desire, such as when you enable GRE tunnels and IPSec that use loopback addresses in their configuration.

Step 2: Enable NetFlow Switching

You should enable NetFlow switching on all interfaces that are to carry ContentFlow traffic. Most NetFlow commands depend on your platform and Cisco IOS Software release. After verification of support for the command in your platform/Cisco IOS Software release, use the commands described in this section to enable NetFlow switching.

To specify IP flow cache, use the following command:

```
R2(config-if)#ip flow-cache feature-accelerate
```

To specify the interface and enter interface configuration mode, use one of the following commands:

```
R2(config)#interface type slot/port-adapter/port
```

or

```
R2(config)#interface type slot/port
```

To enable flow switching on the interface, use the following command:

```
R2(config-if)#ip route-cache flow
```

While the default size of the NetFlow cache meets most of your needs, you can use the following command to increase or decrease the number of entries that are maintained in the cache:

```
R2(config)#ip flow-cache entries number
```

The number of entries that are maintained in the cache can be from 1024 to 524,288, with a default of 64,536.

Step 3: Enable IP Multicast Routing

IP multicast routing must be enabled on all interfaces to the services manager. Use the following command to enable multicast routing on all interfaces:

```
R2(config)#ip multicast routing
```

Use the following command to join a multicast group. Use this command on all interfaces that listen for the services manager multicasts with the group address matching the address that is configured on the services manager:

```
R2(config-if)#ip igmp join-group group-address
```

Step 4: Configure the Router as a Forwarding Agent

Use the commands that are described in this section to configure the router as a Forwarding Agent.

To specify the IP address and IGMP address of the Forwarding Agent, use the following command. The recommended IGMP address is 224.0.1.2:

```
R2(config)# ip casa control-address igmp-address
```

To adjust the memory that is allocated for the affinity pools of the Forwarding Agent, use the following command:

```
R2(config-casa)# forwarding-agent pools initial-affinity-pool max-affinity-pool
```

The default pool size is 5000, with no maximum size restrictions.

To specify the port number, the default of which is port 1637, use the following command:

```
R2(config-casa)# forwarding-agent port-number [password [timeout]]
```

Network Address Translation Overview

Network Address Translation (NAT), as described in RFC 1631, "The IP Network Address Translator (NAT)," was developed to address two key shortcomings facing the Internet: the depletion of IP address space and scaling in routing. By using NAT, your IP network appears to the outside as if it is coming from a different IP address space. This means that you are allowed to use the private IP address ranges reserved in RFC 1918, "Address Allocation for Private Internets," on your network without having to worry about them not being routable in a public space. NAT takes your private addresses and translates them into a routable IP address range, which is normally supplied by your ISP. One other benefit of NAT is a way to gracefully renumber your internal IP network when changing service providers or when you are voluntarily renumbering into a classless interdomain routing (CIDR) block.

If you are running Cisco IOS Software release 12.1(5)T or later, the NAT feature supports all H.225 and H.245 message types, including FastConnect and Alerting, as part of the H.323 version 2 specification, as well as provides full support for NetMeeting Directory (Internet Locator Service).

When you configure a router to use NAT, you configure one interface to the inside of your network and another to the outside of your network. The term *inside* refers to the networks that you own and that must be translated. The term *outside* refers to those networks to which the stub network connects, and are generally not under your control. The following are the different types of addressing that are associated with NAT:

- **Inside local address**—An IP address that is assigned to a host on your inside network

- **Inside global address**—A legitimate IP address that represents one or more of your inside local IP addresses to the outside world

- **Outside local address**—An IP address of an outside host as it appears to your inside network

- **Outside global address**—An IP address that is assigned to a host on the outside network by the owner of the host that is allocated from globally routable address or network space

In a typical implementation, you configure NAT on the exit router between a stub domain and backbone, such as the Internet. When a packet leaves your domain, NAT translates the locally significant source address into a globally unique address. When a packet enters your domain, NAT translates the globally unique destination address into a local address. Remember, if you have more than one exit point on your domain, each NAT must have the same translation table. If NAT runs out of available addresses, the packet is dropped and an ICMP host unreachable message is returned to the originator of the packet.

When your router is configured to use NAT, it must not advertise local networks to the outside. However, routing information that NAT receives from the outside can still be advertised in the stub domain as usual.

When to Use NAT

NAT is a versatile feature that you can use for the following purposes:

- You use private or nonregistered IP addresses on your internal network but want to connect to the Internet. NAT provides the necessary translations of your internal local addresses to globally unique IP addresses before sending packets to the outside network.

- You must change your internal addresses but do not want to do so. In this case, you can use NAT for translation of these addresses.

- You want to do basic load sharing of TCP traffic. With NAT, you can map a single global IP address to many local IP addresses by using the TCP load distribution feature.

- You can use NAT as a practical solution to a connectivity problem only when relatively few hosts in a stub domain communicate outside of the domain at the same time. When this is the case, only a small subset of the IP addresses in the domain must be translated into globally unique IP addresses when outside communication is necessary, and these addresses can be reused when no longer in use.

Configuring IP Services

The next lessons teach you how to configure various IP services, including the following:

- Configuring ICMP redirects

- Configuring the DRP Server Agent

- Configuring HSRP

- Configuring IP accounting

- Configuring NAT

Lesson 17-1: Configuring ICMP Redirects

In this lesson, you configure Ethernet 0 of R2 to disable the sending of ICMP redirects as well as ICMP unreachables. Disabling ICMP redirects has a secondary effect of also disabling the IP Path MTU Discovery (PMTU) mechanism, because PMTU depends on the router to send unreachables. Example 17-1 illustrates a possible configuration for R2 to complete this task.

Example 17-1 *Disabling ICMP Redirects and Unreachables*

```
Configuration items for R2:
R2(config)#interface ethernet 0
R2(config-if)#no ip unreachables
R2(config-if)#no ip redirects
```

Lesson 17-2: Configuring the DRP Server Agent

To configure and maintain the DRP Server Agent, you must perform the following steps:

Step 1   Enable the DRP Server Agent.

Step 2   Optionally limit the source of DRP queries.

Step 3   Optionally configure authentication of DRP queries and responses.

Step 1: Enable the DRP Server Agent

The DRP Server Agent comes disabled by default. Use the following command to enable it:

```
R2(config)#ip drp server
```

In this lesson, you enable the DRP Server Agent on R3. Example 17-2 shows a configuration that you can use to complete this task.

Example 17-2 *Enabling the DRP Server Agent*

```
Configuration items for R3:
R3(config)#ip drp server
```

Step 2: Limit the Source of DRP Queries

You have can limit the source of valid DRP entries as part of your security policy. You can apply a standard IP access list to the interface to define who the Server Agent responds to. If you do not define an access list, the Server Agent answers all DRP queries.

If you define both an access group and a key chain, both security mechanisms must allow access before a request is processed.

Use the following command to limit the source of valid DRP queries by applying a standard IP access list:

```
R2(config)#ip drp access-group access-list-number
```

In this step, you use an access list to limit who can be the source of DRP queries from the host 192.168.254.250. Example 17-3 shows a sample configuration to make this scenario work.

Example 17-3 *Using Access Lists with DRP*

```
Configuration items for R3:
R3(config)#access-list 1 permit 192.168.254.250
R3(config)#ip drp access-group 1
```

Step 3: Configure Authentication of DRP Queries and Responses

As mentioned in the preceding section, you can configure the DRP Server Agent to authenticate DRP queries and responses. You accomplish this by defining a key chain, identifying the keys that belong to the key chain, and specifying how long each key is valid. To identify which key chain to use to authenticate all DRP requests and responses, use the following command:

```
R2(config)#ip drp authentication key-chain name-of-chain
```

To identify a key chain which must match the name that is configured in the preceding command, use the following command:

```
R2config)#key chain name-of-chain
```

Use the following command to identify the key number:

```
R2config-keychain)#key number
```

To identify the key string, use the following command:

```
R2(config-keychain-key)#key-string text
```

To optionally specify the time period during which the key can be received, use the following command:

```
R2(config-keychain-key)#accept-lifetime start-time {infinite | end-time | duration
  seconds}
```

To optionally specify the time period during which the key can be sent, use the following command:

```
R2(config-keychain-key)#send-lifetime start-time {infinite | end-time | duration seconds}
```

To complete this lab, configure authentication for DRP queries and responses by using the key ccie_lab. Example 17-4 shows a sample configuration to make this scenario work.

Example 17-4 *Authenticating DRP*

```
Configuration items for R3:
R3(config)#ip drp authentication key-chain ccie_lab
R3(config)#key chain ccie_lab
R3(config-keychain)#key 1
R3(config-keychain-key)#key-string secret_key
```

Lesson 17-3: Configuring HSRP

To configure Hot Standby Router Protocol (HSRP), perform the following steps:

Step 1 Enable HSRP.

Step 2 Optionally configure HSRP group attributes.

Step 3 Optionally change the HSRP MAC refresh interval.

Step 4 Optionally enable HSRP MIB traps.

Step 5 Optionally enable HSRP for MPLS VPNs.

Step 6 Enable HSRP support of the ICMP redirect message.

Step 1: Enable HSRP

Use the following command to enable HSRP on an interface:

```
R2(config-if)#standby [group-number] ip [ip-address [secondary]]
```

One way of implementing HSRP is to configure load sharing. Figure 17-1 illustrates the topology that you will use for your this lesson.

Figure 17-1 *Multiple HSRP Load Balancing Topology*

```
              192.168.3.3                    192.168.3.4
              HSRP1: 192.168.3.1             HSRP1: 192.168.3.1
              HSRP2: 192.168.3.2             HSRP2: 192.168.3.2
```

In this lesson, half of your clients are configured to use R3 and half of your clients are configured to use R4 as their gateway. In this manner, both routers are used to establish two HSRP groups. Example 17-5 shows you a possible configuration for this step.

Example 17-5 *Configuring Multiple HSRP Groups*

```
Configuration items for R3:
R3(config)#interface ethernet 0
R3(config-if)#ip address 192.168.3.3 255.255.255.0
R3(config-if)#standby 1 ip 192.168.3.1
R3(config-if)#standby 2 ip 192.168.3.2

Configuration items for R4:
R4(config)#interface ethernet 0
R4(config-if)#ip address 192.168.3.4 255.255.255.0
R4(config-if)#standby 1 ip 192.168.3.1
R4(config-if)#standby 2 ip 192.168.3.2
```

Step 2: Configure HSRP Group Attributes

Use the commands described in this section, as needed, to configure other Hot Standby group attributes that affect how the local router participates in HSRP.

To configure the time between hello packets and the hold time before other routers declare the active router to be down, use the following command:

```
R2(config-if)#standby [group-number] timers [msec] hellotime [msec] holdtime
```

Use the following command to set the Hot Standby priority—a value from 1 to 255 with a default of 100, where a higher number is given priority—used in choosing the active router:

```
R2(config-if)#standby [group-number] priority priority
```

To configure a preemption delay, after which the Hot Standby router preempts and becomes the active router, use the following command:

```
R2(config-if)#standby [group-number] preempt [{delay} [minimum delay] [sync delay]]
```

Use the following command to configure the interface to track other interfaces so that if one of the other interfaces goes down, the Hot Standby priority of the device is lowered:

```
R2(config-if)#standby [group-number] track type number [interface-priority]
```

To select an authentication string to be carried in all HSRP messages, use the following command:

```
R2(config-if)#standby [group-number] authentication string
```

To configure the delay period before the initialization of HSRP groups, use the following command:

```
R2(config-if)#standby delay minimum [min-delay] reload [reload-delay]
```

To specify a virtual MAC address for the virtual router, use the following command:

```
R2(config-if)#standby [group-number] mac-address macaddress
```

Use the following command to configure HSRP to use the burned-in address (BIA) of an interface as its virtual MAC address instead of the preassigned MAC address, as on Ethernet and FDDI, or the functional address, as on Token Ring:

```
R2(config-if)#standby use-bia [scope interface]
```

In this step, you enter the required configuration so that if either router becomes unavailable, you ensure that the other router becomes active and assumes the packet-transfer functions of the router that is unavailable. For group 1, make R3 the default active router and R4 the standby router. For group 2, make R4 the default active router and R3 the standby router. Example 17-6 shows the configuration that is necessary to complete these tasks.

Example 17-6 *Tuning HSRP Groups*

```
Configuration items for R3:
R3(config)#interface ethernet 0
R3(config-if)#standby 1 priority 110
R3(config-if)#standby 1 preempt
R3(config-if)#standby 2 preempt
```

continues

Example 17-6 *Tuning HSRP Groups (Continued)*

```
Configuration items for R4:
R4(config)#interface ethernet 0
R4(config-if)#standby 1 preempt
R4(config-if)#standby 2 priority 110
R4(config-if)#standby 2 preempt
```

Step 3: Change the HSRP MAC Refresh Interval

When you run HSRP over FDDI, you can change the interval at which a packet is sent to refresh the MAC cache on learning bridges or switches. HSRP hello packets use the BIA instead of the MAC virtual address. Refresh packets keep the MAC cache on switches and learning bridges current.

You can change the refresh interval on FDDI rings to a longer or shorter interval, thereby using bandwidth more efficiently. If you do not have a learning bridge or switch, you should disable the sending of any MAC refresh packets.

By default, a refresh packet is sent every 10 seconds. Use the following command to change the interval:

```
R2(config-if)#standby mac-refresh seconds
```

Step 4: Enable HSRP MIB Traps

The HSRP Management Information Base (MIB) feature supports Simple Network Management Protocol (SNMP) get operations to allow network devices to get reports about HSRP groups in a network from the network management station.

Enable HSRP MIB trap support from the command-line interface (CLI) so that you can use the MIB to get reports. A *trap* notifies your network management station when one of your routers leaves or enters the active or standby state. When you add an entry in the CLI, the RowStatus for that group in the MIB immediately goes to the active state. Cisco IOS Software only supports a read-only version of the MIB, and set operations are not supported.

Use the next two commands to enable HSRP MIB trap support.

To enable your router to send SNMP traps and informs, and HSRP notifications, use the following command:

```
R2(config)#snmp-server enable traps hsrp
```

To specify the recipient of an SNMP notification operation, and that HSRP notifications are to be sent to the host, use the following command:

```
R2(config)#snmp-server host host community-string hsrp
```

In this step, you configure the HSRP MIB trap feature on R3 and R4. You configure the SNMP host as 192.168.3.254. Example 17-7 illustrates a solution to this scenario.

Example 17-7 *HSRP MIB Trap*

```
Configuration for R3:
R3(config)#snmp-server enable traps hsrp
R3(config)#snmp-server host 192.168.3.254 public hsrp

Configuration items for R4:
R4(config)#snmp-server enable traps hsrp
R4(config)#snmp-server host 192.168.3.254 public hsrp
```

Step 5: Enable HSRP Support for MPLS VPNs

You can still use HSRP in support of an MPLS Virtual Private Network (VPN) when an Ethernet is connected between two provider edge (PE) devices when either of the following conditions are met:

- Your customer edge (CE) device has a default route to the HSRP virtual IP address.

- One or more hosts are configured with the HSRP virtual IP address as their default gateway.

Each VPN is associated with one or more VPN routing/forwarding (VRF) instances. The VRF consists of the following elements:

- An IP routing table

- A Cisco Express Forwarding (CEF) table

- A set of interfaces that make use of the CEF forwarding table

- A set of rules and routing protocol parameters to control the information that is placed in the routing tables

VPN routing information is stored in your IP routing table and your CEF table for each VRF. Each VRF maintains its own set of routing and CEF tables. This is necessary to prevent information from being forwarded outside a VPN and to prevent packets that are outside a VPN from being forwarded to a router within the VPN.

HSRP adds ARP entries and IP hash table entries, also known as *aliases*, using the default routing table instance. Be aware that if a different routing table instance is used when VRF forwarding is configured on an interface, ARP and ICMP echo requests for the HSRP virtual IP address will fail.

HSRP support for MPLS VPNs ensures that the HSRP virtual IP address is added to the correct IP routing table and not to the default routing table.

To use HSRP with MPLS VPNs, perform the following steps:

Step 1   Define the VPN.

Step 2   Enable HSRP.

Use the commands that are described in this section on the PE routers to define the VPN.

To enter VRF configuration mode and assign a VRF name, use the following command:

```
R2(config)#ip vrf vrf-name
```

To create routing and forwarding tables, use the following command:

```
R2(config-vrf)#rd route-distinguisher
```

To create a list of import or export route target communities for the specified VRF, use the following command:

```
R2(config-vrf)#route-target {import | export | both} route-target-ext-community
```

To specify an interface and enter interface configuration mode, use the following command:

```
R2(config)# interface type number
```

To associate a VRF with an interface or subinterface, use the following command:

```
R2(config-if)#ip vrf forwarding vrf-name
```

Figure 17-2 lays out the next topology that you will use for this lesson.

Figure 17-2 *MPLS VPN Topology*

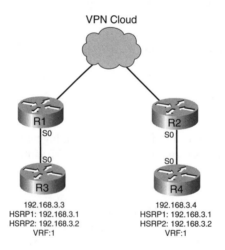

In this lesson, you configure R3 and R4 to function as PEs while continuing to use your previous HSRP configuration on their VRF interfaces. This way, you could configure your CE to use the HSRP virtual IP address as its default route. Configure HSRP to track the interfaces that connect the PEs to the rest of the provider network. Assume that R1 and R2 are correctly configured to act as the PE routers or as one of your service provider's core routers to which your edge devices attach. Example 17-8 illustrates a possible configuration for these requirements.

Example 17-8 *HSRP MPLS VPN Configuration*

```
Configuration items for R3:
R3(config)#ip cef
R3(config)#ip vrf vrf1
R3(config-vrf)#rd 100:1
R3(config-vrf)#route-target export 100:1
R3(config-vrf)#route-target import 100:1
 R3(config-vrf)#exit
R3(config-if)#interface ethernet0
R3(config-if)#ip vrf forwarding vrf1
R3(config-if)#ip address 133.100.3.3 255.255.0.0
R3(config-if)#standby 1 ip 133.100.3.1
R3(config-if)#standby 1 priority 105
R3(config-if)#standby preempt delay minimum 10
R3(config-if)#standby 1 timers 3 1

Configuration items for R4:
R4(config)#ip cef
R4(config)#ip vrf vrf1
R4(config-vrf)#rd 100:1
R4(config-vrf)#route-target export 100:1
R4(config-vrf)#route-target import 100:1
 R4(config-vrf)#exit
R4(config)#interface ethernet0
R4(config-if)#ip vrf forwarding vrf1
R4(config-if)#ip address 133.100.3.4 255.255.0.0
R4(config-if)#standby 1 ip 133.100.3.1
R4(config-if)#standby 1 priority 100
R4(config-if)#standby preempt delay minimum 10
R4(config-if)#standby 1 timers 3 1
```

Step 6: Enable HSRP Support for ICMP Redirect Messages

Use the following command to enable ICMP redirect messages to be sent when HSRP is
configured on an interface:

```
R2(config-if)#standby redirects [enable | disable]
```

You final configuration step in this lesson is to enable ICMP redirects for your two defined
HSRP groups. Example 17-9 shows a solution to these requirements.

Example 17-9 *HSRP with ICMP Redirect*

```
Configuration items for R3:
R3(config)#interface Ethernet0
R3(config-if)#standby redirects

Configuration items for R4:
R4(config)#interface Ethernet0
R4(config-if)#standby redirects
```

Lesson 17-4: Configuring IP Accounting

Use the next two commands to enable IP accounting.

Use the following command to enable basic IP accounting:

```
R2(config-if)#ip accounting
```

To enable IP accounting with the ability to identify IP traffic that fails IP ACLs, use the following command:

```
R2(config-if)#ip accounting access-violations
```

Use the following three optional commands to configure other IP accounting functions.

To set the maximum number of accounting entries to be created, use the following command:

```
R2(config)#ip accounting-threshold threshold
```

To filter accounting information for hosts, use the following command:

```
R2(config)#ip accounting-list ip-address wildcard
```

To control the number of transit records that are stored in the IP accounting database, use the following command:

```
R2(config)#ip accounting-transits count
```

Use the following command to display IP access violations for a specific IP accounting database:

```
R2#show ip accounting [checkpoint] access-violations
```

You must use the **access-violations** keyword to display IP access violations; otherwise, you only see the default display. The default display shows the number of packets that have passed ACLs and were routed toward their destination. The access violations output displays the number of the ACL that failed the last packet for the source and destination pair. The number of packets reveals how aggressive the attack is on a specific destination.

Use the **show ip accounting** command to display the active accounting database. Use the **show ip accounting checkpoint** command to display the checkpointed database. The **clear ip accounting** command clears the active database and creates the checkpointed database.

In the following lesson, you enable IP accounting on R4 based on the source and destination MAC address and based on IP precedence for received and transmitted packets. You also enable identification of the IP address that commits the violation. Example 17-10 shows an example configuration.

Example 17-10 *IP Accounting*

```
Configuration items for R4:
R4(config)#interface Ethernet0
R4(config-if)#ip accounting access-violations
R4(config-if)#ip accounting mac-address input
```

Example 17-10 *IP Accounting (Continued)*

```
R4(config-if)#ip accounting mac-address output
R4(config-if)#ip accounting precedence input
R4(config-if)#ip accounting precedence output
```

Lesson 17-5: Configuring NAT

To configure NAT, you must know your inside local addresses and inside global addresses as well as perform the following optional steps:

Step 1   Translate inside source addresses.

Step 2   Overload an inside global address.

Step 3   Translate overlapping addresses.

Step 4   Provide TCP load distribution.

Step 5   Change translation timeouts.

Step 6   Deploy NAT between an IP phone and the Cisco CallManager.

You also have the option of monitoring and maintaining NAT on your network.

The following sections describe each of these steps.

Step 1: Translate Inside Source Addresses

When translating your IP addresses into IP addresses that are globally unique IP addresses for communications outside your network, you have the following two choices:

- **Static translation**—Used to establish a one-to-one mapping between your inside local address and an inside global address

- **Dynamic translation**—Used to establish a mapping between an inside local address and a pool of global addresses

Configuring Static Translation

Use the commands described in this section to configure static inside source address translation.

To establish static translation between an inside local address and an inside global address, use the following command:

```
R2(config)#ip nat inside source static local-ip global-ip
```

To specify the inside interface and enter interface configuration mode, use the following command:

```
R2(config)#interface type number
```

To mark the interface as connected to the inside, use the next command:

```
R2(config-if)#ip nat inside
```

To specify the outside interface and enter interface configuration mode, use the following command:

```
R2(config)#interface type number
```

To mark the interface as connected to the outside, use the following command:

```
R2(config-if)#ip nat outside
```

While these steps are the minimum that you must configure to implement NAT static translation, you can use multiple inside and outside interfaces if necessary.

Configuring Dynamic Translation

Use the commands described in this section to configure dynamic inside source address translation.

To define a pool of global addresses to be allocated as needed, use the following command:

```
R2(config)#ip nat pool name start-ip end-ip {netmask netmask | prefix-length prefix-
    length}
```

To define a standard access list that permits addresses that require translation, use the following command:

```
R2(config)#access-list access-list-number permit source [source-wildcard]
```

To establish dynamic source translation, specifying the access list that was defined in the preceding command, use the following command:

```
R2(config)#ip nat inside source list access-list-number pool name
```

Once your definitions are configured, apply them to your inside and outside interfaces, as demonstrated in the previous section.

In this lesson, you configure R2 to translate all source addresses that pass through an access list to an address from the pool named ccie-net. The source addresses originates from the 10.10.10.0/24 network and the pool contains addresses from 192.168.2.201 to 192.168.2.215. Example 17-11 gives one solution to this lesson.

Example 17-11 *Dynamic Inside Translation*

```
Configuration items for R2:
R2(config)#ip nat pool ccie-net 192.168.2.201 192.168.2.215 netmask 255.255.255.240
R3(config)#ip nat inside source list 1 pool ccie-net
R2(config)#interface serial 0
R2(config-if)#ip address 192.168.2.1 255.255.255.240
R2(config-if)#ip nat outside
```

Example 17-11 *Dynamic Inside Translation (Continued)*

```
R2(config-if)#exit
R2(config)#interface ethernet 0
R2(config-if)#ip address 10.10.10.1 255.255.255.0
R2(config-if)#ip nat inside
R2(config-if)#exit
R2(config)#access-list 1 permit 10.10.10.0 0.0.0.255
```

Step 2: Overload an Inside Global Address

Overloading a single global address can be used to translate many local addresses to conserve addresses in the inside global address pool. This overloading forces the router to maintain enough information from higher-level protocols, such as TCP or UDP port numbers, to allow it to translate the global address back to the correct local address.

Use the commands described in this section to configure overloading of inside global addresses.

To define a pool of global addresses to be allocated as needed, use the following command:

```
R2(config)#ip nat pool name start-ip end-ip {netmask netmask | prefix-length prefix-
   length}
```

To define a standard access list, use the following command:

```
R2(config)#access-list access-list-number permit source [source-wildcard]
```

To establish dynamic source translation, specifying the access list that was defined with the preceding command, use the following command:

```
R2(config)#ip nat inside source list access-list-number pool name overload
```

Once configured, apply NAT to your inside and outside interfaces, as previously discussed in Step 1.

In this lesson, you add the ability of overloading to NAT. You create a pool of addresses named ccie-net. The pool contains addresses from 192.168.2.201 to 192.168.2.215. You use an access list to allow packets that have a source address from the 10.10.10.0/24 network. If a current translation does not exist, packets that match your access list are translated to an address from the pool. You enable the overload feature to allow the router to use the same global address for any amount of addresses. Example 17-12 gives an example configuration for this scenario.

Example 17-12 *Overloading Inside Global Addresses*

```
Configuration items for R2:
R2(config)#ip nat pool ccie-net 192.168.2.201 192.168.2.215 netmask 255.255.255.240
R2(config)#ip nat inside source list 1 pool ccie-net overload
R2(config)#interface serial0
R2(config-if)#ip address 192.168.2.1 255.255.255.240
R2(config-if)#ip nat outside
 R2(config-if)#exit
```

continues

Example 17-12 *Overloading Inside Global Addresses (Continued)*

```
R2(config)#interface ethernet0
R2(config-if)#ip address 10.10.10.1 255.255.255.0
R2(config-if)#ip nat inside
R2(config-if)#exit
R2(config)#access-list 1 permit 10.10.10.0 0.0.0.255
```

Step 3: Translate Overlapping Addresses

In most cases, NAT is used to translate private IP addresses into legal addresses that are routable on the Internet, but it can also be used to connect two networks that are using the same IP addressing on their internal networks. This scenario is referred to as *overlapping addresses.*

Use the next five commands that are described in this section to configure static SA address translation.

To establish static translation between an outside local address and an outside global address, use the following command:

```
R2(config)#ip nat outside source static global-ip local-ip
```

Once you have configured your outside static, apply NAT to your inside and outside interfaces, as previously discussed in Step 1.

Use the following series of commands to configure dynamic outside source address translation.

To define a pool of local addresses to be allocated as needed, use the following command:

```
R2(config)#ip nat pool name start-ip end-ip {netmask netmask | prefix-length prefix-
  length}
```

To define a standard access list, use the following command:

```
R2(config)#access-list access-list-number permit source [source-wildcard]
```

To establish dynamic outside source translation, specifying the access list that was defined with the preceding command, use the following command:

```
R2(config)#ip nat outside source list access-list-number pool name
```

Once you have configured your dynamic translation, apply NAT to your inside and outside interfaces, as previously discussed in Step 1.

In this lesson, there are addresses on your LAN, in the 192.168.2.0 range, that are being used legitimately by someone else on the Internet. Configure your NAT to allow an extra translation to the 100.100.100.0 range so that you can gain access to that external network. Example 17-13 gives one solution to this problem.

Example 17-13 *Translating Overlapping Addresses*

```
Configuration items for R2:
R2(config)#ip nat pool ccie-net 133.192.168.2.201 192.168.2.215 prefix-length 28
R2(config)#ip nat pool overlap-net 100.100.100.0 100.100.100.255 prefix-length 24
R2(config)#ip nat inside source list 1 pool ccie-net
R2(config)#ip nat outside source list 1 pool overlap-net
R2(config)#interface serial 0
R2(config-if)#ip address 133.100.2.1 255.255.255.240
R2(config-if)#ip nat outside
 R2(config-if)#exit
R2(config)#interface ethernet0
R2(config-if)#ip address 100.100.100.1 255.255.255.0
R2(config-if)#ip nat inside
R2(config-if)#exit
R2(config)#access-list 1 permit 100.100.100.0 0.0.0.255
```

Step 4: Provide TCP Load Distribution

When NAT comes up in everyday conversation, you probably think of it as a translation mechanism that allows your company to access the Internet. NAT has another function that is unrelated to this feature. If your company has multiple hosts that communicate with a heavily utilized host or server, you can use NAT to establish a virtual host on the inside network that coordinates load sharing among multiple real hosts. Allocation is done on a round-robin basis from a rotary pool of real addresses when a new connection is opened from the outside to the inside. Any non-TCP traffic is still passed without translation, unless you have other translations in effect.

Use the commands described in this section to configure destination address rotary translation to allow you to map one virtual host to many real hosts.

To define a pool of addresses that contains the addresses of the real hosts, use the following command:

```
R2(config)#ip nat pool name start-ip end-ip {netmask netmask | prefix-length prefix-
    length} type rotary
```

To define an access list that permits the address of the virtual host, use the following command:

```
R2(config)#access-list access-list-number permit source [source-wildcard]
```

To establish dynamic inside destination translation, specifying the access list that was defined with the preceding command, use the following command:

```
R2(config)#ip nat inside destination list access-list-number pool name
```

Once you have configured TCP load distribution, apply NAT to your inside and outside interfaces, as previously discussed in Step 1.

In this lesson, you configure TCP load distribution to servers with addresses from 10.10.10.2 to 10.10.10.15. You define a virtual address, 10.10.10.1, which distributes connections among the set of real hosts. If an active translation does not already exist, TCP packets from serial interface 0, whose destination matches the access list, are translated to an address from the pool. Example 17-14 illustrates a possible configuration for this lesson.

Example 17-14 *TCP Load Distribution*

```
Configuration items on R2:
R2(config)#ip nat pool real-hosts 10.10.10.2 10.10.10.15 prefix-length 28 type rotary
R2(config)#ip nat inside destination list 2 pool real-hosts
R2(config)#interface serial 0
R2(config-if)#ip address 133.100.32.1 255.255.255.252
R2(config-if)#ip nat outside
R2(config-if)#exit
R2(config)#interface ethernet 0
R2(config-if)#ip address 10.10.10.22 255.255.255.240
R2(config-if)#ip nat inside
R2(config-if)#exit
R2(config)#access-list 2 permit 10.10.10.1
```

Step 5: Change Translation Timeouts

If left to the default value, a dynamic address translation times out after some period of nonuse. When overloading is not in use, simple translation entries time out after 24 hours. Use the following command to change this value:

```
R2(config)#ip nat translation timeout seconds
```

When you use overloading, you have more control over translation entry timeout, because each entry contains more context about the traffic that is using it. Use the remaining commands described in this section to change timeouts on extended entries.

To change the UDP timeout value from the default of 5 minutes, use the following command:

```
R2(config)#ip nat translation udp-timeout seconds
```

To change the DNS timeout value from 1 minute, use the following command:

```
R2(config)#ip nat translation dns-timeout seconds
```

To change the TCP timeout value from 24 hours, use the following command:

```
R2(config)#ip nat translation tcp-timeout seconds
```

To change the Finish and Reset timeout value from 1 minute, use the following command:

```
R2(config)#ip nat translation finrst-timeout seconds
```

To change the ICMP timeout value from 1 minute, use the following command:

```
R2(config)#ip nat translation icmp-timeout seconds
```

To change the Synchronous (SYN) timeout value from 1 minute, use the following command:

```
R2(config)#ip nat translation syn-timeout seconds
```

Step 6: Deploy NAT Between an IP Phone and Cisco CallManager

Communication and registration between a Cisco IP phone and the Cisco CallManager (CCM) use the Selsius Skinny Station Protocol. The Skinny protocol allows messages to flow back and forth between the devices that include IP address and port information used to identify other IP phone users with which a call can be placed.

When using NAT with the CCM and IP phones, NAT must be able to identify and understand the information that is passed within the Skinny protocol. When an IP phone attempts to make a connection with the CCM and its IP address matches your NAT translation rules, NAT translates the original source IP address and replaces it with one from the configured pool. This new address is used to represent the IP phone to the CCM as well as other IP phone users.

Use the following command to specify a port other than the default port on which the CCM is listening for skinny messages:

```
R2(config)#ip nat service skinny tcp port number
```

Monitoring and Maintaining IP Services

Monitoring and maintaining your IP services can be a daunting task. This section gives you an overview of the commands that you can use to monitor and maintain your IP services environment. It includes the following topics:

- Verifying HSRP support for MPLS VPNs
- Displaying system and network statistics
- Clearing caches, tables, and databases
- Monitoring and maintaining the DRP Server Agent
- Clearing the access list counters
- Monitoring the MNLB Forwarding Agent
- Monitoring and maintaining HSRP support for ICMP redirect messages
- Monitoring and maintaining NAT

The following sections take a more in-depth look into each command that you can use to monitor and maintain the IP services on your network.

Verifying HSRP Support for MPLS VPNs

Use the following command to verify that the ARP entry in your router has the correct MAC and IP address for your HSRP group:

```
R2#show ip arp vrf vrf_name
```

Use the following command to verify that the correct IP address is entered into the CEF table for your HSRP virtual address:

```
R2#show ip cef vrf vrf_name
```

Example 17-15 shows the output when you execute these two **show** commands to verify that the HSRP virtual IP address of 10.2.0.1 is in the correct ARP and CEF tables.

Example 17-15 *Verifying ARP and CEF Entries*

```
R2#show ip arp vrf vrf1
Protocol  Address          Age (min)  Hardware Addr   Type   Interface
Internet  10.2.0.1             -      00d0.bbd3.bc22  ARPA   Ethernet0/2
Internet  10.2.0.20            -      0000.0c07.ac01  ARPA   Ethernet0/2

R2#show ip cef vrf vrf1
Prefix              Next Hop           Interface
0.0.0.0/0           10.3.0.4           Ethernet0/3
0.0.0.0/32          receive
10.1.0.0/16         10.2.0.1           Ethernet0/2
10.2.0.0/16         attached           Ethernet0/2
10.2.0.1/32         receive
10.2.0.20/32        receive
224.0.0.0/24        receive
255.255.255.255/32  receive
```

As you can see from this output, the virtual IP address of 10.2.0.1 is in both tables.

Displaying System and Network Statistics

You have the option of displaying specific statistics such as the contents of IP routing tables, caches, and databases. You can then use this information to determine resource utilization and as an aid in solving network issues.

Use the commands described in this section to display specific statistics such as the contents of IP routing tables, caches, and databases.

To display the contents of one or all current access lists, use the following command:

```
R2#show access-lists [access-list-number | access-list-name]
```

To display information regarding compiled access lists, including the state of each compiled access list, use the following command:

```
R2#show access-list compiled
```

To display the contents of current IP access lists, use the following command:

```
R2#show ip access-list [access-list-number | name]
```

To display the active IP accounting or checkpointed database, use the following command:

```
R2#show ip accounting [checkpoint]
```

To display the address of the default router and the address of hosts for which an ICMP redirect message has been received, use the following command:

```
R2#show ip redirects
```

To display IP socket information, use the following:

```
R2#show ip sockets
```

To display statistics on TCP header compression, use the following command:

```
R2#show ip tcp header-compression
```

To display IP protocol statistics, use the following command:

```
R2#show ip traffic
```

To display the status of the standby router, use the following command:

```
R2#show standby [interface [group]] [active | init | listen | standby] [brief]
```

To display HSRP information about delay periods, use the following command:

```
R2#show standby delay [type number]
```

To display TCP statistics, use the following command:

```
R2#show tcp statistics
```

Clearing Caches, Tables, and Databases

You have the option of removing the contents of any particular cache, table, or database. You would use this option when the content of a particular structure has become invalid or when you suspect that the structure is invalid.

To clear the active IP accounting or checkpointed database when IP accounting is enabled, use the following command:

```
R2#clear ip accounting [checkpoint]
```

To clear TCP statistics, use the following command:

```
R2#clear tcp statistics
```

Monitoring and Maintaining the DRP Server Agent

Use the commands described in this section to monitor and maintain the DRP Server Agent.

To clear statistics being collected on DRP requests and responses, use the following command:

```
R2#clear ip drp
```

To display information about the DRP Server Agent, use the following command:

```
R2#show ip drp
```

Clearing the Access List Counters

Each time that a match is made against an access list entry by a packet, the system increases a counter. Use the following command to display the counter:

```
R2#show access-lists
```

Use the following command to clear the counters of an access list:

```
R2#clear access-list counters {access-list-number | access-list-name}
```

Monitoring the MNLB Forwarding Agent

Use the commands described in this section to monitor the status of the MNLB Forwarding Agent.

To display the status of affinities, or connection information, use the following command:

```
R2#show ip casa affinities
```

To display the operational status of the Forwarding Agent, use the following command:

```
R2#show ip casa oper
```

To display statistical information about the Forwarding Agent, use the following command:

```
R2#show ip casa stats
```

To display information about wildcard blocks, use the following command:

```
R2#show ip casa wildcard
```

Monitoring and Maintaining HSRP Support for ICMP Redirect Messages

Use the following commands to display the status of ICMP redirect messages.

To display debug messages for HSRP-filtered ICMP redirect messages, use the following command:

```
R2#debug standby events icmp
```

To display information on ICMP transactions, use the following command:

```
R2#debug ip icmp
```

Monitoring and Maintaining NAT

By default, dynamic address translations time out from the NAT translation table after a set amount of time. You can use the following four commands to clear the entries before the configured timeout.

To clear all dynamic address translation entries from the NAT translation table, use the following command:

```
R2#clear ip nat translation *
```

To clear a simple dynamic translation entry that contains an inside translation or both an inside and outside translation, use the following command:

```
R2#clear ip nat translation inside global-ip local-ip [outside local-ip global-ip]
```

To clear a simple dynamic translation entry that contains an outside translation, use the following command:

```
R2#clear ip nat translation outside local-ip global-ip
```

To clear an extended dynamic translation entry, use the following command:

```
R2#clear ip nat translation protocol inside global-ip global-port local-ip local-port
   [outside local-ip local-port global-ip global-port]
```

Use one of the following two commands to display translation information.

To display active translations, use the following command:

```
R2#show ip nat translations [verbose]
```

To display translation statistics, use the following command:

```
R2#show ip nat statistics
```

Summary

This chapter has reviewed the services for IP that are offered in Cisco IOS Software. IP services allow you to fine-tune the functionality of IP to meet your individual requirements. You began by examining the many optional items that you can use, including ICMP protocol messages, IP source routing, the DRP Server Agent, HSRP, and NAT, among others. You finished the chapter with a look at different ways that you can monitor and maintain your IP services configuration.

Review Questions

1 Why would you use NAT to connect to the Internet?

2 What are ICMP messages used for?

3 What does the Path MTU Discovery feature do?

4 Where would the ICMP redirect message provide the most use?

5 Is it possible to use a single IP address for NAT translations?

6 What four terms are used to describe addresses that are used with NAT?

7 What is CEF?

8 What is the MNLB Forwarding Agent used for?

9 Why would you use the Express TCP Header Compression feature?

10 What are the three states of HSRP?

FAQs

Q — *Is there a way to change the MTU of an interface?*

A — You can use the **mtu** command to set the MTU value that you want on an interface. By using this command, you can also change the value of the IP MTU value so that it continues to match the MTU value of the interface.

Q — *I think that someone is using an IP feature to guide packets around the security measures that I have in place in an attempt to bypass them. Can I configure anything else on my router to help prevent this?*

A — Source routing is an IP option that allows the source IP host to specify a route through the IP network. If source routing is enabled on your router, it forwards the packet according to the specified source route. Although the default in Cisco IOS Software is to perform source routing, you can disable it by using the **no ip source-route global** configuration command.

Q — *I am interested in using the DistributedDirector on my network to redirect users to the closest service. How do I enable my routers to communicate with it?*

A — You can use the DRP Server Agents on a border router, or as a peer to a border router, that support the geographically distributed servers for which DistributedDirector service distribution is desired. Note that, because DistributedDirector makes decisions based on BGP and IGP information, your DRP Server Agents must have access to full BGP and IGP routing tables.

Q — *I want to provide router redundancy on my network without having to use hosts that support the Router Discovery Protocol. Can this be done?*

A — Yes, by using the Hot Standby Router Protocol (HSRP), you can provide high network availability because it has the ability to route IP traffic for your hosts, whether they are on Ethernet, FDDI, or Token Ring networks, without relying on the availability of any single router. You use HSRP to group routers so that they can select an active router and a standby router. The active router is the router that is used to route packets; the standby router is a router that takes over the routing duties when an active router fails, or when your predefined conditions are met.

Q — *Can I use HSRP with MPLS VPNs?*

A — Yes, you can still use HSRP in support of an MPLS VPN when an Ethernet is connected between two provider edge (PE) devices when either of the following conditions are met:

- Your customer edge (CE) device has a default route to the HSRP virtual IP address.

- One or more hosts are configured with the HSRP virtual IP address as their default gateway.

Q — *What accounting features are available in Cisco IOS Software?*

A — IP accounting can provide you with basic IP accounting functions, such as seeing the number of bytes and packets that are switched through the Cisco IOS Software based on the source and destination IP address. One limitation of this is that only IP traffic that uses the device as a transition point can be measured and then, only on the outbound direction; traffic generated by the software or terminating in the software is not included in the accounting statistics.

Q — *What feature is used with a LocalDirector to provide load balancing?*

A — The MultiNode Load Balancing (MNLB) Forwarding Agent is the Cisco IOS Software–based packet redirector component that is included in the MNLD Feature Set built for the LocalDirector. The Forwarding Agent discovers the destination of a connection request and forwards its packets between the client and the chosen destination. This received request is forwarded to the MNLB services manager, the LocalDirector-based component of the MNLD Feature Set for LocalDirector. The services manager makes a decision on load balancing and informs the Forwarding Agent of the most optimal destination. Upon the specification of the destination, the session data is directly forwarded to that destination, without requiring any further participation by the services manager. The MNLD Feature Set for LocalDirector has no limit to the number of Forwarding Agents that you can configure.

Q — *How can I connect two networks that use the same IP address ranges?*

A — You can use NAT to translate connections between two networks that are using the same IP addressing on their internal networks. This scenario is referred to as *overlapping addresses*.

Q — *Is there a feature that I can use to provide load balancing to multiple servers?*

A — You can use NAT to define a virtual IP address for a group of servers for load balancing. Allocation is done on a round-robin basis from a rotary pool of real addresses when a new connection is opened from the outside to the inside. Any non-TCP traffic is still passed without translation, unless you have other translations in effect.

Q — *Can I still use NAT with IP telephony?*

A — Yes, when using NAT with the CCM and IP phones, NAT translates the original source IP address of the IP phone and replaces it with one from the configured pool. This new address is used to represent the IP phone to the CCM as well as to other IP phone users.

PART V

Authentication and Virtual Private Networks

This chapter covers the following topics:

- TACACS+ Versus RADIUS
- Configuring AAA

CHAPTER 18

AAA Services

In this chapter, you will learn the mechanics of configuring advanced authentication, authorization, and accounting (AAA). "Advanced AAA" means that this chapter does not dwell on the basic concepts or installation of AAA. Instead, you will concentrate on practical applications and techniques required for your CCIE Security exam. This book assumes that you are either already familiar with AAA basics or can easily find a good reference on AAA theory and basic configuration. (See Appendix E, "Security-Related RFCs and Publications.")

The introduction portion of this chapter is confined to the discussion of differences between TACACS+ and RADIUS. Otherwise, the main focus of this chapter is configuring AAA. You might wonder why some of the earlier chapters had a fairly large introduction by comparison. This is because you are expected to have a good understanding of routing before configuring any security-related services during your lab examination.

TACACS+ Versus RADIUS

TACACS+ and RADIUS are the two major security server protocols used for AAA. Both authenticate a large number of users by creating a database of usernames and passwords. Many of the features available with these protocols overlap; Cisco designed TACACS+ when RADIUS was already in existence, so it implemented similar characteristics into TACACS+'s own architecture. Both TACACS+ and RADIUS server can be run on UNIX and Windows platforms. Because of the growing popularity of the latter, this chapter concentrates on Windows 2000 implementation of RADIUS and TACACS+ rather than UNIX.

Underlying Protocols

RADIUS uses User Datagram Protocol (UDP) as the protocol for communications between the client and the security server, and TACACS+ uses Transmission Control Protocol (TCP). TACACS+ runs over TCP port 49, and RADIUS over UDP port 1812. However, in some cases port 1645 is used for RADIUS. The fact that these protocols use different communication protocols results in some protocol-specific behavior. TCP, for instance, is connection-oriented, and UDP offers best-effort delivery. TCP makes TACACS+ more scalable, but RADIUS UDP is simpler to implement.

Packet Encryption

With RADIUS, only the user password is encrypted in the NAS-to-server access-request packet. Information such as username, authorized services, and accounting that comprises the remainder of the packet is sent in the clear. Furthermore, client-to-NAS communications are not covered by this encryption method.

In contrast, TACACS+ encrypts the entire packet with the exception of a header. The unencrypted TACACS+ header contains a field specifying whether the payload of that packet is encrypted.

Authentication, Authorization, and Accounting Processes

Authentication and authorization processes for RADIUS are joined because when a RADIUS server successfully authenticates a client, the return packets include authorization information as well. RADIUS accounting, however, can be used independently of authentication and authorization. The RADIUS accounting data can be sent at the start and end of a session.

TACACS+ implements a modular structure, providing separate authentication, authorization, and accounting. This allows a single TACACS+ server to provide each facility independently by relating it to its own databases.

Router Management

RADIUS was not designed by Cisco, so it doesn't understand the IOS command-line interface (CLI). Therefore, RADIUS can't authorize a user to execute commands on a router.

TACACS+, on the other hand, allows authorization on a user or group level for the specific commands you may enter on a router. This can be done in the following two ways:

- By specifying privilege levels for commands on a router and having a TACACS+ server approve a user for a certain privilege level

- By specifying permissible commands for a user or group on a TACACS+ server

For a discussion of privilege levels, review Chapter 15, "Basic Cisco IOS Software and Catalyst 3550 Series Security."

Interoperability

RADIUS offers support for many different vendor-specific attributes aside from the standard ones. Not all vendors implement the complete list of standard attributes, and not all of them stick to the standard attributes alone. RADIUS, therefore, lacks interoperability between vendors. If using multiple vendors is a requirement, verify whether all standard attributes are supported by those vendors, and don't use the vendor-specific attributes not understood by the other vendor.

TACACS+ was created specifically for Cisco and therefore is not commonly used by other vendors.

Traffic

By now you probably realize that because of their inherent differences discussed so far in this chapter, RADIUS and TACACS+ process information between server and client differently and subsequently generate different amounts of traffic. TACACS+, for instance, is capable of a much finer level of control than RADIUS, but at the same time it involves a multistep negotiation process between a client and a server, creating more traffic and taking longer than RADIUS.

Configuring AAA

If you feel that the overview section of this chapter was a little short, don't worry. This section is a comprehensive guide to the following:

- Simplified AAA configuration using RADIUS
- Configuring AAA on a PIX Firewall
- Configuring VPN client remote access
- Authentication proxy with TACACS+
- Privilege levels with TACACS+
- Configuring PPP callback with TACACS+
- Using RADIUS server for PPP callback
- New AAA features

Case Study 18-1: Simplified AAA Configuration Using RADIUS

In this scenario, R8 is configured for AAA. The RADIUS server, host 192.168.1.7, provides some of the basic AAA services for R8. The current topology is shown in Figure 18-1.

Figure 18-1 *R8 and RADIUS Server*

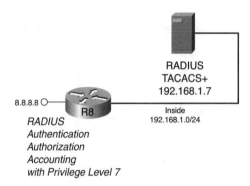

This case study takes you through the following steps:

Step 1 Configure the user and client on the RADIUS server.

Step 2 Enable AAA on R8.

Step 3 Configure authentication with a list.

Step 4 Configure local user database and privilege levels.

Step 5 Specify R8's source interface for RADIUS.

Step 6 Point to the RADIUS server.

Step 7 Configure the default authentication.

Step 8 Configure authorization.

Step 9 Configure accounting.

Step 10 Verify the AAA configuration.

Step 1: Configuring the User and Client on the RADIUS Server

The first step in configuring a user and client on a RADIUS server is inputting the user's information into a RADIUS database. Figure 18-2 shows RADIUS's GUI. The user user1radius is being added to the database.

Figure 18-2 *Adding a User to the RADIUS Server*

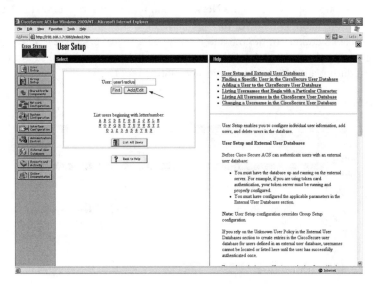

Next, you need to add all the necessary information for the user, including the password and other parameters, as shown in Figure 18-3. In this case study, the password cisco is used for both the CiscoSecure PAP and Separate fields. Choose the group to which the user will be assigned from the drop-down menu at the bottom of the screen. For this case study, the default group has been renamed Radius_Group.

Figure 18-3 *Configuring User Information on the RADIUS Server*

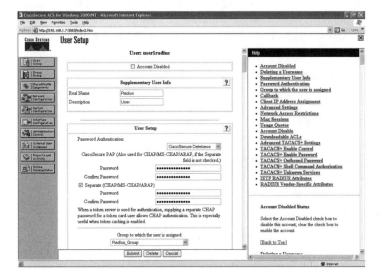

After creating a user account, you need to specify R8 as RADIUS's client under the Network Configuration setup. To get to the Network Configuration setup, click the **Network Configuration** button on the left side of the screen. In Figure 18-4, R8 is identified as the client using its Loopback8 address of 8.8.8.8 and is assigned a key of cisco6727. The Log RADIUS Tunneling Packets from this AAA Client option is checked to allow the server to log the packets rejected during authentication into its accounting reports.

Figure 18-4 *Specifying a RADIUS Client*

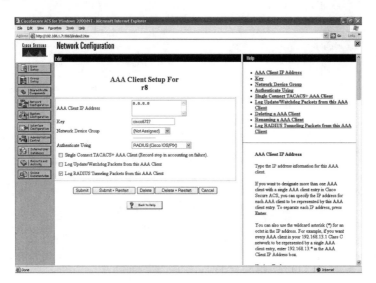

After making any changes to a client setup, including adding a new client, click the **Submit + Restart** button to force the server to reload. Figure 18-5 shows an existing client configuration on the RADIUS server. To add new clients, click the **Add Entry** button.

As soon as the server-side configuration tasks are complete, you need to address the client-side AAA configuration of R8 (discussed in the next step).

Step 2: Enabling AAA on R8

The **aaa new-model** command is used whenever you need AAA services for network security. You will learn about this command in this section and keep reapplying it in further AAA case studies. Remember that AAA elements do not become available for use until you enable AAA with this global command:

```
R8(config)#aaa new-model
```

As soon as you execute the **aaa new-model** command, you can configure other AAA features.

Figure 18-5 *Client List on the RADIUS Server*

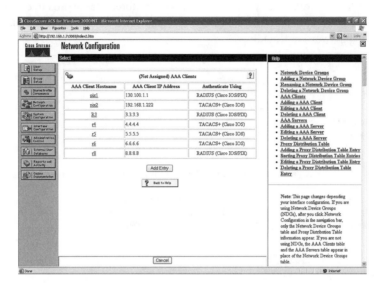

Step 3: Configuring Authentication with a List

Authentication configuration for this case study is divided into the following two parts:

- List authentication
- Default authentication

The general syntax for the **authentication** command is as follows:

```
R8(config)#aaa authentication login {default | list-name} method1 [method2...]
```

Before you become familiar with the numerous methods of authentication, you need to understand the differences between **default** and *list-name*. Whenever the **default** keyword is specified after **login**, it implies that all the router's interfaces, including console and vty lines, accept the authentication methods assigned to the default statement. Conversely, if the *list-name* string is used instead, the methods designated in that authentication command can be applied on a per-interface basis. The list is not actually activated until it is applied to an interface. After it is applied, however, it takes precedence over the default methods for that particular interface.

To apply login authentication to a line, use the following command in line configuration mode:

```
R8(config-line)#login authentication {default | list-name}
```

Make certain that the list names in the global **aaa authentication** command and the line authentication match.

Example 18-1 presents AAA authentication using no_login as the list name and its function on a console port. All users' passwords as well as the line passwords are "cisco."

Example 18-1 *AAA Method List Authentication*

```
R8#show run
hostname R8
!
aaa new-model
aaa authentication login no_login local enable line none
!
username Sam privilege 15 password 7 05080F1C2243
username Jessie privilege 15 password 7 13061E010803
username Alex privilege 15 password 7 030752180500
!
line con 0
password 7 05080F1C2243185E4B52
login authentication no_login
```

Example 18-1 has four different authentication methods configured with the no_login list. There are a total of ten available authentication methods:

- **enable**—Authenticates via the enable password.

- **krb5**—Authenticates using Kerberos 5.

- **krb5-telnet**—Authenticates using Kerberos 5 Telnet authentication protocol for a Telnet connection to the router.

- **line**—Authenticates via the line password.

- **local**—Authenticates using the local username database.

- **local-case**—Authenticates using the case-sensitive local username.

- **none**—No authentication is required.

- **group radius**—Authenticates using the list of all RADIUS servers.

- **group tacacs+**—Authenticates using the list of all TACACS+ servers.

- **group** *group-name*—Authenticates using a group of RADIUS or TACACS+ servers defined by the **aaa group server radius** or **aaa group server tacacs+** command.

Methods are always used sequentially. If the first method returns an error, the next one in line is used, and so on. Remember that as soon as one of the methods denies access with authentication failure, the rest of the methods aren't queried. Likewise, when access is granted by the first method, the second is of no consequence. Only when a method can't respond does AAA use the following one.

In Example 18-1, console authentication is accomplished in the following manner:

- **local**—The first method to be tried.

- **enable**—If local authentication returns an error, a router's enable password is used. See Chapter 15 for a discussion of enable passwords.

- **line**—If the enable password returns an error, the line password (console) takes its turn.

- **none**—If all the previous methods fail, this grants access without authentication.

NOTE   To simplify the AAA configuration in the lab environment, you might want to assign a list specifying local authentication methods such as the one shown in Example 18-1 for your console instead of the default RADIUS or TACACS+ unless instructed otherwise.

Step 4: Configuring Local User Database and Privilege Levels

Chapter 15 covered the syntax for both username and privilege-level commands. To avoid repetition, the commands discussed here are strictly related to the task at hand. For authorization purposes explained in Step 8 of this case study, it is important to ensure that the username-password combination in the local database is an exact replica of the one in the RADIUS server database. Therefore, both user accounts are created with a username of user1radius and a password of cisco. Privilege level 7 is assigned to the user, keeping authorization in mind.

Example 18-2 defines four statements for privilege level 7. The **privilege configure level 7 snmp-server** command allows a level 7 user one specific global configuration command.

Example 18-2 *Local Database of R8*

```
R8#show run
hostname R8
!
aaa new-model
aaa authentication login no_login local enable line none
!
username user1radius privilege 7 password 7 104D000A0618
!
privilege configure level 7 snmp-server
privilege exec level 7 configure
privilege exec level 7 configure terminal
privilege exec level 7 ping
!
```

continues

Example 18-2 *Local Database of R8 (Continued)*

```
line con 0
password 7 05080F1C2243185E4B52
login authentication no_login
```

Step 5: Specifying R8's Source Interface for RADIUS

Remember that when you configured R8 as a client on the RADIUS server, you specified R8's Loopback8 interface as the IP address. The default is to advertise the directly connected interface. If the default is left unaltered, the RADIUS server can't find its client, R8, because the IP address on the server and on the client won't match. To overwrite this behavior and to force RADIUS to use the IP address of another interface for all outgoing RADIUS packets, use the following command:

```
R8(config)#ip radius source-interface interface-name
```

Step 6: Pointing to the RADIUS Server

For R8 to recognize the RADIUS server and make use of its available services, define the following command:

```
R8(config)#radius-server host {hostname | ip-address} [auth-port port-number]
  [acct-port port-number] [timeout seconds] [retransmit retries] [key string]
```

Example 18-3 demonstrates the **radius-server host** command with the arguments used for this specific scenario. The server's IP address of 192.168.1.7 is identified as the host, and authentication and accounting destination UDP port numbers have been assigned as 1645 and 1646, respectively. If you wanted to assign several host entries to a single IP address, you would need to specify different port numbers for each new occurrence.

In this example, no timeout and retransmit values are set with the **radius-server host** command. This means that the global value is used instead. The key is the secret string used between the router and the RADIUS server for mutual authentication. To work, the string must match the one used on the RADIUS server. Therefore, the cisco6727 key is specified on both the server and R8.

Example 18-3 *Configuring Server Specifics on R8*

```
R8#show run
hostname R8
!
! Output omitted for brevity
!
radius-server host 192.168.1.7 auth-port 1645 acct-port 1646 key cisco6727
radius-server retransmit 3
ip radius source-interface Loopback8
```

NOTE   The key needs to appear last in the **radius-server host** command because all spaces within and at the end of the key are recognized as being part of the key. However, any spaces before the key aren't taken into account.

Step 7: Configuring the Default Authentication

It's time to assign the default AAA authentication on R8. Step 3 of this case study discussed the difference between a universal default authentication and authentication via method list. After a default authentication command is assigned, it is applied to all interfaces and lines aside from the console, where no_login list has already been specified.

The general syntax for the **aaa authentication login** command is the same as the one shown in Step 3. The specific command applicable to this scenario is **aaa authentication login default group radius**.

As you know, the **group radius** method tells the access server to consult all RADIUS servers (in case, there is more than one) for authentication.

Step 8: Configuring Authorization

To start the AAA authorization process, you can use the following command syntax:

```
R8(config)#aaa authorization [auth-proxy | network | exec | commands level |
    reverse-access] [default | list-name] [method1] [method2...]
```

Some of the keywords you should already know from Step 3 of this case study. The new keywords symbolize the authorization types, of which **exec**, shown in Example 18-4, is one. Specifying **exec** entitles a user to an EXEC terminal session.

Example 18-4 *Configuring Authorization*

```
R8#show run
hostname R8
!
! Output omitted for brevity
!
aaa new-model
aaa authentication login default group radius
aaa authentication login no_login local enable line none
aaa authorization exec default local if-authenticated
```

The router is told to look in the local database for the authorization method instead of, say, RADIUS because RADIUS is incapable of understanding CLI, as you learned in the introductory section of this chapter. Therefore, privilege level 7, which has been assigned a subset of commands, doesn't mean anything to the RADIUS server.

The **if-authenticated** keyword is another failover method in case the local database doesn't come through. This means that if a user has been successfully authenticated, the user is permitted to enter the shell.

NOTE   The **if-authenticated** method is particularly useful with the callback scenarios.

Step 9: Configuring Accounting

Finally, you need to configure accounting to audit user activity on the network. The full syntax of the **accounting** command is as follows:

```
R8(config)#aaa accounting [system | network | exec | connection | commands level |
    resource | authentication-proxy] [default | list-name] [start-stop | stop-only |
    none] [method1] [method2...]
```

The **aaa accounting** command offers multiple choices when it comes to the accounting type. Here, you concentrate on the **exec** type. As the name suggests, EXEC accounting provides information about user EXEC terminal sessions on the network access server (NAS). The tracked elements include username, date, start and stop times, total session time, the IP address of the access server, and the caller ID for dial-in users.

The available record types are as follows:

- **start-stop**—The most comprehensive record type. It directs the accounting method to send an accounting notice both at the start and end of a session.

- **stop-only**—Indicates the end-of-event accounting notice.

- **none**—Disables accounting.

The choice of methods used for accounting is considerably smaller than that of authentication and authorization. It offers only RADIUS or TACACS+ servers as accounting tools.

Example 18-5 presents the default method list for EXEC accounting that specifies start-stop as the record type and tells R8 to send accounting information to the RADIUS security server.

Example 18-5 *AAA Accounting*

```
R8#show run
hostname R8
!
! Output omitted for brevity
!
aaa new-model
aaa authorization exec default local if-authenticated
aaa accounting exec default start-stop group radius
```

Step 10: Verifying the AAA Configuration

When attempting to access R8 via Telnet, the user encounters the username/password prompt. After the requested information has been input correctly, the user enters the router. To view the current assigned privilege level, the user can issue the **show privilege** command. As a result, level 7 should appear.

To find out which configuration commands are allowed, you can refer to the router's Help menu and confirm that **snmp-server** may be configured by a level 7 user. When the user tries to input an unauthorized command, the router returns an error. This verification procedure is shown in Example 18-6.

Example 18-6 *Telnet User Accessing R8*

```
User Access Verification
Username: user1radius
Password: cisco

R8#show privilege
Current privilege level is 7

R8#config t
Enter configuration commands, one per line.  End with CNTL/Z.

R8(config)#?
Configure commands:
  call          Configure Call parameters
  default       Set a command to its defaults
  end           Exit from configure mode
  exit          Exit from configure mode
  help          Description of the interactive help system
  no            Negate a command or set its defaults
  snmp-server   Modify SNMP parameters

R8(config)#
```

To view the AAA processes as they happen on the router, you may issue **debug** commands such as **debug radius**, **debug aaa authentication**, and **debug aaa authorization**. Their simultaneous output is shown in Example 18-7. You can see that user1radius requests authentication and, after being authenticated, is granted permission to operate at privilege level 7.

Example 18-7 debug *Command Output on R8*

```
R8#debug radius
Radius protocol debugging is on

R8#debug aaa authentication
AAA Authentication debugging is on
```

continues

Example 18-7 debug *Command Output on R8 (Continued)*

```
R8#debug aaa authorization
AAA Authorization debugging is on

R8#
05:40:08: AAA: parse name=tty66 idb type=-1 tty=-1
05:40:08: AAA: name=tty66 flags=0x11 type=5 shelf=0 slot=0 adapter=0 port=66
  channel=0
05:40:08: AAA/MEMORY: create_user (0x826ECEF8) user='NULL' ruser='NULL' ds0=0
  port='tty66' rem_addr='192.1
68.1.100' authen_type=ASCII service=LOGIN priv=1 initial_task_id='0'
05:40:08: AAA/AUTHEN/START (1008895964): port='tty66' list='' action=LOGIN
  service=LOGIN
05:40:08: AAA/AUTHEN/START (1008895964): using "default" list
05:40:08: AAA/AUTHEN/START (1008895964): Method=radius (radius)
05:40:08: AAA/AUTHEN (1008895964): status = GETUSER
05:40:12: AAA/AUTHEN/CONT (1008895964): continue_login (user='(undef)')
05:40:12: AAA/AUTHEN (1008895964): status = GETUSER
05:40:12: AAA/AUTHEN (1008895964): Method=radius (radius)
05:40:12: AAA/AUTHEN (1008895964): status = GETPASS
05:40:13: AAA/AUTHEN/CONT (1008895964): continue_login (user='user1radius')
05:40:13: AAA/AUTHEN (1008895964): status = GETPASS
05:40:13: AAA/AUTHEN (1008895964): Method=radius (radius)
05:40:13: RADIUS: ustruct sharecount=1
05:40:13: Radius: radius_port_info() success=1 radius_nas_port=1
05:40:13: RADIUS: added cisco VSA 2 len 5 "tty66"
05:40:13: RADIUS: Initial Transmit tty66 id 73 192.168.1.7:1645, Access-Request,
  len 97
05:40:13:        Attribute 4 6 08080808
05:40:13:        Attribute 5 6 00000042
05:40:13:        Attribute 26 13 0000000902077474
05:40:13:        Attribute 61 6 00000005
05:40:13:        Attribute 1 13 75736572
05:40:13:        Attribute 31 15 3139322E
05:40:13:        Attribute 2 18 DC34997A
05:40:13: RADIUS: Received from id 73 192.168.1.7:1645, Access-Accept, len 26
05:40:13:        Attribute 8 6 FFFFFFFF
05:40:13: RADIUS: saved authorization data for user 826ECEF8 at 826E446C
05:40:13: AAA/AUTHEN (1008895964): status = PASS
05:40:13: tty66 AAA/AUTHOR/EXEC (2776044849): Port='tty66' list='' service=EXEC
05:40:13: AAA/AUTHOR/EXEC: tty66 (2776044849) user='user1radius'
05:40:13: tty66 AAA/AUTHOR/EXEC (2776044849): send AV service=shell
05:40:13: tty66 AAA/AUTHOR/EXEC (2776044849): send AV cmd*
05:40:13: tty66 AAA/AUTHOR/EXEC (2776044849): found list "default"
05:40:13: tty66 AAA/AUTHOR/EXEC (2776044849): Method=LOCAL
05:40:13: AAA/AUTHOR (2776044849): Post authorization status = PASS_ADD
05:40:13: AAA/AUTHOR/EXEC: Processing AV service=shell
05:40:13: AAA/AUTHOR/EXEC: Processing AV cmd*
05:40:13: AAA/AUTHOR/EXEC: Processing AV priv-lvl=7
05:40:13: AAA/AUTHOR/EXEC: Authorization successful
05:40:13: RADIUS: ustruct sharecount=3
05:40:13: Radius: radius_port_info() success=1 radius_nas_port=1
05:40:13: RADIUS: added cisco VSA 2 len 5 "tty66"
```

Example 18-7 debug *Command Output on R8 (Continued)*

```
05:40:13: RADIUS: Initial Transmit tty66 id 74 192.168.1.7:1646,
  Accounting-Request, len 113
05:40:13:       Attribute 4 6 08080808
05:40:13:       Attribute 5 6 00000042
05:40:13:       Attribute 26 13 0000000902077474
05:40:13:       Attribute 61 6 00000005
05:40:13:       Attribute 1 13 75736572
05:40:13:       Attribute 31 15 3139322E
05:40:13:       Attribute 40 6 00000001
05:40:13:       Attribute 45 6 00000001
05:40:13:       Attribute 6 6 00000007
05:40:13:       Attribute 44 10 30303030
05:40:13:       Attribute 41 6 00000000
05:40:13: RADIUS: Received from id 74 192.168.1.7:1646,
```

To check the accounting record on the RADIUS server, choose **Reports > RADIUS Accounting**. The resulting screen should look similar to Figure 18-6.

Figure 18-6 *RADIUS Accounting*

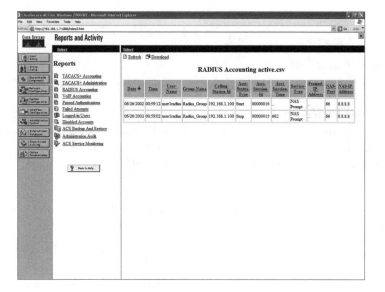

Case Study 18-2: Configuring AAA on a PIX Firewall

In this case study, you configure PIX2 to allow communication between the inside and outside networks and to enable AAA control over the inside network's access and usage by the outside users. Figure 18-7 shows the given topology.

Figure 18-7 *AAA on a PIX Firewall Topology*

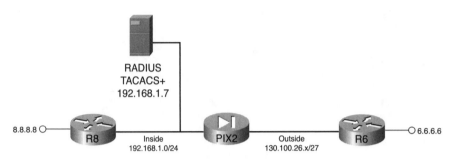

To accomplish this case study's objectives, follow these steps:

Step 1 Configure TACACS+.

Step 2 Initially configure the PIX Firewall.

Step 3 Control connections with access lists.

Step 4 Configure AAA services.

Step 5 Create access via Telnet.

Step 6 Enable SSH access.

Step 1: Configuring TACACS+

As in Case Study 18-1, a AAA server needs to be enabled before any AAA operation can take place. The current server setup is somewhat similar, with two notable differences: TACACS+ instead of RADIUS, with implementation on the PIX instead of a router.

Specifying PIX2 as the TACACS+ Client

In the AAA client setup, follow these steps:

Step 1 Input PIX2's inside interface as the client IP address.

Step 2 Enable the secret key to authenticate PIX2.

Step 3 Choose TACACS+ as the authentication mechanism, as shown in Figure 18-8.

Step 4 Check the Single Connect TACACS+ AAA Client (Record stop in accounting failure) box to allow multiple requests from a client to be transported over a single session rather than establishing a separate session for every TACACS+ request.

Figure 18-8 *AAA Client Setup with TACACS+*

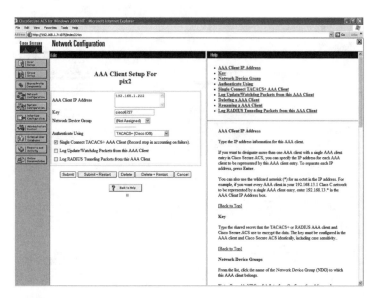

User and Group Setup

The process of specifying user parameters is the same as it was in the RADIUS case study. Refer to Case Study 18-1 if you feel that you need to review the task. In this case study, however, user2tacacs has been assigned to a group called Tacacs_Group. This is done so that the authorization settings can be applied to a group once, and all members of the group are governed by the same rules. To apply the group settings to a user, select the Use Group Settings bullets under the User Setup configuration when configuring user2tacacs.

Figure 18-9 shows the Group Setup screen. You can see that TACACS+ is chosen as the server protocol.

Next, you need to specify the PIX Command Authorization Set, as shown in Figure 18-10. You will find it under the Shared Profile Components. To get there, click the **Shared Profile Components** button on the left side of the screen. In the PIX Command Authorization Set, enter a name and description for your set. Specify whether you want to permit or deny the entry of unmatched commands. If you choose the Deny option, only the commands you enter in the available field are allowed to be entered. Permit, on the other hand, gives free reign over your terminal session to a group user.

Figure 18-9 *Group Setup with TACACS+*

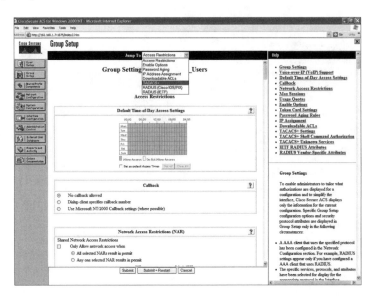

Figure 18-10 *PIX Command Authorization Set*

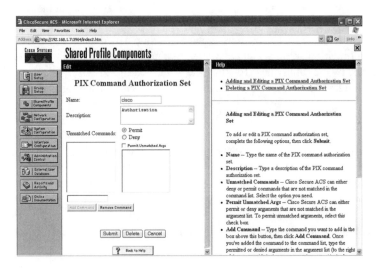

After the PIX Command Authorization Set has been defined, return to the Group Setup screen by clicking the **Group Setup** button on the left side of the screen. You see the screen shown in Figure 18-11. Check the PIX Shell (pixshell) checkbox. In the PIX Command Authorization

Set section, select the Assign a PIX Command Authorization Set for any network device bullet, and choose the configured authorization set, cisco, from the drop-down menu. When you are done, click **Submit + Restart**.

Figure 18-11 *Selecting the PIX Shell*

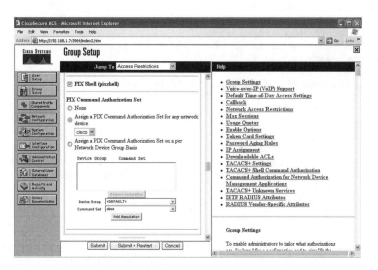

NOTE   If the PIX Shell (pixshell) checkbox does not appear on the Group Settings screen, click the **Interface Configuration** button on the left side of the screen. On the Interface Configuration screen under the TACACS+ Services category, select the PIX Shell (pixshell) checkbox for User, Group, or both. Click the **Submit** button. This causes the PIX Shell (pixshell) option to show up in your Group Settings layout.

Step 2: Initial Configuration of the PIX Firewall

This case study is not meant to serve as a comprehensive guide to general PIX configuration. Instead, it concentrates on the AAA-related tasks that are the focus of this chapter. Nevertheless, initial setup is required for PIX2 to operate and provide the necessary services, including AAA. Example 18-8 shows the fundamental commands to enable the PIX.

Example 18-8 *Initializing PIX2*

```
PIX2(config)#show run
PIX Version 6.2(2)
hostname PIX2
names
```

continues

Example 18-8 *Initializing PIX2 (Continued)*

```
name 130.100.26.6 R6
nameif ethernet0 outside security0
nameif ethernet1 inside security100
nameif ethernet2 DMZ2 security10
nameif ethernet3 DMZ security15
enable password 2KFQnbNIdI.2KYOU encrypted
interface ethernet0 10full
interface ethernet1 auto
interface ethernet2 auto
interface ethernet3 10baset
ip address outside 130.100.26.2 255.255.255.224
ip address inside 192.168.1.222 255.255.255.0
ip address DMZ2 172.16.23.1 255.255.255.0
ip address DMZ 172.16.22.1 255.255.255.0
global (outside) 10 interface
nat (inside) 10 0.0.0.0 0.0.0.0 0 0
static (inside,outside) 130.100.26.7 192.168.1.7 netmask 255.255.255.255 0 0
static (inside,outside) 130.100.26.8 192.168.1.1 netmask 255.255.255.255 0 0
route outside 0.0.0.0 0.0.0.0 R6 1
route inside 8.8.8.0 255.255.255.0 192.168.1.1 1
```

The **nameif** command identifies each interface. You may choose a default name or assign your own, such as DMZ2 for Ethernet2. The security level defaults are accepted in this example—0 for the outside network, 100 for the inside network, and 10 and 15 for the peripherals. Line speeds for a couple of interfaces are explicitly stated to get better performance. IP addresses are assigned to all interfaces.

The PIX Firewall is named with the **hostname PIX2** command. Name recognition is enabled, and R6 is specified as the source of the 130.100.26.6 address. The **global (outside)** and **nat (inside)** statements allow inside IP addresses to be recognized on the outside network. **static (inside,outside)** forms a one-to-one mapping between an internal network address and an external one. Each mapping needs its own dedicated address on the outside network. The default route for the outside network is defined, as well as a network route for the inside network. Finally, the enable password is set to restrict access to privileged mode. Notice that the password appears scrambled because of the **encrypted** keyword at the end of the line.

Step 3: Controlling Connections with Access Lists

Access lists on PIX Firewalls generally control entry rights. The syntax for the PIX access list is as follows:

```
PIX2(config)#access-list acl_id {deny | permit} protocol {source_addr | local_addr}
    {source_mask | local_mask} [operator port] {destination_addr | remote_addr}
    {destination_mask | remote_mask} [operator port] [icmp_type]
```

Access lists can be named or numbered. They can be applied to interfaces. However, their usage in the AAA configuration is what's important here (this is discussed in the next step). When used with AAA services, rather than directly permitting or denying a way in, access lists set up criteria to be matched by the incoming traffic. Permitting certain kinds of traffic causes the access lists to be evaluated by the AAA process. Conversely, denial of the access lists cancels control over that type of traffic by the AAA.

Example 18-9 shows the PIX access lists definition. To identify them by their function, named access lists were chosen for this scenario. You can count three separate access lists. Each of them is identified for future use with authentication, authorization, and accounting.

Example 18-9 *PIX Access Lists*

```
PIX2(config)#show run
!
! Output omitted for brevity
!
access-list inside_authentication_TACACS+ permit tcp any any eq telnet
access-list inside_authentication_TACACS+ permit tcp any any eq www
access-list inside_authorization_TACACS+ permit tcp any any eq telnet
access-list inside_authorization_TACACS+ permit tcp any any eq www
access-list inside_accounting_TACACS+ permit tcp any any eq telnet
access-list inside_accounting_TACACS+ permit tcp any any eq www
```

Step 4: Configuring AAA Services

PIX Firewalls support authentication, authorization, and accounting with RADIUS and TACACS+ servers. More recently, local authentication and authorization also are available. In this case study, PIX2 is set up to refer to the TACACS+ server, 192.168.1.7, for all the authentication, authorization, and accounting services.

Specifying a AAA Server

The first step in the AAA configuration of the PIX is to identify a AAA server. By default, TACACS+, RADIUS, and local servers are specified.

NOTE   You may choose to edit a server's name. In such a case, the newly named server appears in the running configuration along with the default statements. Should you choose to rename a default server, make sure that the name corresponds to the authentication, authorization, and accounting statements. The format of this command is

```
PIX2(config)#aaa-server group_tag protocol auth_protocol
```

The following command enables a AAA server:

```
PIX2(config)#aaa-server group_tag (if_name) host server_ip key timeout seconds
```

The *group_tag* argument is replaced with the name of the server group in the actual configuration.

AAA Authentication Methods

Three major types of AAA authentication methods can be used on PIX Firewalls:

- Console

- Access list

- Include/exclude

You will learn about the first two methods. (Include/exclude is rarely used.)

To force users to authenticate when accessing the PIX Firewall via Telnet, HTTP, Secure Shell (SSH), or serial and enable, consoles use the following command:

```
PIX2(config)#aaa authentication [serial | enable | telnet | ssh | http] console
    group_tag
```

The **telnet** and **ssh** options are discussed in Steps 5 and 6 of this case study. Here you can define **aaa authentication serial console**. This enables authentication for the PIX2 serial console. When this type of authentication is specified, it presumes that a username and password have already been set in the database referred by the *group_tag* argument.

Define the access list match type of AAA authentication. This type is ruled by the criteria defined in the inside_authorization_TACACS+ access list configured in the previous step. The syntax for the command is

```
PIX2(config)#aaa authentication match acl_name [inbound | outbound | if_name
    group_tag]
```

In Example 18-10, the **inside** argument defines the interface name from which to authenticate users. This means that the users on network 192.168.1.0 starting Telnet and web connections from the inside interface are asked for their usernames and passwords before being allowed access.

The example also designates TACACS+ as the server of choice; the inside interface name is placed in parentheses as the server's resident interface, and the **host** argument points to the IP address of the TACACS+ server. The key value, cisco6727, is the same as on the TACACS+ server. The timeout interval accepts the default of 5 seconds. That means that the PIX Firewall retries access to the AAA server within four 5-second intervals before giving up and selecting the next AAA server.

Example 18-10 *AAA Authentication*

```
PIX2(config)#show run
!
! Output omitted for brevity
!
aaa-server TACACS+ protocol tacacs+
aaa-server TACACS+ (inside) host 192.168.1.7 cisco6727 timeout 5
aaa-server RADIUS protocol radius
aaa-server LOCAL protocol local
aaa authentication match inside_authentication_TACACS+ inside TACACS+
aaa authentication telnet console TACACS+
aaa authentication ssh console TACACS+
aaa authentication serial console TACACS+
```

AAA Authorization and Accounting

When authorization with a TACACS+ server is enabled, each time another command is entered, the PIX Firewall sends a username, that command, and its arguments to the TACACS+ server for authorization. The syntax of the **authorization** command is analogous to the **authentication** command from the preceding section, so refer to that section for the meaning of the command arguments:

```
PIX2(config)#aaa authorization match acl_name [inbound | outbound | if_name
    group_tag]
```

The **aaa authorization** command statement lets authorized users access services specified by the ACS server. Similar to the **authentication** command, **aaa authorization** doesn't actually set security policy. Instead, it establishes conditions for traffic selection that need to use the specified services. Example 18-11 shows the command listing for configuring authorization on the network from Figure 18-7.

NOTE   Don't save your configuration until you are sure that the authorization feature works properly. If a configuration mistake locks you out, you can still recover by restarting the PIX Firewall to get back to the previously saved configuration.

The **aaa accounting** command uses an access list to find a match. Although it clearly has its own function, the syntax is identical to the **authentication** and **authorization** commands, with the exception of the **accounting** keyword:

```
PIX2(config)#aaa accounting match acl_name [inbound | outbound | if_name group_tag]
```

Example 18-11 shows the application of the **aaa authorization** and **aaa accounting** commands on PIX2.

Example 18-11 *AAA Authorization and Accounting on PIX2*

```
PIX2(config)#show run
!
! Output omitted for brevity
!
aaa authorization match inside_authorization_TACACS+ inside TACACS+
aaa accounting match inside_accounting_TACACS+ inside TACACS+
```

Step 5: Creating Access Via Telnet

The Telnet interface of the PIX Firewall is created for remote management of the PIX via the console. Telnet interface access is limited to the specified clients within the inside network and is protected by a password (as discussed in the next section).

To assign a permitted host to the Telnet interface, use the following command:

```
PIX2(config)#telnet ip-address [netmask] [if_name]
```

The *ip-address* argument identifies a host to the PIX Telnet console.

Setting a Password for Telnet

For a Telnet session to work, it isn't enough to specify a source host; it also needs a password. You set a Telnet password with the following command:

```
PIX2(config)#passwd password [encrypted]
```

In Example 18-12, the PIX2 configuration lets a host with source IP addresses of 192.168.1.100 and 192.168.1.51 access the inside interface. This example also shows the configuration of the **passwd** command on PIX2. The keyword **encrypted** specifies whether the password appears scrambled or in clear text in the output. You can see that the password cisco has in fact been encrypted and is currently unreadable.

Example 18-12 *Telnet Configuration on PIX2*

```
PIX2(config)#show run
!
! Output omitted for brevity
!
enable password 2KFQnbNIdI.2KYOU encrypted
passwd 2KFQnbNIdI.2KYOU encrypted
telnet 192.168.1.100 255.255.255.255 inside
telnet 192.168.1.51 255.255.255.255 inside
```

Enabling AAA Authentication for Telnet

The "AAA Authentication Methods" section focused on the **aaa authentication serial console** command. There you learned about the serial console version of the command. Here you use the Telnet version of the command. **aaa authentication telnet console** provides user identification for Telnet access by an ACS server. The full syntax is as follows:

```
PIX2(config)#aaa authentication [telnet] console server_tag
```

Modifying the Authentication Prompt

When trying to connect through the PIX Firewall, the AAA services provide a user with a prompt. The user has up to four chances to correctly authenticate. If the username or password doesn't succeed on any of the tries, the firewall drops the session.

The next command allows you to change the login prompt on the PIX for Telnet connections:

```
PIX2(config)#auth-prompt [accept | reject | prompt] string
```

This command has three options:

- **prompt**—Modifies the Telnet authentication request text.

- **accept**—Displays the successful authentication message.

- **reject**—Identifies a login failure.

Example 18-13 shows all three options.

Example 18-13 *Telnet Authentication Prompt*

```
PIX2(config)#show run
!
! Output omitted for brevity
!
aaa authentication telnet console TACACS+
!
auth-prompt prompt You are about to access the Internet
auth-prompt accept Welcome to the Internet
auth-prompt reject Nice Try, Try Again
```

Step 6: Enabling SSH Access

SSH was discussed in Chapter 15. SSH provides strong authentication and encryption capabilities for remote access. It was envisioned as an alternative to Telnet, which sends traffic over the wire in clear text and therefore isn't terribly secure. It is possible to implement

SSH version 1 (SSH v.1) on the PIX Firewall for it to act as a server (never a client), provided that the following components are in place:

- Host name
- Domain name
- Telnet password

Configuring a Host Name, Domain Name, and Telnet Password

In the beginning of this case study, you saw a host name configured on PIX2. This is an integral part of the SSH configuration as well.

You need to configure a domain name for the SSH v.1 on PIX to function. You execute the **domain-name** command in the following manner:

```
PIX2(config)#domain-name name
```

The Telnet password configured in the previous section "Setting a Password for Telnet" is necessary for the SSH configuration as well. Refer to Example 18-12 for its implementation on PIX2.

Generating an RSA Key Pair

Before clients can connect to the PIX Firewall console via SSH, you must generate an RSA key pair for the firewall. You may do so using the following command, where the *modulus* argument is replaced with a bit size of 512, 768, 1024, or 2048:

```
PIX2(config)#ca generate rsa key modulus
```

After you've generated the RSA key, save the key using this command:

```
PIX2(config)#ca save all
```

Identifying an SSH Client

Similar to the way you've identified hosts for Telnet, you can specify source addresses for each would-be SSH client:

```
PIX2(config)#ssh ip-address [netmask] [if_name]
```

You can see that the **telnet** keyword is replaced with **ssh**. The client's source address, mask, and PIX2's receiving interface fill their appropriate spaces in the real configuration.

The next command specifies the idle timeout period in minutes. The SSH connection drops if no activity has been detected for the configured time interval:

```
PIX2(config)#ssh timeout mm
```

Enabling AAA Server Authentication

To specify SSH user authentication by an ACS, use the **aaa authentication console** command with the **ssh** option:

```
PIX2(config)#aaa authentication [ssh] console server_tag
```

Now that the SSH on PIX configuration steps are complete, you can view the results in Example 18-14.

Example 18-14 *SSH on PIX2 Configuration*

```
PIX2(config)# show ca my rsa
% Key pair was generated at: 17:14:26 UTC Jun 26 2002
Key name: pix2.cisco.com
 Usage: General Purpose Key
 Key Data:
  30819f30 0d06092a 864886f7 0d010101 05000381 8d003081 89028181 00d7f87b
  15f565ac 9899dad2 a51d5cd8 a10b367d a79f52fe eaee425d 790b02c3 1f7b8231
  5385eb6f 0771c4aa f1b2975b 3b4455c2 f4b33d7c baf4a5f9 0c6687fc 83c4d7d4
  5d1fdbac dfae4858 09d9081c cc2eb27c 0690bd90 ed3892d1 d0e2543c 079a68c9
  9a8ea939 b98b4418 4d561d69 dd69fecb 7e434234 7fc6160b 5d8398b8 f3020301 0001

PIX2(config)#show run
!
! Output omitted for brevity
!
hostname pix2
domain-name cisco.com
aaa authentication ssh console TACACS+
ssh 192.168.1.100 255.255.255.255 inside
ssh 192.168.1.51 255.255.255.255 inside
ssh timeout 5
```

Case Study 18-3: Configuring VPN Client Remote Access

This case study covers the PIX Firewall configuration process specifically for implementing remote-access VPNs. After you complete the PIX side of the configuration, you set up a remote host using Cisco VPN 3000 Client software versions 2.5/2.6 and Cisco VPN Client version 3.x. When it comes to the PIX configuration, there is virtually no difference between the two versions. The few exceptions that do exist, however, are noted at the appropriate times in this case study.

The firewall configuration for this case study supports the following features:

- Extended Authentication (Xauth) for user authentication
- TACACS+ authorization of user services
- IKE mode configuration for VPN IP address assignment
- Wildcard preshared key for IKE authentication

Another method of IKE authentication is to use a digital certificate instead of a preshared key. This is discussed in Chapter 23, "Cisco PIX Firewall."

Before you begin this case study's PIX configuration procedure, be aware that the entire arrangement of commands from the previous case study remains the same. Figure 18-12 shows the network topology used in this case study.

Figure 18-12 *Network Topology*

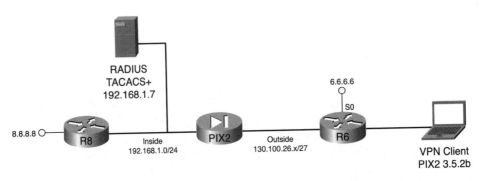

The steps specific to this case study are as follows:

Step 1 Define a AAA server.

Step 2 Configure the IKE policy.

Step 3 Configure Extended Authentication (Xauth).

Step 4 Create a dynamic crypto map.

Step 5 Create access lists.

Step 6 Define the pool of IP addresses.

Step 7 Configure NAT 0.

Step 8 Configure Cisco VPN Client 3.x policy attributes to download to the Cisco VPN Client.

Step 9 Permit IPSec traffic.

Step 10 Configure the Cisco VPN 3000 Client.

Step 1: Defining a AAA Server

Specifying the AAA server is the foremost step of this configuration. You might recall that the TACACS+ server was configured in Case Study 18-2. The statement **aaa-server TACACS+**

(inside) host 192.168.1.7 cisco6727 timeout 5 specifies that the authentication server with the IP address 192.168.1.7 resides on the inside interface and is in the default TACACS+ server group. The key cisco6727 is used between the TACACS+ server and the PIX Firewall to encrypt data between them. Refer to Example 18-10 for the command placement.

Step 2: Configuring the IKE Policy

You read about the concepts of IPSec security associations and IPSec secure communications in the introductory chapters of this book. If you want to learn more about the theory behind IKE, refer to Chapter 19, "Virtual Private Networks." Here, the intent is to give you enough ammunition to enable the necessary IKE functions and create a working solution to VPN client remote access with AAA. The first command you need to set is

```
PIX2(config)#isakmp enable interface-name
```

The interface on which Internet Security Association and Key Management Protocol (ISAKMP) negotiation needs to be established for communication between the IPSec peer and the PIX Firewall is the outside interface, so the syntax applicable to this case study is **isakmp enable outside.**

The next command specifies the parameter by which the PIX Firewall identifies itself to the remote peer when IKE is used to establish IPSec security associations between them. The PIX can be identified by its IP address or its host name. You need to make sure that the identity types are the same for the PIX and its peer whether it's IP address or a host name. The command syntax is as follows:

```
PIX2(config)#isakmp identity {address | hostname}
```

The next set of **isakmp** commands lets you set the rules for negotiating IPSec security associations and enabling IPSec secure communications. There are too many variables available for the **isakmp policy** *priority* command to show the general syntax. For that reason, each **policy** statement used is discussed separately. Keep in mind that each IKE policy is uniquely identified by a *priority* argument. It can be a number in the range of 1 to 65,534, from highest to lowest. In this case study, two policies are defined: policy 10 and policy 20. Their configuration is very similar. Therefore, most **isakmp policy** statements are explained for policy 10 and are simply replicated for policy 20.

The first command in the **isakmp policy** *priority* set is **isakmp policy 10 authentication pre-share**. It specifies the authentication method within an IKE policy and sets it to a preshared key applied by a dynamic crypto map. Dynamic crypto maps are covered in the next section.

The next command, **isakmp policy 10 encryption des**, identifies the policy encryption algorithm. DES and 3DES are the two encryption options available. DES is the chosen algorithm for policy 10. The **isakmp policy 10 hash md5** command indicates the hash algorithm to be used in an IKE policy. Besides MD5, the SHA-1 algorithm is offered as an option.

The **isakmp policy 10 group 2** command is employed to define the Diffie-Hellman group 1 or 2 for an IKE policy. Group 1 uses 768 bits, and group 2 uses 1024 bits. Group 2 is for Cisco VPN Client version 3.x, and group 1 is for Cisco VPN Client 3000 version 2.5/2.6 and earlier.

The **isakmp policy 10 lifetime 86400** command specifies the lifetime of an IKE security association before it expires. The **lifetime** parameter is set in seconds, where 86,400 seconds translates into one day. If two IPSec peers have different lifetimes configured, the shorter of the two is used. Before the current association expires, the new association is renegotiated.

Consider Example 18-15 for the current **isakmp policy** configuration. You can see that IKE policy 20 uses group 1; therefore, policy 20 was created for the version 2.5/2.6 VPN client.

Example 18-15 *IKE Policy Parameters*

```
PIX2#show run
!
! Output omitted for brevity
!
aaa-server TACACS+ (inside) host 192.168.1.7 cisco6727 timeout 5
!
isakmp enable outside
isakmp identity address
isakmp policy 10 authentication pre-share
isakmp policy 10 encryption des
isakmp policy 10 hash md5
isakmp policy 10 group 2
isakmp policy 10 lifetime 86400
isakmp policy 20 authentication pre-share
isakmp policy 20 encryption des
isakmp policy 20 hash md5
isakmp policy 20 group 1
isakmp policy 20 lifetime 86400
```

Step 3: Configuring Extended Authentication (Xauth)

The Extended Authentication (Xauth) feature allows you to create IPSec VPNs using TACACS+ or RADIUS as your user authentication method. In the event of Xauth failure, the IPSec security association isn't established, and the IKE security association is deleted. Before Xauth can be enabled, the **aaa-server** command must be present on the PIX Firewall with the server parameters identified.

Xauth is activated by the following command:

```
PIX2(config)#crypto map map-name client authentication aaa-group_tag
```

Make sure that the *aaa-group_tag* name is the same as the one in the **aaa-server** statement. In this scenario, the crypto map is configured as **crypto map mymap client authentication TACACS+**. This means that Xauth is enabled at the crypto map mymap, and the server used for user authentication is specified in the TACACS+ group.

The following command is used to apply the newly configured crypto map to an interface:

```
PIX2(config)#crypto map map-name interface interface-name
```

This scenario dictates that the crypto map mymap is applied to the outside interface.

Step 4: Creating a Dynamic Crypto Map

A dynamic crypto map can be used when the identity of the remote peer is unknown. When IKE negotiation takes place, the missing parameters are dynamically assigned. Along with the new IPSec security associations, the PIX Firewall installs a temporary crypto map entry. The results of the negotiation are included in that entry. The PIX treats the temporary crypto map entry as a regular one. As soon as the association expires, the entry is removed. The only parameter required for a dynamic crypto map is the transform set. Before a transform set can be included in a crypto map entry, it must be explicitly defined. Transform set configuration is described in the next section.

```
PIX2(config)#crypto dynamic-map dynamic-map-name dynamic-seq-num set transform-set
    transform-set-name1 [transform-set-name9]
```

The sequence number associates certain commands with the dynamic crypto map statement. *transform-set-name1* specifies the name of a transform set. For instance, in this scenario, the dynamic crypto map statement takes on the form **crypto dynamic-map dynmap 10 set transform-set ccie**.

Configuring a Transform Set

Transform sets specify one or both of the available IPSec security protocols—Encapsulating Security Payload (ESP) or Authentication Header (AH)—plus the algorithms to use along with them. The transform set defined in the crypto map protects the data flow during the IPSec security association. While negotiating the association, the peers must agree on a transform set. The set needs to be exactly the same on both peers. The syntax of the command is

```
PIX2(config)#crypto ipsec transform-set transform-set-name transform1 [transform2
    [transform3]]
```

When an ESP protocol is defined in a transform set, as is the case here, you may specify both an ESP encryption transform and an ESP authentication transform by using **crypto ipsec transform-set ccie esp-des esp-md5-hmac**.

transform-set-name was discussed in the preceding section.

Adding the Dynamic Crypto Map Set to a Static Crypto Map Set

When a PIX Firewall peer sends an IKE negotiation request, the PIX checks the request for a crypto map entry match. If no match is found, the PIX rejects the request. To solve this problem, a dynamic crypto map can be referenced in a static crypto map:

```
PIX2(config)#crypto map map-name seq-num [ipsec-isakmp | ipsec-manual] [dynamic
    dynamic-map-name]
```

After you create a dynamic crypto map, such as dynmap in the "Creating a Dynamic Crypto Map" section, you can use the **crypto map ipsec-isakmp dynamic** command to add the dynamic crypto map name set to a static crypto map. This results in a statement resembling **crypto map mymap 10 ipsec-isakmp dynamic dynmap**.

Example 18-16 shows the complete crypto map and transform set configuration for this case study.

Example 18-16 *Crypto Map Statements*

```
PIX2#show run
!
! Output omitted for brevity
!
aaa-server TACACS+ (inside) host 192.168.1.7 cisco6727 timeout 5
crypto ipsec transform-set ccie esp-des esp-md5-hmac
crypto dynamic-map dynmap 10 set transform-set ccie
crypto map mymap 10 ipsec-isakmp dynamic dynmap
crypto map mymap client authentication TACACS+
crypto map mymap interface outside
```

Step 5: Creating Access Lists

The next step is to define an access list for the PIX Firewall local network(s) in need of IPSec protection. The syntax of the PIX access lists was discussed in Case Study 18-2. The specific command used here is **access-list 101 permit ip 192.168.1.0 255.255.255.0 192.168.2.0 255.255.255.0**. It focuses on communication between the two internal networks.

Another necessary step to make the VPN remote client configuration work is to specify an access list to be used with TACACS+ authorization. If you recall, this was done in Case Study 18-2. Refer to Example 18-9 for the output.

Step 6: Defining the Pool of IP Addresses

The next command allocates a pool of local addresses to be assigned to external hosts after they enter the internal network. The syntax is

```
PIX2(config)#ip local pool pool-name start-address-[end-address]
```

The local pool in this scenario consists of IP addresses in the 192.168.2.0/24 network. It is spelled out in the **ip local pool ippool 192.168.2.1-192.168.2.254** command.

Step 7: Configuring NAT 0

Now it's time to make sure that the allocated pool of inside addresses doesn't get translated into outside addresses. During the PIX initial configuration, you designated all inside addresses for the NAT translation with **nat(inside)10 0.0.0.0 0.0.0.0 0 0**. To create an exception, you need to specify a *nat_id* of 0 in an additional statement:

```
PIX2(config)#nat [(if_name)] 0 access-list acl_name
```

To narrow the excluded network to 192.168.2.0, apply access list 101 in the following manner: **nat (inside) 0 access-list 101** (see Example 18-17).

Example 18-17 *Local Address Pool Configuration*

```
PIX2#show run
!
! Output omitted for brevity
!
ip local pool ippool 192.168.2.1-192.168.2.254
access-list 101 permit ip 192.168.1.0 255.255.255.0 192.168.2.0 255.255.255.0
nat (inside) 0 access-list 101
```

NOTE   Although it is possible to accomplish the same task by specifying the network/mask combination instead of an access list, the newer versions of the PIX Firewall highly recommend using the latter for greater security and flexibility.

Step 8: Configuring Cisco VPN Client 3.x Policy Attributes to Download to the Cisco VPN Client

The Cisco VPN 3000 Client needs to receive the policy information such as the DNS, WINS, default domain, and split tunnel mode attributes, from the PIX Firewall. This is made possible by a **vpngroup** command.

The **vpngroup** command on the PIX can set several key Cisco VPN 3000 Client policy attributes. These attributes are combined into a named group. When the Cisco VPN 3000 Client references the same group name, it receives the attributes associated with that group. The **vpngroup** commands used in this example are discussed briefly one-by-one as they are set.

The following command translates into **vpngroup vpn address-pool ippool** to suit the current scenario. The keyword **vpn** is the name of a VPN group. **ippool** is the name of the local pool configured earlier in Step 6:

```
PIX2(config)#vpngroup group_name address-pool pool_name
```

The following command specifies the IP address of the DNS server, which in this case is 156.46.10.10:

```
PIX2(config)#vpngroup group_name dns-server dns_ip_prim [dns_ip_sec]
```

The next command is very similar in syntax and discloses the WINS server information:

```
PIX2(config)#vpngroup group_name wins-server wins_ip_prim [wins_ip_sec]
```

The default domain name is specified in the next command. In this case study, cisco.com is used:

```
PIX2(config)#vpngroup group_name default-domain domain_name
```

The next command allows the VPN client to forward encrypted traffic destined for the corporate network and at the same time access the Internet in the clear. This capability is called *split tunneling*. The PIX Firewall references the access list in its **vpngroup** command to enable a split tunnel. When the client receives the specifications included in the access list, it sends only the traffic specified in that access list via an IPSec tunnel and sends the rest in the clear. When the PIX Firewall receives the encrypted stream on the outside interface, it decrypts the packets and sends them to the access-list-defined internal network.

```
PIX2(config)#vpngroup group_name split-tunnel acl_name
```

Without split tunneling, all traffic between the VPN client and the PIX Firewall is tunneled, so the client doesn't have access to the Internet. With split tunneling enabled, the VPN client can do both. To define split tunneling for the remote client in this case study, use **vpngroup vpn split-tunnel 101**.

The following command forces the VPN client to perform perfect forward secrecy (PFS). This means that each new IPSec security association key is not based on any of the previous keys. If a new Diffie-Hellman exchange is performed every time, none of the previous or subsequent keys are compromised.

```
PIX2(config)#vpngroup group_name pfs
```

The following statement specifies the inactivity timeout for a tunnel:

```
PIX2(config)#vpngroup group_name idle-time idle_seconds
```

The next command specifies the VPN group's preshared key for IKE authentication. It should be the same as the group password entered during the VPN client configuration:

```
PIX2(config)#vpngroup group_name password preshared_key
```

You can view the combination of **vpngroup** commands on PIX2 in Example 18-18.

Example 18-18 *VPN Client Policy Attributes*

```
PIX2#show run
!
! Output omitted for brevity
!
vpngroup vpn address-pool ippool
vpngroup vpn dns-server 156.46.10.10
vpngroup vpn wins-server 10.1.1.1
vpngroup vpn default-domain cisco.com
vpngroup vpn split-tunnel 101
vpngroup vpn pfs
vpngroup vpn idle-time 1800
vpngroup vpn password ********
```

Step 9: Permitting IPSec Traffic

You need to tell the PIX Firewall to implicitly permit any traffic from an IPSec tunnel. Otherwise, the firewall expects any inbound traffic to be explicitly permitted by an access list and therefore performs an inspection. Because the IPSec traffic is already protected, another access list check is unnecessary. This command allows the IPSec inbound sessions to always be permitted:

```
PIX2(config)#sysopt connection [permit-pptp | permit-l2tp | permit-ipsec]
```

Example 18-19 demonstrates the entire PIX Firewall configuration covered in this case study, including the preceding command in the form of **sysopt connection permit-ipsec**.

Example 18-19 *PIX Firewall Configuration for VPN Client Remote Access*

```
PIX2#show run
!
! Output omitted for brevity
!
nat (inside) 10 0.0.0.0 0.0.0.0 0 0
access-list 101 permit ip 192.168.1.0 255.255.255.0 192.168.2.0 255.255.255.0
nat (inside) 0 access-list 101aaa-server TACACS+ (inside) host 192.168.1.7
   cisco6727 timeout 5
sysopt connection permit-ipsec
no sysopt route dnat
crypto ipsec transform-set ccie esp-des esp-md5-hmac
crypto dynamic-map dynmap 10 set transform-set ccie
crypto map mymap 10 ipsec-isakmp dynamic dynmap
crypto map mymap client authentication TACACS+     ← Forces authentication to AAA
crypto map mymap interface outside

ip local pool ippool 192.168.2.1-192.168.2.254

isakmp enable outside
isakmp identity address
isakmp policy 10 authentication pre-share
isakmp policy 10 encryption des
isakmp policy 10 hash md5
isakmp policy 10 group 2
isakmp policy 10 lifetime 86400
isakmp policy 20 authentication pre-share
isakmp policy 20 encryption des
isakmp policy 20 hash md5
isakmp policy 20 group 1
isakmp policy 20 lifetime 86400

vpngroup vpn address-pool ippool
vpngroup vpn dns-server 156.46.10.10
vpngroup vpn wins-server 10.1.1.1
vpngroup vpn default-domain cisco.com
vpngroup vpn split-tunnel 101
vpngroup vpn pfs
vpngroup vpn idle-time 1800
vpngroup vpn password cisco
```

Step 10: Configuring the Cisco VPN 3000 Client

Finally, it's time to configure the remote-peer side of the PIX-to-client VPN connection. This section takes you through a step-by-step configuration procedure, complete with visual examples.

This case study uses Cisco VPN Client version 3.x. Its configuration matches the one of PIX2 already concluded. To perform the client-side configuration, follow these steps:

Step 1   Select **Start** > **Programs** > **Cisco Systems VPN 3.x Client**, and open the VPN Dialer. Click the **New** button, as shown in Figure 18-13.

Figure 18-13   *Cisco Systems VPN Client Main Screen*

Step 2   You see the Connection Entry Wizard dialog box, shown in Figure 18-14. Enter the name of the connection in the space provided. You may enter a description for the connection under the name. Click **Next**.

Step 3   At the next prompt, enter the IP address of the PIX2 outside interface, 130.100.26.2, as shown in Figure 18-15. Click **Next**.

Step 4   In the next dialog box, shown in Figure 18-16, select Group Access Information to input the VPN group options, such as the group name and the shared password already configured on the PIX Firewall. Refer to Example 18-18 to see how the VPN group information was configured on PIX2. Click **Next**.

Figure 18-14 *New Connection Entry Wizard Screen I*

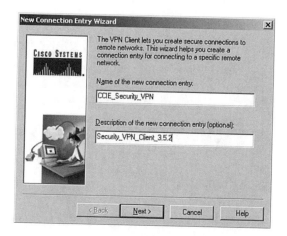

Figure 18-15 *New Connection Entry Wizard Screen II*

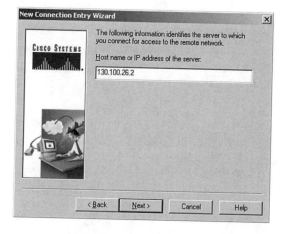

Step 5 The final screen of the New Connection Entry Wizard displays the new connection name, as shown in Figure 18-17. If you are sure that the parameters you've entered are correct, click **Finish**.

Figure 18-16 *New Connection Entry Wizard Screen III*

Figure 18-17 *New Connection Entry Wizard Screen IV*

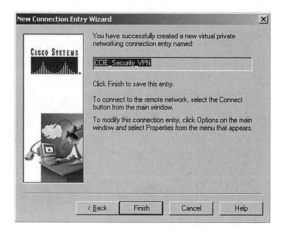

Step 6 Now you can attempt to establish a connection using your new configuration. At the Cisco Systems VPN Client main screen, shown in Figure 18-18, choose the name of the desired connection, CCIE_Security_VPN, from the drop-down menu. Click **Connect**.

Figure 18-18 *Connecting from the Cisco Systems VPN Client Screen*

Step 7 Next you need to enter the username and password to authenticate to the
TACACS+ server, as shown in Figure 18-19. The PIX Firewall commands
that make this possible are

```
aaa-server TACACS+ protocol tacacs+
aaa-server TACACS+ (inside) host 192.168.1.7 cisco6727 timeout 5
crypto map mymap client authentication TACACS+
```

Figure 18-19 *User Authentication for the Connection*

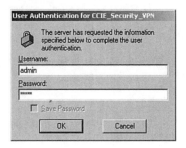

Figure 18-20 shows the phases of the CCIE_Security_VPN connection
establishment.

Figure 18-20 *Connecting to PIX2*

Step 8   View the client authentication on the PIX Firewall by entering the **debug** command. To see the IPSec negotiations of phase 2, enter **debug crypto ipsec 1**. To see the ISAKMP negotiations, enter **debug crypto isakmp 1**. The **debug crypto engine** command shows the traffic that is encrypted. The **debug** command output is shown in Example 18-20. It is followed by the **show uauth** command output, which shows the currently authenticated user and the host IP to which the user is bound.

Example 18-20 debug *Output on PIX2*

```
PIX2# show debug
crypto_isakmp_process_block: src 207.67.1.2, dest 130.100.26.2
VPN Peer: ISAKMP: Added new peer: ip:207.67.1.2 Total VPN Peers:1
VPN Peer: ISAKMP: Peer ip:207.67.1.2 Ref cnt incremented to:1 Total VPN Peers:1
OAK_AG exchange
ISAKMP (0): processing SA payload. message ID = 0

ISAKMP (0): Checking ISAKMP transform 1 against priority 10 policy
ISAKMP:        encryption 3DES-CBC
ISAKMP:        hash SHA
ISAKMP:        default group 2
ISAKMP:        extended auth pre-share
ISAKMP (0): Checking ISAKMP transform 2 against priority 10 policy
ISAKMP:        encryption 3DES-CBC
ISAKMP:        hash MD5
ISAKMP:        default group 2
ISAKMP:        extended auth pre-share
ISAKMP (0): Checking ISAKMP transform 3 against priority 10 policy
ISAKMP:        encryption 3DES-CBC
ISAKMP:        hash SHA
ISAKMP:        default group 2
ISAKMP:        auth pre-share
ISAKMP (0): Checking ISAKMP transform 4 against priority 10 policy
ISAKMP:        encryption 3DES-CBC
ISAKMP:        hash MD5
```

Example 18-20 debug *Output on PIX2 (Continued)*

```
ISAKMP:        default group 2
ISAKMP:        auth pre-share
ISAKMP (0): Checking ISAKMP transform 5 against priority 10 policy
ISAKMP:        encryption DES-CBC
ISAKMP:        hash SHA
ISAKMP:        default group 2
ISAKMP:        extended auth pre-share
ISAKMP (0): Checking ISAKMP transform 6 against priority 10 policy
ISAKMP:        encryption DES-CBC
ISAKMP:        hash MD5
ISAKMP:        default group 2
ISAKMP:        extended auth pre-share
ISAKMP (0): processing KE payload. message ID = 0
ISAKMP (0): processing NONCE payload. message ID = 0
ISAKMP (0): processing ID payload. message ID = 0
ISAKMP (0): processing vendor id payload
ISAKMP (0): received xauth v6 vendor id
ISAKMP (0): processing vendor id payload
ISAKMP (0): remote peer supports dead peer detection
ISAKMP (0): processing vendor id payload
ISAKMP (0): speaking to a Unity client
ISAKMP: Created a peer node for 207.67.1.2
ISAKMP (0): ID payload
        next-payload : 10
        type         : 1
        protocol     : 17
        port         : 500
        length       : 8
return status is IKMP_NO_ERROR
crypto_isakmp_process_block: src 207.67.1.2, dest 130.100.26.2
OAK_AG exchange
ISAKMP (0): processing HASH payload. message ID = 0
ISAKMP (0): processing NOTIFY payload 24578 protocol 1
        spi 0, message ID = 0
ISAKMP (0): processing notify INITIAL_CONTACTIPSEC(key_engine): got a queue event...
IPSEC(key_engine_delete_sas): rec'd delete notify from ISAKMP
IPSEC(key_engine_delete_sas): delete all SAs shared with       207.67.1.2

ISAKMP (0): SA has been authenticated
return status is IKMP_NO_ERROR
ISAKMP (0): sending phase 1 RESPONDER_LIFETIME notify
ISAKMP (0): sending NOTIFY message 24576 protocol 1
ISAKMP/xauth: request attribute XAUTH_TYPE
ISAKMP/xauth: request attribute XAUTH_USER_NAME
ISAKMP/xauth: request attribute XAUTH_USER_PASSWORD
ISAKMP (0:0): initiating peer config to 207.67.1.2. ID = 3403200621
  (0xcad8b86d)
crypto_isakmp_process_block: src 207.67.1.2, dest 130.100.26.2
ISAKMP_TRANSACTION exchange
ISAKMP (0:0): processing transaction payload from 207.67.1.2. message ID =
  2213211724
```

continues

Example 18-20 debug *Output on PIX2 (Continued)*

```
ISAKMP: Config payload CFG_REPLY
return status is IKMP_ERR_NO_RETRANS
ISAKMP (0:0): initiating peer config to 207.67.1.2. ID = 3861414952 (0xe6288428)
crypto_isakmp_process_block: src 207.67.1.2, dest 130.100.26.2
ISAKMP_TRANSACTION exchange
ISAKMP (0:0): processing transaction payload from 207.67.1.2. message ID =
   2213211724
ISAKMP: Config payload CFG_ACK
return status is IKMP_NO_ERROR
crypto_isakmp_process_block: src 207.67.1.2, dest 130.100.26.2
ISAKMP_TRANSACTION exchange
ISAKMP (0:0): processing transaction payload from 207.67.1.2. message ID =
   2213211724
ISAKMP: Config payload CFG_REQUEST
ISAKMP (0:0): checking request:
ISAKMP: attribute     IP4_ADDRESS (1)
ISAKMP: attribute     IP4_NETMASK (2)
ISAKMP: attribute     IP4_DNS (3)
ISAKMP: attribute     IP4_NBNS (4)
ISAKMP: attribute     ADDRESS_EXPIRY (5)
ISAKMP: attribute     APPLICATION_VERSION (7)
ISAKMP: attribute     ALT_DEF_DOMAIN (28674)
ISAKMP: attribute     ALT_SPLIT_INCLUDE (28676)
ISAKMP: attribute     ALT_PFS (28679)
ISAKMP (0:0): responding to peer config from 207.67.1.2. ID = 2516128422
return status is IKMP_NO_ERROR
crypto_isakmp_process_block: src 207.67.1.2, dest 130.100.26.2
OAK_QM exchange
oakley_process_quick_mode:
OAK_QM_IDLE
ISAKMP (0): processing SA payload. message ID = 3061639520

PIX2# show uauth
                       Current    Most Seen
Authenticated Users       1           1
Authen In Progress        0           1
ipsec user 'admin' at 192.168.2.1, authenticated
pix2#
```

Step 9 After you are connected, view your Client Connection Status, as shown in
Figure 18-21. Notice that the client has received an internal IP address from
a local pool.

Step 10 Select the Statistics tab in the Client Connection Status window, as shown in
Figure 18-22, to monitor the network connection and the packet exchange
between the VPN client and the internal network.

Figure 18-21 *Client Connection Status—General*

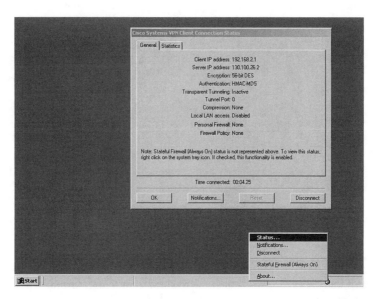

Figure 18-22 *Client Connection Status—Statistics*

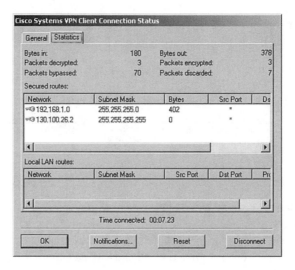

Step 11 Verify your connection by pinging R8's internal address behind the firewall, as shown in Figure 18-23.

Figure 18-23 *Sending ICMP Requests to 192.168.1.1*

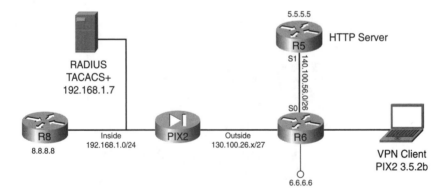

Case Study 18-4: Authentication Proxy with TACACS+

This case study goes through authentication proxy configuration and explains the theory behind it. The topology used here is illustrated in Figure 18-24.

Figure 18-24 *Authentication Proxy Topology*

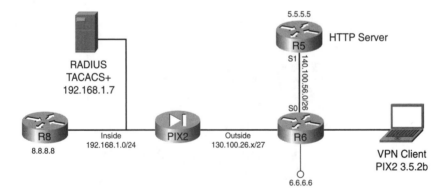

Authentication proxy on a router's interface is designed to intercept an inbound connection request from a user and authenticate it before it goes any further. If the user fails to authenticate at that point, the request for connection is denied. Essentially, the Cisco IOS authentication proxy feature lets a router act in a firewall capacity and apply per-user security policies.

Authentication proxy is triggered when a user tries to log in to the network or access the Internet via HTTP. The proxy checks whether the user has already been authenticated. If so, the authentication proxy doesn't get involved. However, if there is no entry, the authentication proxy prompts the user for a username and password. This causes the user's specific authorization profiles to be automatically obtained from a AAA server and temporarily applied at an inbound interface. Whatever services are permitted in the profile are available to the user for the duration of the connection.

The dynamic user profiles remain active for as long as the user's traffic is detected. After the idle timer expires, the user profile information is removed, and the client's traffic is no longer allowed to pass. The user must initiate another HTTP request to reconnect.

In the event of authentication failure, the user gets four more chances to enter the right username/password combination.

NOTE   Even though after being authenticated the users can access any services for which they are authorized, the authentication proxy itself is triggered by the HTTP connections only. Also, HTTP services must be enabled on the standard HTTP port 80.

To enable authentication proxy with TACACS+, follow these steps:

Step 1   Configure a TACACS+ server.

Step 2   Configure AAA.

Step 3   Configure the HTTP server.

Step 4   Configure the authentication proxy.

Step 5   Apply the authentication proxy to an interface.

Step 6   Verify the authentication proxy.

Step 1: Configuring a TACACS+ Server

This section discusses the server-side configuration tasks to enable the authentication proxy.

Step 1   Define R6 as the TACACS+ client in the manner discussed in earlier case studies, as shown in Figure 18-25. Click **Submit + Restart** when you are done.

Step 2   Click the **Interface Configuration** button on the left, and then click the **TACACS+ (Cisco IOS)** configuration link, as shown in Figure 18-26.

Figure 18-25 *Setting Up R6 as the TACACS+ Client*

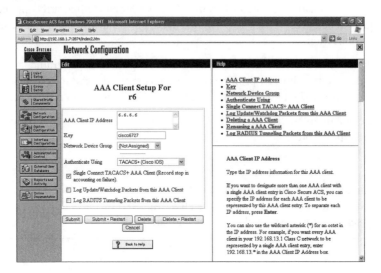

Figure 18-26 *Interface Configuration of the TACACS+ Services*

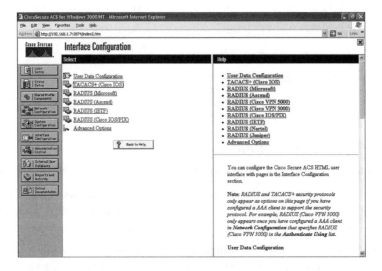

Step 3   As shown in Figure 18-27, under the Interface Configuration setup, choose the
Shell (exec) option in both the User and Group columns. To define the authentication proxy, choose a new service option, and specify the **auth-proxy** keyword. When you are happy with this part of the setup, click **Submit**.

Figure 18-27 *Interface Configuration for the Authentication Proxy*

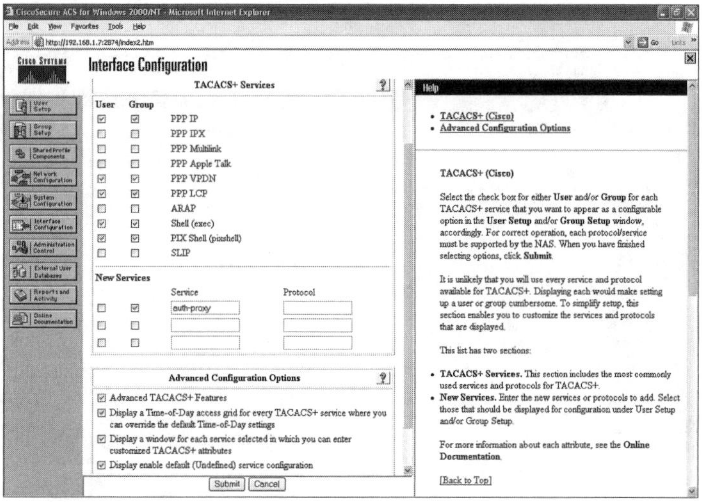

Step 4   Next you enter the Group Setup and define authentication proxy attributes, as shown in Figure 18-28. In the window, create a numbered proxy access list with the **proxyacl#***n* keyword. These access lists only allow the **permit** keyword. The source IP address should be substituted with the keyword **any**. This way, it is replaced with the actual source IP address of the host requesting the proxy authentication. Also, the privilege level for the users must be set to 15.

Step 2: Configuring AAA

On the firewall side (R6), you need to enable the AAA services as covered in other case studies. The **aaa authentication login default group TACACS+** command designates TACACS+ as the authentication method at login.

Specify authentication proxy for authorization with the following command:

```
R6(config)#aaa authorization auth-proxy default group groupname [method1]
   [method2...]
```

In this case, the syntax implemented is **aaa authorization auth-proxy default group tacacs+**.

NOTE   When configuring **aaa authorization auth-proxy**, ensure that **aaa authorization exec** isn't enabled as well. If this rule is violated and both are specified, interference results when the HTTP service tries to authenticate. As a result, the authentication fails.

Figure 18-28 *Authentication Proxy Group Setup*

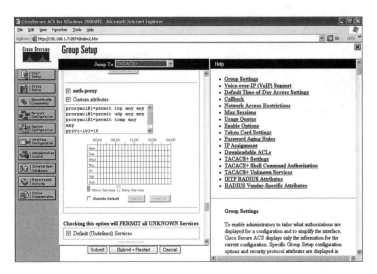

As part of authentication proxy AAA configuration, the following two tasks need to be completed:

- Authentication proxy accounting

- Configuration of TACACS+ server features

Authentication Proxy Accounting

You can also use the authentication proxy to monitor the activity of those using the proxy service. The moment an authentication proxy creates a dynamic user profile, it starts to track the host's traffic. Thus, if it's configured with the **start** option, it can generate an accounting record at that time. When the user traffic diminishes, a "stop" record that includes the total elapsed time is sent to the server. The syntax for the command available since Cisco IOS software Release 12.1T is as follows:

```
R6(config)#aaa accounting auth-proxy default start-stop group tacacs+
```

Configuring TACACS+ Server Features

As part of the AAA configuration, the TACACS+ server features need to be defined. This command specifies a AAA server:

```
R6(config)#tacacs-server host hostname [key string]
```

The *hostname* argument specifies the name or IP address of the server host—130.26.100.7 is used in this example. The optional **key** argument is used for the authentication and encryption between the router and the server. It has to match the key at the TACACS+ server.

The difference between the **key** portion of the **host** command and the universal **tacacs-server key** command shown next is that the universal **key** command dictates the key for all server hosts. The **host key** command, on the other hand, names the key for a specific host and takes precedence over the universal **key** command.

```
R6(config)#tacacs-server key key
```

Example 18-21 demonstrates the AAA portion of the authentication proxy configuration.

Example 18-21 *AAA Configuration*

```
R6#show run
hostname R6
!
aaa new-model
!
! Output omitted for brevity
!
aaa authentication login default group tacacs+
aaa authentication login no_login enable local line none
aaa authentication enable default group tacacs+
aaa authorization auth-proxy default group tacacs+
aaa authorization configuration default group tacacs+
aaa accounting auth-proxy default start-stop group tacacs+
aaa accounting exec default start-stop group tacacs+
!
tacacs-server host 130.26.100.7 key cisco6727
```

Step 3: Configuring the HTTP Server

To enable authentication proxy, the HTTP server also needs to be configured on the router. You do so with the following command:

```
R6(config)#ip http server
```

The authentication proxy uses the HTTP server to communicate with the client for user authentication. Then you need to get the HTTP server to use AAA as the authentication method. Use the following command:

```
R6(config)#ip http authentication aaa
```

Step 4: Configuring the Authentication Proxy

You enable the authentication proxy service itself by entering the following command:

```
R6(config)#ip auth-proxy auth-cache-time min
```

This command sets the idle timer for the authentication proxy. When the specified minutes elapse with no traffic passed, the user authentication entries are removed.

The following command is optional. It displays the name of the router in the authentication login dialog box.

```
R6(config)#ip auth-proxy auth-proxy-banner
```

Next you create rules that govern authentication proxy. The name of the authentication proxy specified in the following command is associated with the HTTP protocol traffic:

```
R6(config)#ip auth-proxy name auth-proxy-name http
```

Without an access list option used with the **ip auth-proxy name** command, as is the case with this scenario, the named authentication proxy rule applies to all HTTP request traffic received at the configured interface, regardless of the source.

Step 5: Applying the Authentication Proxy to an Interface

After the global authentication proxy has been configured, it needs to be applied to the appropriate interfaces. After you enter interface configuration mode, specify the named authentication proxy rule for that interface with this command:

```
R6(config-if)#ip auth-proxy auth-proxy-name
```

Example 18-22 combines the global and interface authorization proxy configuration with the HTTP server configuration.

Example 18-22 *Authentication Proxy Configuration*

```
R6#show run
hostname R6
!
! Output omitted for brevity
!
ip auth-proxy auth-proxy-banner
ip auth-proxy auth-cache-time 5
ip auth-proxy name auth http
!
interface FastEthernet0/0
ip address 130.100.26.6 255.255.255.224
ip auth-proxy auth
!
ip http server
ip http authentication aaa
```

Step 6: Verifying the Authentication Proxy

Figure 18-29 displays the user authentication screen prompted by the authentication proxy. You can see the Username and Password fields. R6's name is displayed per the **authentication-proxy-banner** command.

Figure 18-29 *Authentication Proxy Login Page*

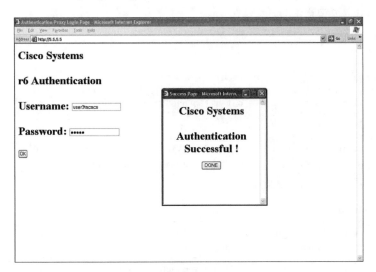

When the user profiles are dynamically added to the interface, the authentication proxy displays a notification of the successful login, as shown in Figure 18-29.

Case Study 18-5: Privilege Levels with TACACS+

This case study uses the topology of the previous study and builds on the tasks already configured (refer to Figure 18-24). This case study is meant to dive deeper into the available authentication, authorization, and accounting commands by following these steps:

Step 1   Enable AAA authentication.

Step 2   Enable AAA authorization.

Step 3   Define privilege levels.

Step 4   Enable AAA accounting.

Step 1: Enabling AAA Authentication

Example 18-23 displays the authentication commands used in this scenario.

Example 18-23 *Authentication Commands on R6*

```
R6#show run
hostname R6
!
```

continues

Example 18-23 *Authentication Commands on R6 (Continued)*

```
! Output omitted for brevity
!
aaa new-model
!
!
aaa authentication login default group tacacs+
aaa authentication login no_login enable local line none
aaa authentication enable default group tacacs+
```

Because the theory behind most of the keywords has already been explained, Table 18-1 is a quick recap of what each command is supposed to accomplish.

Table 18-1 *Authentication Command Summary*

Command	Definition
aaa authentication login default group tacacs+	Specifies the TACACS+ server as the authentication method at login for all interfaces.
aaa authentication login no_login enable local line none	Configures the method list named no_login. It's effective on those interfaces where it's applied, and it overrides the default method. The sequence of authentication methods is as follows: the **enable** password is tried first, and then the local database is consulted, and then the **line** password. Finally, if all these methods return an error, the user is granted permission without authentication.
aaa authentication enable default group tacacs+	Enables user ID and password checking by all TACACS+ hosts for users requesting privileged EXEC level.

Step 2: Enabling AAA Authorization

In Example 18-24, examine the authorization methods specified for R6.

Example 18-24 *AAA Authorization Commands on R6*

```
R6#show run
!
! Output omitted for brevity
!
aaa authorization config-commands
aaa authorization exec default group tacacs+ if-authenticated
aaa authorization commands 3 default group tacacs+
aaa authorization commands 15 default group tacacs+
aaa authorization auth-proxy default group tacacs+
aaa authorization configuration default group tacacs+
```

Table 18-2 briefly describes these authorization methods.

Table 18-2   *Authorization Command Summary*

Command	Definition
aaa authorization config-commands	Defines authorization for all EXEC mode commands, including those related to a specific privilege level. Privilege level configuration is introduced in the following section.
aaa authorization exec default group tacacs+ if-authenticated	Tells the router to contact the TACACS+ server to determine whether the user is permitted to use an EXEC shell. In case of an error from the TACACS+ server, the user is allowed to enter the shell anyway with proper authenticated.
aaa authorization commands 3 default group tacacs+ **aaa authorization commands 15 default group tacacs+**	Consults the TACACS+ server to enable authorization for specific, individual EXEC commands associated with levels 3 and 15.
aaa authorization configuration default group tacacs+	Downloads configurations from the TACACS+ server.

Step 3: Defining Privilege Levels

For the TACACS+ server to authorize the specific level commands, these levels need to be defined. Example 18-25 demonstrates the configuration of privilege level 3.

Example 18-25   *Privilege Levels*

```
R6#show run
!
! Output omitted for brevity
!
privilege configure level 3 snmp-server
privilege configure level 3 config t
privilege configure level 3 config terminal
privilege exec level 3 show start
privilege exec level 3 write memory
privilege exec level 3 config terminal
```

You can see that the user EXEC and global configuration modes at privilege level 3 have been enabled for three commands each.

Step 4: Enabling AAA Accounting

This section of the case study is dedicated to some of the available accounting commands. Up to this point, you haven't really concentrated on the accounting part of the AAA technology. This section offers an extensive list of the accounting commands and their explanations.

Cisco implements a total of seven accounting types:

- Network
- System
- EXEC
- Connection
- Commands
- Resource
- Authentication proxy

Five of them—system, EXEC, connection, resource, and authentication proxy—are used in this scenario. The EXEC and authentication proxy types were discussed in Case Studies 18-1 and 18-4, respectively. The general command syntax was presented in Case Study 18-1. To avoid repetition, only the new material is covered here. If you feel the need to review some of these concepts, refer to the previous case studies. The definitions of the remaining three types are as follows:

- **Connection**—Records all outbound connections made from R6.

- **System**—Informs on the events at the system level, such as when the system reboots or accounting is turned on or off.

- **Resource**—Provides both "start" and "stop" reports for calls that have successfully passed user authentication. It can also provide a "stop" report only for calls that failed authentication. However, the **resource** command isn't used for this purpose here.

All the accounting types specified in this case study use TACACS+ services as their accounting method.

Additional AAA accounting commands are provided in this case study. They are discussed one-by-one in this section.

You might have noticed that the network type of the AAA accounting wasn't specified as one of those used in this case study. However, the following command causes the network records to be nested within EXEC "start" and "stop" records:

```
R6(config)#aaa accounting nested
```

Now the combined start-stop records take the form of EXEC-start, network-start, network-stop, EXEC-stop.

The following command generates an accounting "stop" record for users who failed authentication. It overrides the default of generating records for only those who passed authentication:

```
R6(config)#aaa accounting send stop-record authentication failure
```

The next command presented prevents accounting records from being generated for users who do not have usernames associated with them. Sometimes because of protocol translation, the user's username string is NULL. By default, the Cisco IOS software issues accounting records for all users on the system. The following command ensures that those with the NULL username won't have the accounting records generated for them:

```
R6(config)#aaa accounting suppress null-username
```

The following command forces the interim accounting records for the system users to be sent to the AAA server:

```
R6(config)#aaa accounting update [newinfo] [periodic min]
```

When the keyword **newinfo** is specified, the records are sent every time new information is recorded. When you add **periodic**, interim accounting records are sent periodically as well.

Example 18-26 shows all the AAA accounting commands discussed in this case study.

Example 18-26 *AAA Accounting*

```
R6#show run
!
! Output omitted for brevity
!
aaa accounting suppress null-username
aaa accounting send stop-record authentication failure
aaa accounting nested
aaa accounting update newinfo periodic 5
aaa accounting auth-proxy default start-stop group tacacs+
aaa accounting exec default start-stop group tacacs+
aaa accounting connection default start-stop group tacacs+
aaa accounting system default start-stop group tacacs+
aaa accounting resource default start-stop group tacacs+
```

Case Study 18-6: Configuring PPP Callback with TACACS+

This case study is designed to demonstrate the configuration of router-client to router-callback-server with TACACS+ server. Figure 18-30 displays the topology. R6 acts as a callback client and R8 as a callback server. You learned about the PPP callback feature with local authentication in Chapter 6, "ISDN Connectivity."

Before you implement ISDN callback with TACACS+, your first task is to ensure that the callback feature works without AAA server involvement—that is, via local authentication. Also, you need to test PPP authentication with TACACS+ but without callback. If either of these testing methods fails, your callback with TACACS+ configuration will not work. This case study presumes that both of these tests returned successful results and that it is safe to continue with the configuration in question.

Figure 18-30 *PPP Callback with TACACS+ Topology*

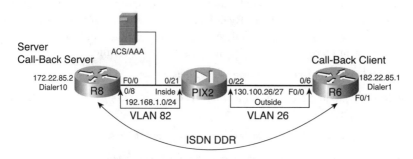

While configuring PPP callback with TACACS+, you follow these steps:

Step 1 Configure the ACS server.

Step 2 Configure the callback client.

Step 3 Configure ISDN on the callback server.

Step 4 Configure AAA on the callback server.

Step 1: Configuring ACS Server

For PPP callback with TACACS+ to work, you need to add the user information stored locally on the router (such as the callback dial string) to the user's profile on the server. Callback dial strings are used to initiate a callback to the user on a specific number for added security or reversal of line charges.

In this scenario, the telephone number is specified by the AAA server instead of letting a user specify his own.

First, you click the **Interface Configuration** button on the left side of the screen. You are taken to the Interface Configuration screen. There you select TACACS+ (Cisco IOS). In the TACACS+ Services section, make sure that the PPP IP and PPP LCP checkboxes are marked. This ensures that the PPP IP and PPP LCP options appear under the User Setup.

Click the **User Setup** button. You see the User Setup screen, shown in Figure 18-31. Under Callback, click the **Callback using this number** option. In the provided field, enter the string needed. Figure 18-31 uses 6666.

Figure 18-31 *Selecting a Callback Option in the User Setup*

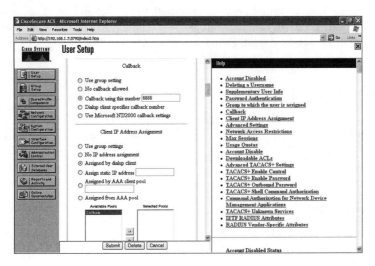

Also, check the options for PPP IP and PPP LCP under the TACACS+ Settings of the User Setup, as shown in Figure 18-32. In the PPP LCP category, check the Callback rotary box and enter the rotary group number that matches the rotary group number configured on your callback server. In this case study, you use the number 10. When you are done, click **Submit** to make the changes take effect.

Figure 18-32 *Selecting TACACS+ Options Under User Setup*

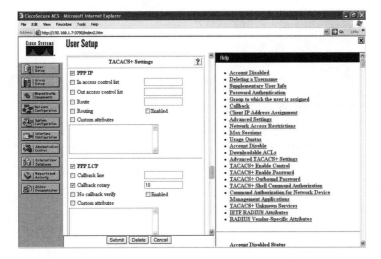

Step 2: Configuring the Callback Client

The initial callback configuration tasks on both the server and the client include the ISDN-related information. All of these commands should already be familiar to you from Chapter 6. Example 18-27 shows the full callback configuration of R6.

Example 18-27 *Callback Client Configuration of R6*

```
R6#show run
hostname R6
!
username R8 password 0 cisco
!
isdn switch-type basic-ni
!
interface BRI0/0
no ip address
encapsulation ppp
dialer pool-member 1
isdn switch-type basic-ni
isdn tei-negotiation first-call
isdn spid1 6661 6666
isdn spid2 6662 6666
no cdp enable
ppp authentication chap
!
interface Dialer1
ip address 172.22.85.2 255.255.255.0
encapsulation ppp
ip ospf cost 65535
ip ospf demand-circuit
dialer pool 1
dialer idle-timeout 60
dialer string 8888
dialer hold-queue 20
dialer-group 1
no peer default ip address
no cdp enable
ppp callback request
ppp authentication chap
ppp chap hostname R6
ppp chap password 0 cisco
!
dialer-list 1 protocol ip permit
```

Notice that the **username** command is configured on the router. This is because R6 authenticates R8 locally via PPP CHAP.

Step 3: Configuring ISDN on the Callback Server

Similar to the client, the callback server ISDN configuration was explained in Chapter 6. Example 18-28 illustrates this part of the callback setup. Note that the rotary group number matches the one in Figure 18-32. Also, no local database is configured in Example 18-28. That is why the **callin** keyword is used with the **ppp authentication chap** command to specify the one-way authentication. You can review the concept of one-way authentication in Chapter 6.

Example 18-28 *Callback Server ISDN Configuration of R8*

```
R8#show run
hostname R8!
isdn switch-type basic-ni
!
interface BRI0/0
no ip address
encapsulation ppp
ip ospf cost 65535
dialer rotary-group 10
isdn switch-type basic-ni
isdn spid1 8881 8888
isdn spid2 8882 8888
no cdp enable
ppp authentication chap
!
interface Dialer10
ip address 172.22.85.1 255.255.255.0
encapsulation ppp
ip ospf cost 65535
dialer in-band
dialer idle-timeout 60
dialer enable-timeout 5
dialer hold-queue 20
dialer-group 1
no peer default ip address
ppp callback accept
ppp authentication chap callin
!
dialer-list 1 protocol ip permit
```

Step 4: Configuring AAA on the Callback Server

You start by enabling AAA in the usual manner with the **aaa new-model** and **tacacs-server host** commands. Then you create a method list to disable authentication on the console port.

When users access the router through dialup via ISDN, the dialup sidesteps the shell entirely and instead starts a network protocol (such as PPP) as soon as the connection is established. Therefore, the **aaa authentication exec** command, which you're already familiar with, is switched with the following syntax:

```
R8(config)#aaa authentication ppp [default | list-name] [if-needed] method1
  [method2...]
```

You can specify a number of PPP login authentication methods. Among them is **group tacacs+**, used in this case study. The specific format of the command applied to this scenario is **aaa authentication ppp default group tacacs+**. This command designates the TACACS+ server as the default method of authenticating the caller.

The **aaa authorization network** command enables authorization for all network-related service requests, such as Serial Line Internet Protocol (SLIP), PPP, PPP Network Control Protocol (NCP), and Apple Remote Access Protocol (ARAP). As a result, the **aaa authorization network default group tacacs+** command used in Example 18-29 defines the network default authorization method, which specifies that TACACS+ authorization is used on serial connections using PPP. Also shown in Example 18-29, the method list is called login.

Example 18-29 *Callback Server AAA Configuration*

```
R8#show run
!
! Output omitted for brevity
!
aaa new-model
aaa authentication login none
aaa authentication ppp default group tacacs+
aaa authorization network default group tacacs+
aaa authorization configuration default group tacacs+
aaa accounting network default start-stop group tacacs+
aaa accounting system default start-stop group tacacs+
!
tacacs-server host 192.168.1.7
tacacs-server directed-request
tacacs-server key cisco6727
```

The last command of the callback server AAA setup is

```
R8(config-if)#dialer aaa
```

The **dialer aaa** command lets the dialer interface access the AAA server and retrieve the user profile from there. Example 18-30 shows how this command fits into the dialer interface configuration.

Example 18-30 *Interface Dialer Configuration with the* **dialer aaa** *Command*

```
R8#show run
!
! Output omitted for brevity
!
interface Dialer10
ip address 172.22.85.1 255.255.255.0
ip ospf cost 65535
encapsulation ppp
dialer in-band
dialer idle-timeout 60
dialer enable-timeout 5
```

Example 18-30 *Interface Dialer Configuration with the* **dialer aaa** *Command (Continued)*

```
dialer hold-queue 20
dialer aaa
dialer-group 1
no peer default ip address
ppp callback accept
ppp authentication chap callin
```

Summary

In this chapter you learned how to configure authentication, authorization, and accounting (AAA). This includes configuring the ACS server, VPN 3000 Client, Cisco router, and PIX Firewall.

AAA is an essential element of network security and an important component of the CCIE Security lab exam. This chapter has given you a broad range of the AAA setup combinations. It serves as a solid base in your preparation for becoming a network security expert.

Review Questions

1 What port does Cisco's implementation of TACACS use?

2 What port(s) does RADIUS use?

3 Which group of ISAKMP is used by VPN Client 3.x?

4 True or false: TACACS+ is not secure?

5 True or false: RADIUS is more secure than TACACS+?

6 Name at least three of the available authentication methods.

7 What do you need to do to enable the PIX Shell (pixshell) option for the Group Setup?

8 What is the syntax for configuring a Telnet password on the PIX Firewall?

9 What are the two ways of assigning a server key on a router?

10 What does the **aaa authorization exec default group tacacs+ if-authenticated** command tell the router to do?

FAQs

Q — *Can RADIUS understand Cisco IOS authorization?*

A — No. RADIUS was developed by Livingston for multivendor use. It doesn't understand Cisco IOS and therefore can't understand different privilege levels for use with command authorization.

Q — *Can TACACS+ understand Cisco IOS authorization?*

A — Yes. TACACS+ is a Cisco product and was designed to understand Cisco IOS, including command authorization.

Q — *Why do I need accounting in AAA?*

A — Accounting is used to track user activity, create billing information, and protect against repudiation by providing a record of user activity.

Q — *What is the reason to assign privilege levels with AAA?*

A — Privilege levels are meant to authorize users at a certain privilege level to a limited set of commands for security purposes.

Q — *Can PIX Firewall use TACACS+ or RADIUS?*

A — Yes. The PIX Firewall software can make equally good use of the TACACS+ and RADIUS-offered services.

Q — *Why do I need SSH authentication?*

A — SSH authentication is deployed to force a user to identify himself before gaining access via Secure Shell.

Q — *Why do I need to use NAT 0 for VPN Client networks?*

A — NAT 0 means "do not translate." In the context of VPN Client networks, it prevents the pool of reserved inside addresses that outside clients use to access the internal network from being translated back into the outside addresses.

Q — *What is the main command to query AAA authorization for callback under interface?*

A — Use the **dialer aaa** command. Don't forget to set it under the interface configuration. Otherwise, your AAA configuration for callback won't work.

This chapter covers the following topics:

- Virtual Private Network (VPN) overview

- IPSec overview

- Tunnel and transport modes

- IPSec operation

- Configuring IPSec in Cisco IOS software and PIX Firewalls

- Certificate Authority (CA) support

CHAPTER 19

Virtual Private Networks

Virtual Private Networks (VPNs) are fast becoming a widely used technology in today's modern networks. The prominence of the public Internet and advances in encryption technologies have acted as a catalyst in the adoption of VPNs. The most common type of VPN is created using the Internet Protocol Security (IPSec) framework of protocols.

This chapter covers the basic theory behind IPSec and then looks at the configuration of a simple IOS-to-IOS and PIX-to-PIX VPN using IPSec. You then delve into the deeper and more technical aspects of these configurations, which might be required for the CCIE Security lab exam.

This chapter also covers the use of preshared keys and certificate authorities before moving on to dynamic multipoint IPSec VPNs.

To be successful with the CCIE Security exam, you need expert-level knowledge of VPNs.

Virtual Private Network (VPN) Overview

A *VPN* can be defined as a method to securely transmit private data over a public infrastructure. In practice, a VPN is effectively an encrypted tunnel over a public network such as the Internet. A tunnel is created between the two VPN endpoints. Data is encrypted before leaving the local VPN endpoint and is decrypted upon arriving at the remote VPN endpoint, ensuring data privacy and security.

Traditional connectivity relies on expensive physical private circuits to connect sites. VPNs rely on the largest, most resilient network in the world—the Internet.

There are two distinct types of VPNs: site-to-site (often separated into intranet and extranet) and remote-access. The following sections describe both types in more detail.

Site-to-Site VPNs

When you have two or more business locations that require connectivity between them, you can either use a traditional connectivity method such as Frame Relay, ISDN, or ATM, or consider implementing a VPN. A site-to-site VPN provides permanent connectivity between two VPN endpoints, effectively directly connecting the two networks. A VPN endpoint device is located at each location; these are responsible for the VPN creation and the delivery of encrypted traffic over the VPN. Where more than two sites need to be linked, site-to-site VPNs are deployed in either hub-and-spoke or full-mesh topologies. Figure 19-1 shows a hub-and-spoke and fully meshed VPN.

Figure 19-1 *Hub-and-Spoke and Fully Meshed VPN*

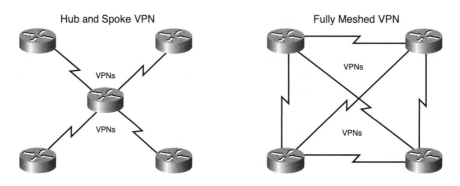

Site-to-site VPNs can be further broken into two subtypes—intranet and extranet:

- *Intranet VPNs* link enterprise customer headquarters, remote offices, and branch offices to a central internal network over a public network such as the Internet using dedicated connections. Intranet VPNs differ from extranet VPNs in that they allow access only to the company's employees.

- *Extranet VPNs* link outside customers, suppliers, partners, or communities of interest to an enterprise customer's network over a shared infrastructure using dedicated encrypted tunnels to ensure data security and privacy. Extranet VPNs differ from intranet VPNs in that they allow access to users outside the enterprise.

The key benefits of site-to-site VPNs over traditional connectivity methods are cost savings and scalability. With traditional connectivity methods, as your business grows, the requirement for extra connectivity requires a large number of private circuits. These private circuits can be either physical lines or logical virtual circuits, but either way, the costs increase greatly with each additional connected site. In an organization that is geographically dispersed or that has international costs, private circuits can be even more prohibitively expensive.

With site-to-site VPNs, connectivity is established between sites using the public Internet connection. The VPN endpoints create the VPN tunnel and transfer encrypted data between the required sites over the existing Internet connection. As you add more sites to the VPN, you must make a configuration change on the VPN endpoint. There might also be a requirement to invest further in the Internet connections at the VPN endpoints to ensure that adequate bandwidth is available for the VPN traffic.

Remote-Access VPNs

Remote-access connectivity is traditionally implemented using a dial-based infrastructure over the Public Switched Telephone Network (PSTN). This design has serious scalability issues that are directly related to cost. The more simultaneous connections you require, the more lines you have to provision into the network access server (NAS). You also have to ensure that adequate interfaces exist on the NAS and that the NAS has sufficient capacity to take the number of required interfaces.

A remote-access VPN typically uses the Internet to provide secure connectivity to remote and home-based users. Remote users connect to the Internet using their Internet service provider (ISP) and then launch a VPN client application to create the VPN tunnel to the central site, ensuring that all communications between the user's PC and the office are passed via a secure encrypted tunnel. After this is established, the user can access network resources as though they were directly connected to the business network, unless access controls have been applied to limit his or her access.

The central site no longer requires a separate dial platform, because each remote-access user enters the corporate network over the public Internet connection. This reduces the number of perimeter entry points to one—the public Internet connection. Because every perimeter access point to a network is considered a security risk, using a remote-access VPN allows security to be improved and more accurately controlled and monitored. In addition, some of the financial savings from not having to provide a dial infrastructure can be used to provide resilience on the main Internet connection in case of failure. A popular method of user connectivity is to use existing ISP flat-rate dial service offerings.

It is important to remember that the use of a remote-access VPN might require the Internet bandwidth at the central site to be increased to support the remote users. This is becoming more of a problem as high-bandwidth connectivity options such as DSL are becoming more available to the home user.

IPSec Overview

IPSec is a developing open framework of protocols from the IETF, as outlined in RFC 2401, *Security Architecture for the Internet Protocol*. (Visit www.ietf.org to search for other IPSec-related RFCs and information.) Cisco has used this framework to incorporate IPSec protocol suite features into its Cisco IOS software and PIX software.

IPSec acts at the network layer, protecting and authenticating IP packets between a VPN endpoint and other participating VPN endpoints running IPSec such as other PIX Firewalls, Cisco routers, the Cisco VPN Client, or the VPN 3000 Concentrator series.

IPSec enables the following VPN features:

- **Data confidentiality**—The IPSec sender can encrypt packets before transmitting them across a network.

- **Data integrity**—The IPSec receiver can authenticate packets sent by the IPSec sender to ensure that the data was not altered during transmission.

- **Data origin authentication**—The IPSec receiver can authenticate the source of the IPSec packets sent. This service is dependent on the data integrity service.

- **Anti-replay**—The IPSec receiver can detect and reject replayed packets.

IPSec consists of the following two main protocols:

- Authentication header (AH)

- Encapsulating Security Payload (ESP)

The following sections describe both protocols in more detail.

Authentication Header (AH)

Authentication header (AH) provides authentication and integrity to packets that are passed between two systems. This is achieved by applying a keyed one-way hash function to the packet to create a digest. A one-way hash takes the message and runs it through the hash algorithm. The result is a hash value that cannot be reversed using the same hash algorithm. This is why it is called a one-way hash. If any part of the packet is changed during transit, the receiver detects this when it performs the same one-way hash function on the packet and compares the value of the digest that the sender supplied. The fact that the one-way hash also involves the use of a shared secret between the two systems means that authenticity can be guaranteed.

NOTE   One important point to remember is that AH does *not* provide encryption. AH also does not function in tunnel mode over NAT. Because of these limiting factors, AH is rarely used in today's VPNs, although it might appear on the lab exam.

The AH function is applied to the entire packet except for any mutable IP header fields that change in transit, such as Time To Live (TTL) fields that are modified by the routers along the transmission path. AH works like this:

1 The IP header and data payload are hashed.

2 The hash is used to build a new AH header, which is prepended to the original packet.

3 The new packet is transmitted to the IPSec peer router.

The peer router hashes the IP header and data payload, extracts the transmitted hash from the AH header, and compares the two hashes. The hashes must match exactly. If even 1 bit is changed in the transmitted packet, the hash output on the received packet changes, and the AH header does not match.

Figure 19-2 illustrates this process.

Figure 19-2 *AH Authentication and Integrity*

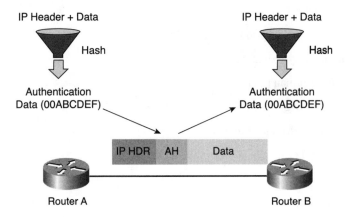

Encapsulating Security Payload (ESP)

Encapsulating Security Payload (ESP) is a security protocol that provides confidentiality (encryption), data origin authentication, integrity, optional antireplay service, and limited traffic flow confidentiality by defeating traffic flow analysis.

ESP differs from AH in that it provides confidentiality by performing encryption at the IP packet layer. It supports a variety of symmetric encryption algorithms, including Data Encryption Standard (DES), Triple DES (3DES), and Advanced Encryption Standard (AES), which you'll learn about in the next section. The default algorithm for IPSec is 56-bit DES. This cipher must be implemented to guarantee interoperability among IPSec products. Cisco products also support the use of 3DES and, more recently, AES for strong encryption. Confidentiality may be selected independent of all other services.

NOTE   A common problem is whether to use AH or ESP. The basic rule is that if you require data confidentiality through encryption, you must use ESP.

In addition to DES, 3DES, and AES, IPSec uses other existing security standards to make up a protocol suite. These are explained in the next sections.

IPSec Protocol Suite

The IPSec protocol suite has several standards that are supported by Cisco IOS software and the PIX Firewall:

- Data Encryption Standard (DES)

- Triple DES (3DES)

- Advanced Encryption Standard (AES)

- Internet Key Exchange (IKE)

- Diffie-Hellman (DH)

- Message Digest 5 (MD5)

- Secure Hash Algorithm (SHA)

- Preshared keys

- RSA signatures

- RSA encryption

- Certificate Authorities (CAs)

Data Encryption Standard (DES)

DES uses a 56-bit symmetric key, ensuring high-performance encryption. DES encrypts and decrypts the data in an IP packet. DES turns clear text into ciphertext via an encryption algorithm and a shared key. The decryption algorithm on the remote end restores clear text from ciphertext using the same key that has already been shared.

Triple DES (3DES)

Triple DES (3DES) is also a supported encryption protocol for use in IPSec on Cisco products. The 3DES algorithm is a variant of the 56-bit DES. 3DES operates similarly to DES in that data is broken into 64-bit blocks. 3DES then processes each block three times, each time with an independent 56-bit key. 3DES effectively doubles encryption strength over the 56-bit DES. 3DES makes the usual dictionary attack methods harder to use, because the clear text after the first decrypt is still considered ciphertext, so it does not match any word in the dictionary.

Advanced Encryption Standard (AES)

AES is is a Federal Information Processing Standard (FIPS) that specifies a cryptographic algorithm primarily intended to replace DES and 3DES as the standard encryption protocol. AES operates using either 128-, 192-, or 256-bit keys and has signifigant performance increases over DES and 3DES because of the way in which the algorithm is written.

Internet Key Exchange (IKE)

IKE is a hybrid protocol that provides utility services for IPSec: authentication of IPSec peers, negotiation of IKE and IPSec security associations, and establishment of keys for encryption algorithms used by IPSec.

NOTE   IKE is synonymous with Internet Security Association and Key Management Protocol (ISAKMP) in Cisco router or PIX Firewall configurations.

IKE negotiates the IPSec *security associations (SAs)*. An SA is a unidirectional relationship between two entities that describes how the entities use security services to communicate securely.

This process requires that the IPSec systems first authenticate themselves to each other and establish ISAKMP (IKE) shared keys.

In phase 1, IKE creates an authenticated, secure channel between the two IKE peers that is the IKE security association.

In phase 2, IKE negotiates the IPSec security associations and generates the required key material for IPSec.

IKE authenticates the peer and the IKE messages between the peers during IKE phase 1. Potential peers in an IPSec session must authenticate themselves to each other before IKE can proceed. The IKE protocol is very flexible and supports multiple authentication methods as part of the phase 1 exchange. The two entities must agree on a common authentication protocol through a negotiation process. IKE phase 1 has three methods to authenticate IPSec peers in Cisco products:

- **Preshared keys**—A key value entered into each peer manually (out of band) used to authenticate the peer.

- **RSA signatures**—Uses a digital certificate authenticated by an RSA signature.

- **RSA encrypted nonces**—Uses RSA encryption to encrypt a nonce value (a random number generated by the peer) and other values.

A common value used by all authentication methods is the peer identity (ID), which helps identify the peer. Some ID values used are as follows:

* The peer's IP address (four octets), such as 172.30.2.2

* The fully qualified domain name (FQDN), such as demo@example.com

Diffie-Hellman (DH)

Diffie-Hellman (DH) is a public-key cryptography protocol. It allows two parties to establish a shared secret key used by encryption algorithms (DES and MD5, for example) over an insecure communications channel. DH is used within IKE to establish session keys. 768-bit (group 1), 1024-bit (group 2), and 1536-bit (group 5) DH groups are supported in the Cisco routers and PIX Firewall. The 1536-bit group is more secure.

Message Digest 5 (MD5)

Message Digest 5 (MD5) is a hash algorithm that authenticates packet data. Cisco routers and the PIX Firewall use the MD5 Hashed Message Authentication Code (HMAC) variant, which provides an additional level of hashing. IKE, AH, and ESP use MD5 for authentication. MD5 uses a 128-bit hash.

Secure Hash Algorithm 1 (SHA-1)

Secure Hash Algorithm 1 (SHA-1) is a hash algorithm that authenticates packet data. Cisco routers and the PIX Firewall use the SHA-1 HMAC variant, which provides an additional level of hashing. IKE, AH, and ESP use SHA-1 for authentication. SHA-1 uses a 160-bit hash.

Preshared Keys

With preshared keys, the same preshared key is configured on each IPSec peer. IKE peers authenticate each other by computing and sending a keyed hash of data that includes the preshared key. If the receiving peer can independently create the same hash using its preshared key, it knows that both peers must share the same secret, thus authenticating the other peer. Configuring preshared keys is easier than manually configuring IPSec policy values on each IPSec peer, yet preshared keys do not scale well because each IPSec peer must be configured with the preshared key of every other peer it establishes a session with.

RSA Signatures

The RSA signatures method uses a digital signature in which each device digitally signs a set of data and sends it to the other party. RSA signatures use a certificate authority (CA) to generate a unique identity digital certificate that is assigned to each peer for authentication. The identity digital certificate is similar in function to the preshared key but provides protection against the generation of a weak preshared key, improved key storage, and scalability.

RSA Encryption

The RSA-encrypted nonces method uses the RSA encryption public key cryptography standard. It requires that each party generate a pseudorandom number (a nonce) and encrypt it in the other party's RSA public key. Authentication occurs when each party decrypts the other party's nonce with a local private key (and other publicly and privately available information) and then uses the decrypted nonce to compute a keyed hash. This system provides for deniable transactions. That is, either side of the exchange can plausibly deny that it took part in the exchange. Cisco IOS software is the only Cisco product that uses RSA encrypted nonces for IKE authentication. RSA encrypted nonces use the RSA public key algorithm.

CAs and Digital Certificates

The distribution of keys in a public key scheme requires some trust. If the infrastructure is untrusted and control is questionable, such as the Internet, distribution of keys is troublesome. RSA signatures are used by certificate authorities (CAs), which are trusted third-party organizations. VeriSign, Entrust, and Netscape are examples of companies that provide digital certificates. A client registers with a CA. After a CA verifies the client's credentials, a certificate is issued. The digital certificate is a package that contains information such as a certificate bearer's identity; the company, device, or individual's name and IP address; the certificate's serial number; the certificate's expiration date; and a copy of the certificate bearer's public key. The standard digital certificate format is defined in the X.509 specification. X.509 version 3 defines the data structure for certificates and is the standard that Cisco supports.

In addition to public CAs such as VeriSign, a company can create its own self-signed CA to authenticate intranet and remote-access VPNs.

Tunnel and Transport Modes

IPSec can be run in either tunnel or transport mode. Each mode has its own particular uses, and care should be taken to ensure that the correct one is selected for the solution.

Tunnel mode is most commonly used between VPN Gateways (or endpoints). This makes the VPN Gateway act as a proxy for the hosts behind it.

Transport mode is used between end stations or between an end station and a gateway if the gateway is being treated as a host, such as an encrypted Telnet session from a workstation to a router. The router is the actual destination.

The following are some examples of when to use tunnel or transport mode (see Figure 19-3):

- Tunnel mode is most commonly used to encrypt traffic between secure IPSec gateways, such as between Cisco router A and PIX Firewall B in Figure 19-3. The IPSec devices proxy IPSec for the devices behind them, such as Terry's PC and the HR servers in the figure. Terry connects to the HR servers securely through the IPSec tunnel set up between the gateways.

- Tunnel mode is also used to connect an end station running IPSec software, such as the Cisco VPN Client, to an IPSec gateway. In this instance, Terry's PC would form an IPSec tunnel with PIX Firewall B.

- Tunnel mode can also be used to set up an IPSec tunnel between Cisco router A and a server, such as the HR server, running IPSec software. Note that Cisco IOS software and the PIX Firewall set tunnel mode as the default IPSec mode.

- Transport mode is used between end stations supporting IPSec, or between an end station and a gateway if the gateway is being treated as a host. For example, transport mode would be run between router A and PIX B in Figure 19-3.

Figure 19-3 *Tunnel and Transport Mode IPSec*

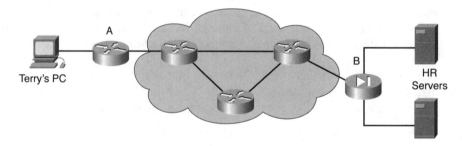

IPSec Operation

IPSec involves many component technologies and encryption methods, but its operation can be broken into five main phases:

1 **Interesting traffic initiates the IPSec process**—Traffic is deemed interesting when the IPSec security policy configured in the IPSec peers starts the IKE process. This is normally traffic that meets a special configured access list in the same way that dial traffic meets a dial access list to initiate a dial-on-demand routing (DDR) connection.

2 **IKE phase 1**—IKE authenticates IPSec peers and negotiates IKE SAs during this phase, setting up a secure channel for negotiating IPSec SAs in phase 2.

3 **IKE phase 2**—IKE negotiates IPSec SA parameters and sets up matching IPSec SAs in the peers.

4 Data transfer—Data is transferred between IPSec peers based on the IPSec parameters and keys stored in the SA database.

5 IPSec tunnel termination—IPSec SAs terminate through deletion or by timing out.

Each phase of this process is described in more detail in the following sections.

Defining Interesting Traffic

Determining what type of traffic is deemed interesting is done as part of formulating a security policy for use of a VPN. The policy is then implemented in the configuration interface for each IPSec peer. For example, in Cisco routers and PIX Firewalls, access lists are used to determine the traffic to encrypt. The access lists are assigned to a crypto policy such that **permit** statements indicate the selected traffic that must be encrypted and **deny** statements specify that the selected traffic must be sent unencrypted. The access list used for IPSec purposes does not permit or restrict access to any network resources. It simply defines which traffic is encrypted and which is not.

IKE Phase 1

The basic purpose of IKE phase 1 is to authenticate the IPSec peers and to set up a secure channel between the peers to enable IKE exchanges. IKE phase 1 performs the following functions:

- Authenticates and protects the identities of the IPSec peers

- Negotiates a matching IKE SA policy between peers to protect the IKE exchange

- Performs an authenticated Diffie-Hellman exchange that results in matching shared secret keys

- Sets up a secure tunnel to negotiate IKE phase 2 parameters

IKE phase 1 occurs in two modes: main mode and aggressive mode.

Main Mode

Main mode has three two-way exchanges between the initiator and receiver:

1 The algorithms and hashes used to secure the IKE communications are agreed on in matching IKE SAs in each peer.

2 The second exchange uses a Diffie-Hellman exchange to generate shared secret key material that generates shared secret keys and to pass nonces, which are random numbers that are sent to the other party and then are signed and returned to prove their identity.

3 The third exchange verifies the other side's identity. The identity value is the IPSec peer's IP address in encrypted form.

The primary outcome of main mode is matching IKE SAs between peers to provide a protected pipe for subsequent protected ISAKMP exchanges between the IKE peers. The IKE SA specifies the following values for the IKE exchange:

- The authentication method used

- The encryption and hash algorithms

- The Diffie-Hellman group used

- The lifetime of the IKE SA in seconds or kilobytes

- The shared secret key values for the encryption algorithms

The IKE SA in each peer is bidirectional.

Aggressive Mode

In aggressive mode, fewer exchanges are done and with fewer packets. On the first exchange, almost everything is squeezed into the proposed IKE SA values: the Diffie-Hellman public key, a nonce that the other party signs, and an identity packet that can be used to verify their identity via a third party. The receiver sends back everything that is needed to complete the exchange. The only thing left is for the initiator to confirm the exchange. The weakness of using aggressive mode is that both sides exchange information before there is a secure channel. Therefore, it is possible to sniff the wire and discover who formed the new SA. However, aggressive mode is faster than main mode.

IKE Phase 2

The purpose of IKE phase 2 is to negotiate IPSec SAs to set up the IPSec tunnel. IKE phase 2 performs the following functions:

- Negotiates IPSec SA parameters protected by an existing IKE SA

- Establishes IPSec security associations

- Periodically renegotiates IPSec SAs to ensure security

- Optionally performs an additional Diffie-Hellman exchange

IKE phase 2 has one mode—quick mode. Quick mode occurs after IKE establishes the secure tunnel in phase 1. It negotiates a shared IPSec policy, derives shared secret key material used for the IPSec security algorithms, and establishes IPSec SAs. Quick mode exchanges nonces that provide replay protection. The nonces generate new shared secret key material and prevent replay attacks from generating bogus SAs.

Quick mode is also used to renegotiate a new IPSec SA when the IPSec SA lifetime expires. Base quick mode refreshes the key material that creates the shared secret key based on the key material derived from the Diffie-Hellman exchange in phase 1.

NOTE	If perfect forward secrecy (PFS) is specified in the IPSec policy, a new Diffie-Hellman exchange is performed with each quick mode, providing key material that has greater entropy (key material life) and thereby greater resistance to cryptographic attacks. Each Diffie-Hellman exchange requires large exponentiations, thereby increasing CPU use and exacting a performance cost.

IPSec Encrypted Tunnel

After IKE phase 2 is complete and quick mode has established IPSec SAs, information is exchanged via an IPSec tunnel. Packets are encrypted and decrypted using the encryption specified in the IPSec SA. SAs are unidirectional, and a pair is created to pass traffic to and from an IPSec peer. This IPSec encrypted tunnel is shown in Figure 19-4.

Figure 19-4 *IPSec Encrypted Tunnel*

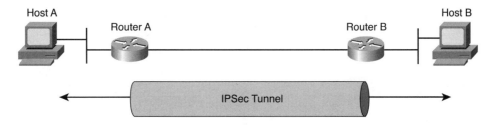

Tunnel Termination

IPSec SAs terminate through deletion or by timing out. An SA can time out when a specified number of seconds have elapsed or when a specified number of bytes have passed through the tunnel. When the SAs terminate, the keys are also discarded. When subsequent IPSec SAs are needed for a flow, IKE performs a new phase 2 negotiation and, if necessary, a new phase 1 negotiation. A successful negotiation results in new SAs and new keys. New SAs can be established before the existing SAs expire so that a given flow can continue uninterrupted.

Configuring IPSec in Cisco IOS Software and PIX Firewalls

Now that you have learned about the concepts behind VPNs and IPSec, you will start looking at the hands-on configuration tasks required to configure IPSec VPNs to the standard required for the CCIE Security lab exam.

You will start by looking at a basic IOS-to-IOS IPSec configuration and a basic PIX-to-PIX IPSec configuration, both using preshared keys. Basic **show** and **debug** commands will be explained for each technology.

You then will expand on these initial configurations and cover more-advanced scenarios.

Case Study 19-1: Configuring a Basic IOS-to-IOS IPSec VPN

This case study sets up an IPSec VPN between two IOS routers using preshared secret keys. Figure 19-5 shows the network topology you have been using throughout this book. For this initial configuration, you will use R4 and R5 to create the IPSec VPN. The requirement of the network configuration is for a VPN to be established between R3 and R4 to facilitate the protected connection from Host A to Host B.

Figure 19-5 *Topology for Configuring a Basic IOS-to-IOS IPSec VPN*

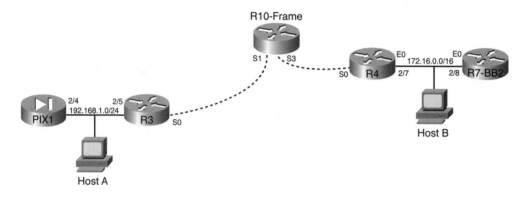

Example 19-1 shows the initial configurations.

Example 19-1 *Initial Configurations*

```
R4
 hostname R4
interface Ethernet0
 ip address 192.168.1.1 255.255.255.0
 no ip directed-broadcast
interface Serial1
 ip address 20.0.0.4 255.0.0.0
ip route 0.0.0.0 0.0.0.0 Serial1
line con 0
 exec-timeout 0 0
 transport input none
line aux 0
line vty 0 4
```

Example 19-1 *Initial Configurations (Continued)*

```
R5
hostname R5
interface Ethernet0
 ip address 172.16.0.1 255.255.0.0
 no ip directed-broadcast
interface Serial0
 ip address 20.0.0.5 255.0.0.0
 no ip directed-broadcast
ip route 0.0.0.0 0.0.0.0 Serial0
line con 0
 exec-timeout 0 0
 transport input none
line aux 0
line vty 0 4
```

R4 and R5 are both set up as the single egress point from the network, so they both have static default routes pointing to their respective serial interfaces.

Both of the routers' serial interfaces are publicly addressed and connected. Before you start the IPSec configuration, you have to ensure that these routers can communicate with each other. For the IPSec peer relationship to be formed, Layer 3 communications must be established between both peers. The best way to check this is to ping the remote IPSec peer from the local IPSec peer at each end, as shown in Example 19-2.

Example 19-2 *Testing Connectivity*

```
R4#ping 20.0.0.5

Type escape sequence to abort.
Sending 5, 100-byte ICMP Echos to 20.0.0.5, timeout is 2 seconds:
!!!!!
Success rate is 100 percent (5/5), round-trip min/avg/max = 4/6/8 ms

R5#ping 20.0.0.4

Type escape sequence to abort.
Sending 5, 100-byte ICMP Echos to 20.0.0.4, timeout is 2 seconds:
!!!!!
Success rate is 100 percent (5/5), round-trip min/avg/max = 4/5/8 ms
```

You can see from Example 19-2 that R4 can ping R5's serial interface and vice versa. This confirms that communication between these peers exists.

Now that you have a working routing configuration, you will add the IPSec components to get to a stage where you have a fully working IPSec configuration. When you reach this point, you will introduce errors to the configuration and compare the results.

You will now look at IPSec's configuration. Like the steps described in the section "IPSec Operation," IPSec configuration also can be broken into steps. Four steps are involved in configuring IPSec:

Step 1   Prepare for IKE and IPSec.

Step 2   Configure IKE.

Step 3   Configure IPSec.

Step 4   Test and verify IPSec.

The next sections describe each of these steps in more detail.

Step 1: Preparing for IKE and IPSec

Configuring IPSec encryption can be complicated. You must plan in advance to configure IPSec encryption correctly the first time and minimize misconfiguration. You should begin this task by defining the IPSec security policy based on the overall company security policy. Here are some planning tasks:

- **Determine IKE (IKE phase 1) policy** — Determine the IKE policies between IPSec peers based on the number and location of the peers.

- **Determine IPSec (IKE phase 2) policy** — Identify IPSec peer details such as IP addresses, IPSec transform sets, and IPSec modes. You then configure crypto maps to gather all IPSec policy details.

- **Check the current configuration** — Use the **show running-configuration**, **show isakmp** [**policy**], and **show crypto map** commands and the many other **show** commands to check the router's current configuration. This is covered later in this chapter when you look at verifying the IKE configuration.

- **Ensure that the network operates without encryption** — Ensure that basic connectivity has been achieved between IPSec peers using the desired IP services before configuring IPSec. You can use the **ping** command to check basic connectivity.

- **Ensure that ACLs are compatible with IPSec** — Ensure that perimeter routers and the IPSec peer router interfaces permit IPSec traffic. To accomplish this task, you need to enter the **show access-lists** command.

Step 2: Configuring IKE

The next major step in configuring Cisco IOS IPSec is to configure the IKE parameters gathered earlier. This section presents the tasks you need to complete to configure IKE policies:

- **Task 1** — Enable or disable IKE with the **crypto isakmp enable** command.

- **Task 2** — Create IKE policies with the **crypto isakmp policy** commands.

- **Task 3**—Configure preshared keys with the **crypto isakmp key** command and associated commands.

- **Task 4**—Verify the IKE configuration with the **show crypto isakmp policy** command.

Enabling or Disabling IKE

The first step in configuring IKE is to enable or disable IKE. IKE is globally enabled and disabled with the **crypto isakmp enable** command. IKE is enabled by default. Use the **no** form of the command to disable IKE.

ISAKMP does not have to be enabled for individual interfaces, but it is enabled globally for all interfaces at the router. You may choose to block ISAKMP access on interfaces not used for IPSec to prevent possible denial-of-service (DoS) attacks by using an ACL statement that blocks UDP port 500 on the interfaces. For example, you would use this command to enable IKE on your router:

```
R4(config)#crypto isakmp enable
```

Creating IKE Policies

The next task in configuring Cisco IOS IKE support is to define a suite of ISAKMP policies. The goal of defining a suite of IKE policies is to establish ISAKMP peering between two IPSec endpoints. Use the IKE policy details you gathered during the planning task.

Use the **crypto isakmp policy** command to define an IKE policy. IKE policies define a set of parameters used during the IKE negotiation. Use the **no** form of this command to delete an IKE policy. The command syntax is as follows:

```
R4(config)#crypto isakmp policy priority
```

The *priority* argument uniquely identifies the IKE policy and assigns it a priority. Use an integer from 1 to 10000, with 1 being the highest priority and 10000 being the lowest.

NOTE   Assign the most-secure policy the lowest-priority number so that the most-secure policy finds a match before any less-secure policies are configured.

The **crypto isakmp policy** command invokes the IKE policy configuration command mode (config-isakmp), where you can set IKE parameters. If you do not specify one of these commands for a policy, the default value is used for that parameter.

While in config-isakmp command mode, the keywords described in Table 19-1 are available to specify the parameters in the policy.

Table 19-1   *config-isakmp Command Mode Keywords*

Keyword	Accepted Values	Default Value	Description
encryption	des 3des	des	Message encryption algorithm.
hash	sha md5	sha	Message integrity (hash) algorithm.
authentication	rsa-sig rsa-encr pre-share	rsa-sig	Peer authentication method.
group	1 2	1	Key exchange parameters (Diffie-Hellman group identifier).
lifetime	Can specify any number of seconds.	86,400 seconds (one day)	ISAKMP-established SA's lifetime. You can usually leave this value at the default.
exit	—	—	Exits config-isakmp mode.

NOTE   Versions of the Cisco IOS software starting from 12.2(13)T might support AES.

You can configure multiple ISAKMP policies on each peer participating in IPSec. ISAKMP peers negotiate acceptable ISAKMP policies before agreeing on the SA to be used for IPSec.

When the ISAKMP negotiation begins in IKE phase 1 main mode, ISAKMP looks for an ISAKMP policy that is the same on both peers. The peer that initiates the negotiation sends all its policies to the remote peer, and the remote peer tries to find a match with its policies. The remote peer looks for a match by comparing its own highest-priority policy against the other peer's received policies in its ISAKMP policy suite. The remote peer checks each of its policies in order of priority (highest-priority first) until a match is found.

A match is made when both policies from the two peers contain the same encryption, hash, authentication, and Diffie-Hellman parameter values, and when the remote peer's policy specifies a lifetime less than or equal to the lifetime in the policy being compared. (If the lifetimes are not identical, the shorter lifetime from the remote peer's policy is used.) Assign the most-secure policy the lowest-priority number so that the most-secure policy finds a match before any less-secure policies are configured.

If no acceptable match is found, ISAKMP refuses negotiation, and IPSec is not established. If a match is found, ISAKMP completes the main mode negotiation, and IPSec SAs are created during IKE phase 2 quick mode.

Configuring Preshared Keys

IPSec peers authenticate each other during ISAKMP negotiations using the preshared key and the ISAKMP identity. The identity can be the router's IP address or host name. Cisco IOS software uses the IP address identity method by default. A command indicating address mode does not appear in the router configuration.

If you choose to use the host name identity method, you must specify the method with the **crypto isakmp identity** global configuration command. Use the **no** form of this command to reset the ISAKMP identity to the default value (address). The command syntax is as follows:

```
R4(config)#crypto isakmp identity {address | hostname}
```

The **address** keyword sets the ISAKMP identity to the IP address of the interface that is used to communicate with the remote peer during ISAKMP negotiations. This keyword typically is used when the peer uses only one interface for ISAKMP negotiations and the IP address is known.

The **hostname** keyword sets the ISAKMP identity to the host name concatenated with the domain name (for example, myhost.domain.com). This keyword should be used if more than one interface on the peer might be used for ISAKMP negotiations, or if the interface's IP address is unknown (such as with dynamically assigned IP addresses).

If you use the host name identity method, you might need to specify the host name for the remote peer if a DNS server is unavailable for name resolution. Here's an example:

```
R4(config)#ip host R5.domain.com 172.30.2.1
```

Configure a preshared authentication key with the **crypto isakmp key** global configuration command. You must configure this key whenever you specify preshared keys in an ISAKMP policy. Use the **no** form of this command to delete a preshared authentication key. The command syntax is as follows:

```
R4(config)#crypto isakmp key keystring address peer-address
R4(config)#crypto isakmp key keystring hostname peer-hostname
```

The *keystring* argument specifies the preshared key. Use any combination of alphanumeric characters up to 128 bytes. This preshared key must be identical at both peers.

The *peer-address* argument specifies the IP address of the remote peer.

The *peer-hostname* argument specifies the host name of the remote peer. This is the peer's host name concatenated with its domain name (for example, myhost.domain.com).

NOTE   A given preshared key is shared between two peers. At a given peer, you could specify the same key to share with multiple remote peers; however, a more secure approach is to specify different keys to share between different pairs of peers.

Example 19-3 shows IKE and preshared keys for R4 and R5. Note that the keystring of cisco1234 matches. The address identity method is specified. The IKE policies are compatible. Default values do not have to be configured.

Example 19-3 *IKE and Preshared Keys*

```
R4(config)#crypto isakmp key cisco1234 address 20.0.0.5
R4(config)#crypto isakmp policy 110
R4(config-isakmp)#hash md5
R4(config-isakmp)#authentication pre-share
R4(config-isakmp)#exit

R5(config)#crypto isakmp key cisco1234 address 20.0.0.4
R5(config)#crypto isakmp policy 110
R5(config-isakmp)#hash md5
R5(config-isakmp)#authentication pre-share
R5(config-isakmp)#exit
```

Verifying the IKE Configuration

You can use the **show crypto isakmp policy** command to display configured and default policies. The resultant ISAKMP policy for R4 is shown in Example 19-4. R5's configuration is identical.

Example 19-4 *IKE Policies*

```
R4#show crypto isakmp policy
Protection suite of priority 110
        encryption algorithm:    DES - Data Encryption Standard (56 bit keys).
        hash algorithm:          Message Digest 5
        authentication method:   Pre-Shared Key
        Diffie-Hellman group:    #1 (768 bit)
        lifetime:                86400 seconds, no volume limit
Default protection suite
        encryption algorithm:    DES - Data Encryption Standard (56 bit keys).
        hash algorithm:          Secure Hash Standard
        authentication method:   Rivest-Shamir-Adelman Signature
        Diffie-Hellman group:    #1 (768 bit)
        lifetime:                86400 seconds, no volume limit
```

Step 3: Configuring IPSec Parameters

The next major step in configuring Cisco IOS IPSec is to configure the IPSec parameters previously gathered. This section describes the tasks used to configure IPSec:

- **Task 1**—Configure transform set suites with the **crypto ipsec transform-set** command.

- **Task 2**—Configure global IPSec security association lifetimes with the **crypto ipsec security-association lifetime** command.

- **Task 3**—Configure crypto ACLs with the **access-list** command.
- **Task 4**—Configure crypto maps with the **crypto map** command.
- **Task 5**—Apply the crypto maps to the terminating/originating interface with the **interface** and **crypto map** commands.

Configuring Transform Set Suites

The first task in configuring Cisco IOS IPSec is to use the IPSec security policy to define a transform set. A *transform set* is a combination of individual IPSec transforms designed to enact a specific security policy for traffic. During the ISAKMP IPSec SA negotiation that occurs in IKE phase 2 quick mode, the peers agree to use a particular transform set to protect a particular data flow. Transform sets combine the following IPSec factors:

- Mechanism for payload authentication: AH transform
- Mechanism for payload encryption: ESP transform
- IPSec mode (transport versus tunnel)

Define a transform set with the **crypto ipsec transform-set** global configuration command. To delete a transform set, use the **no** form of the command. The command syntax is as follows:

```
R4(config)#crypto ipsec transform-set transform-set-name transform1 [transform2
   [transform3]]
```

The *transform-set-name* argument specifies the name of the transform set to create (or modify).

The *transform1, transform2,* and *transform3* options specify up to three transforms. These transforms define the IPSec security protocol(s) and algorithm(s).

This command invokes crypto-transform configuration mode.

You can configure multiple transform sets and then specify one or more in a crypto map entry. The transform set defined in the crypto map entry is used in the IPSec SA negotiation to protect the data flows specified by that crypto map entry's ACL. During the negotiation, the peers search for a transform set that is the same at both peers. When such a transform set is found, it is selected and applied to the protected traffic as part of both peers' IPSec SAs.

When ISAKMP is not used to establish SAs, a single transform set must be used. The transform set is not negotiated.

Transform sets are limited to one AH transform and one or two ESP transforms. Some sample combinations follow.

The following example uses ESP encryption with 56-bit DES. The transform set is called simple:

```
R4(config)#crypto ipsec transform-set simple esp-des
```

The following example uses ESP authentication with MD5 and ESP encryption with 56-bit DES:

```
R4(config)#crypto ipsec transform-set noAH esp-md5-hmac esp-des
```

The following example uses AH authentication with SHA:

```
R4(config)#crypto ipsec transform-set AUTH ah-sha-hmac
```

Follow these steps if you need to change a transform set:

Step 1   Delete the transform set from the crypto map.

Step 2   Delete the transform set from the global configuration.

Step 3   Reenter the transform set with corrections.

Step 4   Assign the transform set to a crypto map.

Step 5   Clear the SA database.

Step 6   Observe the SA negotiation and ensure that it works properly.

An alternative method is to reenter the transform set with the new transforms, as shown in Example 19-5.

Example 19-5 *Transform Sets*

```
! Was the following:
crypto ipsec transform-set R4 esp-des esp-MD5-hmac

! Change it:
R4(config)#crypto ipsec transform-set R4 esp-des
R4(cfg-crypto-trans)#exit
R4(config)#

! Now:
crypto ipsec transform-set R4 esp-des
```

Transform sets are negotiated during quick mode in IKE phase 2 using the transform sets you previously configured. Configure the transforms from most-secure to least-secure as per your policy. IPSec peers agree on one transform proposal per SA (unidirectional).

Configuring Global IPSec Security Association Lifetimes

The IPSec security association lifetime determines how long IPSec SAs remain valid before they are renegotiated. Cisco IOS software supports a global lifetime value that applies to all crypto maps. The global lifetime value can be overridden within a crypto map entry. You can change global IPSec security association lifetime values using the **crypto ipsec security-association lifetime** global configuration command. To reset a lifetime to the default value, use the **no** form of the command. The command syntax is as follows:

```
R4(config)#crypto ipsec security-association lifetime {seconds seconds | kilobytes
    kilobytes}
```

seconds *seconds* specifies the number of seconds a security association lives before expiring. The default is 3600 seconds (one hour).

kilobytes *kilobytes* specifies the volume of traffic (in kilobytes) that can pass between IPSec peers using a given security association before that security association expires. The default is 4,608,000 kilobytes.

Cisco recommends that you use the default **lifetime** values. Individual IPSec SA lifetimes can be configured using crypto maps, which are covered in the "Creating Crypto Maps" section.

Creating Crypto Access Control Lists (ACLs)

Crypto ACLs define which IP traffic is or is not protected by IPSec. This section covers how to configure crypto ACLs.

Crypto ACLs perform the following functions:

- They indicate the data flow to be protected by IPSec.

- They select outbound traffic to be protected by IPSec.

- They process inbound traffic to filter and discard traffic that should have been protected by IPSec.

- They determine whether to accept requests for IPSec SAs for the requested data flows when processing IKE negotiations.

You must use extended IP ACLs to create crypto ACLs. Crypto ACLs identify the traffic flows to be protected. Extended IP ACLs select IP traffic to encrypt by protocol, IP address, network, subnet, and port. Although the ACL syntax is unchanged from extended IP ACLs, the meanings are slightly different for crypto ACLs. **permit** specifies that matching packets must be encrypted, and **deny** specifies that matching packets need not be encrypted. Crypto ACLs behave similar to an extended IP ACL applied to outbound traffic on an interface.

The command syntax for the basic form of extended IP access lists is as follows:

```
access-list access-list-number {permit | deny} protocol source
source-wildcard destination destination-wildcard
```

The **permit** keyword causes all IP traffic that matches the specified conditions to be protected by crypto, using the policy described by the corresponding crypto map entry. The **deny** keyword instructs the router to route traffic in the clear.

source and **destination**, including the wildcards, are networks, subnets, or hosts.

protocol indicates which IP packet type(s) to encrypt.

Any unprotected inbound traffic that matches a **permit** entry in the crypto ACL for a crypto map entry flagged as IPSec is dropped, because this traffic was expected to be protected by IPSec.

If you want certain traffic to receive one combination of IPSec protection (authentication only) and other traffic to receive a different combination (both authentication and encryption), create two different crypto ACLs to define the two different types of traffic. These different ACLs are then used in different crypto map entries that specify different IPSec policies.

CAUTION   Cisco recommends that you avoid using the **any** keyword to specify source or destination addresses. The **permit any any** statement is strongly discouraged, because it causes all outbound traffic to be protected (and all protected traffic sent to the peer specified in the corresponding crypto map entry) and requires protection for all inbound traffic. Then, all inbound packets that lack IPSec protection are silently dropped, including packets for routing protocols, NTP, echo, echo response, and so on.

Cisco recommends that you configure mirror-image crypto ACLs for use by IPSec. Both inbound and outbound traffic are evaluated against the same "outbound" IPSec ACL. The ACL's criteria are applied in the forward direction to traffic exiting your router and in the reverse direction to traffic entering your router. When a router receives encrypted packets back from an IPSec peer, it uses the same ACL to determine which inbound packets to decrypt by viewing the source and destination addresses in the ACL in reverse order.

Creating Crypto Maps

Crypto map entries must be created for IPSec to set up SAs for traffic flows that must be encrypted. This section looks at the purpose of crypto maps, examines the **crypto map** command, and considers sample crypto maps.

Crypto map entries created for IPSec set up security association parameters, tying together the various parts configured for IPSec, including

- Which traffic should be protected by IPSec (crypto ACL)

- The granularity of the traffic to be protected by a set of SAs

- Where IPSec-protected traffic should be sent (who the remote IPSec peer is)

- The local address to be used for the IPSec traffic

- What IPSec security type should be applied to this traffic (transform sets)

- Whether SAs are established manually or via IKE

- Other parameters that might be necessary to define an IPSec SA

NOTE	You can apply only one crypto map set to a single interface.

If you create more than one crypto map entry for a given interface, use each map entry's sequence number (*seq-num*) to rank the map entries: The lower the *seq-num,* the higher the priority. At the interface that has the crypto map set, traffic is evaluated against higher-priority map entries first.

You must use the **crypto map** global configuration command to create or modify a crypto map entry and enter crypto map configuration mode. Set the crypto map entries referencing dynamic maps to be the lowest-priority entries in a crypto map set (that is, to have the highest sequence numbers). Use the **no** form of this command to delete a crypto map entry or set. The command syntax is as follows:

```
R4(config)#crypto map map-name seq-num ipsec-manual
R4(config)#crypto map map-name seq-num ipsec-isakmp [dynamic dynamic-map-name]
R4(config)#no crypto map map-name [seq-num]
```

map-name is the name you assign to the crypto map set, and *seq-num* is the number you assign to the crypto map entry.

The **ipsec-manual** keyword indicates that ISAKMP is not used to establish the IPSec security associations for protecting the traffic specified by this crypto map entry.

ipsec-isakmp indicates that ISAKMP is used to establish the IPSec security associations for protecting the traffic specified by this crypto map entry.

dynamic and *dynamic-map-name* are optional. **dynamic** specifies that this crypto map entry references a preexisting static crypto map. If you use this keyword, none of the crypto map configuration commands are available. *dynamic-map-name* specifies the name of the dynamic crypto map set that should be used as the policy template.

When you enter the **crypto map** command, you invoke crypto map configuration mode with the available commands shown in Example 19-6.

Example 19-6 crypto map *Commands*

```
R4(config-crypto-map)#?
  default        Set a command to its defaults
  description    Description of the crypto map statement policy
  exit           Exit from crypto map configuration mode
  match          Match values.
  no             Negate a command or set its defaults
  reverse-route  Reverse Route Injection.
  set            Set values for encryption/decryption
```

The following command has crypto map configuration mode with the commands and syntax shown in Table 19-2:

```
R4(config)#crypto map
```

Table 19-2 *Crypto Map Configuration Mode Commands and Syntax*

Command	Description
set peer [*hostname* | *ip-address*]	Specifies the allowed IPSec peer by IP address or host name.
set pfs [**group1** | **group2**]	Specifies Diffie-Hellman Group 1 or Group 2.
set transform-set [*set_name(s)*]	Specifies a list of transform sets in order of priority. For an **ipsec-manual** crypto map, you can specify only one transform set. For an **ipsec-isakmp** or **dynamic** crypto map entry, you can specify up to six transform sets.
set security-association lifetime	Sets security association lifetime parameters in seconds or kilobytes.
match address [*access-list-id* | *name*]	Identifies the extended ACL by its name or number. The value should match the *access-list-number* or *name* argument of a previously defined IP-extended ACL being matched.
description	Gives the crypto map a text description.
default	Sets a command to its default value.
reverse-route	Configures reverse route injection.
no	Deletes commands entered in the crypto map.
exit	Exits crypto map configuration mode.

After you define crypto map entries, you can assign the crypto map set to interfaces using the **crypto map** interface configuration command.

NOTE   ACLs for crypto map entries tagged as **ipsec-manual** are restricted to a single **permit** entry; subsequent entries are ignored. The security associations established by that particular crypto map entry are for only a single data flow. To be able to support multiple manually established security associations for different kinds of traffic, define multiple crypto ACLs, and then apply each one to a separate **ipsec-manual** crypto map entry. Each ACL should include one **permit** statement defining what traffic to protect.

Applying the Crypto Map to an Interface

The last step in configuring IPSec is to apply the crypto map set to an interface. Apply the crypto map to the IPSec router's interface connected to the Internet with the **crypto map** command in interface configuration mode. Use the **no** form of the command to remove the crypto map set from the interface. The command syntax is as follows:

```
R4(config-if)#crypto map map-name
```

The *map-name* argument identifies the crypto map set and is the name assigned when the crypto map is created.

As soon as you apply the crypto map, the SAs initialize. Only one crypto map set can be assigned to an interface. If multiple crypto map entries have the same *map-name* but a different *seq-num,* they are considered part of the same set and are all applied to the interface. The crypto map entry with the lowest *seq-num* is considered the highest priority and is evaluated first.

CAUTION   Be aware that applying the crypto map to an interface you are connecting through in-band terminates your session to the router if you do not have IPSec configured on your system. Because of this fact, Telnet sessions to configure IPSec should be used with caution, because it is possible to cut yourself off from Telnet access to the router if you apply the crypto map to the wrong interface. This is something to watch for on the lab exam.

Consider Example 19-7 for R4.

Example 19-7 *Applying a Crypto Map to an Interface*

```
R4(config)#interface serial 1
R4(config-if)#crypto map mymap
R4(config-if)#exit
R4(config)#
```

Example 19-7 shows that the crypto map called mymap has been applied to the Serial 1 interface on the router.

Step 4: Testing and Verifying IPSec

The Cisco IOS software contains a number of **show**, **clear**, and **debug** commands that are useful for testing and verifying IPSec and ISAKMP. You'll learn about them in this section.

You can perform the following actions to test and verify that you have correctly configured the VPN using the Cisco IOS software:

- Display your configured IKE policies using the **show crypto isakmp policy** command.

- Display your configured transform sets using the **show crypto ipsec transform set** command.

- Display the current state of your IPSec SAs with the **show crypto ipsec sa** command.

- View your configured crypto maps with the **show crypto map** command.

- Show the crypto engine information with the **show crypto engine connections active** command.

- Debug crypto engine events with the **debug crypto engine** command.

- Debug IKE and IPSec traffic through the Cisco IOS software with the **debug crypto ipsec** and **debug crypto isakmp** commands.

After you complete these tasks, you have the finished IPSec configurations, as shown in Example 19-8.

Example 19-8 *Finished IPSec Configurations*

```
R4
crypto isakmp policy 110
 authentication pre-share
 hash md5
crypto isakmp key thisshouldbeaverysecurekey address 20.0.0.5
crypto ipsec transform-set MySet esp-des esp-md5-hmac
crypto map MyMap 10 ipsec-isakmp
 set peer 20.0.0.5
 set transform-set MySet
 match address 100
interface Serial1
 ip address 20.0.0.4 255.0.0.0
 crypto map MyMap
access-list 100 permit ip 192.168.1.0 0.0.0.255 172.16.0.0 0.0.255.255

R5
crypto isakmp policy 110
 authentication pre-share
 hash md5
crypto isakmp key thisshouldbeaverysecurekey address 20.0.0.4
crypto ipsec transform-set MySet esp-des esp-md5-hmac
crypto map MyMap 10 ipsec-isakmp
 set peer 20.0.0.4
 set transform-set MySet
 match address 100
interface Serial0
 ip address 20.0.0.5 255.0.0.0
 crypto map MyMap
access-list 100 permit ip 172.16.0.0 0.0.255.255 192.168.1.0 0.0.0.255
```

With this configuration in the routers, you can verify that Host A can successfully ping Host B using the VPN.

IPSec-Related **show** Commands

The preceding section briefly covered the **show** commands that can be used for IPSec. Now that you have the configurations in the working state, this section looks at the output of a few **show** commands to ascertain what a normal configuration shows.

You can use numerous **show** commands to verify IPSec operation. These **show** commands can be split into two groups:

- **show** commands that display information about the IPSec configuration

- **show** commands that display information about the state of the IPSec connections on the router

Display **show** Commands

In this section, you look at the output of three display **show** commands:

- **show crypto ipsec transform-set**

- **show crypto map**

- **show crypto isakmp policy**

The output shown is from R4. The output from R5 in this instance is identical for the **show crypto ipsec transform-set** and **show crypto isakmp policy** commands; it must be for an IPSec peer to be established. The **show crypto map** output for R4 reflects R3 as its peer. On routers configured with multiple peers, this configuration obviously differs between routers, but any IPSec VPNs that exist between R4 and R5 must match exactly in the command's output.

The **show** command in Example 19-9 displays the configured IPSec transform set. Note that you are using esp-des and esp-md5-hmac within the transform set. The default mode for IPSec is tunnel.

Example 19-9 **show crypto ipsec transform-set** *Command*

```
R4#show crypto ipsec transform-set
Transform set MySet: { esp-des esp-md5-hmac  }
   will negotiate = { Tunnel,  },
```

The output in Example 19-10 shows the configured crypto map called MyMap. The information here pertains to the remote IPSec peer and also to the access list that controls the encryption of the IPSec traffic.

Example 19-10 **show crypto map** *Command*

```
R4#show crypto map
Crypto Map "MyMap" 10 ipsec-isakmp
        Peer = 20.0.0.5
        Extended IP access list 100
            access-list 100 permit ip 192.168.1.0 0.0.0.255 172.16.0.0 0.0.255.255
        Current peer: 20.0.0.5
        Security association lifetime: 4608000 kilobytes/3600 seconds
        PFS (Y/N): N
        Transform sets={ MySet, }
```

In Example 19-11, you can see the default policy (priority 65535, which is not shown) and the configured ISAKMP policy of 110. You can see that you are using preshared keys and Diffie-Hellman group 1.

Example 19-11 **show crypto isakmp policy** *Command*

```
R4#show crypto isakmp policy
Protection suite of priority 110
        encryption algorithm:   DES - Data Encryption Standard (56 bit keys).
        hash algorithm:         Message Digest 5
        authentication method:  Pre-Shared Key
        Diffie-Hellman group:   #1 (768 bit)
        lifetime:               86400 seconds, no volume limit
Default protection suite
        encryption algorithm:   DES - Data Encryption Standard (56 bit keys).
        hash algorithm:         Secure Hash Standard
        authentication method:  Rivest-Shamir-Adleman Signature
        Diffie-Hellman group:   #1 (768 bit)
        lifetime:               86400 seconds, no volume limit
```

Informational **show** Commands

As soon as data that matches the IPSec access list has passed the interface that has the crypto map applied to it, the VPN is established. At this point, some additional commands can be entered that show various states of the IPSec components. This section looks at **show crypto engine connections active** and **show crypto ipsec sa**. For this scenario, you will initiate a ping from Host A to Host B, and you will look at the commands on R5.

The output in Example 19-12 shows the two IPSec connections—one inbound (Decrypt) and one outbound (Encrypt). These are linked with the SAs that can be seen in the output from the **show crypto ipsec sa** command. 749 packets have been both encrypted and decrypted. These packets are the ICMP echo and echo replies that the hosts originated.

Example 19-12 show crypto engine connections active *Command*

```
R5#show crypto engine connections active

  ID Interface      IP-Address     State  Algorithm           Encrypt  Decrypt
   1 <none>         <none>         set    DES_56_CBC                0        0
   8 Serial1        20.0.0.5       set    HMAC_MD5+DES_56_CB        0      749
   9 Serial1        20.0.0.5       set    HMAC_MD5+DES_56_CB      749        0

Crypto adjacency count : Lock: 0, Unlock: 0
```

Example 19-13 shows the output of the **show crypto ipsec sa** command. This command presents a lot of information. The first part shows the interface and crypto map name that are associated with the interface. Then the inbound and outbound SAs are shown. These are either AH or ESP SAs. In this case, because you used only ESP, there are no AH inbound or outbound SAs.

You can also see next to the PERMIT statement that a condition met by an ACL initiated the IPSec connection.

Example 19-13 show crypto ipsec sa *Command*

```
R5#show crypto ipsec sa

interface: Serial1
    Crypto map tag: MyMap, local addr. 20.0.0.5

   local  ident (addr/mask/prot/port): (172.16.0.0/255.255.0.0/0/0)
   remote ident (addr/mask/prot/port): (192.168.1.0/255.255.255.0/0/0)
   current_peer: 20.0.0.4
     PERMIT, flags={origin_is_acl,}
    #pkts encaps: 1248, #pkts encrypt: 1248, #pkts digest 1248
    #pkts decaps: 1248, #pkts decrypt: 1248, #pkts verify 1248
    #send errors 1, #recv errors 0

    local crypto endpt.: 20.0.0.5, remote crypto endpt.: 20.0.0.4
    path mtu 1500, media mtu 1500
    current outbound spi: 1DE813F8

    inbound esp sas:
     spi: 0x107624CB(276178123)
       transform: esp-des esp-md5-hmac ,
       in use settings ={Tunnel, }
       slot: 0, conn id: 8, crypto map: MyMap
       sa timing: remaining key lifetime (k/sec): (4607912/3423)
       IV size: 8 bytes
       replay detection support: Y
```

continues

Example 19-13 **show crypto ipsec sa** *Command (Continued)*

```
    inbound ah sas:


    outbound esp sas:
     spi: 0x1DE813F8(501748728)
       transform: esp-des esp-md5-hmac ,
       in use settings ={Tunnel, }
       slot: 0, conn id: 9, crypto map: MyMap
       sa timing: remaining key lifetime (k/sec): (4607912/3423)
       IV size: 8 bytes
       replay detection support: Y


    outbound ah sas:
```

Troubleshooting the IPSec Configuration

In the preceding section, you successfully configured an IPSec VPN between R3 and R4. This was to provide a connection between Host A and Host B over VPN. You then ran various **show** commands and learned what to look for in a working configuration. Now that you have a working configuration, you have a platform to introduce planned errors and watch the results.

This section looks at the most common errors associated with the configuration of IPSec on the Cisco IOS software:

- Incompatible ISAKMP policies

- Differing preshared keys between the IPSec peers

- Incorrect IPSec access lists

- Incorrect crypto map placement

- Routing issues

Incompatible ISAKMP Policies

The ISAKMP policy on each IPSec peer must match for the IPSec VPN to be established. Take a look at the ISAKMP policies for R4 and R5 in Example 19-14. The command to display the ISAKMP policy is **show crypto isakmp policy**.

Example 19-14 **show crypto isakmp policy** *Command*

```
R4#show crypto isakmp policy
Protection suite of priority 110
        encryption algorithm:   DES - Data Encryption Standard (56 bit keys).
        hash algorithm:         Message Digest 5
        authentication method:  Pre-Shared Key
```

Example 19-14 **show crypto isakmp policy** *Command (Continued)*

```
            Diffie-Hellman group:    #1 (768 bit)
            lifetime:                86400 seconds, no volume limit
Default protection suite
            encryption algorithm:    DES - Data Encryption Standard (56 bit keys).
            hash algorithm:          Secure Hash Standard
            authentication method:   Rivest-Shamir-Adleman Signature
            Diffie-Hellman group:    #1 (768 bit)
            lifetime:                86400 seconds, no volume limit

R5#show crypto isakmp policy
Protection suite of priority 110
            encryption algorithm:    DES - Data Encryption Standard (56 bit keys).
            hash algorithm:          Message Digest 5
            authentication method:   Pre-Shared Key
            Diffie-Hellman group:    #1 (768 bit)
            lifetime:                86400 seconds, no volume limit
Default protection suite
            encryption algorithm:    DES - Data Encryption Standard (56 bit keys).
            hash algorithm:          Secure Hash Standard
            authentication method:   Rivest-Shamir-Adleman Signature
            Diffie-Hellman group:    #1 (768 bit)
            lifetime:                86400 seconds, no volume limit
```

You can see from Example 19-14 that both of these routers have two ISAKMP policies, or protection suites. The first has a priority of 110, and the default has a priority of 65535 (this value is not shown). You can also see that the values for the priority 110 suite all match between Routers 4 and 5. This is essential for ISAKMP negotiation.

The values controlled by the ISAKMP policy are

- Encryption algorithm

- Hash algorithm

- Authentication method

- Diffie-Hellman group

- SA lifetime

All these values can be set from ISAKMP configuration mode on the Cisco IOS router. The output in Example 19-15 shows the available commands from ISAKMP configuration mode on the router.

Example 19-15 *Commands Available from ISAKMP Configuration Mode*

```
ISAKMP commands:
  authentication  Set authentication method for protection suite
  default         Set a command to its defaults
```

continues

Example 19-15 *Commands Available from ISAKMP Configuration Mode (Continued)*

```
encryption     Set encryption algorithm for protection suite
exit           Exit from ISAKMP protection suite configuration mode
group          Set the Diffie-Hellman group
hash           Set hash algorithm for protection suite
lifetime       Set lifetime for ISAKMP security association
no             Negate a command or set its defaults
```

In addition to the **show** commands, the command **debug crypto isakmp** is useful when troubleshooting ISAKMP issues. This command actually displays the full ISAKMP exchange as it occurs in the router. The full debug output for a ping from the E0 interface of R4 to the E0 interface of R5 is shown in Example 19-16.

Example 19-16 **debug crypto isakmp** *Command*

```
R4#debug crypto isakmp
00:42:43: ISAKMP (4): beginning Main Mode exchange
00:42:43: ISAKMP (4): sending packet to 20.0.0.5 (I) MM_NO_STATE.
00:42:44: ISAKMP (4): received packet from 20.0.0.5 (I) MM_NO_STATE
00:42:44: ISAKMP (4): processing SA payload. message ID = 0
00:42:44: ISAKMP (4): Checking ISAKMP transform 1 against priority 10 policy
00:42:44: ISAKMP:      encryption DES-CBC
00:42:44: ISAKMP:      hash MD5
00:42:44: ISAKMP:      default group 1
00:42:44: ISAKMP:      auth pre-share
00:42:44: ISAKMP (4): atts are acceptable. Next payload is 0
00:42:46: ISAKMP (4): SA is doing pre-shared key authentication using id type ID
_IPV.4_ADDR
00:42:46: ISAKMP (4): sending packet to 20.0.0.5 (I) MM_SA_SETUP.
00:42:48: ISAKMP (4): received packet from 20.0.0.5 (I) MM_SA_SETUP
00:42:48: ISAKMP (4): processing KE payload. message ID = 0
00:42:50: ISAKMP (4): processing NONCE payload. message ID = 0
00:42:50: ISAKMP (4): SKEYID state generated
00:42:50: ISAKMP (4): processing vendor id payload
00:42:50: ISAKMP (4): speaking to another IOS box!
00:42:50: ISAKMP (4): ID payload
         next-payload : 8
         type         : 1
         protocol     : 17
         port         : 500
         length       : 8
00:42:50: ISAKMP (4): Total payload length: 12
00:42:50: ISAKMP (4): sending packet to 20.0.0.5 (I) MM_KEY_EXCH
00:42:50: ISAKMP (4): received packet from 20.0.0.5 (I) MM_KEY_EXCH
00:42:50: ISAKMP (4): processing ID payload. message ID = 0
00:42:50: ISAKMP (4): processing HASH payload. message ID = 0
00:42:50: ISAKMP (4): SA has been authenticated with 20.0.0.5
00:42:50: ISAKMP (4): beginning Quick Mode exchange, M-ID of 1397342770
00:42:50: ISAKMP (4): sending packet to 20.0.0.5 (I) QM_IDLE
00:42:51: ISAKMP (4): received packet from 20.0.0.5 (I) QM_IDLE
00:42:51: ISAKMP (4): processing SA payload. message ID = 1397342770
```

Example 19-16 debug crypto isakmp *Command (Continued)*

```
00:42:51: ISAKMP (4): Checking IPSec proposal 1
00:42:51: ISAKMP: transform 1, ESP_DES
00:42:51: ISAKMP:   attributes in transform:
00:42:51: ISAKMP:      encaps is 1
00:42:51: ISAKMP:      SA life type in seconds
00:42:51: ISAKMP:      SA life duration (basic) of 3600
00:42:51: ISAKMP:      SA life type in kilobytes
00:42:51: ISAKMP:      SA life duration (VPI) of  0x0 0x46 0x50 0x0
00:42:51: ISAKMP:      authenticator is HMAC-MD5
00:42:51: ISAKMP (4): atts are acceptable.
00:42:51: ISAKMP (4): processing NONCE payload. message ID = 1397342770
00:42:51: ISAKMP (4): processing ID payload. message ID = 1397342770
00:42:51: ISAKMP (4): unknown error extracting ID
00:42:51: ISAKMP (4): processing ID payload. message ID = 1397342770
00:42:51: ISAKMP (4): unknown error extracting ID
00:42:51: ISAKMP (4): Creating IPSec SAs
00:42:51:        inbound SA from 20.0.0.5     to 20.0.0.4     (proxy 172.16.0.0
       to 192.168.1.0    )
00:42:51:        has spi 167445490 and conn_id 5 and flags 4
00:42:51:        lifetime of 3600 seconds
00:42:51:        lifetime of 4608000 kilobytes
00:42:51:        outbound SA from 20.0.0.4    to 20.0.0.5     (proxy 192.168.1.0
       to 172.16.0.0    )
00:42:51:        has spi 102963262 and conn_id 6 and flags 4
00:42:51:        lifetime of 3600 seconds
00:42:51:        lifetime of 4608000 kilobytes
00:42:51: ISAKMP (4): sending packet to 20.0.0.5 (I) QM_IDLE
```

In this output, notice the highlighted section. It shows that the ISAKMP values are acceptable, and then the router continues with the ISAKMP negotiation process.

Example 19-16 shows what the debug output looks like in a working configuration. If you change a value in the ISAKMP policy, though, you change the hash value from MD5 to SHA on R4. Then observe the output from the **debug crypto isakmp** command.

First, look at the newly configured ISAKMP policy on R4 in Example 19-17.

Example 19-17 show crypto isakmp policy *Command*

```
R4#show crypto isakmp policy
Protection suite of priority 110
        encryption algorithm:   DES - Data Encryption Standard (56 bit keys).
        hash algorithm:         Secure Hash Standard
        authentication method:  Pre-Shared Key
        Diffie-Hellman group:   #1 (768 bit)
        lifetime:               86400 seconds, no volume limit
Default protection suite
        encryption algorithm:   DES - Data Encryption Standard (56 bit keys).
```

continues

Example 19-17 **show crypto isakmp policy** *Command (Continued)*

```
        hash algorithm:            Secure Hash Standard
        authentication method:     Rivest-Shamir-Adleman Signature
        Diffie-Hellman group:      #1 (768 bit)
        lifetime:                  86400 seconds, no volume limit
```

The shaded line shows that the hash algorithm has been changed from MD5 to SHA. Now carry out the same ping as before and look at the debug output (see Example 19-18).

Example 19-18 **debug crypto isakmp** *Command*

```
R4#debug crypto isakmp
01:43:48: ISAKMP (7): beginning Main Mode exchange
01:43:48: ISAKMP (7): sending packet to 20.0.0.5 (I) MM_NO_STATE
01:43:48: ISAKMP (7): received packet from 20.0.0.5 (I) MM_NO_STATE
01:43:48: %CRYPTO-6-IKMP_MODE_FAILURE: Processing of Informational mode failed
  with peer at 20.0.0.5
```

You can see from this debug output that there was a failure in the ISAKMP negotiation.

Differing Preshared Keys Between the IPSec Peers

The preshared secret keys must be exactly the same on both the IPSec peers. These keys are compared during ISAKMP phase 1 authentication. Ensure that both routers are using preshared authentication in their ISAKMP policies. This can be done with the **show crypto isakmp** command. Example 19-19 shows the result of the **show crypto isakmp policy** command on Routers 4 and 5.

Example 19-19 **show crypto isakmp policy** *Command*

```
R4#show crypto isakmp policy
Protection suite of priority 110
        encryption algorithm:      DES - Data Encryption Standard (56 bit keys).
        hash algorithm:            Message Digest 5
        authentication method:     Pre-Shared Key
        Diffie-Hellman group:      #1 (768 bit)
        lifetime:                  86400 seconds, no volume limit
Default protection suite
        encryption algorithm:      DES - Data Encryption Standard (56 bit keys).
        hash algorithm:            Secure Hash Standard
        authentication method:     Rivest-Shamir-Adleman Signature
        Diffie-Hellman group:      #1 (768 bit)
        lifetime:                  86400 seconds, no volume limit

R5#show crypto isakmp policy
Protection suite of priority 10
        encryption algorithm:      DES - Data Encryption Standard (56 bit keys).
```

Example 19-19 **show crypto isakmp policy** *Command (Continued)*

```
          hash algorithm:          Message Digest 5
          authentication method:   Pre-Shared Key
          Diffie-Hellman group:    #1 (768 bit)
          lifetime:                86400 seconds, no volume limit
Default protection suite
          encryption algorithm:    DES - Data Encryption Standard (56 bit keys).
          hash algorithm:          Secure Hash Standard
          authentication method:   Rivest-Shamir-Adleman Signature
          Diffie-Hellman group:    #1 (768 bit)
          lifetime:                86400 seconds, no volume limit
```

Check that the authentication method on both routers is set to preshared key; you can see from the shaded lines in the example that it is. If the authentication methods do not match between the routers, the ISAKMP negotiation fails, as outlined in the previous section.

You know that the routers are both using preshared keys as their authentication method. You will now look at the preshared keys on both routers with the **show crypto isakmp key** command (see Example 19-20).

Example 19-20 **show crypto isakmp key** *Command*

```
R4#show crypto isakmp key
Hostname/Address         Preshared Key
20.0.0.5                 thisshouldbeaverysecurekey

R5#show crypto isakmp key
Hostname/Address         Preshared Key
20.0.0.4                 thisshouldbeaverysecurekey
```

Example 19-20 shows the preshared keys for both R4 and R5. You can see that they match. You now will change the key value for R4 to wrongkey. Example 19-21 shows the new output of the **show crypto isakmp key** command on R3.

Example 19-21 **show crypto isakmp key** *Command*

```
R4#show crypto isakmp key
Hostname/Address         Preshared Key
20.0.0.5                 wrongkey
```

This output shows that the preshared key for the IPSec peer 20.0.0.5 is now wrongkey.

After this configuration change, when you try to ping from Host A to Host B, R4 displays the following debug message:

```
%CRYPTO-4-IKMP_BAD_MESSAGE:
IKE message from 20.0.0.5 failed its sanity check or is malformed
```

This informs you that the preshared keys do not match.

Incorrect IPSec Access Lists

The IPSec access list triggers the VPN to be set up between the IPSec peers. This access list operates in a very similar manner to an access list that is used for DDR. With DDR, interesting traffic (as defined by the access list) causes the BRI interface to be raised and the ISDN call placed. The same is true of the IPSec access list. In the initial state, traffic that meets the access list initiates the IPSec process. As soon as the IPSec connection is established, only traffic that meets the IPSec access list is encrypted and delivered through the IPSec tunnel. This is a very important point to remember. It's where the IPSec access list differs from the DDR access list.

In the scenario you have been using in this chapter, you have an access list on both R4 and R5. These access lists mirror each other. The source in the R4 access list is the destination in the R5 access list, and vice versa. The access lists you are using encrypt anything from the local Ethernet network to the remote Ethernet network.

To introduce an error, change the IPSec access list on R4 to have an incorrect source address. Then ping from Host A to Host B. The traffic does not kick off the IPSec process and cannot be routed to the destination.

The current IPSec access list on R4 is shown in Example 19-22.

Example 19-22 *IPSec Access List*

```
R4#show ip access
Extended IP access list 100
    permit ip 192.168.1.0 0.0.0.255 172.16.0.0 0.0.255.255
```

This access list encrypts traffic from the 192.168.1.0/24 network that is destined for the 172.16.0.0/16 network. You will make a subtle change to this access list that will break the IPSec process. You will remove the existing access list and add the following line of configuration:

```
R4(config)#access-list 100 permit ip 192.168.2.0 0.0.0.255
   172.16.0.0 0.0.255.255
```

Note that this line encrypts traffic from the 192.168.2.0/24 network and not the original 192.168.1.0/24 network. After you make this change, Host A attempts to ping Host B. Obviously, this fails.

If you are ever faced with a real-world problem similar to this, your first step should always be to ascertain whether the VPN is established between the IPSec peers. There are various ways to accomplish this on a Cisco IOS router. The easiest way is to use the **show crypto engine connections active** command. This command displays the current state of the IPSec connections (if any). Example 19-23 shows the result of running this command on R3.

Example 19-23 show crypto engine *Command*

```
R4#show crypto engine connections active

 ID Interface      IP-Address      State  Algorithm      Encrypt  Decrypt

Crypto adjacency count : Lock: 0, Unlock: 0
```

You can see that there are no active IPSec connections. If you can verify that relevant traffic has passed the connection that should start the IPSec process, the problem is with the IPSec access list. A simple sanity check of the IPSec access list should be enough to remedy the problem.

Incorrect Crypto Map Placement

On the VPN terminating interface, you have to apply the crypto map. For example, to apply crypto map MyMap to the Serial 1 interface, the command is

```
R4(config-if)#crypto map mymap
```

This command makes the interface a VPN termination point. Any traffic leaving this interface is checked against the IPSec access list. If the traffic matches the IPSec access list, it is encrypted to the standard defined in the related transform set and is delivered to the IPSec peer as defined in the crypto map. A useful command for looking at the crypto map applied to an interface is **show crypto map interface serial 1**. Example 19-24 shows this command run on R4.

Example 19-24 show crypto map *Command*

```
R4#show crypto map interface serial 1
Crypto Map "MyMap" 10 ipsec-isakmp
        Peer = 20.0.0.5
        Extended IP access list 100
            access-list 100 permit ip 192.168.1.0 0.0.0.255 172.16.0.0 0.0.255.255
        Current peer: 20.0.0.5
        Security association lifetime: 4608000 kilobytes/3600 seconds
        PFS (Y/N): N
        Transform sets={ MySet, }
```

You can see from the output in Example 19-24 that crypto map MyMap is applied to the Serial 1 interface. The output of this command also shows the IPSec access list, IPSec peer, SA settings, PFS status, and the related transform set.

If there is a problem with IPSec traffic and you have confirmed that the IPSec access list is correct, the crypto map placement might be a good next thing to check. If the crypto map is not applied to the outbound interface, traffic will never get encrypted for IPSec to forward it to its peer.

If physical as well as logical interfaces are involved in carrying outgoing traffic, the crypto map needs to be applied to both.

One example of this is if you use a GRE tunnel. The GRE tunnel interface uses a tunnel source and tunnel destination. In this case, apply the crypto map to both the tunnel interface and the physical interface that the tunnel traffic is routed over.

Routing Issues

You must address two routing issues—routing to the IPSec peer and routing the required packets to the interface with the crypto map applied. Both these issues can cause problems that result in the failure of the IPSec process.

Layer 3 communication must be established between the IPSec peers. This was covered at the start of this chapter when VPNs were introduced. You learned that a simple ping between the IPSec peers is adequate to confirm this. If the IPSec peers cannot establish Layer 3 communications, the IPSec process will never be complete, and the peers will never be adjacent to each other.

The other routing issue is related to the delivery of the packets from the local router to the remote network over the IPSec tunnel. In this scenario, Host A is on network 192.168.1.0/24 and Host B is on network 172.16.0.0/16 (refer to Figure 19-5 if you need to refresh your memory). For Host A to communicate with Host B, a valid route has to exist in R3's IP routing table to the Host B network address. This follows basic IP routing principles. Looking at the IP routing table shown in Example 19-25, you can see that a default route exists out of the Serial 0 interface.

Example 19-25 show ip route *Command*

```
R4#show ip route
C    20.0.0.0/8 is directly connected, Serial1
C    192.168.1.0/24 is directly connected, Ethernet0
S*   0.0.0.0/0 is directly connected, Serial1
```

Because you are using a static default route, this should not cause a problem with the routing of the packets. Host A sends a packet with a source address of 192.168.1.2 and a destination address of 172.16.0.2. R3 does not have a specific route for the 172.16.0.0/16 network, but the default route directs it at the Serial 0 interface. The crypto map is applied to the Serial 0 interface, and the traffic matches the IPSec access list so that it gets encrypted and tunneled to the destination.

The important part to remember is that you have to ensure that the router forwards the packet to the interface where the crypto map exists. A default route or a specific route for the remote network normally suffices in this situation.

This concludes the explanation of how to configure a basic IOS-to-IOS IPSec VPN. In the next section, you configure a basic PIX-to-PIX IPSec VPN.

Case Study 19-2: Configuring a Basic PIX-to-PIX IPSec VPN

Now that you have covered the basic configuration of an IOS-to-IOS IPSec VPN, this configuration sets up an IPSec VPN between two PIX Firewalls using preshared secret keys.

Figure 19-6 shows the network topology that you have been using throughout this book. For this initial configuration, you will use PIX1 and PIX2 to create the IPSec VPN. The requirement of the network configuration is for a VPN to be established between PIX1 and PIX2 to facilitate the protected connection from Host A to Host B.

Figure 19-6 *Topology for Configuring a Basic PIX-to-PIX IPSec VPN*

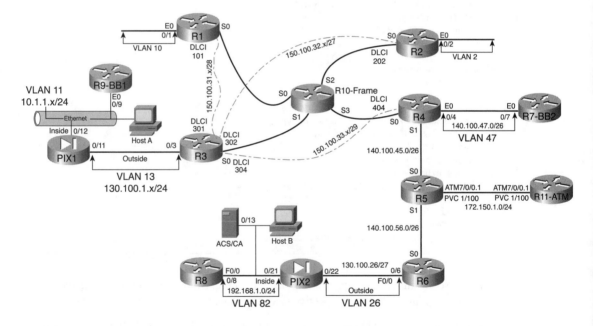

You now will look at the configuration of IPSec on the PIX Firewall. The configuration of IPSec on the PIX follows the same four steps as the configuration of IPSec on IOS routers:

Step 1 Prepare for IKE and IPSec.

Step 2 Configure IKE.

Step 3 Configure IPSec.

Step 4 Test and verify IPSec.

The next sections cover these four steps with a view to the configuration of a Cisco PIX IPSec VPN.

Example 19-26 shows the initial configurations.

Example 19-26 *Initial PIX Configurations*

```
PIX1#write terminal
PIX Version 6.1
nameif ethernet0 outside security0
nameif ethernet1 inside security100
enable password 8Ry2YjIyt7RRXU24 encrypted
passwd 2KFQnbNIdI.2KYOU encrypted
hostname PIX1
interface ethernet0 auto
interface ethernet1 auto
ip address outside 130.100.1.1 255.255.255.0
ip address inside 10.1.1.1 255.255.255.0
global (outside) 1 interface
nat (inside) 1 0.0.0.0 0.0.0.0 0 0
route outside 0.0.0.0 0.0.0.0 130.100.1.3 1

PIX2#write terminal
PIX Version 6.1
nameif ethernet0 outside security0
nameif ethernet1 inside security100
enable password 8Ry2YjIyt7RRXU24 encrypted
passwd 2KFQnbNIdI.2KYOU encrypted
hostname PIX2
interface ethernet0 auto
interface ethernet1 auto
ip address outside 130.100.26.1 255.255.255.224
ip address inside 192.168.1.1 255.255.255.0
global (outside) 1 interface
nat (inside) 1 0.0.0.0 0.0.0.0 0 0
route outside 0.0.0.0 0.0.0.0 130.100.26.6 1
```

Both of these firewalls are set up as the single egress point from the network, so both have static default routes pointing to their respective next-hop routers.

Both next-hop routers are connected via a routing protocol. This provides the connectivity required to form communication between PIX1 and PIX2. Before you start the IPSec configuration, ensure that the PIX Firewalls can communicate with each other. For the IPSec peer relationship to be formed, Layer 3 communications must be established between both peers.

The best way to check this is to ping the remote IPSec peer from the local IPSec peer at each end, as shown in Example 19-27.

Example 19-27 *Result of a Ping Between PIX1 and PIX2*

```
PIX1#ping 130.100.26.1
        130.100.26.1response received -- 0ms
        130.100.26.1response received -- 0ms
        130.100.26.1response received -- 0ms

PIX2#ping 130.100.1.1
        130.100.1.1response received -- 0ms
        130.100.1.1response received -- 0ms
        130.100.1.1response received -- 0ms
```

You can see from the results that PIX1 can ping the outside interface of PIX2 and vice versa. This confirms that communication between these peers exists.

Now that you have a working routing configuration, you will add the IPSec components to get to a stage where you have a fully working IPSec configuration. After you have reached this point, you will then introduce errors to the configuration and compare the results.

Step 1: Preparing for IKE and IPSec

Successful implementation of an IPSec network requires advanced preparation before you start configuring individual PIX Firewalls.

You should begin this task by defining the IPSec security policy based on the overall company security policy. The tasks required are exactly the same as those for the IOS Firewall IPSec VPN:

- Determine IKE (IKE phase 1) policy.

- Determine IPSec (IKE phase 2) policy.

- Check the current configuration.

- Ensure that the network operates without encryption.

- Ensure that ACLs are compatible with IPSec.

Step 2: Configuring IKE

The next major task in configuring the PIX Firewall is to configure the IKE parameters gathered earlier. This section describes the tasks you need to complete to configure IKE policies:

- **Task 1**—Enable or disable IKE with the **isakmp enable** command.

- **Task 2**—Create IKE policies with the **isakmp policy** command.

- **Task 3**—Configure preshared keys with the **isakmp key** command.

- **Task 4**—Verify IKE configuration with the **show isakmp** [**policy**] command.

Enabling or Disabling IKE

Enable or disable IKE (ISAKMP) negotiation for authentication and key exchange with the following command:

```
PIX1(config)#isakmp enable interface-name
```

Specify the PIX Firewall interface on which the IPSec peer will communicate. IKE is enabled by default for individual PIX Firewall interfaces.

Use the **no isakmp enable** *interface-name* command to disable IKE.

You might want to disable IKE on interfaces that do not terminate IKE and IPSec to prevent possible DoS attacks on those interfaces.

NOTE   PIX Firewall version 5.1 and later supports IPSec termination on any interface.

Creating IKE Policies

The next task in configuring IKE support is to define a suite of IKE policies. The goal is to establish IKE peering between two IPSec endpoints. Use the IKE policy details gathered during the planning task.

Use the **isakmp policy** command to define an IKE policy. IKE policies define a set of parameters used during the IKE negotiation:

Step 1   Identify the policy with a unique priority number between 1 and 65000 using the following command:

```
PIX1(config)#isakmp policy name priority
```

Step 2   Specify the encryption algorithm. The default is **des**:

```
PIX1(config)#isakmp policy priority encryption des | 3des
```

Step 3   Specify the hash algorithm. The default is **sha**:

```
PIX1(config)#isakmp policy priority hash md5 | sha
```

Step 4   Specify the authentication method. The default is **rsa-sig**:

```
PIX1(config)#isakmp policy priority authentication pre-share | rsa-sig
```

Step 5   Specify the Diffie-Hellman group identifier. The default is **group 1**:

```
PIX1(config)#isakmp policy priority group 1 | 2
```

Step 6   Specify the IKE security association's lifetime. The default is 86400:

```
PIX1(config)#isakmp policy priority lifetime seconds
```

NOTE	PIX Firewall software has preset default values. If you enter a default value for a given policy parameter, it is not written in the configuration. If you do not specify a value for a given policy parameter, the default value is assigned. You can observe configured and default values with the **show isakmp policy** command.

Configuring Preshared Keys

IPSec peers authenticate each other during ISAKMP negotiations using the preshared key and the ISAKMP identity. The identity can be the PIX Firewall's IP address or host name. Configure the IKE preshared key by completing the following actions:

Step 1   Specify the ISAKMP identity mode as either **address** or **hostname** (optional):

```
PIX1(config)#isakmp identity {address | hostname}
```

The default value is to use the peer's IP address as the identity.

Step 2   Choose **hostname** if the host name is specified in the **isakmp key** command.

Use this setting consistently across peers using preshared keys.

Step 3   Specify name-to-address mapping (optional):

```
PIX1(config)#name ip_address name
```

The **name** command defines name-to-address mapping.

This command is not necessary if the destination host names are already mapped in a Domain Name System (DNS) server.

Step 4   Specify the preshared key:

```
PIX1(config)#isakmp key keystring address peer-address
```

The **isakmp key** command assigns a keystring and the peer address. The pre-shared keystring must be identical at both peers. You can use any combination of alphanumeric characters up to 128 bytes for keystring. You can specify the peer-address as the host or wildcard address. The *keystring* is any combination of alphanumeric characters up to 128 bytes. The *peer-address* should point to the IPSec peer's IP address. A wildcard peer address of 0.0.0.0 may be configured to share the preshared key among many peers. However, Cisco strongly recommends using a unique key for each site-to-site VPN peer. Remote-access VPNs can use the wildcard preshared key, as with a remote-access VPN; you might not know the remote peer's IP address.

You can also use the peer's host name for the preshared key. Preshared keys are easy to configure but are not scalable.

Verifying IKE Phase 1 Policies

The **write terminal** command displays configured policies. A condensed example is shown in Example 19-28. Some of the values for the ISAKMP policy are the defaults and would not show up in your configuration, but they are included here for you to see. Note that the preshared key is cisco1234 and the peer is PIX2 at 192.168.2.2.

Example 19-28 *Verifying IKE Phase 1*

```
PIX1#write terminal
hostname pix1
isakmp enable outside
isakmp key cisco1234 address 130.100.26.1 netmask 255.255.255.255
isakmp policy 10 authentication pre-share
isakmp policy 10 encryption des
isakmp policy 10 hash sha
isakmp policy 10 group 1
isakmp policy 10 lifetime 86400
```

The **show isakmp policy** command displays configured and default policies.

The **show isakmp** command, shown in Example 19-29, displays configured policies much as they would appear with the **write terminal** command.

Example 19-29 **show isakmp** *Command*

```
PIX1(config)#show isakmp
isakmp enable outside
isakmp key cisco1234 address 130.100.26.1 netmask 255.255.255.255
isakmp policy 10 authentication pre-share
isakmp policy 10 encryption des
isakmp policy 10 hash sha
isakmp policy 10 group 1
isakmp policy 10 lifetime 86400
```

Step 3: Configuring PIX Firewall IPSec

The next step in configuring IPSec on the PIX Firewall is to configure the IPSec parameters you determined in Step 1. This section presents the tasks to configure IPSec parameters for IKE preshared keys.

The general tasks and commands used to configure IPSec encryption on the PIX Firewall are as follows. Subsequent sections of this chapter discuss each task in detail.

- **Task 1**—Configure crypto access lists with the **access-list** command.

- **Task 2**—Configure transform set suites with the **crypto ipsec transform-set** command.

- **Task 3**—Configure global IPSec SA lifetimes with the **crypto ipsec security-association lifetime** command (optional).

- **Task 4**—Configure crypto maps with the **crypto map** command.

- **Task 5**—Apply crypto maps to the terminating/originating interface with the **crypto map** *map-name* interface command.

- **Task 6**—Verify IPSec configuration with the various **show** commands.

Use the **sysopt connection permit-ipsec** command in IPSec configurations to permit IPSec traffic to pass through the PIX Firewall without a check of the **conduit** or **access-list** command statements.

By default, any inbound session on a PIX Firewall must be explicitly permitted by a **conduit** or **access-list** command statement. With IPSec protected traffic, the secondary access list check could be redundant. To allow an IPSec authenticated/cipher inbound session to always be permitted, enable **sysopt connection permit-ipsec**. Inbound traffic, even though it bypasses any external conduits or access lists, still is checked by the PIX Adaptive Security Algorithm (ASA), and security is still maintained.

The **no sysopt connection permit-ipsec** command disables this option.

Configuring Crypto Access Lists

The first task in configuring PIX Firewall IPSec is to configure the crypto access lists to select interesting traffic. The PIX crypto access list is the same as an IOS crypto access list, apart from the fact that the PIX uses the full netmask rather than the wildcard mask in the access list.

Configure interesting traffic with crypto access lists. Define a crypto access list with the **access-list** configuration command. To delete an access list, use the **no** form of the command. The command syntax is as follows:

```
PIX(config)#access-list access-list-name deny | permit protocol source
    source-netmask [operator port [port]] destination destination-netmask
    [operator port [port]]
```

access-list-name is name or number of an access list. **deny** does not select a packet for IPSec protection. It prevents traffic from being protected by crypto in the context of that particular crypto map entry. **permit** selects a packet for IPSec protection and causes all IP traffic that matches the specified conditions to be protected by crypto, using the policy described by the corresponding crypto map entry.

protocol is the name or number of an IP protocol. It has to be the keyword **ip** because the PIX can only tunnel based on the IP protocol. The **icmp** keyword cannot be used for IPSec because IKE does not negotiate ICMP.

source and *destination* refer to the address of the network or host where the packet is being sent or from where the packet was received. There are three other ways to specify the source or destination:

- Use a 32-bit quantity in four-part dotted-decimal format.

- Use the keyword **any** as an abbreviation for a *source* and *source-netmask* or *destination-netmask* of 0.0.0.0 0.0.0.0. This keyword is normally not recommended for use with IPSec.

- Use **host** *source* or **host** *destination* as an abbreviation for a *source* and *source-netmask* of 255.255.255.255 or a *destination* and *destination-netmask* of 255.255.255.255.

NOTE   Although the access list syntax is unchanged from access lists applied to PIX Firewall interfaces, the meanings are slightly different for crypto access lists: **permit** specifies that matching packets must be encrypted, and **deny** specifies that matching packets need not be encrypted.

Configuring Transform Set Suites

The next task in configuring PIX Firewall IPSec is to use the IPSec security policy to define a transform set. You define a transform set with the **crypto ipsec transform-set** configuration command. To delete a transform set, use the **no** form of the command. The command syntax is as follows:

```
PIX1(config)#crypto ipsec transform-set transform-set-name transform1 [transform2
    transform3]]
```

The *transform-set-name* argument specifies the name of the transform set to create (or modify). *transform1, transform2,* and *transform3* specify up to three transforms. These transforms define the IPSec security protocol(s) and algorithm(s).

Some additional details for transform sets are as follows:

- Sets are limited to up to one AH and up to two ESP transforms.

- The default mode is tunnel.

- Configure matching transform sets between IPSec peers.

- If you specify an ESP protocol in a transform set, you can specify just an ESP encryption transform or both an ESP encryption transform and an ESP authentication transform.

The PIX Firewall supports the following IPSec transforms:

- AH:

    — **ah-md5-hmac**—AH-HMAC-MD5 transform

    — **ah-sha-hmac**—AH-HMAC-SHA transform

- ESP:

  - **esp-des**—ESP transform using DES cipher (56 bits)

  - **esp-3des**—ESP transform using 3DES (EDE) cipher (168 bits)

  - **esp-md5-hmac**—ESP transform with HMAC-MD5 authentication used with an esp-des or esp-3des transform to provide additional integrity of ESP packets

  - **esp-sha-hmac**—ESP transform with HMAC-SHA authentication used with an esp-des or esp-3des transform to provide additional integrity of ESP packets

Choose from the MD5 or SHA (HMAC keyed hash variants) authentication algorithms to ensure data authentication (using either ESP or AH). The SHA algorithm is generally considered stronger than MD5, but it is slower. The following are examples of acceptable transform combinations:

- esp-des for high-performance encryption

- ah-md5-hmac for authenticating packet contents with no encryption

- esp-3des and esp-md5-hmac for strong encryption and authentication

Configuring Global IPSec Security Association Lifetimes

The IPSec SA lifetime determines how long IPSec SAs remain valid before they are renegotiated. The PIX Firewall supports a global lifetime value that applies to all crypto maps. The global lifetime value can be overridden within a crypto map entry. You can change global IPSec SA lifetime values using the **crypto ipsec security-association lifetime** global configuration command. To reset a lifetime to the default value, use the **no** form of the command. The command syntax is as follows:

```
PIX1(config)#crypto ipsec security-association lifetime {seconds seconds |
  kilobytes kilobytes}
```

seconds *seconds* specifies the number of seconds an SA lives before expiring. The default is 28,800 seconds (8 hours). **kilobytes** *kilobytes* specifies the volume of traffic (in kilobytes) that can pass between IPSec peers using a given SA before that SA expires. The default is 4,608,000 kilobytes (approximately 10 Mbps of traffic for 1 hour).

Configuring Crypto Maps

You must create crypto map entries for IPSec to set up SAs for traffic flows that must be encrypted. This section looks at the purpose of crypto maps, examines the **crypto map** command, and considers sample crypto maps.

Configure the crypto map with the **crypto map** command as follows:

Step 1   Create a crypto map entry in IPSec ISAKMP mode:

```
PIX1(config)#crypto map map-name seq-num ipsec-isakmp
```

Identify the crypto map with a unique crypto map name and sequence number.

Step 2   Assign an access list to the crypto map entry:

```
PIX1(config)#crypto map map-name seq-num match address access-list-name
```

Step 3   Specify the peer to which the IPSec protected traffic can be forwarded:

```
PIX1(config)#crypto map map-name seq-num set peer hostname | ip-address
```

Set the peer host name or IP address.

Specify multiple peers by repeating this command.

The peer is the terminating interface of the IPSec peer.

Step 4   Specify which transform sets are allowed for this crypto map entry:

```
PIX1(config)#crypto map map-name seq-num set transform-set transform-set-name1
   [transform-set-name2, transform-set-name9]
```

Applying Crypto Maps to an Interface

The next task in configuring IPSec is to apply the crypto map set to an interface.

To apply the crypto map to an interface and activate the IPSec policy, use the following command:

```
PIX1(config)#crypto map map-name interface interface-name
```

Consider the following example of applying a crypto map to an outside interface:

```
PIX1(config)#crypto map mymap interface outside
```

IPSec tunnels can be terminated on any interface where you apply a crypto map. This does not mean that you terminate traffic coming from the outside on the inside interface. Traffic terminated on the inside interface is traffic from the inside network. Traffic terminated on the outside is traffic from the outside. Traffic terminated on a DMZ is traffic from the DMZ.

As soon as you apply the crypto map, the SAs should initialize. You can assign only one crypto map set to an interface. If multiple crypto map entries have the same *map-name* but a different *seq-num*, they are considered part of the same set and are all applied to the interface. The crypto map entry with the lowest *seq-num* is considered the highest priority and is evaluated first.

Verifying the IPSec Configuration

The last task in configuring PIX Firewall IPSec is to verify the IPSec configuration accomplished in the previous steps. This section presents the methods and commands used to verify IPSec configuration.

You can view all configured access lists with the **show access-list** command.

View the currently defined transform sets with the **show crypto ipsec transform-set** command:

```
PIX1#show crypto ipsec transform-set [transform-set-name]
```

transform-set-name is optional and shows only the transform sets that have the specified *transform-set-name*.

If no keyword is used, all transform sets configured at the PIX Firewall are displayed.

Use the **show crypto map** command to view the crypto map configuration. If no keywords are used, all crypto maps configured at the PIX Firewall are displayed. The command syntax is as follows:

```
PIX1#show crypto map [interface interface | tag map-name]
```

In this syntax, **interface** *interface* is optional and shows only the crypto map set applied to the specified interface. **tag** *map-name* is also optional and shows only the crypto map set with the specified map name.

Use the **show crypto ipsec security-association lifetime** command to view the current global IPSec SA lifetime.

Step 4: Testing and Verifying IPSec

The last major step in configuring PIX Firewall IPSec is to test and verify the IKE and IPSec configuration accomplished in the previous tasks. This section summarizes the methods and commands used to test and verify VPN configuration.

Test and verify IKE configuration on the PIX Firewall with the commands described in Table 19-3.

Table 19-3   **show** *Commands*

Command	Description
show access-list	Lists the **access-list** command statements in the configuration. Used to verify general access lists' permit IPSec traffic.
show isakmp	Displays configured ISAKMP policies in a format similar to a **write terminal** command.
show isakmp policy	Displays default and any configured ISAKMP policies.

Test and verify IPSec and crypto map configuration on the PIX Firewall with the commands shown in Table 19-4.

Table 19-4 *Commands to Test and Verify IPSec and Crypto Map Configurations*

Command	Description
show crypto map	Displays crypto access lists assigned to a crypto map. Displays configured crypto map parameters.
show crypto ipsec transform-set	Displays configured IPSec transform sets.
show crypto ipsec security-association lifetime	Displays correct global IPSec SA lifetime values.

You can monitor and manage IKE and IPSec communications between the PIX Firewall and IPSec peers with the commands listed in Table 19-5.

Table 19-5 *Commands to Monitor and Manage IKE and IPSec Communications*

Command	Description
show isakmp sa	Displays the current status of ISAKMP SAs.
show crypto ipsec sa	Displays the current status of IPSec SAs. Useful for ensuring that traffic is being encrypted.
clear isakmp sa	Clears ISAKMP SAs.
clear crypto ipsec sa	Clears IPSec SAs.
debug crypto isakmp	Displays ISAKMP (IKE) communications between the PIX Firewall and IPSec peers.
debug crypto ipsec	Displays IPSec communications between the PIX Firewall and IPSec peers.

After all the steps have been completed, you have the finished IPSec configurations. They are shown in Example 19-30.

Example 19-30 *Finished IPSec Configurations*

```
PIX1#write terminal
access-list 100 permit ip 10.1.1.0 255.255.255.0 192.168.1.0 255.255.255.0
crypto ipsec transform-set myset esp-des esp-sha-hmac
crypto map newmap 10 ipsec-isakmp
crypto map newmap 10 match address 100
crypto map newmap 10 set peer 130.100.26.1
crypto map newmap 10 set transform-set myset
crypto map newmap interface outside
isakmp enable outside
isakmp key thisisthekey address 130.100.26.1 netmask 255.255.255.255
isakmp identity address
isakmp policy 10 authentication pre-share
```

Example 19-30 *Finished IPSec Configurations (Continued)*

```
isakmp policy 10 encryption des
isakmp policy 10 hash md5
isakmp policy 10 group 1
isakmp policy 10 lifetime 86400

PIX2#write terminal
access-list 100 permit ip 192.168.1.0 255.255.255.0 19.1.1.0 255.255.255.0
crypto ipsec transform-set myset esp-des esp-sha-hmac
crypto map newmap 10 ipsec-isakmp
crypto map newmap 10 match address 100
crypto map newmap 10 set peer 130.100.1.1
crypto map newmap 10 set transform-set myset
crypto map newmap interface outside
isakmp enable outside
isakmp key thisisthekey address 130.100.1.1 netmask 255.255.255.255
isakmp identity address
isakmp policy 10 authentication pre-share
isakmp policy 10 encryption des
isakmp policy 10 hash md5
isakmp policy 10 group 1
isakmp policy 10 lifetime 86400
```

With this configuration in the firewalls, you can verify that Host A can successfully ping Host B using the VPN.

IPSec-Related **show** Commands

In this working state, this section looks at the output of a few **show** commands to ascertain what a normal configuration shows. You can use numerous **show** commands to verify IPSec operation. These **show** commands can be split into two groups:

- **show** commands that display information about the IPSec configuration
- **show** commands that display information about the state of the IPSec connections on the PIX Firewall

Display **show** Commands

In this section, you look at the output of three display **show** commands:

- **show crypto ipsec transform-set**
- **show crypto map**
- **show crypto isakmp policy**

The output shown is from PIX1. The output from PIX2 is identical for the **show crypto ipsec transform-set** and **show crypto isakmp policy** commands; it must be for an IPSec peer to be established. The **show crypto map** output for PIX2 reflects PIX1 as its peer.

The **show** command in Example 19-31 displays the configured IPSec transform set. Note that you are using esp-des and esp-sha-hmac within the transform set. The default mode for IPSec is tunnel.

Example 19-31 **show crypto ipsec transform-set** *Command*

```
PIX1#show crypto ipsec transform-set

Transform set myset: { esp-des esp-sha-hmac  }
   will negotiate = { Tunnel,  },
```

The output shown in Example 19-32 shows the configured crypto map called newmap. The information here pertains to the remote IPSec peer and also to the access list that controls the encryption of the IPSec traffic.

Example 19-32 **show crypto map** *Command*

```
PIX1#show crypto map

Crypto Map: "newmap" interfaces: { outside }

Crypto Map "newmap" 10 ipsec-isakmp
        Peer = 130.100.26.1
        access-list 100 permit ip 10.1.1.0 255.255.255.0 192.168.1.0 255.255.255.0
  (hitcnt=0)
        Current peer: 130.100.26.1
        Security association lifetime: 4608000 kilobytes/28800 seconds
        PFS (Y/N): N
        Transform sets={ myset, }
```

Example 19-33 shows the default policy (priority 65535, not visible here) and the configured isakmp policy of 10. You can see that you are using preshared keys and Diffie-Hellman group 1.

Example 19-33 **show crypto isakmp policy** *Command*

```
PIX1#show crypto isakmp policy

Protection suite of priority 10
        encryption algorithm:   DES - Data Encryption Standard (56 bit keys).
        hash algorithm:         Message Digest 5
        authentication method:  Pre-Shared Key
        Diffie-Hellman group:   #1 (768 bit)
        lifetime:               86400 seconds, no volume limit
Default protection suite
        encryption algorithm:   DES - Data Encryption Standard (56 bit keys).
```

Example 19-33 show crypto isakmp policy *Command (Continued)*

```
     hash algorithm:           Secure Hash Standard
     authentication method:    Rivest-Shamir-Adleman Signature
     Diffie-Hellman group:     #1 (768 bit)
     lifetime:                 86400 seconds, no volume limit
```

Informational **show** Commands

After data that matches the IPSec access list has passed the interface that has the crypto map applied to it, the VPN is established. At this point, you can enter some additional commands that show various states of the IPSec components. This section looks at **show crypto engine** and **show crypto ipsec sa**. For this test, you will initiate a ping from Host A to Host B and will look at the commands on PIX2.

The output in Example 19-34 shows the firewall's IPSec connection map. You can see that there are two used connections (one inbound and one outbound) and that both are active. This confirms that the VPN is established.

Example 19-34 show crypto engine *Command*

```
PIX2#show crypto engine
Crypto Engine Connection Map:
    size = 8, free = 6, used = 2, active = 2
```

Example 19-35 shows the output of the **show crypto ipsec sa** command. This command presents a lot of information. The first part shows the interface and crypto map name that are associated with the interface. Then the inbound and outbound SAs are shown. These are either AH or ESP SAs. In this case, because you used only ESP, there are no AH inbound or outbound SAs.

You can also see next to the PERMIT statement that a condition met by an access control list (ACL) initiated the IPSec connection.

Example 19-35 show crypto ipsec sa *Command*

```
PIX1#show crypto ipsec sa

interface: outside
    Crypto map tag: newmap, local addr. 130.100.26.1

  local  ident (addr/mask/prot/port): (10.1.1.0/255.255.255.0/0/0)
  remote ident (addr/mask/prot/port): (192.168.1.0/255.255.255.0/0/0)
  current_peer: 130.100.26.1
    PERMIT, flags={origin_is_acl,}
   #pkts encaps: 0, #pkts encrypt: 0, #pkts digest 0
   #pkts decaps: 3, #pkts decrypt: 3, #pkts verify 3
```

continues

Example 19-35 **show crypto ipsec sa** *Command (Continued)*

```
#pkts compressed: 0, #pkts decompressed: 0
#pkts not compressed: 0, #pkts compr. failed: 0, #pkts decompress failed: 0
#send errors 0, #recv errors 0

local crypto endpt.: 130.100.1.1, remote crypto endpt.: 130.100.26.1
path mtu 1500, ipsec overhead 56, media mtu 1500
current outbound spi: 963bff3d

inbound esp sas:
 spi: 0xcbba6d8e(3417992590)
   transform: esp-des esp-sha-hmac ,
   in use settings ={Tunnel, }
   slot: 0, conn id: 1, crypto map: newmap
   sa timing: remaining key lifetime (k/sec): (4607999/28034)
   IV size: 8 bytes
   replay detection support: Y

inbound ah sas:

outbound esp sas:
 spi: 0x963bff3d(2520514365)
   transform: esp-des esp-sha-hmac ,
   in use settings ={Tunnel, }
   slot: 0, conn id: 2, crypto map: newmap
   sa timing: remaining key lifetime (k/sec): (4608000/28025)
   IV size: 8 bytes
   replay detection support: Y

outbound ah sas:
```

Troubleshooting the IPSec Configuration on the PIX Firewall

In the preceding section, you successfully configured an IPSec VPN between PIX1 and PIX2. This was to provide a connection between Host A and Host B over the VPN. You then ran various **show** commands and learned what to look for in a working configuration. Now that you have a working configuration, you have a platform to introduce planned errors and watch the results.

You will look at the most common errors associated with the configuration of IPSec on Cisco PIX Firewalls:

- Incompatible ISAKMP policies

- Differing preshared keys between the IPSec peers

- Incorrect IPSec access lists

- Incorrect crypto map placement

- Routing issues

Incompatible ISAKMP Policies

The ISAKMP policy on each of the IPSec peers must match for the IPSec VPN to be established. Take a look at the ISAKMP policies for PIX1 and PIX2 shown in Example 19-36. The command to display the ISAKMP policy is **show crypto isakmp policy**.

Example 19-36 **show crypto isakmp policy** *Command*

```
PIX1#show crypto isakmp policy

Protection suite of priority 10
        encryption algorithm:   DES - Data Encryption Standard (56 bit keys).
        hash algorithm:         Message Digest 5
        authentication method:  Pre-Shared Key
        Diffie-Hellman group:   #1 (768 bit)
        lifetime:               86400 seconds, no volume limit
Default protection suite
        encryption algorithm:   DES - Data Encryption Standard (56 bit keys).
        hash algorithm:         Secure Hash Standard
        authentication method:  Rivest-Shamir-Adleman Signature
        Diffie-Hellman group:   #1 (768 bit)
        lifetime:               86400 seconds, no volume limit

PIX2#show crypto isakmp policy

Protection suite of priority 10
        encryption algorithm:   DES - Data Encryption Standard (56 bit keys).
        hash algorithm:         Message Digest 5
        authentication method:  Pre-Shared Key
        Diffie-Hellman group:   #1 (768 bit)
        lifetime:               86400 seconds, no volume limit
Default protection suite
        encryption algorithm:   DES - Data Encryption Standard (56 bit keys).
        hash algorithm:         Secure Hash Standard
        authentication method:  Rivest-Shamir-Adleman Signature
        Diffie-Hellman group:   #1 (768 bit)
        lifetime:               86400 seconds, no volume limit
```

You can see from the output in Example 19-36 that both PIXs have two ISAKMP policies, or protection suites. The first has a priority of 10, and the default has a priority of 65535 (although this value is not shown). You can also see that the values for the priority 10 suite all match between PIX1 and Host B. This is essential for ISAKMP negotiation.

The values controlled by the ISAKMP policy are

- Encryption algorithm

- Hash algorithm

- Authentication method

- Diffie-Hellman group

- SA lifetime
- Interface to enable ISAKMP on
- ISAKMP identity method
- ISAKMP peer information

On the Cisco PIX Firewall, these values are all set from global configuration mode with the **isakmp** command. Example 19-37 shows the available options with the **isakmp** command.

Example 19-37 isakmp *Commands*

```
PIX1(config)#isakmp ?
usage: isakmp policy <priority> authen <pre-share¦rsa-sig>
       isakmp policy <priority> encrypt <des¦3des>
       isakmp policy <priority> hash <md5¦sha>
       isakmp policy <priority> group <1¦2>
       isakmp policy <priority> lifetime <seconds>
       isakmp key <key-string> address <ip> [netmask <mask>] [no-xauth]
   [no-config-mode]
       isakmp enable <if_name>
       isakmp identity <address¦hostname>
       isakmp keepalive <seconds> [<retry seconds>]
       isakmp peer fqdn¦ip <fqdn¦ip> [no-xauth] [no-config-mode]
```

The command **debug crypto isakmp** also is of great use when troubleshooting ISAKMP issues. This command displays the full ISAKMP exchange as it occurs in the PIX Firewall. Example 19-38 shows the full debug output for a ping from Host B to the inside interface of PIX1.

Example 19-38 debug crypto isakmp *Command*

```
PIX1#debug crypto isakmp
crypto_isakmp_process_block: src 130.100.26.1, dest 130.100.1.1
OAK_MM exchange
ISAKMP (0): processing SA payload. message ID = 0
ISAKMP (0): Checking ISAKMP transform 1 against priority 10 policy
ISAKMP:      encryption DES-CBC
ISAKMP:      hash MD5
ISAKMP:      default group 1
ISAKMP:      auth pre-share
ISAKMP (0): atts are acceptable. Next payload is 0
ISAKMP (0): SA is doing pre-shared key authentication using id type ID_IPV4_ADDR
return status is IKMP_NO_ERROR
crypto_isakmp_process_block: src 130.100.26.1, dest 130.100.1.1
OAK_MM exchange
ISAKMP (0): processing KE payload. message ID = 0
ISAKMP (0): processing NONCE payload. message ID = 0
ISAKMP (0): processing vendor id payload
ISAKMP (0): processing vendor id payload
ISAKMP (0): remote peer supports dead peer detection
```

Example 19-38 debug crypto isakmp *Command (Continued)*

```
ISAKMP (0): processing vendor id payload
ISAKMP (0): speaking to another IOS box!
return status is IKMP_NO_ERROR
crypto_isakmp_process_block: src 130.100.26.1, dest 130.100.1.1
OAK_MM exchange
ISAKMP (0): processing ID payload. message ID = 0
ISAKMP (0): processing HASH payload. message ID = 0
ISAKMP (0): SA has been authenticated
ISAKMP (0): ID payload
        next-payload : 8
        type         : 1
        protocol     : 17
        port         : 500
        length       : 8
ISAKMP (0): Total payload length: 12
return status is IKMP_NO_ERROR
crypto_isakmp_process_block: src 130.100.26.1, dest 130.100.1.1
OAK_QM exchange
oakley_process_quick_mode:
OAK_QM_IDLE
ISAKMP (0): processing SA payload. message ID = 2342393309
ISAKMP : Checking ipsec proposal 1
ISAKMP: transform 1, ESP_DES
ISAKMP:    attributes in transform:
ISAKMP:       encaps is 1
ISAKMP:       SA life type in seconds
ISAKMP:       SA life duration (basic) of 28800
ISAKMP:       SA life type in kilobytes
ISAKMP:       SA life duration (VPI) of  0x0 0x46 0x50 0x0
ISAKMP:       authenticator is HMAC-SHA
ISAKMP (0): atts are acceptable.
ISAKMP (0): processing NONCE payload. message ID = 2342393309
ISAKMP (0): processing ID payload. message ID = 2342393309
ISAKMP (0): ID_IPV4_ADDR_SUBNET src 192.168.1.0/255.255.255.0 prot 0 port 0
ISAKMP (0): processing ID payload. message ID = 2342393309
ISAKMP (0): ID_IPV4_ADDR_SUBNET dst 10.1.1.0/255.255.255.0 prot 0 port 0
ISAKMP (0): processing NOTIFY payload 24578 protocol 1
        spi 0, message ID = 2342393309
ISAKMP (0): processing notify INITIAL_CONTACT
return status is IKMP_NO_ERROR60
ISAKMP (0): sending NOTIFY message 11 protocol 3
crypto_isakmp_process_block: src 130.100.26.1, dest 130.100.1.1
OAK_QM exchange
oakley_process_quick_mode:
OAK_QM_AUTH_AWAIT
ISAKMP (0): Creating IPSec SAs
        inbound SA from        130.100.26.1to        130.100.1.1(proxy
     172.16.0.0 to      192.168.1.0)
        has spi 2018067353 and conn_id 2 and flags 4
        lifetime of 28800 seconds
```

continues

Example 19-38 debug crypto isakmp *Command (Continued)*

```
         lifetime of 4608000 kilobytes
         outbound SA from        130.100.1.1to        130.100.26.1(proxy
     192.168.1.0 to      172.16.0.0)
         has spi 2776158804 and conn_id 1 and flags 4
         lifetime of 28800 seconds
         lifetime of 4608000 kilobytes
return status is IKMP_NO_ERROR2302: deleting SA, (sa) sa_dest= 130.100.26.1,
   sa_prot= 50, sa_spi= 0xcbba6d8e(3417992590), sa_trans= esp-des esp-sha-hmac ,
   sa_conn_id= 1
```

Notice the shaded section. It shows that the ISAKMP values are acceptable and then the PIX Firewall continues with the ISAKMP negotiation process.

Example 19-38 shows what the debug output looks like in a working configuration. If you change a value in the ISAKMP policy, though, you will change the hash value from MD5 to the default SHA on PIX1 and observe the output from the **debug crypto isakmp** command.

First, look at the newly configured ISAKMP policy on PIX1 in Example 19-39.

Example 19-39 show crypto isakmp policy *Command*

```
PIX1#show crypto isakmp policy

Protection suite of priority 10
        encryption algorithm:   DES - Data Encryption Standard (56 bit keys).
        hash algorithm:         Secure Hash Standard
        authentication method:  Pre-Shared Key
        Diffie-Hellman group:   #1 (768 bit)
        lifetime:               86400 seconds, no volume limit
Default protection suite
        encryption algorithm:   DES - Data Encryption Standard (56 bit keys).
        hash algorithm:         Secure Hash Standard
        authentication method:  Rivest-Shamir-Adleman Signature
        Diffie-Hellman group:   #1 (768 bit)
        lifetime:               86400 seconds, no volume limit
```

The shaded section shows that the hash algorithm has been changed from MD5 to SHA. You now carry out the same ping as before from Host B to PIX1 and look at the debug output, shown in Example 19-40.

Example 19-40 debug crypto isakmp *Command*

```
PIX1#debug crypto isakmp
OAK_MM exchange
ISAKMP (0): processing SA payload. message ID = 0
ISAKMP (0): Checking ISAKMP transform 1 against priority 10 policy
ISAKMP:       encryption DES-CBC
ISAKMP:       hash MD5
```

Example 19-40 debug crypto isakmp *Command (Continued)*

```
ISAKMP:       default group 1
ISAKMP:       auth pre-share
ISAKMP (0): atts are not acceptable. Next payload is 0
ISAKMP (0): Checking ISAKMP transform 1 against priority 65535 policy
ISAKMP:       encryption DES-CBC
ISAKMP:       hash MD5
ISAKMP:       default group 1
ISAKMP:       auth pre-share
ISAKMP (0): atts are not acceptable. Next payload is 0
ISAKMP (0): no offers accepted!
ISAKMP (0): SA not acceptable!
return status is IKMP_ERR_TRANS
```

You can see from this debug output that there was a failure in the ISAKMP negotiation. This is because the ISAKMP values are unacceptable. They are classed as unacceptable because they do not match.

Differing Preshared Keys Between the IPSec Peers

The preshared secret keys must be exactly the same on both IPSec peers. These keys are compared during ISAKMP phase 1 authentication. The first step is to ensure that both PIX Firewalls are using preshared authentication in their ISAKMP policies. This can be done with the **show crypto isakmp** command. The output in Example 19-41 is the result of the **show crypto isakmp** command on both PIX1 and PIX2.

Example 19-41 show crypto isakmp *Command*

```
PIX1#show crypto isakmp
isakmp enable outside
isakmp key ******** address 130.100.26.1 netmask 255.255.255.255
isakmp identity address
isakmp policy 10 authentication pre-share
isakmp policy 10 encryption des
isakmp policy 10 hash md5
isakmp policy 10 group 1
isakmp policy 10 lifetime 86400

PIX2#show crypto isakmp
isakmp enable outside
isakmp key ******** address 130.100.1.1 netmask 255.255.255.255
isakmp identity address
isakmp policy 10 authentication pre-share
isakmp policy 10 encryption des
isakmp policy 10 hash md5
isakmp policy 10 group 1
isakmp policy 10 lifetime 86400
```

Check that the authentication method on both firewalls is set to the preshared key; you can see from the highlighted lines in Example 19-41 that it is. If the authentication methods do not match between the firewalls, the ISAKMP negotiation fails, as outlined in the previous section.

You know that the PIX Firewalls are both using preshared keys as their authentication method. On a Cisco IOS router, you can view the preshared key with the **show crypto isakmp key** command. On the Cisco PIX Firewall, after you enter the preshared key, there is no way to display it. When you look at the on-screen or printed configuration, the preshared key is always replaced with eight stars. So to generate a fault here, you will knowingly change one of the preshared key values to differ from its IPSec peer.

After this configuration change, when you try to ping from Host A to Host B, the VPN is not established because of the failure of the preshared key in the ISAKMP negotiation.

Incorrect IPSec Access Lists

In the scenario you have been using in this chapter, you have an access list on both PIX1 and PIX2. These access lists mirror each other. The source in the PIX1 access list is the destination in the PIX2 access list, and vice versa. The access lists you are using encrypt anything from the local Ethernet network to the remote Ethernet network.

NOTE   It is important to note the slight change in the way access lists are configured on a Cisco PIX Firewall as compared to a Cisco IOS router. On a router, the format for an extended access list contains the source and destination networks along with a wildcard mask. A wildcard mask is the reverse of a subnet mask. The Cisco PIX Firewall implementation of access lists uses subnet masks instead.

For example, an access list to permit anything from 10.1.1.0/24 to 192.168.1.0/24 would be configured as follows:

- Cisco IOS router:

```
Router(config)#access-lists 101 permit ip 10.1.1.0 0.0.0.255 192.168.1.0
  0.0.0.255
```

- Cisco PIX Firewall:

```
PIX(config)#access-list 101 permit ip 10.1.1.0 255.255.255.0 192.168.1.0
  255.255.255.0
```

Note that the Cisco IOS router uses wildcard masks and the PIX uses subnet masks.

To introduce an error, change the IPSec access list on PIX1 to have an incorrect source address. Then, ping from Host A to Host B. The traffic does not kick off the IPSec process and cannot be routed to the destination.

The current IPSec access list on PIX1 is shown in Example 19-42.

Example 19-42 show access-list *Command*

```
PIX1#show access-list
access-list 100 permit ip 10.1.1.0 255.255.255.0
  192.168.1.0 255.255.255.0
```

This access list encrypts traffic from the 10.1.1.0/24 network that is destined for the 192.168.1.0/24 network. You will make a subtle change to this access list that breaks the IPSec process. You will remove the existing access list and add the line of configuration shown in Example 19-43.

Example 19-43 show access-list *Command*

```
PIX1#show access-list
access-list 100 permit ip 10.1.2.0 255.255.255.0
  192.168.1.0 255.255.255.0
```

Note that this encrypts traffic from the 10.1.2.0/24 network and not the original 10.1.1.0/24 network. After you make this change, Host A attempts to ping Host B. Obviously, this fails.

If you are ever faced with a real-world problem similar to this, your first step should always be to ascertain whether the VPN is established between the IPSec peers. There are various ways to accomplish this on a Cisco PIX Firewall. The easiest way is to use the **show crypto engine** command. This command displays the current state of the IPSec connections (if any). Running this command on PIX1 results in the output shown in Example 19-44.

Example 19-44 show crypto engine *Command*

```
PIX1#show crypto engine
Crypto Engine Connection Map:
    size = 8, free = 8, used = 0, active = 0
```

You can see that there are no active IPSec connections. If you can verify that relevant traffic has passed the connection that should start the IPSec process, the problem is with the IPSec access list. A simple sanity check of the IPSec access list should be enough to remedy the problem.

Incorrect Crypto Map Placement

On the VPN terminating interface, you have to apply the crypto map. For example, to apply crypto map newmap to the outside interface, the command is

```
PIX1(config)#crypto map newmap interface outside
```

This command makes the interface a VPN termination point. Any traffic leaving this interface is checked against the IPSec access list. If the traffic matches the IPSec access list, it is encrypted to the standard defined in the related transform set and is delivered to the IPSec peer as defined in the crypto map. A useful command for looking at the crypto map applied to an interface is **show crypto map**. The output in Example 19-45 shows this command run on PIX1.

Example 19-45 show crypto map *Command*

```
PIX1#show crypto map

Crypto Map: "newmap" interfaces: { outside }

Crypto Map "newmap" 10 ipsec-isakmp
        Peer = 130.100.26.1
        access-list 100 permit ip 10.1.1.0 255.255.255.0 192.168.1.0 255.255.255.0
        Current peer: 130.100.26.1
        Security association lifetime: 4608000 kilobytes/28800 seconds
        PFS (Y/N): N
        Transform sets={ myset, }
```

You can see that crypto map newmap is applied to the outside interface. The output also shows you the IPSec access list, IPSec peer, SA settings, PFS status, and the related transform set.

If there is a problem with IPSec traffic and you have confirmed that the IPSec access list is correct, the crypto map placement might be a good next place to check. If the crypto map is not applied to the outbound interface, traffic will never get encrypted for IPSec to forward it to its peer.

Routing Issues

You must address two routing issues—routing to the IPSec peer and routing the required packets to the interface with the crypto map applied. Both these issues can cause problems that result in the failure of the IPSec process.

Layer 3 communications have to be established between the IPSec peers. This was covered at the start of this chapter when VPNs were introduced and you learned that a simple ping between the IPSec peers is adequate to confirm this. If the IPSec peers cannot establish Layer 3 communications, the IPSec process will never be complete, and the peers will never be adjacent to each other.

The other routing issue is related to the delivery of the packets from the local firewall to the remote network over the IPSec tunnel. In this scenario, you can see that Host A is on network 192.168.1.0/24 and Host B is on network 172.16.0.0/16 (refer to Figure 19-6 to refresh your memory). For Host A to communicate with Host B, a valid route has to exist in PIX1's IP routing table to the Host B network address. This follows basic IP routing principles. Looking at the IP routing table in Example 19-46, you can see that a default route exists out of the outside interface to 20.0.0.2.

Example 19-46 show route *Command*

```
PIX1#show route
        outside 0.0.0.0 0.0.0.0 130.100.1.3 1 OTHER static
        outside 130.100.1.0 255.0.0.0 130.100.1.1 1 CONNECT static
        inside 10.1.1.0 255.255.255.0 10.1.1.1 1 CONNECT static
```

Because you are using a static default route, this should not cause a problem with the routing of the packets. Host A sends a packet with a source address of 10.1.1.2 and a destination address of 192.168.1.2. PIX1 does not have a specific route for the 192.168.1.0/24 network, but the default route directs this to the outside interface. The crypto map is applied to the outside interface, and the traffic matches the IPSec access list, so it gets encrypted and tunneled to the destination.

The important part to remember is to ensure that the firewall forwards the packet to the interface where the crypto map exists. A default route or a specific route for the remote network normally suffices in this situation.

At this point, you have seen a sample configuration of both an IOS-based VPN and a PIX-based VPN using preshared keys. The next section expands on this configuration to add different and more-advanced configurations.

Certificate Authority (CA) Support

Now that you have covered the configuration steps and troubleshooting of a simple IOS-to-IOS and PIX-to-PIX VPN using preshared keys, this section moves on to using the same configurations to introduce the use of a CA. IKE phase 1 can be carried out using either preshared keys or a CA. In the previous sections, you configured IKE phase 1 using preshared keys. In this section, you will look at using a CA and RSA certificates to implement IKE phase 1.

In this section, you will follow a setup similar to what you might find in the CCIE Security lab exam. This setup involves using Microsoft 2000 CA Server with Simple Certificate Enrollment Protocol (SCEP) enabled. You will learn about a simple IOS-to-IOS VPN and PIX-to-PIX VPN using CA for IKE phase 1.

NOTE   The SCEP is a Cisco, VeriSign, Entrust, Microsoft, Netscape, and Sun Microsystems initiative that provides a standard way to manage the certificate life cycle. SCEP is important for driving open development for certificate-handling protocols that can interoperate with many vendors' devices.

Configuring CA

There are six simple steps for configuring a CA that are generic to both IOS and PIX configurations:

Step 1   Configure the router/PIX for CA support.

Step 2   Generate local key pairs.

Step 3   Declare the CA.

Step 4   Authenticate the CA.

Step 5   Request your certificate.

Step 6   Save and test the configuration.

You will now look at each of these six steps for both IOS and PIX-based VPNs. The commands differ slightly between the IOS and PIX configuration, but the fundamentals remain the same.

IOS-to-IOS VPN Using CA

This section starts by looking at an IOS-to-IOS VPN using CA for IKE phase 1 authentication. In Case Study 19-1, you covered a VPN configuration between two IOS routers using preshared keys. In this section, you take the same two routers and configuration and work through the configuration necessary for the two routers to use a CA for IKE phase 1.

The next sections describe the six steps defined at the beginning of this section.

Step 1: Configuring the Router for CA Support

The first step in configuring a CA is to carry out some necessary configuration on the routers. For a CA to work, you must ensure that the router can interoperate with it. To do this, you must perform the following tasks:

- **Task 1**—Set the router's time and date.

- **Task 2**—Configure the router's host name.

- **Task 3**—Configure the router's domain name.

- **Task 4**—Configure DNS or a local DNS entry for the CA server.

Setting the Router's Time and Date

Ensure that the router's time zone, time, and date have been set with the **show clock** command in privileged EXEC mode. The clock must be accurately set before you generate RSA key pairs and enroll with the CA server, because the keys and certificates are time-sensitive.

To specify the router's time zone, use the **clock timezone** global configuration command. This command sets the time zone and an offset from Universal Time Code (UTC, displayed by the router). The command syntax is as follows:

```
R4(config)#clock timezone zone hours [minutes]
```

In this syntax, *zone* specifies the time zone to be displayed when standard time is in effect, *hours* is the hours offset from UTC, and *minutes,* which is optional, is the minutes offset from UTC.

The following command sets the time zone to Central Standard Time (CST) in the United States:

```
R4(config)#clock timezone cst -6
```

To set the router's time and date, use the **clock set** privileged EXEC command. The command syntax is as follows:

```
R4#clock set hh:mm:ss day month year
R4#clock set hh:mm:ss month day year
```

hh:mm:ss is the current time in hours (military format), minutes, and seconds. *day* is the current day (by date) in the month. *month* is the current month (by name). *year* is the current year (no abbreviation).

The following command sets the time to 1 second before midnight, December 31, 2003:

```
R4#clock set 23:59:59 31 december 2003
```

You can also optionally set your router to automatically update the calendar and time from a Network Time Protocol (NTP) server with the **ntp** series of commands.

NOTE   Cisco recommends using an NTP server to set the router's time on routers that do not have a clock circuit chip.

Configuring the Router's Host Name

You have to configure the router's host name for CA to work correctly. This is achieved with the **hostname** global configuration command. For example, to set the router's host name to MyRouter, enter the following command:

```
R4(config)#hostname MyRouter
MyRouter(config)#
```

Configuring the Router's Domain Name

A domain name must be installed on the router to create the key pair on the router. To achieve this, use the **ip domain-name** global configuration command. For example, the following configuration sets the domain name to boxingorange.com:

```
R4(config)#ip domain-name boxingorange.com
```

Configuring a Local DNS Entry for the CA Server

It is common to communicate with the CA using a DNS entry rather than an IP address. There are two ways to achieve this. If the CA server has a DNS entry, you can set the router to use a DNS server for name resolution. This is achieved with the **ip name-server** global configuration command. The following configuration sets the DNS server to 172.18.1.120:

```
R4(config)#ip name-server 172.18.1.120
```

The other way to achieve this if the CA does not have a DNS entry is to use the **ip host** command. This is the equivalent of placing an entry in the HOSTS file on a workstation. You can then refer to the name rather than the IP address for local operations on the router. For example, to declare a name of **pkitest1** for the address 172.18.1.121, the following configuration is required:

```
R4(config)#ip host pkitest1 172.18.1.121
```

Step 2: Generating Local Key Pairs

By default, the router does not have a public and private RSA key pair. These are required for the CA to function correctly.

NOTE   Before issuing the command to generate RSA keys, make sure your router has a host name and IP domain name configured (with the **hostname** and **ip domain-name** commands). You will be unable to complete the **crypto key generate rsa** command without a host name and IP domain name.

To generate the key pair, you enter the following global configuration command:

```
R4(config)#crypto key generate rsa
```

When you generate RSA keys, you are prompted to enter a modulus length. A longer modulus offers stronger security but takes longer to generate and longer to use. A modulus less than 512 is normally not recommended. Cisco recommends using a minimum modulus of 1024.

The keys generated are saved in the private configuration in NVRAM, which is never displayed to the user or backed up to another device. You can view the public key but not the private key. The public key is displayed with the command **show crypto key mypubkey rsa**, as shown in Example 19-47.

Example 19-47 show crypto key mypubkey rsa *Command*

```
R4#show crypto key mypubkey rsa
% Key pair was generated at: 18:54:28 UTC Mar 1 1993
Key name: R4.boxingorange.com
 Usage: General Purpose Key
```

Example 19-47 show crypto key mypubkey rsa *Command (Continued)*

```
Key Data:
  30819F30 0D06092A 864886F7 0D010101 05000381 8D003081 89028181 009CC85A
  CAB8E63D C4FE1F6F 708FE97E 776B3243 9A9ABDA0 0A64FF59 28C96C8A 7EB6DE31
  116828FD 8D94D4A9 D79C2C13 44249FA6 EF47EE83 058CD676 55E23691 7ABAF700
  861E36E1 432B5A98 C90EFB8C 4121C317 50B13C31 25740A08 C6F1F860 1DA57535
  946CF196 D3A5700B 2880E33B ECD82E0F 7DA9A745 254EFADE FFD680A4 FF020301 0001
% Key pair was generated at: 18:54:42 UTC Mar 1 1993
Key name: R4.boxingorange.com.server
 Usage: Encryption Key
 Key Data:
  307C300D 06092A86 4886F70D 01010105 00036B00 30680261 00A6CD88 7C7E74E5
  68AE89CD 03C7E016 A6BEC664 0F3CA154 62AD6C11 2FF58387 D60CFFE3 11A41158
  69630435 91CB76BA E13D4135 362FEC62 6B5C2501 837744F3 82684398 DB5AF766
  FF3AD4C7 C01472C2 A4EE3136 6293455D 2C5CF458 6E30AC42 6D020301 0001
```

NOTE   Creating the RSA key pair automatically enables Secure Shell (SSH) access to the router.

Step 3: Declaring the CA

Now that the router is configured and has an RSA key pair, you can declare the CA server. This is done with the **crypto ca identity** global configuration command.

Example 19-48 declares a CA called myca, a Microsoft Windows 2000 CA Server.

Example 19-48 *Declaring the CA Server*

```
R4(config)#crypto ca identity myca
R4(ca-identity)#enrollment mode ra
R4(ca-identity)#enrollment url http://pkitest1:80/certsrv/mscep/mscep.dll
```

The server resolves to the name pkitest1.

Step 4: Authenticating the CA

The router needs to authenticate the CA to verify that it is valid. The router does this by obtaining the CA's self-signed certificate that contains the CA's public key.

To get the CA's public key, use the **crypto ca authenticate** *name* command in global configuration mode. Use the same name that you used when declaring the CA with the **crypto ca identity** command.

If you are using registration authority (RA) mode (using the **enrollment mode ra** command) when you issue the **crypto ca authenticate** command, the RA signing and encryption certificates are returned from the CA as well as the CA certificate.

Example 19-49 shows a CA authentication.

Example 19-49 *CA Authentication*

```
R4(config)#crypto ca authenticate myca
Certificate has the following attributes:
Fingerprint: 93700C31 4853EC4A DED81400 43D3C82C
% Do you accept this certificate? [yes/no]: y
```

NOTE   If you have already authenticated with the CA, you are first prompted to delete the existing CA
certificate as follows:

```
R4(config)#crypto ca authenticate myca
% Please delete your existing CA certificate first.
% You must use 'no crypto ca identity <ip-address>' to delete the CA
   certificate.
```

Step 5: Requesting Your Certificate

At this point, you must obtain your router's certificate from the CA. To do this, you use the
crypto ca enroll *name* global configuration command with the name of the CA you identified
and authenticated. Use the **no** form of this command to delete a current enrollment request.

This command requests certificates from the CA for all your router's RSA key pairs. This task
is also known as *enrolling with the CA.*

During the enrollment process, you are prompted for a challenge password, which the CA
administrator can use to validate your identity. Do not forget the password you use. (Technically,
enrolling and obtaining certificates are two separate events, but they both occur when the
crypto ca enroll command is issued.)

Your router needs a signed certificate from the CA for each of your router's RSA key pairs. If
you previously generated general-purpose keys, this command obtains the one certificate
corresponding to the one general-purpose RSA key pair. If you previously generated special-
usage keys, this command obtains two certificates corresponding to each of the special-usage
RSA key pairs.

Example 19-50 shows a CA enrollment.

Example 19-50 *CA Enrollment*

```
R4(config)#crypto ca enroll myca
% Start certificate enrollment ..
% Create a challenge password. You will need to verbally provide this
   password to the CA Administrator in order to revoke your certificate.
   For security reasons, your password will not be saved in the configuration.
   Please make a note of it.
```

Example 19-50 *CA Enrollment (Continued)*

```
Password: <password>
Re-enter password: <password>

% The subject name in the certificate will be: r1.cisco.com
% Include the router serial number in the subject name? [yes/no]: no
% Include an IP address in the subject name? [yes/no]: no
Request certificate from CA? [yes/no]: yes
% Certificate request sent to Certificate Authority
% The certificate request fingerprint will be displayed.
% The 'show crypto ca certificate' command will also show the fingerprint.
R4(config)#
    Signing Certificate Request Fingerprint:
    0EE481F1 CBB4AF30 5D757610 6A4CF13D
  Encryption Certificate Request Fingerprint:
    710281D4 4DE854C7 AA61D953 CC5BD2B9
%CRYPTO-6-CERTRET: Certificate received from Certificate Authority
```

NOTE   The **crypto ca enroll** command is not saved in the router configuration. If your router reboots after you issue the **crypto ca enroll** command but before you receive the certificate(s), you must reissue the command.

Step 6: Saving and Testing the Configuration

Numerous commands can be issued to verify the CA configuration. You have already learned about the **show crypto key mypubkey rsa** command. Another command that can be used is the **show crypto ca certificates** command.

This command provides the output shown in Example 19-51.

Example 19-51 **show crypto ca certificates** *Command*

```
R4#show crypto ca certificates

Certificate
  Subject Name
    Name: R4.boxingorange.com
        IP Address: 172.30.1.2
    Status: Available
    Certificate Serial Number: 0123456789ABCDEF0123456789ABCDEF
    Key Usage: General Purpose

CA Certificate
  Status: Available
  Certificate Serial Number: 3051DF7123BEE31B8341DFE4B3A338E5F
  Key Usage: Not Set
```

Enabling IKE to Use the Configured CA

Now that the CA is configured and authenticated and you have enrolled with it to obtain a certificate, it is time to configure your Cisco IOS router to use CA for IKE phase 1. The IPSec configuration for R3 is shown in Example 19-52.

Example 19-52 *Cisco IOS IPSec Configuration*

```
R4#write termnial
crypto isakmp policy 110
 authentication pre-share
 hash md5
crypto isakmp key thisshouldbeaverysecurekey address 20.0.0.5
!
!
crypto ipsec transform-set MySet esp-des esp-md5-hmac
!
!
crypto map MyMap 10 IPSec-isakmp
 set peer 20.0.0.5
 set transform-set MySet
 match address 100
!
interface Serial0
 ip address 20.0.0.4 255.0.0.0
 no ip directed-broadcast
 no ip mroute-cache
 crypto map MyMap
!
access-list 100 permit ip 192.168.1.0 0.0.0.255 172.16.0.0 0.0.255.255
```

You can see that you have defined an ISAKMP policy using preshared authentication. To enable the use of the CA you just configured, you have to change the authentication method to be RSA Signatures. Remove the current configuration setting with the command **no authentication pre-share** from config-isakmp mode, and then enter the following command:

```
R4(config-isakmp)#authentication rsa-sig
```

Now use the command **show crypto isakmp policy** to display the configured ISAKMP polices, as shown in Example 19-53.

Example 19-53 **show crypto isakmp policy** *Command*

```
R4#show crypto isakmp policy
Protection suite of priority 110
        encryption algorithm:   DES - Data Encryption Standard (56 bit keys).
        hash algorithm:         Message Digest 5
        authentication method:  Rivest-Shamir-Adleman Signatures
        Diffie-Hellman group:   #1 (768 bit)
        lifetime:               86400 seconds, no volume limit
```

Example 19-53 **show crypto isakmp policy** *Command (Continued)*

```
Default protection suite
        encryption algorithm:  DES - Data Encryption Standard (56 bit keys).
        hash algorithm:        Secure Hash Standard
        authentication method: Rivest-Shamir-Adleman Signature
        Diffie-Hellman group:  #1 (768 bit)
        lifetime:              86400 seconds, no volume limit
```

You can see from Example 19-53 that the protection suite with a priority of 110 is now using RSA Signatures.

NOTE It is worthwhile to note that RSA Signatures is the default authentication method for ISAKMP. Because of this, the configuration line does not show up in the configuration. To check your ISAKMP policy, use the **show crypto isakmp policy** command.

To enable the VPN, simply configure the second router as outlined in this section.

PIX-to-PIX VPN Using CA

Now that you have covered how to configure a CA on a Cisco IOS router, you will move on to the same configuration on a Cisco PIX Firewall.

The configuration of a CA on the Cisco PIX follows the same six steps that CA configuration for IOS does. The next sections explain the PIX-specific commands for the six steps covered in the previous section for IOS.

Step 1: Configuring the PIX for CA Support

The first step in configuring a CA is to carry out some necessary configuration on the PIXs. For a CA to work, you must ensure that the PIX can interoperate with a CA. To do this, you must perform the following tasks:

- **Task 1**—Set the time and date on the PIX.
- **Task 2**—Configure the PIX host name.
- **Task 3**—Configure the PIX domain name.
- **Task 4**—Configure DNS or a local DNS entry for the CA server.

The next sections describe each task in more detail.

Setting the Time and Date on the PIX

Ensure that the PIX Firewall's time and date have been accurately set with the **show clock** command. The clock must be accurately set before you generate RSA key pairs and enroll with the CA server, because the keys and certificates are time-sensitive.

To set the PIX Firewall's time and date, use the **clock set** configuration command. The command syntax is as follows:

```
PIX1(config)#clock set hh:mm:ss day month year
PIX1(config)#clock set hh:mm:ss month day year
```

hh:mm:ss is the current time in hours (military format), minutes, and seconds. *day* is the current day of the month, such as **1**. *month* is the current month expressed as the first three characters of the month, such as **apr** for April. *year* is the current year expressed as four digits, such as **2000**.

The following command sets the time to 1 second before midnight, December 31, 2003:

```
PIX1(config)#clock set 23:59:59 31 dec 2003
```

Cisco's Public Key Infrastructure (PKI) protocol uses the clock to make sure that a certificate revocation list (CRL) is not expired. Otherwise, the CA might reject or allow certificates based on an incorrect timestamp. The certificates themselves are also checked against the time and date to ensure that they are still valid.

NOTE   The lifetime of a certificate and the CRL are checked in GMT time. If you are using IPSec with certificates, set the PIX Firewall clock to GMT time to ensure that CRL checking works correctly.

Configuring the PIX Host Name

You have to configure the PIX host name for CA to work correctly. This is achieved with the **hostname** configuration command. For example, to set the PIX's host name to MyPix, enter the following commands:

```
PIX1(config)#hostname MyPix
MyPix(config)#
```

Configuring the PIX Domain Name

A domain name must be installed on the PIX to create the key pair on the PIX. To achieve this, use the **domain-name** configuration command. For example, the following configuration sets the domain name to boxingorange.com:

```
PIX1(config)#domain-name boxingorange.com
```

Configuring a Local DNS Entry for the CA Server

It is common to communicate with the CA using a DNS entry rather than an IP address.

The way to achieve this is to use the **name** command. This is the equivalent of placing an entry in the HOSTS file on a workstation. You can then refer to the name rather than the IP address for local operations on the PIX. For example, to declare a name of pkitest1 for the address 172.18.1.121, the following configuration is required:

```
PIX1(config)#name 172.18.1.121 pkitest1
```

Step 2: Generating Local Key Pairs

By default, the PIX does not have a public/private RSA key pair. This is required for the CA to function correctly.

To generate the key pair, you enter the following global configuration command:

```
PIX1(config)#ca generate rsa key 1024
```

This command creates an RSA key pair with a key length of 1024 bits.

NOTE   Note that there is a difference here when configuring a key on a Cisco IOS router. In the Cisco IOS software, you are prompted for the key size. On the PIX, you have to specify the key size in the command for the PIX to accept the command.

The keys generated are saved in the private configuration in NVRAM, which is never displayed to the user or backed up to another device. You can view the public key but not the private key. The public key is displayed with the command **show ca mypubkey rsa**. An example is shown in Example 19-54.

Example 19-54 show ca mypubkey rsa *Command*

```
PIX1#show ca mypubkey rsa
% Key pair was generated at: 22:13:22 Nov 22 2002

Key name: PIX1.boxingorange.com
 Usage: General Purpose Key
 Key Data:
  30819f30 0d06092a 864886f7 0d010101 05000381 8d003081 89028181 00d9526e
  9ff221c8 cfd1759e 6379d23d 0e7ee835 893367d5 c7f98944 76312ea7 7445f3bd
  ab0f517c 7532c244 890a09ef e5a02efd bf444e0e dd8f7e02 1fa63c1e 0bf9ffc0
  fc8b9814 adfdc76c bd99e81c 455af200 49830de6 7bfdbb41 193610d5 479fe860
  421bffea 45c36488 e6fafae5 259dcf0b b25999a2 630ab9bd 166ad246 f7020301 0001
PIX1#
```

Step 3: Declaring the CA

Now that you have a key pair generated on the PIX, you have to declare the CA. Remember that the PIX has no granular configuration modes, only config mode, so the identity on the PIX differs from the IOS identity in that a single command declares the CA. For example, to declare a CA called myca (a Microsoft Windows 2000 CA) located on the machine \\pkitest, issue the following command:

```
PIX1(config)#ca identity myca pkitest:/certsrv/mscep/mscep.dll
```

The server resolves to the name pkitest1, which you have created a name entry for. You now have to enable RA mode for the CA server, because it is a Microsoft CA server. You do this by entering the following command:

```
PIX1(config)#ca configure myca ra 2 2
```

Step 4: Authenticating the CA

The PIX needs to authenticate the CA to verify that it is valid. The PIX does this by obtaining the CA's self-signed certificate that contains the CA's public key.

To get the CA's public key, use the **ca authenticate** *ca nickname* command in global configuration mode. Use the same name you used when declaring the CA with the **ca identity** command.

Example 19-55 shows a CA authentication.

Example 19-55 *CA Authentication*

```
PIX1(config)#ca authenticate myca
Certificate has the following attributes:
Fingerprint: 93700c31 4853ec4a ded81400 43d3c82c
```

Step 5: Requesting Your Certificate

The next step is to request signed certificates from your CA for your PIX RSA key pairs using the **ca enroll** command. Before entering this command, have your CA administrator authenticate your PIX Firewall manually before granting its certificates. The command syntax is as follows:

```
PIX1(config)#ca enroll ca_nickname challenge_password [serial] [ipaddress]
```

For the *ca_nickname,* use the nickname entered with the **ca identity** command. *challenge_password* is a required password that gives the CA administrator some authentication when a user calls to ask for a certificate to be revoked. It can be up to 80 characters in length. *serial* specifies the PIX Firewall serial number (optional), and *ipaddress* is the PIX Firewall's IP address (optional).

The **ca enroll** *ca_nickname challenge_password* command requests certificates from the CA for all your PIX Firewall's RSA key pairs. This is called *enrolling with the CA*. This task differs from enrolling with IOS. With IOS, you are prompted for the challenge password. With a PIX, you have to include the challenge password in the **ca enroll** command line.

Your PIX Firewall needs a signed certificate from the CA for each of your PIX Firewall's RSA key pairs. If you already have a certificate for your keys, you cannot complete this command; instead, you are prompted to remove the existing certificate first. If you want to cancel the current enrollment request, use the **no ca enroll** command.

Here's an example of authenticating a CA:

```
PIX1(config)#ca enroll myca mypassword1234567
```

The argument **mypassword1234567** is a password, which is not saved with the configuration.

The **ca enroll** command requests as many certificates as there are RSA key pairs. You need to enable this command only once, even if you have special-usage RSA key pairs.

NOTE   If your PIX Firewall reboots after you issued the **ca enroll** command but before you received the certificates, you must reissue the command and notify the CA administrator.

Step 6: Saving and Testing the Configuration

One very important point with the PIX Firewall is the **ca save all** command. On a PIX, the **write memory** command does not save the key pairs to Flash memory. The **ca save all** command allows you to save the PIX Firewall RSA key pairs, the CA, the RA, the PIX Firewall certificates, and the CA's CRLs in the persistent data file in Flash memory between reloads. The **no ca save all** command removes the saved data from the PIX Firewall's Flash memory. The **ca save all** command itself is not saved with the PIX Firewall configuration between reloads.

Use the **show ca identity** command to view the current CA identity settings stored in RAM, as shown in Example 19-56.

Example 19-56 show ca identity *Command*

```
PIX1#show ca identity

ca identity myca pkitest:80/CERTSRV/MSCEP/MSCEP.DLL
```

Use the **show ca configure** command to view CA communication parameter settings, as shown in Example 19-57.

Example 19-57 show ca configure *Command*

```
PIX1#show ca configure
ca configure myca ra 2 2
```

Use the **show ca certificate** command to verify that the enrollment process was successful and to view PIX Firewall, CA, and RA certificates, as shown in Example 19-58.

Example 19-58 show ca certificate *Command*

```
PIX1#show ca certificate
PIX1(config)#sh ca cert
Type help or '?' for a list of available commands.
PIX1(config)#sh ca cert
RA Signature Certificate
  Status: Available
  Certificate Serial Number: 61058748000000000002
  Key Usage: Signature
    CN = Andrew Mason
    OU = IT
    O = BO
    L = Leeds
    ST = WY
    C = UK
    EA =<16> andrew.mason@boxingorange.com
  Validity Date:
    start date: 14:34:03 UTC Jan 2 2003
    end   date: 14:44:03 UTC Jan 2 2004

CA Certificate
  Status: Available
  Certificate Serial Number: 7ca0b6efcc3376964498c23ba8d82387
  Key Usage: Signature
    CN = labca
    OU = bo
    O = boxing orange
    L = leeds
    ST = west yorkshire
    C = UK
    EA =<16> labca@boxingorange.com
  Validity Date:
    start date: 11:52:36 UTC Jan 2 2003
    end   date: 12:00:09 UTC Jan 2 2005

RA KeyEncipher Certificate
  Status: Available
  Certificate Serial Number: 61058a55000000000003
  Key Usage: Encryption
    CN = Andrew Mason
    OU = IT
    O = BO
    L = Leeds
    ST = WY
    C = UK
    EA =<16> andrew.mason@boxingorange.com
```

Example 19-58 **show ca certificate** *Command (Continued)*

```
   Validity Date:
     start date: 14:34:04 UTC Jan 2 2003
     end   date: 14:44:04 UTC Jan 2 2004

PIX1(config)#
```

Use the **show ca mypubkey rsa** command to view your RSA public key, as shown in
Example 19-59.

Example 19-59 **show ca mypubkey rsa** *Command*

```
PIX1(config)#show ca mypubkey rsa

% Key pair was generated at: 22:13:22 Nov 22 2002

Key name: PIX1.boxingorange.com
 Usage: General Purpose Key
 Key Data:
   30819f30 0d06092a 864886f7 0d010101 05000381 8d003081 89028181 00d9526e
   9ff221c8 cfd1759e 6379d23d 0e7ee835 893367d5 c7f98944 76312ea7 7445f3bd
   ab0f517c 7532c244 890a09ef e5a02efd bf444e0e dd8f7e02 1fa63c1e 0bf9ffc0
   fc8b9814 adfdc76c bd99e81c 455af200 49830de6 7bfdbb41 193610d5 479fe860
   421bffea 45c36488 e6fafae5 259dcf0b b25999a2 630ab9bd 166ad246 f7020301 0001
PIX1(config)#
```

Enabling IKE to Use the Configured CA

Now that the CA is configured and authenticated and you have enrolled with it to obtain a
certificate, it is time to configure your PIX Firewall to use CA for IKE phase 1. The IPSec
configuration for PIX1 is shown in Example 19-60.

Example 19-60 *IPSec Configuration*

```
PIX1#write terminal
access-list 100 permit ip 10.1.1.0 255.255.255.0 192.168.1.0 255.255.255.0
crypto ipsec transform-set myset esp-des esp-sha-hmac
crypto map newmap 10 ipsec-isakmp
crypto map newmap 10 match address 100
crypto map newmap 10 set peer 130.100.26.1
crypto map newmap 10 set transform-set myset
crypto map newmap interface outside
isakmp enable outside
isakmp key thisisthekey address 130.100.26.1 netmask 255.255.255.255
isakmp identity address
isakmp policy 10 authentication pre-share
isakmp policy 10 encryption des
isakmp policy 10 hash md5
isakmp policy 10 group 1
isakmp policy 10 lifetime 86400
```

You can see that you have defined an ISAKMP policy using preshared authentication. To enable the use of the CA you just configured, you have to change this to be RSA Signatures. Remove the current configuration setting with the command **no isakmp policy 10 authentication pre-share**, and then enter this command:

```
PIX1(config)#isakmp policy 10 authentication rsa-sig
```

Now, use the command **show crypto isakmp policy** to display the configured ISAKMP polices, as shown in Example 19-61.

Example 19-61 **show crypto isakmp policy** *Command*

```
PIX1#show crypto isakmp policy
Protection suite of priority 10
        encryption algorithm:   DES - Data Encryption Standard (56 bit keys).
        hash algorithm:         Message Digest 5
        authentication method:  Rivest-Shamir-Adleman Signatures
        Diffie-Hellman group:   #1 (768 bit)
        lifetime:               86400 seconds, no volume limit
Default protection suite
        encryption algorithm:   DES - Data Encryption Standard (56 bit keys).
        hash algorithm:         Secure Hash Standard
        authentication method:  Rivest-Shamir-Adleman Signature
        Diffie-Hellman group:   #1 (768 bit)
        lifetime:               86400 seconds, no volume limit
```

You can see from the configuration that the protection suite with a priority of 10 is now using RSA Signatures.

To enable the VPN, simply configure the second PIX in the same way outlined in this section.

Summary

This chapter covered VPNs with a focus on IPSec. It started with a detailed overview of IPSec before moving on to Cisco IOS and Cisco PIX Firewall IPSec configuration using preshared keys and certificate authorities. This chapter also covered configuration and troubleshooting for a simple site-to-site VPN.

Review Questions

1 What is the main difference between an access list on a Cisco IOS router and an access list on a PIX Firewall?

2 What command creates an RSA key pair on a PIX Firewall with a 1024-bit key length?

3 When using a GRE tunnel with an IOS router, where should you place the crypto map if you want to protect traffic going over the tunnel?

4 What command on a PIX Firewall enrolls a CA that has a CA nickname of myca?

5 What command on the PIX displays the IKE configuration within the router but does not display the default policy settings?

6 What command on the PIX bypasses conduits and access lists for IPSec connections but still checks the traffic against the ASA to maintain security?

7 What encryption and authentication are the defaults for ISAKMP policies?

FAQs

Q — *What is the difference between tunnel and transport mode for IPSec?*

A — Tunnel mode is used when the private IP addresses are used behind the tunnel endpoints. This is because tunnel mode rewrites the IP header with new information. One point to remember is that tunnel mode is not required when you are using GRE tunnels. GRE provides its own tunneling mechanism so that you can use transport mode IPSec in these situation. When you use transport mode, the VPN endpoints must originate and terminate the VPN traffic.

Q — *What is perfect forward secrecy (PFS)?*

A — If PFS is specified in the IPSec policy, a new Diffie-Hellman exchange is performed with each quick mode, providing key material that has greater entropy (key material life) and thereby greater resistance to cryptographic attacks. Each Diffie-Hellman exchange requires large exponentiations, thereby increasing CPU use and exacting a performance cost.

Q — *How do I configure a router or PIX Firewall to use a CA as opposed to a preshared key?*

A — It is most common for people to configure an IPSec VPN using a preshared key. This can be seen with the **show crypto isakmp policy** command on both the router and the PIX Firewall.

It is actually the default setting on both the PIX and IOS software to use RSA signatures as the IKE phase 1 authentication method. To enable this on a device, first you have to create an RSA key pair local on the device and then enroll with a certificate authority. You then have to configure the ISAKMP policy to use the RSA signatures for authentication. This is done in IOS with the command **authentication rsa-sig**.

This command is not displayed in the configuration because it is the default.

This chapter covers the following topics:

- Issues with conventional IPSec VPNs
- Configuring advanced VPNs

CHAPTER 20

Advanced Virtual Private Networks

Now that we have covered the basics of PIX-to-PIX and IOS-to-IOS VPNs using both preshared keys and certificate authorities, this chapter looks at a more-advanced VPN implementation that you might come across on the CCIE Security lab exam.

The standard IPSec implementation that you learned about in Chapter 19, "Virtual Private Networks," presents a number of issues. In this chapter you will learn how to solve some of these issues by using generic routing encapsulation (GRE) tunnels and Dynamic Multipoint IPSec VPN (DMVPN). DMVPN was introduced in Release 12.2(13)T of the Cisco IOS software. You won't be asked to configure it for the CCIE Security Lab exam that uses the Cisco IOS software version earlier than 12.2(13)T. However, the updated exam versions, based on Release 12.2(13)T and later, are likely to implement this feature. To find out the Cisco IOS software release currently used in the CCIE Security Lab exam, consult www.cisco.com/warp/public/625/ccie/.

Issues with Conventional IPSec VPNs

Certain issues arise when you try to achieve full IPSec cloud functionality:

- The inherent nature of IPSec does not allow routing protocol updates to be routed through the IPSec tunnel, because IPSec doesn't encrypt IP multicast/broadcast packets. As a result, whenever there is a change in the topology at the hub or spokes, the other end of the IPSec tunnel cannot be dynamically notified of it.

- Each time a network needs to be added to the list of IPSec participants, a new access list must be defined for user traffic encryption.

- Because IPSec environments are essentially hub-and-spoke networks, the hub router's configuration can grow to the point where it becomes a management nightmare.

- Many hosts' public IP addresses aren't fixed; they change every time a host comes online because of DHCP utilization by a service provider. This is not an ideal situation as far as IPSec is concerned.

• Sometimes remote sites require direct communication with one another, and that means foregoing the hub-and-spoke topology in favor of the full mesh. The issue is that it's very difficult to predict the exact sites to which a spoke might need an occasional direct connection, and directly connecting every site to every other site can become impossible.

Make note of these issues; they are referenced throughout the next sections.

Solving IPSec Issues with GREs

As just mentioned, IPSec does not encrypt IP broadcast/multicast packets and therefore does not allow them to be routed through the IPSec tunnel. Because all dynamic routing protocols except BGP operate based on broadcast or multicast IP packets, this situation creates a problem.

To be able to use dynamic routing over IPSec protected links, you can "run" a routing protocol through a GRE tunnel. GRE tunnels are implemented on routers using a virtual tunnel interface. The GRE tunneling protocol is also designed to handle IP multicast/broadcast packets. The original IP multicast packets are encapsulated into the GRE tunnel unicast packets. This GRE tunnel packet can now be encrypted by IPSec.

An added bonus of GRE encapsulation of the original data packet is that it doesn't need IPSec to encapsulate it into another IP header. Therefore, IPSec can be configured for transport mode, saving 20 bytes. The transport mode restriction of IP source and destination addresses of the encrypted packet matching the IPSec peer addresses isn't an issue, because the same routers are both the IPSec and GRE tunnel endpoints.

As you can see, the combination of GRE tunnels and IPSec transport mode encryption allows dynamic routing protocols to update routing tables on both ends of the encrypted tunnel. In a routing table, the GRE tunnel interface IP address of the opposite end of the tunnel is recorded as the next hop for all prefixes that were learned through that tunnel. Therefore, whenever a change occurs at either end, the other side is automatically notified without any manual intervention so that the encrypted connectivity can continue.

Solving IPSec Issues with DMVPNs

To address the second through fifth issues in the "Issues with Conventional IPSec VPNs" section and still preserve scalability, you can combine multipoint GRE tunnels with Next-Hop Resolution Protocol (NHRP) and IPSec encryption. The solution involves the DMVPN that uses Multipoint GRE/Next-Hop Resolution Protocol (mGRE/NHRP) with IPSec plus a number of new improvements described in the following sections.

Automatic IPSec Encryption Initiation

The DMVPN solution eliminates the need for preconfigured peer IP addresses and crypto access lists, which is the second issue on the list. GRE already has the peer source and destination address either configured or resolved with NHRP (for multipoint GRE tunnels). So IPSec is triggered immediately for the point-to-point GRE or multipoint GRE tunnel (with address resolution via NHRP). The crypto access lists that previously needed to be preconfigured are now automatically derived from the GRE tunnel source and destination addresses.

Dynamic Tunnel Creation for Spoke-to-Spoke Traffic

As mentioned in the "Issues with Conventional IPSec VPNs" section, the conventional solution for spoke-to-spoke communication is full-mesh (issue 5), which often isn't justified. What the DMVPN offers is to designate one router as the hub and all other routers as spokes with tunnels to the hub that are always up. This way, the spokes avoid configuration for direct tunnels to any other spokes. When one spoke wants to communicate with another spoke, the hub router acting as the NHRP server helps the source router resolve the address of the destination router. This allows the two spokes to dynamically create an IPSec tunnel between them (via the single mGRE interface) for direct data transfer. The dynamic tunnels time out after a configured period of inactivity.

The decision to create a direct spoke-to-spoke tunnel versus involving the hub in data forwarding depends on the next-hop IP address of an entry in the routing table.

You can also create a hierarchy of hubs in which each hub supports its own spokes. In this type of architecture, the hubs can be positioned on the same layer or can act as spokes to another higher layer of hubs.

Dynamic NHRP Multicast Definition

Conventionally, NHRP requires manual broadcast/multicast mapping to the tunnel destination addresses to support GRE tunneling of multicast and broadcast IP packets. For each spoke, you need to enter the **ip nhrp map multicast spoke-n-addr** statement on the hub. This brings up the third and fourth issues: the size of the hub configuration and the unknown spoke addresses.

The hub router needs to contain configuration information for every spoke router. This information includes a set of parameters such as a crypto map, a crypto access list, and the spoke router's GRE interface. The trouble is that most of the parameters are the same for each router, with the exception of the IP addresses.

Each set of spoke parameters contains an average of 13 statements. The statement breakdown is as follows:

- Crypto map statements

- One crypto ACL statement

- GRE tunnel interface statements, including the optional tunnel interface bandwidth, delay, and MTU statements

So if you had 300 spoke routers, you would end up with 3900 configuration lines on the hub router. Such a gigantic configuration makes the task of management and troubleshooting very difficult, if not impossible.

You can reduce the configuration size somewhat by employing dynamic crypto maps. This would reduce a 3900-line configuration to 2700 lines. However, in the case of dynamic crypto maps, the spoke router must initiate the IPSec encryption tunnel. Also, if you use the **ip unnumbered** command to minimize the number of GRE tunnels subnets, this might create some issues when troubleshooting.

The DMVPN allows you to configure one multipoint GRE tunnel interface and one IPSec profile on the hub router to encompass all spoke routers. This type of solution maintains a stable configuration size, notwithstanding the number of routers that can potentially be added to the VPN network.

The fourth issue is that IPSec peers require prior knowledge of each other's IP addresses to establish an IPSec tunnel. This is often impossible because of the widespread implementation of dynamic addressing.

One of the possible solutions is to use Tunnel Endpoint Discovery (TED). When TED is used, one IPSec peer sends a special packet to the destination IP address of the original data packet in need of encryption. In theory, this packet should find the peer while traversing the network along the same path that the IPSec tunnel packet will take. When the destination peer receives the packet, it responds, and the two peers can negotiate ISAKMP and IPSec security associations (SAs) and bring up the IPSec tunnel. TED can be used in combination with the GRE tunnels described previously. Although using TED and GRE tunnels together would work, it has an unfortunate restriction: The data packets to be encrypted must have routable IP addresses.

Alternatively, the DMVPN solution offers the same results as TED in an mGRE+IPSec configuration, without the restrictions for private IP addresses and without sending the probe-and-response packets.

Configuring Advanced VPNs

The configuration section of this chapter is divided into two case studies. The first case study teaches you how to modify the conventional IPSec VPN configuration to allow point-to-point GREs. The second case study presents the DMVPN configuration.

Case Study 20-1: Using Dynamic Routing Over IPSec-Protected VPNs

In this case study, using the topology shown in Figure 20-1, you will allow the EIGRP routing information to be forwarded in an encrypted form over the full-mesh GRE tunnel setup.

Loopback interfaces 12.12.12.12, 13.13.13.13, and 14.14.14.14 represent private networks on R2, R3, and R4, respectively.

This case study consists of the following steps:

Step 1 Configure EIGRP routing, loopback interfaces, and full-mesh GRE tunnels.

Step 2 Configure IPSec parameters.

Step 3 Apply IPSec parameters to interfaces.

Step 4 Verify IPSec with GRE configuration.

Figure 20-1 *Basic IPSec Topology*

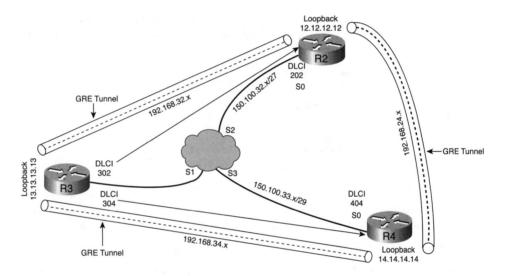

Step 1: Configuring EIGRP Routing, Loopback Interfaces, and Full-Mesh GRE Tunnels

Before getting into the IPSec portion of this case study, you must configure basic routing and interface parameters for all three routers. Especially important to this case study are the following:

- Configuring loopback interfaces
- Setting up GRE tunnels in a full-mesh arrangement
- Configuring EIGRP routing

The following sections describe each of these points.

Configuring Loopback Interfaces

You begin by creating loopback interfaces on R2, R3, and R4. These loopbacks are designed to imitate a private network on each router. Assign the IP addresses in the following manner:

```
R2(config)#interface loopback12
R2(config-if)#ip address 12.12.12.12 255.255.255.255

R3(config)#interface loopback13
R3(config-if)#ip address 13.13.13.13 255.255.255.255

R4(config)#interface loopback14
R4(config-if)#ip address 14.14.14.14 255.255.255.255
```

Also, configure an additional loopback on each router to be referenced as the IP address of a peer on its neighbors and as a GRE tunnel source on a router itself. Use the following commands:

```
R2(config)#interface loopback2
R2(config-if)#ip address 2.2.2.2 255.255.255.255

R3(config)#interface loopback3
R3(config-if)#ip address 3.3.3.3 255.255.255.255

R4(config)#interface loopback4
R4(config-if)#ip address 4.4.4.4 255.255.255.255
```

Setting up GRE Tunnels in a Full-Mesh Arrangement

On each router, set up a GRE tunnel to both of its neighbors. GRE tunnels are implemented on routers using a virtual tunnel interface, as follows:

```
R2(config)#interface tunnel number
```

On R2, Tunnel2 is the GRE tunnel to R3; Tunnel4 is the GRE tunnel to R4. Use Loopback2's IP address as the tunnel source for both tunnels. Use R3's Loopback3 IP address as the tunnel destination for Tunnel2 and R4's Loopback4 IP address as the tunnel destination for Tunnel4. Apply the same rules when configuring GRE tunnels on R3 and R4. All tunnel source and destination addresses need to be reached within the existing infrastructure.

For the tunnel interface IP addresses, use the following:

- 192.168.32.x/24 between R3 and R2
- 192.168.24.x/24 between R2 and R4
- 192.168.34.x/24 between R3 and R4

Configuring EIGRP

On each router, configure the EIGRP parameters. Use the **network** statements to include each GRE tunnel interface and the private network. For more information on configuring EIGRP, review Chapter 9, "EIGRP."

Example 20-1 presents the beginning configuration of R2, R3, and R4, including the features discussed in this step.

Example 20-1 *Beginning Configuration of R2, R3, and R4*

```
R2#show run
version 12.2
!
hostname R2
!
interface Loopback2
 description OSPF Loopback
 ip address 2.2.2.2 255.255.255.255
!
interface Loopback12
 description Loopback for VPN full mesh
 ip address 12.12.12.12 255.255.255.255
interface Tunnel2
 description Basic GRE Crypto to R3
 ip address 192.168.32.2  255.255.255.0
 tunnel source 2.2.2.2
 tunnel destination 3.3.3.3
!
interface Tunnel4
 description Basic GRE Crypto to R4
 ip address 192.168.24.2 255.255.255.0
 tunnel source 2.2.2.2
 tunnel destination 4.4.4.4
!
interface Serial0
 ip address 150.100.32.2 255.255.255.224
 encapsulation frame-relay
 ip ospf authentication message-digest
 ip ospf message-digest-key 5 md5 7 045802150C2E
 ip ospf network point-to-point
 ip ospf hello-interval 65
 ip ospf priority 0
 frame-relay map ip 150.100.32.3 202 broadcast
!
router eigrp 100
 network 12.0.0.0
 network 192.168.24.0
 network 192.168.32.0
 maximum-paths 1
 no auto-summary
 eigrp log-neighbor-changes
!
router ospf 123
 router-id 2.2.2.2
 log-adjacency-changes
 area 0 authentication message-digest
 network 2.2.2.2 0.0.0.0 area 0
 network 150.100.32.0 0.0.0.31 area 0
```

continues

Example 20-1 *Beginning Configuration of R2, R3, and R4 (Continued)*

```
!
R3#show run
version 12.2
!
hostname R3
!
interface Loopback3
 description OSPF Loopback
 ip address 3.3.3.3 255.255.255.255
!
interface Loopback13
 description Loopback for VPN full mesh
 ip address 13.13.13.13 255.255.255.255
!
interface Tunnel2
 description Basic GRE Crypto to R2
 ip address 192.168.32.1 255.255.255.0
 tunnel source 3.3.3.3
 tunnel destination 2.2.2.2
!
interface Tunnel4
 description Basic GRE Crypto to R4
 ip address 192.168.34.1 255.255.255.0
 tunnel source 3.3.3.3
 tunnel destination 4.4.4.4
!
interface Serial0
 no ip address
 encapsulation frame-relay
 no fair-queue
 clockrate 64000
 frame-relay lmi-type ansi
!
interface Serial0.2 point-to-point
 ip address 150.100.32.3 255.255.255.224
 ip ospf authentication message-digest
 ip ospf message-digest-key 5 md5 cisco
 ip ospf hello-interval 65
 ip ospf priority 0
 frame-relay interface-dlci 302
!
interface Serial0.3 point-to-point
 ip address 150.100.33.3 255.255.255.248
 ip ospf authentication message-digest
 ip ospf message-digest-key 5 md5 cisco
 ip ospf hello-interval 65
 ip ospf priority 0
 frame-relay interface-dlci 304
```

Example 20-1 *Beginning Configuration of R2, R3, and R4 (Continued)*

```
!
router eigrp 100
 network 13.0.0.0
 network 192.168.32.0
 network 192.168.34.0
 maximum-paths 1
 no auto-summary
!
router ospf 123
 router-id 3.3.3.3
 log-adjacency-changes
 area 0 authentication message-digest
 network 3.3.3.3 0.0.0.0 area 0
 network 150.100.32.0 0.0.0.31 area 0
 network 150.100.33.0 0.0.0.7 area 0
!

R4#show run
!
version 12.2
!
hostname R4
!
interface Loopback4
 description OSPF Loopback
 ip address 4.4.4.4 255.255.255.255
!
interface Loopback14
 description Loopback for VPN full mesh
 ip address 14.14.14.14 255.255.255.255
!
interface Tunnel2
 description Basic GRE Crypto to R2
 ip address 192.168.24.4 255.255.255.0
 tunnel source 4.4.4.4
 tunnel destination 2.2.2.2
!
interface Tunnel3
 description Basic GRE Crypto to R3
 ip address 192.168.34.2 255.255.255.0
 tunnel source 4.4.4.4
 tunnel destination 3.3.3.3
!
interface Serial0
 ip address 150.100.33.4 255.255.255.248
 ip rip send version 2
 ip rip receive version 2
 encapsulation frame-relay
 ip ospf authentication message-digest
 ip ospf message-digest-key 5 md5 7 104D000A0618
 ip ospf network point-to-point
```

continues

Example 20-1 *Beginning Configuration of R2, R3, and R4 (Continued)*

```
 ip ospf hello-interval 65
 ip ospf priority 0
 frame-relay map ip 150.100.33.3 404 broadcast
 frame-relay lmi-type ansi
!
router eigrp 100
 network 14.0.0.0
 network 192.168.24.0
 network 192.168.34.0
 maximum-paths 1
 no auto-summary
!
router ospf 123
 router-id 4.4.4.4
 log-adjacency-changes detail
 area 0 authentication message-digest
 network 4.4.4.4 0.0.0.0 area 0
 network 150.100.33.0 0.0.0.7 area 0
```

Step 2: Configuring IPSec Parameters

At this point, you are ready to establish basic IPSec parameters. You learned the configuration procedure for basic IPSec in Chapter 19. The IPSec parameters you have to configure for this case study are as follows:

- IKE policy

- IPSec transforms and protocol

- Access lists for encryption

- Crypto map

When defining an IKE policy on R2, R3, and R4, use preshared authentication with **ccie** as a key for all three peers. Identify the peers by their GRE tunnel source IP address. Create a transform called **trvpn** with **esp-des** and **esp-sha-hmac**.

Create an access list to encrypt the private network traffic over the GRE tunnel. When implementing the GRE tunnels, you also have the option to encrypt the GRE tunnel, which means that all traffic going through the GRE tunnel is to be encrypted. This is a very useful solution for the real-life network environment, because it minimizes manual configuration when traffic from hundreds of networks needs to be transported over the GRE tunnel. The access list command for GRE tunnel encryption is as follows:

```
R2(config)#permit gre host tunnel-source host tunnel-destination
```

In this case study, you are required to encrypt traffic to and from the private networks on the three routers. Apply this access list as well as the configured transform set to the crypto map named **vpn**. Identify the peers by their GRE tunnel source IP address.

Example 20-2 shows the IPSec configuration portion of R2, R3, and R4.

Example 20-2 *Configuring IPSec Parameters*

```
R2#show run
!
! Output omitted for brevity
!
crypto isakmp policy 1
 authentication pre-share
crypto isakmp key ccie address 3.3.3.3
crypto isakmp key ccie address 4.4.4.4
!
crypto ipsec transform-set trvpn esp-des esp-sha-hmac
 mode transport
!
crypto map vpn 10 ipsec-isakmp
 set peer 3.3.3.3
 set peer 4.4.4.4
 set transform-set trvpn
 match address 111
!
access-list 111 permit ip 12.12.12.0 0.0.0.255 14.14.14.0 0.0.0.255 log
access-list 111 permit ip 12.12.12.0 0.0.0.255 13.13.13.0 0.0.0.255 log

R3#show run
!
! Output omitted for brevity
!
crypto isakmp policy 1
 authentication pre-share
crypto isakmp key ccie address 2.2.2.2
crypto isakmp key ccie address 4.4.4.4
!
crypto ipsec transform-set trvpn esp-des esp-sha-hmac
 mode transport
!
crypto map vpn 10 ipsec-isakmp
 set peer 2.2.2.2
 set peer 4.4.4.4
 set transform-set trvpn
 match address 111
!
access-list 111 permit ip 13.13.13.0 0.0.0.255 12.12.12.0 0.0.0.255 log
access-list 111 permit ip 13.13.13.0 0.0.0.255 14.14.14.0 0.0.0.255 log
!

R4#show run
!
! Output omitted for brevity
!
crypto isakmp policy 1
 authentication pre-share
```

continues

Example 20-2 *Configuring IPSec Parameters (Continued)*

```
crypto isakmp key ccie address 2.2.2.2
crypto isakmp key ccie address 3.3.3.3
!
crypto ipsec transform-set trvpn esp-des esp-sha-hmac
 mode transport
!
crypto map vpn 10 ipsec-isakmp
 set peer 2.2.2.2
 set peer 3.3.3.3
 set transform-set trvpn
 match address 111
!
access-list 111 permit ip 14.14.14.0 0.0.0.255 12.12.12.0 0.0.0.255 log
access-list 111 permit ip 14.14.14.0 0.0.0.255 13.13.13.0 0.0.0.255 log
```

In Example 20-2, pay attention to the access lists that identify traffic for encryption. The access lists for all three routers specify only the private network packets.

CAUTION Normally, in a full-mesh GRE situation, you need to configure a separate crypto map and access list for each peer. Example 20-2 has only one. This configuration is provided as training for the CCIE Security Lab exam. It helps you save time by avoiding extra typing. Although it is a working configuration, it should never be implemented in a real-life production network.

Step 3: Applying IPSec Parameters to Interfaces

As you learned in Chapter 19, the crypto maps must be applied to every interface through which IPSec traffic will flow. When it comes to GRE tunnels, the **crypto map** statement must be applied on both the physical interface and the tunnel interface, as shown in Example 20-3.

Example 20-3 *Applying IPSec Parameters to Interfaces*

```
R2#show run
!
! Output omitted for brevity
!
interface Tunnel2
 description Basic GRE Crypto to R3
 ip address 192.168.32.2 255.255.255.0
 tunnel source 2.2.2.2
 tunnel destination 3.3.3.3
 crypto map vpn
!
interface Tunnel4
 description Basic GRE Crypto to R4
 ip address 192.168.24.2 255.255.255.0
```

Example 20-3 *Applying IPSec Parameters to Interfaces (Continued)*

```
 tunnel source 2.2.2.2
 tunnel destination 4.4.4.4
 crypto map vpn
!
interface Serial0
 ip address 150.100.32.2 255.255.255.224
 encapsulation frame-relay
 ip ospf authentication message-digest
 ip ospf message-digest-key 5 md5 7 045802150C2E
 ip ospf network point-to-point
 ip ospf hello-interval 65
 ip ospf priority 0
 frame-relay map ip 150.100.32.3 202 broadcast
 frame-relay interface-dlci 202
 crypto map vpn

R3#show run
!
! Output omitted for brevity
!
interface Tunnel2
 description Basic GRE Crypto to R2
 ip address 192.168.32.1 255.255.255.0
 tunnel source 3.3.3.3
 tunnel destination 2.2.2.2
 crypto map vpn
!
interface Tunnel4
 description Basic GRE Crypto to R4
 ip address 192.168.34.1 255.255.255.0
 tunnel source 3.3.3.3
 tunnel destination 4.4.4.4
 crypto map vpn
!
interface Serial0.2 point-to-point
 ip address 150.100.32.3 255.255.255.224
 ip ospf authentication message-digest
 ip ospf message-digest-key 5 md5 cisco
 ip ospf hello-interval 65
 ip ospf priority 0
 frame-relay interface-dlci 302
 crypto map vpn
!
interface Serial0.3 point-to-point
 ip address 150.100.33.3 255.255.255.248
 ip ospf authentication message-digest
 ip ospf message-digest-key 5 md5 cisco
 ip ospf hello-interval 65
 ip ospf priority 0
 frame-relay interface-dlci 304
 crypto map vpn
```

continues

Example 20-3 *Applying IPSec Parameters to Interfaces (Continued)*

```
R4#show run
!
! Output omitted for brevity
!
!
interface Tunnel2
 description Basic GRE Crypto to R2
 ip address 192.168.24.4 255.255.255.0
 tunnel source 4.4.4.4
 tunnel destination 2.2.2.2
 crypto map vpn
!
interface Tunnel3
 description Basic GRE Crypto to R3
 ip address 192.168.34.2 255.255.255.0
 tunnel source 4.4.4.4
 tunnel destination 3.3.3.3
 crypto map vpn
!
interface Serial0
 ip address 150.100.33.4 255.255.255.248
 encapsulation frame-relay
 ip ospf authentication message-digest
 ip ospf message-digest-key 5 md5 7 104D000A0618
 ip ospf network point-to-point
 ip ospf hello-interval 65
 ip ospf priority 0
 frame-relay map ip 150.100.33.3 404 broadcast
 frame-relay lmi-type ansi
 crypto map vpn
```

Step 4: Verifying IPSec with GRE Configuration

To verify whether your configuration is truly functional, you can use several techniques:

- Verifying the crypto map
- Checking the EIGRP routing table
- Monitoring IPSec phase 1 and phase 2 negotiations
- Verifying security associations

The verification commands shown in this section are issued on R3 to keep the examples as brief as possible. The same commands can be issued on two other routers.

Example 20-4 demonstrates the crypto map named vpn configured on R3. Notice the access list 111 definition, peer IP addresses, and interfaces to which the crypto map has been applied (both virtual and physical).

Example 20-4 **show crypto map** *Command on R3*

```
R3#show crypto map

Crypto Map "vpn" 10 ipsec-isakmp
        Peer = 2.2.2.2
        Peer = 4.4.4.4
        Extended IP access list 111
            access-list 111 permit ip 13.13.13.0 0.0.0.255 12.12.12.0 0.0.0.255
            access-list 111 permit ip 13.13.13.0 0.0.0.255 14.14.14.0 0.0.0.255
        Current peer: 2.2.2.2
        Security association lifetime: 4608000 kilobytes/3600 seconds
        PFS (Y/N): N
        Transform sets={ trvpn, }
        Interfaces using crypto map vpn:
                Serial0.2
                Serial0.3
                Tunnel2
                Tunnel4
```

You may issue the **show ip route eigrp** command to view the networks learned via EIGRP. Example 20-5 illustrates such output on R3. Note that the prefixes are learned via tunnel interfaces.

Example 20-5 **show ip route eigrp** *Command Output on R3*

```
R3#show ip route eigrp
D     192.168.24.0/24 [90/310044416] via 192.168.32.2, 00:06:58, Tunnel2
      12.0.0.0/32 is subnetted, 1 subnets
D        12.12.12.12 [90/297372416] via 192.168.32.2, 00:06:58, Tunnel2
      14.0.0.0/32 is subnetted, 1 subnets
D        14.14.14.14 [90/297372416] via 192.168.34.2, 00:06:59, Tunnel4
```

Issue the **debug crypto isa**, **debug crypto ipsec**, and **debug crypto isakmp detail** commands on R3. Then execute an extended ping from R3's 13.13.13.13 to R2's 12.12.12.12, as shown in Example 20-6.

Example 20-6 *Extended Ping from 13.13.13.13 to 12.12.12.12*

```
R3#ping
Protocol [ip]:
Target IP address: 12.12.12.12
Repeat count [5]:
Datagram size [100]:
```

continues

Example 20-6 *Extended Ping from 13.13.13.13 to 12.12.12.12 (Continued)*

```
Timeout in seconds [2]:
Extended commands [n]: y
Source address or interface: 13.13.13.13
Type of service [0]:
Set DF bit in IP header? [no]:
Validate reply data? [no]:
Data pattern [0xABCD]:
Loose, Strict, Record, Timestamp, Verbose[none]:
Sweep range of sizes [n]:
Type escape sequence to abort.
Sending 5, 100-byte ICMP Echos to 12.12.12.12, timeout is 2 seconds:
Packet sent with a source address of 13.13.13.13
```

After issuing the **ping**, watch the **debug** commands shown in Example 20-7, which demonstrate the IPSec session establishment between the two peers.

Example 20-7 debug *Command Output on R3*

```
*Mar  1 00:10:32.475: %SEC-6-IPACCESSLOGDP: list 111 permitted icmp 13.13.13.13 ->
  12.12.12.12 (8/0), 1 packet
*Mar  1 00:10:32.487: IPSEC(sa_request): ,
  (key eng. msg.) OUTBOUND local= 3.3.3.3, remote= 2.2.2.2,
    local_proxy= 13.13.13.0/255.255.255.0/0/0 (type=4),
    remote_proxy= 12.12.12.0/255.255.255.0/0/0 (type=4),
    protocol= ESP, transform= esp-des esp-sha-hmac ,
    lifedur= 3600s and 4608000kb,
    spi= 0x5B4FCC26(1531956262), conn_id= 0, keysize= 0, flags= 0x400C
*Mar  1 00:10:32.499: ISAKMP: received ke message (1/1)
*Mar  1 00:10:32.503: ISAKMP: local port 500, remote port 500
*Mar  1 00:10:32.511: ISAKMP (0:1): beginning Main Mode exchange
*Mar  1 00:10:32.515: ISAKMP (0:1): sending packet to 2.2.2.2 (I) MM_NO_STATE.
*Mar  1 00:10:34.083: ISAKMP (0:1): received packet from 2.2.2.2 (I) MM_NO_STATE
*Mar  1 00:10:34.087: ISAKMP (0:1): processing SA payload. message ID = 0
*Mar  1 00:10:34.091: ISAKMP (0:1): found peer pre-shared key matching 2.2.2.2
*Mar  1 00:10:34.091: ISAKMP (0:1): Checking ISAKMP transform 1 against priority 1
  policy
! R3 is checking for ISAKMP negotiation against the policy it has in its local
  configuration
*Mar  1 00:10:34.095: ISAKMP:      encryption DES-CBC
*Mar  1 00:10:34.099: ISAKMP:      hash SHA
*Mar  1 00:10:34.099: ISAKMP:      default group 1
*Mar  1 00:10:34.099: ISAKMP:      auth pre-share
*Mar  1 00:10:34.103: ISAKMP:      life type in seconds
*Mar  1 00:10:34.103: ISAKMP:      life duration (VPI) of  0x0 0x1 0x51 0x80
*Mar  1 00:10:34.107: ISAKMP (0:1): atts are acceptable. Next payload is 0
! The received attributes are acceptable against the configured set of attributes
*Mar  1 00:10:35.591: ISAKMP (0:1): SA is doing pre-shared key authentication
  using id type ID_IPV4_ADDR
*Mar  1 00:10:35.603: ISAKMP (0:1): sending packet to 2.2.2.2 (I) MM_SA_SETUP..
*Mar  1 00:10:37.631: ISAKMP (0:1): received packet from 2.2.2.2 (I) MM_SA_SETUP
```

Example 20-7 debug *Command Output on R3 (Continued)*

```
*Mar  1 00:10:37.639: ISAKMP (0:1): processing KE payload. message ID = 0
*Mar  1 00:10:39.491: ISAKMP (0:1): processing NONCE payload. message ID = 0
*Mar  1 00:10:39.491: ISAKMP (0:1): found peer pre-shared key matching 2.2.2.2
*Mar  1 00:10:39.515: ISAKMP (0:1): SKEYID state generated
*Mar  1 00:10:39.515: ISAKMP (0:1): processing vendor id payload
*Mar  1 00:10:39.523: ISAKMP (0:1): speaking to another IOS box!
*Mar  1 00:10:39.523: ISAKMP (1): ID payload
        next-payload : 8
        type         : 1
        protocol     : 17
        port         : 500
        length       : 8
*Mar  1 00:10:39.527: ISAKMP (1): Total payload length: 12
*Mar  1 00:10:39.539: ISAKMP (0:1): sending packet to 2.2.2.2 (I) MM_KEY_EXCH
*Mar  1 00:10:39.639: ISAKMP (0:1): received packet from 2.2.2.2 (I) MM_KEY_EXCH
*Mar  1 00:10:39.651: ISAKMP (0:1): processing ID payload. message ID = 0
*Mar  1 00:10:39.651: ISAKMP (0:1): processing HASH payload. message ID = 0
*Mar  1 00:10:39.663: ISAKMP (0:1): SA has been authenticated with 2.2.2.2
! Phase 1 authentication is successful and the SA is authenticated
*Mar  1 00:10:39.667: ISAKMP (0:1): beginning Quick Mode exchange, M-ID of
  1262094673
*Mar  1 00:10:39.691: ISAKMP (0:1): sending packet to 2.2.2.2 (I) QM_IDLE
*Mar  1 00:10:40.111: ISAKMP (0:1): received packet from 2.2.2.2 (I) QM_IDLE
*Mar  1 00:10:40.131: ISAKMP (0:1): processing HASH payload. message ID =
  1262094673
*Mar  1 00:10:40.131: ISAKMP (0:1): processing SA payload. message ID = 1262094673
*Mar  1 00:10:40.135: ISAKMP (0:1): Checking IPSec proposal 1
*Mar  1 00:10:40.139: ISAKMP: transform 1, ESP_DES
*Mar  1 00:10:40.139: ISAKMP:    attributes in transform:
*Mar  1 00:10:40.139: ISAKMP:      encaps is 1
*Mar  1 00:10:40.143: ISAKMP:      SA life typ.!
Success rate is 20 percent (1/5), round-trip min/avg/max = 136/136/136 ms
!
! Output omitted for brevity
!
*Mar  1 00:10:40.943: %SEC-6-IPACCESSLOGDP: list 111 permitted icmp 12.12.12.12 ->
  13.13.13.13 (0/0), 1 packetR3#
```

Note that while the IPSec negotiations are taking place, the extended ping success rate is only
20 percent. When you issue the extended ping after the negotiations are completed the success
rate is 100 percent and the results you receive should match Example 20-8.

Example 20-8 *Extended Ping Results*

```
Type escape sequence to abort.
Sending 5, 100-byte ICMP Echos to 12.12.12.12, timeout is 2 seconds:
Packet sent with a source address of 13.13.13.13
!!!!!
Success rate is 100 percent (5/5), round-trip min/avg/max = 128/129/136 ms
```

Repeat the process shown in Examples 20-6, 20-7, and 20-8 for an extended ping from 13.13.13.13 to 14.14.14.14.

You can now view the established security associations on R3 by issuing the **show crypto isakmp sa** command, as shown in Example 20-9.

Example 20-9 **show crypto isakmp sa** *Command Output on R3*

```
R3#show crypto isakmp sa
dst              src              state         conn-id    slot
2.2.2.2          3.3.3.3          QM_IDLE            1        0
4.4.4.4          3.3.3.3          QM_IDLE            4        0
```

The configuration in this case study does not use the DMVPN solution. In the next case study, you will concentrate on reducing the size of routers' configuration with the help of DMVPN, which makes a tremendous difference in larger topologies.

Case Study 20-2: Configuring DMVPN

This case study uses the same topology as Case Study 20-1. R3 has been elected as hub, and R2 and R4 are spokes for the mGRE structure. The dynamic routing protocol used is RIPv2 instead of EIGRP, but mainly, what needs to change is the IPSec portion of the configuration that makes the DMVPN work. The updated version of the topology is shown in Figure 20-2.

Figure 20-2 *DMVPN Configuration Topology*

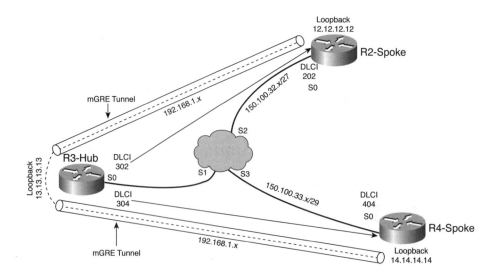

The steps to configure DMVPN are as follows:

Step 1 Configure the IPSec profile.

Step 2 Configure DMVPN on the hub router.

Step 3 Configure DMVPN on the spokes.

Step 4 Verify the DMVPN configuration.

Before you set up the DMVPN-specific parameters, you need to have the **crypto isakmp policy** and **crypto ipsec transform-set** already defined on all your routers, as shown in Example 20-10. Note the 0.0.0.0 address used in the **crypto isakmp** statement on R4. This allows R2 to accept any incoming ISAKMP request from clients that have the pre-shared key.

Example 20-10 **crypto isakmp policy** *and* **crypto ipsec transform-set** *Configuration on R2, R3, and R4*

```
R2#show run
hostname R2
!
crypto isakmp policy 10
 authentication pre-share
 group 2
crypto isakmp key ccie address 0.0.0.0 0.0.0.0
!
crypto ipsec transform-set des-set esp-des esp-sha-hmac
!
interface Loopback12
 ip address 12.12.12.12 255.255.255.0
!
interface Serial0
 ip address 150.100.32.2 255.255.255.224
 encapsulation frame-relay
 ip ospf network point-to-point
 no fair-queue
 frame-relay interface-dlci 202
!
router ospf 1
 log-adjacency-changes
 network 150.100.32.0 0.0.0.255 area 0
!
router rip
 version 2
 network 12.0.0.0
 network 192.168.1.0
 no auto-summary

R3#show run
hostname R3
!
crypto isakmp policy 10
 authentication pre-share
 group 2
```

continues

Example 20-10 **crypto isakmp policy** *and* **crypto ipsec transform-set** *Configuration on R2, R3, and R4 (Continued)*

```
crypto isakmp key ccie address 150.100.32.2
crypto isakmp key ccie address 150.100.33.4
!
crypto ipsec transform-set des-set esp-des esp-sha-hmac
!
interface Loopback3
 ip address 3.3.3.3 255.255.255.255
!
interface Loopback13
 ip address 13.13.13.13 255.255.255.255
!
interface Serial0
 no ip address
 encapsulation frame-relay
 no fair-queue
!
interface Serial0.2 point-to-point
 ip address 150.100.32.3 255.255.255.224
 ip ospf network point-to-point
 frame-relay interface-dlci 302
!
interface Serial0.4 point-to-point
 ip address 150.100.33.3 255.255.255.248
 ip ospf network point-to-point
 frame-relay interface-dlci 304
!
router ospf 1
 log-adjacency-changes
 network 3.3.3.3 0.0.0.0 area 0
 network 150.100.32.0 0.0.0.255 area 0
 network 150.100.33.0 0.0.0.255 area 0
!
router rip
 version 2
 network 13.0.0.0
 network 192.168.1.0
 no auto-summary

R4#show run
hostname R4
!
crypto isakmp policy 10
 authentication pre-share
 group 2
crypto isakmp key ccie address 0.0.0.0 0.0.0.0
!
crypto ipsec transform-set des-set esp-des esp-sha-hmac
!
interface Loopback14
 ip address 14.14.14.14 255.255.255.0
!
interface Serial0
```

Example 20-10 **crypto isakmp policy** *and* **crypto ipsec transform-set** *Configuration on R2, R3, and R4 (Continued)*

```
 ip address 150.100.33.4 255.255.255.248
 encapsulation frame-relay
 ip ospf network point-to-point
 no fair-queue
 frame-relay interface-dlci 404
!
router ospf 1
 log-adjacency-changes
 network 150.100.33.0 0.0.0.255 area 0
!
router rip
 version 2
 network 14.0.0.0
 network 192.168.1.0
 no auto-summary
```

Step 1: Configuring the IPSec Profile

As soon as the prerequisite specifications shown in Example 20-10 are set, you can begin the DMVPN configuration.

The first step of enabling DMVPN is to configure IPSec profiles on all three routers. IPSec profiles are used to create a single template for IPSec policy information, which can then be referenced by name from other parts of the configuration. When you reference an IPSec profile, configuring an entire crypto map becomes unnecessary.

An IPSec profile can consist of IPSec information only. In other words, it does not contain an access list or peering information.

To define an IPSec profile, use the following statement:

```
R2(config)#crypto ipsec profile name
```

You can think of the **crypto ipsec profile** command as being similar in function to a dynamic crypto map. It is designed for tunnel interfaces and defines the IPSec parameters for spoke-hub and spoke-spoke IPSec encryption. After it is entered, this command takes you into crypto map configuration mode.

To select the transform sets for use with the IPSec profile, use the following command syntax:

```
R2(config-crypto-map)#set transform-set transform-name
```

Overall, the only parameter that must be specified in the profile is the transform set. Note that there is no requirement for the **set peer** or **match address** commands. The necessary ingredients are learned directly from the associated GRE tunnel and NHRP mappings.

Several optional commands can be used with the IPSec profile:

```
R2(config-crypto-map)#set identity
R2(config-crypto-map)#set security association lifetime {seconds seconds |
  kilobytes kilobytes}
R2(config-crypto-map)#set pfs [group1 | group2]
```

The **set identity** and **set security association lifetime** commands specify identity restrictions and override the global lifetime value for the IPSec profile, respectively.

The **set pfs** command makes IPSec ask for perfect forward secrecy (PFS) when requesting new security associations for the specific IPSec profile. It makes sense to specify **group2**, as done in this case study, because **group1** is used by default.

Example 20-11 shows the IPSec profile configuration on R2, R3, and R4.

Example 20-11 *IPSec Profile Configuration of R2, R3, and R4*

```
R3#show run
!
! Output omitted for brevity
!
crypto ipsec profile mgreprof
 set transform-set des-set
 set pfs group2

R4#show run
!
! Output omitted for brevity
!
crypto ipsec profile mgreprof
 set transform-set des-set
 set pfs group2

R2#show run
!
! Output omitted for brevity
!
crypto ipsec profile mgreprof
 set transform-set des-set
 set pfs group2
```

Step 2: Configuring DMVPN on the Hub Router

The configuration of the hub router, R3, involves creating the GRE tunnel interface with the **interface tunnel** command. Once inside the interface configuration mode, enter the IP address and maximum transmission unit (MTU) size for the tunnel interface.

Your next task is to configure the NHRP characteristics followed by the GRE tunnel characteristics.

Configuring the NHRP Characteristics

The NHRP configuration is required when the GRE peer address is resolved via NHRP for the multipoint GRE tunnel.

The following command configures the authentication string for an interface using NHRP:

```
R3(config-if)#ip nhrp authentication string
```

The DMVPN solution allows configuring NHRP to dynamically add each spoke to the hub's multicast destination list by using the following command:

```
R3(config-if)#ip nhrp map multicast dynamic
```

The **ip nhrp map multicast dynamic** statement causes NHRP to automatically add spoke routers to the multicast NHRP mappings and register their unicast NHRP mappings when a spoke router initiates the mGRE+IPSec tunnel. This enables dynamic routing over the mGRE+IPSec tunnel, because dynamic routing protocols use multicast packets, as discussed earlier. As a result, this command eliminates the need for a separate multicast mapping configuration statement for each spoke.

To enable NHRP on an interface, use the following command:

```
R3(config-if)#ip nhrp network-id number
```

The *number* argument refers to a globally unique 32-bit network identifier from a nonbroadcast multiaccess (NBMA) network. The available range is from 1 to 4294967295.

To change how long NHRP NBMA addresses are advertised as valid in NHRP responses (the default is 7200 seconds), use the following command:

```
R3(config-if)#ip nhrp holdtime seconds
```

To make RIP advertise the routes back out the mGRE tunnel interface, you need to disable split horizon:

```
R3(config-if)#no ip split-horizon
```

No further changes are needed because RIP automatically uses the originator's IP address as the next hop.

Configuring the mGRE Characteristics

Besides the familiar command that specifies the tunnel source, a few more commands are needed to enable multipoint GRE. To set the encapsulation mode to mGRE for the tunnel interface, enter the following command:

```
R2(config-if)#tunnel mode gre multipoint
```

The **tunnel key** command can be used as a first line of defense to prevent improper configuration or injection of packets from a foreign source:

```
R2(config-if)#tunnel key key-number
```

The *key-number* can range from 0 to 4294967295.

The **tunnel protection** command assigns an IPSec profile to a tunnel interface:

```
R2(config-if)#tunnel protection ipsec profile name
```

This command is configured under the GRE tunnel interface and links that interface with the IPSec profile. It specifies that IPSec encryption takes place after the packet has been encapsulated by the GRE.

Example 20-12 demonstrates the necessary changes made to the R3 configuration to migrate from point-to-point GRE tunnel interfaces on the spoke routers to the mGRE tunnel on R3 by adding the NHRP-related configuration statements. Notice the **ip nhrp map multicast dynamic** command in R3's tunnel configuration. This enables the mapping of multicast routing protocol packets and forwarding them to spoke routers.

Example 20-12 *mGRE Configuration of the Hub Router*

```
R3#show run
!
! Output omitted for brevity
!
interface Tunnel100
 ip address 192.168.1.1 255.255.255.0
 no ip redirects
 ip mtu 1416
 ip nhrp authentication ccie
 ip nhrp map multicast dynamic
 ip nhrp network-id 99
 ip nhrp holdtime 300
 no ip split-horizon
 tunnel source 3.3.3.3
 tunnel mode gre multipoint
 tunnel key 10000
 tunnel protection ipsec profile mgreprof
```

You can see that the R3 configuration is missing the spokes' IP addresses. R3 gets the spoke's external physical interface IP address and the mapping to the spoke's tunnel interface IP address dynamically via NHRP.

Step 3: Configuring DMVPN on the Spokes

The mGRE configuration of spoke routers involves many of the commands introduced in Step 2 of this case study:

- **tunnel interface**
- **ip address**
- **ip mtu**
- **ip nhrp authentication**
- **ip nhrp network-id**
- **ip nhrp holdtime**
- **no ip split-horizon**
- **tunnel source**
- **tunnel mode gre multipoint**
- **tunnel key**
- **tunnel protection ipsec profile**

The new configuration commands include specifying the hub router's address. Spoke routers require a preconfigured address for R3 for the IPSec+GRE tunnel initiation. The NHRP mapping statement to R3 is preset on the spoke:

```
R2(config-if)#ip nhrp map hub-tunnel-ip-address hub-physical-ip-address
```

The following command enables the use of a dynamic routing protocol (RIPv2 in this case) between the spoke and hub and sends multicast packets to the hub router:

```
R2(config-if)#ip nhrp map multicast hub-physical-ip-address
```

As mentioned, the R3 router also acts as the Next-Hop Server (NHS). The spoke is notified of this with the following command:

```
R2(config-if)#ip nhrp nhs hub-tunnel-ip-address
```

The **ip nhrp nhs** command causes the spoke router to send NHRP registration packets to R3 at regular intervals through the mGRE+IPSec tunnel. It provides R3 with the spoke's dynamic IP address information, which in turn allows R3 to tunnel packets back to the spoke routers.

As soon as the IPSec tunnel is set up, the spoke router sends an NHRP registration packet to R3, acting as the NHS. This tells R3 to create an NHRP mapping for the spoke router, so now R3 can forward unicast IP data packets to the spoke router over the mGRE+IPSec tunnel. It also makes dynamic routing possible because R3 adds the spoke router to the NHRP multicast mapping list and therefore allows routing protocol update exchange between itself and the spoke.

As shown in Example 20-13, the configuration of both spoke routers is very similar, with the exception of IP addresses. It simplifies configuration management when the number of spoke routers is considerable.

Example 20-13 *mGRE Configuration of the Spoke Routers*

```
R2#show run
!
! Output omitted for brevity
!
interface Tunnel100
 ip address 192.168.1.2 255.255.255.0
 no ip redirects
 ip mtu 1416
 ip nhrp authentication ccie
 ip nhrp map 192.168.1.1 3.3.3.3
 ip nhrp map multicast 3.3.3.3
 ip nhrp network-id 99
 ip nhrp holdtime 300
 ip nhrp nhs 192.168.1.1
 no ip split-horizon
 tunnel source 150.100.32.2
 tunnel mode gre multipoint
 tunnel key 10000
 tunnel protection ipsec profile mgreprof

R4#show run
!
! Output omitted for brevity
!
interface Tunnel100
 ip address 192.168.1.3 255.255.255.0
 no ip redirects
 ip mtu 1416
 ip nhrp authentication ccie
 ip nhrp map 192.168.1.1 3.3.3.3
 ip nhrp map multicast 3.3.3.3
 ip nhrp network-id 99
 ip nhrp holdtime 300
 ip nhrp nhs 192.168.1.1
 no ip split-horizon
 tunnel source 150.100.33.4
 tunnel mode gre multipoint
 tunnel key 10000
 tunnel protection ipsec profile mgreprof
```

Step 4: Verifying the DMVPN Configuration

Begin the verification portion of your DMVPN configuration by checking to see if Layer 3 is functioning. By issuing the **show ip route ospf** and **show ip route rip** commands, you can ensure that your router is learning the correct prefixes via the correct interfaces, as shown in Example 20-14.

Example 20-14 *Verifying Layer 3 Functionality*

```
R4#show ip route ospf
     3.0.0.0/32 is subnetted, 1 subnets
O       3.3.3.3 [110/65] via 150.100.33.3, 00:00:48, Serial0
     150.100.0.0/16 is variably subnetted, 2 subnets, 2 masks
O       150.100.32.0/27 [110/128] via 150.100.33.3, 00:00:47, Serial0

R4#show ip route rip
     12.0.0.0/24 is subnetted, 1 subnets
R       12.12.12.0 [120/2] via 192.168.1.2, 00:00:21, Tunnel100
     13.0.0.0/32 is subnetted, 1 subnets
R       13.13.13.13 [120/1] via 192.168.1.1, 00:00:21, Tunnel100
```

To view the parameters for each IKE policy, issue the **show crypto isakmp policy** command, as shown in Example 20-15. Notice the **group 2** parameter configured under the **crypto isakmp policy** command. It was set in Step 1 of this case study.

Example 20-15 **show crypto isakmp policy** *Command Output on R4*

```
R4#show crypto isakmp policy
Protection suite of priority 10
        encryption algorithm:   DES - Data Encryption Standard (56 bit keys).
        hash algorithm:         Secure Hash Standard
        authentication method:  Pre-Shared Key
        Diffie-Hellman group:   #2 (1024 bit)
        lifetime:               86400 seconds, no volume limit
Default protection suite
        encryption algorithm:   DES - Data Encryption Standard (56 bit keys).
        hash algorithm:         Secure Hash Standard
        authentication method:  Rivest-Shamir-Adleman Signature
        Diffie-Hellman group:   #1 (768 bit)
        lifetime:               86400 seconds, no volume limit
```

The **show crypto map** command issued on R4 displays the IPSec profile parameters configured as shown in Example 20-16.

Example 20-16 show crypto map *Command Output on R4*

```
R4#show crypto map
Crypto Map "Tunnel100-head-0" 1 ipsec-isakmp
        Profile name: mgreprof
        Security association lifetime: 4608000 kilobytes/3600 seconds
        PFS (Y/N): Y
        DH group:  group2
        Transform sets={
                des-set,
        }

Crypto Map "Tunnel100-head-0" 2 ipsec-isakmp
        Map is a PROFILE INSTANCE.
        Peer = 3.3.3.3
        Extended IP access list
            access-list  permit gre host 150.100.33.4 host 3.3.3.3
        Current peer: 3.3.3.3
        Security association lifetime: 4608000 kilobytes/3600 seconds
        PFS (Y/N): Y
        DH group:  group2
        Transform sets={
                des-set,
        }
        Interfaces using crypto map Tunnel100-head-0:
                Tunnel100
```

You can trigger the IPSec tunnel establishment between the peers by pinging the hub and the other spoke router. Example 20-17 demonstrates the successful results of a ping issued on R4 to R3 and R2 after the IPSec tunnel has been established.

Example 20-17 *Results of the ICMP Requests on R4*

```
R4#ping 13.13.13.13

Type escape sequence to abort.
Sending 5, 100-byte ICMP Echos to 13.13.13.13, timeout is 2 seconds:
!!!!!
Success rate is 100 percent (5/5), round-trip min/avg/max = 168/188/212 ms
R4#ping 12.12.12.12

Type escape sequence to abort.
Sending 5, 100-byte ICMP Echos to 12.12.12.12, timeout is 2 seconds:
!!!!!
Success rate is 100 percent (5/5), round-trip min/avg/max = 164/178/192 ms
```

The **show crypto isakmp sa detail** command displays the ISAKMP security association information built between peers. Example 20-18 demonstrates the security association between R4 and R3.

Example 20-18 show crypto isakmp sa detail *Command Output on R4*

```
R4#show crypto isakmp sa detail
Codes: C - IKE configuration mode, D - Dead Peer Detection
       K - Keepalives, N - NAT-traversal
       X - IKE Extended Authentication
       psk - Preshared key, rsig - RSA signature
       renc - RSA encryption

f_vrf/i_vrf Conn id Local          Remote          Encr Hash Auth DH Lifetime
    Capabilities
        /     1     150.100.33.4   3.3.3.3         des  sha  psk  2  23:54:12
        /     2     150.100.33.4   150.100.32.2    des  sha  psk  2  23:58:37
```

The **show crypto engine connections active** command displays each Phase 2 security association built and the amount of traffic sent, as shown in Example 20-19. Remember that Phase 2
security associations are unidirectional, so each security association shows traffic in one
direction only (encryptions are outbound, and decryptions are inbound).

Example 20-19 show crypto engine connections active *Command Output on R3*

```
R3#show crypto engine connections active

   ID Interface     IP-Address      State  Algorithm          Encrypt  Decrypt
    1 Se2/0.2       150.100.32.3    set    HMAC_SHA+DES_56_CB       0        0
    2 Se2/0.4       150.100.33.3    set    HMAC_SHA+DES_56_CB       0        0
 2000 Tunnel100     192.168.1.1     set    HMAC_SHA+DES_56_CB       0       20
 2001 Tunnel100     192.168.1.1     set    HMAC_SHA+DES_56_CB      15        0
 2002 Tunnel100     192.168.1.1     set    HMAC_SHA+DES_56_CB       0        6
 2003 Tunnel100     192.168.1.1     set    HMAC_SHA+DES_56_CB       8        0
```

The **debug nhrp packet** and **debug nhrp extension** commands display a dump of NHRP
packets and the extensions portion of an NHRP packet, respectively. Example 20-20 demonstrates the output of these commands on R3 after the ping has been issued on R2. Notice the
resolution of the NBMA source and destination addresses, as well as the CCIE key exchange.

Example 20-20 debug nhrp packet *and* debug nhrp extension *Command Output on R3*

```
R3#ping 12.12.12.12

Type escape sequence to abort.
Sending 5, 100-byte ICMP Echos to 12.12.12.12, timeout is 2 seconds:
!!!!!
Success rate is 100 percent (5/5), round-trip min/avg/max = 136/165/188 ms
r3#
*Mar 24 14:48:29.031: NHRP: Receive Registration Request via Tunnel100, packet
  size: 80
*Mar 24 14:48:29.031:   (F) afn: IPv4(1), type: IP(800), hop: 255, ver: 1
```

continues

Example 20-20 **debug nhrp packet** *and* **debug nhrp extension** *Command Output on R3 (Continued)*

```
*Mar 24 14:48:29.031:     shtl: 4(NSAP), sstl: 0(NSAP)
*Mar 24 14:48:29.031: (M) flags: "unique", reqid: 2576
*Mar 24 14:48:29.031:     src NBMA: 150.100.33.4
*Mar 24 14:48:29.031:     src protocol: 192.168.1.3, dst protocol: 192.168.1.
*Mar 24 14:48:29.031: (C-1) code: no error(0)
*Mar 24 14:48:29.031:        prefix: 255, mtu: 1514, hd_time: 300
*Mar 24 14:48:29.031:        addr_len: 0(NSAP), subaddr_len: 0(NSAP), proto_len:
 0, pref: 0
*Mar 24 14:48:29.123: src: 192.168.1.1, dst: 12.12.12.12
*Mar 24 14:48:29.123: (F) afn: IPv4(1), type: IP(800), hop: 255, ver: 1
*Mar 24 14:48:29.123:     shtl: 4(NSAP), sstl: 0(NSAP)
*Mar 24 14:48:29.123: (M) flags: "router auth src-stable", reqid: 1
*Mar 24 14:48:29.123:     src NBMA: 3.3.3.3
*Mar 24 14:48:29.123:     src protocol: 192.168.1.1, dst protocol: 12.12.12.1
*Mar 24 14:48:29.123: (C-1) code: no error(0)
*Mar 24 14:48:29.123:        prefix: 0, mtu: 1514, hd_time: 300
*Mar 24 14:48:29.123:        addr_len: 0(NSAP), subaddr_len: 0(NSAP), proto_len:
 0, pref: 0
*Mar 24 14:48:29.123: Responder Address Extension(3):
*Mar 24 14:48:29.123: Forward Transit NHS Record Extension(4):
*Mar 24 14:48:29.123: Reverse Transit NHS Record Extension(5):
*Mar 24 14:48:29.123: Authentication Extension(7):
*Mar 24 14:48:29.123:   type:Cleartext(1), data:ccie
*Mar 24 14:48:29.343: NHRP: Receive Resolution Reply via Tunnel100, packet size:
 108
*Mar 24 14:48:29.343: (F) afn: IPv4(1), type: IP(800), hop: 255, ver: 1
*Mar 24 14:48:29.343:     shtl: 4(NSAP), sstl: 0(NSAP)
*Mar 24 14:48:29.343: (M) flags: "router auth dst-stable unique src-stable",
 qid: 1
*Mar 24 14:48:29.343:     src NBMA: 3.3.3.3
*Mar 24 14:48:29.343:     src protocol: 192.168.1.1, dst protocol: 12.12.12.1
*Mar 24 14:48:29.343: (C-1) code: no error(0)
*Mar 24 14:48:29.343:        prefix: 24, mtu: 1514, hd_time: 300
*Mar 24 14:48:29.343:        addr_len: 4(NSAP), subaddr_len: 0(NSAP), proto_len:
 4, pref: 0
*Mar 24 14:48:29.343:     client NBMA: 150.100.32.2
*Mar 24 14:48:29.343:     client protocol: 12.12.12.12
*Mar 24 14:48:29.343: Responder Address Extension(3):
*Mar 24 14:48:29.343: (C) code: no error(0)
*Mar 24 14:48:29.343:        prefix: 0, mtu: 1514, hd_time: 300
*Mar 24 14:48:29.343:        addr_len: 4(NSAP), subaddr_len: 0(NSAP), proto_len:
 4, pref: 0
*Mar 24 14:48:29.343:     client NBMA: 150.100.32.2
*Mar 24 14:48:29.343:     client protocol: 192.168.1.2
*Mar 24 14:48:29.343: Forward Transit NHS Record Extension(4):
*Mar 24 14:48:29.343: Reverse Transit NHS Record Extension(5):
*Mar 24 14:48:29.343: Authentication Extension(7):
*Mar 24 14:48:29.343:   type:Cleartext(1), data:ccie
*Mar 24 14:48:29.903: NHRP: Receive Registration Request via Tunnel100, packet
 size: 80
*Mar 24 14:48:29.903: (F) afn: IPv4(1), type: IP(800), hop: 255, ver: 1
*Mar 24 14:48:29.903:     shtl: 4(NSAP), sstl: 0(NSAP)
```

Example 20-20 **debug nhrp packet** *and* **debug nhrp extension** *Command Output on R3 (Continued)*

```
*Mar 24 14:48:29.903:  (M) flags: "unique", reqid: 9060
*Mar 24 14:48:29.903:      src NBMA: 150.100.32.2
*Mar 24 14:48:29.903:      src protocol: 192.168.1.2, dst protocol: 192.168.1.
*Mar 24 14:48:29.903:  (C-1) code: no error(0)
*Mar 24 14:48:29.903:        prefix: 255, mtu: 1514, hd_time: 300
*Mar 24 14:48:29.903:        addr_len: 0(NSAP), subaddr_len: 0(NSAP), proto_len:
   0, pref: 0
*Mar 24 14:48:29.903: Responder Address Extension(3):
*Mar 24 14:48:29.903: Forward Transit NHS Record Extension(4):ping
*Mar 24 14:48:29.903: Reverse Transit NHS Record Extension(5):
*Mar 24 14:48:29.903: Authentication Extension(7):
*Mar 24 14:48:29.903:   type:Cleartext(1), data:ccie
```

The **show ip nhrp** command output shown in Example 20-21 shows R4's NHRP cache. The 12.12.12.0/24 field specifies the IP address and its network mask in the IP-to-NBMA address cache. The **Tunnel100 created 00:00:35** field specifies the interface's type and number and how long ago it was created. The **expire 00:04:04** field shows when the authoritative NBMA address will expire; the value is based on the **ip nhrp holdtime** command, configured for 300 seconds in Step 2 of this case study. The **Type: dynamic** field means that the NBMA address was obtained from the NHRP request packet.

Example 20-21 **show ip nhrp** *Command Output on R4*

```
R4#show ip nhrp
12.12.12.0/24 via 12.12.12.12, Tunnel100 created 00:00:42, expire 00:04:17
Type: dynamic, Flags: router unique used
NBMA address: 150.100.32.2
13.13.13.13/32 via 13.13.13.13, Tunnel100 created 00:00:35, expire 00:04:24
Type: dynamic, Flags: router unique used
NBMA address: 3.3.3.3
14.14.14.0/24 via 14.14.14.14, Tunnel100 created 00:01:09, expire 00:04:04
Type: dynamic, Flags: router authoritative unique local
NBMA address: 150.100.33.4
192.168.1.1/32 via 192.168.1.1, Tunnel100 created 00:03:44, never expire
Type: static, Flags: authoritative used
NBMA address: 3.3.3.3
192.168.1.2/32 via 192.168.1.2, Tunnel100 created 00:01:09, expire 00:04:04
Type: dynamic, Flags: router implicit used
NBMA address: 150.100.32.2
```

Summary

This chapter introduced you to two techniques for configuring IPSec:

- GRE tunnels

- DMVPN

The topics discussed are part of the advanced IPSec configuration. Both the overview and configuration portions of this chapter relied heavily on your thorough understanding and knowledge of concepts discussed in Chapter 19. The DMVPN feature is a recent addition to the security services offered by Cisco. It was introduced with the 12.2(13)T release of the Cisco IOS software. Be sure to check the current CCIE Security Lab equipment list to determine the likelihood of this feature appearing on your exam.

Review Questions

1 Name two issues arising from conventional IPSec configuration.

2 What mechanism is used to accomplish DMVPN?

3 How can you implement dynamic routing protocols over IPSec protected links?

4 When full-mesh GRE tunnels are used, which interfaces need to have a **crypto map** applied?

5 What command specifies that all traffic going through the GRE tunnel is to be encrypted?

6 What are the three components of the DMVPN configuration?

7 In DMVPN, what command issued on the hub router causes NHRP to automatically add spoke routers to the multicast NHRP mappings and register their unicast NHRP mappings when a spoke router initiates the mGRE+IPSec tunnel?

8 What do you do to route RIP over the mGRE tunnel?

FAQs

Q — *Can DMVPN be implemented with multiple routed protocols?*

A — Yes. You can implement multiple routed protocols such as IP and IPX over the DMVPN architecture simultaneously. However, when opting for such a configuration, remember to exercise consistency with the split-horizon issues.

Q — *What routing protocols can be used with DMVPN, and which of them is the most commonly used in enterprise networks?*

A — Possible routing protocols are EIGRP, OSPF, BGP, and RIP. EIGRP is currently the one most commonly used.

Q — *Can you implement redundancy of the NHRP in a DMVPN environment?*

A — Yes. You can configure multiple NHRP servers on multiple hubs for backup.

Q — *What are the current hardware limitations of DMVPN?*

A — The 800 series currently does not support NHRP. NHRP is a DMVPN solution requirement, so DMVPN cannot currently be run on this platform.

This chapter covers the following topics:

- L2F and L2TP overview
- VPDN process overview
- PPTP overview
- Configuring VPDNs

CHAPTER 21

Virtual Private Dialup Networks

A *virtual private dialup network (VPDN)* is a way for a PPP client to gain access to a private network by dialing into an access server. The access server then determines whether it should forward the client's PPP session to a private network server via a virtual tunnel between the access server and the network server. The steps for the VPDN setup process are described in the section "Configuring VPDNs." This technology might or might not be incorporated into the lab exam. It is covered in this book both as part of overall network security and as training material for its possible inclusion in the CCIE Security lab exam in the future.

L2F and L2TP Overview

VPDN is a Layer 2 security technology that is governed by one of two protocols. Layer 2 Forwarding (L2F) Protocol is an older tunneling protocol. Layer 2 Tunneling Protocol (L2TP) is updated and has more features. Both of these protocols are designed to extend the PPP model by separating the Layer 2 (L2) termination point and the PPP termination point from one network access server (NAS) into two different devices. In a typical non-L2F or non-L2TP setup, the Layer 2 termination point and PPP session endpoint reside on the same physical device (the NAS). L2F and L2TP modify this configuration by deploying an L2 endpoint on one device and a PPP endpoint on another, interconnecting them through a tunnel over a network.

A device to which a user has an L2 connection has different names for L2F and L2TP. In L2F the device is called a *NAS*, and in L2TP it is called an *L2TP access concentrator (LAC)*. Similarly, the logical termination point of a PPP session that is tunneled from the client by the LAC or NAS is known by the two different names in L2F and L2TP: *home gateway* and *L2TP network server (LNS)*, respectively. Even though L2TP has largely replaced L2F, the L2F terms NAS and home gateway are still widely used. This can be a bit confusing. Therefore, this chapter attempts to streamline these concepts by consistently referring to the two devices as LAC/NAS and LNS/home gateway.

VPDN Process Overview

Figure 21-1 shows the VPDN process. To help decipher and better understand the later discussion of configuring VPDNs, the VPDN process is described briefly in this section.

Figure 21-1 *VPDN Process*

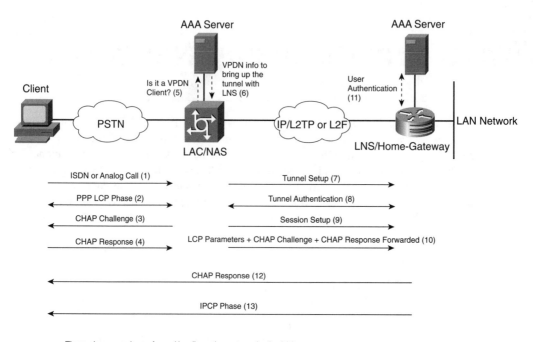

----- These phases can be performed locally on the router or by the AAA server.

Step 1   A dialup client connects to a LAC/NAS through ISDN or analog service.

Step 2   The client and the LAC/NAS negotiate the PPP LCP options such as PAP or CHAP, PPP multilink, compression, and so on.

Step 3   If CHAP has been agreed upon, the LAC/NAS queries the client with a CHAP challenge.

Step 4   The client responds with *username@DomainName* and the password.

Step 5   Using local VPDN configuration or contacting an AAA server, the LAC/NAS determines whether the client is a VPDN user based on the domain name in the CHAP response.

Step 6   If the client is a VPDN user, the LAC attempts to bring up an L2TP or L2F tunnel with the LNS/home gateway according to the information found in its local VPDN configuration or on an AAA server. The authentication process via an AAA server is described in Chapter 18, "AAA Services."

Step 7   Now it's the LNS/home gateway's turn to check the LAC/NAS. The LNS/home gateway verifies the name in the request received from the LAC/NAS and validates it as the potential tunnel peer.

Step 8   The authentication process works both ways: The LAC/NAS needs to authenticate the LNS/home gateway as well. This is done by referencing the local configuration or via an AAA server.

Step 9   The LAC/NAS peers with the LNS/home gateway. Together they form a tunnel in between.

Step 10   The LAC/NAS sends the LCP options negotiated between the client and itself to the LNS/home gateway. It also passes along the client's *username@DomainName* and password.

Step 11   The LNS/home gateway gets involved in the PPP negotiations. It clones the virtual-access interface from a virtual template in its configuration and authenticates the client's LCP options forwarded by the LAC/NAS locally or via an AAA server.

Step 12   The LNS/home gateway sends a CHAP response back to the client.

Step 13   When the IPCP phase is complete, the route is installed, and the PPP session is up between the client and the LNS/home gateway. Chapter 6, "ISDN Connectivity," contains more information on PPP.

The important facts to remember are

- The PPP session is between the two farthest points of the connection: the client and the LNS/home gateway.

- The L2F or L2TP tunnel is formed between the LAC/NAS and the LNS/home gateway. In this implementation, the LAC/NAS's function is to forward the PPP frames.

PPTP Overview

Point-to-Point Tunneling Protocol (PPTP) is an L2 tunneling protocol developed by Microsoft for a Windows-enabled remote client to connect securely to a private corporate network over the public IP network. PPTP is a newer technology and is somewhat of a replacement for VPDN. Unlike in the traditional VPDN architecture, the PPTP client doesn't have to be connected over the dialup services. This is because as far as PPTP is concerned, the client's PC is the PPTP access concentrator (PAC), and the other side of the connection terminates at the PPTP network server (PNS), which is the PIX Firewall. The PIX Firewall has supported PPTP since Release 5.1. PIX's support of PPTP includes PAP, CHAP, and MS-CHAP using local, RADIUS, or TACACS+ AAA. Encryption using the Microsoft Point-to-Point Encryption (MPPE) protocol is supported as well.

Case Study 21-3, later in this chapter, is dedicated to PPTP. You will find out how PPTP relates to the VPDN framework.

Configuring VPDNs

The following case studies discuss the VPDN configuration and various authentication techniques used by VPDN. You will learn how to

- Configure the VPDN to work with local AAA
- Configure TACACS+ authentication and authorization for VPDN
- Configure the PIX Firewall to use PPTP
- Configure the default VPDN group template

Case Study 21-1: Configuring the VPDN to Work with Local AAA

In this case study, you will accomplish the following:

Step 1   Configure R3 as a dialup client.

Step 2   Configure R5 as a LAC.

Step 3   Configure PIX2, which separates the LAC from the LNS.

Step 4   Configure R8 as an LNS to use local AAA to authenticate the tunnel and the user.

Step 5   Verify that the access VPN works properly.

Figure 21-2 shows the VPDN network topology. The tunnel and user authentication occur locally between R5 and R8, the home gateway.

Figure 21-2   *VPDN Topology Using the Local Database*

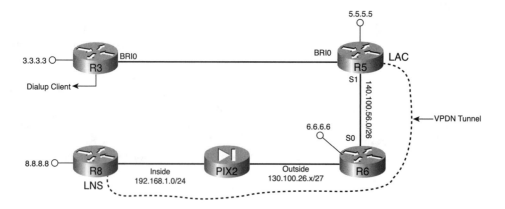

Step 1: Configuring the Client

In this case study, R3 is a dialup client that requires the configuration shown in Example 21-1. There is nothing particularly unusual about the R3 configuration setup. It is a typical dialup client configuration. It is described in detail in Chapter 6. Example 21-1 shows the necessary commands placed on the router. Pay attention to the **ppp chap hostname ccie4460@cisco.com** line. It will be referenced later, in the LNS configuration.

Example 21-1 *R3 as a Dialup Client*

```
R3#show run
hostname R3
!
interface BRI0/0
no ip address
encapsulation ppp
dialer pool-member 1
isdn switch-type basic-ni
isdn spid1 26278037230101
isdn spid2 26278037240101
!
interface Dialer0
ip address negotiated
encapsulation ppp
no ip route-cache
no ip mroute-cache
dialer pool 1
dialer remote-name ccie4460@cisco.com
dialer string 5551313
dialer-group 1
no cdp enable
ppp authentication chap callin
ppp chap hostname ccie4460@cisco.com
ppp chap password 7 03075802031C244F5B1B10110E050A0205282E
!
dialer-list 1 protocol ip permit
!
 ip route 0.0.0.0 0.0.0.0 Dialer 0
```

Step 2: Configuring the LAC/NAS

This step assumes that you know how to configure the LAC for basic dial access, as described in Chapter 6. The dial-related configuration is illustrated in Example 21-2. The client's username and password have been removed from the local AAA database because the LNS/home gateway, not the LAC/NAS, performs username authentication. Another element that has been disposed of is the local IP address. The client is now assigned an IP address from the LNS/home gateway's local IP address pool. This configuration task is presented in Step 4 of this case study.

Example 21-2 *R5's Dialer Access Configuration*

```
R5#show run
hostname R5
!
interface BRI0/0
no ip address
encapsulation ppp
dialer pool-member 1
isdn switch-type basic-ni
isdn spid1 26293867870101
isdn spid2 26293867880101
!
interface Dialer0
ip unnumbered serial 0
encapsulation ppp
no ip route-cache
no ip mroute-cache
dialer pool 1
dialer-group 1
no cdp enable
ppp authentication chap
!
dialer-list 1 protocol ip permit
```

Enabling VPDN to Send L2TP Tunnels

Next, you enable VPDN on R5 with the following command. Enabling VPDN forces a
router to look for tunnel definitions locally and on R8.

```
R5(config)#vpdn enable
```

After the VPDN process has been turned on, you must create a VPDN group. A VPDN
group is a group of VPDN attributes for the LAC/NAS and LNS/home gateway. The following
command associates a VPDN group with the VPDN clients belonging to the cisco.com domain
for this case study:

```
R5(config)#vpdn-group name
```

NOTE   Case Study 21-2 covers a remote AAA solution. VPDN groups aren't needed there.

The next command configures a LAC/NAS to request an L2TP tunnel to an LNS/home
gateway. Placement of this command takes you into a request-dialin VPDN subgroup for
further configuration. Later, you will configure R8 to accept the tunnel.

```
R5(config-vpdn)#request-dialin
```

Now you need to specify which protocol the subgroup will use. As you can see in the following command syntax, you have several choices. In this case, **l2tp** is the correct one:

```
R5(config-vpdn-req-in)#protocol [l2f | l2tp | pppoe | any]
```

The next step in the subgroup configuration is to identify which tunnel the dialup client belongs to by specifying the domain name. Multiple domain names can be assigned to a VPDN subgroup, but here only one is used—cisco.com.

```
R5(config-vpdn-req-in)#domain domain-name
```

Another VPDN group-related command specifies the IP address of the tunnel's end, 130.100.26.8, although multiple IP addresses can be configured to request tunnels to multiple sources.

```
R5(config-vpdn)#initiate-to ip ip-address [limit limit-number] [priority
   priority-number]
```

Finally, you must turn on authentication for L2TP. Each VPDN group is authenticated by its defined name. The name does not need to be the same as the device's host name. The order in which the tunnel is identified and authenticated is as follows:

Step 1   An L2TP tunnel password is consulted (if it is defined).

Step 2   When there is no L2TP tunnel password on the LAC/NAS, the name defined by the following command is used.

Step 3   If the following command is omitted, the host name is used. You see such an instance in Example 21-3, where **local name R5** hasn't been manually entered, but instead is used by the router's default configuration.

```
R5(config-vpdn)#local name host-name
```

Example 21-3 shows the VPDN configuration of the LAC/NAS on R5.

Example 21-3 *VPDN Configuration on R5*

```
R5#show run
!
! Output omitted for brevity
!
vpdn enable
!
vpdn-group 1
 request-dialin
  protocol l2tp
  domain cisco.com
 initiate-to ip 130.100.26.8  priority 1
 local name R5
```

Authenticating and Authorizing the Tunnel

Now it's time to add the local AAA configuration to the LAC/NAS. R5 is supposed to input both R5's and R8's usernames for bidirectional authentication between the LAC/NAS and LNS/home gateway. You accomplish this with the usual **username password** commands.

You learned the intricacies of the AAA commands in Chapter 18. Example 21-4 demonstrates the working AAA configuration for this case study.

Example 21-4 *Local AAA Configuration of the LAC/NAS*

```
aaa new-model
aaa authentication ppp default local
aaa authorization network default local
!
username R5 password 0 cisco
username R8 password 0 cisco
```

Step 3: Configuring the PIX Firewall

As you can see from the network layout diagram, LAC/NAS and LNS/home gateway are separated by PIX2. This means that you need to push your tunnel through it. The general PIX Firewall configuration is described in Chapter 23, "Cisco PIX Firewall." You should feel somewhat comfortable with the PIX by now, after having encountered it in some of the case studies from previous chapters.

Here are a couple of commands you should concentrate on for this case study:

- **static (inside,outside)** manually maps the inside local address to an external global address.

- **access-list** permits L2TP (UDP port 1701) to 130.100.26.8.

View the related PIX configuration in Example 21-5.

Example 21-5 *PIX2 Configuration*

```
PIX2#show run
!
! Output omitted for brevity
!
static (inside,outside) 130.100.26.8 192.168.1.1 netmask 255.255.255.255 0 0
access-list outside_access_in permit udp any host 130.100.26.8 eq 1701
```

Step 4: Configuring the LNS/Home Gateway

The last device to configure for this scenario is the LNS/home gateway. It will also be configured to support local AAA.

Configuring Initial Settings

Start by configuring the local database. This includes setting the administrator access with **username cisco password cisco**. These particular arguments are related strictly to the current case study.

Create a Loopback 100 interface with **interface Loopback100** and assign an IP address to it using **ip address 192.168.100.1 255.255.255.0**.

Remember how you disabled the local IP address pool on the LAC/NAS? Now it's time to specify it on the LNS/home gateway. R8 will assign clients the addresses from that pool with **ip local pool HOME 192.168.100.10 192.168.100.20**. It is a required configuration element.

Configuring Local AAA

Next, you configure local AAA that involves usernames for client and tunnel authentication. It also involves all the usual steps for AAA configuration discussed in Chapter 18. Make sure you specify the PPP authentication as local. Specify that network-related service requests will be authorized by using the local database.

Now, add the tunnel secret (local usernames and passwords) to the database for bidirectional tunnel authentication between R5 and R8 using **username R5 password cisco** and **username R8 password cisco**. These username/password combinations on the LNS/home gateway must be identical to the ones already configured on the LAC/NAS. Remember that the tunnel secret is associated only with the tunnel authentication. It has nothing to do with authenticating a client.

Finally, define the local username to identify the dialup client, R3, with **username ccie4460@cisco.com password cisco**. Example 21-6 demonstrates the AAA configuration with the local database as well as the initial settings described in the previous section.

Example 21-6 *Initial Configuration and AAA on R8*

```
R8#show run
!
! Output omitted for brevity
!
aaa new-model
aaa authentication ppp default local
aaa authorization network default local
!
username cisco password 0 cisco
username R5 password 0 cisco
username R8 password 0 cisco
username ccie4460@cisco.com password 0 cisco
!
interface Loopback100
 ip address 192.168.100.1 255.255.255.0
!
ip local pool HOME 192.168.100.10 192.168.100.20
```

Enabling VPDN to Accept L2TP Tunnels

This section discusses the configuration of the LNS/home gateway for VPDN using L2TP tunnels. First, enable VPDN and create a VPDN group with the **vpdn enable** and **vpdn-group 1** commands, as explained earlier in the section "Enabling VPDN to Send L2TP Tunnels."

The following command lets the LNS/home gateway, R8, accept L2TP tunnels from the LAC/NAS, R5:

```
R8(config-vpdn)#accept-dialin
```

The **accept-dialin** command serves as a reply to a dial-in L2TP tunnel open request from the peer. This is accomplished in the following manner:

1 The peer instigates a dial-in tunnel specified by the **request-dialin** command on R5.

2 The accepting peer consents to a tunnel request.

3 After the L2TP tunnel is established, the dial-in and dial-out calls can use it.

Configure the VPDN protocol in the VPDN subgroup configuration mode with the **protocol l2tp** command. You must enable this command before you can move on.

When the LNS/home gateway accepts the LAC/NAS's tunnel request, it uses the specified virtual template that determines the virtual-access interface settings. You will create the virtual template itself a little later in the process. For now, just remember that you need to reference it under the VPDN **accept-dialin** setup.

```
R8(config-vpdn-acc-in)#virtual-template template-number
```

The *template-number* argument identifies the number of the virtual template that will be used to clone virtual-access interfaces. Only one virtual template is allowed per accept-dialin group.

Next, in VPDN group mode, you specify the host name of the LAC/NAS from which a VPDN tunnel request is accepted. This command should be placed after the **accept-dial** command has already been input:

```
R8(config-vpdn)#terminate-from hostname host-name
```

Only a single host name can be specified per group.

Don't forget the **local name R8** command to make the L2TP tunnel identify itself with the local host name. Example 21-7 shows the VPDN portion of R8's configuration without the virtual-template setup discussed in the next step.

Example 21-7 *VPDN Configuration of the LNS/Home Gateway*

```
R8#show run
!
! Output omitted for brevity
!
vpdn enable
```

Example 21-7 *VPDN Configuration of the LNS/Home Gateway (Continued)*

```
!
vpdn-group 1
 accept-dialin
  protocol l2tp
  virtual-template 1
 terminate-from hostname R5
 local name R8
```

Creating the Virtual Template

As promised, this section covers the virtual template design that is used to clone virtual-access interfaces. A virtual template provides configuration for dynamically created virtual-access interfaces. After the virtual template interface is specified, its configuration is no different than that of a serial interface. You create a virtual template with the following command:

```
R8(config)#interface virtual-template number
```

Make sure you use the same number when referencing the virtual template in accept-dialin mode.

NOTE   Virtual template interfaces are not only applicable for VPDNs. They can be used with virtual profiles, PPP over ATM, PPP over Ethernet, protocol translation, and Multichassis Multilink PPP (MMP).

In the following steps you set up parameters for the virtual template:

Step 1   Specify that the virtual-access interfaces will use Loopback100's IP address with the **ip unnumbered Loopback100** command.

Step 2   After enabling PPP encapsulation, assign an IP address from the home address pool to the client with the **peer default ip address pool HOME** command.

Step 3   Finally, enable CHAP authentication through the local database with the **ppp authentication chap** command.

Example 21-8 demonstrates the setup of the virtual template.

Example 21-8 *Virtual Template Configuration on R8*

```
R8#show run
!
! Output omitted for brevity
```

continues

Example 21-8 *Virtual Template Configuration on R8 (Continued)*

```
 !
interface Virtual-Template1
 ip unnumbered Loopback100
 encapsulation ppp
 no ip route-cache
 no ip mroute-cache
 peer default ip address pool HOME
 ppp authentication chap
 !
interface Loopback100
 ip address 192.168.100.1 255.255.255.0
```

Step 5: Troubleshooting VPDN

The final step in setting up VPDN with local authentication is to verify whether your configuration is working. A number of commands can be issued on R5 and R8 to ensure that the VPDN is set up properly.

Use the commands shown in Table 21-1 to troubleshoot VPDN on LAC R5.

Table 21-1   *Commands to Troubleshoot VPDN on R5*

Command	Description
debug vpdn event	Displays L2TP errors and events that are a part of normal tunnel establishment or shutdown for VPDNs.
debug vpdn l2x-event	Displays messages about events that are part of normal tunnel establishment or shutdown for l2x.
debug vpdn l2x-error	Displays l2x protocol errors that prevent l2x establishment or its normal operation.
debug ppp negotiation	Causes the **debug ppp** command to display PPP packets transmitted during PPP startup, where PPP options are negotiated.
show vpdn tunnel	Displays the details of an active tunnel.

In addition to the commands shown in Table 21-1, you can use the **debug vtemplate** command to troubleshoot VPDN on LAC R8. This command displays cloning information for a virtual-access interface from the time it is cloned from a virtual template to the time the virtual-access interface comes down when the call ends.

Example 21-9 shows the output of the **show vpdn tunnel** command on R5.

Example 21-9 *Debugging the VPDN Operation on R5*

```
R5#show vpdn tunnel
L2TP Tunnel Information Total tunnels 1 sessions 1
LocID RemID Remote Name State Remote Address Port Sessions
    36556 45655 R8 est 130.100.26.8 1701 1
```

Example 21-10 shows the output from the **show vpdn tunnel** command issued on R8, which demonstrates that the tunnel with R5 has been established. The second part of the example shows the caller information, including the address allocated from the pool HOME.

Example 21-10 *Debugging the VPDN Operation on R8*

```
R8#show vpdn tunnel
L2TP Tunnel Information Total tunnels 1 sessions 1
LocID RemID Remote Name State Remote Address Port Sessions
    45655 36556 R5 est 140.100.56.5 1701 1

R8#show caller ip
    Line User IP Address Local Number Remote Number <->
    Vi1 ccie4460@cisco.com \
    192.168.100.10 214 5551212 in
```

Case Study 21-2: Configuring TACACS+ Authentication and Authorization for VPDN

In this case study you will reconfigure the LAC/NAS and LNS/home gateway to query the remote AAA server for the VPDN authentication and authorization tasks. The steps are as follows:

Step 1 Configure the LAC/NAS to point to the TACACS+ server for authentication.

Step 2 Configure the LNS/home gateway to point to the TACACS+ server for authentication.

Step 3 Configure the TACACS+ server.

Figure 21-3 shows the new VPDN network topology.

Figure 21-3 *Access VPN Topology Using Remote AAA*

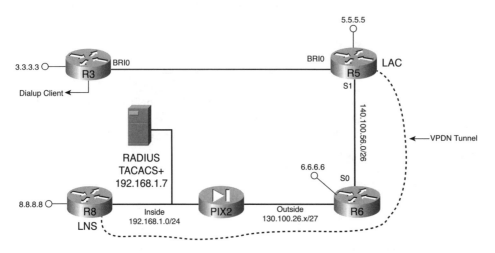

Step 1: Configuring the LAC/NAS

Here you have to change the configuration of the LAC/NAS to delegate the authentication responsibilities to the TACACS+ server at IP address 192.168.1.7. For this, add the new configuration commands and remove the unnecessary ones from the previous case study.

Adding New Commands

Specify that the AAA authentication should take place at the TACACS+ server. Because you will later get rid of the local database as part of the unnecessary command cleanup process, don't specify alternative methods for authentication besides TACACS+. The command to accomplish this is **aaa authentication ppp default group tacacs+**.

The next command should also be familiar from Chapter 18. The **aaa authorization network default group tacacs+** command tells the AAA process to use the TACACS+ server to authorize network-related service requests. To specify the server's IP address and define the secret key, include the command **tacacs-server host 192.168.1.7 key cisco6727**.

Removing Unneeded Commands

VPDN group information should no longer reside on R5. All the tunneling information will now be received from the TACACS+ server. Use the **no vpdn-group 1** command for this.

Another set of commands to delete relates to the local tunnel authentication defined by the **username password** commands. To take out the two **username** commands, enter **no username R5** and **no username R8**. Example 21-11 shows R5's current configuration.

Example 21-11 *LAC/NAS Configuration with TACACS+*

```
R5#show run
!
! Output omitted for brevity
!
aaa new-model
aaa authentication ppp default group tacacs+
aaa authorization network default group tacacs+
!
tacacs-server host 130.100.26.7 key cisco6727
tacacs-server directed-request restricted
tacacs-server key cisco6727
tacacs-server administration
!
vpdn enable
```

Step 2: Configuring the LNS/Home Gateway

The modification of the LNS/home gateway configuration follows the same order as the one from the previous step. The new commands are put in place, and the inapplicable ones are removed. This is done so that the responsibility of authentication is moved from R8 to the TACACS+ server. Now the LNS/home gateway consults the remote server for all its authentication and authorization needs.

Adding the Commands

Similar to the LAC/NAS new configuration, the LNS/home gateway specifies that the AAA authentication for PPP and VPDN uses TACACS+ with the **aaa authentication ppp default group tacacs+** command. No alternative methods are identified in this scenario.

The AAA authorization process for network-related requests should take place on the remote server as well, as specified by the **aaa authorization network default group tacacs+** command.

Point to the server's IP address using the **tacacs-server host 192.168.1.7** command, and attach the **key cisco** argument at the end of the command to assign a shared secret to the router's configuration.

Removing the Commands

Cancel all usernames (except the ones authenticated from the console, of course) from the local database. Besides the usernames related to the tunnel authentication that you remove with the **no username R5** and **no username R8** commands, you need to delete the client's name as well. Use the **no username ccie4460@cisco.com** statement for this.

Unlike in R5's remote AAA setup, here you need to keep the **vpdn-group 1** statement. This is because the virtual-access interfaces defined by the **virtual-template** command need a place from which to be applied.

Example 21-12 displays the new configuration of R8 that fits the needs of this case study.

Example 21-12 *LNS/Home Gateway Configuration for AAA with the TACACS+ Server*

```
R8#show run
!
! Output omitted for brevity
!
aaa new-model
aaa authentication ppp default if-needed group tacacs+
aaa authorization network default group tacacs+
!
vpdn enable
vpdn-group 1
! 1 L2TP VPDN group
 accept-dialin  protocol l2tp
  virtual-template 1
 local name R8
```

Step 3: Configuring the TACACS+ Server

The server configuration is divided into two parts: LAC/NAS- related configuration and LNS/home gateway-related configuration. You learned the server configuration steps in Chapter 18. Now it's a matter of reviewing those tasks and choosing the ones needed for this particular exercise.

Server Configuration for the LAC/NAS

To configure the server for LAC/NAS, follow these steps:

Step 1 In the Welcome screen, click the **User Setup** button.

Step 2 Enter **vpdn_tunnel** in the User box.

Step 3 Click **Add/Edit**.

Step 4 Set up the user as a normal PPP user with the password and/or CHAP password.

Step 5   Click **Submit**. You have now created a user named vpdn_tunnel.

Step 6   Assign the user to group_1.

Step 7   Under TACACS+ Settings, check the PPP/IP and PPP/LCP options.

Step 8   Create another user, cisco.com. The password is cisco.

Step 9   Add this user to group_2.

Step 10   Under the TACACS+ Settings, select the PPP/VPDN service.

Step 11   Underneath, in the appropriate fields, specify that the tunnel ID is **vpdn_tunnel**, the tunnel type is **l2tp**, the IP address list is **130.100.26.8**, and the gateway password and NAS password is **cisco**. Figure 21-4 shows the options for the cisco.com user.

Figure 21-4   *Configuring the cisco.com User on the TACACS+ Server*

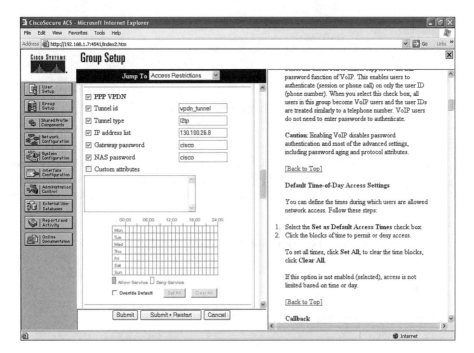

Server Configuration for the LNS/Home Gateway

Set up the ccie4460@cisco.com user as a normal PPP user in the same fashion described in the preceding section. Add the user to group_3. Under the TACACS+ Settings, check the PPP/IP and PPP/LCP service options. The server setup is now complete.

NOTE   You might recall from Chapter 18 that when some of the expected options don't appear under the user or group settings, you need to go into the interface configurations and select the boxes next to the missing options to force them to show up.

Case Study 21-3: Configuring the PIX Firewall to Use PPTP

In this case study, you will configure PIX2 for PPTP with RADIUS authentication without encryption, followed by the RADIUS server configuration. Figure 21-5 presents the topology for this case study.

Figure 21-5 *Topology for the PPTP Configuration Scenario*

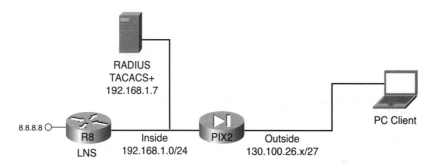

Initial PIX configuration was covered in several prior chapters. It is a working configuration and doesn't need to be covered again here. However, you will see the specific configuration commands needed to enable the PPTP services even if they were previously configured for another reason.

For this case study, you will follow these steps:

Step 1   Specify a local pool of IP addresses.

Step 2   Configure AAA.

Step 3   Implement PPTP.

The following sections describe each step in more detail.

Step 1: Specifying a Local Pool of IP Addresses

Recall that in Chapter 18, the concept of the local IP address pool was explained in Case Study 18-3. (Review that case study if necessary.)

During the PPP IPCP protocol negotiation phase described in Chapter 6, PIX2 assigns a dynamic internal IP address to the PPTP client allocated from the pool. To specify the internal IP address pool for this case study, use the **ip local pool ippool 192.168.2.1-192.168.2.254** command.

Step 2: Configuring AAA

The next step is to identify the RADIUS server as the information source for authentication with two commands: the default **aaa-server RADIUS protocol radius** command and the **aaa-server RADIUS (inside) host 192.168.1.7 cisco6727 timeout 5** command. Both of these statements were used in Case Study 18-3. The only difference is that now you're using RADIUS instead of TACACS+, as described there.

Step 3: Implementing PPTP

You've finally come to the point in your PPTP configuration process where the correlation between it and the VPDN process is explained. On the PIX Firewall, the PPTP is implemented using a number of **vpdn** commands. These commands allow the inbound PPTP connections between a Windows client and PIX2. Remember that only one PIX Firewall interface can have the **vpdn** commands enabled.

The **vpdn** commands on the PIX Firewall are used to implement the L2TP and PPTP server or the PPP over Ethernet (PPPoE) client features. To enable the PPTP function on the PIX Firewall interface, use the following command:

```
PIX2(config)#vpdn enable if_name
```

This command specifies the outside interface because the PPTP traffic is received on it.

Next, set up a VPDN group, and make it accept a dial-in request using PPTP:

```
PIX2(config)#vpdn group group_name accept dialin pptp
```

In this scenario, the *group_name* argument is 1.

You also need to specify the group's PPP authentication type. As mentioned, three types of authentication are available: **PAP, CHAP,** and **MSCHAP.** For this exercise, you will use **CHAP** and **MSCHAP.** The full syntax follows:

```
PIX2(config)#vpdn group group_name ppp authentication [PAP | CHAP | MSCHAP]
```

Next you specify that a PPTP client is to use an inside address allocated by the IP pool. The general syntax is as follows:

```
PIX2(config)#vpdn group group_name client configuration address local
    address_pool_name
```

To tell the PIX Firewall to use a remote AAA server for authentication purposes, use the following command:

```
PIX2(config)#vpdn group group_name client authentication aaa aaa_server_group
```

For this case study's configuration, use a *group_name* argument of **1** and an *aaa_server_group* argument of **radius**.

When used with the **vpdn** commands, the next command allows PPTP traffic to avoid being checked against **access-list** statements:

```
PIX2(config)#sysopt connection permit-pptp
```

Example 21-13 displays the PIX2 portion of this case study's configuration.

Example 21-13 *PPTP Configuration of PIX2*

```
PIX2#show run
!
! Output omitted for brevity
!
ip local pool ippool 192.168.2.1-192.168.2.254
aaa-server TACACS+ protocol tacacs+
aaa-server RADIUS protocol radius

aaa-server RADIUS (outside) host 172.18.124.99 cisco timeout 5
sysopt connection permit-pptp

vpdn group 1 accept dialin pptp
vpdn group 1 ppp authentication pap
vpdn group 1 ppp authentication chap
vpdn group 1 ppp authentication mschap
vpdn group 1 client configuration address local pptp-pool
vpdn group 1 client authentication aaa RADIUS
vpdn enable outside
```

Lesson 21-1: Configuring the Default VPDN Group Template

Beginning with the 12.2(8)T release of the Cisco IOS software, Cisco supports the default VPDN group template feature. As you might guess from the name, the default VPDN group template allows global configuration of one set of group parameters and its subsequent application to actual VPDN groups.

This doesn't mean that the default values have to be applied to all groups without exception. If you were to configure separate settings for a specific VPDN group, they would take precedence over the default ones. Whatever settings are omitted from the specific group configuration, they are borrowed from the default template. In turn, if any settings are missing from the template configuration, the system default values for those settings are used.

Also, there is a way to set up your VPDN configuration so that a specific VPDN group ignores the template's characteristics. Instead, it uses the system defaults for parameters that weren't explicitly stated in its configuration.

The benefits of using a default VPDN group template are obvious. It frees an administrator from the potentially enormous task of configuring, maintaining, and monitoring many separate VPDN group statements. Keep in mind, though, that as soon as an L2TP or L2F tunnel has been established, the changes brought forth with your new template configuration don't take effect until the tunnel is torn down and reactivated.

Before a default template can be configured, the VPDN process and a VPDN group must be in place on the router. The following command changes to template configuration mode, where you can specify the globally controlled parameters:

```
R5(config)#vpdn-template
```

After the **vpdn-template** command has been entered, you can configure the default settings for the VPDN template. Not every command normally available with the VPDN group can be used with the VPDN group template. For more information on where to find the available commands, see Appendix E, "Security-Related RFCs and Publications."

As mentioned, it is possible to make an individual VPDN group disregard the template values for the missing settings. By default, if the VPDN group template is configured on a router, its parameters are automatically applied to a specific VPDN group if no matching parameters exist in the group configuration. For greater flexibility, you can override the default with the following command in VPDN group configuration mode:

```
R5(config-vpdn)#no source vpdn-template
```

To return to the system defaults, use the **source vpdn-template** command.

Summary

This chapter introduced you to the mechanics of VPDNs and some of the L2 protocols that make its operation possible, including L2TP, L2F, and PPTP. With the help of these protocols, a remote client can securely communicate with a private corporate network via a virtual tunnel over a public network. The case studies taught you how to create a working VPDN environment by configuring several Cisco devices, including the following:

- Routers as a client
- LAC/NAS
- LNS/home gateway
- PIX Firewall as a PPTP network server
- Cisco ACS with a VPDN-related configuration

Review Questions

1 What is the PPP session termination point called in L2TP terminology?

2 What are the two termination points of the L2F tunnel?

3 To which configuration mode is a virtual template applied?

4 True or false: LAC/NAS needs to have a local pool of IP addresses defined.

5 Which PPP authentication protocol(s) does PIX Firewall's implementation of PPTP support?

FAQs

Q — *Where is the VPDN technology used the most?*

A — VPDN is ideal for remote dialup users (clients) who can connect to a public network via ISDN or an analog modem and who also require access to a private corporate network.

Q — *What are the port numbers for VPDN in a Cisco implementation?*

A — L2F and L2TP are deployed over UDP port 1701, and PPTP is deployed over UDP port 1723.

Q — *What authentication techniques can VPDN use?*

A — VPDN can authenticate locally and via remote RADIUS or TACACS+ servers.

Q — *In what capacity can VPDN be implemented on the PIX Firewall?*

A — PIX Firewall allows VPDN for inbound connections and implements the L2TP, PPTP, and PPPoE features. When implementing L2TP and PPTP, PIX acts as a server. With PPPoE, the PIX Firewall acts as a client only.

Q — *What is the difference between the VPDN on PIX versus the VPDN on IOS?*

A — VPDN on routers and VPDN on PIX have different functionality. IOS VPDN is used for dialup connections, whereas VPDN on PIX is used for any type of connection. In the PIX VPDN setup, the client is treated as an access concentrator for the PIX's network server.

Firewalls

This chapter covers the following topics:

- Creating a customized firewall
- Configuring TCP intercept
- Context-based access control overview
- Port-to-Application Mapping

CHAPTER 22

Cisco IOS Firewall

This chapter looks at the Cisco IOS Firewall feature set, with the exception of the Cisco IOS IDS, which is covered in detail in Chapter 24, "IDS on the Cisco PIX Firewall and IOS Software." You will be required to implement several of these features on the CCIE Security lab exam. You should know how these features work together and how to modify them to meet your requirements.

The firewall is a network device—most of the time, a network appliance. In this case, however, it is a software enhancement, usually placed at the entrance points to your network to control access to your organization's network assets. With this strategic placement, all traffic entering or exiting your network must pass through the device.

Along with its most popular use, a firewall can also be used to control access to select parts of your network. For example, you can position a firewall at the entry point into your Research and Development network to prevent unauthorized access to your proprietary information.

A firewall's most basic function is to monitor and filter network traffic. Cisco IOS software provides an extensive set of security features, letting you configure a firewall that can meet all your needs, whether you need a simple firewall that is easy to configure and maintain or the flexibility offered by more-elaborate firewalls.

The Cisco IOS Firewall feature set, included in select versions of the Cisco IOS software, combines the existing Cisco IOS Firewall technology with the power of Context-Based Access Control (CBAC). Cisco IOS Firewall features are built around the concept of preventing unauthorized individuals from gaining access to your protected network resources, blocking attacks launched against your network, and, at the same time, allowing your authorized users to access their network resources.

Cisco IOS Firewall features let you configure your Cisco IOS router to act as one of the following:

- An Internet firewall or part of an Internet firewall
- A firewall between groups in your internal network
- A firewall providing secure connections to or from branch offices
- A firewall between your company's network and your company's partners' networks

Creating a Customized Firewall

To create a customized firewall designed to comply with your organization's security policy, you should first determine which of the many features available with the Cisco IOS Firewall are most appropriate. At a minimum, you should consider configuring basic traffic filtering to create a simple firewall. You can create your firewall on a Cisco device by using these Cisco IOS Firewall features:

- Standard access lists and static extended access lists
- Lock-and-key (dynamic access lists)
- Reflexive access lists
- TCP intercept
- CBAC
- Cisco IOS Firewall Intrusion Detection System (IDS)
- Authentication proxy
- Port-to-Application Mapping (PAM)
- Security server support
- Network Address Translation (NAT)
- IPSec network security
- Neighbor router authentication
- Event logging
- User authentication and authorization

Configuring TCP Intercept

IOS's TCP intercept feature can be used to prevent some types of denial-of-service (DoS) attacks, but it should not be used in conjunction with CBAC. The TCP intercept feature implements software to protect servers running TCP from a TCP SYN-flood attack. A TCP SYN-flood attack occurs when a hacker floods a server with a barrage of TCP synchronization (SYN) requests for a connection. These requests are from forged addresses that have unreachable return addresses, resulting in half-open sessions on the server. When the resulting volume of half-open connections reaches a certain threshold, the sessions eventually overwhelm the server and might cause it to start denying service to valid users of your offered services. These services can include a website, e-mail, FTP, printing, and even applications.

TCP intercept can operate in two modes:

- **Passive watch mode**—The software passively watches connection requests and tracks them as they flow through the router. If a connection fails to complete establishment within a configurable interval, the software intervenes and terminates the connection attempt.

- **Active intercept mode**—The software intercepts all requests or only those coming from specific networks or destined for specific servers.

When you enable the TCP intercept feature in active mode, it intercepts the SYN packet from clients to servers that match an extended ACL that you define. The IOS then establishes a connection with the client on behalf of the destination server. If it completes the three-way handshake successfully, it then establishes the connection with the server on behalf of the client. Finally, it joins the two half-connections transparently. This interception keeps connection attempts from unreachable hosts from reaching your server. Be aware, though, that the software continues to intercept and forward packets for the duration of the connection.

When you enable the TCP intercept in passive watch mode, the software allows all connections to pass through to the server, but the connections are watched until they become established. If the connection fails to become established within 30 seconds (the default), the software sends a TCP Reset to the server to prevent too many half-open connections.

When the software encounters an illegitimate request, aggressive timeouts on half-open connections and thresholds on TCP connection requests protect destination servers while still allowing valid requests to establish a connection. You need to understand normal packet flow within your network, because you might want to tune these timers for your environment.

You can also choose to configure the connection rate and threshold of outstanding connections from their default settings.

NOTE   TCP options that are negotiated on handshake are not negotiated by the TCP intercept software, because it does not know what the server can do or will negotiate. (See RFC 1323, "TCP Extensions for High Performance," which has recommendations for window scaling to achieve optimal usage of packet sizes.)

When you are under attack, the TCP intercept feature becomes more aggressive in its protective behavior. If the number of half-open connections exceeds 1100, or if the number of connections arriving in the last minute exceeds 1100, each new arriving request causes the oldest half-open connection to be deleted from the device. The initial retransmission timeout is also reduced to 0.5 seconds, or half the default, reducing the total time the software tries to establish a connection. TCP intercept's aggressive behavior begins and ends based on two factors: total incomplete connections and connection requests during the last 1-minute sample period. Both of these thresholds have default values that you can modify.

The reason for this aggressive behavior is that when a threshold is exceeded, the TCP intercept assumes that your server is under attack. While in aggressive mode, TCP intercept does the following:

- Each new arriving connection causes the oldest half-open connection to be deleted.

- The initial retransmission timeout is reduced to 0.5 seconds, so the total time trying to establish the connection is cut in half. (When not in aggressive mode, the code does exponential backoff on its retransmissions of SYN segments.) The initial retransmission timeout is 1 second. The subsequent timeouts are 2 seconds, 4 seconds, 8 seconds, and 16 seconds. The code retransmits four times before giving up, so it gives up after 31 seconds of no acknowledgment.

- In watch mode, the watch timeout is reduced by half, or 15 seconds, if you are using the default setting.

- You can change the drop strategy from the oldest connection to a random connection with the **ip tcp intercept drop-mode** command.

NOTE   Both factors used to determine the status of aggressive behavior are related and work together. When *either* of the **high** values is exceeded, aggressive behavior begins. When *both* quantities fall below the **low** value, aggressive behavior ends.

Lesson 22-1: Configuring TCP Intercept

To configure TCP intercept, follow these steps:

Step 1   Enable TCP intercept.

Step 2   Optionally set the intercept mode.

Step 3   Optionally set the drop mode.

Step 4   Optionally adjust timers.

Step 5   Optionally adjust the aggressive thresholds.

Step 6   Optionally monitor and maintain TCP intercept.

Step 1: Enabling TCP Intercept

To enable TCP intercept, use the following commands:

```
R2(config)#access-list access-list-number {deny | permit} tcp any destination
    destination-wildcard
R2(config)#ip tcp intercept list access-list-number
```

Because you are in the TCP intercept overview, you can define your ACL to intercept all requests or only those coming from specific networks or destined for specific servers. You typically define your ACL's source as **any** and define specific destination networks or servers. Trying to define the source address can be fruitless, because you cannot possibly know every address a hacker might use, but you can identify the destination to protect your servers.

If an ACL match is not found, the software allows the request to pass with no further action.

In this portion of the lesson, you enable TCP intercept on R2 for all servers on the 100.200.200.0/24 subnet. Example 22-1 contains the configuration for R2 to complete this lesson.

Example 22-1 *Enabling TCP Intercept on R2*

```
Configuration items needed on R2:
R2(config)#ip tcp intercept list 111
R2(config)#ip tcp intercept mode intercept
R2(config)#ip tcp intercept drop-mode random
R2(config)#ip tcp intercept max-incomplete high 800
R2(config)#ip tcp intercept max-incomplete low 700
R2(config)#access-list 111 permit tcp any 100.200.200.0 0.0.0.255
```

Step 2: Setting the TCP Intercept Mode

TCP intercept can operate in either active intercept mode (which is the default) or passive watch mode. You can change this setting to match the requirements outlined in your company's security policy.

Use the following command to set the TCP intercept mode:

```
R2(config)#ip tcp intercept mode {intercept | watch}
```

You now enable TCP intercept to operate in intercept mode. Example 22-2 contains the configuration for R2 to complete this lesson.

Example 22-2 *Setting the TCP Intercept Mode*

```
Configuration items needed on R2:
R2(config)#ip tcp intercept mode intercept
```

Step 3: Setting the TCP Intercept Drop Mode

By default the software drops the oldest half-open connection. You have the option of changing this behavior so that the software drops a random connection instead. You can use the following command to change the default drop behavior:

```
R2(config)#ip tcp intercept drop-mode {oldest | random}
```

In this portion, you set the drop mode to random. Example 22-3 contains the configuration for R2 to complete this lesson.

Example 22-3 *Setting the TCP Intercept Drop Mode*

```
Configuration items needed on R2:
R2(config)#ip tcp intercept drop-mode random
```

Step 4: Changing the TCP Intercept Timers

When you use the default timers with TCP intercept, the software waits 30 seconds for a watched connection to reach an established state before sending a reset to the server. In some cases, you might find this amount of time to be too long or too short. You can use the following command to change this default behavior:

```
R2(config)#ip tcp intercept watch-timeout seconds
```

Another default time causes the software to wait for 5 seconds from the receipt of a reset or FIN-exchange before it ceases to manage the connection. If needed, you can also change this behavior by using the following command:

```
R2(config)#ip tcp intercept finrst-timeout seconds
```

The last timer you can modify is the management of a connection for 24 hours after no activity has been seen on it. To change this value, use the following command:

```
R2(config)#ip tcp intercept connection-timeout seconds
```

Step 5: Changing the TCP Intercept Aggressive Thresholds

You can change the default values of 900 for low and 1100 for high half-open connections used to trigger aggressive mode by using the following commands:

```
R2(config)#ip tcp intercept max-incomplete low number
R2(config)#ip tcp intercept max-incomplete high number
```

You also have the option of changing the threshold for triggering aggressive mode based on the number of connection requests received in the last 1-minute sample period from the default value of 900 for low and 1100 for high. To accomplish this task, use the following commands:

```
R2(config)#ip tcp intercept one-minute low number
R2(config)#ip tcp intercept one-minute high number
```

You also need to change the max-incomplete settings to 700 for the low and 800 for the high. Example 22-4 contains the configuration for R2 to complete this lesson.

Example 22-4 *Adjusting the Aggressive Timers*

```
Configuration items needed on R2:
R2(config)#ip tcp intercept max-incomplete high 800
R2(config)#ip tcp intercept max-incomplete low 700
```

Step 6: Monitoring and Maintaining TCP Intercept

Just like anything else that has to do with security, you need to be able to monitor TCP intercept to determine if it is functioning correctly. You can use one of the following commands to display TCP intercept information:

```
R2#show tcp intercept connections
R2#show tcp intercept statistics
```

CBAC Overview

Context-Based Access Control (CBAC) gives network protection on multiple levels using the following functions:

- Traffic filtering
- Traffic inspection
- Alerts and audit trails
- Intrusion detection

The following sections describe these functions in greater detail.

Traffic Filtering

CBAC can provide intelligent filtering of TCP and UDP packets based on the application-layer protocol session information included in the packet. You can configure CBAC to permit only specified TCP and UDP traffic through your firewall when the connection is initiated from within the network you want to protect. CBAC can inspect traffic for sessions that originate either inside or outside your firewall. CBAC is supported for use on intranet, extranet, and Internet perimeters of your network.

If you do not use CBAC, your filtering of traffic is limited to ACL implementations that examine packets at only the network layer or, at most, the transport layer. You have to use CBAC if you also want to examine packets at the application layer to learn about the session's state. With this feature, you can support protocols that involve multiple channels created as a result of negotiations in the control channel, such as most multimedia protocols and some other protocols (FTP, RPC, and SQL*Net).

You can configure Java blocking with CBAC to filter HTTP traffic based on the server address or to completely deny access to Java applets that are not embedded in an archived or compressed file. Java lets hackers place destructive applications on your network through one of your users. To protect your network and users from this risk, you could require all users to disable Java in their browsers. If this is not a viable solution, you can create a CBAC inspection rule to filter Java applets at your firewall, which allows users to download only applets residing within the firewall and trusted applets from outside the firewall. If your security policy requires extensive content filtering of Java, ActiveX, or virus scanning, you might want to consider purchasing a dedicated content-filtering product.

Traffic Inspection

CBAC inspects traffic that travels through your firewall to obtain and manage state information for TCP and UDP sessions. CBAC uses this state information to create temporary openings in the firewall's ACLs to allow return traffic and additional data connections for permissible sessions. By inspecting these packets at the application layer and maintaining TCP and UDP session information, CBAC detects and prevents certain types of network attacks such as SYN-flooding.

CBAC helps protect your resources against DoS attacks in many ways. CBAC can inspect a packet's sequence numbers in TCP connections to see if they are within expected ranges and can drop any suspicious packets. You also can configure CBAC to drop half-open connections, but this requires processing and memory resources to maintain on your firewall. CBAC can also detect unusually high rates of new connections and issue alert messages.

CBAC can also protect against certain DoS attacks involving the use of fragmented IP packets. Even though your firewall can prevent an attacker from connecting to a given host, the attacker can disrupt services provided by that host. This is accomplished by sending many noninitial IP fragments or by sending complete fragmented packets through a router with an ACL that filters the first fragment of a fragmented packet. These fragments tie up resources on the target host because it stores these fragments as it tries to reassemble the packet.

Alerts and Audit Trails

CBAC can generate real-time alerts and audit trails to keep you informed of different situations. An enhanced audit trail feature uses SYSLOG to track all network transactions, recording time stamps, source host, destination host, ports used, and the total number of transmitted bytes for advanced, session-based reporting. Real-time alerts send SYSLOG error messages to a configured central management console on detection of suspicious activity. You can configure these alerts and audit trail information on a per-protocol basis using CBAC inspection rules.

Intrusion Detection

CBAC provides limited intrusion-detection capability to protect against specific SMTP attacks. This feature reviews SYSLOG messages to monitor for specific attack signatures. When an attack is detected, CBAC resets the offending connection and sends a SYSLOG message with relevant information in it to a configured SYSLOG server.

Intrusion-detection capabilities are beyond the scope of this chapter. They are covered in more detail in Chapter 24.

CBAC Limitations and Restrictions

CBAC does not provide intelligent filtering for all protocols. It does not filter ICMP at all. It works only for the protocols you specify. If you omit a certain protocol for CBAC, or if it can't inspect the traffic, your existing ACLs, if defined, determine how that protocol is filtered. Temporary openings cannot be created for protocols that you do not specify for CBAC inspection.

CBAC cannot protect against attacks originating from within your protected network unless that traffic passes through a router that has the Cisco IOS Firewall feature set deployed on it and is configured to protect against the attack.

CBAC protects against certain types of attacks, but not every type of attack. Determined, skilled attackers might be able to launch effective attacks against your protected networks.

Although CBAC is pretty comprehensive, it has the following restrictions:

- CBAC inspects only IP protocol traffic. Only TCP and UDP packets are inspected; all others should be filtered by an ACL.

- If you have to reconfigure your ACLs when you have CBAC configured, if you configure your ACLs to block TFTP traffic, you cannot netboot over that interface.

- CBAC does not inspect packets originating from or going to your firewall.

- CBAC ignores ICMP Unreachable messages.

- H.323 V2 and RTSP protocol inspection support only the following multimedia client/server applications:

    — Cisco IP/TV

    — RealNetworks RealAudio G2 Player

    — Apple QuickTime 4

- You can use CBAC together with all the other firewall features available in IOS, with the exception of TCP intercept.

- CBAC works with fast switching and process switching.

- With FTP, CBAC does not allow a three-way FTP transfer.

- When CBAC inspects FTP traffic, it allows only data channels with the destination port in the range of 1024 to 65535.

CBAC does not open a data channel if the FTP client/server authentication fails.

CBAC Operation

CBAC creates temporary openings in ACLs placed on your firewall's interfaces. These openings are created when traffic that passes inspection by your ACLS exits your internal network through your firewall. The openings are created to allow returning traffic, normally blocked at the firewall, and additional data channels to enter your internal network back through your firewall. The traffic is allowed back through your firewall only if it is part of a session that triggered CBAC when exiting your firewall.

Throughout this section, the terms *inbound* and *outbound* are used to describe the direction of traffic relative to the router interface on which CBAC is applied. For example, if a CBAC rule is to be used in the inbound direction on an interface, packets entering that interface from the network are inspected. It stands to reason that if a CBAC rule is to be used in the outbound direction on an interface, packets leaving that interface to the network are inspected.

The terms *input* and *output* are used to describe the interfaces at which network traffic enters or exits your firewall router. A packet enters your firewall router via an input interface, is inspected by the firewall software, and then exits your router via the output interface.

When implementing CBAC, you need to specify which protocols you want to be inspected. You also need to specify an interface and the interface direction (in or out) where the inspection originates.

Packets entering the firewall first pass through an inbound ACL on the input interface and an outbound ACL, if defined, on the output interface before CBAC inspects them. If the ACL denies the packet, it is dropped before CBAC inspection occurs.

One item tracked by the CBAC inspection is the sequence numbers that are contained in all TCP packets. If a packet with a sequence number that is not within the expected range is inspected by CBAC, it is dropped.

TCP and UDP inspection can be configured to permit TCP and UDP packets entrance to your internal network through your firewall, even if you do not configure application-layer protocol inspection. Be aware, though, that TCP and UDP inspection do not recognize application-specific commands and might not permit all return packets for an application, particularly if the return packets have a different port number than the previous exiting packet.

NOTE	If you configure both application-layer protocol inspection and TCP or UDP packet inspection, the application-layer protocol inspection takes precedence.

When using TCP and UDP inspection, any packet trying to enter your network must exactly match the corresponding packet that previously exited your network. This means that the entering packet must have the same source/destination address and source/destination port number as the exiting packet, but reversed; otherwise, the entering packet is blocked at the interface. Also, if the sequence number of a TCP packet is outside the window, it is dropped.

When using UDP inspection, only replies are permitted back in through your firewall if they are received within a configurable amount of time after the last request was sent out.

The inspection done by CBAC can recognize application-specific commands (such as illegal SMTP commands) in the control channel and can detect and prevent certain application-level attacks if configured to do so.

You can use Java applet filtering to distinguish between trusted and untrusted applets by defining a list of external sites that you designate as "friendly." If an applet is from a friendly site, your firewall allows it through. If an applet is not from a friendly site, your firewall blocks it. You can alternatively permit applets from all external sites except those you specifically designate as hostile.

Remember that CBAC cannot detect or block encapsulated Java applets. So, if Java applets are wrapped or encapsulated, such as in .zip or .jar format, they are not blocked at your firewall. CBAC also does not detect or block applets loaded from FTP, gopher, HTTP on a nonstandard port, and so forth.

For an operational CBAC implementation, you need to ensure that you have an IP ACL configured appropriately at the interface. Follow these three general rules when evaluating your IP ACLs for your firewall:

- Start with a basic configuration. A basic initial configuration allows all network traffic to flow from your protected networks to the unprotected networks while blocking network traffic from any unprotected networks.

- Permit CBAC traffic to leave the network through your firewall. ACLs that evaluate traffic leaving your protected network should permit traffic that you want CBAC to inspect.

- Use extended ACLs to deny CBAC return traffic entering the network through your firewall; CBAC creates temporary openings for the return traffic. For temporary openings to be created in an ACL, you must use an extended ACL.

Each of these rules is examined in greater detail in the following section.

Basic Configuration

Your Cisco IOS Firewall needs to be configured to allow all network traffic from your protected networks to access unprotected networks while blocking all network traffic (with some exceptions, such as ICMP traffic) from unprotected networks to your protected networks. As with any security implementation, any firewall configuration you do depends on your company's security policy.

Use the following guidelines for configuring the initial firewall ACLs:

- Do not configure an ACL for traffic from your protected networks to unprotected networks, meaning that all traffic from the protected networks can flow through the interface. This helps you simplify the management of your firewall by reducing the number of ACLs you need to apply to interfaces. You still can fine-tune network access for your users on your protected networks as you gain experience with ACL list configuration and firewall operation.

- Configure an ACL that includes entries permitting certain ICMP traffic from unprotected networks. Although an ACL that denies all IP traffic that is not part of a connection inspected by CBAC seems most secure, it is impractical for normal router operation. The router expects to see ICMP traffic from other routers in the network. Additionally, CBAC doesn't inspect ICMP traffic, meaning that specific entries are needed in your ACL to permit return traffic for ICMP commands.

  Include access list entries to permit the following ICMP messages:

  — echo reply

  — time-exceeded

  — packet-too-big

  — traceroute

  — unreachable

- Add an ACL entry that denies any network traffic from a source address matching an address on your protected network. This provides antispoofing protection by preventing a hacker from impersonating a device on your protected network.

- Add an ACL entry denying broadcast messages with a source address of 255.255.255.255 to prevent broadcast attacks.

- By default, the last entry in an extended ACL is an implicit denial of all IP traffic not specifically allowed by other entries in the ACL.

External Interface

Here are guidelines to consider when you are configuring ACLs for an external interface:

- If you use an outbound IP ACL on an external interface, the ACL can be either standard or extended. This outbound ACL should permit only traffic that you want to be inspected by CBAC; traffic not permitted is not inspected by CBAC and is dropped.

- The inbound IP ACL used on the external interface must be an extended ACL. This inbound ACL should be used to deny traffic that you want to be inspected by CBAC, allowing CBAC to create temporary openings for valid return traffic.

Internal Interface

Here are guidelines for you to consider when you are configuring ACLs for an internal interface:

- If you use an inbound IP ACL on an internal interface, the ACL can be either standard or extended. This inbound ACL should permit only traffic that you want to be inspected by CBAC; traffic not permitted is not inspected by CBAC and is dropped.

- The outbound IP ACL used on an internal interface must be an extended ACL. Outbound ACLs should only deny traffic that you want to be inspected by CBAC, allowing CBAC to create temporary openings for valid return traffic. You are not required to configure an extended ACL at both the outbound internal interface and the inbound external interface, but at least one is necessary to restrict traffic flowing through your firewall into your internal protected network.

During a suspected attack, CBAC's DoS feature can take several actions:

- Generate an alert message.

- Protect system resources that can be exploited to impede performance.

- Block packets that originate from suspected attackers.

Like many of the items you will use to enforce your security policy, CBAC uses timeout and threshold values in its operation. It uses these timeout and threshold values to manage session state information, helping determine when to drop sessions that do not become fully established. Setting timeout values that match your network session needs helps you prevent DoS attacks by freeing up system resources, dropping sessions after a specified amount of time, and controlling the number of half-open sessions. CBAC timeouts and thresholds are applied globally across all sessions. When CBAC drops a session, it sends a reset message to the devices at both the session's endpoints (source and destination). When a reset message is received by the system under DoS attack, it releases, or frees up, the processes and resources related to that incomplete session.

One example of when you might want to change the default values is when you want to enable the more-aggressive TCP host-specific DoS prevention that includes the blocking of connection initiation to a host.

Half-Open Sessions

One indication of a DoS attack in progress is an unusually high number of half-open sessions, whether they are absolute or measured as the arrival rate. In the case of TCP, "half-open" means that the session has not reached the established state, and the TCP three-way handshake of SYN, SYN-ACK, ACK has not completed. In the case of UDP, "half-open" means that the firewall has not detected any return traffic.

CBAC measures both the total number of existing half-open sessions and the rate of session establishment attempts. Both TCP and UDP half-open sessions are counted in the total number and rate measurements. Rate measurements are taken several times per minute to ensure an accurate count.

If the total number of existing half-open sessions rises above the **max-incomplete high** threshold, the software begins deleting half-open sessions as needed to accommodate new connection requests. This deletion process continues until the number of existing half-open sessions drops below the **max-incomplete low** threshold.

If the rate of new connection attempts rises above the **one-minute high** threshold, the software begins deleting half-open sessions as needed to accommodate new connection attempts. This deletion process continues until the rate of new connection attempts drops below the **one-minute low** threshold. The rate threshold is measured as the number of new session connection attempts detected in the last 1-minute sample period.

You are given three thresholds when implementing CBAC against DoS attacks:

- The total number of half-open TCP or UDP sessions waiting for a return packet
- The number of half-open sessions based on time
- The number of half-open TCP-only sessions per host

CBAC has two options to use when a threshold is exceeded:

- Send a reset message to the endpoints of the oldest half-open session, freeing up resources needed to service newly arriving SYN packets.
- In the case of half-open TCP-only sessions, CBAC blocks all SYN packets temporarily for the duration configured by the threshold value. When the router blocks a SYN packet, the TCP three-way handshake is never initiated, which prevents the router from using memory and processing resources needed for valid connections.

To use the DoS detection and prevention provided by CBAC, you are required to create a CBAC inspection rule and apply that rule on an interface. You must include the protocols you want to monitor against DoS attacks in this rule. Of course, your job as a security administrator would be much simpler if all DoS attacks were packet-based. Unfortunately, some attacks are based on fragmentation of IP packets. However, CBAC offers you a way to combat these attacks.

If you use a fragmentation inspection feature, your firewall maintains an *interfragment state* for IP traffic. Any noninitial fragments are discarded unless the corresponding initial fragment was permitted to pass through your firewall. Any noninitial fragments received before the corresponding initial fragments are discarded.

CAUTION   Fragmentation inspection can have undesirable effects in certain cases, such as when fragments are received out of order. In this scenario, your firewall discards these out-of-order packets. Because many circumstances can cause out-of-order delivery of legitimate fragments, applying fragmentation inspection in these situations might have a severe performance impact.

Fragmentation inspection is turned off by default, but you can enable it by explicitly including it in an inspection rule using the **ip inspect name** command. Unfragmented traffic is never discarded, because it lacks a fragment state.

CBAC implements a state table to keep track of all this information, as detailed in the following section.

Maintaining Session State Information with a State Table

Whenever a packet is inspected, CBAC updates a state table to include information about the state of the session. Return traffic is permitted back through your firewall only if the state table contains information indicating that the packet belongs to a permissible session. When return traffic is inspected, if the traffic is valid, the state table information is updated as necessary.

Approximating UDP Sessions

Because UDP is a connectionless protocol, it does not include any information in the packet that can be considered actual session information. CBAC can still inspect UDP traffic by approximating a session by examining the information in the packet and determining if the packet is similar to other UDP packets. For example, if the return packet has the same source/ destination addresses and port numbers as a packet that left the router and the packet was detected within the user-configurable UDP idle timeout period, the packet is allowed.

Permitting Return Traffic and Additional Data Connections with ACL Entries

CBAC operates by dynamically creating and deleting ACL entries at the firewall interfaces, in accordance with the information maintained in the state tables. These ACL entries are used to examine traffic returning to your internal network. These entries are used to create temporary openings in your firewall to permit only traffic that is part of a permissible session.

These temporary ACL entries are never saved to NVRAM.

When and Where to Configure CBAC

You should consider configuring CBAC at firewalls protecting your internal networks. CBAC can be used on a firewall that passes traffic such as the following:

- Standard TCP and UDP Internet applications

- Multimedia applications

- Oracle support

CBAC can be used for these applications when you want the application's traffic to be permitted through your firewall when the traffic session is initiated from a particular side of the firewall— most likely from your protected internal network.

A typical implementation of CBAC is configured in a single direction on a single interface, causing traffic to be permitted back into your internal network only if the traffic is part of a valid, existing session. If you wanted to do so, you could configure CBAC to operate in both directions on one or more interfaces. You would configure CBAC in this manner when the networks on both sides of the firewall should be protected, such as with extranet or intranet configurations, and to protect against DoS attacks.

CBAC-Supported Protocols

You can configure CBAC to inspect the following types of sessions:

- All TCP sessions, regardless of the application-layer protocol (sometimes called *single-channel* or *generic TCP inspection*)

- All UDP sessions, regardless of the application-layer protocol (sometimes called *single-channel* or *generic UDP inspection*)

Because application-layer support is included in CBAC, you can configure it to inspect the following:

- CU-SeeMe (only the White Pine version)

- FTP

- H.323 (such as NetMeeting and ProShare)

- HTTP (Java blocking)

- Microsoft NetShow

- UNIX **r** commands (such as **rlogin**, **rexec**, and **rsh**)

- RealAudio

- RTSP (Real-Time Streaming Protocol)

- RPC (Sun RPC, not DCE RPC)

- SMTP (Simple Mail Transport Protocol, but not Extended Simple Mail Transport Protocol [ESMTP])

- SQL*Net

- StreamWorks

- TFTP

- VDOLive

Using IPSec with CBAC

When you enable IPSec on your firewall router that is running CBAC, CBAC can inspect traffic flow if the device is the endpoint for the IPSec connection. If the device is not the IPSec endpoint, and the packet is an IPSec packet, CBAC cannot inspect the packet because the protocol number is not a TCP or UDP number.

Lesson 22-2: Configuring CBAC

To configure CBAC, follow these steps:

Step 1   Pick an interface for CBAC.

Step 2   Configure IP ACLs.

Step 3   Configure global timeouts and thresholds.

Step 4   Define an inspection rule.

Step 5   Apply the inspection rule to an interface.

Step 6   Configure logging and an audit trail.

Step 7   Follow other guidelines for configuring a firewall.

Step 8   Optionally verify CBAC.

Step 1: Picking an Interface: Internal or External

The first and one of the most important steps in configuring CBAC is deciding which interface to place the rule on. Your decision determines how the rest of the configuration will be done. You can configure CBAC on an internal or external interface of your firewall.

Remember that *internal* refers to the side where a session must originate for the traffic to be permitted through your firewall. *External* refers to the side where a session cannot originate. A session that originates from the external side is blocked.

If you are required to configure CBAC in two directions, you should configure CBAC in one direction first, using the appropriate internal and external interface designations. When you configure CBAC for the other direction, you swap the interface designations.

Because your firewall will most likely be configured in one of two basic network topologies, determining which of these topologies is most like your own can help you decide whether to configure CBAC on an internal or external interface.

The first topology you should consider is shown in Figure 22-1. In this simple topology, CBAC is configured for the external serial interface connecting to the Internet. This prevents specified protocol traffic from entering the firewall and the internal network, unless the traffic is part of a session initiated from within your internal network.

Figure 22-1 *Topology with CBAC at the External Interface*

The second topology for your consideration is shown in Figure 22-2. In this topology, CBAC is configured for the internal Ethernet interface. This allows external traffic to access the services in the demilitarized zone (DMZ), such as DNS services, but prevents specified protocol traffic from entering your internal network, unless the traffic is part of a session initiated from within the internal network.

By using these two sample topologies, you should be able to decide whether to configure CBAC on an internal or external interface.

Figure 22-2 *DMZ Topology with CBAC on the Internal Interface*

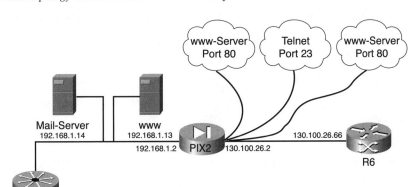

Step 2: Configuring IP ACLs at the Interface

In this portion of the lesson, you define an ACL to be used with CBAC so that it inspects TCP and UDP while allowing ICMP for echo reply, time exceeded, packet too big, trace route, and unreachable. You apply the ACL to your Serial 0 interface, the unprotected interface. Allowed inbound access for specific protocol traffic is provided through dynamic ACLs, which are generated according to the CBAC inspection rules you define. Example 22-5 illustrates the configuration items for R2 that accomplish this task.

Example 22-5 *Defining a CBAC ACL*

```
Configuration items needed for R2:
R2(config)#access-list 111 deny tcp any any
R2(config)#access-list 111 deny udp any any
R2(config)#access-list 111 permit icmp any any echo-reply
R2(config)#access-list 111 permit icmp any any time-exceeded
R2(config)#access-list 111 permit icmp any any packet-too-big
R2(config)#access-list 111 permit icmp any any traceroute
R2(config)#access-list 111 permit icmp any any unreachable
R2(config)#access-list 111 deny ip any any
R2(config)#interface Serial0
R2(config-if)#ip access-group 111 in
```

Step 3: Configuring Global Timeouts and Thresholds

You can use the following commands to configure your CBAC timeouts and thresholds:

To change the length of time that software waits for a TCP session to reach the established state from the default of 30 seconds before dropping the session:

```
R2(config)#ip inspect tcp synwait-time seconds
```

To change the length of time a TCP session is still managed after the firewall detects a FIN-exchange from the default of 5 seconds:

```
R2(config)#ip inspect tcp finwait-time seconds
```

To set the length of time a TCP session is still managed after no activity, the TCP idle timeout, from 1 hour:

```
R2(config)#ip inspect tcp idle-time seconds
```

To change the length of time a UDP session is still managed after no activity, the UDP idle timeout, from the default of 30 seconds:

```
R2(config)#ip inspect udp idle-time seconds
```

To change the length of time a DNS name lookup session is still managed after no activity from the default of 5 seconds:

```
R2(config)#ip inspect dns-timeout seconds
```

To change the number of existing half-open sessions that cause the software to start deleting half-open sessions from the default of 500:

```
R2(config)#ip inspect max-incomplete high number
```

To change the number of existing half-open sessions that cause the software to stop deleting half-open sessions from the default of 400:

```
R2(config)#ip inspect max-incomplete low number
```

To change the rate of new sessions that cause the software to start deleting half-open sessions from the default of 500:

```
R2(config)#ip inspect one-minute high number
```

To change the rate of new sessions that cause the software to stop deleting half-open sessions from 400 per minute:

```
R2(config)#ip inspect one-minute low number
```

To change the number of existing half-open TCP sessions with the same destination host address that will cause the software to start dropping half-open sessions to the same destination host address from the default of 50 sessions and 0 minutes:

```
R2(config)#ip inspect tcp max-incomplete host number block-time minutes
```

In this lesson, you change the CBAC timeouts so that the device waits for 20 seconds for TCP to reach an established state with an idle time of 30 minutes, 1800 seconds. You will also set your UDP idle timeout to 20 seconds. You want to start deleting half-open sessions at 350 sessions and stop deleting them at 250 sessions. Your last item is to start dropping half-open sessions to a single IP address at 75 for 1 minute. Example 22-6 illustrates the configuration items for R2 that accomplish this task.

Example 22-6 *Configuring Global Timeouts*

```
Configuration items needed for R2:
R2(config)#ip inspect tcp synwait-time 20
R2(config)#ip inspect tcp idle-time 1800
R2(config)#ip inspect udp idle-time 20
R2(config)#ip inspect max-incomplete high 350
R2(config)#ip inspect max-incomplete low 250
R2(config)#ip inspect tcp max-incomplete host 75 block-time 1
```

Step 4: Defining an Inspection Rule

Your next required step in configuring CBAC is defining an inspection rule. This rule specifies what application-layer protocols CBAC inspects CBAC at an interface.

Your inspection rule should specify each desired application-layer protocol as well as generic TCP or generic UDP if it is required for your security policy. An inspection rule consists of a series of statements, each listing a protocol and tied together under the same inspection rule name.

You can use the following commands to configure CBAC inspection for an application-layer protocol:

```
R2(config)#ip inspect name inspection-name protocol [alert {on | off}] [audit-trail
    {on | off}] [timeout seconds]
R2(config)#ip inspect name inspection-name rpc program-number number [wait-time
    minutes] [alert {on | off}] [audit-trail {on | off}] [timeout seconds]
```

Table 22-1 lists application *protocol* keywords for the **ip inspect name** command.

Table 22-1   *Application* protocol *Keywords for the* **ip inspect name** *Command*

Application Protocol	Protocol Keyword
CU-SeeMe	**cuseeme**
FTP	**ftp**
H.323	**h323**
Microsoft NetShow	**netshow**
UNIX **r** commands (**rlogin, rexec, rsh**)	**rcmd**

continues

Table 22-1   *Application* protocol *Keywords for the* **ip inspect name** *Command (Continued)*

Application Protocol	Protocol Keyword
RealAudio	**realaudio**
SMTP	**smtp**
SQL*Net	**sqlnet**
StreamWorks	**streamworks**
TFTP	**tftp**
VDOLive	**vdolive**

You can use the following to block all Java applets except applets from friendly locations:

```
R2(config)#ip access-list standard name
R2(config-std-nacl)# deny source [source-wildcard]
```

or

```
R2(config-std-nacl)# permit source [source-wildcard]
```

or

```
R2(config)#access-list access-list-number {deny | permit} protocol source
  [source-wildcard] eq www destination [destination-wildcard]
```

Then apply the ACL to an inspection rule:

```
R2(config)#ip inspect name inspection-name http [java-list access-list] [alert
  {on | off}] [audit-trail {on | off}] [timeout seconds]
```

You can use one or both of the following commands to configure CBAC inspection for TCP or UDP packets:

```
R2(config)#ip inspect name inspection-name tcp [alert {on | off}] [audit-trail
  {on | off}] [timeout seconds]

R2(config)#ip inspect name inspection-name udp [alert {on | off}] [audit-trail
  {on | off}] [timeout seconds]
```

In this portion of the lesson, you define an inspection rule named ccie_cbac that inspects various applications. These applications are CU-SeeMe, FTP, RealAudio, RPC (program number 111000), StreamWorks, VDOLive, and RTSP. Example 22-7 demonstrates a way to configure these options.

Example 22-7 *CBAC Inspection Rule for Application Layer Protocols*

```
Configuration items for R2:
R2(config)#ip inspect name ccie_cbac cuseeme timeout 30
R2(config)#ip inspect name ccie_cbac ftp timeout 30
R2(config)#ip inspect name ccie_cbac realaudio timeout 30
R2(config)#ip inspect name ccie_cbac rpc program-number 111000
R2(config)#ip inspect name ccie_cbac streamworks timeout 30
```

Example 22-7 *CBAC Inspection Rule for Application Layer Protocols (Continued)*

```
R2(config)#ip inspect name ccie_cbac vdolive timeout 30
R2(config)#ip inspect name ccie_cbac rtsp
R2(config)#ip inspect name ccie_cbac h323
```

Step 5: Applying the Inspection Rule to an Interface

Applying your defined inspection rule to an interface is the next step in configuring CBAC.

If you are configuring CBAC for an external interface, apply the rule to your outbound traffic. If you are configuring CBAC for an internal interface, apply the rule to your inbound traffic.

You can use the following command to apply an inspection rule to an interface:

```
R2(config-if)#ip inspect inspection-name {in | out}
```

The next step in this lesson is to apply CBAC to your Ethernet interface. Example 22-8 illustrates the configuration items for R2 that accomplish this task.

Example 22-8 *Applying the CBAC Inspection Rule*

```
Configuration items needed for R2:
R2(config)#interface Ethernet0
R2(config-if)#ip inspect ccie_cbac in
```

Step 6: Configuring Logging and an Audit Trail

You should turn on logging and an audit trail to create a record of network access through your firewall, including illegitimate access attempts and inbound and outbound services. You can use the following commands to configure logging and audit trail functions:

```
R2(config)#service timestamps log datetime
R2(config)#logging host
R2(config)#logging facility facility-type
R2(config)#logging trap level
R2(config)#ip inspect audit-trail
```

Next you configure R2 to log to the SYSLOG server located at 192.168.100.100. You will log error level messages. You will enable audit trail for IP inspect. Example 22-9 lists the configuration items required on R2.

Example 22-9 *Configuring an Audit Trail*

```
Configuration items for R2:
R2(config)#service timestamps log datetime
R2(config)#logging 192.168.100.100
R2(config)#logging trap error
R2(config)#ip inspect audit-trail
```

Step 7: Other Guidelines for Configuring a Firewall

As with any networking device you configure, you should protect access into your firewall by configuring passwords and optionally using user authentication, authorization, and accounting. Refer to Chapter 15, "Basic IOS Software and Catalyst 3550 Series Security," for general guidelines on securing your firewall.

Step 8: Verifying CBAC

After CBAC is configured, you can optionally view and verify your CBAC configuration, status, statistics, and session information by using one or more of the commands described in this section.

To display the contents of all your current IP ACLs, use the following command:

```
R2#show ip access-lists
```

To show a particular configured inspection rule, use the following command:

```
R2#show ip inspect name inspection-name
```

To show the complete CBAC inspection configuration, use the following command:

```
R2#show ip inspect config
```

To show the interface configuration with regards to applied inspection rules and ACLs, use the following command:

```
R2#show ip inspect interfaces
```

To show existing sessions that are currently being tracked and inspected by CBAC, use the following command:

```
R2#show ip inspect session [detail]
```

To show all CBAC configuration and all existing sessions that are currently being tracked and inspected by CBAC, use the following command:

```
R2#show ip inspect all
```

Most of the time, you can tell whether CBAC is inspecting network traffic properly, because your network applications are working as expected. However, in the case of verifying RTSP or H.323 inspection, you can initiate an RTSP- or H.323-based application through your firewall. You can then use the **show ip inspect session** and **show ip access lists** commands to display the dynamic ACL entries and the established connections to these multimedia sessions.

Monitoring and Maintaining CBAC

One way that you can watch for network attacks and investigate network problems is by using **debug** commands and system messages, as described in the following sections.

Debugging CBAC

Several generic **debug** commands are available to you for CBAC.

This command displays messages about software functions called by CBAC:

```
R2#debug ip inspect function-trace
```

This command displays messages about software objects being created or the beginning of the CBAC inspection process:

```
R2#debug ip inspect object-creation
```

This command displays messages about software objects being deleted or the ending of the CBAC inspection process:

```
R2#debug ip inspect object-deletion
```

This command displays messages about CBAC software events, including information about CBAC packet processing:

```
R2#debug ip inspect events
```

This command displays messages about CBAC timer events, such as when a CBAC idle timeout is reached:

```
R2#debug ip inspect timers
```

This command enables the detailed option, which can be used in combination with other options to get additional information:

```
R2#debug ip inspect detail
```

Transport-level **debug** commands are also available for use in monitoring and maintaining CBAC.

This command displays messages about CBAC-inspected TCP events, including details about TCP packets:

```
R2#debug ip inspect tcp
```

This command displays messages about CBAC-inspected UDP events, including details about UDP packets:

```
R2#debug ip inspect udp
```

If you are using application-layer inspection, you can use the following command to provide debugging for application protocols:

```
R2#debug ip inspect protocol
```

Interpreting Syslog and Console Messages Generated by CBAC

CBAC provides syslog messages, console alert messages, and audit trail messages to alert you to network attacks and provide an audit trail that provides details about sessions inspected by CBAC.

The audit trail and alert information can be configured on a per-application basis using the CBAC inspection rules.

DoS Attack Detection Error Messages

CBAC notifies you when it detects a DoS attack. Example 22-10 shows a sample of the error messages generated when a DoS attack is detected.

Example 22-10 *Error Messages from a DoS Attack*

```
%FW-4-ALERT_ON: getting aggressive, count (550/500) current 1-min rate: 250
%FW-4-ALERT_OFF: calming down, count (0/400) current 1-min rate: 0
```

In this example, the %FW-4-ALERT_ON and %FW-4-ALERT_OFF error messages appear together, indicating a separate attack.

The error messages shown in Example 22-11 indicate that a DoS attack has occurred on a specific TCP host.

Example 22-11 *DoS Attack Against a Specific Host*

```
%FW-4-HOST_TCP_ALERT_ON: Max tcp half-open connections (50) exceeded for host
   172.21.127.242.
%FW-4-BLOCK_HOST: Blocking new TCP connections to host 172.21.127.242 for 2 minutes
   (half-open count 50 exceeded)
%FW-4-UNBLOCK_HOST: New TCP connections to host 172.21.127.242 no longer blocked
```

SMTP Attack Detection Error Messages

CBAC can detect and block SMTP attacks in the form of illegal SMTP commands and notify you when the attack occurs. Example 22-12 shows an error message that indicates that an SMTP attack has occurred.

Example 22-12 *SMTP Attack Error Message*

```
%FW-4-SMTP_INVALID_COMMAND: Invalid SMTP command from initiator
   (192.168.12.3:52419)
```

CBAC can also detect a limited number of SMTP attack signatures by examining SYSLOG messages that might indicate a possible attack against your protected network, such as the detection of illegal SMTP commands in a packet. CBAC cannot inspect ESMTP messages. Whenever a signature is detected, CBAC resets the connection.

Table 22-2 defines the SMTP attack signatures that the Cisco IOS Firewall can detect.

Table 22-2   *SMTP Attack Signatures*

Signature	Description
Mail: bad rcpt	Runs on any mail message that has a pipe symbol (	) in the Recipient field.
Mail: bad from	Runs on any mail message that has a pipe symbol (	) in the From: field.
Mail: old attack	Runs when **wiz** or **debug** commands are sent to the SMTP port.
Mail: decode	Runs on any mail message that has :decode@ in the header.
Majordomo	A Majordomo program bug allows remote users to execute arbitrary commands at the server's privilege level.

Example 22-13 shows an error message that is generated when an SMTP attack signature is triggered.

Example 22-13 *SMTP Attack Signature Error Message*

```
02:04:55: %FW-4-TCP_MAJORDOMO_EXEC_BUG: Sig:3107:Majordomo Execute Attack - from
   192.168.25.1 to 192.168.205.1:
```

Java-Blocking Error Messages

CBAC can detect and selectively block Java applets and notify you when a Java applet has been blocked. Example 22-14 shows an error message that might appear when a Java applet is blocked.

Example 22-14 *Java Applet Error Message*

```
%FW-4-HTTP_JAVA_BLOCK: JAVA applet is blocked from (172.21.127.218:80) to
   (172.16.57.30:44673).
```

FTP Error Messages

CBAC can detect and prevent certain types of FTP attacks and notify you when this occurs. Example 22-15 demonstrates the type of error messages you might receive when CBAC detects one of these FTP attacks.

Example 22-15 *FTP Error Messages*

```
%FW-3-FTP_PRIV_PORT: Privileged port 1000 used in PORT command -- FTP client
   10.0.0.1  FTP server 10.1.0.1
%FW-3-FTP_SESSION_NOT_AUTHENTICATED: Command issued before the session is
```

continues

Example 22-15 *FTP Error Messages (Continued)*

```
        authenticated -- FTP client 10.0.0.1
        %FW-3-FTP_NON_MATCHING_IP_ADDR: Non-matching address 172.19.148.154 used in PORT
        command -- FTP client 172.19.54.143  FTP server 172.16.127.242
```

Audit Trail Messages

CBAC provides audit trail messages to record details about inspected sessions. Audit trail information can be configured on a per-application basis using the CBAC inspection rules. You can use the responder's port number, following the responder's address, to determine which protocol CBAC inspected. Example 22-16 shows sample audit trail messages.

Example 22-16 *Sample Audit Trail Messages*

```
    %FW-6-SESS_AUDIT_TRAIL: tcp session initiator (192.168.1.13:33192) sent 22 bytes
      -- responder (192.168.129.11:25) sent 208 bytes
    %FW-6-SESS_AUDIT_TRAIL: http session initiator (172.16.57.30:44673) sent 1599
      bytes -- responder (172.21.127.218:80) sent 93124 bytes
```

Turning Off CBAC

If you want to, you can turn off CBAC by using the **no ip inspect** configuration command. This command removes all CBAC configuration entries and resets all CBAC timeouts and thresholds to their default values. All existing sessions are deleted and their associated dynamic ACLs removed.

Be aware that by turning off CBAC, you might not experience any negative security impact because CBAC creates permit ACLs. When CBAC is disabled, no permit ACLs are maintained, causing no derived traffic to be passed through your firewall. SMTP and Java blocking are exceptions to this rule. With CBAC turned off, unacceptable SMTP commands or Java applets might be permitted through your firewall.

Case Study 22-1: Configuring CBAC on Two Interfaces

Figure 22-3 illustrates the topology you will use for Case Study 22-1.

Figure 22-3 *CBAC Configuration Topology*

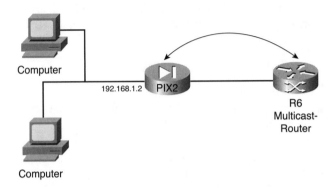

In this case study, you will configure CBAC to inspect the following applications to two servers, 192.168.31.100 and 192.168.31.101, on your internal network while inspecting TCP and UDP traffic going out your network:

- SMTP

- FTP

- HTTP

- CU-SeeMe

- H.323

- RCMD

- RealAudio

- SQLNet

- StreamWorks

- TFTP

- VDOLive

This case study is structured around the following steps:

Step 1 Select an interface.

Step 2 Configure the extended ACL.

Step 3 Configure timeouts.

Step 4 Define the inspection rules.

Step 5 Apply the inspection rule.

Step 6 Configure the audit trail and logging.

Step 1: Selecting the Interface

In this step, you determine which interface to apply your CBAC inspection rules and extended ACL to. You will apply the CBAC inspection rule to the Serial interface and the extended ACL to the Ethernet interface.

Step 2: Configuring the Extended ACL

Next, define your extended ACL and apply it to your serial interface. Example 22-17 lists the configuration items that are required on R3.

Example 22-17 *Configuring the Extended ACL*

```
Configuration items required for R3:
R3(config)#interface Serial0
R3(config-if)#encapsulation frame-relay
R3(config-if)#exit
R3(config)#interface Serial0.1 point-to-point
R3(config-if)#ip address 150.100.31.3 255.255.255.252
R3(config-if)#ip access-group 102 in
R3(config-if)#frame-relay interface-dlci 200 IETF
R3(config-if)#exit
R3(config)#access-list 102 permit icmp any 192.168.31.0 0.0.0.255 echo-reply
R3(config)#access-list 102 permit icmp any 192.168.31.0 0.0.0.255 unreachable
R3(config)#access-list 102 permit icmp any 192.168.31.0 0.0.0.255
  administratively-prohibited
R3(config)#access-list 102 permit icmp any 192.168.31.0 0.0.0.255 packet-too-big
R3(config)#access-list 102 permit icmp any 192.168.31.0 0.0.0.255 echo
R3(config)#access-list 102 permit icmp any 192.168.31.0 0.0.0.255 time-exceeded
R3(config)#access-list 102 deny tcp any host 192.168.31.100 eq smtp
R3(config)#access-list 102 deny ip any any
```

Step 3: Configuring Timeouts

In this step, you change the CBAC timeouts so that the device waits for 35 seconds for TCP to reach an established state with an idle time of 45 minutes. You also set your UDP idle timeout to 45 seconds. You want to start deleting half-open sessions at 400 sessions and stop deleting them at 300 sessions. The last task is to start dropping half-open sessions to a single IP address at 75 for 0 minutes. Example 22-18 illustrates the configuration items for R2 that accomplish this task.

Example 22-18 *Configuring Timeouts*

```
Configuration items needed for R3:
R3(config)#ip inspect tcp synwait-time 35
R3(config)#ip inspect tcp idle-time 2400
R3(config)#ip inspect udp idle-time 45
```

Example 22-18 *Configuring Timeouts (Continued)*

```
R3(config)#ip inspect max-incomplete high 400
R3(config)#ip inspect max-incomplete low 300
R3(config)#ip inspect tcp max-incomplete host 75 block-time 0
```

Step 4: Defining the Inspection Rules

In this step, define your IP inspection rule named mysite. Example 22-19 shows the commands to complete this step.

Example 22-19 *Defining the Inspection Rule*

```
Configuration items required for R3:
R3(config)#ip inspect name mysite tcp idle-time 14400
R3(config)#ip inspect name mysite udp idle-time 1800
R3(config)#ip inspect name mysitedns-timeout 7
R3(config)#ip inspect name mysite cuseeme
R3(config)#ip inspect name mysite ftp
R3(config)#ip inspect name mysite h323
R3(config)#ip inspect name mysite http
R3(config)#ip inspect name mysite rcmd
R3(config)#ip inspect name mysite realaudio
R3(config)#ip inspect name mysite smtp
R3(config)#ip inspect name mysite sqlnet
R3(config)#ip inspect name mysite streamworks
R3(config)#ip inspect name mysite tcp
R3(config)#ip inspect name mysite tftp
R3(config)#ip inspect name mysite udp
R3(config)#ip inspect name mysite vdolive
```

Step 5: Applying the Inspection Rule

In this step, you apply the inspection rule myset to the Ethernet interface. Example 22-20 shows the commands to complete this step.

Example 22-20 *Applying the Inspection Rule*

```
Configuration items required for R3:
R3(config)#interface Ethernet0
R3(config-if)#ip address 192.168.31.3 255.255.255.0
R3(config-if)#ip inspect mysite out
```

Step 6: Configuring the Audit Trail and Logging

In this step, you enable the audit trail and configure the syslog server of 192.168.31.254. Example 22-21 lists the configuration items that are required on R3.

Example 22-21 *Configuring the Audit Trail and Logging*

```
Configuration items required for R3:
R3(config)#ip inspect audit-trail
R3(config)#logging 192.168.31.254
```

Port-to-Application Mapping (PAM)

This section describes the Cisco IOS Firewall Port-to-Application Mapping (PAM) feature. By using PAM, you allow CBAC-supported applications to be run on nonstandard ports. Then you can customize access control for specific applications and services to meet the distinct needs of your networks.

By using the port information, PAM creates a table of default port-to-application mapping information at your firewall. This information allows CBAC-supported services to run on nonstandard ports, bypassing CBAC's limitations of inspecting traffic using only the well-known or registered ports associated with an application.

With PAM, you can also support host- or subnet-specific port mapping, which allows you to apply PAM to a single host or subnet using standard ACLs.

How PAM Works

When PAM is enabled, it generates a table of information that identifies specific applications with specific TCP or UDP port information. When your firewall router first starts up, the PAM table is populated with mapping information defined by the system. As you customize the mapping with information, this table is modified to reflect the new information. The information's overall purpose is to serve as the default port mapping for traffic passing through your firewall.

PAM works in conjunction with CBAC to identify the applications associated with various port numbers as CBAC inspects traffic passing through your firewall.

Entries in the PAM table provide CBAC with three types of mapping information:

- System-defined port
- User-defined port
- Host-specific port

The following sections describe each in more detail.

System-Defined Port Mapping

This table is created upon startup using the well-known or registered port-mapping information. System-defined entries contain all the services supported by CBAC, which requires the system-defined mapping information to function properly. You are not allowed to delete or change the system-defined mapping information. For example, you cannot map HTTP services to port 21 (FTP) or FTP services to port 80 (HTTP). However, you are allowed to override the system-defined entries for specific hosts using the host-specific mapping option.

Table 22-3 lists the default system-defined services and applications that populate the PAM table.

Table 22-3   *System-Defined Port Mapping*

Application Name	Well-Known or Registered Port Number	Protocol Description
cuseeme	7648	CU-SeeMe Protocol
exec	512	Remote Process Execution
ftp	21	File Transfer Protocol (control port)
http	80	Hypertext Transfer Protocol
h323	1720	H.323 protocol (for example, Microsoft NetMeeting, Intel Video Phone)
login	513	Remote login
mgcp	2427	Media Gateway Control Protocol
msrpc	135	Microsoft Remote Procedure Call
netshow	1755	Microsoft NetShow
real-audio-video	7070	RealAudio and RealVideo
rtsp	8559	Real Time Streaming Protocol
shell	514	Remote command
sip	5060	Session Initiation Protocol
smtp	25	Simple Mail Transfer Protocol
sqlnet	1521	SQL-NET
streamworks	1558	StreamWorks Protocol
sunrpc	111	Sun Remote Procedure Call
telnet	23	Telnet
tftp	69	Trivial File Transfer Protocol
vdolive	7000	VDOLive Protocol

User-Defined Port Mapping

The user-defined port mapping is created from user-defined entries in the PAM table. For security reasons, you might be required to run network services or applications that use nonstandard ports. After you have modified a port mapping, you can overwrite that entry later by simply mapping that specific port with a different application. Remember, though, that if you try to map an application to a system-defined port, an error message appears to warn you of the conflict. You can also define a range of ports for an application by establishing a separate entry in the PAM table for each port number in the range. Your user-defined entries are saved with the default mapping information when you save the router configuration.

Host-Specific Port Mapping

You can use the user-defined entries in the mapping table to include host-specific mapping information, which establishes port mapping information for specific hosts or subnets. This mapping allows you to use the same port number for different services on different hosts. Host-specific port mapping also allows you to apply PAM to a specific subnet when that subnet runs a service that uses a port number that is different from the port number defined in the default mapping information. You can also use host-specific port mapping to override a system-defined entry in the PAM table. However, if the host-specific port mapping information is the same as an existing system- or user-defined entry, the new host-specific port changes have no effect.

When to Use PAM

Here are a few examples of when you might want to consider using PAM:

- Use PAM to apply nonstandard port numbers for a service or application.

- Use PAM when a specific host or subnet uses a port number for an application that is different from the default port number established in the PAM table.

- Use PAM when different hosts use the same port number for different applications.

Lesson 22-3: Configuring PAM

Follow these steps to configure PAM:

Step 1   Optionally configure a standard ACL.

Step 2   Enable PAM.

Step 3   Optionally verify PAM operation.

Step 1: Configuring Standard ACLs

If you will use PAM with a specific host or subnet, you must define a standard ACL. You can use the following command to do so:

```
R2(config)#access-list access-list-number permit source [source-wildcard]
```

In this part of the lesson, you define two separate ACLs for the host at 192.168.31.100 and the host at 192.168.31.101. Example 22-22 illustrates the required configuration on R3.

Example 22-22 *Defining ACLs for PAM*

```
Required configuration on R3:
R3(config)#access-list 10 permit 100.100.31.100
R3(config)#access-list 20 permit 100.100.31.101
```

Step 2: Configuring PAM

To configure PAM, use the following command:

```
R2(config)#ip port-map appl_name port port_num [list acl_num]
```

You can use the **list** option to associate this port mapping to the specific hosts in the ACL. If an ACL is included, the hosts defined in that ACL have the application *appl_name* running on port *port_num*.

In this lesson, you have a scenario that requires the same port number to be mapped to different services running on different hosts. Port 8000 is required for HTTP services for host 192.168.31.100, and port 8000 is also required for FTP services for host 192.168.31.101. Example 22-23 illustrates the commands you can use to complete these tasks.

Example 22-23 *Mapping Multiple Services to the Same Port*

```
Required configuration on R3:
R3(config)#ip port-map http port 8000 list 10
R3(config)#ip port-map http ftp 8000 list 20
```

Step 3: Verifying PAM

After PAM is configured, you can verify the port-mapping information using the following command:

```
R2#show ip port-map
```

Monitoring and Maintaining PAM

You can monitor and maintain PAM by displaying the port-mapping information, including the system-defined entries:

```
R2#show ip port-map [appl_name | port port_num]
```

If you include the application name, you see a list of entries by application. If you include the port number, you see the entries by port.

To delete user-defined port-mapping information, use the following command. Remember that this command does not affect the system-defined port-mapping information:

```
R2(config)#no ip port-map appl_name port port_num [list acl_num]
```

Summary

This chapter reviewed the features available to you in the Cisco IOS Firewall feature set. It covered building a custom firewall, TCP intercept, CBAC, and Port-to-Application Mapping.

Review Questions

1 The Cisco IOS Firewall feature set is built around the concept of preventing what?

2 When an attacker opens a large number of half-open TCP connections, this is what type of attack?

3 TCP intercept, by default, drops which connection first?

4 What feature in the Cisco IOS Firewall gives you intelligent filtering of TCP and UDP packets?

5 What is the default setting for the low value of half-open connections before TCP intercept aggressive mode stops?

6 What is spoofing?

7 Can CBAC can be used to prevent SMTP attacks?

8 Which Cisco IOS Firewall feature allows you to run CBAC-supported applications across nonstandard ports?

FAQs

Q — *Why would I want to use a firewall?*

A — A firewall, usually placed at strategic points in your network, lets you provide access control to devices on your network.

Q — *If I implement TCP intercept, do I need to use an ACL?*

A — Yes. TCP intercept intercepts the SYN packets sent to devices you identify. You use an extended ACL to define the devices you want to protect.

Q — *I want to use TCP intercept in my environment, but I don't want the firewall to intercept the SYN packets. Can I still use TCP intercept?*

A — Yes. You can use TCP intercept in watch mode. While TCP intercept is in this mode, it passively watches the connection requests flowing through the firewall. If a connection fails to establish in a defined period of time, the firewall sends a reset to clear the request.

Q — *Why would I implement CBAC instead of using ACLs for access control?*

A — CBAC lets you filter traffic based on the information contained at the application layer. ACLs can only examine packets at either the network or transport layer.

Q — *How does CBAC work with UDP packets, because they do not contain the same information as a TCP packet?*

A — UDP packets are approximated based on a similar packet exiting the network before the packet being received. The UDP header also contains information such as the source and destination addresses and port numbers that can also be used for comparison. If a packet arrives within the user-definable timeout value, it is allowed.

Q — *I need to configure IPSec for VPN connectivity. Can I still use CBAC?*

A — CBAC can be used as long as it is the tunnel endpoint. Otherwise, the packets are not inspected, because an IPSec packet is not a TCP or UDP packet.

Q — *I want to run my HTTP server on port 8080 and still use CBAC for access control. Is this possible?*

A — Yes, but you have to use Port-to-Application Mapping (PAM) to remap the port so that CBAC knows what port it is using.

Q — *I want to map my FTP server to port 80. Can I do this with PAM?*

A — Yes, but you need to use host-specific mapping, because port 80 is a system-defined port. Trying to define it in any other manner will result in an error.

This chapter includes the following topics:

- Security levels and address translation
- TCP and UDP
- Configuring a Cisco PIX Firewall

CHAPTER 23

Cisco PIX Firewall

PIX Firewalls play an important role in the CCIE Security lab configuration as well as in real-life networking security. This chapter concentrates on the firewalling techniques and new features that are available in the PIX release 6.2(2) that might be included in your CCIE Security lab exam.

Instead of going over the general introductory information on PIX Firewalls, it would be more beneficial to examine a few concepts that are pertinent to the configuration of these devices. Each feature presented, both in the introduction and configuration sections, is explained to the extent that is necessary for you to understand it and be able to configure it on your own. If you feel that you need more information on universal PIX topics before you begin the hands-on tasks, refer to Appendix E, "Security-Related RFCs and Publications," for a list of additional resources.

Security Levels and Address Translation

The PIX Firewall treats its interfaces according to the level of trust. The levels range from 0 to 100; 0 is the least trusted and 100 is the most trusted interface. By default, the inside interface is assigned the level of 100 and the outside interface the level of 0 (see Figure 23-1). The inside interface is connected to the network that needs to be protected. The outside interface is attached to the public network (the Internet) that the inside interface needs protection against.

Figure 23-1 *PIX Firewall Interfaces and Security Levels*

This level assignment results in the way the PIX Firewall handles the incoming data. When data travels from the inside interface out, it is implicitly allowed, unless specifically denied by Access Control Lists (ACLs), because the originating interface (inside) is of a higher security level than the receiving interface. Conversely, data destined for the inside interface from the outside or any perimeter interface ranging in priority from 1 to 99 is implicitly denied, unless explicitly allowed by an ACL. This occurs because the originating interface is always of a lower priority than the receiver behind the inside interface.

Regardless of whether the data flow is inbound or outbound, address translation must be in place for any packets to cross the inside or outside boundary. When a session is built through the PIX, a translation slot is created. These translation slots are called *xlates.* Both dynamic translation and static translation are supported and are discussed in further detail in "Lesson 23-1: Configuring the PIX Firewall Basics."

TCP and UDP

As you know, Transmission Control Protocol (TCP) is a connection-oriented protocol, which allows PIX's Adaptive Security Algorithm (ASA) to monitor the state of a TCP session that is established through it. When a packet is sent through the PIX, PIX creates a dynamic entry for the connection that constantly watches the state of that connection and checks all the return packets against that entry.

Because User Datagram Protocol (UDP) is a connectionless protocol, it is more difficult to secure. So ASA handles data transfers from UDP applications similarly to the way that it handles TCP. If a packet is sent from the inside network, the PIX Firewall maintains UDP connection-state information. The subsequent packets are matched against the entry. If the parameters match, the packets going in the reverse direction are accepted. However, if the connection is idle for a short period of time, the dynamic state entry is deleted.

Configuring a Cisco PIX Firewall

You have already encountered the PIX Firewall in several case studies from other chapters. There, the PIX Firewall was a part of a larger topology and played only a supplemental role to another topic. This chapter, on the other hand, is dedicated to the PIX Firewall specifically. Because all services are implemented on one device, the case study format is modified to a lesson format so that the configuration tasks are still separated into their own sections and grouped into logical categories.

Lesson 23-1: Configuring the PIX Firewall Basics

This section helps you to understand and initialize the PIX Firewall. The commands that are described in the subsequent sections are the first and foremost configuration tasks for the PIX. Without them, any more-advanced configuration features would not be functional.

The basics steps that are described in the following subsections are as follows:

Step 1   Changing names and security levels of interfaces

Step 2   Identifying the interface type and speed

Step 3   Specifying the maximum transmission unit (MTU) for an interface

Step 4   Assigning an IP address and subnet mask

Step 5   Outbound connectivity with NAT and PAT

Step 6   Assigning a pool of outside addresses

Step 7   Configuring static NAT

Step 8   Configuring static routes on a PIX Firewall

Step 1: Changing Names and Security Levels of Interfaces

Changing the interface name and its security level is a basic but optional task. System defaults exist that you can accept and do nothing about. However, if you want to have some input in what the interface is called and the level of security that it has, use the following command syntax:

```
PIX2(config)#nameif hardware_id interface security_level
```

System defaults are described in Example 23-1. You can see how each parameter corresponds to the available command argument. For example, **ethernet0** is a *hardware_id* of the **outside** interface with **security0** as its *security_level*.

Example 23-1 *Interface Names and Security Levels: System Defaults*

```
PIX2# show nameif
nameif ethernet0 outside security0
nameif ethernet1 inside security100
nameif ethernet2 intf2 security10
nameif ethernet3 intf3 security15
```

Since the 5.2 release, you can change the default assignment of Ethernet0 as outside and Ethernet1 as inside interfaces. However, the corresponding security levels must remain at 0 and 100, respectively. Perimeter interfaces are different. You are encouraged to change their default *interface-name (intfn)* names to something more meaningful. The security levels of perimeter interfaces can be modified to be from 1 to 99 instead of the default. The default values are 10 for the first perimeter interface, 20 for the second perimeter interface and incremented by 5 for all subsequent interfaces (25, 30, and so on).

NOTE   You should not assign the same security level to two different interfaces. Otherwise, no traffic can flow between them. Also, try not to use dashes when naming interfaces, because they can be misinterpreted when used elsewhere on the PIX. For example, they can be mistaken for an address pool with the DHCP services.

Step 2: Identifying the Interface Type and Speed

After you have renamed an interface or accepted its default, you can bring that interface up because it is shut down by default. Specify the interface speed within the same command. The command format is as follows:

```
PIX2(config)#interface hardware_id hardware_speed [shutdown]
```

The *hardware_speed* options for an Ethernet interface include the following:

- **10baset**
- **100basetx**
- **100full**
- **auto**

Although auto negotiation is the default speed, you should specify the speed of each interface used.

There are still more options for the Gigabit Ethernet interface. The optional **shutdown** keyword administratively disables the interface, if it has been previously enabled. Example 23-2 demonstrates how the PIX interfaces are configured.

Example 23-2 *Specifying Interface Type and Speed*

```
PIX2#show run
interface ethernet0 10full
interface ethernet1 auto
interface ethernet2 auto
interface ethernet3 10baset
```

Step 3: Specifying the Maximum Transmission Unit for an Interface

The next logical step is to specify the MTU size for each of the configured PIX interfaces. When the actual data size is larger than the configured maximum, it must be fragmented before being sent. The available range of MTU values is 64 to 65,535 bytes. Different requirements for those values exist, depending on which PIX version is being used or the media.

PIX Firewall also allows dynamic discovery of the MTU size based on various links along the path by implementing the IP Path MTU Discovery mechanism. The command to set the MTU size is as follows:

```
PIX2(config)#mtu if_name bytes
```

The *if_name* argument specifies which of the PIX interfaces is being ruled by the **mtu** statement. When configuring the MTU size, choose the value of the *bytes* segment. Example 23-3 illustrates the **mtu** command usage on PIX2.

Example 23-3 *Setting the MTU Size on PIX Interfaces*

```
PIX2# show run
interface ethernet0 10full
mtu outside 9000

PIX2# show mtu
mtu outside 9000
mtu inside 1500
mtu DMZ2 1500
mtu DMZ3 1500
```

NOTE   In those cases where the "don't fragment" (DF) bit is set and the data is larger than the defined MTU size, the PIX Firewall does not forward the oversized data but instead notifies the sending host of the problem.

Step 4: Assigning an IP Address and Subnet Mask

Each interface on the PIX Firewall that is involved in traffic handling needs to have an IP address and mask assigned with the following command:

```
PIX2(config)#ip address if_name ip_address [netmask]
```

The *interface_name* argument is, of course, the name used in the **nameif** command. The *ip_address* argument is the address that you give to the interface. The *netmask* argument is the specific subnet mask that is applied to the address. If you omit the mask from your configuration, the firewall assigns a classful mask to the interface, producing an effect that is not always desirable.

You can view the interfaces' IP addresses and masks by using the **show ip** or **show interface** command. In Example 23-4, the inside interface is given a private IP address of 192.168.1.222, and the outside interface is assigned the public address of 130.100.26.2.

Example 23-4 *Configuring Interfaces with IP Addresses and Masks*

```
PIX2# show ip
System IP Addresses:
        ip address outside 130.100.26.2 255.255.255.224
        ip address inside 192.168.1.222 255.255.255.0
        ip address DMZ2 172.16.23.1 255.255.255.0
        ip address DMZ3 172.16.22.1 255.255.255.0
Current IP Addresses:
        ip address outside 130.100.26.2 255.255.255.224
        ip address inside 192.168.1.222 255.255.255.0
        ip address DMZ2 172.16.23.1 255.255.255.0
        ip address DMZ3 172.16.22.1 255.255.255.0

PIX2# show interface ethernet0
interface ethernet0 "outside" is up, line protocol is down
  Hardware is i82558 ethernet, address is 00e0.b600.615f
  IP address 130.100.26.2, subnet mask 255.255.255.224
  MTU 9000 bytes, BW 10000 Kbit full duplex
        0 packets input, 0 bytes, 0 no buffer
        Received 0 broadcasts, 0 runts, 0 giants
        0 input errors, 0 CRC, 0 frame, 0 overrun, 0 ignored, 0 abort
        36 packets output, 2160 bytes, 0 underruns
        0 output errors, 0 collisions, 0 interface resets
        0 babbles, 0 late collisions, 0 deferred
        0 lost carrier, 0 no carrier
        input queue (curr/max blocks): hardware (128/128) software (0/0)
        output queue (curr/max blocks): hardware (0/1) software (0/1)
```

NOTE   If an interface is unused and you did not provide an IP address for it, the PIX Firewall automatically gives it an address of 127.0.0.1 with the subnet mask of 255.255.255.255. The mask of 255.255.255.255 does not permit traffic to flow through the interface, so you must never apply this mask to the utilized interfaces. Also, you must shut down all unused interfaces that still have the 127.0.0.1 address.

Step 5: Outbound Connectivity with NAT and PAT

By now, you should be familiar with the concept of Network Address Translation (NAT). Using a private IP address range on an inside network allows you the freedom of address assignment and adds extra protection because it renders the internal IP addresses unusable by the outside network. As a result, when inside hosts initiate connections with the outside, the PIX Firewall needs to translate their locally significant IP addresses into the globally significant ones.

The function of the following command is to specify an inside IP address or an array of addresses to be translated into the global addresses for communication with the outside network:

```
PIX2(config)#nat (if_name) nat_id local_ip_address [netmask]
```

The *if_name* argument identifies the interface whose IP addresses are in need of translation. The *nat_id* argument is a numeral that associates the specified internal IP address(es) with the outside address or the pool of outside addresses. (Outside address configuration is shown in the next section, "Step 6: Assigning a Pool of Outside Addresses.") The *local_ip_address* argument can define a specific IP address or an entire subnet. You can also use a **0.0.0.0** or simply **0** to indicate that all addresses belonging to an interface are up for translation (see Example 23-5). The *mask* argument in this particular command identifies the number of addresses that you want to translate. For example, if you were to translate only one host, apply the 255.255.255.255 mask to the IP address.

Example 23-5 *NAT Statement on PIX2*

```
PIX2# show nat
nat (inside) 10 0.0.0.0 0.0.0.0 0 0
```

To exclude certain internal addresses from network translation, use the **nat** command with the *nat_id* of **0**, which indicates to the PIX that the IP address(es) appearing behind the 0 in the command line are not meant to be translated.

Step 6: Assigning a Pool of Outside Addresses

After the inside addresses have been identified with the **nat** command, you must specify which outside addresses they are to become once translated. The command format to accomplish this is as follows:

```
PIX2(config)#global (if_name) nat_id [interface | global_ip_address
  [- global_ip_address] [netmask global_mask]]
```

The *if_name* argument in this command signifies the exit interface. The *nat_id* argument must be identical to the one in the **nat** command that you want to reference. If you were to specify the **interface** keyword, the exit interface's own global IP address is used for all inside hosts with the same NAT ID seeking connection to the outside. In such cases, the PAT (Protocol Address Translation) type of translation is used, where multiple hosts can use the same IP address but have different port numbers to make them unique. A single PAT entry allows up to 65,535 hosts to use the same IP address.

An alternative to using the **interface** keyword is to designate a specific IP address or a range of IP addresses separated by a dash in a "from-to" manner. For example, because PAT has some limitations in its application support, you can supplement a single IP address that is identified in one **global** statement with an additional **global** statement for the same NAT ID that provides a pool of IP addresses. This way, the PIX Firewall uses up the addresses in the pool first before touching the PAT address. You can also specify multiple PAT addresses for the same interface.

The rules defined in Example 23-6 state that all inside addresses are to be translated into the public address of the outside interface.

Example 23-6 *Configuring Dynamic NAT*

```
PIX2# show run
global (outside) 10 interface
nat (inside) 10 0.0.0.0 0.0.0.0 0 0
```

Step 7: Configuring Static NAT

In the preceding sections, you learned how to use the **nat** and **global** statements to configure a dynamic method of NAT. Static NAT is a way to assign permanent, one-to-one mappings between an internal network and perimeter or external network addresses. Instead of randomly picking addresses out of the pool, the PIX translates an inside address to the same global address every time that translation is required. This local-to-global address combination is unique and requires a unique registered global address.

Static NAT's most common application is to translate an inside address to an outside address. However, you can use static NAT for the IP address on the lower-security-level interface, such as outside and perimeter, requiring translation to an IP address on a higher-security-level interface, including internal and other perimeter interfaces. Before the release of version 6.2, only static one-to-one translation was available for outside addresses seeking inbound connections via the **alias** command. The Dynamic Outside NAT feature is described in "Lesson 23-6: New Features in PIX Firewall Version 6.2," later in this chapter.

You can use a number of options with the **static** command. The most frequently used options and their sequence are as follows:

```
PIX2(config)#static (internal_if_name, external_if_name) [tcp | udp][global_ip |
    interface] global_port local_ip local_port [netmask mask] [max_conns [emb_limit
    [norandomseq]]]
```

The *internal_if_name* and *external_if_name* arguments are the names that you gave to your higher-security-level and lower-security-level interfaces, respectively. As previously mentioned, this command is generally used for inside-to-outside Network Address Translation, and as such, the sequence of interface names inside the parentheses is *internal_if_name, external_if_name*. If you were to use static translation for a host from the less secure interface, as introduced in the 6.2 release of PIX, the order of the interface names would be reversed, and certain changes are made to the command syntax. The new bidirectional **static** command is presented in "Lesson 23-6: New Features in PIX Firewall Version 6.2," later in this chapter.

The significance of the *global_ip* argument versus the **interface** keyword as well as the *local_ip* and **netmask** concepts was explained earlier in "Step 6: Assigning a Pool of Outside Addresses." When configuring static NAT, port translation is not automatically permitted. To enable PAT, static mapping between ports, known as *port redirection,* is also required. It is accomplished using the *port* arguments. *Local_port* is the port address that needs translation, and *global_port* is the port address that it is translated to.

Recall the **nat 0** command, described in the previous step. You can achieve the nontranslation effect using the **static** command as well if the *global_ip* address that you specified matches the *local_ip* address.

The optional *max_conns* argument sets up the maximum number of connections permitted under the static address translation at the same time. Because network connections over the PIX are accomplished at Layer 3 and translations occur at Layer 4, a number of connections can be open under one translation slot or xlate. The *emb_limit* argument is the limit of embryonic connections. A connection is considered *embryonic* if it has started but has not been completed. Embryonic connections can be used in a flood type of attack.

The **norandomseq** keyword tells the firewall to not randomize the TCP/IP packet's sequence number. Be careful when applying this option because it violates security. Resort to it only if another inline firewall is also randomizing sequence numbers and the combined effect scrambles data.

After you make changes to the NAT-related configuration, you should issue the **clear xlate** command to clean up the existing translation slot.

Figure 23-2 shows the topology of a simple network situation where outside hosts seeking certain services on the inside network using the same outside IP address can do so thanks to port redirection.

Figure 23-2 *Port Redirection*

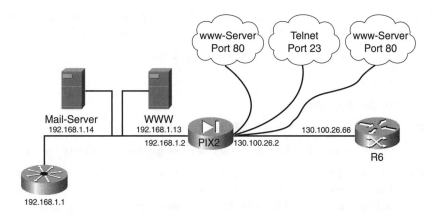

Example 23-7 displays three static NAT statements, which allow access to multiple TCP services located on an internal segment.

Example 23-7 *Configuring Static NAT*

```
PIX2# show static
static (inside,outside) tcp 130.100.26.6 www 192.168.1.13 www
  netmask 255.255.255.255 0 0

static (inside,outside) tcp 130.100.26.6 smtp 192.168.1.14 smtp
  netmask 255.255.255.255 0 0

static (inside,outside) tcp 130.100.26.6 telnet r8 telnet netmask 255.255.255.255 0 0
```
```
PIX2# show xlate
3 in use, 3 most used
PAT Global 130.100.26.6(23) Local 192.168.1.8 (23)
PAT Global 130.100.26.6(25) Local 192.168.1.14 (25)
PAT Global 130.100.26.6(80) Local 192.168.1.13 (80)
```

NOTE   It is common to use static and dynamic NAT in the same configuration. However, be careful that the global address of the **static** command does not overlap with the global address or address range specified with the **nat** command.

Step 8: Configuring Static Routes on a PIX Firewall

You can configure the PIX Firewall to forward traffic by implementing static routes or Routing Information Protocol (RIP). The latter method is described in detail in Chapter 8, "RIP."

The two different types of static routes are as follows:

- Default
- Specific destination

The general command syntax is as follows:

```
PIX2(config)#route if_name ip_address netmask gateway_ip_address [metric]
```

This command states that packets exiting out of this interface destined for a given network go through the interface of a router that is attached to that PIX interface. For default routes, specify the destination network and mask as **0.0.0.0**. If the *metric* argument is substituted with **1**, it means that the router is directly attached to the PIX interface and is the next hop on the way. Remember that only one default route is allowed.

If only one network were attached to the internal interface, one static route would be enough. However, if more networks are behind the internal router, you must enter more specific routes. When creating those routes, specify each different network in its separate statement with the *gateway_ip_address* argument of the directly attached router's interface. The packets intended for those networks are directed back through the router to let the router decide which packet goes to which network. The PIX Firewall is not a router and is not designed to make routing decisions.

Example 23-8 shows the initial configuration of PIX2, including the recently introduced static routes. The **show route** and **show running-config** commands are used to display the output. Notice the use of OTHER and CONNECT in the **show route** output. CONNECT is related to PIX's own interface, and OTHER shows that the gateway is some other device.

Example 23-8 *Initial Configuration of the PIX Firewall*

```
PIX2# show route
        outside 0.0.0.0 0.0.0.0 130.100.26.6 1 OTHER static
        inside 10.0.0.0 255.0.0.0 r8 1 OTHER static
        outside 130.100.26.0 255.255.255.224 130.100.26.2 1 CONNECT static
        DMZ3 172.16.22.0 255.255.255.0 172.16.22.1 1 CONNECT static
        DMZ2 172.16.23.0 255.255.255.0 172.16.23.1 1 CONNECT static
        inside 192.168.1.0 255.255.255.0 192.168.1.222 1 CONNECT static

PIX2# show run
nameif ethernet0 outside security0
nameif ethernet1 inside security100
nameif ethernet2 DMZ2 security10
nameif ethernet3 DMZ3 security15
interface ethernet0 10full
interface ethernet1 auto
interface ethernet2 auto
interface ethernet3 10baset
mtu outside 9000
mtu inside 1500
mtu DMZ2 1500
mtu DMZ3 1500
ip address outside 130.100.26.2 255.255.255.224
ip address inside 192.168.1.222 255.255.255.0
ip address DMZ2 172.16.23.1 255.255.255.0
ip address DMZ3 172.16.22.1 255.255.255.0
global (outside) 10 interface
nat (inside) 10 0.0.0.0 0.0.0.0 0 0
static (inside,outside) tcp 130.100.26.6 www 192.168.1.13 www netmask 255.255.255.255 0 0
static (inside,outside) tcp 130.100.26.6 smtp 192.168.1.14 smtp netmask 255.255.255.255 0 0
static (inside,outside) tcp 130.100.26.6 telnet r8 telnet netmask 255.255.255.255 0 0
route outside 0.0.0.0 0.0.0.0 130.100.26.6 1
route inside 10.0.0.0 255.0.0.0 192.188.1.1 1
```

NOTE   The **show run** command has been made available on the PIX Firewall since version 6.2. You will find it very helpful during your lab exam.

Lesson 23-2: Configuring Network Protection and Controlling Its Access and Use

This section describes several methods of controlling network connectivity on the PIX Firewall. Some of the methods that would fall under this category have already been presented. For example, static NAT and PAT were covered under Step 5 of the preceding section on configuring PIX Firewall basics. Authentication, Authorization, and Accounting were a part of Chapter 18, "AAA Services," along with the new downloadable access list feature.

Several new control techniques were introduced in the 6.2 release and are covered later in this chapter in "Lesson 23-6: New Features in PIX Firewall Version 6.2."

The topics described in the following sections are as follows:

- Using access lists on the PIX Firewall
- Filtering outbound connections
- Protecting against IP spoofing attacks
- Using Flood Guard
- Resetting inbound connections
- Configurable Proxy Pinging

Using Access Lists on the PIX Firewall

After you set up initial connectivity and specify the NAT, you can move on to setting up access lists. You can find several examples of the PIX access lists throughout this book, including in Chapter 16, "Access Control Lists." So by now, you should feel fairly comfortable with using access lists.

Due to the nature of the PIX Firewall and the way that it processes traffic, the PIX access lists have different functionality when they are applied to inbound and outbound traffic. Here, inbound connections are classified as those that originated from the less secure networks bound for the inside, and outbound connections are those that originated from the inside destined for the outside. Even though the command syntax might be the same, the decision-making process on the PIX depends on whether an access list is applied to incoming or outgoing packets. To help you better understand the differences, this section is divided in two subsections: one for inbound and the other for outbound connectivity.

NOTE   The PIX Firewall access lists became available in the version 5.0 release. You should not use the **conduit** command that was available as a substitute to access lists prior to version 5.0 because it is less secure.

Controlling Inbound Access

As you learned earlier in "Security Levels and Address Translation," the PIX Firewall is designed to deny all incoming traffic by default to protect its internal networks from unwelcome outsiders. If you want to allow some inbound connections, you have to explicitly tell the PIX to do so. Therefore, the inbound access lists are used to create an exception to the default rule and permit some inbound traffic.

Access lists produce a match based on the source or destination IP address and/or by the protocol and port number. For more information about controlling user access, refer to Chapter 18. The basic syntax for defining the PIX access list in either direction is as follows:

```
PIX2(config)#access-list acl_id [deny | permit] protocol source_address {source_mask |
    local_mask}[operator port [port]] destination_address {destination_mask | remote_mask}
    [operator port [port]]
```

The *acl_id* argument is the name that identifies a particular access list. Wherever this access list is applied, it is referenced by its *acl_id* argument. The **permit** or **deny** action depends on whether you are applying your access list to inbound or outbound traffic. This section discusses control of inbound connections, and PIX's default behavior is to block all incoming traffic. By allowing certain traffic, you are creating an exception to the default rule, and therefore you should do it carefully by explicitly stating what you would like to permit. Remember that any access list traffic is implicitly denied. The *protocol* argument means **tcp, udp,** or **icmp.**

The following simple rules exist for specifying the *source_address* parameter:

- Use the **any** keyword for an all-inclusive definition.

- For a specific host, add the **host** keyword in front of the IP address.

- For a subnet, mention the network address and appropriate mask. The mask argument is a regular subnet mask, not a wildcard.

Remember the global address that you designated with the **static** command in Lesson 23-1. Now, you can define a *destination_address* argument of the **access-list** command as that global host or network address. The rules for the *source_address* parameter in the preceding list also apply to the *destination_address* parameter.

The *port* argument must appear after the operator argument, which can be one of the following:

- **lt** for less than

- **gt** for greater than

- **eq** for equal

- **neq** for not equal

- **range** for an inclusive range

Omitting the operator and listing the port argument instead is the equivalent of using the **eq** operator. The *port* argument can be the port's numerical value or accepted name.

Once you have created an access list, use the **access-group** command to apply it to an interface (outside, in this case). Although there can be numerous access list lines under a single access list, you can attach only one access list to a single interface with the following command:

```
PIX2(config)#access-group acl_ID in interface if_name
```

The *acl_ID* argument of the **access-group** command must match the one of the access list that you are applying to an interface. For the inbound access lists, the *if_name* argument must be that of the lower-security-level interface that the users are accessing.

Example 23-9 demonstrates the use of the inbound **access-list** and **access-group** commands in combination with the **static** command. You can see that the global addresses that are defined by the two **static** commands are referenced in the *outside_access_in* access list that is assigned to the outside interface. Notice the absence of the **deny** statements because of the implicit **deny any any** statement, which is inherent to access lists.

Example 23-9 *Configuring Inbound Access Control*

```
PIX2# show run
access-list outside_access_in permit icmp any 130.100.26.0 255.255.255.240
access-list outside_access_in permit icmp any host 130.100.26.8
access-list outside_access_in permit tcp any host 130.100.26.7 eq tacacs
access-list outside_access_in permit udp any host 130.100.26.8 eq ntp
access-list outside_access_in permit udp any host 130.100.26.7 eq radius
access-list outside_access_in permit udp any host 130.100.26.7 eq radius-acct
access-list outside_access_in permit udp any host 130.100.26.8 eq 1701
access-list outside_access_in permit udp any host 130.100.26.8 gt 33000
access-list outside_access_in permit udp host 130.100.26.8 any
access-group outside_access_in in interface outside
static (inside,outside) 130.100.26.7 192.168.1.5 netmask 255.255.255.255 0 0
static (inside,outside) 130.100.26.8 192.168.1.7 netmask 255.255.255.255 0 0
```

Controlling Outbound Connectivity

In contrast to the inbound connections, all traffic that originated from the internal network on a higher-security-level interface can flow out the lower-security-level interfaces freely without obstruction, unless you specifically configure it. If you want to impose restrictions on your outbound connections, you must specify an access list using the syntax from "Controlling Inbound Access" with the **deny** action, and then apply it to an outgoing higher-security-level interface with the **access-group** command.

When using the **deny** statement in your access list statements, remember to include the **permit any any** statement at the end of your access list, because the implicit **deny any any** statement renders your interface unusable by traffic.

When assigning an outbound access list to a higher-security-level interface, you can use the available access list arguments to forbid certain users to access the outside networks, restrict access to certain outside services, or a combination of both.

You can use outbound access lists in the context of AAA. To refresh your memory and, perhaps, to give a clearer view of the PIX access list feature, review "Case Study 19-2: Configuring AAA on a PIX Firewall" of Chapter 18.

In Example 23-10, users in the 192.168.1.0 network are prevented from accessing the outside network, as indicated by the 130.100.26.6 IP address. Also, the second line of the **access-list** command keeps all internal users from communicating with the website at address 130.100.26.12 on the outside interface. Finally, the **inside_access_out** access list is applied to an internal interface.

Example 23-10 *Enforcing Access Control for the Outbound Connections*

```
access-list inside_access_out deny tcp 192.168.1.0 255.255.255.0 130.100.26.6
  255.255.255.224
access-list inside_access_out deny tcp any host 130.100.26.12 eq www
access-list inside access out permit any any
access-group inside_access_out in interface inside
```

Filtering Outbound Connections

This section demonstrates some of the additional PIX capabilities of exercising network access control. It discusses filtering selected elements from the outbound connections, such as ActiveX objects, Java applets, and some URLs.

By including ActiveX objects and Java applets in the outbound connections, you can jeopardize network security. This occurs because you can program ActiveX, Java, and JavaScript to remotely load the code that is available. Therefore, the code can be compromised and altered to turn against the network. To avoid this, you need to filter the inbound reply to the outbound traffic requesting ActiveX, Java, and JavaScript from external hosts. Also, you might consider some URLs undesirable, so you can block internal users from accessing those sites.

Filtering ActiveX Objects

PIX Firewall filters ActiveX objects by commenting out the <OBJECT CLASSID> and </OBJECT> tags in the HTML web page. To achieve this, use the **filter activex** command, as follows:

```
PIX2(config)#filter activex port[-port] local_ip mask foreign_ip mask
```

The *port* argument indicates the port (or a range of ports) on which the WWW traffic is received, normally port 80. The *local_ip* and *mask* arguments are changed to the IP address and mask of the internal host or subnet that is requesting services. The *foreign_ip* and *mask* arguments identify a host or subnet to which the request is made. You can substitute both local and foreign addresses and masks with the **0** to indicate any host, as shown in Example 23-11.

Example 23-11 *Blocking ActiveX Objects from Outbound Connections*

```
PIX2# show run
filter activex 80 0.0.0.0 0.0.0.0 0.0.0.0 0.0.0.0
```

NOTE   Specifying 0 for the host or subnet address and mask also applies to the **filter java** and **filter url** commands, which are discussed in the next two sections.

Filtering Java Applets

The **filter java** command allows users to receive a web page with the Java applets disabled. Similar to blocking ActiveX objects, the source is commented out from the HTML web page, so the applet cannot run. The following is the syntax of the **filtering java** command:

```
PIX2(config)#filter java port[-port] local_ip local_mask foreign_ip foreign_mask
```

Because the syntax of the **filter java** command is so close to the **filter activex** command, refer to "Filtering ActiveX Objects" for the arguments description.

NOTE   Sometimes, Java applets are surrounded by <object> tags. In such instances, use the **filter activex** command instead.

Example 23-12 shows the **filter java** command in action. You can see that it disables Java applets on the HTTP port and ports 1024 through 1026 for any source and destination host.

Example 23-12 *Application of Filtering Java Applets*

```
PIX2(config)# show filter
filter java 80 0.0.0.0 0.0.0.0 0.0.0.0 0.0.0.0
filter java 1024-1026 0.0.0.0 0.0.0.0 0.0.0.0 0.0.0.0
```

Filtering URLs for HTTP Requests

You can preclude internal users from accessing certain World Wide Web URLs via HTTP. However, this does not apply to URLs for FTP sites or secure websites (HTTPS). To allow URL filtering, two filtering server applications are currently available: Websense and N2H2. Websense has been included with the PIX-supported application since version 4.2 and N2H2 since version 6.2. Both of these applications are discussed in this section. Other version 6.2 services are discussed in "Lesson 23-6: New Features in PIX Firewall Version 6.2."

When configured on the PIX, the URL-filtering process works in the following manner:

1 An internal user requests access to a website via HTTP.

2 This request is forwarded by the PIX to the web server and to the filtering server (Websense or N2H2) simultaneously.

3 If the HTTP connection is permitted by the filtering server, the PIX Firewall allows it to proceed. However, if the connection is denied, the user encounters the Access Denied screen instead.

Use the following steps to enable URL filtering:

Step 1 Designate an N2H2 or Websense server to use.

The command that is used to identify the URL filtering server depends on whether you are using Websense or the newer N2H2. The syntax for both commands is described in the following paragraph. First, the Websense version of the command is as follows:

```
PIX2(config)#url-server [(if_name)] vendor websense host local_ip [timeout
    seconds] [protocol [TCP | UDP] version 1|4]
```

The *if_name* argument is the name of the PIX interface where URL filtering is enabled. The *local_ip* argument is the IP address of the Websense server. The **timeout** option determines how many seconds the PIX Firewall waits until it stops its connection attempts to the server. You can specify either version 1 or version 4 for the Websense server. TCP can use either version; UDP can only use version 4.

The command syntax to identify the N2H2 server is as follows:

```
PIX2(config)#url-server [(if_name)] vendor n2h2 host local_ip [port number]
    [timeout seconds] [protocol [TCP | UDP]]
```

To translate some of the arguments for the N2H2 server, use the explanation for the corresponding arguments from the Websense command. The only new argument is the port option. It indicates the N2H2 server port on which the PIX Firewall listens for the TCP/UDP replies. The default is 4005. **TCP** is the default protocol.

Example 23-13 illustrates the **url-server** command using Websense. The service is enabled on the inside interface. The filtering server is located at 192.168.1.100 and is using the TCP option of version 4 with the timeout of 5 seconds.

Example 23-13 *Identifying the Filtering Server*

```
PIX2# show run
url-server (inside) vendor websense host 192.168.1.100 timeout 5 protocol TCP version 4
```

Step 2   Enable filtering on the PIX.

The URL-filtering policy configured on the PIX Firewall forces the outbound HTTP traffic to go through the URL-filtering server verification before permitting it to go on. The syntax for the **filter url** command is as follows:

```
PIX2(config)#filter url [http | port[-port]] local_ip local_mask foreign_ip
    foreign_mask [allow] [proxy-block]
```

The HTTP traffic is being filtered by this command. The port argument allows you to specify the numeral for a port (or a range of ports) to filter the HTTP traffic on. The *local_ip* and *mask* arguments identify the user or subnet that is requesting the HTTP connection. The *foreign_ip* and *mask* arguments identify the host or subnet to which the requests are made. You can substitute both local and foreign addresses and masks with the **0** to indicate any host.

The optional **allow** keyword lets the HTTP traffic pass without filtering, in case the main filtering server goes down or an alternative server is not available. If this option is omitted, the outbound World Wide Web traffic cannot pass. The **proxy-block** keyword at the end of the command drops all requests to proxy servers.

You can create exceptions to the URL-filtering policy. The following command excludes the indicated local and foreign hosts from the general filtering rule:

```
PIX2(config)#filter url except local_ip local_mask foreign_ip foreign_mask
```

NOTE   Other optional commands are available for the URL-filtering process. However, they are too specific to be a part of this book or the CCIE Security lab. If you want to learn more about them, check the references shown in Appendix E.

Example 23-14 displays the URL-filtering policy configuration on PIX2. This example was taken from the **show run** command output.

Example 23-14   *Filtering URLs*

```
PIX2# show run
filter url http 0.0.0.0 0.0.0.0 0.0.0.0 0.0.0.0 proxy-block
filter url except 192.168.1.6 255.255.255.255 0 0
```

Several other verification commands are available to aid your URL-filtering configuration. Example 23-15 shows the consecutive outputs of the **show url-server** and **show filter** command. These commands should provide you with the proof that your configuration is correct. The **show filter** command would demonstrate whether all three of your filters—**filter url**, **filter activex**, and **filter java**—are in place.

Example 23-15 *Verifying Filtering Configuration*

```
PIX2# show url-server
url-server (inside) vendor websense host 192.168.1.100 timeout 5 protocol TCP version 4

PIX2# show filter
filter url http 0.0.0.0 0.0.0.0 0.0.0.0 0.0.0.0
filter activex 80 0.0.0.0 0.0.0.0 0.0.0.0 0.0.0.0
filter java 80 0.0.0.0 0.0.0.0 0.0.0.0 0.0.0.0
```

Protecting Against IP Spoofing Attacks

An *IP spoofing attack* is when an attacker pretends to use an authorized address for your network IP address. This type of attack can result in unauthorized access to your network or unauthorized activity outside your network by someone who acts as if they belong to your network. IP spoofing attacks are a threat to network security and therefore need to be protected against.

Under certain conditions, you can implement a technique called *Unicast Reverse Path Forwarding (RPF)* to protect against IP spoofing attacks. Unicast RPF works by doing a route lookup based on the source address versus the usual route lookup based on the destination address.

RPF checks the inbound packets on a specified interface for the IP address of the source. It is disabled by default. When enabled, this feature ensures that the route to the source pre-exists in the PIX local routing table and that the receiving interface matches as well; otherwise, the packet is discarded. RPF works on both inside and outside interfaces to provide protection from ill-intending inside and outside hosts.

NOTE   Do not confuse inside and outside interfaces with outbound and inbound connections for this lesson, although they have been used interchangeably in previous ones. Only the receiving interface, whichever it might be, performs the route check. The outbound interface does not screen the packets.

RPF is performed through ingress or egress filtering. *Ingress filtering* checks packets on the outside interface. *Egress filtering* is implemented on the inside interface. Both filtering methods operate by executing route lookup according to the routing table. Make sure that the necessary routes are available before enabling this feature. The command for Unicast RPF on either interface is as follows:

```
PIX2(config)#ip verify reverse-path interface if_name
```

Example 23-16 shows the **ip verify reverse-path interface** command's usage on PIX2. Note the **route** command that is included in the output. As previously mentioned, you must have the **route** command in place for the packet forwarding using Unicast RPF to function.

Example 23-16 *Reverse Path Forwarding*

```
PIX2# show run
route outside 0.0.0.0 0.0.0.0 130.100.26.6 1
route inside 10.0.0.0 255.0.0.0 r8 1
ip verify reverse-path interface outside
ip verify reverse-path interface inside

PIX2# show ip verify statistics
interface outside: 132 unicast rpf drops
interface inside: 10 unicast rpf drops
interface DMZ2: 0 unicast rpf drops
interface DMZ3: 0 unicast rpf drops
```

NOTE   Although application handling by the PIX Firewall is discussed in "Lesson 23-3: Supporting Specific Protocols and Applications," it is important to explain at this point that Unicast RPF causes each ICMP packet to be checked because no ICMP sessions exist. On the other hand, UDP and TCP have sessions, so the initial packet is the only one scrutinized by reverse route lookup. All subsequent packets belonging to the same session are checked via the existing session state to guarantee that they arrived on the same interface as the initial packet.

Using Flood Guard

The Flood Guard feature is used to protect the AAA services from multiple unanswered login attempts launched by a Denial of Service (DoS) attack. Flood Guard solidifies AAA system use by actively recovering the exhausted TCP user resources. However, it is different from the SYN flood defense mechanism on the PIX.

Although Flood Guard is on by default, you can enable it by using the following command:

```
PIX2(config)#floodguard enable
```

Resetting Inbound Connections

To speed the processing, you can reset any inbound TCP connections for those services that are not allowed by the internal security policy. Two sample circumstances where this might be useful are when the IDENT protocol is in use and with AAA services.

The following sections describe both circumstances in more detail.

IDENT Service

Sometimes, when users try to connect to FTP, HTTP, or POP servers through the PIX Firewall, their connections can take a long time or fail. One of the possible reasons for the delay or failure is that these servers can be using the IDENT protocol for identifying incoming users. When a user requests a service, the server sets off an IDENT connection back toward the client behind the firewall for verification purposes. The IDENT protocol is considered a security violation because it can disclose some of the confidential internal information to an unauthorized outsider, and the PIX intercepts the IDENT connection and denies it. Therefore, the server never receives the response to its request. As a result, the server can decline the user's connection attempt or significantly increase connection time because, not knowing that the PIX refused the IDENT, the server keeps retransmitting its requests until the IDENT timeout period expires.

To solve this problem, you can reset the inbound connections so that when the PIX denies a connection attempt, instead of silently dropping the packet, it sends an RST (a reset flag in the TCP header) back to the outside host, notifying it that the IDENT service is unavailable for the queried user. The PIX also continues to process the original outbound transmission and, thus, significantly reduces the delay caused by the IDENT protocol. To accomplish this on the PIX Firewall, use the **service resetinbound** command, as follows:

```
PIX2(config)#service resetinbound
```

AAA Services

Similarly, you can use the **service resetinbound** command to reset the client that failed authorization to stop it from retransmitting any connection attempts. For more information on AAA services, refer to Chapter 18.

Resetting Connections on the Outside Interface

The **service resetoutside** command is used to reset the denied TCP packets such as IDENT on the PIX Firewall's outside interface. By doing so, the PIX overrides its default behavior and avoids the delay caused by timeout. Use the following command with interface PAT:

```
PIX2(config)#service resetoutside
```

The **service resetinbound** and **service resetoutside** commands introduced in this configuration section are shown in Example 23-17.

Example 23-17 *Service Commands Configuration*

```
PIX2# show service
service resetinbound
service resetoutside
```

Configurable Proxy Pinging

The Configurable Proxy Pinging feature lets you control ICMP access, that is, pinging, to the PIX Firewall interfaces. This feature effectively hides the specified PIX Firewall interfaces on the network. Configurable proxy pinging is executed via an ICMP control list. If no such list exists (by default), all ICMP traffic is implicitly permitted to an interface. With an ICMP control list enabled, the PIX Firewall bases its decision on the first match occurrence followed by an implicit **deny all** statement.

For example, if the first match is explicitly permitted, the ICMP packet is allowed. However, if the packet is denied or unmatched, the PIX Firewall drops it and generates the %PIX-3-313001 syslog message. The following command is used to configure ICMP control lists:

```
PIX2(config)#icmp [permit | deny] [host] source_address [src_mask] [type] if_name
```

Use the **host** keyword to specify that the source is a single host. The *type* parameter defines the ICMP message type. For example, the ICMP control lists from Example 23-18 designate unreachable, echo-reply, mask-reply, and echo message types originating from any source address to either be granted or denied permission to a PIX interface.

Example 23-18 *Configurable Proxy Pinging*

```
PIX2# show icmp
icmp permit any unreachable outside
icmp permit any echo-reply inside
icmp deny any mask-reply inside
icmp deny any echo inside
```

In the first line of the output, notice that the ICMP unreachable message type has been permitted. It is not an arbitrary choice. If you deny ICMP unreachables, you cannot use ICMP Path MTU discovery, which, in turn, can disable IPSec and PPTP traffic.

NOTE   This section discussed ICMP traffic to the PIX. For traffic going through the PIX Firewall, use the **access-list** and **access-group** commands, as described in "Controlling Inbound Access" and "Controlling Outbound Connectivity," earlier in this lesson.

Lesson 23-3: Supporting Specific Protocols and Applications

Certain applications require special handling by the PIX Firewall. Several cases where such handling is necessary are collected and combined into this lesson, including the following:

- Configuring application inspection
- Setting idle timers

- Extending the closing sequence window
- Specifying the maximum TCP segment size

Configuring Application Inspection (Fixup)

You already learned about the ASA earlier in "TCP and UDP," and you saw how ASA is used to track the source and destination ports and addresses of a connection. What was not explained before is the fact that some applications demand a special application inspection function, or fixup. For example, certain applications embed IP addressing information within the user data packet. Consequently, the application inspection is used along with NAT to uncover the location of that information. Now the NAT can translate these hidden IP addresses and change any information that depends upon this translation.

To improve their performance, some applications open an initial session on a well-known port and then negotiate dynamically assigned port numbers for secondary channels. The fixup function supervises sessions to find out the ports numbers of those secondary channels and allows data exchange on these ports for the length of that session.

Some of the application inspection entries and their corresponding port numbers are included in the PIX default configuration. Note that some applications allow you to change their default port assignments, but some do not. The **show fixup** command helps to determine the configurable protocol settings.

Example 23-19 demonstrates the fixup defaults that are present on PIX2.

Example 23-19 *Application Inspection Defaults*

```
PIX2# show fixup
fixup protocol ftp 21
fixup protocol http 80
fixup protocol h323 h225 1720
fixup protocol h323 ras 1718-1719
fixup protocol ils 389
fixup protocol rsh 514
fixup protocol rtsp 554
fixup protocol smtp 25
fixup protocol sqlnet 1521
fixup protocol sip 5060
fixup protocol skinny 2000
```

You can use the following command format to change the default port assignments:

```
PIX2(config)#fixup protocol protocol [port]
```

You can also disable application inspection for a particular protocol by entering **no** in front of the **fixup** command. For example, SMPT **fixup** only allows seven basic SMPT commands. To allow ESMTP (Extended Simple Mail Transfer Protocol) support, turn off the **fixup protocol SMPT** command.

Remember to issue the **clear xlate** command if you make modifications to the fixup configuration. Otherwise, the changes to existing connections do not take effect.

Configuring Idle Timers

You can configure idle timers for connection and translation slots provided for commands shown in Table 23-1. If the specified time has elapsed and the slot has not been used, the resource for the protocol is disengaged and put back into the pool. You can use the following command with a number of options described in Table 23-1:

```
PIX2(config)#timeout option
```

Table 23-1   *Timeout Commands*

Timeout Command	Description
timeout xlate *hh:mm:ss*	Frees the translation slot once the idle timer has expired, a minimum of 1 minute.
timeout conn *hh:mm:ss* [**half-closed** *hh:mm:ss*] [**udp** *hh:mm:ss*] [**rpc** *hh:mm:ss*] [**h323** *hh:mm:ss*] [**sip** *hh:mm:ss*] [**sip_media** *hh:mm:ss*]	Frees the connection slot once the idle timer has expired. Specify **0:0:0** for the *hh:mm:ss* to cause the timer to never expire. The required minimum is 5 minutes. The connection timer precedes the translation timer because the translation timer works only after all connections have timed out.
timeout uauth *hh:mm:ss* [**absolute** | **inactivity**]	Causes users to reauthenticate after either a period of inactivity or an absolute duration.
	The inactivity timer is started after a connection goes idle. If a new connection is established within the specified period, the user does not need to reauthenticate. After the inactivity timer expires, the user must reauthenticate to start a new connection.
	The absolute timer runs continuously. It must be shorter than the xlate timer; otherwise, a user might be reprompted after the session's end. The absolute timer can be used alongside the inactivity timer, but it needs to be set longer than the inactivity timer, or the inactivity timer never comes into play.

Example 23-20 presents the timeout defaults.

Example 23-20 *Default Timeout Values*

```
PIX2# show timeout
timeout xlate 3:00:00
timeout conn 1:00:00 half-closed 0:10:00 udp 0:02:00 rpc 0:10:00 h323 0:05:00 sip
0:30:00 sip_media 0:02:00
timeout uauth 0:05:00 absolute
```

If you have modified the timers and want to return to the default values, issue the **clear timeout** command.

Changing Certain PIX Firewall System Options

You were introduced to the **sysopt connection [permit-ipsec]** command in Chapters 18 and 19. This statement belongs to the series of commands that are used to modify various PIX Firewall security and configuration features. In the following sections, you learn two other commands from the **sysopt** group—**sysopt connection timewait** and **sysopt connection tcpmss**—that impact the behavior of TCP on the PIX.

Accommodating the Simultaneous TCP Session Close

Normally, when the TCP connection is being closed, one side of the connection initiates the closing and the other side acknowledges this process before proceeding with its own shutdown. By default, the PIX Firewall tracks the closing sequence and discharges the connection after two finish (FIN) segments and the acknowledgment (ACK) of the last FIN.

In some end host applications, however, the default behavior is to close the TCP session simultaneously. In such cases, both ends of the connection initiate the closing sequence at the same time. This prevents the connection from being fully terminated by the usual quick-release feature and causes one side of it to remain in the CLOSING state, possibly degrading that end host's performance. The **sysopt connection timewait** command, as follows, modifies the default PIX behavior by extending the closing sequence window to at least 15 seconds so that the simultaneous shutdown gets the chance to run its course:

```
PIX2(config)#sysopt connection timewait
```

Specifying the Maximum TCP Segment Size

Maximum TCP segment size dictates the maximum size of a segment that is sent during the initial TCP proxy connection establishment by either end of the connection. The size of the segment can range from 28 bytes to infinity. The default maximum is 1380 bytes, which is recommended for Ethernet connections. The command syntax for specifying the segment size is as follows:

```
PIX2(config)#sysopt connection tcpmss no_greater_than_bytes
```

This command is on by default, with the maximum value of 1380 bytes. To disable it, set the bytes to 0. You can also specify the minimum value, as shown in Example 23-21.

Example 23-21 *Sysopt Options Configuration*

```
PIX2# show run
sysopt connection timewait
sysopt connection tcpmss minimum 48

PIX2# show sysopt
no sysopt security fragguard
sysopt connection timewait
sysopt connection tcpmss 1380
sysopt connection tcpmss minimum 48
no sysopt nodnsalias inbound
no sysopt nodnsalias outbound
no sysopt radius ignore-secret
no sysopt uauth allow-http-cache
no sysopt connection permit-ipsec
no sysopt connection permit-pptp
no sysopt connection permit-l2tp
no sysopt ipsec pl-compatible
no sysopt route dnat
```

Lesson 23-4: Monitoring the PIX Firewall

This lesson discusses several different ways to record and view the PIX Firewall system messages, including the following:

- Configuring logging
- Configuring the SNMP-related functions
- Responding to IDS syslog messages

Configuring Logging

This section describes ways to record system log (syslog) messages from the PIX Firewall. Syslog messages can display normal system events or error conditions. Furthermore, they can be sent to four possible locations for output: the console, the buffer, an SNMP management station, or a remote syslog server.

The general syntax for the logging command is as follows:

```
PIX2(config)#logging logging_condition
```

Table 23-2 describes the PIX2 logging commands in the order that they appear. Example 23-22, which follows the table, displays several logging commands configured on PIX2. If you need more information on other available syslog commands, see Appendix E.

Table 23-2   *Explanation of the PIX2 Logging Commands*

Logging Command	Description
logging on	Turns the logging process on. If you want any logging to take place, make sure that this command is set, because it notifies the PIX Firewall to start sending messages to all configured output locations.
logging timestamp	Adds a time stamp value to each message that is sent to the syslog server, provided that the system clock has been set on the PIX with the **clock** command.
logging standby	Forces the failover standby unit, which becomes active in the event of the primary PIX Firewall failure in certain configurations, to also send messages. However, this option (disabled by default) creates a lot of traffic on the syslog server.
logging console *severity_level*	Sends syslog messages to the PIX Firewall console and displays them as they happen. This type of messaging can disrupt the PIX Firewall's normal activity, and therefore you should use it with care. For instance, Example 23-22 specifies this service for the emergency level only. It is the highest severity level for system unusable messages equaling 0.
logging monitor *severity_level*	Sends syslog messages to a Telnet console session. The severity level of this command on PIX2 is set to *alerts*, with a value of 1. *alerts* stands one level above *emergencies* with a value of 0.
logging buffered *severity_level*	Causes the syslog messages to be stored and displayed when needed instead of in real time. The severity level used in Example 23-22 is *critical* at Level 2. To display the buffered messages, use the **show logging** command. To erase the previously buffered messages, issue the **clear logging** command.
logging trap *severity_level*	Identifies the severity level (emergencies in Example 23-22) for those messages sent to the syslog server. Additional required commands are discussed later in this section.

continues

Table 23-2   *Explanation of the PIX2 Logging Commands (Continued)*

Logging Command	Description
logging history *severity_level*	Identifies the severity level (emergencies in Example 23-22) for those messages sent to the SNMP host. The SNMP host configuration on the PIX is discussed next in "Configuring the SNMP-Related Functions."
logging host [*interface*] *ip_address* [*protocol/port*]	Names the syslog server that is to receive the syslog messages set by the **logging trap** command. The *interface* parameter identifies the PIX Firewall interface on which the server resides followed by the IP address of the server. The optional protocol argument determines whether the messages sent to this particular server are TCP or UDP. (UDP is the default.)

Example 23-22   *Logging Commands on PIX2*

```
PIX2# show run
logging on
logging timestamp
logging standby
logging console emergencies
logging monitor alerts
logging buffered critical
logging trap emergencies
logging history emergencies
logging host inside 192.168.1.7
```

In Example 23-22, you might have noticed that certain syslog commands specify severity levels. You can identify these levels with a keyword, as was done in Example 23-22, or a corresponding level number (0–7). The severity level causes the PIX Firewall to send all messages at this or a lower (more critical) level to the output location to which it has been assigned.

You already learned how to configure the PIX Firewall for Telnet and SSH in Chapter 18. Example 23-23 is a reminder of this configuration, along with the **terminal width** command, which sets the logging output for the session to 80 characters wide.

Example 23-23   *Configuring Telnet on PIX2*

```
PIX2# show run
telnet 192.168.1.9 255.255.255.255 inside
telnet timeout 5
ssh 192.168.1.9 255.255.255.255 inside
ssh timeout 5
terminal width 80
```

To display the buffered messages, use the **show logging** command, as presented in Example 23-24.

Example 23-24 *Viewing Logging*

```
PIX2# show logging
Syslog logging: enabled
    Facility: 20
    Timestamp logging: enabled
    Standby logging: enabled
    Console logging: level emergencies, 0 messages logged
    Monitor logging: level alerts, 0 messages logged
    Buffer logging: level critical, 1 messages logged
    Trap logging: level emergencies, 0 messages logged
        Logging to inside 192.168.1.7
    History logging: level emergencies, 0 messages logged
101003: (Secondary) Failover cable not connected (this unit)
```

Configuring the SNMP-Related Functions

In the preceding section, you learned how to configure the syslog messages to be sent to the SNMP management station with the **logging history** command. However, because the SNMP functionality has not yet been enabled on PIX2, the **logging** command does not result in anything until the following steps are completed:

Step 1   The PIX Firewall is configured to reply to the management station requests

Step 2   The PIX Firewall is configured to send traps or event notifications to the SNMP station

The commands that are used to accomplish the first step are presented in Table 23-3. Example 23-25 shows the output of the commands on PIX2.

Table 23-3   *PIX Commands to Receive SNMP Requests*

Command	Description
snmp-server host [*if_name*] *ip_addr* [**trap** I **poll**]	Specifies the PIX Firewall interface and the IP address of the SNMP management host. The last optional parameter determines whether the trap or the poll actions are allowed. By naming one, you exclude the other. By default, both options are available.
snmp-server [**contact** I **location**] *text*	Identifies the physical location or the administrator of your PIX Firewall. Both commands are used in Example 23-25.
snmp-server community *key*	Defines the shared read-only password between the SNMP station and its clients (PIX2 is one of them).

Example 23-25 *PIX2 Configuration for Receiving SNMP Requests*

```
PIX2# show run
snmp-server host inside 192.168.1.9
snmp-server location Brookfield, WI
snmp-server contact Mark Sampsonite
snmp-server community 2beornot2be
```

The next step is to ensure that the syslog messages set up by the logging history command are sent to the management station. Issue the following command after configuring the parameters specified in Table 23-3:

```
PIX2(config)#snmp-server enable traps
```

To display the SNMP server configuration, issue the **show snmp-server** command, as shown in Example 23-26.

Example 23-26 *Complete PIX2 Configuration for Sending Syslog Messages to the SNMP Station*

```
PIX2# show snmp-server
snmp-server host inside 192.168.1.9
snmp-server location Brookfield, WI
snmp-server contact Mark Sampsonite
snmp-server community 2beornot2be
snmp-server enable traps
```

IDS Syslog Messages

On the PIX Firewall, you can configure audit policies or rules. An audit policy is applied to an interface and defines a set of actions to be taken as a response to the Cisco Intrusion Detection System (IDS) signature messages. The PIX Firewall performs auditing according to the policy by checking the IP packets as they arrive at an input interface where the policy has been applied. Both inbound auditing and outbound auditing are supported.

An IDS signature is considered to be a part of one of the following available groups:

- Informational
- Attack

In turn, an audit policy can be defined as informational or attack and is identified by a name. For more information on both policy types, consult Chapter 24, "IDS on the Cisco PIX Firewall and IOS Software."

The following is a list of possible configurable audit policy actions that are triggered when an IDS signature match occurs:

- **Alarm**—Upon a signature match in a packet, the PIX Firewall sends a report to all configured syslog servers. It is the default action.

- **Drop**—Causes the offending packet to be dropped.

- **Reset**—Besides dropping the offending packet, it also closes an active connection to which the packet belonged.

If a matched signature does not trigger an action that causes the packet to be dropped, the same packet can then trigger other signatures.

Table 23-4 displays the list of commands that you can use to configure audit policies and their appropriate actions. Commands in the table appear in the same order as they appear in Example 23-27, which follows the table.

Table 23-4   *Audit Policy Commands*

Audit Policy Command	Description
ip audit name *audit_name* **attack [action [alarm] [drop] [reset]]**	Configures an audit policy that applies to signatures of the attack type followed by the list of available actions—alarm, drop, and reset. If a policy is defined without actions, the configured default actions are used instead (this is explained further later in this table). The *audit_name* argument is the name given to the audit policy.
ip audit name *audit_name* **info [action [alarm] [drop] [reset]]**	Configures an audit policy that applies to signatures of the informational type followed by the list of available actions—alarm, drop, and reset.
ip audit interface *if_name* *audit_name*	Applies an audit policy from the **ip audit name** command or a set of default actions to an interface. Both the attack- and the informational-type policies can be applied per interface, but only one of each kind.
ip audit info [action [alarm] [drop] [reset]]	Indicates the default actions for informational signatures in the event that no specific actions are defined by the **ip audit name info** command. If actions are omitted from the default command as well, the PIX processes informational signatures with no particular response.
ip audit attack [action [alarm] [drop] [reset]]	Indicates the default actions for attack signatures in the event that no specific actions are defined by the **ip audit name attack** command. If actions are omitted from the default **attack** command, the PIX processes attack signatures with no particular response, similar to the **ip audit info** command previously described.
ip audit signature *signature_#* **disable**	Each IDS signature is recognized by a known number. (See Appendix E for reference.) This command excludes a particular signature from an audit policy.

Example 23-27 *IDS Signature Use Configuration*

```
PIX2# show run
ip audit name IDS attack action alarm drop reset
ip audit name IDS_Info info action alarm drop reset
ip audit name ccie attack action alarm drop reset
ip audit interface outside IDS_Info
ip audit interface outside IDS
ip audit interface inside IDS_Info
ip audit interface inside ccie
ip audit info action alarm
ip audit attack action alarm
ip audit signature 1006 disable
ip audit signature 2000 disable
ip audit signature 2003 disable
ip audit signature 2004 disable
ip audit signature 2009 disable
ip audit signature 2150 disable
ip audit signature 2151 disable
ip audit signature 6052 disable
```

Lesson 23-5: Using the PIX Firewall as a DHCP Server

You can configure the PIX Firewall to act as a Dynamic Host Configuration Protocol (DHCP) server on its inside (and only the inside!) interface. This means that it can provide network configuration parameters for the connected clients through the use of DHCP. The parameters the client is supplied with include ways to access the enterprise network and the network services to use, for example, the DNS server.

Table 23-5 describes commands that are used to configure the DHCP server on the PIX. These commands are presented in the order in which you would implement them.

Table 23-5   *DHCP Server Commands*

DHCP Server Command	Description
dhcpd address *ip1*[-*ip2*] [*if_name*]	Specifies the DHCP address pool from which addresses are assigned to clients. You should substitute the *if_name* parameter with the inside interface name because it is the only interface that is currently supported for DHCP services. Make sure that the IP address of the interface itself belongs to the same subnet as the pool.
dhcpd dns *dns1* [*dns2*]	Identifies the IP address of a DNS server to be used by the DHCP clients. It is an optional command and is capable of supporting up to two DNS servers.
dhcpd wins *wins1* [*wins2*]	Identifies the IP address of a WINS server to be used by the DHCP clients. It is an optional command and is capable of supporting up to two WINS servers.

Table 23-5   *DHCP Server Commands (Continued)*

DHCP Server Command	Description
dhcpd lease *lease_length*	Specifies the period of time, in seconds, during which the temporary DHCP services granted to a client are valid.
dhcpd domain *domain_name*	Identifies the optional DNS domain name for a client.
dhcpd auto_config [*client_if_name*]	Enables the PIX Firewall to automatically configure DNS, WINS, and domain name values from the DHCP client to the DHCP server. If the user also specifies *dns*, *wins*, and *domain* parameters, the CLI parameters overwrite the *auto_config* parameters. The optional *client_if_name* parameter specifies the PIX's outside interface.
dhcpd ping_timeout *timeout*	Assigns a ping timeout value, in milliseconds, before an IP address can be given to a client.
dhcpd enable inside	Allows the DHCP daemon to listen to the clients' requests on the inside interface because it is the only one currently supported.

Example 23-28 shows the DHCP server configuration on PIX2. Notice that the inside interface IP address matches the subnet that is allocated to the DHCP pool. The **show dhcpd statistics** and **show dhcpd binding** commands display the statistics and binding information, respectively, that is associated with the **dhcpd** commands.

Example 23-28   *DHCP Server Configuration*

```
PIX2# show run
ip address inside 192.168.1.222 255.255.255.0
dhcpd address 192.168.1.200-192.168.1.220 inside
dhcpd dns 156.46.20.10 156.46.20.20
dhcpd wins 172.16.1.100 172.16.1.101
dhcpd lease 3600
dhcpd ping_timeout 750
dhcpd domain cisco.com
dhcpd auto_config outside
dhcpd enable inside

PIX2# show dhcpd statistics

Address pools        1
Automatic bindings   1
Expired bindings     0
Malformed messages   0

Message              Received
BOOTREQUEST          0
DHCPDISCOVER         1
DHCPREQUEST          5
```

continues

Example 23-28 *DHCP Server Configuration (Continued)*

```
DHCPDECLINE            0
DHCPRELEASE            0
DHCPINFORM             0

Message               Sent
BOOTREPLY              0
DHCPOFFER              1
DHCPACK                4
DHCPNAK                1

PIX2# show dhcpd binding

IP address       Hardware address        Lease expiration        Type

  192.168.1.200    0100.0795.f29a.7a            3237 seconds      Automatic
```

Lesson 23-6: New Features in PIX Firewall Version 6.2

The current PIX Firewall release version 6.2 introduced a number of new features and services that were previously unavailable with other versions. This section familiarizes you with those new features that are the most beneficial in preparing for your CCIE Security lab exam. The features are as follows:

- Bidirectional NAT

- Forwarding multicast transmissions

- Using TurboACL

- Using Network Time Protocol

- Enabling Auto Update support

All of these features fall under the categories discussed in previous lessons of this chapter and follow the same order within this lesson as their parent categories within the chapter.

Configuring Bidirectional NAT

In "Lesson 23-1: Configuring the PIX Firewall Basics," the concept of dynamic NAT and PAT was discussed. Normally, the concept is applied to the outbound traffic, where the internal addresses require translation into the valid outside address. The PIX Firewall version 6.2 release offers NAT and PAT for connections going in the opposite direction. So now, you can use address translation for traffic moving from a less secure to a more secure interface.

Bidirectional NAT works in the following manner:

1 When the PIX Firewall receives a packet on one of its less secure interfaces, it searches the connections database for an existing xlate entry.

2 If there is no xlate entry, it consults the configuration file for a NAT policy.

3 The new xlate is created according to the set policy. As a result, the PIX can replace the outside address with the address that is valid on the inside.

4 The follow-up packets can now be correctly translated because of the newly established xlate entry in the database.

Example 23-29 illustrates the **nat** and **global** commands, which are needed to configure outside dynamic NAT. Note that the syntax used here is identical to the one that you learned in Lesson 23-1. The only differences are (a) the address pool is now defined on the inside interface and (b) the outside addresses are now initiating the translation.

Example 23-29 *Using Outside Dynamic NAT*

```
PIX2# show run
nat (outside) 1 172.16.1.1 255.255.255.0 outside
global (inside) 1 192.168.2.1-192.168.2.10
```

NOTE   If two private networks have overlapping address space and require mutual translation, use the **static** command, as described in Lesson 23-1.

Bidirectional NAT Using the **static** Command

When using static NAT to access the interface of a higher security level from an interface of a lower security level, you must use access lists in conjunction with the **static** command. The syntax for bidirectional static NAT is as follows:

```
PIX2(config)#static [(prenat_interface, postnat_interface)] {mapped_address | interface}
    real_address [dns] [netmask mask] [norandomseq] [connection_limit [em_limit]]
```

Because the syntax applies to bidirectional NAT, the *prenat interface* is the interface in need of translation and the *postnat interface* is the interface that provides the translation. This is in contrast with the traditional version of the **static** command presented in Step 7 of Lesson 23-1, which only allows the inside-to-outside translation. The *real_address* is the IP address that gets translated to the *mapped_address*. The optional **dns** keyword signifies that DNS replies that match the xlate are translated. The rest of the keywords and arguments were discussed in Step 7 of Lesson 23-1.

Forwarding Multicast Transmissions

The new Stub Multicast Routing (SMR) feature allows the PIX Firewall to act as a "stub router," which in turn acts as a proxy agent in the IGMP transactions between the LAN client hosts and the multicast (MC) router. Essentially, the PIX Firewall can now forward the IGMP messages between hosts that are registered in a multicast group and MC routers that route multicast data to the hosts.

Allowing Hosts to Receive Multicast Transmissions

You must configure the PIX Firewall as a stub router whenever it separates the internal hosts and the MC router. Figure 23-3 illustrates such a situation.

Figure 23-3 *Multicast Forwarding by the PIX Firewall*

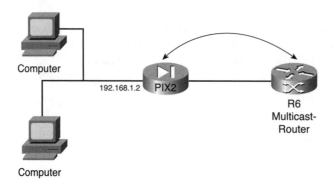

The configuration tasks include allowing the PIX to forward the IGMP reports from the hosts to the router and permitting the multicast transmissions from the router to the hosts. The configuration steps are placed in their logical order in Table 23-6.

Table 23-6 *Configuring Multicast—Host Side*

Command	Description
multicast interface *if_name*	Enables multicast forwarding on an interface. The hosts are most likely connected to the inside interface, but you need to enable multicast on both inside and outside interfaces.
igmp max-groups *n*	After you enter the **multicast interface** *if_name* command, you are placed in the multicast subcommand mode that is most likely for the inside interface. All the following commands belong to that mode. This command specifies the maximum number of IGMP groups that are allowed for the given interface. Available values range from 0 to 2000.
igmp forward interface *out_if_name*	Enables IGMP reports to be received on a specified (inside) interface and forwarded out of another (less secure) interface whose name replaces the *out_if_name* argument.
igmp join-group *group_address*	Attaches the interface that is connected to the hosts (inside) to the multicast group identified by the *group_address* argument. This is an optional command and is useful in those instances when a client cannot respond using IGMP, but still needs to receive multicast transmissions so the PIX Firewall can act on behalf of that client.

Table 23-6   *Configuring Multicast—Host Side (Continued)*

Command	Description
access-list *acl_ID* **permit igmp any** *destination_addr destination_mask*	Configures an access list that limits IGMP traffic to certain allowed multicast groups that are identified by the *destination_address* and *destination_mask* arguments.
igmp access-group *acl_ID*	Applies the newly configured IGMP access list to the interface (inside).

Example 23-30 displays all the commands listed in Table 23-6.

Example 23-30   *Enabling Multicast on the Host-Connected PIX Interface*

```
PIX2# show run
access-list inside_multicastACL permit igmp any 224.0.0.0 255.255.255.0
multicast interface outside
multicast interface inside
  igmp max-groups 1
  igmp forward interface outside
  igmp access-group inside_multicastACL
  igmp join-group 224.1.1.1
```

Forwarding Multicasts from a Transmission Source

Once you have enabled the host-side interface of the PIX Firewall to receive multicast transmissions, you must configure the PIX Firewall to forward multicasts from the source router. To accomplish this task, first enable multicast on the router-connected interface (outside) using the **multicast interface** command that was described in Table 23-6.

Next, create a static route from the inside source to the next-hop router interface with the following command:

```
PIX2(config)#mroute source_address source_mask in-if-name destination_address
  destination_mask out-if-name
```

The *source* part of the command arguments specifies information about the multicast source. The *destination* part defines parameters of the Class D address/mask for the multicast transmission from the source.

Example 23-31 illustrates the multicast configuration on PIX2. In the output, the commands from the preceding section are combined with the command that you just learned.

Example 23-31   *Configuring PIX2 for Multicast Forwarding*

```
PIX2# show run
access-list inside_multicastACL permit igmp any 224.0.0.0 255.255.255.0
multicast interface outside
```

continues

Example 23-31 *Configuring PIX2 for Multicast Forwarding (Continued)*

```
multicast interface inside
  igmp max-groups 1
  igmp forward interface outside
  igmp access-group inside_multicastACL
  igmp join-group 224.1.1.1
mroute 192.16.1.1 255.255.255.255 inside 230.1.1.2 255.255.255.255 outside
```

Using TurboACL

Understanding TurboACL depends heavily on understanding the PIX Firewall access lists. For a more detailed review, see "Lesson 23-2: Configuring Network Protection and Controlling Its Access and Use."

You already know that one access list can have numerous entries. When a packet is examined and searched for an entry match, the PIX Firewall does so in a linear fashion. After a match is located, a packet is processed according to the action designated by the match: drop or forward. This type of search process becomes increasingly inefficient as the access list gets longer because of the time it takes to locate a match. TurboACL allows the PIX Firewall to compile ACLs into tables that can reduce the search time.

TurboACLs only improve performance of long access lists, those of 19 entries or more. As a result, when enabled, TurboACL checks all existing access lists and only marks those that contain 19 or more entries for turbo-compilation.

TurboACL is memory intensive. The amount of required resources depends on the complexity and the size of an access list. Also, whenever a TurboACL entry is changed, a data table needs to be recompiled, requiring considerable CPU time.

TurboACL is turned off by default. You can enable it per access list and globally. Once enabled globally, you can disable it per access list as well. The syntax for the TurboACL command is as follows:

```
PIX2(config)#access-list compiled
```

If you disable a TurboACL with the **no** argument, all existing compiled tables are destroyed and all access lists on the PIX are again processed in the usual linear manner. Example 23-32 demonstrates the global TurboACL command along with the short access list.

Example 23-32 *TurboACL Feature*

```
PIX2# show run
access-list compiled
access-list inside_multicastACL permit igmp any 224.0.0.0 255.255.255.0

PIX2# show access-list
access-list compiled
access-list inside_multicastACL turbo-configured; 1 elements
access-list inside_multicastACL permit igmp any 224.0.0.0 255.255.255.0 (hitcnt=0)
```

Using Network Time Protocol

You learned about the Network Time Protocol (NTP) in Chapter 15, "Basic Cisco IOS Software and Catalyst 3550 Series Security." Here, you learn how to configure NTP on the PIX Firewall. Starting with the PIX version 6.2 release, you can enable the firewall to receive its system time from the centralized source, such as the NTP version 3 server.

Table 23-7 lists the commands that are necessary to enable NTP client services on the PIX.

Table 23-7 *NTP Commands*

NTP Command	Description
ntp server *ip_address* [**key** *number*] **source** *if_name* [**prefer**]	Identifies the IP address of the NTP server. The key option needs to match the number specified with the **authentication-key** command. The **interface** keyword and *name* argument indicate the PIX interface, which sends packets to the time server. The **prefer** keyword designates the server that is named in the command as a preferred server if multiple servers are used.
ntp authenticate	Enables authentication for NTP messages.
ntp trusted-key *number*	Specifies one or more key numbers. These numbers must correspond with the keys that are defined by the command used in the following command. As a result of enabling NTP authentication and defining shared keys, the NTP server is now required to provide the matching key numbers in its packets for added security.
ntp authentication-key *number md5 value*	Configures authentication keys to be used with other NTP commands, such the **trusted-key** and **ntp server** commands.
clear ntp	Removes NTP configuration.

Example 23-33 illustrates the NTP configuration on the PIX Firewall. The **show** commands that are used display various aspects of NTP. Use the **show ntp** command to see the current NTP configuration, the **show ntp status** command to view the NTP clock information, and the **show ntp associations detail** command for the configured network time server associations. In the **ntp authentication-key** command, notice that the *value* parameter appears scrambled in the output of the **show ntp** command.

Example 23-33 *NTP on PIX2*

```
PIX2# show ntp
ntp authentication-key 6727 md5 ********
ntp authenticate
ntp trusted-key 6727
ntp server r8 key 6727 source inside prefer

PIX2# show ntp status

Clock is synchronized, stratum 4, reference is 192.168.1.1
```

continues

Example 23-33 *NTP on PIX2 (Continued)*

```
nominal freq is 99.9984 Hz, actual freq is 100.0006 Hz, precision is 2**6
reference time is af3bf5f5.0d1923cb (02:39:49.051 UTC Mon Mar 1 1993)
clock offset is -8.7785 msec, root delay is 1.66 msec
root dispersion is 8.91 msec, peer dispersion is 0.09 msec

PIX2# show ntp associations detail

192.168.1.1 configured, authenticated, our_master, sane, valid, stratum 3
ref ID 127.127.7.1, time af3bf5ea.253ebe6b (02:39:38.145 UTC Mon Mar 1 1993)
our mode client, peer mode server, our poll intvl 64, peer poll intvl 64
root delay 0.00 msec, root disp 0.03, reach 377, sync dist 0.946
delay 1.66 msec, offset -8.7785 msec, dispersion 0.09
precision 2**18, version 3
org time af3bf5f5.0aa3185b (02:39:49.041 UTC Mon Mar 1 1993)
rcv time af3bf5f5.0d1923cb (02:39:49.051 UTC Mon Mar 1 1993)
xmt time af3bf5f5.0c95cafb (02:39:49.049 UTC Mon Mar 1 1993)
filtdelay =    1.66    1.62    1.60    1.69    1.62    1.60    1.65    1.60
filtoffset =  -8.78   -8.83   -8.86   -8.91   -8.96   -9.03   -9.07   -9.15
filterror =    0.02    0.99    1.97    2.94    3.92    4.90    5.87    6.85
```

Enabling Auto Update Support

The Auto Update feature allows the PIX Firewall to retrieve its configurations and software images from a centralized location. It also provides centralized basic monitoring support of the PIX.

You can accomplish this monitoring support in one of the following two ways:

- The PIX initiating connection with the Auto Update server

- The Auto Update server initiating connection with the PIX

In either case, you must configure the PIX Firewall to enable communication between it and the central location.

Specifying the Auto Update Server Information

First, enable PIX to recognize the Auto Update server by specifying the server's information on the PIX. You can only define one Auto Update server. The command syntax is as follows:

```
PIX2(config)#auto-update server url [verify-certificate]
```

The format of the *url* argument is as follows:

```
http[s]://[user:password@]location[:port]/pathname
```

You can choose HTTP or HTTPS, in which case SSL is used. When logging in to the server, the *user:password* combination is used to verify identity. *Location* is the IP address of the server. The *port* argument is optional. If unspecified, the PIX uses the default port assignments for HTTP or HTTPS. *Pathname* is the name of the resource on the server.

If the **verify-certificate** keyword is configured, the PIX verifies the certificate that is returned by the Auto Update server.

Managing Auto Update Support

As previously mentioned, the PIX server can request communication with an Auto Update server. This is accomplished by polling the server. For the PIX Firewall to poll the server, you must specify the identification strategy by which the server recognizes the firewall. Several methods of identification are available, as you can see in the following command syntax:

```
PIX2(config)#auto-update device-id hardware-serial | hostname | ipaddress [if_name] |
    mac-address [if_name] | string text
```

Example 23-34 uses the **hostname** option, which causes the PIX Firewall to present its host name to the server as a means of identification.

If there has been no communication between the PIX and the server for a period of time, you can prevent the PIX from starting any new connections to the server by using the following command:

```
PIX2(config)#auto-update timeout period
```

Example 23-34 demonstrates the Auto Update feature configuration on PIX2. Note that in the **auto-update server** command, the user and password have been replaced with asterisks for the output of the **show running-config** command. The lower portion of the example displays the **show auto-update** command, which shows the Auto Update server, poll time, and timeout period.

Example 23-34 *PIX2 Auto Update Feature Configuration*

```
PIX2# show run
auto-update device-id hostname
auto-update timeout 60
auto-update server https://********@192.168.1.100/cisco/pix verify-certificate

PIX2# show auto-update
Server: https://192.168.1.100/cisco/pix
Certificate will be verified
Poll period: 720 minutes, retry count: 0, retry period: 5 minutes
Timeout: 60 minutes
Device ID: host name [PIX2]
Next poll in 588.36 minutes
```

Summary

Cisco PIX Firewall is an important technology featured on the CCIE Security Lab exam. This chapter's goal was to familiarize you with the array of configuration options available for the PIX Firewall, particularly its 6.2 release. The lessons in this chapter present configuration options that offer a wide range of PIX Firewall services.

Review Questions

1   What is the translational slot on the PIX Firewall called?

2   What is the default security level for the outside interface?

3   On the PIX Firewall, inbound traffic is filtered and outbound traffic is allowed by default. True or false?

4   You can configure syslog messages to be sent to which location(s)?

5   The IP address of the inside interface does not need to belong to the same subnet as the pool of its DHCP addresses. True or false?

6   How many entries must an access list have to become turbo-compiled?

FAQs

Q — *Is there a way to filter e-mail content on the Cisco Secure PIX Firewall?*

A — No. The PIX Firewall does not perform content filtering at the application layer because it does not inspect the data portion of the TCP packet. This is a job for a mail server.

Q — *Sometimes users who are connecting to an FTP server get very slow response times. What could be causing this?*

A — The IDENT protocol on the server could be the root of the problem. If the **service resetinbound** command is not configured on the PIX, the server has no way of knowing that PIX denied its IDENT request as a security violation.

Q — *Does the PIX Firewall support inbound port mapping?*

A — Yes. The current version of PIX supports inbound port redirection; this support began with PIX Software version 6.0. However, earlier PIX software versions do not support port mapping.

Q — *Can two different default routes be configured on the PIX Firewall, such as for load balancing?*

A — No. PIX cannot handle load balancing. That would require a more intelligent level of routing that the PIX is not designed for. A gateway router should be used for this purpose.

PART **VII**

Intrusion Detection

This chapter covers the following topics:

- Cisco IOS software intrusion detection
- Cisco PIX Firewall intrusion detection
- Cisco IOS software and PIX IDS signatures
- Configuring Cisco IDS

CHAPTER 24

IDS on the Cisco PIX Firewall and IOS Software

This chapter looks at the intrusion detection capabilities of Cisco IOS software and the Cisco PIX Firewall. It starts by looking at the IDS signatures that are supported on both the Cisco PIX Firewall and Cisco IOS software. Then it looks at the steps required to configure IDS on the Cisco PIX Firewall and Cisco IOS software.

Cisco IOS Software Intrusion Detection

Intrusion detection has been available as part of specific releases of Cisco IOS software from Release 12.05(T). IDS capabilities were available only on midrange to high-end router platforms. More recently, with the introduction of Cisco IOS Release 12.2 and the increase in processor capabilities of the lower routers, IDS functionality in the Cisco IOS software now includes the following platforms:

- Cisco 830

- Cisco 1700

- Cisco 2600

- Cisco 3600

- Cisco 7100

- Cisco 7200

As soon as the Cisco IOS software IDS features are installed and enabled on the router, it acts as a network IDS sensor. The router passively monitors and analyzes all packet flow through the router and checks this data against the installed and configured IDS signatures.

NOTE   IDS causes a significant performance impact on the router. This should not be a problem for low-bandwidth Internet connections, but LAN-to-LAN connections, especially over Fast Ethernet, might suffer.

If suspect activity is detected, the router can be configured to do the following:

- **Send an alarm to a management platform**—In this instance, either a Syslog server or a Cisco Post Office Protocol (POP)-compatible product, such as Cisco Secure Intrusion Detection Director (CSIDD) or Cisco Secure Policy Manager (CSPM), can receive the alarm.

- **Drop the packet**—The packet is dropped from the router and is not forwarded to its destination interface.

- **Reset the TCP connection**—The reset function sends a packet with the RST (reset) flag set to both the source and destination. This terminates the current session between the hosts.

The 59 default IDS signatures are available for use with the Cisco IOS IDS. These can be disabled on a signature-by-signature basis if the requirements do not fit the network design. They are listed in Table 24-1, shown later.

The Cisco IOS software IDS features can improve perimeter security by adding perimeter visibility of network intrusion attempts. Network-based IDSs, such as the Cisco IDS Sensor, listen to traffic passing on the network segment, whereas a router-based IDS receives and processes all inbound and outbound traffic to and from a network.

The Cisco IOS software IDS complements an existing Cisco Secure IDS installation. It can act as a perimeter-based sensor reporting as the IDS sensor does, to the IDS Director.

Cisco PIX Firewall Intrusion Detection

Intrusion detection on the Cisco PIX Firewall became available with Release 5.2(1) of the PIX operating system. Intrusion detection is available on all current PIX platforms.

The configuration of IDS on the PIX Firewall is very limited in comparison to the configuration available on the Cisco IOS software IDS. The PIX Firewall supports only Syslog. It has no knowledge of the POP used by the CSIDD or CSPM.

The PIX Firewall is always used as a network device to separate trusted networks from untrusted networks and to provide adaptive security for the networks behind it. The IDS feature on the PIX Firewall lets administrators enforce perimeter intrusion detection on a device that is already providing security services.

Many Internet sites employ PIX Firewalls to protect the hosted network that exists behind the PIX. The inclusion of IDS in this device allows security administrators to gather intrusion data and proactively act on any suspected vulnerabilities. This functionality used to be available only using a network-based IDS sensor connected to the protected VLANs in the hosted solution.

When suspect activity is identified, the Cisco PIX Firewall operates much like the Cisco IOS software IDS in that it can either send an alarm, drop the connection, or reset the session. (Refer to the preceding section for an explanation of these three options.)

PIX, as with the Cisco IOS IDS, supports the 59 default IDS signatures, which are discussed in the next section.

Cisco IOS Software and PIX IDS Signatures

The Cisco Network Security Database contains a comprehensive list of intrusion detection signatures. The Cisco Secure Intrusion Detection System (CSIDS) range of sensors and modules uses the full list of signatures.

The Cisco IOS software IDS and Cisco Secure PIX Firewall IDS use a cut-down number of intrusion detection signatures from the Network Security Database. These signatures are representative of the most common network attacks and information-gathering scans that are commonly found in an operational network.

The Cisco IOS software and PIX Firewall IDS software were designed with flexibility in mind. This allows individual signatures to be disabled where false positives exist.

Table 24-1 is a complete list of the 59 Cisco IOS software and Cisco PIX Firewall IDS signatures. The signatures are listed by order of their signature number in the Cisco Secure Encyclopedia (CSEC). After each signature's name is an indication of the kind of event that can trigger it (Info or Attack) and the type of signature it is (Atomic or Compound):

- Info signatures identify activity—that is, information gathering. An example is a port scan.

- Attack signatures identify activity that portrays an attempted network attack. Such an attack could be a denial of service attempt or an attempted exploit against a known SMTP vulnerability.

- Atomic signatures detect data patterns as simple as an attempt to access a specific port on a specific host. Atomic signatures that are marked with an asterisk (*) are allocated memory for session states by CBAC.

- Compound signatures detect complex data patterns, usually over a period of time.

The CSEC and current signatures can be found online at www.cisco.com/cgi-bin/front.x/ csec/idsHome.pl (note that you need a Cisco.com login and password to access this page).

Table 24-1 *59 Cisco IOS Software IDS and PIX Firewall IDS Signatures*

ID	Name	Trigger	Type
1000	IP options—Bad Option List	Triggered by the receipt of an IP datagram in which the list of IP options in the header is incomplete or malformed.	Info, Atomic
1001	IP options—Record Packet Route	Triggered by the receipt of an IP datagram in which the IP options list for the datagram includes option 7 (Record Packet Route).	Info, Atomic
1002	IP options—Timestamp	Triggered by the receipt of an IP datagram in which the Timestamp option is chosen (option 4).	Info, Atomic
1003	IP options—Security	Triggered by the receipt of an IP datagram in which the options list for the datagram includes option 2 (Security options).	Info, Atomic
1004	IP options—Loose Source Route	Triggered by the receipt of an IP datagram in which the options list for the datagram includes option 3 (Loose Source Route).	Info, Atomic
1005	IP options—SATNET ID	Triggered by the receipt of an IP datagram in which the options list for the datagram includes option 8 (SATNET stream identifier).	Info, Atomic
1006	IP options—Strict Source Route	Triggered by the receipt of an IP datagram in which the IP options list for the datagram includes option 2 (Strict Source Routing).	Info, Atomic
1100	IP Fragment Attack	Triggers when any IP datagram is received with the More Fragments flag set to 1 or if an offset is indicated in the Offset field.	Attack, Atomic
1101	Unknown IP Protocol	Triggers when an IP datagram is received with the Protocol field set to 134 or greater. These protocol types are undefined or reserved and should not be used.	Attack, Atomic
1102	Impossible IP Packet	Triggers when an IP packet arrives with the source equal to the destination address. This signature catches a *land attack,* which you can learn more about in the document "Security Advisory: TCP Loopback DoS Attack (land.c) and Cisco Devices" on the Cisco Systems website.	Attack, Atomic

Table 24-1   *59 Cisco IOS Software IDS and PIX Firewall IDS Signatures (Continued)*

ID	Name	Trigger	Type
2000	ICMP Echo Reply	Triggers when an IP datagram is received with the Protocol field in the header set to 1 (ICMP) and the Type field in the ICMP header set to 0 (Echo Reply).	Info, Atomic
2001	ICMP Host Unreachable	Triggers when an IP datagram is received with the Protocol field in the header set to 1 (ICMP) and the Type field in the ICMP header set to 3 (Host Unreachable).	Info, Atomic
2002	ICMP Source Quench	Triggers when an IP datagram is received with the Protocol field in the header set to 1 (ICMP) and the Type field in the ICMP header set to 4 (Source Quench).	Info, Atomic
2003	ICMP Redirect	Triggers when an IP datagram is received with the Protocol field in the header set to 1 (ICMP) and the Type field in the ICMP header set to 5 (Redirect).	Info, Atomic
2004	ICMP Echo Request	Triggers when an IP datagram is received with the Protocol field in the header set to 1 (ICMP) and the Type field in the ICMP header set to 8 (Echo Request).	Info, Atomic
2005	ICMP Time Exceeded for a Datagram	Triggers when an IP datagram is received with the Protocol field in the header set to 1 (ICMP) and the Type field in the ICMP header set to 11 (Time Exceeded for a Datagram).	Info, Atomic
2006	ICMP Parameter Problem on Datagram	Triggers when an IP datagram is received with the Protocol field in the header set to 1 (ICMP) and the Type field in the ICMP header set to 12 (Parameter Problem on Datagram).	Info, Atomic
2007	ICMP Timestamp Request	Triggers when an IP datagram is received with the Protocol field in the header set to 1 (ICMP) and the Type field in the ICMP header set to 13 (Timestamp Request).	Info, Atomic
2008	ICMP Timestamp Reply	Triggers when an IP datagram is received with the Protocol field in the header set to 1 (ICMP) and the Type field in the ICMP header set to 14 (Timestamp Reply).	Info, Atomic

continues

Table 24-1 *59 Cisco IOS Software IDS and PIX Firewall IDS Signatures (Continued)*

ID	Name	Trigger	Type
2009	ICMP Information Request	Triggers when an IP datagram is received with the Protocol field in the header set to 1 (ICMP) and the Type field in the ICMP header set to 15 (Information Request).	Info, Atomic
2010	ICMP Information Reply	Triggers when an IP datagram is received with the Protocol field in the header set to 1 (ICMP) and the Type field in the ICMP header set to 16 (ICMP Information Reply).	Info, Atomic
2011	ICMP Address Mask Request	Triggers when an IP datagram is received with the Protocol field in the header set to 1 (ICMP) and the Type field in the ICMP header set to 17 (Address Mask Request).	Info, Atomic
2012	ICMP Address Mask Reply	Triggers when an IP datagram is received with the Protocol field in the header set to 1 (ICMP) and the Type field in the ICMP header set to 18 (Address Mask Reply).	Info, Atomic
2150	Fragmented ICMP Traffic	Triggers when an IP datagram is received when the Protocol field in the header is set to 1 (ICMP) and either the More Fragments flag is set to 1 (ICMP) or an offset is indicated in the Offset field.	Attack, Atomic
2151	Large ICMP Traffic	Triggers when an IP datagram is received when the Protocol field in the header is set to 1 (ICMP) and the IP length is greater than 1024.	Attack, Atomic
2154	Ping of Death Attack	Triggers when an IP datagram is received when the Protocol field in the header is set to 1 (ICMP), the Last Fragment bit is set, and (IP offset * 8) + (IP data length) > 65535. In other words, the IP offset (which represents the starting position of this fragment in the original packet and which is in 8-byte units) plus the rest of the packet is greater than the maximum size of an IP packet.	Attack, Atomic
3040	TCP—no bits set in flags	Triggers when a TCP packet is received with no bits set in the Flags field.	Attack, Atomic
3041	TCP—SYN and FIN bits set	Triggers when a TCP packet is received with both the SYN and FIN bits set in the Flags field.	Attack, Atomic

Table 24-1   *59 Cisco IOS Software IDS and PIX Firewall IDS Signatures (Continued)*

ID	Name	Trigger	Type
3042	TCP—FIN bit with no ACK bit in flags	Triggers when a TCP packet is received with the FIN bit set but with no ACK bit set in the Flags field.	Attack, Atomic
3050	Half-open SYN Attack/SYN Flood	Triggers when multiple TCP sessions have been improperly initiated on any of several well-known service ports. Detection of this signature is currently limited to FTP, Telnet, HTTP, and e-mail servers (TCP ports 21, 23, 80, and 25, respectively).	Attack, Compound
3100	Smail Attack	Triggered by the very common "smail" attack against SMTP-compliant e-mail servers (frequently sendmail).	Attack, Compound
3101	Sendmail Invalid Recipient	Triggered by any mail message with a pipe (l) symbol in the Recipient field.	Attack, Compound
3102	Sendmail Invalid Sender	Triggered by any mail message with a pipe (l) symbol in the From: field.	Attack, Compound
3103	Sendmail Reconnaissance	Triggers when **expn** or **vrfy** commands are issued to the SMTP port.	Attack, Compound
3104	Archaic Sendmail Attacks	Triggers when **wiz** or **debug** commands are issued to the SMTP port.	Attack, Compound
3105	Sendmail Decode Alias	Triggered by any mail message with =decode@ in the header.	Attack, Compound
3106	Mail Spam	Counts the number of Rcpt to: lines in a single mail message and alarms after a user-definable maximum has been exceeded (the default is 250).	Attack, Compound
3107	Majordomo Execute Attack	A bug in the Majordomo program allows remote users to execute arbitrary commands at the server's privilege level.	Attack, Compound
3150	FTP Remote Command Execution	Triggers when someone tries to execute the **FTP SITE** command.	Attack, Compound
3151	FTP SYST Command Attempt	Triggers when someone tries to execute the **FTP SYST** command.	Info, Compound
3152	FTP CWD ~root	Triggers when someone tries to execute the **CWD ~root** command.	Attack, Compound

continues

Table 24-1   *59 Cisco IOS Software IDS and PIX Firewall IDS Signatures (Continued)*

ID	Name	Trigger	Type
3153	FTP Improper Address Specified	Triggers if a **port** command is issued with an address that is not the same as the requesting host.	Attack, Atomic[*]
3154	FTP Improper Port Specified	Triggers if a **port** command is issued with a data port specified that is less than 1024 or greater than 65535.	Attack, Atomic[*]
4050	UDP Bomb	Triggers when the UDP length specified is less than the IP length specified.	Attack, Atomic
4100	Tftp Passwd File	Triggered by an attempt to access the passwd file (typically /etc/passwd) via TFTP.	Attack, Compound
6100	RPC Port Registration	Triggers when attempts are made to register new RPC services on a target host.	Info, Atomic[*]
6101	RPC Port Unregistration	Triggers when attempts are made to unregister existing RPC services on a target host.	Info, Atomic[*]
6102	RPC Dump	Triggers when an RPC dump request is issued to a target host.	Info, Atomic[*]
6103	Proxied RPC Request	Triggers when a proxied RPC request is sent to the portmapper of a target host.	Attack, Atomic[*]
6150	ypserv Portmap Request	Triggers when a request is made to the portmapper for the YP server daemon (ypserv) port.	Info, Atomic[*]
6151	ypbind Portmap Request	Triggers when a request is made to the portmapper for the YP bind daemon (ypbind) port.	Info, Atomic[*]
6152	yppasswdd Portmap Request	Triggers when a request is made to the portmapper for the YP password daemon (yppasswdd) port.	Info, Atomic[*]
6153	ypupdated Portmap Request	Triggers when a request is made to the portmapper for the YP update daemon (ypupdated) port.	Info, Atomic[*]
6154	ypxfrd Portmap Request	Triggers when a request is made to the portmapper for the YP transfer daemon (ypxfrd) port.	Info, Atomic[*]
6155	mountd Portmap Request	Triggers when a request is made to the portmapper for the mount daemon (mountd) port.	Info, Atomic[*]

Table 24-1   *59 Cisco IOS Software IDS and PIX Firewall IDS Signatures (Continued)*

ID	Name	Trigger	Type
6175	rexd Portmap Request	Triggers when a request is made to the portmapper for the remote execution daemon (rexd) port.	Info, Atomic[*]
6180	rexd Attempt	Triggers when a call to the rexd program is made. The remote execution daemon (rexd) is the server responsible for remote program execution. This might indicate an attempt to gain unauthorized access to system resources.	Info, Atomic[*]
6190	statd Buffer Overflow	Triggers when a large status monitor (statd) request is sent. This could be an attempt to overflow a buffer and gain access to system resources.	Attack, Atomic[*]
8000	FTP Retrieve Password File	SubSig ID: 2101 Triggered by the string "passwd" issued during an FTP session. Might indicate someone attempting to retrieve the password file from a machine to crack it and gain unauthorized access to system resources.	Attack, Atomic[*]

Configuring Cisco IDS

This section looks at the tasks required to configure Cisco intrusion detection on the Cisco router and Cisco PIX Firewall. This section concentrates on intrusion detection from an Internet and, specifically, a hosted solution point of view. You will start by looking at a Cisco IOS IDS configuration that is located on a corporate router that provides Internet access to an organization. You will then look at the Cisco Secure PIX Firewall IDS that is deployed to protect a corporate website hosted at an Internet service provider (ISP).

Case Study 24-1: Configuring the Cisco IOS Software IDS

Routers connect networks. The Internet connection point of nearly all companies is through a routing device. In this section, you look at the configuration of the Cisco IOS software IDS for a router that is acting as the Internet connection point for a large company. This company has other WAN links to other sites. All Internet-bound traffic is routed through the central site. The Internet connection is provided for Internet browsing and e-mail only. No Internet servers are located at any corporate site. The router has been configured with Context-Based Access Control

(CBAC) to allow back through the firewall only what originated from the inside on the corporate network. Network Address Translation (NAT) has been used in an overload fashion. NAT overload is also known as Port Address Translation (PAT). In light of this, theoretically, from the outside, nothing on the inside should be visible.

Because all Internet traffic comes through this connection to the corporate network, it has been decided to configure intrusion detection on this router to provide a further layer of security against any external threats. This case study focuses on R6, as shown in Figure 24-1.

Figure 24-1   *Corporate Internet Connection*

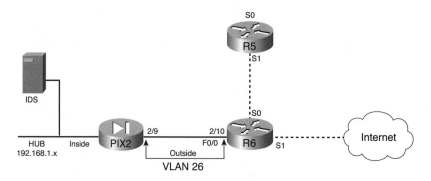

To configure intrusion detection on the Cisco IOS software IDS, you have to ensure that you are using the correct Cisco IOS software version. You must be using Cisco IOS Release 12.0(5)T or later with the IDS included.

By following these steps, you configure intrusion detection to use Syslog logging and to protect the router's outside interface:

Step 1   Enter the following commands in global configuration mode:

```
ip audit notify log
ip audit name ids info action alarm
ip audit name ids attack action alarm drop reset
```

The first line configures the IDS to use Syslog logging. With the Cisco IOS software IDS, you have the option of using Syslog or the Cisco Secure IDS Director. The second and third lines specify the IDS profile called ids. This profile is set to alarm for informational messages and to alarm, drop, and reset sessions for attack messages.

Step 2   After the IDS profile has been created, you have to apply it to an interface. Enter the following configuration line from interface configuration mode for the interface you want to apply the policy to:

```
ip audit ids in
```

The **ip audit ids** in command applies the IDS policy ids to the interface for inbound traffic. This is similar to the **ip access-group** command, which applies access lists either inbound or outbound to interfaces.

You can use the following **show** commands on the router to look at the configuration of IDS:

- **show ip audit configuration**
- **show ip audit interface**
- **show ip audit name**

The **show ip audit configuration** command displays the global configuration settings for IDS on the router. You can see from the command output in Example 24-1 that this router is using Syslog logging and not the NetRanger Director.

Example 24-1 show ip audit configuration *Command*

```
R6#show ip audit configuration
Event notification through syslog is enabled
Event notification through Net Director is disabled
Default action(s) for info signatures is alarm
Default action(s) for attack signatures is alarm
Default threshold of recipients for spam signature is 250
PostOffice:HostID:0 OrgID:0 Msg dropped:0
          :Curr Event Buf Size:0  Configured:100
Post Office is not enabled - No connections are active
Audit Rule Configuration
 Audit name ids
    info actions alarm
    attack actions alarm drop reset
```

The **show ip audit interface** command displays interface-specific information about IDS for every interface IDS is configured on. Example 24-2 shows that the IDS profile ids is configured inbound on the Fast Ethernet 0/0 interface on the router.

Example 24-2 show ip audit interface *Command*

```
R6#show ip audit interface
Interface Configuration
 Interface Serial 1
  Inbound IDS audit rule is ids
    info actions alarm
    attack actions alarm drop reset
  Outgoing IDS audit rule is not set
```

The **show ip audit name** command displays the IDS information for the specific IDS profile. Example 24-3 shows the configuration of the IDS profile called ids configured for the example.

Example 24-3 show ip audit name *Command*

```
R6#show ip audit name ids
Audit name ids
    info actions alarm
    attack actions alarm drop reset
```

Disabling a Signature in the Cisco IOS Software IDS

Within the Cisco IOS software IDS, you can disable specific signatures. Normally this feature is used if an instance of network activity results in numerous false positives. The command to disable a signature on Cisco IOS IDS is as follows, where 1101 is the number of the signature you want to disable:

```
ip audit signature 1101 disable
```

Refer to Table 24-1 to review the signatures.

This concludes the simple configuration of the Cisco IOS software IDS. As you can see, the configuration of IDS on Cisco IOS is fairly straightforward. You have to ensure that the router is successfully logging to a Syslog server. Numerous Syslog servers are available for both UNIX and Windows platforms.

Case Study 24-2: Configuring the Cisco Secure PIX Firewall IDS

It is very common for hosted solutions that are located in an ISP to be behind a firewall. This firewall separates the hosted solution from the main ISP public network and provides NAT and stateful inspection of packets to protect the hosted network from various external attacks. This makes the firewall an ideal place to implement IDS.

IDS technologies operate by passively listening to traffic to ascertain if the traffic is genuine or if it matches a known attack signature. This can be a problem in a shared network environment, because the last thing you want is your IDS alerting constantly because of traffic destined for other networks. This can be true of a hosted solution from an ISP, because the public Ethernet connection that forms the outside interface of the PIX Firewall can be in the same broadcast domain as numerous other hosted networks. However, all ISPs should use switches to provide Ethernet connectivity. The switch ensures that only the required unicast traffic is delivered to each hosted network. The nature of static NAT translation causes the outside switches to send unicast traffic for every host behind the firewall to the port where the firewall's outside interface is physically connected. This removes potential false positives on the IDS from traffic that is directed toward other hosted networks. However, because the switch implements a single broadcast domain throughout the Layer 3 domain, you might still get false positives for broadcast-based attacks.

This section looks at a very simple hosted Internet solution and the commands that are required to install IDS on the firewall. Figure 24-2 shows this simple network. This case study uses PIX2 from the network topology you have been using throughout this book.

Figure 24-2 *Simple Hosted Network*

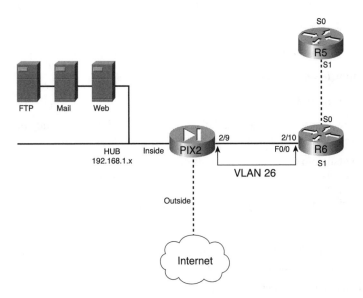

Figure 24-2 shows a simple model in which the hosted firewall's outside interface is connected to the Internet and the inside interface provides access to the protected network. This simple network has a web server, mail server, and FTP server. To enable IDS on the PIX Firewall, the software on the PIX must be Release 5.2 or later.

IDS configuration on the PIX is carried out with one command that has numerous variables associated with it. This command is **ip audit**. The important point to remember is that the alarm action with both the info and attack signatures uses the current configured Syslog server. This means that Syslog has to be configured and working on an inside interface. Syslog is enabled with the **logging** commands.

The following lines configure IDS on the PIX's outside interface. Remember that the outside interface is the Internet-facing interface. You could also configure IDS on the inside interface to catch any servers that might have been compromised, because they would initiate outbound attacks against other devices on the Internet. The following commands are all entered in global configuration mode:

```
ip audit info action alarm
ip audit attack action alarm
ip audit name idsattack attack action alarm drop reset
ip audit name idsinfo info action alarm
ip audit interface outside idsinfo
ip audit interface outside idsattack
```

The first two lines of the configuration are configured by default and apply to all interfaces. This configuration causes an alarm on info or attack signatures when you configure a policy without specific actions. The third and fourth lines specify IDS policies named idsattack and idsinfo. The fifth and six lines apply these named IDS policies to the outside interface.

You can use the following **show** commands on the PIX to look at the IDS configuration:

- **show ip audit info**
- **show ip audit attack**
- **show ip audit interface**
- **show ip audit name**

The **show ip audit info** command displays the global info IDS policy on the firewall. You can see from Example 24-4 that the global info IDS policy is to alarm.

Example 24-4 show ip audit info *Command*

```
pixfirewall# show ip audit info
ip audit info action alarm
```

The **show ip audit attack** command displays the global attack IDS policy on the firewall. You can see from Example 24-5 that the global attack IDS policy is to alarm.

Example 24-5 show ip audit attack *Command*

```
pixfirewall# show ip audit attack
ip audit attack action alarm
```

The **show ip audit interface** command displays the specific IDS policy that has been applied to an interface. Example 24-6 shows that the named IDS policies idsinfo and idsattack have been applied to the PIX's outside interface.

Example 24-6 show ip audit interface *Command*

```
pixfirewall# show ip audit interface outside
ip audit interface outside idsinfo
ip audit interface outside idsattack
```

The **show ip audit name** command displays the IDS policy that is specified in a named policy. Example 24-7 shows that the IDS policy idsinfo is set to alarm.

Example 24-7 show ip audit name *Command: idsinfo*

```
pixfirewall# show ip audit name idsinfo
ip audit name idsinfo info action alarm
```

Example 24-8 shows that attack signatures are alarmed, dropped, and reset.

Example 24-8 **show ip audit name** *Command: idsattack*

```
pixfirewall# show ip audit name idsattack
ip audit name idsattack attack action alarm drop reset
```

After IDS has been configured, you can monitor the Syslog information to identify any security issues. The log data shown in Example 24-9 is extracts from an actual Internet-facing PIX Firewall. You can see that the IDS on the PIX has intercepted quite a few items of suspicious activity.

Example 24-9 *Excerpted Log Data from the Internet-Facing PIX Firewall*

```
IDS:3041 TCP SYN+FIN flags from 24.15.59.98 to 194.73.134.2 on interface outside
IDS:3041 TCP SYN+FIN flags from 24.15.59.98 to 194.73.134.6 on interface outside
IDS:3041 TCP SYN+FIN flags from 24.15.59.98 to 194.73.134.7 on interface outside
IDS:3041 TCP SYN+FIN flags from 24.15.59.98 to 194.73.134.20 on interface outside
IDS:3041 TCP SYN+FIN flags from 24.15.59.98 to 194.73.134.21 on interface outside
IDS:3041 TCP SYN+FIN flags from 24.15.59.98 to 194.73.134.22 on interface outside
IDS:3041 TCP SYN+FIN flags from 24.15.59.98 to 194.73.134.23 on interface outside
IDS:3041 TCP SYN+FIN flags from 24.15.59.98 to 194.73.134.24 on interface outside
IDS:3041 TCP SYN+FIN flags from 24.15.59.98 to 194.73.134.26 on interface outside
IDS:3041 TCP SYN+FIN flags from 24.15.59.98 to 194.73.134.25 on interface outside
IDS:3041 TCP SYN+FIN flags from 24.15.59.98 to 194.73.134.27 on interface outside
IDS:3041 TCP SYN+FIN flags from 24.15.59.98 to 194.73.134.28 on interface outside
IDS:3041 TCP SYN+FIN flags from 24.15.59.98 to 194.73.134.30 on interface outside
IDS:3041 TCP SYN+FIN flags from 24.15.59.98 to 194.73.134.29 on interface outside
IDS:3041 TCP SYN+FIN flags from 24.15.59.98 to 194.73.134.100 on interface outside
```

The following message could indicate that the IP address 137.39.5.35 is trying to overcome the packet-filtering security policy. It could indicate an attack, so further investigation is warranted:

```
IDS:2001 ICMP unreachable from 137.39.5.35 to 194.73.134.7 on interface outside
```

The following message indicates that a successful ICMP echo reply (ping) was sent from the IP address 64.225.249.26:

```
IDS:2000 ICMP echo reply from 64.225.249.26 to 194.73.134.2 on interface outside
```

This is an informational message. It is important to note that ICMP echo reply messages might occur very frequently in your network, especially if you are using an ICMP-based network-monitoring tool. It might be worthwhile to disable this signature, as outlined in the following section.

Although you do not have to configure a Syslog server on the outside, it is important to check the Syslog messages when you are configuring IDS, because this is an excellent way to confirm that the configuration is working as you expect.

Disabling a Signature in the Cisco Secure PIX Firewall IDS

Within the Cisco Secure PIX Firewall IDS, you can disable specific signatures. This feature is normally used if there is an instance of network activity that results in numerous false positives. The command to disable a signature on Cisco PIX Firewall IDS is as follows, where 1101 is the number of the signature you want to disable:

```
ip audit signature 1101 disable
```

NOTE   The **ip audit signature disable** command is the same for both the PIX IDS and the Cisco IOS IDS.

This concludes our simple configuration of the Cisco PIX IDS. As you can see, the configuration of IDS on the PIX is fairly straightforward. You have to ensure that the PIX is successfully logging to a Syslog server. Numerous Syslog servers are available for both UNIX and Windows platforms.

Summary

In this chapter, you examined the intrusion detection capabilities of the Cisco IOS software and the Cisco Secure PIX Firewall. Both of these devices run 59 signatures that represent the most common network-based intrusion issues found in today's networks. The chapter started by looking at how Cisco IOS software and the PIX handle IDS. Next you saw the 59 default signatures that the Cisco IOS software IDS and PIX Firewall IDS use. You then covered the configuration steps necessary to configure the IDS functionality in Cisco IOS and the Cisco Secure PIX Firewall.

Review Questions

1   By default, when IDS on Cisco IOS software is enabled, are all the default signatures enabled or disabled?

2   True or false: Implementing IDS on a Cisco PIX Firewall affects the firewall's throughput performance.

3   What command disables the ICMP Echo Reply signature, ID = 2000?

4   What type of signature identifies information-gathering activity?

5   In what version of the PIX OS was intrusion detection introduced?

6   What type of signature detects complex data patterns, usually over a period of time?

7 What command displays interface-specific information about IDS for every interface IDS is configured on?

8 What type of signature identifies activity that portrays an attempted network attack?

9 What type of signature detects data patterns as simple as an attempt to access a specific port on a specific host?

10 What command displays the global configuration settings for IDS on the router?

FAQs

Q — *What is the main difference between Cisco Secure IDS and Cisco IOS/PIX IDS?*

A — The main difference between Cisco Secure IDS and Cisco IOS/PIX IDS is that Cisco IOS/PIX IDS uses a cut-down 59-signature database consisting of the most common exploit attempts, whereas the Cisco Secure IDS uses the ful Cisco Network Security Database of signatures. Another major difference is that Cisco Secure IDS is not in the data path; therefore, it does not interfere with or affect network performance.

Q — *What is the main difference between the Cisco IOS software IDS and the PIX Firewall IDS?*

A — The main difference between the Cisco IOS software IDS and the PIX Firewall IDS is that the Cisco IOS IDS can send alerts via POP to the IDS management platform of your choice, either the CSIDD or the CSPM.

This chapter covers the following topics:

- Preventing denial-of-service attacks

- Layer 2 VPN (L2VPN)

- Configuring ISP services

CHAPTER 25

Internet Service Provider Security Services

Internet service providers (ISPs) offer a multitude of services. Covering all those services would require several more books of the same size as the one before you. Therefore, this chapter concentrates only on those aspects related directly to network security in general and the CCIE Security lab exam in particular.

Preventing Denial-of-Service Attacks

As you know, denial-of-service (DoS) attacks are a common and serious threat for modern networks, especially those with access to the Internet. Cisco IOS software offers several useful features to fight DoS. Among them are the two discussed in this section: rate limiting using committed access rate and reverse path forwarding.

Committed Access Rate (CAR)

Committed access rate (CAR) is a quality of service (QoS) feature that implements classification and policing through rate limiting. Packet classification means that the 8 (0 through 7) type of service (ToS) bits in the IP header are used to classify packets as belonging to an assigned category. These categories are as follows:

- **0**—Routine
- **1**—Priority
- **2**—Immediate
- **3**—Flash
- **4**—Flash override
- **5**—Critical ECP
- **6**—Internetwork control
- **7**—Network control

In turn, those categories are placed in classes according to their priority. There are six available priority classes (the last two ToS categories are reserved for internal network use). They determine how the devices on the network treat the traffic.

Packets can be classified based on a variety of factors. The selection criteria can be specified in a CAR access list and include, but are not limited to, the following:

- Physical port

- Source or destination MAC address

- Source or destination IP address

- Application port

- IP protocol type

Also, the packets can be categorized externally, such as by a customer. CAR lets you either accept the external classification or override it through reclassification.

Along with the classification feature, CAR can be used to police traffic. This function lets you enforce a rate limit, or, in other words, let traffic access the specified bandwidth only. You can configure the action the router takes when traffic exceeds the allowable limit. Then, packets can either be dropped or marked down in their priority level.

Reverse Path Forwarding (RPF)

You were introduced to the concept of unicast Reverse Path Forwarding (RPF) in Chapter 23, "Cisco PIX Firewall." Although configuration is, of course, different because in this chapter it's applied to the router rather than the PIX, the theory is very similar.

The DoS attack is often caused by the attacker's using a spoofed IP source address, which makes it extremely hard to recognize, filter, and subsequently track down and punish the attacker. By implementing unicast RPF, you can ensure that the only packets getting through are the ones whose source IP address already exists in your router's routing table. If you, as an ISP, create this policy in your network, it will in turn protect your customers as well.

Layer 2 VPN (L2VPN)

To provide VPN services to multiple clients, ISPs have to implement tunneling so that their customers' VLAN and Layer 2 protocol configurations remain separate from those of other customers. Even though several Cisco devices support tunneling features, only the Catalyst 3550 switch is covered in this chapter because it is the device used in the CCIE Security lab environment. The Catalyst 3550 switch can provide the necessary services through 802.1Q tunneling and Layer 2 protocol tunneling.

802.1Q

If the requirement is to keep all customers' VLANs separated, an ISP would have to provide a unique block of VLAN ranges so that the VLANs belonging to different customers don't overlap. This could lead to certain configuration restrictions for a customer and running out of VLAN ranges for a service provider.

To solve this dilemma, the IEEE 802.1Q tunneling feature was introduced. By implementing 802.1Q tunneling, a service provider can maintain multiple-VLAN clients through the use of a single VLAN per client. The customer's VLAN IDs remain unchanged due to the hierarchical structure of the 802.1Q tunnel. A port that allows a single VLAN to encompass multiple VLANs within it is called a *tunnel port*. As you might guess, each customer needs its own dedicated tunnel port that supports all its VLANs. On the customer side, the edge port is configured as an 802.1Q trunk port that is linked to the ISP's tunnel port.

Layer 2 Protocol Tunneling

The customers' role in implementing a VPN tunnel is to make certain that their topology is properly set up. This includes scaling their networks at all remote locations to include correct information in each VLAN's spanning tree across the board. To make this possible, a client uses Cisco Discovery Protocol (CDP) to discover neighbors and VLAN Trunking Protocol (VTP) to maintain uniform VLAN architecture at their local and remote sites.

With protocol tunneling, when the Layer 2 protocol customer traffic reaches the inbound side of the service provider edge switch, the protocol packets are encapsulated with a special MAC address of the tunnel port. These packets are then forwarded across the provider's network to the outbound edge-switch interfacing the destination side of the customer without having been processed by the ISP's intermediate switches. This allows clients at all sites to synchronize their VLAN and spanning tree configuration and allows CDP to discover neighbors as if they were directly connected, ignoring the service provider network in between.

When 802.1Q tunneling is employed without Layer 2 protocol tunneling, the proper STP, CDP, and VTP information is not propagated transparently through the service provider on to the remote customer network. As a result, the customer's Layer 2 information is mixed up with that of the service provider. Conversely, with protocol tunneling enabled, Layer 2 protocols belonging to a customer are separated from those of the service provider and its other customers. Layer 2 protocol tunneling can also be used independently of 802.1Q tunneling.

Configuring ISP Services

The case studies presented in this section deal with the configuration aspects of the concepts already discussed. These are only a few of the services that ISPs can offer, but they are important to your preparation for the lab exam.

Case Study 25-1: DoS Prevention Through Rate Limiting

The topology for this case study is very simple. A router named R8 is connected to the Internet. Your job is to configure R8 in such a way that it is protected from attacks by limiting the rate of traffic. Case Study 25-2, which is devoted to RPF, also uses the topology shown in Figure 25-1. Although RPF and CAR can be implemented together, the RPF case study does not include the rate-limiting configuration.

Figure 25-1 *DoS Prevention Topology*

As you know, you can set up a policy to limit an interface's input and/or output transmission rate. After the traffic matches a criterion, the router takes action based on whether that traffic conforms to or exceeds the rate limit. You can configure multiple rate policies on an interface, each corresponding to its own types of traffic. Higher priority, for instance, might be entitled to a higher rate limit than the rest. The policies are examined in the order in which they were entered until a match is found. The default action is to send, so if there is no match, the traffic is forwarded.

To complete this case study, you follow these steps:

Step 1   Configure CAR for all IP traffic.

Step 2   Configure CAR policies.

Step 1: Configuring CAR for All IP Traffic

Because CAR is applied to an interface, you start by entering interface configuration mode. In this case, it is FastEthernet0/0.

The following command sets up an overall rate-limiting policy independent of traffic type:

```
R8(config-if)#rate-limit [input | output] bps burst-normal burst-max conform-action
    action exceed-action action
```

The **input** and **output** options determine whether the packets in question are sent or received on this interface. When applying this command to the configuration, change the *bps* argument to the average rate in bits per second. The *bps* value must be in increments of 8 kbps and must range between 8000 and 2,000,000,000. The average rate is determined by a long-term average of the transmission rate.

burst-normal specifies the normal burst size in bytes. The requirement is that the minimum *burst-normal* value equals the chosen *bps* divided by 2000. Logically, then, *burst-max* is the excess burst size in bytes.

Following the rate arguments are the **conform-action** and **exceed-action** keywords, with appropriate *action*s assigned to them. Which of these actions is taken depends on whether the traffic follows or breaks the rules defined by the rate arguments. Table 25-1 lists the available actions.

NOTE   Traffic falling under the average rate set by the *bps* argument always conforms.

Table 25-1   **conform-action** *and* **exceed-action** *Options*

Action	Description
continue	Points to the next **rate-limit** command
drop	Drops the packet
set-prec-continue *new-prec*	Specifies the precedence level and points to the next **rate-limit** command
set-prec-transmit *new-prec*	Specifies the precedence level and forwards the packet
transmit	Forwards the packet

In this case study, the general CAR policy is defined in the following terms:

- It is applied to incoming traffic.
- The average rate is set at 8,000,000 bps; the normal burst rate and excess burst rate are 16,000 and 24,000, respectively.
- In the case of conforming, the traffic is assigned an IP precedence of 5 and is transmitted.
- As soon as the limit is exceeded, the packets are dropped.

The preceding set of guidelines results in the configuration shown in Example 25-1.

Example 25-1 *Setting up the CAR for All IP Traffic*

```
R8#show run
!
! Output omitted for brevity
!
interface FastEthernet0/0
ip address 192.168.1.1 255.255.255.0
```

continues

Example 25-1 *Setting up the CAR for All IP Traffic (Continued)*

```
rate-limit input 8000000 16000 24000 conform-action set-prec-transmit 5
  exceed-action drop
no cdp enable
no ip route-cache
```

Step 2: Configuring CAR Policies

Configuring CAR policies for each class of traffic essentially means expanding on the **rate-limit** command. All keywords and arguments of the **rate-limit** command stay the same, with the addition of the **access-group** option. Here is the exact syntax:

```
R8(config-if)#rate-limit [input | output] access-group [rate-limit] acl-number bps
  burst-normal burst-max conform-action action exceed-action action
```

The **access-group** argument points to the policy defined in an **access-list** command. Access lists used to create parameters for traffic matching can be standard, extended, or special rate-limit lists. You can configure as many **rate-limit** commands as there are policies specified by access lists, because the **access-group** keyword references the same ID number as an access list.

Example 25-2 shows two CAR policies applied to incoming traffic that matches criteria from two different access lists, 100 and 102. One of the access lists controls web traffic, and the other controls FTP.

Example 25-2 *Configuring CAR Policies*

```
R8#show run
!
! Output omitted for brevity
!
interface FastEthernet0/0
ip address 192.168.1.1 255.255.255.0
rate-limit input access-group 100 2000000 24000 32000 conform-action
  set-prec-transmit 5 exceed-action set-prec-transmit 0
rate-limit input access-group 102 10000000 24000 32000 conform-action
  set-prec-transmit 5 exceed-action drop
!
access-list 100 permit tcp any any eq www log
access-list 102 permit tcp any any eq ftp log
access-list 102 permit tcp any any eq ftp-data log
```

From the two **rate-limit** commands, you can conclude that all web traffic is to be transmitted. However, the IP precedence for web traffic that conforms to the first rate policy is set to 5. For excessive web traffic, the IP precedence is set to 0 (best effort). FTP traffic is transmitted with an IP precedence of 5 if it conforms to the second rate policy. If the FTP traffic exceeds the rate policy, it is dropped.

Remember that in the first step of this case study, you set up a general policy for all IP traffic. Therefore, any remaining traffic that does not fall under access lists 100 and 102 is limited to 8 Mbps, with a normal burst size of 16,000 bytes and an excess burst size of 24,000 bytes.

You can view your configuration by issuing the **show interfaces rate-limit** command, as shown in Example 25-3.

Example 25-3 show interfaces rate-limit *Command*

```
R8#show interfaces fastEthernet 0/0 rate-limit
FastEthernet0/0
  Input
    matches: access-group 100
      params:  2000000 bps, 24000 limit, 32000 extended limit
      conformed 1 packets, 247 bytes; action: set-prec-transmit 5
      exceeded 0 packets, 0 bytes; action: set-prec-transmit 0
      last packet: 117808ms ago, current burst: 0 bytes
      last cleared 00:09:34 ago, conformed 0 bps, exceeded 0 bps
    matches: access-group 102
      params:  10000000 bps, 24000 limit, 32000 extended limit
      conformed 0 packets, 0 bytes; action: set-prec-transmit 5
      exceeded 0 packets, 0 bytes; action: drop
      last packet: 1180548ms ago, current burst: 0 bytes
      last cleared 00:05:58 ago, conformed 0 bps, exceeded 0 bps
    matches: all traffic
      params:  8000000 bps, 16000 limit, 24000 extended limit
      conformed 0 packets, 0 bytes; action: set-prec-transmit 5
      exceeded 0 packets, 0 bytes; action: drop
      last packet: 1180552ms ago, current burst: 0 bytes
      last cleared 00:05:23 ago, conformed 0 bps, exceeded 0 bps
```

So far the discussion has focused on the incoming traffic. Example 25-4 shows the CAR policy creation for outgoing traffic to limit SYN packets.

Example 25-4 *Rate Limiting for SYN Packets*

```
R8#show run
!
! Output omitted for brevity
!
interface FastEthernet0/0
rate-limit output access-group 113 45000000 100000 200000 conform-action transmit
  exceed-action drop
!
access-list 113 permit tcp any any syn
```

Case Study 25-2: DoS Prevention Through RPF

The topology for this case study is taken from the preceding scenario, so refer to Figure 25-1 to refresh your memory. For this case study, assume that the CAR configuration described in the preceding case study has been canceled. (You can do this by including the **no** keyword in front of the **rate-limit** command.)

As you might already know, unicast RPF is an effective way to prevent distributed DoS attacks that use source IP address spoofing. You should apply it on the router's input interface. With unicast RPF enabled, the router performs the reverse route lookup made possible by implementing the Cisco Express Forwarding (CEF) feature on the router. As part of its operation, CEF generates the Forwarding Information Base (FIB). The router then uses the FIB to look up the preexisting route along with all its associated interfaces. Remember that besides the packet's source IP address, an interface on which the packet arrived must match as well; otherwise, the packet is dropped.

To enable CEF on the router, enter the following command in global configuration mode:

```
R8(config)#ip cef
```

After CEF is specified globally, select the input interface on the router—in this instance, FastEthernet0/0. In interface configuration mode, use the following command to allow unicast RPF to function:

```
R8(config-if)#ip verify unicast reverse-path
```

The preceding command should look familiar from your past experience with configuring RPF on PIX Firewalls in Chapter 23. The most notable difference is that PIX Firewalls have no interface configuration mode, so you have to specify the interface at the end of the **ip verify** command line.

Example 25-5 demonstrates unicast RPF configuration on R8.

Example 25-5 *Configuring Unicast RPF on the Input Interface*

```
R8#show run
!
! Output omitted for brevity
!
ip cef
!
interface Serial0/0
 ip address 207.67.1.1 255.255.255.0
 ip verify unicast reverse-path
 no ip proxy-arp
 no ip mroute-cache
 no cdp enable
```

You can verify the unicast RPF operation with the help of the **show cef interface** command. Example 25-6 shows the output of this command for the FastEthernet0/0 interface.

Example 25-6 **show cef interface** *Command Output*

```
R8#show cef interface serial 0/0 detail
Serial0/0 is down (if_number 8)
  Corresponding hwidb fast_if_number 8
  Corresponding hwidb firstsw->if_number 8
  Internet address is 207.67.1.1/24
  ICMP redirects are always sent
  Per packet load-sharing is disabled
  IP unicast RPF check is enabled
  Inbound access list is not set
  Outbound access list is not set
  IP policy routing is disabled
  Interface is marked as point to point interface
  Hardware idb is Serial0/0
  Fast switching type 4, interface type 60
  IP CEF switching disabled
  IP Feature Fast switching turbo vector
  Input fast flags 0x4000, Output fast flags 0x0
  ifindex 4(4)
  Slot 0 Slot unit 0 Unit 0 VC -1
  Transmit limit accumulator 0x0 (0x0)
  IP MTU 1500
```

Case Study 25-3: Configuring L2VPN

Figure 25-2 shows two remote routers—R1 and R10—that belong to the same client. Both routers have interfaces that participate in VLAN10 and VLAN11. The routers are separated by 3550-A and 3550-B switches. Your assignment is to create an L2VPN tunnel between R1 and R10 so that the VLANs of both routers can communicate with their counterpart.

In this case study, you complete the following steps:

Step 1   Configure routers.

Step 2   Configure switches.

Step 3   Verify your configuration.

Figure 25-2 *L2VPN Topology*

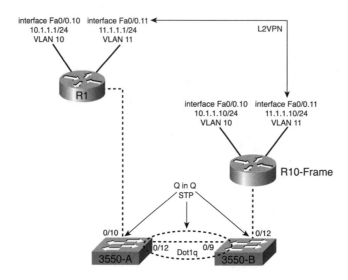

Step 1: Configuring Routers

The first step in L2VPN configuration is to enable the router side of the connection. You can start by creating two subinterfaces on each of the routers: one for VLAN10 and the other for VLAN11. After entering subinterface configuration mode, you need to specify a VLAN encapsulation format for each subinterface. Because you are defining 802.1Q as the encapsulation standard, you must place the following command in every subinterface configuration:

```
R1(config-if)#encapsulation dot1q vlanid
```

vlanid is the VLAN number for a subinterface.

Remember to assign an IP address to each subinterface. Understandably, subinterfaces that belong to the same VLAN need to be in the same subnet. For ease of management, you can also add a description indicating in which VLAN the subinterface is participating.

Example 25-7 shows the beginning configuration of R1 and R10, including the **encapsulation** command. Notice the consistency between the IP addresses of both routers.

Example 25-7 *Enabling VLANs on R1 and R10 and Specifying the VLAN Encapsulation Format*

```
R1#show run
!
! Output omitted for brevity
!
interface FastEthernet1.1
 description VLAN 10
```

Example 25-7 *Enabling VLANs on R1 and R10 and Specifying the VLAN Encapsulation Format (Continued)*

```
 encapsulation dot1Q 10
 ip address 10.1.1.1 255.255.255.0
!
interface FastEthernet1.2
 description VLAN 11
 encapsulation dot1Q 11
 ip address 11.1.1.1 255.255.255.0

R10#show run
!
! Output omitted for brevity
!
interface FastEthernet2/0.1
 encapsulation dot1Q 10
 ip address 10.1.1.10 255.255.255.0
!
interface FastEthernet2/0.2
 encapsulation dot1Q 11
 ip address 11.1.1.10 255.255.255.0
```

Step 2: Configuring Switches

The switch configuration can be divided into two parts—tunnel port configuration and trunk port configuration.

Tunnel Port Configuration

The tunnel port physically connects the service provider switch to the client. In Figure 25-2, the 3550-A switch is connected to R1 via its GigabitEthernet0/10 interface, and 3550-B is connected to R10 via its GigabitEthernet0/12 interface. In this section, you will enable tunnel port functionality for both interfaces.

First, you enter the interface configuration mode of the interface that will be configured as the tunnel port. Because subsequent configuration of 3550-A's and 3550-B's tunnel ports is identical, this section explains the configuration of 3550-A. You will see the configuration of both switches' tunnel ports in the next example.

After you specify the needed interface, you can begin configuring the 802.1Q-related tasks. The following command specifies the default VLAN, which is reserved by the service provider for a particular customer:

```
3550-A(config-if)#switchport access vlan vlan-id
```

Next, you specify the interface as an 802.1Q tunnel port with the following command:

```
3550-A(config-if)#switchport mode dot1q-tunnel
```

Now that the 802.1Q configuration of the tunnel ports is complete, you can configure Layer 2 protocol tunneling parameters by adding the following command to your interface configuration:

```
3550-A(config-if)#l2protocol-tunnel [cdp | vtp | stp]
```

Example 25-8 demonstrates the tunnel port setup of the 3550-A and 3550-B switches. Notice that the customer VLAN ID is 100 and that Layer 2 protocol tunneling is specified for CDP, VTP, and STP in both cases.

Example 25-8 *Tunnel Port Configuration*

```
3550-A#show run
!
! Output omitted for brevity
!
interface GigabitEthernet0/10                            ←to R1
switchport access vlan 100
switchport mode dot1q-tunnel
l2protocol-tunnel cdp              ←pass CDP, VTP, and STP to R1
l2protocol-tunnel vtp
l2protocol-tunnel stp

3550-B#show run
hostname 3550-B
!
! Output omitted for brevity
!
interface GigabitEthernet0/12                            ←to R10
switchport access vlan 100
switchport mode dot1q-tunnel
l2protocol-tunnel cdp              ←pass CDP, VTP, and STP to R10
l2protocol-tunnel vtp
l2protocol-tunnel stp
```

Trunk Port Configuration

It's time to enable trunk port functionality on 3550-A's GigabitEthernet0/12 and 3550-B's GigabitEthernet0/9 interfaces that link the two switches. Again, the first step is to enter interface configuration mode. Then enter the following command:

```
3550-A(config-if)#switchport trunk [allowed vlan vlan-list] | [encapsulation
  [dot1q | isl | negotiate]]
```

allowed vlan *vlan-list* specifies which VLANs are allowed to pass traffic through this interface. Although you can choose to specify the exact VLANs, the default is **all** (which is used in this case study).

The next parameter is **encapsulation**. Of the available options, this example employs **dot1q**. If this type of encapsulation is enabled, both tagged and untagged traffic is allowed.

Recall the **switchport mode** command introduced in the preceding section. Here you use it again; however, this time, you indicate that the interface will act in the trunk capacity. The syntax is as follows:

```
3550-A(config-if)#switchport mode trunk
```

NOTE   Along with dot1q-tunnel and trunk modes, the **switchport mode** command offers access and dynamic options.

Example 25-9 demonstrates the trunk port configuration of switches 3550-A and 3550-B.

Example 25-9 *Trunk Port Configuration*

```
3550-A#show run
!
! Output omitted for brevity
!
interface GigabitEthernet0/10                        ←to R1
 switchport access vlan 100
 switchport mode dot1q-tunnel
 l2protocol-tunnel cdp
!
interface GigabitEthernet0/12                      ←to 3550-B
 switchport trunk encapsulation dot1q
 switchport mode trunk

3550-B#show run
hostname 3550-B
!
! Output omitted for brevity
!
interface GigabitEthernet0/9                        ←to 3550-A
 switchport trunk encapsulation dot1q
 switchport mode trunk
!
interface GigabitEthernet0/12                       ←to R10
 switchport access vlan 100
 switchport mode dot1q-tunnel
 l2protocol-tunnel cdp
```

Step 3: Verifying the L2VPN Configuration

Now that you have completed the necessary tasks to enable 802.1Q tunneling and Layer 2 protocol tunneling, you need to make sure that your configuration is successful.

You can start by issuing the **show interfaces** command to view the interface configuration on the switches. Example 25-10 shows the output of the **show interfaces gigabitEthernet 0/**port-number **switchport** command.

Example 25-10 **show interfaces switchport** Command Output

```
3550-A#show interfaces gigabitEthernet 0/10 switchport
Name: Gi0/10
Switchport: Enabled
Administrative Mode: dot1q-tunnel
Operational Mode: dot1q-tunnel
Administrative Trunking Encapsulation: negotiate
Operational Trunking Encapsulation: native
Negotiation of Trunking: Off
Access Mode VLAN: 100 (VLAN0100)
Trunking Native Mode VLAN: 1 (default)
Administrative private-vlan host-association: none
Administrative private-vlan mapping: none
Operational private-vlan: none
Trunking VLANs Enabled: ALL
Pruning VLANs Enabled: 2-1001

3550-B#show interfaces gigabitEthernet 0/12 switchport
Name: Gi0/12
Switchport: Enabled
Administrative Mode: dot1q-tunnel
Operational Mode: dot1q-tunnel
Administrative Trunking Encapsulation: dot1q
Operational Trunking Encapsulation: native
Negotiation of Trunking: Off
Access Mode VLAN: 100 (VLAN0100)
Trunking Native Mode VLAN: 1 (default)
Administrative private-vlan host-association: none
Administrative private-vlan mapping: none
Operational private-vlan: none
Trunking VLANs Enabled: ALL
Pruning VLANs Enabled: 2-1001
```

The **switchport** keyword at the end of the **show interfaces** command displays the administrative and operational status of a switching port. Compare Example 25-10 to Example 25-11, where the **show interfaces gigabitEthernet 0/**port-number **trunk** command is issued for the trunk ports of both switches. You might notice that this command displays the trunk port statistics. Although the **switchport** options can be used to examine both the trunk and tunnel interfaces, the **trunk** option applies only to the trunk ports. Also, when looking for the active trunk port information, you don't have to specify an interface number; issuing the **trunk** keyword is sufficient.

Example 25-11 **show interfaces trunk** *Command Output*

```
3550-A#show interfaces gigabitEthernet 0/12 trunk

Port        Mode          Encapsulation  Status        Native vlan
Gi0/12      on            802.1q         trunking      1

Port        Vlans allowed on trunk
Gi0/12      1,-4094

Port        Vlans allowed and active in management domain
Gi0/12      1,100

Port        Vlans in spanning tree forwarding state and not pruned
Gi0/12      1,100

3550-B#show interfaces gigabitEthernet 0/9 trunk

Port        Mode          Encapsulation  Status        Native vlan
Gi0/9       on            802.1q         trunking      1

Port        Vlans allowed on trunk
Gi0/9       1,-4094

Port        Vlans allowed and active in management domain
Gi0/9       1,100

Port        Vlans in spanning tree forwarding state and not pruned
Gi0/9       1,100
3550-B#
```

The next logical step is to verify the Layer 2 protocol tunneling operation on the switches. To do this, issue the **show l2protocol-tunnel** command. It displays information about Layer 2 protocol tunnel ports. Note that it applies only to ports that have Layer 2 protocol tunneling enabled. Example 25-12 shows the output of this command on the two switches.

Example 25-12 **show l2protocol-tunnel** *Command Output*

```
3550-A#show l2protocol-tunnel
COS for Encapsulated Packets: 5

Port    Protocol       Threshold         Counters Encap     Decap
                       (cdp/stp/vtp)     (cdp/stp/vtp       cdp/stp/vtp)
-----------------------------------------------------------------------
Gi0/10  cdp stp vtp    ----/----/----    105/0/0            0/0/0

3550-B#show l2protocol-tunnel
COS for Encapsulated Packets: 5
```

continues

Example 25-12 show l2protocol-tunnel *Command Output (Continued)*

```
Port    Protocol       Threshold        Counters Encap     Decap
                       (cdp/stp/vtp)    (cdp/stp/vtp       cdp/stp/vtp)
-----------------------------------------------------------------------
Gi0/12  cdp stp vtp    ----/----/----   76/0/0             0/0/0
```

Now you can move on to the routers for configuration verification. Issue ICMP requests to ensure interconnectivity. Ping the subinterfaces of the remote router, as shown in Example 25-13.

Example 25-13 *Results of ICMP Requests*

```
R1#ping 11.1.1.10

Type escape sequence to abort.
Sending 5, 100-byte ICMP Echos to 11.1.1.10, timeout is 2 seconds:
.!!!!
Success rate is 80 percent (4/5), round-trip min/avg/max = 1/1/4 ms

R1#ping 11.1.1.10

Type escape sequence to abort.
Sending 5, 100-byte ICMP Echos to 11.1.1.10, timeout is 2 seconds:
!!!!!
Success rate is 100 percent (5/5), round-trip min/avg/max = 1/1/4 ms
R1#
```

After pinging the remote router subinterfaces, you can check the ARP table to ensure that the router can see them. Example 25-14 shows R1's ARP table.

Example 25-14 show arp *Command Output*

```
R1#show arp
Protocol  Address       Age (min)  Hardware Addr   Type   Interface
Internet  10.1.1.10            1   0030.7bbf.0438  ARPA   FastEthernet1.1
Internet  11.1.1.10            0   0030.7bbf.0438  ARPA   FastEthernet1.2
Internet  11.1.1.1             -   00d0.06ff.c0e2  ARPA   FastEthernet1.2
Internet  10.1.1.1             -   00d0.06ff.c0e2  ARPA   FastEthernet1.1
R1#
```

Finally, you can issue the **show cdp neighbor** command to check which neighbors are directly connected. Example 25-15 shows that R1's direct neighbor is R10.

Example 25-15 **show cdp neighbor** *Command Output*

```
R1#show cdp neighbor
Capability Codes: R - Router, T - Trans Bridge, B - Source Route Bridge
                  S - Switch, H - Host, I - IGMP, r - Repeater

Device ID        Local Intrfce     Holdtme    Capability  Platform  Port ID
R10              Fas 1.1           143        R           2600      2/0.1
R10              Fas 1.2           173        R           2600      2/0.2
```

Summary

This chapter provided information on some of the security-related services commonly offered by ISPs that you might encounter on the CCIE Security lab exam:

- DoS prevention with CAR and unicast RPF

- L2VPN

The DoS prevention service provides protection from DoS attacks, such as ICMP and SYN floods, by enforcing rate limiting or allowing only IP packets that originated from verified sources. The L2VPN feature provides VPN support at Layer 2.

Review Questions

1 Name two features offered by CAR.

2 What sort of information must preexist on the router to allow a packet with unicast RPF?

3 Name the two tunneling techniques under L2VPN.

4 What is the command syntax to implement unicast RPF on a router?

5 Which Layer 2 protocol parameters can be specified with Layer 2 protocol tunneling?

FAQs

Q — *Why does the router drop packets and report an exceeded rate even though the conformed rate is less than the configured rate? What Committed Access Rate (CAR) factors influence these decisions?*

A — Don't forget about the normal burst and extended burst values. A traffic policer uses them to make sure that the configured Committed Information Rate (CIR) is reached. If you want good throughput, set these values high enough. If they are configured too low, the achieved rate might be much lower than the configured rate. If you want to monitor the current burst and determine whether the displayed value is consistently close to the limit (BC) and extended limit (Be) values, issue the show **interface rate-limit** command.

Q — *What are the optimal criteria for selecting Committed Burst (BC) and Excess Burst (Be) values?*

A — Unlike a traffic shaper, a policer such as CAR does not buffer excess packets for later transmission. All it does is drop or forward the packets. To avoid unnecessary throughput degradation caused by occasional traffic bursts, you need to properly configure the normal burst and extended burst values. You can apply a rule to burst parameters that is similar to the buffering rule. The recommendation is that buffering or burst should be equal to the TCP round-trip time (RTT) multiplied by bit rate.

Table 25-2 shows the recommended formulas for calculating the normal and extended burst values.

Table 25-2 *Burst Rate Formulas*

Burst Type	Formula
Normal burst	RTT × rate
Extended burst	2 × normal burst

For example, the following calculates the burst for a TCP session with a policing rate of 64 Kbps and a TCP RTT of .15 seconds:

Burst = RTT × rate = .15 [sec] × (64000/8) [bytes/sec] = 1200 [bytes]

Extended burst = 2 × normal burst = 2 × 1200 [bytes] = 2400 [bytes]

Q — *What technologies does Cisco offer service providers so that they can supply Layer 2 services more effectively?*

A — It depends on the underlying infrastructure. If Layer 2 VPN is the prevailing service, Cisco offers a pure Layer 2 infrastructure using 802.1q VLANs and Spanning Tree Protocol for the most cost-effective solution.

For increasing network traffic, the service provider can opt for a more scalable solution based on Multiprotocol Label Switching (MPLS). L2VPN is simpler but is not scalable, unlike MPLS/IP.

PART VIII

Sample Lab Scenarios

This chapter covers the following topics:

- Practice Lab Format
- How the Master Lab compares to the CCIE Security lab exam
- CCIE Practice Lab 1: Building Layer 2
- CCIE Practice Lab 2: Routing
- CCIE Practice Lab 3: Configuring Protocol Redistribution and Dial Backup
- CCIE Practice Lab 4: Configuring Basic Security
- CCIE Practice Lab 5: Dial and Application Security
- CCIE Practice Lab 6: Configuring Advanced Security Features
- CCIE Practice Lab 7: Service Provider
- CCIE Practice Lab 8: All-Inclusive Master Lab

CHAPTER 26

Sample Lab Scenarios

You have finally come to the point in this book where you can test your readiness for the real-life CCIE Security lab exam. This chapter is not meant to provide easy answers to the fill-in-the-blank questions, nor does it serve as a cheat sheet for the exam. The goal of this chapter is to prepare you for the format of the CCIE Security lab exam through the use of seven practical labs plus one master lab that combines most of the topics covered in the other labs. If you can configure the first seven labs and the final master lab in the required amount of time by following all the rules with no extraneous assistance, you most likely will be able to undertake the "real deal" with a high degree of confidence.

No single source—including this book—can or should claim to be a one-stop solution for CCIE lab preparation. Although this chapter assumes that you have successfully read and understood all the preceding chapters, its concepts are not confined to this book only. Also, this chapter does not include every single concept discussed in the previous pages. However, this does not mean that it's safe to skip the topics that are not part of any of the practice labs. It is impossible to account for all the variables and future updates to the exam. Try to think of the practice labs in this chapter as a study guide instead of a take-home test.

After all, the point of this book is not to give away the answers, but to help you realize the complexity of the CCIE Security lab exam and serve as one of the sources you use in your studies.

To view the comprehensive directory of topics that might be included on the CCIE Security exam and other suggested printed material, visit the Cisco website at www.cisco.com/en/US/learning/ or www.cisco.com/warp/public/625/ccie/.

For a list of additional study resources, see the Appendix E, "Security-Related RFCs and Publications."

Practice Lab Format

The practice labs you see in this chapter follow the general layout of the chapters in this book. Each lab topic refers to its parent chapter, so you can easily look back for clarification. However, it is highly recommended that you rely on your own knowledge as much as possible, even if it takes you longer. Also, do not begin the master lab until you have successfully configured all the other labs. The master lab is a true test. Ideally, it would take you 8 hours to complete it—the same as the real CCIE Security lab exam.

If you don't finish the first seven training labs, you most likely would not be able to achieve the 8-hour goal of the master lab, which would result in a failing grade. However, even if your first attempt takes longer than 8 hours, keep practicing until you can meet the requirement. Each of the seven practice labs suggests a time period in which you are reasonably expected to finish it. If you are way off the mark, repeat the lab until you get close to the recommended schedule. Remember, these are all general guidelines. You are the only one who can judge your own abilities, readiness, study methods, and pace.

The seven practice labs are placed in a logical progression, starting with what is considered fairly basic and moving to the more-complex. Most of the time, each successive lab relies on the one before it for groundwork configuration. This is yet another reason why you shouldn't skip any steps. Having said this, some technologies cannot work in conjunction with some others, so they cancel each other out. There is no way of knowing which of the two conflicting technologies will be covered on the CCIE Security lab exam. Therefore, you should practice both. In such cases, you need to reconfigure some of the elements of your practice labs to make room for the new ones. While you are working on any of the practice labs, your concern is that particular lab. Don't worry about the configuration of any of the previous or following labs.

It is highly recommended that you not check the lab solutions until you are done with the labs and you want to verify your configuration, or until you've hit a roadblock and feel you can't go on unless you look up the answer to your dilemma. After you are done with each lab, you can verify the correctness of your configuration by checking the solutions on the CD-ROM included with this book.

How the Master Lab Compares to the CCIE Security Lab Exam

As noted earlier, the master lab in this book follows the same format as the real CCIE lab. Because you have only 8 hours to complete the lab, some of the components on the CCIE lab exam are preconfigured. However, the practice labs in this book are designed for individual self-study, so you are the one who will preconfigure them.

To accommodate for this discrepancy, the master lab has a prestaging section following the equipment list that lists the required preconfigured elements. During the CCIE exam, you should make a point of checking all the preconfigured elements to ensure that they are consistent and in line with the timed portion of your test. In this book's master lab, all configuration of lab equipment (except for a few devices, such as the backbone routers and Frame Relay) is included with the timed portion of the lab so that you can brush up on your typing. This forces you to think on your feet to complete all the steps in the given amount of time.

You should finish the prestaging portion before moving on to the timed part of the lab setup. Other than the configuration examples in the prestaging section, the labs do not offer any configuration solutions. This is done so that you can rely on your own wits, just like you will during the real CCIE exam.

Throughout the master lab, you are expected to maintain full functionality of all steps configured. In other words, if one configuration step breaks something that was configured earlier, you must make sure that it is fixed. This rule applies to the CCIE Security lab exam as well. This is different from the seven practice labs, in which you don't have to worry about configuring the other labs unless otherwise noted.

You might find the master lab to be more difficult in some ways than the real CCIE lab. It is not meant to scare you off. Instead, it's designed to prepare you so that you are not taken aback like so many other CCIE candidates when they realize too late that they are unprepared for the exam.

Each step in the master lab lists the number of minutes in which you can be expected to complete it. All steps combined amount to 8 hours, which is a stretch goal. Overall, if you finish the master lab in less than 10 hours, you've done well. Good luck!

TIP   The one-day lab format puts your typing skills to the test. If you are a slow typist, try practicing the alias EXEC commands for building shortcuts to the Cisco IOS software commands; otherwise, your typing speed will be a hindrance.

CCIE Practice Lab 1: Building Layer 2

Equipment List

- One Frame Relay switch: four serial ports
- Two backbone routers: one Ethernet interface
- Three lab routers: one Ethernet interface and one serial interface
- One lab router: one Ethernet interface and two serial interfaces
- One lab router: one Ethernet interface
- One lab router: two serial interfaces and one ATM interface
- One lab router: one serial interface, one ATM interface, and one Ethernet interfaces
- One reverse Telnet router: 14 asynchronous connections
- One Catalyst 3550 switch: 17 Ethernet interfaces, software release 12.1.12c-EA1a (ED); Software feature sets: C3550 EMI IOS CRYPTO IMAGE AND CMS FILES
- Two PIX Firewalls: two Ethernet interfaces, software release 6.2.2
- One ACS/Win2K CA server: one Ethernet interface, ACS server release 3.0.2

All lab routers use Cisco IOS software Releases 12.2.13b or 12.2.13T. The software feature set for both releases is IP/FW PLUS IPSEC 56. Not all physical interfaces available on lab routers and switches are used in this lab. Figure 26-1 shows the network connections diagram. 0/X numbers next to the interfaces indicate their respective switchports.

Figure 26-1 *Layer 2 Lab Topology*

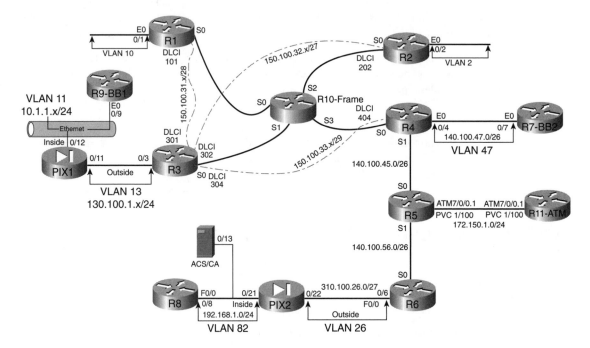

Prestaging: Configuring the Frame Relay Switch

Configure the Frame Relay switch to operate in the environment shown in Figure 26-1. This is part of the preconfigured portion of the lab. Follow Example 26-1 to set up your Frame Relay switch.

Example 26-1 *Frame Relay Switch Configuration*

```
R10#show run
version 12.2
!
hostname R10
  !
  frame-relay switching
  !
```

Example 26-1 *Frame Relay Switch Configuration (Continued)*

```
!
interface Serial0
 no ip address
 encapsulation frame-relay
 clockrate 125000
 frame-relay lmi-type ansi
 frame-relay intf-type dce
 frame-relay route 101 interface Serial1 301
!
interface Serial1
 no ip address
 encapsulation frame-relay
 clockrate 64000
 frame-relay lmi-type ansi
 frame-relay intf-type dce
 frame-relay route 301 interface Serial0 101
 frame-relay route 302 interface Serial2 202
 frame-relay route 304 interface Serial3 404
!
interface Serial2
 no ip address
 encapsulation frame-relay
 clockrate 64000
 frame-relay lmi-type ansi
 frame-relay intf-type dce
 frame-relay route 202 interface Serial1 302
!
interface Serial3
 no ip address
 encapsulation frame-relay
 clockrate 64000
 frame-relay lmi-type ansi
 frame-relay intf-type dce
 frame-relay route 404 interface Serial1 304
!
```

Prestaging: Configuring the First Backbone Router, R9-BB1

Match the configuration of the first backbone router to the output shown in Example 26-2. Configure two loopback interfaces and the Ethernet interface. Configure RIP routing and advertise the three local networks. Set up two static routes, both the default route and the route to the external network pointing to the PIX1 internal interface.

Example 26-2 *Backbone Router 1 Configuration*

```
R9#show run
version 12.2
!
hostname R9
 !
 ip subnet-zero
 no ip finger
 !
key chain lab
 key 2
  key-string ccie
!
 interface Loopback9
  ip address 9.9.9.9 255.255.255.0
  !
 interface Loopback19
  ip address 19.19.19.19 255.255.255.0
  !
 interface Ethernet0
  ip address 10.1.1.9 255.255.255.0
 ip rip authentication mode md5
 ip rip authentication key-chain lab
  no cdp enable
  !
 router rip
  version 2
  network 9.0.0.0
  network 10.0.0.0
  network 19.0.0.0
  no auto-summary
  !
router bgp 9
 bgp log-neighbor-changes
 network 9.9.9.9 mask 255.255.255.255
 network 10.1.1.0 mask 255.255.255.0
 neighbor 130.100.1.3 remote-as 1234
!
 ip classless
 ip route 130.100.1.0 255.255.255.0 10.1.1.1
 ip http server
 !
  line con 0

  transport input none
 line aux 0
 line vty 0 4
```

Prestaging: Configuring the Second Backbone Router, R7-BB2

Configure the second backbone router, R7, as shown in Example 26-3. Configure keys and name the key string ccie, because it is scrambled in the output. Configure loopback interfaces and set up BGP in autonomous system 1560. Advertise local networks via BGP and select R4 to become a peer. Use cisco as the BGP password.

Example 26-3 *Device Name Configuration*

```
R7#show run
version 12.2
!
hostname R7
 !
 ip subnet-zero
 no ip domain-lookup
 !
 key chain ccie
 key 6727
  key-string 7 03520C5951
 !
 interface Loopback1
 ip address 7.1.1.7 255.255.255.0
 !
 interface Loopback2
  ip address 17.1.1.7 255.255.255.0
 !
 interface Loopback3
  ip address 27.1.1.7 255.255.255.0
 !
 interface Loopback4
  ip address 37.1.1.7 255.255.255.0
 !
 interface Loopback100
  ip address 209.112.65.1 255.255.255.0
 !
 interface Loopback101
  ip address 209.112.66.1 255.255.255.0
 !
 interface Loopback102
  ip address 209.112.67.1 255.255.255.0
 !
 interface Loopback103
  ip address 209.112.68.1 255.255.255.0
 !
 interface Loopback104
  ip address 209.112.69.1 255.255.255.0
 !
 interface Loopback105
  ip address 209.112.70.1 255.255.255.0
```

continues

Example 26-3 *Device Name Configuration (Continued)*

```
!
interface Loopback200
 ip address 156.46.1.1 255.255.255.0
!
interface Loopback201
 ip address 156.46.2.1 255.255.255.0
!
interface Loopback202
 ip address 156.46.3.1 255.255.255.0
!
interface Loopback203
 ip address 156.46.4.1 255.255.255.0
!
interface Loopback204
 ip address 156.46.100.1 255.255.252.0
!
interface Loopback444
 ip address 140.100.9.1 255.255.255.224
!
interface Loopback777
 ip address 7.7.7.7 255.255.255.255
!
interface Loopback6727
 description Test Loopback for RIPv2
 ip address 67.67.67.1 255.255.255.0
!
interface Ethernet0
 ip address 140.100.47.7 255.255.255.192
 ip rip send version 2
 ip rip receive version 2
 ip rip authentication mode md5
 ip rip authentication key-chain ccie
!
 router rip
 version 2
 network 67.0.0.0
 network 140.100.0.0
 no auto-summary
!
router bgp 1560
 no synchronization
 bgp router-id 7.7.7.7
 bgp log-neighbor-changes
 network 7.1.1.0 mask 255.255.255.0
 network 7.7.7.7 mask 255.255.255.255
 network 17.1.1.0 mask 255.255.255.0
 network 27.1.1.0 mask 255.255.255.0
 network 37.1.1.0 mask 255.255.255.0
 network 140.100.47.0 mask 255.255.255.192
 network 156.46.1.0 mask 255.255.255.0
 network 156.46.2.0 mask 255.255.255.0
 network 156.46.3.0 mask 255.255.255.0
```

Example 26-3 *Device Name Configuration (Continued)*

```
 network 156.46.4.0 mask 255.255.255.0
 network 156.46.100.0 mask 255.255.252.0
 network 209.112.65.0
 network 209.112.66.0
 network 209.112.67.0
 network 209.112.68.0
 network 209.112.69.0
 network 209.112.70.0
 neighbor 140.100.47.4 remote-as 456
 neighbor 140.100.47.4 description R4
 neighbor 140.100.47.4 password 7 06050C28491A5D4F55
 neighbor 140.100.47.4 version 4
 no auto-summary
!
!
line con 0
line aux 0
line vty 0 4
```

Now that you've completed the preset portion of this practice lab, you can move on to the timed portion.

Lab Rules

- Follow the timed portion instructions carefully.

- Do not use any static routes or floating routes unless you're specifically told to do so.

- Propagate specific routes only when instructed.

- Do not modify the vty line configuration unless specifically instructed.

- Your reference materials include Chapters 4, 5, and 7 of this book, the Cisco Documentation CD-ROM, and any other resources you might find useful.

- It is recommended that you read through the entire lab before beginning.

- It is recommended that you make an accurate network illustration.

- Refer to Figure 26-1 to see the physical topology of the Layer 2 Lab.

Timed Portion

Complete this lab in 1 hour.

Section 1: Prepping the Lab

Step 1 Access server: Configure the reverse Telnet router so that all routers, switches, and PIX Firewalls can be accessed via reverse Telnet. Configure all devices with the password cisco.

Step 2 IP address assignment: Follow the IP address assignment guidelines for the physical interfaces shown in Figure 26-1. Configure one loopback interface for each lab router. Use the router number as the loopback interface number and its IP address byte content. For instance, R3's loopback interface should be named Loopback3, with an IP address of 3.3.3.3. Use the /24 subnet for all loopback interfaces.

Step 3 Allow for full IP reachability to all physical and loopback interfaces unless noted otherwise.

Step 4 Document your already-accomplished steps. Continue documenting further steps.

Section 2: Layer 2 Switching

Step 1 Connect R1, R2, R3, R4, R6, R7, R8, and R9, as well as PIX1, PIX2, and the ACS/CA server to the Catalyst switch.

Step 2 Associate an IP address of 192.168.100.1 with the Catalyst 3550-A VLAN82.

Step 3 Create separate VLANs for the Backbone 1 and Backbone 2 segments, as shown in Figure 26-1.

Step 4 Configure R1's Ethernet segment as VLAN10, R2's as VLAN2, R3's as VLAN13, R6's as VLAN26, and R8's as VLAN82 on the Catalyst 3550-A. Follow Figure 26-1 for VLAN assignment of the remaining devices.

Step 5 Configure a sniffer/analyzer on port 0/24 to be able to monitor all traffic on VLAN26.

Step 6 Configure a full-duplex 802.1Q trunk on port 0/5.

Step 7 Do not propagate STP for VLAN26 and VLAN13 down the trunk.

Step 8 Set the VTP password to ccie.

Step 9 Combine the 0/20 and 0/23 interfaces into an EtherChannel.

Section 3: Frame Relay

Step 1   Follow Figure 26-1 to configure the Frame Relay network. R1, R2, and R4 traffic goes through R3 unless noted otherwise.

Step 2   Configure traffic shaping on the PVC between R1 and R3 to respond to BECNs. The carrier provided is 32 kbps. The R3 local port speed is 64 kbps and the R1 local port speed is 512 kbps.

Section 4: ATM

Step 1   Configure R5 and R11, which connect back-to-back for classical IP over ATM. Make sure they can ping each other.

Step 2   Configure R5 in such a way that when it pings R11 it doesn't use Inverse ARP.

CCIE Practice Lab 2: Routing

Equipment List

- One Frame Relay switch: four serial ports
- Two backbone routers: one Ethernet interface
- Four lab routers: one Ethernet interface and one serial interface
- One lab router: one Ethernet interface
- One lab router: one Ethernet interface and two serial interfaces
- One lab router: two serial interfaces
- One reverse Telnet router: 13 asynchronous connections
- One Catalyst 3550 switch: 12 Ethernet interfaces
- Two PIX Firewalls: two Ethernet interfaces

Not all physical interfaces available on lab routers and switches are used in this lab. Figure 26-2 shows the network connections diagram. 0/*X* numbers next to the interfaces indicate their respective switchports.

Figure 26-2 *Routing Lab Configuration*

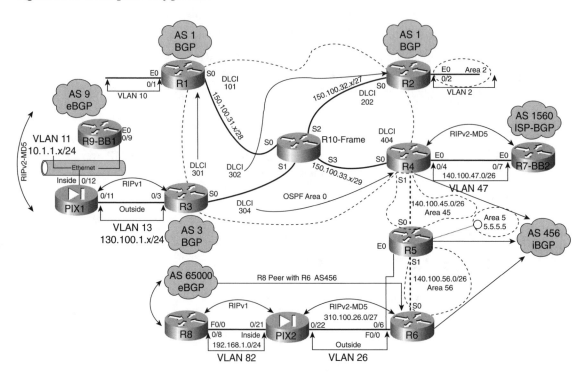

Lab Rules

- Do not begin Lab 2 until you have finished Lab 1.

- Follow the timed portion instructions carefully.

- Do not use any static routes or floating routes unless you're specifically told to do so.

- Propagate specific routes only when instructed.

- Do not modify the vty line configuration unless specifically instructed.

- Your reference materials include Chapters 8, 10, and 12 of this book, the Cisco Documentation CD-ROM, and any other resources you might find useful.

- It is recommended that you read through the entire lab before beginning.

- It is recommended that you make an accurate network illustration.

- Refer to Figure 26-2 to see the physical topology of the Routing Lab.

Timed Portion

Complete this lab in 4 hours.

Section 1: Prepping the Lab

Use the device configuration and documentation from the preceding lab. No changes need to be made. Note that not all the equipment from the preceding lab is used in this one.

Section 2: Configuring RIP

Step 1   Configure RIPv2 with MD5 authentication on R4 going to the second backbone router. Use the key information from the Backbone 2 router configuration shown previously in Example 26-3. Force R4 to send and receive only version 2 updates to and from the R7.

Step 2   Configure RIPv1 on R3's Ethernet port connecting to PIX1's outside interface. Configure RIPv2 with MD5 authentication between PIX1 and Backbone 1.

Step 3   Configure RIPv1 on R8's Ethernet port connecting to PIX2's inside interface. Configure RIPv2 with MD5 authentication between PIX2 and R6.

Section 3: Configuring OSPF

Step 1   Configure the Frame Relay network to be in OSPF Area 0.

Step 2   Configure the link between R4 and R5 to be in OSPF Area 45. The link between R5 and R6 is in OSPF Area 56.

Step 3   Modify the OSPF Hello time on R3's serial link to 65 seconds.

Step 4   Configure five loopback addresses on R3—3.3.3.3, 3.3.3.13, 3.3.3.23, 3.3.3.33, and 130.100.100.1. Add 3.3.3.3 to OSPF Area 0. Introduce 3.3.3.13 and 3.3.3.23 into OSPF without using the **network** statement. Do not include 3.3.3.33 and 130.100.100.1 in OSPF.

Step 5   Secure OSPF communication for every applicable link. Don't use clear-text authentication.

Step 6   Put R5's loopback interface 5.5.5.55/32 in OSPF Area 45. Advertise this route to all other routers except R1.

Step 7   Configure VLAN2 to be in OSPF Area 2 and to send link-state type 7s to any new OSPF routers that will appear on VLAN2.

Step 8   Configure R8 to receive all OSPF routes from R6 through PIX2. R8 should be able to ping every loopback address from R1 to R7.

Section 4: Configuring BGP

Step 1   R7 is configured to be in AS 1560, as shown in Example 26-3. R4, R5, and R6 are in autonomous system 456. Configure a secure EBGP peering from R4 to R7.

Step 2   Peer R4 with R5, and peer R5 with R6; do not configure a peer from R4 to R6. Ensure that R4, R5, and R6 are receiving the loopback routes from the second backbone router.

Step 3   Configure R4 to represent the 209.112.0.0 loopbacks as one route to the rest of the internetwork; suppress all other more-specific subnets.

Step 4   Place R8 in autonomous system 65000. Establish an EBGP peering between R8 and R6. Accommodate your configuration so that PIX2 allows the peering via a GRE tunnel. Make R8's internal IP address visible on the outside of PIX2. Ensure that R8 receives and can reach all routes from R7.

Step 5   Advertise R8's loopback without using a **network** statement. Ensure that it can be seen by all other routers.

Step 6   Configure BGP to prevent AS65000 AS-path from advertising to R7. Avoid using access lists.

Step 7   Place R1 in autonomous system 1, R2 in autonomous system 2, and R3 in autonomous system 3. Configure R1, R2, and R3 to appear as if they belong to the same autonomous system—1234. Allow R4 to receive R1's, R2's, and R3's routes from autonomous system 1234. Make sure destinations advertised by R8 and R7 (including the BGP loopbacks) can be reached by R1, R2, and R3.

Step 8   R9 is in autonomous system 9. Create a peering between R9 and its neighbor in autonomous system 3 through PIX1 without using a GRE tunnel. Use an IP address of 10.1.1.9 in R3's **neighbor** statement for autonomous system 9.

Step 9   Limit the number of prefixes received by R9 from R3 to 100.

Step 10   Make autonomous system 9 appear as autonomous system 93 to R4.

Step 11   Ensure that R9 can reach prefixes advertised by R7.

CCIE Practice Lab 3: Configuring Protocol Redistribution and Dial Backup

Equipment List

- One Frame Relay switch: four serial ports
- Two backbone routers: one Ethernet interface
- Three lab routers: one Ethernet interface and one serial interface
- One lab router: one Ethernet interface
- One lab router: one Ethernet interface and two serial interfaces
- One lab router: one Ethernet interface, one serial interface, and one ISDN interface
- One lab router: two serial interfaces and one ISDN interface
- One reverse Telnet router: 13 asynchronous connections
- One Catalyst 3550 switch: 12 Ethernet interfaces
- Two PIX Firewalls: two Ethernet interfaces

Not all physical interfaces available on lab routers and switches are used in this lab. Figure 26-3 shows the network connections diagram. 0/*X* numbers next to the interfaces indicate their respective switchports.

Lab Rules

- Do not begin Lab 3 until you have finished Labs 1 and 2.
- Follow the timed portion instructions carefully.
- Do not use any static routes or floating routes unless you're specifically told to do so.
- Propagate specific routes only when instructed.
- Do not modify the vty line configuration unless specifically instructed.
- Your reference materials include Chapters 6, 9, and 13 of this book, configuration guides, the Cisco Documentation CD-ROM, and any other resources you might find useful.
- It is recommended that you read through the entire lab before beginning.
- It is recommended that you make an accurate network illustration.
- Refer to Figure 26-3 to see the physical topology of the Redistribution Lab.

Figure 26-3 *Redistribution Lab Configuration*

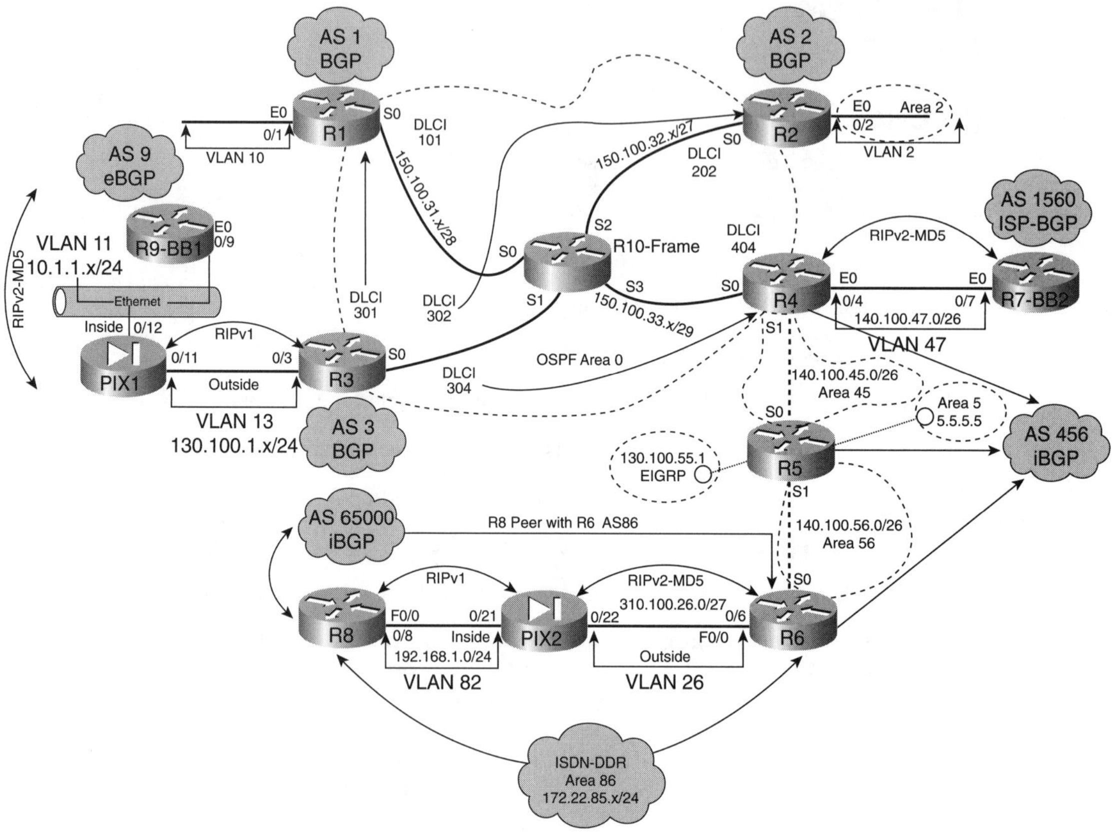

Timed Portion

Complete this lab in 4 hours.

Section 1: Prepping the Lab

Step 1 Use the device configuration and documentation from the preceding lab. Changes that need to be made are discussed in the applicable sections. Note that not all the equipment from the preceding lab is used in this one.

Step 2 Make sure that whenever you redistribute any protocols, both PIX Firewalls receive all routes and those routes are visible in the PIX routing table.

Section 2: Redistributing RIP

Step 1   On R4, redistribute routes received via RIP from R7 into OSPF.

Step 2   R6 should be able to ping R7's loopback interfaces.

Section 3: Redistributing EIGRP

Step 1   Add another loopback to R5 with an IP address of 130.100.55.1/24. Place the loopback in the EIGRP domain.

Step 2   Redistribute the EIGRP route into OSPF.

Step 3   Verify that the EIGRP address can be reached from the OSPF domain.

Step 4   All OSPF, EIGRP, and RIP routes involved in the preceding steps should be seen by R8. Ensure that R7 can reach all R8's loopbacks.

Section 4: Redistributing OSPF

Step 1   Ensure that all newly redistributed routes are visible on R3.

Step 2   Make sure that complete end-to-end connectivity exists between R8 and the two backbone routers.

Section 5: Configuring DDR with ISDN

Step 1   Add the ISDN interfaces between R6 and R8 to OSPF Area 86. R6 is allowed to place a call to R8, but not vice versa. Do not configure IP addresses on R6 and R8's BRI interfaces. Configure dial pools on R6 and R8 instead. Verify that you can ping the local ISDN interfaces before you move on.

Step 2   Configure the link to drop after 45 seconds of inactivity.

Step 3   Configure CHAP authentication between the routers with a password of cisco.

Step 4   The ISDN link should not be brought up unless the OSPF routes are lost or an OSPF topology change is detected.

CCIE Practice Lab 4: Configuring Basic Security

Equipment List

- One Frame Relay switch: four serial ports
- Two backbone routers: one Ethernet interface

- Three lab routers: one Ethernet interface and one serial interface
- Two lab routers: one Ethernet interface and two serial interfaces
- One lab router: one Ethernet interface
- One lab router: two Ethernet interfaces and one serial interface
- One reverse Telnet router: 13 asynchronous connections
- One Catalyst 3550 switch: 16 Ethernet interfaces
- Two PIX Firewalls: two Ethernet interfaces
- One HTTP/FTP server: one Ethernet interface

Not all physical interfaces available on lab routers and switches are used in this lab. Figure 26-4 shows the network connections diagram. 0/*X* numbers next to the interfaces indicate their respective switchports.

Figure 26-4 *Basic Security Lab Configuration*

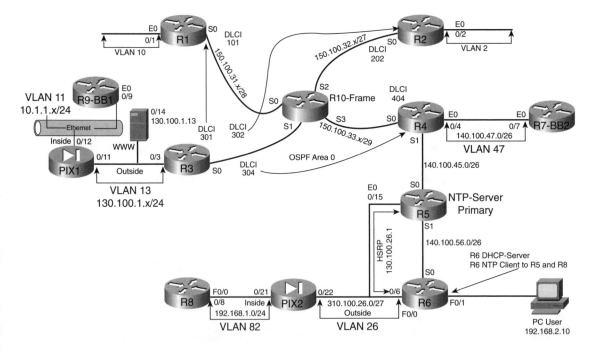

Lab Rules

- Do not begin Lab 4 until you have finished Labs 1, 2, and 3.
- Follow the timed portion instructions carefully.
- Do not use any static routes or floating routes unless you're specifically told to do so.
- Propagate specific routes only when instructed.
- Do not modify the vty line configuration unless specifically instructed.
- Your reference materials include Chapters 15, 16, and 17 of this book, the Cisco Documentation CD-ROM, and any other resources you might find useful.
- It is recommended that you read through the entire lab before beginning.
- It is recommended that you make an accurate network illustration.
- Refer to Figure 26-4 to see the physical topology of the Basic Security Lab.

Timed Portion

Complete this lab in 4 hours.

Section 1: Prepping the Lab

Use the existing configuration of all devices in the lab as your base. Make the necessary changes and additions along the way per specific instructions or as implied. Note that not all the equipment from the preceding lab is used in this one. Also, new devices are added in this lab.

Section 2: Configuring Access Control

Step 1   Prevent the loopback on R6 from reaching R1. Make sure that this network is advertised to all other routers.

Step 2   Create an outbound filter on R7, blocking only the even subnets from the loopback range of 209.112.65.1 to 209.112.70.1.

Step 3   Assume that a web server is placed on VLAN13 with an IP address of 130.100.1.13. Apply an inbound access list to R3 to allow only routing protocols, pings, and web traffic to enter the router and gain access to the server.

Step 4   Assume that an FTP server located on VLAN13 has an IP address of 130.100.1.13. Apply an access list on R3 to allow only users located on the inside of the PIX2 network access to FTP and secure web traffic. Make sure that files can be transferred properly.

Step 5   Apply an outbound list to the R2 serial interface, limiting departing traffic to routing protocols, pings, and WWW.

Step 6   Configure R6 to be able to ping all networks, but block R6 from requesting the traceroute through R5.

Section 3: IP Services

Step 1   Set up HSRP between R5 and R6. R6 should be the primary default gateway. If R6 loses its serial connection, R5's Ethernet0 interface becomes the default gateway. Make HSRP secure.

Step 2   Configure R6 as a DHCP server. Configure the router to allow hosts on its Ethernet segment to resolve their IP addresses from the DHCP server.

Step 3   Configure R6 such that when a user Telnets to R6 using R6's IP address, the user actually accesses R5.

Step 4   Set up R8 so that when user admin Telnets to it, the user can enter only **show start**, **show ip route**, and **telnet** commands.

Step 5   Set up R8 as the HTTP server and the FTP client.

Step 6   Configure R5 for a secure Telnet session. Verify the success of your configuration using R6.

Step 7   Set up R8 as a DRP Server Agent. Use ccie as an authentication key chain. Limit the agent's response to DRP quires from R6.

Step 8   Disable ICMP redirects on R6. Disable domain lookups. Disable ICMP mask reply. Disable proxy ARP.

Step 9   Disable the CDP service on R6 for all interfaces using a single command.

Step 10   Set up R6 so that only the host 192.168.1.10 can view this router's management statistics.

Section 4: Catalyst Security

Step 1   Configure the Catalyst 3550-A so that only R3 and R8 can Telnet to it.

Step 2   Configure port 0/19 on the switch as secure. Set the maximum value to 10.

Step 3   Exercise storm control on port 0/18.

CCIE Practice Lab 5: Dial and Application Security

Equipment List

- One lab router: one Ethernet interface

- One lab router: one serial interface and one ISDN interface

- One lab router: two Ethernet interfaces and one serial interface

- One lab router: one ISDN interface

- One reverse Telnet router: six asynchronous connections

- One Catalyst 3550 switch: seven Ethernet interfaces

- One PIX Firewall: two Ethernet interfaces

- One ACS server: one Ethernet interface

- One PC: one Ethernet interface, Cisco Systems VPN Client 3000 (version 3.6.3)

Not all physical interfaces available on lab routers and switches are used in this lab. Figure 26-5 shows the network connections diagram. 0/*X* numbers next to the interfaces indicate their respective switchports.

Lab Rules

- Do not begin Lab 5 until you have finished Labs 1, 2, 3, and 4.

- Follow the timed portion instructions carefully.

- Do not use any static routes or floating routes unless you're specifically told to do so.

- Propagate specific routes only when instructed.

- Do not modify the vty line configuration unless specifically instructed.

- Your reference materials include Chapters 6, 18, 19, 21, and 23 of this book, the Cisco Documentation CD-ROM, and any other resources you might find useful.

- It is recommended that you read through the entire lab before beginning.

- It is recommended that you make an accurate network illustration.

- Refer to Figure 26-5 to see the physical topology of the Dial and Application Security Lab.

Figure 26-5 *Dial and Application Security Lab Configuration*

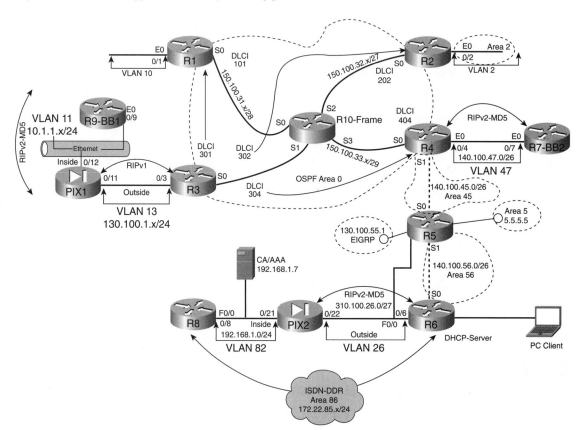

Timed Portion

Complete this lab in 11 hours.

Section 1: Prepping the Lab

Use the existing configuration of all devices in the lab as your base. Make the necessary changes and additions along the way per specific instructions or as implied. Note that not all the equipment from the preceding labs is used in this one. Also, new devices are added to this lab.

Section 2: AAA Using RADIUS

Step 1   Configure the ACS server to run RADIUS services. Use user1 as a username, cisco as a key, and R8's loopback address as a source for authentication.

Step 2   Set up R8 to authenticate against the RADIUS server.

Step 3   Permit a user to issue pings, access global configuration mode, and configure an SNMP server on R8.

Step 4   Create an authentication list with an appropriate method, and apply it to R8's console line.

Step 5   Configure authorization on R8 to allow the assigned permissions. Make your last authorization method allow unrestricted user entrance to the shell if all other methods fail. Do not use "none."

Step 6   Configure accounting on R8 to record user activity from the time of login until the time of logout. Verify that the accounting records are functioning on the ACS server.

Section 3: Configuring AAA on the PIX Firewall

Step 1   Configure TACACS+ services on VLAN82's ACS server. Specify PIX2 as a client. Assign user2 to a group. Use cisco6727 as the key. Authorize the use of Shell. Do not restrict command privileges.

Step 2   On PIX2, set up matching criteria for authentication, authorization, and accounting based on Telnet and WWW traffic regardless of source or destination.

Step 3   Identify the TACACS+ server on PIX2 and point to it for all AAA services. Configure all console authentication options. Configure authentication, authorization, and accounting to refer to the matching criteria specified earlier.

Step 4   Limit Telnet access to PIX2 to hosts on the network 192.168.1.0 using cisco6727 as a password.

Step 5   Change all three login prompts for Telnet users to reflect your personality.

Step 6   Configure PIX2 to accept SSH sessions from hosts 192.168.1.100 and 192.168.1.1.

Section 4: Configuring VPN Client Remote Access

Step 1   Configure PIX2 for IPSec negotiations for a VPN client.

Step 2   Configure a VPN client to authenticate against the TACACS+ server.

Step 3   Make sure that the client can reach the private network behind the PIX2 Firewall.

Section 5: Authentication Proxy with TACACS+

Step 1 Configure the TACACS+ server to allow R6 to act as the authentication proxy.

Step 2 Configure AAA services for authentication proxy on R6 so that they all refer to the TACACS+ server for necessary information and resources.

Step 3 Allow all system activity to be captured by the AAA server from beginning to end.

Step 4 Enable an authentication proxy named auth on R6. Force user authentication entries to be removed after an inactivity period of 5 minutes. Be sure that no conflicting services are enabled, causing authentication to fail.

Step 5 Verify that your configuration is working properly by attempting to authenticate through R6.

Section 6: Privilege Levels with TACACS+

Step 1 Enable R6's Telnet interface to permit login by trying the TACACS+ server first, then the local database, and, finally, the line password. All other requests for authentication should go through the TACACS+ server.

Step 2 Configure authorized users to have access to either the highest or the intermediate control level.

Step 3 Allow users at the intermediate level to configure an SNMP server, save the configuration, and view the saved configuration. Remember that all authorization decisions should come from the TACACS+ server.

Step 4 Configure all types of accounting to monitor user activity from beginning to end. Do not monitor activity of users who do not have usernames associated with them. For all other users, configure accounting information to be sent every 4 minutes.

Section 7: PPP Callback with TACACS+

Step 1 In this scenario, R6 is a client, and R8 is a server.

Step 2 Configure the TACACS+ server to allow callback. Specify the telephone number on the TACACS+ server.

Step 3 Use the TACACS+ server for all AAA services, including those that are callback-related.

Step 4 Make sure that all activity is recorded.

Step 5 Use appropriate debugs to verify whether the callback is working.

Section 8: Configuring the VPDN to Work with Local AAA

Step 1   Configure R3 as a dialup client. Assign it a username and domain name of your choice.

Step 2   Configure R5 as a LAC. Keep in mind that you will set up R8 as the LNS in the next step. Accommodate the VPDN portion of your configuration for local authentication. Configure a general set of rules to be applied to all specific VPDN instances on the router. Choose L2TP as the tunneling protocol. Configure local authentication and authorization for the tunnel.

Step 3   Make sure that the configuration of PIX2 allows the L2TP tunnel to be established.

Step 4   Configure R8 behind PIX2 as the LNS. Use local AAA to authenticate the tunnel and the user. Assign a range of 11 possible IP addresses for the client. Create a loopback interface with an IP address of 192.168.100.1 to be used by the virtual-access interface.

Step 5   Execute the appropriate debugs to verify that the access VPN works properly.

Section 9: Configuring TACACS+ Authentication and Accounting for VPDN

Step 1   Reconfigure the LAC and LNS to query the remote AAA server for the VPDN authentication and accounting tasks. Modify R5's and R8's configuration to point to the TACACS+ server for client and tunnel authentication.

Step 2   Configure the TACACS+ server to authenticate the tunnel and the user.

Step 3   Make sure that R5 can ping 192.168.1.1.

Section 10: Configuring PIX2 to Use PPTP

Step 1   Modify the PIX2 configuration to enable PPTP.

Step 2   Have the client authenticate against the TACACS+ server. Assign a range of 50 possible IP addresses for the client.

CCIE Practice Lab 6: Configuring Advanced Security Features

Equipment List

- One Frame Relay switch: four serial ports
- Two backbone routers: one Ethernet interface
- Three lab routers: one Ethernet interface and one serial interface
- One lab router: one Ethernet interface
- One lab router: one Ethernet interface and two serial interfaces
- One lab router: one Ethernet interface, one serial interface, and one ISDN interface
- One lab router: two serial interfaces and one ISDN interface
- One reverse Telnet router: 13 asynchronous connections
- One Catalyst 3550 switch: 14 Ethernet interfaces
- Two PIX Firewalls: two Ethernet interfaces
- One ACS server: one Ethernet interface
- One IDS/Syslog server: one Ethernet interface

Not all physical interfaces available on lab routers and switches are used in this lab. Figure 26-6 shows the network connections diagram. 0/X numbers next to the interfaces indicate their respective switchports.

Lab Rules

- Do not begin Lab 6 until you have finished Labs 1, 2, 3, 4, and 5.
- Follow the timed portion instructions carefully.
- Do not use any static routes or floating routes unless you're specifically told to do so.
- Propagate specific routes only when instructed.
- Do not modify the vty line configuration unless specifically instructed.
- Your reference materials include Chapters 6, 19, 20, 22, 23, and 24 of this book, the Cisco Documentation CD-ROM, and any other resources you might find useful.
- It is recommended that you read through the entire lab before beginning.
- It is recommended that you make an accurate network illustration.
- Refer to Figure 26-6 to see the physical topology of the Advanced Security Lab.

Figure 26-6 *Advanced Security Lab Configuration*

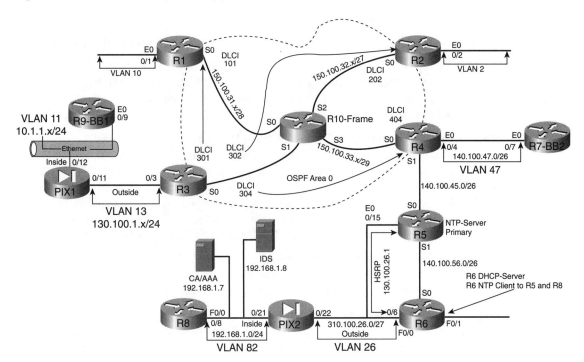

Timed Portion

Complete this lab in 11 hours.

Section 1: Prepping the Lab

Use the existing configuration from the other labs. Make the necessary changes and additions along the way per specific instructions or as implied. Note that not all the equipment from the previous labs is used in this one.

Section 2: Configuring IOS Firewall

Step 1   Configure address translation on R6 as if you have only one available IP address. Choose the best method to use only an IP address of your S0 interface to make NAT work. Everything from the 130.100.26.x network must be translated into 140.100.56.6. For example:

— WWW server 130.100.26.10

— Telnet server 130.100.26.11

— FTP server 130.100.26.12

Configure R6 such that all these services can be reached from the outside using a single IP address.

Step 2 On R6, configure CBAC to inspect TCP, UDP, FTP, HTTP, and SMTP traffic. Apply the configuration to the FastEthernet0/0 interface. Make sure that ICMP traffic can get through.

Step 3 On R8, configure CBAC for all TCP and HTTP traffic to be inspected. Configure max half open sessions to be 950. Configure min half open sessions to be 300. Configure Max incomplete half open sessions per host to not go over 132. In case of a violation, configure a 15-minute lockout. Configure the DNS timeout to be 50 seconds. Allow Java applets from Loopback8's network. Set the idle timeout for TCP connections to 130 seconds. The access list and CBAC should be applied on Ethernet0.

Step 4 Configure Loopback12 on R2 with an IP address of 121.121.121.121. Configure Loopback12 on R1 with the same IP address. Configure the two routers so that both Loopback12 interfaces can communicate and ping one another.

Step 5 Configure R6 to deny HTTP traffic Monday through Friday between the hours of 8 a.m. and 6 p.m. Allow UDP traffic on Saturday and Sunday from noon to 8 p.m. only.

Step 6 Configure an extended access list to allow only R1 and R2 networks to Telnet to R6. Make sure all other processes aren't interrupted.

Section 3: PIX Firewall

Step 1 ICMP echo replies should return to PIX1's inside network.

Step 2 Assume that there is a host on an inside network of PIX1 with an IP address of 192.168.1.192. Make the host's IP address appear on the outside as is.

Step 3 Configure the PIX2 outside interface to disregard pings without using an access list.

Step 4 When PIX2 inside hosts request FTP, POP, or HTTP services, speed up the response to their requests.

Step 5 Configure both PIX Firewalls to block Java and ActiveX applets from outside networks.

Step 6 Configure PIX2 to send critical/monitor alerts and history emergencies to syslog server 192.168.1.7.

Step 7   Configure PIX2 to allow only one SNMP workstation to view stats on the PIX.

Step 8   Configure NTP/MD5 authentication on PIX2.

Step 9   Prevent PIX2 from allowing IP spoofing on the outside.

Step 10   When configuring your mail server, configure PIX2 to not respond to DATA, HELO, MAIL, NOOP, QUIT, RCPT, and RSET. Configure all necessary components so that anyone can send e-mail to a mail server behind PIX2 with an inside IP address of 192.168.1.125.

Step 11   Configure PAT translation on PIX1.

Step 12   Configure the PIX2 firewall to retrieve its configurations and software images from a centralized location with an IP address of 192.168.1.100.

Step 13   Configure PIX2 such that, when users on the inside network boot their machines, they get the dynamic IP address and WINS, DNS, and default gateway information assigned by PIX2.

Section 4: Cisco IOS IDS

Step 1   Assume that an IDS sensor is placed on the PIX2 internal segment with an IP address of 192.168.1.8. Make sure PIX2 allows the IDS traffic through.

Step 2   Configure IDS on R6. Specify the NetRanger organization ID as 6666, sensor ID as 43, and Director ID as 123.

Step 3   Send messages to Syslog and Director at 192.168.1.8.

Step 4   Monitor everything coming from the 140.100.x.x network.

Step 5   Configure the notification queue size to be 180.

Step 6   Audit signatures that are triggered by an e-mail with a suspiciously large number of recipients.

Step 7   Disable signatures that are triggered on the very common smail attack against e-mail servers.

Step 8   Disable signatures that are triggered when any IP datagram is received with an offset value less than 5 but greater than 0.

Step 9   Disable signatures caused by the ping-of-death attack.

Step 10   Configure TCP connections to reset upon info and attack.

Section 5: IPSec VPN

Step 1 Assume that a DHCP server is located on the same segment as R8's FastEthernet0/0 interface. Configure R8 to dynamically assign an IP address to itself without applying it manually.

Step 2 Configure loopback networks 11.11.11.x and 12.12.12.x on R1 and R2, respectively, so that they discover IPSec endpoints without explicitly stating the peer's IP address, as in **crypto isakmp key cisco address x.x.x.x**. Make sure that only 11.11.11.11 and 12.12.12.12 trigger IPSec tunnel and discovery events.

Step 3 Configure a full mesh between R3, R4, R6, and R8:

- R3 loopback 13.13.13.13

- R4 loopback 14.14.14.14

- R6 loopback 16.16.16.16

- R8 loopback 18.18.18.18 to be encrypted across the network

Use the following guidelines for your configuration:

- isakmp

- Preshared authentication with ccie key

- md5 hash

- isakmp lifetime 2000 seconds

- des-esp and des-sha-hmac transform set

- Configure IPSec in a transport mode

Step 4 Make sure that only these loopbacks trigger IPSec negotiations.

Step 5 Configure a fully meshed GRE tunnel between the routers from Step 2 and route their private loopbacks through that tunnel. Use EIGRP for routing. Make sure all these loopbacks can ping one another.

Step 6 Make sure that R6, R8, and R4 can ping each others' loopbacks that are being encrypted through R3. Make appropriate changes to PIX2 to allow for this.

Section 6: DDR-IPSEC

Step 1 Make sure that in case of a failure, ISDN becomes active with all IPSec encryption and is still operational.

Step 2   Configure PIX1 IPSec to PIX2 to encrypt the inside network. Make sure that the inside networks can ping each other. Use the most common encryption method.

Section 7: IPSec VPN with CA

Step 1   Configure PIX2 NTP/MD5 as a client to R8.

Step 2   Configure PIX2 to receive a digital certificate from the CA server. Use the following guidelines for your configuration:

      — isakmp

      — rsa-sig authentication

      — md5 hash

      — des-esp transform set

Step 3   Configure R5 to receive a digital certificate from the CA server.

Step 4   Make sure that R5 and PIX2 are enrolled with the CA and are using it to establish IPSec. Verify whether R5's loopback 15.15.15.15 can ping 192.168.1.8 (R8's FastEthernet0/0).

CCIE Practice Lab 7: Service Provider

Equipment List

- Two lab routers: one Ethernet interface
- One lab router: one serial interface
- One lab router: two Ethernet interfaces and one serial interface
- One reverse Telnet router: six asynchronous connections
- Two Catalyst 3550 switches: two Ethernet interfaces

Not all physical interfaces available on lab routers and switches are used in this lab. Figure 26-7 shows the network connections diagram.

Figure 26-7 *Service Provider Lab Configuration*

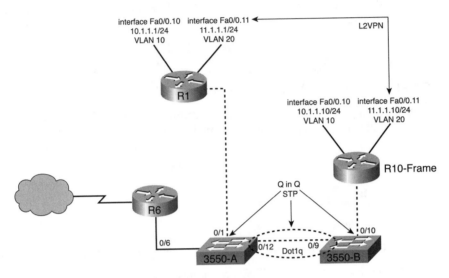

Lab Rules

- Do not begin Lab 7 until you have finished Labs 1, 2, 3, 4, 5, and 6.

- Follow the timed portion instructions carefully.

- Do not use any static routes or floating routes unless you're specifically told to do so.

- Propagate specific routes only when instructed.

- Do not modify the vty line configuration unless specifically instructed.

- Your reference materials include Chapters 4, 15, 17, and 25 of this book, configuration guides, the Cisco Documentation CD-ROM, and any other resources you might find useful.

- It is recommended that you read through the entire lab before beginning.

- It is recommended that you make an accurate network illustration.

- Refer to Figure 26-7 to see the physical topology of the Service Provider Lab.

Timed Portion

Complete this lab in 4.5 hours.

Section 1: Prepping the Lab

Use the existing configuration of all devices in the lab as your base. Make necessary changes and additions along the way per specific instructions or as implied. Note that not all the equipment from the previous labs is used in this one. Also, new devices are added to this lab.

Section 2: QoS

Step 1 Configure R6 serial 0/0 to prevent DoS TCP SYN Attacks to R6 from the outside.

Step 2 Configure an access list to block all outside network addresses that could possibly be used to hack your network. (See RFC 2267 or RFC 2827.)

Step 3 Limit the ICMP rate to approximately 500 kbps on R6's serial 0/0 interface.

Step 4 Guarantee all secure web traffic a bandwidth of approximately 300 kbps going out of R6.

Section 3: L2VPN

Step 1 On R1 and R10, configure subinterfaces to belong to VLAN10 and VLAN20. Assign at least one subinterface of each router to each VLAN.

Step 2 The subinterfaces of both routers should be able to reach each other over 3550-A and 3550-B.

Step 3 Configure your switching such that neither switch has knowledge of VLAN10 and VLAN20.

Step 4 Verify your configuration by making sure that VLAN10 and VLAN20 on R1 can reach their counterparts on R10.

CCIE Practice Lab 8: All-Inclusive Master Lab

Equipment List

- One Frame Relay switch: four serial ports
- Two backbone routers: one Ethernet interface
- Three lab routers: one Ethernet interface and one serial interface

- One lab router: one Ethernet interface and two serial interfaces
- One lab router: one Ethernet interface, two serial interfaces, and one ATM interface
- One lab router: two Ethernet interfaces, one serial interface, and one BRI interface
- One lab router: one Ethernet interface and one BRI interface
- One lab router: one ATM interface
- One reverse Telnet router: 16 asynchronous connections
- One Catalyst 3550 switch: 24 Ethernet interfaces
- One Catalyst 3550 switch: two Ethernet interfaces
- Two PIX Firewalls: two Ethernet interfaces
- One ACS/CA server: one Ethernet interface
- One HTTP/FTP server: one Ethernet interface
- One PC: one Ethernet interface

The following list specifies the software versions used for this practice lab:

- Cisco IOS Software release 12.2.13b or 12.2.13T. The software feature set for both releases is IP/FW PLUS IPSEC 56.
- Catalyst 3550 Software release: 12.1.12c-EA1a (ED); Software feature sets: C3550 EMI IOS CRYPTO IMAGE AND CMS FILES
- PIX Firewall Software release 6.2.2
- ACS Server release 3.0.2
- Cisco Systems VPN Client 3000 (version 3.6.3)

Prestaging: Configuring the Frame Relay Switch

Configure the Frame Relay switch to operate in the environment shown in Figure 26-8. This is part of the preconfigured portion of the lab. Follow Example 26-4 to set up your Frame Relay switch.

Figure 26-8 *Frame Relay Switch Configuration*

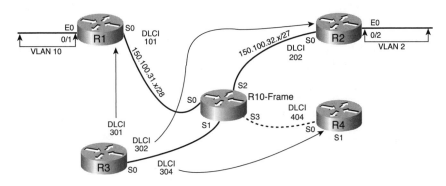

Example 26-4 *Frame Relay Switch Configuration*

```
R10#show run
version 12.2
!
hostname R10
 !
 !
 frame-relay switching
 !
 !
 interface Serial0
  no ip address
  encapsulation frame-relay
  clockrate 125000
  frame-relay lmi-type ansi
  frame-relay intf-type dce
  frame-relay route 101 interface Serial1 301
 !
 interface Serial1
  no ip address
  encapsulation frame-relay
  clockrate 64000
  frame-relay lmi-type ansi
  frame-relay intf-type dce
  frame-relay route 301 interface Serial0 101
  frame-relay route 302 interface Serial2 202
  frame-relay route 304 interface Serial3 404
 !
 interface Serial2
  no ip address
  encapsulation frame-relay
  clockrate 64000
```

continues

Example 26-4 *Frame Relay Switch Configuration (Continued)*

```
  frame-relay lmi-type ansi
  frame-relay intf-type dce
  frame-relay route 202 interface Serial1 302
 !
interface Serial3
 no ip address
 encapsulation frame-relay
 clockrate 64000
 frame-relay lmi-type ansi
 frame-relay intf-type dce
 frame-relay route 404 interface Serial1 304
 !
```

Prestaging: Configuring the First Backbone Router, R7-BB1

Match the configuration of the first backbone router to the output shown in Example 26-5.
Configure two loopback interfaces and the Ethernet interface. Configure RIP routing, and
advertise the three local networks. Set up two static routes—the default route and the route
to the external network pointing to the PIX1 internal interface.

Example 26-5 *Backbone Router 1 Configuration*

```
R9#show run
version 12.2
!
hostname R9
 !
 ip subnet-zero
 no ip finger
 !
 no ip dhcp-client network-discovery
 !
key chain lab
 key 2
  key-string ccie
!
 interface Loopback9
  ip address 9.9.9.9 255.255.255.0
  !
 interface Loopback19
  ip address 19.19.19.19 255.255.255.0
  !
 interface Ethernet0
  ip address 10.1.1.9 255.255.255.0
  ip rip authentication mode md5
  ip rip authentication key-chain lab
  no cdp enable
  !
 router rip
```

Example 26-5 *Backbone Router 1 Configuration (Continued)*

```
      version 2
      network 9.0.0.0
      network 10.0.0.0
      network 19.0.0.0
      no auto-summary
      !
 router bgp 9
  bgp log-neighbor-changes
  network 9.9.9.9 mask 255.255.255.255
  network 10.1.1.0 mask 255.255.255.0
  neighbor 130.100.1.3 remote-as 1234
 !
  ip classless
  ip route 130.100.1.0 255.255.255.0 10.1.1.1
  ip http server
  !
   line con 0
   transport input none
  line aux 0
  line vty 0 4
  !
```

Prestaging: Configuring the Second Backbone Router, R7-BB2

Configure the second backbone router, R7, as shown in Example 26-6. Configure keys and name the key string ccie, because it is scrambled in the output. Configure loopback interfaces and set up BGP in autonomous system 1560. Advertise local networks via BGP, and select R4 to become a peer. Use cisco as the password in BGP.

Example 26-6 *Device Name Configuration*

```
R7#show run
version 12.2
!
hostname R7
 !
 ip subnet-zero
 no ip domain-lookup
 !
 key chain ccie
 key 6727
  key-string 7 03520C5951
 !
 interface Loopback1
 ip address 7.1.1.7 255.255.255.0
 !
```

continues

Example 26-6 *Device Name Configuration (Continued)*

```
interface Loopback2
 ip address 17.1.1.7 255.255.255.0
!
interface Loopback3
 ip address 27.1.1.7 255.255.255.0
!
interface Loopback4
 ip address 37.1.1.7 255.255.255.0
!
interface Loopback100
 ip address 209.112.65.1 255.255.255.0
!
interface Loopback101
 ip address 209.112.66.1 255.255.255.0
!
interface Loopback102
 ip address 209.112.67.1 255.255.255.0
!
interface Loopback103
 ip address 209.112.68.1 255.255.255.0
!
interface Loopback104
 ip address 209.112.69.1 255.255.255.0
!
interface Loopback105
 ip address 209.112.70.1 255.255.255.0
!
interface Loopback200
 ip address 156.46.1.1 255.255.255.0
!
interface Loopback201
 ip address 156.46.2.1 255.255.255.0
!
interface Loopback202
 ip address 156.46.3.1 255.255.255.0
!
interface Loopback203
 ip address 156.46.4.1 255.255.255.0
!
interface Loopback204
 ip address 156.46.100.1 255.255.252.0
!
interface Loopback444
 ip address 140.100.9.1 255.255.255.224
!
interface Loopback777
 ip address 7.7.7.7 255.255.255.255
!
interface Loopback6727
 description Test Loopback for RIPv2
 ip address 67.67.67.1 255.255.255.0
```

Example 26-6 *Device Name Configuration (Continued)*

```
!
interface Ethernet0
 ip address 140.100.47.7 255.255.255.192
 ip rip send version 2
 ip rip receive version 2
 ip rip authentication mode md5
 ip rip authentication key-chain ccie
!
router rip
 version 2
 network 67.0.0.0
 network 140.100.0.0
 no auto-summary
!
router bgp 1560
 no synchronization
 bgp router-id 7.7.7.7
 bgp log-neighbor-changes
 network 7.1.1.0 mask 255.255.255.0
 network 7.7.7.7 mask 255.255.255.255
 network 17.1.1.0 mask 255.255.255.0
 network 27.1.1.0 mask 255.255.255.0
 network 37.1.1.0 mask 255.255.255.0
 network 140.100.47.0 mask 255.255.255.192
 network 156.46.1.0 mask 255.255.255.0
 network 156.46.2.0 mask 255.255.255.0
 network 156.46.3.0 mask 255.255.255.0
 network 156.46.4.0 mask 255.255.255.0
 network 156.46.100.0 mask 255.255.252.0
 network 209.112.65.0
 network 209.112.66.0
 network 209.112.67.0
 network 209.112.68.0
 network 209.112.69.0
 network 209.112.70.0
 neighbor 140.100.47.4 remote-as 456
 neighbor 140.100.47.4 description R4
 neighbor 140.100.47.4 password 7 06050C28491A5D4F55
 neighbor 140.100.47.4 version 4
 no auto-summary
!
line con 0
line aux 0
line vty 0 4
```

Prestaging: Configuring the Reverse Telnet Router

Configure the reverse Telnet router so that all routers, switches, and PIX Firewalls can be accessed via reverse Telnet. Configure all devices with the password cisco. Follow Example 26-7 for access server configuration.

Example 26-7 *Access Server Configuration*

```
RAS#show run
hostname RAS
!
ip host r3 2003 1.1.1.1
ip host r6 2006 1.1.1.1
ip host r5 2005 1.1.1.1
ip host r4 2004 1.1.1.1
ip host pix2 2016 1.1.1.1
ip host pix1 2015 1.1.1.1
ip host r10 2010 1.1.1.1
ip host r9 2009 1.1.1.1
ip host r8 2008 1.1.1.1
ip host r7 2007 1.1.1.1
ip host r2 2002 1.1.1.1
ip host r1 2001 1.1.1.1
ip host CAT3550A 2011 1.1.1.1
ip host CAT3550B 2012 1.1.1.1
!
!
interface Loopback0
ip address 1.1.1.1 255.255.255.255
!
line con 0
 exec-timeout 0 0
 privilege level 15
line 1 16
 no exec
 no exec-banner
 exec-timeout 0 0
 exec-character-bits 8
 transport input all
line aux 0
line vty 0 4
 exec-timeout 0 0
 privilege level 15
 password cisco
 no login
!
end
```

Now that you've completed the prestaging portion of the lab, you can move on to the next timed portion that you are actually being tested on.

Lab Rules

- Follow the instructions carefully.

- Wipe out all configurations left over from the practice labs.

- Do not use any static routes or floating routes unless you're specifically told to do so.

- Propagate specific routes only when instructed.

- Do not modify the vty line configuration unless specifically instructed.

- Your only available reference material is the Cisco Documentation CD-ROM. Do not consult anyone or anything other than the mentioned resources.

- It is recommended that you read through the entire lab before beginning.

- It is recommended that you make an accurate network illustration.

Figure 26-9 shows the physical topology of the Master Lab.

Figure 26-9 *Master Lab Physical Layout*

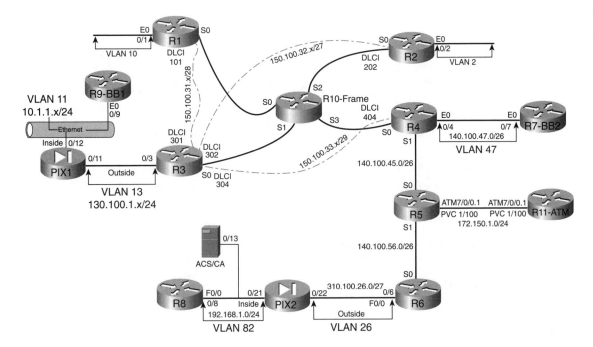

Timed Portion

Complete this lab in 8 hours.

Section 1: Beginning Configuration (6 Minutes)

Step 1   IP address assignment: Follow the IP address assignment guidelines for physical interfaces shown in Figure 26-2. Configure one loopback interface for each lab router. Use the router number as the loopback interface number and its IP address byte content. For instance, R3's loopback interface should be named Loopback3, with an IP address of 3.3.3.3. Use the /24 subnet for all loopback interfaces. (6 minutes)

Step 2   Allow for full IP reachability to all physical and loopback interfaces unless noted otherwise.

Step 3   Document the already-accomplished steps. Continue documenting further steps.

Section 2: Layer 2 Switching (15 Minutes)

Step 1   Connect R1, R2, R3, R4, R5, R6, R7, R8, and R9, as well as PIX1, PIX2, and the ACS/CA server, to the Catalyst switch. (5 minutes)

Step 2   Associate an IP address of 192.168.100.1 with the Catalyst 3550-A VLAN82. (1 minute)

Step 3   Create separate VLANs for Backbone 1 and Backbone 2 segments, as shown in Figure 26-9. (2 minutes)

Step 4   Configure R1's Ethernet segment as VLAN10, R2's as VLAN2, R3's as VLAN13, R5's and R6's as VLAN26, and R8's as VLAN82 on the Catalyst 3550-A. Refer to Figure 26-1 for VLAN assignment of the remaining devices. (4 minutes)

Step 5   Configure a sniffer/analyzer on port 0/24 to monitor all traffic on VLAN26. (2 minutes)

Step 6   Set the VTP password to ccie. (1 minute)

Section 3: Frame Relay (5 Minutes)

Refer to Figure 26-8 to configure the Frame Relay network. R1, R2, and R4 traffic goes through R3 unless noted otherwise.

Section 4: ATM (3 Minutes)

Configure R5 and R11, which connect back-to-back for classical IP over ATM. Configure R5 in such a way that when it pings R11 it doesn't use Inverse ARP. Make sure they can ping each other.

Section 5: RIP (17 Minutes)

Step 1   Configure RIPv2 with MD5 authentication on R4 going to the second backbone router. Use the key information from the R7-BB2 router configuration shown in Example 26-6. Force R4 to send and receive only version 2 updates to and from R7. (5 minutes)

Step 2   Configure RIPv1 on R3's Ethernet port connecting to PIX1's outside interface. Configure RIPv2 with MD5 authentication between PIX1 and R9-BB1. (6 minutes)

Step 3   Configure RIPv1 on R8's Ethernet port connecting to PIX2's inside interface. Configure RIPv2 with MD5 authentication between PIX2 and R6. (6 minutes)

Section 6: OSPF (23 Minutes)

Step 1   Configure the Frame Relay network to be in OSPF Area 0. (5 minutes)

Step 2   Configure the link between R4 and R5 to be in OSPF Area 45. The link between R5 and R6 is in OSPF Area 56. Make sure all routes are visible to and from Area 0. (8 minutes)

Step 3   Configure five loopback addresses on R3—3.3.3.3, 3.3.3.13, 3.3.3.23, 3.3.3.33, and 130.100.100.1. Add 3.3.3.3 to OSPF Area 0. Introduce 3.3.3.13 and 3.3.3.23 into OSPF without using the **network** statement. Do not include 3.3.3.33 and 130.100.100.1 in OSPF. (2 minutes)

Step 4   Configure MD5 authentication of all OSPF neighbor adjacencies. (8 minutes)

Section 7: BGP (43 Minutes)

Step 1   R7 is configured to be in autonomous system 1560, as shown in Example 26-6. R4, R5, and R6 are in autonomous system 456. Configure a secure EBGP peering from R4 to R7. (5 minutes)

Step 2   Peer R4 with R5, and peer R5 with R6; do not configure a peer from R4 to R6. Ensure that R4, R5, and R6 are receiving the loopback routes from the second backbone router. (5 minutes)

Step 3 Configure R4 to represent the 209.112.0.0 loopbacks as one route to the rest of the internetwork; suppress all other more-specific subnets. (2 minutes)

Step 4 Place R8 in autonomous system 65000. Establish an EBGP peering between R8 and R6. Accommodate your configuration so that PIX2 allows the peering via a GRE tunnel. Make R8's internal IP address visible on the outside of PIX2. Ensure that R8 receives and can reach all routes from R7. (10 minutes)

Step 5 Advertise R8's loopback without using a **network** statement. Ensure that it can be seen by all other routers. (1 minute)

Step 6 Configure BGP to prevent AS65000 AS-path from advertising to R7. Avoid using access lists. (1 minute)

Step 7 Place R1 in autonomous system 1, R2 in autonomous system 2, and R3 in autonomous system 3. Configure R1, R2, and R3 to appear as if they belong to the same autonomous system—1234. Allow R4 to receive R1's, R2's, and R3's routes from autonomous system 1234. Make sure destinations advertised by R8 and R7 (including the BGP loopbacks) can be reached by R1, R2, and R3. (6 minutes)

Step 8 R9 is in autonomous system 9. Create a peering between R9 and its neighbor in autonomous system 3 through PIX1 without using a GRE tunnel. Use an IP address of 10.1.1.9 in R3's **neighbor** statement for autonomous system 9. (8 minutes)

Step 9 Limit the number of prefixes received by R9 from R3 to 100. (1 minute)

Step 10 Make autonomous system 9 appear as autonomous system 93 to R4. Ensure that R9 can reach prefixes advertised by R7 and R8, including all summarized loopbacks. (4 minutes)

Section 8: Redistributing Protocols (5 Minutes)

On R4, redistribute routes received via RIP from R7 into OSPF. R6 should be able to ping R7's loopback interfaces.

Section 9: ISDN and DDR (10 Minutes)

Step 1 Add the ISDN interfaces between R6 and R8 to OSPF Area 86. R6 is allowed to place a call to R8, but not vice versa. Do not configure IP addresses on R6's and R8's BRI interfaces. Configure dial pools on R6 and R8 instead. Verify that you can ping the local ISDN interfaces before you move on. Configure the link to drop after 45 seconds of inactivity. Configure CHAP authentication with a password of cisco between the routers. R3 should not make a call unless the OSPF routes are lost or an OSPF topology change is detected.

Section 10: Access Control (16 Minutes)

Step 1   Prevent the loopback on R6 from reaching R1. Make sure this network is advertised to all other routers. (2 minutes)

Step 2   Create an outbound filter on R7, blocking only the even subnets from the loopback range of 209.112.65.1 to 209.112.70.1. (2 minutes)

Step 3   Assume that a web server is placed on VLAN13 with an IP address of 130.100.1.13. Apply an inbound access list to R3 to allow only routing protocols, pings, and web traffic to enter the router and gain access to the server. (4 minutes)

Step 4   Assume that an FTP server located on VLAN13 has an IP address of 130.100.1.13. Apply an access list on R3 to allow only users located inside the PIX2 network access to FTP and secure web traffic. Make sure that files can be properly transferred. (4 minutes)

Step 5   Configure R6 to be able to ping all networks, but block R6 from requesting the traceroute through R5. (4 minutes)

Section 11: IP Services (18 Minutes)

Step 1   Set up HSRP between R5 and R6. R6 should be the primary default gateway. If R6 loses its serial connection, R5's Ethernet0 interface becomes the default gateway. Make HSRP secure with MD5 authentication. (4 minutes)

Step 2   Configure R6 as a DHCP server. Configure the router to allow hosts on its Ethernet segment to resolve their IP addresses from the DHCP server. Make sure the DHCP lease never expires. (3 minutes)

Step 3   Set up R8 so that when user "admin" Telnets to it, the user is allowed to enter only **show start**, **show ip route**, and **telnet** commands. (4 minutes)

Step 4   Configure R5 for a secure Telnet session. Verify the success of your configuration using R6. (5 minutes)

Step 5   Set up R6 so that only host 192.168.1.10 can view this router's management statistics. (2 minutes)

Section 12: Catalyst Security (6 Minutes)

Step 1   Configure the Catalyst 3550-A so that only R3 and R8 can Telnet to it. (2 minutes)

Step 2   Configure port 0/19 on the switch as secure. Set the maximum value to ten MAC addresses. (4 minutes)

Section 13: AAA Using RADIUS (17 Minutes)

Step 1   Configure the ACS server to run RADIUS services. Use user1 as a username, cisco as a key, and R8's loopback address as a source for authentication. (4 minutes)

Step 2   Set up R8 to authenticate against the RADIUS server. (3 minutes)

Step 3   Permit a user to issue pings, access global configuration mode, and configure an SNMP server on R8. (4 minutes)

Step 4   Create an authentication list with an appropriate method, and apply it to the console line of R8. (2 minutes)

Step 5   Configure authorization on R8 to allow the assigned permissions. Make your last authorization method allow unrestricted user entrance to the shell if all other methods fail. Do not use "none." (2 minutes)

Step 6   Configure accounting on R8 to record user activity from the time of login until the time of logout. Verify that the accounting records are functioning on the ACS server. (2 minutes)

Section 14: Configuring AAA on the PIX Firewall (26 Minutes)

Step 1   Configure TACACS+ services on VLAN82's ACS server. Specify PIX2 as a client. Assign user2 to a group. Use cisco6727 as the key. Authorize the use of Shell. Do not restrict command privileges. (8 minutes)

Step 2   On PIX2, set up matching criteria for authentication, authorization, and accounting based on Telnet and WWW traffic regardless of source or destination. (6 minutes)

Step 3   Identify the TACACS+ server on PIX2 and point to it for all AAA services. Configure all console authentication options. Configure authentication, authorization, and accounting to refer to the matching criteria specified in Step 2. (5 minutes)

Step 4   Limit Telnet access to PIX2 to hosts on the network 192.168.1.0 using cisco6727 as a password. (1 minute)

Step 5   Change all three login prompts for Telnet users to reflect your personality. (2 minutes)

Step 6   Configure PIX2 to accept SSH sessions from hosts 192.168.1.100 and 192.168.1.1. (4 minutes)

Section 15: Authentication Proxy with TACACS+ (18 Minutes)

Step 1 Configure the TACACS+ server to allow R6 to act as an authentication proxy. (8 minutes)

Step 2 Enable an authentication proxy named "auth" on R6. Force user authentication entries to be removed after an inactivity period of 5 minutes. Configure AAA services for authentication proxy on R6 so that they all refer to the TACACS+ server for necessary information and resources. Make sure all system activity is captured by the AAA server from beginning to end. Verify that your configuration is working properly by attempting to authenticate through R6. (10 minutes)

Section 16: Privilege Levels with TACACS+ (16 Minutes)

Step 1 Enable R6's Telnet interface to permit login by trying the TACACS+ server first, and then the local database, and, finally, the line password. All other requests for authentication should go through the TACACS+ server. (4 minutes)

Step 2 Configure authorized users to have access to either the highest or the intermediate control level. (2 minutes)

Step 3 Allow users at the intermediate level to configure an SNMP server, save the configuration, and view the saved configuration. Remember that all authorization decisions should come from the TACACS+ server. (5 minutes)

Step 4 Configure all types of accounting to monitor user activity from beginning to end. (5 minutes)

Section 17: PPP Callback with TACACS+ (10 Minutes)

Step 1 In this scenario, R6 is a client, and R8 is a server. Configure the TACACS+ server to allow callback. Specify the telephone number on the TACACS+ server. Use the TACACS+ server for all AAA services, including those that are callback-related. (8 minutes)

Step 2 Record all activity. (2 minutes)

Section 18: Cisco IOS Firewall (60 Minutes)

Step 1 Configure address translation on R6 as if you have only one available IP address. Choose the best method to use only an IP address of your S0 interface to make NAT work. Everything from the 130.100.26.x network must be translated into 140.100.56.6. For example:

— WWW server 130.100.26.10

       — Telnet server 130.100.26.11

       — FTP server 130.100.26.12

Configure R6 such that all these services can be reached from the outside using a single IP address. (10 minutes)

Step 2   On R6, configure CBAC to inspect TCP, UDP, FTP, HTTP, and SMTP traffic. Apply the configuration to the FastEthernet0/0 interface. Make sure that all previously configured services are still working. (10 minutes)

Step 3   On R8, configure CBAC for all TCP and HTTP traffic to be inspected. Configure max half open sessions to be 950. Configure min half open sessions to be 300. Configure Max incomplete half open sessions per host to not go over 132. In case of a violation, configure a 15-minute lockout. Configure the DNS timeout to be 50 seconds. Allow Java applets from Loopback8's network. Set the idle timeout for TCP connections to 130 seconds. The access list and CBAC should be applied on Ethernet0. Make sure that all previously configured services are still working. (15 minutes)

Step 4   Configure Loopback12 on R2 with an IP address of 121.121.121.121. Configure Loopback12 on R1 with the same IP address. Configure the two routers so that both Loopback12 interfaces can communicate and ping one another. (10 minutes)

Step 5   Configure R6 to deny HTTP traffic Monday through Friday between the hours of 8 a.m. and 6 p.m. Allow UDP traffic on Saturday and Sunday from noon to 8 p.m. only. (10 minutes)

Step 6   Configure an extended access list to allow only R1 and R2 networks to Telnet R6. Make sure that all other processes aren't interrupted. (5 minutes)

Section 19: PIX Firewall (45 Minutes)

Step 1   ICMP echo replies should return to PIX1's inside network. (5 minutes)

Step 2   Assume that a host on an inside network of PIX1 has an IP address of 192.168.1.192. Make the host's IP address appear on the outside as is. (2 minutes)

Step 3   Configure the PIX2 outside interface to disregard pings without using an access list. (2 minutes)

Step 4   When PIX2 inside hosts request FTP, POP, or HTTP services, speed up the response to their requests. (2 minutes)

Step 5   Configure both PIX Firewalls to block Java and ActiveX applets from outside networks. (4 minutes)

Step 6   Configure PIX2 to send critical/monitor alerts and history emergencies to syslog server 192.168.1.7. (5 minutes)

Step 7   Configure PIX2 to allow only one SNMP workstation to view stats on the PIX. (3 minutes)

Step 8   Configure NTP/MD5 authentication on PIX2 as a client to R8. (6 minutes)

Step 9   Prevent PIX2 from allowing IP spoofing on the outside. (1 minute)

Step 10 When configuring your mail server, configure PIX2 to not respond to DATA, HELO, MAIL, NOOP, QUIT, RCPT, and RSET. Configure all necessary components so that anyone can send e-mail to a mail server behind PIX2 with an inside IP address of 192.168.1.125. (5 minutes)

Step 11 Configure PAT translation on PIX1. (1 minute)

Step 12 Configure the PIX2 Firewall to retrieve its configurations and software images from a centralized location with an IP address of 192.168.1.100. (4 minutes)

Step 13 Configure PIX2 such that, when users on the inside network boot their machines, they get the dynamic IP address and WINS, DNS, and default gateway information assigned by PIX2. (5 minutes)

Section 20: Cisco IOS IDS (14 Minutes)

Step 1   Assume that an IDS Sensor placed on the PIX2 internal segment has an IP address of 192.168.1.8. Make sure that PIX2 allows the IDS traffic through. Configure IDS on R6. Specify the NetRanger organization ID as 6666, sensor ID as 43, and Director ID as 123. (5 minutes)

Step 2   Send messages to Syslog and Director at 192.168.1.8. (1 minute)

Step 3   Monitor everything coming from the 140.100.x.x network. Configure the notification queue size to be 180. (2 minutes)

Step 4   Audit signatures that are triggered by an e-mail with a suspiciously high number of recipients. Disable signatures that are triggered on the very common smail attack against e-mail servers. Disable signatures that are triggered when any IP datagram is received with an offset value less than 5 but greater than 0. Disable signatures caused by the ping-of-death attack. (4 minutes)

Step 5   Configure TCP connections to reset upon info and attack. (2 minutes)

Section 21: IPSec VPN (53 Minutes)

Step 1   Assume that a DHCP server is located on the same segment as R8's FastEthernet0/0 interface. Configure R8 to dynamically assign an IP address to itself without applying it manually. (1 minute)

Step 2   Configure loopback networks 11.11.11.x and 12.12.12.x on R1 and R2, respectively, so that they discover IPSec endpoints without explicitly stating the peer's IP address, as in **crypto isakmp key cisco address x.x.x.x.** Make sure that only 11.11.11.11 and 12.12.12.12 trigger IPSec tunnel and discovery events. (10 minutes)

Step 3   Configure a full mesh between R3, R4, R6, and R8:

— R3 loopback 13.13.13.13

— R4 loopback 14.14.14.14

— R6 loopback 16.16.16.16

— R8 loopback 18.18.18.18 to be encrypted across the network

Use the following guidelines for your configuration:

— isakmp

— Preshared authentication with cisco key

— md5 hash

— isakmp lifetime 2000 seconds

— des-esp and des-sha-hmac transform set

— Configure IPSec in a transport mode

Make sure that only these loopbacks trigger IPSec negotiations. (20 minutes)

Step 4   Configure a fully meshed GRE tunnel between the routers from Step 3 and route their private loopbacks through that tunnel using EIGRP. Make sure that all these loopbacks can ping one another. Make sure that R6, R8, and R4 can ping each others' loopbacks that are being encrypted through R3. Make the appropriate changes to PIX2 to accommodate for this. (10 minutes)

Step 5   Configure PIX1 IPSec to PIX2 to encrypt the inside network. Make sure that the inside networks can ping each other. Use the most common encryption method. (12 minutes)

Section 22: IPSec VPN with CA (17 Minutes)

Step 1   Configure PIX2 to receive a digital certificate from the CA server. (10 minutes)

Use the following guidelines for your configuration:

— isakmp

— rsa-sig authentication

— md5 hash

— des-esp transform set

Step 2   Configure R5 to receive a digital certificate from the CA server. Make sure that R5 and PIX2 are enrolled with the CA and are using it to establish IPSec. Verify whether R5's loopback 15.15.15.15 can ping 192.168.1.8 (R8's FastEthernet0/0). (7 minutes)

Section 23: Configuring VPN Client Remote Access (15 Minutes)

Step 1   Configure PIX2 for IPSec negotiations for a VPN client. (10 minutes)

Step 2   Configure a VPN client to authenticate against the TACACS+ server. Make sure that the client can reach the private network behind the PIX2 Firewall. (5 minutes)

Section 24: QoS (12 Minutes)

Step 1   Configure R6 serial 0/0 to prevent DoS TCP SYN Attacks to R6 from the outside. (3 minutes)

Step 2   Configure an access list to block all outside network addresses commonly used to hack your network. (See RFC 2267 or RFC 2827.) (5 minutes)

Step 3   Limit the ICMP rate to approximately 500 kbps on R6's serial 0/0 interface. (2 minutes)

Step 4   Guarantee all secure web traffic a bandwidth of approximately 300 kbps going out of R6. (2 minutes)

Section 25: L2VPN (10 Minutes)

Step 1   On R1 and R10, configure subinterfaces to belong to VLAN10 and VLAN20. Assign at least one subinterface of each router to each VLAN. (4 minutes)

Step 2 The subinterfaces of both routers should be able to reach each other over 3550-A and 3550-B. Configure your switching such that neither switch has any knowledge of VLAN10 and VLAN20. Verify your configuration (See Figure 26-10) by making sure that VLAN10 and VLAN20 on R1 can reach their counterparts on R10. (6 minutes)

Figure 26-10 *Final Topology*

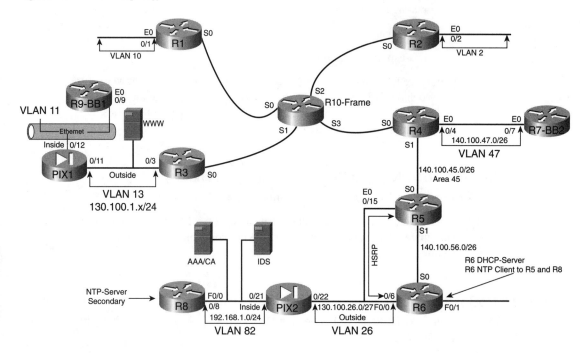

Summary

This chapter let you practice what you've learned from reading this book. The seven practice labs and the final master lab included the topics covered on the CCIE Security lab exam. Along with the current covered topics, some of the possible future additions to the lab were offered.

PART IX

Appendixes

This appendix covers the following topics:

- Installing Solaris
- Applying patches
- Securing network services
- Securing your startup scripts
- Enabling logging
- Performing optional security tasks

Basic UNIX Security

When it comes to UNIX-flavored operating systems, you have many choices. Because of this, trying to explain how to secure each of these would require a book in itself or, more likely, several books. This appendix covers basic ways to secure a Sun Solaris operating system. Covering this subject in detail is also outside the scope of this book, so this appendix covers the most basic items required to achieve a system that is both secure and manageable. The good news is, even though the commands between different versions of UNIX-based software, and even Solaris itself, might be different, the basic concepts are pretty much equivalent.

When it comes to determining which items to configure on your UNIX system, the role the device plays in your overall network, as well as the services it offers to network users, can tell you which items to be concerned with. For example, if a device will not offer web services, there is no need to run a web server on it. One of the best approaches you can take is to run only the services that are absolutely necessary for the box to function.

Because of its popularity and versatility, maintaining a UNIX system can become a daily task. This is because of new exploits that are developed, patches to fix the exploits and other items, and one of the most cumbersome tasks—reviewing the Syslog files that the system generates.

Securing the Solaris operating system is much like any other task you undertake to configure the Cisco IOS software. You must perform certain tasks to build a solid foundation for future security refinements:

- Installing the OS
- Applying the patches
- Securing the network services
- Securing the startup scripts
- Enabling logging
- Miscellaneous security-related tasks

Installing Solaris

Because installing Solaris is the first step, it is one of the most vital. You want to be sure that you select the latest version of the Solaris OS, or at least the latest that your applications will support. Like most manufacturers, Sun continues to develop improvements and added features in its OS as well as its security. You should install the OS in a secure lab environment, or at least isolated from the network, with all the patches that will be applied downloaded and scanned for viruses on a second device. Installing a machine while it is connected to a nonsecure network makes it possible for an attacker to exploit any vulnerability with the OS before you've had time to patch it.

Sun makes the installation of the Solaris OS very easy through a menu-based installer. The first choice that many power users seem to make is installing everything available without concern for security. By choosing to install only the required software and options, you can increase your security by reducing the amount of software to patch as well as any possible exploits associated with that software. You should be as frugal as possible during this task, because you can always add later any software packages you might have forgotten. Remember that even the Core System Support option installs many services you might not need for proper operation of your system.

Partitioning your drive is mostly up to you and any policies your company might have in place. This subject is often debated. Some users believe that a large file system with only / as a partition is optimal, and others insist on using the long-recommended four partitions of /, /usr, /var, and /opt. Generally, the /usr and /opt partitions are used to install applications, and the /var partition is used for system logging and protects your root (/) partition by preventing overfilling. The /swap partition is created automatically during the initial installation, but it can be modified to complement the amount of memory you have installed on your system.

Applying Patches

After you've finished the initial installation and you've rebooted the system, you can start installing all the recommended patches. Patches for Solaris come in the form of patch clusters and can be found on Sun's website at www.sunsolve.sun.com. If you are a Sun service contract customer, you can also find maintenance updates (MUs) here.

When you install patches, a failure is not always a catastrophic condition. If your patch installation fails with a "return code 2" message, the patch has already been installed on your system. A "return code 8" message indicates that the package to which the patch applies is not installed on your system. Any other failures should be investigated and the problem corrected before you attempt to reinstall the patch.

Installing the latest patches from Sun helps you continue to protect your system from the many vulnerabilities that have been discovered since your distribution CD-ROM was produced. Failure to maintain the patches on your system can expose your system to attack through unpatched vulnerabilities. The up side is that there are many automated tools on the Internet that you can use to scan your system for known vulnerabilities.

Securing Network Services

The /etc/inetd.conf file is where you begin configuring most of the network services for your computer. You can stop these services by placing a pound sign (#) in front of the services that are not required for operation. One method you can use to do this is to comment out everything in the inetd.conf file (after making a backup, of course) and add them back as you need them. You should comment out the following services:

- **ftp**—Allows a user to transfer files to or from a host.

- **tftp**—Allows remote users to transfer files from a host without requiring a login.

- **systat**—Invokes **/bin/ps -auxww**, which shows you processes running as well as the user it runs as.

- **rexd**—Allows remote users to run RPC programs on a host.

- **ypupdated**—Updates Network Information Service (NIS) information.

- **netstat**—Invokes **/bin/netstat -a**, which shows which ports a machine is listening on.

- **rstatd**—Extracts performance statistics from the kernel through programs such as perfmeter.

- **rusersd**—Returns a list of users on a network.

- **sprayd**—Records the packets sent by spray and sends a response to the packets' originator.

- **walld**—Handles rwall and shutdown requests.

- **shell**—Allows remote users to run arbitrary commands on a host via the Berkeley rsh utility.

- **exec**—Allows remote users to execute commands on a host without needing to log in.

- **talk**—Allows two users on different systems to communicate with each other.

- **comsat**—Used for incoming mail notification via biff.

- **rquotad**—Returns quotas for a user of a local file system that is mounted by a remote machine over the NFS.

- **name**—The TCP/IP trivial name service protocol.

- **uucp**—Allows remote users to transfer files to or from a host using the UNIX-to-UNIX Copy Program (UUCP) protocol.

- **sadmind**—Coordinates distributed system administration remotely.

- **login**—Allows remote users to use the Berkeley rlogin utility to log in to a host without supplying a password.

- **finger**—Remotely obtains information about a user such as the terminal the user is logged in to, the shell, the login directory path, if there is unread e-mail, and the contents of the .plan and .project files.

- **chargen**—Outputs a rotating sequence of printable characters for testing tty devices and other situations in which known and varying sequence is desired.

- **echo**—Relays back all data sent to it to test connectivity.

- **time**—Prints the current time and date.

- **daytime**—Returns the current date and time in ASCII.

- **discard**—Discards the incoming data stream.

- **telnet**—Allows a remote user to connect to a host.

- **imap**—Used for the IMAP4 remote mail access protocol server.

- **pop3**—Used for the POP-3 remote mail access protocol server.

- **dtspc**—Used for the Common Desktop Environment (CDE) subprocess control.

- **fs**—Provides a font server.

- **kcms**—Provides remote access to the Kodak Color Management System (KCMS) profiles.

- **all rpc services**—Provides remote procedure call (RPC) services as protocols to be used in cooperative processing, such as in a client/server environment.

After you have commented out these services, you need to restart your inetd daemon. You have the option of replacing the standard inetd.conf with one that just includes Telnet and FTP. This can be replaced with Secure Shell (SSH) under ideal circumstances if these two services are required.

The following sections discuss some of the most often used services and ways to secure them.

FTP

You can use the /etc/ftpusers file to restrict the listed users from using the FTP service to connect to your system. If you use SSH to replace FTP, you can use the secure copy (**scp**) command as a more secure method to transfer files instead of FTP.

rlogin and rsh

If rlogin or rsh is required in your environment, removing the entry from the pam.conf file causes rlogin and rsh to ignore the $HOME/.rhosts and /etc/hosts.equiv files to require the user to always enter a password for access. Although rlogin and rsh always require the user to enter a password, you should use SSH if possible.

Remote Procedure Call (RPC)

rpcbind allows an RPC caller to locate an RPC service. Standard RPC is not secure because it uses AUTH_UNIX authentication, which means that it depends on the remote system's IP address and the remote user's ID (UID) for identification. As you may know, a malicious user can easily forge or change either of these forms of identification. You should be able to safely disable RPC by renaming /etc/rc2.d/S71RPC on your servers without affecting your users. Use secure-RPC if you have to run RPC services.

Network File System (NFS)

NFS is another facility that has many vulnerabilities. With NFS, any file system that you list in the /etc/dfs/dfstab file is exported to the world by default.

To provide a more secure implementation of NFS, you can include a list of NFS clients, or a netgroup, with the **-o rw** or **-o ro** options. You can include the **nosuid** option to disable setuid programs on any mount that you identify as not required for operation.

Do not run your NFS mount through the rpcbind program. This makes the mount daemon see any request as if it were local to the system and allow it. You can use an rpcbind replacement that disables request forwarding or install the latest Sun rpcbind patches, which also disable forwarding. Use fsirand to randomize the inode numbers on all your NFS servers.

If you do not need to use the NFS facility, you can remove the export file, /etc/dfs/dfstab, and rename the /etc/rc3.d/S15nfs.server file to disable the NFS server daemon. If you want to prevent a machine from being an NFS client, you can rename the /etc/rc2.d/S73nfs.client file.

Securing Your Startup Scripts

The startup scripts on your system reside in the /etc/rc2.d and /etc/rc3.d directories. Many of the services here are not required for proper operation of your system and pose potential security vulnerabilities. Preventing a script from starting is as simple as replacing the capital S with any other letter or, in the case of a kill script, replacing the capital K with a number. Here are some common services that you might not require and, in most cases, can safely disable:

- **Automounter**—/etc/rc2.d/S74autofs
- **Sendmail**—/etc/rc2.d/S88sendmail and /etc/rc1.d/K57sendmail
- **SNMP**—/etc/rc2.d/S76snmpdx
- **Autoinstall**—/etc/rc2.d/S72autoinstall
- **Cachefs**—S73cachefs.daemon

Enabling Logging

Logging is one tool that you, as a system administrator, can use daily. Logging provides you with a means to determine if your system is operating optimally, determine a chain of events for problems, and, if handled properly, provide forensic evidence if your system has been compromised.

By default, a Solaris system logs to the /var/adm directory. At a minimum, you can enable additional logging by creating two additional log files—/var/adm/sulog to log unsuccessful su attempts, and /var/adm/loginlog to log consecutive failed login attempts.

These files are by no means the extent of logging you can enable on a Solaris system. You can configure your syslogd in a way that allows you to examine the activities of each daemon that can write to the specified log level. To enable this enhanced logging, the end of your /etc/syslog.conf file should contain the following:

```
kern.debug/var/log/all/kern.log
user.debugvar/log/all/user.log
mail.debug               /var/log/all/mail.log
daemon.debug             /var/log/all/daemon.log
auth.debug               /var/log/all/auth.log
syslog.debug             /var/log/all/syslog.log
lpr.debug                /var/log/all/lpr.log
news.debug               /var/log/all/news.log
uucp.debug               /var/log/all/uucp.log
cron.debug               /var/log/all/cron.log
local0.debug             /var/log/all/local0.log
local1.debug             /var/log/all/local1.log
local2.debug             /var/log/all/local2.log
local3.debug             /var/log/all/local3.log
local4.debug             /var/log/all/local4.log
local5.debug             /var/log/all/local5.log
local6.debug             /var/log/all/local6.log
local7.debug             /var/log/all/local7.log
```

Remember that you must create the white space between the type and action using only tabs, not spaces. You must have created the files you listed as the store of logging information before your syslogd can write to them.

The more information you log to files, the faster they need to be rotated before the file becomes too large to browse or fills the /var partition. You can use /usr/bin/newsyslog to rotate your log files for you. All logging information you capture should be archived for a specified period of time.

One other item you can enable for logging is authentication messages. You can uncomment the following line in your /etc/syslog.conf to accomplish this:

```
#auth.notice ifdef('LOGHOST', /var/log/authlog, @loghost)
```

Remember that you must create the referenced file before you can store information there.

Performing Optional Security Tasks

You can implement several tasks to provide a more complete security solution for your Solaris systems. You can choose to implement a few of them or none of them; it all depends on your company's security requirements.

Executing Code from the Stack

Several of today's exploits depend on the many security holes introduced by one system flaw: the ability to execute code from the stack. Many of these exploits use a bug known as a *buffer overflow*. The exploit code overflows a buffer in a way that lets the buffer overflow write code into the stack space. After this code is placed in the stack space, the exploit can execute arbitrary code on the target system.

You can secure your system against a stack-based buffer overflow by adding the following to the /etc/system file:

```
set noexec_user_stack=1
set noexec_user_stack_log=1
```

The first line prevents the execution of any code on your stack. You should be aware that using this line might cause some of your programs, which run code from your stack legitimately, to no longer function. A good rule of thumb to follow about the use of this line is that if your system is designed for a single purpose and needs to be as secure as possible, you should use this option. The second line logs any attempt by someone who tries to run an exploit using this method.

Verifying Installation Information

You should verify that the following contain the items you specified during installation:

- Verify that your /etc/hostname.*interface* file contains only the host name of your machine.

- Verify that your /etc/inet/hosts file contains only the following entries, unless your specific requirements dictate otherwise:

```
127.0.0.1              localhost
local IP address       hostname
IP address     loghost
```

NOTE   You can add a few other specific entries to your /etc/inet/hosts file. These entries should specify hosts that will be used for a specific reason, such as a logging host or your DNS server. If you have a central logging host, add an entry for it as well. In these cases, your file might look similar to this:

```
127.0.0.1              localhost
IP address        hostname          loghost
IP address        hostname          dns
```

This configuration can prevent certain types of attacks, such as DNS, against your system. The major disadvantage of using this approach is that for every host configured this way, you must have a policy to ensure that the information is kept consistent and correct.

Setting the umask

The default umask setting makes too many files world-readable by default. On a standalone system that has only one user, this setting might be fine, but the general recommendation is to change your umask to 027. You should allow your system to run for some time to determine if this change is practical for your environment. This change makes any file created by normal system operation not world-readable by default. If you encounter a problem with this setting, you can create a group that contains a list of users who might require access to read files created by system daemons.

Securing the Root Account

With access to the root account, anyone can make any change to your system. Access to this account should be limited to a few select individuals, with others granted only temporary access using su. The following are general rules for securing the root account:

- Set a very secure password for the root account.

- Be sure root has a umask setting of 077 or 027.

- Be sure root has a safe search path, as in /usr/bin:/sbin:/usr/sbin.

- Ensure that root is the only account that can access the console, on systems that are not used for user workstations, by ensuring that the following line in /etc/default/login is not commented out:

```
CONSOLE=/dev/console
```

Avoiding TCP Shortcomings

The following are recommendations for TCP settings for your system:

- Set your TCP initial sequence number generation parameters to protect against session hijacking and spoofing.

- In the file /etc/default/inetinit, set TCP_STRONG_ISS=2.

Locking Unneeded User Accounts

Solaris provides support for older versions by continuing to create many accounts that are no longer used. You should consider removing, locking, or commenting out these accounts unless your requirements dictate otherwise. These accounts include, but are not limited to, the following:

- sys
- uucp
- nuucp
- smtp
- listen

You can lock these accounts by putting *LK* in the Password field of your /etc/shadow file.

Login Banner

You can change your /etc/motd file to contain a banner to warn unauthorized users about inappropriate and unauthorized use of your system.

Routing

With today's robust networks, most Solaris systems are not used for routing anymore, but routing is still enabled by default. You can disable routing using the following:

```
#touch /etc/notrouter
```

Unless your system has specific requirements, you can remove the SUNWsndmr and SUNWsndmu sendmail packages to prevent exploits designed against mail.

Disabling Stop-A

Stop-A lets a user stop the entire system and bring it down to a command line. As soon as the user has access to the command line, exploits may be run to upgrade privileges or run arbitrary code. You can disable the Stop-A abort sequence by making the following change to your /etc/default/kbd file:

```
KEYBOARD_ABORT=disabled
```

Improving Electrically Erasable Programmable Read-Only Memory (EEPROM) Security

You can improve your system's security by requiring an EEPROM password before booting from a CD-ROM or tape drive. You can set the password by performing the following:

```
#eeprom security-mode=full
New password: password
Retype new password: password
```

Do not make this password the same as your root password. Setting the security level to full requires a user to enter a password to boot the system. You can use the Command keyword, instead of the full keyword, to provide protection without the need for a boot password. If someone has physical access to your machine, they can replace its EEPROM to gain access to your system. Fortunately, by replacing the machine's EEPROM, the person also changes the hostid. You should record all your hostids and periodically check this list against the system's to verify that none of your EEPROMs have been replaced.

Auditing File Security

File ownership is one way an unauthorized user can gain access to files he normally would not have access to. You should examine all your file ownership and protections. You can check for world-writeable files on your system by using the following command:

```
find  /  -local  !  -type  1  -perm -0002 -ls >  /var/log/world-writeable-files
```

You can also use the following commands to examine setUID, setGID, and group-writeable to determine what files need to have these set:

```
find  /  -local  !  -type  1  -perm  -4000  -ls >  /var/log/suid-files
find  /  -local  !  -type  1  -perm  -2000  -ls >  /var/log/sgid-files
find  /  -local  !  -type  1  -perm  -0020  -ls >  /var/log/group-writeable-files
find  /  -local  !  -type  1  -perm  -0001  -ls >  /var/log/world-executable-files
```

A thorough examination of these results can be used to restrict file permissions as much as possible. Only the programs that require the setUID/setGID should remain set. Only programs that are required to be group/world-executable should be executable in this manner, and all other programs should have this setting changed. You can use a third-party product, such as Tripwire, to track the changes made to the files.

You can configure all file systems, except where requirements do not allow it, to be mounted as read-only and nosuid to prevent changes to files and programs that often result from unauthorized access or attempts to corrupt data.

The default configuration of Solaris permits group write permission of the /etc directory. Unless your specific requirements state otherwise, you can prevent this by using the following:

```
chmod -R g-w /etc
```

SSH

SSH is a program that can be used for secure communications with the Solaris system. It encrypts all communications streams to the system and can replace Telnet and FTP, among other less-secure programs. SSH comes with its own logging and access control, such as TCP Wrapper. You can obtain SSH from a variety of sources, such as www.ssh.com and openssh.com.

Tripwire

As mentioned, Tripwire, when used for accounting purposes, can keep track of changes to files. This helps you in auditing and monitoring any changes made to files on your system during normal operation.

Physical Security

Physical security of your system is just as important as the security you implement on your network. It would be a waste of resources to secure your network against any type of attack if an unauthorized user could walk up to your system and remove it. If an unauthorized user can gain physical access to your system, it is only a matter of time before the user has all the information contained on the machine, including any locally stored user accounts and passwords. A good physical security implementation should include limited access to the devices under protection, as well as securable or separate environmental controls, such as power and air conditioning.

Summary

This overview was intended to give you a basic introduction to UNIX security. By no means is it meant to answer every security scenario you might encounter. Continued education and mailing lists are excellent sources you can use to keep on top of the latest security vulnerabilities and countermeasures. Remember that a good security practice you can use in your day-to-day operations is to remove all privileges and access for your users and grant only the privileges and access they require to complete their assigned job requirements.

This appendix includes the following topics:

- Installing the OS
- Securing network services
- Checklist for enabling baseline security
- Applying patches
- Enabling auditing and logging
- Using file systems

Basic Windows Security

It is a well publicized fact that the history of Windows security is tarnished. These security events have contributed to the ongoing development of security within Windows operating systems and applications. Vendors now take Windows security seriously because they know that security is a major contributing factor when choosing an operating system.

A Windows operating system (OS) can be either a network operating system or a desktop operating system. As a Windows desktop operating system, you can use Windows 95, 98, Me, NT4 Workstation, 2000 Professional, or XP. As a Windows server operating system, you can use either Windows NT4 Server or 2000 Server.

Since the early days of MS-DOS and the initial versions of Windows, which barely included any meaningful security, improvements have been made to secure not only the operating system itself but also users, file systems, resources, and network access.

Compliance with the National Computer Security Centre (NCSC) C2 rating has been achieved in Windows NT; however, this is somewhat limited in a real working environment. This C2 rating dictates that Windows NT must be a stand-alone system with no networking enabled. A network-attached Windows NT system is not a C2-certified system. The C2 security policy is known as DAC (Discretionary Access Control) and dictates that specific access is governed by a user's privilege. Under Windows NT, this specifies that users of the system own objects, have control over the protection of the objects they own, and are accountable for all their access-related actions. This specific access is governed by a user's privilege. Unlike other C2-rated operating systems, such as versions of IBM OS/400 and Digital OpenVMS, Windows NT is the first PC/desktop operating system to achieve this security rating.

More recently, Windows 2000 has received the Common Criteria (CC) Certification. The CC Certification is a globally recognized standard for evaluating the security of IT-related products. You can find more information on this certification on Windows 2000 at the following website:

www.microsoft.com/windows2000/server/evaluation/news/bulletins/cccert.asp

An out-of-the-box installation of a Windows operating system is not secure. Over time, many bugs and exploits have been identified and publicized, and like other operating systems, patches and updates are released. To maintain a secure stance in a networked environment, the administrator must keep current with these service packs and fixes. Like any network- or Internet-connected operating system, the Windows OS is only as secure as the administrator makes it.

You can find the latest security patches and vulnerability information by starting at www.microsoft.com/security/ and browsing to the relevant section.

The modern Windows security model dictates that any legitimate user must log on and be validated before using the system and network resources. User accounts are assigned to groups of users, who are then assigned to resources. A user base in a Windows environment can either be local to a machine, a member of a domain model, or a member of an Active Directory model.

Securing a networked Windows (NT and 2000) operating system is much like any configuration task that you undertake to secure other operating systems. You must follow certain tasks to build a solid foundation for future security refinements. These tasks include the following:

- Installing the OS
- Securing network services
- Applying the patches
- Enabling auditing and logging

Installing the OS

Installing the Windows operating system is the first step and, therefore, is one of the most vital stages. Obviously, the version of Windows that you select must be appropriate for your hardware and applications. To ensure a successful installation, you should check the Microsoft Hardware Compatibility List (HCL) for hardware compatibility. Like most manufacturers, Microsoft continues to make improvements and develop added features in its OS as well as its security. You should install the OS in a secure lab environment, or at least isolated from the network, with all patches that are to be applied downloaded and scanned for viruses on a second device. Installing on a machine while it is connected to a nonsecure network makes it possible for an attacker to exploit any vulnerability with the OS version before you have had time to apply patches.

As with other operating systems, many power users choose to install everything that is available, without concern for security. By choosing to install only the required software and options, you can increase your security by reducing the amount of software that needs to be patched as well as by minimizing possible exploits that are associated with that software. As stated in Appendix A, "Basic UNIX Security," you should be as frugal as possible during this task because you can install any additional software packages that you might have forgotten at a later time. Remember that a default installation includes many services that you might not need for proper operation of your system. If the system that you are installing for does not need to participate in a domain environment, always use the member server mode. This server mode assumes that you do not need the server to synchronize user information with other servers or to authenticate users to a domain. This server mode keeps a local user base rather than one that has been synchronized with other servers on your network and domain. If you were installing a web server, for example, you would install it as a member server.

Securing Network Services

Microsoft recently released and made freely available several tools to aid you in securing a Windows server. These tools include the Microsoft Baseline Security Analyzer (MBSA), Hfnetchk, IIS Lockdown Wizard, UrlScan, and others, as described in this section.

The MBSA tool allows you to scan Windows NT4, 2000, and XP computers for security misconfiguration. This tool also scans for installed application services, such as Internet Information Server (IIS), SQL Server, and Exchange Server as well as their configurations. In addition to scanning for security misconfiguration, MBSA also notifies the administrator of any service packs that are required to bring the Windows installation up to date with the latest security fixes. MBSA can also scan system misconfigurations for Internet Explorer (IE) 5.01 and later, Office 2000 and 2002, and Windows Media Player 6.4 and later.

The MBSA tool also includes a command-line tool called Hfnetchk. *Hfnetchk* is a free tool available from Microsoft that assists you in keeping current with the various service packs and hot fixes that are released by Microsoft. From a central location, Hfnetchk can be executed from a command line and can scan and evaluate the service pack and hot fix level of Windows NT4, 2000, and XP as well as various popular application services such as IIS and Exchange Server. See Microsoft Knowledge Base article Q303215 for a list of supported Windows operating systems and applications (search for the document number at support.microsoft.com). Hfnetchk works by downloading an XML file from Microsoft that contains information about which hot fixes and service packs are currently available for each product. Hfnetchk determines a Windows installation patch level by evaluating the Registry and file information and comparing that to the information that is described in the XML file.

Microsoft has also released two other tools that are specifically designed for securing IIS installations. These tools are the IIS Lockdown Wizard and UrlScan. Both tools work together and provide the administrator with the ability to secure the IIS-based web services.

The official hot fix, service pack, and security bulletin resource is located at the following website:

www.microsoft.com/technet/treeview/default.asp?url=/technet/security/current.asp

Checklist for Enabling Baseline Security

Within Windows 2000, you can create domain security policies and distribute these to other servers within the domain using the Security Configuration Tool Set. Within Windows NT4, you can use the Security Configuration Manager (SCM) utility to consolidate all security-related settings into a single inf file. You can use this file to distribute a security configuration to any number of servers.

The following is a checklist of steps to follow in creating a baseline level of security with a Windows NT 4 Server and Windows 2000–based server running either on its own or as part of a domain:

☐ Verify that all disk partitions are formatted with the NT File System (NTFS). By using NTFS, you benefit from security controls and protection that are not inherit in FAT16 and FAT32 file systems (See "NTFS" in this appendix). On an existing system, you can convert from FAT to NTFS using the Convert utility and the following command:

CONVERT drive_letter /FS:NTFS

Windows 2000 and XP now incorporate a built-in optional file system called Encrypting File System (EFS).

☐ Verify that the Administrator account has a strong password. Windows 2000 allows a password of up to 127 characters, and Windows NT4 Server allows a password of up to 14 characters. For maximum protection, make sure the Administrator account password is at least 9 characters long and that it includes at least 1 punctuation mark or nonprinting ASCII character in the first 7 characters. You should not synchronize or use the Administrator password across multiple servers.

☐ Disable unnecessary application services. During or after installing your Windows operating system, be sure to deselect or remove any unnecessary application services. In particular, decide whether the server is to run any web services. If not, be sure to deselect or remove IIS. IIS is a commonly exploited service on servers that are running a Windows operating system. Avoid installing applications on the server that are not required to fulfill its task, for example, client software, e-mail software, and office software.

☐ Disable unnecessary network services. If the server will not be participating in a network utilizing NetBIOS services (for example, WINS), unbind and remove the WINS service in Network properties. Also, disable NetBIOS over TCP/IP in TCP/IP properties. This removes any services that are listening on NetBIOS ports, which are commonly exploited on servers that are running a Windows operating system. By disabling NetBIOS services, you effectively close the following ports:

— UDP port 137 (name services)

— UDP port 138 (datagram services)

— TCP port 139 (session services)

Remember that certain applications and services depend on NetBIOS and can no longer operate after these services have been disabled; therefore, it is important to verify that any clients and applications no longer need NetBIOS. For example, pre-Windows 2000 computers are unable to browse, locate, or create file- and print-share connections to a Windows 2000 server with NetBIOS disabled.

☐ Disable or delete unnecessary accounts. Within Windows 2000 and XP, review any inactive accounts for users or applications that use the Computer Management snap-in. In Windows NT 4, use User Manager. Disable any nonactive accounts, and delete accounts that are no longer required.

☐ Protect files and directories. From a default installation of a Windows NT4 or 2000 operating system, you must make a number of file system permission changes to secure the operating system files themselves. The definitive list of files and directories that require modification for a secure Windows environment are available in the NSA Windows NT Systems Security Guidelines, produced by Trusted System Services (see nsa2.www.conxion.com/index.html).

☐ Disable the Guest account. The Guest account is disabled by default on servers that are running Windows NT4 Server and Windows 2000.

☐ Protect the Registry from anonymous access. A default installation of Windows NT4 and 2000 does not restrict user access to the Registry. See the Microsoft Knowledge Base article "How to Restrict Access to the Registry from a Remote Computer" (visit support.microsoft.com/ and search for article Q153183).

☐ Apply appropriate Registry Access Control Lists (ACLs). Clean-installed Windows 2000 servers have secure default ACLs applied to Registry entries; however, upgrades from previous versions (for example, Windows NT4 Server) do not modify the previous security settings. Refer to the article "Default Access Control Settings in Windows 2000," for the necessary modifications (see www.microsoft.com/TechNet/prodtechnol/windows2000serv/maintain/security/secdefs.asp).

☐ Restrict access to public Local Security Authority (LSA) information. The LSA handles aspects of security administration on the local computer, including access and permissions. Perform the following Registry edit under Windows NT4 Server and Windows 2000 to implement restrictions for anonymous users and to restrict the amount of public information they can obtain about the LSA component:

```
Hive
HKEY_LOCAL_MACHINE \SYSTEM

Key
CurrentControlSet\Control\LSA

Value Name
RestrictAnonymous

Type
REG_DWORD

Value
1
```

CAUTION   Accessing and modifying the Registry can be a hazardous operation that could result in an unstable or unusable system.

☐ Set stronger password policies. Within Windows NT4 Server, use the Account Policy Manager, and within Windows 2000, use the Domain Security Policy or Local Security Policy snap-in to enforce strong passwords on users. In Windows 2000, you can load a snap-in through the Microsoft Management Console (MMC). Microsoft makes the following recommendations:

— Set the minimum password length to 8 characters.

— Set a minimum password age that is appropriate to your network (typically from 1 to 7 days).

— Set a maximum password age that is appropriate to your network (typically no more than 42 days).

— Set a password history maintenance (using the Remember passwords option) of at least 6.

☐ Set account lockout policy. Within Windows NT4 Server and Windows 2000, the administrator can enable an account lockout policy. This disables an account after an administrator-specified number of login failures. Within Windows NT4 Server, use User Manager for Domains and select the Account Policy option. Within Windows 2000, use the Domain Security Policy or Local Security Policy snap-in.

The Windows NT Server Resource Kit includes a tool that allows you to adjust some account properties that are not accessible through the normal management tools. This tool, passprop.exe, allows you to lock out the Administrator account. The */adminlockout* switch allows you to lock out the Administrator account.

☐ Configure the Administrator account. Default installations of Windows NT4 Server and Windows 2000 contain an Administrator login account, which is similar to the UNIX root account. You should rename this account to something different from the obvious. For example, do not use admin, supervisor, root, and so on. Adding a decoy account, such as administrator, admin, or root, with no privileges would throw off a hacker or at least create enough activity in the security logs and audit trails to alert the real administrator. Enable account lockouts on Administrator accounts, but be sure that other Administrator accounts are available to unlock any locked accounts.

☐ Remove all unnecessary shares. Be sure to remove any unnecessary shares to directories (folders) or files. By default, in Windows NT4 Server and Windows 2000 installations, all drives are shared for administrative purposes. This could potentially be exploited, so to secure your systems, remove this share by using Windows Explorer.

☐ Set appropriate ACLs on all necessary file shares. Newly created shares, by default, allow all users the Full Control permission. All legitimate shares that are resident on a server should have the appropriate ACLs applied. See "NTFS," later in this appendix, for an explanation of NTFS permissions.

☐ Install antivirus software and updates. You must install antivirus software and keep current with the latest virus signatures on all Internet and intranet systems. More security antivirus information is available on the Microsoft TechNet security website (visit www.microsoft.com/technet/ and click Security in the navigation menu).

Applying Patches

As explained earlier in this appendix, Microsoft has produced tools to determine service pack and hot fix requirements. You should keep informed of newly released service packs and update your OS as soon as possible. When this book was written, the most recent service pack for Windows 2000 is Service Pack 3; for Windows NT4 Server, it is Service Pack 6a. Microsoft service packs are cumulative, which means that they contain the fixes that were included in previous versions of the service pack plus any new fixes. Hot fixes are released as interim fixes until the next service pack becomes available. In addition to Windows service packs, *Security Roll Up Packages* are available. These packages are a collection of all the security fixes packaged into one post–service pack update. Currently, versions are available for Windows NT4 Server and Windows 2000.

In Windows 2000 and XP, Microsoft has implemented a utility called Windows Update. This utility notifies the system user of crucial security and product updates and offers to automatically download and install these updates in an online environment. A Security Notifications Bulletin service is also now available from Microsoft. This service enables users and administrators to subscribe and receive by e-mail accurate information informing them of new security issues, threats and attacks, and details of fixes. You can subscribe to this service at the following website:

register.microsoft.com/regsys/pic.asp

As mentioned earlier, you should lab test any new service packs and make a full backup of your system before implementing them.

Enabling Auditing and Logging

Auditing and logging provide the ability to track user account activity, track logon and logoff date and time, see what files have been accessed, and determine what web pages have been viewed. Enabling auditing and logging allows you to track these events and provides the administrator with important security information, as follows:

- **Event logs**—These logs are built into Windows NT4 Server, Windows 2000, and Windows XP and consist of the System Event Log, the Application Event Log, and the Security Event Log. The Event Viewer utility is used to view the logs and apply filters. The System Event Log tracks errors, warnings, and information about the operating system itself, its services, and the hardware it is running on. The Application Event Log tracks application events and history. The Security Log tracks security events such as user activity, any access attempts, failures and successes, and the accessing of files and directories.

- **IIS logs**—These logs are specific to Internet Information Server and are more comprehensive than the standard event logs. IIS logs provide website, time and date, access, and page information.

Auditing of specific user events includes logon/logoff, use of user rights, user right and group management, security policy changes, file and object access, restart/shutdown, and system and process tracking. These audited events appear in the Security Log in Event Viewer. Within Windows NT4 Server, these events are configured in User Manager for Domains and Policies. In Windows 2000, use the Group Policy snap-in within the Microsoft Management Console (MMC) and the Audit Policies within the MMC.

Enabling file and directory auditing provides security monitoring over what resources are being accessed. Monitoring files and directories in any network operating system environment is critical. Auditing and monitoring are only effective if the administrators actually review this information; otherwise, serious events could go unnoticed. File and directory auditing is granular in the sense that it allows the administrator to track a specific user's access to a specific directory or file. To enable file and directory auditing, follow these steps:

Step 1   Use Windows Explorer to navigate the file system.

Step 2   Right-click the object.

Step 3   Choose Properties.

Step 4   Select the Security tab.

Step 5   Click Auditing.

Any configured auditing events appear in the security log. For Special Permissions, select Advanced under the Security tab.

File Systems

When planning for and installing a Windows operating system, only one choice exists for a secure installation: NTFS. FAT and FAT32 provide no file system security. You simply cannot apply permissions to files or directories under FAT and FAT32. In this section, you cover the common file systems in turn and the security implications of each.

FAT

The FAT file system, which uses a 16-bit table, is the simplest file system that is supported in a Windows and desktop environment. FAT first appeared in Microsoft DOS and ingeniously took its name from the system's terminology: File Allocation Table. FAT served as the definitive PC/desktop file system for several years until hard disk technology began to develop beyond the limitations of this file system.

FAT under DOS and Windows supports a maximum partition size of 2 GB. Under Windows NT, FAT supports partitions of up to 4 GB. Due to its 32-KB cluster size, FAT does not make efficient use of hard disk space.

FAT16 provides no file or directory security permissions. Since the introduction of FAT32, FAT is now commonly referred to as FAT16. The next section describes FAT32 in more detail.

FAT32

FAT32 shipped with Windows 95 OEM Release 2 (OSR2) and brought with it several advantages over the previous file system. Unlike FAT, which uses a 16-bit file system and a total of 65,525 entries, FAT32 uses a 32-bit file system and supports billions of entries. The FAT32 file system is no longer restricted to a 32-KB cluster size, uses a new default cluster size as small as 4 KB, and supports partition sizes up to 2 terabytes (TB) in size.

FAT32 is more robust than the previous version of FAT. It can recover from a single point of failure by including a backup copy of critical data structures.

Initially, FAT only allowed 8-character filenames and 3-character extensions, so the introduction of Windows 95 and the ability to support 255-character filenames was of great benefit. Currently, Windows 95 OEM Release 2 (OSR2), 98, Me, 2000, and XP are the only Microsoft operating systems that can access FAT32 volumes. MS-DOS, the original version of Windows 95, and Windows NT4 cannot recognize a FAT32 partition.

Neither FAT16 nor FAT32 support proper file system security permissions. For example, you cannot restrict access to a file or folder by user or group membership.

NTFS

NTFS was originally designed for Windows NT and supports file-level system security. Its design goals were to provide not only reliability and recoverability but also added platform functionality, POSIX (portable operating system interface for computing) support, and the removal of previous file system limitations.

Recoverability is addressed through transaction logging against the file system so that in the event of a failure, the file system can be rolled back to the last commit point to recover consistency. Under NTFS, multiple copies of the master file table are stored. These attributes make the file system ideal for use in file servers, high-end systems, and large disk volumes. NTFS is capable of providing physical disk fault tolerance by the following three methods:

- Disk Mirroring (RAID-1) is configured with two mirrored disks connected to one controller.

- Disk Duplexing (RAID-1) is configured with two mirrored disks connected to two controllers.

- Disk Striping with Parity (RAID-5) is configured with at least 3 and no more than 32 NTFS-formatted disks, where data is striped across all disks along with parity information. The parity stripe is used to reconstruct missing or bad data striped during a read or write operation.

RAID-0 is supported under NTFS; however, RAID-0 provides no redundancy in the event of a failure, when data would have to be restored from backup. Data is striped across at least 3 and no more than 32 NTFS disks and provides increased disk performance.

NTFS supports platform and file-system security models based on local and network user accounts and user groups. You can manipulate these security attributes using the standard Windows Explorer interface.

POSIX is supported under NTFS. NTFS makes no distinction between uppercase and lowercase filename characters; however, POSIX uses a full case-sensitive mode of operation. MS-DOS and Win32 systems, on the other hand, use the case-insensitive mode operation under NTFS.

With NTFS, various limitations of the FAT16 and FAT32 file systems have been removed. NTFS can support disk and volume sizes up to 16 exabytes (EB) of data. Like FAT32, NTFS supports filenames of up to 255 characters, excluding any of the following:

> / [ ] ; = " \ : | , * .

NTFS does not support removable media, such as floppy disks, due to the overhead that the file system uses. As described earlier, file system encryption is now built into Windows 2000 and XP in the form of EFS. Disk-editing tools that are available from third-party vendors can enable you to read an NTFS volume without an access check. EFS addresses this issue by providing file encryption.

Two versions of NTFS currently exist: NTFS4.0, which is native to Windows NT4, and NTFS5.0, which is native to Windows 2000 and Windows XP.

NTFS Permissions

NTFS permissions together build an Access Control List (ACL) that dictates a user's level of access to a file, folder, or share. There are two categories of permissions, as follows:

- **Standard**—Standard permissions are preset and frequently used for files and folders.

- **Special**—Special permissions provide finer granularity to files and folders.

Folder permissions govern access to a folder and the files and subfolders within that folder. Permissions can be assigned to a user or group of users. Table B-1 illustrates the folder permissions that are available and the type of access that is granted to the user.

Table B-1   *NTFS Folder Permissions*

NTFS Folder Permission	Access Description
List	View the folder contents
Read	View the folder contents, open files, view files, view folder attributes and permissions
Read & Execute	Same as Read, plus the ability to navigate through all files and subfolders
Write	Same as Read, plus the ability to create new files and folders and change folder attributes
Modify	Combined access of Read & Execute and Write, plus the ability to delete the folder
Full Control	Same access as Modify, plus the ability to change permissions, take ownership, and delete folders and files

File permissions govern access to a file. Permissions can be assigned to a user or group of users. Table B-2 illustrates the file permissions that are available and the type of access that is granted to the user.

Table B-2   *NTFS File Permissions*

NTFS File Permission	Access Description
Read	Open the file and view its attributes, ownership, and permissions
Read & Execute	Same as Read, plus the ability to run and execute applications
Write	Same as Read, plus the ability to change file content and attributes
Modify	Same as Read & Execute and Write combined, plus the ability to delete the file
Full Control	Same as Modify, plus the ability to change permissions and take ownership

When dissimilar permissions are assigned between a folder and the files within it, the NTFS file permissions override or take priority over the NTFS folder permissions. A user account that has access to a file can access that file even though the parent folder does not state permission. For example, if the folder had no list permission assigned for the user, a UNC format request would be needed to open the file directly because the user would be unable to list it or see it.

Universal Naming Convention (UNC) is a method of locating a file or share over a network. A UNC name specifies a shared folder and file that are accessible over a network as opposed to a folder and file that are identified by a drive letter and path. For example, a UNC path to the file index.html on a server called webserver would be \\webserver\index.html.

By default, NTFS permissions are inherited. Permissions that are assigned to a parent folder are inherited by all files and subfolders within it. Consequently, by assigning permissions to a subfolder within a parent folder, all subfolders and files within the new subfolder are inherited from it.

Every file or folder has an owner, usually the initial creator. An owner has full control of the file or folder and can assign other users permissions to it. However, a user who has the appropriate permissions can take ownership of the file or folder.

Share-Level Security

NTFS permissions are assigned to folders and files, and they can be assigned to shares. Shared drives and folders provide network access to files. In a similar way that folders and files are assigned NTFS permissions, share permissions are assigned to govern what access a user can receive to a specific share. Table B-3 illustrates the share permissions that are available and the type of access that is granted to the user.

Table B-3   *NTFS Share Permissions*

NTFS Share Permission	Access Description
Read	Display the contents of the folder, open files, display attributes, and run and execute applications
Change	Same as Read, plus the ability to create new folders and files within the shared folder or drive, open and change files, change file attributes, and delete folders and files
Full Control	Same as Change, plus the ability to take ownership of files and change file permissions

Combined Security

You can assign multiple NTFS permissions to a user account directly or to a group that the user is a member of. Note that NTFS permissions are cumulative. The effective user permissions are a least-restrictive combination of the direct user permissions and any group permissions that the user has inherited through group membership. For example, if a user is assigned Read access to a specific file and a group that the user is a member of dictates that all users within the group have Write permissions, the effective permission to the file is Read and Write.

In any instance, Deny or No Access overrides all other permissions. For example, if a user is a member of two groups, one allowing full control to a folder and the other denying access to the folder, the user is denied permission. Administrators are encouraged not to use this permission and instead to simply not assign permission that would provide access to a folder or file.

When combining share permissions and NTFS permissions, the most restrictive applies.

The steps for determining effective NTFS permissions are as follows:

Step 1   Determine effective shared permissions by choosing the least restrictive of all shared permissions. The exception is the Denied permission, which overrides Allow.

Step 2   Determine effective NTFS permissions by choosing the least restrictive of all shared permissions. The exception is the Denied permission, which overrides Allow. Also, file permissions take precedence over folder permissions.

Step 3   Combine the results of Steps 1 and 2, and choose the most restrictive permission out of share and NTFS. If there is no overlap, then no permissions are effective.

Summary

This overview provides a basic introduction to Windows security and is not intended to answer every security scenario that you might see. The guidelines for installing and securing the OS and network services, applying patches, enabling auditing and logging, and using file systems outline fundamental practices to use when administering a Windows networking environment. Remember to access the Microsoft website to keep current on the latest hot fixes and patches.

This appendix covers the following topics:

- ISDN switch types
- ISDN cause code fields
- ISDN cause values
- ISDN bearer capability values
- ISDN progress field values

ISDN Error Codes and Debugging Reference

One of the most frustrating things you run into when working with ISDN is the error messages you receive upon a failure or during a debugging session. Unless you work with ISDN on a daily basis, chances are these messages will seem like a foreign language to you. Fortunately, you can memorize a few of these message codes to get you by in most situations you will encounter; the only problem is deciding which ones to memorize. As you work with ISDN more in your environment, you will gain an understanding of which of the numerous codes you need to remember.

This appendix lists the most common ISDN switch types you will work with on Cisco equipment, ISDN cause codes, cause values, bearer capability values, and progress description field values that are valid within the **debug** commands available to you.

ISDN Switch Types

Matching the ISDN switch type to the one your service provider uses is one of the most important steps you will complete in your configuration of ISDN. If your switch type does not match, your link will either fail to operate or will operate in an unstable manner. Currently, the ISDN interface supports 19 different ISDN switch types. Table C-1 lists the most common switch types you are likely to encounter when working with Cisco ISDN equipment in North America.

Table C-1 *Common ISDN Switch Types*

Keyword	Switch Description
basic-5ess	AT&T basic rate switches
basic-dms100	NT DMS-100 basic rate switches
basic-ni1	National ISDN-1 switches
None	No switch is defined
primary-5ess	AT&T 5ESS switch type for the U.S. (ISDN PRI only)
primary-dms100	NT DMS-100 switch type for the U.S. (ISDN PRI only)

You use basic when configuring a BRI. You use primary when configuring a PRI.

ISDN Cause Code Fields

Whenever you start an ISDN debug session, one of the first things you notice is that any failure or error appears as a line of gibberish. This gibberish is actually the ISDN cause code. It is composed of fields that are normally displayed in the following format:

I = 0x $y1$ $y2$ $z1$ $z2$ [$a1$ $a2$]

Table C-2 describes these fields to help you decode these messages.

Table C-2 *ISDN Cause Code Fields*

Cause Code Field	Value Description
$0x$	Indicates that the values that follow are in hexadecimal.
$y1$	8—ITU-T standard coding.
$y2$	0—User
	1—Private network serving local user
	2—Public network serving local user
	3—Transit network
	4—Public network serving remote user
	5—Private network serving local user
	6—International network
	A—Network beyond internetworking point
$z1$	The class (the more-significant hexadecimal number) of the cause value. See Table C-3 for detailed information about possible values.
$z2$	The value (the less-significant hexadecimal number) of the cause value. See Table C-3 for detailed information about possible values.
$a1$	(Optional) A diagnostic field that is always 8.
$a2$	(Optional) A diagnostic field that is one of the following values:
	0—Unknown
	1—Permanent
	2—Transient

ISDN Cause Values

Now that you have the class and value of the cause value (in hexadecimal, of course), you need a way to decode this to help you further isolate your problem. Table C-3 describes these values, referred to as the *cause information element*. If you are using the **debug isdn q931** command to obtain your output, drop the highest bit of the cause value (for example, 0x90 becomes 0x10) before consulting this table. (The notes referred to in the Diagnostics column appear after the table.)

Table C-3   *ISDN Cause Values*

Decimal Value	Hex Value	Cause	Diagnostic	Explanation
1	01	Unallocated (unassigned) number	Note 10	ISDN number is sent to the switch in the correct format; however, the number is not assigned to any destination equipment.
2	02	No route to specified transit network	Transit network identity (Note 9)	ISDN exchange is asked to route the call through an unrecognized intermediate network.
3	03	No route to destination	Note 10	Call was routed through an intermediate network that does not serve the destination address.
6	06	Channel unacceptable		Service quality of the specified channel is insufficient to accept the connection.
7	07	Call awarded and being delivered in an established channel		User is assigned an incoming call that is being connected to an established call channel.
16	10	Normal call clearing	Note 10	Normal call clearing has occurred.
17	11	User busy		Called system acknowledges the connection request but is unable to accept the call because all B channels are in use.
18	12	No user responding		Connection cannot be completed because the destination does not respond to the call.
19	13	No answer from user (user alerted)		Destination responds to the connection request but fails to complete the connection within the prescribed time. The problem is at the remote end of the connection.
21	15	Call rejected	Note 10—User-supplied diagnostic (Note 4)	Destination can accept the call but rejected the call for an unknown reason.

continues

Table C-3   *ISDN Cause Values (Continued)*

Decimal Value	Hex Value	Cause	Diagnostic	Explanation
22	16	Number changed	Note 10—User-supplied diagnostic (Note 4)	ISDN number used to set up the call is not assigned to any system.
26	1A	Nonselected user clearing		Destination can accept the call but rejected the call because it was not assigned to the user.
27	1B	Designation out of order		Destination cannot be reached because the interface is not functioning correctly, and a signaling message cannot be delivered. This might be a temporary condition, but it could last for an extended period of time.
28	1C	Invalid number format		Connection could not be established because the destination address was presented in an unrecognizable format or because the destination address was incomplete.
29	1D	Facility rejected	Facility identification (Note 1)	Facility requested by the user cannot be provided by the network.
30	1E	Response to STATUS ENQUIRY		Status message was generated in direct response to the prior receipt of a status enquiry message.
31	1F	Normal, unspecified		Reports the occurrence of a normal event when no standard cause applies. No action is required.
34	22	No circuit/channel available		Connection cannot be established because no appropriate channel is available to take the call.
38	26	Network out of order		Destination cannot be reached because the network is not functioning correctly, and the condition might last for an extended period of time. An immediate reconnect attempt will probably be unsuccessful.

Table C-3   *ISDN Cause Values (Continued)*

Decimal Value	Hex Value	Cause	Diagnostic	Explanation
41	29	Temporary failure	Facility identification (Note 1)	Error occurred because the network is not functioning correctly. The problem will be resolved shortly.
42	2A	Switching equipment congestion		Destination cannot be reached because the network switching equipment is temporarily overloaded.
43	2B	Access information discarded	Discarded information element identifier(s) (Note 5)	Network cannot provide the requested access information.
44	2C	Requested circuit/ channel unavailable		Remote equipment cannot provide the requested channel for an unknown reason. This might be a temporary problem.
47	2F	Resources unavailable, unspecified		Requested channel or service is unavailable for an unknown reason. This might be a temporary problem.
49	31	Quality of service unavailable	See Table C-2	Requested quality of service cannot be provided by the network. This might be a subscription problem.
50	32	Requested facility not subscribed	Facility identification (Note 1)	Remote equipment supports the requested supplementary service by subscription only.
57	39	Bearer capability not authorized	Note 3	User requested a bearer capability that the network provides, but the user is not authorized to use it. This might be a subscription problem.
58	3A	Bearer capability presently unavailable		Network normally provides the requested bearer capability, but it is unavailable at the present time. This might be due to a temporary network problem or a subscription problem.

continues

Table C-3 *ISDN Cause Values (Continued)*

Decimal Value	Hex Value	Cause	Diagnostic	Explanation
63	3F	Service or option unavailable, unspecified	Note 3	Network or remote equipment was unable to provide the requested service option for an unspecified reason. This might be a subscription problem.
65	41	Bearer capability not implemented		Network cannot provide the bearer capability requested by the user.
66	42	Channel type not implemented	Channel Type (Note 6)	Network or the destination equipment does not support the requested channel type.
69	45	Requested facility not implemented	Facility Identification (Note 1)	Remote equipment does not support the requested supplementary service.
70	46	Only restricted digital information bearer capability is available		Network is unable to provide unrestricted digital information bearer capability.
79	4F	Service or option not implemented, unspecified		Network or remote equipment is unable to provide the requested service option for an unspecified reason. This might be a subscription problem.
81	51	Invalid call reference value		Remote equipment received a call with a call reference that is not currently in use on the user-network interface.
82	52	Identified channel does not exist	Channel identity	Receiving equipment is asked to use a channel that is not activated on the interface for calls.
83	53	A suspended call exists, but this call identity does not		Network received a call resume request. The call resume request contained a Call Identify information element that indicates that the call identity is being used for a suspended call.

Table C-3   *ISDN Cause Values (Continued)*

Decimal Value	Hex Value	Cause	Diagnostic	Explanation
84	54	Call identity in use	Channel identity	Network received a call resume request. The call resume request contained a Call Identify information element that indicates that it is in use for a suspended call.
85	55	No call suspended		Network received a call resume request when there was not a suspended call pending. This might be a transient error that will be resolved by successive call retries.
86	56	Call having the requested call identity has been cleared	Clearing cause	Network received a call resume request. The call resume request contained a Call Identity information element, which once indicated a suspended call. However, the suspended call was cleared either by timeout or by the remote user.
88	58	Incompatible destination	Incompatible parameter (Note 2)	Indicates that an attempt was made to connect to non-ISDN equipment.
91	5B	Invalid transit network selection		ISDN exchange was asked to route the call through an unrecognized intermediate network.
95	5F	Invalid message, unspecified		Invalid message was received, and no standard cause applies. This is usually because of a D-channel error. If this error occurs systematically, report it to your ISDN service provider.
96	60	Mandatory information element is missing	Information element identifier(s) (Note 5)	Receiving equipment received a message that did not include one of the mandatory information elements. This is usually due to a D-channel error. If this error occurs systematically, report it to your ISDN service provider.

continues

Table C-3 *ISDN Cause Values (Continued)*

Decimal Value	Hex Value	Cause	Diagnostic	Explanation
97	61	Message type nonexistent or not implemented	Message type	Receiving equipment received an unrecognized message, either because the message type was invalid or because the message type was valid but not supported. The cause is either a problem with the remote configuration or a problem with the local D channel.
98	62	Message not compatible with call state, or message type nonexistent or not implemented		Remote equipment received an invalid message, and no standard cause applies. The cause is a D-channel error. If this error occurs systematically, report it to your ISDN service provider.
99	63	Information element nonexistent or not implemented	Information element identifier(s) (Notes 5, 7)	Remote equipment received a message that includes information elements, which were not recognized. This is usually because of a D-channel error. If this error occurs systematically, report it to your ISDN service provider.
100	64	Invalid information element contents	Information element identifier(s) (Note 5)	Remote equipment received a message that includes invalid information in the information element. This is usually because of a D-channel error.
101	65	Message not compatible with call state	Message type	Remote equipment received an unexpected message that does not correspond to the current state of the connection. This is usually because of a D-channel error.
102	66	Recovery on timer expires	Timer number (Note 8)	Error-handling (recovery) procedure was initiated by a timer expiration. This is usually a temporary problem.

Table C-3   *ISDN Cause Values (Continued)*

Decimal Value	Hex Value	Cause	Diagnostic	Explanation
111	6F	Protocol error, unspecified	Timer number (Note 8)	Unspecified D-channel error when no other standard cause applies.
127	7F	Internetworking, unspecified		Event occurred, but the network does not provide causes for the action it takes. The precise problem is unknown.

Note 1—The coding of facility identification is network-dependent.

Note 2—An incompatible parameter is composed of an incompatible information element identifier.

Note 3—The format of the diagnostic field for causes 39, 3A, and 41 is shown in the ITU-T Q.850 specification, Table 3b/Q.850.

Note 4—The user-supplied diagnostic field is encoded according to the user specification, subject to the maximum length of the cause information element. The coding of user-supplied diagnostics should be done in such a way that it does not conflict with the coding described in Table C-2.

Note 5—Locking and nonlocking shift procedures described in the ITU-T Q.931 specification apply. In principle, information element identifiers are in the same order as the information elements in the received message.

Note 6—The following coding is used:
Bit 8—Extension bit
Bits 7 through 5—Spare
Bits 4 through 1—According to Table 4-15/Q.931 octet 3.2, channel type in ITU-T Q.931 specification

Note 7—When only the locking shift information element is included and no variable-length information element identifier follows, it means that the codeset in the locking shift itself is not implemented.

Note 8—The timer number is coded in IA5 characters. The following coding is used in each octet:
Bit 8—Spare "0"
Bits 7 through 1—IA5 character

Note 9—The diagnostic field contains the entire transit network selection or network-specific facilities information element, as applicable.

Note 10—See Table C-2 for the coding that is used.

ISDN Bearer Capability Values

As you might suspect, bearer capabilities are also encoded in a *bearer capability value*. Table C-4 lists the ISDN bearer capability values you might see during a debugging session. These messages have the following format:

- 0x8890 for 64 kbps
- 0x8890218F for 56 kbps

Table C-4   *ISDN Bearer Capability Values*

Capability Value Field	Value Description
0x	Indicates that the values that follow are in hexadecimal
88	ITU-T coding standard; unrestricted digital information
90	Circuit mode, 64 kbps
21	Layer 1, V.110/X.30
8F	Synchronous, no in-band negotiation, 56 kbps

ISDN Progress Field Values

Even the progress of an ISDN call is encoded into an ISDN progress field, except that the values are in binary instead of hexadecimal. Table C-5 lists the values used in the Progress Description field contained in the ISDN progress indicator information element.

Table C-5   *ISDN Progress Description Field Values*

Bits	Decimal Number	Description
0000001	1	Call is not end-to-end ISDN; further call progress information may be available in-band
0000010	2	Destination address is non-ISDN
0000011	3	Origination address is non-ISDN
0000100	4	Call has returned to the ISDN
0001000	8	In-band information or appropriate pattern now available
0001010	10	Delay in response at destination interface

All other values you might see in the Progress Description field are reserved.

Summary

After browsing the tables in this appendix, you should see why you might not want to memorize every error you might receive. Although all these values are commonly referred to as errors, some of them you will see in the normal operation of an ISDN call, such as the normal call clearing message. Only time and experience can help you figure out which of these values are the most important, because each environment has its own unique characteristics.

This appendix covers the following topics:

- The software configuration register
- The break sequence
- Using the software configuration register for password recovery
- Renaming software to recover a password
- Replacing software to recover a password
- Password recovery through resetting a device
- Using hardware settings to recover a password
- Password recovery on the Cisco Secure IDS Sensor
- Password recovery on the Cisco Secure PIX Firewall
- Password recovery for ACS on UNIX
- Password recovery for ACS on NT
- Password recovery on VPN Concentrators
- How to simulate a Break key sequence

Password Recovery on Cisco IOS, CatalystOS, and PIX

Although it is not a topic you like to think about, at one time or another in your career you will need to perform password recovery on some type of Cisco device. This appendix gives you an overview of the various methods you can use to recover a forgotten password. These methods include changing configuration register variables and replacing the software with a password-recovery version, as some devices require.

The Software Configuration Register

Most of the Cisco devices you will deal with in your day-to-day operations require a change in the software configuration register variable to facilitate password recovery. This group of variables has other functions as well and can be used to customize your devices to your individual needs.

These devices have a 16-bit software register that is stored in nonvolatile memory (NVM). Table D-1 describes each of the 16 software configuration memory bits, and Table D-2 lists the details of the boot field.

Table D-1   *Software Configuration Bit Meanings*

Bit Number	Hex	Meaning
00–03	0x0000–0x000F	Boot field
06	0x0040	Ignore NVM contents
07	0x0080	Original equipment manufacturer (OEM) bit enabled
08	0x0100	Break disabled
10	0x0400	IP broadcast with all 0s
11–12	0x0800–0x1000	Console line speed
13	0x2000	Boot default ROM software if network boot fails
14	0x4000	IP broadcasts do not have network numbers
15	0x8000	Enable diagnostic messages and NVM contents

Table D-2   *Details of the Boot Field*

Boot Field	Meaning
00	Stays at the system bootstrap prompt (ROM monitor) on a reload of the power cycle
01	Boots the first system image in onboard flash
02–F	Specifies a default netboot filename
	Enables boot system commands that override the default netboot filename

A boot filename is formed as part of the automatic configuration process. The boot filename starts with "cisco" and links the octal equivalent of the boot field number, a dash, and the processor-type name. Table D-3 lists the default boot filenames or actions for the processor. Remember that if you define a **boot system** command in your router's configuration, it overrides the default netboot filename selected in the configuration register.

Table D-3   *Default Boot Filenames*

Action/Filename	Bit 3	Bit 2	Bit 1	Bit 0
Bootstrap monitor	0	0	0	0
Default software	0	0	0	1
cisco2-*processor*	0	0	1	0
cisco3-*processor*	0	0	1	1
cisco4-*processor*	0	1	0	0
cisco5-*processor*	0	1	0	1
cisco6-*processor*	0	1	1	0
cisco7-*processor*	0	1	1	1
cisco10-*processor*	1	0	0	0
cisco11-*processor*	1	0	0	1
cisco12-*processor*	1	0	1	0
cisco13-*processor*	1	0	1	1
cisco14-*processor*	1	1	0	0
cisco15-*processor*	1	1	0	1
cisco16-*processor*	1	1	1	0
cisco17-*processor*	1	1	1	1

processor represents the processor family. For instance, on IGS-based platforms, this is igs. On RSP-based platforms, this is RSP.

You can use bit 8 to control the console Break key. By setting bit 8, you cause the processor to ignore the console Break key. By clearing bit 8, you force the processor to interpret a break as a command to force the system into the bootstrap monitor, halting normal operation. You can send a break within the first 60 seconds of a system reboot, regardless of the configuration settings.

You can use bit 10 to control the host portion of the Internet broadcast address. By setting bit 10, you cause the processor to use all 0s for broadcasts; clearing bit 10 causes the processor to use all 1s for broadcasts. Bit 10 works in conjunction with bit 14, which you can use to control the network and subnet portions of the broadcast address. Table D-4 illustrates the combined effect of bits 10 and 14.

Table D-4   *Configuration Register Settings for Broadcast Address Destination*

Bit 14	Bit 10	Address (*net host*)
Off	Off	*1s 1s*
Off	On	*0s 0s*
On	On	*net 0s*
On	Off	*net 1s*

You can use bit 13 to determine the response to a bootload failure. By setting bit 13, you cause the server to load the operating software from ROM after five unsuccessful attempts to load a boot file from the network. By clearing bit 13, you cause the server to continue attempting to load a boot file from the network indefinitely.

You can use bits 11 and 12 to determine the baud rate of the console terminal. Table D-5 shows the bit settings you can use for the four available baud rates.

Table D-5   *System Console Terminal Baud Rate Settings*

Baud	Bit 12	Bit 11
9600	0	0
4800	0	1
1200	1	0
2400	1	1

The Break Sequence

Before you start the password-recovery process, you need to be aware that the Break key sequence of the most common operating systems depends on the software you use. Table D-6 shows the standard Break key sequences you use with a variety of software.

Table D-6 *Standard Break Key Combinations*

Software	Platform	Operating System	Key Combination or Procedure
Hyperterminal	IBM-compatible	Windows 2000	Ctrl-Break
Hyperterminal (version 595160)	IBM-compatible	Windows 95	Ctrl-F6-Break
Kermit	Sun workstation	UNIX	Ctrl-\l Ctrl-\b
MicroPhone Pro	IBM-compatible	Windows	Ctrl-Break
Minicom	IBM-compatible	Linux	Ctrl-a f
ProComm Plus	IBM-compatible	DOS or Windows	Alt-b
Telix	IBM-compatible	DOS	Ctrl-End
Telnet to Cisco	IBM-compatible	—	Ctrl-]
Teraterm	IBM-compatible	Windows	Alt-b
Terminal	IBM-compatible	Windows	Break Ctrl-Break
Tip	Sun workstation	UNIX	Ctrl-], then Break or Ctrl-c ~#
VT 100 Emulation	Data general	—	F16
Windows NT	IBM-compatible	Windows	Break-F5 Shift-F5 Shift-6 Shift-4 Shift-b (^$B)
Z-TERMINAL	Macintosh	Apple	Command-b
—	Break-Out Box	—	Connect pin 2 (X-mit) to +V for half a second
—	Cisco to aux port	—	Ctrl-Shift-6, then b
—	IBM-compatible	—	Ctrl-Break

Using the Software Configuration Register for Password Recovery

Two different methods exist for recovering a password using the software configuration register method. One uses the **config-register** or **confreg** command, and the other uses the **o/r** command. Which method you use depends on the platform and device you are performing the procedure on.

Using config-register or confreg for Password Recovery

This section describes the procedure used to recover a password using the **config-register** or **confreg** command. If you used the **enable password** command to configure your privileged EXEC mode, you can recover it using a utility such as the free GetPass password-recovery utility, available from Boson at www.boson.com/promo/utilities/getpass/getpass_utility.htm. It is written for use against the enable password hash, displayed when you enable the **service password encryption** command, but if you used the **enable secret** command to configure the password, you must set a new one. A new utility called tomas, available at packetstormsecurity.org/cisco/tomas.zip, might be able to brute-force an enable secret.

The following steps assume that you are performing password recovery on a Cisco router. You can adapt these steps to other Cisco devices that use the software configuration register, such as the Catalyst 8540 or the Catalyst 3550, by replacing the default prompts of the device you are working with. To set the software configuration register so that you may recover the password, follow these steps:

Step 1   Attach a terminal or a PC with terminal emulation to the router's console port.

Step 2   If you still have access to your router, use the **show version** command and record the settings of the current software configuration register.

If you don't have access to your router, you may safely assume that it is currently set to 0x2102.

Step 3   Using the power switch, power-cycle your router by turning it off and then back on.

If you are performing this on a Cisco 6400, you must pull out and then replace the Node Route Processor (NRP) or Node Switch Processor (NSP) card.

If you are performing this on the Cisco 6x00 using NI-2, you must pull out and then replace the NI-2 card.

Step 4   Press the **Break** key sequence (use Table D-6 to determine this) on your terminal keyboard within 60 seconds of power-up to put your router into ROM Monitor mode (ROMMON).

Step 5   Enter the **confreg 0x2142** command at the rommon prompt to tell the device to boot from Flash while ignoring the configuration stored in nonvolatile random-access memory (NVRAM).

Step 6   Reset the device by entering the **reset** command at the rommon prompt to reboot your router while ignoring its saved configuration.

Step 7   Enter **no** after each setup question, or press **Ctrl-c** to skip the initial setup procedure if desired. Be aware that if you decide to run through the initial setup procedure and write the new configuration to NVRAM, you will lose your other configuration.

Step 8   Enter the **enable** command at the Router> prompt to change to privileged EXEC mode with the Router# prompt.

Step 9   Enter the **configure memory** or **copy startup-config running-config** command to copy your existing configuration stored in NVRAM into memory.

Step 10   Enter the **write terminal** or **show running-config** command to show your router's configuration. In this configuration, you should note which interfaces need to be brought back up because they are all in the shutdown state. You can also see the currently configured passwords in either an encrypted or unencrypted format. If your passwords are stored in their unencrypted form, you can reuse them. If your passwords are stored in their encrypted format, the password encryption algorithm used determines if you can recover them. If the encrypted password is preceded by the number 7, you can use a utility such as GetPass to recover the original password. If the encrypted password is preceded by the number 5, you might need to reset it if a utility such as tomas cannot recover it.

Step 11   If you must reset your password, enter the **configure terminal** command to make the change. You should now have a prompt similar to the following:

```
hostname(config)#
```

Step 12   Enter the appropriate command, such as **enable secret** *password,* to change the password.

Step 13   If you have not already done so, enter the **configure terminal** command to enter configuration mode to bring all required interfaces back up. Enter the appropriate command, such as **interface ethernet0/0**, to enter interface configuration mode. Enter the **no shutdown** command for every interface you want to activate. You can verify the state of your interfaces by issuing the **show ip interface brief** command after exiting configuration mode. Every interface you want to use should have an "up up" status.

Step 14 Enter the **config-register 0x2102** command or the value you recorded previously.

Step 15 Press **Ctrl-z** or **End** to leave configuration mode. Your prompt should now be as follows:

```
hostname#
```

Step 16 Enter the **write memory** or **copy running-config startup-config** command to save your new configuration to NVRAM.

The following steps are specified for use on the Catalyst 4000 switch with a Sup III processor. They illustrate another method of using the **confreg** command:

Step 1 Attach a terminal or a PC with terminal emulation to the console port.

Step 2 Power-cycle your device and press **Ctrl-c** within 5 seconds to prevent your device from autobooting. This places the device in ROM Monitor mode.

Step 3 Enter the **confreg** command at the prompt, and do the following to initiate password recovery:

Enter **y** when you see the following prompt:

```
do you wish to change the configuration? y/n  [n]:
```

Enter **n** for the following prompts:

```
enable  "diagnostic mode"? y/n  [n]:
enable  "use net in IP bcast address"? y/n  [n]:
disable "load ROM after netboot fails"? y/n  [n]:
enable  "use all zero broadcast"? y/n  [n]:
enable  "break/abort has effect"? y/n  [n]:
```

Enter **y** when you see the following prompt:

```
enable  "ignore system config info"? y/n  [n]:
```

Enter **n** for the following prompts:

```
change console baud rate? y/n  [n]:
change the boot characteristics? y/n  [n]:
```

Enter **y** after you verify the output and see the following prompt:

```
do you wish to save this configuration? y/n  [n]:
```

Step 4 Enter **reset** to cause the module to reboot and ignore its saved configuration as you instructed.

Step 5 After you press the **Enter** key, you can use the **configure memory** or **copy startup-config running-config** command to copy the saved configuration into memory from NVRAM.

Step 6 Use the **show ip interface brief** command to verify that all the interfaces you are using are in the "up up" state.

Step 7   Issue the **write terminal** or **show running-config** command to display your saved configuration for the module.

Step 8   Reset your passwords by entering configuration mode using the **configure terminal** command. If you used the **enable secret** command to set your password, you must issue the **no enable secret** command before you can set a new password.

Step 9   Change your configuration register value back to 0x2102 using the **config-register** command. Use the **config-register** command at the config prompt to change and verify the configuration register value.

Step 10 Issue the **write mem** command to save your new passwords to NVRAM.

Using o/r for Password Recovery

This section describes the procedure used to recover a password using the **o/r rommon** command. Use the following commands to perform password recovery on older Cisco routers and Cisco IOS software that does not support the **config-register** or **confreg** commands:

Step 1   Attach a terminal or a PC with terminal emulation to the router's console port.

Step 2   Power-cycle your router by using the power switch to turn it off and then back on.

Step 3   Press the **Break** key sequence within 60 seconds of the power-up to put your router into ROMMON.

Step 4   Record the current value stored in the configuration register by entering **o** at the > prompt.

Step 5   Change the value stored in the configuration register by entering **o/r 0x2142** at the > prompt to boot from Flash without loading the configuration.

Step 6   Enter **i** at the > prompt to reboot your router while ignoring its stored configuration.

Step 7   Enter **no** after each setup question, or press **Ctrl-c** to skip the initial setup procedure if desired. Be aware that if you decide to run through the initial setup procedure and write the new configuration to NVRAM, you lose your other configuration.

Step 8   Enter **enable** at the Router> prompt to enter privileged EXEC mode. Your prompt changes to the Router# prompt.

Step 9   Enter the **write terminal** or **show running-config** command to show your router's configuration. In this configuration, you should note which interfaces will need to be brought back up, because they will all be in shutdown state. You can also see the currently configured passwords in an encrypted or unencrypted format. If your passwords are stored in their unencrypted form, you can reuse them. If your passwords are stored in their encrypted format, the password encryption algorithm used determines if you can recover them. If the encrypted password is preceded by the number 7, you can use a utility such as GetPass to recover the original password. If the encrypted password is preceded by the number 5, you might need to reset it if a utility such as tomas cannot recover it for you.

Step 10 If you must reset your password, enter the **configure terminal** command to make the change. You should now have a prompt similar to the following:

```
hostname(config)#
```

Step 11 Enter the appropriate command, such as **enable secret** *password,* to change the password.

Step 12 If you have not done so already, enter the **configure terminal** command to enter configuration mode and bring all required interfaces back up. Enter the appropriate command, such as **interface ethernet0/0**, to enter interface configuration mode. Enter the **no shutdown** command for every interface you want to activate. You can verify the state of your interfaces by issuing the **show ip interface brief** command after exiting configuration mode. Every interface you want to use should have an "up up" status.

Step 13 Enter the **config-register 0x2102** command or the value you recorded previously.

Step 14 Press **Ctrl-z** or **End** to leave configuration mode. Your prompt should now be as follows:

```
hostname#
```

Step 15 Enter the **write memory** or **copy running-config startup-config** command to save your new configuration to NVRAM.

Renaming Software to Recover a Password

Some Cisco devices, such as the Catalyst 2900XL, 3500XL, 2950, and 3550 series of switches, require you to rename your configuration file that contains the password definitions for your device. By following these steps, you can recover your passwords:

Step 1 Attach a terminal or a PC with terminal emulation to the router's console port.

Step 2 Unplug the power cable to reset your device.

Step 3   Before reconnecting the power cord, hold down the mode button, located on the left side of your switch's front panel. Do not release the mode button until a second or two after the LED above port 1x is no longer illuminated. The following appears on your terminal:

```
The system has been interrupted prior to initializing the flash file system.
```

The following commands initialize the Flash file system and finish loading the operating system software:

flash_init

load_helper

boot

Step 4   Enter the following commands to finish initializing your device:

flash_init

load_helper

Step 5   Enter the **dir flash:** command; do not forget the : (colon symbol). The switch displays the contents of the file system on your terminal.

Step 6   Enter the **rename flash:config.text flash:config.old** command to rename the configuration file that contains the password definitions for your device.

Step 7   Enter the **boot** command to boot your system.

Step 8   Answer **no** by entering **n** when you are prompted to start the Setup program.

Step 9   Enter privileged EXEC mode by using the **enable** command.

Step 10   Enter the **rename flash:config.old flash:config.text** command to rename your configuration file using its original name.

Step 11   Copy the configuration file into memory by issuing the **copy flash:config.text system:running-config** command.

Step 12   Reset your passwords by entering configuration mode using the **configure terminal** command. If you used the **enable secret** command to set your password, you must issue the **no enable secret** command before you can set a new password.

Step 13   Enter the **write memory** command to save your new running configuration to the configuration file.

Replacing Software to Recover a Password

Some Cisco devices require you to replace the current software you have on the device with a special version of software. This special version of software erases the contents of NVRAM, so you do not have to enter a password to gain access to your device. By following these steps, you can recover your passwords on the Cisco Catalyst 5000 ATM module:

Step 1   Download the special ATM recovery image (one such image is atm_911.gbi) and a copy of your original or the latest ATM module image. If your LANE module does not have an external console connection, you must perform this procedure through remote means, such as Telnet.

Step 2   Use the **download** command to download the ATM module recovery image from the Catalyst 5000 supervisor console.

Step 3   When you see the "module online" message, your unknown password is disabled, and the contents of NVRAM are erased.

Step 4   If you want to save your original configuration without your unknown password, continue with Step 5; otherwise, skip ahead to Step 9.

Step 5   Use the **session** command to gain access to the ATM module you are performing this procedure on. Enter the **session** *ATM slot #* command.

Step 6   Use the **enable** command to gain access to privileged EXEC mode. You are not prompted for a password.

Step 7   Use the **write memory** command to save your original configuration to NVRAM, minus the passwords.

Step 8   Use the **exit** command to exit the module.

Step 9   If you want to enter a new configuration for your ATM module, or you just completed Steps 5 through 8, you must download your original ATM image using the **download** command from the Catalyst 5000 supervisor module.

Step 10 When you see the "module online" message, you may use the **session** command to gain access to your ATM module.

Step 11 Use the **enable** command to gain access to privileged EXEC mode. You are not prompted for a password.

Password Recovery Through Resetting the Device

Some older Cisco Catalyst devices with older Catalyst operating systems (CatOSs), such as the Catalyst 5000, 5500, 2926G, and 2926 series of switches, require you to reset the device to recover a password. This is possible because the CatOS ignores your password settings for

30 seconds after the device completes the initialization, giving you this amount of time to complete the password-recovery procedure. Follow these steps to accomplish this method of password recovery:

Step 1   Attach a terminal or a PC with terminal emulation to the switch's console port.

Step 2   Power-cycle your switch by turning it off and then back on.

Step 3   Press **Enter** when you are prompted for your password to enter a null password. You might have to wait a few minutes after your reset before you see the first password prompt.

Step 4   Enter privileged EXEC mode by entering the **enable** command at the prompt.

Step 5   Press **Enter** when you are prompted for the enable password to enter a null password.

Step 6   You can now change your passwords by using the **set password** and **set enablepass** commands.

Using Hardware Settings to Recover a Password

A few of the older Cisco devices or modules, such as the Catalyst 1200 series of switches, require you to modify hardware settings to recover a password. There are two ways to accomplish this:

- By shorting the jumper settings by hand

- By changing the jumper settings through software

The following sections cover the steps necessary to accomplish both of these methods.

Manually Shorting Jumper Settings

The following procedure causes your device to fail and stop running software. This is similar to accessing ROMMON mode on a router. Use these steps when manually shorting jumper settings:

Step 1   Remove the switch's cover.

Step 2   Locate pins JP17 and short across them. These pins are located to the right of the LEDs and to the left of the Reset button.

Step 3   After you short the pins, reboot your switch. Your switch initializes to a boot prompt.

Step 4 When you reach the boot prompt, you can use the **ifconfig** command to define an IP address and download Network Management Processor (NMP) and Data Movement Processor (DMP) software to your device.

If these steps do not accomplish password recovery, your hardware is probably defective.

Using Software to Change Jumper Settings

Using software to change jumper settings erases the NVRAM configuration and allows you to modify your soft jumper settings. To use this method on LANE/MPOA modules, you must have a separate console connected to the module in question, as well as one connected to the supervisor module. Follow these steps to facilitate the password-recovery process:

Step 1 Reset the module by issuing the **reset** *slot_num* command from the supervisor module.

Step 2 When you see the following prompt, press the **Esc** key to display the soft jumper configuration menu:

```
Hit ESC key within 3 seconds to enter SOFT-JUMPER config menu.
```

Step 3 Select the Modify Jumper Configuration menu by choosing option 2. You are not required to press **Enter** when selecting from this menu.

Choosing this option displays information for the current jumper configuration and asks if you want to change it.

Step 4 Continue to answer **n** to all questions until you see the following line:

```
DMON jumper ................Disabled. Want to change (y/n/q/e/d)?
```

Step 5 Enter **e** to enable debug monitor mode.

Step 6 Exit the menu by entering **q**.

Step 7 The programmable ROM boot continues with the startup.

Step 8 Again reset the module from the supervisor. The module displays the DMON> prompt, indicating that it is in debug monitor mode.

Step 9 Enter the debug monitor **mwl** command (multiple write of long words).

Step 10 You need to enter information for the start address, count, and data. This information should be entered as follows to erase the configuration stored in NVRAM:

```
Start Addr? 20000000
Count? 0006ffff
Data? ffffffff
```

Do not exceed the 6ffff count. You can enter **q** to exit the **mwl** command at any time.

Step 11 Enter **q** or **f** to debug the monitor to undergo the usual boot-programmable ROM path.

Step 12 When you see the following message, press the **Esc** key immediately:

```
Hit ESC key within 3 seconds to enter SOFT-JUMPER config menu.
```

Step 13 Select the Modify Jumper Configuration menu by choosing option 2.

Choosing this option again displays information for the current jumper configuration and asks if you want to change it.

Step 14 Continue to answer **n** to all questions until you see the following line:

```
DMON jumper ................Disabled. Want to change (y/n/q/e/d)?
```

Step 15 Enter **d** to disable debug monitor mode.

Step 16 Enter **q** to quit the menu and to boot to the Cisco IOS software prompt as usual. You no longer have a configuration stored in your NVRAM, but you can reconfigure your device as required.

Password Recovery on the Cisco Secure IDS Sensor

The username/password that comes on a Solaris-based Cisco Secure IDS Sensor appliance is netrangr/attack. If you changed the username/password from this default and you don't remember what it is, you have to perform password recovery. You can follow the procedure outlined in this section to accomplish this task.

Before you can start the password-recovery process, you need the following items:

- The Solaris Device Configuration Assistant disk, or boot disk. If you do not currently have a copy of this diskette, you can download it from the Sun support website at soldc.sun.com/support/drivers/dca_diskettes/.

- The Solaris for Intel (x86) CD-ROM

- Console access to the workstation

After you have these items, you can follow these steps to recover the password:

Step 1 Insert your boot disk into the floppy drive.

Step 2 Insert your Solaris CD into the CD-ROM drive.

Step 3 Turn off your workstation and wait 10 seconds before turning it back on.

Step 4 Your system boots from the boot disk. After it runs through some configuration, it displays the Configuration Assistant screen.

Step 5 Press the **F3** key to initiate a partial scan of your system for boot devices. A list of these devices is displayed when the scan is complete.

Step 6 Make sure your CD-ROM device appears in the list of devices, and press the **F2** key to continue.

Step 7 Select the CD-ROM drive from the list of possible boot devices that appears.

Step 8 Press the **Spacebar** to place an X next to your CD-ROM device.

Step 9 Press the **F2** key to boot your system from the CD-ROM.

Step 10 Choose option 2, Jumpstart install selection, when prompted. Your system continues its boot process.

Step 11 Select the appropriate language when prompted on the next two screens.

Step 12 Press **Ctrl-c** to stop the installation script and to gain access to a prompt when the Solaris Installation screen appears.

Step 13 Enter **mount -F ufs /dev/dsk/c0t0d0s0 /mnt** at the prompt to mount the / partition with a mount point of /mnt.

Step 14 Enter **cd /mnt/etc** to change the working directory to the newly created mount point.

Step 15 You are now ready to remove the root password, but first you must set your shell environment so that you can read data correctly. Enter the following at the prompt to complete this step:

TERM=ansi

export TERM

Step 16 You can now edit the shadow file to remove the root password by entering **vi shadow** at the prompt. The entry you will modify should look similar to the following:

```
root:gNyqp8ohdfxPI:10598::::::
```

The : is a field separator. Your encrypted password is the second field.

Step 17 Delete the second field to remove the password for the root user.

Step 18 Enter **:wq!** to commit your changes to disk and to quit your editing session of the file.

Step 19 Remove your disk and CD-ROM from the appropriate drives.

Step 20 Reboot the system by entering **init 6** at the prompt.

Step 21 When prompted for a username, enter **root**.

Step 22 Because this account no longer has a password, press **Enter** when prompted for a password.

Step 23 You can now use the **passwd** command from a terminal prompt to set a new password for the root account.

Password Recovery on the Cisco Secure PIX Firewall

This section details the steps necessary to recover a lost password on a Cisco Secure PIX Firewall through software Release 6.2. This procedure removes only the password and, if you are employing them, Telnet and console **aaa authentication** commands.

To use the password-recovery procedure for the PIX, you must have the appropriate PIX Password Lockout Utility, which depends on the software version you are currently running on your PIX. If you do not have this file, you can download it from the Cisco.com website. In addition to the PIX Password Lockout Utility (such as np62.bin for Release 6.2 of the PIX software), you need the following:

- rawwrite.exe for devices with a floppy drive or a TFTP Server for devices without a floppy drive.

- A terminal or a PC with terminal emulation software attached to the PIX's console port.

As you might guess, the procedure is different for a PIX with a floppy drive versus a PIX without one, as described in the next sections.

A PIX with a Floppy Drive

The following steps allow you to recover a password on a PIX with a floppy drive:

Step 1   Place the appropriate password-recovery file on a floppy using the rawrite.exe file on your PC. Follow the software's prompts to get the floppy ready for the PIX.

Step 2   Connect a terminal or a PC with terminal emulation software to the PIX console port.

Step 3   Insert the PIX Password Lockout Utility disk you created earlier into the PIX's floppy drive.

Step 4   Reset the PIX by pressing the Reset button on the front panel.

Step 5   Eject the disk, and press the Reset button again to reboot the PIX when you see the following message:

```
Erasing Flash Password. Please eject diskette and reboot.
```

Step 6   When you see the password prompt, press **Enter**.

The default Telnet password returns to "cisco" when this process is complete. You no longer have a default enable password.

Step 7   Run the **passwd** and **enable password** commands to place new passwords on your PIX. Save your new configuration by issuing the **write memory** command.

A PIX Without a Floppy Drive

The following steps are designed for use on a PIX without a floppy drive:

Step 1   Connect a terminal or a PC with terminal emulation software to the PIX console port.

Step 2   Press the **Break** or **Esc** key immediately after you power on your PIX Firewall and the startup messages start to appear. The monitor> prompt appears after you successfully interrupt the boot process.

Step 3   Use the **interface** command to specify which interface ping traffic will travel across. If you have only two interfaces on your PIX, the **monitor** command defaults to the inside interface.

Step 4   Specify an IP address by using the **address** command for the previously identified interface.

Step 5   Specify the IP address of the remote TFTP server containing the appropriate PIX password-recovery file by issuing the **server** command.

Step 6   Specify the filename of the PIX password-recovery file by using the **file** command.

Step 7   If required to gain access to the remote TFTP server, specify the IP address of the gateway by entering the **gateway** command.

Step 8   Use the **ping** command to verify connectivity to the remote TFTP server.

Step 9   Start the download by issuing the **tftp** command.

Step 10   During loading of the password-recovery file, you see messages asking if you want to erase the passwords and, if used, the **aaa authentication** commands for Telnet and console access. Answer **y** to the appropriate prompts.

The default Telnet password after this process is complete returns to "cisco." You no longer have an enable password.

Step 11   Use the **passwd** and **enable password** commands to place new passwords on your PIX. Save your new configuration by issuing the **write memory** command.

Password Recovery for ACS on UNIX

If you lose your password for ACS running on Solaris, you can reset it by entering the following commands from the command line:

```
$BASE/CLI/DeleteProfile -p 9900 -u superuser
$BASE/CLI/AddProfile -p 9900 -u superuser -a 'member = administrator \n
  privilege = web "password" 15 '
```

Remember to replace *password* with your new password.

Password Recovery for ACS on NT

If you lose your password for ACS running on NT, you can recover it by editing the NT Registry. Remember to back up the NT Registry before completing this task.

For earlier versions of ACS, you can modify the requirement for local login using a username and password in the NT Registry. You can search for and change the allowAutoLocalLogin key to 1 by using the regedit utility. This allows local login, but do not forget to recycle the services.

For later ACS versions, 2.6 and 3.0, you can use the regedit utility to remove the users in the following key:

> HKEY_LOCAL_MACHINE\SOFTWARE\Cisco\CiscoAAA##\CSAdmin\Administrators

In this location, you see all the administrators who have been created. After deleting the users and exiting the Registry, you no longer are prompted for a username and password. Use the ACS GUI to add the required administrator profiles.

Password Recovery on VPN Concentrators

Password recovery on the Cisco VPN concentrators depends on the series of concentrator you have—3000 or 5000—as described in the following sections.

Password Recovery on the Cisco 3000 Series VPN Concentrator

Recovering a password on a Cisco 3000 series VPN concentrator depends on the version of software you are running. For software version 2.5 or earlier, you need to contact the Cisco TAC for assistance in recovering a password. On concentrators running software version 2.5.1 or later, follow these steps to recover the password:

Step 1 Connect a terminal or a PC with terminal emulation to your VPN concentrator.

Step 2 Press **Ctrl-c** within 3 seconds of seeing a line of three dots after the diagnostics check is complete to display a menu that allows you to reset the system passwords to their defaults.

The factory default passwords for the Cisco VPN 3000 series are as follows:

Username: **admin**

Password: **admin**

Password Recovery on the Cisco 5000 Series VPN Concentrator

Follow these steps to recover a password on a Cisco 5000 series VPN concentrator:

Step 1   Power off your device and place the rotary dial switch on the back at position 9. Power your device back on.

Step 2   When your device finishes initializing, you can use the default password of letmein to log in within 5 minutes.

Step 3   Use the command-line interface (CLI) to configure a new password by using the following commands:

configure General

Password = [*string*]

EnablePassword = [*string*]

Note that by saving your changes, you cause the device to reboot automatically. Let your device boot up completely before proceeding to the next step.

Step 4   Power off your device and return the rotary dial switch to position 0. Power your device back on.

Step 5   After your device is finished initializing, you can log in with your new password.

How to Simulate a Break Key Sequence

This section is included in case your terminal emulator does not support the Break key or if a bug prevents it from sending the correct signal, as with old versions of Hyperterminal running under Windows NT:

Step 1   Connect your terminal or a PC with terminal emulation to your router with the following terminal settings:

1200 baud rate

No parity

8 data bits

1 stop bit

No flow control

You should not see any output on your screen unless you have previously changed your router's console port to these settings.

Step 2   Power-cycle your router by turning it off and then back on.

Step 3   Press the **Spacebar** for 10 to 15 seconds to generate a signal similar to the **Break** sequence.

Step 4   Disconnect your terminal or PC with terminal emulation and reconnect it with a 9600 baud rate. You should now be in ROM Monitor mode.

Summary

By using the steps outlined in this appendix, you should be able to recover the password with any Cisco device you will be likely to encounter in your job as a network security administrator. Some of these procedures work across multiple devices, and others are designed for a specific device. Experiment with them until you discover the technique that works best for you.

Security-Related RFCs and Publications

This appendix provides a list of security-related RFCs and publications that you can use as background reading for your Security CCIE lab exam preparation.

Requests for Comments

A Request for Comments (RFC) is a document that outlines a plan or proposal that the author wants to get feedback on. The Internet Engineering Task Force (IETF) uses RFCs as the basis for documenting Internet standards. RFCs enable the Internet community, not just people who write documents, to be involved in the standard-setting process.

RFCs are freely available from the IETF website at www.ietf.org. They are numbered sequentially in date submission order, so newer RFCs have higher RFC numbers.

This section includes a list of security-related RFCs. You do not need to read every RFC, but you can use these RFCs as a reference point for detailed information on a specific RFC topic.

In the following list, the RFC number is presented first, followed by the RFC title and then the author.

- 3445, "Limiting the Scope of the KEY Resource Record." Massey, December 2002.

- 3414 "User-based Security Model (USM) for version 3 of the Simple Network Management Protocol (SNMPv3)." U. Blumenthal and B. Wijnen, December 2002. (Obsoletes RFC 2274 and 2574.)

- 3365, "Strong Security Requirements for Internet Engineering Task Force Standard Protocols." J. Schiller, August 2002.

- 3268, "Advanced Encryption Standard (AES) Ciphersuites for Transport Layer (TLS)." P. Chown, June 2002.

- 3218, "Preventing the Million Message Attack on Cryptographic Message Syntax," E. Rescorla, January 2002, informational.

- 3211, "Password-Based Encryption for CMS," P. Gutmann, December 2001.

- 3207, "SMTP Service Extension for Secure SMTP over Transport Layer Security," P. Hoffman, February 2002. (Obsoletes RFC 2487.)

- 3206, "The SYS and AUTH POP Response Codes," R. Gellens, February 2002.

- 3185, "Reuse of CMS Content Encryption Keys," S. Farrell and S. Turner, October 2001.

- 3183, "Domain Security Services Using S/MIME," T. Dean and W. Ottaway, October 2001.

- 3168, "The Addition of Explicit Congestion Notification (ECN) to IP." K. Ramakrishnan, S. Floyd, and D. Black, September 2001.

- 3163, "ISO/IEC 9798-3 Authentication SASL Mechanism," R. Zuccherato and M. Nystrom, August 2001.

- 3161, "Internet X.509 Public Key Infrastructure Time-Stamp Protocol (TSP)," C. Adams, P. Cain, D. Pinkas, and R. Zuccherato, August 2001.

- 3156, "MIME Security with OpenPGP," M. Elkins, D. Del Torto, R. Levien, and T. Roessler, August 2001. (Updates RFC 2015.)

- 3128, "Protection Against a Variant of the Tiny Fragment Attack (RFC 1858)," I. Miller, June 2001. (Updates RFC 1858.)

- 3127, "Authentication, Authorization, and Accounting: Protocol Evaluation," D. Mitton, M. St. Johns, S. Barkley, D. Nelson, B. Patil, M. Stevens, and B. Wolff, June 2001.

- 3118, "Authentication for DHCP Messages," R. Droms and W. Arbaugh, Eds., June 2001.

- 3114, "Implementing Company Classification Policy with the S/MIME Security Label." W. Nicolls, May 2002.

- 3112, "LDAP Authentication Password Schema," K. Zeilenga, May 2001.

- 3097, "RSVP Cryptographic Authentication—Updated Message Type Value," R. Braden and L. Zhang, April 2001. (Updates RFC 2747.)

- 3090, "DNS Security Extension Clarification on Zone Status," E. Lewis, March 2001. (Updates RFC 2535.)

- 3083, "Baseline Privacy Interface Management Information Base for DOCSIS Compliant Cable Modems and Cable Modem Termination Systems," R. Woundy, March 2001.

- 3079, "Deriving Keys for Use with Microsoft Point-to-Point Encryption (MPPE)," G. Zorn, March 2001.

- 3078, "Microsoft Point-To-Point Encryption (MPPE) Protocol," G. Pall and G. Zorn, March 2001.

- 3062, "LDAP Password Modify Extended Operation," K. Zeilenga, February 2001.

- 3058, "Use of the IDEA Encryption Algorithm in CMS," S. Teiwes, P. Hartmann, and D. Kuenzi, February 2001.

- 3041, "Privacy Extensions for Stateless Address Autoconfiguration in IPv6," T. Narten and R. Draves, January 2001.

- 3039, "Internet X.509 Public Key Infrastructure Qualified Certificates Profile," S. Santesson, W. Polk, P. Barzin, and M. Nystrom, January 2001.

- 3029, "Internet X.509 Public Key Infrastructure Data Validation and Certification Server Protocols," C. Adams, P. Sylvester, M. Zolotarev, and R. Zuccherato, February 2001.

- 3013, "Recommended Internet Service Provider Security Services and Procedures," T. Killalea, November 2000.

- 3008, "Domain Name System Security (DNSSEC) Signing Authority," B. Wellington, November 2000. (Updates RFC 2535.)

- 2994, "A Description of the MISTY1 Encryption Algorithm," H. Ohta and M. Matsui, November 2000.

- 2984, "Use of the CAST-128 Encryption Algorithm in CMS," C. Adams, October 2000.

- 2977, "Mobile IP Authentication, Authorization, and Accounting Requirements," S. Glass, T. Hiller, S. Jacobs, and C. Perkins, October 2000.

- 2953, "Telnet Encryption: DES 64 bit Output Feedback," T. Ts'o, September 2000.

- 2952, "Telnet Encryption: DES 64 bit Cipher Feedback," T. Ts'o, September 2000.

- 2951, "TELNET Authentication Using KEA and SKIPJACK," R. Housley, T. Horting, and P. Yee, September 2000.

- 2950, "Telnet Encryption: CAST-128 64 bit Cipher Feedback," J. Altman, September 2000.

- 2949, "Telnet Encryption: CAST-128 64 bit Output Feedback," J. Altman, September 2000.

- 2948, "Telnet Encryption: DES3 64 bit Output Feedback," J. Altman, September 2000.

- 2947, "Telnet Encryption: DES3 64 bit Cipher Feedback," J. Altman, September 2000.

- 2946, "Telnet Data Encryption Option," T. Ts'o, September 2000.

- 2945, "The SRP Authentication and Key Exchange System," T. Wu, September 2000.

- 2944, "Telnet Authentication: SRP," T. Wu, September 2000.

- 2943, "TELNET Authentication Using DSA," R. Housley, T. Horting, and P. Yee, September 2000.

- 2942, "Telnet Authentication: Kerberos Version 5," T. Ts'o, September 2000.

- 2941, "Telnet Authentication Option," T. Ts'o, Ed., J. Altman, September 2000. (Obsoletes RFC 1416.)

- 2898, "PKCS #5: Password-Based Cryptography Specification Version 2.0," B. Kaliski, September 2000.

- 2865, "Remote Authentication Dial In User Service (RADIUS)," C. Rigney, S. Willens, A. Rubens, and W. Simpson, June 2000. (Obsoletes RFC 2138.) (Updated by RFC 2868.)

- 2853, "Generic Security Service API Version 2: Java Bindings," J. Kabat and M. Upadhyay, June 2000.

- 2845, "Secret Key Transaction Authentication for DNS (TSIG)," P. Vixie, O. Gudmundsson, D. Eastlake, and B. Wellington, May 2000. (Updates RFC 1035.)

- 2831, "Using Digest Authentication as an SASL Mechanism," P. Leach and C. Newman, May 2000.

- 2830, "Lightweight Directory Access Protocol (v3): Extension for Transport Layer Security," J. Hodges, R. Morgan, and M. Wahl, May 2000.

- 2829, "Authentication Methods for LDAP," M. Wahl, H. Alvestrand, J. Hodges, and R. Morgan, May 2000.

- 2828, "Internet Security Glossary," R. Shirey, May 2000.

- 2827, Network Ingress Filtering: Defeating Denial of Service Attacks Which Employ IP Source Address Spoofing," P. Ferguson and D. Senie, May 2000. (Obsoletes RFC 2267.)

- 2818, "HTTP Over TLS," E. Rescorla, May 2000.

- 2817, "Upgrading to TLS Within HTTP/1.1," R. Khare and S. Lawrence, May 2000. (Updates RFC 2616.)

- 2785, "Methods for Avoiding the 'Small-Subgroup' Attacks on the Diffie-Hellman Key Agreement Method for S/MIME," R. Zuccherato, March 2000.

- 2773, "Encryption Using KEA and SKIPJACK," R. Housley, P. Yee, and W. Nace, February 2000. (Updates RFC 0959.)

- 2755, "Security Negotiation for WebNFS," A. Chiu, M. Eisler, and B. Callaghan, January 2000.

- 2747, "RSVP Cryptographic Authentication," F. Baker, B. Lindell, and M. Talwar, January 2000. (Updated by RFC 3097.)

- 2744, "Generic Security Service API Version 2: C-bindings," J. Wray, January 2000. (Obsoletes RFC 1509.)

- 2743, "Generic Security Service Application Program Interface Version 2, Update 1," J. Linn, January 2000. (Obsoletes RFC 2078.)

- 2726, "PGP Authentication for RIPE Database Updates," J. Zsako, December 1999.

- 2725, "Routing Policy System Security," C. Villamizar, C. Alaettinoglu, D. Meyer, and S. Murphy, December 1999.

- 2716, "PPP EAP TLS Authentication Protocol," B. Aboba and D. Simon, October 1999.

- 2712, "Addition of Kerberos Cipher Suites to Transport Layer Security (TLS)," A. Medvinsky and M. Hur, October 1999.

- 2709, "Security Model with Tunnel-Mode IPsec for NAT Domains," P. Srisuresh, October 1999.

- 2695, "Authentication Mechanisms for ONC RPC," A. Chiu, September 1999.

- 2659, "Security Extensions for HTML," E. Rescorla and A. Schiffman, August 1999.

- 2634, "Enhanced Security Services for S/MIME," P. Hoffman, Ed., June 1999.

- 2633, "S/MIME Version 3 Message Specification," B. Ramsdell, Ed., June 1999.

- 2632, "S/MIME Version 3 Certificate Handling," B. Ramsdell, Ed., June 1999.

- 2623, "NFS Version 2 and Version 3 Security Issues and the NFS Protocol's Use of RPCSEC_GSS and Kerberos V5," M. Eisler, June 1999.

- 2619, "RADIUS Authentication Server MIB," G. Zorn and B. Aboba, June 1999.

- 2618, "RADIUS Authentication Client MIB," B. Aboba and G. Zorn, June 1999.

- 2617, "HTTP Authentication: Basic and Digest Access Authentication," J. Franks, P. Hallam-Baker, J. Hostetler, S. Lawrence, P. Leach, A. Luotonen, and L. Stewart, June 1999. (Obsoletes RFC 2069.)

- 2612, "The CAST-256 Encryption Algorithm," C. Adams and J. Gilchrist, June 1999.

- 2595, "Using TLS with IMAP, POP3 and ACAP," C. Newman, June 1999.

- 2587, "Internet X.509 Public Key Infrastructure LDAPv2 Schema," S. Boeyen, T. Howes, and P. Richard, June 1999.

- 2585, "Internet X.509 Public Key Infrastructure Operational Protocols: FTP and HTTP," R. Housley and P. Hoffman, May 1999.

- 2577, "FTP Security Considerations," M. Allman and S. Ostermann, May 1999.

- 2560, "X.509 Internet Public Key Infrastructure Online Certificate Status Protocol—OCSP," M. Myers, R. Ankney, A. Malpani, S. Galperin, and C. Adams, June 1999.

- 2559, "Internet X.509 Public Key Infrastructure Operational Protocols—LDAPv2," S. Boeyen, T. Howes, and P. Richard, April 1999. (Updates RFC 1778.)

- 2554, "SMTP Service Extension for Authentication," J. Myers, March 1999.

- 2541, "DNS Security Operational Considerations," Eastlake, March 1999.

- 2528, "Internet X.509 Public Key Infrastructure Representation of Key Exchange Algorithm (KEA) Keys in Internet X.509 Public Key Infrastructure Certificates," R. Housley and W. Polk, March 1999.

- 2527, "Internet X.509 Public Key Infrastructure Certificate Policy and Certification Practices Framework," S. Chokhani and W. Ford, March 1999.

- 2521, "ICMP Security Failures Messages," P. Karn and W. Simpson, March 1999.

- 2511, "Internet X.509 Certificate Request Message Format," M. Myers, C. Adams, D. Solo, and D. Kemp, March 1999.

- 2510, "Internet X.509 Public Key Infrastructure Certificate Management Protocols," C. Adams and S. Farrell, March 1999.

- 2504, "Users' Security Handbook," E. Guttman, L. Leong, and G. Malkin, February 1999.

- 2485, "DHCP Option for the Open Group's User Authentication Protocol," S. Drach, January 1999.

- 2484, "PPP LCP Internationalization Configuration Option." G. Zorn, January 1999.

- 2480, "Gateways and MIME Security Multiparts," N. Freed, January 1999.

- 2479, "Independent Data Unit Protection Generic Security Service Application Program Interface (IDUP-GSS-API)," C. Adams, December 1998.

- 2478, "The Simple and Protected GSS-API Negotiation Mechanism," E. Baize and D. Pinkas, December 1998.

- 2459, "Internet X.509 Public Key Infrastructure Certificate and CRL Profile," R. Housley, W. Ford, W. Polk, and D. Solo, January 1999.

- 2444, "The One-Time-Password SASL Mechanism," C. Newman, October 1998. (Updates RFC 2222.)

- 2440, "OpenPGP Message Format," J. Callas, L. Donnerhacke, H. Finney, and R. Thayer, November 1998.

- 2420, "The PPP Triple-DES Encryption Protocol (3DESE)," H. Kummert, September 1998.

- 2419, "The PPP DES Encryption Protocol, Version 2 (DESE-bis)," K. Sklower and G. Meyer, September 1998. (Obsoletes RFC 1969.)

- 2411, "IP Security Document Roadmap," R. Thayer, N. Doraswamy, and R. Glenn, November 1998.

- 2410, "The NULL Encryption Algorithm and Its Use with IPsec," R. Glenn and S. Kent, November 1998.

- 2408, "Internet Security Association and Key Management Protocol (ISAKMP)," D. Maughan, M. Schertler, M. Schneider, and J. Turner, November 1998.

- 2407, "The Internet IP Security Domain of Interpretation for ISAKMP," D. Piper, November 1998.

- 2406, "IP Encapsulating Security Payload (ESP)," S. Kent and R. Atkinson, November 1998.

- 2403, "The Use of HMAC-MD5-96 within ESP and AH," C. Madson and R. Glenn, November 1998.

- 2402, "IP Authentication Header," S. Kent and R. Atkinson, November 1998.

- 2385, "Protection of BGP Sessions via the TCP MD5 Signature Option," A. Heffernan, August 1998.

- 2350, "Expectations for Computer Security Incident Response," N. Brownlee and E. Guttman, June 1998.

- 2323, "IETF Identification and Security Guidelines," A. Ramos, April 1998.

- 2316, "Report of the IAB Security Architecture Workshop," S. Bellovin, April 1998.

- 2312, "S/MIME Version 2 Certificate Handling," S. Dusse, P. Hoffman, B. Ramsdell, and J. Weinstein, March 1998.

- 2311, "S/MIME Version 2 Message Specification," S. Dusse, P. Hoffman, B. Ramsdell, L. Lundblade, and L. Repka, March 1998.

- 2289, "A One-Time Password System," N. Haller, C. Metz, P. Nesser, and M. Straw, February 1998.

- 2268, "A Description of the RC2(r) Encryption Algorithm," R. Rivest, March 1998.

- 2246, "The TLS Protocol Version 1.0," T. Dierks and C. Allen, January 1999.

- 2243, "OTP Extended Responses," C. Metz, November 1997.

- 2228, "FTP Security Extensions," M. Horowitz and S. Lunt, October 1997. (Updates RFC 0959.)

- 2222, "Simple Authentication and Security Layer (SASL)," J. Myers, October 1997. (Updated by RFC 2444.)

- 2203, "RPCSEC_GSS Protocol Specification," M. Eisler, A. Chiu, and L. Ling, September 1997.

- 2202, "Test Cases for HMAC-MD5 and HMAC-SHA-1," P. Cheng and R. Glenn, September 1997.

- 2196, "Site Security Handbook," B. Fraser, September 1997. IETF FYI #8.

- 2195, "IMAP/POP AUTHorize Extension for Simple Challenge/Response," J. Klensin, R. Catoe, and P. Krumviede, September 1997. (Obsoletes RFC 2095.)

- 2179, "Network Security For Trade Shows," A. Gwinn, July 1997.

- 2144, "The CAST-128 Encryption Algorithm," C. Adams, May 1997.

- 2104, "HMAC: Keyed-Hashing for Message Authentication," H. Krawczyk, M. Bellare, and R. Canetti, February 1997.

- 2085, "HMAC-MD5 IP Authentication with Replay Prevention," M. Oehler and R. Glenn, February 1997.

- 2084, "Considerations for Web Transaction Security," G. Bossert, S. Cooper, and W. Drummond, January 1997.

- 2082, "RIP-2 MD5 Authentication," F. Baker and R. Atkinson, January 1997.

- 2025, "The Simple Public-Key GSS-API Mechanism (SPKM)," C. Adams, October 1996.

- 2015, "MIME Security with Pretty Good Privacy (PGP)," M. Elkins, October 1996. (Updated by RFC 3156.)

- 1991, "PGP Message Exchange Formats," D. Atkins, W. Stallings, and P. Zimmermann, August 1996.

- 1968, "The PPP Encryption Control Protocol (ECP)," G. Meyer, June 1996.

- 1964, "The Kerberos Version 5 GSS-API Mechanism," J. Linn, June 1996.

- 1961, "GSS-API Authentication Method for SOCKS Version 5," P. McMahon, June 1996.

- 1948, "Defending Against Sequence Number Attacks," S. Bellovin, May 1996.

- 1929, "Username/Password Authentication for SOCKS V5," M. Leech, March 1996.

- 1915, "Variance for The PPP Connection Control Protocol and the PPP Encryption Control Protocol," F. Kastenholz, February 1996.

- 1910, "User-Based Security Model for SNMPv2," G. Waters, Ed., February 1996.

- 1864, "The Content-MD5 Header Field," J. Myers and M. Rose, October 1995. (Obsoletes RFC 1544.)

- 1858, "Security Considerations for IP Fragment Filtering," G. Ziemba, D. Reed, and P. Traina, October 1995.

- 1848, "MIME Object Security Services," S. Crocker, N. Freed, J. Galvin, and S. Murphy, October 1995.

- 1847, "Security Multiparts for MIME: Multipart/Signed and Multipart/Encrypted," J. Galvin, S. Murphy, S. Crocker, and N. Freed, October 1995.

- 1828, "IP Authentication Using Keyed MD5," P. Metzger and W. Simpson, August 1995.

- 1824, "The Exponential Security System TESS: An Identity-Based Cryptographic Protocol for Authenticated Key-Exchange (E.I.S.S.-Report 1995/4)," H. Danisch, August 1995.

- 1810, "Report on MD5 Performance Touch," June 1995.

- 1760, "The S/KEY One-Time Password System," N. Haller, February 1995.

- 1750, "Randomness Recommendations for Security," D. Eastlake, S. Crocker, and J. Schiller, December 1994.

- 1734, "POP3 AUTHentication command," J. Myers, December 1994.

- 1731, "IMAP4 Authentication Mechanisms," J. Myers, December 1994.

- 1704, "On Internet Authentication," N. Haller and R. Atkinson, October 1994.

- 1675, "Security Concerns for Ipng," S. Bellovin, August 1994.

- 1636, "Report of IAB Workshop on Security in the Internet Architecture—February 8–10, 1994," R. Braden, D. Clark, S. Crocker, and C. Huitema, June 1994.

- 1535, "A Security Problem and Proposed Correction with Widely Deployed DNS Software," E. Gavron, October 1993.

- 1511, "Common Authentication Technology Overview," J. Linn, September 1993.

- 1510, "The Kerberos Network Authentication Service (V5)," J. Kohl and C. Neuman, September 1993.

- 1507, "DASS—Distributed Authentication Security Service," C. Kaufman, September 1993.

- 1472, "The Definitions of Managed Objects for the Security Protocols of the Point-to-Point Protocol," F. Kastenholz, June 1993.

- 1457, "Security Label Framework for the Internet," R. Housley, May 1993.

- 1446, "Security Protocols for version 2 of the Simple Network Management Protocol (SNMPv2)." J. Galvin and K McCloghrie, April 1993.

- 1424, "Privacy Enhancement for Internet Electronic Mail: Part IV: Key Certification and Related Services," B. Kaliski, February 1993.

- 1423, "Privacy Enhancement for Internet Electronic Mail: Part III: Algorithms, Modes, and Identifiers," D. Balenson, February 1993.

- 1422, "Privacy Enhancement for Internet Electronic Mail: Part II: Certificate-Based Key Management," S. Kent, February 1993.

- 1421, "Privacy Enhancement for Internet Electronic Mail: Part I: Message Encryption and Authentication Procedures," J. Linn, February 1993. Proposed.

- 1412, "Telnet Authentication: SPX," K. Alagappan, January 1993.

- 1411, "Telnet Authentication: Kerberos Version 4," D. Borman, Ed., January 1993.

- 1355, "Privacy and Accuracy Issues in Network Information Center Databases," J. Curran and A. Marine, August 1992.

- 1352, "SNMP Security Protocols." J. Galvin, K. McCloghrie, and J. Davin, July 1992.

- 1321, "The MD5 Message-Digest Algorithm," R. Rivest, April 1992.

Publications

Many publications are available on the topic of network security. Some of these are relevant to the CCIE Security exam and some are not. A good understanding of the theory is required to become accomplished with hands-on configuration, and every CCIE candidate should have a well-established book collection.

Cisco has compiled a list of books that are relevant to the CCIE Security exam. This list can be found at the following website:

www.cisco.com/en/US/learning/le3/le2/le23/le476/learning_certification_type_home.html

These books include the following:

- *Applied Cryptography: Protocols, Algorithms, and Source Code in C,* 2nd ed., Bruce Schneier, Wiley & Sons, October 1995.

- *Big Book of IPsec RFCs: Internet Security Architecture,* compiled by Peter Loshin, Morgan Kaufmann, November 1999.

- *Building Cisco Remote Access Networks,* Catherine Paquet, Ed., Cisco Press, August 1999.

- *Cisco Internetwork Troubleshooting,* Laura Chappell and Dan Farkas, Eds., CCIE No. 3800, Cisco Press, August 1999.

- *Cisco IOS Dial Solutions,* Cisco Press, August 2001.

- *Cisco IOS Network Security,* Cisco Press, August 2001.

- *Cisco Secure Internet Security Solutions,* Andrew Mason and Mark Newcomb, Cisco Press, May 2001.

- *Cisco Secure Virtual Private Networks,* Andrew Mason, Cisco Press, December 2001.

- *Designing Network Security,* Merike Kaeo, Cisco Press, May 1999.

- *Digital Certificates: Applied Internet Security, Jalal Feghhi and Peter Williams,* Addison Wesley, September 1998.

- *Enhanced IP Services for Cisco Networks,* Donald Lee, Cisco Press, September 1999.

- *Firewalls and Internet Security: Repelling the Wily Hacker,* William Cheswick and Steven M. Bellovin, Addison-Wesley, Professional Computing, April 1994.

- *Inside Internet Security: What Hackers Don't Want You to Know,* Jeff Crume, Addison-Wesley, August 2000.

- *Internet Cryptography,* Richard E. Smith, Addison Wesley, July 1997.

- *Internet Security Protocols: Protecting IP Traffic,* Uyless Black, Prentice Hall, July 2000.

- *Internetworking Troubleshooting Handbook,* Cisco Press, February 2001.

- *IPSec: The New Security Standard for the Internet, Intranets, and Virtual Private Networks,* Naganand Doraswamy and Dan Harkins, Prentice Hall, July 1999.

- *Maximum Security: A Hacker's Guide to Protecting Your Internet Site and Network,* Anonymous, Sams Publishing, December 2002.

- *MPLS and VPN Architectures,* Ivan Pepelnjak and Jim Guichard, Cisco Press, October 2000.

- *Network Security: Private Communication in a Public World,* Charlie Kaufman, Radia Perlman, and Mike Speciner, Prentice Hall, April 2002.

- *Top-Down Network Design,* Priscilla Oppenheimer, Cisco Press, December 1998.

White Papers

In addition to the previous list of publications, Cisco has identified four key white papers that you should read and understand for the CCIE Security exam. These white papers, listed as follows, are available at Cisco.com:

- Characterizing and Tracing Packet Floods Using Cisco Routers:

    www.cisco.com/warp/public/707/22.html

- Defining Strategies to Protect Against UDP Diagnostic Port Denial of Service Attacks:

    www.cisco.com/warp/public/707/3.html

- Strategies to Protect Against Distributed Denial of Service:

    www.cisco.com/warp/public/707/newsflash.html

- Strategies to Protect Against TCP SYN Denial of Service Attacks:

    www.cisco.com/en/US/tech/tk648/tk364/
    technologies_tech_note09186a00800f67d5.shtml

You can also find numerous security-related documents at the following Cisco Security Technical Tips web page:

    www.cisco.com/en/US/support/index.html

Answers to the Review Questions

Chapter 4

1 What is the purpose of the VLAN Trunking Protocol?

Answer: VTP manages the addition, deletion, and renaming of VLANs from a centralized location.

2 How are nonroutable protocols affected by VLANs?

Answer: Because a router is required for inter-VLAN communications, it is not possible for nonroutable protocols to communicate outside of their VLANs.

3 How does the Catalyst 3550 switch, with Layer 3 software installed, deal with packets that are for an unknown destination?

Answer: If a default route is configured, or you are using a routing protocol to receive routing information, the 3550 switch can send the packet to the default gateway for delivery; otherwise, it is dropped.

4 Why would you configure an interface as a trunk?

Answer: A trunk is an interface that is a member of all VLANs in the VLAN database unless you specifically prohibit its membership to certain VLANs. This is the only way that an interface can be a member of multiple VLANs and see the traffic on them.

5 Why would you see an untagged packet on a switch that is configured with VLANs?

Answer: The native VLAN, the one configured on the port, does not need a tag because it is assumed that any packet received on it is for the configured VLAN.

6 Why would you use PAgP?

Port Aggregation Protocol (PAgP) allows an EtherChannel to be formed dynamically without having to configure both sides of the channel.

7 What is a routed port?

Answer: A routed port is a physical port that acts like a port on a router without requiring you to have a router.

8   What is a designated port?

Answer: A designated port is an elected forwarding port that is logically closer to the root switch.

9   What can prevent an alternate or root port from becoming the designated port after a unidirectional link failure?

Answer: The Loop Guard feature provides this protection.

10   What can prevent packets with an unknown destination MAC address from being flooded to every port on a switch?

Answer: Port blocking can provide this protection for unicast and multicast packets.

Chapter 5

1   What kind of technology is Frame Relay?

Answer: Frame Relay is a packet-switched technology.

2   Describe the difference between SVCs and PVCs.

Answer: An SVC (switched virtual circuit) is created for each data transfer and is terminated when the data transfer is complete. SVCs have a setup and teardown time associated with them. A PVC (permanent virtual circuit) is a permanent network connection that does not terminate when the transfer of data is complete. Previously not widely supported by Frame Relay equipment, SVCs are gaining in popularity in many of today's networks.

3   What is the data-link connection identifier (DLCI)?

Answer: The DLCI is a value that is assigned to each virtual circuit and DTE device connection point in the Frame Relay WAN. Two different connections can be assigned the same value within the same Frame Relay WAN—one on each side of the virtual connection—but two virtual circuits cannot share the same DLCI on a local host.

4   Describe how LMI Frame Relay differs from basic Frame Relay.

Answer: LMI Frame Relay adds a set of enhancements, referred to as *extensions*, to the features that are supported by basic Frame Relay. Key LMI extensions provide the following functionality:

- Global addressing
- Virtual circuit status messages
- Multicasting

Chapter 6

1 Which protocol series does ISDN use to communicate from the local terminal equipment to the ISDN switch in the central office?

Answer: E series, I series, Q series

2 True or false: The S reference point is an interface between NT1 and NT2.

Answer: False

3 What is an ISDN switch type?

A. A global configuration parameter

B. An interface configuration parameter

C. Either a global or an interface communication parameter

Answer: C

4 True or false: Access lists can be used to define interesting traffic.

Answer: True

5 What is the correct command syntax for assigning interesting traffic to an interface?

Answer: dialer-group

6 OSPF demand circuit is designed to stifle what?

A. Hellos

B. Routing updates

C. LSAs

D. All of the above

Answer: A, C

7 True or false: PAP encapsulation is more secure than CHAP.

Answer: False

Chapter 7

1 How many bits are used for VPI at UNI?

Answer: 8

2 What form of addressing does a PVC use?

Answer: VPI/VCI pair

3   What are two forms of ATM global addresses?

Answer: E.164 and NSAP

4   Automatic ATM address registration is enabled via what?

Answer: ILMI

5   Is specifying an AAL5SNAP encapsulation type a mandatory configuration step in the RFC 2684 configuration using PVCs?

Answer: No

Chapter 8

1   Manual summarization is supported in which version of RIP?

Answer: RIPv2

2   How long is the invalid timer's default period, in seconds?

Answer: 180

3   What is the correct syntax for creating an authentication key?

Answer: `Router(config-keychain)#key key-number`

4   Fill in the blanks: By default, a Cisco router listens to _____ messages but sends _____ messages.

Answer: First blank: RIPv1 and RIPv2; second blank: RIPv1

5   When RIP is used for routing in nonbroadcast network environments, do you need to turn split horizon on or off?

Answer: Off

Chapter 9

1   What algorithm does EIGRP use to decide which route is put into the routing table?

Answer: Diffusing Update Algorithm (DUAL)

2   Besides the routing table, what other tables does EIGRP use in its operation?

Answer: Neighbor table and topology table

3   What default metric values does EIGRP use?

Answer: EIGRP uses bandwidth and delay as the default metrics in its calculations. It does not, by default, use MTU, load, or reliability. This means that EIGRP uses a calculation of 256(bandwidth × delay) in calculating its metric.

4   Why does EIGRP use protocol-dependent modules?

Answer: EIGRP uses protocol-dependent modules to provide support for multiple routable protocols. Each protocol-dependent module handles the specific tasks for that particular protocol.

5   How do you update automatic redistribution between IGRP and EIGRP?

Answer: If you use the same autonomous system when defining both IGRP and EIGRP, automatic redistribution is enabled.

6   What is a passive route in EIGRP?

Answer: A passive route is one that is in the "ideal" state. EIGRP computations are completed, and the route is placed in the routing table.

7   What is the default hello interval for a low-speed T1 circuit?

Answer: 60 seconds

8   When using authentication with EIGRP, what is protected, and how is it protected?

Answer: MD5 is used to sign a routing update so that a receiving EIGRP router can confirm that the packet came from another MD5-configured router. This helps protect your router from receiving unsigned routing updates.

9   Are GRE tunnels point-to-point or point-to-multipoint?

Answer: Point-to-point

Chapter 10

1   Why are loopback interfaces advertised as /32 in OSPF?

Answer: Loopback interfaces are considered host routes in OSPF.

2   What are the route types used with OSPF?

Answer: Intra-area routes, inter-area routes, external routes Type 1, and external routes Type 2

3   Why do I receive the "cannot allocate router id" error message?

Answer: OSPF chooses the highest IP address as its router ID. If none of your interfaces are in the up/up mode and configured with an IP address, OSPF returns this error message. Using a loopback interface prevents this error.

4   Why do I receive the "unknown routing protocol" error message?

Answer: This message is most frequently caused by your selection of Cisco IOS Software that does not support OSPF.

5   What do the states DR, BDR, and DROTHER mean in the **show ip ospf** interface command output?

Answer: DR means designated router, BDR indicates backup designated router, and DROTHER means a router that is neither the DR nor the BDR.

6   Which router is responsible for generating the network LSA?

Answer: The DR generates a network LSA, which is used to list all routers on that network.

7   Why do neighbors show a state of 2-WAY/DROTHER when issuing the **show ip ospf neighbor** command?

Answer: To reduce the amount of flooding on broadcast media, such as Ethernet, FDDI, and Token Ring, the router gets a full status with only DR and BDR, and it shows 2-WAY for all other routers.

8   Why is it difficult to identify the DR or BDR on a serial link?

Answer: This is normal. On point-to-point and point-to-multipoint networks, no DRs or BDRs exist.

9   What special commands are required to run OSPF over BRI/PRI links?

Answer: Implementation for this scenario is easier if you use the dialer map command with the broadcast keyword. To prevent the circuit from being established only for routing-related traffic, you can also configure the circuit as a demand circuit.

Chapter 11

1   What is IS-IS?

Answer: The IS-IS routing protocol is a link-state routing protocol from the OSI protocol suite.

2   What is Dual IS-IS?

Answer: Dual IS-IS, also known as Integrated IS-IS, allows you to carry IP routing information as well as CLNS information. Dual IS-IS can be implemented using both or just IP.

3   What is the difference between a NET and an NSAP?

Answer: The NSAP is the full address of a system (IS or ES) in CLNS and determines the area address in IP-only IS-IS. The NSAP with the N-selector set to 0 is the NET.

4 Which of the following packets are used in IS-IS?

A. IIHs—IS-to-IS hello packets

B. EIHs—ES-to-IS hello packets

C. LSPs—link-state packets

D. FSNPs—Fragmented Sequence Number packets

E. CSNPs—Complete Sequence Number packets

F. PSNPs—Partial Sequence Number packets

Answer: A, C, E, and F

5 What algorithm does IS-IS use to determine "best" routes?

Answer: IS-IS uses the SPF algorithm.

6 Which of the following are the three modes of operation that Integrated IS-IS can run in?

A. CLNS only

B. OSI only

C. IP only

D. Hybrid—CLNS with IP

E. IPX only

Answer: A, C, and D

7 How can I tell who is acting as the PSN in a multiaccess network?

Answer: By issuing the show clns is-neighbor command, you can determine the PSN by examining the circuit ID field. The ID in front of the dot is the PSN.

8 How many Level-2 IS-IS areas can I configure on a single router?

Answer: One. However, you can configure up to 29 Level-1 areas.

Chapter 12

1 What are the applications of a route map in BGP?

Answer: Route maps can be applied on incoming or outgoing routing information to or from a neighbor. They also influence route redistribution decisions. Route maps are used to permit or deny a route and also to alter attributes of a route with set statements.

  2 What is the purpose of MD5 authentication in BGP?

  Answer: MD5 authentication in BGP can be used to protect against spoofing, denial-of-service attacks, and man-in-the-middle attacks. When MD5 is implemented, the BGP peer knows that information it received is from the correct source and was not altered in transit.

  3 Why is the **maximum-prefix** command needed?

  Answer: To prevent an autonomous system from being bombarded with a multitude of networks from an external neighbor, you can limit the number of networks that your autonomous system is willing to receive. This command is useful when preventing an ISP from being flooded with unnecessary routes from a customer or vice versa.

  4 Why should private autonomous system filtering be used?

  Answer: Networks that aren't meant to be seen on the Internet can be assigned an autonomous system number from the reserved range of 64512 to 65535 and are considered private. Therefore, they should never be seen outside the customer's realm. Private autonomous system filtering prevents private autonomous system information from being propagated to the service provider and beyond.

  5 Where do you use the **next-hop-self** command?

  Answer: next-hop-self changes BGP default behavior, because sometimes routers don't know how to reach the router that is automatically advertised as the next hop. To solve this problem, a router may specify its own IP address as the next-hop attribute instead of the one automatically selected. These situations include the following:

  - **In IBGP or IBGP-like confederation scenarios, the next hop is the EBGP router that injected the route into the autonomous system.**

  - **When a route is announced on a multiaccess medium (such as Ethernet or Frame Relay), the next hop is usually the IP address of the router interface connected to that medium, which originated the route.**

Chapter 13

  1 What metric is used by RIP?

  Answer: The hop count is the metric of choice for the RIP routing protocol.

  2 Which routing protocols can redistribute static routes automatically without any additional configuration?

  Answer: Both RIP and IGRP routing protocols can automatically redistribute static routes.

3 What happens if you do not include a match statement with a route map?

Answer: If you do not define a match criteria, everything passing through the route map matches.

4 Which RFC is written to cover redistribution between OSPF and BGP?

Answer: RFC 1403 covers the topic of redistribution of routes between OSPF and BGP.

5 Why do you need to filter routes when redistributing between two EIGRP autonomous systems?

Answer: You can create a routing loop if the same routes are allowed back into the routing table for routes that originated from this autonomous system.

Chapter 14

1 What are the three ways to ensure security in your network environment?

Answer: Integrity ensures that some type of control must exist to ensure that business-critical items are accurate and in a workable condition. Confidentiality ensures that access restrictions are enforced so that only authorized personal are allowed to see or use sensitive items. Availability ensures that services are available when needed.

2 What two security protocols provide data authentication?

Answer: Authentication Header (AH) and Encapsulating Security Protocol (ESP) provide data authentication.

3 What three types of VPNs are supported by Cisco devices?

Answer: The three types of VPNs supported by Cisco devices are remote-access, intranet, and extranet.

4 What three types of security server protocols are currently supported by Cisco devices?

Answer: The three types of security server protocols currently supported by Cisco devices are Remote Authentication Dial-In User Service (RADIUS), Terminal Access Controller Access Control Server (TACACS+), and Kerberos.

5 What product is the same as an electronic ID?

Answer: A digital signature is an electronic ID.

6 What three types of attacks is an IDS designed to protect against?

Answer: The three types of attacks an IDS is designed to protect against are access, denial of service, and reconnaissance.

7 What two types of traffic analysis procedures are available on Cisco's IDS products?

Answer: Profile-based and signature-based are the two types of traffic analysis procedures available on Cisco's IDS products.

8 Why would a company need a risk assessment?

Answer: A risk assessment identifies what needs to be protected, what it needs protection from, and how to protect it. It also sets a value on the items that need securing and gives you a means to determine if the cost to implement the security solution is a valid expenditure.

Chapter 15

1 What is the NTP standard time zone?

Answer: UTC

2 What is the secure alternative to Telnet?

Answer: SSH

3 Which command(s) protect(s) the privileged EXEC mode on a router?

Answer: enable password and enable secret

4 How many privilege levels exist?

Answer: 16: 0 through 15

5 What does the **exec-timeout 0 0** command indicate?

Answer: Never times out

6 You can disable the Cisco Discovery Protocol (CDP) globally or per interface. True or false?

Answer: True

7 You can exercise storm control on the 3550 switch ports for which type(s) of traffic?

Answer: Unicast, multicast, and broadcast

Chapter 16

1 What feature allows you to provide access control on a network device that determines what traffic is permitted to enter or exit your network?

Answer: This feature is the Access Control List (ACL).

  2 How is the 3550 switch able to filter IP packets?

     Answer: This switch bridges the packet, then routes the packet internally, applies IP ACLs, and then bridges the packet again to send it to its destination.

  3 How are entries in an ACL processed?

     Answer: When a device starts evaluating the ACE entries in an ACL, the device tests the packet against each ACE in the order in which you entered it.

  4 What type of ACL is used to control traffic entering a Layer 2 interface?

     Answer: The port ACL is used to filter traffic on a Layer 2 interface.

  5 Which ACL grants a user access to a specific source or destination based on a user authentication process?

     Answer: Lock-and-key uses the dynamic ACL to grant access on a user-by-user basis.

  6 What is a Switched Virtual Interface?

     Answer: A Switched Virtual Interface (SVI) is a Layer 3 interface to a VLAN.

  7 What criteria are used to define an ACL?

     Answer: Typically, you use the source address, the destination address, or the upper-layer protocol of a packet to define your matching criteria.

  8 When you use a VLAN map with a router ACL and one of your packet flows matches a deny statement of a VLAN, what happens to the packet flow?

     Answer: The packet is denied, regardless of the configuration of your router ACL.

  9 What is the function of a VLAN map?

     Answer: The VLAN map is used to configure filtering in a VLAN.

  10 Which ACL can provide filtering based on the IP upper-layer protocol "session" information?

     Answer: You can use the reflexive ACL, also known as IP session filtering, to accomplish this.

Chapter 17

  1 Why would you use NAT to connect to the Internet?

     Answer: NAT provides you with a way to translate illegal or private addresses to a legal, routable address for connecting to an external network.

2 What are ICMP messages used for?

Answer: ICMP is used to provide a type of maintenance functionality to TCP/IP. ICMP messages include error and information messages that are used to inform devices of different items.

3 What does the Path MTU Discovery feature do?

Answer: With Path MTU Discovery, a device can discover the smallest MTU that is supported along a transmission path to avoid the fragmentation associated with sending a packet that is larger than the smallest MTU.

4 Where would the ICMP redirect message provide the most use?

Answer: You can use ICMP redirect in situations where multiple exit points exist to inform an originating device of a shorter path to the nearest exit. It can also be useful when a device has a misconfigured IP protocol stack.

5 Is it possible to use a single IP address for NAT translations?

Answer: By using the overload feature, you can use a single IP address to translate multiple addresses.

6 What four terms are used to describe addresses that are used with NAT?

Answer: The four terms are inside local address, inside global address, outside local address, and outside global address.

7 What is CEF?

Answer: Cisco Express Forwarding (CEF) is one of the advanced Layer 3 IP switching technologies that is available with Cisco IOS Software.

8 What is the MNLB Forwarding Agent used for?

Answer: The MultiNode Load Balancing (MNLB) Forwarding Agent is the Cisco IOS Software–based packet redirector component that works in conjunction with a LocalDirector for load balancing.

9 Why would you use the Express TCP Header Compression feature?

Answer: You can use the Express TCP Header Compression feature to reduce network overhead and speed transmission of TCP packets.

10 What are the three states of HSRP?

Answer: The three states are dormant, active, and passive.

Chapter 18

1 What port does Cisco's implementation of TACACS use?

Answer: In Cisco, TACACS implementation is used over port 49 TCP only.

2 What port(s) does RADIUS use?

Answer: RADIUS can be implemented over port 1812 TCP/UDP and port 1813 TCP/ UDP for accounting. The Cisco specification for RADIUS uses UDP only. In some implementations, RADIUS can also be deployed over port 1645.

3 Which group of ISAKMP is used by VPN Client 3.x?

Answer: VPN Client 3.x uses Diffie-Hellman group 2 of 1024 bits.

4 True or false: TACACS+ is not secure.?

Answer: False. TACACS+ is very secure, because it encrypts a packet's entire payload.

5 True or false: RADIUS is more secure than TACACS+.?

Answer: False. When compared with TACACS+, RADIUS is less secure, because it encrypts only the user password. The rest of the packet is transmitted in clear text— including username, authorized services, and accounting information.

6 Name at least three of the available authentication methods.

Answer: There are ten possible authentication methods:

enable

krb5

krb5-telnet

line

local

local-case

none

group radius

group tacacs+

group group-name

7 What do you need to do to enable the PIX Shell (pixshell) option for the Group Setup?

Answer: If the PIX Shell (pixshell) checkbox does not appear on your Group Settings screen, click the Interface Configuration button on the left side of the screen. On the Interface Configuration screen under the TACACS+ Services category, select the PIX Shell (pixshell) checkbox for User, Group, or both.

8 What is the syntax for configuring a Telnet password on the PIX Firewall?

Answer: `PIX(config)#`**passwd** `password` `[encrypted]`

9 What are the two ways of assigning a server key on a router?

Answer: Globally or per server host.

10 What does the **aaa authorization exec default group tacacs+ if-authenticated** command tell the router to do?

Answer: It tells the router to contact the TACACS+ server to determine whether the user is permitted to use an EXEC shell. In case of an error from the TACACS+ server, the user is allowed to enter the shell anyway, provided that he or she has been properly authenticated.

Chapter 19

1 What is the main difference between an access list on a Cisco IOS router and an access list on a PIX firewall?

Answer: The main difference between PIX and IOS ACLs is that the PIX ACL uses the network mask, and the IOS router uses a wildcard mask in the ACL.

2 What command creates an RSA key pair on a PIX Firewall with a 1024-bit key length?

Answer: ca generate rsa key 1024

3 When using a GRE tunnel with an IOS router, where should you place the crypto map if you want to protect traffic going over the tunnel?

Answer: With GRE tunnels, you should always place the crypto map on both the logical (GRE) interface and the physical interface that the tunnel leaves the router on. Without the crypto map placement on both of these interfaces, the crypto access list is not matched, and the VPN is not triggered.

4 What command on a PIX firewall enrolls a CA that has a CA nickname of myca?

Answer: ca enroll myca

5   What command on the PIX displays the IKE configuration within the router but does not display the default policy settings?

   Answer: The command that does this is show isakmp. The show isakmp command displays the ISAKMP configuration that has been entered. The show isakmp policy command displays all the configured ISAKMP policies.

6   What command on the PIX bypasses conduits and access lists for IPSec connections but still checks the traffic against the ASA to maintain security?

   Answer: sysopt connection permit-ipsec

7   What encryption and authentication are the defaults for ISAKMP policies?

   Answer: The default encryption in an ISAKMP policy is DES, and the default authentication in an ISAKMP policy is SHA.

Chapter 20

1   Name two issues arising from conventional IPSec configuration.

   Answer: IPSec does not allow routing protocol updates to be routed through the IPSec tunnel, because IPSec doesn't encrypt IP multicast/broadcast packets.

   Each time a new network needs to be added to the list of IPSec participants, a new access list must be defined for user traffic encryption.

   The hub router's configuration can become enormous.

   Changing public IP hosts' addresses because of DHCP utilization by a service provider

   Occasional requirement for a full-mesh configuration

2   What mechanism is used to accomplish DMVPN?

   Answer: mGRE/NHRP

3   How can you implement dynamic routing protocols over IPSec protected links?

   Answer: By using GRE tunnel interfaces

4   When full-mesh GRE tunnels are used, which interfaces need to have a **crypto map** applied?

   Answer: Both tunnel and physical interfaces

5   What command specifies that all traffic going through the GRE tunnel is to be encrypted?

   Answer: `Router(config)#`**`permit gre host`** `tunnel-source` **`host`** `tunnel-destination`

6   What are the three components of the DMVPN configuration?

Answer: IPSec profiles, hub configuration, spokes configuration

7   In DMVPN, what command issued on the hub router causes NHRP to automatically add spoke routers to the multicast NHRP mappings and register their unicast NHRP mappings when a spoke router initiates the mGRE+IPSec tunnel?

Answer: `Router(config-if)#ip nhrp map multicast dynamic`

8   What do you do to route RIP over the mGRE tunnel?

Answer: Turn off split horizon.

Chapter 21

1   What is the PPP session termination point called in L2TP terminology?

Answer: L2TP network server

2   What are the two termination points of the L2F tunnel?

Answer: NAS and home gateway

3   To which configuration mode is a virtual template applied?

Answer: VPDN group accept-dialin

4   True or false: LAC/NAS needs to have a local pool of IP addresses defined.

Answer: False

5   Which PPP authentication protocol(s) does PIX Firewall's implementation of PPTP support?

Answer: PAP, CHAP, MS-CHAP

Chapter 22

1   The Cisco IOS Firewall feature set is built around the concept of preventing what?

Answer: The Cisco IOS Firewall feature set is built around the concept of preventing unauthorized access to your protected network resources.

2   When an attacker opens a large number of half-open TCP connections, this is what type of attack?

Answer: This is a DoS attack, designed to deny legitimate users access to your resources.

3 TCP intercept, by default, drops which connection first?

Answer: TCP intercept drops the oldest half-open connection first.

4 What feature in the Cisco IOS Firewall gives you intelligent filtering of TCP and UDP packets?

Answer: Context-Based Access Control (CBAC) gives you intelligent filtering of TCP and UDP packets.

5 What is the default setting for the low value of half-open connections before TCP intercept aggressive mode stops?

Answer: 900 half-open connections is the default.

6 What is spoofing?

Answer: Spoofing is when an attacker forges a packet's IP address, usually during a DoS attack of some type.

7 Can CBAC can be used to prevent SMTP attacks?

Answer: Yes. CBAC monitors commands sent across the defined SMTP port.

8 Which Cisco IOS Firewall feature allows you to run CBAC-supported applications across nonstandard ports?

Answer: Port-to-Application Mapping (PAM) can be used to map applications to nonstandard ports.

Chapter 23

1 What is the translational slot on the PIX Firewall called?

Answer: The translational slot is called the *xlate*.

2 What is the default security level for the outside interface?

Answer: The default security level for the outside interface is 0.

3 On the PIX Firewall, inbound traffic is filtered and outbound traffic is allowed by default. True or false?

Answer: True

4 You can configure syslog messages to be sent to which location(s)?

Answer: Syslog messages can be sent to the console, an SNMP management station, or a remote syslog server.

5   The IP address of the inside interface does not need to belong to the same subnet as the pool of its DHCP addresses. True or false?

Answer: False

6   How many entries must an access list have to become turbo-compiled?

Answer: An access list is required to have 19 entries to become turbo-compiled.

Chapter 24

1   By default, when IDS on Cisco IOS software is enabled, are all the default signatures enabled or disabled?

Answer: By default, they are all enabled.

2   True or false: Implementing IDS on a Cisco PIX Firewall affects the firewall's throughput performance.

Answer: True

3   What command disables the ICMP Echo Reply signature, ID = 2000?

Answer: ip audit signature 2000 disable

4   What type of signature identifies information-gathering activity?

Answer: Info signature

5   In what version of the PIX OS was intrusion detection introduced?

Answer: PIX OS 5.2

6   What type of signature detects complex data patterns, usually over a period of time?

Answer: Compound signature

7   What command displays interface-specific information about IDS for every interface IDS is configured on?

Answer: show ip audit interface

8   What type of signature identifies activity that portrays an attempted network attack?

Answer: Attack signature

9   What type of signature detects data patterns as simple as an attempt to access a specific port on a specific host?

Answer: Atomic signature

10 What command displays the global configuration settings for IDS on the router?

Answer: show ip audit

Chapter 25

1 Name two features offered by CAR.

Answer: Classification and rate limiting

2 What sort of information must preexist on the router to allow a packet with unicast RPF?

Answer: Source IP address and incoming interface

3 Name the two tunneling techniques under L2VPN.

Answer: 802.1Q tunneling and Layer 2 protocol tunneling

4 What is the command syntax to implement unicast RPF on a router?

Answer: `Router(config-if)#ip verify unicast reverse-path`

5 Which Layer 2 protocol parameters can be specified with Layer 2 protocol tunneling?

Answer: cdp, stp, vtp

INDEX

Numerics

3DES (Triple DES) 432, 636
802.1Q tunneling 881

A

AAA 428, 436, 448–449
    configuring on PIX Firewall 581, 583, 585–593
    configuring with RADIUS 569–581
    user account verification 449–451
    VPDN configuration 752–761
access attacks 436
access control lists. *See* ACLs
access-list command 756
accounting, Tripwire 967
accounts
    locking 965
    root account, modifying 964
ACEs (access control entries) 477
    applying to interfaces 496–497
    entry order 496
    implicity deny statement 495
ACLs (access control lists) 428, 443, 477, 480–483.
    See also advanced ACLs
    ACEs 477
        entry order 496
        implicit deny statement 495
    applying to interfaces 496, 497, 501
    assigning to vtys 445
    Cisco PIX Firewall configuration 824–826
    configuring 498
    crypto 477
        functions of 477
        implementing 478–479
    defining 495
    defining criteria 498–500
    displaying information 514–515
    IP, testing Layer 4 information 493
    lock-and-key 506–507
        configuring 484–487
    logging 494–495, 511–512
    named extended IP ACLs
        configuring 482
        creating 503

time range function 483–484
named MAC extended IP ACLs,
    configuring 482
named standard IP ACLs
    configuring 482
    creating 503
numbered extended IP ACLs
    configuring 481
    creating 502, 503
numbered standard IP ACLs
    configuring 481
    creating 502
port, configuring 490, 491
reflexive 507–511
    configuring 488–489
router configuration 490
size limitations 517–518
time range function
    implementing 504–506
troubleshooting 516–517
TurboACL, configuring on PIX
    Firewall 6.2 850
unsupported features on
    Catalyst 3550 switch 518
VLAN map entries
    creating 513
    removing 514
ACS, password recovery 1011
active routers (HSRP) 527
active state (EIGRP) 250
ActiveX objects, filtering 827
address mapping, configuring on Frame Relay
    105–108
address translation, xlates 814
addressing, IS-IS 333
    NSAP format 333–334
    requirements 334–335
adjacencies 328
    configuring on IS-IS 324–325
adjusting MTU packet size 526
administrative distance 398
    configuring on OSPF networks 300–301
advanced ACLs 482–483
    defining 495
    lock-and-key, configuring 484–487, 506–507
    logging 494–495
    port ACLs, configuring 490–491

C

D

M

Q-R

S

U

V

W-X-Y-Z